PENGUIN REFERENCE

# THE PENGUIN DICTIONARY OF ARCHITECTURE AND LANDSCAPE ARCHITECTURE

John Fleming's *Robert Adam and His Circle in Edinburgh and Rome* was awarded the Bannister Fletcher Prize and the Alice Davis Hitchcock Medal. He is an FRSL. John Fleming has collaborated with Hugh Honour on *The Penguin Dictionary of Decorative Art* and *A World History of Art*, which was awarded the Mitchell Prize.

Hugh Honour is the author of *Neo-Classicism* and *Romanticism,* both published by Penguin in the 'Style and Civilization' series of which he and John Fleming are the editors. He has also written *Chinoiserie: The Vision of Cathay, The Companion Guide to Venice* and *The Image of the Black in Western Art, from the American Revolution to World War I,* for which he received the Anisfield–Wolf Book Award in Race Relations. He is an FBA and an FRSL.

Sir Nikolaus Pevsner was from 1949 to 1955 Slade Professor of Fine Art and a Fellow of St John's College, Cambridge. In 1959 he became Professor of the History of Art at Birkbeck College, University of London, and remained there until his retirement in 1969, when he became Emeritus Professor. He was made a CBE in 1953 and received a knighthood in 1969. From its inception he edited the *Pelican History of Art and Architecture* and wrote most of the *Buildings of England* volumes, as well as editing the whole series. He wrote many other books, including *The Englishness of English Art, An Outline of European Architecture* and *Pioneers of Modern Design,* all of which are published in Penguin. He died in 1983.

# THE PENGUIN DICTIONARY OF
# ARCHITECTURE AND LANDSCAPE ARCHITECTURE

*John Fleming*
*Hugh Honour*
*Nikolaus Pevsner*

## FIFTH EDITION

PENGUIN BOOKS

Published by the Penguin Group
Penguin Books Ltd, 27 Wrights Lane, London w8 5tz, England
Penguin Putnam Inc., 375 Hudson Street, New York, New York 10014, USA
Penguin Books Australia Ltd, Ringwood, Victoria, Australia
Penguin Books Canada Ltd, 10 Alcorn Avenue, Toronto, Ontario, Canada m4v 3b2
Penguin Books (NZ) Ltd, Private Bag 102902, NSMC, Auckland, New Zealand

Penguin Books Ltd, Registered Offices: Harmondsworth, Middlesex, England

The Penguin Dictionary of Architecture first published 1966
Second edition 1972
Third edition 1980
Fourth edition 1991
Fifth edition published as The Penguin Dictionary of
Architecture and Landscape Architecuture simultaneously in
Great Britain and in the USA as a Penguin hardback 1998
Published in paperback in Penguin Books 1999

3

# FOREWORD TO THE FOURTH EDITION

This is the first edition to be published since the death of Nikolaus Pevsner, whose loss we acutely feel. From the book's inception, now more than twenty-five years ago, he was the guiding spirit and it was only at his repeated insistence that his name appears last on the title-page – 'alphabetical order, please! That is correct,' he would say. He wrote the entries for medieval and nineteenth- and twentieth-century architects, as well as the European and American national entries and most of the stylistic ones. He was assisted by Sabrina Longland in connection with definitions of medieval terms and by Enid Caldecott in connection with modern technical terms. We wrote the rest of the book. But for the third edition specialists contributed entries for Australian, Byzantine, Canadian, Russian and South African architecture and also for the entry on windows, all being signed by their authors, to whom we are most grateful. Sarah Pearson revised and in some instances re-wrote entries for the techniques of roof-construction.

For this fourth edition we have made additions to the national entries to take account of recent developments and have also re-written the Chinese, Indian, Japanese and other Asian entries. Its increased size is, however, due mainly to the addition of entries for many contemporary architects, some of whom had not even begun their careers when the first edition went to press. We have also revised many entries in the light of the increased and more accurate knowledge of the history of architecture published in recent years. And we have appended very brief bibliographies to most of the biographical entries as well as some others (for those cited in abbreviated form full titles are given on pp. 639–44). Over the years we have received much help and advice and we should like to acknowledge that given us by Bruce Boucher, Adrian Edwards, Eileen and John Harris, Ruth Kamen, Alastair Laing, Renato Pedio, Rupert Scott, John Shearman and Sir John Summerson. We are also grateful to the Royal Commission on Historical Monuments (England) for permission to reproduce the cruck drawing (Fig. 39).

JOHN FLEMING    HUGH HONOUR

*January 1990*

# FOREWORD TO THE FIFTH EDITION

We have substantially revised and expanded the text for this new edition, partly because of the number of contemporary architects who have recently become prominent internationally but mainly in order to include landscape architecture. For the latter we have written over 100 entries, both on individual landscape architects and theorists and on such topics as Business Parks, Motorways, Parkways, Theme Parks and Public Parks. We have also revised the old entries on 'Capability' Brown, Downing, Le Nôtre, Olmsted and others.

On architecture many of the old entries have been revised and more than 100 new entries have been added on contemporary architects and on such general topics as Historical Preservation, Mission Style, Ornament, Prehistoric Architecture, Proportion, Restoration and Urban Design, as well as on such terms of recent coinage as Barrier Free Design, Computer Aided Design, Critical Regionalism, Deconstructivism, Green, Environmental or Sustainable Architecture, Façadism, Intelligent Building, Shopping Malls and Tensile or Membrane Structures.

Many old friends have helped us with this edition as they did with previous editions, and we would like to thank especially Bruce Boucher, Giuseppe Chigiotti, Eileen and John Harris, Alastair Laing, Jane Oldfield, Alex Tzonis and Mary Wall. We are much indebted to John Dixon Hunt in connection with landscape architecture and, in connection with Historical Preservation, to Muija Yang of the Unesco World Heritage Centre in Paris and to Elizabeth Llewellyn of the World Monuments Fund in London.

As always our publishers have been unfailingly supportive, especially Peter Carson, Ravi Mirchandani, Alice Roberts, Ellah Allfrey and Simon Winder in London and Cassia Farkas and Hugh Rawson in New York. To the meticulous editorial care of Annie Lee and to the skill of the draughtsman Alan Fagan we are greatly indebted.

JOHN FLEMING    HUGH HONOUR

*January 1998*

CROSS-REFERENCES AND ABBREVIATIONS: Cross-references are indicated by printing the key word in CAPITALS. Abbreviations are used in the bibliographies for works of which the full titles are given on pp. 639–44.

# A

**Aalto**, Hugo Alvar Henrik (1898–1976). Among the most important C20 architects and pre-eminent in his native Finland, Aalto started *c*. 1923–5 in a typically Scandinavian 'National Romantic' idiom derived from Lars SONCK and Eliel SAARINEN combined with the Nordic classicism of ASPLUND. Then he turned decisively to Modernism with his Turun Sonomat Building, Turku (1927–9), followed by the remarkable library at Viipuri (1927, 1930–35), the Paimio Sanatorium (1929–33) and the Sumila Factory with workers' housing at Kotka (1936–9). He possessed a strong feeling for materials and their characters, which, Finland being a country of forests, inspired him to use timber widely. He invented bent plywood furniture (1932) and timber figured prominently in his Finnish Pavilion at the Paris Exhibition of 1937 and in the Villa Mairea at Noormarkku (1938–41). However, Aalto's most original works date from after the Second World War. By then he had evolved a language entirely his own, quite unconcerned with current clichés, yet in its vigorous display of curved walls and single-pitched roofs, in its play with brick and timber, in harmony with the international trend towards plastically more expressive *ensembles*. And with his earlier sensitive response to the vernacular undiminished, he continued to explore his conception of architecture as an intermediary between human life and the natural landscape. The principal works are Baker House, Massachusetts Institute of Technology, Cambridge, Massachusetts (1947–9), with a curved front and staircases projecting and climbing diagonally; the Village Hall and Civic Centre, Säynätsalo (1949–59); the Helsinki University of Technology, Espoo (1949–66); the Pensions Institute, Helsinki (1952–7), a more straightforward job; the Vuoksenniska Church, Imatra (1956–9); the public libraries at Seinäjoki (1963–5) and at Rovaniemi (1963–8); the Mount Angel Library, St Benedict, Oregon (1970), and the Finlandia Concert Hall, Helsinki (1970–75), his last and one of his finest buildings.

M. Quantrill, *A.A. A Critical Study*, Helsinki 1983; G. Schildt, *A.A.*, 3 vols, London/New York 1984, 1986, 1991; R. Weston, *A.A.*, London 1995.

**Abacus**. The flat slab on the top of a CAPITAL: in Greek Doric a thick square slab; in Greek Ionic, Tuscan, Roman Doric and Ionic, square with the lower edge moulded; in Corinthian and Composite with concave sides and the corners cut off. *See* Fig. 86.

**Abadie**, Paul (1812–84). French architect. His Sacré Cœur, Montmartre, Paris (begun 1874), is the best-known example of French neo-Romanesque architecture though later than St Pierre de Montrouge, Paris, by VAUDREMER. The Sacré Cœur was inspired by St Front, Périgueux, which Abadie restored (disastrously).

*Entre archéologie et modernité. P.A. architecte*, exh. cat. Paris 1988/90.

**Abbey**. A MONASTERY governed by an abbot or abbess.

**Abbot**, Stanley William (1905–75), *see* PARKWAY.

**ABC**. The most important CON-STRUCTIVIST group outside Russia, established in Switzerland in 1924 by LIS-SITSKY, Hannes MEYER, STAM and others. It disbanded in 1939.

S. Ingbarman, *ABC. International Constructivist Architecture 1922–1939*, Cambridge, Mass., 1994.

**Abercrombie**, Sir Patrick (1879–1957). English town planner responsible for the influential though never executed Greater London Plan of 1945. HOLFORD's plan for the City of London formed the inner core of Abercrombie's plan.

G. E. Cherry (ed.), *Pioneers of British Planning*, London 1981.

**Abraham**, Raimund (b.1933), *see* AUSTRIAN ARCHITECTURE.

**Abramovitz**, Max (b.1908). American architect, a partner of Wallace K. HARRISON from the late 1930s until 1976. He designed the Philharmonic Hall for Harrison's Lincoln Center, New York (1962). His Assembly Hall (1963) and Krannert Center, University of Illinois, Urbana (1969), are notable.

*The Architecture of M.A.*, Champaign, Urbana 1963.

**Abutment**. Solid masonry placed to counteract the lateral thrust of a VAULT or ARCH. *See* Fig. 6.

**Abyssinian architecture**, *see* ETHI-OPIAN ARCHITECTURE.

**Acanthus**. A plant with thick, fleshy, scalloped leaves used on carved ornament of Corinthian and Composite CAPITALS and on other mouldings. *See* Fig. 1.

Fig. 1 Acanthus

**Achaemenid architecture**, *see* PER-SIAN ARCHITECTURE.

**Acropolis**. The citadel of a Greek city, built at its highest point and containing the chief temples and public buildings, as at Athens.

**Acroteria**. Plinths for statues or ornaments placed at the apex and ends of a PEDIMENT; also, more loosely, both the plinths and what stands on them. *See* Fig. 2.

**Adam**, Robert (1728–92), the greatest British architect of the later C18, was equally if not more brilliant as a decorator, furniture designer, etc., for which his name is still a household word. He is comparable in his chaste and rather epicene elegance with his French contemporary SOUFFLOT, but without Soufflot's chilly solemnity. He was a typically hardheaded Scot, canny and remorselessly ambitious, yet with a tender, romantic side to his character as well. Both facets were reflected in his work, which oscillates between a picturesque version of neo-classicism and a classicizing version of neo-Gothic. His work has an air of unceremonious good manners, unpedantic erudition and unostentatious opulence which perfectly reflects the civilized world of his patrons. Appreciating that it would be bad manners, and bad business, to make any violent break with established traditions, he devised a neo-classical style lighter and more gaily elegant than that of the Palladians who preceded or the Greek Revivalists who succeeded him. He avoided startling innovations such as the Greek Doric for classical buildings or the picturesquely asymmetrical for Gothic ones. He answered the current demand for a new classicism by enlarging the repertory of decorative motifs and by a more imaginative use of contrasting room plans derived largely from Imperial Roman Baths. In

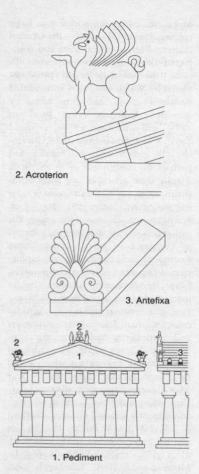

**2. Acroterion**

**3. Antefixa**

**1. Pediment**

Fig. 2 Acroterion, antefixa and general view

his cunning variation of room shapes and in his predilection for columned screens and apses to give a sense of spatial mystery, no less than in his neo-Gothic castles – so massively romantic outside and so comfortably classical within – he answered the taste for the picturesque. He became the architect *par excellence* to the Age of Sensibility, as BURLINGTON

had been to the English Augustan period. His influence spread rapidly all over England and beyond, as far as Russia and America. His output was enormous, and only the unlucky Adelphi speculation robbed him of the fortune he would otherwise have made.

His father, William Adam (1689–1748), was the leading architect of his day in Scotland and developed a robust, personal style based on VANBRUGH, GIBBS and the English Palladians, e.g. Hopetoun House, near Edinburgh (1721–6), and Duff House, Banff (1735–41). His brothers John (1721–92) and James (1732–94) were also architects, and all three trained in their father's Edinburgh office: Robert and James attended Edinburgh University as well. Robert Adam's early work is no more than competent, e.g. Dumfries House (designed 1750–54). His genius emerged only after his Grand Tour (1754–8), most of which was spent in Rome studying Imperial Roman architecture under CLÉRISSEAU, with whom he also surveyed Diocletian's palace at Split in Dalmatia (later published by him as *Ruins of Spalatro*, 1764).

In 1758 he settled in London, where he was joined by his brother James after a similar Grand Tour with Clérisseau (1760–63). The columnar Admiralty Screen, London (1759–60), gave immediate proof of his ability and originality, but all his other early commissions were for the internal transformation of old houses or the completion of houses already begun by other architects. Nevertheless, his style rapidly matured, and the interiors of Harewood House (1758–71), Kedleston Hall (1760–70), Syon House (1762–69), Osterley Park (1761–80), Luton Hoo (1767–70), Newby Hall (1767–74), and Kenwood (1767–9) are perhaps his masterpieces of interior design. His meticulous attention to detail is revealed no less in the jewel-like finish of the painted decorations and very shallow stucco work than in the care he lavished on every part of each room from the carpets to the keyhole guards. No previous architect had attempted such comprehensive schemes of interior decoration. Although individual decorative motifs are often small in scale they are woven together with such skill that the general effect is rarely finicking, and although the same artistic personality is evident in each room the effect of a series is never monotonous. They perfectly illustrate those qualities for which he and James expressed their admiration in the introduction to their *Works in Architecture* (1773; 2nd vol. 1779; 3rd vol. 1822): movement or 'rise and fall, the advance and recess and other diversity of forms' and 'a variety of light mouldings'. His neo-classicism is most evident in the planning of Syon, with its varied geometric shapes (basilican hall, rotunda, projected central Pantheon, etc.), and on the south front of Kedleston, modelled on a Roman TRIUMPHAL ARCH.

His originality and ingenuity in planning culminated in his London houses of the 1770s – e.g. 20 St James's Square, 20 Portman Square – in which, however, the decoration became increasingly shallow and linear, tending towards the flippancy and frippery for which he was much criticized towards the end of his life.

Between 1768 and 1772 he and James embarked on their most ambitious enterprise, the Adelphi, a vast palatial group of houses on the banks of the Thames (now destroyed). Unfortunately the speculation failed and they were saved from bankruptcy only by the expedient of a lottery and by loans from their elder brother John in Edinburgh.

Partly as a result of the Adelphi fiasco the quality of Robert Adam's work declined sharply after 1775. But it recovered amazingly during the last decade

of his life under the stimulus of large commissions in Edinburgh – the General Register House (begun 1774 and completed, with modifications, after his death), the University (begun 1789, completed by W. H. PLAYFAIR to modified designs 1817–34, the dome added by Rowand Anderson (1834–1921) in 1887), and Charlotte Square (designed 1791). The entrance front to the University is his most monumental building and perhaps his masterpiece as an architect. To the same period belong most of his sham castles, e.g. Culzean Castle (1777–92) and Seton Castle (1789–91), which were much in advance of their date. His earlier neo-Gothic style, e.g. the interiors of Alnwick Castle (*c*.1770, now destroyed), had been similar in its sophisticated elegance to his neo-classical style. Now he developed a much bolder manner. At Culzean he took full advantage of a dramatic site on the Ayrshire coast for a martial display of round towers and battlements embracing rooms of feminine delicacy inside. The charm of the place lies in this contrast, which would have been greatly relished by the C18 Man of Sensibility, who could here enjoy the chilling horror of storms at sea from an eminently safe and civilized interior.

J. Rykwert, *The Brothers A. The Men and the Style*, London 1985; J. Gifford, *W.A. (1689–1748)*, Edinburgh 1989; D. Howard (ed.), *W.A.*, Edinburgh 1990; D. King, *The Complete Works of R. and J.A.*, London 1991; S. Parissien, *A. Style*, London 1992; A. A. Tait, *R.A. Drawings and Imagination*, Cambridge 1992; Summerson 1991; Colvin 1995.

**Addorsed**. Term applied to two figures, usually animals, placed symmetrically back to back; often found on CAPITALS.

**Adler**, Dankmar (1844–1900), *see* SULLIVAN, Louis Henry.

**Adobe**. Unbaked mud brick dried in the sun, often containing chopped straw and pounded earth as a reinforcement. It was used for building from very early times, e.g. 5th millennium BC at Hassuna, Iraq, and later in many parts of the world, notably in Africa, Central Asia and Iran, Spain and South America, Mexico and south-west USA, *see* PUEBLO. It has recently been revived by architects in Australia, Egypt and the USA, e.g. FATHY; PREDOCK. *See also* COB and PISÉ.

Davey 1961; J. Dethier, *Architecture du terre ou l'avenir d'un tradition millénaire Europe–Tiers Monde–États Unis*, Paris 1980; J. L. Bourgeois, *Spectacular Vernacular. The A. Tradition*, New York 1989; O. Romero and D. Larkin, *A. Building and Living with Earth*, Boston 1994.

**Adyton** or **Adytum**. The inner sanctuary of a Greek temple whence oracles were delivered; also, more loosely, any private chamber or sanctuary.

**Aedicule**. Properly a canopied niche or shrine framed by two columns supporting an ENTABLATURE and PEDIMENT, set in a temple and containing a statue; but also, more loosely, the framing of a door, window or other opening with two columns, piers or pilasters supporting a gable, lintel, plaque, or an entablature and pediment.

**Aegricane**, *see* BUCRANE.

**Aeolic capital**, *see* ORDER.

**Aesthetic Movement**. A late C19 English and American artistic movement in reaction against 'Philistine' taste. It derived from the 'art for art's sake' theories of Gautier, Baudelaire and, in England, Walter Pater, though it had no counterpart in France or elsewhere in continental Europe. The opening of the Grosvenor Gallery, London, in 1877 marked its apogee with Whistler and Oscar Wilde to the fore. Its chief influence was on painting and the decorative arts; in architecture its leading exponent was GODWIN. Other architects associated with it, notably ASHBEE and LETHABY, more properly belong to the ARTS AND CRAFTS. The two movements overlapped and had something in common. In the USA it had much less influence on architecture than on interior design and decoration.

J. D. Kornwolf in *In Pursuit of Beauty. Americans and the A.M.*, New York 1986; E. Aslin, *The A.M.*, London 1969.

**Affronted**. Term applied to two figures, usually animals, placed symmetrically facing each other; often found on CAPITALS. *See* Fig. 3.

Fig. 3 Affronted

**Afghanistan architecture**, *see* INDIAN AND PAKISTANI ARCHITECTURE; ISLAMIC ARCHITECTURE.

**African architecture**, *see* COPTIC ARCHITECTURE; EGYPTIAN ARCHITECTURE; ETHIOPIAN ARCHITECTURE; ISLAMIC ARCHITECTURE; SOUTH AFRICAN ARCHITECTURE.

**Agger**. Latin term for the built-up foundations of Roman roads; also sometimes applied to the banks of hill-forts or other earthworks.

**Aggregate**. Crushed stone, sand and other granular material forming the main constituent in CONCRETE, MORTAR and PLASTER.

**Agora**. The open space in a Greek or Roman town used as a market-place or general meeting-place, usually surrounded by porticos as in a FORUM.

**Agostino di Duccio** (1418–81). Italian architect, primarily a sculptor but worked with ALBERTI on the Tempio Malatestiano at Rimini, where his extremely individual and exquisitely refined relief sculpture is best seen. Equally sculptural and equally masterly is the façade he designed for the oratory of S. Bernardino at Perugia (1457–61). Very different in feeling is his monumental Porta S. Pietro or Porta delle Due Porte at Perugia (1473–81).

S. Hesse, *Die Fassade des Oratoriums San Bernardino in Perugia*, Göppingen 1992; Heydenreich 1996.

**Ahmad Ustad** or Ustad Ahmad Lahori (1580?–1649), known as Ahmad Mi'mar. He was chief architect to Shah Jahan at the vast Red Fort palace complex in Delhi and also at Agra (*see* INDIAN ARCHITECTURE).

**Aichel**, Jan Blazej Santini (1667–1723), *see* SANTINI-AICHEL, Jan Blazej.

**Aida**, Takefumi (b.1937). Japanese architect of the first post-war generation alongside KUROKAWA and MAKI. He made his name with his playful Toy Block Houses in Hofu and Tokyo in the late 1970s and early 1980s but went on to develop a more poetic approach, with parallel white walls creating layered spaces which he called an 'architecture of fluctuation'. His Saito Memorial Hall, Shibaura Institute of Technology, Omiya (1990), is the prime example, though the Tokyo War Dead Memorial Park, Tokyo (1988), is more convincing.

*T.A. Buildings and Projects*, New York 1989.

**Aillaud**, Émile (1902–88). French architect notable for his housing estates outside Paris, e.g. Les Courtillières, Pantin, formed of huge serpentine curves (1955–60), and La Grande-Borne, Grigny (1964–71). Also remarkable were La Noé, Chanteloup-les-Vignes (1971–5), and the Quartier Picasso, Nanterre (1974–8).

J.-F. Dhuys, *L'Architecture selon E.A.*, Paris 1983.

**Air-conditioning**. Mechanical systems for ventilating and controlling, especially lowering, the temperature and humidity of enclosed spaces were developed in the early C19 in the USA. By 1889 Carnegie Hall, New York, had an air-cooling system using blocks of ice and in 1904 a system using ammonia was installed in the New York Stock Exchange. But the first true air-conditioning system was invented by Willis Haviland Carrier (1876–1950) in 1902–6 and the first large office building to be completely air-conditioned was the Milam Building, San Antonio, Texas, in 1928. The PSFS Building, Philadelphia, of 1932 by HOWE and LESCAZE was the second. Individual room air-conditioners were being manufactured by the late 1920s but individual window-mounted air-conditioners were mass-produced only after the Second World War.

M. Ingels, *W. H. Carrier. Father of A.-C.*, Garden City 1952; Banham 1984; Elliott 1992.

**Air house** or **air-inflated** or **air-supported structures**, *see* PNEUMATIC STRUCTURES.

**Aisle**. In a longitudinally planned building, e.g. a BASILICA or a Christian church, that part parallel to the main space or nave and divided from it by a colonnade or arcade or, in rare cases, by a screen wall.

An aisle is usually of lesser height than the nave and is sometimes surmounted by a gallery and sometimes by clerestory lighting. *See* Fig. 13.

**Akkadian architecture**, *see* SUMERIAN AND AKKADIAN ARCHITECTURE.

**Alabaster**. A fine-grained form of gypsum or limestone, white or reddish or yellowish white and translucent. It was used, cut into thin laminae, for church windows in the Middle Ages, notably in Italy, e.g. San Vitale, Ravenna.

**Alan of Walsingham**. Sacrist of Ely Cathedral at the time when the new Lady Chapel was begun (1321) and the tower over the Norman crossing collapsed (1322) and was replaced by the celebrated octagon. From the documents it is almost certain that the bold idea of replacing the square crossing tower by a larger octagon was his, though the execution of the timber vaults and lantern is now recognized as the work of William Harley the King's Master Carpenter.

Harvey 1984.

**Álava**, Juan de (d.1537). *see* JUAN DE ÁLAVA.

**Alberti**, Leone Battista (1404–72). Italian playwright, musician, painter, mathematician, scientist and athlete as well as architect and architectural theorist, he came nearer than anyone to the Renaissance ideal of a 'complete man'. Aristocratic by temperament, he was the first great dilettante architect, though he did not dedicate himself to architecture until after 1450. He confined himself to designing, and had nothing to do with the actual building of his works. But his few buildings are masterpieces and his *De re aedificatoria* (1452, fully published 1485) is the first architectural treatise of the Renaissance. It crystallized current ideas on proportion, the orders, and ideal (symbolic) town planning. (English translation

by J. Rykwent, *On the Art of Building in Ten Books*, Cambridge, Mass. 1988.) But though he began with theory his buildings are surprisingly unpedantic and undogmatic. They progressed from the nostalgically archaeological to the boldly experimental. Perhaps his dilettante status allowed him greater freedom than his professional contemporaries. He designed only six buildings and saw only two of them completed (the *tempietto* in San Pancrazio and the façade of S. Maria Novella, both in Florence). To some extent he was indebted to BRUNEL-LESCHI, to whom (among others) he dedicated his treatise *Della pittura* (1436), but whereas Brunelleschi's buildings were elegantly linear his were massively plastic. Architectural beauty he defined as 'the harmony and concord of all the parts achieved in such a manner that nothing could be added, or taken away, or altered except for the worse' and ornament as 'a kind of additional brightness and improvement of Beauty'. By ornament he meant the classical vocabulary of orders, columns, pilasters and architraves which he always used correctly and grammatically but frequently out of context, e.g. his columns always support architraves (not arches), but are frequently merely decorative and without real structural purpose. His most notable and influential achievement was the adaptation of classical elements to the wall architecture of the Renaissance.

The illegitimate son of a Florentine exile, he was probably born in Genoa. Educated in the humanist atmosphere of Padua, he later studied law at Bologna University and visited Florence for the first time in 1428. In 1432 he went to Rome, where he joined the Papal civil service which apparently allowed him ample time for both travel and the cultivation of his various talents. He became Papal adviser for the restoration of Rome

(1447–55) and may have collaborated there with Bernardo ROSSELLINO. In 1450 he was commissioned to transform the Gothic church of S. Francesco, Rimini, into a memorial to the local tyrant, Sigismondo Malatesta, his wife and courtiers. It was subsequently called the Tempio Malatestiano. He designed a marble shell to encase the old building, the front freely based on a Roman triumphal arch (symbolizing the triumph over death), the side walls pierced by deep arched niches each containing a sarcophagus. The front was never finished, and it is now difficult to visualize how he intended to mask the upper part of the old Gothic façade. As it stands it is a magnificent fragment, one of the noblest and most poignant evocations of the grandeur, *gravitas* and decorum of Roman architecture. His next work was another addition to a Gothic church, the completion of the façade of S. Maria Novella, Florence (1456–70). Entirely coated with an inlay of different coloured marbles, it owes as much to the C11–12 church of S. Miniato, Florence, as to any Roman building, though the central doorway is derived from the Pantheon. But the whole design is based on a complex geometrical arrangement of squares, and is thus the first instance of the use of HARMONIC PROPORTIONS in the Renaissance. The upper part of the façade is in the form of a pedimented temple front linked to the sides by great scrolls which were to be much copied in later periods. It was commissioned by Giovanni Rucellai, whose name is inscribed across the top with typical Renaissance confidence. For the same patron he designed the façade of Palazzo Rucellai, Florence (begun after 1452, completed by 1460, under Rossellino's supervision), and the exquisite, casket-like little marble-clad shrine of the Holy Sepulchre (1467) in S. Pancrazio, Florence. The Palazzo Rucellai, with

its rusticated walls articulated by three superimposed orders of pilasters (Ionic and Corinthian very freely interpreted), is indebted to Brunelleschi's Palazzo di Parte Guelfa. But it has certain novelties, e.g. square-headed door-cases, a vast cornice instead of eaves, and double windows with pilasters and a central column supporting an architrave beneath the rounded cap. The exquisite adjustment of the proportions distinguishes it from the palace designed in emulation of it at Pienza by Rossellino.

S. Sebastiano (1460 onwards) and S. Andrea (1470), both at Mantua, are the only buildings which Alberti designed entire, though neither was completed during his lifetime. For S. Sebastiano he chose a centralized Greek cross plan and designed a massively austere façade as a pilastered temple front, perhaps to be approached up a wide flight of steps. The entablature is broken with a rounded-headed window (derived from the Roman arch of Tiberius at Orange), which increased its severity by reducing the pilasters from six to four. This alteration and his complete rejection of columns mark his increasing tendency to stray from correct classical usage in the creation of a more logical wall architecture. The church was completed, with further alterations, after his death. At S. Andrea his plans were carried out more faithfully, though the dome he designed to cover the crossing was never executed. The façade is a combination of a pedimented temple front and a triumphal arch, with shallow pilasters in place of columns and a deep central recess framing the main door. Inside he abandoned the traditional aisle structure for a barrel-vaulted nave flanked by side chapels. Interior and exterior are carefully integrated. The sides of the nave, with pilastered solids and arched recesses alternating, repeat the rhythmical pattern and the triumphal arch of the façade on exactly the same scale. These two buildings herald a new and less archaeological attitude to antiquity. They reach forward from the Early to the High Renaissance and beyond.

Wittkower 1988; F. Borsi, *L.B.A.*, Oxford 1977; R. Tavernor, *L.B.A. and the Art of Building. History, Context and Interpretation*, London 1994; J. Rykwert and E. Engel, *L.B.A.*, Milan 1994; Heydenreich (1974) 1996.

**Alberts**, Ton (b.1927), *see* DUTCH ARCHITECTURE; ENVIRONMENTAL ARCHITECTURE.

**Albini**, Franco (1905–77). Italian architect trained in Milan. His interior of the Palazzo Bianco Museum, Genoa, and of the treasury of Genoa Cathedral (1951 and 1954) established him as a display architect. His principal buildings were the municipal office, Genoa (1952–61), and the Rinascente department store, Rome (with Franca Helg, 1957–62). His stations for the Milan Metropolitana (1962 onwards) are also notable.

F. Moschini, *F.A.*, London 1979; S. Leet, *F.A.*, Princeton 1989; F. Rossi Prodi, *F.A. (1905–1977)*, Rome 1997.

**Alcázar**. A Spanish fortified palace, the most notable examples being those of Segovia, Seville and Toledo (*see* SPANISH ARCHITECTURE).

**Alchymia**. The second of the Italian 'new wave' design groups (*see* ARCHIZOOM), formed in Milan in 1977 by MENDINI and others, some of whom left before it closed in 1991.

**Alcove**. 1. A recess or niche in a wall or an extension or recess (sometimes vaulted) to a room, e.g. for a bed. 2. A secluded bower or summerhouse in a garden.

**Aldrich**, Henry (1648–1710). Dean of Christ Church, Oxford, he was a virtuoso and architect of distinction. Only two buildings are certainly by him, or largely by him: All Saints', Oxford (1706–10, steeple revised 1717–20 by HAWKSMOOR, whom Aldrich knew), and Peckwater Quad, Christ Church (built by William Townesend 1707–14). Peckwater Quad is a remarkable early example of PALLADIANISM. Aldrich also designed Christ Church Library (built 1717–38) but his designs were completely recast by George Clarke (1661–1736) after Aldrich's death. The Fellows' Building, Corpus Christi College (1706–12), has been attributed to Aldrich; also, with less probability, Trinity College Chapel (1691–4) and Queen's College Library (1693–4). He wrote a Vitruvian–Palladian treatise which was posthumously published in 1789 as *Elementa architecturae civilis*.

Harris 1990; Summerson 1991; Colvin 1995.

**Aleijadinho**, António Francisco Lisboa (1730 or 1738–1814). The greatest Brazilian sculptor and architect. A mulatto (the illegitimate son of a Portuguese architect), he worked in the rich gold-mining province of Minas Gerais, and combined barbarically rich and contorted sculptural decoration with the more dignified architectural forms of traditional Lusitanian church design. His masterpieces are São Francisco, Ouro Preto (1766–94), and the monumental scenic staircase in front of Bom Jesus de Matozinhos, Congonhas do Campo (1800–1805).

Kubler and Soria 1959.

**Alen**, William van (1883–1954), *see* ART DECO.

**Aleotti**, Giovanni Battista (1546–1636). Italian early Baroque architect working in Parma (the hexagonal S. Maria del

Quartiere, 1604–19) and Ferrara (University façade, 1610). He is notable for his Teatro Farnese, Parma (1618–28, damaged in 1944 but restored), which was larger and more magnificent than any previous theatre and combined PALLADIO's and SCAMOZZI's innovations in theatre design with a U-shaped auditorium and wide open, rectangular proscenium arch.

L. Magagnato, *Teatri italiani del Cinquecento*, Venice 1954; DBI 1960.

**Alessi**, Galeazzo (1512–72). The leading High Renaissance architect in Genoa. Born in Perugia and trained in Rome where he was much influenced by MICHELANGELO, he settled in Genoa by 1548. He was adept at turning difficult sloping sites to advantage, and made great play with monumental staircases, colonnades and courtyards on different levels. His several palaces, notably Villa Cambiaso (1548), Palazzo Cambiaso (1565, now Banco d'Italia), and Palazzo Parodi (1567), set the pattern for Genoese domestic architecture. He also built the imposing S. Maria di Carignano, Genoa (1549–52), based on BRAMANTE's design for St Peter's. In Milan he designed Palazzo Marino (1557), now the Municipio, of which the courtyard is an outstanding example of MANNERIST architecture. The *salone maggiore* is also remarkable but was damaged in 1943 and is heavily restored. (The façade facing Piazza della Scala is by Luca Beltrami, 1889.) Other works by him in Milan include SS. Paolo e Barnaba (1561–7) and the façade of S. Maria presso S. Celso (completed by Martino BASSI after he left Milan in 1569).

N. A. H. Brown, *The Milanese Architecture of G.A.*, New York 1982; Lotz (1974) 1996.

**Alexander**, Christopher (b.1936). English architect, trained at Cambridge and Harvard; founded the Center of Environmental Structures, Berkeley, California, in 1967. A controversial but influential theorist, especially of urban design, he published with Serge Chermayeff *Community and Privacy. Toward a New Architecture of Humanism* (1963), advocating HILBERSEIMER's de-urbanizing regionalism and low-rise high-density housing, followed by his *Notes on the Synthesis of Form* (1964) and *The Oregon Experiment* (1975), which set out a co-operative planning experiment for a 15,000-student campus. *A Pattern Language: Towns, Buildings, Construction* (1977) consists of 253 design precepts enabling clients to design for themselves. In *The Timeless Way of Building* (1979) he repudiated the rationalism he had previously advocated. His *A New Theory of Urban Design* followed in 1987. Among his projects, those for user-designed apartment buildings at St Quentin-en-Yvelines, France (1974), and for housing at Mexicali, Mexico (1976), should be mentioned. His Eishin Gakuen High School, Iruma, Japan, dates from 1985–7.

S. Grabow, *C.A. The Search for a New Paradise in Architecture*, Boston–Henley–London 1983.

**Alfieri**, Benedetto (1699–1767). Piedmontese nobleman (uncle of the poet), began as a lawyer, turned to architecture, and succeeded JUVARRA as royal architect in Turin (1739). He was largely employed in completing Juvarra's work in the Palazzo Reale, Turin, and elsewhere. The Teatro Regio, Turin, was begun by Juvarra but is largely by Alfieri (1736–40). His main independent building is the vast parish church at Carignano (1757–64), with a severe façade and very rich interior on a peculiar kidney-shaped plan. He also designed the noble west portico of Geneva Cathedral in a surprisingly radical classicizing style (1752–6).

Pommer 1967; A. Bellini, *B.A.*, Milan 1978; C. Cancro, *B.A. (1699–1767) L'opera completa*, Milan 1980.

**Algardi**, Alessandro (1598–1654). Born in Bologna but settled in Rome, best known as a sculptor, representing the sobriety of Bolognese classicism in opposition to BERNINI. His reputation as an architect rests on the Villa Doria-Pamphili in Rome, of which he had the general direction. (The attribution of the design to his assistant Giovanni Francesco Grimaldi (1606–90) is now not accepted.)

J. Montagu, *A.A.*, London 1985.

**Alicatado**. Spanish term meaning 'cut work' applied to wall decorations composed of mosaics of variously coloured geometrically shaped pieces of glazed pottery in use from the C12 (e.g. Alhambra, Granada, and Alcázar, Seville) but soon superseded by uniformly shaped TILES. By the C15 it was used only to surround tilework.

**Alignment**. 1. An arrangement in a straight line. 2. Theoretically the lines establishing the position of a construction. 3. In a survey, the ground plan showing the direction of a route or highway. 4. In prehistoric architecture, an alley of standing stones or MEGALITHS as at Carnac, France.

**Allée**. French term for a walk of gravel, sand or turf, bordered by PALISADES, hedges or trees with branches trained to meet overhead and exclude sunlight (*allée couverte*), especially one in a geometrically laid-out garden or park. It is to be distinguished from an AVENUE.

**Allio**, Domenico dell' (d.1563), *see* AUSTRIAN ARCHITECTURE.

**Allio**, Donato Felice d' (*c.*1677–1761), *see* AUSTRIAN ARCHITECTURE.

**Alliprandi**, Giovanni Battista (1665–*c.*1720), *see* CZECH ARCHITECTURE.

**Almonry**. The room in a MONASTERY in which alms are distributed.

**Almquist**, Osvald (1884–1950). With Gunnar ASPLUND a pioneer of modern functionalist architecture in Sweden, e.g. his hydro-electric power plants near Hammersfors and Krangfors (1925–8).

B. Linn, *O.A. Ein Arkitekt och Hans Arbete*, Stockholm 1967.

**Almshouse**. A house or, more usually, a group of houses built and endowed by private charity for the aged and poor – replacing, after the dissolution of the monasteries in England, monastic houses where alms and hospitality were dispensed. Many were built in Elizabethan and Stuart times, often as personal memorials to their founders. In type they range from those built round a courtyard with hall and chapel, to a simple row of cottages. The larger ones often have gables over the street front. The Penrose Almshouses, Barnstaple (1627), have a gabled gatehouse. The more splendid and conspicuous foundations were often those of bishops and archbishops, e.g. Abbot's Hospital, Guildford (begun 1619). John NASH's Blaise Hamlet (1811) consists of ten almshouses.

W. H. Godfrey, *The English A. with Some Account of its Predecessor, the Medieval A.*, London 1955; B. Bailey, *A.*, London 1988.

**Alphand**, Jean-Charles-Adolphe (1817–91). French landscape architect, trained as an engineer. He worked with HAUSSMANN on the rebuilding of Paris, designing the PUBLIC PARKS which are notable for the organic irregularity of their layout in contrast to that of Haussmann's urban designs. The first was the Bois de Boulogne, a former hunting forest with a network of alleys radiating from *rond-points*, which he transformed from 1852 onwards into an English-style landscape park with meandering carriageways, paths and lakes. The Parc des Buttes-Chaumont, laid out in 1864–9, is smaller but more remarkable, with streams, waterfalls, a lake, a temple perched on a hill and grottoes of concrete simulating stone on the site of a disused quarry that had become a rubbish dump. His work was continued by Éduard-François ANDRÉ, whose *L'Art des jardins* (1879) advocated the English LANDSCAPE GARDEN for public parks.

W. Robinson, *The Parks, Promenades and Gardens of Paris*, London 1869.

**Alsop**, William (b.1947), *see* ENGLISH ARCHITECTURE.

**Altana**. A covered terrace or loggia raised above the roof, like a BELVEDERE. Venetian in origin and usually of wood, it was intended for drying clothes and is still so used in Venice. It later became a feature of C15–16 domestic architecture in Rome.

**Altar**. An elevated slab or other structure, usually rectangular or round and of stone, for religious rites, sacrifices or offerings. In Ancient Egypt, Greece and Rome altars took many different forms. The Christian altar is a table or slab on supports consecrated for celebration of the sacrament; usually of stone. In the Middle Ages portable altars could be of metal. After the Reformation communion tables of wood replaced altars in England.

**Altar frontal**, *see* ANTEPENDIUM.

**Altar-tomb**. A post-medieval term for a tomb resembling an altar with solid sides but not used as one. *See* TOMB-CHEST.

**Alternative architecture**. Loosely defined term for various forms of owner-built houses, usually of cheap, recycled materials and often based on geodesic and similar structures, mainly in the USA in the 1960s, e.g. houses constructed of dismantled truck and automobile bodywork at Drop City, Colorado, *c*.1966.

**Aluminium** or **aluminum**. A metallic element extracted from bauxite. Silvery white, corrosion-resistant and extremely light in weight, ductile and malleable, it can be spun, pressed or cast. Discovered by Sir Humphrey Davy in 1807, it was not manufactured until a suitable flux was found in 1890. In 1909 Alfred Wilm discovered an alloy which led to Duralumin, used for Zeppelins in the First World War. Its development in architecture followed, notably with FULLER's Dymaxion House (1927, though not realized until 1945–6), Frey and Kocher's Aluminaire House, Syosset, NY (1931, now reconstructed at the New York Institute of Technology, Central Islip, Long Island), and, in answer to the urgent demand for prefabricated mass-housing after the Second World War, the aluminium bungalow programme of 1945 in England and Charles Goodman's National House in the USA using modular components. It was later exploited by PROUVÉ (Aluminium House, 1953) and more recently for cladding, e.g. by FOSTER at the Sainsbury Centre for the Visual Arts, Norwich (1974–7).

J. Peter, *A. in Modern Architecture*, New York 1956; M. Pawley, *Theory and Design in the Second Machine Age*, Oxford 1990; W. Schafke, *A.: das Metall der Moderne – Gestalt, Gebrauch, Geschichte*, Cologne 1991.

**Alure**. An alley or place to walk in, especially behind a parapet or round the roof of a church.

**Álvares**, Afonso (*fl.*1551–75), *see* PORTUGUESE ARCHITECTURE.

**Álvares**, Baltasar (*fl.*1570–1620), *see* PORTUGUESE ARCHITECTURE.

**Álvares**, Mario Roberto (b.1913). Leading contemporary Argentine architect notable for his Centro Cultural General San Martín (1953–64), Belgrano Day School (1964) and the metal and glass office building for SOMISA (1966–77), all in Buenos Aires.

M. Trabuco, *M.R.A.*, Buenos Aires 1965.

**Amadeo** or **Omodeo**, Giovanni Antonio (1447–1522). Born in Pavia, Italy, and primarily a sculptor, he was working at the Certosa there by 1466; then he worked in Milan (MICHELOZZO's Portinari Chapel in S. Eustorgio), where he encountered the Early Renaissance style. The immediate result was the Colleoni Chapel (1470–73) attached to S. Maria Maggiore, Bergamo – based on the Portinari Chapel but encrusted with Renaissance ornamentation in Gothic profusion. He designed the elaborate façade of the Certosa outside Pavia (1491 onwards). He may have been involved in BRAMANTE's great choir at S. Maria delle Grazie, Milan (begun 1493). The Gothic dome over the crossing of Milan Cathedral was built after designs by Amadeo and Dolcebuono, with advice from FRANCESCO DI GIORGIO.

R. V. Schofield *et al.* (eds.), *G.A.A. Documenti*, Como 1989; Heydenreich and Lotz (1974) 1996.

**Ambo**. A stand raised on two or more steps, for the reading of the Epistle and the Gospel; a prominent feature in early medieval Italian churches. Sometimes two were built, one for the Epistle and one for the Gospel, on the south and north sides respectively. After the C13 the ambo was replaced by the PULPIT.

**Ambry**, *see* AUMBRY.

**Ambulatory**. A semicircular or polygonal aisle enclosing an APSE or a straight-ended sanctuary; originally used for processional purposes.

**Ambulatory church**. In Early Christian and Byzantine architecture a church in which a domed centre bay is enveloped on three sides by AISLES. *See also* CROSS-DOMED CHURCH.

**American architecture**, *see* BRAZILIAN ARCHITECTURE; MESO-AMERICAN ARCHITECTURE; MEXICAN ARCHITECTURE; PERUVIAN ARCHITECTURE; UNITED STATES ARCHITECTURE.

**Ammanati**, Bartolomeo (1511–92). A Florentine sculptor and architect, he began under SANSOVINO in Venice, then played a part with VASARI and VIGNOLA at the Villa Giulia, Rome (1551–5). He enlarged the Palazzo Pitti, Florence (1568–70), with a powerful though almost grotesquely rusticated garden façade and courtyard (begun 1560). His finest work was the very graceful Ponte S. Trinità, Florence (1558–70, destroyed 1944 but rebuilt). He completed the Palazzo Grifoni, Florence (1557), and supervised the building of MICHELANGELO's vestibule stairway in the Laurenziana, Florence. Outside Florence he designed the Tempietto della Vittoria near Arezzo (1572). In Lucca he designed part of the Palazzo Provinciale (1578) with a handsome Serlian loggia and in Rome the Collegio Romano (*c.*1582–5).

M. Kiene, *B.A. architetto (1511–92)*, Milan 1995; Lotz (1974) 1996.

**Amphiprostyle**. Term applied to a temple with porticos at each end, but without columns along the sides. *See* Fig. 4.

**Amphitheatre**. An elliptical or circular space surrounded by rising tiers of seats, as used by the Romans for gladiatorial contests, the Colosseum, Rome, of AD 70–80 being the most famous. The earliest known all-masonry amphitheatre is that at Pompeii of *c.*80 BC. Examples survive all over the Ancient Roman world, from Germany (Trier, *c.*AD 100)

Fig. 4 Amphiprostyle

and France (Arles and Nîmes, late CI) to North Africa (El Djem, early C3). In landscape architecture an amphitheatre is an area of similar form but with turfed terraces instead of seats.

**Amsterdam School**, *see* DUTCH ARCHITECTURE; EXPRESSIONISM; KLERK, Michel de.

**Anastylosis**. Recently coined technical term for the process of rebuilding an ancient temple or other structure according to its original tectonic system with its original materials, using new blocks of stone (clearly indicated as such) only when necessary for support, as at the Khmer temple complex at Banteay Srei, Cambodia.

**Anathyrosis**. The smooth marginal dressing of the outer contact band of a masonry joint, the central portion being left roughened and sunk so as to avoid contact.

**Ancones**. 1. Brackets or CONSOLES on either side of a doorway, supporting a CORNICE. 2. The projections left on blocks of stone, such as the drums of a column, to hoist them into position.

**Anderson**, Sir Robert Rowand (1834–1921), *see* ADAM, Robert.

**Ando**, Tadao (b.1941). Self-taught Japanese architect whose early work is remarkable for its poetic reinterpretation of traditional (*sukiya* style) vernacular Japanese domestic architecture for small urban residences, e.g. Azuma House, Sumiyoshiku, Osaka (1976), Matsumoto House, Ashiya (1977), and Glass Block House, Osaka (1978). He went on to design public and commercial complexes with the same minimalist purity but in larger and more open spatial compositions, notably in his Rokko Housing I, Kyoto (1983), Festival, Naha, Okinawa (1984), Time's I, Kyoto (1984), Galleria Akka, Osaka (1988) and Collezione, Tokyo (1990). His later work, which includes Christian churches as well as a Buddhist sanctuary, and numerous museums and art galleries, is outstanding for its sensitive integration with the natural environment, e.g. Church on the Water, Tomamu (1988), Children's Museum, Himeji (1989), and Water Temple, Awaji Island (1991), all of which make imaginative use of sheets of water. His Forest of Tombs Museum, Kaomachi, Kamaoto (1992), Chikatsu-Asuka Historical Museum, Minami-Kawachi, near Osaka (1994), and the Benesse House and Museum of Contemporary Art, Naoshima (1992–5), are remarkable for their use not only of light, wind and water but also of earth as an architectural element, part of them often being underground. Ando has been influential not only in Japan both by his prolific writings and constantly evolving architecture, of which the Japanese Pavilion at the Expo '92, Seville, his Vitra Seminar Building, Basel (1995) and the Benetton Factory, Villorba di Treviso, Italy (1996), are examples in Europe.

K. Frampton, *T.A.*, New York 1991; M. Furuyama, *T.A.*, Zürich 1993; E. Dal Co (ed.), *T.A. Complete Works*, London 1995; R. Pare, *T.A. The Colour of Light*, London 1996.

**André**, Édouard-François (1840–1911).

French landscape architect and theorist. Trained in horticulture, he began to work under ALPHAND on the public parks in Paris in 1860. Outside France he worked in England (Sefton Park, Liverpool, 1867–72), in the Netherlands (Waldam Castle, Goor, 1886, where he revived the C17 Dutch-style garden) and in Italy and Lithuania, where he laid out grounds in the English style. His *L'Art des jardins* (Paris 1879) was used as a manual for adapting the principles of the English landscape garden to public parks.

D. Imbert, *The Modernist Garden in France*, London 1993.

**Andrea di Cione** (*fl.*1343–68), *see* ORCAGNA.

**Andrea Pisano** (d.1348/9), *see* PISANO, Andrea.

**Andreu**, Paul (b.1938). French architect responsible for planning Charles de Gaulle Airport, Paris, notably Terminal 1 (1969–74). From 1984 he was associated with SPRECKELSEN at La Défense, Paris, collaborating on the Grand Arche (1986–9). He was also responsible for the conception of Kaohsiung Airport, Taiwan; Manila Airport, Philippines; al-Dawha Airport, Qatar; and for the French terminal of the Channel Tunnel.

S. Salat and F. Labbé, *P.A., metamorphose du cercle*, Paris 1990.

**Andrews**, John (b.1933). Australian architect, trained in Sydney and under J. L. SERT at Harvard. He made his name with Scarborough College, University of Toronto, Canada (1962–9), designed to accommodate 5,000 people in a self-sufficient institution. This was followed by students' housing at Guelph University, Canada (1965–8), Seaport Passenger Terminal, Miami, Florida (1967), and the Gund Hall Graduate School of Design, Harvard University, Massachusetts (1968), which Philip JOHNSON called

'one of the six greatest buildings of the C20'. Of his recent buildings the American Express Tower, Sydney (1976), the Canadian National Tower, Toronto (1977) and the Merlin Hotel, Perth (1984), should be mentioned.

P. Drew, *The Third Generation. The Changing Meaning of Architecture*, New York 1972; J. Taylor and J. Andrews, *J.A. Architecture, a Performing Art*, Melbourne 1982.

**Ang**. In Chinese roof construction a long transverse bracket arm with the function of a lever. An *ang ton* is placed directly under a roof sloping downwards to the eaves.

**Anglo–Saxon architecture**, *see* ENGLISH ARCHITECTURE.

**Angular capital**. An IONIC capital with all four sides alike, and the volutes turned outwards as in a Corinthian capital. A C16 innovation, probably due to SCAMOZZI and frequently employed until the late C18, when rejected as incorrect.

**Anhalt-Dessau**, Leopold Friedrich Franz, Fürst von (1740–1817). German hereditary prince and patron of architecture and, especially, landscape architecture. After a Grand Tour, admiring the natural landscape of southern Italy and the landscape gardens of England, he began in 1765 to create, with two professional landscape architects, Johann Friedrich Eyserbeck (1734–1818) and Johann Georg Schoch (1758–1826), a 150 sq. km. (58 sq. mile) *Gartenreich* (garden kingdom) of farms, woods and pleasure grounds near Dessau. At Wörlitz he had a country house built in the English neo-Palladian style by ERDMANSDORF. The surrounding park was laid out in the English style also (the first in Germany), with a neo-Gothic building (also the first in Germany), a miniature Vesuvius, numerous classical temples and a lake with an island dedicated to J. J. Rousseau like that in GIRARDIN's park at Ermenonville.

H. Günther (ed.), *Gärten der Goethezeit*, Leipzig 1993; R. Christ, *Dessau und des Wörlitzer Gartenreich*, Rostock 1997; U. Bode *et al.*, *Den Freunden des Natur und Kunst. Das Gartenreich des F. v. A.D.*, Ostfildern 1997.

**Annular**. Ring-shaped, as in an annular barrel vault or annular passage.

**Annulet**, *see* SHAFT-RING.

**Anreith**, Anton (1754–1822), *see* SOUTH AFRICAN ARCHITECTURE.

**Anse de panier**, *see* ARCH.

**Anta**. A PILASTER of which the base and CAPITAL do not conform with the ORDER used elsewhere on the building; it is usually placed at the ends of the projecting walls of a temple PORTICO or pronaos. If there are columns between the *antae* they are called columns *in antis*; the portico and temple itself may also be called *in antis*, as distinct from being PROSTYLE.

**Antechurch** or **forechurch**. An appendix to the west end of a church, resembling a porch or a NARTHEX, but several bays deep and usually consisting of nave and aisles.

**Antefixae**. Ornamental blocks on the edge of a roof to conceal the ends of the tiles. *See* Fig. 2.

**Antelami**, Benedetto (active 1177–?1233). Italian sculptor and probably an architect also. Attributed to him are the Baptistery, Parma (1196–1216, completed 1270), the cathedral of Borgo San Donnino, now Fidenza (1179–96 and 1214–18), and S. Andrea at Vercelli (1219–25/6). This church already has features pointing in the direction of French Gothic. The transition from Romanesque to Gothic is obvious in his sculpture.

A. C. Quintavalle, *B.A.*, Milan 1990.

**Antependium** or **altar frontal**. A decorative, detachable covering for the front of an altar as distinct from the front itself. Antependiums are of various materials: painted wood, ivory, embroidered silk or other textiles, gold, silver or other metals, e.g. the gold antependium from Basel Cathedral of *c.*1022/4 (Musée de Cluny, Paris) or that in the Palatine Chapel, Aachen, also of gold, of *c.*1020. If the covering is continued round the sides and back it is called a PALIOTTO.

**Anthemion**. Ornament reminiscent of a honeysuckle flower alternating with palm leaves or PALMETTES, common in Ancient Greek and Roman architecture. *See* Fig. 5.

Fig. 5 Anthemion

**Anthemios of Tralles**. Geometrician and theorist rather than architect, he is known for sure to have designed only one building, but that among the greatest in the world: Hagia Sophia, Constantinople (AD 532–7). The dates of his birth and death are unknown. Born at Tralles in Lydia, he came of a Greek professional middle-class family; his father was a physician. In 532 Justinian chose him to design the new church of Holy Wisdom (Hagia Sophia) to replace a predecessor which had been burnt in riots. This vast undertaking was completed in the incredibly brief period of five years, to the gratification of Justinian, who claimed to have surpassed Solomon. Anthemios described architecture as 'the application of geometry to solid matter', and his great work with its dome 32.6 m. (107 ft) in diameter is remarkable as a feat of engineering (even though the dome collapsed in 558). But it is also much more, for by the cunning use of screened aisles and galleries around the central area of the church he concealed the supports of the dome which thus seems to float above the building, creating an atmosphere of mystery emphasized by the contrast between the light central space and the dark aisles. He was assisted by ISIDORUS OF MILETUS.

Krautheimer 1986; R. J. Mainstone, *Hagia Sophia*, London 1988; R. Mark and A. S. Cakmak, *The Hagia Sophia*, Cambridge 1992.

**Anticlastic**. Of a surface, having curvatures in opposite senses (concave and convex) in different directions through any point, e.g. as in a HYPERBOLIC PARABOLOID ROOF.

**Antis, in**, *see* ANTA; PORTICO.

**Antoine**, Jacques-Denis (1733–1801). A leading architect in the reign of Louis XVI. His masterpiece is the Mint, Paris (1768–77) – huge, solemn, and very Roman, though he did not visit Italy until 1777. He built a number of Parisian *hôtels*, notably the Hôtel de Jaucourt (1782), and outside Paris, the Château de Herces near Houdan (1772) and the Chapelle de la Visitation at Nancy (1785).

Braham 1980; Kalnein 1995.

**Antonelli**, Alessandro (1798–1888). Professor of Architecture at Turin from 1836 till 1857. His most famous works are the crazily high, externally classical and internally iron-supported towers of the so-called Mole Antonelliana at Turin (originally intended as a synagogue and 167.5 m (about 550 ft) high) and of the cathedral of Novara 140 m. (about 420 ft) high). The former was designed in 1863, the latter in 1840.

Meeks 1966; F. Rosso, *A.A.*, Florence 1989.

**Antonio di Vincenzo** (*c*.1350–1401/2), *see* ITALIAN ARCHITECTURE.

**Antunes**, João (1683–1734), *see* PORTUGUESE ARCHITECTURE.

**Apadana** or **apadhana**. In ancient Persia a free-standing columned hall apparently serving as a throne-room. Outstanding was the hundred-columned apadana built in Persepolis under Darius I (*see* PERSIAN ARCHITECTURE). The apadana often had a portico, and was itself mostly square in plan.

**Apartment** or **flat**. A room or set of rooms for domestic use, on one floor, usually one of several within a large building. If on more than one floor it is called a DUPLEX. The earliest were the *insulae* of Ancient Rome (*see* ROMAN ARCHITECTURE). In C17 France the term was used for suites of rooms within grand houses, notably the Parisian three-room suite of antechamber, chamber and closet. From the early C18 onwards apartment houses for middle-class occupation were being built in France and England as well as tenements or rooming houses of low-rental rooms. C19 tenements were of two types, gallery access and common-stair access (*see* Henry ROBERTS). By the 1890s skyscraper apartment blocks were being built in New York, e.g. the Dakota Apartment Building (1884) followed by the Ansonia (1899–1904). Though later denigrated, the post-Second World War TOWER BLOCKS contributed notably to slum clearance in England. Among C20 apartment buildings the Unité d'Habitation, Marseille (1955), by LE CORBUSIER, is outstanding.

J. F. Geist and K. Kurvers, *Das Berliner Mietshaus 1740–1989*, Munich 1989; F. Loyer, *Paris XIX^e Siècle. L'Immeuble et la rue*, Paris 1989.

**Apex stone**. The top stone in a GABLE end, sometimes called the *saddle stone*.

**Apollodorus of Damascus** (active AD 97–130). Born in Syria, he went to Rome and became official architect to Trajan (AD 97–117), accompanying him on his military campaigns and designing or inspiring almost all the buildings erected under him. His first recorded work was the stone-and-wood bridge over the Danube at Dobreta (AD 104). But his masterpieces were naturally in Rome itself: an ODEON circular in plan (probably that built by Domitian in the Campus Martius), the Baths of Trajan and Trajan's Forum. The latter, with its imposing axial planning and subtle play of symmetry, illustrates his style, a brilliant compromise between the Hellenistic and the pure Roman traditions. He also planned the markets at the extreme end of the Quirinal hill, and was probably involved in work at the port of Rome (Fiumicino) and at Civitavecchia. The TRIUMPHAL ARCHES at Ancona and Benevento have been attributed to him. Though he was on less happy terms with Hadrian, he collaborated with him on at least one project, and dedicated to him his treatise on the construction of engines of assault, *Poliorketa*. But, according to Dio Cassius, Hadrian banished him from Rome in about AD 130, and later condemned him to death because of his harsh criticism of the Temple of Venus and Rome.

MacDonald 1965; Ward-Perkins 1981.

**Apophyge**. The slight curve at the top and bottom of a column where the SHAFT joins the CAPITAL or base.

**Applied column**, *see* ENGAGED COLUMN.

**Apron**. A raised panel below a window-sill, sometimes shaped and decorated.

**Apse**. Ancient Roman in origin (found in both religious and secular contexts), an apse is a semicircular or polygonal extension to, or termination of, a larger rectangular space. Often opposite an entrance, it usually has a rounded vault. In Ancient Roman BASILICAS the praetor's chair stood in it. In Early Christian basilicas it was the place of the clergy and bishop and was frequently elevated, with a passage under the seating (e.g. Hagia Irene, Constantinople). In the C9 a bay was inserted between the apse and transept, reducing the former to an adjunct of the chancel. Aisles might also terminate in apses, as could transepts. Double-ended churches would have a counter-apse. With the C12 broken-ended chevets became commoner, and ultimately the Gothic urge towards spatial amalgamation abolished the distinction between chancel and apse in favour of a deep polygonal or square-ended choir. *See also* CONCH; EXEDRA.

**Apsidiole** or **absidiole**. A small, projecting apsidal chapel.

**Apteral**. An adjective describing a classical-style building with columns at the end, but not along the sides.

**Aqueduct**. An artificial channel for carrying water, usually an elevated masonry or brick structure supported on arches; invented by the Ancient Romans, e.g. the C1 BC Pont du Gard near Nîmes in France and the early C1 to C2 aqueduct at Segovia, Spain, which still carries the town's water supply.

Ward-Perkins 1981.

**Arabesque**. Intricate and fanciful surface decoration generally based on geometrical patterns and using combinations of flowing lines, tendrils, etc., covering the surface with a network of zigzags, spirals, etc. Human figures were not used, as they were in GROTESQUE ornament. The origin of arabesque ornament is disputed, but the name derives from the belief that it was typically Saracenic, especially that on Venetian Saracenic metalwork. The development of arabesque ornament is contemporary with that of STRAPWORK at Fontainebleau, France, in 1533–5, but the nature of the connection between them is unknown.

P. Ward-Jackson in *Victoria & Albert Museum Bulletin*, July 1967.

**Araeostyle**. With an arrangement of columns spaced four diameters apart. *See also* DIASTYLE; EUSTYLE; PYCNOSTYLE; SYSTYLE.

**Arau**, *see* BELGIAN ARCHITECTURE.

**Arcade**. A range of arches carried on piers or columns, either free-standing or blind, i.e. attached to a wall. In southern Europe cloisters and courtyards were often 'arcaded' along one or more sides and on one or more floor levels, e.g. Certosa, Pavia, Italy (1429–73). Streets and piazzas or plazas or 'places' (in France) might be arcaded, as in Ancient Rome or in medieval and Renaissance Bologna where many still survive. *See also* SHOPPING ARCADE.

**Arch**. The spanning of an opening by means other than that of a LINTEL. The most primitive form was made by COR-BELLING. True arches are curved and so constructed with wedge-shaped blocks over the opening that the downward thrust of the weight of their own material and of that above is converted into outward thrusts resisted by the flanking material. There are many different types.

*Anse de panier* is a French term for an arch whose curve resembles that of the handle of a basket; also called *basket arch*. It is formed by a segment of a large circle continued left and right by two segments of much smaller circles.

*Basket arch* or *three-centred arch, see* above.

A *catenary arch* is like an inverted CATENARY.

*Corbel arch, see* false arch.

*Depressed arch, see* four-centred arch.

A *diaphragm arch* is a transverse arch, either plain or moulded in section, separating one bay of a roof or vault from the next, across the nave of a church. They were probably used to prevent fire spreading from one section of a wooden roof to another.

*Discharging arch, see* relieving arch.

A *drop arch* is pointed with a span greater than its radii.

An *elliptical arch* is a half ellipse from a centre on the SPRINGING LINE.

*Equilateral arch, see* pointed arch.

A *false* or *corbel arch* is one constructed by progressive cantilevering or corbelling from the two sides with horizontal joints.

A *four-centred* or *depressed arch* is a late medieval form – an arch of four arcs, the two outer and lower ones springing from centres on the springing line, the two inner and upper arcs from centres below the springing line.

A *horseshoe arch* is often found in Islamic buildings; it can be either a pointed or a round horseshoe.

*Keel arch, see* ogee arch.

A *lancet arch* is pointed, with radii much larger than the span.

An *ogee arch* is pointed and usually of four arcs, the centres of two inside the arch, of the other two outside; this produces a compound curve of two parts, one convex and the other concave. Introduced *c.*1300 it was popular throughout the late Middle Ages and in England especially in the early C14; also called a *keel arch*. In a *nodding ogee arch* the apex projects beyond the vertical plane of the wall or supporting member.

A *pointed arch* is produced by two curves, each with a radius equal to the span and meeting in a point at the top; also called an *equilateral arch*.

A *quadrant arch* is an internal buttress similar in both form and function to an external flying buttress.

A *raking* or *rampant arch* has one impost higher than the other.

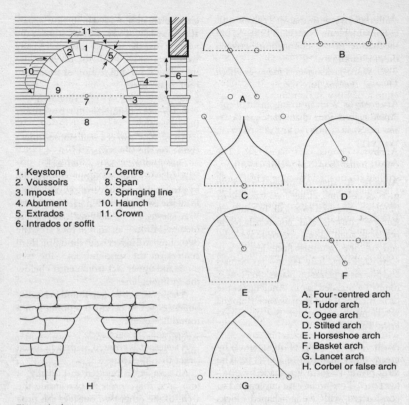

1. Keystone
2. Voussoirs
3. Impost
4. Abutment
5. Extrados
6. Intrados or soffit
7. Centre
8. Span
9. Springing line
10. Haunch
11. Crown

A. Four-centred arch
B. Tudor arch
C. Ogee arch
D. Stilted arch
E. Horseshoe arch
F. Basket arch
G. Lancet arch
H. Corbel or false arch

Fig. 6 Arch

A *relieving arch* is usually of rough construction placed in a wall, above an arch or any opening, to relieve it of much of the superincumbent weight; also called a *discharging arch*.

A *rowlock arch* has bricks or small VOUSSOIRS in separate concentric rings.

A *segmental arch* is a segment of a circle drawn from a centre below the springing line.

A *segmental pointed arch* is drawn from two centres below the springing line.

A *shouldered arch* consists of a lintel connected with the jambs of a doorway by corbels. The corbels start with a concave quadrant and continue vertically to meet the lintel.

A *skew arch* has jambs not at right-angles to its faces.

A *stilted arch* has its springing line raised by vertical PIERS above the IMPOST level.

A *strainer arch* is one inserted, in most cases, across a nave or an aisle to prevent the walls from leaning.

A *Tudor arch* is a late medieval pointed arch whose shanks start with a curve near to a quarter circle and continue to the apex in a straight line.

*See* Fig. 6.

**Arch façade**. A façade in the form of a large screen hollowed out into a series of deep, unornamented arches. In England it appears first in Norman churches and most dramatically in the west façade of Lincoln Cathedral and at the abbey church of Bury St Edmunds.

**Archer**, John Lee (1791–1852), *see* AUSTRALIAN ARCHITECTURE.

**Archer**, Thomas (*c*.1668–1743). The only English Baroque architect to have studied continental Baroque at first hand. His buildings are unique in England in showing an intimate appreciation of BERNINI and BORROMINI. He came of good family and made a four-year Grand Tour after Oxford, returning home in 1695. A Whig, he was successful at Court and in 1703 obtained the lucrative post of Groom Porter. His buildings date between then and 1715, when he acquired the even more profitable post of Controller of Customs at Newcastle, whereupon he gave up architecture. The north front of Chatsworth, Derbyshire (1704–5), and the garden pavilion at Wrest Park, Bedfordshire (1709–11), are his best surviving secular buildings but his reputation rests mainly on his three churches – Birmingham Cathedral (1710–15); St Paul, Deptford, London (1713–30); and St John, Smith Square, London (1713–30), with its spectacular and much-maligned towers. Heythrop House, Oxfordshire (1707–10), was his most grandiloquent effort but it was burnt and largely rebuilt in 1870.

Summerson 1991; Colvin 1995.

**Archigram**. An English group formed in 1961 by Peter Cook (b.1936) with Michael Webb (b.1937) and David Green (b.1937), who were later joined by Ron Herron (1930–94), Dennis Crompton (b.1935) and Warren Chalk (1927–88). Their fantastic space-age visions of a flex-ible, disposable Pop architecture with clip-on technology, all in rapturous candy-colours, were unrealized but became very influential, notably their designs for Plug-in City (1964), Instant City (1968) and Urban Mark (1972). Cook's Montreal Tower project was a remarkable prototype design, though the machine-look was anticipated by Michael Webb in his Furniture Manufacturers project of 1957, which resembled an automobile engine. Archigram disbanded in 1975, their Capsule at Expo '70, Osaka, being almost their only realized project. However, Ron Herron was later to create the Imagination Building, London (1989), a six-storey atrium in which something of Archigram's spirit lived on.

H. Lachmayer, P. Schoenig and D. Crimpton, *A Guide to A. 1961–1974*, London 1994; *A.*, exh. cat., Centre Pompidou, Paris 1994; R. Banham, *The Visions of Ron Herron*, London 1994.

**Architectonic**. Pertaining to architecture or expressing in another artistic form (music, sculpture, painting) the spatial and other qualities peculiar to architecture.

**Architects' Collaborative (TAC)**, *see* GROPIUS, Walter (1883–1969).

**Architects' Co-Partnership**. A group of English architects founded in 1939 and refounded in 1945. An anonymous team approach and a preference for industrial building materials characterize their work. The Dunlop Semtex Rubber Factory, Brynmawr, Wales (1946–53), with Ove ARUP, was outstanding. Their later work includes the Biochemistry Building, Imperial College, London (1961–4), and the Wolfson Building, Trinity College, Cambridge (1972).

**Architecture**. The art and science of designing structures and their surroundings in keeping with aesthetic, functional or other criteria. The distinction made between architecture and building, e.g. by RUSKIN, is no longer accepted. Architecture is now understood as encompassing the totality of the designed environment, including buildings, urban spaces and landscape. Architectural theory goes back to VITRUVIUS and the lost Ancient Greek writings on which he relied. It has continued ever since with a number of cultural, psychological and symbolic as well as spatial, structural and other interpretations, e.g. FUNCTIONALISM which was integral to MODERNISM. The aesthetics of architecture cannot be readily distinguished from those of the other arts (poetry, music, sculpture, painting), and many questions remain to preoccupy architects: what does architecture express? what does it represent? and with what means (symbolic or otherwise) can it do this?

**Architecture Parlante**. Term for the expressiveness sought by French revolutionary architects, notably LEDOUX and BOULÉE, with a 'narrative' architecture whose purpose and character would be made evident not by symbols but by structure and form. The term has been much used by POST-MODERNISTS.

**ArchiteXt**, *see* JAPANESE ARCHITECTURE.

**Architrave**. The lintel extending from one column or pier to another; also, the lowest of the three main parts of an ENTABLATURE; also, more loosely, the moulded frame surrounding a door or window (if this frame turns away at the top at right angles, rises vertically and returns horizontally, forming a shoulder, it is called a *shouldered architrave*). *See* Figs. 47, 51, 86.

**Architrave-cornice**. An ENTABLATURE from which the FRIEZE is elided.

**Archivolt**. The continuous architrave moulding of the face of an arch, following its contour; also the INTRADOS or underside of an arch.

**Archizoom**. Italian 'new wave' group in Florence 1966–73 and Milan 1974. Mainly concerned with interior design, they heralded later developments with 'anti-design' and 'banal-design'. *See also* ALCHYMIA.
A. Branzi, *The Hot House*, London 1985.

**Arcosolia**, *see* CATACOMB.

**Arcuated**. A term applied to a building dependent structurally on the use of arches or the arch principle, in contrast to a TRABEATED building.

**Arena**. The central open space of an AMPHITHEATRE; also, more loosely, any building for public contests or displays in the open air.

**Arets**, Wiel (b.1955), *see* DUTCH ARCHITECTURE.

**Ariss**, John, the first professional architect in North America, emigrated from England in or shortly before 1751, when he advertised in the *Maryland Gazette* as being 'lately from Great Britain' and ready to undertake 'Buildings of all Sorts and Dimensions . . . either of the Ancient or Modern Order of Gibbs, Architect'. His work is unrecorded, but some of the finer Virginian houses were probably designed by him, e.g. Mount Airey, Richmond County (1755–8); they are English Palladian, with Gibbsian overtones.
Pierson and Jordy 1970; Whiffen and Koeper 1981.

**Ark**, *see* ECHAL.

**Armenian architecture**, *see* BYZANTINE ARCHITECTURE.

**Arnolfo di Cambio** (*c.*1245–*c.*1310). A Florentine sculptor and mason. Assistant of Nicola PISANO in 1266, he is already called a *subtilissimus magister* in 1277. He signed works of decorative architecture and sculpture combined in 1282, 1285 and 1293. The architectural forms used are truly Gothic, aware of French precedent, and contain trefoil-headed and trefoil-cusped arches. In 1296 the new cathedral of Florence was begun; Arnolfo was master mason. His design is recognizable in the nave and aisles, but the present centralizing east end with its three polygonal apses is by Francesco TALENTI, though it only enlarged and pushed considerably farther east the east end as intended by Arnolfo, perhaps under the influence of Cologne. It is curious that Arnolfo, in the earliest source referring to him (though as late as *c.*1520), is called a German. Several other buildings have been attributed to Arnolfo, among them, with convincing arguments, S. Croce (begun 1294/5), the Florentine Badia (begun 1284), and the tower of the Palazzo Vecchio (*c.*1310).

A. M. Romanini, *A. di C. e lo 'stil novo' del gotico italiano* (1969), Florence 1980; White 1987.

**Aronco**, Raimondo d' (1857–1932), *see* SOMMARUGA, Giuseppe.

**Aronson**, Shlomo (b.1936), *see* ISRAELI ARCHITECTURE AND LANDSCAPE ARCHITECTURE.

**Arquitectonica**. American partnership founded in Miami, Florida, in 1977 by Bernardo Fort-Brescia (b.1951) and his wife Laurinda Hope Spear (b.1950). They began with the Spear House, Miami (1976–8) and the Palace, Miami (1979–82), but made their name with the colourful neo-Modern residential block the Atlantis, Miami (1978–82). It has a 'sky-patio' punched through the façade and was featured in the popular TV serial *Miami Vice*. They went on to build Mulder House (1983–5) and Banco di Credito (1983–8), both in Lima, Peru; the North Dade Justice Center, Miami (1984–7); the Center for Innovative Technology, Herndon, Virginia (1985–8); the Rio Shopping Center, Atlanta, Georgia (1988), to both of which Martha SCHWARTZ contributed as landscape architect; the Banque de Luxembourg, Luxembourg (1989–94), their 'All Star Resorts' at Walt Disney World, Florida (1994), and the US Embassy, Lima (1993–5). In 1995 they won the competition for a hotel and entertainment complex at 42nd Street and Eighth Avenue, New York, with a design which will convert Times Square into a symbolized rocket crashing into Disneyland.

E. Dunlop and M. Vignelli (eds.), *A.*, New York 1991; P. Johnson (intro.), *A.*, Washington, DC 1991.

**Arris**. A sharp edge produced by the meeting of two surfaces at a corner or an angle.

**Arruda**, Diego (active 1508–31). The leading practitioner of the MANUELINE STYLE in Portugal. His main work is the nave and chapterhouse of the Cristo church, Tomar (1510–14), with its almost surrealist sculptured decoration: sails and ropes around the circular windows, mouldings of cork floats threaded on cables, buttresses carved with patterns of coral and seaweed. His brother Francisco (active 1510–47) was mainly a military architect, but built the exotic, almost Hindu, tower at Belem (1515–20).

Kubler and Soria 1959.

**Art Deco**. The fashionable Jazz Age style concurrent with INTERNATIONAL MODERN in the 1920s and 1930s. The name derives from a Paris exhibition of decorative and industrial art in 1925. It is characterized by unfunctional 'modernism' – e.g. streamlining motifs in architecture. The French architect Robert Mallet-Stevens (1886–1945) was its chief European exponent in architecture, e.g. his cubistic apartments and other buildings in rue Mallet-Stevens, Paris (1926–7). In the USA the style found its most notable expression in skyscrapers (e.g. the Chrysler building, New York, 1928–30, by William Van Alen, 1882–1954) and cinemas, etc., notably Radio City Music Hall, Rockefeller Center, New York (*c.*1932). In England the Hoover Factory, London, by Wallis, Gilbert & Partners (1931–5), is notable though only the façade survives. In landscape architecture and garden design GUÉVRÉKIAN was outstanding.

B. Hillier, *A.D.*, Minneapolis 1971; R. H. Bletter and C. Robinson, *Skyscraper Style – A.D. New York*, New York 1975; P. Bayer, *A.D. Architecture, Design, Decoration and Details from the Twenties and Thirties*, London 1992.

**Art Nouveau**. The name of a shop opened in Paris in 1895 to sell objects of modern, i.e. non-period-imitation, style. The movement away from imitation of the past had started in book production and textiles in England in the 1880s (*see* MACKMURDO), and had begun to invade furniture and other furnishings about 1890. Stylistically, the origins lay in the designs of William MORRIS and the English ARTS AND CRAFTS. One of the principal centres from 1892 onwards was Brussels (*see* HANKAR; HORTA; van de VELDE). In France the two centres were Nancy, where in Emile Gallé's glass Art Nouveau forms occurred as early as the 1880s, and Paris, e.g. GUIMARD, JOURDAIN. Art Nouveau forms are characterized by the ubiquitous use of undulation like waves or flames or flower stalks or flowing hair. Some artists kept close to nature, others, especially van de Velde, preferred abstract forms as being a purer expression of the dynamics aimed at. The most important representatives of Art Nouveau are: in America, Louis C. Tiffany (1848–1933) and SULLIVAN in the interior of the Auditorium Building, Chicago, and elsewhere; in Germany (where it is called *Jugendstil*), Hermann Obrist (1863–1927) and August Endell (1871–1925), whose Elvira Studio, Munich (1897–8), was notable; in Austria, HOFFMANN and OLBRICH, who designed the Sezession Building in Vienna; and in Italy (where it is called *Stile Liberty* or *floreale*), Raimondo d'Aronco (1857–1932), Ernesto Basile (1857–1932) and SOMMARUGA. In architecture by far the greatest is GAUDÍ. It has rightly been pointed out that Art Nouveau has a source and certainly a parallel in the paintings and graphic work of Gauguin, Munch, and some others. The climax in Britain, and at the same time the beginning of the end, is the work of Charles R. MACKINTOSH of Glasgow, in whose architecture and decoration the slender curves and the subtle opalescent colours of Art Nouveau blend with a new rectangular crispness and pure whiteness of framework. Vienna took this up at once, and found from it the way into the C20 emphasis on the square and the cube (*see* LOOS; HOFFMANN; LECHNER).

Nicoletti 1978; Loyer 1979; F. Russell, *A.N. Architecture*, London 1979; E. A. Borisowa and G. J. Sternin, *Jugendstil in Russland . . .*, Stuttgart 1988; F. Dierkens and J. Vandenbreelen, *A.N. in Belgium, Architecture and Interior Design*, Tielt 1991; J. Shimonura, *A.N. Architecture. Residential Masterpieces*, London 1992.

**Artesonado**. Spanish term for wooden coffered ceilings and doors richly decorated in MUDÉJAR style with inlaid geometrical patterns. The finest examples are C15–16 (throne room, Aljafería, Saragossa, and Alhambra, Granada). From Spain it was transmitted to South America. The term is, however, loosely applied in Spain to various types of wooden ceilings and panelling.

**Arts and Crafts**. A late CI9 English movement to revive handicrafts and reform architecture by using traditional building crafts and local materials (*see* VERNACULAR ARCHITECTURE). It was born in the wake of the 1851 Great Exhibition in London and in opposition to the machine-made furnishings etc. made possible by the Industrial Revolution. Inspired by RUSKIN and MORRIS, it may be said to have started when Morris met Philip WEBB in 1856, though DEVEY had anticipated it architecturally at Penshurst, Kent, in 1850. In 1859–60 Webb built for Morris his famous Red House, Bexley Heath, Kent, which exemplified the aims of the movement – informality, modesty, structural integrity, etc. Webb was followed by Norman SHAW and Eden NESFIELD and the movement culminated with ASHBEE, LETHABY, VOYSEY and the early LUTYENS, though others should be mentioned, notably Ernest Newton (1856–1922) and his Lethaby-influenced houses (Redcourt, Haslemere, Surrey, 1895); Edward Schroeder Prior (1852–1932) and his butterfly-plan houses (The Barn, Exmouth, Devon, 1896–9); Halsey Ricardo (1854–1928) and his colourful, tile-covered houses (8 Addison Road, London, 1905–7); M. Hugh Baillie Scott (1865–1945) and his rough-cast and open-planned houses with inglenooks etc. inside (Blackwell School, Bowness-on-Windermere, Cumbria, 1900); and, in Scotland, Robert LORIMER and George Walton (1867–1933), an associate of MACKINTOSH. His The Leys, Elstree, Hertfordshire, of 1901 should be mentioned.

Gardens of the type advocated by William Robinson and Gertrude JEKYLL, with an abundance of free-growing 'old-fashioned' flowering plants – with no carpet-bedding and no exotics – provided the perfect setting for such houses. The movement also played a notable part in early GARDEN CITIES AND GARDEN SUBURBS with Shaw's Bedford Park, London (1877), and the work of Voysey there and of Baillie Scott at Hampstead Garden Suburb and of UNWIN's partner Raymond Barry Parker (1867–1941) at Letchworth Garden City.

The movement contributed notably to church building with Lethaby's All Saints, Brockhampton, Herefordshire (1900–1902), and Prior's St Andrew, Roker, Durham (1906–7). More typically Arts and Crafts are Holy Trinity, Sloane Street, London (1888), by John Dando Sedding (1838–91), and St Cyprian's, Clarence Gate, London (1902–3), by COMPER.

In England the movement declined after 1900 but it was influential in Europe, mainly in Germany through Hermann Muthesius (1861–1927), whose *Das englische Haus* (1904–5) is a classic and whose Haus Freudenberg, Berlin (1907–8), outdoes Baillie Scott; and through the DEUTSCHER WERKBUND, thus influencing BEHRENS, OLBRICH, and the early BAUHAUS. In the USA the movement's influence was felt as early as the 1870s with RICHARDSON, but its outstanding exponent was Frank Lloyd WRIGHT, founder member of the Chicago Arts and Crafts Society in 1897. McKIM and WHITE and also George Washington Maher (1864–1926) should also be mentioned, as well as, on the west coast, GREENE & GREENE and even perhaps MAYBECK, Julia MORGAN and John Galen Howard (1864–1931), whose School of Architecture for UCLA at Berkeley, California, and shingle style houses are notable.

J. D. Kornwolf, *M.H. Baillie Scott and*

*the A. and C. Movement*, Baltimore and London 1972; M. Richardson, *Architects of the A. and C. Movement*, London 1981; D. Hawkes, *Modern Country Homes in England: The A. and C. Architecture of Barry Parker*, London 1986; W. Kaplan, *'The Art that is Life': The A. and C. Movement in America 1875–1920*, Boston 1987; P. Stansky, *Redesigning the World: William Morris, the 1880s and the A. and C.*, Princeton 1988; E. Cumming and W. Kaplan, *The A. and C. Movement*, London 1991; P. Davey, *A. and C. Architecture*, London 1994; D. Haigh, *Baillie Scott. The Artistic House*, London 1995; I. Anscombe, *A. and C. Style*, London 1996; Winter 1997.

**Arup**, Ove (1895–1988). English architect trained in engineering in Germany and Denmark. He was engaged first in civil engineering and became involved in architecture in 1936–9 when working in London with TECTON, with whom he pioneered new ideas in concrete construction (e.g. the Penguin Pool, London Zoo). In 1946 he was involved with the ARCHITECTS' CO-PARTNERSHIP at the Brynmawr Rubber Factory. From 1949 his consulting practice became known for its fresh approach to difficult structural problems and collaborated with leading architects, e.g. the SMITHSONS' Secondary Modern School, Hunstanton (1950–51), Norfolk. In 1963 a partnership of architects and engineers, including Peter RICE, was formed and called Arup Associates. This multi-professional team was responsible for Point Royal, Bracknell, Berkshire (1964), new buildings for Corpus Christi College, Cambridge (1965–71), Somerville College, Oxford (1965–75), Gateway House, Basingstoke, Hampshire (1973–6), with notable landscaping, and the aluminium-clad Festival Hall, Liverpool (1982–4). Among Arup's own works of these years the trimly elegant Kingsgate Footbridge,

Durham (1967), the Runnymede Bridge, Surrey (1978), and the Kylesku Bridge, Scotland (1984), were notable. As consultants Arup Associates were involved in UTZON's Sydney Opera House, FOSTER's Hongkong and Shanghai Bank, Hongkong, PIANO and ROGERS' Centre Pompidou, Paris, and GRIMSHAW's Eurostar Railway Terminal, Waterloo Station, London. They designed a number of notable High Tech buildings, e.g. Lloyds' offices, Chatham, Kent (1983), and the Broadgate Development, London (first phase 1984–8, second phase 1988–91), for which they were responsible for the overall planning as well, as they were also for Stockley Park, Heathrow, near London (1985), the most ambitious English BUSINESS PARK so far.

M. Brawne, *A. Associates*, London 1983; P. Rice, *An Engineer Imagines*, London 1994; D. Sommer *et al.*, *O.A. and Partners. Engineering and the Built Environment*, Basel 1994.

**Asam**, Cosmas Damian (1686–1739) and Egid Quirin (1692–1750). German architects, brothers who always worked together as architects though sometimes separately as decorators (Cosmas Damian was a fresco-painter and Egid Quirin a sculptor). Sons of a Bavarian painter, they did not emerge from provincial obscurity until after visiting Rome (1712–14). As a result of this Roman training they remained essentially Baroque rather than Rococo architects. They seem to have admired the juicier C17 Italians rather than their elegant and frivolous contemporaries. They decorated many important churches (e.g. Michelfeld; Einsiedeln, 1727; St Jacobi, Innsbruck; Osterhofen; Freising Cathedral, 1723–4; St Maria Victoria, Ingolstadt; Aldersbach), but designed and built only four, in which, however, they carried to unprecedented lengths the melodramatic effects of concealed lighting, spatial illusionism, and other tricks which they had picked up in Rome. Their emotionalism is seen at its wildest in the fantastic *tableau vivant* altarpieces at Rohr (1717–23) and Weltenburg (1716–35). They attempted something better in St John Nepomuk, Munich (1735–8), a church which is attached to their house and was entirely paid for by them. This is a tiny but sensational church, a masterpiece of German Baroque in which architecture and decoration are successfully combined to achieve an intense atmosphere of religious fervour. Their last work, the Ursulinenkirche, Straubing (1738–40), is almost equally good.

Hitchcock 1968; B. Rupprecht, *Die Brüder A. Sinn und Sinnlichkeit in bayerischen Barock*, Regensburg 1980; K. Harries, *The Bavarian Rococo Church*, New Haven/London 1983; B. Bushart and B. Rupprecht (eds.), *C.D.A. Leben und Werk*, Munich 1986; H. J. Sauermost, *Die A. als Architekten*, Munich 1986.

**Asbestos**. An incombustible chemical-resistant fibrous mineral; a form of impure magnesium silicate. By the 1870s fire-resistant fabrics were being woven with it and its use, in combination with cement, as a building material followed, especially for fire-proofing, electrical insulation, etc. In 1900 Ludwig Hatschek produced the first asbestos-cement sheets, which were being manufactured on a large scale by 1910. Corrugated roofing sheets were in use during the First World War. The first asbestos-cement pipes were made in England in 1927. Recently the use of asbestos has been limited by its proven health hazard (mesothelioma being caused by asbestos exposure) and it has now been largely superseded, e.g. by glass-reinforced concrete.

**Ashbee**, Charles Robert (1863–1942). More a social reformer than an architect.

His model was MORRIS and he became a leading member of the ARTS AND CRAFTS movement. In 1888 he founded his Guild and School of Handicraft in the East End of London. The guild moved into the country, to Chipping Campden in Gloucestershire, in 1902. The First World War killed it. His best architectural designs were for houses in Cheyne Walk, London – Nos. 72–3 (1897, destroyed in the Second World War) and Nos. 38 and 39 (1899–1901). As adviser to the Military Governor in Palestine from 1918 he was instrumental in preserving the visual integrity of Jerusalem. *See also* ISRAELI ARCHITECTURE.

A. Crawford, *C.R.A.*, London 1985.

**Ashlar**. Hewn blocks of masonry wrought to even faces and square edges and laid in horizontal courses with vertical joints, as opposed to rubble or unhewn stone straight from the quarry. It was in use in Ancient Egypt by 3,000 BC.

**Ashlar piece**, *see* ROOF.

**Aslin**, Charles Herbert (1893–1959), *see* INDUSTRIALIZED BUILDING.

**Asphalt**. A mixture of BITUMEN and sand, clay or other minerals such as limestone. It melts and flows stiffly when heated and sets hard. Used for roofing, waterproofing, for damp-courses, etc., or for paving streets, walks, etc.

**Asplund**, Gunnar Erik (1885–1940). The most important Swedish architect of the C20, he collaborated with LEWERENTZ as a landscape architect from 1915 onwards at the Woodlands Cemetery, Stockholm, where his Woodlands Chapel of 1918–20 is remarkable in fusing classicism with northern vernacular architecture. His principal work, in the Scandinavian classical style first developed by the Danes, was the Stockholm City Library (1920–28) with its high circular reading room rising as a drum above the rest of the *ensemble*. With his work for the Stockholm Exhibition of 1930 he changed to the Central European Modern, but instead of treating it in the relatively massive manner then current, he lightened up his forms by means of thin metal members, much glass, and some freer forms of roof, etc., thereby endowing the style with a grace and translucency which had a great international impact. But Asplund was never demonstrative or aggressive. His buildings always observe a noble restraint. The finest of them are the extension of the Town Hall of Göteborg (1934–7), with its beautifully transparent courtyard, and the Woodlands Crematorium, Stockholm (1935–40), which may well be called the most perfect example of genuine C20 monumentality and religious architecture in existence.

C. Caldenby and O. Hultin, *A. 1885–1940*, New York 1985; D. Cruikshank (ed.), *G.A.*, London 1988; C. St John-Wilson, *G.A. Architect 1885–1940. The Dilemma of Classicism*, London 1988; C. Constant, *The Woodland Cemetery. Towards a Spiritual Landscape*, Stockholm 1994.

**Asprucci**, Antonio (1723–1808). A notable early neo-classical architect in Rome. His masterpiece is the interior of Villa Borghese, Rome (1782 onwards), and the elegant temples, sham ruins, and other follies in the park, where he was succeeded by Luigi Canina (1795–1856).

M. Chiarini in *DBI* 1962.

**Assyrian architecture**, *see* SUMERIAN AND AKKADIAN ARCHITECTURE.

**Astragal**. 1. A small half-round moulding, often decorated with a bead and reel enrichment. 2. In the USA and Scotland, a glazing bar. 3. A strip of wood or metal along the edge of a door to cover the gap between it and the door frame, to reduce noise and draughts. *See* Figs. 7, 51.

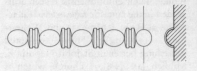

Fig. 7 Astragal

**Asturian architecture**, *see* SPANISH ARCHITECTURE.

**Astylar**. A term applied to a façade without columns or pilasters.

**Atelier 5**, *see* SWISS ARCHITECTURE.

**Atlantes**. Supports in the form of carved male figures, used especially by German Baroque architects instead of columns to support an ENTABLATURE. The Roman term is *telamones*. *See also* CARYATID.

**Atrium**. 1. In Etruscan and Roman architecture, an inner court open to the sky and surrounded by small rooms covered with tiled roofs sloping inwards to a rectangular opening, e.g. House of the Silver Wedding, Pompeii. 2. In Early Christian and medieval architecture, an open court in front of a church, usually a colonnaded quadrangle, e.g. S. Ambrogio, Milan, *c.*1080–1128. 3. In Renaissance architecture, an entrance hall. 4. In late C19 and C20 architecture, a covered courtyard within or between buildings, usually on several levels and often acting as a central light-well and communal area or concourse, e.g. George Herbert Wyman's Bradbury Building, Los Angeles, 1893. Since the 1960s atriums have proliferated following ROCHE's Ford Foundation Headquarters, New York (1963–8), and PORTMAN's Hyatt Regency Hotel, Atlanta, Georgia (1987). The latter has a spectacularly high, skylighted atrium with interior exposed elevators in glass shafts overlooking a garden-like space with sidewalk café, coffee-shop and lounges providing the animation and movement of an open-air plaza.

W. Blaser, *A. 5,000 Years of Open Courts*, Basel 1985; R. Saxon, *The A. Comes of Age*, London 1994.

**Attached column**, *see* ENGAGED COLUMN.

**Attic base**. The base of an IONIC column consisting of two large rings of convex mouldings (the lower of greater diameter) joined by a spreading concave moulding, used in Athens in the C5 and C4 BC.

**Attic storey**. 1. A storey above the ENTABLATURE or main cornice of a building and in strictly architectural relation to it, as, e.g., in Roman TRIUMPHAL ARCHES. 2. Also, more loosely, the space within the sloping roof of a house or the upper storey of a building if less high than the others, i.e. a GARRET.

**Atwood**, Charles B. (1849–95), *see* BURNHAM, Daniel Hudson.

**Aubert**, Jean (d.1741). French architect who began under Jules HARDOUIN-MANSART, then became Court Architect to the Duc de Bourbon-Condé for whom he worked at the Palais Bourbon, Paris (1722–9, demolished), and at Chantilly. His stables (planned 1719, built 1721–35) and interior decoration at the Petit Château, Chantilly (finished 1722), are outstanding, as is his Hôtel de Biron, Paris (1728–30, now the Musée Rodin), and the interior decoration at the Hôtel de Lassay (after 1725). They epitomize the Régence Style.

Kalnein 1995.

**Auditorium**. 1. A room for an audience, as in a theatre. 2. A building for public meetings or theatrical performances, e.g. SULLIVAN's Auditorium Building, Chicago.

**Aula**. In Ancient Roman architecture a court or hall, especially an open court attached to a house. The term is sometimes used for a hall or meeting-place in later architecture, especially in university and other educational buildings.

**Aulenti**, Gae (b.1927). Italian architect who made her name internationally with her transformation of the Gare d'Orsay, Paris, into a museum (1982–5) and her Italian pavilion for Expo '92 in Seville.

**Aumbry** or **ambry**. A cupboard or recess used to keep sacred vessels in.

**Austin**, Henry (1804–91), *see* UNITED STATES ARCHITECTURE.

**Australian architecture** of the colonial period (1788–1850) is an extension of English Georgian architecture in its imperial phase. The first leading architects were Francis Howard GREENWAY in New South Wales and John Lee Archer (1791–1852), who had been trained by John RENNIE, in Tasmania. Archer's St John's Church in Hobart was completed in 1835. John Verge (1782–1861) built some of the best country and town houses, notably Camden Park, New South Wales (1831), and Elizabeth Bay House, Sydney (1832), with a fine elliptical staircase and hall.

Climate, the abundance of land, the availability of convict labour to work in stone, and the taste of military officers, many of whom had served in India and became settlers, favoured the rise of spacious single-storey residences and indeed mansions (Panshanger, Tasmania, of c.1838, architect unknown, is a good example), often with wide verandas, thus making possible a characteristic integration of the roof with the Doric columnar support.

In public architecture the purposes and the needs of a penal colony determined the priority of types: barracks, churches, gaols, court houses, hospitals, customs houses, naval docks and warehouses were built handsomely to the taste of the governing class with convict labour and skills. The ruins of Port Arthur, Tasmania, in an isolated coastal setting, provide a spectacle of penal architecture unrivalled elsewhere.

During this Indian summer of the Georgian Rule of Taste the first examples of neo-Gothic were comparatively severe. The popularity of verandas led to a demand for ornamental ironwork, imported at first mainly for town houses, and the development of local manufactures, culminating in the exceptionally rich ironwork of the Victorian period.

Apart from the siting of public buildings and some grid-planning in the central areas, urban development clung to the line of the main highways, still a characteristic of smaller Australian towns. A landmark in the history of town planning is Adelaide, laid out by Colonel Light from 1837. The idea of a green belt for new towns had been recently advocated by T. J. Mazlen (1832) and others in England, but Light was the first to carry it out on a spacious scale on all sides, averaging a mile in depth. By exploiting the course of the Torrens River and reserving the heights of North Adelaide and the opposing North Terrace of the city for the residences of the gentry, he achieved a plan which rivals Edinburgh New Town in its feeling for landscape.

The beginning of the Victorian period (1851–1900) coincided with the discovery of gold and the rapid expansion of pastoralism. The new optimism is expressed in government buildings, cathedrals, banks, and a spate of civic and municipal town halls with impressive porticos and high towers. Government House in Melbourne (1872–6), by William Wardell (1823–99), who also designed the large St Patrick's Cathedral (begun 1863), was based on the plan of Osborne House on the Isle of Wight. The high tower derives from the Capitol in Rome. The Anglican cathedral of St Paul's was designed after 1877 by William BUTTERFIELD in England; some changes were made and the spires are later, but the interior with its use of coloured marble is highly original. The dome of the Law Courts in Melbourne (1877–82) is modelled on GANDON's Four Courts in Dublin. The Catholic cathedral of Adelaide, St Francis Xavier's (begun 1870 and still unfinished), reputedly goes back to a design by PUGIN. (It was built to a design by his son E. W. Pugin.)

In Sydney the dominant Victorian architect was Edmund Blacket (1817–83) whose Sydney University (1854–60) is Gothic in style but Palladian in plan. The opulence of the period is best studied in the town and country houses, built for the leading squatting families.

The collapse of the Land Boom in 1892–3, the two world wars, and the intervening Depression slowed down the building mania. A COLONIAL REVIVAL began in Sydney c.1910 with William Hardy Wilson (1881–1955), whose Eryldene, Gordon (1913–14), is typical of the late Georgian style he emulated, with columnar verandas and sash-windows with shutters and fanlights. Later the growth of American influence led to the award by competition for the plan of Canberra to Walter Burley GRIFFIN, formerly with Frank Lloyd WRIGHT in Chicago, who arrived in 1913 and remained until 1935. By allowing no building on the surrounding hills and by spaciously separating the centres of civic growth, he achieved a grandiose landscape plan on which geometry is imposed but splendidly relieved by the irregular and dominant lake in the centre. Also notable are Griffin's Capitol Theatre in

Melbourne (1921–4) and Castlecrag housing, Sydney (1921–35).

A breakthrough for the modern school of architects, hitherto hampered by the conservatism of government and commercial patronage, was the Academy of Science, Canberra (1958–9), by Sir Roy Grounds (1905–81). Grounds was subsequently appointed the architect of the National Gallery of Victoria (1962–7) and the Victorian Arts Centre in Melbourne (1961–85). In Sydney, Harry Seidler (b.1923), who had studied under GROPIUS at Harvard and came to Australia in 1948, has had an extensive industrial and commercial practice; the Australia Square Tower (1967), financed by private enterprise, is a handsome and conspicuous civic landmark. His Australian Embassy in Paris (1977–9) is also notable. In Melbourne the 1970s Collins Place development has two tower blocks by I. M. PEI. More recently, the Australian architect John ANDREWS, after making a reputation in Canada and the USA, has worked extensively in Canberra (student residences for the National University, 1971–4, and for the College of Advanced Education, 1973–5), in Sydney (Hooker Tower, 1971–4, and American Express Tower, 1976) and in Brisbane (Chemical Engineering building, University of Queensland, 1973–5). In Canberra the New Parliament House (1980–88) was designed by the 'Philadelphia School' Romualdo GIURGOLA.

Though small-scale, the work of Glen MURCUTT is outstanding for its combination of Miesian clarity and other qualities of Modernism with the revival of traditional Australian corrugated-iron construction, e.g. Magney House, Bingie Point, Moruya, New South Wales (1983–4). Likewise notable in their disdain for 'good taste' are Edmond & Corrigan (Maggie Edmond, b.1946; Peter Corrigan, b.1941), e.g. their additions to Keysborough parish, Melbourne (1975–81), and their recent extension to the Institute of Technology, Melbourne (1994). The most famous modern building in Australia is, of course, the Sydney Opera House by UTZON (with Ove ARUP), who won the competition in 1957. The circumstances leading to his resignation or dismissal occasioned a *cause célèbre* in which he was supported by almost the entire architectural profession in Australia. Although not finished to his design, it illustrates splendidly the triumph of an idea over practical, political and bureaucratic difficulties, and has become one of the rare buildings to capture the popular imagination. [J. Burke]

**Austrian architecture**. Austria originated in the Ostmark (Eastern Marches) established in 803 by Charlemagne after he had subdued the Bavarians in 788. When the Hungarian invasion had been halted (955), the Ostmark was renewed and remained in the hands of the Babenberg dynasty from 976 to 1246. After that Austria passed to the Habsburgs. The archbishopric of Salzburg was created in 789; additional bishoprics came much later: Gurk in 1070, Seckau in 1218, and Vienna only in 1480.

Of pre-Romanesque architecture in Austria little is known. Salzburg Cathedral (767–74) was, according to excavations, nearly 61 m. (200 ft) long and had a straightforward Early Christian basilica plan with one apse. Romanesque buildings are in an interesting mixture of elements from Bavaria and Lombardy, although West Germany (especially Hirsau, the centre of Cluniac architecture for Germany) and even France also play a part. Bavarian influence means basilican churches with pillars (Hirsau stood for columns – see St Paul im Lavanttal in Austria), no transepts, and three parallel apses, while Lombardy was the source of much of the best decoration; it is to be found at Klosterneuburg (1114–33), Gurk (1140s–c.1200; crypt of a hundred marble columns), Millstatt, and even the portal of St Peter at Salzburg (c.1240). Another source of ornament was Normandy (zigzag, etc.) via Worms, Bamberg and Regensburg – see St Stephen, Vienna; St Pölten; and the Karner at Tulln. Karners are charnel-houses with chapels, centrally planned, and they are an Austrian speciality. The largest church of the C12 was Salzburg Cathedral as rebuilt in 1181 onwards. It was as long as Old St Peter's in Rome, and had double aisles, round towers over apses in the end walls of the transepts, two (older) west towers, and an octagonal crossing tower.

Cistercian colonization was actively pursued in Austria, and Viktring (built 1142–1202) is indeed an early and faithful follower of Fontenay, the earliest preserved house in France; it has, for example, the pointed tunnel vaults of Fontenay. On the other hand Heiligenkreuz (begun c.1150–60) has rib vaults with heavy square ribs, a Lombard characteristic. Heiligenkreuz received a choir in 1295, of the hall type. This is of course fully Gothic, and HALL CHURCHES are characteristic of the German Late Gothic. The hall choir was suggested by an earlier Cistercian hall choir in Austria: Lilienfeld (1202–30), also nearly entirely Gothic. This is an extremely early case of the hall elevation and one which established Austria as one of the sources of German hall churches. Zwettl, also Cistercian, received its splendid hall choir with ambulatory and low radiating chapels much later (1343–83). From here influences again reached out to south and south-west Germany. The friars, the most active order of the later C13 and the C14, went in for halls too.

The principal achievement of the C14 and C15 is of course St Stephen in Vienna,

not a cathedral originally. The hall chancel is of 1304–40, the glorious south tower of 1359–1433. Connections in the early C14 were principally with Bohemia (Vienna) and Bavaria (Franciscan church, Salzburg, begun 1408; by Hans STET-HAIMER). Developments in architecture in the later C15 and early C16 were as great and important as they were in sculpture: intricate vaults, with star, net, and even rosette motifs, are characteristic, and culminate in the stucco ribs with vegetable details of Laas (c.1515–20) and Kötschach (1518–27) in Carinthia. Supports may be twisted piers (Salzburg Castle, 1502) or even tree-trunk piers (Bechyně Castle, across the Bohemian border). The first notable secular buildings are also of these late years: the Bummerlhaus at Steyr (1497), the Goldenes Dachl at Innsbruck (completed 1500), and the Kornmesserhaus at Bruck on the Mur (1499–1505). The arcading here suggests Venetian influence.

But Italian influence was very soon to mean something quite different from the Gothic of the Kornmesserhaus. The portal of the Salvator Chapel in Vienna of just after 1515 is entirely Lombard Renaissance and must be the work of a sculptor from there. Similar works, especially funerary monuments, picked up the new forms at once. In architecture the next examples are the portal of the Arsenal at Wiener Neustadt (1524) and the elegant courtyard of the Portia Palace at Spittal (c.1540); comparison with the much heavier courtyard of the Landhaus at Graz (1556–65; by Domenico dell'Allio, d.1563) shows a characteristic development. The stage after this is represented by the courtyard of the Schalla-burg near Melk (1572–1600) with caryatids, etc. – what would in Britain be called Elizabethan. On the whole, Austria is less rich in first-rate Renaissance buildings than Bohemia. The Hofkirche at

Innsbruck (1553–63) is a Gothic hall, though with slender columns instead of piers. The only fully Italian building in the ecclesiastical field is Salzburg Cathedral, by Santino SOLARI, with two west towers and a crossing dome, and this is of 1614–28. The cathedral, the Archiepiscopal Palace and the Franciscan church show a very complete development of Italianate C17 stucco decoration.

In Vienna a remarkable number of churches were built and rebuilt, but they appear minor when one measures them by the achievements of the Austrian Baroque of c.1690–1730. The great names are first the theatrical designer and engineer Lodovico Burnacini (1636–1707), who designed the wildly Baroque Trinity Monument on the Graben in 1687; then Domenico MARTINELLI of the two Liechtenstein palaces of c.1700; and then FISCHER VON ERLACH and HILDEBRANDT. Little need be said about them here – of Fischer's brilliant centralizing church plans at Salzburg (Trinity, 1694–1702; Collegiate, 1694–1707), heralded by those of G. ZUCCALLI of 1685; of his Karlskirche in Vienna with its fantastic Trajan's Columns; of his restrained and courtly decoration; and of Hildebrandt's brilliant spatial interlocking and his fiery decoration (Upper Belvedere, Vienna, 1714–24). Meanwhile the great abbeys in the country were as busy rebuilding as the towns and the nobility: Melk (1702–14; by PRANDTAUER); St Florian (1686–1705; by CARLONE and then Prandtauer); Göttweig (begun 1719; by Hildebrandt); Klosterneuburg (begun 1730; by Donato Felice d'Allio (c.1677–1761)). Particularly splendid are the libraries in the abbeys (Altenburg, 1740; Admont, c.1745).

The Louis XVI or Robert ADAM style of the later C18 is represented in Vienna by the Academy of the Sciences (1753; by JADOT DE VILLE ISSY) and the Josephinum (1783; by Isidore Canevale (1730–86)). The Gloriette, a large-scale eye-catcher in the park of Schönbrunn by Johann Ferdinand von Hohenburg (1732–1816), is, in spite of its early date (1775), in a neo-Cinquecento style. Neo-Grecian at its most severe are the Theseustempel (1820–23) and the Burgtor (1824), both by NOBILE (the latter originally designed by CAGNOLA).

C19 historicism is in full swing with the perfectly preserved Anif Castle near Salzburg (begun 1838), the church of Altlerchenfeld, Vienna (1848–61), by Eduard van der Nüll (1812–68), in neo-Romanesque, and the Arsenal (1849–56) by Christian Friedrich Ludwig von Förster (1797–1863) and others, also in a neo-Romanesque style. Shortly after, Vienna established herself as one of the centres of historicism on a grand scale with the abolition of the fortress walls of inner Vienna and the making of the Ringstrasse (begun 1859). Along this wide green belt a number of majestic public buildings were erected in various period styles: the Votivkirche (begun 1856) by Heinrich von Ferstel (1828–83), in Gothic; the Opera (begun 1861) by van der Nüll and August Siccard von Siccardsburg (1813–68), in free Renaissance; the Town Hall (1872–83) by Friedrich von Schmidt (1825–91) in symmetrical Gothic; the Museums (begun 1872) by SEMPER and Karl von Hasenauer (1833–94), in Renaissance to Baroque; the Academy (begun 1872–3; by Theophil von HANSEN), in Renaissance; the Parliament (begun 1873, also by von Hansen), in pure Grecian; the Burgtheater (begun 1873; again by Semper and Hasenauer) in Renaissance; the University (by Ferstel) in a mixed Italian and French C16 style; and, finally, the Neue Hofburg (1872 and 1881 onwards; by Semper and Hasenauer), again in Renaissance. There are also large blocks of flats in the monumental, strung-out composition.

Vienna was one of the most important centres in the world when it came to abandoning historicism and creating a new idiom for the C20. The leaders were Otto WAGNER, whose Postal Savings Bank (1904) is remarkably fresh and enterprising, his pupil OLBRICH, whose Secession (1898) blazed the trail – though more towards ART NOUVEAU than towards the C20 – and the two even younger men, HOFFMANN and LOOS, whose domestic work was almost equalled by that of Josef Frank (1885–1967), e.g. his Wittbrandgasse house, Vienna (1913–14). When the C20 style began to settle down, and be accepted in the mid-twenties, a mild variety of it was applied to the many blocks of working-class flats, some of them vast, which the municipality of Vienna erected, e.g. the Karl-Marx-Hof (1927) by Karl Ehn (1884–1957).

After the Second World War, building recovered slowly but by the mid-1960s Austrian architects had regained their former leading position internationally with Hans HOLLEIN and Gustav Peichl (b.1928), notable for his Austrian State Radio (ORF) studios (1968–81) and enormous Kunsthalle at Bonn (1985–92), and, more recently, with COOP HIMMELBAU and the Viennese group Haus-Rucker-Co formed in 1967 and active since then also in Düsseldorf and New York. Also notably active in the USA is Raimund Abraham (b.1933). The Yugoslav-born Boris Podrecca (b.1940) made his name internationally with his Basler Insurance Offices, Vienna (1991–3), and the Dirnhirmgasse School, Vienna (1994).

**Avant-corps**. Part of a building projecting prominently from the main block or CORPS DE LOGIS.

**Avenue**. Term of French derivation introduced by EVELYN for: 1. A way of approach or access to a building, usually in the country and marked on either side by regularly planted trees. 2. From the C19, a wide street in a town, with or without trees. *See also* BOULEVARD.

**Averlino**, Antonio, *see* FILARETE.

**Axial plan**. Of a building planned longitudinally or along an axis, i.e. not CENTRALLY PLANNED, e.g. a basilica as opposed to an octagon.

**Axis**. An imaginary straight line about which the earth or any other body rotates; or, in architecture, an imaginary straight line passing centrally through a composition, ground-plan or façade so as to give an impression of balance.

**Axonometric projection**. A geometrical drawing showing a building in three dimensions. The plan is set up truly to a convenient angle, and the verticals projected to scale, with the result that all dimensions on a horizontal plane and all verticals are to scale, but diagonals and curves on a vertical plane are distorted. *See* Fig. 8.

K. Kline, *Projective Geometry*, New York 1956.

**Aymonino**, Carlo (b.1926). Italian architect best known for his city-centre planning: Turin and Bologna (1962); Reggio Emilia (1971); Florence (1978); Terni (1985); Scandicci (1989); San Donà di Piave (1990); via Ostiense, Rome (1991); and for his publications: *Origine e sviluppo della città moderna* (Padua, 1971); *Il significato della città* (Bari 1975); *Piazze d'Italia. Progettare gli spazi aperti* (Milan 1988). His Gallaratese 2 Complex, Milan (1967–73), included a notable apartment building by Aldo ROSSI.

C. Conforti, *C.A. L'architettura non è un mito*, Rome (1980) 1983; P. Eisenman and G. Giucci, *C.A.*, London 1996.

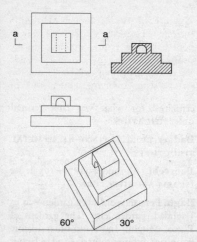

60°   30°

Fig. 8 Axonometric projection Plan;
Section aa; Elevation

**Aztec architecture**, *see* MESOAMERI-
CAN ARCHITECTURE.

**Azulejos**. Glazed pottery TILES usually
painted in bright colours with floral and
other patterns, much used on the outsides
and insides of Spanish, Portuguese and
Central and South American buildings.

**Azuma**, Takamitsu (b.1933). Japanese
architect who began as assistant to
SAKAKURA but developed a self-
consciously individual style of 'oppo-
sitional harmonies', e.g. Satsuki
Kindergarten, Osaka (1969–73). He was
a founder of the ArchiteXt group in 1971
which broke with the METABOLISTS and
argued for discontinuity and contradiction.

Bognar 1985.

# B

**Babylonian architecture**. No notable buildings survive from Babylon's first period of predominance under Hammurabi (*fl.*1792–1750 BC), but from its second so-called neo-Babylonian period of between 612 and 539 BC excavations in Iraq have revealed the city's plan and the foundations of brick-built temples, palaces, fortifications, etc. These include a ZIGGURAT, the biblical Tower of Babel, and sections of the glazed brick processional way and Ishtar Gate, now reconstructed in the Staatliche Museum, Berlin.

**Bacini**. Painted and glazed earthenware plates and bowls of *c.*1200 embedded as decoration on façades and exteriors of Italian Romanesque churches, campanili and occasionally other buildings, e.g. S. Piero in Grado, Pisa; SS. Giovanni e Paolo, Rome.

**Back-to-back housing**. A cost-saving system of building houses in blocks with no space between those facing in opposite directions, much adopted in the industrial towns of C19 Britain. Most have now been demolished.

**Backsteingotik**, *see* GERMAN ARCHITECTURE.

**Bacon**, Henry (1866–1924), *see* UNITED STATES ARCHITECTURE.

**Bacon**, Edmund Norwood (b.1910). American architect and town planner responsible for the post-Second World War development of Philadelphia, 1946–70. His 1963 plan for the City Center was notable. However, as an early exponent of URBAN RENEWAL, he was to be much

criticized for what was later termed GENTRIFICATION.

**Badger**, Daniel D. (1806–84), *see* METAL STRUCTURES.

**Baerveld**, Alexander (1877–1930), *see* ISRAELI ARCHITECTURE.

**Bagh**. Persian word for a garden – as in Baghdad, garden city. The gardens of Persia, Moghul India and other Islamic countries differ both in size and in layout but the term *chahar bagh* defines a single type divided into four quadrants, e.g. that of the Taj Mahal, Agra.

**Baguette** or **bagnette**. A small moulding of semicircular section, like an ASTRAGAL; also a frame with a small BEAD MOULDING.

**Bähr**, Georg (1666–1738). The leading Baroque architect in Dresden, Germany. He began as a carpenter and in 1705 became Ratszimmermeister (master carpenter to the city) in Dresden. But he had already begun to study mechanics (he invented a *camera obscura* and a mechanical organ) and his first building was begun the same year, the parish church of Loschwitz (1705–8) on an elongated octagonal plan. Two Greek cross plan churches followed, at Schmiedeberg (1713–16) and Forchheim (1719–26) both in the Erzegebirge. His masterpiece was the Frauenkirche in Dresden (1722–38: destroyed 1944), by far the grandest Protestant church in Germany. Bähr's first design for it dates from as early as 1722, a Greek cross plan with octagonal galleries, deriving from VISCARDI's Mariahilfkirche at Freystadt (1700–1708). But in 1726 this design was revised in favour of a square ground-plan with a circular arrangement of piers, with angle turrets flanking the dome on all four sides. The dome was also redesigned to increase its height and pitch, thus producing a very bold silhouette. The interior resembled a centrally planned theatre with curving galleries and a richly decorated organ (by Gottfried Silbermann 1732–6) as the main feature. The Dreikönigskirche in Dresden Neustadt (1732–9) originally designed by PÖPPELMANN was supervised by Bähr.

Hempel 1965.

**Bailey**. An open space or court of a stone-built castle; also called a *ward*. *See also* MOTTE-AND-BAILEY.

**Baillairgé**, Thomas (1791–1859), *see* CANADIAN ARCHITECTURE.

**Baillie Scott**, Hugh Mackay (1865–1945), *see* ARTS AND CRAFTS.

**Baird**, John (1798–1859), *see* METAL STRUCTURES.

**Bakema**, Jacob Berend (1914–81). Dutch architect in partnership with Johannes Hendrik van den Broek (1898–1978) from 1948. He became influential for his shopping streets and centres, notably De Lijnbaan, Rotterdam (1949–54), and Amstleven, Amsterdam (1961). Also notable were his Buikslotermeer, Amsterdam (1962), the Rathaus, Terneuser (1963–72), the Netherlands Pavilion 'Osaka Tower' for Expo '70, Osaka, and the Psychiatric Hospital, Middelharnis (1973–4). He published his work with Van den Broek as *Architectengemeenschop van den Broek en Bakema* (Stuttgart (1976) 1981).

G. Gibitosi and A. Izzo, *Van den Broek/B.*, Rome 1976.

**Baker**, Sir Herbert (1862–1946), was born in Kent and remained an English

countryman. Baker's most interesting work belongs to South Africa. He went out early, gained Cecil Rhodes's confidence, and built Groote Schuur for him in 1890 in the traditional Dutch Colonial idiom, and later private houses in Johannesburg, some very successful in an Arts and Crafts way (Stonehouse, 1902). His most prominent buildings were the Government House and Union Buildings in Pretoria (1905 onwards and 1910–13). Side by side with his friend LUTYENS he was called in at New Delhi, and was responsible there for the Secretariat Building (1912 onwards). His style is as imperially classical as Lutyens's but much weaker, less original, and less disciplined. This is especially evident in his later London buildings (Bank of England, 1921; India House, 1925; South Africa House, 1930). He was more at ease where he could use a less elevated style and a great variety of materials. This is why the War Memorial Cloister at Winchester College (1922–4) is one of his most successful buildings. He published *Architecture and Personalities* (1944). See also SOUTH AFRICAN ARCHITECTURE.

D. E. Greig, *H.B. in South Africa*, Cape Town and London 1970; R. G. Irving, *Indian Summer. Lutyens, B. and Imperial Delhi*, London 1981; M. Keath, *H.B. Architecture and Idealism 1892–1913. The South African Years*, Cape Town 1992.

**Balcony**. A platform projecting from a wall, enclosed by a railing or balustrade, supported on brackets or columns or cantilevered out. A small, decorative balcony projecting from a window-sill, sometimes to hold flowerpots, is called a *balconette*.

**Baldachin** or **baldacchino**. A canopy over a throne, altar, doorway, etc. It may be portable, suspended from a ceiling, projecting from a wall or free-standing on columns or other supports. *See also* CIBORIUM.

**Baldessari**, Luciano (1896–1982), *see*
ITALIAN ARCHITECTURE.

**Balinese architecture**, *see* INDONESIAN
ARCHITECTURE.

**Balistraria**. In medieval military architecture, the cross-shaped opening in
BATTLEMENTS and elsewhere for the use
of the crossbow.

**Ballflower**. A globular three-petalled
flower enclosing a small ball; a decoration
in use in the first quarter of the C14. *See*
Fig. 9.

**Balloon framing**. A simplified US version of European timber-frame construction, introduced in Chicago *c.* 1830–35.
It superseded the traditional LOG CABIN.
A skeleton of light machine-cut uprights
or studs is attached to the joists or horizontal members by nails to form a cage
or crate, with clapboard covering also
nailed so that the whole is held together
by nails. The studs run from sill to roof
plate, spaced about 40 cm (16 inches)
apart. The substitution of nails for mortice
and tenon joints, which enabled skilled

Fig. 9 Ballflower

workers to be replaced by unskilled
labourers, depended on the early C19
availability of cheap, mass-produced
machine-made nails. It was an early
form of INDUSTRIALIZED BUILDING, the
standardized parts being assembled on
the site, and became the standard technique in North America for any small
to medium-sized building. It was succeeded by Western or platform framing
in which shorter members were used; *see*
Fig. 10.

Giedion 1962; G. Giordano, *La
moderna tecnica delle costruzioni in legno*,
Milan 1964; Condit 1968.

**Ballu**, Théodore (1817–85). French
architect. His best-known building is
Holy Trinity, Paris (1863–7), a design in
the Early Renaissance of Italy and France.

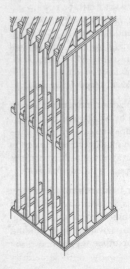
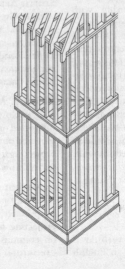

Fig. 10 Balloon frame and
Western or platform frame

He completed GAU's Ste Clotilde, Paris.

M. Decouchy, *T.B.*, Paris 1875; Benevolo 1971.

**Baltard**, Louis-Pierre (1764–1846). French architect. He built the Law Courts at Lyon (1836–41) which, with its long row of giant Corinthian columns, is a belated representative of the Empire style. Baltard taught first at the École Polytechnique, then at the École des Beaux Arts.

**Baltard**, Victor (1805–74), son of Louis-Pierre Baltard. His most famous work was Les Halles, Paris (1854–66, demolished), an important urban development. His church St Augustine (1862–71) is externally a domed building of the Early French Renaissance but internally proclaims its iron construction.

Benevolo 1971.

**Baluster**. A short post or pillar in a series supporting a rail or COPING and thus forming a *balustrade*. See Fig. 109.

**Balustrade**, *see* BALUSTER.

**Band** or **plat band**. An unmoulded, projecting STRING COURSE.

**Banded column**. A column broken by plain or rusticated blocks of stone. *See* RUSTICATED COLUMN.

**Banquette**. 1. In military architecture, a raised way running along the inside of a parapet or bottom of a trench, on which soldiers stand when firing. 2. A raised footpath or sidewalk, e.g. at the side of a bridge, joined to the parapet but above road level. 3. A recessed window-seat or a long low bench against a wall or built into a wall.

**Baptistery**. A room or building for Christian baptismal rites. Pre-Constantinian baptisteries were no more than a room with a tub for immersion, sometimes with a canopy over it, as at Dura-Europos, Syria, of *c*.230. Early Christian baptisteries were usually separate from the church and followed the pattern set by Constantine *c*.315 at the Lateran, Rome, i.e. a small centrally planned building, usually circular or octagonal, with a central FONT and sufficient space around it for officiating clergy, sometimes with an ambulatory and central dome. Notable early examples survive in Italy at Pisa (1153–1265), Parma (1196–1270) and Florence (C11–13).

**Bar tracery**, *see* TRACERY.

**Barabino**, Carlo Francesco (1768–1835), *see* ITALIAN ARCHITECTURE.

**Barbaro**, Daniele (1513–70), *see* PROPORTION.

**Barbican**. An outwork defending the entrance to a castle.

**Barelli**, Agostino (1627–79). Born in Bologna, where he designed the Theatine church of S. Bartolomeo (1653), he later introduced the Italian Baroque style to Bavaria. He designed the Theatine church of St Cajetan, Munich (1663), completed by Enrico ZUCCALLI, on the model of S. Andrea della Valle, Rome. He also built the squarish central block of the electoral palace at Nymphenburg outside Munich (1663), completed by EFFNER in 1717–23.

N. Lieb, *München. Die Geschichte seiner Kunst*, Munich (1971) 1977.

**Bargeboards** or **vergeboards**. Projecting boards placed against the incline of the gable of a building, hiding the ends of the horizontal roof timbers; sometimes decorated. *See* Fig. 11.

**Barlow**, William Henry (1812–1902), *see* ENGLISH ARCHITECTURE.

**Barn**. A covered building for the storage of grain and other agricultural produce. Medieval barns were sometimes

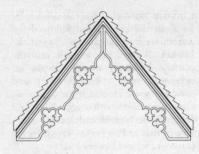

Fig. 11 Bargeboards

extremely large and their enormous roofs of CRUCK CONSTRUCTION gave them considerable architectural distinction. William Morris said the C13 Great Coxwell barn was 'as noble as a cathedral'. The Cholsey barn of *c.*1200 (demolished 1815) was the largest in Europe, the second largest being that at Vaulerand in France. Tithe-barns for the storage of the priest's tithe were a feature of many ecclesiastical estates.

E. Enderby *et al.*, *B. The Art of a Working Building*, London 1992; M. Kirk, *The B. Silent Spaces*, London 1994.

**Barnes**, Edward Larrabee (b.1915). American architect, trained under GROPIUS and BREUER at Harvard. His early work was recognized retrospectively, in the 1980s, as having been germinal in its concern with environment and community, notably his remarkable Haystack Mountain School of Crafts on Deer Island, Maine (1958–62), a seemingly artless composition of shingled cottages dispersed on a dramatic site. He was effective also in urban environments, e.g. New England Merchants National Bank, Boston (1963–70); the Walker Art Center, Minneapolis (1971); the IBM Building, 590 Madison Avenue, New York (1973–83), with its remarkable atrium which created one of the most successful metropolitan public spaces

anywhere. Also notable are his Library, Music and Art Building for the Emma Willard School, Troy, NY (1963–71); his campuses for the State University of New York at Potsdam (1962–78) and Purchase (1966–77); his 599 Lexington Avenue skyscraper, New York (1981–6) and the Dallas Museum of Art, Dallas, Texas (1983).

P. Blake, *E.L.B. Architect*, New York 1994.

**Baroque architecture**. The architecture of the C17 and part of the C18. It is characterized by exuberant decoration, expansive curvaceous forms, a sense of mass, a delight in large-scale and sweeping vistas, and a preference for spatially complex compositions. The term applies fully to the C17 in Italy (notably BERNINI and BORROMINI) and to the C17 and part of the C18 in Austria, Germany and Spain, but with limitations to the C17 in France and the late C17 and early C18 in England. For all these latter cases the term Baroque Classicism has sometimes been adopted to denote that they are instances of the Baroque tempered by classical elements. This is especially evident in England, where the swelling forms of Baroque plans and elevations were never favoured. *See also* ENGLISH ARCHITECTURE; FRENCH ARCHITECTURE; GERMAN ARCHITECTURE; ITALIAN ARCHITECTURE; RUSSIAN ARCHITECTURE; SPANISH ARCHITECTURE.

**Barragán**, Luis (1902–88). Mexican architect and landscape architect who, after travelling in Spain and France, where he attended lectures by Le Corbusier, settled in Mexico City in 1936. His early work combined the severe, geometrical forms he admired in Le Corbusier with Mexican vernacular elements and resulted in an individual style, e.g. his own house in Tacubaya (1947). His later work continued to recall the Mexican *pueblo*, especially in colour and in the settings he created for it, indeed he became almost as much a landscape architect as a designer of buildings, making much use of water and light and lush vegetation to offset the geometrical severity of his strikingly planar architecture. Most of his work is in or on the outskirts of Mexico City, e.g. El Pedregal, where between 1945 and 1950 he transformed a large area of barren lava outcrop into a series of tropical gardens interspersed with forecourts, sheets of water, fountains and ranch-like houses of which the most important volumes are external. Notable examples of his dramatic, highly coloured wall-architecture include the Egerstrom House and Stables, San Cristobal, Los Clubes, Mexico City (1967–8), and the Meyer House, Bosque de Las Lomas, Mexico City (1978–83). The Satellite City Towers (1957 with Mathias Goeritz) should also be mentioned.

Walker and Simo 1994; L. Noelle, *L.B.: Bosquejo y creatividad*, Mexico City 1995; R. Rispa (ed.), *B. The Complete Works*, London 1996.

**Barrel vault**, *see* VAULT.

**Barrett**, Nathan F. (1845–1919), *see* COMPANY TOWN.

**Barrier-free** or **universal design**. Design for handicapped accessibility, considering the needs of those with visual, hearing and mental disabilities as well as those with physical mobility problems, e.g. buildings with alternatives to stepped entrances and internal steps and staircases. It became compulsory by federal law in the USA after 1990.

A. Peloquin, *B.-F. Residential Design*, New York 1994; J. Holmes-Siedle, *B.-F. Design*, London 1996.

**Barrow** and **long barrow**, *see* MEGALITH, TUMULUS.

**Barry**, Sir Charles (1795–1860). The most versatile of the leading Early Victorian architects in England, an excellent planner and an energetic, tough and hardworking man. With some inherited money he travelled in 1817–20 through France, Italy, Greece, Turkey, Egypt and Palestine, studying buildings and doing brilliant sketches. In 1823 he won the competition for St Peter's, Brighton, and then for some years did 'pre-archaeological' Gothic churches, i.e. an inventive rather than a correct interpretation of the style. In 1824 he designed the Royal Institution of Fine Arts in Manchester – Grecian this time – and he followed this up with the Manchester Athenaeum (1836). But the Travellers' Club in London (1829–31) was Quattrocento, and this meant the start of the neo-Renaissance for England. With the Reform Club of 1837 his Renaissance turned Cinquecento, and with Bridgewater House (1847) a free, not to say debased, Cinquecento. This development from the reticent to the spectacular and from low to high relief permeates his work in general – see, now in the northern Renaissance field, the development from Highclere, Hampshire (1837), itself far busier than his early work, to the Halifax Town Hall, West Yorkshire (1859–62), which is asymmetrical and a jumble of motifs. It was completed by Barry's son Edward M. Barry (1830–80), who built the Charing Cross and Cannon Street Hotels, London.

But Sir Charles's *magnum opus* is, of course, the Houses of Parliament, won in competition in 1835–6 and begun in 1839; it was formally opened in 1852. Its ground plan is functionally excellent, its façade to the Thames still symmetrical in the Georgian way, but its skyline completely asymmetrical and exceedingly well balanced with its two contrasting towers and its flèche. Most of the close Perpendicular detail and nearly all the

Barthélèmy, Jacques-Eugène

internal detail is by PUGIN, who was commissioned by Barry for the purpose.

A. Barry, *The Life and Works of Sir C.B.*, London 1867; J. M. Crook and H. M. Port, *The History of the King's Works*, vol. vi, London 1973; H. M. Port, *The Houses of Parliament*, London 1976; Hitchcock 1977; Colvin 1995.

**Barthélèmy**, Jacques-Eugène (1799–1868), *see* FRENCH ARCHITECTURE.

**Bartizan**. A small turret projecting from the angle on the top of a tower or parapet. *See* Fig. 12.

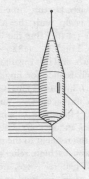

Fig. 12 Bartizan

**Basement**. The lowest storey of a building, usually below or partly below ground level or, if beginning at ground level, of less height than the storey above. It is a living-space, as distinct from a CELLAR.

**Basevi**, George (1794–1845). English architect; he was articled to SOANE and in 1816–19 was in Italy and Greece. His first buildings are Grecian, but his best-known building, the Fitzwilliam Museum at Cambridge (1836–45, completed with some alterations by C. R. COCKERELL in 1845–8), already shows the trend towards classical harmony becoming, with clustered giant columns and a heavy attic, more dramatic and indeed Baroque. It is the same trend which

distinguishes the BEAUX ARTS style in France from the Empire style. Early in his career (*c.*1825), Basevi also designed Belgrave Square (minus the corner mansions), London, and later Thurloe Square (1839–45) and Pelham Crescent and Pelham Place (now Egerton Place) (1833 onwards), London, and a number of country houses in various styles.

Colvin 1995.

**Basile**, Ernesto (1857–1932). Italian ART NOUVEAU architect. His principal works are the Villa Igeia Hotel, Palermo (1901), the Villino Florio, Palermo (1900–1902, destroyed 1962), and the new parliament building in Rome (1902–26), a vast extension to Bernini's Palazzo di Montecitorio.

DBI (1965); Nicoletti 1978.

**Basilica**. An Ancient Roman colonnaded hall for public use (e.g. the basilicas of Trajan and Augustus, Rome; the basilica of Constantine, Trier, Germany, survives almost intact), later adopted as a building type for EARLY CHRISTIAN churches. The term indicated function and not form, but Ancient Roman basilicas were often oblong buildings with aisles and galleries and with an apse opposite the entrance which might be through one of the longer or shorter sides. It was from public buildings of this type that Early Christian churches evolved (not from pagan religious architecture) and by the C4 they had acquired their essential characteristics: oblong plan; longitudinal axis; a timber roof, either open or concealed by a flat ceiling; a termination, either rectangular or in the form of an apse; and usually a nave with two or more aisles, the former higher and wider than the latter, lit by clerestory windows and with or without a gallery. *See* Fig. 13.

Ward-Perkins 1981; Krautheimer 1986.

**Basket arch**, *see* ARCH.

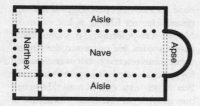

Fig. 13 Basilica

**Bassi**, Martino (1542–91). Milanese architect who succeeded ALESSI at S. Maria presso S. Celso, Milan, and from 1573 onwards rebuilt the Early Christian rotunda, S. Lorenzo, Milan. He became architect at the cathedral, Milan, in 1587. From 1578 he also worked at the Sacro Monte, Varallo.

R. Wittkower, *Gothic v. Classic*, New York 1974; Lotz (1974) 1996.

**Bastard**, John (1688–1770) and William (c.1689–1766). English provincial architects notable for rebuilding the centre of Blandford, Dorset, in a vernacular Baroque style after a fire in 1731.

Summerson 1991; Colvin 1995.

**Bastide**. 1. In France a small fort, sometimes converted later for domestic use in the south of France. 2. In south-west France, a new town, usually fortified, laid out in C13–14 on a regular standardized plan, e.g. Monpaziers and Molière (Dordogne), Villeréal (Lot-et-Garonne).

A. Laurat *et al.*, *B. Villes nouvelles du Moyen-Âge*, Toulouse 1988.

**Bastille**. A tower or bastion of a fortress. The famous prison-fortress in Paris, taken during the Revolution on 14 July 1789, was called the Bastille and the name has since been used generally for a prison.

**Bastion**. A projection at the angle of a fortification, from which the garrison can see and defend the ground before the ramparts.

**Bastle** or **bastel-house**. A defensible farmhouse, accommodating animals on the ground floor, usually vaulted, and human beings above, found along the upland areas of the Scottish border, mostly dating from 1550–1650.

**Bath stone**. Building stone from the oolite formation near Bath but also quarried elsewhere in England and used throughout her architectural history. It is of fine grain, cream in colour; soft when quarried but hardens on exposure.

**Batten**. A light strip of wood used over a seam between boards.

**Batter**. The inclined face of a wall, thicker at the base and sloping towards the top to increase stability.

**Battlement**. A PARAPET with alternating indentations or EMBRASURES and raised portions or *merlons*; also called *crenellation*. See Fig. 14.

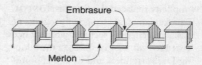

Fig. 14 Battlements

**Baudot**, Anatole de (1834–1915). French architect, a pupil of LABROUSTE and VIOLLET-LE-DUC. His St Jean de Montmartre in Paris (1894–1902) is the first building where all the structural members, including the vaulting ribs, are of exposed reinforced concrete. Yet the character remains Gothic. It can be called the most successful demonstration of the union of old and new advocated by Viollet-le-Duc in his *Entretiens*. Actually reinforced concrete is not strictly correct. The ribs were of bricks pierced with steel rods, the cells of reinforced cement.

Collins 1965; Hitchcock 1977.

**Bauhaus**. The Grand-Duke of Saxe-Weimar had founded a school of arts and crafts at Weimar in 1906. He appointed VAN DE VELDE to the directorship – a very progressive move; for van de Velde believed in teaching in workshops rather than studios. When van de Velde left Germany, he suggested GROPIUS as his successor, and Gropius took over in 1919. He reorganized the school and called it the Bauhaus. According to its first manifesto the school was to teach crafts, and all artists and architects were to work together towards the great goal of 'the building of the future'. The manifesto was enthusiastic in tone and had on its cover an Expressionist vision of a cathedral, a woodcut by Feininger. This first phase of the Bauhaus, inspired by MORRIS, MUTHESIUS and the ARTS AND CRAFTS movement, and sustained by the Expressionist mood of post-war Germany, did not last long. The aim now became industrial design, and stark cubic simplicity replaced the EXPRESSIONISM. This fundamental change of programme was accelerated by lectures which Theo VAN DOESBURG gave in 1922 introducing DE STIJL ideas and by the appointment of László Moholy-Nagy (1895–1946), the theorist and Constructivist designer, in 1923. The result was a memorandum by Gropius issued in 1924 and called *Art and Technology – A New Unity*. However, in the same year, political changes led to the dissolution of the Bauhaus in Weimar. At that moment the Burgomaster of Dessau offered the school a new field of activity. A new building was designed by Gropius and built in 1925–6, one of the paradigmatic masterpieces of the INTERNATIONAL MODERN style. In 1926 the Bauhaus received recognition as the State School of Art of Anhalt. This seemed to secure the future. A department of architecture was established, and Hannes MEYER became its

head. In 1928, Gropius resigned and suggested Hannes Meyer as his successor. Meyer was politically far more radical than Gropius. He organized the department of architecture, but was dismissed for political reasons in 1930. His successor was MIES VAN DER ROHE. However, the growth of National Socialism in Anhalt led to his dismissal and, in 1932, to the closure of the school. Mies tried to carry on in Berlin, converting the school into a private enterprise. But in 1933 that also was closed by the Nazis.

The Bauhaus was the most important school of art of the C20. Its most significant achievement was that to the very end artists and craftsmen, and in the end architects too, worked together. At the start of the Bauhaus the *Vorkurs*, as built up by Johannes Itten, comprised them all. The intention of the *Vorkurs* was to stimulate a theoretically and practically sound sense of form and colour. Later the Bauhaus became the only art school in which designs for industrial products were developed. Moreover, Gropius's own style of architecture became almost automatically a symbol of the programme of the school. But, when all is said, the most impressive fact about the Bauhaus is that Gropius succeeded in keeping together in happy co-operation such dissimilar artists as Kandinsky, Feininger, Klee and Schlemmer.

After 1933 the staff dispersed, nearly all emigrating to the USA and carrying with them the Bauhaus ideals. In 1935 Gropius published *The New Architecture of the Bauhaus*. In 1937 Moholy-Nagy became director of the New Bauhaus in Chicago, which failed. He then set up an independent school of design later renamed the Chicago Institute of Design. In 1951–6 MaxBILL (1908–94) revived the Bauhaus programme at the influential Design School at Ulm.

H. Wingler, *The B.: Weimar, Dessau,*

*Berlin and Chicago*, Cambridge, Mass., 1969; G. Naylor, *The B. Reassessed. Sources and Design Theory*, London 1985; C. Engelmann and C. Schädlich, *Die B.-bauten in Dessau*, Berlin 1991; M. Droste, *B.*, London 1993; E. Firgacs, *The B. Idea and B. Politics*, Budapest 1995.

**Baulk-tie**, *see* ROOF.

**Baumeister**, Richard (1833–97), *see* URBAN DESIGN.

**Bautista**, Francisco (1594–1679). A Spanish Jesuit priest who built churches for his order in Madrid and Toledo. That in Madrid, S. Isidro el Real (1629), based on the plan of the Gesù in Rome, with a somewhat severe façade, is the most interesting. The church had considerable influence in Spain.

Kubler and Soria 1959.

**Bawa**, Geoffrey (b.1919). Sri Lankan architect, trained in London but practising in Colombo. His sensitive adaptation of modern techniques to traditional Sri Lankan architecture characterizes his buildings, often set in lush gardens designed for them, e.g. the Bentota Beach Hotel (1969), the University of Ruhunu, Matara (1980–86), the New Parliament building Sri Jayawardenapura, Kotte (1982), and the Triton Hotel, Ahungalla (1982), all in Sri Lanka.

B. B. Taylor, *G.B.* (Singapore 1986), London 1995.

**Bay**. A vertical division of the exterior or interior of a building marked not by walls but by fenestration, an order, buttresses, units of vaulting, roof compartments, etc.

**Bay leaf garland**. Classical decorative motif used to enrich TORUS mouldings, etc. *See* Fig. 15.

**Bay window**. An angular or curved projection of a house front filled by fenestration. If curved, also called a *bow window*.

Fig. 15 Bay leaf garland

If on an upper floor only, called an *oriel* or *oriel window*.

**Baylis**, Douglas (1916–71). American landscape architect of the CALIFORNIA SCHOOL who promoted its principles in the periodical *Landscape Architecture*. He began with CHURCH and from 1946 was in partnership with his wife. Their more notable works include the Civic Center Plaza and Washington Square, San Francisco; the grounds of IBM Headquarters, San José, California, and the Monterey Freeway, California.

**Bazar**. 1. Persian word for 'market' (*suq* in Arabic), usually an irregular conglomeration of alleys, roofed or covered with awnings (rarely open to the sky), lined with shops and entered through gates that can be closed at night. In most Islamic cities development was haphazard over the centuries. The colonnaded streets of Hellenistic/Roman cities in Anatolia and Syria (e.g. Aleppo) were converted into bazars after the Muslim conquest. Soon after taking Constantinople in 1453 Mehmet II ordered the construction of a bazar of which the central part survives. Bazars were sometimes built in conjunction with MOSQUES and MADRASAS so that the rent paid by the shopkeepers could finance the pious foundations, e.g. complex of Sultan Hasan, Cairo (1356–61). In Central Asia a many-domed structure of austere dignity called a *charsu* (four markets) was devised to cover the crossings, e.g. at Bukhara, Uzbekistan, where three were incorporated in a commercial district which included a CARAVANSERAI and warehouses (1562–87). Similar buildings were erected in Iran, e.g. Kirman (1596–1606), and in India, e.g. Fatehpur Sikri (1573–4). The most imposing bazar is at Isfahan, Iran (1619–20), where a lofty portal consisting of an IWAN flanked by arched galleries on two storeys, encrusted with ceramic tiles, gives access to the royal bazar, a large caravanserai and a 2 km. (1¼ mile) long bazar with a sequence of *charsu*.

M. Scharabi, *Der B.*, Tübingen 1985.

2. In the early C19 the word bazar or bazaar was adopted in the West for markets in which objects were sold to benefit charities, later for any shop selling miscellaneous goods.

**Bazhenov**, Vasily Ivanovich (1738–99). An early neo-classical architect, probably the most visionary Russian architect of any period. He was unlucky in his career, and his genius has to be judged on the basis of only half-a-dozen buildings and several projects. Of humble birth, he began under Ukhtomsky in Moscow and CHEVAKINSKY in St Petersburg, later studying in Paris and Italy (early 1760s). In 1767 Catherine II commissioned him to design a great palace, embracing the existing monuments, in the Moscow Kremlin. It never rose above its massive foundations, but the plans and scale model already show him at his maturity – great Ionic colonnades binding the upper storeys above a severe rustication – and it established his reputation. His next commission was also frustrated – a remodelling of Catherine's palace and park at Tsaritsyno, near Moscow, in a most inventive mock-Gothic (with classical and Old Russian elements not far below the surface). His lesser structures survive, but the palace was dismantled on the verge of completion and the task given to KAZAKOV. Of his other possible essays in Gothic the church at Cherkizovo-Starki is especially interesting for its originality and early date (founded 1759).

Out of court favour, Bazhenov turned to private Moscow patrons: the Pashkov House (1784), the circular bell-tower of the Skorbyashchenskaya church, and the Yushkov House with its dramatic rounded and colonnaded corner. With Paul's accession he produced his last and strangest public assignment: a moated neo-classical fortress, the 'St Michael Castle' in St Petersburg, an uningratiating yet fascinating building (the severity of its forms now somewhat masked with decorative additions by Vincenzo Brenna, 1745–1820). Its large detached pavilions are Bazhenov's final masterpiece. [R. R. Milner-Gulland]

Hamilton 1983.

**BBPR**, *see* ROGERS, Ernesto Nathan.

**Bead and reel**, *see* ASTRAGAL.

**Bead moulding**. A small cylindrical moulding enriched with ornament resembling a string of beads; used in the Romanesque period.

**Beakhead**. A Norman decorative motif consisting of a row of bird, animal or human heads biting a ROLL MOULDING. *See* Fig. 16.

Fig. 16 Beakhead moulding

**Beam**. In roof construction a transverse, horizontal timber (*see* ROOF). In the body of a building a main horizontal timber supporting floor or ceiling JOISTS. A *dragon beam* is set diagonally and projecting at the corner of a building to support the joists of a JETTY on two adjacent sides.

**Beaux Arts style**. A very rich classical style favoured by the École des Beaux Arts, Paris, in late C19 France, e.g. GARNIER's Opéra, Paris (1861–75), and much imitated elsewhere, e.g. Palais de Justice, Brussels, 1866–83, by Joseph Poelaert (1817–79). It was also very influential in the USA, where many of the leading late C19 architects had been trained at the École des Beaux Arts, e.g. HUNT, McKIM, RICHARDSON.

A. Drexler (ed.), *The Architecture of the École des B.A.*, New York 1977; D. D. Egbert, *The B.A. Tradition in French Architecture*, Princeton 1980; Middleton 1982.

**Becerra**, Francisco (*c.*1545–1605), *see* PERUVIAN ARCHITECTURE.

**Beckhard**, Herbert (b.1926), *see* BREUER, Marcel.

**Bed moulding**. A small moulding between the CORONA and the FRIEZE in any ENTABLATURE.

**Beehive house**. A primitive structure, circular in plan and built of rough stones set in projecting courses to form a dome. They are still inhabited in south-east Italy (Apulia), where they are called *trulli*. The finest example of beehive construction is the tomb called the 'Treasury of Atreus' at Mycenae (C13 BC).

**Beer**, Georg (d.1600), *see* SCHICKHARDT, Heinrich.

**Beer**, Michael (d.1666). German architect, born at Au in the Bregenzerwald, the founder of the Vorarlberger school of architects which included, besides the Beer family, the MOSBRUGGER family and the THUMB family. The latter intermarried with the Beer family. The long series of buildings by this school, mostly for Benedictine monasteries in southwest Germany and Switzerland, was eventually to mark the triumph of German over Italian elements in south German Baroque architecture (i.e. over the domination of such Italians as ZUCCALLI and VISCARDI from the Grisons). Michael Beer is known to have worked at the abbey church at Kempten (1652–4) and he was probably responsible for its design, which attempted a fusion of the longitudinal and centralized types of church. It has a curious, large-domed octagon between nave and chancel. His son Franz Beer (1660–1726) became one of the leading architects of the Vorarlberg school. He began at Obermarchtal abbey church, where he and Christian THUMB took over after the death of Michael THUMB in 1690. The influence of the Thumbs is still evident in his next building, Kloster Irsee (1699–1704). But he achieved an individual style and also great elegance and lightness at the abbey church at Rheinau in Switzerland (1704–11), where he emphasized verticality by setting the galleries well back from the pilaster ends of the internal buttresses which typify the Vorarlberg type of church. His style culminated in the Cistercian abbey church of St Urban in the Canton of Lucerne (1711–15) and at the Benedictine abbey church at Weingarten (1715–23), though his responsibility at the latter is uncertain. (He refused to direct the building operations, and the design was probably a collaboration with Johann Jakob Herkommer (1648–1717) and perhaps also Caspar MOSBRUGGER.) In 1717 he reconstructed the Premonstratensian abbey church at Weissenau near Ravensburg. Two plans (unexecuted) for the abbey church at Einsiedeln are attributed to him. His eldest daughter married Peter THUMB. Johann Michael Beer (1696–1780) designed the choir and east façade of the abbey church at St Gallen (1760–69) and Ferdinand Beer (1731–89) designed the administrative block of the monastery at St Gallen.

W. Oechslin (ed.), *Die Vorarlberger*

*Barockbaumeister*, exh. cat. Bregenz 1978; N. Lieb and F. Dieth, *Die Vorarlberger Barock-Baumeister*, Munich and Zürich (1960) 1983.

**Behnisch**, Gunter (b.1922). German architect who made his name with his and Frei OTTO's structures at the Olympiapark, Munich (1967–72). He is notable especially for his numerous and imaginative schools, colourful and relaxed, eminently friendly and welcoming, which range from the Vogelsang-schule, Stuttgart (1959), to the circular Progymnasium 'Auf dem Schäfersfeld', Lorsch (1973); the Kindergarten, Stuttgart-Luginsland (1991); the Geschwester-Scholl School, Frankfurt-am-Main (1993–4); and the St Benno Roman Catholic School, Dresden (1992–6). His playful Hysolar Institute, Stuttgart (1987), was acclaimed by Deconstructivists. More imposing are his Postmuseum, Frankfurt-am-Main (1990); the new Parliament Building, Bonn (1992); the State Insurance Agency, Schleswig-Holstein (LVA), Lübeck (1992–7); and the Central Administrative Building, Landesgirokasse, Stuttgart (1992–7).

J. K. Schmitt and U. Zoller, *B. & Partners. Bauten 1952–1992*, Stuttgart 1994; D. Gauzin-Muller, *B. & Partners. Vom Munchner Olympiapark zum Bonner Parliament*, Stuttgart 1995.

**Behrens**, Peter (1868–1940). German architect and designer who started as a painter but after 1890 was attracted by design and crafts, under the direct or indirect influence of the teachings of MORRIS. He designed typefaces, was one of the founders of the Vereinigte Werkstätten at Munich, and for them designed table glass among other things. In 1899 Ernst Ludwig, Grand Duke of Hesse, called him to Darmstadt (*see* OLBRICH). The house he designed for himself there in 1900–1901 is original, vigorous, and

even ruthless. In 1907 he was among the founders of the DEUTSCHER WERK-BUND, became architect to the AEG in Berlin, and designed for them factories (notably the Berlin turbine building of 1908–9), shops, products, and even stationery. The factories are among the earliest anywhere to be taken seriously architecturally and designed without any recourse to period allusions. For more representational jobs he used a more representational style which has been called a 'scraped classicism' (Haus Wiegand, Berlin-Dahlem, 1911–12; offices in Düsseldorf for Mannesmann, 1911–12; German Embassy, St Petersburg, 1911–12). Around 1910 GROPIUS, LE COR-BUSIER and MIES VAN DER ROHE were all working in his office. After the First World War his style paid tribute first to the then current EXPRESSIONISM (offices for I. G. Farben, Höchst, 1920–24), then to the INTERNATIONAL MODERN (AEG's Berolinahaus and Alexander-haus, Alexanderplatz, Berlin, 1928–31; warehouse for the State Tobacco Administration, Linz, Austria, 1930). In 1925 he designed 'New Ways', 508 Wellingborough Road, Northampton – the earliest example of the C20 style in England. (The house incorporates a room designed by MACKINTOSH in 1907.)

A. Windsor, *P.B. Architect and Designer*, London 1981; T. Buddensieg, *Industriekultur, P.B. and the A.E.G. 1907–1914*, Cambridge, Mass., 1984.

**Bélanger**, François-Joseph (1744–1818). The most elegant Louis XVI architect and a leading French landscape gardener. Trained in Paris, he visited England in 1766. The following year he joined the Menus Plaisirs and in 1777 designed his masterpiece, the exquisite neo-classical Bagatelle in the Bois de Boulogne, Paris, which he built for the king's brother in sixty-four days to win a bet with Marie-

Antoinette. The garden, laid out between 1778 and 1780, was the most famous *jardin anglais* of the period. It was followed in 1784 by the *jardin anglo-chinois* at another of his pavilions, the Folie Saint James at Neuilly, and in 1786 by the last of his great landscape gardens, Méréville. He also designed the exquisite pavilion in the garden of the Hôtel de Brancas, Paris (1771) and some interiors of great elegance, e.g. Hôtel de Mlle Desvieux, Paris (1788). In 1813 he designed a remarkable glass and iron dome for the Halle au Blé in Paris to replace the no less remarkable glass and wood dome of Legrand and Molinos of 1782.

Braham 1980; M. K. Deming, *La Halle au blé de Paris 1762–1813* . . . , Brussels 1984.

**Belcher**, John (1841–1913), *see* ENG-LISH ARCHITECTURE.

**Belfast roof**, *see* ROOF.

**Belfry**. Generally the upper room or storey in a tower in which bells are hung, and thus often the bell-tower itself, whether it is attached to or stands separate from the main building. Also the timber frame inside a church steeple to which bells are fastened. Derived from the Old French *berfrei* (tower), the word has no connection with 'bell'.

**Belgian architecture**. In the Middle Ages the southern Netherlands belonged to the archdiocese of Cologne; hence Romanesque building drew its inspiration chiefly from Germany. The earliest building of major importance, St Gertrude at Nivelles (consecrated 1046), is, side by side with St Michael at Hildesheim, the best-preserved Ottonian church in the German orbit. The former St John at Liège was built to a central plan like Charlemagne's church at Aachen, the former Liège Cathedral had a west as well as an east chancel, St Bartholomew, also at

Liège, has a typically German unrelieved façade block with recessed twin towers (cf. especially Maastricht), and the cathedral of Tournai has a trefoil east end (i.e. transepts with apsidal ends) on the pattern of St Mary in Capitol at Cologne; its group of five towers round the crossing may also be derived from Cologne.

Tournai had a great influence on the Early Gothic architecture of France (Noyon, Laon): the east end was rebuilt c. 1242, no longer on a German pattern but on that of such High Gothic cathedrals as Soissons and Amiens. The Gothic style in present-day Belgium was, in fact, imported from France; borrowings also occurred from Normandy and Burgundy, and as in other countries the Cistercians were among the pioneers. Orval of the late C12 is still Transitional, Villers (1210–72) is fully Gothic, as are the principal church of Brussels, Ste Gudule (begun before 1226, the façade C15), the beautiful chancel of St Martin at Ypres (begun 1221), and Notre Dame at Tongres (begun 1240). Later Gothic architecture in the southern Netherlands first drew mainly on French inspiration, dominant at Hertogenbosch (c. 1280–1330) and in the chancel of Hal in the C14. But in the C15 Belgium, admittedly influenced by French Flamboyant as well as German *Sondergotik* (*see* GERMAN ARCHITECTURE), developed a splendid style of her own. The principal buildings are Notre Dame at Antwerp (completed 1518), St Rombaut at Malines, St Peter at Louvain (begun 1425), and the Sablon Church at Brussels. Characteristic features are complicated lierne vaults of German derivation, proud towers – that of Antwerp 93 m. (306 ft) high, that of Malines about 98 m. (320 ft) and intended to be about 164 m. (530 ft) – and exceedingly elaborate Flamboyant fitments, such as rood screens.

The most spectacular castle is that of

Ghent (inscribed 1180), with its oblong keep and its many towers along the curtain wall. But the sphere in which Belgium is in the forefront of European building is in the town halls and guild halls of her prosperous towns. The Cloth Hall at Ypres (1202–1304, destroyed 1915, replaced by a replica), 134 m. (440 ft) long, was the grandest such building in all Europe, and there is the town hall of Bruges (tower c.1376–1482, 107 m. (350 ft) high), then, ornately and lacily decorated, those of Brussels (begun 1402), Louvain (1448–63), Ghent (1517), and Oudenarde (1525–30). Interiors were as rich as exteriors – see, for example, the magnificent chimney-piece in Courtrai Town Hall (1526). The names of the master masons are now mostly known: the Keldermans are the most familiar, notably Rombout (c.1460–1531). There are also plenty of medieval town houses preserved; Romanesque buildings are mostly in stone (Tournai), Gothic most often in brick, frequently with crow-stepped gables (as early as the C13).

The Renaissance appeared in occasional motifs in paintings as early as 1500 and was more widely represented after 1510. The most important date for the promotion of the Renaissance spirit is 1517, when Raphael's cartoons for tapestries in the Sistine Chapel reached Brussels, where the tapestries were to be made. In the same year the Stadtholderess Margaret of Austria had additions built to her palace at Malines in the Renaissance style. Their relative purity is exceptional; the usual thing in the twenties and thirties is a happy-go-lucky mixing of Renaissance with traditional motifs, sometimes quite restrained (The Salmon, Malines, 1530–34), but mostly exuberant (The Greffe, Bruges, with its fabulous chimney-piece, 1535–7; the courtyard of the former Bishop's Palace, Liège, 1526). In churches the Renaissance was confined to details;

the proportions and the vaults remained Gothic (St Jacques, Liège, 1513–38). A very influential element in architectural decoration was introduced in Antwerp in the forties and spread all over northern Europe – the combination of STRAP-WORK, inspired by Fontainebleau, and GROTESQUES, inspired by Ancient Roman excavations. Cornelis FLORIS and later Hans Vredeman de VRIES were its most eminent practitioners.

But Floris also designed the Antwerp Town Hall (1561–6), and this, though provided with a big, dominating gable in the northern style, is in its motifs entirely developed from BRAMANTE and SERLIO, i.e. the Italian (and French) Cinquecento. The former Granvella Palace in Brussels (c.1550) is also classical Cinquecento. However, the Jesuits, in their churches, clung to the Gothic well into the C17; an exception is St Charles Borromeo at Antwerp (1615–21), with a broad MANNERIST façade and a tunnel-vaulted interior with arcades on columns in two tiers. True C17 architecture came in under the influence of Italy and France (domes such as Notre Dame de Montaigu, begun 1609; St Pierre, Ghent, begun 1629; Notre Dame de Hanswyck, Malines, begun 1663), and after c.1650 developed into a characteristic Belgian Baroque, inspired largely by Rubens. Church façades are without towers and covered with sumptuous and somewhat undisciplined decoration (St Michael, Louvain, 1650–66; St John Baptist, Brussels, 1657–77; St Peter, Malines, 1670–1709). Typical of the situation about 1700 are the houses round the Grand' Place in Brussels built after the bombardment of 1695 and with their gables basically still rooted in the Belgian past.

Of the C18 and early C19 little need be said; this period was dominated by French classicism (Royal Library, Brussels, c.1750; Palais des Académies, Brussels,

1823–6). But in the later C19 Belgium found the way back to an exuberant Baroque. The cyclopean BEAUX ARTS STYLE Palais de Justice, Brussels (1866–83), by Joseph Poelaert (1817–79), is one of the most Baroque buildings of its time in Europe, though Poelaert could also work in a wild Gothic (Laeken church, begun 1862). A generation later Belgium for the first time in her architectural history, and only for a few years, proved herself a pioneer; this was when attempts were being made to establish ART NOUVEAU as a viable architectural style. By far the most important architect in this movement was Victor HORTA of Brussels, and the key buildings are the Hôtel Tassel (designed 1892), the Hôtel Solvay (1895–1900), and the Maison du Peuple (1895–9), all of them with much of the undulating-line ornament of Art Nouveau, but also with a daring use of iron both externally and internally. Paul HANKAR developed a striking variant to Horta's style, while Henry VAN DE VELDE, though Belgian, belongs to international rather than Belgian Art Nouveau.

Few Belgian architects were known internationally in the early C20, apart from van de Velde and Louis Van der Swaelman (1883–1929), see GARDEN CITY AND GARDEN SUBURB. But in the late 1960s and 1970s Belgium regained some of its former influence with Maurice Culot (b. 1939) and Lucien KROLL. In Brussels in 1968 Culot formed ARAU (Atelier du Recherche et d'Action Urbaine) to plead for the renovation and restoration of the architectural substance when urban renewal is necessary, as then in Brussels, where the city centre was being destroyed to make room for anonymous European Community office blocks. Lucien Kroll's advocacy of 'creative participation' in building resulted most notably in his Student Centre at Wolluvé Saint-Lambert, Louvain (1969–77), the only

major European example of *ad hoc* architecture.

**Bell**, Edward Ingress (1837–1914), *see* WEBB, Sir Aston.

**Bell**, Henry (1647–1711). English amateur architect, like PRATT, notable for his rebuilding of King's Lynn, Norfolk, e.g. the Customs House (1683).

Summerson 1991; Colvin 1995.

**Bell capital**, *see* CAPITAL.

**Bell gable**, *see* BELLCOTE.

**Bellcote** or **bellcot**. A framework on a roof to hang one or more bells from, usually at the west end of a towerless church. Often found on Early English churches and sometimes known as a bell gable or bell-turret.

**Bellini**, Mario (b.1935). Italian architect who made his name with his *Pianeta Ufficio* systems furniture (1974) and later as an architect with a large office and industrial complex in via Kuliscioff, Milan (1984–8). This impressive and sophisticated (historicizing in detail) building was followed by a series of distinguished works in Italy and Japan including the elegant Design Centre, Tokyo (1992). Also notable are his Primary School, Giussana, Milan (1991–5); the Risonare Vivre Club, Kobuchizawa, Japan (1992); and his projected Presidential complex and tower for the Citadel, Moscow (1995).

A. Ranzani (ed.), *M.B. Architetture 1982–1995*, Basel 1996.

**Bellot**, Dom Paul (1876–1944), *see* EXPRESSIONISM.

**Bellus**, Emil (1899–1979), *see* SLOVAK ARCHITECTURE.

**Belluschi**, Pietro (1899–1994). Born in Italy, trained in Rome, he emigrated to the USA in 1923 and settled in the northwest where he made his name with his extensions to the Portland Art Museum in 1932–8. His Equitable Savings and Loan Building (now the Far West Federal Bank), Portland (1944–8), was a paradigmatic International Style building with glass curtain walls. But he became known mainly as a church builder: Zion Lutheran Church, Portland (1950); First Presbyterian Church, Cottage Green, Oregon (1951); Central Lutheran Church, Boston (1957); Trinity Church, Concord, Massachusetts (1964); and more than thirty others in which he succeeded in preserving the traditional image of a church without resorting to any historicizing features. From 1951 to 1965 he was Dean of Architecture and Planning at Massachusetts Institute of Technology, Cambridge, Massachusetts. Of his later work the Julliard School of Music, Lincoln Center, New York (1970), was notable.

L. Gubitosi and A. Izzo, *P.B. Building and Plans*, Rome 1974; M. L. Clausen, *P.B. Modern American Architect*, Cambridge, Mass., 1994.

**Beltrami**, Luca (1854–1933), *see* SOMMARUGA, Giuseppe.

**Belvedere**, *see* GAZEBO.

**Bema**. The Greek word means a speaker's tribune or a platform. 1. A raised stage for the clergy in the apse of Early Christian churches. 2. In Eastern usage, a space raised above the nave level of a church, which is shut off by the ICONOSTASIS and contains the altar. 3. In synagogues, the elevated pulpit from which are read the Pentateuch and Torah. Rabbinical authorities differ over its correct position: Maimonides (1204) maintains that the centre is correct, as does Moses Isserles of Cracow (c16), but Joseph Karo (1575) prescribed no fixed place. In modern times it has often been moved forward near the Ark for practical reasons. It is usually wooden and rectangular, and

sometimes has a curved front and back, also open sides approached by steps.

**Beman**, Solon Spencer (1853–1914). American architect who was brought to Chicago from New York in 1879 by G. M. Pullman to design his COMPANY TOWN with the landscape architect Nathan F. Barrett (1845–1919), who planned the street and park system. Pullman (1880–95) was later acclaimed internationally as a model industrial development together with his Ivorydale, Ohio (1883–8). His buildings were in a variety of vernacular styles, e.g. surviving houses at Florence Square, South Forestville, Chicago. His Studebaker (now Fine Arts) Building, Chicago (1884), combines a glazed front with historicizing terracotta cladding and his Grand Central Station, Chicago (1890) an iron and glass train-shed with a neo-Romanesque clock-tower.

**Bench-ends**, *see* PEW.

**Benedetto da Maiano** (1442–97). Italian architect and sculptor, the younger brother of GIULIANO DA MAIANO, with whom he collaborated at the S. Fina chapel in the Collegiata in S. Gimignano (1466). Though primarily a sculptor, he was equally notable as an architect if the attribution to him of the portico of S. Maria delle Grazie, Arezzo (1490–91), is correct. It is supremely elegant and airy, very different in feeling from Giuliano da SANGALLO's Palazzo Strozzi in Florence, with the construction of which he was certainly involved.

G. Pampaloni, *Palazzo Strozzi*, Rome 1963.

**Benedictine architecture**, *see* CLUNY.

**Benjamin**, Asher (1773–1845), *see* UNITED STATES ARCHITECTURE.

**Bens**, Adolf (1894–1982), *see* CZECH ARCHITECTURE.

**Bentley**, John Francis (1839–1902).
English architect, a pupil of Henry Clutton. Converted to Catholicism in 1861,
he set up on his own in 1862. After a
number of years spent mostly on designs
for church furnishings and on additions
and alterations, he built the Convent of
the Sacred Heart at Hammersmith,
London (1868 onwards), with a scrupulous simplicity and near-bareness; the serried chimneys are particularly impressive.
Wider success came much later. Among
the most memorable buildings are Holy
Rood, Watford, Hertfordshire, a rich
Gothic church, but also most intelligently
thought out (1883–90), and St Francis at
Bocking, Essex (1898). In 1894 he was
commissioned to design Westminster
Cathedral, London (1895–1903). The
style here is Byzantine, the material brick
with ample stone dressings and concrete
for the domes. No iron is used: Bentley
called it 'that curse of modern construction'. The campanile, asymmetrically
placed, is the tallest church tower in
London. The interior is superbly large in
scale and extremely sparing in architectural detail, although according to Bentley's intention it should have been
covered with mosaics and slabs of variegated marble (and this is gradually being
done). However, Philip WEBB admired
it bare as it was.

W. Scott-Moncrieff, *J.F.B.*, London
1924; J. Browne and T. Deane, *Westminster Cathedral. Building of Faith*,
London 1995.

**Berg**, Max (1870–1947), *see* CONCRETE;
GERMAN ARCHITECTURE.

**Berkel**, Ben van (b.1957), *see* DUTCH
ARCHITECTURE.

**Berlage**, Hendrik Petrus (1856–1934).
Dutch architect who studied at the
Zürich Polytechnic, then worked under
CUYPERS. The building that made him

famous, and is indeed a milestone in the
development of Dutch architecture away
from C19 HISTORICISM, is his Amsterdam Stock Exchange (1897–1903), now
a cultural centre. It does not mark a break
with the past, but the treatment of period
forms, derived from the Romanesque as
well as the C16, is so free and the detail
so original that it amounted to a profession
of faith in an independent future.
Specially characteristic are certain
chunky, rather primeval details and others
that are jagged and almost Expressionist.
Berlage's style, indeed, prepared the way
for the EXPRESSIONISM of the so-called
School of Amsterdam (*see* KLERK; OUD).
He was equally forward-looking in
URBAN DESIGN, e.g. his 'new south' area
of Amsterdam (1902–20). Berlage
designed one building in England, the
office building Holland House, Bury
Street, City of London (1910–14). His
last major works, the Nationale-
Nederlander offices, The Hague (1918–
27, enlarged by DUDOK 1953–4 following Berlage's plan), and the Gemeente-
museum, The Hague (1919–35), are less
personal in style. His writings have been
translated by J. Boyd White as *Thoughts
on Style 1885–1909* (Santa Monica, California, 1995).

P. Singelenberg, *H.P.B.: Idea and Style.
The Quest for Modern Architecture*, Utrecht
1972; S. Polano, *H.P.B. (1856–1934).
Opera completa*, Milan 1987; J. Van der
Werf, *Beurs van B.*, Amsterdam 1994.

**Berm**. The level area separating ditch
from bank on a hill-fort or barrow; a
narrow ledge or shelf, as along a slope; the
shoulder of a road. The latter is sometimes
raised artificially by adjacent landowners
as a protection against traffic noise, pollution, etc.

**Bernard de Soissons**, *see* JEAN
D'ORBAIS.

**Bernini**, Gianlorenzo (1598–1680). The dominating figure in Roman Baroque art. Primarily a sculptor, like MICHELANGELO, he was almost as universal a genius, being painter and poet as well as architect. He was born in Naples of a Neapolitan mother and Florentine father, Pietro Bernini, a late Mannerist sculptor of the second rank. The family settled in Rome c.1605. Bernini spent the whole of his working life there, and no other city bears so strong an imprint of one man's vision and personality. His buildings and sculpture perfectly express the grandeur, flamboyance, and emotionalism of the Counter-Reformation. He was already famous as a sculptor by the age of twenty, but his long and almost uniformly successful career as an architect began with the election of Urban VIII (Barberini) in 1623. He was appointed architect to St Peter's six years later. But most of his important buildings belong to his middle age, mainly during the pontificate of Alexander VII (Chigi, 1655–67). By then his fame was so great that Louis XIV begged him to come to Paris to enlarge the Louvre. Unlike his neurotic contemporary and rival BORROMINI, who accused him of stealing some of his designs, he was well-balanced and extrovert in temperament, polished and self-assured in manner. Yet he was devout and deeply religious: an ardent follower of Jesuit teaching. He combined to an exceptional degree a revolutionary artistic genius with the organizing ability of a man of affairs.

His first commissions (1624) were for the renovation of S. Bibiana and the baldacchino in St Peter's. Though interesting as an experiment, S. Bibiana suffers from a lack of assurance most uncharacteristic of its author and in striking contrast to the daringly original baldacchino (1624–33) he erected under della Porta's dome in the centre of St Peter's. With its gigantic bronze barley-sugar columns, buoyant scrolls and dynamic sculpture, this showy masterpiece is the very symbol of the age – of its grandeur, luxury and lack of restraint. And by its glorification of the twisted columns used in Constantine's basilica and traditionally connected with the Temple of Jerusalem it celebrates the continuity of the Church and its triumph over the Reformation.

Various other commissions followed: the façade and staircase of Palazzo Barberini, the remodelling of Porta del Popolo, the Cornaro Chapel in S. Maria della Vittoria (1645–52). In the latter polychrome marbles, exaggerated perspective, and every trick of lighting and scenic illusion are exploited to heighten the dramatic effect of his marble group of the Ecstasy of St Teresa, placed as if behind a proscenium arch above the altar. But not until he was almost sixty did he get the chance to show his skill as a designer of churches, first at Castelgandolfo (1658–61), then at Ariccia (1662–4), and, finally and most brilliantly, at S. Andrea al Quirinale in Rome (1658–70), which perfectly realizes his conception of a church as a unified architectural setting for the religious mysteries illustrated by the sculptural decoration.

Of his two great secular buildings in Rome, Palazzo di Montecitorio (1650 onwards) and Palazzo Odescalchi (1664 onwards), the latter is by far the more important. It is composed of a richly articulated central part of seven bays with giant composite pilasters, between simple rusticated receding wings of three bays, and marks a decisive break with Roman tradition. It was very influential and became the model for aristocratic palaces all over Europe. Unfortunately, the composition was ruined by later alterations and enlargements. Bernini's last great secular enterprise, for the Louvre in Paris of 1664–6, was never carried out but was nevertheless influential, especially his third project for the east façade. His gift for the monumental and colossal found supreme expression in the Piazza of St Peter's (1656 onwards). The conception is extremely simple and extremely original – an enormous oval surrounded by colonnades of free-standing columns with a straight entablature above. This not only helped to correct the faults of MADERNO's façade by giving it the impression of greater height but expressed with overwhelming authority and conviction the dignity, grandeur and majestic repose of Mother Church. Bernini himself compared his colonnades to the motherly arms of the Church 'which embrace Catholics to reinforce their belief'. The Piazza was to have been enclosed by a third arm, unfortunately never built, and the intended effect of surprise and elation on passing through the colonnades has now been idiotically destroyed by opening up the via della Conciliazione. The free-standing colonnades of the Piazza have been widely copied, from Greenwich to St Petersburg. Bernini's last great work, the Scala Regia in the Vatican (1663–6), epitomizes his style – his sense of scale and movement, his ingenuity in turning an awkward site to advantage, his mastery of scenic effects (optical illusions, exaggerated perspectives, concealed lighting), and his brilliant use of sculpture to dramatize the climaxes of his composition. He here achieved the perfect Baroque synthesis of the arts.

F. Borsi, *B. architetto*, Milan 1980; Wittkower 1982; Varriano 1986; Waddy 1990.

**Berthault**, Louis-Martin (*c.* 1770–1823). French architect, pupil of PERCIER, notable as the designer of gardens for the Empress Josephine at Malmaison and for Louis XVIII at Compiègne, where he introduced a new style of irregular layout incorporating formal areas with an emphasis on flowering plants.

M.-B. D'Arneville, *Parcs et jardins sous le Premier Empire: reflets d'une société*, Paris 1981.

**Bertotti-Scamozzi**, Ottavio (1719–90), the leading Palladian-Revival architect in Italy, built numerous houses in and around Vicenza, notably Palazzo Pagello-Beltrame (1780) and Palazzo Franceschini (1770, now the Questura), distinctly neo-classical versions of PALLADIO. He is more important as the editor of Palladio's work: *Le fabbriche e i disegni di Andrea Palladio raccolti e illustrati* (1776–83) and *Le terme dei Romani, disegnate da A. Palladio* (1797).

L. Olivato, *O.B.-S. studioso di Andrea Palladio*, Vicenza 1976; C. Kamm-Kyburz, *Der Architekt O.B.-S. 1719–1790*, Berne 1983.

**Béton brut**. 'Concrete in the raw', that is, concrete left in its natural state when the FORMWORK has been removed. Sometimes special formwork is used to show clearly the timber graining on the concrete surface. Also called *board-marked concrete*.

**Bianchi**, Pietro (1787–1849), *see* ITALIAN ARCHITECTURE.

**Bianco** or **Bianchi**, Bartolommeo (*c.* 1590–1657). Italian architect, born in Como, but working in Genoa by 1619 when he began Palazzo Durazzo-Pallavicini. His best building is the University (1630–36), where he took full advantage of a steeply sloping site to produce a masterpiece of scenic planning with dramatic staircases and colonnaded courtyards on four levels.

Wittkower 1982.

**Bibiena**, *see* GALLI DA BIBIENA.

**Bidonville**. A loosely defined term for an aggregation of owner-built housing of scrap materials, usually metal; a mid- to late C20 phenomenon on the outskirts of cities in undeveloped or recently developing countries, e.g. Lima, Caracas and São Paulo in South America; Bombay and Calcutta in India. It is to be distinguished from ALTERNATIVE ARCHITECTURE.

**Bifora** or **biforate window**, *see* WINDOW.

**Bigelow**, Jacob (1787–1879). American physician and botanist who designed Mount Auburn cemetery, Boston (begun 1811), as a 29-hectare (72-acre) landscape park that could serve also as a place of recreation for the public. It was the first rural CEMETERY and the first PUBLIC PARK in the USA.

B. Linden-Ward, *Silent City on a Hill: Landscapes of Memory and Boston's Mount Auburn Cemetery*, Columbus, Ohio 1988.

**Bill**, Max (1908–94), *see* BAUHAUS; SWISS ARCHITECTURE.

**Billet**. A Romanesque moulding of Ancient Roman origin consisting of several bands of raised short cylinders or square pieces placed at regular intervals. *See* Fig. 17.

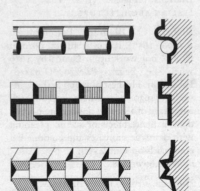

Fig. 17 Billet

**Bindesbøll**, Michael Gottlieb Burkner (1800–1856), *see* DANISH ARCHITECTURE.

**Biomorphic**. Term for non-geometrical forms based on natural shapes. Used mainly for the abstract paintings and sculptures of Hans Arp and only rarely applicable to architecture; *but see* ORGANIC ARCHITECTURE.

**Bird's beak moulding**. Moulding used in Ancient Greek architecture and thought to resemble, in section, the beak of a bird.

**Bird's mouth**. A notch or re-entrant V-shaped incision down or along an external angle in stone or other facing material, to break a sharp edge. Similarly, in a rafter or other timber member in ROOF construction, a notch to form a joint with a purlin or plate.

**Bitumen**. A smooth, hard, solid or semi-solid, black or brownish black resinous mineral which melts when heated and sets hard. Similar to pitch and tar. It was used as a mortar for bricklaying and waterproofing in ancient Mesopotamia, replaced by lime-based mortars in Ancient Greek and Roman times. It only began to be widely used in Europe in the C19 when it was imported from Trinidad. Limestone impregnated with bitumen, known as Rock Asphalt, was used for road surfaces in the late C18 when it was mined at Ragusa (Sicily), Limner (Germany) and Val de Travers (Switzerland). *See also* ASPHALT.

**Blacket**, Edmund T. (1817–83), *see* AUSTRALIAN ARCHITECTURE.

**Blade**, *see* CRUCKS.

**Blind arch**. An arch within a wall framing a recessed flat panel, not an opening; used ornamentally to vary a plain expanse of masonry or to decrease the dead weight of a wall. A series of such blind arches, as often found in Romanesque and Gothic buildings, is called a *blind arcade*. *See* Fig. 6.

**Blind** or **blank tracery**. Tracery applied to the surface of walls, wood panels, etc., in Gothic buildings.

**Blind window**. The elements of a window (the surround, mullion, etc.) applied to a wall without any aperture. It was used as a decorative device and is found from the Middle Ages onwards. It was often used in the later periods to give symmetry to the façade of an asymmetrically planned building.

**Block capital**, *see* CAPITAL.

**Blocked**. Term applied to columns, etc. with regular projecting blocks as in a GIBBS SURROUND or a RUSTICATED COLUMN.

**Blocked column**, *see* COLUMN.

**Blocked rustication**, *see* RUSTICATION.

**Blocking course**. In classical architecture, the plain course of stone surmounting the CORNICE at the top of a building; also a projecting cornice of stone or brick at the base of a building.

**Blom**, Piet (b.1934), *see* DUTCH ARCHITECTURE.

**Blomfield**, Sir Reginald (1856–1942). English architect, a pupil of SHAW, he promoted first an English and then a French (Beaux Arts) classicism about which he wrote influential histories (1897 and 1911). The elevations for the west side of Piccadilly Circus, London, of *c.*1913 are his, as was also the more scholarly Carlton Club, Pall Mall, London (1921, destroyed 1940). As a garden designer he is notable for having reintroduced formal bedding, etc., opposing ROBERTSON's and JEKYLL's informality.

R. A. Fellows, *Sir R.B. An Edwardian Architect*, London 1985.

**Blondel**, Jacques-François (1705–74). A minor French architect (not related to Nicolas-François Blondel) but a very influential writer, theorist and teacher, becoming Professor at the Académie Royale de l'Architecture in 1762. Conservative in taste, he exalted the French tradition as exemplified by MANSART and PERRAULT. His publications include *De la distribution des maisons . . .* (1737); *L'Architecture française* (1752–6) known as the 'Grand Blondel' of which only four of the projected eight volumes appeared; *Discours sur la nécessité de l'étude de l'architecture* (1754) and *Cours d'architecture* (1771–7), which contains his public lectures and the substance of his teaching. The last two volumes were published posthumously by his pupil Pierre Patte (1723–1812). Of his buildings nothing survives except three sides of the Place d'Armes at Metz.

W. Herrmann, *Laugier and Eighteenth Century French Theory*, London 1962; Braham 1980; Rykwert 1980; Picon 1992.

**Blondel**, Nicolas-François (1617–86). French engineer and mathematician, more interested in the theory than the practice of architecture. He expounded the rigidly classical and rationalist doctrines of the French Academy in his *Cours d'architecture* (1675, augmented ed. 1698). The Porte St Denis, Paris (1671), is his best surviving building.

Blunt 1982.

**Blore**, Edward (1787–1879). An English topographical and antiquarian draughtsman before he became a practising architect. His great chance came in 1816 on meeting Walter Scott, then about to rebuild Abbotsford, to which Blore later contributed. After that he extended his practice considerably. Much was restoration. Among his original buildings are the domestic parts of Lambeth Palace, London (1829–48), the Pitt Press, Cambridge (1831–2), Worsley Hall, Lancashire (1840–45, demolished), Great Moreton Hall, Cheshire (1841–6), and Thicket Priory, Yorkshire (1844–7).

Colvin 1995.

**Blum**, Hans (*fl.*1550). Blum published the most influential German treatise on the orders: *Quinque Columnarum Exacta descriptio atque delineatio . . .* (Zürich 1550) and thus provided German architects with their first grammar in the classical language of architecture. It was based on SERLIO and often reprinted. Later editions (*Ein kunstrych Buoch von allerly Antiquiteten . . .* Zürich *c.*1560, *Warhafte Contrafacturen etlich alt u. schoner Gebauden . . .* Zürich 1562) contain designs by Blum for churches, triumphal arches, etc. An English edition appeared in 1601.

Hitchcock 1981; Harris 1990.

**Bo**, Jorgen (b.1919), *see* DANISH ARCHITECTURE.

**Bo Bardi**, Lina (1914–92), *see* BRAZILIAN ARCHITECTURE.

**Board-marked concrete**, *see* BÉTON BRUT.

**Boasted work**. Stonework roughly blocked out preparatory to carving; also masonry finished with a boaster chisel.

**Boberg**, Ferdinand (1860–1946), *see* SWEDISH ARCHITECTURE.

**Böblinger**. A family of south German masons of which the two most important members were Hans Senior and Matthäus. Hans (1412–82) was a journeyman at Konstanz in 1435, then became foreman under Matthäus ENSINGEN at St Mary, Esslingen, and in 1440 master mason of this church. Matthäus (d.1505) was one of Hans's sons and was probably trained in Cologne. He was later at Esslingen with his father, and then at Ulm where, after three years, he became master mason of the Minster (1480). He

was successor there to Ulrich and Matthäus Ensingen, and replaced Ulrich's design for the west tower with one of his own. His steeple was completed in 1481–90 and became the highest church tower in Europe at 162 m. (530 ft). However, in 1492 Matthäus had to resign from the post and leave the town after cracks had appeared in the tower. He was called to a number of other places for consultation or to provide designs and supervise. Thieme and Becker's *Künstler-Lexikon* mentions eight more members of the family.

Baum 1956; Bucher 1979.

**Bodley**, George Frederick (1827–1907), was of Scottish descent and George Gilbert SCOTT's first pupil (1845–*c.*1850). Mostly but not exclusively a church architect, he always worked in the Gothic style; in his earlier works he was influenced by the French C13, later by English models. His style is as competent and knowledgeable as Scott's, but distinguished by a never-failing taste, including the choice of those who were to do furnishings and fitments. An early patron of MORRIS, he also started the stained glass artist C. E. Kempe on his notable career. Among his earliest works are St Michael, Brighton (1859–61), St Martin, Scarborough (1861–2), and All Saints, Cambridge (1863–4). In 1869 he went into partnership with Thomas Garner (1839–1906), another pupil of Scott's; the partnership lasted till 1898, though after 1884 the partners designed and supervised jobs individually. Among their most lavish works is Holy Angels, Hoar Cross, Staffordshire (1871–7). St Augustine, Pendlebury (1870–74), Manchester, on the other hand, is one of the most monumental by virtue of its simplicity; instead of aisles, it has passages through internal buttresses, a motif derived from Albi and Spain and often repeated by the younger generation. Perhaps the noblest of all

Bodley's churches is that of Clumber (1886–9), now standing forlorn in the grounds of the demolished mansion. Bodley also designed the chapel of Queens' College, Cambridge (1890–91), and buildings for King's College, Cambridge (1893). His last commission was for Washington Cathedral, Washington, DC, for which he prepared designs (1906–7). The cathedral was begun in 1910 under Henry Vaughan (d.1917) and completed in 1990. Among his pupils were C. R. ASHBEE and Sir Ninian COMPER (*see* ARTS AND CRAFTS).

Clarke 1969; Hitchcock 1977.

**Bodt**, Jean de (1670–1745). A Huguenot who left France after the revocation of the Edict of Nantes in 1685, was trained as an architect in Holland and after working for a time in England settled in 1698 in Berlin, where he soon became the most important architect after SCHLÜTER. In 1701 he built the Fortuna Portal of the Potsdam Stadtschloss (retained by KNOBELSDORFF in his rebuilding of 1744) and completed NERING's Arsenal in Berlin (*c.*1706) and Parochialkirche, modifying both designs. In about 1710 the east front of Wentworth Castle, South Yorkshire, was built to his designs for the Earl of Strafford. (The Earl of Strafford was ambassador to the King of Prussia 1706–11.) In 1728 he settled in Dresden, where he was appointed Superintendent of the Royal Works and thus was in charge of PÖPPELMANN's work at the Japanisches Palais. But all his own ambitious projects for buildings in Dresden and elsewhere in Saxony remained on paper.

Colombier 1956; Hempel 1965.

**Boffrand**, Gabriel Germain (1667–1754), the greatest French Rococo architect, began as a sculptor, studying under Girardon in Paris (1681), but soon turned to architecture. He became the pupil and later the collaborator of J. HARDOUIN-MANSART. In 1711 he became Premier Architect to the Duc de Lorraine, for whom he built the *château* of Lunéville (1709–15) and its chapel (1720–23). Nearly all his work in Nancy has been demolished. He made a large fortune, mainly by the speculative building of Parisian *hôtels* (e.g. Hôtels Amelot de Gournay, 1712; de Seignelay, 1713; de Torcy, 1714), but he lost the bulk of it in the Mississippi Bubble of 1720. Like his contemporary de COTTE he had great influence outside France, especially in Germany (e.g. on the Residenz, Würzburg). His virtuosity is well seen in the Hôtel de Montmorency, Paris, built round an oval court with rooms of various shapes and sizes, including a pentagon. The elevations, as always with Boffrand, are of the utmost simplicity and reticence, while the interior is of course very luxurious. His finest interior is probably that of the pavilion he added (*c.*1733–40) to the Hôtel de Soubise (now the Archives Nationales), Paris. His Rococo ideal of elegant informality and sophisticated simplicity was realized in his Château de Saint Ouen, a brilliant and original conception consisting of a tiny Trianon-like pavilion of three rooms, set in a spacious courtyard formed by the guests' apartments, offices, stables, etc. He published *Livre d'architecture contenant les principes généraux de cet art* in 1745.

M. Gallett and J. Garms, *G.B. 1667–1754*, Paris 1986; Kalnein 1995.

**Bofill**, Ricardo (Levi) (b.1939). Spanish architect who founded the workshop 'Taller de Arquitectura' in Barcelona in 1962 and quickly became known for his low-cost housing complexes in a provocative mixture of brightly painted brick and other regional Spanish vernacular materials and styles, e.g. the Xanadu apartments, Calpe (1967); the indigo, violet and pink tourist complex La

Muralla Roja, Alicante (1969–72), and the Walden 7 residential complex, Sant Just Desvern, near Barcelona (1970–75). These were followed by enormous classicizing Post-Modern housing and commercial developments in France: Les Arcades du Lac, St Quentin-en-Ivelines, near Paris (1978–83); Les Espaces d'Abraxas, Marne-la-Vallée, near Paris (1978–82); La Place Nombre d'Or, Montpellier (1978–84); Les Colonnes de St Christophe, Cergy Pontoise, Paris (1981–6); and Les Echelles du Baroque, Montparnasse, Paris (1983–6). Rhetorical, even megalomaniac, they nevertheless succeed in introducing a sense of grandeur and monumentality into public spaces. His later work is more restrained, e.g. Shepherd School of Music, Rice University, Houston, Texas (1992); INEFC, Monjuic, Barcelona (1991). He has published L'Architecture d'un homme (Paris 1978) and, with N. Vernon, L'Architecture des villes (Paris 1995).

J. A. Warren, R.B. Taller de Arquitectura, New York 1989.

**Bogardus**, James (1800–1874). An American inventor of many things in many fields, Bogardus concerns us here for his cast-iron façades of commercial buildings which he promoted as being fireproof, transportable and efficient. The earliest was his own factory in New York, built in 1848 (see METAL STRUCTURES). He published Cast-Iron Buildings. Their Construction and Advantages (New York 1856), anticipating that by Daniel D. BADGER of 1865. Three of his buildings survive in New York: 85 Leonard Street, 254 Canal Street and 63 Nassau Street. His iron façades played an important role in the development of prefabricated building parts. Even more interesting was his proposed design for the New York exhibition of 1853 which has a central tower from which the roofs were suspended on the principle of suspension bridges.

Condit 1968; Benevolo 1971; M. Gayle, Cast-Iron Architecture in New York, New York 1974.

**Bohigas**, José Oriol (b.1927), see SPANISH ARCHITECTURE.

**Böhm**, Dominikus (1880–1955). German church architect, e.g. St Johann, Neu-Ulm (1921–7); the parabolic concrete vaulted church at Bischofsheim (1926); St Engelbert, Cologne-Riehl (1930–32). His later work is more conventional, e.g. St Maria Königin, Cologne-Marienburg (1954).

A. Hoff, H. Muck and R. Thomas, D.B. Leben und Werk, Munich/Zürich 1962; G. Stalling, Studien zu D.B., Berne/Frankfurt 1974.

**Böhm**, Gottfried (b.1920). Son of Dominikus Böhm, whose practice he inherited. He developed an extremely dramatic, sculptural style, e.g. the Town Hall, Bensberg (1963–9), and the Pilgrimage Church, Neviges (1963–8), but later abandoned this for lighter, airier, glass and steel buildings, e.g. the Landesamt für Datenverarbeitung und Statistik, Düsseldorf (1969–76), the Gemeindezentrum, Rheinberg (1977–80) and Zublinhaus, Stuttgart (1981–4). Later he compromised rather uneasily with such large-scale complexes as Bremerhaven University (1982–9).

S. Raev, G.B. Bauten und Projeckte 1950–1980, Cologne 1982; S. Raev, G.B., Lectures, Buildings and Projects, Stuttgart 1987.

**Boileau**, Louis-Auguste (1812–96). French architect. One of the first to use iron construction in church architecture. His only familiar work is St Eugène in Paris (1854–5), earlier than BALTARD's St Augustine and VIOLLET-LE-DUC's defence of iron in the Entretiens. However, earlier still than St Eugène is the

Ste Geneviève Library by LABROUSTE. St Eugène was the model for the church of Vésinet (1863). Boileau also wrote a book on the use of iron in architecture, *Nouvelle forme architecturale* (Paris 1853).

Hitchcock 1977; C. Behnisch and G. Hartung, *Eisenkonstruktionen des 19 Jahrhunderts*, 1982.

**Boiserie**. French term for wood panelling or other fitted woodwork for an interior scheme of decoration (*see* PANEL). The term is usually applied to French C17 and especially C18 panelling elaborately decorated with shallow relief carvings of foliage etc., notably by such Rococo ornamental sculptors as François-Antoine Vassé (1681–1736), Jules Degoullons (1671–1738), François Roumier (d.1748) and Jacques Verberckt (1704–71). They also carried out ecclesiastical schemes, notably choir stalls with panelling – e.g. in Notre Dame, Paris, and Orléans Cathedral. In C18 Germany boiseries were often combined with STUCCO decorations on the ceiling to form unified schemes of decoration, e.g. at the Residenz, Munich, and the Amalienburg at Nymphenburg, where the stucco work is by J. B. ZIMMERMANN and the boiseries by the Paris-trained Wenzelaus Miroffsky (d.1759) and Joachim Dietrich (d.1753) – probably to designs by the architect François CUVILLIÉS. It is seldom known to what extent the ornamental sculptors were responsible for the design of their boiseries and how much the supervising architects, such as GABRIEL, HARDOUIN-MANSART and de COTTE, were involved.

A. Laing in A. Blunt (ed.), *Baroque and Rococo Architecture and Decoration*, London 1978; B. Pons, *Les Sculpteurs ornementistes parisiens et l'art décoratif des Bâtiments de roi*, Strasbourg 1985; B. Pons, *Architecture and Panelling. The James A. de Rothschild*

*Bequest at Waddesdon Manor*, London 1997.

**Boito**, Camillo (1836–1914). Italian architect, brother of Verdi's librettist, an ardent exponent of neo-Romanesque though a moderate in the RESTORATION controversy. His hospital at Gallarate (1871) and entrance to the Padua museum are notable.

Meeks 1966; G. Zucconi, *L'invenzione del passato C.B. e l'architettura medievale 1855–1890*, Venice 1997.

**Bolection moulding**. A moulding used to cover the joint between two members with different surface levels. It projects beyond both surfaces. *See* Fig. 18.

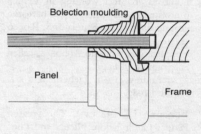

Fig. 18 Bolection moulding

**Bollard**. A thick post of wood, metal or stone for securing ropes and hawsers, usually on a ship or wharf but also elsewhere; also, by analogy, similarly shaped posts used in series to limit vehicular access to an area, sometimes with intervening chains.

**Bolles-Wilson** (Julia Bolles, b.1948; Peter Wilson, b.1950), *see* GERMAN ARCHITECTURE.

**Bomarzo**, Duke of (*c*.1513–84), *see* ORSINI, Pier Francesco 'Vicino', Duke of Bomarzo.

**Bon** or **Buon**, Bartolomeo (*c*.1405–*c*.1467). Venetian sculptor-architect, son of Giovanni Bon (*c*.1362–1443), with whom he worked at the Ca' d'Oro (1424–31) and then on the Porta della Carta, Doges' Palace (1438–43), where Late Venetian Gothic reached its apogee. His portals at S. Giovanni e Paolo (1458–63) and Madonna dell'Orto (1460–66) are more classicizing, as is his upper storey of the Arco Foscari in the Doges' Palace (1460–64). His unfinished Ca' del Duca (Palazzo Corner), Grand Canal, would have been precociously Renaissance (only the basement is by him). The Arsenal Gate (1460–62) has been attributed to him.

McAndrew 1980; Lieberman 1982; Howard 1987.

**Bon** or **Bono**, Bartolomeo (d.1529). Lombard architect working in Venice (unrelated to his namesake), where the ground floor of the Scuola di S. Rocco (1516–24) is his best-known work. It was completed by Antonio Abbondi, called Scarpagnino (d.1549).

McAndrew 1980; Lieberman 1982; Howard 1987.

**Bonanno** (*fl.* late C12). The greatest Pisan sculptor before Nicola and Giovanni PISANO and, like them, also an architect. The campanile or Leaning Tower at Pisa, begun in 1173, is his most notable building. His role in the design and construction of Pisa Cathedral (*see* BUSCHETO) and the baptistery (*see* DIOTISALVI) is controversial. His bronze doors for Pisa Cathedral were completed in 1180 (destroyed by fire in 1595) but those of 1185 for Monreale Cathedral, Sicily, survive. Those for the Porta di S. Ranieri, Pisa Cathedral, are attributed to him. They are of controversial date.

*DBI* 1969.

**Bonatz**, Paul (1877–1956). German architect notable for his Stuttgart railway station (1911–27), inspired by Eliel SAARINEN's Helsinki station, and for his work with Fritz Todt (1891–1942) on the

Autobahn system (1935–40), especially the bridges, which he designed. His other works ranged from the University Library, Tübingen (1910–12), to the Kunstmuseum, Basel, Switzerland (1931–6), and the Opera House, Ankara, Turkey (1947–8). He published *Leben und Bauen* (Stuttgart 1950).

N. Bongartz *et al.*, *P.B. 1877–1956*, Stuttgart 1977; M. Roser, *P.B. Wohnhause*, Stuttgart 1991.

**Bonavia**, Santiago (d.1759), *see* SPANISH ARCHITECTURE.

**Bond**, *see* BRICKWORK.

**Bond stone**, *see* PARPEN.

**Bonnet tile**. A curved tile used for joining plain tiles along the hip of a roof.

**Bonneuil**, Étienne de (*fl.*1287–8), *see* SCANDINAVIAN ARCHITECTURE.

**Bonomi**, Joseph (1739–1808). Born and trained in Italy, he came to England in 1767 at the invitation of the ADAM brothers, for whom he worked. But by the 1780s he was practising independently. His masterpiece is the small but very imposing church of St James, Great Packington, Warwickshire (1789–90). It is extremely severe: plain brick outside, Greek Doric inside with smooth, painted ashlar. It is the only building in England which can be compared with the contemporary work in France by Ledoux and in Prussia by Gilly. Bonomi's other work is less original. His large country house Roseneath (1803–6) outside Glasgow was demolished in 1961. His son Ignatius (c.1787–1870) was an architect in Durham, designing both country houses (e.g. Burn Hall, 1821–34) and a number of churches including the neo-Norman Duddo (1832) and Oxenhope (1849) in Northumberland and West Yorkshire. He retired in 1855. His second son, also Joseph (1796–1878), designed the flax mill of Marshall & Co., Leeds, the most grandiose Egyptian-style building in Europe (1842).

Meadows, *J.B. Architect (1739–1808)*, exh. cat. London 1988; Summerson 1991; Colvin 1995.

**Borromini**, Francesco (1599–1667). The most original genius of Roman High Baroque architecture and the jealous rival of his almost exact contemporary BERNINI. A late starter, lonely, frustrated and neurotic, he eventually committed suicide. Born at Bissone on Lake Lugano, the son of a mason, he worked in Milan before going to Rome in late 1619. He remained there for the rest of his life. Befriended by his distant relation MADERNO, he found employment as a stone-carver at St Peter's, mainly on decorative *putti*, festoons, etc., e.g. the wrought-iron gates to the Cappella del S. Sacramento (1627), which are after his designs. After Maderno's death (1629) he continued under Bernini, later becoming his chief assistant and occasionally contributing to the designs both at St Peter's and at Palazzo Barberini. But their relationship was uneasy. Himself a first-rate craftsman, Borromini despised Bernini's technical shortcomings; Bernini's success rankled. The two men parted for good in 1634 when Borromini's great opportunity came with the commission for S. Carlo alle Quattro Fontane. Despite its miniature size, S. Carlo (1637–41) is one of the most ingenious spatial compositions ever invented and displays Borromini's mastery of his art and revolutionary disregard for convention. The oval plan, emphasized by the honeycomb dome, is based on geometric units (equilateral triangles), but the swaying rhythm and sculptural effect of the undulating walls and restless, intertwined plastic elements produce an almost voluptuous effect. The concave-convex-concave façade was begun in 1665. S. Carlo was quickly followed by S. Ivo della Sapienza (1643–60). Borromini's triangular planning system here produced a star-hexagon, which he worked out vertically with dynamic effect. The fantastic dome culminates in an extraordinary ZIGGURAT-like spiral feature.

His style reached its zenith at S. Ivo. Later buildings were either left unfinished or inhibited by complexities of site or by his having to take over plans by previous architects. Unfinished works include S. Maria dei Sette Dolori (1642–8); the interior remodelling of S. Giovanni in Laterano (1646–9), which still lacks the intended nave vaulting; and S. Andrea delle Fratte (1653–65), where the dome is still without its lantern though the drum-like casing and three-storey tower outdo even S. Ivo in fantasy. At S. Agnese in Piazza Navona (1653–7) he took over from Carlo RAINALDI, changing the character of his interior designs by seemingly minor alterations and completely redesigning the façade on a concave plan. The dramatic grouping of high drum and dome framed by elegant towers is one of his best and most typical compositions, though he was dismissed as architect before its completion and further changes were made (notably in the pediment). An awkward site cramped his style at the Oratory of St Philip Neri (1638–50), remarkable for its ingenious dual-purpose façade uniting chapel and monastic buildings. His domestic architecture is fragmentary but no less startling – *trompe l'œil* arcade at Palazzo Spada, river front and loggia at Palazzo Falconieri, grand *salone* at Palazzo Pamphili (after 1647) and the library at the Sapienza. The latter was the prototype of many great C18 libraries. His Villa Falconieri at Frascati (*c.*1644) was altered by FUGA.

He became increasingly unorthodox, and his last work, the Collegio di

Propaganda Fide (1647–64), shows a remarkable change of style towards monumentality and austerity, the capitals, for example, being reduced to a few parallel grooves. Its façade in via di Propaganda – heavy, oppressive, nightmarish – is unlike anything before or since. Reproached in his own day for having destroyed the conventions of good architecture, Borromini had little immediate influence in Italy except superficially in ornamentation. (His revolutionary spatial concepts were to bear abundant fruit later on in central Europe.) His style was too personal and eccentric, especially in its combination of Gothic and post-Renaissance elements. His Gothic affinities were noted by his contemporaries (e.g. Baldinucci), and indeed they went beyond a partiality for medieval features such as the SQUINCH, for his geometrical system of planning and emphasis on a dynamic skeleton brought him close to the structural principles of Gothic. Yet his blending of architecture and sculpture and his voluptuous moulding of space and mass tie him to the Italian anthropomorphic tradition.

J. Connors, *B.'s Roman Oratory*, Cambridge, Mass., 1980; A. Blunt, *B.*, London 1979; Wittkower 1982; P. Portoghesi, *B. nella cultura europea*, Rome (1964) 1982; Varriano 1986; M. Raspe, *Das Architektursystem B.*, Munich 1994.

**Bosche**, Theo (1940–94), *see* VAN EYCK, Aldo.

**Boss**. An ornamental knob or projection covering the intersection of ribs in a vault or ceiling; often carved with foliage. See Figs 19, 119.

**Bosquet**. French term for a small irregularly planned wood or shrubbery such as was often incorporated in the layout of geometrically planned gardens from the mid-C17 to the C18 as a contrasting,

Fig. 19 Boss

apparently natural, shaded area with paths meandering through it. Sometimes, as at Versailles, it was enclosed by a 3 m. (10 ft) high clipped hornbeam hedge (*charmille*) above and slightly over which the free-growing trees projected.

**Botta**, Mario (b.1943). Swiss architect, trained under SARPA and worked under both LE CORBUSIER and KAHN. He became the leading member of the Italo-Swiss 'Ticino School'; *see* SWISS ARCHITECTURE. His early, small-scale single-family houses are notable for their sensitive response to the regional vernacular and to the landscape, e.g. houses at Cadenazzo (1970–71), Ligornetto (1976), Pregassona (1979) and Stabio (1981), likewise his schools such as that at Morbio Inferiore (1972–7). His later buildings are exceptional both in scale and in their free use of modern construction techniques and their bold and colourfully patterned façades, e.g. the fortress-like Banca dell Gottardo, Lugano (1988); the sharply angled, severely triangular Watari-um, Tokyo (1990); the broken cylindrical Commercial and Residential Building, Lugano (1991); the Museum of Modern Art, San Francisco (1994); the cathedral at Evry, near Paris (1995); the Tamaro Chapel, Rivera (1996), and the Tinguely Museum, Basel (1996). In 1997 he published *Ethik des Bauens – The Ethics of Building* (Basel/Boston/Berlin).

S. Wrede, *M.B.*, New York 1987; J. Petit, *B. Traces d'architecture*, Lugano 1994; E. Pizzi, *M.B. The Complete Works 1960–85 and 1985–1990*, Zürich 1994.

**Boulevard**. A wide street with trees along the sides and also sometimes down the middle, notably those laid out by HAUSSMANN in Paris. The old French word *boloart*, from which *boulevard* derives, meant the horizontal portion of a rampart and hence the promenade laid out on a disused or demolished rampart. The first in Paris was opened by Louis XIV in 1670 and went from the Porte St Denis to the Bastille, occupying the site of ancient walls levelled by Vauban. This and other early boulevards were intended as promenades and not for use by heavy traffic as were to be those later created by Haussmann. The latter became a feature of C19 city planning not only in France. In C20 USA the term has come to denote any wide main thoroughfare, e.g. Sunset Boulevard, Los Angeles.

**Boullée**, Étienne-Louis (1728–99). A leading French neo-classical architect, he probably had more influence than LEDOUX, though he built little (the Hôtel Alexandre, Paris, 1763–6, is the most interesting survivor), and his treatise on architecture remained unpublished until as recently as 1953, for he had many and important pupils, such as J.-N.-L. DURAND who wrote the most influential treatise of the Empire period. His best designs date from the 1780s and 1790s and are, if anything, even more megalomaniac than Ledoux's – e.g. a 152 m. (500 ft) high spherical monument to Newton – and they are also, like Ledoux's, expressive or *parlantes* in intention despite their apparently abstract, geometrical simplicity. In his treatise he pleads for a felt, as much as reasoned, architecture, and for character, grandeur and magic.

H. Rosenau, *B. and Visionary Architecture*, London 1976; Braham 1980; P. Madec, *B.*, Paris 1986; J. P. Mouillesceaux and A. Jacque, *Les Architectes de la Liberté 1789–1799*, Paris 1989; J. M.

Pérouse de Montclos, *E.-L.B.*, Paris 1994; Kalnein 1995.

**Bourgeau**, Victor (1809–88), *see* CANADIAN ARCHITECTURE.

**Bow window**, *see* BAY WINDOW.

**Bowstring roof**, *see* ROOF.

**Bowtell**. A term in use by the C15 (e.g. William of Worcester's notes; masons' contracts) for a convex moulding. A form of ROLL MOULDING usually three-quarters of a circle in section; also called *edge roll*. *See* Fig. 20.

**Box**. A small country house, e.g. a shooting box. A convenient term to describe a compact minor dwelling, e.g. a rectory.

**Box-frame**. A box-like form of concrete construction, where the loads are taken on cross-walls. This is suitable only for buildings consisting of repetitive small cells, such as flats or hostels. Sometimes called *cross-wall* construction. *See* Fig. 21.

**Box-pew**, *see* PEW.

Fig. 20 Bowtell

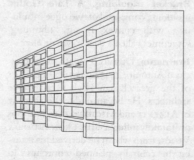

Fig. 21 Box-frame

**Boyceau**, Jacques de la Barauderie
(d.*c.*1633). Influential French designer
and theorist of French-style gardens. He
was a Huguenot, fought in the civil war,
became a gentleman of the royal chamber
under Henri IV and supervisor of gardens
under Louis XIII. For Marie de Médicis
he probably designed (with Claude MOL-
LET) the Luxembourg gardens in Paris,
which had the first recorded PARTERRE
DE BRODERIE. His posthumously published *Traité de jardinage* (Paris 1638) raised
garden design to a fine art with its curricu-
lum for the education of a gardener –
geometry, draughtsmanship, architecture
and artistic theory as well as horticulture
– and with its attention to the placing of
statues, fountains, etc., the management
of sloping sites and the proportional
relationships between open and planted
spaces.

F. Hazelhurst, *J.B. and the French
Garden*, Athens, Georgia 1966.

**Boytac**, Diego (*fl.*1490–1525), *see*
PORTUGUESE ARCHITECTURE.

**Brace**. A subsidiary timber, curved or
straight, set diagonally to strengthen a
timber frame. *See also* ROOF.

**Bracket**. A small supporting piece of
stone or other material, often formed of
scrolls or VOLUTES, to carry a projecting
weight. *See also* ANCONES; CORBEL.

**Bracket moulding**. A Late Gothic
moulding composed of two ogee mouldings with convex facings adjoining,
sometimes called a *double ogee* or *brace*.

**Bramante**, Donato (Donato di Pascuc-
cio d'Antonio, 1443/4–1514). The first
of the great Italian High Renaissance
architects. He began under the shadow
of ALBERTI and MICHELOZZO, and was
profoundly influenced by LEONARDO DA
VINCI, from whom he derived his interest in centrally planned churches. In
Rome he evolved a classic style of

imposing monumentality which was to
have a deep and lasting effect on the
development of Italian architecture.
PALLADIO declared that he 'was the first
who brought good architecture to light'.
He was born near Urbino, where he
probably met the leading artists at the
humanist court of Federigo da Montefeltro, Piero della Francesca, and FRAN-
CESCO DI GIORGIO, to whom he
presumably owed his interest in the problems of perspective. He is first recorded
in 1477 painting perspective decorations
on the façade of Palazzo del Podestà,
Bergamo, and he later (1481) made a
drawing which was engraved as a perspective model for painters. He entered the
service of Duke Ludovico Sforza *c.*1479,
for whom he worked at Vigevano as both
decorative painter and architect. His first
building of importance is S. Maria presso
S. Satiro, Milan (begun 1482). Here he
encased the tiny C9 Cappella della Pietà
in a drum decorated with niches flanked
by slender pilasters, and crowned it with
a rather chunky octagonal lantern. He
entirely rebuilt the rest of the church on
a Latin cross plan. Alberti's influence is
apparent in the design for the façade
(never completed), the use of shallow
pilasters on the side wall and the barrel-
vaulted nave. There was no room for a
chancel so he feigned one in *trompe l'œil*
painting and relief (still deceptive if seen
from the right spot). Above the crossing
he built a dome with coffered interior,
the first since Roman times. He also built
an octagonal sacristy, very richly decorated with carvings. In 1488 he was
appointed consultant to Pavia Cathedral
but only the crypt was carried out according to his proposals. The great centrally
planned east end of S. Maria delle Grazie,
Milan, in which Leonardo was involved
with him, was begun in 1493, spacious
and airy internally, but with a lavish use
of elegant but rather finicking carving on

the exterior of the apses and the sixteen-sided drum which encases the dome (though much of this ornament may have been added without the warrant of his designs). For S. Ambrogio, Milan, he designed the Canons' Cloister (1492, only one wing built) and a further group of four cloisters (1497, two completed after 1576 to his plans). In the Canons' Cloister he used slender Corinthian columns with high friezes and boldly projecting impost blocks, and four columns in the form of tree trunks with the stumps of sawn-off branches protruding from the cylinders, a motif which was a learned reference to the origin of the orders as well as a personal emblem of Ludovico Sforza.

In 1499 the French invasion of Lombardy and the fall of the Sforzas forced him to flee to Rome, then the artistic centre of Italy. Apart from some frescoes, his first work in Rome was a cloister at S. Maria della Pace (1500), astonishingly different from anything he had previously designed. It has sturdy Doric piers and attached Ionic columns derived from the Colosseum on the ground floor, and an open gallery on the first with alternate Corinthian columns and Composite piers supporting not arches but an architrave. The effect is wholly Roman in its quiet gravity. He became still graver and more Roman in his next building, the circular Tempietto of S. Pietro in Montorio, Rome (commissioned 1502, built c. 1504–after 1510), the first great monument of the High Renaissance and the first to show the correct use of the Doric order since antiquity, which has a majestic solemnity belying its small size. Surrounded at the base by a Tuscan Doric colonnade with a correct classical entablature, it has no surface decorations apart from the metopes and the shells in the niches. It was intended to have been set in the centre of a circular peristyle which would have provided the perfect spatial foil to

its solidity, for it is conceived in terms of volume rather than space, like a Greek temple. Here the Renaissance came closer to the spirit of antiquity than in any other building.

The election of Pope Julius II in 1503 provided Bramante with a new and wholly congenial patron who commissioned him to draw up a vast building plan for the Vatican and St Peter's. A range of buildings later incorporated in the Cortile di S. Damaso was promptly begun, with three tiers of superimposed arcades. Though massive, this was relatively modest in comparison with the scheme for the Cortile del Belvedere, a huge courtyard on three levels measuring about 290 m. by 70 m. (950 ft by 225 ft), flanked by arcaded buildings, with a theatre at the lower end and a museum for classical antiquities with a central exedra closing the upper court. Work began at the museum end, but only the first storey was completed to his designs (much altered later). The only one of his works in the Vatican which survives intact is the handsome spiral ramp enclosed in a tower of the Belvedere (c. 1505). For St Peter's he proposed a church that would have been the *ne plus ultra* in centralized planning – a Greek cross with four smaller Greek crosses in the arms, roofed by a vast central dome as large as the Pantheon's with four smaller domes and four corner towers, all standing isolated in an immense *piazza*. The foundation stone was laid in 1506 and building was begun but little was completed before the Pope's death in 1513 brought all work to a halt. (There are analogies between his designs for St Peter's and the 'Ninfeo' at Genazzano now attributed to him.) The choir for S. Maria del Popolo, Rome (1505–9), is small in scale but grand in conception, with a massively coffered vault and shell-capped apse. Its combination of painting, sculpture and architecture anticipated

Raphael's Chigi Chapel and the Baroque concept of the *Gesamtkunstwerk*. The Santa Casa at Loreto (begun 1509) is almost as Roman as the Cortile del Belvedere, though heavily and richly decorated with sculptures by Andrea Sansovino, Tribolo, Baccio Bandinelli, G. B. della Porta and others. He also designed and began Palazzo Caprini, Rome (1502–10, later altered out of recognition), with a heavily rusticated basement and five pedimented windows between coupled half-columns on the upper floor, a design which was to be among the most influential in Renaissance architecture. The house was later acquired by RAPHAEL, who inherited his position as leading architect in Rome.

A. Bruschi, *B.*, London 1977; L. Patetta, *L'architettura del quattrocento a Milano*, Milan 1987; Heydenreich and Lotz 1996.

**Bramantino** (*fl.* 1503–36), *see* SUARDI, Bartolomeo.

**Branch tracery**, *see* TRACERY.

**Brattishing**. An ornamental cresting on the top of a screen or cornice usually formed of leaves, Tudor flowers or miniature battlements.

**Brazilian architecture and landscape architecture**. Brazil was settled by the Portuguese early in the C16 and remained a Portuguese colony till 1807. The country became an independent empire in 1822, and a republic in 1889. Architecture during the colonial centuries remained dependent on Portugal; one of the earliest Baroque churches is S. Bento at Rio of 1652. The centres of the Baroque, however, are S. Salvador de Bahia and the towns of Minas Gerais, where gold was discovered in the late C17. At Bahia the Terceiros church of 1703 is exuberantly CHURRIGUERESQUE; so is the decoration of the church of S. Francisco (1708 onwards). The architec-

tural climax of Brazilian Baroque, however, is Ouro Preto near Belo Horizonte, with its many churches of the second half of the C18, mostly with two façade towers and elongated central plans. To the same group belongs the church of Bom Jesus at Congonhas do Campo (1777): sculpture here and in several of the Ouro Preto churches is by ALEIJADINHO.

A revulsion from the Baroque came only after 1815. French artists immigrated, including A. J. V. Grandjean de Montigny (1776–1850), who finished the Customs House at Rio in 1820. A little later, but still French Classical, is the theatre at Recife by Louis Vauthier (*c.*1810–77), and the rather more American-Colonial-looking theatre at Belém do Pará (1868–78) with its attenuated giant portico. The neo-Baroque is best illustrated by the opera house at Manáus of 1890–96.

While all this had been first colonial and then peripheral, Brazil became one of the leading countries of the world in architecture after the Second World War. The Modern Movement had been introduced by the white cubic houses built from 1928 onwards by Gregori Warchavchik (1896–1972), who had published his *Manifesto on Modern Architecture* in 1925. LE CORBUSIER visited Brazil briefly in 1929, and again in 1936, in connection with the proposed new Ministry of Education at Rio. The building was begun to an amended plan by a group of young Brazilian architects in 1937. Among them were both Lucio COSTA and Oscar NIEMEYER, now the most famous Brazilian architects. Niemeyer was especially important for his early buildings at Pampulha, a club, a dance hall and a casino of 1942, and a church of 1943. They were the earliest buildings in any country resolutely and adventurously to turn away from the international rationalism then just being accepted by progressive authorities and clients in most countries. Instead, Niemeyer introduced parabolic curves in elevation, a tower with tapering sides, passages under canopies snaking their way from one building to another, a pair of monopitch roofs slanting downward to where they meet. Other architects whose names have become familiar are Marcelo and Milton Roberto (1908–64 and 1914–53), Rino Levi (1901–65) and Affonso Eduardo Reidy (1909–64), whose Pedregulho Housing development (1947–55) and Museum of Modern Art, Rio (1954–7), are outstanding. The Italian-born Lina Bo Bardi (1914–92), who settled in São Paulo in 1946, should also be mentioned. Her Art Museum (1959–68) and Pompeia Factory Sports Complex (1977), both in São Paulo, were notable.

Lucio Costa's name became a household word overnight when in 1956 he won the competition for the plan of Brasilia, the new capital of Brazil. The principal buildings there are by Niemeyer: the hotel, the brilliant president's palace, the palaces of the three powers, and the ministry buildings. Niemeyer's centrally planned cathedral was dedicated in 1970. The landscape architect Roberto BURLE MARX contributed notably to the setting.

**Breeze block**. A cheap building block made with coke breeze, i.e. coke and coke cinders and cinder dust. Joinery can be nailed or screwed to them. Now superseded by CLINKER BLOCKS.

**Brenna, Vincenzo** (1745–1820), *see* CAMERON, Charles.

**Bressumer** or **breastsummer**. A horizontal timber which carries a wall above, such as the beam supporting a projecting gable or the lintel of a wide opening like a fireplace.

**Brettingham**, Matthew (1699–1769).

An undistinguished English architect, but had a large practice and built Holkham Hall, Norfolk, to KENT's designs. He later claimed to have designed it himself. Few of his own works survive; Langley Hall, Norfolk (c. 1745), is probably the best. In London he designed several important town houses: Norfolk House (1748–52, demolished 1938), York House, Pall Mall (1761–3, demolished), and No. 5, St James's Square (1749). His son Matthew (1725–1803) was also an architect, equally successful and equally undistinguished.

Summerson 1991; Colvin 1995.

**Breuer**, Marcel (Laiko) (1902–81). Born in Hungary, he studied at the BAUHAUS from 1920. In 1925 he was put in charge of the joinery and cabinet workshop, and in that year designed his first tubular steel chair. He went to London in 1935, to Harvard in 1937, and was in a partnership with GROPIUS (1937–40). His independent practice in America started effectively only after the Second World War. He was first commissioned to design private houses in New England. A sympathy with natural materials (rubble, timber), derived perhaps from his Bauhaus days, had already been apparent in some of his work in England and was evident in his own house at New Canaan, Connecticut (1951, remodelled 1981 by Breuer's former partner Herbert Beckhard (b. 1926)). Later his practice spread to other countries (Bijenkorf, Rotterdam, with Elzas, 1953; Unesco, Paris, with ZEHRFUSS and NERVI, 1953–8), and his style then followed the rather less rational, more arbitrary trend of architecture in general (Abbey of St John, Collegeville, Minnesota, 1953–61, and the Lecture Hall for New York University on University Heights, Bronx, New York, 1956–61). The Whitney Museum of American Art, New York (1963–6), the Housing and Urban Development Headquarters Building, Washington, DC (1963), and the IBM complex at Boca Raton, Florida (1967–77) were his last important works. He published *Sun and Shadow. The Philosophy of an Architect* (ed. P. Blake) in 1956.

C. Jones (ed.), *M.B. 1921–1961 Buildings and Projects*, London 1962; T. Papachristou, *M.B. Neue Bauten und Projekte*, Stuttgart 1970; D. Masello, *Architecture without Rules. The Houses of M.B. and Herbert Beckhard*, London and New York 1993.

**Brickwork**. Bricks made from sun-dried or fired clay were being used in the Tigris and Euphrates valleys for building at least as early as 3000 BC and from there spread to Egypt, Persia and India, e.g. at Mohenjo-Daro, Pakistan (*c*.2000 BC). Fired bricks were used at Nimrud (883–859 BC) but the finest early example of kiln-baked bricks is the Ishtar Gate from Babylon, *c*.575 (Staatliche Museen, Berlin), *see* GLAZED BRICKS. Greatly developed in the Ancient Roman world, though often disguised by marble and other cladding, brickwork was exploited for decorative as well as structural use in Islamic Asia, notably at the Tomb of the Samanids, Bokhara, Uzbekistan (*c*.914–43). In Europe brickwork declined in the early Middle Ages and did not recover until the C13. For glass bricks, developed in the late C19, *see* GLASS. *See also* TERRACOTTA.

For English brickwork the terminology is as follows: A *header* is a brick laid so that the end only appears on the face of the wall, while a *stretcher* is a brick laid so that the side only appears on the face of the wall. A *closer* is half a header and is sometimes used to finish the brickwork of every other course at the end of a wall or against an opening.

*English bond* is a method of laying bricks so that alternate courses or layers on the

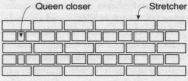

English bond

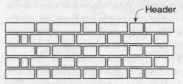

Flemish bond

Fig. 22  Brickwork

face of the wall are composed of headers or stretchers only. *English garden wall bond* is a method of laying bricks so that three courses of stretchers alternate with one course of headers on the face of the wall. *Flemish bond* is a method of laying bricks so that alternate headers and stretchers appear in each course on the face of the wall. *Heading bond* is composed of headers only. *Monk bond* is a variation of Flemish bond, two stretchers and one header being repeated in one course. *Nogging* is the name given to brickwork used to fill the spaces between the timbers in a timber-framed building. *See* Fig. 22.

**Bridge**. A built construction spanning a river, canal, ravine, etc. or connecting two points at a height above the intervening ground and allowing free passage beneath. The main types are: *girder bridges*, resting on supports at either end; *arch bridges*, borne on arches or arched vaults (*see also* AQUEDUCT; VIADUCT); *suspension bridges*, with the framework hung from high masts (e.g. TELFORD's Menai Straits Bridge of 1819–26), and *cantilever bridges*. There are three main types of movable bridges: the simple *drawbridge*, the *swing bridge*, which moves horizontally, and the *bascule bridge*, which moves vertically on the see-saw principle (e.g. Tower Bridge, London). The earliest surviving bridge of any length is that of Martorell in Spain, *c.*219 BC, with a centre arch 40 m. (130 ft) across. Cast iron was used for bridges from 1779 (first at Coalbrookdale, England) and the C19 introduction of railways led to swift developments in bridge-building, notably by George Stephenson (1781–1848), Robert Stephenson (1803–59) and BRUNEL in England, EIFFEL in France, and John A. Roebling (1806–69) in the USA. Roebling's most famous bridge is the Brooklyn Bridge, New York, begun in 1867 and completed by his son Washington in 1883. The outstanding bridges of the early C20 reflect developments in concrete construction, notably those by FREYSSINET, HENNEBIQUE, MAILLART and, more recently, MORANDI, ARUP, CALATRAVA and VAN BERKELL. *See also* CLAPPER BRIDGE.

R. Mainstone, *Developments in Structural Form*, London 1975; C. Jurecka, *Brücken Historische Entwicklungen – Faszination der Technik*, Vienna and Munich 1979; F. Leonhardt, *Brücken – Ästhetik und Gestaltung*, Stuttgart 1982; D. P. Billington, *The Tower and the B. The New Art of Structural Engineering*, Princeton 1983.

**Bridgeman**, Charles (d.1738). English landscape architect and from 1728 Royal Gardener. A plan of the garden he designed for VANBRUGH's Eastbury Park, Dorset (begun 1718), reveals his mastery of a tightly-knit geometrical layout. But his later, innovatory works are marked by his incorporation of parterres, straight avenues and geometrically planned ponds or lakes in parks where most of the space was given up to irregularly planted woods and wide areas of grass, sometimes pasture or arable land. Exploiting such natural features as low hills and winding streams,

and opening up views of the surrounding country by means of the HA-HA, he became one of the creators of the English LANDSCAPE GARDEN, notably at Stowe, Buckinghamshire (begun 1713), and Claremont, Surrey (begun *c.*1725). He collaborated with architects who designed temples etc. for parks, e.g. with Vanbrugh at Stowe, of which he commissioned a set of large prints published posthumously. None of his layouts has survived intact, their geometrical elements having been obliterated e.g. by KENT at Stowe and Claremont. But in Kensington Gardens, London, the Round Pond (1728) and lake, the Serpentine (1731), exemplify the two, old and new, styles in which he worked.

P. Willis, *C.B. and the English Landscape Garden*, London 1978.

**Brinkman**, Johannes Andreas (1902–49). Notable Dutch architect ranking with RIETVELD, DUIKER, OUD and STAM in the inter-war period of DE STIJL. His most famous building was the Van Nelle Factory, Rotterdam (1926–30), with Stam and Cornelius Van der Vlugt (1894–1936). His White Houses (1927–8) and the Fegenoord Stadium, Rotterdam (1934–6), were notable.

J. Geurst and J. Molenaar, *Van der Vlugt, Architect 1894–1936*, Delft 1983; Curtis 1996.

**Brise-soleil**. A sun-break or check; now frequently an arrangement of horizontal or vertical fins, used in hot climates to shade the window openings.

**Broach spire**, *see* SPIRE.

**Broach-stop**, *see* STOP-CHAMFER.

**Broch**. A prehistoric Scottish stronghold, in form a circular double-walled drystone tower with a central court. The best preserved is the Broch of Mousa on Shetland.

Brodrick, Cuthbert

**Brodrick**, Cuthbert (1822–1905). An English (Yorkshire) architect whose capital work is the Leeds Town Hall (1853–8), a grand edifice with a many-columned dome, influenced by COCKERELL and WREN. More original is his Leeds Corn Exchange (1861–3), elliptical in plan, Italian Renaissance in style, and with little in the way of enrichment. He also did the wondrously big and heavy Grand Hotel at Scarborough in a style paying tribute to the then fashionable French Renaissance (1863–7), and the Town Hall of Hull (1862–6).

T. B. Wilson, *Two Leeds Architects: C.B. and George Corson*, Leeds 1937; Hitchcock 1977.

**Broek**, Johannes Hendrik van der (1898–1978), *see* BAKEMA, Jacob Berend.

**Broken pediment**, *see* PEDIMENT.

**Brongniart**, Alexandre-Théodore (1739–1813). French neo-classical architect, born in Paris and trained under J.-F. BLONDEL. In 1765 he began his very successful independent practice, designing the theatre at Caen (destroyed) and the Hôtel de Montesson, Paris. For his private houses he adopted a graceful and unpedantic neo-classical style, the nearest equivalent in architecture to the sculpture of Clodion, who was several times employed to decorate them (e.g. Hôtel de Condé, Paris, designed 1780). For the Capuchin convent in the Chaussée d'Antin, now Lycée Condorcet (1780–82, façade rebuilt 1864), he developed a much more severe manner, designing a colonnade of Paestum Doric columns for the cloister. In 1804 he was entrusted with the new cemetery of Père-Lachaise in Paris and its *jardin anglais* layout was very influential. His last important work was the Paris Bourse, an appropriately grandiose Corinthian building in the Imperial Roman style (begun 1807, altered and enlarged 1895).

Braham 1980; *A.-T.B. 1739–1813*, exh. cat., Musée Carnavalet, Paris 1985; *A.-T.B., 1739–1813 architecture et décor*, Paris 1986.

**Brooks**, James (1825–1901). An English Gothic-Revival church architect whose directness of approach is comparable to BUTTERFIELD's; but, where Butterfield is obstinate and perverse, Brooks excels by a simplicity which LETHABY called big-boned. His favourite material was stock brick, his favourite style that of the early C13 with lancet windows and apse. His principal churches are all in London: first a group in the poor north-eastern suburbs (St Michael, Shoreditch, 1863; Holy Saviour, Hoxton, 1864; St Chad, Haggerston, 1867; St Columba, Haggerston, 1867); and then, a little more refined, three individual masterpieces, among the best of their date in the country: the Ascension, Lavender Hill (1874); the Transfiguration, Lewisham (1880, recently mutilated by the insertion of a *mezzanine* floor above the arcades); and All Hallows, Gospel Oak (1889), all in London. The latter was intended to be vaulted throughout.

Clarke 1969; Hitchcock 1977; Dixon and Muthesius 1978.

**Brosse**, Salomon de (*c.*1571–1626). French architect born at Verneuil, where his maternal grandfather Jacques Androuet DU CERCEAU was building the *château*. His father was also an architect. He settled in Paris *c.*1598, and was appointed architect to the Crown in 1608. Unlike his relations in the Du Cerceau family and his predecessor BULLANT he conceived architecture in terms of mass and not merely of surface decoration. This plastic sense is evident in his three great *châteaux* of Coulommiers (1613), Luxembourg (begun 1615, enlarged and

72

altered C19), and Blérancourt (1612–19, one pavilion survives). The latter is the finest, and was revolutionary in its day, being a free-standing symmetrical block designed to be seen from all sides. In 1618 he began the Palais du Parlement at Rennes, to which his feeling for sharply defined masses and delicacy of classical detail gives great distinction. (There are some C19 alterations.) In 1623 he built the Protestant Temple at Charenton. His frenchified classicism is epitomized in the façade of St Gervais, Paris (1623), which combines VIGNOLA's Gesù scheme with L'ORME's frontispiece at Anet with three superimposed orders. He was the most notable precursor of François MANSART, whom he anticipated in some ways.

R. Coope, *S. de B. and the Development of the Classical Style in French Architecture from 1565 to 1630*, London 1972.

**Brown**, Lancelot (nicknamed Capability) (1716–83). The most famous English landscape architect. He began as a gardener in his native Northumberland and in 1741 became head gardener and supervisor of building work at Stowe, Buckinghamshire, where he collaborated with KENT in improving what was already one of the most famous LANDSCAPE GARDENS. From 1749 he was widely employed as a consultant for laying out parks, designing their temples, Gothic gateways, bridges, etc., including additions to extant buildings as well as a few complete and large buildings, notably Croome Court, Worcestershire (1751–3), and, in collaboration with his son-in-law H. HOLLAND, Claremont House, Surrey (1771–4). He described his landscaping work as 'place making', the exploitation of a site's potentialities – what he called its capability, hence his nickname – to create a perfectly integrated environment. Very soon he developed an artfully informal manner,

planning numerous parks with wide expanses of closely cropped rolling land, clumps of trees, streams and serpentine lakes which provided a perfect setting for the neo-Palladian country seat, placed directly on grassland without any formal approaches. He did away with parterres, stone steps, balustrades, etc., although sometimes allowing space for a flower garden. A thick planting of trees served to conceal the bounds of the idyllic park as well as any disturbing features in the unimproved landscape beyond. His probably apocryphal remark on his lake at Blenheim, 'Thames, Thames, you will never forgive me,' sums up his attitude. His parks were less an alternative to geometrically planned gardens than an alternative to raw nature which proved irresistibly appealing not only in England but also on the European continent (especially Germany) and North America. In England his parks were increasingly criticized from the 1770s, by CHAMBERS for their similarity to common pastureland, later by KNIGHT, PRICE and others of the PICTURESQUE school for their mannered artificiality, lack of variety and tendency to create a single mood of somnolent tranquillity. The best preserved are at Warwick Castle (*c.*1750), Croome Court, Worcestershire (1751–3), Bowood, Wiltshire (1761), Blenheim, Oxfordshire (1765, much altered), Dodington, Gloucestershire (1764), Ashburnham, Sussex (1767), and Nuneham Courtenay, Oxfordshire (1778).

D. Stroud, *C.B.*, London (1950) 1975; R. Turner, *C.B. and the C18 English Landscape*, London 1985; T. Hinde, *C.B. The Story of a Master Gardener*, London 1986; Summerson 1991; Colvin 1995.

**Brunelleschi**, Filippo (1377–1446). The first Italian Renaissance architect and one of the greatest, as elegant and refined as Botticelli and as springlike. Far less dogmatic and antiquarian than his immediate successors, e.g. ALBERTI and MICHELOZZO, he was less concerned with the revival of antiquity than with practical problems of construction and the management of space. He, more than anyone else, was responsible for linear PERSPECTIVE, and a preoccupation with the linear conquest of space characterizes his architecture. In his buildings the horizontals are marked by thin lines which seem to follow the guides of a perspective framework, while the verticals, columns and fluted pilasters have a spidery, linear attenuation.

Born in Florence, he began as a goldsmith and sculptor, joining the Arte della Seta in 1398, then working for a goldsmith in Pistoia (silver altar, Pistoia Cathedral, c.1399), and competing in 1401–2 for the second bronze door of the Florence Baptistery (he tied with Ghiberti but refused to collaborate with him). In 1404 he was admitted as a master to the Goldsmiths' Guild, and in the same year his advice was sought about a buttress for the cathedral in Florence. (A visit to Rome he is said to have made with Donatello after 1402 is now discounted.) He continued as a sculptor for a while, but gradually turned his attention exclusively to architecture. In 1415 he repaired the Ponte a Mare at Pisa; in 1417 he advised on the projected dome of Florence Cathedral. His first major works, all in Florence, date from 1418 onwards – a domed chapel in S. Jacopo sopr'Arno (destroyed), the Barbadori Chapel in S. Felicità (partly destroyed), the Palazzo di Parte Guelfa (much altered, but the prototype Early Renaissance palace), and S. Lorenzo. While these were in progress he began, in 1420, to build his masterpiece, the dome of Florence Cathedral (see Fig. 41), and in 1419 the Ospedale degli Innocenti in Florence.

At S. Lorenzo he began with the sacristy (finished 1428), a cube roofed by a very elegant dome with narrow ribs radiating from the central lantern, a type of construction he called *a creste e vele* (with crests and sails), which neatly expresses its appearance of canvas stretched over the quadrant ribs. The whole interior is painted white, while taut bands of grey *pietra serena* outline the main architectural members; this is the first instance of this strikingly effective decorative scheme. The church itself he designed as a basilica, adding shallow transepts and also chapels attached to the side aisles. But he drew his inspiration not from Imperial Rome so much as the Tuscan Romanesque or proto-Renaissance of the C11–12.

He was commissioned to build the cathedral dome in partnership with Ghiberti, who gradually slipped out of the picture. The dome is Gothic in outline with elegantly curved white ribs springing up to the centre, but it is essentially Renaissance in its engineering technique – herringbone brickwork in the Roman manner. The skeleton was completed in 1436, and a further competition held for the lantern – won this time by Brunelleschi alone. In 1438 he designed the semicircular tribunes with shell-capped niches and coupled Corinthian columns which stand beneath the drum.

The Ospedale degli Innocenti, Florence (designed 1419, built 1421–44), is often claimed as the first Renaissance building. It consists of an arcade of slender, even spindly, Corinthian columns with blue-and-white glazed terracotta plaques between the arches, and a first floor with widely spaced pedimented windows above the centre of each arch. The wide spacing of the arches harks back to C11 and C12 Tuscan work, but the detail is distinctly Roman.

In 1429 he began the Pazzi Chapel in the cloister of S. Croce, Florence. The plan is more complex than that of the S. Lorenzo Sacristy: an atrium in the ratio of 1:3, the main building 2:3, and a square chancel. (It was built on the foundations of an earlier chapter-house.) The interior decoration is more forceful than S. Lorenzo, with virile semicircular arcs of *pietra serena*, Corinthian pilasters, and, in the spandrels, glazed terracotta reliefs. The façade is odd, closer to the tribune of a basilica than a temple portico – slender Corinthian columns supporting a blank attic storey with shallow carved rectangular panels and coupled pilasters. It was not completed until long after Brunelleschi's death and may not have been designed by him. (A second visit to Rome he is said to have made in 1433 is now also discounted.) S. Maria degli Angeli, Florence, was his most archaeological design, though unfortunately building stopped after three years and only the lower parts of the walls remain. It was the first centrally planned church of the Renaissance (an octagon with eight chapels surrounding the central space, sixteen-sided outside with flat walls and deep niches alternating). At S. Spirito, Florence (begun 1436), he reverted to the basilican Latin cross plan, but gave it an entirely new centralized emphasis by running an aisle round the whole church (the west section never built). Once again the proportions are straightforward – an arrangement of cubes, half-cubes, and double cubes – creating that balance and feeling of tranquil repose which was among the chief aims of Renaissance architects. The classical ornamentation is correct and vigorous though sometimes employed in a slightly unorthodox fashion. Several other works have been attributed to him, notably the centre of Palazzo Pitti, Florence, which he may have designed shortly before his death. Though astylar it is clearly an Early Renaissance building, with its massive rusticated stonework inspired by Roman work and with proportions governed by a simple series of ratios.

Brunelleschi became the first Renaissance architect almost by accident. He seems to have been drawn towards Ancient Rome less for aesthetic than for practical, engineering reasons. An eclectic empiricist, he hit by instinct on those ideas which were to be developed by his successors. Perhaps his greatest merit was to have preserved Early Renaissance architecture from the dry pedantry of archaeology and Revivalism.

E. Battisti, *F.B.*, (Milan 1976) London 1981; H. Saalman, *F.B. The Buildings*, London 1993.

**Brutalism** or the **New Brutalism**. A term coined in England in 1954 to characterize the style of LE CORBUSIER at the moment of Marseille and Chandigarh, and the style of those inspired by such buildings: in England the SMITHSONS and STIRLING and GOWAN; in Italy Vittoriano Viganò (Istituto Marchiondi, Milan, 1953–9); in America Paul RUDOLPH; in Japan MAYEKAWA, TANGE, and many others. Brutalism nearly always uses concrete exposed at its roughest (BÉTON BRUT) and handled with overemphasis on big chunky members which collide ruthlessly.

R. Banham, *The New Brutalism*, London 1966.

**Bryce**, David (1803–76), *see* SCOTTISH ARCHITECTURE.

**Bryggman**, Erik (1891–1955), *see* FINNISH ARCHITECTURE.

**Bucrane** or **bucranium**. In classical architecture, a sculptured ox-skull, usually garlanded, often found in the METOPES of a Doric frieze. A similar relief of a ram's or goat's head or skull is called an *aegricane*. *See* Fig. 23.

Fig. 23 Bucrane

**Buddhist railing**. A barrier of stone carved to resemble a wooden fence, with horizontal slats woven through the verticals, made to surround a STUPA (as at Sanchi in India), but also carved in relief as a symbol. *See* Fig. 113.

**Building line**. A notional line marking the minimum limit in distance of buildings from a street, or defining the limit of frontages.

**Building systems**, *see* INDUSTRIALIZED BUILDING.

**Bulfinch**, Charles (1763–1844). American architect who came of a wealthy, cultivated Boston family. He graduated at Harvard and was, on his European journey in 1785–7, advised by JEFFERSON. His principal works are the Beacon Monument (1791) in Boston, a Doric column 20 m. (60 ft) high; the State House in Boston (1795–8); and the Court House, also in Boston (1810). They are perhaps the most dignified American public buildings of their time. In Boston extensive street planning and the building of terraces of houses with unified façades was also done under Bulfinch's chairmanship, notably Tontine Crescent (1793, demolished 1858). In his church plans (Holy Cross, Boston, 1805; New South Church, Boston, 1814; Church of Christ, Lancaster, Massachusetts, 1816) he was influenced by WREN, in his secular work

by CHAMBERS and ADAM. From 1817 to 1830 Bulfinch was in charge of work on the Capitol in Washington.

H. Kirker, *The Architecture of C.B.*, Cambridge, Mass., 1969; Whiffen and Koeper 1981.

**Bulgarian architecture**, *see* BYZANTINE ARCHITECTURE.

**Bullant**, Jean (*c.*1520/25–78). French architect whose early, rather pedantic classical style was based on L'ORME and the study of antiquity (he visited Rome *c.*1540–45), but it rapidly acquired MANNERIST complexities and, finally, in his late works for Catherine de' Medici, showed a fantasy similar to that of his rival DU CERCEAU. Much of his work has been destroyed. His additions to the Château d'Écouen illustrate his characteristically pedantic accuracy in classical details and no less characteristic misunderstanding of the spirit that stood behind them, as witness his most unclassical use of the colossal order. Mannerist features are striking in his bridge and gallery at Fère-en-Tardenois (1552–62) and in the Petit Château at Chantilly (*c.*1560). Of his work for Catherine de' Medici only his additions to Chenonceau survive – the western arm of the forecourt and gallery over the bridge (*c.*1576). He published *Reigle générale d'architecture* (1563) and *Petit traicté de géometrie* (1564).

Blunt 1982.

**Bullet**, Pierre (1639–1716). French architect, a pupil of N.-F. BLONDEL. He began in the classical academic tradition and did not display much originality until towards the end of his career at the Hôtels Crozat and d'Évreux in the Place Vendôme, Paris (1702–7). Built on irregular corner sites, they foreshadow the freedom and fantasy of Rococo architects in the shape and disposition of rooms. He wrote a theoretical treatise, *L'Architecture pratique* (1691).

Blunt 1982.

**Bull's eye window**. A small circular window like an ŒIL-DE-BŒUF.

**Bungalow**. A detached, single-storey house in its own plot of land. The term first occurs in 1784 as an anglicization of the Hindu word '*bangla*' and was given to lightly constructed dwellings with verandas erected for English officials in mid-C19 Indian cantonments and hill stations. Later the term was used for similarly light, simple dwellings built as second homes in England and America. In England the pioneer examples were at Westgate-on-Sea and Birchington (1869–82). So many of these were later built by unqualified designers that certain areas became known as 'bungaloid growths'.

A. D. King, *The B.: The Production of a Global Culture*, London (1984) 1995; C. Lancaster, *The American B. 1880–1920s*, New York 1985.

**Bunning**, James Bunstone (1802–63), *see* LABROUSTE, Pierre-François-Henri.

**Bunshaft**, Gordon (1909–90). American architect, chief designer for SKIDMORE, OWINGS & MERRILL from 1937 onwards. He was responsible for much of the firm's outstanding work, notably Lever House, New York (1952), the Manufacturers' Trust Building, New York (1954), the Marine Midland Building, 140 Broadway, New York (1967), and the National Commercial Bank, Jeddah, Saudi Arabia (1977–84).

C. H. Krinsky, *G.B. of SOM*, New York 1988.

**Buon**, Bartolomeo (*c*.1405–*c*.1467), *see* BON, Bartolomeo.

**Buontalenti**, Bernardo (1531–1608). Florentine Mannerist architect, painter and sculptor, and also a prolific designer of masques, fireworks (hence his nickname 'delle Girandole') and other entertainments for the Tuscan Grand Ducal court. He was even more sophisticated and stylish than his contemporaries AMMANATI and VASARI, e.g. the fantastic *trompe l'œil* altar steps in S. Stefano (1574–6), the perverse Porta delle Suppliche at the Uffizi (*c*.1580), and the grottoes in the Boboli Gardens (1583–8), all in Florence. But this preciosity and sense of fantasy was necessarily restrained in his major works, of which the most notable are the *galleria* and *tribuna* of the Uffizi (1584), the Villa di Artimino at Signa (1594), the façade of S. Trinità (1592–4), the Fortezza del Belvedere (1590–95) and the Palazzo Nonfinito (1593–1600), all in Florence, and the Loggia dei Banchi in Pisa (the design of 1605 was executed by Puglioni). He also produced a fantastic design for the façade of the cathedral at Florence (1587) and carried out much engineering work for the Grand Duke, notably at the harbour of Leghorn and a canal between Leghorn and Pisa (1571–3). His grand-ducal villa at Pratolino (1569–75) was destroyed in the C19.

I. M. Botto in *DBI* 1972; A. Fara, *B.B. Baumeister aus Florenz*, Basel 1990.

**Burgee**, John (b.1937), *see* JOHNSON, Philip.

**Burges**, William (1827–81). English architect, trained in engineering, then in the offices of Blore and Matthew Digby WYATT. He travelled in France, Germany and Italy, and was always as interested in French as in English Gothic forms. In 1856, he won, with Henry Clutton (1819–93), the competition for Lille Cathedral, but in the event the building was not allotted to them. In 1859 he added the east end to Waltham Abbey, Essex, where for the first time the peculiar massiveness and heavy-handedness of his detail comes out. He was a great believer in plenty of carved decoration, and specialized much less in ecclesiastical work than the other leading Gothic Revivalists. His principal works are Cork Cathedral (1862–76), still in a pure French High Gothic; the substantial addition to Cardiff Castle (1868–85); the remodelling of Castell Coch near Cardiff (1875–91); the Harrow School Speech Room (1872); and his own house in Melbury Road, Kensington (1875–80). Hartford College, Connecticut, was also built to his designs (1873–80).

J. M. Crook, *W.B. and the High Victorian Dream*, London 1981.

**Burghausen**, Hans von (d.1432), *see* STETHAIMER.

**Burle Marx**, Roberto (1909–94). Brazilian landscape architect, the son of a German father and a Brazilian mother of French descent. In 1928/9 he spent eighteen months in Berlin, studying painting, music and Brazilian flora in the Dahlem botanic garden. After returning to Brazil he studied painting at the National Academy, then directed by the architect Lucio COSTA, who commissioned him to design his first garden. By 1937 he was working as a landscape architect for clients of Costa and NIEMEYER, with whom he made his name internationally in 1939 at the New York World's Fair by designing the exotic garden court for their Brazilian Pavilion. The free forms and brilliant colours he used have affinities with contemporary, especially Surrealist, paintings, as do his plans with the biomorphic compositions of such artists as Arp and Miró. His gardens were in accord with Niemeyer's expressive architecture. He said that his aim was to rid gardens of European features and 'the romantic approach, since gardens must keep pace with human progress'. He made great use of Brazilian plants (many of which he had brought in

from the jungle himself) in exuberant, painterly but also sculptural compositions with as much sensitivity to space as to form. Of his private gardens, the extensive Monteiro House garden at Correias, Rio de Janeiro (1947), the intimate Carlos Somlo garden, Rio de Janeiro (1948), and his own at San Antonio da Bica are among the more notable. His public works include the roof-garden for Niemeyer's Ministry of Education (1938), Pendregulho Housing (1947–55), and the Museum of Modern Art (1954–7), all in Rio de Janeiro; East and West Parks and Canal Development, Caracas (1956); Botanical Garden, São Paolo (1961); Sousa Hospital, Rio de Janeiro (1966), and the 5 km. (3 mile) long promenade of the Copacabana Beach, Rio de Janeiro (1970). He was associated with Costa in the planning of Brasilia (1960), for which he designed parks and other landscaping. He was also active in the campaign to preserve the rain forests.

H. Adams, *R.B.M. The Unnatural Art of the Garden*, MoMA, New York 1991; Walker and Simo 1994.

**Burlington**, Richard Boyle, 3rd Earl of (1694–1753), was the patron and high priest of English PALLADIANISM and a gifted architect in his own right. He first visited Italy in 1714–15, but his conversion to Palladianism came after his return to London, which coincided with the publication of CAMPBELL's *Vitruvius Britannicus* and LEONI's edition of Palladio's *Four Books of Architecture*. He immediately replaced GIBBS with Campbell as architect of Burlington House and set out once more for Italy to study the master's buildings at first hand. He returned (1719) with his protégé William KENT, and for the next thirty years dominated the architectural scene in England. The widespread fashion for Palladio was largely due to his influence. He financed Kent's

*Designs of Inigo Jones* (1727) and in 1730 published Palladio's drawings of Roman *thermae*. But there was a marked difference between his own and his followers' interpretation of the master. For him Palladianism meant a return to the architecture of antiquity as explained and illustrated by Palladio, and he avoided, whereas his followers blindly accepted, all the non-classical and Mannerist features in the master's style. Cold, intellectual and aristocratic, he was described by Pope as a 'positive' man, and both the strength and weakness of Palladianism derive from his obsessive, puritanical urge to preach absolute classical standards – those just and noble rules which were in due course to 'Fill half the land with imitating fools' (Pope). His fastidious but dogmatic character is equally evident in his buildings, which became increasingly dry and pedantic. They have a staccato quality – an over-articulation or over-emphasis of individual features – suggesting a formula-loving mind. His *œuvre* appears to have consisted of about a dozen buildings designed mostly for himself or friends, beginning in 1717 with a garden pavilion – the Bagno (demolished) – at Chiswick, where he built his best-known work, the ornamental villa based on Palladio's Rotonda (*c.*1723–9). His only other important works to survive are the Dormitory, Westminster School, London (1722–30, rebuilt 1947), Northwick Park, Worcestershire (1730), and the Assembly Rooms, York (1732, refronted 1828). This latter is an exact model of Palladio's Egyptian Hall, based on VITRUVIUS. In addition to his independent work, he may be credited as part author of several buildings by his protégé Kent, notably Holkham Hall, Norfolk.

Wittkower 1974; Summerson 1991; C. Carré, *Lord B. (1694–1753) le connaisseur, le mécène, l'architecte*, Clermont-Ferrand (1985) 1993; J. Harris, *The Palladian Revival. Lord B., His Villa and Garden at Chiswick*, London 1994; D. Arnold (ed.), *Belov'd by Ev'ry Muse. R.B. 3rd Earl of Burlington and 4th Earl of Cork (1694–1753)*, London 1994; P. D. Kingsbury, *Lord B.'s Town Architecture*, London 1995; T. Barnard and J. Clark (eds.), *Lord B.: Architecture, Art and Life*, London 1995; Colvin 1995.

**Burmese architecture**. In Burma as elsewhere in South-East Asia durable materials were reserved for religious buildings, which are the only ones surviving from before the C19. As Buddhism has been, since an early period, the main national religion, STUPAS (confusingly known in Burma as pagodas) abound. The most sacred and famous, the Shwedagon in Rangoon, is traditionally said to have been founded in C5 BC but has been enlarged several times (finally in 1768) to its present height of 104 m. (342 ft) from its tiered platform. Covered in gold and encrusted with precious stones, its present characteristically Burmese form, with a spreading base from which a hemisphere merges into a spire, is probably a magnification of that given it in the C14. There are remains of C5–8 stupas and temples at the site of the city of Sri Ksetra, near Prome. But the largest group of ancient Burmese buildings is at Pagan, in a bend of the Irrawaddy, a city founded probably in C2 AD, much developed after 1044 and covering an area of 90 sq. km. (35 sq. miles) by 1287, when it was sacked by Mongols under Kublai Khan. Of its numerous surviving buildings the most notable are the Ananda temple (begun 1090), with a spiky, many-spired exterior constructed of stone on a Greek-cross plan with four porticos leading to two narrow vaulted concentric corridors for passage round a solid central block against which 10 m. (30 ft) high statues of the Buddha stand; the elegant stucco-decorated Schwegugyi temple, smaller but with more interior space (1131); the Kubyaukgy temple (1215, restored 1468), a brick-built imitation of the Mahabodi shrine at Bodh Gaya, India; and the massive brick Mingalazedi stupa, begun in 1274. After the fall of Pagan, the building of stupas continued at Pegu, Mingun and Rangoon. In 1857 a new capital was founded at Mandalay in northern Burma with an extensive, very intricately decorated wood-built royal palace, of which only a single pavilion survived destruction in the Second World War, in a square enclosure surrounded by walls and a moat. Buildings dating from the British occupation (beginning in south Burma in 1824) are numerous in Rangoon but undistinguished.

**Burn**, William (1789–1870), see SCOTTISH ARCHITECTURE; SHAW, Richard Norman.

**Burnacini**, Lodovico Ottavio (1636–1707), see AUSTRIAN ARCHITECTURE.

**Burnet**, John (1814–1901), see SCOTTISH ARCHITECTURE.

**Burnett**, Sir John (1857–1935), see EDWARDIAN ARCHITECTURE.

**Burnham**, Daniel Hudson (1846–1912). American architect, from an old Massachusetts family. His father moved to Chicago, and there, after several false starts, the son went into an architect's office, where he met J. W. ROOT. The two went into partnership, an ideal pair: Root was poetic and versatile, Burnham practical and a skilled administrator. Burnham and Root have an important share in the evolution of the so-called CHICAGO SCHOOL. Their best-known buildings are the Montauk building (1881–2, demolished), which heralded the advent of the skyscraper; the Monadnock building (1889–91), still a load-bearing masonry structure, though severely direct and unornamented; the Masonic Temple (1890–92, demolished), with its twenty-two storeys the tallest building in the world at the time it was built and with a complete steel skeleton (as introduced slightly before by HOLABIRD & ROCHE); the Reliance building, Chicago (1890, extended 1894); One South Culvert Building, Baltimore (1901); and the Flat-iron building in New York (1902). Burnham was made Chief of Construction for the World's Columbian Exposition in Chicago, which took place in 1893. Buildings were designed by HUNT, McKIM, Mead and WHITE, Charles B. Atwood (1849–95), POST, SULLIVAN, and others. The most monumental of them were classical and columnar, and this demonstration of BEAUX ARTS ideals cut short the life of the Chicago School. Though his Union Station, Washington, DC (1907), should be mentioned, Burnham was to concentrate more and more on town and area planning: his plans for the District of Columbia (1901–2) are the start of comprehensive town planning in America. They were followed by the plans for Chicago (1906–9) and many others.

T. S. Hines, *B. of Chicago: Architect and Planner*, New York 1979; Zukowsky 1988.

**Burton**, Decimus (1800–1881). English architect, the son of James Burton (1761–1837), a successful London builder. As early as 1822–3 he designed Grove House (now Nuffield Lodge, 1822–4) and the Colosseum (1823–7, demolished 1875) in Regent's Park, London. The Colosseum had a dome larger than that of St Paul's, and an elevator. It housed a panorama of London. In 1824–5 he began various additions and improvements to Hyde Park, London, including the Hyde Park Corner screen. Constitution Arch followed in 1827–8. He designed several housing estates, e.g. at Tunbridge Wells, Kent (1828 onwards), the centre of Fleetwood, Lancashire (1836–43); the great metal and glass palm house at Chatsworth, Derbyshire (with PAXTON, 1836–40, demolished 1920), and Kew, London (1841–8 with R. Turner, ironmaster in Dublin); several villas in Regent's Park, London; the Athenaeum, London (1827–30) and several country houses now mostly altered or demolished.

G. R. Williams, *D.B.*, London 1984; Summerson 1991; Colvin 1995.

**Buscheto** or **Busketus** or **Boschetto**. His name is recorded in documents of 1104 and 1110, and the Latin inscription on his sarcophagus, embedded in the façade of Pisa Cathedral, ascribes the building to him. Pisa Cathedral was begun in 1063 and consecrated, perhaps unfinished, in 1116. Nothing else is known about him, but the key role he appears to have played in the creation of Pisan Romanesque architecture has led to much speculation.

P. Sanpaolesi, *Il duomo di Pisa e l'architettura romanica delle origine*, Pisa 1975.

**Bush-hammering**. A method of obtaining an even, rough, 'rusticated' texture on concrete after it has set, by using a bush-hammer (a mechanically operated percussion tool) with a specially grooved head which chips the surface.

**Business park**. Buildings for offices, research establishments and sometimes light industry, with centralized facilities in a designed landscape setting, outside a town but close to major transport routes. It differs from an INDUSTRIAL PARK, from which it developed in the USA in the 1970s, in that space is let or sold subject to an overall masterplan. The most ambitious so far is Stockley Park, Heathrow, London, designed in 1985 by ARUP

ASSOCIATES: 395 acres of wasteland of which two-thirds were transformed into a park with artificial hills, streams and lakes and the rest into enclosures inspired by C17 French gardens in which the individually designed buildings (by FOSTER, SOM, ROGERS and others) are disposed. Other notable business parks include Bishop Ranch, San Ramon, California (MPA design, 1983–7); and Riverside Office Park, Bedford View, Johannesburg (Environmental Design Partnership, 1985–90).

A. Philipps, *The Best of B.P. Design*, London 1993.

**Butterfield**, William (1814–1900). English High-Church Gothic-Revivalist, aloof in his life (a bachelor with a butler) and studious in his work. The peculiar aggressiveness of his forms – one jarring with the other – and of his colours – stone and multicoloured brick in stripes or geometrical patterns – was tolerated by the purists of the Cambridge Camden movement and their journal *The Ecclesiologist*, partly because he was their personal friend (he drew much for the *Instrumenta ecclesiastica* of 1847), partly because he must have had a great power of conviction. His earliest church (and parsonage) of importance was Coalpitheath, Gloucestershire (1844). This was followed by St Augustine's College, Canterbury, quieter than most of his work. The eruption of his fully developed personal style came with All Saints, Margaret Street, London (1849–59), a ruthless composition in red brick of church and accessory buildings on three sides of a small courtyard. The steeple is slender, noble, north German Gothic, and asymmetrically placed. St Matthias, Stoke Newington, London, followed in 1850–52 – yellow brick, with a nave crossed by two transverse arches; then St Alban's, Holborn, London, in 1863; Keble College, Oxford, in 1867–75; the Rugby School buildings in 1870–86; and many others. Nearly all his work, apart from that for colleges and schools, was ecclesiastical. An exception is the robustly utilitarian County Hospital at Winchester (1863). His early cottages (c.1848–50) are also remarkably free from HISTORICISM. They provided the pattern for WEBB's Red House.

P. Thompson, *W.B.*, London 1971; Hitchcock 1977.

**Buttress**. A mass of masonry or brickwork projecting from or built against a wall to give additional strength, usually to counteract the lateral thrust of an arch, roof or vault.

*Angle buttresses*. Two meeting at an angle of 90° at the angle of a building.

*Clasping buttress*. One which encases the angle.

*Diagonal buttress*. One placed against the right angle formed by two walls, and more or less equiangular with both.

*Flying buttress*. An arch or half-arch transmitting the thrust of a vault or roof from the upper part of a wall to an outer support or buttress.

*Lateral buttress*. A buttress standing at the corner of a building on axis with one wall.

*Pier buttress*. An exterior pier which counteracts the thrust of a vault or arch.

*Setback buttress*. A buttress set slightly back from the angle. *See* Fig. 24.

**Bye**, Arthur Edwin Jnr (b.1919). American landscape architect who has laid out private gardens, notably that of F. L. WRIGHT's Roland Reisley House, Pleasantville, NY, as well as cemeteries, campuses and business parks, all with locally indigenous plants on apparently natural undulating ground. He is the author of *Art into Landscape. Landscape into Art* (1983) and *Abstracting the Landscape* (1990).

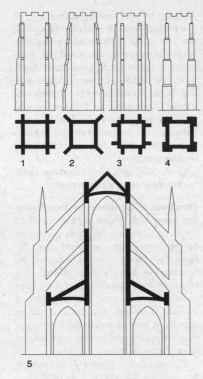

Fig. 24 Buttress: 1. Angle buttress 2. Diagonal buttress 3. Setback buttress 4. Clasping buttress 5. Flying buttress

**Byrd**, William II (1674–1744). A gentleman farmer and famous diarist who was the creator of the earliest recorded landscape garden in America. On several visits to England from 1706 onwards he encountered the theory and practice of the new style of landscaping and later laid out the grounds of his estate, Westover, Virginia, with irregular plantations of trees, a grotto and probably a ha-ha.

**Byzantine architecture**. The culmination of Early Christian architecture. This style developed after AD 330 when Constantine established the Imperial capital at

Byzantium (renamed Constantinople) on the Bosphorus. The arts in Rome were then at a low ebb, but no efforts were spared to make the new capital as traditionally Roman as possible. Such a building as the aqueduct of Valens differs little from those built in the West during the previous 300 years. But gradually a new and original style emerged. Classical concepts, such as the ORDERS, were no longer observed; classical detail of all kinds was coarsened and the lush relief decorations popular in Rome were abandoned in favour of flat, rather lacy ornaments. Early C5 churches in Cilicia (e.g. Kandirli and Cambazli), built in a mixture of Syrian and Roman styles, suggest that some of the new influences came from the East. The later C5 church of St John in Studion, Constantinople, also shows a tendency to depart from classical precepts. Yet classicism, or at least a desire to recapture the splendours of the classical past, was to remain a force of recurrent importance throughout Byzantine art, especially in the secular arts where the taint of paganism probably mattered less to early Christians. Very little is known of Byzantine domestic architecture, but recent excavations have revealed that the Imperial Palace in Constantinople was among the greatest buildings of its time.

In the C5 two forms of church were evolved: the BASILICA and the centrally planned church reserved for the shrines of martyrs. The latter, called *martyria*, were usually built on a Greek cross plan and were domed – the combination of a dome with a square base being a Byzantine introduction from the Near East. It was the achievement of C6 architects to combine these two forms of church and to create interiors in which a wholly unclassical play of void and solid, dark and light, produced an effect of mystery which is perhaps the most striking feature of the Byzantine church. The outstanding

masterpiece of Byzantine church architecture, Hagia Sophia, Constantinople (built AD 532–7 by ANTHEMIOS OF TRALLES and ISIDORUS OF MILETUS), shows this quality to perfection. But it was the mathematical and intellectual rather than the emotive qualities of Hagia Sophia that impressed contemporaries. 'Through the harmony of its measurements it is distinguished by indescribable beauty,' wrote Procopius. The same author commented that 'a spherical-shaped Tholos standing upon a circle makes it exceedingly beautiful'. At this time mathematics was considered the highest of the sciences, and Anthemios was a notable mathematician who believed that architecture was 'the application of geometry to solid matter'.

By the C9 symbolism began to play a greater part in Byzantine church architecture. The church was now regarded as a microcosm of all earth and sky, as the setting of Christ's life on earth, and at the same time as the image of the liturgical year. This complex triple symbolism was expressed in painted or mosaic decorations where the very colours used had an emblematic significance. The mystique of numbers also found reflection in church design. To the Byzantine these intellectual concepts were as important as the air of mystery created by screens and galleries dividing the well-lit central area from those surrounding it. The typical Byzantine CROSS-IN-SQUARE church plan (a Greek cross inscribed in a square and capped by a central dome and subsidiary domes) provided a perfect background for the display of this elaborate painted or mosaic decoration.

As early as the C5 the Byzantine style began to influence architecture in Italy, especially Ravenna (S. Giovanni Battista, S. Croce, and the so-called Mausoleum of Galla Placidia). The basilican S. Apollinare in Classe, Ravenna (*c.*536–50), and the octagonal S. Vitale, Ravenna (c. 526–47), are among the greatest and least altered of all Byzantine buildings. Though erected by Byzantine architects, and probably by Byzantine masons as well, both reveal slight Western peculiarities, notably in the decoration of the exterior. Later, Western buildings began to show more radical departures from Byzantine precedents – e.g. S. Marco, Venice, with its very rich marble-clad exterior.

The C7–9 marked a prolonged crisis for Byzantine civilization, under threat not only from external enemies (Persians, Arabs, Bulgars, etc.) but from the protracted and enigmatic internal schisms of the Iconoclast controversy – whose resolution in favour of the holy images (843) had not only theological but important aesthetic consequences for East Christian art and architecture, henceforth to be comprehensively and organically linked. The Middle Byzantine (i.e. C9–12) decorative system – representations of sacred persons and events, disposed with the more 'heavenly' scenes in the higher and eastern parts of the building, utilizing glass mosaic or true fresco and tempera panel-paintings (icons) – predicated appropriate architectural forms, of which the cross-in-square church, whose elements were picturesquely massed so as to culminate in a central dome on a tall drum resting (via pendentives or squinches) on four columns or piers, developed in this age as the characteristic type. To the basic quincunx of the ground-plan various additions or modifications could be made: these normally included three apses to the east and one or more narthexes (porches) to the west; subsidiary domes were often placed over the corner-bays.

The cross-in-square church-type – particularly suitable for smaller buildings – proliferated and refined itself throughout the middle and late (i.e. post-1261)

Byzantine periods; in Russia it outlived the Fall of Constantinople (1453) by at least two centuries. Its spread coincided with greater attention not only to the interior but to the exterior surfaces of the masonry: polychrome brick, stone and plaster-work, ceramic inlays, chiselled mouldings, low-relief sculpture, pseudo-Kufic 'lettering' become common decorative features. Though this can lead in late examples to fussiness, it generally gives Byzantine architecture a renewed liveness and joyful picturesqueness of total effect (cf. C14 examples such as Holy Apostles, Salonica or Pammakaristos, Constantinople). A small but important group of C11–12 churches (Hosios Loukas, Dafni, etc.) are built on a grander scale, their comparatively wide domes supported on an octagon of piers. Basilican plans do not entirely die out; most such churches are small, but an example impressive in its C11 remodelling is St Sofia at Ohrid, Macedonia. The later Byzantine period has also left us some scanty remains of domestic architecture: the palace known as Tekfur Saray in Constantinople, several monastic *ensembles* (notably on Mount Athos).

At no stage is it easy to define the geographical scope of Byzantine architecture, and the problem becomes particularly acute from the middle Byzantine period onwards: while the actual frontiers of the Empire tended to contract, its missionary activity and cultural prestige grew throughout Eastern and (more sporadically) Western Europe. 'Provincial' architecture from Aachen to Armenia, from Sicily to the White Sea, exhibits a wide variety of forms that are in obvious respects related to the Byzantine heritage, while they can with equal justice be placed in the context of the early development of national traditions. The religious division of Europe into Roman Catholic and Orthodox did not make itself deeply evident until the Western sack of Constantinople (1204), after which the cultural community of the East Christian world tends to be more closely felt. While, however, Constantinople continued to the end to be the chief focus for cultural endeavour in Eastern Europe and the chief repository (in particular) of classicizing tendencies in art and architecture, the history of so-called Byzantine architecture is by the late Middle Ages more and more to be read in the variety of surviving monuments originating beyond the direct sphere of Constantinopolitan influence – though this was capable of reasserting itself at any time up to the Fall. We shall therefore briefly examine each of the main national schools of East Christian architecture in turn.

The Transcaucasian states (Armenia and Georgia), Christian since the C4, preserve an exceptional wealth of building in fine local stone from all periods. Both basilican and (very inventive) centralizing plans are met with throughout, but particularly outstanding are some well-preserved domed churches from the beginning of C6 (St Hripsime at Etchmiadzin, Armenia, and Dzhvari at Mtskheta, Georgia); they seem more closely related to the Near-Eastern church architecture of Syria than to anything in Constantinople, and the extent to which Armenian builders actually originated (rather than followed) certain developments in Byzantine and even Western European architecture has been the subject of much inconclusive debate. By the beginning of the C11 great domed basilicas such as the cathedral of Ani, Armenia, and Sveti-Tskoveli, Mtskheta, have developed vaulting systems and decorative features that startlingly foreshadow the vocabulary of Romanesque and even Gothic church architecture. The massing of forms in smaller churches (e.g. Metekhi at Tbilisi, Georgia, 1278) has a more Byzantine feel.

But certain features remain characteristic of the architecture of the region: low-relief patterned carving (sometimes figurative – notably at Aghthamar, Armenia, C10) and prominent mouldings; faceted domes on high polygonal drums; a tendency for the external ground-plan to conceal rather than reveal the inner articulation. Independent Armenian architecture was extinguished with Armenia itself in the late Middle Ages, but in Georgia impressive (though no longer innovative) churches were still being produced in the C17 (Ananuri). Both countries preserve a certain amount of early secular building (e.g. the C13 monastic refectory of Hagartsin, Armenia; many fortresses in Georgia).

In Bulgaria, an independent and powerful state from the C7 to the early C11, excavations have revealed remarkable and extensive remains of the early palace complex at Pliska and the so-called Round Church at Preslav. The Byzantine coastal outpost of Mesembria (Nesebur) preserves, despite earthquake damage, a wealth of middle to late Byzantine churches; from the second period of Bulgarian independence (C13–14) many small cross-in-square and basilican churches survive in the capital, Turnovo, and elsewhere. After the Turkish conquest Bulgaria is notable for the quality of its vernacular wooden houses (at Arbanasi, Plovdiv, Ohrid – now in Macedonia – etc.).

Serbia became a unified state in the late C12, and a large number of interesting buildings survive from that time until Turkish domination became complete in 1459. Characteristic of the great C13 monastic churches such as Studenica, Mileševo, and Sopoćani (the Raška School) is the combination of Romanesque exterior features, derived through the Dalmatian coast, with the full and magnificent interior decorative scheme of an Orthodox domed basilica. The last and most ambitious of this series is Dečani (1327), said to contain the largest surviving area of medieval fresco-painting in the world. In the C14 Serbia expanded southwards, and the cross-in-square plan, often multi-domed, becomes usual. A magnificently ingenious variant of this is the pyramidically tiered church of Gračanica (1320). In the reduced Serbian state of C15 architectural activity and innovation continue with a series of buildings (the Morava School) of tall, narrow proportions, an abundance of external decoration and a trefoil ground-plan at the east end derived from churches on Mount Athos. The most remarkable and monumental work of the Morava School is probably the fortress-monastery of Manasija (1407). At Smederevo, the last capital, an extensive citadel with walls recalling those of Constantinople was built (1444 onwards).

Romanian architecture in the old heartlands of Wallachia and Moldavia carried on where Serbian architecture left off. No masonry churches survive from before the C14; though there are early examples at Cozia and Curtea-de-Argeş (St Nicholas) in Wallachia and at Radauţi in Moldavia, the 'golden age' of Romanian architecture starts in the post-Byzantine period at the turn of the C15–16 and lasts into the C17. In comparison with Serbian Morava architecture, Romanian churches are even more ornate, casket-like, elongated, tall, narrow, and fancifully adorned, with the occasional admixture of imported decorative features (e.g. Gothic window tracery). Most notable and original is a group of Moldavian churches decorated between c.1520 and 1600 with complete cycles of frescoes on the exterior (pro-

tected by overhanging eaves) as well as inside. The most bizarrely impressive building is the monastic cathedral at Curtea-de-Argeş (1517), representing a post-Byzantine mannerism whose extreme forms are equalled only in the near-contemporary St Basil's in Moscow (no direct connection is to be postulated).

RUSSIAN ARCHITECTURE is dealt with separately; Byzantine masons and mosaicists worked in C11 Kiev, and cross-in-square forms established themselves firmly from an early stage: the Byzantine heritage was not fully worked out until the post-Petrine modern age.

Finally, it must be noted that certain Greek areas (Trebizond, Cyprus and the 'monastic republic' of Mount Athos) remained independent of Constantinople in the late Byzantine period, and developed their own architectural traditions – notably the Athonite monastic cathedral-type, with cross-arms ending in semicircular apses, that was to provide the basic ground-plan for late Serbian and Romanian churches.

The Fall of Constantinople (1453) and Turkish conquest of the Balkans brought Byzantine architecture in the former Empire to an effective end; church architecture became extremely modest, externally visible domes a rarity. Turned in on itself, Orthodox architecture in the next four centuries developed aesthetic originality in only one direction: the vernacular art of elaborately carved wooden iconscreens, whose charm could only partially compensate for the rapid decline not only in architectural form, but in the decorative schemes of wall-paintings and icons. [R. R. Milner-Gulland]

Krautheimer 1986; C. Mango, *B.A.*, London 1986.

# C

**Cable moulding**. A Romanesque moulding imitating a twisted cord. *See* Fig. 25.

Fig. 25 Cable moulding

**Cable structures**, *see* OTTO, Frei.

**Cabled fluting**, *see* FLUTING.

**CAD**, *see* COMPUTER AIDED DESIGN.

**Caen stone**. Stone from Caen, Normandy, used in English medieval buildings.

**Cagnola**, Marchese Luigi (1762–1833). Italian neo-classical architect who played a leading role in the Napoleonic transformation of Milan, designing the severe Ionic Porta Ticinese (1801–14) and the much richer Arco della Pace (1806–38). He also designed a Pantheon-like parish church at Ghisalba (*c.*1830), a fantastic campanile crowned with CANEPHORAE supporting a dome at Urgnano (*c.*1820), and his own many-columned Grecian villa Inverigo (begun 1813).

Meeks 1966; G. Mezzanotte, *Architettura neoclassica in Lombardia*, Naples 1966; P. Favole in *DBI* 1973.

**Caisson**. 1. An air chamber, resembling a well, driven down to a firm foundation stratum in the soil and filled with concrete. It is used for construction below water (e.g. for the piers of a bridge) or on water-logged ground. 2. A sunken panel in a flat or vaulted ceiling (*see* COFFERING).

**Calatrava**, Santiago (b.1951). Spanish architect trained in Valencia and Zürich. He is as inventive and resourceful a concrete engineer as TORROJA and NERVI and as ebullient a designer as CANDELA. He made his name in 1987 with the 140 m. (460 ft) long Bach de Roda bridge at Barcelona, supported by an enormous but elegant fin-like sloping pylon with cables strung like a harp. His later bridges include those at Merida (1988) and Seville (1992). His railway stations at Lucerne (1989), Zürich (1990) and Lyons-Satolas (1994) are sculpturally moulded concrete constructions, gestural in their evocation of movement. Also notable are his 250 m. (820 ft) high telecommunications tower, the Torre de Montjuic, Barcelona (1989–92), and the Gallery and Heritage Square project, BCE Place, Toronto (1987–92). More recently he has been commissioned to design the cathedral of St John the Divine, New York.

M. McQuaid, *S.C. Structures and Expressions*, MoMA, New York 1993; D. Sharp (ed.), *S.C.*, London 1994; A. Tzonis and L. Lefaivre, *Movement in Structure. The Work of S.C.*, Basel/Berlin 1995; S. Polano, *S.C. Opera completa*, Milan 1996.

**Caldarium**. The hot-room in a Roman bath, *see* THERMAE.

**Calderini**, Guglielmo (1837–1916), *see* ITALIAN ARCHITECTURE.

**Caldwell**, Alfred (b.1903). American landscape architect who began under

JENSEN in Chicago and adopted his 'Prairie Style', e.g. for Eagle Point Park, Dubuque, Iowa, and Lincoln Park, Chicago (c.1936). From 1938 he was closely associated with the German refugee architects who had settled in Chicago, collaborating with MIES VAN DER ROHE on the layout of the Illinois Institute of Technology and with HILBERSEIMER on the Lafayette Park Development, Detroit (1955–9). He developed the latter's theories of regional planning both in practice – e.g. the single-storey farmhouse he built for himself at Bristol, Wisconsin (1948–73) – and in writing, with a strong socially conscious emphasis, *Architecture and Nature. The Work of Alfred Caldwell* (Boston 1984).

**Caliduct**. A pipe for conveying heat, usually hot air. A term invented by Sir Henry Wotton (*Elements of Architecture*, 1624).

**California School**. American landscape architects, notably BAYLIS, CHURCH, ECKBO and HALPRIN, working in California independently of one another and in individual styles from the late 1930s but all answering local demands for private gardens, often with swimming-pools, that extended the space of living quarters. Although designed for the American West Coast temperate climate that favoured out-of-doors living, their widely publicized gardens had world-wide influence.

**Callicrates** was the leading architect in Periclean Athens, and with ICTINUS designed the Parthenon (447–438 BC). He probably designed and built the exquisite little Ionic temple of Athena Nike on the Acropolis, Athens (448–after 421 BC). He also built the south and central portion of the Long Walls from Athens to Piraeus, and perhaps restored part of the city walls.

R. Carpenter, *The Architects of the Parthenon*, Harmondsworth 1970.

**Calotte**, *see* DOME.

**Camarin**. A small chapel behind and above the high altar in Spanish churches. It is usually visible from the nave. The earliest example is in the church of the Desamparados in Valencia (1647–67).

**Camber**. Of a horizontal timber, usually a tie-beam or a collar-beam (*see* ROOF), in which the centre is higher than the ends.

**Cambio**, Arnolfo di (c.1245–c.1310), *see* ARNOLFO DI CAMBIO.

**Cambodian architecture**, *see* KHMER ARCHITECTURE.

**Came**. A soft metal strip grooved at the side, used to divide adjacent pieces of glass in a STAINED GLASS window or in LEADED LIGHTS.

**Camelot**, Robert (1903–92), *see* ZEHRFUSS, Bernard-Louis.

**Cameron**, Charles (1745–1812). The son of a London mason, he became a pupil of WARE c.1764, went to Rome in 1768 and published *The Baths of the Romans* in 1772. Nothing more is known of him until he was summoned to Russia in 1779 by Catherine the Great. He lived there for the rest of his life. For Catherine he created several magnificent apartments in RASTRELLI's palace at Tsarskoe Selo near St Petersburg, to which he also made extensive additions, e.g. the Agate Pavilion and Cameron Gallery. The grounds had already been laid out in the English style from 1771, the earliest of its kind in Russia and one of the largest anywhere, but Cameron introduced improvements, giving the lakes more natural outlines and adding monuments and obelisks. For the Grand Duke Paul he built the great palace at Pavlovsk (1782–5) and the circular Doric peripteral Temple of Friendship in the English Park. In about 1787 he was superseded as architect-in-chief by his pupil Vincenzo Brenna (1745–1820), and when Catherine died in 1796 he was dismissed from royal service. But he stayed on in Russia, building for private patrons, e.g. the Razumovsky Palace at Baturin in the Ukraine (1799–1802, unfinished). He returned to favour after the death of Paul I, and in 1805 designed the naval hospital and barracks at Kronstadt. He was an admirer and close follower of CLÉRISSEAU and Robert ADAM, especially in interior decoration, though lacking Adam's finesse.

T. Talbot-Rice and A. A. Tait (eds.), *C.C.*, exh. cat., Edinburgh and London 1967–8; A. Kuchamov, *Pavlosk, Palace and Park*, Leningrad 1975; D. Shvidkovsky, *The Empress and the Architect: British Architecture of the Court of Catherine the Great*, London 1996.

**Campanile**. The Italian word for a bell-tower, usually separate from the main building. The earliest surviving Italian campanili are at Ravenna – circular and probably of the C9. The earliest recorded campanile was square and was attached to St Peter's in Rome. It went back to the mid C8.

**Campbell**, Colen (1676–1729). Little is known about him until 1715, when the first volume of *Vitruvius Britannicus* appeared and he built Wanstead House (1713–20, now demolished), which became the model for large English Palladian country houses. With Baldersby Park, North Yorkshire (1720–28), he initiated the neo-Palladian villa. He was probably responsible for Lord BURLINGTON's conversion to PALLADIANISM and was commissioned to remodel Burlington House, London (1718–19). Mereworth Castle, Kent (1722–5), is perhaps the best of the English versions of Palladio's Rotonda design.

Houghton Hall (1721, Norfolk, interior by KENT executed by Ripley with modifications by GIBBS) is enormous and imposing, but Ebberston Lodge, near Scarborough (1718), and Compton Place, Eastbourne (1726–7), are more elegant and refined.

H. E. Stutchbury, *The Architecture of C.C.*, Manchester 1967; Harris 1990; Summerson 1991; Colvin 1995.

**Campen** or **Kampen**, Jacob van (1595–1657). A wealthy and erudite painter-architect and the leading exponent of Dutch PALLADIANISM, an unpretentious, placid and economic form of classicism characterized by its use of brick mixed with stone and its straightforward, almost diagrammatic use of pilasters. He studied in Italy and probably knew SCAMOZZI, who certainly influenced him greatly, rather more indeed than Palladio. Van Campen's style is epitomized in his masterpiece the Mauritshuis, The Hague (1633–5), entirely Palladian in plan, with giant Ionic pilasters, raised on a low ground floor and supporting a pediment, crowned with a typically Dutch hipped roof rising in a slightly concave line from the eaves. His great Town Hall in Amsterdam (now the Royal Palace: 1648–55), built entirely of stone, is heavier but very imposing – the grandest of all town halls. More original is the Nieuwe Kerk in Haarlem (1645–9), of the Greek CROSS-IN-SQUARE type. He also designed the Coymans house on the Keizersgracht, Amsterdam (1624), the earliest example of Palladianism in Holland, the Noorde inde Palace, The Hague (1640), and the Accijnhuis and theatre in Amsterdam (1637). With Christian Huygens he was responsible for the general conception of decoration by Jordaens and others in Pieter POST's Huis-ten-Bosch. His domestic style had great influence through his followers Post, Arend van 's GRAVESANDE and Philip VINGBOONS. And it was later introduced into England by Hugh MAY and others.

K. Freemantle, *The Baroque Town Hall of Amsterdam*, Utrecht 1959; Kuyper 1980.

**Campionesi**. Italian (Lombard) sculptors and architects from Campione di Lugano, active from the late C12 to the C14 in northern Italy. In Modena Cathedral the late C12 rood screen is attributed to Anselmo di Campione, the Porta Regia (1209–31) to his son Ottavio, the completion of the campanile and the pulpit (1319) to Enrico. At S. Maria Maggiore, Verona, the baptistery (1340, later moved to the exterior) is inscribed to Giovanni di Campione, also one of the porches (1351). Campionesi also worked at the cathedrals of Milan, Monza and Trent.

A. M. Romanini, *L'Architettura gotica in Lombardia*, Milan 1964.

**Campo Baeza**, Alberto (b.1946), *see* MINIMALISM and SPANISH ARCHITECTURE.

**Campo santo**. Italian term for a Christian cemetery, usually with reference to an ancient burial ground, walled and enclosed. That at Pisa of 1278–83 by Giovanni di Simone (*fl.*1277), with its cloister-like interior, is the most famous.

**Campus**. A self-contained architectural composition of separate university buildings in a park-like setting with residential accommodation, libraries, classrooms, etc., for a community of students and teachers. The first, which broke away from the medieval quadrangle arrangement of university colleges, was Downing College, Cambridge, by WILKINS, begun in 1806. This seems to have been unknown to RAMÉE when he planned Union College, Schenectady, NY, in 1813 and to JEFFERSON when he conceived the University of Virginia at Charlottesville, 1817–26. These began a long tradition in the USA, from OLMSTED's University of California, Berkeley, in 1863 and Stanford University, California, 1886–91, to the University of California at Santa Cruz by CHURCH and others in 1960–62 and the University of New Mexico by ECKBO in 1962–92. In the USA the term *campus* is often used loosely for all university complexes, irrespective of their design and including those in cities; also for any park-like grounds attached to public buildings.

R. P. Dober, *C. Planning*, New York 1964; P. V. Turner, *C.: An American Planning Tradition*, Cambridge, Mass., 1984.

**Canadian architecture and landscape architecture**. History and geography combined to make Canada a colony first of France, then of Britain and finally, a nation entirely dependent for its continuing existence – unacknowledged as the fact may be – on the armed forces of a benevolent neighbouring power. Its architecture manifests these circumstances.

Not that it is necessarily impoverishing to follow rather than lead. Excesses and exaggerations can thereby be successfully avoided. The best of the past is oftenest preserved where pressure for innovation is least. In architecture, as in speech, colonies preserve forms longer than mother countries. Occasionally too, striking combinations of new and old can result from colonial conditions. All of which principles are demonstrable in Canadian architectural history.

For example, the parish church architecture evolved in mid-C17 French Canada constituted for all intents and purposes a genuinely creative response to colonial conditions. Its fusion of a Romanesque tradition, common from Carolingian times on, with certain up-to-date C17 Baroque details has a few parallels in France in locales where conditions roughly approximated those in Quebec, but is not a copy of anything in France. A good many examples of this architecture are known from old photographs and drawings – e.g. the parish church at St Laurent, Île d'Orléans, begun 1695, façade reconstructed 1708 by Jean Maillou (1668–1753, Royal Architect of New France), demolished 1864; Ste-Anne-de-Beaupré (built 1689 by master-mason Claude Baillif, demolished 1878); the old parish church of Les Trois-Rivières with Louis Quinze interior (1710, burnt out 1908). The best extant example is the chapel of the Ursuline Convent in Quebec, with its *récollette* retable executed 1734–9 by Noël Levasseur (1680–1740) and his cousin Pierre-Noël (1690–1770).

So distinctive was this church-type that after the Cession of 1763 it was successfully revived as a symbol of French resistance to assimilation in the form of a standard plan devised by Abbé Pierre Conefroy (1752–1816) which was applied in over thirty parish churches around Montreal, the region most threatened with assimilation. Good surviving examples are the churches of Lacadie (1801) and St Mathias, Rouville (1813). Conefroy's own church at Boucherville still stands, built in 1813, but considerably altered by later additions. This body of architecture is one of the earliest examples anywhere of typically C19 architectural eclecticism for associative reasons.

In the C19 parish organization remained the chief institution ensuring survival of a distinctive French culture in North America: accordingly, the C19 parish churches of Quebec constituted its most notable architecture. In the Quebec region, Thomas Baillairgé (1791–1859) created a body of architecture worthy in many respects of a place in any history of world architecture, even though his

climactic effort, the façade of the Basilica of Quebec, was abortive (1844–6). St Joseph Lauzon (1830–32, enlarged by insertion of an extra section in the nave, 1954) is a good representative example of Baillairgé's single-spired church type; of his twin-towered façades Deschambault (1834–8) is characteristic (this design also includes deliberate reminiscences of the 1803 Anglican cathedral of Quebec and the 1666–1807 Jesuit church in Quebec). Best-known and indeed a unique *pièce d'occasion* is the triple-towered façade of Ste-Famille, Île d'Orléans, resulting from Baillairgé's addition of a central spire in 1843 to mark the centenary of the original 1743 twin-towered structure.

Montreal's two major C19 churches are also important examples of eclectic architectural symbolism. Notre Dame, the 1722 parish church built by the Sulpicians, was replaced in 1824–9 by one of the continent's earliest and largest Gothic Revival churches, designed by an Irishman from Brooklyn, James O'Donnel (1774–1830). It was commissioned, apparently, with a view to asserting French Catholic presence in the English Protestant part of Montreal by a design supposed to resemble the medieval cathedral of Notre Dame in Paris – the whole concept being related to the Bourbon restoration and the Gothic Revival of 1815–35 in France. The cathedral of St Jacques was one of the last examples of the medieval practice of architects being sent to copy other buildings for associative reasons. Its genesis was in a visit to Rome by the diocesan architect, Victor Bourgeau (1809–88), commissioned by the Bishop of Montreal, Ignace Bourget, in 1870 for the purpose of reproducing St Peter's on a reduced scale as a new Montreal cathedral to symbolize Canadian support for the Holy See in its contest with Italian liberalism. Built in 1875–85 by Joseph Michaud (1822–1902) with

Bourgeau's collaboration, this replica of St Peter's may still be seen in the heart of Montreal.

The bulk of English Canada's architectural history consists of later styles. Already in 1750 a typical variant of Gibbs's parish church-type with Palladian detail had appeared in Halifax – St Paul's, whose frame was prefabricated in Boston (almost totally altered by remodellings in 1812 and 1867). But the bulk of these churches date from the Loyalist time after the American Revolution when they had ceased to appear, for obvious reasons, in the old colonies. Typical were churches like St Mary's, Auburn, Nova Scotia (1790); St Stephen's, Chester, Nova Scotia (1795), in the diocese of the violently anti-American bishop Charles Inglis; Holy Trinity, Quebec (designed in 1803 by Major William Rose, one of a typical family of soldiers and Empire administrators), and St George, Kingston, Ontario (designed in 1859 by George Browne of Belfast). C18 Baroque was likewise perpetuated in public buildings in early Upper Canada as a symbol of devotion to the Old Empire, e.g. Kingston's City Hall (1843 by George Browne); Victoria Hall, Cobourg (1856–60 by Kivus Tully of Belfast); Osgoode Law Courts, Toronto (1829 and later, original design by John Ewart); and St Lawrence Hall, Toronto (1850 by William Thomas).

A Late Gothic Revival superseded Georgian in English Canada from c.1840, shading into Italianate predominance by c.1860, thence into miscellaneous picturesqueness. Ecclesiologist architects designed cathedrals for St John's, Newfoundland (1846–85, substantially by the two Gilbert SCOTTS) and Fredericton (1843, substantially completed to designs by BUTTERFIELD), but these are more transplanted English than Canadian architecture. The most striking Canadian examples of picturesque mid-C19 styles come in a body of polychromatic brick farmhouses in southern Ontario from the 1870s to 1890s, their distinctive decorative detail deriving from a revealing complex of British origins – High Gothic Revival of medieval polychromy by Pugin, Butterfield and Ruskin plus characteristic Nonconformist middle-class industrial and commercial architecture as well as housing and small shop-fronts, throughout the Midlands, Ulster and Lowland Scotland. The Late Victorian similarly persisted in Canada a good generation after losing its dominance in Britain. Edward Lennox's Casa Loma, Toronto (1911), for example, is essentially the kind of adapted Scottish Baronial employed in Sir James Gowans's houses in Edinburgh in the 1870s and '80s (not to mention Balmoral Castle).

Landscape architecture was initially confined to small French-style gardens of which that of the Sulpician Seminary, Montreal (c.1680), survives. After the American Revolution LANDSCAPE GARDENS were created for the richer Loyalists who had crossed the US border and settled in Canada. From the early C19 the publications of LOUDON provided models for smaller-scale layouts. The major developments of landscape architecture began in the early C20 with MAWSON from England and TODD from the USA who designed the notable garden suburbs round Montreal. In the 1950s the French urban designer Jacques Gréber (1882–1962), who had previously worked in the USA, planned the remarkable network of parks and gardens of the National Capital Region of Ottawa.

A change in the design of public buildings became evident in the work of the versatile Ernest Cormier (1885–1980), whose Art Deco building for the University of Montreal (1928–55), classicizing Supreme Court, Ottawa (1938–50), and curtain-wall National Printing Bureau, Hull (1950–58), should be mentioned. Works like the Malton International Airport, Toronto (1963–6), the Union Railway Station, Ottawa (1969), and the New National Gallery of Canada, Ottawa (1976), all by John C. Parkin (b.1922); the City Hall, Toronto (1958–64), by Viljo Revell (1910–64); and, more recently, Simon Fraser University, Burnaby, British Columbia (1963–5), and Lethbridge University, Alberta (1971), by Arthur ERICKSON, or Scarborough College, Ontario (1962–9 with additions 1972), and Student Housing Complex, Guelph University, Ontario (1965–8), by John ANDREWS, must certainly count as major examples of current *avant-garde* modes. All major Canadian cities have examples of modern urban layouts and total environments: Place Ville-Marie, Montreal (1960 by I. M. PEI for William Zeckendorf), Dominion Centre, Toronto (1963–9 by MIES VAN DER ROHE) and the Robson Square development, Vancouver (1979) by OBERLANDER, being the best-known. Also famous internationally, as a result of Expo '67, was Moshe SAFDIE's Habitat, a seminal example of mass housing. He has since designed the Museum of Civilization, Quebec (1981–6), the National Gallery of Canada, Ottawa (1983–8), an extension to the Montreal Museum (1987–92), and the Library Square and Federal Tower, Vancouver (1992–5). St Mary's Church, Red Deer, Alberta (1968), and the Kehewen (1975) and later schools in Alberta, all by Douglas Cardinal (b.1934), are notable, more so than his later Canadian Museum of Civilization, Hull, Quebec (1983–9). More recently the City Hall, Mississauga, Toronto (1986–8), by Edward JONES in a classicizing Post-Modern style *à la* Ledoux is outstanding, as are also the 'organic' buildings by John and Patricia Patkau (b.1947;

b.1950), notably their Canadian Clay and Glass Gallery, Waterloo, Ontario (1988–92), Seabird Island School, Agassiz (1988–91), and the Strawberry Vale School, Victoria (1992–6), both British Columbia.

Special conditions in Canada have resulted in a number of outstanding works of historic architecture. University College, the main and for long the only building of Toronto University, designed in 1856 by William Frederick Cumberland (1821–81), a classmate and friend of John Ruskin at Oxford, has been compared to the Oxford Museum, designed on Ruskin's principles by Deane and Woodward; but University College is a better example of those principles, and an earlier one – a major monument of High Victorian picturesque eclectic style, as well as the typical High Victorian formal block with centre and corner towers. The design for the Dominion Parliament Buildings in Ottawa (1859, completed 1866, destroyed by fire in 1916 except for the Library, and rebuilt in a chastened vein), by Thomas Fuller (1822–98), clearly followed the mode of University College but Gothicized the detail to conform with Westminster Palace and express continuity of tradition between Old Britain and New Canada. Thus came into being a Canadian national style, carried through in many other government buildings all over the country, and most dramatically in the '*château*-style' hotels erected by the Canadian Pacific Railroad and its competitors from the 1880s into the 1930s. Its most representative examples are Château Frontenac, Quebec, and the Empress, Victoria, both dating from the 1890s and early C20, both deliberately composed as symbols of Canadian nationality marking the eastern and western entrances to the country by sea – and with Scottish castle details making both, as more than one critic has suggested, climactic monuments to Canada's status as a 'Scotch colony' in those first five decades when Canadian politics, business, railroading, journalism and homesteading were decisively dominated by Scottish immigrants.

Finally, any history of Canadian architecture should refer to the remarkable body of domestic architecture by Samuel Maclure of Victoria (1867–1929) in response to a curious social situation existing in the capital of British Columbia between 1890 and 1930 whereby an entire governing class effectively withdrew from concern with practical affairs to create an ideal world of retirement and refined leisure, the very image of *rentier* capitalism at its height. For this clientele, Maclure created a series of remarkable houses, mostly Tudor in detail, perfectly manifesting the values and lifestyles of an expatriate British aristocracy. Most still survive, typical examples being the Biggarstaff Wilson and John J. Shallcross houses in Victoria (1905–6 and 1907) and the Hon. Walter C. Nicol house in Sidney (1925). With his partner Cecil Croker Fox, Maclure also designed a number of mansions and public buildings for magnates in booming Vancouver, e.g. Boys Residential School, now RCMP headquarters (1914).

The impressive restorations undertaken by successive Canadian governments after the Second World War should be mentioned, notably Fort Louisbourg on Cape Breton Island, Nova Scotia, and the Hudson's Bay Post at Lower Fort Garry, Manitoba. [A. Gowans]

**Cancelli**. In early Christian architecture, a latticed screen or grille separating the choir from the main body of a church.

**Candela**, Felix (1910–97), was born in Spain but lived in Mexico from 1939. He was one of the most resourceful concrete engineers of the age, notably for SHELL

vaulting, and was also important architecturally. He was inspired initially by TORROJA. Among his most significant works, both in Mexico City, are the Church of Our Lady of Miracles (1953–5), an extreme example of mid-century EXPRESSIONISM, and the Cosmic Ray Pavilion, University City (1952), which is a tiny four-legged shed with a HYPERBOLIC PARABOLOID roof only about 0.5 cm. (1 inch) thick at the ridge. Later buildings by Candela are the Chapel of the Missionaries of the Holy Spirit at Coyoacán (1956, with Enrique de la Mora) with a simple saddle-shaped canopy on rough stone walls; the restaurant at Xochimilco (1958, with Joaquin Alvarez Ordóñez) placed in the water gardens like an eight-petalled flower of paraboloids; the Market Hall at Coyoacán (1956, with Pedro Ramirez Vásquez and Rafael Mijares), with the mushroom-shaped umbrellas which Candela later used at the John Lewis warehouse, Stevenage, Hertfordshire (1963, with Yorke, Rosenberg and Mardall); and the Olympic Stadium, Mexico City (1968). From 1971 to 1978 he taught at the University of Illinois, Chicago.

C. Faber, *C. The Shell Builder*, New York and London 1963; H. Ursula (ed.), *Zum Werk von F.C.*, Cologne 1992; J. A. Starezewski, *F.C. The Structure and Form of Reinforced Concrete Shells*, Ann Arbor 1993.

**Candi**. Javanese term for an ancient temple or shrine (*see* JAVANESE ARCHITECTURE).

**Candid**, Peter; or Peter de Wit or de Witte (1548–1628). MANNERIST painter and architect, born in Bruges. He was the son of a Flemish sculptor, Elias de Witte, with whom he went to Florence *c.*1573. He studied painting in Italy, perhaps under VASARI, and worked as a painter both in Florence and Rome. In 1586 he settled in Munich under the patronage of Duke Wilhelm V and Maximilian I, who had already attracted thither Friedrich SUSTRIS and the Mannerist sculptor Hubert Gerhard. Candid was involved as an architect in the later stages of the building of the Munich Residenz.

Hitchcock 1981.

**Candilis**, Georges (1913–95). French architect and town planner who worked with LE CORBUSIER from 1945 to 1948 and in 1950 founded a partnership with Shadrach Woods (1923–73) in Tangier. They worked extensively in North Africa, e.g. town plan for Casablanca (1952). Their most notable works were the town plans for Bagnols-sur-Cèze (1956–61) and Toulouse-le-Mirail, France (1960, carried out 1964–7), and the Free University complex, Berlin (1967–79).

A. Josic and S. Woods, *G.C. Ein Jahrzeit Architekten und Stadtplannung*, Stuttgart/Bern 1968; G. Candilis, *Bâtir la vie. Un architecte témoin de son temps*, Paris 1977.

**Canephora**. A sculptured female figure carrying a basket on her head.

**Canevale**, Isidore (1730–86), *see* HUNGARIAN ARCHITECTURE.

**Canina**, Luigi (1795–1856), *see* ASPRUCCI, Antonio.

**Canopy**. A hood suspended or projected over a door, window, tomb, altar, pulpit, niche, etc.

**Canterbury**, *see* MICHAEL OF CANTERBURY.

**Cantilever**. A horizontal projection (e.g. a step, balcony, beam or canopy) supported by a downward force behind a fulcrum. It is without external bracing

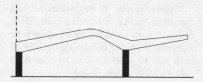

Fig. 26  Cantilever beam

and thus appears to be self-supporting. *See* Fig. 26.

**Cantoria**. Italian term for a singers' gallery, sometimes a prominent feature in Italian Renaissance churches, e.g. those of marble with reliefs by Andrea della Robbia and Donatello (Museo dell'Opera del Duomo, Florence).

**Cap**. The crowning feature of a windmill, usually a domical roof; also an abbreviation for CAPITAL.

**Cap house**. A small roofed superstructure to a stair leading to a parapet walk.

**Cape Dutch architecture**, *see* SOUTH AFRICAN ARCHITECTURE.

**Capital**. The head or crowning feature of a column, pier or pilaster. In Classical architecture capitals have canonical forms, i.e. Doric, Ionic, Composite, Corinthian (*see* ORDER). Terms commonly used for other capitals are modern and descriptive (and sometimes ambiguous).

*Aeolic capital. See* ORDER.

*Basket capital.* A Byzantine form, hemispherical or approximately so, decorated with a wicker design like a basket.

*Bell capital.* A form of capital of which the chief characteristic is a reversed bell between the SHAFT or NECKING and the upper moulding. The bell is often enriched with carving.

*Block capital, see* cushion capital.

*Crocket capital.* An Early Gothic form, consisting of stylized leaves with endings rolled over, similar to small VOLUTES.

*Cube capital, see* cushion capital.

*Cushion capital.* A Romanesque and Byzantine capital cut from a cube, with its lower parts rounded off to adapt it to a circular shaft; the remaining flat face of each side is generally a LUNETTE. Also called a *block* or *cube capital.*

*Lotus capital.* An ancient Egyptian type, like a lotus bud or flower.

*Palm capital.* An ancient Egyptian type, like the crown of a palm tree.

*Papyrus capital.* An ancient Egyptian type, like a bundle of papyrus stalks.

*Protomai capital.* A capital with half-figures, usually animals, projecting from its four corners.

*Scalloped capital.* A development of the *block* or *cushion capital* in which the single lunette on each face is elaborated into one or more truncated cones.

See also AFFRONTED; DOSSERET; STIFF-LEAF; WATERLEAF. See Figs. 27, 86.

**Capstone**. The coping stone on top of a wall.

**Caracol** or **caracole**. A spiral staircase (*see* STAIR).

**Caratti**, Francesco (d.1677). Italian architect born at Bissone near Como; went in 1652 to Prague, where he became the leading architect. His masterpiece is the Černin Palace (begun 1668), with a row of thirty giant attached Corinthian columns and a rusticated basement which breaks forward to provide bases for the columns and bulges out into a central porch. The strong chiaroscuro created by the projections makes this façade one of the most exciting of its time. He also built the Mary Magdalen Church, Prague (begun 1656), and the east wing of the palace at Roudnice (1665).

Hempel 1965.

**Caravanserai**. A stopping place for caravans, i.e. groups of merchants and others travelling together, for protection against

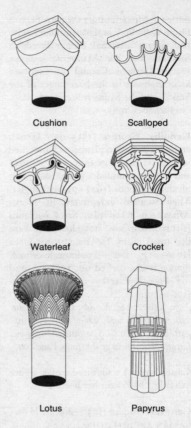

Cushion      Scalloped

Waterleaf      Crocket

Lotus      Papyrus

Fig. 27 Capital

robbers, in open country or in towns of Islamic central and west Asia and North Africa; alternatively called a *khan, ribat* or *funduq.* Built normally of adobe or brick along the major trade routes and pilgrimage routes to Mecca, at a day's journey (about 25 km. or 15 miles) from one another, they were usually rectangular enclosures with large courtyards, a fountain or well, sleeping accommodation, kitchens, often a mosque, occasionally a *hammam.* Exteriors were fortified. Entrance portals, high enough for loaded camels, were often imposing with reliefs in brickwork. In plan they differ regionally. The earliest to survive in part include Ribat-i Malik (1068–80), on the road between Samarkand and Bukhara, Uzbekistan, and Ribat Sharaf (completed 1154) between Nishapur and Merv, Iran. Numerous caravanserais were built in Anatolia in the C13, e.g. Sultan Han, near Kayseri. Ottoman C15 caravanserais were exceptionally large, e.g. Khan al-Qutaifah. Urban caravanserais served exclusively for storage (not lodging) and several are notable works of architecture: Khan Mirjan, Baghdad (1359), with magnificent vaulted hall; C17 Khan al-Sabun, Aleppo, and the As'ad Pasha Khan, Damascus (1753), with a many-domed interior in striped dark and light stonework.

Hillenbrand 1994.

**Carcase** or **carcass**. The skeleton or load-bearing structure of a building, especially of a timber-framed building, by analogy to furniture for which the term indicates the main structure to which the veneers are applied.

**Cardinal**, Douglas J. (b.1934), *see* CANADIAN ARCHITECTURE.

**Cardo**. The principal north–south street in an Ancient Roman town or military camp, *see* CASTRUM.

**Carlone**, Carl Martin (1616–67), *see* HUNGARIAN ARCHITECTURE.

**Carlone**, Carlo Antonio (d.1708), is the most important member of a large family of Italian artists working in Austria and south Germany. His masterpiece is the richly stuccoed interior of the Italianate Priory Church of St Florian (1686–1705). Other works include the Jesuitenkirche zu den Neun Chören der Engel, Vienna (1662), with a rather secular street façade, and the charming little pilgrimage church of Christkindl (begun 1706), which was finished by PRANDTAUER, who was much indebted to Carlone.

Brucker 1983.

**Carolingian architecture** takes its name from Charlemagne (King from 768, Emperor 800–814) and his descendants and the style extends in time from the late C8 into the C10, and in space through those countries which formed part of Charlemagne's Empire, especially France, Germany and the Netherlands. Anglo-Saxon architecture in England and Asturian architecture in Spain stand outside this style, which is composite and the result of conflicting trends in these formative centuries of Western civilization. Charlemagne himself promoted a renaissance of Roman – i.e. Constantinian – Christianity. This is evident in poetry, in script, in illumination, and also in the plans and elevations of certain churches which follow Early Christian examples (St Denis, Fulda, etc.). But indigenous characteristics also make themselves felt and point forward to the ROMANESQUE. In this category are prominent towers, strongly stressed west ends and east ends (Centula, plan for St Gall), and also heavier, more massive members. The most spectacular building preserved from Charlemagne's time is the Palatine chapel at Aachen, designed by Odo of Metz, begun in 792 and dedicated 805. *See also* GERMAN ARCHITECTURE; FRENCH ARCHITECTURE.

Conant 1979.

**Carpenter's Gothic**. Contemporary term for the early GOTHIC REVIVAL in England, e.g. designs by Batty LANGLEY; later used in the USA for C19 building with much exterior woodwork incorporating Gothic motifs.

A. de C. and D. B. McArdle, *C.G.*, New York (1978) 1983.

**Carpet-bedding**, *see* PARTERRE.

**Carport**. An open shed with lean-to roof for an automobile, e.g. as in WRIGHT's Usonian houses.

**Carr**, John (1723–1807). An English late and provincial exponent of PALLADIANISM, working mainly in Yorkshire. He began life as a mason in his father's quarry near Wakefield, and in his twenties built Kirby Hall to the design of Lord BURLINGTON and Roger MORRIS. He was later associated with Robert ADAM in the building of Harewood House (begun 1759). From then onwards he designed and built many large country houses. He was unoriginal, but could be refined and dignified in a quiet way, e.g. Denton Park (c.1778) and Farnley Hall (c.1786). His largest and perhaps his best work is the Crescent at Buxton (1780–90), where he very successfully combined the younger WOOD's invention of the monumental residential crescent with the arcaded ground floor surmounted by giant pilaster order used by Inigo JONES at Covent Garden.

J. Carr, *The Works in Architecture of J.C.*, York 1973; I. Hale (ed.), *J.C.*, Hull 1973; Summerson 1991; Colvin 1995.

**Carrel** or **carol**. A niche in a cloister where a monk might sit and work or read; sometimes applied to BAY WINDOWS.

**Carrère**, John Merven (1858–1911). American architect, trained at the École des Beaux Arts, Paris. He worked for McKIM, MEADE & WHITE until 1885 when he went into partnership with Thomas Hastings (1860–1929). They worked in a Beaux Arts style on the grandest scale, e.g. New York Public Library (1897–1911). Their Senate Office Building and Carnegie Institute, Washington, DC, are also notable.

H. H. Reed, *The New York Public Library. Its Architecture and Decoration*, New York 1986.

**Carrier**, Willis Haviland (1876–1950), *see* AIR-CONDITIONING.

**Cartouche**. An ornamental panel in the form of a scroll or sheet of paper with curling edges, usually bearing an inscription and sometimes ornately framed.

**Carvalho**, Eugenio dos Santos de (1711–60), *see* PORTUGUESE ARCHITECTURE.

**Caryatid**. A sculptured female figure used as a column to support an entablature or other similar member, as on the Erechtheum, Athens. The term is also applied loosely to various other columns and pilasters carved wholly or partly in the form of human figures: ATLANTES (male caryatids), CANEPHORAE (females, carrying baskets on their heads), HERMS (three-quarter-length figures on pedestals), telamones (another name for atlantes), and TERMS (tapering pedestals merging at the top into human, animal, or mythical figures). *See* Fig. 28.

**Case Study Houses**. A programme sponsored by John Entenza and *Arts and Architecture* magazine in Los Angeles 1945–62 to promote inexpensive well-designed houses using the latest techniques and materials. The most notable were those by EAMES, Craig Ellwood (b.1922) and Pierre Koenig (b.1925), the latter's Case Study House no. 22 of 1959 at Woods Drive, Los Angeles, being made world-famous by a night-time photograph of it by Julius Shulman.

M. E. McCoy, *C.S.H. 1945–62*, Los Angeles 1977; E. Smith, *Blueprints for Modern Living: History and Legacy of the C.S.H.*, Los Angeles.

**Casemate**. A vaulted room, with EMBRASURES, built in the thickness of the ramparts or other fortifications, and used as a barracks or battery, or both.

**Casement**. 1. The hinged SASH of a window, attached to the upright side of

Fig. 28 Caryatid

the window-frame. 2. The wide concave moulding in door and window JAMBS and between COMPOUND columns or piers, found in Late Gothic architecture. The term was in use by the middle of the C15 (William of Worcester's notes).

**Casement window**. A metal or timber window with the sash hung vertically and opening outwards or inwards.

**Casino**. 1. An ornamental pavilion or small house, usually in the grounds of a larger house. 2. In the C18 a dancing saloon, today a building for gambling.

**Cassels**, Richard, *see* CASTLE, Richard.

**Cast iron**. Cast or 'grey' IRON has a higher percentage of carbon in the alloy than wrought iron (up to 5 per cent, whereas wrought iron has less than 0.5 per cent). Of low ductility, it is shaped or cast in moulds, usually of compressed sand. First developed in China, it was used in Europe from the C14 (in America from the C17) for domestic utensils, etc. From the late C17 it was also used for railings, screens, entrance gates, etc., e.g. at Hampton Court, London, by James Tijou, in 1693; also in buildings as a reinforcement, e.g. in PERRAULT'S Louvre colonnade, Paris, of 1670. By the early C18 it was being used for structural members, e.g. the slender iron pillars supporting the galleries in WREN'S St Stephen's Chapel, Westminster, London, of 1714; but it was not widely accepted for structural use until the 1780s and 1790s following the construction in England of the Iron Bridge at Coalbrookdale, Shropshire in 1775–6 and Benyon, Bage and Marshall's iron-framed flax mill at Shrewsbury, Shropshire, in 1796–7. By the 1840s there were 'cast iron districts' in New York, *see* BOGARDUS, METAL STRUCTURES and INDUSTRIALIZED BUILDING. It was also exploited for street lamps and STREET FURNITURE. The most notable factories producing such work in cast iron were the Carron Ironworks in Scotland, the Coalbrookdale Company, Shropshire, and the Tule Ironworks in Russia.

L. Aitchison, *A History of Metals*, London 1960; E. G. and J. Robertson, *C.I. Decoration. A World Survey*, London (1977) 1994.

**Cast stone**. Stone aggregate bonded with cement and used like solid stone for masonry. Cast stone lintels were used at Carcassonne, France, in 1138.

**Castellamonte**, Carlo Conte di (1560–1641). Italian architect trained in Rome. He became architect to the Duke of Savoy in 1615 and played a large part in developing the city plan of Turin, where he designed Piazza S. Carlo (1637) and several churches. He began Castello di Valentino, Turin (1633), completed in the French style with a high hipped roof (1663) by his son Amadeo (1610–83), who succeeded him as court architect.

G. Brino *et al.*, *L'opera di C. e A. di C.*, Turin 1966; Wittkower 1982.

**Castellated**. Decorated with BATTLE-MENTS and TURRETS.

**Castle**. A fortified habitation. The planning and building of castles is primarily directed by the necessities of defence; it rarely extends as a whole into architecture proper, though certain features may. In the earlier Middle Ages the principal elements of castles were the donjon or KEEP and the hall in France and England, the Bergfrid and the Palas in Germany. The keep is a tower spacious enough to act as living quarters in time of war for the lord or governor and the garrison; the Bergfrid is a tower of normal proportions; the Palas is the hall-range. The earliest dated donjon is at Langeais (*c.*990), the earliest surviving major hall at Goslar (mid CII).

England built some hall-keeps, i.e. keeps wider than they are high (Tower of London). In France and Italy in the early C13 Roman precedent led to symmetrical compositions with angle towers and a gatehouse in the middle of one side. Some castles of Edward I in Britain took this over, and where in the late Middle Ages castles were still needed (south coast, Scottish border), they were often symmetrically composed. The rule in Britain at this time, however, was that castles could be replaced by unfortified manor houses. Towards the end of the Middle Ages the spread of firearms changed the castle into the fortress, with low BASTIONS for mounting cannon and no towers. *See also* CURTAIN WALL.

*Fortress Elements*

*Casemate.* Vaulted chamber in a bastion for men and guns.

*Cavalier.* Raised earth-platform of a fortress used for look-out purposes or gun placements.

*Counterscarp.* The face of the ditch of a fortress sloping towards the defender.

*Demi-Lune, see Half-Moon.*

*Glacis.* The ground sloping from the top of the rampart of a fortress to the level of the country around.

*Half-Moon.* Outwork of a fortress, crescent-shaped or forming an angle.

*Hornwork.* Outwork of a fortress with two demi-bastions.

*Ravelin.* Similar to a *Half-Moon.*

*Redoubt.* Small detached fortification.

*Scarp.* The side of the ditch of a fortress sloping towards the enemy.

*Sconce.* Detached fort with bastions.

**Castle**, Richard (*c.*1690–1751). A German, formerly Cassels, who settled in Ireland in 1727–8, worked for PEARCE on the Parliament House, Dublin, and became the leading architect of his day in Ireland. His surviving works conform to English PALLADIANISM without any trace of his foreign origin: e.g. Tyrone House (1740–45) and Leinster House (1745–51) in Dublin, and his two great country houses, Carton, Kildare (1739–45), and Russborough, Wicklow (1742–55).

Summerson, 1991; Colvin 1995.

**Castrum** (Latin). Roman military camp, built on a common rectangular layout throughout the Empire. A castrum was surrounded by a rampart and a wall with towers, and crossed by two main streets, the *cardo* and *decumanus*, running between four gates – the *porta praetoria, porta dextra, porta sinistra* and *porta decumana*. The headquarters (*praetorium*) lay at their intersection, and the barracks, armoury and other essential military buildings in the four quarters made by the streets. Camps were strategically placed along the *limes* to secure the border.

**Cat walk**. A narrow walking way round the upper walls of a high building, giving access to the roof and eaves for maintenance.

**Catacomb**. An underground cemetery, sometimes on several levels, consisting of linked galleries with shelf-tombs (*loculi*) and chambers (*cubicula*) with tomb niches (*arcosolia*). The word *catacumbas* (of uncertain derivation) was first applied in the c5 to the Christian cemetery initiated some two hundred years earlier beneath the church of S. Sebastiano on the Appian Way outside Rome. It was later extended to cover the many similar Early Christian cemeteries in and around Rome and in Naples, Sicily and North Africa, which vary in plan (e.g. originally gridiron in Rome and radial in Syracuse). Paintings on the walls of the Roman catacombs are among the earliest (c3–4) examples of Christian art. Christians had, however, preferred open-air cemeteries from the c3, and catacombs were rarely used for burials after the c6. The term catacomb is also applied to other and later subterranean cemeteries (e.g. the c18 catacombs of Paris), including those of non-Christian cults.

Krautheimer 1986.

**Cataneo**, Pietro (*fl.*1546–67). Italian architect notable mainly as the author of *I quattro primi libri di architettura* (Venice 1554), enlarged as *L'Architettura* (Venice 1567), evidently influenced by the as yet unpublished writings of his compatriot from Siena FRANCESCO DI GIORGIO MARTINI. He was the first writer to describe URBAN DESIGN as a central task of the architect, recommending rectangular or regularly polygonal plans centralized on a cathedral which, like all Christian churches, should be built on a Latin cross plan to symbolize the death of Christ.

*DBI* 1979; Kruft 1994.

**Catenary**. The curve formed by a chain or rope uniformly loaded along its length and freely suspended from two points horizontally separated. For catenary arch, *see* ARCH.

**Cathedra**. The bishop's chair or throne in his cathedral church, originally placed behind the high altar in the centre of the curved wall of the APSE.

**Cathedral**. Bishop's church, from CATHEDRA.

**Caul** and **caulcole**. The main stalk of a leaf on a Corinthian capital (*see* ORDER) from which grow the lesser stalks or caulcoles (Latin *cauliculi*) supporting the VOLUTES.

**Caus** or **Caux**, Salomon de (*c.*1577–1626). A French garden designer and hydraulic engineer who worked in England 1611–12 and then at Heidelberg, Germany, where he laid out for the Elector Palatine elaborate formal gardens featuring waterworks and grottoes of the fantastic kind illustrated in his *Les Raisons des forces mouvantes*, 1615. His son or nephew Isaac (*fl.*1612–55) went to England with him, settled there (naturalized 1634) and designed similarly elaborate gardens (one of his grottoes survives at Woburn Abbey, Bedfordshire). As an architect he was associated with Inigo JONES and the *c*.1636 rebuilding of the south front of Wilton House, Wiltshire, where he laid out the gardens as illustrated in his *Wilton Gardens, New and Rare Inventions of Water-Works* (reprinted 1982 (London/New York) with an introduction by John Dixon Hunt). The south front was gutted by fire in 1647/8 and the interior was rebuilt by WEBB.

C. S. Maks, *S. de C.*, Paris 1935; R. Strong, *The Renaissance Garden in England*, London 1979; Colvin 1995; Mowl and Earnshaw 1995.

**Causeway**. A roadway on a raised embankment, usually across low wet ground, a bog or marsh.

**Cavalier**. In military architecture, a raised earth-platform of a fortress, for look-out purposes or gun placements.

**Cavetto moulding**. A hollow moulding, about a quarter of a circle in section. *See* Fig. 29.

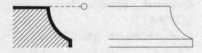

Fig. 29 Cavetto moulding

**Ceiling**. A timber or plaster surface covering the underside of a roof or floor, concealing the structural members. If of wood it is often decorated by carving, sometimes with inset oil paintings. If of plaster it can be decorated by mouldings and low reliefs or by painting, as in the Sistine Chapel, Rome, by Michelangelo. Later ceilings were sometimes painted to give an illusion of their being open to the heavens, e.g. by POZZO.

**Cell**. One of the compartments of a groin or rib VAULT, in the Romanesque period usually of plastered rubble, in the Gothic period of neatly coursed stones; the earliest known example is St Denis of 1140–44. Also called a *web*.

**Cella**. The main body of a classical temple (containing the cult image), as distinct from the portico, etc.

**Cellar**. A room below or partly below ground for storage, etc. as distinct from a basement, which is a living-space.

**Celure**. The panelled and adorned part of a wagon roof (*see* ROOF) above the ROOD or the altar.

**Cement**. 1. A binder which sets to hold together the materials of concrete, mortar, etc. and hardens as a solid mass. 2. A rendering used for facing exterior walls, also known as STUCCO. Various types of the latter were available in England from the 1770s, notably Wark's (1765) and Liardet's (1773), of which the patents were acquired by the ADAM brothers and much used by them. Later 'Parker's Stucco' or 'Roman Cement' (patented 1796–1819) was used by NASH, notably for his Regent's Park and Regent Street buildings in London. In 1794 Joseph Aspdin discovered Portland Cement and patented it in 1824. It was used in C19 and early C20 England as an economic rendering in imitation of Portland stone. Portland Cement is also known as Hydraulic Cement as it hardens under water.

Davey 1961.

**Cemetery**. An enclosed burial-ground as distinct from a CATACOMB, COLUMBARIUM, MAUSOLEUM or NECROPOLIS.

Cemeteries are found in Buddhist and Islamic as well as Christian countries where the first was the CAMPO SANTO at Pisa in 1277. The earliest Christian public cemeteries outside towns were built by Protestants, for doctrinal as well as practical (hygienic) reasons, in Germany (Kassel, 1526) and Switzerland (Geneva, 1536). The earliest monumentally planned cemeteries were created by English Protestants in India, at Surat in 1646 and Calcutta in 1767 where the Park Street Cemetery was laid out with tree-lined avenues of classically inspired tombs. Later, burial grounds in Catholic Europe were condemned as insalubrious and new cemeteries decreed by enlightened despotisms in France in 1776 and the Austrian Empire in 1784. This prompted architects such as BOULLÉE and DELAFOSSE to design ambitious projects, though little action was taken until after the French Revolution when the Montmartre cemetery was begun in 1795 in a disused quarry outside Paris. In 1804 Napoleon prohibited burials in churches and required every urban community to establish a public cemetery at least 40 m. (130 ft) outside its boundaries. The Paris cemetery later named Père Lachaise was opened the same year, laid out by BRONGNIART. It was much admired and led to a number of garden or 'rural' cemeteries in Europe and the USA, e.g. BIGELOW's Mount Auburn, Boston, in 1831, David Bates Douglas's Green-Wood Cemetery, Brooklyn, New York (1838 onwards), and OLMSTED's Mountain View, Oakland, California, in 1864. Lawn cemeteries with graves flush with the ground in wide areas of mown grass, as advocated by DOWNING and first realized at Cincinnati in 1855 by Adolphus Strauch (1822–83), provided a more easily maintained alternative which culminated at the Forest Lawn Cemetery, Glendale, California (1906 onwards). In Britain the first non-denominational cemeteries were laid out like landscape gardens, notably Kensal Green, London, in 1832, designed by John Griffith (1796–1888), and in 1842 J. C. LOUDON published On the Laying Out, Planting and Managing of Cemeteries (republished 1981 with an introduction by J. C. Curl). More formal grid-plans were preferred elsewhere, usually with a wide axial avenue from entrance to funeral chapel, with few if any trees, e.g. Brescia, Italy (1815) with a solemn Greek Doric entrance; Staglieno outside Genoa (1844–51) with a Doric Pantheon. Lawn cemeteries have preponderated in the C20, notably those in north-eastern France by LUTYENS for the missing and killed of the First World War. At Enskede, near Stockholm, an area of pinewood and old gravel pits was transformed by ASPLUND and LEWERENTZ into the Forest Cemetery, begun in 1917 and developed until 1941 when a remarkable crematorium by Asplund was incorporated, the whole forming an outstanding example of C20 landscape design synthesizing regular and informal traditions, Christian beliefs and a Nordic cult of nature. Also notable was the City of the Dead, Zale Cemetery at Ljubljana, Slovenia (1938–40), by PLEČNIK. The San Cataldo Cemetery near Modena, Italy, by Aldo ROSSI (designed 1971–6, built 1980–85), is notable among post-Second World War cemeteries.

Meeks 1966; S. French in D. E. Stannard (ed.), Death in America, Philadelphia 1975; J. S. Curl, A Celebration of Death, London 1980; R. A. Etlin, The Architecture of Death, Chicago 1984; H. Colvin, Architecture and the After-Life, London 1991.

**Cenotaph**. A monument to a person or persons buried elsewhere.

**Centerbrook Architects**, see MOORE, Charles.

**Centering**. Wooden framework used in arch and vault construction; it is removed (or 'struck') when the mortar has set.

**Centrally planned**. Of a building which radiates from a central point, as distinct from one on an AXIAL PLAN, i.e. a circular or octagonal building or one on a Greek Cross plan as opposed to a BASILICA. The Ancient Greek THOLOS is an early instance. The Pantheon, Rome; St Sophia, Istanbul; and Bramante's and Michelangelo's plans for St Peter's are other notable examples. *See* Fig. 30.

**Cerda**, Ildefonso (1815−76), *see* URBAN DESIGN.

**Ceylon (Sri Lanka)**, *see* SRI LANKAN ARCHITECTURE.

**Chaînes**. Vertical strips of rusticated masonry rising between horizontal string mouldings and cornice, dividing a façade into bays or panels; much used in C17 French domestic architecture.

**Chair-rail** or **dado-rail**. A moulding round a room to prevent chairs, when pushed back against the walls, from damaging their surface.

**Chaitya**. A Sanskrit word for a sacred mound, especially a Buddhist STUPA.

**Chaitya arch**. An English term for a recurrent motif in Indian Buddhist and Hindu architecture, resembling in miniature the arches (derived from the cross-section of a vaulted wooden building) which crown the entrance to CHAITYA HALLS.

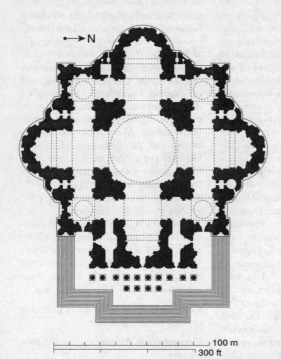

Fig. 30 Centrally planned: Michelangelo's St Peter's, Rome

100 m
300 ft

**Chaitya hall**. An early Indian Buddhist or Hindu temple or shrine, in form not unlike a Christian BASILICA, having a long hall divided into a central nave with side aisles by two rows of columns, terminating in a part-circular or apsidal end to allow a passage way round the votive CHAITYA or STUPA. The earliest were free-standing timber structures, none of which survives. Rock-cut chaitya halls imitate them. In plan they remained constant, but the entrance façade evolved from the simple C2 BC screens to later and increasingly elaborate porticos with horseshoe windows and flanked by niches for Buddha images, e.g. that of 50–70 AD at Karli, Maharashtra. *See* Fig. 31.

**Chalet**. A Swiss herdsman's hut or mountain cottage. The term is now loosely applied to any house built in the Swiss vernacular style, usually of wood.

**Chalgrin**, Jean-François-Thérèse (1739–1811). French architect, a pupil of SERVANDONI and BOULLÉE and Rome scholar (1758–63). He began in the rather epicene neo-classical manner then cur-

rent (e.g. in the work of SOUFFLOT), and reintroduced the basilican plan in his St Philippe-du-Roule, Paris (designed 1768 and built by 1774), with an imposing Doric portico. But much of the elegance of Chalgrin's design has not survived later alterations. In 1776 he completed Servandoni's St Sulpice, Paris, designing the north tower and the exquisite baptistery at its base. His masterpiece, the Arc de Triomphe, Paris (1806–35), is more Romantic-Classical in the style of Boullée, with its imperial symbolism and megalomaniac scale. He did not live to see it finished, and the sculptural decoration by Rude and others gives it a distinctly C19 appearance. He rebuilt the Odéon, Paris, in 1807, following the original designs by Joseph Peyre and Charles de WAILLY.

T. W. Gaehtgens, *Napoleon's Arc de Triomphe*, Göttingen 1974; Braham 1980.

**Chamber tomb**, *see* MEGALITH.

**Chamberlin, Powell & Bon**. A London partnership (Peter Hugh Girard Chamberlin, 1919–78, Geoffry C.

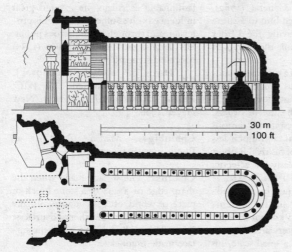

Fig. 31 Chaitya hall: Karli, India

Hamilton Powell, b.1920, and Christopher Bon, b.1921). The partners won the competition in 1952 for a City of London housing estate round Golden Lane, including the Barbican Arts Centre (1978). The whole redevelopment was finished in 1982. Their building for New Hall, Cambridge (begun 1960), is decidedly *outré* in its forms, as much of their work tends to be, e.g. at the University of Leeds (1972–5).

**Chambers**, Sir William (1723–96). The greatest official architect of his day in England, born in Göteborg, Sweden, the son of a Scottish merchant. At sixteen he joined the Swedish East India Company and for nine years made voyages to India and China. His architectural training began in 1749 in Paris under J.-F. Blondel, and was continued in Italy from 1750 until 1755, when he settled in London. He was an immediate success. His appointment (1756) as architectural tutor to the Prince of Wales established him in royal favour, and he became successively Architect to the King, jointly with Robert Adam (1760), Comptroller (1769), and Surveyor General (1782). In 1770 the king allowed him to assume a knighthood on receiving the Order of the Polar Star from the King of Sweden.

His career was that of a supremely successful official and his buildings are extremely competent; fastidious in ornament, impeccable in the use of orders, but rather academic, despite his famous Pagoda in Kew Gardens, and much less spectacular than those of his rival Robert Adam. His style is scholarly but eclectic, based on English Palladianism smoothed out and refined by the neoclassicism of Soufflot and his contemporaries, whom he had known in Paris and with whom he afterwards kept in touch. Usually best on a small scale, his

scholarly finesse is well illustrated by two of his earlier works, the Casino at Marino, Dublin (1757–69), an exemplary combination of strictly classical elements to fit a Greek cross plan, and the Pagoda at Kew (1757–62), in which he aspired to similar archaeological accuracy in another manner. He was notable for his staircases, e.g. Gower House, London (*c*.1769, destroyed), Melbourne House, London (*c*.1772, destroyed), and Somerset House, London. His country houses are neo-Palladian in plan and composition – e.g. Lord Bessborough's villa, now a school, at Roehampton, London (*c*.1760), and Duddingston House, Edinburgh (1762–4) – while the Strand façade of his largest and best-known work, Somerset House, London (1776–86), is a conscious imitation of a Palladian composition by Inigo Jones on the site. The courtyards and river façade display more vivacity and originality, and some of the interior decoration equals anything by Adam for refinement, particularly in the Strand block in which some rooms represent the earliest examples of a mature Louis XVI style in England. Though never as fashionable as Adam, he exerted great influence both as official head of his profession and through his numerous pupils. His *Treatise on Civil Architecture* (1759) became a standard work.

J. Harris, *Sir W.C.*, London 1970; J. Harris and M. Snodin (eds.), *Sir W.C. Architect to George III*, London/New Haven 1996.

**Chambiges**, Martin (d.1532), *see* French architecture.

**Chamfer**. The surface made when the sharp edge or arris of a stone block or piece of wood, etc., is cut away, usually at an angle of 45° to the other two surfaces. It is called a *hollow chamfer* when the surface made is concave.

**Champneys**, Basil (1842–1935), *see* ENGLISH ARCHITECTURE.

**Chancel**. That part of the east end of a church in which the main altar is placed; reserved for clergy and choir. From the Latin word *cancellus*, which strictly means the screen that often separated it from the body of the church. The term more usually describes the space enclosed and is applied to the whole continuation of the nave east of the CROSSING.

**Chancel arch**. The arch at the west end of a CHANCEL.

**Chantry chapel**. A chapel attached to, or inside, a church, endowed for the celebration of Masses for the soul of the founder or for the souls of such others as he may order. Many were built in C13–15 Europe, including such exceptional examples architecturally as the Capilla del Condestable, Burgos Cathedral, Spain (*c.*1486–94) and King Henry VII's Chapel, Westminster Abbey, London (1502/3–13).

**Chapel**. 1. A small chamber containing an altar, usually for worship of a particular saint and usually forming part of a church or other religious building but sometimes a separate detached building. *See also* LADY CHAPEL. 2. In England places of worship built for Christian denominations outside the established church (e.g. Congregational, Methodist, Wesleyan) are called Dissenting or Nonconformist Chapels or Meeting-Houses. They are seldom distinguished architecturally and owed little to any conscious rejection of architectural styles associated with the established church.

**Chapterhouse**. The place of assembly for abbot or prior and members of a monastery for the discussion of business or for reading the chapters of the monastic rule. It is reached from the CLOISTERS, to whose eastern range it usually belongs, and in England is often polygonal in plan. *See* Fig. 79. In cathedrals it usually belongs to the secular canons.

**Chareau**, Pierre (1883–1950). French architect and designer notable for his Maison de Verre, Paris (1928–32 with Bernard Bijoet, 1889–1979), in which mass-produced components were assembled on a flexible plan, incorporating exposed metal structure, moving screens, retractable staircases and a façade of glass bricks. He emigrated to the USA in 1940. The innovatory quality of his Maison de Verre was only recognized posthumously in the 1960s.

M. Velley and K. Frampton, *P.C. Architect and Craftsman (1883–1950)*, London 1965; B. B. Taylor, *P.C. (1883–1950) Designs and Architecture*, Cologne 1992.

**Charmille**, *see* BOSQUET.

**Charnel house** or **ossuary**. A building or vault in which human bones are preserved, usually those exhumed from a churchyard to make room for later graves. C13 examples include several centrally planned two-storey structures in a late Romanesque style, e.g. at Jak, Hungary; Dreikönigskapelle, Tulln, Austria; Bratislava Cathedral, Slovakia. The crypts of churches were often adopted (e.g. the C13 Holy Trinity Church, Rothwell, Northamptonshire England), and sometimes in Catholic Europe their walls were covered with decorative patterns of skulls as reminders of mortality.

**Charterhouse**. A Carthusian monastery. The Carthusians were a contemplative order, founded by St Bruno in 1086 at Chartreuse, France, and their monasteries have individual cells for the monks, not dormitories as in Benedictine monasteries. The Certosa at La Verna, Italy, and the Certosa di Galluzzo near Florence are notable examples.

**Chatri**. Pillared pavilions surmounted by a dome, a feature of Indo-Islamic architecture which first appeared in the early C16, often round the drum of a domed building. *See* Fig. 32.

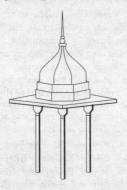

Fig. 32 Chatri

**Chattra**. In early Buddhist sculpture and architecture, a stone parasol, often crowning a STUPA; if more than one, superimposed one on another, called a *chattravalli*. *See* Fig. 113.

**Chedi**. In THAI ARCHITECTURE, a STUPA.

**Chelles**, Jean de and Pierre de, *see* JEAN DE CHELLES.

**Chemetoff**, Alexandre (b.1950) and Paul (b.1928), *see* FRENCH ARCHITECTURE.

**Chequer-work**. A method of decorating walls or pavements with alternating squares of contrasting materials (e.g. stone, brick, flint) to produce a chessboard effect.

**Chermayeff**, Serge (1900–1996). Russian architect in partnership with MENDELSOHN 1933–6 in England. In 1940 he emigrated to the USA, where he experimented with wood-frame structures and became an influential teacher and theorist, notably with Christopher

ALEXANDER with whom he published *Community and Privacy* (1963). In 1971 he published with Alexander Tzonis *Shape of Community*.

R. Plunz (ed.), *Design and the Public Good: Selected Writings (1930–1980) by S.C.*, Cambridge, Mass., 1982.

**Chersiphron** (*fl.c.*560 BC), *see* GREEK ARCHITECTURE.

**Chevakinsky**, Savva (1713–1770s). Appointed architect to Tsarskoe Selo in 1745, he was responsible (with A. Kvasov) for most of the work there apart from RASTRELLI's, e.g. the Rococo Hermitage. His greatest surviving work is the St Nicholas Marine Cathedral (1752) in St Petersburg, the finest Late Baroque church in Russia. Though overshadowed by Rastrelli, he had his own lively artistic personality. [R. R. Milner-Gulland]

**Chevet**. The French term for the east end of a church, consisting of APSE and AMBULATORY with or without radiating chapels.

**Chevron**. A Romanesque moulding forming a zigzag; so called from the French word for a pair of rafters giving this form. *See* Fig. 33.

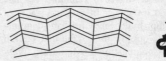

Fig. 33 Chevron

**Chiattone**, Mario (1891–1957), *see* SANT'ELIA, Antonio.

**Chiaveri**, Gaetano (1689–1770). Late Baroque architect, born in Rome but worked mainly in northern Europe – St Petersburg (1717–27), Warsaw and Dresden (*c.*1737–48). His masterpiece was the Hofkirche in Dresden (begun 1738, damaged 1944, restored), a Roman

Catholic church intended to rival the grandeur of BÄHR's Lutheran Frauenkirche. It has a very elegant campanile with an open-work top section which provided the perfect foil to the solidity of Bähr's dome, as did also the exterior of the church itself with its rhythmically advancing and receding walls crowned by numerous statues. Chiaveri provided plans for the river front of the royal palace in Warsaw (1740, only partly adopted) and somewhat theatrical designs for a royal palace in Dresden (*c*.1748, not executed). He published a volume of engraved designs: *Ornamenti diversi di porte e finestre* (1743–4).

Hempel 1965.

**Chicago School**. A term of disputed definition, perhaps best understood as referring to a group of architects working in Chicago between *c*.1880 and *c*.1910 and their development of utilitarian multi-storey buildings (SKYSCRAPERS) characterized by their external expression of the skeleton frame and the repetitious use of identical fenestration for storeys of similar plan and also by an emphasis on verticality – e.g. JENNEY, RICHARDSON, BURNHAM & ROOT, HOLABIRD & ROCHE, SULLIVAN, WRIGHT, and others.

Condit 1964.

**Chicago window**. A window occupying the full width of a bay and divided into a large fixed sash flanked by a narrow movable sash on each side, as in the Marquette building by HOLABIRD & ROCHE (1894) and SULLIVAN's Carson Pirie & Scott store (1899–1904) in Chicago.

**Chigi**. Japanese term for the scissors-like finials on the roof of a Shinto temple.

**Chimney bar**. The bar above the fireplace opening which carries the front of the CHIMNEY-BREAST.

**Chimney-breast**. The stone or brick structure projecting into a room and containing the fireplace and flue.

**Chimney-piece**, *see* MANTELPIECE.

**Chimney shaft**. A high chimney with only one flue.

**Chimney-stack**. Masonry or brickwork containing several flues, projecting above the roof and terminating in chimney-pots.

**Chinese architecture and landscape architecture**. Features that characterize the architecture of China, and the rest of East Asia, are already evident in the remains of two Shang dynasty (*c*.1750–1045 BC) cities excavated beneath modern Zhengzhou and Anyang (Henan province) – the former a rectangle covering some 5 sq. km. (2 sq. miles) surrounded by a vast earthwork estimated at having been some 10 m. (33 ft) high and 20 m. (65 ft) wide. The more important buildings were set on raised platforms and were of wooden trabeated construction, with walls of light material serving simply as protective screens. Paintings, relief carvings and little pottery models dating from the Han dynasty (*c*.202 BC TO AD 220) record such buildings and also indicate the importance given to tiled roofs. Underground tombs of the Han period reveal that the technique of tunnel vaulting with brick and stone had been mastered, but most of their stone elements imitate trabeated wooden construction, notably columns crowned by spreading consoles or brackets to carry beams. Stone was used for fortifications and for bridges, the earliest surviving being that built 605–17 at Zhaoxian (Hebei province) with a flattened arch spanning 37.5 m. (123 ft). Otherwise the earliest stone buildings are PAGODAS erected after the introduction of Buddhism from India. The twelve-sided pagoda built *c*.520 in the Songshan monastery (near Luoyang,

Henan province) is derived from an Indian SIKHARA. The much larger seven-storey square-plan Great Wild Goose pagoda at Xian (Henan province) owes more to Han dynasty watchtowers (known from pottery models) and the corbels supporting its roofs simulate woodwork. By the time of the Song dynasty (960–1279) pagodas had been given a wholly Chinese form – tall towers of uniform width or very slightly tapering with roofs marking each storey – followed until the late C19, sometimes of stone or brick but usually of wood with ceramic tiles (the earliest surviving wooden example, of 1058, is at Yingxian, Shanxi province).

Few wooden buildings survive from before the C16 in China. But Chinese styles and structural techniques were adopted for Buddhist monasteries in C7–8 Japan, where very fine examples have been preserved (*see* JAPANESE ARCHITECTURE). By this time a complex system of wooden construction had been devised to carry heavy ceramic-tiled ROOFS (pitched, gambrel or hipped), with the ridge-pole resting on a framework of columns joined horizontally by tie-beams and purlins, with elaborate corbels to spread the load, especially under wide-spreading eaves. A single storey was normal (libraries were the main exception, e.g. that of the C11 in the Longxing monastery at Zhengding in Hebei province), but the appearance of an upper floor was sometimes given by a lean-to roof immediately above the level of the entrance, either extending the interior space or covering an open colonnade. In 1103 Li Jie, an architect of the imperial Board of Works, published *Methods and Designs of Architecture* which formulated a system of proportions, derived from the vertical breadth of a bracket arm, to govern the size and spacing of columns and beams, and also described the various

types of carved ornament. The treatise was officially prescribed for use throughout the empire.

The earliest surviving wooden building in China is the great hall of 847 in the Foguang monastery on Mount Wutai in Shanxi province. Song dynasty buildings include the large temple of the Holy Mother (1023–32) at Jinci near Taiyuan in Shanxi province. The Daoist Yongle temple (Shanxi province) built under the Yuan dynasty (1260–1368) is architecturally simple but provides a clear example of the normal system of axial planning, with a gate-house, large hall and two smaller halls on axis. (It was dismantled and faithfully re-erected 1959–63.) Architectural principles overruled religious differences even in the exteriors of mosques (e.g. in Beijing and Xian), though pagodas were reserved for Buddhist establishments. The only exceptions were lamaist monasteries, which followed TIBETAN precedents (e.g. in Beijing and at Chengde in Hebei province). And although the vast majority of early Chinese temples were extensively restored or entirely rebuilt under the Ming (1368–1644) and Qing (1644–1912) dynasties their essential original forms were maintained. The temple of Confucius at his birthplace Qufu in Shandong province was built to replace its predecessor destroyed by fire in 1724 and is unusual only in that it has ten marble columns wreathed round with dragons supporting the eaves of its lower roof on the south front. The residence of the descendants of Confucius next to it, dating partly from the Ming period, is virtually the only surviving large non-imperial palace – an axial succession of halls similar to temples approached through courtyards flanked by smaller buildings, with a garden at the north end.

Apart from the Great Wall, which was given its present appearance 1368–1500, the imperial palace or 'Forbidden City' in Beijing (literally 'northern capital') is the major architectural achievement of the Ming and Qing dynasties, indeed one of the most impressive in the world. With three huge courtyards dominated by buildings on high platforms, the plan follows a very ancient tradition. It was begun in 1407, but the Grand Ancestral Shrine erected in 1464 to replace a predecessor destroyed by fire is the only survivor among its many buildings dating entirely from the Ming period; the others are C18 reconstructions and much of their decoration is still later. But respect for tradition gives to the whole complex a stylistic unity extending from the great ceremonial halls in the southern half to the imperial living quarters and the numerous small houses for widows and concubines, each composed of detached buildings set round a courtyard (similar to private houses elsewhere in the city, though very few now survive). At Shengyang in the north-east, a palace complex was constructed 1625–32, with buildings similar to those of the imperial palace in Beijing, though smaller and less obsessively symmetrical in planning, for the Manchu rulers of the Qing dynasty who were to supplant the Ming as emperors of China in 1644; it survives intact with few later alterations.

From an early period great importance was given to LANDSCAPE ARCHITECTURE, as to landscape painting, inspired by philosophical (Confucian) and religious (Daoist) beliefs as well as aesthetic delight in the natural world. Outside the Han capital Changan (near modern Xian) the emperor Wu (140–86 BC) had an artificial lake made to evoke the Daoist Islands of the Blest. Informally planned parks were laid out for emperors of the later dynasties, e.g. for the Southern Song at Hangzou, for the Yuan, Ming and Qing at and near Beijing where several

survive including the Bei Hain park around an artificial lake and the more extensive Summer Palace with numerous buildings also around a lake (begun 1153, periodically elaborated and given its present form in the late C19), as well as the formally planned ceremonial enclosure of the Temple of Heaven in Beijing. At Chengde (ancient Je-hol) in east Hebei province, the emperor Kangxi in 1703 had a park 25 km. (15½ miles) in circumference laid out with a palace by a lake, summer houses and temples among gentle hills. Throughout the country temples and monasteries were normally set in gardens. Writers, artists and others also made gardens in the spirit of landscape paintings with water, trees and curiously shaped rocks framed by the columns and trellis-work of covered walks, and some, probably dating back to the C16 in origin, survive at Suzou in Jiangsu province. Imperial building work continued with a marked decline in the quality of decorative detail until shortly before the end of the régime: the Summer Palace, Yiheyuan, outside Beijing, begun 1888 as a replacement for its predecessor sacked by European troops in 1860; in the city itself the great circular Hall of Annual Prayers (popularly called the Temple of Heaven), with its blue tiled roofs, was begun after 1889 as the replica of an early C15 building that had been destroyed by fire.

In the mid C18 an addition to the imperial summer palace Yuanmingyuan (of which only ruins survive) was built under the supervision of Jesuits in an Italianate Baroque style. This was a unique instance of Western influence in the imperial period, though Europeans erected buildings in their own styles for their own use, e.g. the Baroque Catholic church of Xuanwu Men, Beijing (1657), the red-brick Gothic Holy Trinity church, Shanghai, by George Gilbert SCOTT and William Kidner (1866–9), the French Gothic Catholic cathedral, Shanghai (1896–1910), as well as consulates, banks, etc. in the treaty ports. Many more such buildings went up after the Republican Revolution of 1911, most prominently in Shanghai. The Chinese-based British firm Palmer & Turner provided designs in an enterprising range of styles – in Shanghai the overblown BEAUX ARTS style Hong Kong and Shanghai Bank (1921–3), the simplified ART DECO style Peace Hotel (1926–8) and the half-timbered Tudor style Sassoon Villa (1930). European styles were also taken up by a few Chinese architects, e.g. the pidgin-neo-Georgian lecture hall of Nanjing University. But there was also a politically inspired Chinese revival, e.g. the Sun Yat Sen mausoleum begun 1926 by Lu Yan-zhi (1894–1929) and the Central Museum of 1937, both in Nanjing. Attempts were also made to apply Chinese decorative features to Western-style buildings: the Municipal Government Building, Shanghai (1930), is among the worst examples, the Zhongshan hospital, Shanghai (1937), among the best. The INTERNATIONAL MODERN style was introduced for a few private houses in the 1930s and for hotels since 1949. But this term can hardly be applied to the recent proliferation of high-rise blocks throughout the country, built economically to accommodate the urban populations: they are purely utilitarian. The most prominent post-Second World War public buildings date from the time of close Sino-Russian alliance and Soviet influence is evident – the daunting Great Hall of the People and Museum of Chinese History (both 1959) which have massive colonnaded façades and a few discreet Chinese decorative details on either side of Tiananmen square, Beijing. The Memorial Hall of Chairman Mao (1977) in the same square is smaller and more recognizably Chinese even though

it is flat roofed. The most interesting recent buildings are hotels for foreign tourists, ranging in styles from Chinese to nondescript Western but including the Xiangshan Hotel outside Beijing of 1979–83 by M. I. PEI. The Ju'er Hutong Courtyard Housing Project, initiated in Beijing in 1987 by Liangyong Wu (b.1922), is a remarkable inner-city rehabilitation and participatory design project.

**Chinoiserie.** European imitations or evocations of Chinese art which first appeared in the C17, became very popular in the C18 – especially in England, Germany, France and Italy – and lingered on into the C19. Numerous PAGODAS, pavilions, bridges, etc. were built in Europe in parks and gardens that were sometimes believed to have been laid out like those in China. Of the larger buildings in the style, the teahouse at Potsdam (1754–7), the pavilion at Drottningholm, Sweden (1763–9), the Palazzina La Favorita, Palermo (1799), and the interior of the Royal Pavilion, Brighton (1802–21), are the most important.

O. Siren, *China and the Gardens of Europe* (1950), intr. H. Honour, Washington DC, 1990.

**Chochol**, Josef (1880–1956), *see* CZECH ARCHITECTURE, CUBIST ARCHITECTURE.

**Choir**. The part of a church where divine service is sung, usually part of the chancel, with stalls for the singers.

**Choir screen**. A partition of wood or stone, elaborately carved, separating the choir and chancel from the nave and transepts of a church. It corresponds approximately to the ICONOSTASIS in a Byzantine church.

**Chromium**. A silvery metallic element obtained from chrome ironstone by smelting. Discovered in 1798 by a French chemist, Vauquelin, but little used, despite its colour, brilliance and resistance to corrosion, until the First World War for projectile coverings. In 1925 it was introduced commercially and taken up by innovative designers and architects both in Europe and the USA, e.g. by MIES VAN DER ROHE for the columns and other elements of the Barcelona Pavilion in 1929. Chromium is usually electroplated on metal above a coating of nickel: chromium plating now seems to typify the period.

**Chullpa**. A burial tower of stone or adobe, cylindrical or square in form, found in parts of the southern Andes, especially around Lake Titicaca, just before and after the Inca conquest.

**Church**. An edifice or place of assembly set apart for Christian worship. The earliest known is that at Dura Europos, Syria, *c*.250, a private house in which two rooms were united to make an assembly hall. Another room had a basin or font, surmounted with a canopy, for baptism and there may have been a room for the celebration of the Eucharist on an upper floor. The prototype for the first great churches erected after the legalization of Christianity in 313 was found not in pagan temples but in the secular BASILICA; *see also* EARLY CHRISTIAN ARCHITECTURE and MARTYRIA. The basilican church plan continued in medieval architecture and centrally planned churches were exceptional, until they became prominent with St Sophia in Constantinople and BRAMANTE's and MICHELANGELO's St Peter's in Rome.

**Church**, Thomas Dolliver (1902–78). American landscape architect, the leading member of the CALIFORNIA SCHOOL. He began in 1929 designing small easily maintained private gardens conceived as outdoor rooms, with much use of timber

decks, patterned pavements, groundcover plants in place of turf lawns, and various illusionistic devices to increase apparent size. With their carefully planned sunlit and shaded areas and organically shaped swimming-pools, his gardens provided an ideal setting for the Californian upper-middle rich lifestyle, as in his Donnell Residence garden, Sonoma County, California (1948), and his Phillips Residence garden, Napa Valley, California (1954). The following year he published *Gardens are for People* (reprinted with texts by G. Hall and M. Laurie, New York 1983). Illustrated with his designs, this had world-wide influence. His larger institutional works were less original but include the landscaping for WURSTER's Valencia Public Housing Project, San Francisco (1939–43), Park Merced, San Francisco (1947–9), the General Motors Research Center, Detroit (1949–59) and campus plans for the University of California, Berkeley (1961) and Stanford University, Palo Alto (1969). His assistants included BAYLISS and HALPRIN, who formed with ECKBO the nucleus of the California School of which he remained the undogmatic doyen. He published *Your Private World: A Study of Intimate Gardens* (San Francisco 1969).

Walker and Simo 1994.

**Churriguera**, José Benito de (1665–1725). The eldest of three Spanish architect brothers, the others being Joaquin (1674–1724) and Alberto (1676–1750). They came of a family of Barcelona sculptors specializing in elaborately carved retables and began in this way themselves; hence their peculiar architectural style with its lavish piling up of surface ornamentation, now known as the Churrigueresque style. Some of its more fantastic and barbaric features may have been inspired by native art in Central and South America. José Benito settled early in Madrid as a carver of retables (e.g. Sagrario in Segovia Cathedral) and did not turn architect until 1709, when he laid out the town of Nuevo Baztán, the most ambitious and original urban scheme of its period in Spain. His brother Joaquin's best works date from the next decade, e.g. the patio of the Colegio de Anaya and Colegio de Calatrava at Salamanca. The youngest brother, Alberto, was the most talented, but did not emerge as an architect in his own right until after the death of his two elder brothers. The Plaza Mayor at Salamanca (begun 1729) is his first great work. San Sebastian, Salamanca, followed in 1731, but seven years later he left Salamanca and resigned as architect in charge. His last works are small but among his best: e.g. the parish church at Orgaz (1738) and the portal and façade of the church of the Assumption at Rueda (1738–47).

Kubler and Soria 1959.

**Churrigueresque style**. The lavish over-decorated style named after the CHURRIGUERA family, though the term is often extended to include all the more florid, Late Baroque architecture in Spain and Spanish America, especially Mexico. Pedro de RIBERA and Narciso TOMÉ were its best practitioners in Spain, where it was popular mainly in Castille.

J. M. Pla Dalman, *La arquitectura barroca española y el Churriguerismo*, Madrid 1951.

**CIAM** or **Congrès International d'Architecture Moderne**. Founded in 1928, it became the chief instrument for disseminating Modernist ideas of architecture and town planning. Dominated in the 1930s by LE CORBUSIER, it emphasized functionalism and rational planning. CIAM had two periods of great influence: 1930–34 and 1950–56. The so-called 'Athens Charter' issued by CIAM in 1933 set out segregated planning principles for urban design in which the primary functions were identified as 'residential, work, recreation and traffic' – COSTA's Brasilia was to be its great exemplar. In the 1950s the younger generation (represented by 'Team 10' and including BAKEMA and VAN EYCK, the SMITHSONS and CANDILIS) rejected the ideals of the older generation, introducing the 'cluster planning' concept at the 10th Congress (1956), *see* URBAN DESIGN. The last meeting of CIAM took place in 1959.

A. Smithson, *Team 10 Primer*, Cambridge, Mass., 1963; M. Steinman, *CIAM: Dokumente 1928–1939*, Basel and Stuttgart 1979.

**Ciborium**. A canopy raised over the high altar. It is normally a dome supported on columns. *See also* BALDACHIN.

**Cill**, *see* SILL.

**Cima recta**, **cima reversa**, *see* CYMA RECTA; CYMA REVERSA.

**Cimborio**. The Spanish term for a LANTERN admitting light over a crossing tower (*see* CROSSING) or other raised structure above a roof.

**Cincture**. A small convex moulding round the SHAFT of a column.

**Cinquefoil**, *see* FOIL.

**Circus**. 1. In Roman architecture a long oblong building with rounded ends and with tiered seating on both sides and at one end; if used for horse-racing, a hippodrome. 2. In the C18 a circular or nearly circular range of houses, e.g. that by WOOD in Bath, Somerset. 3. In modern town planning a circular road or street junction, e.g. Piccadilly Circus, London.

**City Beautiful Movement**. Term derived from the title of a book by Charles Mulford Robinson (1869–1917), *Modern Civic Art, or the City Made Beautiful* (1903), and used in the USA for a nationwide endeavour to dignify city centres with boulevards, squares and monumental BEAUX ARTS style public buildings, usually financed by public subscriptions. The movement began in the 1850s with the founding of civic Improvement Societies in New England. In 1892 R. M. HUNT founded the Municipal Art Society 'to provide adequate sculptural and pictorial decoration for the public buildings of the city of New York and to promote in every way the beautifying of its streets and public places'. The buildings and layout of the World's Columbian Exposition, Chicago 1893, were products of these ideas and became the main source of inspiration for the following two decades. Major projects included the McMilland Plan for Washington DC, by BURNHAM, McKIM and F. L. OLMSTED Jr (1901–2), C. GILBERT's design for the surroundings of the Minnesota State Capitol, St Paul (1903–6), and the ambitious plans by Burnham and Edward H. Bennett for San Francisco (1904–5) and Chicago (1906–9). Although none was fully implemented, few American cities were untouched by the movement.

W. H. Wilson, *The C.B.M.*, Baltimore 1989.

**Ciriani**, Henri (b.1936), *see* FRENCH ARCHITECTURE.

**Cistercian architecture**. The Cistercian Order was founded in 1098. It was named after Cîteaux in Burgundy. The third abbot, and the one to establish the rules of the Order, was the Englishman Stephen Harding. The most famous Cistercian is St Bernard of Clairvaux (1090–1153), named after Clairvaux, the second mother abbey of the Order. The other two were Pontigny and Morimond, all in Burgundy. The Order pleaded for reform, and an exacting life. One of the rules was to settle in wild country and to colonize and cultivate it. The Cistercians became extremely successful landowners.

They settled in near and far countries. At the time of the death of St Bernard there were 339 houses, in 1200 about 525 (including nunneries). Whereas the Cluniacs (*see* CLUNY) did not impose rules of architectural planning, a Cistercian house is at once recognizable by plan and elevation in whatever country it may be. Both plans and elevations, at least up to about 1150, were kept demonstratively simple. Choirs had straight ends, chapels extending east of the transepts ended straight too. The standard plan had two to each transept, but there could be up to four. Apses are rare (except in Spain). Details were simple too, but great efforts were made to achieve fine workmanship. The earliest completely preserved church is Fontenay in Burgundy (1139–47), the grandest preserved Burgundian church Pontigny (c.1140–1200). England possesses the finest ruins: Fountains, Rievaulx, Kirkstall, Roche, Tintern, etc. The best-known Italian houses are Casamari, Fossanova and Chiaravalle; the best-known Spanish ones Moreruela, La Oliva, Poblet and Santas Creus; the best-known in Germany Eberbach, Ebrach, Maulbronn, Bronnbach, Walkenried and Riddagshausen; in Austria Heiligenkreuz, Lilienfeld and Zwettl.

W. Braunfels, *Abendländische Klosterbaukunst*, Cologne (1969) 1978; P. Fergusson, *Architecture of Solitude. C. Abbeys in Twelfth Century England*, Princeton 1984; C. Norton and D. Parks (eds.), *C. Art and Architecture in the British Isles*, London 1986; R. Stalley, *The C. Monasteries of Ireland*, New Haven and London 1987; S. Tobin, *The C., Monks and Monasteries of Europe*, Huntington 1995.

**Citadel**. In military architecture, a fort with from four to six bastions. It was usually sited at a corner of a fortified town but connected with it, e.g. Lille or Arras.

**Cladding**. A lightweight external covering or skin applied to a structure for protective or aesthetic purposes, the load-bearing function of the wall being taken by some other element of the structure. *See also* CURTAIN WALL; FRAMED BUILDING; METAL STRUCTURES.

M. Rostron, *Light C. of Buildings*, London 1964; A. Brooks, *C. of Buildings*, London 1990.

**Clapboard**. In the USA and Canada the term for WEATHERBOARD.

**Clapper bridge**. A bridge made of large slabs of stone, some built up to make rough PIERS and other longer ones laid on top to make the roadway.

**Clarke**, George (1661–1736), *see* ALDRICH, Henry.

**Clarke**, Gilmore David (1892–1982). American landscape architect, the designer of the first true PARKWAY – from the Bronx Park to Kensico Dam, New York (1913–25). He later designed several others including Merritt Parkway, Connecticut (1934–40), Palisades Interstate Parkway, New Jersey (1950), and was chief landscape architect for the Westchester Park System stretching north from New York City (1923–33). With his partner Michael Rapuano he was one of the planners of the New York World's Fairs (1939 and 1964) and the gardens surrounding the UN Headquarters, New York (1947–52).

**Clason**, Isak Gustaf (1856–1930), *see* SWEDISH ARCHITECTURE.

**Clasp**, *see* INDUSTRIALIZED BUILDING.

**Classicism**. A revival of or return to the principles of Greek or (more often) Roman art and architecture. The word 'classic' originally signified a member of the superior tax-paying class of Roman citizens. It was later applied, by analogy, to writers of established reputation; and in the Middle Ages it was extended to all Greek and Roman writers and also to the arts of the same period, though always with an implication of 'accepted authority'. The various classical revivals were thus attempts to return to the rule of artistic law and order as well as evocations of the glories of Ancient Rome. Although most phases of medieval and later European art have to some extent been influenced by antiquity, the term 'classicism' is generally reserved for the styles more consciously indebted to Greece and Rome.

The first of these revivals was the CAROLINGIAN *renovatio* of the C8–9 – a politically, no less than aesthetically, inspired return to late Imperial Roman art and architecture. The Tuscan C11 Proto-Renaissance represents a somewhat similar attempt to revive Roman architectural forms. The few monuments produced under it exerted considerable influence on the earliest works of BRUNELLESCHI and thus the initial phase of the RENAISSANCE proper. But from the C16 onwards the Renaissance reinterpretation of antiquity was to exert almost as much influence on classicizing architects as antiquity itself. For it was during the Renaissance that writers began to evolve a classical theory of architecture based largely on the confused and confusing treatise of VITRUVIUS, which had been rediscovered in 1414. Throughout the C17 architectural theory remained essentially classical, though practising architects often paid no more than lip-service to it. But there was a practical as well as a theoretical return to classical standards in late C17 France (notably in the work of PERRAULT and MANSART). And in early C18 England such architects as Colen CAMPBELL, Lord BURLINGTON and William KENT led a return to classicism by way of Inigo JONES and PALLADIO. This PALLADIANISM has sometimes been interpreted as the first phase of the late C18 neo-classical movement.

This movement, generally referred to as neo-classicism, began in the 1750s as a reaction against the excesses of the Late BAROQUE and ROCOCO and as a reflection of a general desire for established principles based on laws of nature and reason. In art and architecture these also embodied the 'noble simplicity and calm grandeur' which Winckelmann regarded as the prime qualities of Greek art. Fresh attention was given to surviving antique buildings in Europe and Asia Minor. PIRANESI's etchings inspired a new vision of Roman architecture, emphasizing its formal and spatial qualities. Classically 'incorrect' motifs were rejected in favour of those more archaeologically correct. But the mere copying of Greek and Roman buildings was rarely practised and never recommended. Theorists like LAUGIER and LODOLI demanded rational architecture based on first principles, not one which imitated Roman grandeur.

These new ideas were bound up with a nascent primitivism – a belief that architecture, like society, had been at its purest and best in its simplest and most primitive form. This led to an appreciation of the severity of Greek DORIC, made possible by the publications of James STUART and others and by the discovery of the early Doric temples in Sicily and at Paestum – though for the more fundamentalist architects (e.g. C. A. Ehrensvärd in Sweden) even the latter were insufficiently plain, sturdy and masculine. It also led to the creation of an architecture of pure geometrical forms – the cube, pyramid, cylinder and sphere – which found its most extreme expression in the designs of BOULLÉE, LEDOUX and GILLY, and in buildings by SOANE in England, LATROBE in the USA and ZAKHAROV in Russia. But if few late C18 architects took neo-classical prin-ciples to their logical conclusion equally few remained entirely immune to them.

Neo-classical buildings are solid and rather severe. Decoration, including classical enrichments, is restrained and sometimes eliminated altogether. The orders are used structurally rather than ornamentally, with columns supporting entablatures and not merely applied to the walls. Volumetric clarity is emphasized both internally and externally by unbroken contours. The Baroque organic principle by which a façade is unified by interlocking its various parts (so that the wings flow out of the central block and the main storey into those above and below) is rejected in favour of an inorganic one by which the masses are rigidly defined and, sometimes brutally, juxtaposed.

In the early C19 these severe neo-classical ideas were abandoned in favour of styles richer in decoration, more picturesque in composition and more literary in their allusions to the past. In France, under the Empire, the richly luxurious and dramatically expressive Roman Imperial style was revived as propaganda for the régime. Architects once more played for effect rather than sought to express visually a high intellectual idea. Thus the classical tradition survived, in Europe and the USA and in various European colonies in Asia and Africa, throughout the C19, but simply as a form of HISTORICISM – whether Greek, Roman or Renaissance (*see* GREEK REVIVAL). And although many individual buildings in these styles are of high quality (notably those by BARRY, ELMES, SMIRKE, PLAYFAIR, STRICKLAND, SCHINKEL, KLENZE, HITTORF, etc.) they show little further development. Ironically enough, the leading tenets of the neo-classicists (logical construction, truth to materials, etc.) were taken up and developed in an anti-classical way by the architects of the GOTHIC REVIVAL.

By the late C19 these historicizing styles had come full circle from neo-classical austerity, logical simplicity and purity to the lavish and heavily ornamented BEAUX ARTS STYLE which persisted well into the C20, especially in the USA with Paul CRET and others. In the 1920s and 1930s classicism was once again purged of superfluous ornament in a so-called 'stripped' style superficially similar to late C18 neo-classicism and much promoted for official buildings by the Fascist and Nazi regimes, from which it got a bad name (*see* ITALIAN ARCHITECTURE; GERMAN ARCHITECTURE). At the same time, however, there were many architects who were indifferent or averse to Modernism without any political or ideological motives and were able to draw inspiration freely from Ancient Roman, Renaissance and also C17–18 versions of classicism, e.g. Philip Trammell Shutze (1890–1982), whose Citizens and Southern National Bank, Atlanta, Georgia (1929), has an interior of Imperial Roman grandeur. More recently POST-MODERNISM led to the revival of classical elements in the work of several notable architects, from STIRLING and OUTRAM in England to STERN and others in the USA, and, in Europe, BOFILL, BOTTA, ROSSI and several others. Contemporaneously, however, there was also a return to a more nostalgic interpretation of classicism, e.g. in England with Quinlan Terry (b.1937) and other late NEO-GEORGIAN architects and in the USA with John Blatteau (b.1943), whose opulent Banqueting Hall for the State Department (1982) and Riggs National Bank (1991), both Washington, DC, are notable.

**Cleat**. A batten, brace or clamp of wood or metal fixed to a rafter or other surface to strengthen or support it. It may also be a wedge-shaped piece of wood or metal attached to a surface to prevent it slipping or to act as a support, e.g. for a bracket. In metalwork it is a supporting bracket.

**Clerestory** or **clearstory**. The upper stage of the main walls of a church above the aisle roofs, pierced by windows; the same term is applicable in domestic building. In Romanesque architecture it often has a narrow wall-passage on the inside.

**Clérisseau**, Charles-Louis (1721–1820). A French neo-classical draughtsman and architect who exerted a wide influence through his pupils and patrons, William CHAMBERS, Robert and James ADAM, and Thomas JEFFERSON. He also provided designs (not executed) for Catherine the Great. His own buildings are uninspired, e.g. the Palais de Justice, Metz (1776–89).

Braham 1980; T. J. McCormick, *C.-L.C. (1721–1820)*, Cambridge 1990; V. Chevtchenko *et al.* (eds.), *C.-L.C. (1721–1820) Dessins du musée de l'Hermitage Saint-Petersbourg*, Paris 1995, Kalnein 1995.

**Clerk**, Simon (d.c.1489). Master mason of Bury St Edmunds Abbey, Suffolk, from 1445 at the latest, and also of Eton College, c.1455–60 (in succession to his brother John), and King's College Chapel, Cambridge, from 1477 to 1485. Of his work at Bury St Edmunds nothing survives; at Eton and Cambridge he continued work, that is, he did not initiate, and so his style remains unknown to us. He is named here as an example of the way distinguished masons were given responsibility in several places.

Harvey 1984.

**Cleveland**, H. W. S. (1814–1900). American landscape architect who worked with OLMSTED at Prospect Park, Brooklyn, New York, from 1867 until he settled in Chicago in 1869. His major works date from the 1870s: Milwaukee's Juneau Park (1873) and the Twin Cities metropolitan park system, Minneapolis (1877–95), a remarkable urban open-space network. In 1871 he published *Landscape Architecture as Applied to the Wants of the West* (reprinted Pittsburgh 1965), in which he defined landscape architecture as the art of arranging land so as to adapt it most conveniently, economically and gracefully to any of the varied wants of civilization.

**Clinker block**. A cheap building block made of clinker (i.e. fused ash from furnaces). It has superseded the BREEZE BLOCK.

**Clocher**. The French term for a bell-tower.

**Cloister**. An enclosed space in a MONAS-TERY, in form a quadrangle or open court, surrounded by roofed or vaulted passages or ambulatories, with an open arcade or colonnade on the interior sides and plain walls on the others. In a monastery the cloister connects the church with the domestic buildings, usually south of the nave and west of the transept. It first appears in the famous AD 820 plan for St Gall, Switzerland. Several Roman-esque and later medieval examples are notable both architecturally and for their sculptured ornamentation, e.g. St Trophime, Arles, France (C12). The central open space is usually arranged as a garden with walks, often with a central well or fountain, and may also serve as a burial ground. In some respects a cloister is comparable to the VIHARA in an Indian Buddhist monastery.

R. Rey, *L'Art des cloîtres romans*, Toulouse 1955; Braunfels 1973.

**Cloister vault**. American term for a domical VAULT rising direct on a square or polygonal base, the curved surfaces separated by GROINS or RIBS. It is not a true dome. That of S. Maria del Fiore, Florence, by Brunelleschi is the best-known example. *See* Fig. 41.

**Cluny**. A Burgundian monastery founded in 910. It generated the reform of the Benedictine Order, and the militancy of the Church in the C11. Urban II, who summoned Europe to the First Crusade, was once a monk there, as were later Popes such as Gregory VII and Paschal II. In the early C12 the abbey church of Cluny, of which little survives, was the largest in all Europe (*see* FRENCH ARCHITECTURE). It was built in the characteristic Burgundian style; but this style was not, as with the CISTERCIANS, mandatory upon its daughter-houses; these took their character from the locality. La Charité-sur-Loire, Vézelay, St Martial in Limoges, Moissac and St Martin-des-Champs in Paris are among the best-known of them. The mother-house in England was Lewes, the chief houses in Switzerland were Romainmôtier and Payerne, and in Germany, Hirsau. Around 1200 the Order had about 1,500 establishments.

J. Evans, *Romanesque Architecture of the Order of C.*, Farnborough, (1938) 1972; M. Eschapasse, *L'Architecture bénédictine en Europe*, Paris 1963; Conant 1979.

**Cluster planning**, *see* URBAN DESIGN.

**Clustered pier**, *see* COMPOUND PIER.

**Clutton**, Henry (1819–93), *see* BENTLEY, John Francis; BURGES, William.

**Coade stone**. An 'artificial stone' marketed by Eleanor Coade (1733–1821) of Lambeth from 1769 and, after her death, by William Croggon until *c.*1840. Finer than STUCCO and other available compositions, it was a type of pottery (stoneware) and was widely used for all kinds of architectural ornament from capitals and key-stones to whole doorways (as still *in situ* in Bedford Square, London). The fan-vaulted screen in St George's Chapel, Windsor, by Henry Emlyn (1787), is of Coade stone.

A. Kelly, *Mrs C.'s Stone*, London 1990.

**Coates**, Wells (Windemut) (1895–1958). English architect notable chiefly for his Lawn Road Flats in Hampstead (1932–4) and Palace Gate flats (1937–9), London, pioneer work in England in INTERNATIONAL MODERN style. He founded MARS (Modern Architectural Research Group) in 1933.

S. Cantacuzino, *W.C.*, London 1978; L. Cohn (ed.), *W.C. Architect and Designer 1895–1958*, Oxford 1979.

**Cob**. Walling material made of clay mixed with straw, gravel and sand. It can be used with or without formwork (*see* PISÉ).

**Cobb**, Henry (b.1926). American architect, trained at Harvard and a partner of I. M. PEI since 1956. He was responsible for the design of several of the firm's notable buildings, e.g. the John Hancock Tower, Boston (1966–76).

**Cockerell**, Charles Robert (1788–1863), English architect, son of S. P. COCKERELL, studied under his father and assisted Sir Robert SMIRKE. From 1810 to 1817 he was abroad, first in Greece, Asia Minor and Sicily, then in Italy. Keenly interested in archaeology, he was excellent at classical and modern languages; in Greece he worked on the discoveries of Aegina and Phigaleia. However, Cockerell combined his passion for Greek antiquities with a great admiration for WREN, and the result is a style which is the English parallel of the Paris BEAUX ARTS STYLE of about 1840: grander than before, fond of giant orders and sudden solecisms, yet still firmly disciplined. Cockerell is an architects' architect, and PUGIN hated him passionately. Among his buildings the following only

can be referred to: the Cambridge University (now Law) Library (1837–42) with its splendid coffered tunnel vault; the Taylorian (Ashmolean) building in Oxford (1841–5); various branch buildings for the Bank of England, whose architect he became in 1833 (e.g. those in Manchester and Liverpool, both begun in 1845); and a number of insurance office buildings (e.g. the Liverpool & London and Globe Insurance, Dale Street, Liverpool, of 1855–7). He was Professor of Architecture at the Royal Academy, the recipient of the first Gold Medal of the Royal Institute of British Architects, and a member of the academies of Paris, Rome, Munich, Copenhagen, etc. He also wrote on the iconography of the west front of Wells Cathedral.

D. Watkin, *The Life and Work of C.R.C.*, London 1974.

**Cockerell**, Samuel Pepys (1753–1827). English architect who began in TAYLOR's office along with NASH. He acquired numerous surveyorships – Admiralty, East India Company, St Paul's, Foundling Hospital, etc. – but is remembered for his fantastic country house, Sezincote, Gloucestershire (1805), the first Indian-style building in England. Elsewhere he showed French influence of an advanced kind, e.g. the west tower of St Anne's, Soho, London. In 1792 he restored Tickencote church in the Norman style, thus anticipating C19 restorations.

Colvin 1995.

**Coderch**, José Antonio (1913–84), *see* SPANISH ARCHITECTURE.

**Codussi** or **Coducci**, Mauro (*c.*1440–1504). Italian architect. Born near Bergamo, he had settled in Venice by 1469 and was largely responsible, with LOMBARDO, for replacing Venetian Gothic with a classicizing style achieving a remarkable synthesis of the Veneto-

Byzantine and Renaissance. His earliest-known work is S. Michele in Isola (1468–77), the first Renaissance church in Venice, with a façade derived from ALBERTI's Tempio Malatestiano but capped by a semicircular pediment of Veneto-Byzantine inspiration. Between 1480 and 1500 he completed S. Zaccaria, begun in 1458 by Antonio Gambello (d.1481), with its very tall façade on which columns and niches are piled up on one another, and with classical ornament in most unclassical profusion. He was more restrained in S. Giovanni Crisostomo (1494–1504). Palazzo Zorzi a San Severo (c.1480), Palazzo Corner-Spinelli (c.1485–90) and Palazzo Vendramin-Calergi (begun c.1502) have been attributed to him; also the east wing of the Doges' Palace (1485 onwards), formerly attributed to Antonio Rizzo (c.1430–1499/1500) who designed the Scala dei Giganti in the courtyard. In 1492–1504 he rebuilt S. Maria Formosa on the plan of its C12 predecessor (exterior and dome are C16 and C17). His surviving masterpiece is the great double staircase at the Scuola di S. Giovanni Evangelista (1498). His staircase at the Scuola di S. Marco (1490–95) was destroyed in the C19 but his upper storey of the façade begun by Lombardo survives. He also designed the campanile of S. Pietro di Castello (1482–8). The clock tower in Piazza S. Marco has been attributed to him.

L. O. Puppi and L. Puppi, *M.C. e l'architettura veneziana del primo rinascimento*, Milan 1977; McAndrew 1980; Lieberman 1982; Howard 1987; V. Palli, *M.C. Architetto bergamesco 1440?–1504*, Zogna (Bergamo) 1992.

**Coenen**, Jo (b.1949), *see* DUTCH ARCHITECTURE.

**Coffering**. Decoration of a ceiling, a vault, or an arch SOFFIT, consisting of sunken square or polygonal ornamental panels. *See also* CAISSON; LACUNAR.

**Coffin**, Marian Cruger (1880–1957). The first woman to establish a practice as landscape architect in the USA. She was engaged mainly in designing large informal gardens for rich clients, e.g. the E. F. Hutton and Marshal Field estates on Long Island. She also laid out the campus of the University of Delaware and the New York Botanical Garden. Her own garden at New Haven was remarkable in creating an illusion of spaciousness in a very limited area.

**Coia**, Jack (1898–1981), *see* SCOTTISH ARCHITECTURE.

**Coignet**, François (1814–88), *see* CONCRETE.

**Cola da Caprarola** (Cola di Matteucci) (*fl.*1499–1519), *see* LEONARDO DA VINCI.

**Collar-beam**, *see* ROOF.

**Collar roof**, *see* ROOF.

**Collcutt**, Thomas Edward (1840–1924), *see* ENGLISH ARCHITECTURE.

**Colonia**, Juan, Simón, Francisco, *see* SIMÓN DE COLONIA.

**Colonial Revival**. The late C19–20 revival of American vernacular C18 brick and clapboard domestic architecture in the USA. It was promoted by Robert Swain Peabody (1845–1917) with his Denny House, Brush Hill, Milton, Massachusetts (1878) and his 'Massachusetts Building' (adapted from the early C18 Hancock House, Boston) for the Columbian Exposition, Chicago (1893), which provided a model for moderate-sized houses in New England, especially at coastal resorts. The more elaborate and original SHINGLE STYLE was developed at the same time and some architects worked in both styles, e.g. McKIM, MEAD & WHITE. Local variants were derived from colonial period buildings in Pennsylvania and the southern states. In the West a MISSION REVIVAL style began in the 1890s, followed by a Spanish Colonial Revival style with much relief ornament and over-wrought iron from the 1920s, e.g. Sherwood House, La Jolla, California (1925–8).

The same term – Colonial Revival – is applied to similar styles elsewhere. In Australia, where the federation of former colonies into states in 1901 inspired a new sense of national identity, the revival of the simple late Georgian style of houses built for the first British settlers was initiated in Sydney by William Hardy Wilson (1881–1955), with columned verandas, sash windows with shutters and fanlights, e.g. Eryldene at Gordon, New South Wales (1913–14). In South Africa, on the other hand, the vernacular 'Cape Dutch' style evolved for homesteads from the C17 had barely died out when H. BAKER from England began to exploit it with considerable refinement in his house for Cecil Rhodes (1893) and was soon followed by local architects.

A. Axelrod (ed.), *The C.R. in America*, New York 1985.

**Colonial style**, *see* UNITED STATES ARCHITECTURE.

**Colonnade**. A row of columns carrying an entablature or arches.

**Colossal order**. Any ORDER whose columns rise from the ground through several storeys, sometimes called a giant order.

**Columbarium**. An ancient Roman burial place, so called because it was constructed with niches or shelves on every wall for urns with ashes, like dovecotes or *columbaria*. Though pagan, they were open to all regardless of religion but they were avoided by the early Christians, who abhorred cremation; *see* CATACOMB.

**Column**. An upright structural member, square, round or rectangular and usually slightly tapering. It can be isolated, engaged or attached to a wall. Normally intended as a support but sometimes erected independently as a monument. In classical architecture it consists of a shaft, capital and, except in Greek Doric, a base (*see* ORDER). A *blocked column* has alternate rectangular blocks and circular drums. For the twisted column which appears in Baroque architecture, *see* SOLOMONIC COLUMN.

**Columna rostrata** or **rostral column**. In Roman architecture, an ornamental column decorated with ships' prows to celebrate a naval victory. *See* Fig. 34.

Fig. 34 Columna rostrata

**Colvin**, Brenda (1897–1981). English landscape architect who began by designing private gardens but made her name after the Second World War with her remarkable 'ecological environments', e.g. for Shotton Steelworks, Cheshire (1958), Rugely Power Station, Staffordshire (1962), and the Timpley Reservoir, Worcestershire (1962). Her major project, a thirty-year programme for the transformation of the landscape surrounding the Gale Common Power Station, Eggsborough, Yorkshire, makes use of fly-ash waste from coal-fired power stations to create a hill with grassed terraces leading up to fields and woods, thus limiting both climatic and visual pollution. She was one of the founders of the British Institute of Landscape Architects in 1929 and her *Land and Landscape* (London (1947) 1970) became a standard work.

S. Harvey (ed.), *Reflections on Landscape. The Lives and Works of Six British Landscape Architects*, Aldershot 1987.

**Common rafter**, *see* ROOF.

**Communion table**, *see* ALTAR.

**Community architecture**. An English movement for low-tech labour-intensive user-designed and user-built housing. Foreshadowed theoretically by Yona FRIEDMAN and by Ralph ERSKINE's 'participatory design process' at Byker in 1969–80, it was pioneered in the 1970s by Walter Segal (1907–85) with timber-frame construction self-built housing, providing architectural skills and services to poor and run-down communities on whose participation it depends. Schemes for both new housing and the rehabilitation of old housing followed in the 1980s. The precepts of Christopher ALEXANDER may be associated theoretically with the movement.

N. Waites and C. Knevitt, *C.A.: How*

*People are Creating their Own Environment*, London 1987; J. McKean, *Learning from Segal*, Basel/Boston/Berlin 1989; G. Towers, *Building Democracy. C.A. in the Inner Cities*, 1995.

**Company town**. A planned settlement for industrial workers. In C18 France housing was provided for workers in royal factories, notably the grandiose saltwork town at Chaux begun by LEDOUX in 1775. But the term 'company town' is usually reserved for one built by private enterprise. It is a C19 to early C20 phenomenon. In 1800 the English social reformer Robert Owen (1771–1856) began to build a village with a school, infirmary, community centre and co-operative shop as well as living accommodation for employees in his cotton mill at New Lanark, Scotland, which soon became a showplace. Accommodation for workers was necessarily provided where factories were far from urban centres, especially in the USA, normally limited to dormitories of a rudimentary kind though sometimes well planned, as at Lowell, Massachusetts, begun in 1822. In mid-C19 England, villages for workers were built by such paternalistic factory owners as Edward Akroyd and Sir Titus Salt, the former at Copley Hill (1847–53) and Akroydon (begun 1859), near Halifax, West Yorkshire, the latter at Saltaire near Shipley, West Yorkshire (1854–72). The emphasis was on physical and moral well-being with churches, schools and libraries but no pubs. At Guise in France, J. B. Godin, influenced by Charles Fourier, established around his iron-foundry the extensive *Familistière* that he bequeathed to his workers as a co-operative concern. But company towns were more usually built simply to provide healthier and more easily controlled workers' accommodation than the slums of industrial towns, e.g. Kronenberg near Essen, Germany, founded by Alfred Krupp (1873).

In 1880–84 the American railroad manufacturer George M. Pullman (1831–97) built for his employees the town named after him near Chicago, designed by BEMAN in a garden suburb planned by N. F. Barrett (1845–1919). In England the Quaker chocolate manufacturer Cadbury created Bourneville near Birmingham (begun 1879) and the soap manufacturer W. H. Lever (later Viscount Leverhulme) Port Sunlight near Liverpool (begun 1888), with vernacular-style cottages on tree-lined streets evoking a pre-industrial village. Later the chocolate manufacturer Rowntree created New Earswick near York, planned with UNWIN (begun 1902). In the USA from the late C19 until the Depression numerous company towns were built, often far from the great cities, e.g. Tyrone, New Mexico. Here as elsewhere they were architecturally traditional. But KOTERA designed c.1912 a town for the Bata shoe factory at Zlin (now Gottwaldov, Czech Republic), realized by Frantisek Lydie Gahura (1891–1958) in the International Modern style that was adopted also for Bata at East Tilbury, Essex (1933), the earliest popular housing of this type in England. At Sumila in Finland a cellulose factory with housing for employees by AALTO was built (1936–9). After the Second World War public and private transport have made company towns redundant.

J. S. Garner, *The Model C.T. Urban Design through Private Enterprise in C19 New England*, Amherst, Mass., 1984; M. Crawford, *Building the Working Man's Paradise*, London 1995.

**Compass roof**, *see* ROOF.

**Comper**, John Ninian (1864–1960). English architect, a pupil of BODLEY, he continued the ARTS AND CRAFTS tradition in a series of crisp and noble Late Gothic Revival churches – from St Cyprian's, Clarence Gate, London (1902–3), St Mary's, Wellingborough (1904–31), All Saints Convent, London Colney (1923–7), to St Philip's, Cosham, Portsmouth (1937). He was knighted in 1950.

A. Symondson, *Sir N.C. The Last Gothic Revivalist*, London 1988.

**Compluvium**. Rectangular opening in the atrium of an Ancient Roman house towards which the roof sloped, throwing off rainwater into a shallow cistern or impluvium in the floor.

**Composite order**, *see* ORDER.

**Composition** or **compo**. A mixture of whiting, resin and size used from the C18 onwards for moulded ornaments on ceilings, mouldings and panels (notably in BOISERIE), fixed with glue or panel pins. It is also a generic term for various C18 English plaster mixtures used as substitutes for STUCCO, mostly containing gypsum and size.

**Compound pier**. A pier with several SHAFTS, attached or detached, or demi-shafts against the faces of it; also called a *clustered* pier. *See* Fig. 35.

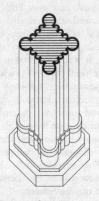

Fig. 35 Compound pier

**Computer Aided Design** or **CAD**. The use of a computer with visual display unit to assist in the design and/or construction process. It allows the architect to see and manipulate two- and three-dimensional representations of a design, the computer carrying out more complex and more detailed analysis and calculations than was previously possible. The consequences of analysis and any resultant changes in design are made immediately evident and the architect is left free to exercise unprogrammable judgements, e.g. of taste. Complicated three-dimensional perspective views can be produced and the point of view changed at will, some systems even allowing for binocular vision so that the architect can obtain an impression of walking inside the projected structure. The architect can thus create a building's form while anticipating the loads on the structure. Its use varies; some architects confine its application to the realization of their designs while others use it throughout the design process, the computer sometimes even becoming the conceptual starting point for a design.

F. E. Perkins, *Hands on CAD*, London 1989; N. Johnson, *AutoCAD: the Computer Reference*, London 1991; D. Raker and H. Rice, *Inside AutoCAD*, London 1992; F. A. Penz, *Computers in Architecture*, London 1992.

**Conch**. A semicircular niche surmounted by a half-dome.

**Concourse**. 1. An open space where several roads or paths meet, as in a French geometrically laid-out park. 2. In a building, an open space for accommodating crowds, as in a railway terminal or a hotel atrium.

**Concrete**. Concrete is 'mortar mixed with small stones to produce a hard monolithic mass' (P. Collins, *Concrete*, 1959). It was used in Ancient ROMAN ARCHITECTURE and became a determining factor in its development. Unlike modern concrete, which can be mixed and poured, Ancient Roman concrete had to be laid in courses as it dried out quickly. But about the time of Augustus (early AD CI) a slow-drying mortar was discovered and this revolutionized architecture. Combined with the arch and vault it enabled Ancient Roman architects to cover, without any internal support, spaces far larger and of far greater flexibility of form than had been possible before. It brought about an architecture of space rather than of mass. The earliest example is Nero's Golden House by SEVERUS. Trajan's Market and the Pantheon, Rome, are other notable examples.

After the fall of the Roman Empire it was almost forgotten and only revived in the late C18. The revival started in France, where the word for concrete is *béton*. Among the pioneers in the late C18 and early C19 are F. Cointereau and F. M. Lebrun. The story became more consistent only after 1850. The leaders were François Coignet (1814–88), who in 1864 built the shell of the church of Le Vésinet of concrete. Meanwhile experiments had gone on with iron reinforcement of the concrete. LOUDON in 1832 mentioned concrete floors with embedded iron lattice work. Joseph Monier (1823–1906) made flowerpots with reinforcement in the 1860s and columns and beams in 1877, and in 1873 William E. Ward (1821–1900) built a large house entirely of concrete in Port Chester, NY. Scholarly calculations began in the 1870s in the USA (W. E. Ward, T. Hyatt) and Germany (WAYSS, KOENEN). But the breakthrough was due to François HENNEBIQUE who started factories with a framework of reinforced concrete in 1895 and was soon kept busy. Hennebique's

American counterparts were Ernest L. RANSOME and, after 1905, Albert KAHN of Detroit, who pioneered industrial methods of standardization and team design in his factories for the Ford Motor Company, General Motors, and others. The first exposed concrete (or rather reinforced cement and steel rods piercing bricks) appeared in the church of St Jean de Montmartre in Paris (1894–1902), by BAUDOT, a pupil of VIOLLET-LE-DUC. The next step in the history of concrete was taken by MAILLART in 1905. Maillart recognized that concrete could be handled for bridges, not trabeated but arcuated, arch and roadway being a structural unity. A few years later, in 1910–13, Max Berg (1870–1947) built the grandiose dome of the Hala Ludowe at Wroclaw (formerly Jahrhunderthalle, Breslau) of reinforced concrete. In 1919 PERRET, who only very rarely departed from tabeated concrete construction, built the vast Esders clothing workshop in Paris with elegantly slender transverse arches. A unity of pier and vault could also be achieved by what is called mushroom slabs. These were developed by Maillart in Switzerland from 1910 onwards, and concurrently in America. Reinforced concrete also made it possible to build very far-projecting canopies, for instance in GARNIER's designs for an industrial city, published in 1917. In 1916 FREYSIN-NET began his airship hangars at Orly. They were of parabolic section with a transversely pleated surface. The greatest masters of concrete in our day were – needless to say – NERVI and CANDELA. *See also* PRE-STRESSED CONCRETE; REINFORCED CONCRETE.

Collins 1959; Davey 1961; Mainstone 1975; J. Faber and D. Alsop, *Reinforced C. Simply Explained*, London 1979; C. Stanley, *Highlights in the History of C.*, London 1979; L. G. Mallinson, *An Historical Examination of C.*, D.O.E., London

1986; A. Allen, *Reinforced C. Design to BS 8110*, London 1988.

**Condominium**. A building or building complex, usually residential and of low density, in which each unit is individually owned but subject to group control and restrictions.

**Cone mosaic**. The earliest known form of architectural ORNAMENT, found in Sumerian temples at Uruk (Iraq) of 3500–3000 BC. Zigzag and other geometrical patterns were formed by embedding in the mud plaster walls and pilasters thousands of small clay cones (about 10 cm. (4 inches) long) with black, red or buff-coloured tops.

**Conefroy**, Abbé Pierre (1752–1816), *see* CANADIAN ARCHITECTURE.

**Confessio**. In early medieval churches a subterranean chamber or recess located below or near the altar and sheltering a relic.

**Conoid**. In form like a cone, a term commonly used in connection with the lower part of a medieval vault where the ribs converge, forming approximately an inverted half-cone.

**Conservation**, *see* HISTORIC PRESERVATION.

**Conservatory**, **greenhouse** or **winter garden**. A glazed building either detached from or attached to a house and opening out of it. The earliest were C17 glass and stone structures, e.g. at Versailles, Paris (1684–6), Kew, London (1761, by CHAMBERS), and the Jardin des Plantes, Paris, by MOLINOS (1795). The great development of conservatories came with the introduction of the wrought-iron glazing bar and metal structures. The first iron and glass conservatory was of 1789 at Stuttgart-Hohenheim. LOUDON built iron and glass greenhouses from 1817 onwards and they culminated in PAXTON's enormous and famous curvilinear iron and glass conservatory at Chatsworth, Derbyshire (1836–40), that at Kew by BURTON (1844–8) and that at Lyon in 1847 by Hector Horeau (1801–71). The oldest surviving example is the Camellia House at Wollerton Hall, Nottinghamshire, by T. Clarke of 1823.

J. Hix, *The Glasshouse*, London (1974) 1996; S. Koppelkman, *Glasshouses and Wintergardens of the Nineteenth Century*, London 1981; Kohlmaier and Von Sartory, *Houses of Glass. A Nineteenth-Century Building Type*, Cambridge, Mass., 1986; M. Wood and A. S. Warren, *Glasshouses. A History of Greenhouses, Orangeries and C.*, London 1988; P. Marston, *The Book of the C.*, London 1992.

**Console**. An ornamental bracket with a compound curved outline and usually of greater height than projection. *See* ANCONES; BRACKET; CORBEL; MODILLION.

**Constructivism**. Less a movement – still less a style – than a whole aesthetic (in some respects anti-aesthetic) ideology, crystallized in Soviet Russia *c*.1920 from ideas already adumbrated by early practitioners of Modernism (*see* INTERNATIONAL MODERN; MALEVICH; TATLIN). Though potentially embracing all the arts, its most important achievements were in architecture and design: in the 1920s and early 1930s the VESNIN brothers, LISSITSKY, K. MELNIKOV, N. Ladovski, I. LEONIDOV and many others produced an outstandingly advanced and functionally effective series of (mostly) public buildings, as well as *avant-garde* exhibition designs and theatrical sets, in the Constructivist spirit of utilitarian simplicity and respect for the logic of materials. Russian Constructivism spawned many competing factions and theoretical '-isms', some extremely iconoclastic (e.g. A. Gan's slogan 'Art is

dead!', 1922); the suppression of artistic groupings in the USSR in 1932 signalled a change of Soviet artistic policy that would lead to the return of heavy pseudo-Renaissance pastiche styles for a couple of decades (cf. RUSSIAN ARCHITECTURE). But the Constructivist heritage has lived on to the present, to some extent in Russia, more obviously in the West, whither it was largely disseminated through the BAUHAUS and the ABC group (1922–39) which included Lissitsky, H. MEYER, STAM, etc. [R. R. Milner-Gulland]

C. Lodder, *Russian C.*, London and New Haven 1983; S. O. Khan-Magomedov, *Pioneers of Soviet Architecture: The Search for New Solutions in the 1920s and 1930s*, London 1987; S. Ingberman, *ABC. The International C. Architecture 1922–1939*, Cambridge, Mass., 1994.

**Contamin**, Victor (1840–93), *see* DUTERT, Charles-Louis-Ferdinand.

**Contant d'Ivry**, Pierre (1698–1777), *see* VIGNON, Pierre-Alexandre.

**Continuous imposts**, *see* IMPOST.

**Conurbation**. A term used in England to denote a group of towns linked together geographically, and possibly by their function, to form a continuous urban region, e.g. the towns of the Black Country or the Potteries. The word was first used by Patrick GEDDES about 1910.

**Cook**, Peter (b.1936), *see* ARCHIGRAM.

**Cooley**, Thomas (1740–84), *see* IRISH ARCHITECTURE.

**Coop Himmelblau**. An Austrian group formed in 1968 by Wolf D. Prix (b.1942), Helmut Swiczinsky (b.1944) and Rainer Michael Holzer, who left in 1971. Influenced by HOLLEIN and by HAUS-RUCKER-CO they developed an aggressive approach with the Reiss bar (1977), Flammenflügel bar (1980) and

Roter Engel bar (1981), all in Vienna. Their Merz-Schule project (1981), roof conversion, Falkestr. 6, Vienna (1983–8), Funder Factory, S. Veit, Kärnton (1985–9), realize better their radical aims. In 1988 they took part in the Deconstructivist Exhibition in New York. Of their later work the UFA Kinozentrum, Dresden (1994), and the Research Centre, Seibersdorf, Austria (1993–5), should be mentioned. They published *Architektur Muss Brennen* (Graz) in 1980.

Klotz 1986; W. Werner, *C.H. The Power of the City*, Darmstadt 1988; K. Offerman, *C.H.*, Stuttgart 1989; W. Prix, *C.H.*, London 1994.

**Coping**. A capping or covering to a wall, either flat or sloping to throw off water.

**Coptic architecture**. The Copts were Christian Egyptians, converted *c*.C2. They broke away from the Church in 451, established their own hierarchy in the C6 and in the C7 sided with the Muslims against the Byzantine emperor, preserving their independence as a church and people. Their architecture forms a unique category of Early Christian architecture and includes the earliest Christian monasteries, e.g. the White Monastery near Sohag, Egypt, of *c*.440. Though primitive in plan and construction, the ornamentation of early Coptic buildings is often sophisticated, with Corinthian capitals, Byzantine basket capitals, etc. (examples in the Coptic Museum, Cairo). By the C7 a standard type of Coptic church had developed with barrel-vaulted nave and aisles supported by piers, a forechoir resembling a transept and a chancel with three square apses, later with domes. The C12 church of Deir-Baramus at Wadi'n Natrun, Egypt, is a good example. Later C11–12 Coptic churches remained basilican, with numerous chapels and cells, e.g. Abu Sargeh (St Sergius), Cairo. The C12 rock-hewn churches at Lalibela in northern Ethiopia are exceptional, *see* ETHIOPIAN ARCHITECTURE.

Krautheimer 1986; A. J. Butler, *The Ancient C. Churches of Egypt*, London 1986.

**Corazzi**, Antonio (1792–1877), *see* POLISH ARCHITECTURE.

**Corbel**. A projecting block, usually of stone, supporting a beam or other horizontal member. A series, each one projecting beyond the one below, can be used in constructing a vault or arch.

**Corbel arch**, *see* ARCH.

**Corbel course**. A continuous projecting course of stones supporting beams or other horizontal members.

**Corbel-ring**, *see* SHAFT-RING.

**Corbel table**. A projecting course of masonry supported by a range of CORBELS, forming a parapet; often found in Norman buildings.

**Corbelling**. Brick or masonry courses, each built out beyond the one below like a series of corbels, to support a BARTIZAN, chimney-stack, projecting window, etc., or to form a rough ARCH, vault or dome.

**Corbie steps** or **crow steps**. Steps on the COPING of a gable, used in Flanders, Holland, north Germany and East Anglia, and also in C16 and C17 Scotland.

**Cordemoy**, Jean-Louis de. An early French neo-classical theorist about whom very little is known except that he was a priest (prior of St Nicholas at La Ferté-sous-Jouars) and was not, as is sometimes said, identical with L. G. de Cordemoy (1651–1722). His *Nouveau traité de toute l'architecture* (1706) was the first to preach truth and simplicity in architecture and to insist that the purpose of a building should be expressed in its form. His ideas anticipated and probably influenced those of LAUGIER and LODOLI.

Herrmann 1962; R. Middleton in *Journal of the Warburg and Courtauld Institutes*, 1962; Rykwert 1980.

**Cordon**. In military architecture, the rounded stone moulding or band below the parapet of the revetment of the rampart, going all round the fort.

**Coretti**. Small galleries like the boxes of a theatre, often inserted into the choir wall of Baroque churches.

**Corinthian order**, *see* ORDER.

**Cormier**, Ernest (1885–1980), *see* CANADIAN ARCHITECTURE.

**Cornette**, Benoit (b.1955), *see* FRENCH ARCHITECTURE.

**Cornice**. In classical architecture, the top, projecting section of an ENTABLATURE; also any projecting ornamental moulding along the top of a building, wall, arch, etc., finishing or crowning it. That along the sloping sides of a pediment is called a raking cornice. *See* Figs. 51, 86.

**Corona**. The vertical-faced projection in the upper part of a CORNICE, above the BED MOULDING and below the CYMATIUM, with its SOFFIT or undersurface recessed to form a drip.

**Corporate Modernism**. A development of INTERNATIONAL MODERNISM in the USA in the 1950s epitomized by such glass-and-metal curtain-walled skyscraper offices as SOM's Lever House (1952) and Union Carbide Building (1955–60), both in New York. Emery Roth & Sons built seventy such anonymously detailed, blandly profiled, bulky glass-and-metal office buildings in Manhattan between 1950 and 1970, usually of the set-back type, e.g. the Colgate-Palmolive Building (1954–6) and Tower East (1962). They were seen as symbols of corporate status and reflections of the proprietors' progressive outlook.

A. Drexler, *Buildings for Business and Government*, MoMA, New York 1959; S. Rattenbaum, *Mansions in the Clouds: The Skyscraper Palazzi of Emery Roth*, New York 1986.

**Corps de logis**. The French term for the main building forming a self-contained dwelling, as distinct from the wings, pavilions, service quarters, stables, etc.

**Correa**, Charles Mark (b.1930). Indian architect trained in the USA at MIT. In 1956 he returned to India and moved steadily away from MODERNISM towards a flexible approach drawing on Indian vernacular architecture and building practice. He uses local and traditional materials and forms with great sensitivity, e.g. Gandhi Ashram Memorial Museum, Ahmedabad (1958–63). This was followed by the ECIL Office Complex, Hyderabad (1965–8); the Kanchenjunga Apartments, Bombay (1970–83); the Bharat Bhavan, Bhopal (1975–81); the National Crafts Museum, New Delhi (1975–90); and the Vidhan Bhavan, State Assembly, Bhopal (1980 onwards). He has also been active in urban design, e.g. his project for the Bombay low-income housing estate at Belapur for 2 million people (1983–6). Among his recent works the Jawahar Kala Cultural Centre, Jaipur (1986–92), and the Centre for Astronomy and Astrophysics, Pune (1988–92), are notable. The former is inspired by the mandalas in ancient Vedic texts and creates a mysterious complex of spaces, a mystic labyrinth. He published *The New Landscape* (London 1989) and *The Ritualistic Pathway: Five Projects. A Portfolio of Architecture* (London/Delhi 1992).

H. U. Khan (ed.), *C.C.*, Singapore/London 1987; V. Baht and P. Scriver, *After the Masters: Contemporary Indian Architecture*, Ahmedabad 1990; K. Frampton, *C.C.*, London 1996.

**Cortile**. The Italian term for a courtyard, usually internal and surrounded by ARCADES.

**Cortona**, Pietro Berrettini da (1596–1669). Italian painter and architect, second only to BERNINI in the history of Roman Baroque art, was born at Cortona, the son of a stone mason. Apprenticed to the undistinguished Florentine painter Commodi, he went with him to Rome c.1612 and settled there. He can have received only superficial training in architecture, if any at all. First patronized by the Sacchetti family, for whom he designed the Villa del Pigneto (1626–36, now destroyed, but a landmark in villa design), he was soon taken up by Cardinal Francesco Barberini and his cultivated circle. Thereafter he had architectural and pictorial commissions in hand simultaneously. His first important building, SS. Martina e Luca, Rome (1634–69), is also the first great, highly personal, and entirely homogeneous Baroque church, conceived as a single plastic organism with a single dynamic theme applied throughout. It is notable especially for the pliable effect given to the massive walls by breaking them up with giant columns: these are not used to define bays or space, as they would have been by a Renaissance architect, but to stimulate the plastic sense. The decoration is extremely rich, even eccentric (e.g. the wildly undulating forms of the dome coffering), with here and there Florentine MANNERIST traits. In contrast to Bernini he excluded figure sculpture entirely; he also excluded colour and had the interior painted white throughout.

His use of concave and convex forms in the façade of S.Maria della Pace, Rome (1656–9), is typically Baroque. More original is his application of theatre design to the *piazza*: he treated it as an auditorium, the side entrances being arranged as if they were stage doors and the flanking houses as if they were boxes. The gradual elimination of Mannerist elements from his style and his tendency towards Roman simplicity, gravity and monumentality are apparent in the façade of S. Maria in Via Lata, Rome (1658–62). Comparison between his early and late works, notably the dome of S. Carlo al Corso, Rome (begun 1668), illustrates his remarkable progress from eccentricity and complexity, with effervescent decoration, to serene classical magnificence. Most of his grander and more ambitious schemes remained on paper (Chiesa Nuova di S. Filippo, Florence; Palazzo Chigi, Rome; Louvre, Paris). Though equally great as painter and architect he said that he regarded architecture only as a pastime.

Wittkower 1982; Varriano 1986.

**Cosmati work**. Decorative work in marble with inlays of coloured stones, mosaic, glass, gilding, etc., much employed in Italian Romanesque architecture, especially in and around Rome and Naples, C12–13. Roman marble workers of this period were known collectively as the Cosmati from the name Cosma, which recurs in several families of marble workers.

E. Hutton, *The C. The Roman Marble Workers of the XIIth and XIIIth Centuries*, London 1950.

**Costa**, Lúcio (b.1902). Born at Toulon in France. Brazilian architect, planner and architectural historian. He was the leading member of the team which, with LE CORBUSIER as consultant, produced the Ministry of Education, Rio de Janeiro (1937–43). The block of flats in Eduardo Guinle Park (1948–54) is his. As a planner he suddenly rose to fame by winning the competition for Brasilia, the new capital (Nova Cap) of Brazil, in 1957. The plan is a formal one, yet not at all formal in the BEAUX ARTS sense. It has the shape of a bow and arrow or a bird, the head being the square with the two houses of parliament and the parliamentary offices, the tail being the railway station. Close to this are sites for light industry; nearer the head, but on the way along the straight monumental axis towards the station, follows the quarter of hotels, banks, theatres, etc., which lies at the junction of body and wings. The long curved wings (or the bow proper) are for housing; this area is divided into large square blocks, called *superquadre*, each with its freely arranged high slabs of flats, schools, church, etc.

It exemplifies the urban planning principles promoted by CIAM in the 'Athens Charter' and provides an impressive setting for NIEMEYER's buildings.

J. O. Gazenco and M. M. Scarone, *L.C.*, Buenos Aires 1959; F. Bullrich, *New Directions in Latin American Architecture*, New York 1969; D. Epstein, *Brasilia. Plan and Reality*, Berkeley, California, 1973.

**Cottage**. 1. A small, one-storey dwellinghouse in a village or open country, usually for agricultural labourers. In C16–17 England cottages were simple mud, clay-lump or turf cabins and very few, if any, survive. The earliest known English cottages were built for weavers following the C17 boom in the cloth industry. This led to some notable vernacular architecture in such villages as Bibury, Gloucestershire, and Burford, Oxfordshire. In the late C18 the cottage was discovered by such writers as James Malton, whose *Essay on British Cottage Architecture* (1798) emphasized its asymmetricality and irregularity, its hips, gables and dormers and its construction of brick, half-timbering and thatch. These qualities were taken up by exponents of the PICTURESQUE, e.g. NASH, and exploited in the COTTAGE ORNÉE. In the late C19

the Old English cottage was revived by DEVEY and ARTS AND CRAFTS architects but in a different spirit from that of the *cottage ornée*. 2. In the USA the term 'cottage' refers to a summer residence at a watering place, usually small but sometimes large and sumptuously furnished and equipped.

C. Hussey, *The Picturesque*, London 1924; M. W. Barley, *The English Farmhouse and C.*, London 1961; A. Clifton-Taylor, *The Pattern of English Building*, London 1962; Summerson (1953) 1991.

**Cottage ornée**. An artfully rustic building emulating the Old English COTTAGE. Usually asymmetrical in plan, often with thatched roof, much use of fancy weatherboarding and very rough-hewn wooden columns to support verandas, porches, etc. A product of the PICTURESQUE cult of the late C18 and early C19 in England, it might serve merely as an ornament in a park or as a lodge or a dependant's dwellinghouse. Some, intended for the gentry, were on a larger scale. Numerous designs for *cottages ornées* were published, e.g. PAPWORTH's *Designs for Rural Residences* (1818). By this date it had become as popular as the small *villa* for the middle-class. Later C19 cottages designed by DEVEY and ARTS AND CRAFTS architects were different in spirit and the term *cottage ornée* is inappropriate for them.

C. Hussey, *The Picturesque*, London 1924; S. Lyall, *Dream Cottages*, London 1988; Summerson (1953) 1991.

**Cotte**, Robert de (1656/7–1735), an early French Rococo architect, was instrumental in the diffusion abroad, especially in Germany, of French architectural and decorative fashions. He began under his brother-in-law J. HARDOUIN-MANSART, who established him professionally and whom he later succeeded as Premier Architecte (1709). His main work for the Crown was remodelling the choir of Notre Dame, Paris (completed 1714), with decoration by Pierre LE PAUTRE. His Parisian *hôtels* date from 1700 onwards, the most notable among those that survive being the Hôtel de Bouvallais (*c.*1717) and the redecoration of François MANSART's Hôtel de Toulouse, now the Banque de France, in which the gallery (1718–19) is a Rococo masterpiece (the decoration is by François-Antoine Vassé). His monastic buildings for the Abbey of Saint Denis (1700–1725, only the east and south ranges built during his lifetime) and the façade of Saint Roche, Paris (finished 1736/8), should also be mentioned. He also worked extensively outside Paris (e.g. Palais Rohan, Strasbourg, 1727–8, built 1731–62), and was frequently consulted by German patrons, e.g. for extensions to the *château* at Bonn and for Schloss Clemensruhe at Poppelsdorf, Bonn (1715); his designs or advice were not always accepted (e.g. at Schloss Brühl, Schloss Schlessheim and the Residenz at Würzburg).

R. Neuman, *R. de C. (1656/7–1735) and the Perfection of Architecture in C18 France*, Chicago/London 1994.

**Coupled roof,** *see* ROOF.

**Cour d'honneur.** The front court of a palace or *château* where honoured guests might alight from their carriages and be formally received.

**Course.** A continuous layer of stones, bricks, etc., in a wall. A *lacing course* binds the facing to the core of the wall.

**Court style,** *see* RAYONNANT.

**Courtonne,** Jean (1671–1739), *see* FRENCH ARCHITECTURE.

**Covarrubias,** Alonso de (1488–1570). Spanish mason and decorative sculptor in a limpid, playful Early Renaissance style, though for structural members he still adhered to the Gothic tradition. He appears first as one of the nine consultants for Salamanca Cathedral in 1512, a sign of remarkably early recognition. From 1515 he did decorative work at Sigüenza. The church of the Piedad at Guadalajara (1526) is now in ruins, but the Chapel of the New Kings at Toledo Cathedral (1531–4) survives complete and is a delightful work. The fine staircase of the Archbishop's Palace at Alcalá is of *c.*1530, the richly tunnel-vaulted Sacristy at Sigüenza of 1532–4. Covarrubias was master mason of Toledo Cathedral and architect to the royal castles (1537 onwards); see the courtyard of the Alcázar at Toledo.

Kubler and Soria 1959.

**Cove** or **coving.** A large concave moulding, especially that produced by the arched junction of wall and ceiling in a 'cove ceiling'. In a ROOD SCREEN the concave curve supporting the projecting ROOD LOFT is called the coving.

**Cover fillet.** A moulded strip used to cover a joint in panelling, etc.

**Cowl.** A metal covering, like a monk's hood, fixed over a chimney or other vent, and revolving with the wind to improve ventilation.

**Crabtree,** William (1905–91), *see* ENGLISH ARCHITECTURE.

**Cradle roof,** *see* ROOF.

**Craig,** James (1744–95), *see* SCOTTISH ARCHITECTURE.

**Cram,** Ralph Adams (1863–1942). American neo-Gothic architect, he admired BODLEY and took up his Perpendicular Gothic at All Saints, Ashmont (1891), St Thomas's, New York (1905–13, with GOODHUE), and the Chapel and Graduate College, Princeton University (1911 onwards, with Ferguson). His Cathedral of St John the Divine, New York (begun 1911), essays French Gothic, while his Rice University Administration Building, Houston, Texas (1912), is 'Byzantine Gothic'. He published *The Gothic Quest* (1907) and *The Substance of Gothic* (1917).

D. S. Tucci, *R.A.C. American Medievalist*, Boston 1975; A. M. Daniel, *The Early Architecture of R.A.C. 1889–1902*, 1980; R. Muccigrosso, *American Gothic. The Mind of R.A.C.*, 1980.

**Cramp**. A metal pin or other device to bind together stones of the same course. *See* DOWELL.

**Credence**. A small table or shelf near the altar, on which the Sacraments are placed.

**Crenellation**, *see* BATTLEMENT.

**Crepidoma**. The stepped base of a Greek temple.

**Crescent**. A semi-elliptical row of houses. Invented by John WOOD the younger at the Royal Crescent, Bath (1767–75), which was followed by John CARR's Crescent at Buxton (1780–90), where Wood's invention of a monumental residential crescent was combined with an arcaded ground floor. John Palmer (*c.*1738–1817) went further with his concave–convex Lansdowne Crescent, Bath (1789–93). Crescents became a feature of C19 town planning though usually without emulating the most original feature of Wood's crescent, i.e. its facing what appears to be unlimited parkland, trees being planted in the foreground to conceal the city beyond.

**Crest** or **cresting**. An ornamental finish along the top of a screen, wall or roof; usually decorated and sometimes perforated.

**Cret**, Paul (1876–1945). French Beaux Arts architect who settled in the USA in 1903. He built the Pan-American Union (1912–13), the Folger Shakespeare Library (1932) and the Federal Reserve Board Building (1935), all in Washington, DC. Also notable are his Indianapolis Public Library, Indianapolis (1914), and the Cincinnati Union Terminal, Cincinnati, Ohio (1933), now the Museum Center.

E. G. Grossman, *The Civic Architecture of P.C.*, Cambridge, Mass. 1996.

**Cretan and Mycenaean architecture**. Excavations have revealed the earliest examples of European architecture at Knossos and Phaestos in Crete. Although many of the discoveries are of controversial significance, and most of the proposed reconstructions are unconvincing, enough survives to reveal certain general characteristics. At both Knossos and Phaestos there were elaborate palaces, richly coloured and decorated with selinite revetments, destroyed in the (probably seismic) catastrophe of *c.*1700 BC which marks the first break in Cretan history. The palaces built to replace them were more carefully integrated with the surrounding landscapes; they had hanging gardens, cool courtyards and colonnaded walks. Planning seems to have been wilfully asymmetrical, and long corridors linked a bewildering series of tiny rooms with the courtyards and pillared halls. Decorations proliferated, and both interiors and exteriors were boldly and brightly painted in a manner which must have been almost jazzy. Another dramatic destruction occurred *c.*1400 BC; shortly afterwards Crete seems to have come under Mycenaean control.

The Mycenaeans of the Greek mainland developed the MEGARON and also the *tholos* or BEEHIVE tomb, of which the best surviving example is the so-called 'Treasury of Atreus' at Mycenae (C15 BC). Between 1400 and 1200 BC, when the Mycenaeans held the upper hand in the Greek world, they produced an architecture of great monumentality and sophistication. The great cyclopean walls surviving at Mycenae and Tiryns reveal their engineering abilities. They developed the fortified acropolis as the civic and religious centre of the city. They began to use stone sculpture (e.g. the Lion Gate at Mycenae) as well as painting for decoration and, for especially fine rooms, incrustations of alabaster. But their most important achievement was in monumental planning. Abandoning the haphazard systems of the palaces at Knossos and Phaestos, they enhanced the majestic impact of the acropolis at Mycenae by arranging a succession of courtyards, staircases and rooms on a single axis. The Mycenaeans were overthrown and their buildings destroyed by incursions from the north in the C12 BC but two Mycenaean architectural elements – the *megaron* and the acropolis – were destined to survive in GREEK ARCHITECTURE.

**Crinkle-crankle wall**. A serpentine or continuously snake-like curving or undulating wall.

**Critical regionalism**. A term coined in 1981 and quickly given currency by architectural critics though never precisely defined. It is an attitude or approach rather than a theory, in reaction against the consumerist Post-Modern hedonism of the Reagan and Thatcher years. Consciously 'regional', it seeks to combine a response to the local with a certain universality, avoiding the vernacular, sentimental or picturesque while affirming the importance of environmental, cultural and societal values. Architects such as CODERCH or BARRAGÁN might be instanced as precursors and BOTTA, SIZA or ANDO as exemplary of its aims in their syntheses of the local and the general.

K. Frampton in H. Foster (ed.), *The Anti-Aesthetic. Essays on Postmodern Culture*, Port Townsend, Washington 1983; S. Amourgis (ed.), *C.R. The Pomona*

*Meeting Proceedings*, Pomona, California, 1991.

**Crocket**. A decorative hook-like spur of stone carved in various leaf shapes and projecting at regular intervals from the angles of spires, pinnacles, canopies, gables, etc., in Gothic architecture. Also used in Gothic capitals in place of leaves and volutes (*see* CAPITAL; Fig. 36).

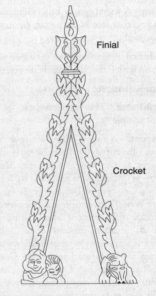

Fig. 36 Crockets

**Crocket capital**, *see* CAPITAL.

**Cromlech**, *see* MEGALITH.

**Cronaca**, Simone del Pollaiuolo (1457–1508). A Florentine but, like Giuliano da SANGALLO with whom he was to be closely associated, he spent several years in Rome when young (1475–85). He collaborated with Giuliano da Sangallo at the sacristy of S. Spirito, Florence, and with BENEDETTO DA MAIANO at Palazzo Strozzi, Florence, for which he designed the magnificent and famous cornice (1490–1504). His masterpiece is S. Francesco (S. Salvatore) al Monte, Florence (1487–1504) – extremely elegant yet robust and dignified. The Palazzo Guadagni in Florence (1503–6) has been attributed to him.

Goldthwaite 1980; Heydenreich 1996.

**Cross**. One of the most ancient symbolical ornamental devices, found in many cultures from prehistoric times. In ancient Egypt a form of cross called an *ankh*, composed of a T surmounted by a loop, was the symbol of life. The *swastica*, a cross in which the arms are bent at right angles in the same relative direction, is of similarly ancient origin (supposedly a solar symbol), notably in ancient India. A cross became the main Christian symbol when it was adopted by the Emperor Constantine in the early c4, signifying specifically 'Triumph over Death'. It has been used in ornament and has also determined the plans of churches. There were two main types: (1) The Latin cross, with a long arm and a shorter one placed more than halfway up; (2) the Greek cross, with equal arms fixed on a short handle, as represented in Byzantine art from the c5, which signified the thaumaturgical power of Christ. The Greek cross plan was used mainly for Byzantine and Italian Renaissance churches, the Latin cross plan for churches in northern Europe from the Middle Ages onwards. For ornamental use the Christian Church developed various types of cross, sometimes in association with saints (e.g. St Andrew's cross, St Anthony's cross), sometimes by a process of decorative elaboration (e.g. clover-leaf cross). For the main types of cross, *see* Fig. 37.

**Cross-domed church**. In early Christian and Byzantine architecture, a church plan whose core, enveloped on three sides by aisles and galleries, forms a cross. The

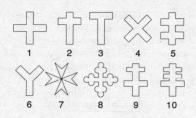

1. Greek cross
2. Latin cross
3. St Anthony's cross
4. St Andrew's cross
5. Double cross
6. Forked cross
7. Maltese cross
8. Clover-leaf cross
9. Cross of Lorraine
10. Papal cross

Fig. 37 Cross

core is surmounted by a dome in the centre and four barrel vaults resting on four corner piers. Sometimes called an *ambulatory church*.

**Cross-in-square**, cross-inscribed, *croix inscrite* or quincunx. The most widely spread Byzantine church plan, of obscure origin. The Nea, completed in 880, is said to have been the first example in Constantinople. It is composed of nine bays. The centre bay is a large square, the corner bays are small squares and the remaining four bays are rectangular. The tall central bay is domed (resting on four piers or columns), the corner bays are either domed or groin- or barrel-vaulted and the rectangular bays are usually barrel-vaulted.

**Cross-rail**. A main horizontal member of a timber-framed wall placed between the WALL-PLATE at the top and the SILL at the bottom (*see* TIMBER-FRAMING).

**Cross-vault**, *see* VAULT.

**Cross-window**. A window with one MULLION and one TRANSOM. *See* Fig. 38.

**Crossing**. The space at the intersection of the nave, chancel and transepts of a

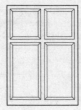

Fig. 38 Cross-window

church; often surmounted by a crossing tower or dome.

**Crow steps**, *see* CORBIE STEPS.

**Crowe**, Dame Sylvia (1901–97). English landscape architect who began as a garden designer but from 1945 was engaged mainly in public works, as planning consultant for the NEW TOWNS (1948–58) – notably Basildon, Harlow, Warrington and Washington – and for the surroundings of nuclear power stations, notably Trausfynydd, Snowdonia, and Wylfa, Anglesey. As consultant to the Forestry Commission she brought about major changes in the upland landscape. Her Commonwealth Garden at Canberra, Australia (1966), and her roof-garden for the Scottish Widows' Fund offices in Edinburgh (1976), were remarkable. Her publications, *Tomorrow's Landscape* (1956), *Garden Design* (1958, 1994), *The Landscape of Power* (1960), *Forestry in the Landscape* (1966) and, with M. Mitchell, *The Pattern of Landscape* (1988), contributed notably to the development of environmental planning in the UK.

S. Harvey (ed.), *Reflections on Landscape. The Lives and Work of Six British Landscape Architects*, Aldershot 1987.

**Crown**. The top part of an ARCH including the keystone, *see* Fig. 6.

**Crown glass**. Early window glass made by blowing and spinning, the glass becoming a flat, circular disc with a bullion at the centre.

**Crown-post**, *see* ROOF.

**Cruciform**. Shaped like a cross, as in the plan of a Christian church.

**Cruck construction**. A category of medieval architecture, of obscure origin, which culminated in such great roofs as those of the C13 Great Coxwell BARN and of Westminster Hall, London (1395–6), where the roof has a span of slightly over 21 m. (67 ft). It is a multi-tiered construction, combining the hammerbeam and the arch-brace-and-collar type of ROOF. In cruck construction the CRUCKS or blades extend from the ground or low side-walls to the ridge of the roof. They are the chief load-bearing members that support the roof.

N. W. Alcock, *Cruck Construction: An Introduction and Catalogue*, London 1981.

**Crucks**. Pairs of inclined timbers known as blades, usually curved, in CRUCK CONSTRUCTION. There are several types. *Base* blades rise from ground level to a tie- or collar-beam (*see* ROOF) upon which the roof truss is carried; in timber buildings they support the walls. *Full* blades rise from ground level to the apex of a building; they serve as the main members of a roof truss and in timber buildings they support the walls. *Jointed* blades are formed from more than one timber; the lower member normally rises from ground level and acts as a wall-post; it is usually elbowed at the wall-plate level and jointed just above. *Middle* blades rise from halfway up the walls to a tie- or collar-beam upon which the roof truss is supported. *Raised* blades rise from halfway up the walls to the apex. *Upper* blades are supported on a tie-beam and rise to the apex. *See* Fig. 39.

**Crusader castles**. The mainly C12 military architecture of the Crusaders in the

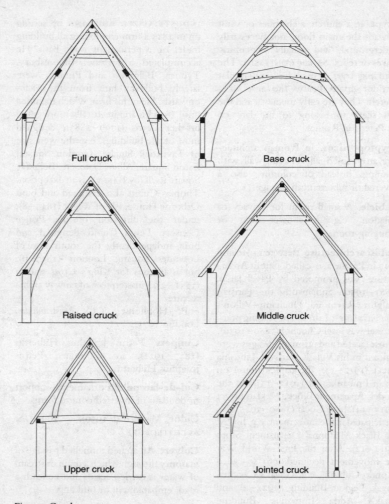

Full cruck

Base cruck

Raised cruck

Middle cruck

Upper cruck

Jointed cruck

Fig. 39 Crucks

Holy Land between 1099 and 1291 when the Crusaders had a permanent presence on the Levantine coast. It was notable for pilgrim forts, coast fortifications and, especially, strategic inland castles of which the most remarkable is the Krak des Chevaliers in Syria, built to secure the Homs Gap by the Knights Hos-pitallers 1150–1200. It survives almost intact.

H. Kennedy, *C.C.*, Cambridge 1994; B. Kühnel, *C. Art of the Twelfth Century or an Art Historical Notion?*, Berlin 1994; J. Folda, *The Art of the C. in the Holy Land, 1098–1187*, Cambridge 1995.

**Crypt**. In a church, a chamber or vault beneath the main floor, not necessarily underground, and usually containing graves or relics. *See also* CONFESSIO. The term *ring crypt* is used for semicircular corridor crypts below the apse of a church. They are early medieval and the first seem to belong to the late C6 (St Peter's in Rome).

**Cryptoporticus**. In Roman architecture, an enclosed gallery having walls with openings instead of columns; also a covered or subterranean passage.

**Cubicle**. A small room for privacy or isolation, e.g. a shower-room or changing-room.

**Cubist architecture**. Between 1910 and 1917 in Prague a so-called 'Cubist Architecture' was promoted by Pavel Janák (1882–1956), anticipating the Parisian sculptor Raymond Duchamp-Villon's '*maison cubiste*' of 1912. The leading practitioner was Josef Chochol (1880–1956), whose faceted and prismatic designs were realized in his Villa Kovarovic, Libusina Street (1912–13), the triplex house on Rasin Embankment (1912–13) and the Hodek Apartment Block, Neklan Street (1913–14). Josef Gočár (1880–1945) also participated in the movement, e.g. his 'At the Black Madonna' Department Store (1911–12). After the First World War the movement declined into so-called 'Rondo Cubism', e.g. Gočár's Czechoslovak Legion Building (1921–2) and Janák's Adria Insurance Building (1922–5).

A. V. Vegesack (ed.), *Czech Cubism*, London 1992; R. Svacha, *The Architecture of New Prague 1895–1945*, Cambridge 1995.

**Cubitt**, Thomas (1788–1855), began as a carpenter and became the greatest London speculative builder and developer. He took the crucial step towards INDUSTRIALIZED BUILDING by setting up in 1815 a firm employing all building trades on a permanent wage basis. He accumulated a fortune. Bloomsbury, Tyburn, Belgravia and Pimlico were largely built by him from the 1820s onwards. He or his firm, which included until 1832 his architecturally more gifted brother Lewis (1799–1883), designed most of the buildings, e.g. the west side of Tavistock Square, Gordon Square, Eaton Square, Albert Gate, etc. Belgrave Square itself (by BASEVI) is an exception. Thomas Cubitt also designed and built Osborne House, Isle of Wight (1845–8), under the direction of the Prince Consort. Lewis Cubitt designed and built independently the south side of Lowndes Square, London (1837–9), but is famous for King's Cross station (1851–2), a masterpiece of railway architecture.

P. Hobhouse, *T.C. Masterbuilder*, London 1971.

**Cuijpers**, Petrus Josephus Hubertus (1827–1921), *see* CUYPERS, Petrus Josephus Hubertus.

**Cul-de-lampe**. An ornamental support or pendant of inverted conical form.

**Culot**, Maurice (b.1939), *see* BELGIAN ARCHITECTURE.

**Culvert**. An arched tunnelled passage of masonry through which a drain or stream of water is carried across and beneath a road, embankment or building.

**Cumberland**, William Frederick (1821–81), *see* CANADIAN ARCHITECTURE.

**Cupola**. A DOME, especially a small dome on a circular or polygonal base crowning a roof or turret.

**Curtail step**. The lowest step in a flight, with a curved end which projects beyond the newel.

**Curtain wall**. 1. In medieval architecture, the outer wall of a castle, surrounding it and usually punctured by towers or BASTIONS. 2. A non-load-bearing wall which can be applied in front of a framed structure to keep out the weather. In 1917 Willis Polk (1867–1924) gave the Hallidie Building in San Francisco a continuous curtain wall of steel and glass which hung in front of the main frame, thus separating 'structure' from 'cladding'. There are now many types manufactured from a variety of materials; sections may include windows and the spaces between. *See* Fig. 40.

Hart, Henn and Sontag 1985.

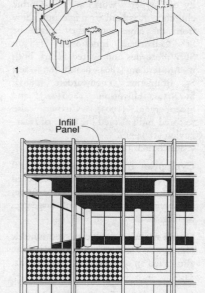

Fig. 40 Curtain wall: 1. Medieval 2. Non-load-bearing

**Curvilinear tracery**, *see* TRACERY.

**Cushioned frieze**. A frieze with a convex profile, also called a pulvinated frieze.

**Cusp**. Projecting points formed at the meeting of the FOILS in Gothic TRACERY, etc. *See* Fig. 56.

**Cutaway**. A diagrammatic drawing of a building showing both inside and outside elements from an oblique angle. *See* Fig. 41. *See also* AXONOMETRIC PROJECTION.

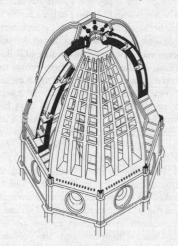

Fig. 41 Cutaway: Brunelleschi's domical vault, Florence Cathedral

**Cutwater**. The wedge-shaped end of a pier of a bridge, so constructed to break the current of water.

**Cuvilliés**, François (1695–1768). French born, he became one of the most accomplished German Rococo architects. Though he derived inspiration from the French Rococo, his decoration is much more exuberant than anything in France. His masterpiece, the Amalienburg in the park of Nymphenburg near Munich, has an easy elegance and gossamer delicacy which makes it the supreme secular monument of the Rococo. Born at Soignies-en-Hainaut, he entered the service of the exiled Elector Max Emanuel of Bavaria in 1708. As court dwarf, he travelled in the Elector's train through France, and in 1714 accompanied him on his return to Munich. Too small for the army, he began by working as a military architect and showed such promise that he was sent to Paris (1720–24) to study under J.-F. BLONDEL. In 1725 he was appointed Court Architect in Munich with EFFNER. For the Elector's brother he replaced SCHLAUN as architect at Schloss Brühl near Cologne (1728) and designed the beautiful little house of Falkenlust in the park. His first work in Bavaria was the decoration of the Reiche Zimmer in the Residenz, Munich (1729–37, partly destroyed). In 1733 he provided designs for the abbey church of Schäftlarn and for Palais Königsfeld (now the Archbishop's Palace), Munich. His next work was the Amalienburg (1734–9). It is a single-storey building with a large circular room in the centre which makes the garden façade curve outwards gracefully. The carved wood and silvered decorations in the main rooms are of exquisite refinement and the colour schemes are remarkably subtle – a cool watery blue background in the centre, citron yellow in one of the side rooms, and straw yellow in the other. In 1747 he provided plans for Wilhelmstal, near Kassel (erected by C.-L. DU RY). His last major work was the Residenztheater, Munich (1751–3; partly destroyed 1944, restored 1958), one of the last insouciant extravaganzas of the Rococo, liberally decorated with exquisitely carved *putti*, caryatids, swags, trophies of musical instruments, and those frothy cartouches which characterize the style. In 1767 he completed the façade of the Theatine church of St Cajetan in Munich. He published a *Livre de cartouches* in 1738.

H. R. Hitchcock, *Rococo Architecture in Southern Germany*, London 1968; W. Braunfels, *F.C. (1695–1768). Der Baumeister der galanter Architektur des Rokoko*, Munich 1986.

**Cuypers**, Petrus Josephus Hubertus (1827–1921), the most important Dutch architect of the C19, studied at the Antwerp Academy and in 1850 became City Architect at Roermond. In 1852 he set up a workshop there for Christian art. In 1865 he went to Amsterdam, where he built his two most famous buildings, both in the Dutch brick Renaissance style, and both restrained and without the exuberance of others working in the northern Renaissance styles. The two buildings are the Rijksmuseum (1877–85) and the Central Station (1881–9). But the majority of Cuypers's works are neo-Gothic churches. It is hard to single out a few from the large total: they might be St Catharina, Eindhoven (1859); St Wilibrordus and Sacred Heart, both in Amsterdam (1864–6 and 1873–80); St Bonifatius, Leeuwarden (1881); St Vitus, Hilversum (1890–92); and Steenbergen (1903). Cuypers also restored and enlarged the castle of Haarzuylen (1894–6).

Hitchcock 1977.

**Cyclopean masonry**. In pre-classical Greek architecture, masonry composed of very large irregular blocks of stone; also any polygonal masonry of a large size. *See* Fig. 103.

**Cyma recta**. A double-curved moulding, concave above and convex below; also called an *ogee moulding*. *See* Figs. 42, 51.

**Cyma reversa**. A *cyma recta* in reverse; also called a *reverse ogee moulding*. See Figs. 42, 51.

**Cymatium**. The top member of a CORNICE in a classical ENTABLATURE.

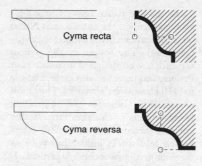

Cyma recta

Cyma reversa

Fig. 42 Cyma recta; cyma reversa

**Czech architecture**. The architecture of Bohemia and Moravia, contiguous regions that had been at times independent kingdoms, part of the Habsburg empire from the C16 to 1918 when incorporated in Czechoslovakia with Slovakia, from which they separated in 1992 as the Czech Republic. Medieval buildings are stylistically German. The oldest Christian buildings date from the C10 (Rotunda, Hradshin, Prague, excavated). The principal Romanesque buildings of the C12 and early C13 are St George at Prague, the crypt of Doksany and Strahov Abbey in Prague. At Třebíč in the mid C13 French Gothic influence begins to make itself felt. Its climax is Prague Cathedral, begun in 1344 by Matthias of Arras and inspired by Narbonne. It was continued after Matthias's death (d.1353) by Peter PARLER (choir completed 1385 and much of the south transept before he died in 1399), and his work is the architectural parallel to Charles IV's great epoch in Bohemian history. Charles made Prague the capital of the Empire, added large, boldly planned areas to the city, and built not far from Prague his castle Karlstejn (1348–67). Peter Parler represents a stylistic link with south Germany which was never to snap. With the flowing tracery in its windows, the complicated rib vaults, the flying ribs and the superb

portrait heads on the triforium, Prague Cathedral blazed the trail for the architecture of the C15 and early C16 in Germany and Austria. Peter Parler was also the architect of the chancel of Kolin, added to a hall nave of c.1280 – the first in Bohemia, and of course derived from Germany. Parler also began the cathedral-like church of St Barbara, Kutná Hora, in 1388. Yet another important church of Charles's time is the octagonal Karlov church in Prague.

Of the other Late Gothic churches the most notable are those of Třeboň, Český Krumlov, Olomouc, Plzeň, Brno, Most (Brüx) of 1517, and finally Louny (Laun) of 1529 etc. by Benedikt RIETH.

For by then Rieth had reached his full maturity. His (though begun by M. Rajsek) are also the fabulously intertwined vaults of Kutná Hora, but his centre was of course Prague. On the Hradshin a predecessor, in the 1480s, had done the amazing oratory in the cathedral with its intricate decorative ribs in the form of branches and twigs. This may or may not be by Rajsek. Rieth's *magnum opus* is the Vladislav Hall on the Hradshin (1493–1502). This combines another intertwined vault with windows of pure Italian Renaissance forms and other details in an insouciant mixture of Latest Gothic and Renaissance.

The last years of the C15 are an early date for Renaissance features in the East, later, it is true, than the years of King Matthias in Hungary, but earlier than the earliest examples in Poland – and indeed in Austria and Germany. Only one generation later Paolo della Stella (d.1552) and Bonifaz Wohlmut (d.1579) built the Belvedere (1534–63) in the Hradshin gardens in the purest and most elegant Cinquecento style. It is of a precociousness as astonishing as Rieth's work. However, with the one exception of Hrezda castle near Prague, a star-shaped hunting-lodge of 1555 with exquisite wholly Italian stucco decoration, it remained alone, and the common development is more similar to the German and the Polish so-called Renaissance. The number of buildings and such features as portals is great. The Schwarzenberg Palace on the castle hill has shaped gables and diamond-cut ashlar blocks (1545 onwards), the Ball Court on the Hradshin (1567–9 by Wohlmut) rich sgraffito decoration. The same technique of decoration appears in a house of 1555 at Telč, whose crazy gable is reminiscent of Poland. Among the most characteristic features are colonnaded courtyards, in two or even three tiers (Bučovice, Velké Losiny).

Count Waldstein, the ambitious general, led architecture back to Italian grandeur and simplicity with his vast palace in Prague and especially its Loggia corresponding in height to three storeys of the palace (1623–34, by Andrea Spezza (d.1628) and others). Vienna has nothing to compare with it or with the Franco-Italian Schloss Troya, Prague (1679–96) by Jean-Baptiste MATHEY; but the two largest palaces of the second half of the C17 are in the same vein as contemporary work in Vienna (and Hungary). They are the Lobkowicz Palace at Roudnice (1655) and the Černin Palace in Prague (begun 1668), both by Francesco CARATTI. The Černin Palace is twenty-nine windows wide and four storeys high, with no pavilions or other projections, but with the heaviest diamond rustication on the ground floor and serried attached giant columns above. Also notable are the Collegium Clementinum, Prague (1654–8), and the monastery at Kladno (1663–8) by Carlo Lurago (c.1618–84). The change from this massed display to the splendidly curvaceous Bohemian C18 style was due to two members of the Bavarian DIENTZENHOFER family:

Christoph and Kilian Ignaz. Christoph's principal work is the church of St Niklas on the Kleinseite (Malá Strana) at Prague (1703–11). The source of the style is GUARINI, who designed a church near Prague, and there are also close relations to HILDEBRANDT's work. The most characteristic features of Christoph Dientzenhofer's churches are façades curving forward and backward, interlocked oval spaces inside, and skew or three-dimensional arches. A particularly bold motif is the diagonally set façade towers of Kilian Ignaz Dientzenhofer's St John Nepomuk on the Rock (1730). Among domestic buildings there is much influence from FISCHER VON ERLACH in the early C18 (Liblice Castle by Alliprandi, 1699). A layout of exceptional boldness was that of Kuks, built from 1707 onwards for Count Sporck. A palace, no longer extant, faced a vast block of almshouses across a valley in which was a race-course, and extremely Baroque sculpture adorns the terrace of the almshouses and extends into the dense woods near by. The most interesting architect of these years was Jan Blazej SANTINI-AICHEL with his re-modellings of Gothic churches in a queer Baroque-Gothic all his own, though inspired by Rieth and BORROMINI.

The best examples of the turn to neo-classicism are the neo-Palladian mansion of Kačina (1802) by Christian Friedrich Schuricht (1753–1832) and the beautiful saloon in the Rohan Palace, Prague, of 1807 by Louis Joseph Montoyer (c.1749–1811). The style carries on to the colonnade, baths, etc. of the Chotek gardens at Kroměříž (Kremsier) of the 1830s and 1840s. Little needs singling out between 1850 and 1900, foremost the National Theatre (1868–84) and the Rudolfinum (1884) in Prague by Josef Zítek (1832–1909). Both are Italianate, the theatre richer, the Rudolfinum more restrained and refined.

For the C20 Jan Koteřa (1871–1923), a pupil of Otto WAGNER in Vienna, was very influential, notably through Josef Gočár (1880–1945) and Josef Chochol (1880–1956), who promoted c.1910–14 a weird Expressionist, so-called CUBIST ARCHITECTURE, of which Chochol's apartment block in Neklan Street, Prague, of 1913–14 is a remarkable surviving example. In 1920 the commission to reconstruct Prague Castle and its gardens as a presidential palace for the new republic went to another Wagner pupil, Jože PLEČNIK. The INTERNATIONAL MODERN style was going strong before 1930 when MIES VAN DER ROHE built his most important European period house – the Tugendhat house – at Brno, where an exhibition of Modern Culture had been held in 1928. A very notable group of small houses was designed and built for this 1928 exhibition by Jan Visek, Jaroslav Grunt and Bohuslav Fuchs (1895–1972), whose Vesna girls' school and boarding school at Brno of 1929–30

is an outstanding early example of the International Style, as are also the Machnac Sanatorium at Trenčianske Teplice (1929–32) by Joromír Krejcar (1895–1949), the Ministry of Pensions, Prague, designed in 1928 by Josef Havlíček (1899–1961) and Karel Honzík (1900–1966), and the Electricity Company building, Prague, by Adolf Bens (1894–1982) of 1926 with its large, glazed inner courtyard. Only a few years later came the plans for the industrial centres of Hradec Králové (which were directed by Gočár) and for Zlin, now Gottwaldov, the town of the Bata shoe factory.

Of post-independence work the rehabilitation of the Town Hall, Benesov (1993–5), and the reconstruction of the Lvi dvur restaurant at the Castle, Prague (1994–5), by Josef Pleskot (b.1952) should be mentioned.

**CZWG Architects** (formed 1975), *see* ENGLISH ARCHITECTURE.

# D

**Dado**. 1. In classical architecture, the portion of a PLINTH or PEDESTAL between the base and CORNICE; also called a *die*. *See* Fig. 91. 2. In modern architecture, the finishing of the lower part of an interior wall from floor to waist height.

**Dado-rail**, *see* CHAIR-RAIL.

**Dagger**. A TRACERY motif of the Decorated style: a lancet shape, rounded or pointed at the head, pointed at the foot, and cusped inside. *See* Fig. 43.

Fig. 43 Dagger

**Dagoba**, *see* STUPA; SRI LANKAN ARCHITECTURE.

**Dahlerup**, Jens Vilhelm (1836–1907), *see* DANISH ARCHITECTURE.

**Dais**. A raised platform at one end of a medieval hall, where the head of the house dined with his family circle.

**Dance**, George (1741–1825). English architect, the son of George Dance senior (1695–1768, architect of the Mansion House, London, 1739–42). Went at seventeen to Italy for seven years with his brother Nathaniel, the painter, winning a gold medal at Parma in 1763 with some surprisingly advanced neo-classical designs. His early buildings are equally original and advanced, and might almost suggest an acquaintance with his more *avant-garde* French contemporaries, LEDOUX and BOULLÉE, because of his

use of the elements of architecture as a means of expression rather than of abstract geometrical design. His first building after his return from Italy was the exquisitely pure and restrained All Hallows, London Wall (1765–7). This was followed by his daring and highly imaginative Newgate Prison, London (1770–80, demolished), the most original and dramatic building of its period in England. His ability appears to have been quickly recognized, despite his unorthodoxy, for he was elected a founder member of the Royal Academy in 1768. His later buildings show no decline in originality or imagination: indeed, some of them anticipate SOANE – e.g. the Council Chamber of the Guildhall, London (1777, destroyed), in which the dome was treated like a parachute with fine lines radiating from the glazed opening in the centre, and the library of Lansdowne House, London (1788–91, completed by SMIRKE), which was lit by concealed windows in the semi-domed *exedrae* at either end of the long flat-vaulted room. After the turn of the century his style became increasingly austere and at Stratton Park, Hampshire (1803–6, only the portico survives) and the College of Surgeons, London (1806–13), he foreshadowed the Greek Revival of Smirke and WILKINS. But his principal artistic legatee was his pupil Soane. His unorthodoxy was exhibited in such works as the neo-Gothic south front of the Guildhall, London (1788–9), and the Tudor Gothic exterior of Ashburnham Place, Sussex (1813–17, demolished).

D. Stroud, *G.D. Architect 1741–1825*, London 1971; Summerson 1991; S. Jeffery, *The Mansion House*, London 1993; Colvin 1995.

**Dancing steps**. Shaped steps on a turn, the tapered end being widened to give a better foothold; also called *danced stairs* or *balanced winders*.

**Danish architecture and landscape architecture**. (For medieval and earlier architecture in Denmark, *see* SCANDI-NAVIAN ARCHITECTURE.) The Renaissance made itself felt late and slowly in Denmark. A house like Hesselagergård of *c.*1550 has semicircular gables on the Venetian pattern, but otherwise shows little of a true understanding of the Renaissance. The two great castles or country palaces of the Danish kings, Frederick II's Kronborg and Christian IV's Frederiksborg, date from 1574–85 and *c.*1602–20 respectively. In style they derive from the Netherlands, and Antonius van Obbergen (1543–1611) and Hans Steenwinckel the elder (*c.*1545–1601), working at Kronborg Castle, Helsingfors (Elsinore) and Hans and Lourens van Steenwinckel (1587–1639 and *c.*1585–1619), the architects of Frederiksborg, were in fact Dutchmen. Rosenborg in Copenhagen, a summer palace, dates from 1606–17, the delightful Exchange in Copenhagen by the Steenwinckels, from 1619–25. Its spire, in the form of three entwined dragons' tails, is a landmark. The style of all these buildings is close to that of the Netherlanders who built at Danzig or Emden, and not too distant from that of Jacobean England. The same style in ecclesiastical architecture appears in Holy Trinity, Kristianstad in Sweden of 1618 etc., probably by the Steenwinckels. The church is a hall church with very slim piers and still has the shaped gables of the Netherlandish style. The burial chapel of Christian IV attached to Roskilde Cathedral was begun even a few years earlier (1614)

and has Netherlandish gables of a slightly more advanced type and in addition Gothic windows, a case of Revival rather than Survival.

In 1662 the area of Copenhagen east of Kongens Nytorv and towards the new Citadel was laid out with a grid of straight streets, and in the course of the late C17 and the C18 this area filled up with private palaces and houses as stately as those of the best quarters of Paris during the same period. Their style throughout is the classical style which by then had begun to dominate Denmark and Scandinavia, usually Dutch in inspiration, e.g. the Charlottenborg Palace, Copenhagen (1672–83), in the new area mentioned above, and the Church of Our Saviour, Copenhagen (1682–96), by Lambert van Haven (1630–95), of which the interior recalls de KEYSER's churches in Amsterdam. The former Sophie-Amalienborg in Copenhagen of 1667–73, on the other hand, is an attempt at the Italian villa in Denmark.

Openness to influences from several countries remained characteristic throughout the C18. Frederiksborg (1707–9) and Fredensborg (*c.*1720) were Italian in inspiration (both were much altered later), Christiansborg, the former royal palace in Copenhagen, was south German, as was the charming Hermitage, Dyrehaven, north of Copenhagen, of 1734 by Laurids de Thura (1706–59). The finest mid-C18 building in Denmark is the Amalienborg in Copenhagen by EIGTVED, laid out in 1750–54 as an octagonal 'place' with four palaces at the diagonals and four streets branching off in the main directions. The style is French, the quality of the highest. Eigtved also designed the Frederiks church, magnificent, with a dominating dome on a high drum, but this was not carried out; Laurids de Thura made another, more classical design, and Nicholas-Henri

Jardin (1720–99), called in from France, a third, in its detail even more classical, with a giant portico of detached columns and columns round the drum.

The neo-classical phase of the classical revival began remarkably early in Denmark, where the Moltke Chapel at Karise of 1761–6 and the Chapel of Frederik V in Roskilde Cathedral (final design 1774) by Caspar Frederik Harsdorff (1735–99) are among the purest works of their date anywhere. The leader of the Greek Revival in Denmark was Christian Frederick HANSEN (1756–1845), his principal works being the Law Courts on the Nytorv of 1803–16 and the Church of Our Lady of 1810–26, both in Copenhagen. All on his own is Gottlieb Bindesbøll (1800–1856), whose Thorvaldsen Museum in Copenhagen of 1839–47 is as original within the Greek Revival as the work of Greek THOMSON in Glasgow. For later historicist revival architecture the best examples are the Copenhagen University Library of 1855–61 in the RUNDBOGENSTIL by Johan Daniel Herholdt (1818–1902), with elegant exposed iron members inside; the Italian Renaissance style Royal Theatre of 1872–4 by Jens Vilhelm Dahlerup (1836–1907), the Magasins du Nord of 1893 onwards by Albert Christian Jensen (1847–1913) with French pavilion roofs, and the French Baroque-style Frederik church, Copenhagen, of 1876–94 by Ferdinand Meldahl (1827–1908), following the style of Jardin's design.

From the 1890s onwards, however, some Danish architects joined the vanguard of those who endeavoured to get away from Victorian obtrusiveness and from Historicism. The Copenhagen Town Hall by Martin Nyrop (1849–1921) was begun in 1893 and is as important as BERLAGE's Exchange in Amsterdam as an example of the imaginative treatment of elements from various styles

of the past to achieve an original whole. KLINT's famous Grundtvig church, Copenhagen, which was begun finally only in 1919, straddles the gap between traditionalism and post-First World War EXPRESSIONISM. But the Grundtvig church is an exception in Denmark. The way to the C20 was as a rule not via a free Gothic but via Classicism. The paramount examples are the Faborg Museum, Copenhagen, of 1912–15 by Carl Petersen (1874–1923) and the Copenhagen Police Headquarters of 1919–24 by Hack Kampmann (1856–1920) and Aage Rafn (1890–1953). Then Denmark entered its moderate, sensitive C20 style, illustrated at its most Danish in Aarhus University of 1931 onwards by Kay Fisker (1893–1965) with the landscape architect SORENSEN, at its most international by the impeccable work of Arne JACOBSEN and a few others, notably Jorgan Bo (b.1919) at his Louisiana Art Museum, Humlebeck near Copenhagen (1958–71), Hening Larsen (b.1929) at his École des Hautes Études Commercials, Copenhagen (1985–9) and Ministry of Foreign Affairs, Riyadh, Saudi Arabia (1982–5) and Johan Otto von Spreckelsen (1929–87), whose posthumously completed Grande Arche de la Défense, Paris (1982–9), is striking. Only UTZON broke with Danish restraint in his rhapsodic design for the Sydney Opera House (begun 1956). His Bagsvaerd church, Copenhagen, of 1974–6 is no less remarkable, as are also his influential courtyard housing schemes in Fredensborg of 1962–3 – two- or three-storey mass housing with closed alleys to create privacy and segregation of traffic.

**D'Aronco**, Raimondo (1857–1932), *see* ITALIAN ARCHITECTURE; SOMMARUGA, Giuseppe.

**Daub.** Mud or clay smeared on to some rigid structure, usually of interwoven branches or lathes, as in WATTLE AND DAUB, to exclude draughts and give a smooth finish. It is rarely preserved unless accidentally baked.

**Davis**, Alexander Jackson (1803–92) was born in New York, joined Ithiel Town (1784–1844) as a draughtsman and became his partner in 1829. Town had already designed the Connecticut State Capitol with a Greek Doric portico in 1827. The partners now designed more capitols of the same type, but with domes a little incongruously rising over the middle of the longitudinal blocks (Indiana, 1831; N. Carolina, 1831; Illinois, 1837; Ohio, 1839). They are among the grandest of the Greek-Revival buildings in America. Their United States Custom House, New York (1833–42, now the Federal Hall Memorial Museum), should also be mentioned. But Davis could also do collegiate Gothic (New York University, Washington Square, 1832 onwards) and other versions of Gothic, e.g. Lyndhurst, Tarrytown, NY (1838–42 and 1865–7), and was versed in the cottage style too, e.g. Gatehouse, Blithewood, Barrytown, NY (1836–51). Indeed his reputation was founded on his picturesque, irregularly designed and planned villas for romantic settings, notably on the Hudson River, e.g. Montgomery Place, Tarrytown, NY, where DOWNING advised on the landscape garden. At the same time he was interested in modern materials – he did an iron shop-front as early as 1835 – and was in fact an exceptionally versatile designer. In 1853–57 he planned the layout of the 140 hectare (350 acre) Llewellyn Park, West Orange, New Jersey, a hilly site transformed into a residential community with winding carriage ways connecting 2–4 hectare (5–10 acre) sites for fifty villas, twenty of which he designed himself. He was one of the founders of

the American Institute of Architects.

R. H. Newton, *Town and D. Architects. Pioneers in American Revivalist Architecture 1812–1870*, New York 1942; W. Andrews, *Architecture, Ambition and Americans. A Social History of American Architecture*, New York (1947) 1978; A. Peck (ed.), *A.J.D. American Architect 1803–1892*, New York 1992.

**De Bodt**, Jean (1670–1745), see BODT, Jean de.

**De Brosse**, Salomon (c.1571–1626), see BROSSE, Salomon de.

**De Carlo**, Giancarlo (b.1919). Italian architect and theorist. In the mid-1950s he was one of the rebels who formed Team 10, see CIAM. His first important building, the students' residence for Urbino University (1962–6), illustrates his sensitive adaptation of a contemporary idiom to an historic context. His later university buildings in Urbino, e.g. the Faculty of Education Building (1968–76), were equally carefully integrated into the townscape. At his Matteotti housing, Terni (1971–4), he explored a 'participatory design process'. Later he very successfully adapted Venetian vernacular architecture for his housing along a new canal at Mazzorbo, Venice (1980). Though a rebel among 'Modernists', his theories as well as his work distance him from contemporaries such as Leon KRIER.

B. Zucchi, *G.D.C.*, London 1992.

**De Caux** or **De Caus**, Isaac (*fl.*1612–55) and Salomon (c.1577–c.1626), see CAUS or CAUX, Isaac de and Salomon de.

**De Cotte**, Robert (1656/7–1735), see COTTE, Robert de.

**De Key**, Lieven (c.1560–1627), see KEY, Lieven de.

**De Keyser**, Hendrick (1565–1621), *see* KEYSER, Hendrick de.

**De Klerk**, Michel (1884–1923), *see* KLERK, Michel de.

**De Meuron**, Pierre (b.1950), *see* HERZOG, Jacques.

**De Rossi**, Giovanni Antonio (1616–95). A prolific Roman High Baroque architect. His most important work is in the domestic field, e.g. the grandiose Palazzo Altieri, Rome (1650–54 and 1670–76), and the smaller, more elegant Palazzo Asti-Bonaparte, Rome (*c*.1665), which set a pattern for C18 architects in Rome. In his ecclesiastical work he showed a preference for oval plans and lavish sculptural decoration. His Cappella Lancellotti in S. Giovanni in Laterano, Rome (*c*.1680), and S. Maria in Campo Marzo, Rome (1676–86), are minor masterpieces of Roman High Baroque.

Wittkower 1982.

**De Sanctis**, Francesco (1693–1740). Italian architect who designed the Spanish Steps in Rome (1723–5), the vast and fabulous external Baroque stairway of elegant, curvilinear design, mounting from Piazza di Spagna to S. Trinità dei Monti; a masterpiece of scenic town planning.

N. A. Mallory, *Roman Rococo Architecture from Clement XI to Benedict XIV (1700–1758)*, New York 1978.

**De Stijl**. Dutch art and architecture movement founded in 1917 by the theorist Theo VAN DOESBURG. The architects OUD, RIETVELD, DUIKER, Cornelis Van Eesteren (1897–1988) and Robert van't Hoff (1887–1979) were prominent members but the painter Mondrian dominated the movement and the group's early buildings were influenced by his theories, e.g. van't Hoff's concrete cubistic houses of 1914–16 near Utrecht. They were also influenced by Frank Lloyd WRIGHT. Rietveld's Schröder house, Utrecht (1924), epitomizes De Stijl architecture. Van Doesburg lectured at the Bauhaus in 1921 and at about this date Oud left the group, which was joined by others, notably LISSITSKY, through whom Constructivism became a strong influence. After van Doesburg's death (1931) the group disbanded. It was very influential, more so than its achievements in architecture would warrant.

H. L. C. Jaffé, *D.S. 1917–1931. The Dutch Contribution to Modern Art*, Amsterdam 1956; C. P. Warnecke, *D.S. 1917–1931. The Ideal as Art*, Cologne 1994.

**De Wailly**, Charles (1730–98), *see* WAILLY, Charles de.

**Deane**, Thomas (1792–1871), *see* RUSKIN, John and WOODWARD, Benjamin.

**Decastyle**. Of a PORTICO with ten fronted columns.

**Deck**, Odile (b.1953), *see* FRENCH ARCHITECTURE.

**Decker**, Paul (1677–1713). German Baroque architect famous for his book of engraved designs: *Fürstlicher Baumeister, oder: Architectus civilis* (1711, 2nd edition with supplementary plates 1716). He worked under SCHLÜTER in Berlin from 1699, later settling in Nuremberg and finally, in 1712, in Bayreuth. Little is known of his work and he appears to have built nothing of importance. But his magnificent and fantastic designs, illustrating the most extravagant type of Baroque architecture and decoration (the latter derived from Bérain through Schlüter) had considerable influence on later German and Austrian architecture, e.g. FISCHER VON ERLACH. Decker's posthumous *Architectura Theoretica-Practica* (1720) is a handbook to ornament.

E. Schneider, *P.D. der Altere (1677–1713), Beiträge zu seinem Werk*, Düren 1937.

**Deconstructivism** or **Deconstructionism**. Terms used in, respectively, the USA and Europe for a development in architectural theory and practice in the 1980s, to some extent a reaction to the POMO hedonism of the Reagan and Thatcher years. Deconstructivism alludes to Russian CONSTRUCTIVISM as a point of departure, Deconstructionism to the literary theory and critical methodology of the French philosopher Jacques Derrida (b.1930) which suggested how the call for an architecture that expresses meaning and communicates might be answered. Derrida had applied his theories to the visual arts in his *The Truth in Painting* (Paris 1978, Chicago 1988) and in the mid-1980s he was involved with TSCHUMI in the Parc de la Villette, Paris, which explored Deconstructionist concepts of dissociation. Similar 'strategies' had been evident earlier in the work of architects not all of whom might wish to be associated with Deconstructivism, e.g. GEHRY. Deconstructivism was launched in 1988 in New York at MoMA with an exhibition sponsored by Philip JOHNSON. Designs by EISENMAN, HADID, SITE, LIBESKIND, COOP HIMMELBLAU and OMA as well as Tschumi were exhibited. The catalogue discussed Deconstructivism in terms of 'disruption, dislocation, deflection, deviation and distortion', and was not concerned in any simple sense with fragmentation or the taking apart of constructions. Deconstructionism is based on the assumption that architecture is a language, amenable to the methods of linguistic philosophy. Few Deconstructivist buildings have been realized, though Eisenman's Wexner Center for the Visual Arts, Columbus, Ohio (1986), and Hadid's Vitra Firehouse, Weil am Rhein, Germany (1993), should be mentioned.

P. Johnson and M. Wigley, *D. Architecture*, New York 1988; P. Brunette and D. Wills (eds.), *D. and the Visual Arts. Art, Media, Architecture*, Cambridge 1994.

**Decorated style** or 'Dec'. Historical division of English Gothic architecture 1240–1360 (*see* ENGLISH ARCHITECTURE).

N. Coldstream, *The D.S. Architecture and Ornament 1240–1360 (from Henry III to Edward II)*, London 1994.

**Deinocrates**, a Hellenistic architect, contemporary with Alexander the Great, appears to have been the architect, with Paeonius, of the temple of Artemis at Ephesus (*c*.356 BC). He is credited with the town plan of Alexandria and various other important undertakings, some of them rather fanciful, e.g. the project to transform Mount Athos into a colossal statue of the king.

R. Martin, *L'Urbanisme dans la Grèce antique*, Paris 1956.

**Delafosse**, Jean-Charles (1734–91). French architect known mainly for his ornamental designs in a rather ponderous version of the Louis XVI style, with much use of heavy swags and chunky Greek frets. Two of the houses he built in Paris survive – Hôtel Titon and Hôtel Giox (nos. 58 and 60 rue du Faubourg-Poissonnière) of 1776–80, both discreetly decorated with his favourite type of ornament.

Kaufmann 1955; Braham 1980.

**Del Duca**, Giacomo (*c*.1530–1604). Italian sculptor and architect, and assistant to MICHELANGELO for whom he carved the sculptural decoration on Porta Pia, Rome (1562–5). The dome of S. Maria di Loreto, Rome, was added by him *c*.1575. In 1584–6 he designed the garden at Villa Farnese, Caprarola, and the main exterior entrance stairway.

DBI 1988.

**Della Porta**, Giacomo (1533–1602), *see* PORTA, Giacomo della.

**Delorme**, Philibert (1500/15–1570), *see* L'ORME, Philibert de.

**Demi-column** or **half-column**. A column half sunk into a wall; a type of ENGAGED COLUMN, to be distinguished from a PILASTER.

**Demilune**. In military architecture, a detached crescent-shaped or triangular outwork, built in the moat.

**Dentil**. A small square block used in series in Ionic, Corinthian, Composite, and more rarely Doric CORNICES. *See* Figs. 51, 86.

**Department store**. A large shop or store with different departments. The first was the Bon Marché, Paris (1850), later enlarged by BOILEAU and EIFFEL with glass and iron extensions. The Haughwout Store, New York (1857, demolished), was the first with passenger elevators. Notable later department stores include SULLIVAN's Carson Pirie Scott Building, Chicago (1899–1904), JOURDAIN's La Samaritaine, Paris (1901–10, renovated 1926–30), and MENDELSOHN's Shocken Stores in Stuttgart (1926) and Chemnitz (1928).

**Dependency**. In the USA an outbuilding or a subordinate group of structures that serves as an adjunct to a central building, a feature of large estates, especially in Virginia where it included schools, slave quarters, burial grounds, etc.

**Depressed arch**, *see* ARCH.

**Dereham**, Elias of, *see* ELIAS OF DEREHAM.

**Desornamentado**. The severe, unornamented style of Juan de HERRERA which became the official style of Philip II's reign in Spain (1555–98).

**Desprez**, Jean-Louis (1743–1804), *see* SWEDISH ARCHITECTURE.

**Deutscher Werkbund**. A German association of *avant-garde* manufacturers, architects, artists and writers founded in Munich in 1907, inspired by BEHRENS and others and guided by similar ideas to those of the Deutsche Werkstätten, founded in Dresden in 1898, i.e. to create a national art without any stylistic imitation, based on sound construction and the co-operation of artisan, artist and architect. It was very influential in early industrial design. Their 1914 exhibition in Cologne included notable buildings by GROPIUS, TAUT and van de VELDE. Their influential 1927 experimental housing at Stuttgart (Weissenhofseidlung) was supervised by MIES and included buildings by LE CORBUSIER, OUD and STAM. By that date, however, its ideas had been taken over by Gropius for the BAUHAUS. Closed in 1934, it reopened in 1945 in East Germany and later in West Germany, but its pioneering days were over.

L. Burckhardt (ed.), *The W.: History and Ideology 1907–33*, New York 1980; R. Pommer and C. F. Otto, *Weissenhof and the Modern Movement in Architecture*, Chicago 1990; F. J. Schwartz, *The W.*, New Haven/London 1996.

**Devey**, George (1820–86). English architect; trained as a watercolourist under J. S. Cotman, he anticipated the ARTS AND CRAFTS movement in his love and knowledge of vernacular building – e.g. his cottages and other estate buildings at Penshurst, Kent (1850). His later buildings – Betteshanger (1856–61), St Alban's Court, Nonington (1864), and Hall Place, Leigh (begun 1871), all in Kent – are larger and lack the informality and spontaneity of his cottages. Though a pioneer he had little influence (except through VOYSEY) and was overshadowed by MORRIS and WEBB despite their Red House (1860) being much less pure in its use of the vernacular.

M. Girouard, *The Victorian Country House*, London 1979; J. Allibone, *G.D. Architect (1820–1886)*, Cambridge 1990.

**Dézailler d'Argenville**, Antoine-Joseph (1680–1765), *see* LE BLOND, Jean-Baptiste-Alexandre and LE NÔTRE, André.

**Di xue**. Chinese term for a moon door, the circular doorway in a garden wall symbolizing heaven and also serving as the frame for a vista.

**Diaconicon**. In Byzantine architecture, a room attached to or enclosed in a church; in Early Christian times, utilized for the reception of the congregation's offerings and serving as archive, vestry and library; later used only for the latter functions (also, a sacristy).

**Diaper work**. All-over surface decoration of a small repeated pattern such as lozenges or squares. *See* Fig. 44.

 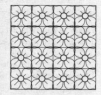

Fig. 44 Diaper work

**Diaphragm arch**. A transverse arch (*see* VAULT) across the nave of a church, carrying a masonry gable. Diaphragm arches divide wooden roofs into sections and were probably used to prevent fire spreading.

**Diastyle**. With an arrangement of columns three diameters apart. *See also* ARAEOSTYLE; EUSTYLE; PYCNOSTYLE; SYSTYLE.

**Die**. The part of a PEDESTAL between the plinth and the cornice, also called the DADO. *See* Fig. 91.

**Dientzenhofer**, Christian or Christoph, *see* DIENTZENHOFER, Kilian Ignaz.

**Dientzenhofer**, Georg (1643–89). The eldest member of an important Bavarian family of Baroque architects. His main works are the Cistercian abbey church at Waldsassen (1685–1704, with A. Leuthner); the nearby pilgrimage church at Kappel (1685–9), built on an unusual trefoil plan with three minaret-like towers to symbolize the Trinity; and the façade of St Martin, Bamberg (1686–91).

**Dientzenhofer**, Johann (1663–1726), the son of Georg, studied first in Prague then in Italy (1699–1700). His Italianate cathedral of Fulda (1704–12) reflects BORROMINI's remodelling of S. Giovanni in Laterano. His most impressive church is that of the Benedictine abbey of Banz (1710–18), where his brother Leonhard (d.1707) had built the conventual buildings; it has a complex ground plan based on a series of ovals and derived perhaps from GUARINI. His masterpiece is Schloss Pommersfelden, one of the largest and finest of German Baroque palaces, built in the remarkably short period of seven years (1711–18), with vastly imposing staircase (for which the patron, Lothar Franz von Schönborn, sought advice of HILDEBRANDT and also contributed ideas of his own), marble hall, gallery, hall of mirrors, and numerous richly stuccoed apartments.

**Dientzenhofer**, Kilian Ignaz (1689–1751), the most distinguished member of the Dientzenhofer family, was the son of Christian or Christoph (1655–1722, a brother of Johann who settled in Prague, where he built several churches, notably St Niklas on the Kleinseite, 1703–11, and St Margeretha, Břevnov, 1708–15). Trained first under his father, then under HILDEBRANDT, Kilian Ignaz soon became the leading Baroque architect in Prague. His style is sometimes a little theatrical, and he makes much play with contrasting concave and convex surfaces. His first independent building is the pretty little Villa Amerika, Prague (1717–20), with an almost Chinese roof in two tiers and very elaborate window surrounds. He also built the Palais Sylva-Tarouca, Prague (1749), on a much larger scale. His originality is best seen in his churches: the Thomaskirche, Prague (1723), with its intentionally jarring details; St Johann Nepomuk am Felsen, Prague (1730), with diagonally set towers on either side of the façade, a device he used again at St Florian, Kladno (c.1750), and St Niklas in the Old City in Prague (1732–7). His many other churches are notable for the variety of their Baroque plans – a circle at Nitzau, pure oval at Deutsch-Wernersdorf, a succession of ovals at St Mary Magdalen, Karlovy Vary (1733–6), an elongated octagon with straight sides at Ruppersdorf, and with convex inner and concave outer sides at Hermsdorf (near Hallstadt) and star-shaped for the Chapel of St Mary of the Morning Star above Wockersdorf. He added a bold dome and towers to his father's St Niklas (1737–51). At the abbey church of Unter-Rotschow (1746–7) he showed for the first time a tendency towards classical restraint.

C. Norberg-Schultz, *K.I.D. e il barocco boemo*, Rome 1968; M. Vilimkova and J. Brucker, *D., Rosenheim* 1989; *Die D. Barock Baukunst in Bayern und Böhmen*, exh. cat., Rosenheim-Prague 1991.

**Dietterlin**, Wendel (1551–99). German architect and engraver important mainly for his publication *Architectura und Ausstheilung der V. Seuln* (1593–4), with plates which represent the northern MANNERIST conception of architectural decoration at its most bizarre – with frantically

interlaced STRAPWORK etc. The complete edition of 1598 has additional plates which are sober by comparison.

**Diglyph**, *see* TRIGLYPH.

**Dinkeloo**, John (1918–81), *see* ROCHE, Eamonn Kevin.

**Diocletian window**, *see* THERMAL WINDOW.

**Diotisalvi** (*fl.*C12), *see* ITALIAN ARCHITECTURE.

**Dipteral**. A term applied to a building with a double row of columns on each side.

**Discharging arch**, *see* ARCH.

**Disneyland**, *see* THEME PARK.

**D'Isola Oneglia**, Aimano (b.1928), *see* GABETTI, Roberto (b.1925).

**Distemper**. Paint composition consisting of whiting, size and colouring matter, used for painting walls.

**Distyle in antis**. In classical architecture, a PORTICO with two columns between pilasters or ANTAE.

**Diwan** or **divan**. In Islamic architecture a royal reception chamber or 'government office'.

**Dixon**, Jeremy (b.1939). English architect in partnership from 1989 with Edward JONES. Previously Dixon had realized several notable housing projects in London: St Mark's Road, Kensington (1975); Lanark Road, Maida Vale (1982), and at Dudgeon's Wharf, Isle of Dogs (1972–89). His works in partnership with Jones include the Henry Moore Foundation, Leeds (1993); two residential towers for Robert Gordon University, Aberdeen (1993–4); the postgraduate study centre and housing, Darwin College, Cambridge (1994); the J. Sainsbury's supermarket, Plymouth (1994); the Science

Building, University of Portsmouth (1996), and the renovation of the Royal Opera House, Covent Garden, London (in progress 1997), including the north-east corner of Inigo JONES's square and adjacent streets. The latter project is not-ably 'site specific', shifting in style from a classical to a contemporary idiom (for the square and adjacent streets), from the Barryesque (for the opera house fly-tower) to an interpretive reconstruction of the Floral Hall, thus maintaining the neighbourhood character without recourse to pastiche.

**Dodecastyle**. Of a PORTICO with twelve frontal columns.

**Dobson**, John (1787–1865), English architect. The architectural character of the centre of Newcastle, as laid out from *c.*1835 onwards by the enterprising builder and developer Richard Grainger (1797–1861), is due to Dobson. He studied in London under the water-colourist John Varley and afterwards returned to Newcastle. He could work in the Gothic style, but was at his best in a very restrained Grecian or classical, e.g. Eldon Square, Newcastle (1835, now demolished). His most important build-ings are along the triangle of Grey Street–Market Street–Grainger Street (built *c.*1835–7) and the well-known Central Railway Station (1849–50). His Royal Arcade (1831–2) has been demolished, but his entrance to Newcastle General Cemetery (1836) survives. Of his country houses Nunnykirk (1825) and Meldon Park (1832) are Grecian; Beaufront Castle (1837–41) Gothic; and Lilburn Tower (1829–37) Tudor – all in North-umberland.

T. Faulkner and A. Greg, *J.D.*, New-castle 1987.

**Doesburg**, Theo van (Christian Emil

Maria Kupper, 1883–1931), *see* VAN DOESBURG, Theo.

**Dog-leg staircase**, *see* STAIR.

**Dogtooth**. Early English ornament con-sisting of a series of four-cornered stars placed diagonally and raised pyramidally. *See* Fig. 45.

Fig. 45 Dogtooth

**Dolmen**, *see* MEGALITH.

**Dome**. A vault of even curvature erected on a circular base or drum. The section can be segmental, semicircular, pointed or bulbous. Its origins are remote. From PREHISTORIC times and in many parts of the world, round huts and TENTS were constructed with frameworks of saplings joined at the centre and covered with some kind of thatch, matted materials or skins, and this domical form was probably transposed into more durable shelters of rammed earth or mud-brick. Round houses at Khirokitia, Cyprus (*c.*5800 BC) had mud-brick walls and may have been roofed with domes of the same material. Sepulchral chambers were covered with rough false domes of stone by CORBEL-LING in the 5th millennium in northern Europe and this system was refined to give an even surface in the almost conical beehive interior of the so-called Treasury of Atreus (*c.*1300 BC) (*see* THOLOS). In Italy, where the Etruscans had vaulted subterranean tomb chambers with cor-belled false domes, the development of CONCRETE in Imperial Rome facilitated the construction of large, true hemi-spherical domes above ground, notably over the octagonal room in Nero's

Domus Aurea (54–68) and the Pantheon (118–29). Domes of concrete or, where the necessary materials were unavailable, brick or stone were built throughout the Roman empire over temples, mausolea, baths, palaces and, from the C4 onwards, Christian churches, especially MAR-TYRIA. In Iran Zoroastrian FIRE TEMPLES were crowned with stone domes from about the C2 and in the palace at Firuza-bad, Iran, c.226–41, three ceremonial rooms were vaulted with large domes of rubble, faced with plaster, supported on squinches (see below), the earliest recorded instance of a form later adopted in Europe. Byzantine domes were composed of brick, stone, timber or a combination of materials – bricks and terracotta tiles for Hagia Sophia, 532–7.

The function of a dome was protective but it could also symbolize the vault of the heavens, and thus acquired religious and regal significance comparable to that of the hemispherical but solid STUPAS erected over Buddhist relics and the can-opies and parasols sheltering Asian rulers with pretensions to universal authority. Cosmic symbolism was sometimes made explicit by the decoration of the interior surface with stellar patterns or astrological figures. The exteriors of religious or royal buildings were similarly marked by a dome and since a hemispherical or saucer dome (see below) is barely visible from ground level it was raised on a drum and/ or constructed with a double-shell (see below).

If a dome is erected on a square base, members must be interposed between the square and the circle. They can be pendentives or squinches. A *pendentive* is a spherical triangle; its curvature is that of a dome whose diameter is the diagonal of the initial square. The triangle is carried to the height which allows the erection on its top horizontal of the dome proper. A *squinch* is either an arch or arches of

increasing radius projecting one in front of the other, or horizontal arches pro-jecting in the same manner. If squinches are placed in the corners of the square and enough arches are erected on them they will result in a suitable base-line for the dome. In all these cases the dome will have the diameter of the length of one side of the square. It can be placed direct on the circular base-line, when this is achieved, or a drum, usually with windows, can be interpolated. If the dome has no drum and is segmental, it is called a *saucer* dome. If it has no drum and is semicircular, it is called a *calotte*.

Another method of developing a dome out of a square is to take the diagonal of the square as the diameter of the dome. In this case the dome starts as if by penden-tives, but their curvature is then con-tinued without any break. Such domes are called *sail vaults*, because they resemble a sail with the four corners fixed and the wind blowing into it.

In Islamic buildings the area between the square or polygonal base and the dome, often composed of or decorated with MUQARNAS, is called the *zone of transition*.

A *domical vault* is not a dome proper. If on a square base, four webs (CELLS) rise to a point separated by GROINS, known in the US as a cloister vault, *see* Fig. 41. The same can be done on a polygonal base.

An *umbrella*, *parachute*, *pumpkin* or *melon dome* is a dome on a circular base, but also divided into individual webs, each of which, however, has a base-line curved segmentally in plan and curved in elev-ation. *See* Fig. 46.

A *double-shell* dome has a space between the vaulting and the exterior which serves as a protective surface, e.g. Dome of the Rock, Jerusalem, completed 691. The outer shell could also be given a profile distinct from and more conspicuous than that of a hemispherical or segmental vault,

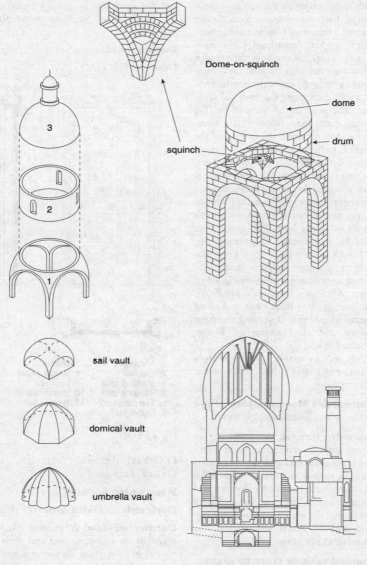

Dome-on-squinch

dome

drum

squinch

sail vault

domical vault

umbrella vault

Double-shell dome, Gur-i Mir, Samarkand

Fig. 46 Dome

without necessitating the vertical extension of the interior space. Such domes became a feature of Islamic architecture. The Gur-i Mir, Samarkand, Uzbekistan (*c.*1400–1404), has a bulbous ribbed outer dome covered with ceramic tiles rising some 14 m. (45 ft) above the hemispherical vault, both springing from the same base. The point of the dome of the Taj Mahal, Agra, India (1630–53), is some 30 m. (100 ft) above the ceiling of the interior. In Europe, where the construction of domes ceased in the Middle Ages, the first significant double-shell dome is that designed by BRUNELLESCHI and built of brick for the cathedral in Florence (1434), though strictly it is a domical vault on an octagonal base. This system was used for true domes of masonry, e.g. St Peter's, Rome (1588–93). From the early C17 the outer shell was usually supported on a timber framework. WREN's dome of St Paul's, London (1675–1709), has three shells: a brick vault, a cone of chain-girdled brick supporting the stone lantern and the exterior of timber sheathed in lead.

*See also* GEODESIC DOME, ONION DOME, PANTHEON DOME and TENSILE STRUCTURES.

**Doménech I Montaner**, Lluis (1849–1923), *see* SPANISH ARCHITECTURE.

**Domestic Revival**. A movement in British and US architecture in the 1870s and 1880s associated with the ARTS AND CRAFTS revival of VERNACULAR styles and techniques, notably by VOYSEY and DEVEY (later by Norman SHAW, Philip WEBB and the early LUTYENS) in England and by RICHARDSON and the SHINGLE STYLE in the USA.

**Domical vault**, *see* CLOISTER VAULT.

**Domus**. In Roman architecture, a house for a single well-to-do family, as distinct from the huts or tenements of the poor

and the apartment houses (INSULAE) of the middle class. *See* ROMAN ARCHITECTURE.

**Donjon**, *see* KEEP.

**Door**, *see* Fig. 47.

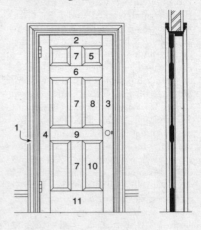

1. Architrave
2. Top rail
3. Shutting stile
4. Hanging stile
5. Top panel
6. Frieze rail
7. Muntin
8. Middle panel
9. Lock rail
10. Bottom panel
11. Bottom rail

Fig. 47 Door

**D'Orbay**, François (1631–97), *see* ORBAY, François d'.

**Doric order**, *see* ORDER.

**Doric style**, *see* GREEK ARCHITECTURE.

**Dormer window**. A window placed vertically in a sloping roof and with a roof of its own. It usually serves sleeping quarters, hence the name. Also called a LUCARNE. The gable above a dormer window is often formed as a pediment and called a *dormer head*.

**Dorter**, *see* MONASTERY.

**Dortsman**, Adriaan (d.1682), *see* DUTCH ARCHITECTURE.

**Doshi**, Balkrishna Vithaldas (b.1927). Indian architect who was trained in Bombay and worked under LE COR-BUSIER (1951–7) and L. KAHN (1962–72). In 1958 he opened his own office (Vastu–Shilpa Consultants) in Ahmedabad and from 1977 to 1993 was in partnership with C. STEIN as Stein, Doshi & Bhalla. His brick and concrete Centre for Environmental Planning and Technology, Ahmedabad (1967–81), now includes his most striking building, the Hussain–Doshi Gufa art gallery (1993), a sprawling, partly underground, organic structure recalling wattle and daub vernacular mud buildings with an interior evocative of natural cave complexes. Apart from his own office, San-garth at Ahmedabad (1981), which foreshadowed the Hussain–Doshi Gufa, his buildings are more conventional, e.g. Indian Institute of Management, Bangalore (1977–83); Ghandi Labour Institute, Ahmedabad (1980–84); National Institute of Fashion Technol-ogy, New Delhi (1991–5). His Vidhyad-har Nagar town plan of 1984 and Aranya Township Low-cost Housing, Indore (1988), were notable.

W. J. R. Curtis, *B.D. An Architecture for India*, Ahmedabad 1988.

**Dosseret**. The French term for an additional high block or slab set on top of an ABACUS and placed between it and the SPANDREL of the arch above; also called a *super-abacus*. Common in Byzantine work, and found in some Romanesque buildings. *See* IMPOST BLOCK; Fig. 48.

**Dotti**, Carlo Francesco (*c*.1670–1759). A leading Late Baroque architect in Bol-ogna. His sanctuary of the Madonna di S. Luca, Bologna (1723–57), is a master-

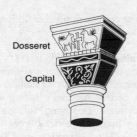

Fig. 48 Dosseret

piece of dramatic grouping, with a domed church built on an elliptical plan and a boldly undulating colonnade sweeping out from the main façade.

A. M. Matteucci, *C.F.D. e l'architettura bolognese del settecento*, Bologna 1969.

**Dou**. In Chinese and Japanese architec-ture a notched timber block supporting the next higher bracket in a structural system using multiple bracket arms, *see* GONG.

**Double cone moulding**. A Roman-esque motif, formed by the continuous horizontal juxtaposition of cones alter-nately base to base and vertex to vertex.

**Double-framed roof**, *see* ROOF.

**Double-pile house**. An English C17 type: a rectangular block two rooms deep, the two rows of rooms usually being sep-arated by a corridor running the length of the house, e.g. Thorpe Hall, Cam-bridgeshire (1653–6) by Peter MILLS. The type was adumbrated in JONES's Queen's House, Greenwich.

**Double-return stairs**, *see* STAIR.

**Dovetailing**. A method of jointing woodwork. Wedge-shaped projections at the end of one member fit into corre-sponding cut-out sections at the end of another.

**Dowell**. A metal pin between stones of

different courses to prevent shifting; *see also* CRAMP.

**Downing**, Andrew Jackson (1815–52), the son of a nurseryman and from the beginning an enthusiast for landscape and plants, became America's leading writer on landscape gardening, cottages and country houses, America's REPTON or LOUDON. His chief writings are *A Treatise on the Theory and Practice of Landscape Gardening Adapted to North America* (1841); *Cottage Residences* (1842); *Notes about Buildings in the Country* (1849); and *The Architecture of Country Houses* (1850). He advised variety in the design of picturesque villas and cottages, especially in wood, thus promoting an early STICK STYLE he called 'board-and-batten' of which he recommended a 'bracketed' version as an alternative to the Italian villa, Tudor parsonage and other European importations. These so-called 'Downing houses', with ample verandas and bay windows, constitute an original American type later taken up by DAVIS and NOTMAN.

For gardens and landscaping, although much influenced by English writings, he advocated a style better suited to North American conditions, as in his own Newburgh Garden, NY, with fine trees, a flower garden with gravel paths and box edging, wide lawns and views of the river Hudson, now known only from descriptions. His recommendations in *The Horticulturist*, which he edited, were widely followed and appreciation of the American landscape, notably of the Hudson valley, was greatly stimulated by him. His only garden to have survived unaltered is Springside, Poughkeepsie, NY (1850–52). That at Davis's Montgomery Place owed much to his advice. For the last two years of his life he was in partnership with VAUX, with whom he designed the grounds of the White House and Smithsonian Museum, Washington, DC. He helped to establish the New York City Park Commission which was to instigate the creation of Central Park, New York, designed by OLMSTED and Vaux.

Hitchcock 1977; J. M. Haley (ed.), *Pleasure Grounds: A.J.D. and Montgomery Place*, Tarrytown, NY, 1988; G. B. Tatum and E. B. MacDougall (eds.), *Prophet with Honor. The Career of A.J.D. 1815–1852*, Washington, DC 1990; D. Schuyler, *Apostle of Taste. A.J.D. 1815–1852*, Baltimore 1996; J. K. Major, *To Live in the New World. A.J.D. and American Landscape Gardening*, Cambridge, Mass., 1997.

**Doxiadis**, Constantinos (1913–75). Greek architect and urban designer and theorist. He was involved in planning Islamabad, Pakistan (1960–61), and in the Detroit plan and Great Lakes Megalopolis scheme (1964–71). His theory of 'ekistics' and 'Ecumenopolis' or 'World City of Tomorrow' were expounded in his *Ekistics. An Introduction to the Science of Human Settlements* (London 1968) and *Ecumenopolis: The Inevitable City of the Future* (New York 1979). He also published *Architecture in Transition* (New York 1963), *Urban Renewal and the Future of the American City* (New York 1966) and *Architectural Space in Ancient Greece* (Cambridge, Mass., 1972).

**Dragon beam**, *see* BEAM.

**Dravidian architecture**. A term for south INDIAN ARCHITECTURE.

**Dressings**. Stones worked to a finished face, whether smooth or moulded, and used around an angle, window, or any feature.

**Drip**. A projecting member of a cornice, etc., from which rainwater drips and is thus prevented from running down the face of the wall below.

**Drip-joint**. A joint between two pieces of metal on a roof, acting as a water conductor and preventing water from penetrating between the metal.

**Dripstone**, *see* HOOD-MOULD.

**Dromos**. A long uncovered passage leading to an underground THOLOS or chamber tomb, as at the Treasury of Atreus, Mycenae, Greece (*c.* 1300 BC). *See* Fig. 115.

**Drop**. The lower projecting end of a newel (*see* STAIR).

**Drop arch**, *see* ARCH.

**Drop ornament**. A carved ornament in the form of a pendant.

**Drop tracery**. A border of pendant tracery on the SOFFIT of a Gothic arch.

**Drops**. English term for GUTTAE.

**Drum**. 1. A vertical wall supporting a DOME, CLOISTER VAULT or CUPOLA; it may be circular, square or polygonal in plan and is usually interposed between the dome, cloister vault or cupola and a system of supporting PENDENTIVES, SQUINCHES, ARCHES or other supports. 2. A cylindrical block of stone forming a column.

**Dry masonry**. Masonry laid without mortar.

**Du Cerceau**. A family of French architects and decorators. Jacques Androuet the elder (*c.* 1520–*c.* 1585) was the founder of the dynasty; he is, and always was, more famous for his engravings than for his buildings, none of which survives. The *châteaux* of Verneuil (1568) and Charleval (1570, abandoned unfinished 1574) were probably the best. But he was essentially an inventor of ornament, not an architect, and indulged in the most wanton and grotesque designs, generally in a Late MANNERIST style. His first *Livre*

*d'architecture* (Paris, 1559) reveals his personal vein of fantasy and lack of refinement. It had considerable influence, and some of the more practical designs may even have been built. But he was best known for his *Les plus excellents bastiments de France* (1576–79). His son Baptiste (*c.* 1545–90) succeeded LESCOT as architect at the Louvre in 1578. In 1584 he became Architecte Ordinaire du Roi but had to leave Paris the following year as a Protestant refugee. He provided designs for the Pont Neuf, Paris (1578), and may have designed the Hôtel d'Angoulême, now Lamoignon, Paris (1584). His younger brother Jacques II (1550–1614) was, with Louis MÉTEZEAU, the favourite architect of Henry IV. He became Architecte du Roi in 1594 and probably designed the pavilions of the Place des Vosges, Paris. Baptiste's son Jean (*c.* 1590– after 1649) became Architecte Ordinaire du Roi in 1617. He built the *escalier en fer de cheval* at Fontainebleau (1634) and designed two of the most typical Louis XIII Parisian *hôtels* – the Hôtel Sully (1625–9) and the Hôtel de Bretonville (1637–43). They are both remarkable for the richness of their elaborately carved decoration – sculptural friezes, pediments with scrolls and masks, and allegorical figures in niches.

Blunt 1982; R. Coope, *Salomon de Brosse and the Development of the Classical Style in French Architecture from 1565 to 1630*, London 1972; D. A. Chevalley, *Der grosse Tuilerientwurf in der Überlieferung Ducerceaus*, Bern and Frankfurt 1973.

**Du Ry**, Paul (1640–1714). He came of a family of French architects and was the grandson of Charles (*fl.* 1611–36), the son of Mathurin (*fl.* 1639) and nephew of de BROSSE. A Huguenot, he left France after the revocation of the Edict of Nantes in 1685 and settled in Kassel, Germany, where he built the Oberneustadt to house other Huguenot refugees. This trim piece of urban layout included the simple, centrally planned Karlskirche (1698–1710, badly damaged but restored). In his post of Oberbaumeister in Kassel he was succeeded by his son, Charles-Louis (1692–1757), who built the Mint and the Militarkasino (both destroyed). Simon-Louis (1726–99), the son of Charles-Louis, was an architect of greater importance. He began under his father, then studied under the Swedish court architect Carl Hårleman in Stockholm (1746–8) and Jacques-François BLONDEL in Paris before beginning a tour of Italy from which he returned in 1756. His first work was at Schloss Wilhelmstal near Kassel, where he was involved in completing the building begun according to designs of CUVILLIÉS and added the two severely simple little lodges (1756–8). In Kassel he was responsible for laying out the spacious rectangular Friedrichsplatz with the austerely Palladian Fredericianum (1768–79), which is important as the first ever museum-library building designed as such. At Wilhelmshöhe, outside Kassel, he built the south and north wings of the vast and imposingly classical Schloss (1786–90), completed later by H. C. JUSSOW, and probably some of the follies in the Park (e.g. Der Mulang, a Chinese village and the 'Felseneck'). He was also responsible for numerous buildings in Kassel, most of which were destroyed in 1945.

Kaufmann 1955; Hempel 1965; H. K. Boehlke, *S.-L.D.R. Ein Wegbereiter klassizistischer Architekte in Deutschland*, Kassel 1980.

**Duany & Plater-Zyberg Architects Inc.** An American partnership known as D/PZ, formed in Miami, Florida, in 1980 by Andres Duany (b.1950) and Elizabeth Plater-Zyberg (b.1950) who were founder members of ARQUITECTONICA

(1976–80). They made their name in 1978 with their controversial plan for Seaside, Florida, a 32-hectare (80-acre) beachfront development which rejected current trends in favour of what they termed 'traditional American urbanism' or TND (Traditional Neighborhood Development) to create a strong neighbourhood identity. Acclaimed by some as the 'New Urbanism', reviving the vernacular and classical traditions and reintegrating them into the mainstream of modern architecture, Seaside was spurned by others for its 'historicist and escapist esthetics'. Later works include Windsor House, Windsor, Florida (1990), and Tahiti Beach House, Coral Gables, Florida (1991). They published *Towns and Town-Making Principles* (New York 1991).

A. Kreiger and W. Lennertz (eds.), *A.D. and E.P.-Z.: Towns and Town-Making Principles*, New York 1991; P. Katz, *The New Urbanism: Towards an Architecture of Community*, New York 1993.

**Duban**, Félix (1798–1870). French architect who, with LABROUSTE, VAUDOYER and VIOLLET LE DUC, was one of the outstanding exponents of 'romantic' Historicism, notably with his restorations at the *château* at Blois from 1844 onwards. His Hôtel Portalès-Gorgier, Paris (1837–8), and his work at the École des Beaux-Arts, Paris, especially the Quai Malaquais façade (1861), were notable.

S. Bellenger and F. Hamon (eds.), *F.D. 1798–1870. Les couleurs de l'architecture*, Paris 1996.

**Dudok**, Willem Marinus (1884–1974), Dutch architect, was municipal architect to the small town of Hilversum near Amsterdam from 1916. He designed many schools and other public buildings, and his style appears to be complete as early as 1921 (Dr Bavinck School, Public

Baths): exposed brick; asymmetrical compositions of rectangular blocks, usually with a tower; long bands of low windows. The style reached its climax with the Hilversum Town Hall of 1924–31, internationally one of the most influential buildings of its date. Of Dudok's later buildings, the Utrecht Theatre (1938–41) and the Royal Dutch Steel Works at Velsen (Ijmuiden, 1948) are the most notable.

Hitchcock 1977; M. Cramer et al., *W.M.D. 1884–1974*, Amsterdam 1981; H. J. Schurrmans, *W.M.D. Architect 1884–1974, Stadsbaummeester van Wereldallurs*, Baarn 1993; E. Mattie, *Functionalism in the Netherlands*, Amsterdam 1994; H. van Bergeijk, *W.M.D. 1884–1974 (Werkkatalog)*, Basel 1995; D. Langmead, *W.M.D. A Bio-Biography*, London 1996; P. Jappelli and G. Menna, *W.M.D. (1884–1974), Architetture e città*, Naples 1997.

**Duiker**, Johannes (1890–1935). Dutch architect and member of the DE STIJL movement. His main works were the Zonnestraal Sanatorium, Hilversum (1926–8), the Open-Air School, Amsterdam (1929–36) and the Handelsblad-Cineac Cinema, Amsterdam (1934). His Grand Hotel Gooiland, Hilversum (1934–6), was carried out after his death by Bernard Bijvoet (1889–1979).

J. Molema, *J.D.*, Rotterdam 1989.

**Duplex apartment** or **maisonette**. A self-contained dwelling on two floors connected by its own internal stairs, forming part of an apartment house or block of flats.

**Durand**, Jean-Nicolas-Louis (1760–1834), French architect who was probably the most widely influential architectural theorist of the early C19, not only in France but also in Germany. He was trained partly under BOULLÉE and partly

under the civil engineer Rodolphe Perronet (1708–94, designer of the Pont de la Concorde, Paris). He built little (Maison La Thuile, Paris, 1788, destroyed in C19) but he was employed on festival decorations during the Revolution and submitted numerous projects for public buildings to the Convention. In 1795 he was appointed professor of architecture at the new École Polytechnique, which replaced and was modelled on the royal school of military engineering, retaining this post until 1830. He published in 1800 *Recueil et parallèle des édifices en tout genre* in which public buildings of various periods and countries (including non-European) were illustrated according to his theory of modular proportions. But his major work is the two-volume *Précis et leçons d'architecture* (1802–5, frequently reprinted and translated into German) in which he stated a rationalist ideal of utilitarian functionalism. 'One should not strive to make a building pleasing, since if one concerns oneself solely with the fulfilment of practical requirements, it is impossible that it should not be pleasing,' he wrote. 'Architects should concern themselves with planning and with nothing else.' Yet he abandoned neither the use of historical ornament nor the principle of strictly symmetrical planning.

Hitchcock 1977; W. Szambien, *J.-N.-L.D. 1760–1834*, Paris 1984; S. Villari, *J.-N.-L.D. (1760–1834) Art and Science of Architecture*, (1987) New York 1990.

**Durbar**. A public audience given by a ruler in India and thus in Indian architecture the hall or open-air space intended for it.

**Dutch architecture and landscape architecture**. The oldest preserved buildings in the northern Netherlands belong to the CAROLINGIAN fringe. They are the WESTWORK of St Mary at Maastricht and the Valkhof Chapel at

Nijmegen, which was built in strict imitation of Charlemagne's palace chapel at Aachen. The ROMANESQUE style proper appears first at Deventer, St Peter at Utrecht and the more impressive abbey church of Susteren (c. 1060 onwards), the latter clearly dependent on Werden and Essen. A little later is the grand westwork of St Servatius at Maastricht, again German in type. Even more patent is the German origin of the trefoil-shaped early C12 chancel of Rolduk (Cologne). The mature and late Romanesque of the Rhineland is represented by St Mary at Maastricht and the splendid Roermond Abbey, begun as late as 1219–20. It was Cistercian but shows nothing of Cistercian architectural customs. Its nearest parallel is at Neuss, and, just as in such churches of the Rhineland, a general Romanesque mood is combined with French Early Gothic motifs.

The GOTHIC style was accepted late. The cathedral of Utrecht was begun in 1254. Its style is derived from that of Soissons via the chancel of Tournai only completed in 1255. The vaulting pattern of ambulatory and radiating chapels shows the dependence. The smaller Buur church at Utrecht has the French High Gothic type of piers and was started shortly after 1253. Halls were occasionally built on the Westphalian pattern (Zutphen), but the type of the major later medieval churches, the large number and size of which testifies to the prosperity of Holland, is basilican and remarkably simple, with an inner elevation of arcade and clerestory divided by no more than a triforium, a blind triforium or a narrow wall passage. To this type belong the major churches of Breda, Delft (New Church), Dordrecht, Haarlem, The Hague (Great Church), Leiden, all begun in the late C14. The New Church in Amsterdam followed later. All these churches have an ambulatory, but the majority leave out the radiating chapels. Some have very large transepts. The Great Church in The Hague has a specially airy hall nave, which continued inspiring architects into the C17. The only church of richly decorated interior and exterior is St John at Hertogenbosch, started again in the late C14. Of other typical features of the Dutch Gothic the widespread use of brick must be remembered, also with patterns on the façade (as in north Germany) and the great prominence of Late Gothic west steeples with pretty and daring openwork details (Utrecht Cathedral, C14; Zierikzee, 1453 onwards, mostly destroyed; Amersfoort St Mary, later C15; Rhenen, begun 1492).

Concerning secular architecture the earliest noteworthy structures are the circular castles or enclosures of Leiden, Egmond, Teilingen, etc. They are of the late C11 and C12, and some have had as their centre a keep. The most spectacular secular building is the Great Hall of the Binnenhof at The Hague, built in the second half of the C13 and more akin to Westminster Hall than to continental great halls. For the late Middle Ages the lively façades of some town halls (Middelburg, 1412–1599, rebuilt after 1945) and houses with stepped gables are characteristic.

Holland has some fine Early Renaissance monuments of the 1530s built by Italians, notably the tower of Ijsselstein church (1532–5) by Alessandro Pasqualini (d. before 1559) of Bologna and the courtyard of Breda castle (begun 1536) by Tommaso Vincidor (c. 1495–1560) also of Bologna. Buildings such as the town halls of Nijmegen (c. 1555) and The Hague (1564–5) show how the new Renaissance motifs are absorbed into the native traditions. Soon, however, out of tradition and the enjoyment of the multifariousness of available Renaissance motifs and the modifications and distortions they were capable of, a boisterous national style with ornate gables and extensive play with brick and stone mixtures was developed. It culminates in the work of Lieven de KEY at Haarlem (Meat Hall, 1602–3, tower New Church, 1613) and in Leiden (Town Hall, 1593–7) and the churches by Hendrick de KEYSER in Amsterdam, which are extremely interesting for their centralizing Protestant plans. This style, as exemplified by buildings like the Kloveniersdoelen at Middelburg (c.1607–10) had immense influence along the German seaboard as far as Gdansk (Danzig) and in Denmark. Architects from the Netherlands are found in most of these places.

At the same time as in England and France classical restraint replaced these 'Jacobean' displays. In the newly independent and staunchly Protestant United Provinces or Dutch Republic (liberated from Spanish rule by 1609) this may have been due partly to a Calvinist demand for sobriety. The first signs of a change were Honselersdijk of 1621–c.1630 and Rijswijk of 1630, both inspired from France and both by unknown architects. But at a time between these two country houses of the Stadtholder, Jacob van CAMPEN began his activity; his are the most important classical buildings in Holland. His earliest is the Coymans house in Amsterdam (1624), and in the thirties and forties plenty more outstanding classical buildings appeared, especially van Campen's Mauritshuis in The Hague (1633–5), his magnificent Amsterdam Town Hall, now Royal Palace (begun 1648), and his Nieuwe Kerk at Haarlem (1645–9). Other architects also contributed to this noble and restrained style: Pieter POST with Huis-ten-Bos, The Hague (begun 1645), the Weigh-house at Leiden (1657) and the Town Hall of Maastricht (begun 1659) with its splendid entrance hall, Arend van 's GRAVESANDE with the octagonal Mare church at Leiden

(1638–48), Adriaan Dortsman (d.1682) with the circular Lutheran church in Amsterdam (1668–71) and Justus VINGBOONS with the ambitious Trippenhuis in Amsterdam (1662), built as a private house for two brothers. Altogether no other town in Europe is as rich as Amsterdam in prosperous private houses. They allow us to see the whole development from the time of de Keyser into the late C18.

In the C17, the Golden Age of Dutch art, a distinctive style of LANDSCAPE ARCHITECTURE was developed. Gardens were laid out on geometrically rigid plans, almost invariably flat, often bordered and intersected by canals, mainly as settings for flowering and especially exotic plants rather than trees though the larger ones were sometimes linked to wooded parks. The earliest, designed by the Stadtholder Prince Frederick Henry of Orange for himself in the 1620s, were soon followed by those of rich merchants whose suburban properties lined the waterways (now known only from descriptions and visual images). Such gardens, providing an alternative to late C16 intricacy and C17 French grandiosity, established a style followed in Germany and especially in England after 1688 when William of Orange and his consort began their reign as William III and Mary II. French influence became evident in extensive late C17 layouts with strong central axes as at Het Loo, Gelderland, Holland (1686–95), designed for William and Mary by Jacob ROMAN in collaboration with the French refugee D. MAROT, but including a characteristically Dutch enclosed garden (recently restored).

The palace at Het Loo shows, nevertheless, the French influence that became paramount in Dutch architecture from this time. The most notable examples include the beautiful town hall of Enkhuisen of 1686–8 by Steven Vennecool (1657–1719), and then such remarkably ambitious private (or formerly private) houses as the Middelburg Library of 1733 (by J. P. van Baurscheidt Jun. of Antwerp), the Royal Library at The Hague of 1734–6 (by Marot) and Felix Meritis in Amsterdam. The latter, by J. Otten Husley (1738–94), is of 1778, hence on the way to neo-classicism. The Pavilion at Haarlem for Henry Hope, the banker, followed in 1785–8. The best early neo-classical church is St Rosalia in Rotterdam of 1777–9 (by Jan Giudice). This is on the pattern of the palace chapel of Versailles, while the ballroom in the Knuiterdijk Palace in The Hague of the 1820s (by Jan de Greef) is on the pattern of the Vitruvian Egyptian Hall and of its English imitators.

The first third of the C19 was unquestioningly classical and more or less Grecian (Scheveningen, Pavilion, 1826; Leeuwarden, Law Courts, 1846). Then about 1840 neo-Gothic made a late start (Catholic Church, Harmelen, 1838; Gothic Hall behind the Knuiterdijk Palace, The Hague 1840; Riding School, The Hague, 1845; former station, Rotterdam, 1847). Concurrently neo-Romanesque appears, though more rarely (Coolsingel Hospital, Rotterdam, 1842 onwards). As in other countries the Gothic soon turns from the romantic to the archaeologically accurate, and the best examples of this serious-minded Gothicism are the churches by CUYPERS. But Cuypers is famous for his large neo-1600 buildings, clearly disposed and resourcefully detailed (Rijksmuseum and Central Station Amsterdam, 1877–85 and 1881–9).

From there a way into the C20 was found by the brilliant and typically Dutch BERLAGE. His Exchange in Amsterdam of 1897–1903 is in style transitional between Historicism and the C20. From Berlage, whose detail tends to be arty-crafty and often very curious, one line went to Johann Melchoir van der Mey (1878–1949) and his crazy Scheepvarthuis in Amsterdam (1913–17) and to the EXPRESSIONISM of the Amsterdam School; another line went into the Rationalism of DE STIJL and the INTERNATIONAL MODERN, notably the Van Nelle Tobacco Factory, Rotterdam (1926–30), by Johannes Andreas BRINKMAN and Johannes Hendrik van de Broek (1898–1978), who was later in partnership with Bakema (see below). Cubistic but fantastic is Gerrit RIETVELD's Schroeder house at Utrecht of 1925, cubic and rational and extremely well grouped the buildings of DUDOK. OUD's work during and after the Second World War represents a turn away from Rationalism which took place in other countries as well. A noteworthy Dutch achievement after the Second World War was the rebuilding of the centre of Rotterdam, with the Lijnbaan shopping centre (1953–5) by van der Broek and BAKEMA. More influential has been the work of Aldo VAN EYCK, especially his Children's Home, Amsterdam (1958–60), Arnhem Pavilion (1966) and his later urban renovation work, notably at Zwolle (1975–7) with Théo Bosch. Among prominent contemporary architects Herman HERTZBERGER and Piet Blom (b.1934) were widely acclaimed for, respectively, the Old Age Home, Amsterdam (1975), and 't Speelhuis, Helmund (1975–8). More recently Rem KOOLHAAS has become influential internationally with his OMA (Office for Metropolitan Architecture), formed in 1975, and their subsequent promotion of a cool contextualism, for example the Parliament extension in The Hague (1978) and projects for the Berlin 1984 Bauaustellung. In 1978 he published *Delirious New York* (New York and London). Also notable internationally were Tom Alberts (b.1927) with his remarkable ENVIRONMENTAL, Green or Sustainable NMB Bank in Amsterdam (1978–88); Jo Coenen (b.1949) with his Netherlands Architecture Institute, Rotterdam (1988–94); Wiel Arets (b.1955) with his AZL Pensionfund Building, Heerlen (1995); Erick van Egeraat (b.1956) who was one of the co-founders in 1980 of MECANOO, notable for their Prinsenland housing, Rotterdam (1988–93); and Ben van Berkel (b.1957) who made his name with the Erasmus Bridge, Rotterdam (1990–96).

**Dutch gable**, *see* GABLE.

**Dutert**, Charles-Louis-Ferdinand (1845–1906). French architect who, with the engineer Victor Contamin (1840–93), designed the Palais des Machines for the International Exhibition of 1889 in Paris (demolished in 1905). It was a remarkable example of the use of metal and glass in architecture. In 1896 he designed the Nouvelles Galeries du Musée d'Histoire Naturelle, Paris.

S. Durant and A. Low, *Palais des Machines. F.D.*, London 1994.

**Dwarf gallery**. A wall-passage with small arcading on the outside of a building; usual in Romanesque architecture, especially in Italy and Germany.

**Dymaxion**, *see* FULLER, Richard Buckminster.

# E

**Eames**, Charles (1907–78). An American designer, he was a universal artist. He designed furniture (the famous Eames Chair of 1940–41, developed in collaboration with Eero SAARINEN), made films (*Black Top*, 1950), and built his own house at Santa Monica in California (1949), No. 8 in John Entenza's CASE STUDY programme and a much admired masterpiece of INDUSTRIALIZED BUILDING. Windows and doors were prefabricated standard items from a manufacturer's catalogue. Yet, with these elements Eames succeeded in achieving a light, grid-like effect of Japanese finesse. The metal frames are filled in with transparent and translucent glass and stucco.

J. Steele, *E. House Pacific Palisades 1949, C.E.*, London 1994; P. Kirkham, *C. and Ray E. Designers of the* C20, Cambridge 1995; D. Albrecht et al., *The Work of C. and R. E. A Legacy of Invention*, New York 1997.

**Early Christian architecture**. The first Christian structures date from after AD 200 and were of three types: meeting-houses, CATACOMBS and MARTYRIA. The meeting-house comprised an assembly room for celebrating the Eucharist, a baptistery and various other rooms, as at Dura Europos in Syria of 200–230, the earliest known. After the recognition of Christianity by Constantine in 313 the modest meeting-houses were gradually replaced by churches for which the model was found in Roman administrative meeting-halls, not in pagan temples. Thus evolved the Christian BASILICA, e.g. the C4 Lateran Basilica

and Old St Peter's in Rome. At first, however, Constantinian church architecture varied from aisleless halls to centralized buildings (e.g. S. Costanza, Rome, *c*.350; S. Lorenzo, Milan, *c*.370; S. Gereon, Cologne, *c*.380) though the latter were usually martyria. With the banning of all heathen cults in 391 Christianity became the official religion of the Roman Empire and the basilica attained its canonical form, e.g. S. Maria Maggiore, Rome, 432–40. Outside Italy early Christian architecture developed similarly (e.g. S. Demetrios, Salonika, C5; S. Leonidas, Corinth-Lechaion, late C5–6), sometimes with regional variations as at the very imposing ruined church of four basilical cross-arms meeting in an octagon at Qal'at Si'man, Syria, *c*.480–90. *See also* COPTIC ARCHITECTURE. For subsequent developments, *see* BYZANTINE ARCHITECTURE.

Krautheimer 1986.

**Early English** or 'E.E.'. Historical division of English medieval architecture *c*.1190–*c*.1250. *See* ENGLISH ARCHITECTURE.

**Earth Art**, *see* LAND ART.

**Earth building**. A house of unburnt ADOBE, COB or PISÉ, usually owner built and maintained. Its thick walls provide insulation against heat, cold and sound but require a protective coating to prevent damage by rain.

**Earth-sheltered building**, *see* ENVIRONMENTAL, GREEN OR SUSTAINABLE ARCHITECTURE.

**Easter sepulchre**. A recess with TOMB-

CHEST, usually in the north wall of a CHANCEL; the tomb-chest was designed to receive an effigy of Christ for Easter celebrations.

**Eaves**. The underpart of a sloping roof overhanging a wall or flush with it. Eaves may have a horizontal *fascia* which carries the gutter.

**Echal**. In a synagogue, the fitting enclosing the Ark or cupboard in which are kept the rolls of the Law; often of wood. An ornate example of the C18 exists in London at Bevis Marks, in the form of a large tripartite REREDOS.

**Echinus**. A convex moulding below the ABACUS of a Doric CAPITAL. *See* Fig. 86. Also the moulding, covered with EGG AND DART, under the cushion of an IONIC capital.

**Eckbo**, Garrett (b.1910). American landscape architect trained at the University of California, Berkeley, and at Harvard where with his fellow students KILEY and ROSE he rebelled against the historicist teaching of garden design. Inspired by GROPIUS, who became professor of architecture there in 1937, he sought to evolve a distinctively modern style, especially for the surroundings of working-class housing. After returning to California in 1939 he worked for the Farm Security Administration designing settlements for migrant workers and from 1942 to 1945 for war and public housing developments. From 1945 onwards, in partnership with Robert Royston (b.1918) until 1958 and with Edward A. Williams (b.1914) until 1973, he designed numerous private gardens in the CALIFORNIA SCHOOL style, differing from those by CHURCH in their use of exotic plants and sometimes modern industrial materials, with sophisticated detailing. But he became increasingly engaged on housing developments, urban plazas, environ-

ments for industrial buildings and power stations, campuses and parkways, mainly in California, e.g. José Del Valle Park, Lakewood (1955), Downtown Mall, Fresno (1963), Union Bank Square, Los Angeles (1964–8), though he has worked elsewhere in the USA and in England, Hawaii, the Philippines and India (Lodhi Park, New Delhi, 1968, with J. A. STEIN). The open spaces with trees, ponds and plenty of stone seating that he designed for the University of New Mexico, Albuquerque (1962–78), are among his most successful creations. Both as a teacher and as the author of *Landscape for Living* (New York 1950), followed by many other publications, he has had great influence. *See also* EDAW.

Walker and Simo 1994; M. Treib and D. Imbert, *G.E. Modern Landscapes for Living*, Los Angeles 1997.

**Eclectic**. A term applied to works of art and especially C19 and C20 architecture combining elements from two or more historical styles.

**École des Beaux Arts**, *see* BEAUX ARTS STYLE.

**Ecological architecture**, *see* ENVIRONMENTAL, GREEN OR SUSTAINABLE ARCHITECTURE.

**EDAW**. An American corporation of landscape architects that grew out of the partnership of ECKBO, Francis Dean, Don Austin and Edward A. Williams, all of whom had withdrawn by 1973 but allowed their initials to be used as the acronym for an increasingly large firm with offices in all five continents. It has been engaged in all types of landscape architecture, from the design of private gardens to vast schemes for the protection of natural environments. Notable works include the reorganization of the monumental core of Washington, DC (from 1976), the resort areas of Disney World,

Orlando, Florida, and of EuroDisney, Marne-la-Vallé, France (1992), Clarke Quay redevelopment, Singapore; LuLu Island theme park and resort off Abu Dhabi; and Eco City, a satellite of Tokyo (1994).

*Process Architecture* 120 (1994); Walker and Simo 1994.

**Edge roll**, *see* BOWTELL.

**Edicula**, *see* AEDICULE.

**Edwardian architecture**. An historical period of English architecture *c.*1890– 1914, named after Edward VII (reigned 1901–10). *See* ENGLISH ARCHITECTURE.

**Eesteren**, Cornelis van (1897–1988), *see* DUTCH ARCHITECTURE.

**Effner**, Joseph (1687–1745), born in Munich, was the son of the chief gardener to Max Emanuel, Elector of Bavaria, who sent him to be trained as an architect in Paris under BOFFRAND (1706–15). In 1715 he was appointed Court Architect. He was in Italy in 1718. Between 1719 and 1725 he completed ZUCCALLI's Schloss Schleissheim and designed the magnificent monumental staircase. He also completed Agostino BARELLI's Schloss Nymphenburg outside Munich (1717– 23), converting Barelli's Italianate villa into a German Baroque palace and adding several exquisite little pavilions in the park; the Pagodenburg (1717–19, classical exterior with chinoiserie interior), the Roman Badenburg (1719–21), and the precociously picturesque Magdalenklause (1725–8). At the Munich Residenz he was in charge of the new Grottenhof from 1715 where the sparkling Ahnengalerie or Gallery of Ancestors (1726–31) was designed by him, though the ceiling is by CUVILLIÉS. His only later building of note is the Preysing palace in the Residenzstrasse, Munich (1727–34).

Hempel 1965; P. Stadler, *J.E. (1687–*

*1745): Hofbaumeister Max Emanuels*, exh. cat., Dachau 1987.

**Egas**, Enrique de (d. probably 1534), was the son either of Hanequin of Brussels, who built the upper parts of the towers of Toledo Cathedral and the Portal of the Lions (1452), or of Egas Cueman, his brother, a sculptor who died in 1495. In 1497 Enrique became master mason of Plasencia Cathedral – where work, however, soon stopped and was later continued by JUAN DE ÁLAVA and Francisco de COLONIA – and in 1498 of Toledo Cathedral. Enrique's masterpieces are the hospitals of Santiago de Compostela (1501–11) and Toledo (1504–14), where the north Italian Early Renaissance appears early and at its most delightful. He was consulted at the Seo of Saragossa in 1505, and at Seville Cathedral in 1512 and 1525, and also on cathedral projects at Malaga (1528) and Segovia (1529). He was also connected with the designs for the Royal Chapel at Granada (begun *c.*1504), and designed Granada Cathedral (begun 1523, but soon turned Renaissance from Enrique's Gothic by SILOE).

Kubler and Soria 1959.

**Egeraat**, Erick van (b.1956), *see* DUTCH ARCHITECTURE.

**Egg and dart** or **egg and tongue**. An OVOLO MOULDING decorated with a pattern based on alternate eggs and arrowheads. *See* Fig. 49.

Fig. 49  Egg and dart

**Egyptian architecture**. As Herodotus pointed out, the Ancient Egyptians regarded the dwellinghouse as a temporary lodging and the tomb as a permanent abode. Houses were built of clay, sometimes but not always in the form of baked bricks; tombs and temples reproduced the elements of this domestic architecture on the grandest possible scale and in the most durable materials. Thus the bundles of papyrus stalks used as supports in mud huts were transformed into the majestic carved stone papyrus columns of the temples. No efforts were spared to secure the permanence of the tombs and their attendant temples by such devices as the use of the living rock and the steep BATTER of walls to resist earthquake shocks. The result is an architecture of impersonal and to this day daunting monumentality. Features peculiar to ancient Egyptian architecture include the PYRAMID, the OBELISK, the steeply battered PYLON, the symbolical lotus column, and incised relief decoration without any structural relevance.

The earliest large-scale work in stone is the funeral complex at Saqqara, built by the architect IMHOTEP for King Zoser, founder of the third dynasty (2780–2680 BC or, according to an alternative chronology, 2686–2613 BC) – a vast stepped pyramid almost 60 m. (200 ft) high, surrounded by a columned processional hall and other buildings to provide a habitation for the dead king and a realistic stage-setting for ritual, all enclosed by a niched limestone wall. The stepped pyramid was superseded by the regular pyramid, of which the most famous examples are at Giza, built for kings of the fourth dynasty (c.2680–2565 or 2613–2498 BC). The collapse of the Old Kingdom (c.2258 or 2181 BC) created the first break in the history of Ancient Egyptian architecture. There was a temporary revival in the period of the Middle Kingdom (2134–1786 or 2040–1782 BC): earlier styles were slightly simplified and less durable materials were used (as in the pyramid of Sesostris I at

Lisht). But not until the New Kingdom period (1570–1085 BC) were great buildings once again erected. The most notable monuments are the mortuary temple of Queen Hatshepsut at Deir el Bahari (c.1480 BC) by Senmut, with its pillared halls, colonnades, and gigantic ramps connecting the different levels; the magnificent temple of Amon at Karnak (c.1570–1085 BC); and the many-columned temple of Amon-Mut-Khonsu at Luxor (c.1570–1200 BC).

In the reign of Amenhotep IV (1379–1362 BC), who changed his name to Akhenaten to declare his monotheistic devotion to the sun god Aten and proscribed the worship of the old state gods at Thebes, a new capital city named Akhetaten was founded some 320 km. (200 miles) down the Nile at a site now known as Tell el Amarna. It had a huge precinct with open-air temples – a striking departure from tradition – surrounded by a garden city with royal palaces and spacious houses for courtiers and officials, separated from the workers' quarters on a tight grid-plan. After Akhenaten's death, the city was demolished, polytheism restored and the capital moved back to Thebes where old temples were enlarged in the traditional style. Under Rameses II (1304–1247 BC) the great temple at Abu Simbel was hacked out of the living rock, with four 20 m. (65 ft) high statues on its front and chambers extending some 55 m. (175 ft) into the cliff-face. The funeral temple of Rameses II, the Ramesseum, at Thebes, though largely in ruins, with its daunting hypostyle hall, is just as imposing. It is also of structural interest for the barrel vaults of its storerooms. Rameses III (1298–1168) was the last pharaoh to build on a megalomaniac scale and his temple at Medinet Habu is no smaller than the Ramesseum and better preserved. By his time the power and wealth of Egypt were already in decline.

The final revival took place under the rule of the Ptolemies, whom Alexander the Great had established on the Egyptian throne. Numerous temples survive from this period (323–30 BC), still built in the traditional manner, e.g. the temples of Horus at Edfu and the temples on the island of Philae. Other buildings were, however, HELLENISTIC.

Alexandria, founded by Alexander 332 BC, was developed as a metropolis laid out on a grid plan, with magnificent buildings known from descriptions though a few traces survive: royal palaces, the museum and library (founded c.300 BC, severely damaged 47 BC, destroyed 651 AD), and on the island of Pharos the white marble tower some 100 m. (328 ft) high built as a landmark c.280 BC and used as a lighthouse from CI BC, one of the 'wonders of the ancient world'. There are similarly few remains of the buildings erected after the Roman annexation of Egypt in 30 BC and from the succeeding centuries. Christianity was introduced in diverse forms from the mid-CI and from the time of Constantine large churches were built, all subsequently destroyed though smaller Coptic churches and monasteries of the C5 and later survive; see COPTIC ARCHITECTURE.

A new era began with the Arab conquest in 641. Their first capital was Fostat of which little remains earlier than the Mosque of Ibn Tulun c.877–9, of a sober grandeur unsurpassed in Islamic architecture. The Fatimid Caliphs – Shiites descended from the Prophet's sister, Fatima – whose first power centre was in Tunisia (remains of palace and much restored mosque at Mahdiya begun 912), conquered Egypt in 969 and founded, adjacent to Fostat, the new capital city of Cairo (al-Qahira, 'the triumphant'). They built magnificent palaces (destroyed), the great congregational al-

Azhar Mosque (960–73), the equally grandiose al-Hakim Mosque (990–1013), both with prominent minarets and domes and façades of unprecedented monumentality, also smaller religious structures including *mashads* (places of pilgrimage); e.g. that at Aswan, notable for its early form of MUQARNAS vaulting below the dome, and numerous MAUSOLEA. The city walls of Cairo with the dauntingly massive Bab al-Nasr and other gateways of the late CII were their final major architectural achievement.

The rule of the Fatimids was brought to an end in 1171 by Salah al-Din (Saladin), an adversary of the Shiites as of the Crusaders, who returned Egypt to Sunnite orthodoxy and converted the al-Azhar Mosque into its educational centre. Many of the finest Islamic buildings in Egypt were constructed under the succeeding Mamluk Sultans (descendants of slaves from Central Asia enrolled in Muslim armies), who ruled Syria, western Arabia and much of Anatolia as well from 1260. They include in Cairo the vast complexes – mosque, madrasa, hospital, bazaar, founder's tomb-chamber – named after the Sultans Qala'un (1283–5), al-Nasir Muhammad (1295–1304), Salar and Sanjar al-Jawli (begun 1303), Hasan (begun 1356), Qa'itbay (1472–4), as well as the mosques of al-Maridami (1339–40) and Mu'ayyad Shaykh (begun 1415) – all characterized by lavish ornament and the sometimes fantastic elaboration of their multi-storeyed minarets. In 1517 Egypt became part of the Ottoman empire and although some local architectural traditions survived there were no more patrons as generous as the Mamluk Sultans. Architecture came under the influence of Istanbul even after the country regained virtual independence under Muhammad Ali, founder of the huge mosque in the citadel, Cairo (1820–57).

In the late C19 and early C20 both Cairo and Alexandria were greatly enlarged according to European notions of urban design and new buildings were mainly in European styles, including the International Modern. But mid-C20 Egypt was in the forefront of those newly independent North African countries seeking an architectural identity, notably with Hassan FATHY and Abdel Wahad EL-WAKIL.

**Egyptian hall.** A hall with an internal PERISTYLE as derived by PALLADIO from VITRUVIUS. It was especially popular with neo-Palladian architects, e.g. Lord BURLINGTON's Assembly Rooms in York. It has no direct connection with Egyptian architecture.

**Egyptian Revival.** The art of Ancient Egypt interested Europeans from the Renaissance onwards, but the first large-scale imitations (apart from pyramids and obelisks) date from the late C18 and were purely decorative, beginning with the interior of the English coffee-house in Rome by PIRANESI, who published engravings of it in 1769. In France, Napoleon's Egyptian campaign of 1798 stimulated a taste for Égyptiennerie manifested in the decorative arts and a few built structures, notably a fountain of 1809 in rue de Sèvres, Paris. The publication by one of the *savants* who took part in the campaign, Vivant Denon's *Voyage dans la basse et haute Égypte* (Paris 1802, reprinted London 1802), with the first extensive corpus of accurate illustrations of Egyptian monuments, inspired several free imitations in England, beginning with the Egyptian Hall for exhibitions, Piccadilly, London, 1811–12 (demolished), by Peter Frederick Robinson (1776–1858). As the debt of Greece to Egypt was generally acknowledged, windows of trapezoid shape like Egyptian doors were sometimes inserted in GREEK REVIVAL buildings (e.g. by BINDESBØLL and THOMSON). But explicitly Egyptian palm-, lotusbud- and Hathor-columns were used for their associations on a limited range of buildings (the flax mill of Marshall & Co., Leeds, by J. BONOMI II in 1842, the elephant house of 1858 in the Antwerp zoo) and also for cemetery entrances (Sharrow Vale, Sheffield, 1836; Highgate, London, 1839–42) and many later both in England and the USA. Egyptian motifs were taken up in the 1920s by ART DECO architects and designers, e.g. Carreras cigarette factory, Hampstead Road, London (1928), by A. G. Porri.

R. Carrott, *The E.R.*, Berkeley 1978; J. S. Curl, *Egyptomania* (1980), Manchester 1993; J. M. Humbert, *Egyptomania. Egypt in Western Art 1720–1930*, Paris 1994.

**Ehn**, Karl (1884–1957), *see* AUSTRIAN ARCHITECTURE.

**Ehrenkrantz**, Ezra (b.1933), *see* INDUSTRIALIZED BUILDING.

**Ehrensvard**, Carl August (1745–1800), *see* SWEDISH ARCHITECTURE.

**Eiermann**, Egon (1904–70). German architect and a pupil of POELZIG. By concentrating on industrial buildings, Eiermann managed to carry the INTERNATIONAL MODERN of the thirties through the Nazi years in Germany. Of his many post-war factories one of the finest is at Blumberg (1951). Also remarkable was his Mattheus Kirche, Pforzheim (1953). His international fame was established by the German Pavilion at the Brussels Exhibition of 1958, a perfect blend of crisp, clear, cubic, transparent blocks and their grouping in a landscape setting. The solution to the problem of grouping the new Kaiser-Wilhelm Gedächtniskirche at Berlin (1959–62) with the dramatic neo-Romanesque ruin of the old is more questionable. Other buildings of special importance are the offices of the Essener Steinkohlen-Bergwerke, Essen (1958–60); the wholesale warehouses, etc., for Messrs Neckermann at Frankfurt (1958–61); and the German Embassy, Washington (1961–3). In 1968 he designed an office block for an Italian firm in Frankfurt with towers like inverted chalices.

W. Schirmer (ed.), *E.E. Bauten und Projekte*, Stuttgart 1984; K. Feireiss (ed.), *E.E. Die Kaiser-Wilhelm-Gedächtnis Kirche*, Berlin 1994.

**Eiffel**, Gustav (1832–1923), the French engineer, is famous chiefly for the Eiffel Tower, built for the Paris Exhibition of 1889. At 308 m. (1,010 ft), the tower was the highest building in the world until the Chrysler and then the Empire State buildings were erected in New York. The Eiffel Tower in its immensely prominent position in the centre of Paris marks the final acceptance of metal, in this case iron, as an architectural medium. Eiffel's iron bridges are technically and visually as important as the Eiffel Tower (Douro, 1876–7; Garabit Viaduct, 1880–84). He was also engineer to the Bon Marché store in Paris (1876), and to the Statue of Liberty in New York, both of which have remarkable iron interiors.

M. Besset, *G.E. 1832–1923*, Paris 1957; R. Barthes, *La Tour E.*, Paris 1961; J. Harriss, *The Tallest Tower. E. and the Belle Époque*, Boston, Mass., 1975; B. Lemoine, *G.E. 1832–1923*, Paris 1986.

**Eigtved**, Nils (1701–54). Danish Rococo architect famous for the Amalienborg in Copenhagen, the finest C18 urban group outside France. Trained in Dresden and Warsaw under Carl Friedrick PÖPPELMANN (1725–33), he also visited Paris and Rome before settling in Copenhagen in 1735. As court architect he laid out an entire new section of the city with the octagonal Amalienborg (1750–54) and its four palaces set diagonally at its centre. He designed the Frederiks church on axis with it but his designs were greatly altered in execution. His Rococo interiors (1734 onwards) in the royal palace of Christiansborg were destroyed in 1794.

K. Voss, *Arkitekten N.E. 1701–1754*, Copenhagen 1971.

**Eisenman**, Peter (b.1932). American architect associated with the NEW YORK FIVE since 1972. He took their concern with 'form' and disdain for function to its furthest limits, his designs for single-family houses being conceived almost as abstract sculptures, e.g. House VI (Frank House), West Cornwall, Connecticut (1972) and House X, Bloomfield in Hills, Michigan (1975–8). In the 1970s he became known as an influential *avant-garde* theorist and taught at Harvard, Princeton, Yale and the Institute for Architecture and Urban Studies, New York, which he founded in 1967 and directed. Meantime he was moving away from neo-Modernism and in 1988 exhibited with the DECONSTRUCTIVISTS. He had already designed the Wexner Center for the Visual Arts, Columbus, Ohio (1983–6), still among America's most prominent Deconstructivist buildings, followed by the Greater Columbus Convention Center, Columbus, Ohio (1989–93); the Koizumi Lighting Theatre/IZM, Tokyo, with Kojiro Kitayama (1990); and the NC Building, Tokyo (1992) which embodied his conception of 'textual geology in architecture' and appears to be on the point of collapse, shifting and slipping as if frozen during an earthquake. His Aronoff Center, New York (1991–6), resembles a row of interlocking showboxes about to topple over. He published *House of Cards* (Oxford 1978); *Moving Arrows, Eros and other Errors* (Oxford

1986), and *The Formal Basis of Modern Architecture* (Berlin 1996).

Jencks 1988; Klotz 1988; J. F. Bédard (ed.), *Cities of Artificial Excavation. The Work of P.E. 1978–88*, Montreal 1994; P. Ciorra, *P.E. Bauten und Projekte*, Stuttgart 1995; C. C. Davidson (ed.), *Eleven Authors in Search of a Building*, New York/London 1997.

**El-Wakil**, Abdel Wahed (b.1943). Egyptian architect trained under Hassan FATHY in Cairo. His early work, e.g. Halawa House (1972–5), Hamdy House (1978) and Chourbaggy House (1984), all near Cairo, follows the modernized vernacular style pioneered by Fathy, with some personal interpretations. His later buildings are often on a grand scale, e.g. Sulaiman Palace, Jeddah, Saudi Arabia (1981). His mosques, of massive wall and vault construction, are imposing, e.g. Quiblatain and Quba Mosques, Medina, Saudi Arabia, the Island Mosque (1986), the Cornice Mosque (1986) and the King Saud Mosque (1987), all in Jeddah.

**Eldem**, Sedad Hakki (1908–88), *see* TURKISH ARCHITECTURE.

**Elevation**. The external faces of a building; also a drawing made in projection on a vertical plane to show any one face (or elevation) of a building. *See* Fig. 50.

**Elevator** or **lift**. An apparatus for trans-porting freight or passengers vertically, consisting of a platform or chamber suspended in a shaft, moving vertically in guides and serving two or more floors of a building. It was crucial in the development of the SKYSCRAPER. Steel operated hoists and other primitive forms of the elevator were in use by the early C19 (BURTON's Colosseum, London, in 1823; WILLARD's Bunker Hill Monument, Boston, in 1844). Elisha Graves Otis exhibited a 'safety elevator' in New York in 1854 and in 1857 the Haughwout Department Store, New York (now demolished), and in 1859 the Fifth Avenue Hotel, New York (now demolished), had passenger elevators. Hydraulic elevators were introduced in the 1860s. The ten-storey Equitable Building, New York (1868–71, now demolished), by POST was the first office building with elevators. In the 1880s an electric elevator was exhibited by Siemens in Germany and the first installed in Baltimore in 1887. By 1897 there were over 5,000 elevators of various kinds in New York. In 1903 traction elevators were introduced by the Otis Elevator Company. *See also* ESCALATOR.

Elliott 1994.

**Elias of Dereham** or **Durham** (d.1245) was Canon of Salisbury and Wells and a confidant of Archbishops Hubert Walter

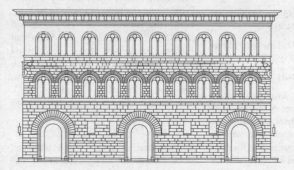

Fig. 50 Elevation: Michelozzo's Palazzo Medici-Riccardi, Florence

and Stephen Langton, Bishop Jocelyn of Wells, Bishop Hugh of Lincoln, Bishop Poore of Salisbury, and Bishop des Roches of Winchester. He was present at the sealing of Magna Carta and at the translation of the relics of Thomas à Becket in 1220. He was, in addition, in charge of the King's Works at Winchester Castle and Clarendon Palace, and '*a prima fundatione rector*' of Salisbury Cathedral. *Rector* sounds like administrator rather than designer, but he was also paid for making a vessel for Salisbury Cathedral and is called *artifex* in connection with the new shrine of Thomas à Becket; so he was certainly something of an artist, and it is likely that he was, like ALAN OF WALSINGHAM a hundred years later, a man capable also of designing buildings and of discussing details constructively with the master masons.

Harvey 1984.

**Eliot**, Charles (1859–97), *see* PARKWAY.

**Elizabethan architecture**. A period of English Early Renaissance architecture from 1558 to 1603, followed by Jacobean architecture 1603–25; *see* ENGLISH ARCHITECTURE.

**Ell**. In the USA a single-storey lean-to-wing containing a kitchen. Ells were added in the C17 to WEATHERBOARDED, timber-framed buildings in New England.

**Elliot**, Archibald (1760–1823), *see* SCOTTISH ARCHITECTURE.

**Elliot**, James (1770–1810), *see* SCOTTISH ARCHITECTURE.

**Elliptical arch**, *see* ARCH.

**Ellis**, Peter (1804–84). English architect now famous as a pioneer of the modern office building. His Oriel Chambers in Water Street, Liverpool, of 1864, with its façade glazed throughout in the form of angular oriels separated by very slender mullions, foreshadows the Chicago skyscraper of twenty years later. The back is almost entirely of glass, cantilevered out in front of the frame, itself of cast iron with brick arches. The back of his office block, No. 16 Cook Street, Liverpool (1866), is even more advanced, consisting of a wall and spiral staircase entirely of glass except for the thinnest of iron mullions.

Hitchcock 1977.

**Elmes**, Harvey Lonsdale (1814–47). English architect, son of James Elmes (1782–1862), architect and writer, a champion of the Elgin Marbles, of Keats, and of Wordsworth. James wrote on prison reform, and in 1823 edited the life and works of Wren. Harvey was a pupil of his father and in 1836 won the competition for St George's Hall, Liverpool (designed 1840). Even though, in its grouping and its massing of columns, it is no longer of Grecian purity, the building is convincedly classical. The interior was completed brilliantly by C. R. COCKERELL in 1851–4.

Colvin 1995.

**Ely**, *see* REGINALD OF ELY.

**Embattled**. Furnished with BATTLEMENTS; or a moulding with an indented pattern.

**Emberton**, Joseph (1889–1956). An early exponent of Modernism in England. His Yacht Club, Burnham-on-Crouch (1931), was the only example from England in the 'International Style' exhibition in New York in 1932. His Universal House, Southwark (1933, demolished 1960), had a vitriolite glass façade, with rounded corners. Also notable are his Simpson's, Piccadilly, London (1936), and Pleasure Beach (1935) and Casino (1939), Blackpool.

R. Ind, *J.E.*, London 1982.

**Embrasure**. A recess for a window, door, etc., or a small opening in the wall or PARAPET of a fortified building, usually splayed on the inside.

**Empire style**, *see* CLASSICISM.

**Encaustic tiles**. Earthenware tiles glazed and decorated, much used in the Middle Ages and in Victorian churches for flooring.

**Enceinte**. In military architecture, the main enclosure of a fortress, surrounded by the wall or ditch.

**Endell**, August (1871–1925), *see* ART NOUVEAU.

**Enfilade**. The French system of aligning internal doors in a sequence so that a vista is obtained through a series of rooms when all the doors are open. They are usually placed close to the windows. The arrangement was introduced *c.*1650 and became a feature of Baroque palace planning.

**Engaged column**. A structural column attached to, or partly sunk into, a wall, usually non-loadbearing; also called an *applied column* or *attached column*. *See also* DEMI-COLUMN.

**Engel**, Carl Ludwig (1778–1840). German but active from 1815 in Finland. He knew SCHINKEL's work and had lived several years in St Petersburg. These are the two sources of his neo-classical style. His main buildings are the Senate (1818–22), the Old Church (1826), the University (1818–32), the Cathedral (1830–40) and the University Library (1836–44), all at Helsinki. The cathedral is strictly centrally planned, a Greek cross with four porticos outside, a quatrefoil inside. Above the centre is a tall dome. The university library has two splendid oblong reading-rooms with detached giant columns all round.

J. M. Richards, *A Guide to Finnish Architecture*, London 1966; N. E. Wickberg, *E.*, exh. cat., Berlin 1970.

**English architecture and landscape architecture**. For pre-Christian buildings see MEGALITH and PREHISTORIC ARCHITECTURE. Apart from Hadrian's Wall (*c.*122–33) little survives from the Roman occupation (55 BC–AD 407). Excavations have proved in places as distant from one another as Tintagel in Cornwall and Whitby in Yorkshire that early monastic establishments were of the Egyptian coenobitic type with separate detached huts clustered round a centre with the church and probably a refectory. At Abingdon it must have been the same, and Nendrum is an Irish example. The type reached England via Ireland. Of the same C7 are also the earliest surviving Anglo-Saxon churches. They fall into two groups, one in the south-east, characterized by apses and a triple arcade dividing the choir from the nave, the other in the north, with long, tall, narrow nave and straight-ended chancel: the first group includes St Pancras and St Martin at Canterbury, Reculver and Bradwell-on-Sea; the latter, Monkwearmouth, Jarrow and Escomb. None of these has aisles, but instead they had side chambers, called *porticus*. Towers did not exist, but there were west porches. Between the two groups stand Brixworth in Northamptonshire, larger than the others and with aisles, and Bradford-on-Avon in Wiltshire. But the typically Anglo-Saxon decoration of Bradford, with its pilaster-strips, flat blank arches, triangles instead of arches – the whole applied like the timbering of timber-framed work – is as late as the C10 and is indeed the most prominent decorative feature of later Anglo-Saxon architecture. Towers seem to have made their appearance in the C10 too; they are either at the west end or placed centrally between nave and chancel. Highly decorated examples are to be found at Earls Barton and Barton-on-Humber. Transepts also appear, and aisles become a little more frequent. That churches of timber, which must have been the rule in the earliest centuries, still went on as late as the C11 is proved by Greensted in Essex, which can be dated c.1013. Many churches of the later C11 have Anglo-Saxon side by side with Norman motifs; the mixture is called the *Saxo-Norman overlap*.

What is called Norman architecture in England is not the art of Normandy but that brought by William the Conqueror to England, i.e. really what on the Continent is called Romanesque. The Norman style in fact begins just before the Conquest, with Westminster Abbey as rebuilt by Edward the Confessor. This is a close parallel to such buildings in Normandy as Jumièges, Mont St Michel, and the churches of Caen: internally with arcade, gallery (ample or small, with large or sub-divided openings towards the nave), CLERESTORY, and open timber roof; externally with two façade towers and a square crossing tower (Canterbury, Southwell). The volume of building was enormous. Nearly every cathedral and abbey church was rebuilt, and most of the bishops and abbots came from Normandy. But apart from the system of Normandy, there are also interesting variations of diverse origin: the mighty single west tower of Ely on the pattern of Germany; the giant niches of the façades of Tewkesbury and Lincoln, also on German patterns; the gallery tucked in below the arch of the arcade (Jedburgh); and the giant round piers of Tewkesbury and Gloucester, perhaps on a Burgundian pattern (as at Tournus). Ornament is prevalently geometrical (zigzag, CRENEL-LATION, chain, reel, and similar motifs). Figure sculpture is rarely concentrated on the portals as in the French royal domain (York, chapterhouse of St Mary); its connections are rather with the west of France and with Lombardy.

In only one respect does England appear to lead in the European Romanesque style; in the VAULTING of Durham Cathedral. For while England has no parallel to the mighty tunnel vaults of so many French naves and the groin vaults of so many German naves, Durham was rib-vaulted from the beginning (1093), and hers seem to be the earliest rib vaults not only of northern Europe but possibly of Europe altogether. While it may be that some of the elementary rib vaults of Lombardy are in fact of earlier date, those of Durham are without question infinitely more accomplished, and they and their descendants in France (Caen, St Étienne, Beauvais) led to the triumphant adoption of rib vaulting at St Denis and in the whole Gothic style, first in France and then everywhere.

The Gothic style reached England first by means of the CISTERCIAN Order. Its first English buildings of c.1130–60, however, though provided with pointed arches, have Burgundian Cistercian sources of a Romanesque kind, and where rib vaults first appear, they are derived from Durham rather than France. Cistercian churches go Gothic very gradually about 1160–80 (Roche), and a few non-Cistercian churches take part in this development (Ripon). But the real, the only fully convinced, beginning of Gothic architecture in England is the east end of Canterbury Cathedral, begun by WILLIAM OF SENS in 1174 and brought to completion in 1185 by William the Englishman. Sens and Paris Cathedrals are the precursors, the retrochoir at Chichester and the nave of the Temple Church the immediate successors. Also immediately follows the retrochoir at Winchester, a hall choir, a form liked in England (on the pattern of Anjou churches, as it reappears at Salisbury, the Temple and Barking Abbey.

But real, thoroughly English Gothic,

i.e. the so-called Early English style, begins with Wells *c.*1175–1239 and Lincoln *c.*1190–1280. Here there is more stress on horizontals than in France, there are straight east walls (not radiating chapels), and the details also keep right away from the central French development. The chancel of Lincoln in particular with its crazy vault has no French parallel and begins a distinguished series of figured vaults which precedes those of any other country. The first star vaults are in the Lincoln nave, and the acme of this system is Exeter of the late C13. Less original but equally impressive are Salisbury of 1220–*c.*1266 and the east transept of Durham.

Durham Cathedral lies on the castle hill and late C11 as well as C12 domestic parts survive. Altogether, although English castles are primarily castles with keeps, like the French donjons (the Tower in London, Colchester, Rochester, etc.), these keeps were not normally used domestically, but great halls, chapels, etc. were also built. A reform of the defensive system was brought about by the Crusades, in England as (a little earlier) in France. Emphasis was now laid on the defence not of one tower but of the whole wall with its many smaller towers, and often even on more than one concentric wall, on the pattern ultimately of the walls of Constantinople. Such castles are Dover, the Tower of London and the splendid late C13 castles of Wales (Conway, Caernarvon, Harlech, Beaumaris).

In church architecture the late C13 marks the change from the Early English to the Decorated style. This lasted into the second half of the C14, and is characterized first and foremost by the OGEE, a double or S-curve, which occurs chiefly in arches and in the TRACERY of windows. The other main characteristic is a maximum of decoration covering surfaces (e.g. in foliage DIAPERS) and encrusting arches, gables, etc.; the leaves are not naturalistic but stylized, with nobbly forms reminiscent of certain seaweeds. Spatially the Decorated style favours the unexpected vista, especially in diagonal directions. Principal works are the east parts of Bristol Cathedral (begun in 1298) and Wells Cathedral (*c.*1290–*c.*1340), the Lady Chapel and the famous Octagon at Ely (1321–53), and screens (Lincoln), funerary monuments (Edward II, Gloucester Cathedral; Percy Tomb, Beverley), stalls (Exeter), etc. No other country has anything as novel, as resourceful and as lavish as the English Decorated style, though when a similar direction was taken by Peter PARLER at Prague, it is likely that English influence played a determining part. The start at Prague was in 1353.

At that time, however, England was already turning her back on the Decorated. The Perpendicular style, beginning in London *c.*1335 and reaching a full climax in the Gloucester chancel in 1337–57, is the very reverse of the Decorated. Perpendicular is characterized by the stress on straight verticals and horizontals, by slender, vertically subdivided supports and large windows, by window tracery with little fantasy and inventiveness. The signature tune is the panel motif, which is simply arched but with the arch cusped. This occurs in rows and tiers everywhere in the tracery, and almost as frequently in blank-wall decoration. In vaulting the Perpendicular first favours lierne VAULTS, therein following the inventions of the Decorated, and later fan VAULTS, introduced about 1350–60 either in the cloisters at Gloucester or in the chapterhouse at Hereford. For the Early Perpendicular the chancel of Gloucester Cathedral is the most important work; for the time about 1400 the naves of Canterbury (1379–1405 by Henry

YEVELE) and Winchester (c.1360 but mostly c.1394–1410); for the Late Perpendicular St George's Chapel at Windsor (begun 1474), King's College Chapel at Cambridge (1446–61, 1477–85 and 1508–15) and the chapel of Henry VII at Westminster Abbey (1503–19) and its predecessor, the chancel vault of Oxford Cathedral (c.1478 onwards). But for the Perpendicular style parish churches are as significant as the major buildings so far noted. The grandest of these are in Suffolk and Norfolk, in Somerset (especially towers), and in the Cotswolds, demonstrating the riches which the wool and cloth trade made for the middle class. The Perpendicular style, once it had been established, went on without major changes for 250 years, and it can be argued that the Elizabethan style in England is more Perpendicular than it is Renaissance.

It was in Henry VII's Chapel that the first works in England in the Italian Renaissance style were put up, the tombs of the Lady Margaret and Henry VII by Pietro Torrigiani of Florence (1512–18). Henry VIII and his court favoured the new style which was impressively promoted in the crafts by Holbein's designs. But the Renaissance in England remained till about 1550 a matter of decoration, and it was coarsened as soon as it fell into native hands. The Protector Somerset in Somerset House was the first to understand Italian or rather by then French Renaissance principles more fully, and from Somerset House the Elizabethan style proceeded. It combines the symmetry of façades, as the Renaissance had taught it, and Renaissance details, with Netherlandish decorative motifs (STRAPWORK) and the Perpendicular belief in very large windows with MULLIONS and TRANSOMS. Longleat (mainly 1568 onwards, by SMYTHSON) is the first complete example: others are Burghley House

(1552–87), Montacute (1580–99), Wollaton (1580–85) and Hardwick (1591–7). The first fifteen years of the reign of James I brought no change. Among the principal buildings are Hatfield (1607–12), Audley End (1603–16), Bramshill (1605–12). Plans of houses are often of E or H shape, if they do not have internal courtyards as the largest have. Windows are usually very large and may dominate the walls. Gables, straight or curved in the manner of the Netherlands, are frequent. Wood and plaster decoration is rich and often over-extravagant. Ecclesiastical architecture was almost at a standstill, and even the ample Jacobean-looking church furnishings are usually Jacobean only in style but as late as the 1630s.

By then the greatest revolution in English architecture had, however, already taken place, the revolution achieved by Inigo JONES. His Queen's House at Greenwich was begun in 1616, his Banqueting House in Whitehall in 1619. Jones's strictly Palladian Classicism was continued by John WEBB, Sir Roger PRATT, and Hugh MAY. Another contributing factor was the domestic architecture of Holland, which influenced England first in a semi-classical form with Dutch gables. The Jones style was too pure and exacting to find favour immediately outside the most cultured circles. The universal acceptance of classical architecture came only with the time of WREN, but in domestic building the so-called Wren type of house – quite plain, with a middle pediment, a pedimented doorway, and a hipped roof – is not a creation of Wren. Stuart churches are a rarity. They also become more frequent only at the time of Wren and are largely the result of the Fire of London. They are of a wide variety of plans, longitudinal or central or a synthesis of the two, and also of a wide variety of elevational features, especially in the steeples. The range of forms used by Wren is immense. It goes from the noble classical simplicity of the dome of St Paul's to the dramatic Baroque of the west towers of St Paul's and of Greenwich and the Hampton Court plans, to the brick domesticity of Kensington Palace and even to the Gothic Revival of a few of the city churches.

HAWKSMOOR, Wren's favourite pupil, and the ingenious VANBRUGH followed Wren's lead in working towards a synthesis of Baroque and Gothicism or a general medievalism. The emergence of the English-style LANDSCAPE GARDEN in about 1715–20 with BRIDGEMAN and KENT (later and more extensively with BROWN and REPTON) was not unconnected with this medievalism, which was much stronger than in any other country. The fact that the architects of the generation after Vanbrugh and Hawksmoor returned to the Palladianism of Jones is only at first sight a contradiction. Palladian houses and picturesque grounds must be seen as the two sides of the same coin. The architects in question are men such as Colen CAMPBELL, Lord BURLINGTON, and KENT (the latter, however, much inspired by the Vanbrugh style as well). GIBBS continued rather in the Wren vein: he is chiefly remembered for his churches, which had much influence in America as well as in England. Palladianism ruled until modified by the more elegant and varied style of Robert ADAM, but essentially the Palladian tradition maintained its hold until the 1820s (NASH's Regent's Park terraces).

Georgian architecture is classical in its major exteriors; but on the smaller domestic scale it still has the sensible plainness of the Queen Anne style. Interiors are more elaborate than exteriors; here also Palladianism was the rule at first, but it was handled with greater freedom and verve. A brief phase of ROCOCO followed about the middle of the century:

then the enchantment of Robert Adam's delicate decoration captured nearly everybody. Grecian interiors were rare until about 1820, but Victorian licence and exuberance are already heralded in certain Regency interiors (Brighton Pavilion).

But Victorian architecture is not all licence and exuberance. At the other end of the scale is the respect for the past, a Historicism taken very seriously as a matter of religious or social responsibility. The licence is usually paramount in domestic, the seriousness in ecclesiastical architecture. Not that Historicism did not dominate domestic architecture too, but there it was taken in a less demanding way. Victorian church architecture is almost entirely Gothic, though in the 1840s there was a passing fashion for neo-Norman and neo-Early-Christian or neo-Italian-Romanesque (T. H. WYATT, Wilton). The revived Gothic was treated as a rule correctly (SCOTT); but some of the very best (PEARSON) were able to allow themselves freedom within the Gothic *ensemble*. The Gothic phase most readily imitated was first Perpendicular (Houses of Parliament), then from *c.*1840 onwards, thanks chiefly to PUGIN, the so-called Second Pointed or Middle Pointed, i.e. the style of *c.*1250–1300, and then from the seventies onwards, again Perpendicular (BODLEY). At the end of the century Historicism began to break down, and Norman SHAW could use domestic C17 elements in a church (St Michael, Bedford Park) and John Dando Sedding (1838–91) yet freer, but always sensitively handled, elements, e.g. Holy Redeemer, Clerkenwell, London (1887–8).

In secular architecture the possibility of using Gothic side by side with classical had already been handed down from Wren and Hawksmoor via the Rococo Gothic of Horace Walpole's Strawberry Hill and the romantic Gothic of James

WYATT's Fonthill. Other styles had also occasionally been tried, though not seriously (CHINOISERIE, also the Indian of S. P. Cockerell). But Gothic was given publicly the same weight as classical only with BARRY's Houses of Parliament (1836–68). At the same time Barry introduced a neo-Quattrocento (Travellers' Club) a neo-Cinquecento (Reform Club) and a neo-Elizabethan (Highclere, 1837). So by c.1840 a wide range of historical possibilities were accepted. To them in the late fifties the French Renaissance with its prominent pavilion roofs was added.

Quite separate from all this was the great engineering development. England had been first in the Industrial Revolution (and the size of the new mansions and size and frequency of the new churches bear witness to England's unprecedented industrial and consequently commercial prosperity). The first iron bridges belong to England (TELFORD, BRUNEL), and the largest iron and glass conservatories (PAXTON, BURTON). In BUNNING's Coal Exchange (1846–9) iron and glass first appeared with architectural ambitions, and only two years after its completion Paxton's Crystal Palace was entirely of iron and glass, the whole 550 m. (1,800 ft) length of it. But iron and glass in architecture remained after that confined to exhibition buildings, train sheds (notably St Pancras station, London, of 1864–8 by the engineer William Henry Barlow (1812–1902), with a single span of 74 m. (243 ft) rising to 30 m. (98 ft) high), and, on the fringe of architecture, to warehouses and office buildings. The functional self-sufficiency of these new materials and the shunning of over-decoration which followed from their convinced use, however, made them unpopular with the High Victorian architects. But from 1877 onwards William MORRIS fought publicly for sim-

plicity, for truth to materials and against over-decoration, though he did so in a militant anti-industrial spirit. Hence those who were convinced by Morris's teachings were less attracted by an alliance with industry and commerce than by an application of Morris's principles to the human scale of domestic architecture. The leaders were Morris's friend Philip WEBB and the more richly endowed Norman SHAW. They, from the sixties onwards, built houses for a small section of the middle class which were fresher and aesthetically more adventurous than anything done at the same time abroad (see ARTS AND CRAFTS). Working-class architecture, on the other hand, i.e. housing provided by manufacturers and then by trusts (Peabody Trust), remained grim and was only humanized when HOWARD's garden city principle had begun to be applied to factory housing (notably at Bourneville) despite the introduction, several decades earlier, of PUBLIC PARKS, notably by LOUDON, PENNETHORNE and PAXTON. About 1900 England was still leading both in the planning conception of the garden suburb and in the architecture of the so-called DOMESTIC REVIVAL. This, in the work of VOYSEY, and the early work of LUTYENS, was beginning to move out of historicism towards a greater independence of period motifs and towards that simplicity and directness which in the commercial field had already been achieved by the CHICAGO SCHOOL.

The pre-First World War years were notable for the work of MACKINTOSH, BENTLEY, COMPER, HOLDEN and the eccentric Harrison TOWNSEND, though the eclectic Aston WEBB was perhaps more representative of the Edwardian period as typified by such stylistically heterogeneous buildings as the Imperial Institute, London (1887–93, demolished 1957), by Thomas Collcutt (1840–1924), the Rylands Memorial Library, Manchester (1890–99), by Basil Champneys (1842–1935), or the Ashton Memorial, Lancaster (1904–9), by John Belcher (1841–1913). However, when radical innovation became the demand of the more go-ahead architects England lagged behind France, Germany and Austria and contributed only occasionally in the later 1920s and a little more frequently in the 1930s with the work of a few adherents of the INTERNATIONAL MODERN movement, in particular the ARCHITECTS' CO-PARTNERSHIP, COATES, FRY, Francis Yorke (1906–62), Owen WILLIAMS and Joseph EMBERTON. The Boots factory, Beeston, Nottinghamshire (1930–32, 1935–8), Peckham Health Centre, London (1935), by Williams, and the Royal Corinthian Yacht Club, Burnham-on-Crouch (1931), by Emberton, are notable *incunabula* of Modernism, as is also the Peter Jones store, Sloane Square, London (1935–9) by William Crabtree (1905–91). The remarkable work of TECTON of these years was outstanding.

In the immediate aftermath of the Second World War the contributions of the London County Council under MATTHEW and MARTIN to mass-housing and schools were notable as were, slightly later, the public buildings of LASDUN, Sir Basil Spence (1907–76) and others. The NEW TOWNS created with the collaboration of landscape architects such as COLVIN, CROWE and JELLICOE were notable and forward-looking. Already by the late 1950s the first of several reactions against Modernism made itself felt with BRUTALISM in the early work of STIRLING and the SMITHSONS, followed by the more radical, unproductive but influential ARCHIGRAM. The 1970s were notable for ERSKINE's work at Newcastle-on-Tyne, which anticipated the COMMUNITY ARCHITECTURE pro-

moted by SEGAL and others. A few years later POST-MODERNISM found talented exponents in England, e.g. Jeremy DIXON and Edward JONES though they later repudiated it, Terry FARRELL and the colourful John Outram (b.1934), whose Harp Central Heating building at Swanley, Kent (1984) and Blackwell Pumping Station, Isle of Dogs, London (1988) were striking. However, recent English architecture is notable mainly for HIGH TECH as developed by FOSTER, ROGERS, ARUP Associates, Michael and Patty HOPKINS, Nicholas GRIMSHAW and others, among whom the structural engineer Peter RICE played a significant role. High Tech is unusual for being exclusively English – the only English architectural movement of international significance this century – though some of its major achievements have been for foreign clients. It can be seen as the culmination of several Modernist trends and as sparking off such reactionary, traditionalist responses as the NEO-GEORGIAN development at Richmond Riverside (1985–8) by Quinlan Terry (b.1937), comparable to François Spoerry's Port Grimaud in France and Port Liberté, New York. Less theatrical and nostalgic were China Wharf (1986–8) and Cascades (1987–8), Docklands Development, London, by CZWG Architects (N. Campbell, b.1947; R. Zogolovitch, b.1947; R. Wilkinson, b.1947; P. Gough, b.1946).

More recently Ian Ritchie (b.1947) and William Alsop (b.1947) have made their names internationally, the former with the National Museum of Science, Technology and Industry, La Villette, Paris (1985 with Peter Rice), the B8 Building, Stockley Park, Heathrow, London (1989–90), and the Cultural Centre, Albert, France (1991): the latter with the Ferry Terminal, Hamburg (1990–91), and the huge Local Government Offices,

Marseille (1991–4), which was hailed in France as the most innovative building since PIANO & ROGERS's Pompidou Centre in Paris. Zaha HADID, practising in London, has been widely acclaimed, but unfortunately few of her remarkable DECONSTRUCTIVIST projects have been realized as yet.

**English bond**, *see* BRICKWORK.

**Enneastyle**. A portico with nine columns, or other disposition of nine columns.

**Ensingen**, Ulrich von (d.1419), and his son Matthäus (d.1463), the two most important members of a south German family of masons. Ulrich was sufficiently distinguished by 1391 for him to put his name forward as master mason to the cathedral authorities at Milan. In 1392 he became master mason for Ulm Minster (begun 1377). He changed plan and elevation boldly and designed the west tower with its splendid porch. The upper parts of the tower were built to a changed design by Matthäus BÖBLINGER. In 1394 Ulrich went after all to Milan, but was not satisfied or able to convince the authorities, and so left in 1395. In 1397 he was appointed master mason at Ulm for life. In 1399, in addition to his job at Ulm, he was put in charge of the continuation of the west tower at Strasbourg. Here it was he who started the single tower instead of the two originally projected and built the enchanting octagon stage. The spire, however, is by his successor Johann HÜLTZ. He also worked at the Frauenkirche, Esslingen, from 1398 onwards, and probably designed the west tower, which was carried out (and probably altered) by Hans BÖBLINGER.

Ulrich had three sons who became masons. One of them is Matthäus, who first worked under his father at Strasbourg, then became master mason at Berne, where he designed the new minster in 1420–21. From Berne he also undertook the job of master mason at Esslingen, but was replaced there in 1440 by Hans Böblinger. From 1446 he was master mason at Ulm. Of his sons three were masons.

L. Mojon, *Der Münsterbaumeister M.E.*, Bern 1967; Frankl 1972; R. Wortmann, *600 Jahre Ulmer Münster*, Ulm 1977; B. Schock-Werner, in Recht 1989.

**Entablature**. The upper part of an ORDER, consisting of ARCHITRAVE, FRIEZE and CORNICE. *See* Figs. 51, 86.

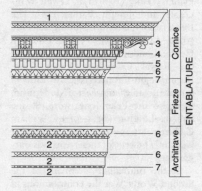

1. Cyma recta    5. Dentils
2. Fascia    6. Cyma reversa
3. Modillions    7. Astragal
4. Ovolo

Fig. 51 Entablature: Corinthian

**Entasis**. The very slight convex curve used on Greek and later columns to correct the optical illusion of concavity which would result if the sides were straight. Also used on spires and other structures for the same reason.

**Entresol**, *see* MEZZANINE.

**Environmental, green or sustainable architecture**. The growing concern with environmental and ecological questions in the 1960s and 1970s, alerted notably by McHarg's passionate appeals, led to the search for an architecture that is environmentally compatible or 'sustainable'. Buildings constructed of earth, wood or other natural material (not involving pollution in its treatment), that are energy-efficient (e.g. that exploit solar energy for heating etc. with effective insulation) and that make little or no impact on the nature of a site and its resources, were designed with these 'green' issues and their solution in mind. Notable attempts to meet some or all of them were made by the German architect Thomas Herzog (b.1941) at his small-scale but highly effective Burghardt House, Regensburg (1977–9), by the American partnership 'Jersey Devil' at Hill House, La Honda, California (1977–9), an earth-sheltered building partly underground and covered with a layer of earth and turf, the energy efficiency being increased by insulation, and by the Dutch architects Ton Alberts (b.1927) and Max van Huut (b.1947) at their large-scale MB bank headquarters, Amsterdam (1978–88) and by the English group 'Future Systems' (founded in 1979 by Jan Kaplicky, b.1937) with their Green Building project (1990 with Arup) and Hauer-King House (1995), London. Also significant were the architectural-urbanistic projects initiated in the USA, notably by Paolo Soleri at Arcosanti, Arizona, where his concept of Arcology or 'Architecture Coherent with Ecology' was put into practice from 1970 onwards and, more recently, the Laredo Demonstration Blueprint Farm, Texas, where a new building typology was evolved in 1987 by a group of architectural and ecological pioneers at the Center for Maximum Potential Building Systems, Austin, Texas. Old buildings have also begun to be refurbished to make them 'sustainable', an exemplary instance of this being Post's Audubon Building, New York (originally Schermerhorn Building 1891), which was restored and refurbished in 1990–92 by the National Audubon Society (for the protection and maintenance of vital habitats and ecosystems).

R. and B. Vale, *G.A.*, London 1991; A. St John, *Sourcebook for S. Design*, Boston 1993; K. Yeang, *Designing with Nature: The Ecological Basis of Architectural Design*, London 1994; B. Edwards, *Towards a S.A.*, London 1996; S. and J. Baggs, *The Healthy House. Creating a Safe, Healthy and Environmentally Friendly Home*, London 1996.

**Environmental control**. The regulation of temperature, humidity, lighting, etc. inside a building by mechanical means, e.g. by air-conditioning. Such services are now almost as important as structure in architectural design.

**Environmental design**. A term coined in the 1950s for those aspects of design related to the control of the artificial environment in a building. Passive control, e.g. thick-walled courtyard design in arid climate, is to be distinguished from active control, e.g. air-conditioning, including solar-powered systems. Integrated Environmental Design or IED introduced permanent supplementary artificial lighting systems, by day as well as night, and the use of tinted and reflective glass to minimalize solar heat. After the 1973–4 energy crisis sophisticated IED systems were invented to reduce energy consumption in artificial environments, sometimes sealed from the polluted urban atmosphere, controlled by computer in intelligent buildings. Unacceptable environmental characteristics became known as a 'sick building syndrome'.

Banham 1969; R. Knowles, *Energy and Form*, Cambridge, Mass., 1975; C. Day, *Places of the Soul. Architecture and E.D. as a Healing Art*, London 1990.

**Eosander (von Göthe)**, Johann Friedrich (1670–1729). German architect, a pupil of TESSIN, he succeeded SCHLÜTER in Berlin, where he was employed at Charlottenburg from 1702 onwards. The domed tower is his as well as much of the interior. He doubled the size of the Royal Palace in Berlin (1706–13). The only surviving fragment – the portal – is by Eosander after Schlüter's design. In 1722 he went to Dresden, where he built the Ubigau palace (1724–6).

R. Biederstedt, *J.F.E. Grundzüge einer Bibliographie*, Stockholm 1961; Hempel 1965; G. Peschen, *Das Königliche Schloss zu Berlin*, Munich 1993.

**Equilateral arch**, *see* ARCH.

**Erdmannsdorf**, Friedrich Wilhelm Freiherr von (1736–1800). German neo-classical architect inspired by the English neo-Palladians, then fashionable at Frederick the Great's Potsdam, rather than by Palladio himself. He decided to become an architect when travelling in England in 1763. His work is elegant and polite, very different from the radical and severe neo-classicism of his exact contemporary LEDOUX. In 1765–6 he travelled in Italy with his patron the Prince of ANHALT-DESSAU and met both Winckelmann and CLÉRISSEAU. He also visited England again. On his return to Germany he built the neo-Palladian country house at Wörlitz (1768–73) and laid out with the Prince of Anhalt-Dessau the remarkable LANDSCAPE GARDEN (begun 1771), the earliest in Germany. His later buildings in Dessau have all been destroyed: the Schlosstheater (1777), Schloss Georgium (*c.*1780) and the Stables and Riding School (1790–91).

*F.W. von E., 1736–1800*, exh. cat., Wörlitz 1986; H.-J. Kadetz, *F.W. von E. 1736–1800. Wegbereiten des deutschen Frühklassizismus in Anhalt-Dessau*, East Berlin 1986.

**Erickson**, Arthur Charles (b.1924). Canadian architect notable for his pragmatic and eclectic large-scale public projects, the Simon Fraser University, Burnaby, British Columbia (1963–5), Lethbridge University, Alberta (1971), and the Government Offices and Courthouse complex, Vancouver (1973–80), a huge and remarkable urban layout.

E. Iglauer, *Seven Stones. A Portrait of A.E. Architect*, Seattle 1981; *The Architecture of A.E.*, London 1988.

**Erith**, Raymond (1904–73), *see* NEO-GEORGIAN.

**Erskine**, Ralph (b.1914). Born in England, he settled in Sweden in 1939 and opened an architectural practice in 1946 at Drottningholm. He excelled in low-cost housing, e.g. at Fors in Dalecarlia (1950–53), at Tibro (1959–64) and Kiruna (1959–65). He became known internationally for his Byker housing at Newcastle upon Tyne (1969–80), where the residents were closely consulted throughout the 'participatory design process'. At Byker two-storey terrace houses with irregular small windows and other openings are ranged behind an immense outer wall eight storeys high and one kilometre long. This defensive conception was later developed by Erskine for a new town at Resolute Bay, Canada (1973 onwards). His best-known recent works include the colourful Lilla Bommen, Gothenburg (1987–90), and the Ark at Hammersmith, London (1991), a commercial office building with communal spaces.

S. Ray, *R.E.*, Bari 1978; D. Lasdun, *Architecture in the Age of Scepticism*, London 1984; M. Egelius, *R.E. Architect*, Stockholm 1990; H. Pearman, *The London Ark*, London 1993; R. P. Collymore, *The Architecture of R.E.*, London 1994.

**Ervi**, Aarne (1910–77), *see* FINNISH ARCHITECTURE.

**Erwin von Steinbach** (d.1318) is one of the most famous medieval architects, because Goethe wrote his prose poem *Von deutscher Baukunst* (1772) on Strasbourg Cathedral, and especially its façade and steeple, round Erwin's name. The Chapel of the Virgin (1275–1319, destroyed 1682; fragment in the Musée de l'Œuvre de Notre Dame, Strasbourg) bore an inscription saying that 'Master Erwin built this work'. He is mentioned in documents as master of works at Strasbourg from 1284 onwards and on his tomb he is called the 'Gubernator' of the fabric. However, the steeple was not built during his lifetime. But it is likely that the west façade and the famous drawing for it of *c.*1275, known as '*dessin B*', are by Erwin (Musée de l'Œuvre de Notre Dame, Strasbourg).

Recht 1989.

**Escalator** or **moving stairway**. A development of the conveyor belt used in mines and factories for moving freight horizontally or vertically. The first passenger escalator consisted of an inclined and continuously circulating belt on which passengers stood. Steps were added later. In 1892 an experimental belt escalator was exhibited by Jesse W. Reno in Brooklyn, New York, and a stepped version was patented by G. H. Wheeler in the same year. This was later acquired by the Otis Elevator Company, who exhibited their stepped escalator in Paris in 1900. Escalators are used mainly in railway and airway terminals, department stores and other public buildings.

Elliott 1994.

**Escarp** or **scarp**. In military architecture, the bank or wall immediately in front of and below the rampart. It is often the inner side of the fosse or ditch.

**Eseler**, Nicolaus (*c.*1400–1492), *see* GERMAN ARCHITECTURE.

**Esonarthex**, *see* NARTHEX.

**Espagnolette**. An elongated and hinged fastening used on double French doors and windows. Despite the name, it appears to have been of French, not Spanish, origin and to have come into use in the early C17.

**Esplanade**. 1. An open and level stretch of pavement or grass used as a public promenade, especially along the shore of a lake, river or the sea. 2. In military architecture, the GLACIS of the counterscarp, hence the open ground separating the citadel of a fortress from the town.

**Estipite**. A type of PILASTER tapering towards the base, extensively used in Spanish post-Renaissance architecture.

**Ethiopian architecture**. Stone buildings of C1 BC to AD C5 are known from excavations at Aksuma, notably the Ta'akha Mariam palace, a multi-storey monumental rectangular structure which had two large interior courtyards, several smaller courts on different levels and hundreds of rooms. A similar but smaller structure has been excavated at Enda Mika'el, Aksum. Several remarkable carved stone *stelae* of the same date survive intact. The COPTIC rock-hewn churches at Lalibela, notably the Biet Giorgis of the C11–13, have ornamental similarities.

**Etruscan architecture**. The main building materials were wood, rubble, clay (sometimes baked); stone was used only for the foundations of temples and secular buildings, for fortifications, and for tombs. As the Romans were anxious to erase all memory of the Etruscans very few of their buildings survive above ground level. Their most notable surviving constructions are city walls dating from the C6 to the C4 BC (Tarquinia, Chiusi, Cortona, etc.) – sometimes with handsome if rather heavy arched gateways – though most of these are later (e.g. Falerii Novi, c.250 BC; Perugia, c.300 BC). After the C5 BC temples were built on a plan derived from Greece, but with rather widely spaced, stocky, wooden, unfluted columns, wooden beams, and richly modelled terracotta facings and ACROT-ERIA applied to them. Underground tombs were usually hewn out of the living rock; their interiors were very elaborately painted and occasionally decorated with stucco reliefs (e.g. Tomb of the Stucchi, Cerveteri, C3 BC).

Boethius 1978.

**Eulalius** designed the Church of the Holy Apostles, Constantinople (536–45, destroyed), the prototype Greek cross-plan church with five domes. It inspired S. Marco, Venice, and S. Front, Périgueux.

**Eustyle**. With an arrangement of columns two and a quarter diameters apart. *See also* AEROSTYLE; DIASTYLE; PYCNO-STYLE; SYSTYLE.

**Evelyn**, John (1620–1705). English architectural writer and garden theorist, a founder of the Royal Society, famous as a diarist. His first publication, *Fumifugium* (1661), proposed to remedy London's foul air by rational urban design and the provision of SQUARES with trees and flowering plants. This was followed by *Sylva* (1664), a treatise on forestry, mainly practical but also extolling the natural beauty of trees. The same year he published *A Parallel of the Ancient Architecture with the Modern* (1664), a translation of FRÉART's *Parallèle*, recommending the establishment of university faculties of architecture and with an appendix defining classical terminology. It became a standard text. He also translated two French treatises on gardening and garden

layouts, and prepared an encyclopaedic work on the subject, *Elysium Britannicus* (unpublished). Inspired by the French and Italian gardens he had admired on his travels (1643–52), he laid out his own grounds at Sayes Court, Deptford, Kent, and those of his brother at Wotton House, Surrey, from 1652 onwards and the more grandiose Albury Park, Surrey, from 1677. He advised on planning the parks of Cornbury House, Oxfordshire (1664 and 1680), and Euston Hall, Suffolk (1671), with long straight avenues, a word he introduced into English. None of these layouts survived the vogue for LAND-SCAPE GARDENS which his frequently reprinted writings on trees and forestry had helped to initiate.

T. O'Malley and J. Wischke (eds.), *J.E.'s 'Elysium Britannicus' and European Gardening*, Dumbarton Oaks, Washington, DC 1997.

**Exedra**. In classical architecture, a semi-circular or rectangular extension of a building forming internally a recess with raised seats; also, more loosely, any APSE or niche or the apsidal end of a room or a room opening full width into a larger, covered or uncovered space.

**Exonarthex**, *see* NARTHEX.

**Expressionism**. The style dominant in northern Europe about 1905–25. In architecture it is partly a continuation of ART NOUVEAU and was itself continued after the Second World War, e.g. by BRUTALISM. Buildings should not be confined to functioning well but create sensations of freely shaped abstract sculpture. GAUDÍ in his late work was the greatest architect of Expressionism. In Holland Expressionism is represented by the Amsterdam School, notably by the housing estates of Michel de KLERK and most wildly by van der Mey's Scheepvarthuis of 1913–17, both in Amsterdam.

In Denmark the Grundtvig church in Copenhagen (1913–26), by KLINT is gothicizing Expressionism. In Germany the most radical architectural Expressionism was never built, notably the fantastic sketches by Hermann Finsterlin (1887–1973), which often do not look like buildings at all, Bruno TAUT's utopian projects and POELZIG's House of Friendship for Istanbul (1916) and sketches for the Salzburg Festival Theatre (1920). The style of the latter was only once allowed to appear in reality: in the remodelling of a circus in Berlin as the Grosses Schauspielhaus (1918–19, destroyed). The Einstein Tower at Potsdam by MENDELSOHN (1919–21), the Chile-Haus in Hamburg (1922–3) by Fritz Höger (1877–1949), Quarr Abbey, Isle of Wight (1908–14) by Dom Paul Bellot (1876–1944), a virtuoso in brick, and St Engelbert, Cologne-Riehl (1930–32), by Dominikus BÖHM, are notable Expressionist buildings. Even GROPIUS and MIES VAN DER ROHE for a short time sacrificed on the altars of Expressionism: Gropius in his monument to the revolutionaries who were killed in the March Riots (1912), Mies in his glass skyscrapers of 1919–21 and the monument to Liebknecht and Rosa Luxemburg (1926).

W. Pehnt, *E. Architecture*, London 1973; W. de Wet, *E. in Holland: Die Architektur des Amsterdam Schüle*, Stuttgart 1986.

**Extrados**. The outer curved face of an arch or vault. *See* Fig. 6.

**Eyck**, Aldo van (b.1918), *see* VAN EYCK, Aldo.

**Eye-catcher** or **gloriette**. A decorative building, such as a sham ruin, usually built on an eminence in a landscape park to terminate a view or otherwise punctuate the layout. *See also* FOLLY.

**Eyre**, Wilson (1858–1944). American architect working in Philadelphia in a free, eclectic and personal version of the SHINGLE STYLE, e.g. C. B. Moore house, 1321 Locust Street, Philadelphia (1891) and Mask and Wig Club, Philadelphia (1893). His later Colonial Revival houses were equally picturesque, e.g. W. T. Jeffries house, Glen Riddle, Pennsylvania (1917).

V. J. Scully, *The Shingle Style and the Stick Style*, New Haven 1971.

**Eyserbeck**, Johann Friedrich (1734–1818), *see* ANHALT-DESSAU, Leopold Friedrich Frans, Fürst von.

# F

**Fabric**. The load-bearing structure of a building, its brick, concrete or timber or metal carcase or frame as well as the infill panels. Sometimes the term is used to include the cladding, windows, glazing, roof-covering and doors if attached to the structure. The term 'urban fabric' is now used for a complex of streets, open spaces and buildings.

**Façade**. The front or face of a building, usually emphasized architecturally.

**Façadism**. A recently coined term for a conservation principle giving paramountcy to street façades. It assumes the primacy of exterior design to which the interior and plan conform. It is used disparagingly when the preservation of historical buildings in urban redevelopment is questioned, as being an artificial and nostalgic return to the past.

J. Richards, *F.*, London 1994.

**Faïence**. The French name for tin-glazed earthenware or maiolica, used for household utensils and also for TILES for pavements and floors, interior and exterior wall cladding, sometimes also for applied architectural ornament, e.g. BACINI.

**Falconetto**, Giovanni Maria (1468–1535). Italian architect who anticipated SANSOVINO's and PALLADIO's Classicism in his remarkable Loggia Cornaro, Padua (1524). A top storey was added *c.*1530 when the Odeon Cornaro was built. His town gates at Padua – Porta S. Giovanni (1528) and Porta Savanarola (1530) – are also distinguished as is also his Monte di Pietà, Padua (1531–5).

L. Puppi *et al.*, *Alvise Cornaro e il suo tempo*, Padua 1980; B. Boucher, *Palladio*, London 1994; Lotz 1995.

**Faloci**, Pierre-Louis (b.1949), *see* FRENCH ARCHITECTURE.

**False arch**, *see* ARCH.

**False gallery**, *see* GALLERY.

**Fan vault**, *see* VAULT.

**Fanlight**. 1. A window, often semicircular, over a door, in Georgian and Regency buildings, with radiating glazing bars suggesting a fan. 2. Also, less commonly, the upper part of a window hinged to open separately.

**Fanzago**, Cosimo (1591–1678). Italian architect, born at Clusone near Bergamo, who settled in 1608 in Naples, where he became the leading Baroque architect. Trained as a sculptor, he also worked as a decorator and painter, and was interested less in planning than in decoration. His exuberant style is epitomized in the fantastic Guglia di S. Gennaro (1631–60), and in such effervescent façades as those of S. Maria della Sapienza (1638–41), S. Giuseppe degli Scalzi (*c.*1660), and his vast unfinished Palazzo Donn'Anna (1642–4). His earlier buildings are more restrained and elegant, e.g. the arcades of the Certosa di S. Martino above Naples (1623–31).

Blunt 1975; Wittkower 1982.

**Farrand**, Beatrix Cadwalader Jones (1872–1959). American landscape architect of independent means but no less professional in her outlook than her aunt, the novelist Edith Wharton. Her main work was the Dumbarton Oaks garden,

Washington, DC (1921–47), planned in an Italian Renaissance style but planted freely in the JEKYLL manner. Other private gardens included the Abby Aldrich Rockefeller Garden, Seal Harbor, Maine (1926–50), and, in England, part of the Dartington Hall garden, Devon (1933–8). She also laid out several US university CAMPUSES, notably Princeton (1913–41) and Yale (1924–47).

D. K. McGuire and L. Fern (eds.), *B.J.F. (1872–1959): Fifty Years of American Landscape Architecture*, Dumbarton Oaks, Washington, DC 1982; D. Balmor *et al.*, *B.F.'s American Landscapes*, New York 1985; J. Brown, *Beatrix: The Gardening Life of B.J.F.*, New York 1995.

**Farrell**, Terry (b.1938). English architect whose early, light-hearted TV-AM Building, London (1983), and elegantly Post-Modern-Classical Henley Royal Regatta Headquarters, Henley-on-Thames (1985), were followed by the dramatic and imposing large-scale development at Charing Cross, London (1990–93). The giant glazed railway shed arches and the seven to nine storeys of office space suspended above and insulated from the railway tracks successfully dominate the prominent site. His colourful Vauxhall Cross, Albert Embankment, London (1990–93), and J. Sainsbury's Supermarket, Harlow (1994), are equally remarkable on a smaller scale.

K. Powell, *T.F. & Co.*, London 1993.

**Fascia**. 1. A plain horizontal band projecting slightly from the surface of a wall or, more usually, in an ARCHITRAVE. In an architrave of the Ionic or Corinthian order two or more fascias over-sailing each other and sometimes separated by narrow mouldings are usual, *see* Figs. 51, 86. 2. A board or plate covering the end of roof rafters.

**Fatimid architecture**, *see* EGYPTIAN ARCHITECTURE.

**Fathy**, Hassan (1900–1989). Egyptian architect notable as a pioneer in the use of traditional materials and methods and for his sensitive adaptation of local vernacular styles. He became known internationally for his village of New Gournia near Luxor (1945–8), largely ADOBE built, of which he gave a full account in his influential book *Architecture for the Poor* (Chicago 1973). By then he had already built several remarkable small houses in or near Cairo, notably the Said House, el-Marg (1942), and the Nasr House (1945), followed by several others, e.g. Munastirili House (1950) and Stoppleare House, Luxor (1952). His housing complexes at Bariz in the Kharga Oasis (1964) and at Sidi Crier on the Mediterranean coast (1971) were never fully realized. Of his later work the Riad House (1973) and Samy House (1979), both in Cairo, should be mentioned, also the Presidential Rest House, Garf Hussein (1981), and the Villa Andreoli, Medinet el Fayoum (1984). He published *Natural Energy and Vernacular Architecture*, Chicago 1984. *See also* EL-WAKIL, Abdel Wahed.

D. Rastorfer, *H.F.*, London 1985; J. M. Richards (ed.), *H.F.*, Singapore 1985; J. Steele, *H.F.*, London 1988; K. Kaiser, *Architekten H.F.*, Stuttgart 1990.

**Faubourg**. A suburb or quarter of a medieval city outside the walls.

**Federal style**. A chronological rather than stylistic term for North American arts from the establishment of the Federal Government in 1789 to *c*.1830.

I. Craig, *The Federal Presence*, Cambridge 1984; W. Garrett, *Classic America. The F.S. and Beyond*, New York 1992.

**Fehling**, Hermann (1909–96), *see* GERMAN ARCHITECTURE.

**Fehn**, Sverre (b.1924), *see* NORWEGIAN ARCHITECTURE.

**Fellner**, Jacob (1722–80), *see* HUN-GARIAN ARCHITECTURE.

**Fenestration**. The arrangement of windows in the exterior walls of a building.

**Feng shui**. Chinese term (wind-water) for systems of auspicious planning of living spaces and tombs based on the belief that currents of vital spirit or 'cosmic breath' running through the earth influence human fortunes. The main principles, evolved before C3 BC and later elaborated with variations, range from simple rules for orientation (houses to face south and be protected from the west) and devices to deflect evil spirits, believed to travel in straight lines (masonry screens built inside court entrances), to the complex relationships of buildings to prevailing winds and the waters, hills and valleys of surrounding country. Although discountenanced in the People's Republic, Feng shui principles are still observed by Chinese communities elsewhere. A specialist advised on the siting and such matters as the angle of elevators in FOSTER's Hong Kong and Shanghai Bank. Some of Feng shui's basic principles are in accord with C20 Western environmental studies.

P. Waring, *The Way of F.S.*, London 1993; E. Lip, *F.S. Environments of Power*, London 1995.

**Fenoglio**, Pietro (1865–1927), *see* ITALIAN ARCHITECTURE.

**Feretory**. A shrine for relics designed to be carried in processions; kept behind the high altar.

**Fergusson**, James (1808–86), *see* ORNAMENT.

**Ferme ornée**. Literally an ornamental farm, a French term adopted in C18 England to describe a LANDSCAPE GARDEN incorporating farmland. The hierarchical relationship between garden or pleasure ground, orchard and agricultural land in the layout of an estate had been discussed in mid-C17 England by the agronomist Samuel Hartlib and his friends. From 1715 SWITZER advocated 'mixing the useful and profitable parts of gardening with the pleasurable', e.g. by surrounding arable fields, paddocks, vegetable plots, etc. with hedgerows of ornamental plants, describing such a combination as an 'ornamental farm' in 1713 and a *ferme ornée* in 1742. The most famous examples were Woburn Farm, Surrey, laid out by its owner Philip Southcote from 1735 – and far more ornamental than agricultural – the Leasowes, Warwickshire, laid out by its owner, the poet William Shenstone, in 1745–63. In France the term was first used in this sense by WATELET in 1774.

**Ferro-concrete**, *see* REINFORCED CONCRETE.

**Ferstel**, Heinrich von (1828–83), *see* AUSTRIAN ARCHITECTURE.

**Festoon**. A carved ornament in the form of a garland of fruit and flowers, tied with ribbons and suspended at both ends in a loop; commonly used on a FRIEZE or panel and also called a *swag*. See Fig. 52.

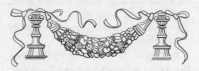

Fig. 52 Festoon

**Fielded panel**, *see* PANEL.

**Fieldstone**. The American word for RUBBLE.

**Figini**, Luigi (1903–84), and **Pollini**, Gino (1903–82). Figini and Pollini in 1926 established with TERRAGNI and a few others RATIONALISM or 'Gruppo 7', the first Italian group with an ostensibly modern programme. Their best-known works were done for Olivetti at Ivrea (headquarters building 1948–50). The church of the Madonna dei Poveri at Milan (1952–6) shows the development from the rational International Style of the thirties to the freer forms of the second half of the century. Of their later buildings, the church of SS. Giovanni e Paolo, Milan (begun 1966) may be mentioned.

C. Blasi, *F. e P.*, Milan 1963; V. Savi, *L.F. and G.P. Architects*, (1980) 1990.

**Figueroa**, Leonardo de (1650–1730), Spanish architect, the creator of the Sevillian Baroque style, was the first to make use of the cut-brick construction in white or yellow walls surrounded with red trim so intimately associated with the city. His style is rich in an abundance of glazed tiles, patterned columns, SALOMÓNICAS, ESTÍPITES, tassels, foliated brackets, undulating cornices, statues of saints and caryatids and mermen. All his works are in Seville: e.g. Hospital de Venerables Sacerdotes (1687–97); Magdalena church (1691–1709); Salvador church (1696–1711); and the very ornate west entrance to S. Telmo (1724–34). S. Luis, the richest and finest Baroque church in Seville (1699–1731), is usually attributed to him. His son Ambrosio (1700–1775) maintained his style in Seville (S. Catalina, 1732; chapel of the Cartuja, 1752–8; and Sacrament chapel in El Arahal, 1763–6), and the family tradition was carried on over the threshold of the neoclassical period by his grandson Antonio Matías (c. 1734–96?), who built the elegant campanile at La Palma del Condado (1780).

Kubler and Soria 1959.

**Filarete**, Antonio Averlino (c. 1400–1469). Italian architect who built little but played an important part in the diffusion of the Early Renaissance style. Born in Florence, he adopted the Greek name Filarete (lover of virtue) fairly late in life. He began as a sculptor and executed a bronze door for St Peter's (1443) in Rome. In 1451 he was commissioned by Francesco Sforza to build the Ospedale Maggiore in Milan, which he designed on a very elaborate symmetrical plan. He built only the first storey of the central block, a sturdy basement carrying an elegant Brunelleschian arcade, begun in 1456. While in Milan he completed his *Trattato d'architettura*, which VASARI called the most ridiculous book ever produced; it circulated widely in manuscript but was not printed until the C19. (A modern edition, edited by A. M. Finoli and L. Grassi, was published in Milan 1972.) Owing little to VITRUVIUS or ALBERTI, it is a highly original work written as a dialogue and inspired partly by Platonic philosophy, about which he seems to have learned from the Greek scholar at the Sforza court, Francesco da Tolentino called Filelfo. One of its novelties was the association of the Greek orders (he admitted neither the Tuscan nor the Composite) with the classes of society for whom buildings were intended. It also includes numerous designs for hopelessly impractical buildings and plans for two ideal cities, Sforzinda inland and Plousiapolis on the coast, which were to be blessed with every amenity, including a ten-storey tower of Vice and Virtue, with a brothel on the ground floor and an astronomical observatory on the top.

I. Patetta, *L'architettura del quattrocento a Milano*, Milan 1987; Onians 1988; F. Welch, *Art and Authority in Renaissance Milan*, London 1995; Heydenreich (1974) 1996.

**Fillet**. A narrow, flat, raised band running down a shaft between the flutes in a column or along an arch or a ROLL MOULD-

ING; also the uppermost member of a CORNICE, sometimes called a *listel*. *See* Fig. 53.

**Fingerplate**. A metal plate, rectangular or oval in form, fixed above and/or below a door handle to protect the door surface from finger marks.

**Finial**. A formal ornament at the top of a canopy, gable, pinnacle, etc.; usually a detached foliated FLEUR-DE-LIS form. *See* Fig. 36.

**Finlay**, Ian Hamilton (b.1925). Scottish poet, artist and designer of gardens who created from 1966 onwards a highly personal landscape garden on bare moorland at Stonypath (later called Little Sparta), near Dunsyre, south-west of Edinburgh. Inscriptions on stone in fine Roman lettering together with architectural fragments and other artefacts are interspersed among carefully sited trees and shrubs to create a uniquely allusive and evocative environment. In 1982 he transformed part of the grounds of the Kröller-Müller Museum, Otterloo, Holland, into a Sacred Grove of Five Columns by placing at the feet of five trees the circular stone bases of classical columns inscribed with the names of Corot, Lycurgus, Michelet, Robespierre and Rousseau. His other works include Stockton Park, Luton, Bedfordshire (1986–91), and the 'Stone Drums' entrance to the Harris Museum, Preston, Lancashire (1989).

Y. Abruoux, *I.H.F. A Visual Primer*, London (1985) 1992; P. Simig and F. Zdenek, *I.H.F. Works in Europe 1972–1995*, Ostfildern 1995.

**Finnish architecture**. Although Finland lies between Sweden and Russia, Eastern inspiration remained very sporadic right down to the beginning of the C19. The principal influence came throughout the centuries from Sweden and north Germany. Nothing exists that

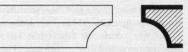

Fig. 53  Fillet

is older than the C13; the earliest buildings are village churches. Brick soon became the favourite material – apart of course from wood. In the village churches detail is elementary. The only large church is the cathedral of Turku (Åbo), which dates from the C14. Star vaults and ornamented brick gables came from Germany, detached wooden campanili (such as also exist in England) from Sweden. The extremely copious wall-paintings have their parallel in Sweden too.

Gothic plan types survived very long, and there is no Early Renaissance decoration. The turn to a classical style came only with the C17, and then again on Swedish patterns. The best early example is the manor house of Sarvlax of 1619, with giant pilasters already of a classical kind. Then in the late C17 the churches – being all Protestant – adopted cruciform and other central plans, again in connection with Swedish patterns (St Katharine, Stockholm). Wood, however, remained the favourite material.

The first climax of Finnish architecture came immediately after the country had become Russian. Helsinki was made the capital in 1812, and a plan for a new centre was made in 1817 (by J. A. Ehrenstrom). Thus C19 Helsinki is a planned town with streets as wide as in the Russian provinces and a large central square. The main buildings around this square are all the work of C. L. ENGEL. They are in a neoclassical idiom of mixed SCHINKEL and St Petersburg elements. They culminate in the cathedral of 1830–40. But even as late as 1848 a large church in the country was still built of wood (Kerimaki).

The second climax falls into the years between c.1850 and c.1910. They are the years of a national romanticism. Like Sweden, like Russia, like Hungary, Finland looked to a romanticized and very colourful past for inspiration. Alex Gallén, the painter, and of course Sibelius, are the best-known representatives of this trend. In architecture it is exemplified by the National Museum at Helsinki (1904–10) by Eliel SAARINEN, Armas Lindgren (1874–1929) and Hermann Gesellius (1874–1916), and Tampere Cathedral (1899–1907), by Lars Sonck (1870–1956). They are quite irregular in outline, use assorted motifs of the past freely and emphasize boldly local materials. Saarinen won the competition for the Helsinki railway station (1905–14) with a blend of a rational plan with motifs partly curvaceous and fantastical and partly (already) rectangular. The latter motifs come close to those used in the same years by OLBRICH and BEHRENS.

Finland achieved independence at last in 1917. AALTO was nineteen then and the much less known Erik Bryggman (1891–1955) twenty-six. A mere twelve years later Aalto had, with the Paimio Sanatorium and the Viipuri Library (Viipuri was taken away from Finland by Russia in 1940), achieved international fame within the current central European modern style. But Aalto was not just one of many. His strong personality had come through already by 1937, and in his work from 1947 onwards he is one of the leaders of a style of free curves, unexpected skylines, bold rhythms of glass and windowless walls. He liked to use timber and hard red brick. Side by side with him are others, first Bryggman, whose Cemetery Chapel at Turku of 1939 is as bold and novel as anything by Aalto himself, and then a younger generation led by Viljo Revell (1910–64; Toronto City Hall). The place to see the high

standard of recent Finnish architecture at its most concentrated is Tapiola outside Helsinki, a 'new town' of c.17,000 inhabitants, planned as a 'garden city' by Aarne Ervi (1910–77) and carried out from 1952 onwards with many buildings also by him (1962–74) and by Reima Pietilä (1923–93), whose Kaleva Church, Tampere (1959–66), and central buildings in Hervanta New Town, near Tampere (1979), were followed by the lavish palace and administrative complex for the Emir of Kuwait (1970–81). More recently the German Embassy, Helsinki (1986–93), and Mannisto Church, Kuopio (1986–92), both by Juha Leiviskä (b.1936); the extension to the Stockmann building, Helsinki (1984–9), by Kristian Valter Gullichsen (b.1932); Rovaniemi Airport (1988–92) and the Chancery of the Finnish Embassy, Washington, DC (1990–94), by Mikko Heikkinen (b.1949) and Markku Komonen (b.1945), are notable.

**Finsterlin**, Hermann (1887–1973), see EXPRESSIONISM.

**Fioravanti**, Aristotele (c.1415–86), see RUSSIAN ARCHITECTURE.

**Fire temple**. A Zoroastrian place of worship in which the sacred fire, symbol of the god Ahura Mazda, is kept alight, usually in a square open-sided pavilion with a domed roof supported on four columns and called a *chahar taq* (four arches). In Iran the remains of some fifty survive, probably dating from the Sassanian period (224–642) when Zoroastrianism was the state religion, e.g. at Yazd (still active) and Chak Chak. After the Muslim invasion in 651 some fire temples were converted into mosques by filling the opening on one side to make a QIBLA wall, e.g. at Qurva and Yazd-i Khast, and they appear to have provided the model for such Islamic buildings as the Mausoleum of the Samanids at Bukhara, Uzbekistan, and the domed prayer-halls of Iranian mosques. *See* Fig. 54.

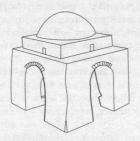

Fig. 54 Fire temple

**Fireproof construction.** In pre-C19 buildings masonry-bearing walls and arches were used to reduce the amount of wood and other inflammable material. When iron and steel frames were introduced in the C19 the metal was protected from fire by tile cladding or with concrete or plaster.

**Fischer**, Johann Michael (1692–1766), the most prolific of south German Rococo architects, built no less than twenty-two abbeys and thirty-two churches. Though less gifted than his contemporaries NEUMANN and ZIMMERMANN, he had great sensitivity to spatial relationships and could obtain monumental effects. His masterpiece is the Benedictine abbey church at Ottobeuren (1748–67), with a fine soaring façade and magnificently rich interior frothing with effervescent decoration. The smaller church at Rott-am-Inn (1759–63) shows a tendency towards greater restraint and provides a perfect setting for the statues by Ignaz Günther. Other works include St Anne, Munich (1727–39), on an oval plan; the abbey church at Diessen (1732–9); the church at Berg-am-Laim (1735–43); the Benedictine abbey at Zwiefalten (1741–65),

even larger than Ottobeuren and still richer inside; and finally, the Brigittine abbey church at Altomünster (1763–6).

Hitchcock 1958; N. Lieb, *J.M.F. Baumeister und Raumschöpfer im späten Barock Suddeutschlands*, Regensburg 1982; G. Dischinger and F. Peter (eds.), *J.M.F. (1692–1766) Werkverzeichnis*, Tübingen 1995.

**Fischer**, Karl von (1782–1820). German architect, the precursor of KLENZE in Munich where his Prinz Karl Palais (1803), the layout of the Karoliner Platz (1808) and the National Theatre (1811–18, rebuilt by Klenze 1823) are notable.

I. Springorum-Kleiner, *K.V.F. 1781–1820*, Munich 1982.

**Fischer**, Theodore (1862–1938). German exponent of an original late Rundbogenstil or neo-Romanesque as bold as RICHARDSON's, e.g. the church of the Redeemer, Munich (1899–1901), Garrison Church, Ulm (1908–12), University of Jena (1905–8). In a different vein his workers' village, Gmundersdorf, Reutlingen (1903–15), was a remarkable early garden suburb. Smooth and restrained are his museums at Kassel (1909–12) and Wiesbaden (1912–15).

W. Nerdinger, *T.F.*, Munich 1988.

**Fischer von Erlach**, Johann Bernhard (1656–1723), a leading Baroque architect in Austria, was more restrained and intellectual than his rival HILDEBRANDT, but also more courtly and traditional. Born near Graz, he began as a sculptor and stucco worker, then went to Italy probably in 1674 and perhaps received some training in architecture under Carlo FONTANA in Rome. In 1685 he settled in Vienna. There he was eventually appointed Court Architect in 1704. His first building of note is Schloss Frain in Moravia (1690–94), with an imposing oval hall. Italian influence, especially that of BORROMINI, is very evident in his three churches in Salzburg, the Dreifaltigkeitskirche (1694–1702), Kollegienkirche (1694–1707), and Ursulinenkirche (1699–1705). His masterpiece, the Karlskirche in Vienna (begun 1716), is a unique design with no antecedents and no successors, but his Roman memories are again quite explicit, notably in the opening theme of a Pantheon portico framed by a couple of Trajan's columns, expressive of his conscious striving after imperial grandeur. His secular buildings include the façade and monumental staircase, with its monumental ATLANTES, of the Stadtpalais of Prinz Eugen, Vienna (1695–8); the Palais Batthyány-Schönborn, Vienna (c.1700); the Palais Clam Gallas, Prague (1707–12); the Palais Trautson, Vienna (1710–16); and finally, the Hofbibliothek in the Hofburg, Vienna, which he began the year of his death (1723) and which was finished by his son Joseph Emanuel (1693–1742). This library is one of the most imposing interiors in Europe and illustrates his imperial manner at its grandiloquent best. He assumed the title 'von Erlach' on being knighted by the Emperor. His wide scholarship found expression in his *Entwurf einer historischen Architektur* (published Vienna 1721), which was the first architectural treatise to include and illustrate Egyptian, Chinese and Islamic buildings, and which thus exerted a great influence on various later architectural exoticisms.

H. Aurenhammer, *J.B.F. von E.*, London 1973; H. Keller (ed.), *F. von E., Entwurf einer historischen Architektur* (1721) 1978; Brucker 1983.

**Fisker**, Kay (1893–1965), *see* DANISH ARCHITECTURE.

**Flagg**, Ernest (1857–1947). American Beaux Arts architect. His Corcoran Art Gallery, Washington, DC (1892–7), was followed by his New York skyscraper the Singer Tower (1907, demolished 1968). The smaller Singer Loft Building, New York (1904), with its remarkable coloured terracotta, glass and metal façade, survives. His Flagg Court, Bay Ridge, NY (1933–6), is also notable.

M. Bacon, *E.F. Beaux Arts Architect and Urban Reformer*, Cambridge, Mass., 1986.

**Flagstone**. A large flat slab of sandstone or other rock capable of being split into 'flags' suitable for paving.

**Flamboyant**. The late Gothic style in France. In Flamboyant TRACERY the bars of stonework form long wavy divisions (*see* FRENCH ARCHITECTURE).

**Flank**. In military architecture, the side of a BASTION returning to the courtine from the face.

**Flashing**. Metal, usually lead or zinc, covering to protect and reinforce the angles of a roof and the joints between roof and chimneys, dormers, gables, etc.

**Flat**, *see* APARTMENT.

**Flat arch**, *see* ARCH.

**Flèche**. A slender spire, usually of wood, rising from the ridge of a ROOF; also called a *spirelet*.

**Flemish bond**, *see* BRICKWORK.

**Fleur-de-lis**. French for lily-flower; originally the royal arms of France.

**Fleuron**. A decorative carved flower or leaf.

**Flight**. A series of stairs unbroken by a landing.

**Flint work**, *see* KNAPPED FLINT.

**Flitcroft**, Henry (1697–1769). English architect, a protégé of Lord BURLINGTON, who procured him various posts in the Office of Works, where he eventually succeeded KENT as Master Mason and Deputy Surveyor. He was known as 'Burlington Harry'. Competent but uninspired, he was little superior to the 'imitating fools' who, according to Pope's prophecy, followed Lord Burlington's just and noble rules. His colossal east front at Wentworth Woodhouse, Yorkshire (c.1735–70), the longest façade in England, illustrates the empty pomposity into which PALLADIANISM declined: Woburn Abbey, Bedfordshire, is equally derivative (1747–61). His town houses are more successful, notably 10 St James's Square, London (1735). St Giles-in-the-Fields, London (1731–3), is an unflattering imitation of St Martin-in-the-Fields.

Summerson 1991; Colvin 1995.

**Floris**, Cornelis (1514/20–75). Primarily a sculptor and ornamentalist (*see* GROTESQUE) but also the leading MANNERIST architect in the southern Netherlands. He visited Rome c.1538. The tall, grave and classicizing Antwerp Town Hall (1561–6) is his masterpiece. Other notable works include the House of the German Hansa, Antwerp (c.1566), and the rood screen in Tournai Cathedral (1572). His style was widely diffused (and debased) by the engravings of Hans Vredeman de VRIES.

Tafuri 1966.

**Flötner** or **Flettner**, Peter (c.1485–1546). German Renaissance architect, sculptor, goldsmith, and an influential ornamental designer. He published at Nuremberg innumerable engraved designs for furniture, arabesques, etc. In 1518 he was working at the Fugger chapel in St Anna, Augsburg, and later travelled in Italy before settling in Nuremberg in 1522. His rather fanciful version of the Renaissance style can be seen in the fountain in the market-place at Mainz (1526), but his masterpiece as an architect was

the Hirschvogelsaal in Nuremberg (1534, destroyed), the earliest and perhaps most accomplished example of Renaissance domestic architecture in Germany.

Hitchcock 1981; M. Angerer, *P.F. Entwürfe*, Kiel 1984.

**Flowing tracery**, *see* TRACERY.

**Flush bead moulding**. An inset bead or convex moulding, its outer surface being flush with adjacent surfaces. *See* Fig. 55.

Fig. 55 Flush bead moulding

**Flushwork**. The decorative use of KNAPPED FLINT in conjunction with dressed stone to form patterns, such as TRACERY, initials, etc.

**Fluting**. Shallow, concave grooves running vertically on the SHAFT of a column, PILASTER, or other surface; they may meet in an ARRIS or be separated by a FILLET. If the lower part is filled with a solid cylindrical piece it is called *cabled fluting*. *See* Fig. 86.

**Flying buttress**, *see* BUTTRESS.

**Flying façade**. The continuation of the façade wall of a building above the roof-line, especially in Mayan architecture.

**Foil**. A lobe or leaf-shaped curve formed by the CUSPING of a circle or an arch.

The number of foils involved is indicated by a prefix, e.g. trefoil, multifoil. *See* Fig. 56.

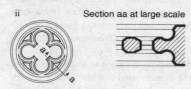

Section aa at large scale

Fig. 56 i. Detail of flowing tracery showing elaborate use of cusping. ii. Foil

**Foliated**. Carved with leaf ornament.

**Folly**. A costly but useless structure built to satisfy the whim of some eccentric and thought to show his folly; usually a tower or a sham Gothic or classical ruin in a landscaped park intended to enhance the view or picturesque effect. *See also* EYE-CATCHER.

**Fomin**, Ivan (1872–1936), *see* RUSSIAN ARCHITECTURE.

**Font**. A receptacle for baptismal water in a BAPTISTERY or church. Originally a large basin at floor level for immersion baptism, fonts became smaller when immersion baptism was abandoned. They then took the form of large bowls, often of bronze or stone, standing directly on the floor or supported by a pedestal.

**Fontaine**, Pierre-François-Léonard (1762–1853), French architect, the son and grandson of architects, became Napoleon's favourite architect and was largely responsible, with his partner PERCIER, for the creation of the Empire style. He studied in Paris under Antoine-François Peyre (1739–1823), then in Rome 1786–90. Percier joined him in Paris the following year, and they remained together until 1814. Their decorative style is well illustrated at Malmaison, where they worked for Napoleon from 1802 onwards, Joséphine's tented bedroom being completed in 1812. They extended the north wing of the Louvre to the Tuileries, and built the beautifully detailed Arc du Carrousel (1806–7) between the Tuileries and the Grande Galerie. Their joint works also include the rue de Rivoli, Paris (1801); the fountain in the Place Dauphine, Paris (1802); and much restoration and decoration at the royal *châteaux* (Fontainebleau, Saint-Cloud, Compiègne, Versailles) and at the Louvre, notably the Salle des Cariatides. Their influence spread rapidly throughout Europe mainly by means of their publications: *Palais, maisons, etc., à Rome* (1798) and especially their *Recueil de décorations intérieures* (1801). The most notable of Fontaine's independent works are the Chapelle Expiatoire, Paris (1816–26), the restoration of the Palais Royal, Paris (1814–31, including the Galerie d'Orléans (1825–34), a remarkable early shopping ARCADE), and the Hôtel-Dieu, Pontoise (1823–7).

M. L. Biver, *P.F., premier architecte de l'empereur*, Paris 1964; Braham 1980.

**Fontana**, Carlo (1638–1714). Italian architect, born near Como but settled in Rome *c.*1655. He began as assistant to CORTONA, RAINALDI, and BERNINI, working under the latter for ten years. His accomplished but derivative style is best seen in the façade of S. Marcello al Corso, Rome (1682–3), and in the many chapels he built in Roman churches: Cappella Cibo in S. Maria del Popolo (1683–7); baptismal chapel in St Peter's (1692–8). Less successful is the Jesuit church and college at Loyola in Spain. He restored and largely rebuilt SS. Apostoli, Rome (1702), and completed Bernini's Palazzo di Montecitorio, Rome, including the main entrance (1694–7). His secular buildings are undistinguished, e.g. Palazzo Spreti, Ravenna (1700), and Ospizio di S. Michele, Rome (1700–1703). By industry and perseverance he became undisputed leader of his profession in Rome and was largely responsible for the classicizing, bookish academicism into which the Baroque style declined. He had an enormous influence all over Europe through his numerous pupils, who included FISCHER VON ERLACH and HILDEBRANDT in Austria, GIBBS in England, and PÖPPELMANN in Germany.

A. Braham and H. Hager, *C.F. The Drawings at Windsor Castle*, London 1978; Wittkower 1982.

**Fontana**, Domenico (1543–1607). Italian architect, born near Lugano, settled in Rome *c*.1563, and became architect to Sixtus V (1585–90), under whom he laid the foundations of Baroque Rome (Vatican obelisk 1586, four streets radiating from S. Maria Maggiore). His *magnum opus* is the Lateran Palace in Rome (1586), followed by the Vatican Library (1587–9). He assisted Giacomo della PORTA in building the dome of St Peter's. In 1592 he settled in Naples, where he was appointed 'Royal Engineer' and obtained many large commissions including the Royal Palace (1600–1602).

Wittkower 1982.

**Fontana**, Giacomo (1710–73), *see* POLISH ARCHITECTURE.

**Footing**. The projecting base of a pier or wall. Continuous wall footings are a continuous projection below a wall, forming a base to distribute the wall's load. Single column footings are isolated bases below a pier.

**Forderer**, Walter-Maria (b.1928), *see* SWISS ARCHITECTURE.

**Forechurch**, *see* ANTECHURCH.

**Forestier**, Jean-Claude-Nicolas (1861–1930). French landscape architect. From 1887 he worked under ALPHAND in and around Paris, where he was to be employed until the end of his life: Bois de Vincennes (1887); Avenue de Breteuil (1900 onwards); Parc de Bagatelle (1905 onwards); Champ de Mars (1908–28). After Morocco became a French protectorate in 1912 he collaborated with Henri Proust (1874–1959) on plans for developing the main towns, leaving their old centres intact, with notable results, e.g. Fez. At the Exposition des Arts Décoratifs, Paris 1925, he was in charge of the exhibition of gardens by various designers, notably GUÉVRÉKIAN and MALLET-STEVENS. In Spain he laid out the subtropical Parque Maria Luisa, Seville, with much use of Islamic-style ceramics (1911), and the area round the hill of Montjuich, Barcelona, for the international exhibition of 1929–30 (preserved as a public park). In the Argentine the 8 km. (5 mile) Avenue Costanera along the river Plate was the only part of his design for Buenos Aires to be realized. His *Grandes villes et systèmes des parcs* (1908) has been republished with additional material by B. Leclerc, D. Imbert *et al.* (Paris 1997).

B. Leclerc (ed.), *J.-C.-N.F. 1861–1930. Du jardin au paysage urbain*, Paris 1990; D. Imbert, *The Modernist Garden in France*, London 1993.

**Formeret**. In a medieval VAULT, the rib

against the wall, known also as a *wall rib*.

**Formwork**. Commonly called *shuttering*, this is the temporary form that 'wet' concrete is poured into; it is constructed of braced timber or metal. When the formwork is removed, the concrete is found to have the texture of the material imprinted upon its surface. The formwork may be re-used if the type of construction is suitable, as in walls or repeating floor BAYS.

**Förster**, Christian Friedrich Ludwig von (1797–1863), *see* AUSTRIAN ARCHITECTURE; URBAN DESIGN.

**Fortalice**. A small fortification, often a tower only.

**Fortress**, *see* CASTLE.

**Forum**. In Roman architecture, a central open space usually surrounded by public buildings and colonnades: it corresponds to the Greek AGORA.

**Fosse**. A ditch or moat, whether dry or wet, used in defence.

**Foster**, Norman (b.1935). Leading English HIGH TECH architect. He was in partnership with Richard ROGERS as 'Team 4' until 1967. His work is notable for its crisp and clean elegance and the precision of its sophisticated engineering approach. He made his name with the serpentine, suspended, tinted solar glass skinned Willis–Faber–Dumas Insurance Offices, Ipswich, Suffolk, (1970–75), and the space-age hangar-like Sainsbury Centre for the Visual Arts, Norwich (1976–8). His brightly painted metal and glass Renault Distribution Centre, Swindon, Wiltshire (1980–83), led the way to a remarkable sequence of large-scale and often spectacular works: the Hongkong & Shanghai Bank Headquarters, Hong Kong (1979–86); Stansted Airport Terminal, Essex (1989–91); the ITN Headquarters, London (1989); the Century

Tower, Tokyo (1992); the Business Promotion Centre, Duisberg, Germany (1993); Faculty of Law Building, Cambridge (1993–5); Commerzbank Headquarters, Frankfurt-am-Main (1994–7); the Chek Lap Koh Airport Terminal, Hong Kong (1995–8); office building, Mühlheim, Germany (1996). But he can be equally effective and impressive on a small scale, e.g. the suavely elegant aluminium and concrete Médiathèque, Nîmes, France (1984–93), and the Sackler Gallery, Royal Academy, London (1989–91). He was knighted in 1990 and awarded the OM in 1997.

D. Sudjic, *N.F., Richard Rogers, James Stirling*, London 1986; A. Benedetti (ed.), *N.F.*, Bologna 1988; I. Lambot, *N.F. Buildings and Projects of Foster Associates*, London 1990; D. Treiber, *N.F.*, London 1995.

**Foundation**. 1. The supporting ground underneath a building. 2. The lower part of a structure which meets the ground and transfers all loads to it. Low-rise buildings usually have shallow foundations of reinforced concrete; high-rise buildings are often on deep foundations such as piles.

**Four-centred arch**, *see* ARCH.

**Fourier**, Charles (1782–1827), *see* COMPANY TOWN; URBAN DESIGN.

**Fowke**, Francis (1823–65). English engineer and architect notable for his Royal Albert Hall, London, designed 1864, with its great metal and glass dome and terracotta ornamentation. It was built 1866–71 after his death by Henry Young Darracott Scott (1822–83). Fowke's other buildings are notable as examples of Historicism: Royal Scottish Museum, Edinburgh (designed 1858, built 1861 onwards), and the Victoria and Albert Museum, London (designed 1860, built 1863 onwards), of which only a part, now the inner courtyard, survives, Lombard Early Renaissance in style.

J. Physick, *The V. & A. Museum. The History of Its Building*, London 1982.

**Foyer**. The vestibule or entrance hall of a theatre.

**Frame construction**, *see* FRAMED BUILDING.

**Frame house**. In the USA a sawn-timber house of FRAMED construction, usually covered with SHINGLES or WEATHERBOARDING. It appeared first on the East Coast in the C17 when European influence was strong, e.g. Boardman House, Sangus, Massachusetts (1868).

**Framed building**. A structure whose weight is carried by the framework instead of by load-bearing walls. The term includes modern METAL and REINFORCED CONCRETE structures, as well as TIMBER-FRAMED (half-timbered) buildings. In the former the frame is usually encased within a FACING (or CLADDING) of light material; in the latter the infilling may be of WATTLE AND DAUB, brick, etc.

**Francesco di Giorgio Martini** (1439–1501/2), Italian Early Renaissance theorist, wrote a treatise which, though not printed until the C19, exerted considerable influence, especially on LEONARDO DA VINCI, who owned a copy of it. He was born in Siena, the son of a poultry dealer, and trained as a sculptor and painter. In 1476 he moved to Urbino and entered the service of Federigo da Montefeltro, who employed him as a medallist and military engineer. He wrote *c.*1482 his *Trattato di architettura civile e militare*, based partly on VITRUVIUS (whom he translated or had translated) and ALBERTI, but showing a more practical attitude to the problems of architectural symbolism. Much of it is devoted to church planning: he produces a symbolic rationalization of the church with a long nave and centralized east end, and he also deals with the placing of the altar in a centralized church or tribune, stating the case for a central position to symbolize God's place in the universe, and for a peripheral position to symbolize his infinite distance from mankind.

His work as an architect is poorly documented. He probably contributed to the design of Palazzo Ducale, Urbino (perhaps the exquisitely beautiful loggia looking out over the surrounding hills). In 1485 he provided a model for the Latin cross church of S. Maria del Calcinaio, Cortona (completed 1516), a masterpiece of Early Renaissance clarity, harmony and repose. He also provided a design for the austerely simple Palazzo del Comune, Jesi (1486; but much altered). Many other works have been attributed to him: S. Maria degli Angeli, Siena; S. Bernardino, Urbino; and Palazzo Ducale, Gubbio. He was also renowned as a designer of fortifications and war machinery.

A. S. Weller, *F. di G.*, Chicago 1943; R. Papini, *F. di G.M. architetto*, Florence 1946; P. Rotondi, *Il Palazzo Ducale di Urbino*, Urbino 1950; F. P. Fiore and M. Tafuri (eds.), *F. di G. architetto*, Milan 1993; Heydenreich 1996.

**Francke**, Paul (1538–1615), *see* GERMAN ARCHITECTURE.

**Frank**, Josef (1885–1967), *see* AUSTRIAN ARCHITECTURE.

**Frater**, *see* MONASTERY.

**Fréart de Chambray**, Roland (1606–76), *see* LEMERCIER, Jacques.

**Freed**, James Ingo (b.1930). German-born American architect, trained in Chicago under MIES VAN DER ROHE and joined I. M. PEI as a partner in 1956. He was responsible for the design of the firm's New York Convention Center (1985) and, notably, the United States

Holocaust Museum, Washington, DC (1986–93). This remarkable building combines in uneasy harmony several contradictory currents in contemporary architecture, creating a work that is 'abstractly symbolic' without being scenographic. His Public Library, San Francisco (1992–6), followed.

**Freestone**. Any stone that cuts well in all directions, especially fine-grained limestone or sandstone.

**French architecture and landscape architecture**. For pre-Christian buildings *see* PREHISTORIC ARCHITECTURE; ROMAN ARCHITECTURE. The earliest Christian buildings, e.g. the baptisteries of Aix and Marseille Cathedrals, dating from the C5, are of the same Early Christian type as baptisteries of C5 in Italy. The origin of the plan types is Imperial Roman. Of the Merovingian period the two most interesting buildings are the so-called crypt of Jouarre near Meaux and the baptistery of St Jean at Poitiers. The former was not a crypt at all, but an attachment to a church. It was much changed in the C11 and C12, but the columns and the coarsely sub-Roman capitals are probably of the late C7. St Jean is also essentially of the C7, and still has a pediment of Roman descent, with a group of oddly triangular and semicircular windows. Chronicles tell us of more civilized and more Italo-Early Christian buildings (Tours, Clermont Ferrand, both C5) with aisles, columns, transepts and apses. Such buildings must have continued or been revived in the CAROLINGIAN age. However, nothing of any ambition has survived. Germigny-des-Prés is tiny, though with its central plan of Byzantine origin (via Spain?) interesting. The excavations of St Denis have revealed a building of Early Christian type there, with aisles, transepts and apse. It was consecrated in 775. In 790–99 Centula

(St Riquier) was built. All we know of it is deduced from texts and parallels with other buildings. It was of revolutionary novelty in plan and elevation, with a WESTWORK, nave and aisles, transepts, a chancel and an apse, and with towers of identical details, perhaps of timber, over the west as well as the east crossings. They were flanked by round stair turrets. The result must have been as proud and as lively as any of the later German Romanesque cathedrals on the Rhine.

The Romanesque style can be said to have started in the C10, when two new types of plans were evolved, both to become Romanesque standard and both devised to allow for the placing of more altars. One is connected with the second building of CLUNY Abbey, the centre of a much-needed monastic reform. This was consecrated in 981 and had chancel aisles flanking the east apse, and moreover apsidal chapels on the east sides of the transept. In contrast to this so-called staggered plan is the plan with ambulatory and radiating chapels which seems to have been derived from such a crypt as that of St Pierre-le-Vif at Sens and to have been adopted in the late C10 or anyway about 1000. Early examples are Tournus and Notre Dame de la Couture at Le Mans. The building to popularize it all over present-day France was, it seems, St Martin at Tours (begun after 997, now largely demolished). From here it became one of the distinguishing features of a small but important group of late C11 to early C12 churches in the country. They are or were St Martial at Limoges, St Sernin at Toulouse and to a lesser degree St Foy at Conques. Their other characteristics are transepts with aisles and, in elevation, galleries and tunnel VAULTS.

The vaulting of the main spaces of churches was a practical as well as an aesthetic need. A stone vault increases security against fire when a church is struck by lightning, and at the same time creates a spatial unity which a timber ceiling on stone walls can never achieve. Yet most French churches before the later CII had timber ceilings (St Remi at Reims 1005–49, Jumièges in Normandy c.1040–67, St Étienne, c.1060–81, and Ste Trinité, 1062–c.1130, at Caen). The great exception to the rule is St Philibert at Tournus in Burgundy, which has early CII vaults of such a variety and used in such a variety of ways that it appears to us a laboratory of vaulting. There are tunnel vaults longitudinal and transverse, groin vaults and half-tunnels.

Tournus has a separate forechurch or antechurch, two-storeyed, aisled and of three bays in depth. Such an antechurch, though single-storeyed, had already been done at Cluny and was repeated when in 1088 a new church was begun at Cluny. This was, with its antechurch and its two pairs of east transepts, to be the largest church of Europe, c.183 m. (600 ft) long. In elevation it differed from the Tours-Toulouse type. It had a blind triforium, clerestory windows and a pointed tunnel vault. Pointed arches are by no means an invention of Gothic builders. The details at Cluny and elsewhere in Burgundy show signs of an appreciation of the ancient Roman remains in the area. Autun Cathedral, consecrated in 1132, has much in common with Cluny. Vézelay (c.1104–32 and later) on the other hand is inspired by the Rhineland. It has no gallery or triforium and groin instead of tunnel vaults.

Tunnel vaults are the most usual system of vaulting in Romanesque France. The regions to which we must now turn have them as their norm. They are Auvergne (Clermont-Ferrand, Issoire), similar to the Tours–Toulouse type, but more robust in detail and built with the local volcanic materials, Poitou with HALL CHURCHES of steep and narrow proportions (the finest by far is St Savin-sur-Gartempe), and Provence (Arles, St Paul-trois-Châteaux), also tall and narrow but with clerestory lighting. Provençal churches are often aisleless. Where they have aisles, groin vaults or half-tunnels are used.

Exceptions are two regions, Normandy and the Angoumois and Périgord. The former was slow in taking to major vaulting. After the Conquest anyway the weight of Norman activity and ambition shifted to England, and here at the end of the CII rib vaulting was introduced, a technically superior form of groin vaulting (Durham). The churches of Caen took it over about 1115–20 in sexpartite forms. The Angoumois and Périgord on the other hand placed their faith in vaults of a different type, inspired, it seems, by Byzantium – either direct or via Venice. They kept away from aisles, and put on their solid outer walls domes on PENDENTIVES. Cahors, Angoulême and Périgueux are the foremost examples. Angers Cathedral, begun c.1145, is of this type too, but in its details it is unmistakably Gothic, though a Gothic deliberately different from that of the Royal France which was the Angevins' enemy.

The Gothic of Royal France, i.e. the Gothic sooner or later for most of Europe, begins at St Denis and Sens about 1140. It is characterized by the combining of pointed arch and rib vault into a system of great logic and structural ingenuity. St Denis moreover has an ambulatory and chapels of a suppleness which makes all Romanesque east ends appear elementary additions of separate parts. Both St Denis and Sens have two-tower façades. This motif which became a Gothic feature is derived from such Norman buildings as St Étienne at Caen, just as the rib vault with the sophisticated profiles of St Denis had its origin in Norman architecture.

St Denis also possessed the first of the Gothic figure portals, with column-like figures standing erect in the jambs. At St Denis they are not preserved, but they are at Chartres in the west front, where they date from c.1145–50.

The great Early Gothic cathedrals are Sens, c.1140; Noyon, 1145–1228; Laon, c.1160–c.1230; Paris, 1163–1250. They have the sexpartite rib vaults of Caen and show a development to higher proportions, thinner members, larger openings, and less inert wall. At Noyon and Laon CROCKET capitals begin to appear, a symbol of the resilience and freshness of the Early Gothic style. Noyon and Laon have four-tier elevations inside, i.e. galleries as well as triforia. This represents a quickening of rhythm and a further opening of the wall.

Chartres, as rebuilt from 1194, turned Early Gothic into High Gothic. Its quadripartite rib vaults, tall arcades, tall clerestory windows, flying buttresses and its replacement of the gallery by a low triforium band all convey a sense of greater coherence, a yet quicker rhythm and yet more open walling. The system created at Chartres was taken over for the rebuilding of the cathedrals of Reims (1211 onwards) and Amiens (1220–70), and the abbey church of St Denis (1231 onwards), with the scale and the daring of slender supports and large openings ever increasing, until Beauvais reached a height of c.48 m. (155 ft). Bar TRACERY started at Reims; so did naturalistic foliage, the convincing concomitant of the High Gothic mood. Of the major cathedrals of these years, only Bourges stands apart, a very individual synthesis of conservative Early Gothic with the most boldly High Gothic elements. The greatest subtlety and refinement but also a first step away from High Gothic clarity appear in St Urbain at Troyes of 1262 and St Nazaire at Carcassonne of c.1270.

The later C13 cathedrals built as a sign of the spreading of royal power to the south and the west followed the lead of Reims and Amiens. Only in a few provinces did regional features manage to hold their own. Thus Poitou and also Anjou persisted with hall churches, even if their proportions and their spatial feeling changed in the Gothic direction. In the south a type established itself, probably on a Catalan pattern, with high proportions and chapels between internal buttresses instead of aisles (Albi, 1282–1390).

The greatest part of the C14 in France was a period of less architectural progress and this changed only gradually after about 1375, when Flamboyant tracery began to establish itself – more than two generations after flowing tracery had become usual in England. The Flamboyant style, as the French call it, i.e. French Late Gothic, got a firm foothold only in the C15, although even then it remained more a matter of decoration than of plan and elevation. The richest province is Normandy (St Ouen, Rouen, and the west porch of St Maclou, Rouen, of c.1500–1514). Other notable examples are the church of Brou, Bourg-en-Bresse (1516–32) and the west front of Troyes Cathedral (c.1507) by Martin Chambiges (d.1532), who was master mason at Beauvais and Sens Cathedrals from 1490.

Castle building is first characterized by the KEEP or donjon, turning very early from square or oblong to round or rounded. In consequence of the experience of eastern fortification during the Crusades the keep was given up about 1200 and systems were designed instead where defence is spread along the whole CURTAIN WALL, which is sometimes doubled and has many towers. Shortly after 1200 (Louvre, Dourdan) this new system was occasionally regularized and made into a symmetrical composition of four ranges with angle towers round a square or oblong courtyard. In the course of the C15 the manor house or country house (Plessis-lès-Tours, 1463–72) began to replace the castle. The Flamboyant style created many splendid and ornate public and private buildings in the towns, such as the Law Courts of Rouen (1499–1509) and, the finest of all private houses, the House of Jacques Cœur at Bourges (1442–53).

The Renaissance arrived early in France, but in a desultory way. Italians were working in Marseille in 1475–81. Odd Quattrocento details in painting occur even earlier. They also appear in architectural decoration (Easter Sepulchre, Solesmes, 1496). The earliest example of a systematic use of Quattrocento pilasters occurs at the Château de Gaillon (1502–10). With François I full acceptance of such motifs as this is seen at Blois (1515–24) and in other *châteaux* along the Loire. The most monumental of them is Chambord (1519–47), a symmetrical composition with a square main building having an ingenious double-spiral staircase in the centre and tunnel-vaulted corridors to north, south, west and east with standard lodgings in the corners. The largest of the *châteaux* of François I is Fontainebleau (1528 onwards) by Gilles LE BRETON (d. 1553), and here, in the interior (Gallery of François I, 1532–40), Mannerism in its most up-to-date Italian form entered France (*see* Francesco PRIMATICCIO). At the same time gardens were laid out in the Italian style at Amboise, Blois, Gaillon and Fontainebleau. By the middle of the C16 France had developed a Renaissance style of her own, with French characteristics and architects. The most important of them were LESCOT, who began the rebuilding of the Louvre in 1546, and L'ORME. L'Orme introduced the dome and proved himself an ingenious technician as well as a creator of grand compo-

sitions (Anet, 1541–63). BULLANT at Écouen (1538–55) appears as L'Orme's equal. His use of giant columns, internationally very early, had a great influence on France.

The wars of religion shook France so violently that little on a large scale could be built. The palace of Verneuil (begun *c.*1568) was built slowly, while the palace of Charleval (begun 1570) was abandoned very soon. Both are by the elder DU CERCEAU, and both show an overcrowding of the façades with restless and fantastical detail. The typically French pavilion roofs make their appearance here. Another example of the restlessness of these years is the Town Hall at Arras (1510 onwards).

With Henri IV things settled down. His principal contributions are *places* in Paris, i.e. town planning rather than palace architecture. The Place des Vosges (1605 onwards) survives entirely, the Place Dauphine fragmentarily, and the Place de France, the first with radiating streets (an idea conceived under Sixtus V in Rome), was never built. The elevations are of brick with busy stone DRESSINGS, a style which remained typical up to about 1630 (earliest part of Versailles, 1624). Henri IV's ideas on *places* as focal points of monumental town planning were taken up enthusiastically under Louis XIV and Louis XV, and reached their climax in the Paris of Napoleon III (Louis XIV: Place des Victoires, Place Vendôme, layout of Versailles). Henri IV and his queen Marie de Médicis were also interested in landscape architecture and it was for them that J. BOYCEAU and C. MOLLET created the first PARTERRES DE BRODERIE, which remained a distinguished feature of French gardens for a century.

The leading architects under Louis XIV were at the start François MANSART and LE VAU, then PERRAULT and Jules HARDOUIN-MANSART. François

Mansart (like Corneille in literature and Poussin in painting) guided France into that classical style to which she remained faithful till beyond 1800, though it looks as if Salomon de BROSSE, the important architect under Louis XIII, had in his last work, the Law Courts at Rennes (begun 1618), preceded Mansart. Mansart is of the same fundamental importance in *châteaux* (Blois, 1635–8), town *hôtels* (Vrillière, begun 1635; Carnavalet, 1660), and churches. In church architecture de Brosse had started on tall façades crowded with Italian columns (St Gervais, 1623). Mansart toned them down to something closer to the Roman Gesù pattern, and he established the dome as a feature of ambitious Parisian churches (Visitation, 1632; Minims, 1636). His grandest church is the Val-de-Grâce, begun in 1645 and continued by LEMERCIER. But Lemercier had preceded Mansart in the field of major domed churches: his Sorbonne church with its remarkably early giant portico of detached columns was begun in 1635. Le Vau was a more Baroque designer than Mansart, as is shown by his liking for curves, and particularly for ovals, externally and internally. His first Paris house is the Hôtel Lambert (1642–4), his first country house Vaux-le-Vicomte (1657–61), with its domed oval central saloon, where Louis XIV's team of Le Vau, Lebrun (the painter) and LE NÔTRE appeared together for the first time. From 1662 Le Nôtre worked at Versailles, where he created the largest and grandest of French formal gardens, though his park at Dampierre (1675–86) is perhaps finer.

In 1665 Louis XIV called BERNINI to Paris to advise him on the completion of the Louvre. But Bernini's grand Baroque plans were discarded in favour of Perrault's elegant, eminently French façade with its pairs of slender columns and straight entablature in front of a long loggia (1667–70). The king's architect during Louis XIV's later years was Hardouin-Mansart. He was not a man of the calibre of the others, but he was a brilliant organizer, and it fell to him vastly to enlarge and to complete Versailles (1678 onwards). The magniloquent grandeur of the interiors is his but also the noble simplicity of the Orangery and the informal layout of the Grand Trianon (1690s). He also designed the truly monumental Dôme-des-Invalides (1680–91). In Mansart's office the Rococo was created by younger designers (e.g. Pierre LEPAUTRE) about 1710–15. It became essentially a style of interior decoration, notably in BOISERIES. Otherwise the difference between the C17 and C18 *hôtel* or country house is greater finesse and delicacy of detail, and a more cunning planning of cabinets and minor rooms, and a decrease in scale, e.g. additions to the Palais Royale, Paris (1717–20), by Gilles Marie Oppenordt (1672–1742); Hôtel de Matignon, Paris, by Jean Courtonne (1671–1739). BOFFRAND and de COTTE were both very influential in Germany. The most impressive major work of the mid-century is perhaps the planning and building of the new centre of Nancy by HÉRÉ (1752).

From the middle of the C18 onwards France turned to Classicism, first with some theoretical writings (Cochin, 1750, LAUGIER, 1753), then in actual architecture too. A moderate, still very elegant Classicism prevails in the work of GABRIEL (Place de la Concorde, 1753–75, Petit Trianon, designed 1761). More radical is SOUFFLOT's Panthéon (1757–90) with its exquisite dome (inspired by Wren's St Paul's) resting on piers of Gothic structural daring, its Greek-cross shape and its arms accompanied by narrow aisles or ambulatories, the separation from the arms being by columns carrying straight lintels. The last quarter of the C18 saw even more radical endeavours towards architectural reform. They were made mostly by young architects back from the French Academy in Rome. There they found inspiration not only in classical antiquity but even more in its bewitching interpretation by PIRANESI. One such was M.-J. PEYRE, whose influential (*Œuvres d'architecture* came out in 1765. But the most influential of all – BOULLÉE – had not been in Rome. His Hôtel de Brunoy of 1772 belongs to the earliest examples of the new simplicity and rectangularity. Others are the Mint (1768–77) by J.-D. ANTOINE (1733–1801), the Hôtel de Salm (1782) by Pierre Rousseau (1751–1810), and CHALGRIN's brilliant St Philippe-du-Roule of 1768–77. But Boullée's influence was exerted less by what he built than by drawings he made for a future book. They and LEDOUX's buildings at Arc-et-Senans and in Paris together with his published drawings represent a new radicalism of form and at the same time a megalomania of scale. Boullée's most influential follower was J.-N.-L. DURAND, not because of his buildings but because of the publications which came out of his lecture courses at the École Polytechnique. They were used abroad as much as in France (*see* e.g. SCHINKEL). Durand's two books were issued in 1800 and 1802–9. But the most successful architects of the years of Napoleon's rule were PERCIER and FONTAINE. In their works and in e.g. the Bourse (1807) by A.-T. BRONGNIART, the façade of the Palais Bourbon (1803–7) by Bernard Poyet (1742–1824) and the Madeleine (1804–45) by P.-A. VIGNON the style of Boullée and Ledoux became less terse and demanding and more rhetorical and accommodating. Side by side with this classical development from Revolution to Empire runs the development of Romanticism in the form of the *jardin anglais* and its furnishings. Examples are

the Bagatelle by BÉLANGER of 1778 and the part of Versailles where Marie-Antoinette's Dairy was built in 1782–6 by Richard MIQUE. In these developments RAMÉE's and WATELET's writings were influential as well as the latter's example at his own Park. Later at Malmaison and Compiègne BERTHAULT reintroduced formal areas with flowering plants for the Empress Josephine and Louis XVIII respectively.

The interaction between classical and Gothic went on in the C19. The grand chapel of Louis XVIII at Dreux was built classical in 1816–22, but enlarged Gothic in 1839. Ste Clotilde, Paris (1846–7), by F. C. GAU, is serious neo-Gothic; so is Notre Dame de Bon Secours outside Rouen (1840–47) by J.-E. Barthélémy (1799–1868), and in the 1840s also VIOLLET-LE-DUC began his highly knowledgeable if drastic restorations. Medieval scholarship reached its acme with his publications. Meanwhile HITTORF began St Vincent de Paul, Paris (1824), in a classical turning Early Christian. His later work is in a free Italianate, and in his two circuses of 1839 and 1851 he used glass and iron domes. The understanding among architects of what role iron could play was wider in France than in Britain. LABROUSTE's Ste Geneviève Library of 1838–50 is of a very pure, refined Italian Renaissance outside but has its iron framework exposed inside. Viollet-le-Duc in his *Entretiens* pleaded for iron, and already before their publication, in 1854–5, L.-A. BOILEAU had built St Eugène essentially of iron.

Concerning façades rather than structure, the French Renaissance was now added to the *répertoire*, first in the enlargements of the Louvre by Louis Visconti and H.-M. LEFUEL (1853 onwards), then in the façade of St Augustin by Victor BALTARD. The church (1862–71) again has iron inside. Shortly after, the full

Baroque triumphed in GARNIER's Opéra of 1861–75, a masterpiece of BEAUX ARTS architecture. Those less ready for lush displays now rediscovered the Romanesque (VAUDREMER, 1864 etc.; ABADIE, Sacré Cœur, 1874 etc.) and with this sparked off the style of RICHARDSON in America and with it the great rise of American architecture. Contemporaneously Paris was being transformed urbanistically by HAUSSMANN, whose improvements also involved ALPHAND as designer of public parks, assisted later by ANDRÉ, whose influence persisted into the next century through FORESTIER.

But while Paris remained leading in the development of iron and steel (Halles des Machines by DUTERT and Eiffel Tower, both for the exhibition of 1889), in architecture proper she produced nothing to emulate the English ARTS AND CRAFTS or the American CHICAGO SCHOOL. France came into her own again only about 1900 with the ART NOUVEAU structures of GUIMARD and its ART DECO and other derivatives by Henri-Frédéric Sauvage (1873–1932), and the pioneer designs of PERRET and Tony GARNIER. From them the way was open to the INTERNATIONAL MODERN of the 1920s in the hands of LE CORBUSIER, Robert Mallet Stevens (1886–1945) and André Lurçat (1894–1970) with which the 'Modernist' gardens of GUÉVRÉKIAN may be associated. Lurçat designed the villa Hefferlin, Ville-d'Avray (1932). His 1945 town plan for Maubeuge is remarkable, his residential complexes at St Denis (1952–8) less so. Jean PROUVÉ was the most interesting French experimenter in structure, together with Bernard ZEHRFUSS, who collaborated on the CNIT building (1958) and Unesco building (1958) in Paris with BREUER and NERVI.

The housing developments of Georges CANDILIS near Nîmes and on the south-east littoral should be mentioned, as well as those by AILLAUD outside Paris and, more recently, those by BOFILL at Montpellier and near Paris. The large-scale neo-Mediterranean vernacular resort town of Port Grimaud near St Tropez (1967–75) by François Spoerry (b.1912) is startling and was derided by Modernists as a fake fishing village. But in 1984 Spoerry was commissioned to design the New England vernacular Port Liberté in New York harbour. Outstanding among recent buildings in Paris – apart from the Centre Pompidou by PIANO and ROGERS – are the apartments 'Le Cour d'Angle' at St Denis (1982–3) by Henri Ciriani (b.1936), the Conservatoire de Musique (1984) by Christian de PORTZAMPARC, the enormous Institut du Monde Arabe (1987) by Jean NOUVEL, the layout and buildings of the Parc de la Villette (1985 onwards) by Bernard TSCHUMI, the Ministère de Finances, Paris (1983–9) by Paul Chemetov (b.1928) with B. Huidobro, and the new Bibliothèque Nationale (1992–6) by Dominique PERRAULT. Among younger architects to have become prominent may be mentioned ODBC or Decq et Cornette (Odile Decq, b.1953, and Benoit Cornette, b.1955), notable for their Banque Populaire de l'Ouest, Rennes (1989–90), and Valode et Pistre (Denis Valode, b.1946, and Jean Pistre, b.1951), whose Usine L'Oréal, Aulney sous Bois (1993), made their name. Outstanding also is the landscape architect Bernard LASSUS, both as a designer and a theorist. Jacques Simon (b.1930) is also notable, e.g. his Place Saint-John Perse, Reims.

**French window**, *see* WINDOW.

**Fresco.** A term often used loosely for all types of wall and ceiling painting, *see* MURAL PAINTING. Strictly it refers to that type in which the pigments are applied to fresh (*fresco*) lime plaster while it is still wet. The pigments, ground in water, are absorbed into the plaster and thus permanently fixed. Pigments applied later are said to be painted *a secco*. Of very ancient origin – known in rudimentary forms in Mycenaean Crete and Ancient Greece – the technique was perfected in Italy towards the end of the C13 by Giotto. Though used mainly for pictorial decorations on interior walls and ceilings, e.g. Michelangelo's Sistine Chapel ceiling, it was also used for exterior façades, e.g. by Giorgione in Venice (fragments in Ca' d'Oro, Venice). The latter are to be distinguished from SGRAFFITO decorations.

**Fret**. A geometrical ornament of horizontal and vertical straight lines repeated to form a band, e.g. a *key pattern* or *meander*. See Fig. 57.

Fig. 57 Fret

**Freyssinet**, Eugène (1879–1962). French architect and one of the leading CONCRETE designers of his generation. His fame rests principally on the two airstrip hangars at Orly (1921–3). They were of parabolic section, with a transversely folded surface and over 60 m. (200 ft) high. They were destroyed in 1944. Freyssinet also designed important concrete bridges, e.g. those at Plougastel (1925–30), Esbly (1946–50) and the St Michel bridge at Toulouse (1959). His Basilica Pius X, Lourdes (1956–8), should also be mentioned. He published *Une Révolution dans les techniques de béton* (Paris 1926).

G. Günschel, *Grosse Konstrukteure. F. – Maillart – Dischinger – Finsterwalder*, Berlin, Frankfurt, Vienna 1966; J. Fernandez Ordoñez, *E.F.*, Barcelona 1978.

**Friedberg**, Marvin Paul (b.1931). American landscape architect and urban planner working in New York. He made his name with urban playgrounds and recreational areas which differ strikingly from city parks in having predominantly hard surfaces (concrete or granite), subdivided into human-scale spaces at various levels linked by steps, with few if any trees or shrubs, e.g. Jacob Riis Plaza (1965), Camper Plaza (1967), Cadman Plaza (1970), River Plaza (1972), all in New York. For the city of Niagara Falls, NY, he laid out a tree-lined mall and – inside a vast 53 × 47 m. (175 × 155 ft) glasshouse designed by PELLI – a winter garden with pools and tropical plants. Also notable are his Pershing Park in Pennsylvania Avenue, Washington, DC (1979), the Transpotomac Canal Center, Alexandria, Virginia (1988), and the Olympic Plaza, Calgary, Alberta, Canada (1988). His partnership has also provided master-plans for large urban developments, e.g. Monroe Center, Grand Rapids, Michigan (1976), and the Central Business District, Poughkeepsie, NY (1979).

Lyall 1991; Walker and Simo 1994.

**Friedman**, Yona (b.1923), *see* URBAN DESIGN.

**Frieze**. 1. The middle division of an ENTABLATURE, between the ARCHITRAVE and CORNICE; usually decorated but may be plain. *See* Figs. 51, 86. 2. The decorated band along the upper part of an internal wall, immediately below the cornice.

**Frigidarium**. The cool room in an Ancient Roman bath, *see* THERMAE; the largest and most richly decorated, with the swimming-pool and gymnasium.

**Frisoni**, Donato Giuseppe (1683–1735). He was born at Laino, between Como and Lugano in northern Italy, and began as a stucco-worker. In this capacity he was employed in 1709 on the vast palace at Ludwigsburg, Germany. In 1714 he succeeded the previous architect there (Johann Friedrich Nette, 1672–1714) and became responsible for the final form of the palace with its imposing second CORPS DE LOGIS (1725–33) and the tre-foil-shaped Court church. He also designed the elegant small banqueting house, Favorite, on the hill opposite (begun 1718). But perhaps his major achievement is the town plan of Ludwigsburg, very unusual for its inte-gration of the palace and its garden with a regular system of streets.

Hempel 1965.

**Fritsch**, Theodor (1844–1931), *see* URBAN DESIGN.

**Frontal**. The covering for the front of an altar (*see* ANTEPENDIUM).

**Frontispiece**. The main façade of a building or its principal entrance BAY.

**Fry**, Edwin Maxwell (1899–1987). One of the pioneers in England of the INTER-NATIONAL MODERN of the 1930s. His early buildings were private houses, dat-ing from 1934 onwards. From 1934 to 1936 he was in partnership with GROP-IUS. The most important outcome of this is the Impington Village College, Cam-bridgeshire (1936). Of his later, post-war work done in partnership with his wife Dame Jane Drew (1911–96) and specializing in tropical architecture and design, the university and other buildings at Ibadan, Nigeria, and housing at Chan-digarh, India (1951–4), where he was senior architect with LE CORBUSIER, should be mentioned. He published with his wife *Tropical Architecture in the Dry and Humid Zones* (London 1966).

H. A. N. Brockman, *F., Drew, Knight, Cramer. Architecture*, London 1978.

**Fuchs**, Bohuslav (1895–1972), *see* CZECH ARCHITECTURE.

**Fuga**, Ferdinando (1699–1781), Italian architect, born in Florence and died in Naples. But his principal works are all in Rome, e.g. Palazzo della Consulta (1732–7), the façade of S. Maria Mag-giore (1741–3), and Palazzo Corsini (1736 onwards), in which his sophisti-cated Late Baroque style is seen at its elegant best. In 1751 he settled in Naples, where he received several important commissions (Albergo de' Poveri, Chiesa dei Gerolamini), but his early virtuosity had by then faded to a tame Classicism and his late works are notable mainly for their size.

Blunt 1971; E. Kieren (ed.), *F.F. e l'architettura romana del settecento*, exh. cat., Rome 1988.

**Fuksas**, Massimiliano (b.1944), *see* ITALIAN ARCHITECTURE.

**Fujii**, Hiromi (b.1935), *see* DECON-STRUCTIVISM.

**Fulcrum**. A support about which free rotation is possible or about which rotation occurs.

**Fuller**, Richard Buckminster (1895–1983). American engineer and inventor who, after working in a variety of com-mercial jobs, started work in 1922 on structural systems for cheap and effective shelter, light in weight as well as quick to erect. The first was his Dymaxion House project of 1927, intended for low-cost mass-production and derived from the techniques of aircraft and vehicle con-struction. (He used the term *Dymaxion* to describe his concept of the maximum performance per gross energy input.) He later developed a bathroom unit (1937), a circular aluminium single-unit *Dymaxion* dwelling known as the Wichita House, produced by the Beech Aircraft Corpor-ation at their Wichita factory (1945–6) and the Autonomous Living Package (1949). They were all notable contributions to INDUSTRIALIZED BUILDING. His main concern, however, was with covering large spans. The result was his GEODESIC DOMES developed after the Second World War. They were made by him on the SPACE-FRAME principle in many different materials: timber, plywood, aluminium, paper board, PRE-STRESSED CONCRETE, and even bamboo. The best-known are the Union Tank Car repair shop, Baton Rouge, Louisiana (1958) (with a diameter of 118 m. (384 ft)), the Climatron, St Louis (1960), the US pavilion at the Montreal Exhibition (1967), and the weather radome, Mount Fuji, Tokyo (1973). He also developed a system known as Tensegrity Structures, spatial skeletal structures utilizing distinct elements in compression and tension rods, the latter being joined together only via elements in compression.

He was an inspiring teacher and had wide and considerable influence especially in the USA but also elsewhere. He published *Ideas and Integrities. A Spontaneous Autobiographical Disclosure* (Englewood Cliffs, NJ 1963), *Intuition* (New York 1972) and *Critical Path* (New York 1981), and his writings were collected and edited by J. Meller as *The Buckminster Fuller Reader* (London 1970).

R. W. Marks and R. B. Fuller, *The Dymaxion World of B.F.*, Garden City, NY, (1960) 1973; J. Ward (ed.), *The Artifacts of R.B.F.*, New York 1985; L. S. Sieden, *B.F.'s Universe. An Appreciation*, New York 1989; M. Pawley, *B.F.*, London 1996.

**Fuller**, Thomas (1822–98), see CANADIAN ARCHITECTURE.

**Functionalism**. The theory best known from SULLIVAN's dictum that 'form follows function', i.e. that the form of a building can be derived from full knowledge of the purpose it is to serve, later extended to the proposition that an architect's primary aim should be to ensure that a building functions well and that nothing should interfere with its fitness to fulfil its purpose. Functionalism has a long history in architectural theory, notably in the C18 and C19 with CORDEMOY, LODOLI, DURAND and VIOLLET LE DUC and later with Otto WAGNER and Adolf LOOS. It culminated in the early C20 with MODERNISM when it was thought that the form which most closely follows function, as in the design of aeroplanes, is also the most beautiful.

E. R. de Zurko, *Origins of F. Theory*, New York 1957; J. M. Richards, *The F. Tradition*, London 1958.

**Furness**, Frank (1839–1912). A Philadelphia architect who for a short time employed SULLIVAN. Furness's style is very idiosyncratic, comparable in mood to that of TEULON and Bassett Keeling (1836–86) in England. It must be called Gothic, but all features are gross and some are original. The Provident Life and Trust Company, Philadelphia (1876–9; 1888–90, demolished *c.*1950), and the National Bank, Philadelphia (1883–4, demolished), were remarkable. The earlier Pennsylvania Academy of Fine Arts, Philadelphia (1872–6) survives.

Hitchcock 1977; J. F. O'Gorman, *The Architecture of F.F.*, Philadelphia (1973) 1987; G. E. Thomas, M. J. Lewis and J. A. Cohen, *F.F. The Complete Works*, New York 1991.

**Furttenbach**, Josef (1591–1667), see GERMAN ARCHITECTURE.

**Fusuma**. A sliding door or screen in Japanese architecture.

**Future Systems** (founded 1979), see ENVIRONMENTAL, GREEN OR SUSTAINABLE ARCHITECTURE.

**Futurism**. Italian *avant-garde* movement

launched in Milan in 1908 by the poet Marinetti and inspired by the dynamism of the modern city. The Futurists aimed to replace the culture of the past with a utopia based on the machine and new technologies. The leading Futurist architect SANT'ELIA issued a Manifesto of Futurist Architecture in 1914 but the First World War prevented the realization of its aims except on paper. His drawings and those of Mario Chiattone (1891–

1957) of 1912–14 created a remarkable vision of the metropolis of the future, complete with multi-level highways and flyovers amid stepped-back skyscrapers. However, Futurism came to an end in 1916 and an attempt to revive it after the war foundered in its alliance with Fascism.

M. W. Martin, *F. Art and Theory*, New York (1968) 1977; C. Tisdall and A. Bozzola, *F.*, London/New York 1977.

# G

**Gabetti**, Roberto (b.1925). Italian architect in partnership since 1950 with Aimano d'Isola Oreglia (b.1928) in Turin. They made their name with the playfully 'neo-Liberty' Bottega di Erasmo Bookshop, Turin (1953–4), and went on to develop more innovative designs and concepts in such works as the Società Ippica Torinese, Nicholino, Turin (1959–60); Olivetti residential complex, Ivrea (1969–70); Conca Bianca condominium, Sestrière (1976–9); the experimental solar-heated Orbessano apartments, Turin (1982–5), which were used as a case study for the EC's Project Monitor in 1987; the Carmelite monastery, Quart, Val d'Aosta (1984–9), and the SNAM offices and gardens, San Donato, Milan (1985–91).

F. Cellini and C. Donato, *G. & I. Progetti e architetture 1950–1985*, Milan 1985; P. Zermani, *G. & I.*, Bologna 1989; C. Olmo, *G. & I.*, Turin 1993; F. Dal Co (ed.), *G. & I. Architetture*, Milan 1995.

**Gable**. The triangular upper portion of a wall at the end of a pitched roof corresponding to a pediment in classical architecture. It can be used non-functionally, e.g. on the portal of a Gothic cathedral. It normally has straight sides, but there are variants. A crow-stepped or corbie-stepped gable has stepped sides. A Dutch gable (characteristic of *c.*1630–50) has curved sides crowned by a pediment (*see* Fig. 58). A hipped gable has the uppermost part sloped back. A shaped gable (characteristic of *c.*1600–1650) has multi-curved sides (*see* Fig. 58).

**Gable roof**, *see* ROOF.

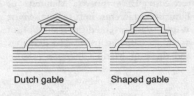

Dutch gable    Shaped gable

Fig. 58 Gable

**Gablet**. A decorative motif in the form of a small gable, as on a buttress, above a niche, etc. For gablet roof, *see* ROOF.

**Gabriel**, Ange-Jacques (1698–1782). The greatest C18 architect in France and perhaps in Europe. His genius was conservative rather than revolutionary: he carried on and brought to its ultimate perfection the French classical tradition of François MANSART, by-passing, as it were, the Rococo. He resembled his great contemporary CHARDIN in his solid unostentatious good taste, which reached its highest pitch of refinement in small intimate buildings such as his Hermitage or Pavillon de Pompadour at Fontainebleau (begun 1749) and in his great masterpiece, the Petit Trianon in the park at Versailles (designed 1761, built 1762–4). His father was a successful architect, Jacques Gabriel (1667–1742), who built several good Parisian *hôtels*, notably the Hôtel Peyrenc de Moras (1723–4), the Place Royale at Bordeaux (1731–55) and the two palaces at Rennes (1731–62), the former a masterpiece of Rococo urbanism. His Palais des États, Dijon (1731–6), is also notable. In 1735 he succeeded de COTTE as Premier Architecte and Director of the Academy. Ange-

Jacques Gabriel was trained in Paris under his father and never went to Italy. He worked under and with his father for the Crown, and in due course succeeded him as Premier Architecte. In this position he built exclusively for the king, Louis XV, and Mme de Pompadour. Additions and alterations to the various royal palaces – Fontainebleau, Compiègne, Versailles – took up most of his time. They were sometimes Rococo to match existing work. His theatre and the projected reconstruction of the Marble Court at Versailles are extremely elegant. His largest commissions outside Versailles were for the École Militaire, Paris (1768–73), and the layout of the Place de la Concorde, Paris (1753–75); while the two great palaces (Hôtel de Crillon and Ministère de la Marine, 1757–75) flanking his rue Royale – their façades with screens in the style of PERRAULT's great east front of the Louvre – are his most successful buildings on the monumental scale. The Pavillon Français, Versailles (1750), the small hunting-boxes or Pavillons de Butard (1750) and de la Muette (1753–4) and the Petit Château at Choisy (1754–6) foreshadow the civilized intimacy of his masterpiece. The Petit Trianon may owe something to the sober dignity of English PALLADIANISM, but the extreme elegance and refinement of this perfectly proportioned cubical composition is wholly French and achieves a serenity and distinction different in kind and quality from any other contemporary building.

C. Tadgell, *A.-J.G.*, London 1978; Braham 1980; M. Gallet and Y. Bottineau, *Les G.*, Paris 1982; Kalnein 1995.

**Gadrooned**. Decorated with convex curves; the opposite of fluted (*see* FLUTING).

**Gahura**, Frantisek Lydia (1891–1958), *see* COMPANY TOWN.

**Galilee**. A large porch, vestibule or occasionally a chapel, originally for penitents and usually at the west end of a church. Sometimes called a NARTHEX or PARADISE.

**Galilei**, Alessandro Maria Gaetano (1691–1737), born in Florence and trained there, went to England in 1714–19 (designed Castletown, Co. Kildare, Eire, built by PEARCE 1722, and the portico for Kimbolton Castle, 1718–19). In 1731 he won the competition for the façade of S. Giovanni in Laterano, Rome, with a somewhat tight and severely classical design (executed 1733–6). He also designed the Corsini Chapel there (1732–5) and the façade of S. Giovanni dei Fiorentini, Rome (1734).

Wittkower 1982.

**Gallery**. In church architecture, an upper storey over an aisle, opening on the nave. Also called a *tribune* and often, wrongly, a TRIFORIUM. A *false gallery* is a middle storey comparable in height to a gallery but opening into the roof space over the aisles without external windows. Found as an exterior feature with continuous small open ARCADING in medieval Italian and German churches, and sometimes called a DWARF GALLERY.

In secular architecture: 1. A platform or mezzanine supported on columns or brackets and overlooking the main interior space of a building, e.g. a theatre. 2. A long room, often on an upper floor, for recreation or entertainment and sometimes used for the display of paintings, etc. (hence the modern term 'art gallery'). In England such rooms were often called 'long galleries'. The most famous is the Galerie des Glaces, Versailles (begun 1678), widely copied in palace architecture. 3. In Italy a shopping ARCADE is called a *galleria*.

**Galleting**. Inserting into mortar courses,

while still soft, small pieces of stone, chips of flint, etc., sometimes for structural but usually for decorative reasons.

**Galli da Bibiena**. The leading family of QUADRATURA painters and theatrical designers in early C18 Italy. They came from Bibiena near Bologna. Several members of the family were spirited draughtsmen and accomplished painters of *trompe l'œil* architecture; a few were architects as well. Ferdinando (1657–1743) designed the church of S. Antonio Abbate, Parma (1712–16), with a very effective double dome. In 1711 he published his important *L'architettura civile preparata sulla geometria e ridotta alle prospettive*. His brother Francesco (1659–1731) became the greatest designer of theatres and established a long-surviving tradition. His main theatres (only partly surviving) are the Opera House, Vienna, and theatres of Nancy, Verona (Teatro Filarmonico) and Rome (Teatro Aliberti, 1720). One of Ferdinand's sons, Giuseppe (1696–1757), worked as a theatrical designer in Vienna and in Dresden (1747–53) and in 1746–8 designed the wonderfully rich interior of the theatre at Bayreuth; while another son, Antonio (1700–1774), designed several theatres in Italy, of which only four survive: Teatro Rinnovati, Siena (1753); Teatro Comunale, Bologna (1756–63), Teatro Scientifico, Palazzo dell'Accademia Virgiliana, Mantua (begun 1767), and Teatro Lauro Rossi, Macerata (executed by C. Morelli). Antonio also built the chapel in the Immacolata, Sabbioneta (*c*.1770), with a remarkable dome decorated internally with an open, detached network of stucco ornamentation. A third son, Alessandro (1686–1748), became Architect-General to the Elector Palatine in Mannheim, where he built the opera house (1737, destroyed) and began the fine Jesuit church (1738–56). The very

elaborate stage designs by members of the family may have exerted some influence on JUVARRA and PIRANESI.

H. A. Mayor, *The B. Family*, New York 1945; Wittkower 1982.

**Gallo**, Francesco (1672–1750). Italian architect working in Piedmont. He completed VITOZZI's pilgrimage church at Vicoforte, adding the enormous and spectacular dome (begun 1728). His ingeniously planned Sant'Ambrogio, Cuneo (1703–43), the Jesuit College, Mondovì (begun 1713, now the Palazzo di Giustizia) and S. Filippo, Mondovì (1734–50), S. Croce and S. Bernardino, Cavallermaggiore (1737–43), should also be mentioned.

Pommer 1967.

**Gambello**, Antonio (d.1481), *see* CODUSSI, Mauro.

**Gambrel roof**, *see* ROOF.

**Gameren**, Tylman van (d.1706), *see* TYLMAN VAN GAMEREN.

**Gandon**, James (1743–1823). English architect, a pupil of CHAMBERS, he became the leading neo-classical architect in Dublin. He was of French Huguenot descent and his work is sometimes surprisingly advanced and close to his *avant-garde* French contemporaries, e.g. Nottingham County Hall (1770–72), of which the façade survives. In 1781 he went to Dublin to supervise the construction of the Custom House on the Liffey (completed 1791, interior destroyed 1921). But his masterpiece is the Four Courts, also on the Liffey (1786–1802, interior destroyed 1922), where he took over from Thomas Cooley (1740–84). Also in Dublin are his portico of the Bank of Ireland (1785) and the King's Inns (begun 1795 but later enlarged). He published, with J. Woolfe, two supplementary volumes to *Vitruvius Britannicus* in 1769 and 1771.

E. McParland, *J.G. Vitruvius Hibern-*

*icus*, London 1985; Summerson 1991; Colvin 1995.

**Ganghofer**, Jorg (d.1488), *see* GERMAN ARCHITECTURE.

**Garbhagriha**. The small unlit shrine in a Hindu temple.

**Gardella**, Ignazio (b.1905). Italian architect who, though not a member of Gruppo 7 or MIAR, combined in his early work their RATIONALISM with traditional and even vernacular elements, e.g. the Anti-Tuberculosis Dispensary, Alessandria (1936–8). This fusion was realized again in his immediate post-Second World War works such as his apartments for Borsalino, Alessandria (1950–51), and the Casa alle Zattere, Venice (1953–8). Among his later works the S. Enrico a Bolgiano church, Metanopoli, Milan (1962–6), is notable, as are also the Alfa Romeo office building, Arese (1969); the Architectural Faculty Building, Genoa (1975–90); the Teatro Carlo Felice, Genoa (1982–91 with Aldo ROSSI), and the Esselunga Office Building, Sesto Fiorentino (1991–3).

G. C. Argan, *I.G.*, Milan 1959; P. Zernani, *I.G.*, Rome 1991; J. Rykwert intro., *I.G.*, Heinz Gallery, London 1994.

**Garden city and garden suburb**. The garden city scheme, conceived by Ebenezer HOWARD in 1898, was first translated into reality at Letchworth (begun 1903) by Raymond UNWIN and Barry PARKER, in the form of English cottages within an arcadian setting of trees, gardens and winding roads. It had been foreshadowed by their New Earswick Model Village, York, begun the previous year. The first garden suburbs in England were Bedford Park, London (begun 1877, by Norman SHAW), Port Sunlight (1888 onwards) and Bourneville, Birmingham (mainly 1893 onwards), but the finest English specimen is the Hampstead

Garden Suburb in London, started in 1906. In Germany the most interesting garden city is that planned by Richard RIEMERSCHMID and Heinrich TESSENOW in 1907 at Hellerau near Dresden (begun in 1909), though Theodor FISCHER's Gmindersdorf, Reutlingen (1903–15), should be mentioned as well as MUTHESIUS's Neudorf, Strasbourg (1912–14), and Ernst MAY's Römerstadt, Frankfurt (1926–8). In Belgium the Kappeleveld garden suburb, Woluwe, was laid out in 1922 by Louis Van der Swaelman (1883–1929), whose Boitefort and Cité Floreal, Brussels, are also notable. Howard's garden city programme was later taken up by Clarence STEIN in the USA. See Fig. 59. *See also* COMPANY TOWN; NEW TOWNS; RADBURN PLANNING.

G. Benoit-Lévy, *La Cité-jardin*, Paris 1904; W. L. Creese, *The Search for Environ-*

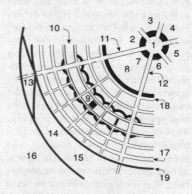

1. Garden
2. Museum and gallery
3. Hospital
4. Library
5. Theatre
6. Concert hall
7. Town hall
8. Central park
9. School
10. Grand Avenue
11. Boulevard Columbus
12. Boulevard Newton
13. Railway station
14. Allotments
15. Dairy farms
16. Large farms
17. First Avenue
18. Fifth Avenue
19. Railway line

Fig. 59 Garden city (after Howard 1898)

ment. *The G.C.: Before and After*, London and New Haven (1960) 1966, Baltimore 1992; R. Fishman, *Urban Utopias in the Twentieth Century*, New York 1977; K. P. Arbold, *Gartenstadt. Vom Sofakissen zum Stadtebau. Die Geschichte der Deutschen Werkstatten und der Gartenstadt Hellerau*, Dresden 1991; S. V. Ward (ed.), *The G.C. Past, Present and Future*, London 1992.

**Garderobe**. Wardrobe. Also the medieval name for a lavatory.

**Gargoyle**. A water spout projecting from a roof, or the PARAPET of a wall or tower, and carved into a grotesque figure, human or animal.

**Garner**, Thomas (1839–1906), *see* BODLEY.

**Garnier**, Jean-Louis-Charles (1825–98). A French architect, he won the Grand Prix of the Academy in 1848, and went to Rome in the same year and to Athens in 1852. Back in Paris in 1854, he worked under BALLU. In 1861 he won the competition for the Opéra, and the building was completed in 1875. Prominently placed in one of HAUSSMANN's many grand *points de vue*, it is the most splendid incarnation of the Second Empire and a masterpiece of the BEAUX ARTS STYLE. The exterior, the ample staircase, the glittering foyer are frankly Baroque, and openly endeavour to beat the Baroque at its own game. At the same time Meyerbeer, Wagner, Verdi could not be heard in more sympathetic surroundings, since the building is most intelligently planned for its particular purpose of combining a setting for opera with a setting for social display. The same is true, in its own intentionally more meretricious way, of the Casino at Monte Carlo (1879–85), which had great influence in Europe on lighthearted resort architecture. Garnier's own villa at Bordighera (1874), with its asymmetrically placed tower, is Italianate and not Baroque.

M. Steinhauser, *Die Architektur der Pariser Oper*, Munich 1970; A. Drexler (ed.), *The Architecture of the École des Beaux-Arts*, New York 1972; C. C. Mead, *C.G.'s Paris Opera. Architectural Empathy*, Cambridge, Mass., 1992; F. Patureau, *Le Palais Garnier dans la société parisien 1875–1914*, Munich 1992.

**Garnier**, Tony (1869–1948). French architect and urban designer, who won the Prix de Rome in 1899 and spent much of his time not measuring and studying ancient buildings, but working on the designs for a Cité Industrielle. These designs were submitted in 1904, exhibited, and finally published in 1917. They represent a completely new approach to town planning, in radical opposition to the academic principles of town planning as taught by the École des Beaux Arts, principles of symmetry and imposed monumentality. Garnier instead gave himself a site that was imaginary and yet realistic, since it resembled the country near his native Lyon: he decided that his town should have 35,000 inhabitants, located industry, railway lines, station, town centre and housing, and related them rationally to each other. Moreover, he proposed that all the buildings should be made essentially of CONCRETE. He designed small houses of quite novel cubic simplicity placed among trees, and some major buildings with the large CANTILEVERS which REINFORCED CONCRETE had just begun to make possible, with glass and concrete roofs, etc. In 1905 Garnier was called by the newly elected mayor, Édouard Herriot, to Lyon to be municipal architect. He built the slaughterhouse in 1909–13, the stadium in 1913–16 and laid out the Quartier des États Unis, 1920–35.

D. Wiebenson, *T. G. The Cité Industri-*

*elle*, London 1969; Hitchcock 1977; R. Jullian, *T.G. (1869–1948). Utopiste et constructeur*, Paris 1987; A. Gerihex and O. Cinqualle (eds.), *T.G. L'œuvre complète*, Paris 1989.

**Garth**. A medieval term for an enclosed area, usually a garden enclosed by cloisters in a monastery.

**Gärtner**, Friedrich von (1792–1847). German architect, the son of an architect, studied at the Munich Academy, then for a short time with WEINBRENNER, and after that in Paris with PERCIER and FONTAINE. In 1815–17 he was in Italy, and in 1818–20 in Holland and England. After that he held a chair at the Munich Academy. On a second journey to Italy in 1828 he was introduced to King Ludwig I of Bavaria, and from then was, side by side and in competition with KLENZE, the king's favourite architect. Gärtner's speciality was what the Germans call the RUNDBOGENSTIL, the style of round arches, be they Italian Romanesque or Italian Quattrocento: it is said that it was King Ludwig rather than Gärtner who favoured this post-classical style. In Munich Gärtner built the Ludwigskirche (1829–40), the State Library (1831–40), and the University (1835–40), all three in the Ludwigstrasse, and at its south end the Feldherrenhalle, a copy of the Loggia dei Lanzi in Florence (1840–44) and an essay in the Tuscan Gothic. In 1835–6 Gärtner was in Athens, where he designed the palace of the new king, a son of Ludwig. In 1839 he was commissioned by Ludwig I of Bavaria to design the Pompeiian House at Aschaffenburg (1841–8).

O. Hederer, *F. von G. (1792–1847). Leben-Werk-Schüler*, Munich 1976; Hitchcock 1977; W. Nerdinger (ed.), *F. von G., Ein Architekenleben 1791–1847*, Munich 1992.

**Gau**, Franz Christian (1790–1853). German architect, born in Cologne, went to Paris in 1810, and in 1815 with a Prussian grant to Rome, where he became a friend of the Nazarenes (Overbeck, Cornelius, etc.). In 1818–20 he was in Egypt and Palestine, but returned to Paris in 1821. Gau was more widely known during his lifetime as an Egyptian scholar than as an architect. Yet his Ste Clotilde (1846–57; completed by BALLU) is the one outstanding neo-Gothic church in Paris. The style is a rich High Gothic, the façade has two towers with spires like St Nicaise at Reims, and the roof construction is of iron.

Hitchcock 1977.

**Gaudí y Cornet**, Antonio (1852–1926), Spanish architect, born at Reus (Tarragona), where his father was a coppersmith and pot- and kettle-maker. So he grew up acquainted with metals, and it is not surprising that the savagery of his ornamental invention appeared first in metal railings and gates. Nor was the architecture of the building for which these were designed – the Casa Vicens at Barcelona – tame or imitative in the sense of C19 Historicism. The house, built in 1878–80, is in fact a nightmarish farrago of Moorish and Gothic elements; indeed, Moorish and Gothic – and in addition, it seems, Moroccan – are the sources of Gaudí's style. The Casa Vicens was followed in 1883–5 by El Capricho, a house at Comillas in northern Spain – equally crazy and less dependent on any past style.

In 1883 Gaudí was put in charge of the continuation of a large church in Barcelona, the Sagrada Familia, begun as a conventional neo-Gothic building. He did the crypt in 1884–91 and began the transept façade in 1891. By then he had been taken up by Count Güell, an industrialist who remained his faithful patron.

His town house, the Palacio Güell (now a theatre museum), dates from 1885–9, and here there first appeared the parabolic arches and the wild roof excrescences which were to become part of Gaudí's repertoire. But far more fiercely extravagant than anything he or any architect had done before were the designs for the chapel of Sta Coloma de Cervelló which Gaudí began to build in 1889 for one of Count Güell's estates: it was never completed. It has an entirely free, asymmetrical, jagged plan, with pillars set at a slant, warped vaults, an indescribable interplay of exterior and interior, and ostentatiously crude benches. For the Parque Güell, a park at Barcelona, begun in 1900, similar motifs were used, and in addition the snakily undulating back of a long seat running along the sides of a large open space was faced with bits of broken tile and crockery in arbitrary patterns as effective as any invented by Picasso (who lived at Barcelona during these very years, 1901–4).

In 1903 Gaudí began the upper part of the transept of the Sagrada Familia. The lower part had gradually reached an ever freer interpretation of Gothic motifs, but the turrets at the top defeated comparison with anything architectural from the past or the present. Instead, comparisons with termite hills or with crustaceous creatures come at once to mind. The ceramic facing is similar to that in the Parque Güell. Aesthetically as surprising and socially more so than any earlier building are Gaudí's two blocks of luxury flats, the Casa Batlló and the Casa Milá (both begun 1905); for here was acceptance by wealthy Barcelonians of Gaudí's unprecedented architecture. The façades undulate, rise and fall, and are garnished with fantastical top excrescences and sharp, piercing, aggressive wrought-iron balconies. Moreover, the rooms have no straight walls, no right angles. The principles

behind ART NOUVEAU (see HORTA; MACKINTOSH; MACKMURDO; van de VELDE), usually confined to decoration and mostly two-dimensional decoration, could not well be pushed to a further architectural extreme. But see SPANISH ARCHITECTURE.

G. R. Collins, A.G., London 1960; E. Casanelles, A.G. A Reappraisal, New York 1967; R. Descharnes and C. Prévost, G. the Visionary, New York (1969) 1971; O. Bohigas, Arquitectura Modernista, Barcelona, Barcelona (1968) 1973; G. R. Collins and J. Bassegoda-Nouelle, The Designs and Drawings of A.G., Princeton 1983; C. Kent and D. Prindle, Park Güell, New York 1992.

**Gazebo**. A small look-out tower or summerhouse with a view, usually in a garden or park but sometimes on the roof of a house; in the latter case it is also called a *belvedere*.

**Geddes**, Sir Patrick (1854–1932). If Raymond UNWIN was the greatest British urban designer of his day in practice, Geddes was the greatest in urban design theory, a theory which he established in the present much-widened sense of the word, with emphasis laid on the necessity of preliminary surveys, on 'diagnosis before treatment', and on the dependence of acceptable urban design on sociological research bordering on biological work. Geddes was, in fact, a trained biologist and zoologist though he never took a degree. He was Professor of Botany at Dundee from 1889 to 1918, and of Sociology at Bombay from 1920 to 1923. He was knighted shortly before his death. His principal works on URBAN DESIGN are *City Development* (1904) and *Cities in Evolution* (1915).

P. Boardman, *The Worlds of P.G. (1854–1932)*, London 1978; H. Meller, *P.G. Social Evolutionist and City Planner*, London 1990.

**Gehry**, Frank (b.1929). Influential Canadian-born American architect. Trained in Los Angeles and at Harvard, he settled in Santa Monica, California, in 1962. For so *avant-garde* an architect he developed late, but his challenging, often radically subversive approach to architecture was fully realized in his own house at Santa Monica in 1978–9. This anticipated later DECONSTRUCTIVIST concepts of a building as a fractured collage and also exploited contemporary vernacular techniques and cheap industrial materials such as corrugated iron, chain-link fencing, common plywood and interior asphalt flooring. In this way it recalls the 'Dirty Realism' of contemporary sculptors such as his friend Richard Serra. The Norton House, Venice, California (1982–4), was less brash but also welcomed and reflected its chaotic environment. It includes a free-standing studio modelled on the lifeguard stations on nearby beaches. With the California AeroSpace Museum, Los Angeles (1983–4), and the Chiat-Day on Main Street, Venice, California (1984–91), Gehry turned to Disneyland for stimulation if not inspiration, the Chiat-Day façade being split into two incompatible halves by a giant pair of binoculars the full height of the building and forming the automobile entrance (designed in collaboration with Claes Oldenburg and Coosju van Bruggen). His 'sculptural' approach became more sophisticated in the Schnabel House, Brentwood, California (1986–9), where copper, lead-coated or stucco-covered metal panels were used as cladding for an apparently arbitrary but exhilarating composition of non- or even anti-functional elements. The Vitra Design Museum, Basel, Switzerland (1987–9), was also intended to be clad in metals and 'look like an old oil can' but the Swiss client insisted on a smooth plaster finish. Nevertheless, this remarkable building, with its seeming confusion of curved and slanting, of softly swelling and sharply angular forms, challenged all and any conventions and rules. In contrast the Loyola Law School, Los Angeles (1984–93), creates a lively urban space with three large and four small buildings detailed in ways that evoke the past, one even having a pedimented roof and free-standing columns. Of his later projects the University of Toledo Arts Building, Toledo, Ohio (1990–92), the shimmering stainless steel Frederick R. Weisma Art Museum, Minneapolis (1990–93), the limestone clad American Center, Paris (1993–4), the Minden Ravensberg Electric Company Offices, Bad Oeynhausen, Germany (1991–5), the Nationale-Nederlanden Building, Prague (1994–6), and the Guggenheim Museum, Bilbao, Spain (1994–7), are notable. His Disney Concert Hall, Los Angeles, was begun in 1989 but abandoned.

J. Pastier, *American Architecture of the 1980s*, Washington, DC; J. Steele, *Los Angeles Architecture, the Contemporary Condition*, London 1993; C. Jencks (ed.), *F.G. Individual Imagination and Cultural Conservatism*, London 1995; Curtis 1996; F. Dal Co *et al.*, *F.G. Architetture*, Milan 1997.

**Genelli**, Hans Christian (1763–1823), *see* GILLY, Friedrich.

**Genga**, Girolamo (*c.*1476–1551). Late Italian Renaissance painter and architect from Urbino. His buildings are heavier and more scenographic than RAPHAEL's, e.g. additions to Villa Imperiale, Pesaro (1535), which recall the Villa Madama, Rome. It has elaborate and very fine illusionistic architectural painted decorations, also by Genga with a team of assistants. His only other building of importance is S. Giovanni Battista, Pesaro (1543 onwards), similarly solemn and monumental. The Villa Imperiale was built for the Duke of Urbino and was influential, e.g. on the Villa Giulia, Rome, through AMMANATI.

Tafuri 1966; A. Pinelli and O. Rossi, *G. architetto. Aspetti della cultura urbinata del primo '500*, Rome 1971; M. Groblewski, *Die Kirche San Giovanni Battista in Pesaro von G.G.*, Regensburg 1976.

**Gentrification**, *see* URBAN RENEWAL.

**Geodesic dome**. A hemispherical SPACE-FRAME construction of lightweight rods joined to form hexagons, developed by Buckminster FULLER.

B. van Loon, *G.D.*, London 1994.

**Geoffrey de Noiers** (active *c*.1200), was called *constructor* of the choir of St Hugh at Lincoln Cathedral (begun 1192). The term may mean only supervisor, but more probably he is the designer of this epoch-making building. The design is, in spite of Geoffrey's name, entirely English, not merely in its proportions and the curious layout of the east chapels, but especially in its vault, the earliest vault whose ribs make a decorative (and a very wilful) pattern rather than simply express their function.

N. Pevsner, *The Choir of Lincoln Cathedral*, Oxford 1963.

**Geometric staircase**, *see* STAIR.

**Geometrical tracery**, *see* TRACERY.

**Georgian architecture**. Historical division of English architecture 1714–1830 (reigns of George I, II, III and IV), *see* ENGLISH ARCHITECTURE. Also the architecture of Georgia, formerly USSR, *see* BYZANTINE ARCHITECTURE.

**Gerbier**, Sir Balthazar (1592–1663), a Dutch-born Huguenot who settled in England in 1616, was courtier, diplomat, miniaturist and pamphleteer as well as architect. He almost certainly designed the York Water Gate, Victoria Embankment Gardens, London (1626–7), a direct imitation of the Fontaine de Médicis at the Luxembourg in Paris. Nothing else by him survives. He designed Hampstead Marshall (*c*.1660), completed by William WINDE.

H. R. Williamson, *Four Stuart Portraits*, London 1949; Summerson 1991; Colvin 1995.

**German architecture and landscape architecture**. For pre-Christian buildings *see* PREHISTORIC ARCHITECTURE; LONGHOUSE; ROMAN ARCHITECTURE. Of Early Christian buildings little was known until recently except the rotunda of St Mary on the Würzburg fortress and the traces of the grand basilica of St Boniface at Fulda, both C8. Excavations have now told us of small aisleless churches with straight-ended chancels, much as in northern England.

But all this is small fry in comparison with Charlemagne's buildings, especially the happily preserved palace chapel of Aachen and the large abbey church of Centula (St Riquier), only known from descriptions and derivations. Aachen was a palace of the Emperor, Ingelheim was another. Both were spacious, axially planned, and apparently aware of Imperial Roman plans. The large Aachen chapel dedicated in 805 is externally a polygon of sixteen sides, and internally has an ambulatory round an octagonal centre; above the ambulatory is a gallery and on top of the octagon a domical VAULT. Details are amazingly pure in the Roman tradition, as indeed is so much – script, poetry, illumination – that issued from the Emperor's circle. This applies also, e.g., to the curious gatehouse of Lorsch Abbey. At Aachen the most original feature is the WESTWORK, and as for Centula, consecrated in 799, all is original – a westwork with a tower repeating the shape of the crossing tower, transepts emanating from the crossing, and transept-like wings off the westwork, a chancel and an apse. As original is the vellum plan for St Gall Abbey, datable to about 820. This has a west as well as an east apse and a pair of round campanili, the earliest church towers of which we have a record.

Centula can be called the pattern from which the German Romanesque style derived. The years of development are the late C10 – with the westwork of St Pantaleon in Cologne, consecrated in 980, and the nunnery church of Gernrode (begun 959–63). At St Michael in Hildesheim of c.1010–33 the Romanesque style is complete. Its climax is the great cathedrals and abbeys of the Rhineland dating from the mid-C11 to the early C13: Speier 1030–61 and later, Mainz 1009, 1181 and later, Maria Laach 1093–1156 and Worms late C11 and C12. Internationally speaking the mid-C11 was the time of the great superiority of the work in the Empire over work in England, Italy, and most parts of France, as it was the time of the Salians, the most powerful of the emperors. The principal buildings are the following: the hall-range of the palace of Goslar of c.1050 not matched anywhere, Speier Cathedral already mentioned, with its ruthlessly grand inner elevation and the groin vaults which the nave received about 1080–90, the first major vaults in Germany. The decoration is inspired by northern Italy, the elevational system probably inspired by the Roman basilica of Trier. Trier Cathedral is another of the masterpieces of these years – a lengthening of a centrally planned Roman building. The west front has the first so-called dwarf gallery, i.e. an arcaded wall-passage, earlier than any in Italy. But the most coherent major building of these years is St Mary-in-Capitol (c.1040–65) at Cologne, built on a trefoil plan for the east end and with tunnel vaults. The details are very severe – e.g. BLOCK CAPITALS, as had been

introduced at St Pantaleon and at Hildesheim. Beneath is a crypt of many short columns; Speier has another. The trefoil east end became the hallmark of the Romanesque school of Cologne. Cologne before the Second World War had more Romanesque churches than any other city in Europe. They go on into the early C13, when motifs tend to get fanciful and decoration exuberant – baroque, as it has been called. The west end of Worms, completed c.1230, shows this at its most outré, but also shows that now the French Gothic began to make its mark.

But we cannot leave the Romanesque without referring to a developing liking for HALL CHURCHES in Westphalia (Kirchlinde c.1175) and also in Bavaria (Waldersbach c.1175) and to the style promoted by the Congregation of Hirsau, i.e. the German Cluniacs. Their churches are not much like French Cluniac churches. The main church at Hirsau was begun in 1082; specially good other Hirsau-type churches are Alpirsbach and Paulinzella, the latter of 1112–32. The Hirsau type had an antechurch (like Cluny) with two west towers, nave arcades with columns, mostly with plain block capitals, and two slim towers over the east bays of the aisles.

Now for the relation to the Gothic in France which had been created there about 1135–40. Germany did not take any notice of it until about 1200 with Gelnhausen (c.1200–1230), the 'PARADISE' of the abbey church of Maulbronn (c.1210–20), St Gereon at Cologne (1219 onwards) and Limburg on the Lahn (consecrated 1235). The result here is a mixture, resourceful and entertaining, but impure and not guided by any understanding of what Gothic architecture really is about. That changed suddenly and very dramatically with St Elizabeth at Marburg, started in 1235, the church of the Virgin at Trier, started a few years later (a centrally planned building making ingenious use of French elements) and Cologne Cathedral, started in 1284. St Elizabeth with its rib vaults and bar-tracery presupposes Reims, started in 1211, but with its trefoil east end derived from Cologne. The church after a change of plan was built as a hall church, and that is a motif of Westphalian derivation. It became the hallmark of the Late Gothic in Germany. Cologne Cathedral is French in general and in particular. Amiens and Beauvais are closest to it. It was to be the largest and the highest of all High Gothic cathedrals, but only the east end was built, and that was conse-crated only in 1322. The rest is mostly C19.

To proceed with German Gothic development one must watch for the spread of the hall church. One group is hall chancels of Austrian abbeys – Lilien-feld (consecrated 1230), Heiligenkreuz (consecrated 1295) and Zwettl (begun 1343). Meanwhile Westphalia turned from Romanesque to Gothic halls (Osna-brück, 1256–92, nave at Münster, c.1267 onwards). Halls also established them-selves in north-east and east Germany and especially in the architecture of the Friars. An early example (c.1240) is the Frankfurt Blackfriars.

The full maturity of the German hall church is reached in south Germany from 1351, the date when the chancel of Schwäbisch-Gmünd was begun, prob-ably by Heinrich PARLER, and through the C15 into the C16. The architects spreading this Late Gothic style (called *Sondergotik*) were the PARLER family, with Peter, the greatest, who in 1353 became the Emperor Charles IV's archi-tect of Prague Cathedral and introduced here complicated rib vaults and inciden-tally amazing portrait sculpture (in the triforium). A Michael Parler worked at Ulm, a Johann was called to Milan, another Johann appears at Freiburg, but the fantastic spire with its filigree tracery all over is earlier than that Parler. Altogether we hear of more architects' names now (*see* ENSINGEN; BÖBLINGER; HEINZELMANN) and also of the statutes of masons' lodges. There are many out-standing Late Gothic parish churches in south Germany and Austria, such as St Martin at Landshut (and the Salzburg Greyfriars) by Hans STETHAIMER, Nördlingen (1427 onwards) and Dinkelsbühl (1448 onwards) by Nicolaus Eseler (c.1400–1492), Amberg (1420 onwards), the Frauenkirche in Munich (1468 onwards) by Jörg von Ganghofer (d.1488) and the chancel of St Lorenz in Nuremberg (begun 1439) by Heinzel-mann and RORICZER. Nor is north Ger-many poor in Late Gothic churches.

But the pride of north Germany is its brick churches, in an impressive and very simplified Gothic (called *Backsteingotik*), and its brick town halls such as those of Lübeck and Stralsund and the over-whelming one, mainly of the late C14, at Torun (Thorn) in the territory of the Prussian Knights. Their castles are as overwhelming, especially the C14 Mal-bork (Marienburg).

Altogether Germany is rich in Late Gothic secular work. At the castle at Meissen the rebuilding of 1471–c.1485 demonstrates the transition from castle to palace. So does, on an even grander scale, the work of Benedict RIETH VON PIEST-ING on the Hradchin at Prague. The Vla-dislav Hall belongs to the years 1493–1502. Its curvaceous rib vaults are the acme of German Late Gothic fantasy.

But the Vladislav Hall also has motifs of the Italian Renaissance. The infiltration started in fact earlier in Bohemia, Hun-gary and Poland than in Germany. In Germany Dürer and Burkmayr used Renaissance detail elegantly in 1508, and in 1509 the Fuggers of Augsburg founded a chapel in St Anna, Augsburg, which was intended to look north Italian as an ensemble. In the second quarter of the C16 much decoration *à la* Como or Pavia can be found (Georgentor, Dresden 1534). Ensembles however remained rare – e.g. the Johann-Friedrichs-Bau (1533– 6), Schloss Hartenfels, Torgau, by Konrad Krebs (1491–1540). The purest is part of the Stadtresidenz at Landshut (1537–43) inspired by GIULIO ROMANO, to whom it has been attributed. But soon, in any case, purity was no longer the ideal. As the wholly national Elizabethan style emerges in England, so does the so-called German Renaissance in Germany, with gables, stubby columns and coarse, more Flemish than Italian, decoration. Examples are the Town Halls of Leipzig (1556) and Rothenburg (1573–8), the Lusthaus, Stuttgart (1584–93, demolished), by George Beer (d.1600) and SCHICKHARDT, the Plassenburg, Kulmbach (1559 onwards), and the Pellerhaus in Nuremberg (1602–7, gutted but rebuilt), by Jacob WOLFF. There are, however, also some more international-looking buildings, i.e. buildings of French (Schloss Aschaffenburg 1605– 14, gutted 1944 but rebuilt, by RIDINGER) or Flemish (Ottheinrichsbau, Heidelberg, 1556–9 with a formal garden by S. DE CAUX; Town Hall portico, Cologne, 1567–70) or Italian inspiration (St Michael, Munich, 1583–92 by SUSTRIS, Hans Krumpper (*c.*1570–1635) and others). The most original churches about 1600 are Protestant and north German: those of Wolfenbüttel by Paul Francke (1538–1615) and Bückeburg (1613–23). But all this has little to do with the Renaissance.

Just as in England with Inigo Jones, a true understanding of the High Renaissance came only after 1600 and even then very rarely, e.g. Josef Furtenbach (1591– 1667), important mainly for his publications. The key building is Elias HOLL's Augsburg Town Hall of 1615–20. But then – and this singles out Germany – the Thirty Years War interrupted this organic development.

It left the country devastated and impoverished, and when building again became possible, the situation in the country – and indeed taste – had changed. The most important architectural events took place in the Catholic south, and the source of inspiration was Italy, and at first even the architects were Italian, as, e.g., BARELLI and ZUCCALLI, who built the Theatinerkirche in Munich (1663–88), or Carlo Lurago (*c.*1618–84), who built Passau Cathedral (*c.*1668), followed by the VORARLBERGER SCHOOL. About 1700, Germans replaced the Italians. Of the first generation are SCHLÜTER, who built the Palace and the Arsenal in Berlin, the great FISCHER VON ERLACH in Vienna and PÖPPELMANN of the Zwinger in Dresden (1709 onwards). All three were born about 1660. HILDEBRANDT in Vienna was a little younger. While Fischer von Erlach, despite his ingenious plans with their centralizing tendencies and their ovals, is a classicist at bottom, Hildebrandt represents the BORROMINI and GUARINI party in Europe, as do the DIENTZENHOFERS in Franconia and Bohemia (Johann: Banz 1710–18; Christoph: Břevnov near Prague 1708–15; Kilian and Christoph Ignaz: the two St Nicholases, Prague, 1730s). The Fischer–Hildebrandt antinomy is equally patent in Dresden, but here it is a Catholic–Protestant antinomy: BÄHR's Protestant Frauenkirche begun 1722, the town church *v.* CHIAVERI's Catholic church of 1738 onwards, the Court church.

As for other northern centres Frederick the Great's early Sanssouci at Potsdam (1745–7) with KNOBELSDORFF looked to Rococo France (even if not with such abandon as CUVILLIÉS's Amalienburg at Nymphenburg near Munich of 1734–9), his later buildings, including the Gothic Nauener Gate at Potsdam of 1755, to England. The Rhineland naturally looked to France, but even there – Brühl, Bruchsal – in the end the greatest German architect of the century won.

He is, needless to say, Balthasar NEU-MANN, and his masterworks are the Episcopal Palace of Würzburg (1720–44), still in some elements guided by Hildebrandt, and the splendid churches of Vierzehnheiligen (1742 onwards) and Neresheim (1747 onwards). Neumann lived at Würzburg, i.e. in Franconia. The three greatest Bavarian church builders were ASAM, ZIMMERMANN and J. M. FISCHER, all born between 1685 and 1695. The Asam brothers, also painters and sculptors, are the most Italian – influenced by Borromini, and rich in their brown and gold decoration (Weltenburg; St John Nepomuk, Munich). Fischer (Ottobeuren, Zwiefalten, Rott) is all large and light in colours and ingenious in planning as well. Zimmermann is primarily remembered – rightly so – for the Wies church (1745–54). There were two Zimmermann brothers as well, the other being a painter, and the *unisono* of all the arts is of course one of the most characteristic features of the Baroque. The great abbeys of south Germany and even more Austria show that in all their sumptuous parts (see e.g. Melk, St Florian, Klosterneuburg).

No wonder then that the total reaction against the Rococo was a Protestant and a north German initiative. Heralded by ERDMANSDORF's and ANHALT-DESSAU's neo-Palladian *Schloss* and English-style park at Wörlitz in 1768–73, the Danish-born LANDSCAPE GARDEN and PUBLIC PARK theorist HIRSCHFELD of Kiel University pioneered a movement which was to culminate in 1789 with RUMFORD and SCKELL's Englischer Garten in Munich, the first public park. In architecture, Friedrich GILLY of Berlin was similarly influenced by recent developments in France and England (he never went to Italy). What London meant to him we do not know, but Paris meant the most radical innovators of Europe – the Odéon, the Théâtre Feydeau, the rue des Colonnes. Gilly died too young to build more than negligibly, but his designs for a National Monument to Frederick the Great and for a National Theatre prove him to be one of the few architects of genius of the period.

SCHINKEL was his pupil, again one of the greatest of the period in all Europe, less brilliantly endowed perhaps, but of rare competence and as resourceful as Gilly. He started as a painter, especially as a theatrical painter, in the romantic vein. His design of 1810 for a mausoleum for Queen Luise is Gothic. When after Napoleon's defeat building started again, he built in a pure but highly original Grecian. The New Guard House, the Theatre, the Old Museum (all in Berlin and all designed in 1816–22) are among the noblest of the Greek Revival anywhere. He became Superintendent of Building in Prussia and his influence stretched far, even into Scandinavia and Finland. Later in life he experimented with more original forms – centrally planned churches, façades of public buildings of exposed brick and functional bareness (Academy of Architecture of 1831–6, designs for a library and a bazaar). When he visited England in 1826, his principal interests were industrial products and the new huge mills. The landscape architect Peter Joseph LENNÉ often worked in association with Schinkel, notably at Potsdam where he created the great landscape park encompassing buildings by both Schinkel and PERSIUS. He went on to transform the Tiergarten in Berlin into a public park and followed it with several others, being succeeded by PUCKLER-MUSKAU.

KLENZE, Schinkel's opposite number in Bavaria, was more accommodating but equally resourceful. His *œuvre* already comprises the full HISTORICISM of the c19: the Greek (Glyptothek, Munich and Walhalla, Regensburg), the Quattrocento and Cinquecento parts of the Royal Palace, Munich, the Early Christian of the church of All Saints, Munich, the originality of the Hall of Liberation above Kelheim. As for c19 Historicism Germany made the RUND-BOGENSTIL one of her specialities. In the Italian Renaissance vein SEMPER did such buildings as the Dresden Gallery (1847 onwards) and the Dresden Opera. The difference between the first and second Opera (1838 onwards and, after a fire, 1871 onwards) is that between c19 neo-Renaissance and neo-Baroque. The neo-Baroque appeared at its best in the Houses of Parliament, Berlin, by Paul Wallot (1841–1912) (1884 onwards). Compare then the Parliament with Ludwig von Hoffmann's Supreme Court at Leipzig (1887 onwards), and you will get a first idea of the development from ornateness to simplicity.

Germany was indeed one of the leading countries in overcoming Historicism and establishing the new functional style of the c20, in which the DEUTSCHER WERKBUND played a notable role. Foreshadowed by such buildings as the Wertheim Department Store, Berlin (1896–7), by Alfred Messel (1853–1909), and OLBRICH's Tietz Department Store, Düsseldorf (1908), the key works are by Peter BEHRENS of *c*.1904–14, buildings including the famous factories for the AEG. Behrens's pupils were GROPIUS and MIES VAN DER ROHE. Gropius's *magnum opus* remains the BAUHAUS building at Dessau. Mies's greatest work

was done after his emigration to Chicago. Other leaders in the so-called INTER-NATIONAL MODERN were Max Berg (1870–1947) of the Centennial Hall at Wroclaw (Breslau) of 1913 – the first (apart from bridges) to take into account the possibilities of arcuated concrete – and MENDELSOHN of the Einstein Tower of 1919–20.

But the Einstein Tower is pre-the-International-Modern of Mendelsohn. It belongs to that EXPRESSIONISM to which for a brief moment even Gropius and Mies fell victim. Most convincedly Expressionist in the years about 1920 were Dominikus BÖHM, POELZIG, SCHAR-OUN, and to some extent Hugo HÄRING, e.g. the Garkau farm buildings of 1923, and Heinrich Tessenow (1876–1950), e.g. the Sächsische Landeschule, Dresden, of 1925–7. After 1933 the most prominent buildings were Nazi, e.g. the Haus der Deutsches Kunst, Munich (1933–7) by Paul Ludwig Troost (1878–1934), the Autobahn (1935–40) by Fritz Todt (1891–1942) and BONATZ, who designed the bridges, etc. for it, and the new Berlin Chancellery and Nuremberg party rally buildings, etc. by SPEER. In the immediate post-war period came the Expressionist revival with Scharoun's Berlin Philharmonie concert hall (1956–63) and Gottfried BÖHM's Bensberg Town Hall (1963–9), carried on into the 1980s by Hermann Fehling (1909–96) and Daniel Gogel (b.1927) with their observatory at Gaveling, Munich (1976–80). Neo-Expressionism also informed the brilliant structural conceptions of Frei OTTO and Gunther BEHNISCH (though the latter was to develop in a different direction), while the International Modern tradition was carried on by EIER-MANN and HENTRICH. More recently Oswald Mathias UNGERS and Josef Paul Kleihues (b.1933) have taken up a new 'rationalistic' approach (*see* NEO-

RATIONALISM) which Kleihues, as planning director of IBA (Internationale Bauaustellung, Berlin, 1979–84), promoted; he went on to refurbish and renovate the Hamburger Bahnhof, Berlin (1992–6), as an art gallery and to design the Museum of Contemporary Art, Chicago (1992–6). Thomas Hertzog (b.1941) has made notable contributions to ENVIRONMENTAL ARCHITECTURE and during the last decade several young architects and landscape architects have become prominent internationally, e.g. Axel Schultes (b.1943), whose Kunstmuseum, Bonn (1986–92), led to his commission in 1993 for a new government ministerial quarter in Berlin; and Bolles–Wilson (Julia B. Bolles, b.1948; Peter L. Wilson, b.1950), whose New City Library, Munster (1991–5) and New Government Office, Munster (1995–6) are notable. Outstanding among landscape architects is Peter LATZ, whose Landschaftspark Duisberg Nord, begun in 1991, initiated the 'narrative park'.

**Gesellius**, Herman (1874–1916), *see* FINNISH ARCHITECTURE.

**Gesso**. A composition of gypsum or chalk and size, sometimes with other materials. It provides a smooth absorbent white surface. The term is sometimes used for *plaster of Paris*, a white gypsum powder that forms a paste when mixed with water and hardens into a solid: used by sculptors for moulds and casts.

**Giant order**, *see* COLOSSAL ORDER.

**Gibberd**, Sir Frederick (1908–84). English architect, one of the first to accept the INTERNATIONAL MODERN style of the 1930s (Pulman Court, Streatham, London, 1934–5). His best-known works after the Second World War are the plan and some of the chief buildings for the New Town of Harlow, Essex (1947), the terminal buildings for London Airport (1950–69), the Roman Catholic Cathedral, Liverpool (1960), and the Central London Mosque, Regent's Park (1969).

**Gibbs**, James (1662–1754). The most influential London church architect of the early C18. In contrast to his predominantly Whig and neo-Palladian contemporaries, he was a Scot, a Catholic, and a Tory with Jacobite sympathies, and had the unique advantage of training under a leading Italian architect, Carlo FONTANA. Born in Aberdeen he went to Rome *c.*1703 to study for the priesthood, but left the Scots College after a year. He stayed on in Rome until 1709, and appears to have studied painting before turning to architecture. His first building, St Mary-le-Strand, London (1714–17), is a mixture of WREN and Italian Mannerist and Baroque elements. Rather surprisingly, he was then taken up by Lord BURLINGTON, though only to be dropped in favour of Colen CAMPBELL, who replaced him as architect of Burlington House. He had no further contact with the neo-Palladians and remained faithful to Wren and his Italian masters, although he absorbed into his eclectic style a few Palladian features. St Martin-in-the-Fields, London (1722–6), is his masterpiece, and was widely imitated, especially in its combination of temple-front portico and steeple rising from the ridge of the roof. The monumental side elevations of recessed giant columns and giant pilasters have windows with his characteristic GIBBS SURROUND.

His best surviving secular buildings are outside London: the Octagon, Twickenham (1720); Sudbrooke Lodge, Petersham (*c.*1720); Ditchley House (1720–25); and the Senate House (1722–30) and King's College Fellows' Building at Cambridge (1724–49). Several of these display his ebulliently Italian Baroque style of interior decoration at its sumptuous best. His last and most original building, the Radcliffe Library, Oxford (1737–49), is unique in England in showing the influence of Italian Mannerism. He exerted great influence both in Britain and in America through his *Book of Architecture* (1728), one of the plates from which probably inspired the White House in Washington.

T. Friedman, *J.G.*, New Haven and London 1984; Harris 1990; Summerson 1991; Colvin 1995.

**Gibbs surround**. The surround of a doorway or window consisting of alternating large and small blocks of stone, quoinwise, or of intermittent large blocks; sometimes with a narrow raised band connecting up the verticals and along the face of the arch. Named after the architect James GIBBS though used by other architects, e.g. PALLADIO; CAMPBELL. *See* Fig. 60.

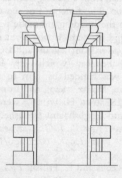

Fig. 60 Gibbs surround

**Gigliardi**, Domenico, *see* ZHILYARDI, Domenico.

**Gil de Hontañón**, Juan (d.1526) and Rodrigo (d.1577). Spanish architects, father and son. Juan is the designer of the last two Gothic cathedrals of Spain, Salamanca and Segovia: at Salamanca he

was consulted in 1512 (with eight others) and made master mason; at Segovia he started the new building in 1525. An earlier work of his is the cloister of Palencia Cathedral (begun 1505). He was consulted in 1513 for Seville Cathedral and designed the new lantern, etc., also still Gothic (1517–19).

Rodrigo appears first in 1521 at Santiago, probably as an assistant of JUAN DE ÁLAVA; then, in 1526, as one of the five architects consulted on the projected vast collegiate church of Valladolid (the others are his father, his master, Francisco de COLONIA, and Riaño). He was master mason at Astorga Cathedral (from 1530), where he built the nave; at Salamanca Cathedral (from 1537), where the transepts must be his; at the cloister of Santiago (from 1538), where he followed Álava; at Plasencia Cathedral (1537 or 1544), where the contributions of various masons are obscure; and at Segovia Cathedral (from 1563), where the east end is his. His finest secular work is the PLATERESQUE façade of the University at Alcalá de Henares (1537–53). He also wrote a book on architecture which is known only at second-hand.

Kubler and Soria 1959.

**Gilbert**, Cass (1859–1934). American architect known for his Woolworth Building, New York (1910–13), which initiated a series of Gothic skyscrapers including the Chicago Tribune Tower of 1923–5. Until 1930 the Woolworth Building was the highest building in America. Gilbert also designed the Minnesota Capitol, St Paul (1895–1905), the United States Customs House, New York (1901–7), and the Chamber of Commerce, Washington, DC (1924–5).

S. L. Irish, *C.G.'s Career in New York City*, Ann Arbor 1990.

**Gill**, Irving John (1870–1936). American architect, working in California after training in Chicago under SULLIVAN 1890–93 alongside WRIGHT. He started his own practice in San Diego in 1893. His early buildings experimented with various styles, notably SHINGLE but also PRAIRIE, English cottage vernacular, Spanish Mission and others, though always adhering to ARTS AND CRAFTS principles even when he evolved his own style *c.*1907 with the Laughlin House, Los Angeles, and the La Jolla Women's Club, La Jolla (1914). The Dodge House, Los Angeles (1916, demolished 1970), and the Horatio West apartments, Santa Monica (1919), illustrate his developed style, emphatically cubic and with large concrete blocks. It is curiously similar to advanced work in Europe of the same years.

E. McCoy, *Five California Architects*, New York 1960; D. Gebhard, *Architecture in Southern California*, Los Angeles 1965; W. Kaplan, *The Art that is Life; The Arts and Crafts Movement in America 1875–1920*, Boston 1987–8.

**Gilles le Breton** (d.1553), *see* LE BRETON, Giles.

**Gilly**, Friedrich (1772–1800), came of a French Huguenot family which had moved to Berlin in 1689, and was the son of the architect David Gilly (1748–1808). In spite of his neo-classical convictions he started as a Gothic enthusiast, drawing the Marienburg in West Prussia (1794). The king bought one of the drawings and gave young Gilly a four-year travel grant which, because of the war, he could not take up. In 1796 the idea of a national monument for Frederick the Great was revived. The king had died in 1786, and in the following year the monument had first been suggested: Hans Christian Genelli (1763–1823) at once submitted a Greek Doric temple, a very early case of faith in Grecian ideals (*but see* LEDOUX and SOANE). Gilly now designed a great

funerary precinct and in its centre, raised on a high platform, a much larger Greek Doric temple – a Parthenon for the Prussian king. The precinct is strikingly original and strikingly severe in its forms. It is true that Gilly leant on the most recent work of young Parisian architects and their model PIRANESI (e.g in the tunnel-vaulted triumphal arch), but the absolutely unmoulded cubic shapes are all his.

The year after, he took up his grant, but went to France and England instead of Italy: what he drew in Paris shows the sympathies already indicated by the monument. On his return in 1798 Gilly was made Professor of Optics and Perspective at the newly founded Academy of Architecture. In the same year he did his design for a national theatre for Berlin; in spite of certain motifs derived from Paris it is perhaps the most unimitative design of the age. It seems easier to reach the C20 from this unrelieved geometrical shape than from anything between Gilly and 1890. The functions of the various parts of the building are made perfectly clear, and the semicircular front in particular, taken from Legrand and Molinos's Théâtre Feydeau (which Gilly drew in Paris), was handed by him to Moller (Theatre, Mainz, 1829), and from there reached SEMPER. His writings were translated into English and published as F. Neumayer (intro.), *F.G. Essays on Architecture 1796–1799* (Chicago/Malibu 1994).

H. Reelfs and K. Frössli, *F.G. 1772–1800 . . .*, exh. cat., Berlin 1984; Watkin and Mellinghoff 1987.

**Ginzburg**, Moisei (1893–1946), *see* RUSSIAN ARCHITECTURE.

**Giocondo**, Fra Giovanni (1433–1515). Italian architect and Dominican friar, born in Verona. The Palazzo del Consiglio, Verona (1476–93), used to be attributed to him. He was in Naples 1489–

93, where he succeeded GIULIANO DA MAIANO at Poggioreale, then in Paris 1495–1505, where he was responsible for the construction of a bridge over the Seine *c*.1500. In 1511 he published the first illustrated edition of VITRUVIUS. He produced a plan for St Peter's (1505–12) and was appointed architect to St Peter's with RAPHAEL in 1514.

V. Fontana, *Fra G.G. Architetto 1433–1515*, Vicenza 1988; Heydenreich 1996.

**Giotto di Bondone** (*c*.1266–1337) was appointed master mason to the cathedral and city of Florence in 1334 on account of his fame as a painter. His architectural work was limited to the campanile of the cathedral, which he began in that year. It seems certain that only the first storey of the socle was finished when he died. It was completed, with alterations, by Andrea PISANO and Francesco TALENTI in the 1340s and 1350s.

Trachtenberg 1971; White 1987.

**Giovanni di Simone** (*fl*.1277), *see* CEMETERY.

**Giovanni Pisano**, *see* PISANO, Nicola.

**Girardin**, Louis-René, Marquis de Vauvray (1735–1808), *see* LANDSCAPE GARDEN.

**Girder**. A metal (iron or steel) BEAM. A box girder is of hollow rectangular or other closed cross-section with transverse plates or other diaphragm members at intervals for strengthening.

**Giuliano da Maiano** (1432–90). Italian architect and sculptor, the elder brother of BENEDETTO DA MAIANO. He began as a wood-carver (choirstalls in Pisa Cathedral, cupboards in New Sacristy, Florence Cathedral 1463–5) but later worked mainly as an architect and was appointed architect to Florence Cathedral from 1477 until his death. He helped to diffuse the Early Renais-

sance style of BRUNELLESCHI and MICHELOZZO throughout Tuscany and beyond to the Marches and Naples. He designed the chapel of S. Fina in the Collegiata at S. Gimignano (1466), Palazzo Spannochi, Siena (begun 1473), and Palazzo Venier, Recanati (1477, much altered later). His masterpiece is the cathedral of Faenza (1474–86). At Naples he designed the Palazzo di Poggio Reale (*c*.1488, destroyed) and the quadrangular Porta Capuana (*c*.1485) and, probably, the Piccolomini, Terranova and Tolosa chapels in S. Anna di Monteoliveto, Naples.

D. Lamberini *et al.* (eds.), *G. di M. e la bottega dei Maiano*, Florence 1994; F. Quintero, *G. di M. e l'architettura del Rinascimento in Toscana e nell'Italia centrale*, Rome 1995; Heydenreich 1996.

**Giulio Romano** (Giulio Pippi or Giuliano Giannuzzi, 1499–1546), Italian architect and painter, born in Rome. He began, as both painter and architect, in the classical shadow of RAPHAEL, under whom he was trained. He worked on the painted and stucco decorations at the Villa Madama and may have contributed to its design. But he rapidly developed a strongly personal and dramatically forceful MANNERIST style. His first building, the Palazzo Adimari Salviati, Rome (begun *c*.1520 but much altered later), the Villa Lante on the Gianicolo, Rome (begun 1520/21, now the Finnish Academy), and the Palazzo Stati Maccarani in Piazza S. Eustachio, Rome (begun 1522/3, now Palazzo di Brazza), already display his originality, especially the Palazzo Maccarani, which is extremely wilful and eccentric in its use of the classical repertory of form. (Palazzo Cicciaporci, Rome, was for long attributed to him, erroneously.) In 1524 he went to work for Federigo Gonzaga at Mantua, where all his most notable buildings were constructed. Palazzo Te (1524–34) was designed for Federigo's honeymoon and as a summer villa. One storey high, it is built around an enormous courtyard and looks on to a garden terminated by a semicircular pilastered colonnade. Much in the plan derives from Ancient Rome by way of Raphael's Villa Madama, but the careful interrelation of house and garden is new. Still more revolutionary were the façades: one of them smooth, with the SERLIAN MOTIF repeated as a blind arcade towards the garden; the others excessively rough with irregular rustication, Tuscan columns, massive keystones and wilfully misused classical details (the centre triglyph of each inter-columniation looks as if it had slipped out of place). He decorated the interior with frescos, mainly of an erotic nature. One room gives a key to his strange personality: it has only one door and no windows and the walls and ceiling are painted to represent the Fall of the Titans, so that the shape of the room is entirely effaced and the visitor finds himself engulfed in a cascade of boulders and gigantic nude figures some 4 m. (14 ft) high.

On the façade of his own house in Mantua (c.1544) he again indulged in a truculently licentious misuse of classical detail, but this time with a different intention. It is elegantly aloof and sophisticated instead of oppressive and neurotic. For the Palazzo Ducale, Mantua, he designed the 'appartamento di Troia' (1536–9), with its elaborate stucco decorations, and the adjacent Cortile della Cavallerizza (1539 onwards), with coupled twisted columns on the first floor and much heavy rustication, one wing being pierced by arches and square windows to afford a view across the nearby lake. He also designed the abbey church of San Benedetto Po in Polirone (1540 onwards) and remodelled Mantua Cathedral (1545 onwards) with double aisles supported by sturdy Corin-thian columns whose repeated drum-beat monotony draws the visitor towards the high altar – another instance of his pre-occupation with the effect a building would make rather than with the perfec-tion of its form. The Palazzo Italiano at Landshut, Bavaria (1537 onwards), has been attributed to him.

E. Verheyen, *The Palazzo del Te in Mantua*, Baltimore 1977; C. L. Frommel *et al.*, *G.R.*, Milan 1989; *G.R. (Atti del Convegno, Mantua 1989)*, Mantua 1991; D. Ferrari and A. Belluzzi, *G.R. Repertorio di fonti documentarie*, Rome 1992; Lotz 1996.

**Giurgola**, Romualdo (b.1920). Italian-born American architect, trained in Rome and New York. He was a disciple and then a colleague of L. KAHN at the University of Pennsylvania (1954–71) and became the leading member of the Philadelphia School. Less solemn than Kahn, his dexterity is evident in the juxta-position of his Liberty Bell Pavilion and Penn Mutual Tower in Philadelphia (1975). The Graduate Studies Center, Bryn Mawr, Pennsylvania, followed in 1980 when he also began his major work, the Australian Parliament Building, Can-berra (1980–88). He was involved with LEGORETTA at Solana, IBM Southlake and Village West, Dallas, Texas (1988–90). More recently he designed the IBM Palisades Advanced Business Institute, Palisades, NY (1990), and the ANA Hotel, The Rocks, Sydney, Australia (1992).

K. Frampton, *Mitchell/G. Architects*, New York 1983; H. Beck (ed.), *Parliament House, Canberra*, Sydney 1988.

**Glacis**. In military architecture, the ground sloping from the top of the para-pet of the covered way till it reaches the level of the open country, so that every part of it can be swept by the fire of the ramparts.

**Glass**. Although manufactured in the East Mediterranean from c.2500 BC for small solid objects and vessels, glass was not used in architecture until Imperial Roman times and then for windows only in the houses of the rich. From the C4 church windows were sometimes filled with coloured glass and in the early Middle Ages the technique of 'stained glass' was developed by fitting together pieces of various shapes and colours with strips of lead, at first in geometrical patterns and from the mid-C11 in figurative compositions (five windows in Augsburg Cathedral in Germany). Stained glass was brought to its peak of excellence on a par with mural painting in C12–13 France (first at St Denis, then Bourges, Chartres, Le Mans, etc.), Italy (Florence, Siena) and England (Canterbury, York, etc.), in symbiotic relationship with Gothic architecture as taller churches both created and satisfied demands for larger windows: in the Sainte-Chapelle, Paris (1243–8), stonework is reduced to a lacy mesh of tracery. Larger pieces of coloured glass were made in the C14, some with a yellow surface stain on which designs could be effectively picked out in black enamel. Windows admitted more light, though still conceived as areas to be looked at rather than seen through. Glass was, however, too costly to be much used in domestic buildings (mainly in small greenish translucent panels): windows were more often filled with linen or parchment if not left void to be closed by wooden shutters. The invention of clear crystal glass in early C16 Venice and its production in panels for windows from the mid-C17 was quickly exploited by architects. The Galerie des Glaces at Versailles (begun 1678) depended for its effect on the tall clear glass windows giving a view of the park along one side and, on the other, similarly framed mirrors made by backing sheets of glass with an amalgam of mercury and tin, a technique perfected in France. The use of clear glass for windows and mirrors transformed the design of interiors. Several panels of glass supported on a grid of wooden glazing bars were, however, still needed for windows until the mid-C18 when larger, tougher and more clearly transparent pieces of plate or sheet glass became available, giving more light inside and also affecting exteriors. Once again the technique of glass-making developed in symbiosis with architectural design.

Glass was used as a building material from the late C18, first for CONSERVATORIES, then in vaults and domes (see BÉLANGER, FONTAINE) and then for complete structures (PAXTON's Crystal Palace, London, 1851, and VOIT's Glaspalast, Munich, 1853–4, both burnt down in the 1930s), supported by metal frameworks (see METAL STRUCTURES). The large-span glazed roof was developed in the mid-C19 for railway stations (Paddington Station, London, 1854), covered markets (Les Halles, Paris, 1852–9, demolished), shopping arcades (Galleria Vittorio Emanuele, Milan, 1864–7) and stores (Bon Marché, Paris, 1876), culminating in the vast Galerie des Machines for the Paris 1889 exhibition (destroyed 1905) by DUTERT and CONTAMIN. The use of glass walling by ELLIS in England and the architects of the Chicago School in the US, followed by the introduction of the glazed CURTAIN WALL led to the continuous glass façades of BEHRENS, GROPIUS, TAUT, etc., and the glass-clad skyscrapers of MIES VAN DER ROHE. Already in 1914 glass had been hailed as the building material of the future by P. Schibert in his *Glasarchitektur*, Berlin. Reflective tinted solar-control glass that admits light but limits the transmission of heat is nowadays much used for office buildings, e.g. FOSTER's Willis Faber building, Ipswich (1975). Glass bricks for

construction were made from the late
CI9, at first rhomboid and used mainly
for decorative effect (e.g. by GUIMARD),
from the 1920s quadrilateral and adopted
in FUNCTIONALIST buildings (e.g. by
CHAREAU and Taut). Glass slabs and glass
tubing, etc. were also exploited structurally by LE CORBUSIER, F. L. WRIGHT
and others.

W. Blaser, *Filigrane Architektur*, Basel
1980; E. Schild, *Zwischen Glaspalast und
Palais des Illusions*, Brunswick/Wiesbaden
1983; G. Robinson and B. Sartory, *House
of G.*, Cambridge, Mass., 1986; D. Button
and B. Pye, *G. in Building*, London 1993;
M. Wigginton, *G. in Architecture*, London
1994; T. Riley, *Light Structures*, New
York 1995.

**Glazed bricks**. Polychrome glazed
bricks were developed in the ancient
Near East (Assyria) in the late 2nd millennium BC and were used for wall decoration on a large scale at Khorsabad (C8 BC)
and Babylon (*c*.575 BC) and Susa (C5 BC).
Those from Khorsabad and Susa are now
in Berlin (Staatliche Museen) and Paris
(Louvre).

W. Andrae, *Coloured Ceramics from
Assur*, London 1925.

**Glemme**, Erick (1905–59). Swedish
landscape architect in the Stockholm Park
Department, for which he designed
additions to the city's central open space,
the Kungsträdgarden, as well as three
major developments: the 4 km. (2½ mile)
Norr Malstrand lakeshore promenade
and park, including open-air theatres,
garden rooms, playgrounds, etc. (1941–
3); the renovation of the hilly Tegner
Grove as a landscape garden (1941); and
the transformation of the Vasa Park into
a series of rock gardens (1947).

**Gloriette**, *see* EYE-CATCHER.

**Glyph**. A vertical channel in a TRIGLYPH.

**Glyptoteca**. A building to display sculpture; a sculpture gallery.

**Gočár**, Josef (1880–1945), *see* CUBIST
ARCHITECTURE; CZECH ARCHI-
TECTURE.

**Godefroy**, Maximilien (1765–1840?).
French *émigré* architect who introduced
Parisian NEO-CLASSICAL ideals to the
USA. He was trained in Paris where he
probably knew LEDOUX. He arrived in
America in 1805. His chief works are the
advanced neo-classical, Unitarian
Church in Baltimore (1817–18) and the
Commercial and Farmer's Bank in Baltimore (1812–13) of which only the doorway survives. His masterpiece is the Battle
Monument in Baltimore (designed 1810,
built 1814–27), the first great civic
monument in the USA and a precursor
of MILLS's Washington Monuments in
Baltimore and Washington. But Godefroy's neo-classical ideals did not prevent
him from indulging in neo-Gothic, e.g.
the chapel of St Mary's Seminary, Baltimore (1807). He left America in 1819,
settling first in London, unsuccessfully,
and in 1827 returned to France.

R. L. Alexander, *The Architecture of
M.G.*, Baltimore 1974; Hitchcock 1977.

**Godwin**, Edward William (1833–86).
English architect, born in Bristol, where
in 1862 he designed a warehouse in a
massive style with rows of round-arched
openings, rather similar to the warehouses
of Boston, Massachusetts. In the same
year he moved to London, having won
the competition for Northampton Town
Hall. This, built 1861–4, is Gothic. So are
Congleton Town Hall, Cheshire (1864–
6), and Dromore Castle, Limerick (1866–
73). But Godwin was not content to be
a revivalist. His 'art furniture' of 1871 and
later is inspired by Japan, but at the same
time decidedly original. In architecture
this originality could be even bolder, e.g.

White House, Tite Street, Chelsea, London, built for Whistler in 1877–9 (demolished) and the even more original designs for 44 Tite Street (1878, modified in construction). Later on Godwin was engaged in theatrical decoration.

D. Harbron, *The Conscious Stone. The Life of E.W.G.*, London 1949; Hitchcock 1977; E. Aslin, *E.W.G. Furniture and Interior Decoration*, London 1986.

**Goff**, Bruce Alonzo (1904–82). An extreme individualist and typically American loner, Goff always practised in the mid-West, usually for clients of moderate means, and only towards the end of his life became more widely known. His work is mainly residential but is otherwise unclassifiable in its maverick originality. He delighted in combining opposites – flowing, free-form curves with complicated geometrical configurations, organic materials with standard prefabricated parts. Notable are his Ford House, Aurora, Illinois (1948), a radially divided circle in plan, constructed of curved steel ribs and standard Quonset-hut members; Bavinger House, Norman, Oklahoma (1949–55), a continuous snail-like spiral of open spaces suspended from a steel mast and cables; Glen Harder House, near Mountain Lake, Minnesota (1970), like an Indian encampment; the Price House, Bartlesville, Oklahoma (1956–76), formed of interlocking polygons; and the Barby II Residence, Tucson, Arizona (1974–6). The Japanese Pavilion, Los Angeles County Museum, California, was completed by his assistant Bart Prince (b.1947), who has become the most notable American exponent of organic architecture, with strong regional connotations, e.g. his own house and studio, Albuquerque, New Mexico (1988); the Hight Residence, Mendocino County, California (1994–5), and the Sziklai Residence, Carefree, Arizona (1997).

D. DeLong, *The Architecture of B.G. Buildings and Projects 1916–1977*, New York 1977; J. Cook, *The Architecture of B.G.*, London 1978; D. G. DeLong, *B.G. Toward Absolute Architecture*, Cambridge, Mass., 1988; C. Mead, *Space for the Continuous Present in the Residential Architecture of B.G.*, Albuquerque 1989; C. Mead, *Houses by B.G. An American Architecture for the Continuous Present*, Albuquerque 1991; P. Saliga and M. Woolever, *The Architecture of B.G. 1904–1982. Design for the Continuous Present*, Munich/Chicago 1995.

**Gogel**, Daniel (b.1927), *see* GERMAN ARCHITECTURE.

**Goldberg**, Bertram (1913–97). German-born American architect, trained at the Bauhaus in 1932–3. He settled in Chicago in 1934 and began developing prefabricated housing and industrial units for the US government, culminating in his Unishelter Prefabricated Unit Houses of 1950. His Marina City, Chicago (1959–64), marked a new departure with its dramatic 'corn cob' towers. Their organically moulded forms, made possible by concrete shell construction, were repeated in his Raymond Hilliard Housing (1964–6) and Prentice Women's Hospital (1970–75), both in Chicago. His middle-income urban agglomerate, River City, Chicago (designed 1976, built 1981–7), was unfortunately never fully built as planned, only the first of the projected five phases of the complex being completed.

L. Legner, *The New Architecture of B.G.*, Chicago 1984.

**Golden section**. An irrational proportion, probably known to the Ancient Greeks (perhaps Euclid) and thought to be divine by Renaissance theorists, notably Luca Pacioli (*De divina proportione*, 1479, published 1509). It may be defined as a line cut in such a way that the smaller section is to the greater as the greater is to the whole. This cannot be worked out mathematically, hence its fascination. Approximately it would be 5:8.

M. Boissavlievitch, *Le Nombre d'or et l'esthétique scientifique de l'architecture*, Paris 1952; O. Hageneier, *Der goldene Schnitt*, 1977.

**Goldfinger**, Ernö (1902–87). Hungarian-born architect who settled in Paris (1920–34) and then in London where his apartment blocks, Balfron Tower, Poplar (1965–7), and Trellick Tower, Kensington (1967–72), were notable, though later denigrated. His own house in Willow Road, Hampstead (1937–9), became a Goldfinger museum in 1996.

**Golosov**, Ilya A. (1883–1945), *see* RUSSIAN ARCHITECTURE.

**Gondouin** or **Gondoin**, Jacques (1737–1818). French neo-classical architect trained under J.-F. BLONDEL and at the French Academy in Rome (1761–4), then travelled in Holland and England. His masterpiece is the École de Chirurgie in Paris (1769–75), designed as a temple of Aesculapius. The street façade is in the form of an Ionic colonnade (correctly Greek in detail) with a TRIUMPHAL ARCH motif in the centre giving access to a square court on the far side of which a Corinthian portico leads into the semi-circular anatomy theatre covered by a half Pantheon-dome. The building also included a small hospital, library, laboratories, etc. Monumental in design and practical in plan it is one of the finest and most advanced public buildings of its period anywhere. The anatomy theatre became the prototype for the Chamber of Deputies in the Palais Bourbon (1795–7 but rebuilt 1828–33) and for many later legislative buildings including LATROBE's House of Representatives in the Capitol at Washington. Gondouin established a

successful private practice but was ruined by the Revolution and went into hiding. Under the Empire he re-emerged and designed the column in the Place Vendôme, Paris (completed 1810), first of the giant columns to be erected in the early C19 from Baltimore to St Petersburg.

Braham 1980.

**Gong**. In Chinese architecture the bow-shaped arms of the multiple bracket-arm structural system. The lower and shorter brackets support the longer ones at their end points on DOU or shaped blocks. Introduced into Japan with Buddhist architecture and elaborated for visual effect, e.g. Yakushiji pagoda, Nara.

**Gontard**, Karl Philip Christian von (1731–91). German architect working in Bayreuth, Berlin and Potsdam where he was responsible for the Rococo interior of Johann Gottfried Büring's Neues Palais, Sanssouci (1765–9). His Military Orphanage (1771–8) and Brockes House (1776), both in Potsdam, are very imposing. Also notable is his Spittel-kolonnade, Berlin (1776).

H. J. Giersberg, *Friedrich als Bauherr . . .* , Berlin 1986.

**González de León**, Teodoro (b.1926). Mexican architect and landscape architect who worked with LE CORBUSIER in Paris 1948–9, later with PANI in Mexico. From 1968 he has been intermittently in partnership with ZABLUDOVSKY and developed an architecture of massive linearity with Mayan echoes, e.g. Delegación Chauhtémac, Mexico City (1972–3); INFONAVIT headquarters, Mexico City (1975); and Mexican Embassy, Brasilia (1975). His later large-scale public commissions tend towards the rhetorical, e.g. Tabasco Government Center, Villahermosa (1986–8), but his tropical landscape garden, Parque Tomás Garrido,

Villahermosa (1984–7) is outstanding in its evocative power. His Supreme Court, Mexico City (1987–92), is notable, as are the curvilinear Fondo de Cultura Económica (1990–92) and Conservatorio Nacione de Música (1994), both in Mexico City.

L. Noelle (ed.), *G. de L. La voluntad del creador*, Bogota 1994.

**Goodhue**, Bertram Grosvenor (1869–1924). American church architect, rather more versatile than his partner CRAM at St Thomas's, New York (1905–13). His St Vincent Ferrer church, New York (1914–18), the Rockefeller Chapel, University of Chicago (1918–28), and St Bartholomew's, New York (1914–19), inspired by BENTLEY's Westminster Cathedral, are notable. His masterpiece is the Nebraska State Capitol, Lincoln (1920–32). The National Academy of Science, Washington, DC (1919–24), is also by him.

R. Oliver, *B.G.G.*, New York and London 1983.

**Gopura**. The elaborate high gateway to a Hindu temple, usually very richly decorated with sculpture. Notable examples survive in southern India. *See* Fig. 61.

**Gorge cornice**. In Ancient Egyptian architecture, the hollow-and-roll moulding. It is also found in Persian architecture.

**Gothic architecture**. The architecture of the pointed arch, the RIB VAULT, the FLYING BUTTRESS, the walls reduced to a minimum by spacious arcades, by GALLERY or TRIFORIUM, and by spacious CLERESTORY windows. These are not isolated motifs; they act together and represent a system of skeletal structure with active, slender, resilient members and membrane-thin infilling or no infilling at all. The motifs are not in themselves Gothic inventions. Pointed arches had existed in ROMANESQUE Burgundy,

Fig. 61 Gopura

southern France, and also Durham. Rib vaults had existed in Durham too; and the principle of flying buttresses as half-arches or half-tunnel vaults under the roofs of aisles or galleries above aisles is also found in French and English Romanesque. Even the verticalism of Gothic churches is only rarely more pronounced than that of, say, St Sernin at Toulouse or Ely (both Romanesque churches). The earliest completely Gothic building is the lower part of the east end of St Denis Abbey, dating from 1140–44 (*see* Abbot SUGER). For the development of the style in France and then in all other countries, *see* FRENCH ARCHITECTURE; ENGLISH ARCHITECTURE; GERMAN ARCHITECTURE; SPANISH ARCHITECTURE, etc.

**Gothic Revival**. The movement to

revive the Gothic style belongs chiefly to the late C18 and the C19. Before the late C18 it must be distinguished from the Gothic Survival, an unquestioning continuation of Gothic forms, which is of course largely a matter of out-of-the-way buildings. Of major buildings mostly churches are concerned, and St Eustache in Paris and the chapel of Lincoln's Inn in London were completed well within the C17. By then, however, the new attitude of Revival had also appeared – the conscious choice of the Gothic style in contrast to the accepted current style. The first cases are those of the finishing of Gothic buildings, cases of Gothic for the sake of conformity (flèche, Milan Cathedral; façade, S. Petronio, Bologna), but soon the choice was also made for new buildings, though rarely before c.1720. Then cases multiply, at least in England (HAWKSMOOR). Sanderson Miller (1717–80) began building sham castles in the 1740s, and with Arbury Hall, Warwickshire (c.1760–70), by Henry Keene (1726–76) and especially Horace Walpole's Strawberry Hill, near London (c.1750–70), the Gothic Revival became a fashion. It affected France and Germany in the later C18, and a little later also Italy, Russia, America, etc. With the growth of archaeological knowledge, the Gothic Revival became more competent but also more ponderous (see HISTORICISM). For churches Gothic remained the accepted style well into the C20 (Episcopalian Cathedral, Washington, DC, begun to a design by BODLEY in 1907). Of public buildings, the epoch-making one was the Houses of Parliament in London (BARRY and PUGIN, 1836–65): other major examples are the Town Hall, Vienna (1872–83), by Friedrich von Schmidt (1825–91); the Houses of Parliament, Budapest (1883–1902), by Imre Steindl (1839–1902); the Law Courts, London (1866–82), by STREET; the University,

Glasgow (1866–71), by Sir Giles Gilbert SCOTT, and the Rijksmuseum, Amsterdam (1877–85), by CUYPERS. *See also* CARPENTER'S GOTHIC.

K. Clark, *The G.R.*, London (1928) 1962; P. Frankl, *The G.*, Princeton (1960) 1966; Clarke 1969; G. German, *G.R. in Europe and Britain*, London 1973; W. Andrews, *American G.*, New York 1975; C. Baur, *Neugotik*, Munich 1981; M. McCarthy, *Origins of the G.R.*, London 1987; M. J. Lewis, *The Politics of the German G.R. August Reichensperger*, Cambridge, Mass. 1993.

**Gowan**, James (b.1923), *see* STIRLING, James.

**Grain elevator**. A silo or other building for storing grain and equipped with mechanical lifting devices. Large and imposing grain elevators of reinforced concrete were built in the late C19 and early C20 in the USA, notably at Minneapolis, Buffalo and Duluth. They were greatly admired by early C20 *avant-garde* architects, being compared by GROPIUS to the monumental temple architecture of Ancient Egypt.

D. R. Torbert, *A Century of Minnesota Architecture*, Minneapolis 1958; Banham 1986; L. Maher-Kiplinger, *G.E.*, New York 1996.

**Granite**. A hard igneous grey or dark pink rock consisting of feldspar, mica and quartz, found in all parts of the world. It takes a high polish, like MARBLE, and has been used for building as well as sculpture since Ancient Egyptian times, notably for obelisks and columns. The colossal monolithic columns used for the portico of the Pantheon in Rome are of Egyptian granite.

Davey 1965.

**Grassi**, Giorgio (b.1935), *see* ITALIAN ARCHITECTURE; NEO-RATIONALISM.

**Graves**, Michael (b.1934). Leading

POST-MODERN architect in the USA of the generation after VENTURI. He emerged in 1969 as one of the NEW YORK FIVE and developed towards a colourful and sophisticated neo-Historicism, e.g. his Plocek House at Warren, NJ (1982). His Public Services Building, Portland, Oregon (1980–82), made him famous internationally though his Humana Tower, Louisville, Kentucky (1986), surpasses it. His extremely personal use of 'classical' and 'vernacular' elements can be both elegant and idiosyncratic, e.g. the Environmental Education Center, Liberty State Park, Jersey City (1983), the San Juan Capestrano Library, California (1983). More provocative are his recent buildings for Disney in California and Florida, the Team Disney Building, Burbank (1991), the Dolphin and Swan hotels at Disney World, Orlando, Florida (1989–90), and the new hotel New York at Euro-Disney, Marne-la-Vallée, France (1992).

K. Nichols and P. Burke, *M.G. Buildings and Projects*, Princeton 1988; A. Buck and M. Vogt (eds.), *M.G.*, Berlin 1994; K. Nichols (ed.), *M.G. Buildings and Projects 1990–1994*, New York 1995.

**Gravesande**, Arent van's (d.1662). A follower of van CAMPEN and a leading exponent of Dutch Classicism. His style was already well developed in his earliest known building, the Sebastiaansdoelen in The Hague (1636). His mature work is all in Leiden, where he was municipal architect – the Cloth Hall (1639), the Bibliotheca Thysiana and his masterpiece the Marekerk (1638–48), an octagonal domed church with Ionic columns supporting the drum of the dome. He later began a variant of this design in the Oostkerk at Middelburg (1646).

Kuyper 1980.

**Gray**, Eileen (1879–1976). English designer and architect who lived in Paris from 1902 onwards. She began as a lacquerwork and furniture designer and only later worked as an architect, in a simple elegant modern style influenced by LE CORBUSIER, e.g. villas at Roquebrune (1926–9) and Castellar (1932–4). At the Paris International Exhibition in 1937 she showed an ambitious project for a holiday centre in Le Corbusier's Pavillon des Temps Nouvelles. She became famous in the 1970s, mainly for her furniture.

B. Loye, *E.G. 1879–1976*, Paris 1984; P. Adam, *E.G.*, London 1985; P. Garner, *E.G. Designer and Architect*, Cologne 1993; S. Hecker and C. F. Muller, *E.G. (1879–1976)*, Barcelona 1993.

**Gréber**, Jacques (1882–1962), *see* CANADIAN ARCHITECTURE.

**Greek architecture**. Commenting on the buildings on the Acropolis at Athens, Plutarch remarked: 'They were created in a short time for all time. Each in its fineness was even then at once age-old; but in the freshness of its vigour it is, even to the present day, recent and newly wrought.' No better description of the aims and achievements of Greek architects has ever been written. Their ambition was to discover eternally valid rules of form and proportion; to erect buildings human in scale yet suited to the divinity of their gods; to create, in other words, a classically ideal architecture. Their success may be measured by the fact that their works have been copied on and off for some 2,500 years and have never been superseded. Though severely damaged, the Parthenon remains the most nearly perfect building ever erected. Its influence stretches from the immediate followers of its architects to LE COR-BUSIER. Greek architecture was, however, predominantly religious and official. Whereas temples and public buildings were of the greatest magnificence, private houses seem to have been fairly simple single-storey affairs, built of cheap materials.

Although the technique of constructing arches was known to the Greeks and the materials used for building temples, after the C6 BC, were normally stone or marble, their architecture was TRABEATED and preserved many of the techniques of wooden construction. A deep respect for tradition led them to preserve as decorative elements in their stone buildings many of the constructional elements of wooden ones: TRIGLYPHS representing the end of cross-beams, GUTTAE the pegs used for fastening them, and METOPES the space between them. They derived much from other Mediterranean civilizations – the plan of the temple from Asia Minor or Mycenae (*see* MEGARON), the columnar form from Egypt.

But the Doric temple form evolved in the late C7 BC was as original as it was typically Greek in its bold simplicity, unity of design, and use of decoration to emphasize (never to mask) structure. The earliest Doric temple to survive is that of Hera at Olympia (*c.*580 BC); it originally had wooden columns, which were gradually replaced in stone. Fragments from the temple of Artemis at Korkyra, Corfu (*c.*580 BC), reveal that sculpture was already used for the pediments. Other notable early Doric temples include the Temple C at Selinunte (Selinous) in Sicily (mid C6 BC), the so-called Basilica at Paestum (*c.*530 BC), and the temple of 'Concord' at Agrigento in Sicily (*c.*500–470 BC). In all these the columns are rather stocky and primitive-looking, partly because their smooth stucco coverings have flaked off. Much greater refinement marks the temple of Hephaistos (Theseum), Athens (mid-C5 BC). The summit was reached at the Parthenon (447–432 BC), with its perfect proportions and nicely balanced relation of

sculpture to architecture. Here, as in other Doric temples, great pains were taken to correct optical illusions by the subtle use of ENTASIS. The temple to Athena Nike (*c.*425 BC) and the Erechtheum (421–406 BC), also on the Acropolis, reveal a tendency towards the exquisite; and the latter, with its graceful Ionic capitals and wonderful CARYATIDS, also points towards a new appreciation of architectural movement.

The so-called Dorian people who dominated most of mainland Greece and the western colonies regarded Doric as their national architectural style. Ionians of the Aegean islands and the coast of Asia Minor developed the more delicate Ionic ORDER, as in the temple of Artemis at Ephesus (*c.*560–550 BC) by the Cretan architect Chersiphron of Knossos, whose son Metagenes completed the building. It first appeared on the mainland in the buildings they contributed to the sanctuary at Delphi. And probably for political as much as aesthetic reasons, in the C5 BC the Athenians, then allied with the eastern Greeks against the Persians, admitted the Ionic order for the Erechtheum on the Acropolis in Athens (dedicated to the ancestor Dorians shared with the Ionians). The Ionic order was otherwise used on the mainland for interiors, notably in the temple of Apollo Epikourios at Bassae (late C5), which also included one column with a Corinthian capital, at the end of the CELLA. Until the HELLENISTIC period, the Corinthian order was used exclusively for interiors, e.g. Great Tholos at Delphi (*c.*375 BC), temple of Athena Alea at Tegea (*c.*360 BC), Tholos of Epidauros (*c.*350 BC). The only exception was the Choragic Monument of Lysicrates in Athens (late C4 BC), a kind of enlargement of a bronze offering table. This little building, with an almost overbred elegance (which had great appeal in the C18), illustrates the final stage of Greek architectural development on the eve of the Macedonian conquest by Philip and his son Alexander the Great. A tendency towards superhuman monumentality as well as lavish ornamentation culminated in the Mausoleum at Halicarnassus (modern Bodrum) in 355–330 BC, where the role of the sculptors was greater than that of the architect.

Although the main Greek achievement was in the evolution of the Doric temple, many other types of religious buildings were of great beauty. The grandest were the theatres, notably that of Dionysus under the Acropolis in Athens (C5 BC, but much altered) and that at Epidauros (c.350 BC), which reveal as perfect a command of acoustics as of visual effects. Theatres of this type were much imitated, especially in Asia Minor, during the HELLENISTIC period. See also CRETAN AND MYCENAEAN ARCHITECTURE.

For later architecture in Greece see BYZANTINE ARCHITECTURE and, for C19 developments, Theophil and Hans Christian HANSEN. Stamathios Kleanthis (1802–62), a pupil of SCHINKEL, and Lyssander Kaftanzoglou (1812–62) rivalled the Hansens with such buildings as the former's Byzantine Museum, Athens, and the latter's Polytechneion, Athens, designed in the 1850s (built 1862–80). In the C20 notable contributions to URBAN DESIGN were made by DOXIADIS and to contemporary regionalism (Cycladic, Macedonian, etc.) by Dimitris Pikionis (1887–1968), with such buildings as his Elementary School, Lycabettus, Athens (1932); Experimental School, Salonika (1935); and Church of St Dimitrios Lombardiaris, Athens (1951–7), with the adjoining park and promenade facing the Acropolis. He was followed by Aris Konstantinides (1913–93) with his social housing projects and hotels at Epidauros, Poros and Kalam-

baka. The industrial architecture of Takis Zenetos (1926–77) should be mentioned (e.g. the Fix and Vianil factories, Athens, of 1957 and 1964), also the hotels and other work by Nikos Valsamakis (b.1924), e.g. the Hotel Amalia, Nauplia (1980) and the Banque de Credit, Athens (1978–91). More recently Susanna and Dimitris Andonakakis (b.1935 and 1933) have worked the same regional vein with distinction, as at their Museum on Chios (1965), their universities at Rethimnion and Canea (Khania), Crete (1981–2), and numerous private houses, e.g. the Tzirtilakis House, Canea, Crete (1992).

**Greek cross plan**. A centralized plan based on a CROSS with four equal arms. The two axes are at right angles and have identical, balancing elements on each of the axes around the central elements, e.g. San Marco, Venice.

**Greek key pattern,** see FRET.

**Greek Revival**. Greek as against Roman architecture became known to the West only about 1750–60 (see CLASSICISM). It was at first regarded as primitive and imitated by only a few architects. The earliest example is a garden temple at Hagley by 'Athenian' STUART (1758). A Grecian fashion began only in the 1780s. Among the earliest believers in the positive value of the simplicity and gravity of the Greek C5 were LEDOUX and SOANE. The Greek Revival culminated in England and France in the 1820s and 1830s, even, with the HANSENS, in Athens itself. In Germany it continued into the mid-C19 and in the USA it flourished especially in the period 1815–60. (See also GILLY; HAMILTON; PLAYFAIR; SCHINKEL; SMIRKE; STRICKLAND; WILKINS; etc.)

Crook 1972; Honour 1977 and 1979; Middleton and Watkin 1977; R. G. Kennedy, *G.R. America*, New York 1989.

**Green**. A piece of grassy land situated in or near a town or village and used by the public for recreation.

**Green architecture**, *see* ENVIRONMENTAL, GREEN OR SUSTAINABLE ARCHITECTURE.

**Green-belt**. An area of park, agricultural land or wild country surrounding a village or town and providing protection. LOUDON proposed a prototype green-belt for London in 1829 and later in the C19 it was taken up by GARDEN CITY planners and was widely adopted for new towns in the UK and USA. The name Greenbelt was given to one of three new towns founded in Maryland in 1937 by the Resettlement Administration as part of F. D. Roosevelt's New Deal; *see* Clarence STEIN.

**Greene & Greene**. South Californian architects: Charles Sumner Greene (1868–1957) and Henry Greene (1870–1954). They specialized in massive timber construction and followed the ARTS AND CRAFTS movement in exposing joints. Their œuvre was almost exclusively domestic. Their very low-pitched roofs are reminiscent of Frank Lloyd WRIGHT and the Prairie Style. They particularly liked the juxtaposition of timber with boulders. Examples of their work are the J. H. Cuthbertson House of 1902, Blacker House of 1907 and Gamble House of 1908–9, all in Pasadena, California, and the Pratt House of 1909 in Ojai, California.

Jordy 1970; R. L. Makinson, *C. and H.G. and Their Work*, 1978; and *G. & G. Architecture as a Fine Art*, Santa Barbara (1977) 1985; R. Winter, 1997.

**Greenhouse**, *see* CONSERVATORY.

**Greenway**, Francis Howard (1777–1837). A pupil of NASH, he was active first in Bristol and Clifton, England, where he designed the Assembly Rooms (1806, completed by Joseph Kay). Declared insolvent in 1811, he was accused of forgery in 1812 and condemned to death but transported to Australia instead. The verdict was for fourteen years, but he was at once recommended by a retired admiral to Governor Macquarie and very soon found himself busy designing buildings in and around Sydney. He became Acting Civilian Architect in 1816. His principal buildings belonged to only five or six years: the lighthouse and Macquarie Tower; the churches of St Matthew, Windsor, St Luke, Liverpool, and St James, Sydney; the Government House at Sydney, the Hight Park Barracks and the Liverpool Hospital. Greenway's style appeared at first to be Late Georgian, but individual motifs occur, especially in St Matthew. But his success did not, alas, last long. After quarrelling with Macquarie he was less busy.

M. H. Ellis, *F.G. His Life and Times*, Sydney and San Francisco (1949) 1966; M. Herman, *Early Australian Architects (1788–1850) and their Work*, Sydney and London 1954.

**Gregotti**, Vittorio (b.1927). Italian architect and theorist associated with NEO-RATIONALISM. He published his influential *Il territorio dell'architettura* in 1965 and demonstrated his theories in practice with a structurally articulate architecture that is both topographically and climatically determined, notably in large-scale urban projects. His University of Palermo Science Department buildings (1969–88) and the University of Calabria complex at Cosenza (1974–80) were remarkable, as was his Montedison Research Centre, Naples (1977–89). During the 1980s he published notable mega-architectural theories which he later realized at the Belém Cultural Centre, Lisbon (1988–92). In 1992 he also remodelled the Olympic Stadium, Barcelona, with great effect.

M. Tafuri, *V. G. Buildings and Projects*, Milan (1981) 1988; M. Tafuri, *G. Associati 1973–88*, Milan 1989; G. Vragnaz, *G. Associati*, Milan 1990.

**Grid**. A framework or network of horizontal and vertical lines forming squares of uniform size, like a chequerboard.

**Grid plan**, *see* URBAN DESIGN.

**Griffin**, Walter Burley (1876–1937). An American PRAIRIE SCHOOL architect, he worked for Frank Lloyd WRIGHT in Chicago 1901–5 and then on his own, contributing notably to the Rock Crest Rock Glen development, Mason City, Iowa (1908–17). In 1912 he won the competition for a new capital city at Canberra, settled in Australia and created at Canberra a gigantic GARDEN CITY (only the centre still bears the imprint of his conception). He also planned the community suburb of Castlecrag, Sydney (1921–35), and designed some notable buildings, e.g. Newman College, Melbourne (1915–18); Capitol Theatre, Melbourne (1921–4), before settling in 1935 in Lucknow, India, where he provided plans for the university campus, the Pioneer Press and a number of houses for Indian clients.

M. L. Peisch, *The Chicago School of Architecture: Early Followers of Sullivan and Wright*, New York 1964; J. Birrell, *W.B.G.*, Brisbane 1964; D. L. Johnson, *The Architecture of W.B.G.*, Melbourne 1977; M. Maldre, *W.B.G. in America*, Chicago 1996.

**Griffith**, John (1796–1888), *see* CEMETERY.

**Grimaldi**, Giovanni Francesco (1606–80), *see* ALGARDI, Alessandro.

**Grimshaw**, Nicholas (b.1939). English architect and an imaginative and resourceful exponent of High Tech. His Waterloo International Railway Terminal, London (1988–93), serving Channel Tunnel rail traffic, established his reputation. This lightweight and supple-seeming structure of steel and glass avoids all historical references; the structure itself is its theme. His earlier works included the remarkable Sports Hall for IBM, Hampshire (1980–82); the Financial Times Printing Works, London (1987–8); and the British Pavilion for Expo '92, Seville (1992). His Igus GmbH Factory, Cologne (1993); the Western Morning News Building, Plymouth (1990–93); the Compass Centre, Heathrow Airport, London (1994); and the RAC Regional Centre, Bristol (1995), followed.

R. Moore, *N.G. Buildings and Projects*, London 1994; G. Amory, *Architecture, Industry and Innovation. The Early Work of N.G. & Partners*, London 1995; R. Moore (ed.), *Structure, Space and Skin. The World of N.G. & Partners*, London 1995.

**Groin**. The curved line or sharp edge formed by the intersection of vaulting surfaces.

**Groin vault**, *see* VAULT.

**Gropius**, Walter (1883–1969). German architect who studied at the Colleges of Technology of Berlin and Munich. He received his introduction to the C20 problems of architecture and the responsibilities of the architect in the office of Peter BEHRENS, who believed in the architect's duty to provide well-designed buildings for working in, and also well-designed everyday products. He spent the years 1907–10 with Behrens. The outcome of this was that Gropius, as soon as he had established a practice of his own (1910), produced his proto-Modern housing at Golzengüt and submitted a memorandum to a powerful potential client on the mass-producing of housing and equipment. One year later he built, with Adolph Meyer (1881–1929), the Fagus factory at Alfeld, which was one of the earliest buildings in any country to be in full command of the elements of architecture which were to constitute the INTERNATIONAL MODERN style: glass CURTAIN WALLING, unrelieved cubic blocks, corners left free of visible supports. For the Werkbund Exhibition at Cologne in 1914, Gropius produced, also with Adolph Meyer, a Model Factory and Office Building, equally radical in its statement of new principles. Apart from Behrens, Frank Lloyd WRIGHT was now a source of inspiration; for two publications about him had appeared in Berlin in 1910 and 1911. On the strength of the Werkbund Exhibition building, Henry van de VELDE, then head of the School of Arts and Crafts at Weimar, advised the Grand Duke to make Gropius his successor. Gropius accepted and, when the First World War was over, settled down at Weimar to convert the school into a completely new establishment, for which he coined the name BAUHAUS (House of Building). This name alludes to Gropius's conviction that, as with the medieval cathedral, the building ought to be the meeting-place of all arts and crafts teaching; all should work towards this ultimate unity. He also believed that all artists should be familiar with crafts, and that the initial training of artists and craftsmen should be one and the same – an introduction to form, colour and the nature of materials. This part of the teaching programme, first worked out by Johannes Itten, was known as the Basic Course (*Vorkurs*).

Gropius, in the first years of the Bauhaus, was propelled by the ideas of William MORRIS on the one hand, by the enthusiasm of the EXPRESSIONISTS on the other. There are, indeed, a few works by him belonging to these first years which are entirely Expressionist in style, notably the jagged concrete monument to those killed in the March Rising (1921) and the large log-house for the timber manufacturer Adolf Sommerfeld (1921–2, destroyed), the latter equipped by Bauhaus staff and students. But then in 1923, stimulated by contacts with the Dutch group of DE STIJL (led by Theo van Doesburg), Gropius returned to the ideals of his early years. The Bauhaus turned from emphasis on craft to emphasis on industrial design, and Gropius's own style followed once again the line laid down by the Fagus factory. The principal monument of this change is the Bauhaus's own new premises at Dessau (1925–6), functionally planned and detailed, the paradigmatic masterpiece of what was later to become known as the International Modern style. It survived the Second World War intact. Other important designs of these flourishing years in Germany are those for a Total Theatre (1926) and the long slabs of 'rational' housing for Siemensstadt (1929).

The rising tide of National Socialism killed the Bauhaus, but Gropius had already left it in 1928. After Hitler assumed power, Gropius left Germany and, following a short spell of partnership with Maxwell FRY in London (1934–7) – the most influential outcome of which was the Impington Village College near Cambridge and the English edition of his *The New Architecture of the Bauhaus* (London 1935) – he went to Harvard, where his principal job was once again teaching. His and Konrad WACHSMANN's General Panel system was a notable experiment in prefabricated housing and in 1945, in accordance with his faith in co-operative work, he started his own firm as TAC (The Architects' Collaborative) – a group of younger men working with him in full freedom. Of the achievements of this cooperative the Harvard Graduate Center (1949), a block of flats for the Berlin Hansa quarter (Interbau

Exhibition 1957) and the Pan Am Building, New York (1958–63), may be mentioned, together with Gropius's own US Embassy, Athens, of 1957–61 and the ceramic factory at Rosenthal-am-Rotbuhl in Selb, Germany (1964).

M. Franciscono, *W.G. and the Creation of the Bauhaus in Weimar*, Chicago and London 1971; R. R. Isaacs, *W.G. Der Mensch und sein Werk*, Berlin 1983–4; H. Probst and C. Schadlich, *W.G.*, Berlin 1986; D. Sharp, *Bauhaus Dessau 1925–6. W.G.*, London 1993; P. Berdini, *W.G.*, Barcelona 1994.

**Grosch**, Christian Henrik (1801–65), *see* NORWEGIAN ARCHITECTURE.

**Grotesque**. Fanciful ornamental decoration composed of small, loosely connected motifs, not unlike ARABESQUES but including human figures, monkeys, sphinxes, etc. It derived from Ancient Roman decorations, either painted or in low relief, which came to light in the Renaissance after being buried for centuries in subterranean ruins known as *grotte*, hence the name *grotesques*. At first details only were used, but in 1516 complete schemes were revived by Raphael in the Vatican and these became famous when Raphael used them *c.*1519 to decorate the Vatican Logge, largely executed by Giovanni da Udine, who decorated the Villa Madama, Rome, in a similar manner (1520–21). Within a few years engravings of grotesques were in circulation. By the mid C16, grotesques had spread from Italy to the rest of Europe and during the next 300 years were widely used, often in combination with STRAPWORK.

P. Ward-Jackson in *Victoria & Albert Museum Bulletin*, April and July 1967; N. Dacos, *La Découverte de la Domus Aurea et la formation des G. à la Renaissance*, London and Leiden 1971; A. Chastel, *La G.*, 1988.

**Grotto**. An artificial cavern, usually with fountains and other water-works and decorated with rock- and shellwork, also sculpture, ceramic reliefs and panels, etc. Known to have been a feature of Ancient Roman gardens, the grotto was revived in the Renaissance, notably by MANNERIST architects such as BUONTALENTI, e.g. grottoes in the Boboli Gardens, Florence (1583–8). The most celebrated later example was that created for Alexander Pope, with incrustations of minerals, shells and pieces of glass on its walls in a tunnel beneath the road that separated his house from his garden at Twickenham, Middlesex (1719–25). In more rustic forms they became features of numerous LANDSCAPE GARDENS. Thomas Wright (1711–86) published engravings of *Six Original Designs of Grottos*, London 1753; others were illustrated by C. C. L. HIRSCHFELD.

B. Jones, *Follies and G.*, London (1955) 1974; N. Miller, *Heavenly Caves*, New York 1982; Lotz 1996.

**Grout**. A thin fluid MORTAR used to fill joints or other voids, e.g. between paving stones to keep them firmly in place.

**Gruen**, Victor (1903–80). German architect, trained under BEHRENS, who emigrated to the USA in 1938 where he specialized in eye-catching shop designs, e.g. his Grayson Store, Seattle (1940–41), and later invented the 'shopping centre' sited out of town for car-owners, e.g. his Northland Shopping Center, Detroit (1952). His Southdale Center, Minneapolis (1956), was the prototype enclosed suburban shopping mall. His plan for Fort Worth, Texas (1955), was notable and in 1964 he published *Heart of our Cities*.

C. Tunnard, *Man-Made America*, New Haven 1963.

**Gruppo 7**, *see* RATIONALISM.

**Guadet**, Julien (1834–1908), French architect and theorist trained under LABROUSTE at the École des Beaux Arts, Paris, with which he was to be closely associated throughout his career, winner of the Rome prize in 1864, instructor in one of the three official *ateliers* from 1871 and professor of architectural theory from 1894. Of his relatively few buildings the most prominent is the Hôtel des Postes in rue du Louvre, Paris (1881–6), a metal construction masked by a stone façade with chunky engaged pilasters in a free interpretation of Doric. He was of greater significance for his writings. His inaugural lecture as professor of theory expounded the rational doctrine of the École as taught during the previous decades. It was reprinted in his influential four-volume *Eléments et théories de l'Architecture* (1901–4, 6th edn 1929–30). Intended as a textbook for students, this provided solutions to all the problems they might encounter, from the choice of paper for drawings to the 'composition' of buildings, which he defined as the putting together, welding and uniting of walls, openings, vaults and roofs. He went on to give the first thorough study of building types, with examples taken from the whole history of architecture. However, the purpose of a building remained, for him, its controlling factor and he wrote that 'the architect must first of all determine the content from which he can then derive the container'. This might suggest a precocious functionalism but he accepted that most buildings would in fact be clothed in an historical style as demanded by the patron. Thus he became known as the BEAUX ARTS theorist. Yet his pupils included Auguste PERRET and Tony GARNIER. His son Paul (1873–1931) designed for himself an astylar house in Paris (1912), built in concrete with the assistance or Perret.

Banham 1960; Collins 1965; D. D.

Egbert, *The Beaux Arts Tradition in French Architecture*, Princeton 1980; Kruft 1994.

**Guarini**, Guarino (1624–83), Italian architect, born in Modena and a Theatine father, well known as a philosopher and mathematician, before he won fame as an architect. (He expanded Euclid and even foreshadowed Monge in his learned *Placita philosophica* of 1665.) Since he was first a mathematician and second an architect, his complex spatial compositions are sometimes difficult to understand. All his important surviving buildings are in Turin, where he spent the last seventeen years of his life. His admiration of BORROMINI is very obvious in Collegio dei Nobili (1678) and Palazzo Carignano (1679), especially the latter with its oval saloon and undulating façade in the style of S. Carlo alle Quattro Fontane. To inflate Borromini's miniature church to palatial grandiloquence was daring enough, yet his originality had already carried him even further in the Cappella della SS. Sindone (1667–90, damaged by fire 1997) and in S. Lorenzo (1668–87). Both churches are crowned with fantastic and unprecedented cone-shaped domes. That of SS. Sindone is built of superimposed segmental arches that diminish in span as they ascend, the abstract geometric poetry of this free construction being emphasized by the diaphanous light which filters through the grids. The S. Lorenzo dome is equally unusual: it is composed of interlocking semicircular arches forming an octagon on a circular drum. The inspiration for this odd conception may have come from Hispano-Moresque architecture, perhaps from the similar dome in the mosque of al Hakim at Cordoba, Spain (AD 965), or, more likely, from French Gothic, which he certainly studied when in France. (He was also the first architect to write positively about the engineering achievements of

Gothic architects in his own treatise.) Guarini's structural ingenuity was not confined to domes, and his other experiments, notably those with banded vaults and diagonal, forward-tilted, or three-dimensional arches, were to be very influential in Germany and Austria. None of his important buildings outside Turin has survived: e.g. SS. Annunziata and Theatine Palace in Messina (1660); Ste Anne-la-Royale, Paris (1662 onwards); St Mary of Altötting, Prague (1679); and S. Maria Divina Providencia, Lisbon. This last represented a radical reformulation of the standard Counter-Reformation church in terms of interpenetrating ovals and circles, influential in Central Europe. His influence was greatly increased by his *Architettura civile*, published posthumously in 1737: engravings from it were known from 1668 onwards.

Wittkower 1982; H. A. Meek, *G.G. and his Architecture*, New Haven and London 1988.

**Guas**, Juan (d.1496). A Spanish mason of French descent, probably the designer of S. Juan de los Reyes at Toledo (1477 onwards). Towards the end of his life Guas was master mason of Segovia and Toledo Cathedrals. It is likely that the wildly Late Gothic façade of S. Gregorio at Valladolid is his (1487–96).

Kubler and Soria 1959.

**Gucewicz**, Wawrzyniec (1753–98), *see* POLISH ARCHITECTURE.

**Guedes**, Amancio d'Alpoim Miranda (b.1925), *see* SOUTH AFRICAN ARCHITECTURE.

**Guêpière**, Pierre-Louis-Philippe de la (c.1715–73). French architect who, alongside PIGAGE, introduced Louis XVI taste and standards into Germany. In 1750 he published *Recueil de projets d'architecture* and in the same year was summoned to

Stuttgart, where he succeeded Leopoldo Retti as Directeur des Bâtiments in 1752 and designed the interiors of Retti's Neues Palais (destroyed). His masterpieces are the small and exquisite La Solitude (1763–7) outside Stuttgart and Mon Repos (1764–7) near Ludwigsburg. The interior of the latter was partially modified c.1804 in an Empire style. He returned to France in 1768 but built nothing of note there. His designs for the Hôtel de Ville at Montbéliard were executed after his death with considerable alterations. He published *Recueil d'esquisses d'architecture* in 1762.

Colombier 1956; H. A. Klaiber, *Der Württemberg Oberbaudirektor P. de la G.*, Stuttgart 1959; H. J. Wörner, *Architektur der Frühklassizismus in Suddeutschland*, Munich 1979.

**Guévrékian**, Gabriel (1900–1970). Armenian architect, born in Istanbul and trained in Paris under MALLET-STEVENS. He first attracted international notice in 1925 at the Exposition des Arts Décoratifs, Paris, with a Modernist ART DECO 'garden of water and light'. In 1927 he laid out a similarly 'Modernist' garden at Hyères, France, with alternate squares of ceramic tile pavement and pyramidal flowerbeds in a triangular space (reconstructed 1990). Both gardens were influential on designers seeking an alternative to historicizing and naturalistic schemes. His Villa Heim, Neuilly, Paris (1927–8), was Art Deco in style inside and out, set in a garden subdivided into small spaces and with terrace gardens on each of its three storeys and a roof-garden – an unprecedented synthesis of house and garden. He was Secretary General of CIAM from 1928 until 1933, when he went to Iran where he became Chief Architect and Planner in Tehran and designed the Ministry of Industry, a theatre and several private houses. In 1937 he settled in England, where his urban design projects were abandoned because of the war. Later he collaborated in the reconstruction of Saarbrücken, Germany, but soon emigrated to the USA where he devoted himself to teaching.

E. Vitou, G.G., Paris 1987; D. Imbert, *The Modernist Garden in France*, London 1993.

**Guilloche**. A pattern of interlacing bands forming a plait and used as an enrichment on a moulding. *See* Fig. 62.

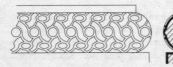

Fig. 62 Guilloche

**Guimard**, Hector (1867–1942), French architect and professor at the École des Arts Décoratifs from 1894 to 1898. He is the best of the French ART NOUVEAU architects. At the beginning of his career (in 1893) he was influenced, it seems, by HORTA. His most remarkable building is the block of flats called Castel Bérenger in Paris (1894–1912). The use of metal, faïence and glass-bricks is bold and inventive, though the exterior is of less interest. On the other hand his Métro stations (1899–1904) are nothing but exterior – open metal arches in extreme Art Nouveau shapes – a daring thing for an architect to design, and perhaps an even more daring thing for a client to accept.

F. L. Graham, *H.G.*, New York 1970; Y. Brunhammer and G. Naylor, *H.G.*, London 1970; M. Rheims and G. Vigne, *H.G. 1867–1942*, New York 1988; F. Caccin *et al.*, *G.*, Paris 1992–3.

**Gullichsen**, Kristian Valter (b.1932), *see* FINNISH ARCHITECTURE.

**Gumpp**, Johann Martin (1643–1729). The most important member of an Austrian family of architects working in Innsbruck, where he was Hofkammerbaumeister and a pioneer exponent of the Baroque. His main works are the Fugger-Taxis palace (1679–80), the remodelling of the old Government House (1690–92) and the Spitalkirche (1700–1701). His son Georg Anton (1682–1754) followed him as master mason to the Innsbruck court and was responsible for the boldly unconventional Landhaus (1725–8).

M. Krapf, *Die Baumeister G.*, Vienna and Munich 1979–80.

**Guttae**. Small drop-like projections carved below the TENIA under each TRIGLYPH on a Doric ARCHITRAVE. *See* Fig. 86.

**Gwathmey**, Charles (b.1938). American architect who began with the NEW YORK FIVE, of which his own residence and studio at Amagansett, NY (1963–5), was exemplary. In 1968 he formed Gwathmey, Siegel & Associates with Robert Siegel (b.1939). Their main works are the Whig Hall, Princeton (1970); the East Campus Student and Academic Center, Columbia University, New York (1976); the De Menil House, East Hampton (1979–84); the American Museum of the Moving Image, Astoria, NY (1988); the Busch–Reisinger Fine Arts Library, Harvard University, Cambridge, Massachusetts (1990); the Disney World Convention Center, Orlando, Florida (1991), and the Disney Contemporary Resort, Lake Buena Vista, Florida (1991); the extension to F. L. WRIGHT'S Guggenheim Museum, New York (1992); and the Science, Industry and Business Library, New York (1996).

P. Arnell and T. Bickford, *C.G. and R.S. Buildings and Projects 1964–84*, New York 1984; B. Collins and D. Kaprow,

*G.S. & Ass. Buildings & Projects 1982–92*, New York 1993.

**Gymnasium**. In Ancient Greece and Rome a place for physical exercise and training, larger than a PALAESTRA. English has taken over the athletic, German, French and Italian the educational connotations of the word.

J. Delorme, *Gymnases. Étude sur les monuments consacrés à l'éducation dans la Grèce ancienne*, Paris 1960.

**Gynaeceum**. In an Ancient Greek (or Roman) house, the apartments reserved for women. In Byzantine architecture, the women's gallery in a church.

# H

**Haag**, Richard (b.1923). American landscape architect. His two most notable works are strikingly different from one another: Gasworks Park, Seattle (1970–78) and Bloedel Reserve, Bainbridge Island in Puget Sound, Washington (begun 1985). The former is a recreational area on a promontory jutting into Lake Union, where he made a prominent feature of derelict gasworks which a conventional designer would have demolished; the latter is a series of gardens with a large oblong pool, surrounded by tall clipped hedges, between an artificially natural landscape garden and a truly wild bird sanctuary. His Battelle Seattle Research Center, Seattle (1967–72), and Jordan Park, Everett Marina Park, Washington (1970–72), should also be mentioned.

Lyall 1991; Cerver 1995.

**Ha-ha**. A walled ditch dividing a garden or park from the fields outside without interrupting the view. A ha-ha is invisible except close to, hence its name, derived from the supposed exclamation of surprise on encountering it. It consists of a sunken retaining wall on the garden side, deep enough to obstruct intruding animals, and a sloping bank on the other, visually uniting the garden with the neighbouring fields. French in origin – a primitive form was mentioned by A. J. Dézaillier d'Argenville in his *La Théorie et la pratique du jardinage* (1709) and by SWITZER and others – it was taken up and developed by C18 English landscape architects, notably KENT and BRIDGEMAN whose ha-ha survives at Rousham.

**Hacienda**. In Spain and Spanish-speaking countries in Central and South America, a low, sprawling house with projecting roof and spacious verandas or porches, such as was traditional for an owner's house on a large estate or plantation. It was later developed for domestic architecture, e.g. in south-western USA, and more recently by such architects as BARRAGÁN and LEGORETTA.

**Hadfield**, George (1763–1826), was born in Leghorn and trained at the Royal Academy Schools, London, winning the Gold Medal (1784) and studying in Italy 1790–91. In 1795 he went to America to supervise the construction of the new Capitol in Washington, replacing Étienne Sulpice (called Stephen) Hallet (c.1760–1825). He disapproved of the design (by Thornton) and Hallet's revisions, but the radical alterations he suggested, such as the introduction of a colossal order, were not approved and he was dismissed in 1798. He continued to practise in Washington and impressed his neo-classical taste on the new city, e.g. the City Hall (1820, now the District of Columbia Courthouse), United States Bank (1824), Fuller's Hotel, Gadsby's Hotel, Van Ness's mausoleum (1826) and the imposing Paestum portico of Arlington House (1818), one of the most splendid examples of the Greek Revival in America.

Whiffen and Koeper 1981; Colvin 1995.

**Hadid**, Zaha (b.1950). Born in Baghdad, trained in London (1972–8) she worked with KOOLHAAS until 1982 when she won a competition for a Club House in Hong Kong. Her provocative but remarkable 'fragmented' design was later included in the New York DECONSTRUCTIVIST exhibition, 1988. The project was never realized, nor were her equally remarkable designs for an office building in Berlin (1986) and for the Cardiff Bay Opera House, Wales (1994). Her built works to date are the interior of the Monsoon Restaurant, Sapporo, Japan (1990); the Vitra Fire Station, Weil-am-Rhein, Germany (1989–93) and an apartment building in Kreuzberg, Berlin (1987–94). In 1994 she published *Lines* (London).

E. Blum, *Ein Haus, ein Aufruhr*, Wiesbaden 1997; M. Mönninger, *Z.H. Projekte 1990–1997*, Stuttgart 1997.

**Hagioscope**, *see* SQUINT.

**Halfpenny**, William (Michael Hoare, d.1755). English architect to whom Holy Trinity, Leeds (1722–7), and the Redland Chapel, Bristol (1740–43), have been erroneously attributed, but he published some twenty architectural manuals for country gentlemen and builders which were enormously successful and influential. His designs are mostly Palladian but also include some rather hamfisted attempts at Rococo sophistication, CHINOISERIE, GOTHIC REVIVAL, etc. *Practical Architecture* (1724), *A New and Compleat System of Architecture* (1749) and *Rural Architecture in the Chinese Taste* (*c.*1750) are among the best of his books.

Harris 1990; Colvin 1995.

**Half-timbering**, *see* FRAMED BUILDING; TIMBER-FRAMING.

**Hall**. 1. A large room for assembly or entertaining. 2. An entrance room or corridor. 3. The principal and largest room in a medieval palace or residence, communal and multipurpose, e.g. West-

minster Hall, London (begun 1097–9, remodelled 1395–1402).

M. Thompson, *The Medieval H. The Basis of Secular Domestic Life 600–1600*, Aldershot 1995.

4. A manor house. 5. A public building e.g. city hall, town hall and guildhall, of which magnificent medieval examples survive, notably in Belgium and Germany.

M. Damus, *Das Rathaus – Architektur und Sozialgeschichte von Gründerzeit zur Postmoderne*, Berlin 1988.

**Hall**, William Hammond (1846–1934). American civil engineer and landscape architect notable for the layout of Golden Gate Park, San Francisco (1871–6), with winding carriage roads, lawns, lakes and a botanical garden on what had been barren sand dunes which he succeeded in stabilizing. It was the first of the great PUBLIC PARKS in the USA after OLMSTED and VAUX's Central Park in New York.

R. H. Clary, *The Making of Golden Gate Park: The Early Years 1865–1906*, San Francisco 1979.

**Hall church**. A German type of church in which nave and aisles are of approximately equal height. Thus the nave is not lit from above but from the large windows of the aisles. Transepts and a distinct chancel are omitted. The earliest example is the C11 Chapel of St Bartholomew in Paderborn: the finest by STETHAIMER. *See*. Fig. 63.

**Hallet**, Étienne Sulpice (called Stephen) (*c.*1760–1825), *see* HADFIELD, George; THORNTON, William.

**Halprin**, Lawrence (b.1916). American landscape architect working in San Francisco, first under CHURCH and from 1943 independently. His private gardens are exemplary CALIFORNIA SCHOOL designs. His public works are notable for

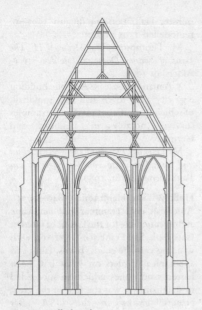

Fig. 63  Hall church

their imaginative use of concrete, stone and water, e.g. Lovejoy Plaza, Portland, Oregon (1966), with variations in level to offset sculptures that can be climbed over and pools that invite splashing and wading; the dramatic Freeway Park, Seattle, Washington (1970–76); the poetic F. D. Roosevelt Memorial Garden, Washington, DC (begun 1974); and the severe Walter and Elise Haas Promenade on a hill overlooking the old city of Jerusalem (1984–6). In 1963–5 he participated notably in the pioneering environmental-architectural project for a condominium at Sea Ranch on the northern Californian coast. Planned for an experimental community as 'a place where wild nature and human habitation could interact in a kind of intense symbiosis', this low-density development makes as minimal as possible an intrusion on the landscape with buildings (by

MOORE and others) in unadorned, unpainted local redwood recalling the vernacular forms of rough barns and sheep sheds formerly in the area. Sea Ranch appears to have been sited and laid out quite casually, as befitting an 'organic community' in harmonious relation with the natural lie of the land. Together with his partners, Halprin has also been involved in URBAN RENEWAL, e.g. with WURSTER at Ghiradelli Square, San Francisco (1962–5), as well as down-town shopping malls for Minneapolis (1962–7) and Charlottesville, Virginia (1972–5). His theories of design process and motion expounded in lectures, films and books have been widely influential: *RSVP Cycles: Creative Processes in the Human Environment* (New York 1970); *Taking Part: A Workshop Approach to Creativity* (Cambridge, Mass. 1972).

T. Itoli, *The Third Generation Architect and Concept*, Tokyo 1974; Lyall 1991; P. Walker and M. Simo, *Invisible Gardens*, Cambridge, Mass. 1994.

**Hamilton**, Thomas (1784–1858). Scottish architect and the leading GREEK REVIVAL architect in Edinburgh alongside W. H. PLAYFAIR. His masterpiece is the Royal High School, Edinburgh (1825–9). It is as forceful and dramatic – and as accomplished – as any Greek Revival building anywhere. But he was never able to repeat this success and his later work lacks impetus, e.g. the Assembly Rooms, Ayr (1827–30), the Burns Monument on Calton Hill, Edinburgh (1830), the Dean Orphanage, Edinburgh (1833–6), and the ingenious, refined but unconvincing Royal College of Physicians, Edinburgh (1843–6).

J. Rock, *T.H. Architect 1784–1858*, exh. cat., Edinburgh 1984; Summerson 1991; Colvin 1995.

**Hammam**. Arabic for steam-bath, which in Islamic countries usually consisted of a changing-room, latrines and a steam-room, or two of each for men and women who were otherwise accommodated on alternate days. Though heated by the HYPOCAUST system, hammams differ from Ancient Roman THERMAE both in their less grandiose proportions and in the greater importance given to the changing-room and steam-room. The cooling-room was often omitted altogether. The earliest surviving hammams are in the remains of c8 Umayyad palace complexes and are richly decorated, e.g. Khirbat al-Mafjar, Jordan, with carved stucco work and fine mosaic pavements. Public hammams were probably utilitarian but they became an urban architectural feature throughout Islam: by the c12 Damascus had fifty-seven. Many survive and are still in use, e.g. the Cagalogu Hammami of 1741 in Istanbul, Turkey. Their exteriors are austere but the steam-rooms often have marble floors and columns and tiled walls. After the introduction of piped water they began to be abandoned.

In c19 Europe imitations of hammams with steam-rooms and Islamic style decorations, called Turkish baths, were built and recommended for their physical regenerative effects. One opened in Jermyn Street, London, in 1862 and was followed by others in Europe and the USA.

Hillenbrand 1995.

**Hammerbeam**, *see* ROOF.

**Hankar**, Paul (1859–1901). Belgian architect, a contemporary of HORTA, to whose ART NOUVEAU style he developed a striking variant, e.g. Maison Ciamberlani (now Bulgarian embassy), Brussels (1897).

F. Loyer, *P.H. La Naissance de l'Art Nouveau*, Brussels 1986.

**Hanna/Olin Landscape Architects**, *see* OLIN, Laurie (b.1939).

**Hans von Burghausen** (d.1432), *see* STETHAIMER or SETTHEIMER, Hans.

**Hansen**, Theophil von (1813–91). Danish architect whose father, Christian Frederick (1756–1845), was the leading GREEK REVIVAL architect in Denmark (*see* DANISH ARCHITECTURE). Theophil became a leading exponent of c19 HISTORICISM, specializing in Italian Renaissance but equally at home with Greek Revival and Venetian Byzantine. He was trained in Copenhagen and travelled to Berlin, Munich, Italy and Greece and settled there, in Athens, for eight years (1838–46). His elder brother, Hans Christian Hansen (1803–93), had been in Athens since 1833, became the Royal Architect and built Athens University (1839–50) in an appropriate Greek Revival style. Theophil Hansen's buildings in Athens, also Greek Revival, date from some years later – the Academy (1859–87) and Library (1885–92). In 1846 he had settled in Vienna, where he spent the rest of his life. In 1851 he married the daughter of Ludwig Förster, with whom he had collaborated on the Army Museum in the Arsenal in Vienna (1850) and who was mainly responsible for the Ring and the consequent urban development in Vienna. Hansen designed several of the more prominent public buildings on or near the Ring: Heinrichshof (1861–3, destroyed 1945); Musikverein (1867–9); Academy of Art (1872–6); Parliament (1873–83); Stock Exchange (1874–7).

Paulsson 1958; J. Travlos, *Neo-Classical Architecture in Greece*, Athens 1967; R. Wagner-Rieger, *Der Architekt T. von H.*, Vienna 1977; R. Wagner-Rieger and M. Reissberger, *T. von H. Die Wiener Ringstrasse*, Wiesbaden 1980; H. Lund and A. L. Thygesen, *C.F.H.*, Copenhagen 1995.

**Hara**, Hitoshi (b.1936). A maverick among contemporary Japanese architects,

Hara's work defies categorization. Pursuing what he calls an 'architecture of modality' inspired by natural phenomena, he has created a bewilderingly varied series of buildings, from his own Hara House, Tokyo (1974), a 'house-within-a-house' in which the exterior is relocated indoors, to the vast Yamato International Building, Tokyo (1987), resembling an Aegean Island Shangri-la, and the glittering Umeda Sky Building, Osaka (1993), a sleek, metal-clad skyscraper surmounted by a futuristic Arcadia recalling ISOZAKI's 'City of the Air'.

Y. Futagawa (ed.), *H.H. GA Architect 13*, Tokyo 1993.

**Hardenberg**, Herbert Janeway (1847–1918), *see* HOTEL.

**Hardouin-Mansart**, Jules (1646–1708), French architect, the grandnephew of François MANSART, by whom he may have been trained, owed more to LE VAU, whose grand manner he and Lebrun brought to perfection in the Galerie des Glaces at Versailles. He understood perfectly the artistic needs of Louis XIV's court and excelled as an official architect, being competent, quick and adaptable. (He was appointed Royal Architect in 1675, Premier Architecte in 1685, and Surintendant des Bâtiments in 1699.) His meteoric career aroused jealousy, and Saint-Simon accused him of keeping tame architects in a backroom to do all his work for him. He was certainly lucky in having such gifted assistants as Pierre Lassurance (1650–1724) and Pierre LE PAUTRE, but he had real ability himself and a vivid sense of the splendour and visual drama required for a royal setting. From 1678 onwards he was in charge of the vast extensions to Versailles. These were disastrous externally, for he filled in the central terrace of Le Vau's garden façade and trebled its length. The stables, orangery, Trianon and chapel are more successful (the latter being finished by Robert de COTTE). His Baroque tendencies reached their height in the Invalides Chapel in Paris (1680–91), while the Place Vendôme (1698 onwards) illustrates his genius for the spectacular in town planning. Towards the end of his life, notably in a number of rooms at Versailles, Trianon and Marly, redecorated under his direction in the 1690s, he veered away from Baroque splendours towards a lighter and more elegant style which marks the first step towards the Rococo.

G. Cattani and P. Bourget, *J.H.-M.*, Paris 1956; Blunt 1982; R. W. Berger, *A Royal Passion. Louis XIV as Patron of Architecture*, Cambridge 1994.

**Hardwick**, Philip (1792–1870). The son of Thomas Hardwick (1752–1829), the architect of St Mary's, Marylebone Road, London (1813–17). He trained under his father, went to Paris in 1815 and spent a year in Italy (1818–19) before joining his father in London. His œuvre does not seem to have been large, but it is of high quality and varied interest. His most famous building was Euston station in London, with its majestic Greek Doric propylaea (1836–9), which became famous when it was infamously destroyed by the British Transport Commission in 1962. The station building was quite independent of the propylaea, whose spiritual function was that of a worthy introduction to that miracle of human ingenuity, the London-to-Birmingham railway. The range of stylistic possibilities open to Hardwick was great, and he was remarkably good at all of them: a monumentally plain, strictly utilitarian Classicism of brick and short Tuscan columns for the St Katherine's Dock warehouses, London (1827–8); and at the time most unusual restrained English Baroque for the Goldsmiths' Hall, London (1829–35); Jacobean for Babraham Hall, Cambridgeshire (1831); and a convincing and unaffected Tudor for Lincoln's Inn Hall and Library, London (1842–5). On the latter, PEARSON was assistant, and it is possible that the refined detailing is his; at all events, the building is effortlessly convincing and has no longer the character of romantic make-believe of early C19 Tudor imitations. He virtually stopped practising in the mid-1840s when his son Philip Charles (1822–92) took over. He retired completely in 1861.

A. and P. Smithson, *The Euston Arch*, London 1968; Colvin 1995.

**Hargreaves**, George (b.1952). American landscape architect, from 1983 principal of Hargreaves Associates, San Francisco. His works, which are always site-specific in a cultural-historical as well as a physical and ecological sense, range from the frequently illustrated Harlequin Plaza, Greenwood, Colorado (1983), which makes a surrealist effect in front of the mirror glass walls of office buildings and a distant view of the Rocky Mountains, to Byxbee Park, Palo Alto, California, as much land art as landscape architecture, sealing a landfill of garbage at the edge of San Francisco Bay (1988–92). His Fiddlers Green Amphitheater, Englewood, California (1983–5), Candlestick Point Cultural Park, San Francisco (1985–93), three public parks in San José, California, notably the Guadaloupe River Park (1985–94), and the Waterfront development, Louisville, Kentucky (begun 1990), are also notable.

Lyall 1991.

**Häring**, Hugo (1882–1958). German architect and theorist of ORGANIC ARCHITECTURE. He began as an Expressionist, e.g. farm and estate buildings at Gurkau, near Lübeck (1924–5). Also notable were his mass-housing developments, e.g. Siemensstadt, Berlin (1929–31).

H. Lauterbach *et al.* (eds.), *H.H.*, Stuttgart 1965; J. Joedicke (ed.), *H.H. das andere Bauen*, Stuttgart 1983.

**Harleman**, Carl (1700–1753), *see* SWEDISH ARCHITECTURE.

**Harling**. Scots term for ROUGHCAST.

**Harmonic proportions**, *see* PROPORTION.

**Harris**, E. Vincent (1879–1971), *see* NEO-GEORGIAN.

**Harrison**, Austen (1891–1976), *see* ISRAELI ARCHITECTURE.

**Harrison**, Peter (1716–76). The only architect of distinction in pre-Revolutionary America. Born in England, he married an American heiress, emigrated in 1740, and settled in Newport, Rhode Island, as a trader in wines, rum, molasses and mahogany. He presumably taught himself architecture but quickly acquired competence in the Palladian style, as his first work shows – Redwood Library, Newport (1748–50), a timber building imitating rusticated stone. Other buildings show Gibbsian influence: King's Chapel, Boston (1749–54); Synagogue, Newport (1759–63). But he returned to Inigo JONES and the English Palladians for inspiration in his later works: Brick Market, Newport (1761–72), and Christ Church, Cambridge, Massachusetts (1760). He settled in New Haven, Connecticut, in 1761, and became Collector of Customs there in 1768, suffering some persecution in his later years as a loyalist and government official.

C. Bridenbaugh, *P.H. First American Architect*, Chapel Hill 1949; Whiffen and Koeper 1981.

**Harrison**, Thomas (1744–1829). A Yorkshire architect, he designed some of the best and most gravely imposing neo-classical buildings in England. He was trained in Rome (1769–76) but never went to Greece. His masterpiece is Chester Castle, a complex of public buildings on which he worked for most of his life, though they were largely designed between 1786 and 1790. He won the commission in competition in 1785. The Prison, Exchequer Court, and Grand Jury Rooms were built 1788–91, the Shire Hall 1791–1801, the barracks and armoury wings 1804 onwards and the great Doric Propylaeum 1810–22. His other buildings include the Lyceum Club, Liverpool (1800–1802), and the former Portico Library (now Lloyds Bank), Manchester (1802–6).

Crook 1972; Summerson 1991; Colvin 1995.

**Harrison**, Wallace Kirkman (1895–1981). American architect. With Raymond HOOD and others he was responsible for the Rockefeller Center, New York (1931–40), and with his partner Max ABRAMOVITZ headed the team, which included LE CORBUSIER, for the United Nations Headquarters, New York (1947–53). The mammoth New York State Center at Albany (1962–78), the Lincoln Center, New York (1962–8) and the domed University of Illinois Assembly Hall, Champaign-Urbana (1963), were also theirs. Harrison designed the new Metropolitan Opera House for the Lincoln Center.

V. Newhouse, *W.K.H. Architect*, New York 1989.

**Harsdorff**, Caspar Frederik (1735–99), *see* DANISH ARCHITECTURE.

**Hasegawa**, Itsuko (b.1941). Japanese architect. Trained in Yokohama, she worked with SHINOHARA until 1979 when she set up her own practice in Tokyo. Spirited and lighthearted, she has brought a fresh sense of fun to contemporary Japanese architecture, using glass

and a variety of metals to create shimmering forms and spaces and what she calls 'naturalistic symbols'. Among her notable works are the AONO Building, Matsuyama (1982); the Shonandai Culture Centre, Fujisawa, Tokyo (1989); Cona Village, Amagasaki (1990); STM House, Tokyo (1991); Elementary School in Busshoji-mura, Oshima-machi (1993); the Sumida Cultural Centre, Tokyo (1994), finished with perforated aluminium in layers of translucent lacy screens; the ballooning Gymnasiums, Hikone (1995); and the Museum of Fruit, Yamasaki (1995).

A. Botella *et al.*, *I.H.*, London 1993; *Recent Buildings and Projects*, Basel/Boston/Berlin 1997.

**Hasenauer**, Karl von (1833–94), *see* SEMPER, Gottfried.

**Haunch**. Part of an arch, roughly midway between the springing line and crown, where the lateral thrust is strongest. *See* Fig. 6.

**Haus-Rucker-Co.**, *see* AUSTRIAN ARCHITECTURE.

**Haussmann**, Baron Georges-Eugène (1809–91). A French Protestant from Alsace who became a lawyer and civil servant. He was ruthless, canny and obstinate. Napoleon III made him Prefect of the Seine Department in 1853 and entrusted to him his sweeping plans for city improvement. Haussmann kept the post till 1870 and did as much as, or perhaps more than, the emperor expected. Haussmann's improvements – with those of J. C. A. ALPHAND as the designer of parks – follow the traditional principles of French town planning as established by Henri IV and developed by Louis XIV, and finally – Haussmann's direct model – by the so-called Artists' Plan of 1797: long straight boulevards meeting at *rond-points* are the principal motifs. It is often said that Haussmann made these boulevards to obtain good firing-lines in case of a revolution, but he was at least as much guided by traffic considerations (e.g. the connecting of railway stations) and was without doubt also passionately devoted to vistas towards monuments or monumental buildings such as the Arc de Triomphe or the Opéra. In 1890–93 he published his *Mémoires* (3 vols.).

D. H. Pinkney, *Napoleon III and the Rebuilding of Paris*, Princeton 1958; Loyer 1987.

**Haveli**. In Indian architecture, a courtyard house with tall rooms, small openings and interpenetrating levels.

**Haviland**, John (1792–1852). American architect. He was a pupil of James ELMES and went to live in Philadelphia in 1816. In 1818–19 he brought out *The Builder's Assistant*, the first American book to illustrate the ORDERS of columns. His *magnum opus* is the Eastern Penitentiary at Cherry Hill, Philadelphia (1821–9), much imitated in Europe. It has battlements, whereas Haviland's Institute for the Deaf and Dumb (1824) has classical features and The Tombs in New York (1836–8, Law Courts and Prison, in one) is neo-Egyptian. He was precocious in his use of cast iron in the Miners' Bank (1829–30), Pottsville, Pennsylvania, though he used it only as a decorative sheathing for the brick walls; *see* METAL STRUCTURES.

S. Tutman and R. Moss, *Biographical Dictionary of Philadelphia Architects, 1700–1930*, Boston 1985.

**Havliček**, Josef (1899–1961), *see* CZECH ARCHITECTURE.

**Hawksmoor**, Nicholas (1661–1736), the most original of English Baroque architects except VANBRUGH, came from a family of Nottinghamshire farmers. At eighteen he became WREN's amanuensis and was closely associated with him at Greenwich Hospital and other buildings until his death. Vanbrugh also found him an able assistant and employed him from 1690 onwards, notably at Castle Howard, Yorkshire, and Blenheim Palace, Oxfordshire. Indeed, he became more than just an assistant to both Wren and Vanbrugh, though it is impossible now to assess how much they owed to him. It was presumably his expertise that enabled the untrained Vanbrugh's designs to be realized. His independent works have great originality, and only his dour, capricious character and lack of push denied him greater opportunities and worldly success. Vigorous, odd, bookish, yet massively plastic in feeling, his style is a highly personal Baroque amalgam of Wren, classical Rome, and Gothic. Like Vanbrugh, but unlike Wren, his passion was for dramatic effects of mass, and he has been criticized for heaviness as a result. He began working on his own *c*.1702 at Easton Neston, Northamptonshire, a compact rectangular building with a giant order all round; it combines Wren's grandeur and urbanity, and in some details foreshadows Vanbrugh. In 1711 he was appointed Surveyor under the Act for Building Fifty New Churches, and the six he designed himself form the bulk of his œuvre. All of them are minor masterpieces: St Alphege, Greenwich (1712–14, gutted 1941, restored); St Anne's, Limehouse (1714–30, restored after fire, 1851–4), with its medieval steeple in classical dress; St George-in-the-East, Wapping Stepney (1714–29, gutted 1941 and exterior restored as a shell 1960–64); St Mary Woolnoth (1716–24, interior altered by BUTTERFIELD 1875–6 when the galleries were removed), with its square within a square plan; St George's, Bloomsbury (1716–30), the most grandiose and least odd of all his buildings;

and Christchurch, Spitalfields (1714–29, spire altered 1822–3 and interior 1851 and 1866 when the galleries were removed; restoration in progress), as perverse and megalomaniac as anything by Vanbrugh. His other buildings are only slightly less notable – the quadrangle, hall and Codrington Library at All Souls College, Oxford (1716–35), and the west tower of Westminster Abbey (1718), all in his neo-Gothic manner; and finally, the grim and austere circular mausoleum at Castle Howard (1729–36), where he returned to Rome and BRAMANTE for inspiration.

Summerson 1991; K. Downes, *H. (1661–1736)*, London (1970) 1994; Colvin 1995.

**Hayberger**, Gotthard (1699–1764), *see* HUEBER, Joseph.

**Header**, *see* BRICKWORK.

**Hecatompedon**. The name given to the NAOS of the Parthenon in Athens which measures 100 Doric ft by 50 Doric ft, and hence to any similarly proportioned buildings.

**Hecker**, Zvi (b.1931), *see* ISRAELI ARCHITECTURE.

**Heikkinen**, Mikko (b.1949), *see* FINNISH ARCHITECTURE.

**Heinzelmann**, Konrad (d.1454), was at Ulm in the 1420s. He was called to Nördlingen in 1429 as master mason to design and build the church of St George, then to Rothenburg in 1428 to work on the church of St Jakob. In 1439 he went to Nuremberg, and there designed and began the beautiful chancel of St Lorenz.

Frankl 1972.

**Hejduk**, John (b.1929), *see* NEW YORK FIVE.

**Helix**. A spiral motif, especially the inner spiral of the volute of a Corinthian capital.

**Hellenistic architecture**. The architec-ture of the Hellenistic kingdoms created out of the empire conquered by Alexander the Great (356–323 BC). Several of the finest surviving buildings are on the west coast of modern Turkey. The tendency towards greater elegance and elaboration in small buildings (e.g. the Choragic Monument of Lysicrates, Athens) and a more richly sculptural and monumental style for large ones (e.g. the Mausoleum of Halicarnassus and the Ionic temple of Artemis at Ephesus), already evident in early C4 GREEK ARCHITECTURE, was accelerated. The greatest Hellenistic city was Alexandria, laid out on a regular grid plan with numerous vast and very splendid buildings, none of which survives. The Ionic temple of Athena Polias, Priene (*c.*335 BC), and of Artemis Leukophryene at Magnesia by HERMOGENES (*c.*150 BC) are representative of the style. Doric temples were still built, but the columns became much more slender and motifs from the Ionic order were introduced, as in the Temple of Hera Basileia at Pergamom (*c.*150 BC). The richer Corinthian order was more to the taste of the new civilization: at Athens the great temple of Olympian Zeus (begun 174 BC, though not completed until AD 131) is the first Corinthian building on the grand scale, and provides a piquant contrast to the sober solemnity of the Parthenon on the Acropolis above it.

Many of the finest Hellenistic buildings are civic rather than religious: the Bouleuterion or Council House at Miletos (*c.*170 BC) and various colonnaded walks like the recently restored Stoa of Attalos in the Athenian AGORA (*c.*150 BC). A new interest was also manifested in urban planning. At Pergamom (*c.*190–133 BC) a library, large theatre, palace, barracks and several temples (including the remarkable Altar of Zeus *c.*165 BC, now Staatliche Museen, Berlin) were visually related to one another and placed scenographically to take full advantage of a terraced hill-top site. Grid planning was more usual, as at Priene, but with greater attention than before to monumental effects and the creation of vistas. Inventiveness was shown also in the planning of sanctuaries, notably that of Asclepios on Kos and the Temple of Apollo at Didyma (begun 313 BC). Military engineering was brought to a new height of efficiency and many forts and walls, with handsome crisply cut masonry and sometimes with arched gateways, survive both in Greece and in Asia Minor (e.g. Priene). Excavations have revealed that private houses were built on a much grander scale than before. Techniques of construction developed in the Hellenistic kingdoms included the KEYSTONE arch and the TUNNEL VAULT (used mainly for tombs but occasionally for substructures and passages) both of which were later exploited by the Romans.

The Hellenistic style survived the conquest of Asia Minor by the Romans; indeed, Imperial Roman architecture may be regarded as its logical development. The main buildings of the two great Syrian sites, Baalbek (the very rich Temple of Bacchus, courts and portico, c.AD 120–200) and Palmyra (Temple of the Sun, c.AD 1; Temple of Baal, AD 131), are predominantly Hellenistic in feeling, though their vaults, arches and domes are typically Roman.

**Helm**. The termination of a spire or tower, especially the bulbous onion-dome type found in central and eastern Europe.

**Helm roof**, *see* ROOF.

**Hemicycle**. A semicircular structure, e.g. the rounded end of a church or an apse-like recess as sometimes found on a façade.

**Hemicycle buttress**. In Ancient Roman architecture, a semicircular buttress, often very large and concealed by other masonry. It might have an additional function to that of its structural purpose.

**Hennebique**, François (1842–1921). French architect and one of the pioneers of concrete architecture. He first used REINFORCED CONCRETE in 1879. His most important patents are of 1892. In 1894 he built at Viggen in Switzerland the first bridge of reinforced concrete, in 1895 at Roubaix the first grain elevator. His concrete and glass factories begin in 1894. For an exhibition at Geneva in 1896 he built a cantilevered concrete staircase, and for a small theatre at Morges in 1899 cantilevered galleries. In a small theatre at Munich in 1903 he was allowed to leave the concrete frame exposed. His own crazy concrete villa at Bourg-la-Reine dates from 1904. In 1900 he designed the glass and metal roofs for the Grand Palais and Petit Palais, Paris. In Rome he designed the reinforced concrete Ponte Risorgimento over the Tiber for the 1911 exhibition.

Collins 1959; Pevsner 1968.

**Henostyle-in-antis**. A portico with one column between *antae*.

**Henri Deux style**, *see* FRENCH ARCHITECTURE; HISTORICISM.

**Henry of Reyns**, Master of the King's Masons to Windsor Castle in 1243, and later to Westminster Abbey. He was dead, it seems, by 1253. This means he was King's Master Mason when Westminster Abbey was begun and so was probably its designer. Reyns sounds temptingly like Reims, and Reims Cathedral is, in fact, the stylistic source of much at Westminster (tracery, the wall-passages in the east chapels), together with work at Amiens, Royaumont and the Sainte

Chapelle in Paris, only just completed when the abbey was begun. However, there are other features, such as the large gallery and the ridge-rib of the vault, which are entirely English and may make it more likely that Henry was an Englishman who had worked at Reims. Judging by style, Henry may also have designed the King's Chapel at Windsor Castle (built *c.*1240).

Webb 1965; Harvey 1984.

**Henselmann**, Herman (1905–95), *see* GERMAN ARCHITECTURE.

**Hentrich**, Helmut (b.1905). German architect, studied at Freiburg, Vienna and Berlin, and in New York under Norman Bel Geddes 1930–31. He was with Hubert Petschnigg from 1954 in a partnership known as HPP. Among their most prominent buildings are the Thyssen building at Düsseldorf (Dreischeibenhaus) of 1957–60, the Aweta building at Ludwigshafen of 1960–63, the Klöckner-Humboldt Haus at Deutz of 1961–4, the Bonhoeffer church at Düsseldorf of 1964–5, the University buildings at Bochum begun in 1961 and the Europacentre, Berlin (1963–6). Their Finland House at Hamburg was the first high block in suspension construction in Europe (1966), followed by their Standard Bank, Johannesburg, with OVE ARUP (1967–9). Recent buildings: Concert Hall, Düsseldorf (1978), and Town Hall at Rheydt (1981–4).

H. B. Adams, *H.P.P.*, Düsseldorf 1989.

**Heptastyle**. Of a portico with seven fronted columns.

**Héré de Corny**, Emmanuel (1705–63). French architect who designed the Place Royale (Place Stanislas) in Nancy, the finest example of Rococo urbanism anywhere. He was probably trained under BOFFRAND in Lunéville and Paris but returned *c.*1740 to Nancy to become architect to Stanislas Leszynski, ex-king of Poland, for whom all his work was carried out – the Château de la Malgrange (1739–40), Place Royale (1752 onwards, with the Place de la Carrière leading into the Hemicycle) and the Hôtel de Ville (1752–5), all in Nancy. The Place Royale owes much to the superb ironwork by Lamour. Héré's lantern and interior of St Jacques, Lunéville (1730–47), are also notable. Héré published his works in *Recueil des plans . . .* (1750) and *Plans et élévations de la Place Royale de Nancy* (1753).

J. Rau, *E.H. Premier architecte von Stanislas Leszynski in Lothringen (1705–1763)*, Berlin 1972; A. France-Lanord, *E.H. Architecte du Roi Stanislas*, Nancy 1984; Kalnein 1995.

**Herholdt**, Johan Daniel (1818–1902), *see* DANISH ARCHITECTURE.

**Herigoyen**, Emanuel Joseph von (1746–1817), *see* GERMAN ARCHITECTURE.

**Herland**, Hugh (*c.*1330–1411). English carpenter in the king's service probably from *c.*1350, and in charge of the king's works in carpentry from 1375, when William Herland, presumably his father, died. His *magnum opus* is the hammerbeam roof of Westminster Hall, done in the 1390s; it has a span of about 21 m. (67 ft). He also worked for William of Wykeham (with WILLIAM OF WYNFORD) at New College, Oxford, and probably at Winchester College.

Harvey 1984.

**Herm**. Originally, a rectangular pillar terminating in a head or bust (usually of Hermes), used to mark boundaries, etc. in Ancient Greece. The form was adopted by Renaissance and post-Renaissance architects.

**Hermelin**, Sven (1900–1984), *see* SWEDISH ARCHITECTURE AND LANDSCAPE ARCHITECTURE.

**Hermogenes** (*c.*150 BC). Architect and influential architectural theorist of the Hellenistic period. He was probably born at Priene, where he designed an altar. Critical of the Doric ORDER, because 'the distribution of the triglyphs and metopes is troublesome and unharmonious', he designed two important Ionic temples – that of Dionysos at Teos and the large pseudodipteral temple of Artemis Leukophryene at Magnesia on the Meander. He commented on these works in writings which are lost but were known to and quoted by VITRUVIUS.

J. Onians, *Art and Thought in the Hellenistic Age*, London 1979; Lawrence 1983.

**Herrera**, Juan de (1530–97). Spanish architect, he travelled abroad, mainly in Italy, from 1547 to 1559. He was appointed to succeed Juan Bautista de TOLEDO at the Escorial in 1563, though he did not design any additions until after 1572: the infirmary and chapel (1574–82) were his main contributions. But his majestic if sometimes rather solemn and Italianate style is best seen at the Royal Gardens at Aranjuez (1569), at the Exchange at Seville (1582), and in his designs for Valladolid Cathedral (*c.*1585), which were only partly executed but had enormous influence, e.g. on Salamanca, Mexico, Puebla and Lima Cathedrals. The severity and lack of ornament of Herrera's style became the official style during Philip II's reign – known as *estile desornamentado*.

Kubler and Soria 1959; G. Kubler, *Building the Escorial*, Princeton 1982; C. Wilkinson-Zerner, *J. de H. Architect to Philip II of Spain*, New Haven/London 1993.

**Herringbone work**. Stone, brick or tile work in which the component units are laid diagonally instead of horizontally. Alternate courses lie in opposite directions, forming a zigzag pattern along the wall-face.

**Herron**, Ron (1930–94), *see* ARCHIGRAM; ENGLISH ARCHITECTURE.

**Hertzberger**, Herman (b.1932). Dutch architect who, together with VAN EYCK and BAKEMA, joined Team 10 and with them edited *Forum* from 1959 to 1963. His early Het Studenthuis, Amsterdam (1958–66), was Brutalist in its use of materials but already displayed the egalitarian concerns which, following the '68 student uprisings, were to mark his later work, the Montessori School, Delft (1966–78), the Old People's Home, Amsterdam (1967–75), and especially his famously innovative office building, Centraal Beheer, Apeldorn (1968–72). He there abandoned the 'open plan' office for a cellular complex consisting of balconies and rooms opening informally off a bi-axial atrium or circulation hall. This created a friendly honeycomb of work spaces and social spaces. His Lindenstrasse apartment building for IBA, Berlin (1984–6) and Vredenburg Music Centre, Utrecht (1973–8), developed the same concept and his Ministry of Social Welfare, The Hague (1979–90), attempted a further advance in 'friendly' architecture and planning. His later buildings were less innovative: the Theatre Centre Spui, The Hague (1986–93); the School and Library, Breda (1991–3), the Benelux Offices, The Hague (1990–93), and the Chassé Theatre, Breda (1992–5). His *Lessons for Students in Architecture*, Rotterdam 1991, has become a classic text in several languages.

A. Luchinger, *H.H.*, Stuttgart 1987; W. Reinink, *H.H. Architect*, Rotterdam 1991; H. van Bergeijk, *H.H.*, Basel/Berlin 1997.

**Herzog**, Jacques (b.1950). Swiss architect trained under Aldo ROSSI in Zürich

Herzog, Thomas

and in partnership with Pierre de Meuron (b.1950) since 1978. Their Minimalist private gallery for Goetz, Munich (1992), was followed by the Ricola Chocolate and Caramel Factory and Storage Building, Mulhouse (1993), and the equivocal copper-clad Signal Box at Basel railway station (1995).

P. Blum (ed.), *Architecture of H. & de M.*, New York 1994; G. Mack, *H. & de M. 1989–1991*, Basel 1996.

**Herzog**, Thomas (b.1941), *see* ENVIRONMENTAL, GREEN OR SUSTAINABLE ARCHITECTURE; GERMAN ARCHITECTURE.

**Hewn stone**. The American term for ASHLAR.

**Hexastyle**. Of a portico with six frontal columns.

**High Gothic architecture**, *see* GOTHIC ARCHITECTURE.

**High Renaissance architecture**, *see* MANNERISM; RENAISSANCE.

**High-rise building**, *see* SKYSCRAPER.

**High Tech**. A concept of or approach to architecture, rather than a style. Based on engineering and on construction and other (e.g. space) technologies, it shares with MODERNISM a belief that a building should exhibit the method and materials of its construction and express a C20 Machine Aesthetic. Unlike BRUTALISM, it favoured lightweight materials and flexibility. It was developed by English architects in the 1970s, notably by FOSTER and ROGERS. High Tech buildings are characterized by exposed structure (of steel and other metals), exposed services (pipes and air ducts, etc.), by a smooth, impervious skin (often of glass) and by flexibility to create, internally, service zones and not rooms or sequences of rooms. The origins of High Tech may be sought in PAXTON's

Crystal Palace and other C19 engineering structures, more recently in the work and theories of Buckminster FULLER, the plug-in fantasies of ARCHIGRAM and the tensile structures of Frei OTTO. The Centre Pompidou, Paris (1977), by PIANO and Rogers and the Sainsbury Centre for the Visual Arts, Norwich (1977), by Foster were High Tech's first notable buildings. Lloyd's of London (1986) and the Hong Kong Bank Headquarters, Hong Kong (1986) by Rogers and Foster respectively are among the latest. Also notable are several works by M. HOPKINS, by ARUP Associates and by Nicholas GRIMSHAW.

C. Davies, *H.T. Architecture*, London 1989.

**Hilbersheimer**, Ludwig (1995–1967). German-born American architect and urban designer and theorist. In 1925 he published *Grosstadtbauten*, advocating high-rise city planning, followed by *Grosstadtarchitektur* in 1927, when he also contributed to the Weissenhof experiment at Stuttgart with MIES VAN DER ROHE and others. From 1928 he was at the BAUHAUS and between 1932 and 1936 designed several notable housing developments in Berlin. In 1938 he emigrated to the USA, becoming Professor of Town Planning at the Illinois Institute of Technology, Chicago. Abandoning his early centralized city-plan in favour of horizontally planned, decentralized, low-rise high-density urban developments, he became very influential in urban design and a vigorous exponent of regionalism. But although his theories, especially regarding regionalism and courtyard housing, were taken up by others, they were seldom to be realized.

R. Pommer *et al.*, *In the Shadow of Mies. L.H. Architect, Educator and Urban Planner*, New York 1988; K. M. Hays, *Modernism and the Posthumanist Subject. The Architec-*

*ture of Hannes Meyer and L.H.*, Cambridge, Mass. 1992.

**Hild**, Joszef (1789–1867), *see* HUN-GARIAN ARCHITECTURE.

**Hildebrandt**, Johann Lukas von (1668–1745). The leading Baroque architect in Austria alongside FISCHER VON ERLACH, he was born in Genoa, the son of a captain in the Genoese army and an Italian mother. Italian always remained his first language. He studied with Carlo FON-TANA in Rome before settling in Vienna. He was appointed Court Architect in 1700 and knighted by the emperor in 1720. He succeeded Fischer von Erlach as First Court Architect in 1723. His style is lighter than SCHLÜTER's and more Italianate than Fischer von Erlach's, livelier too and homelier, with typically Viennese charm. He much admired GUARINI, as his early (1699) Dominican church at Gabel in north Bohemia shows. It has Guarini's characteristic three-dimensional arches and a complicated and imaginative Guarinesque plan (concave corners hidden by convex balconies etc.). The influence of BORROMINI is evident in much of the carved decoration of his masterpiece, the Lower and Upper Belvedere in Vienna, built for Prince Eugene (the former completed 1714–15, the latter built 1720–24). His secular buildings are notable for their oval and octagonal rooms (Palais Schwarzenberg in Vienna, begun 1697; Summer Palace Ráckeve in Hungary, 1701–2; Palais Starhemberg-Schönborn in Vienna, 1706–17) and for their ingeniously planned and spatially dramatic ceremonial staircases (Palais Daun-Kinsky of 1713–16 and the Upper Belvedere in Vienna, Schloss Mirabell in Salzburg of 1721–7 and his addition to the Palais Harrach in Vienna of 1727–35). In 1711 he was consulted about the great staircase at Johann DIENTZENHO-FER's Pommersfelden Palace and added

the three-storey gallery there. From 1720 to 1723 and again from 1729 to 1744 he collaborated with NEUMANN on the rebuilding of the Residenz at Würzburg, contributing the designs for the lavishly decorated upper part of the central pavilion facing the gardens and the interiors of the Imperial hall and chapel. Though primarily a secular architect Hildebrandt built several churches including the Church of the Seminary at Linz (1717–25) with its boldly *mouvementé* façade, the parish church of Gollersdorf (1740–41) and probably the Piaristenkirche in Vienna (plan dated 1698, begun 1716 but later modified by K. I. DIENTZEN-HOFER), octagonal in plan and bright, rhythmical and Borrominesque inside. In 1719 he began the palatial enlargement of Göttweig abbey, magnificently sited above the Danube.

B. Grimschitz, *J.L. von H.*, Vienna 1959; Hempel 1965; H. and G. Auremhammer, *Das Belvedere in Wien*, Vienna and Munich 1971; Brucker 1983.

**Hindu architecture**, *see* INDIAN ARCHITECTURE.

**Hip**. The external angle formed by the meeting of two sloping roof surfaces. *See* ROOF; Fig. 100.

**Hipped roof**, *see* ROOF.

**Hippodamos of Miletos** (*fl. c.* 500–440 BC). Town planner, political theorist and philosopher interested in the problem of urbanism. According to Aristotle (*Politics*), he originated the art of town planning and devised an ideal city to be inhabited by 10,000 citizens, divided into three classes (soldiers, artisans and husbandmen), with the land also divided into three (sacred, public and private). The gridiron plan associated with his name had been in use since the C7 BC in Ionia though not in Attica. And his social ideas were hardly forward looking. But he seems to have been the first to appreciate that a town plan might formally embody and clarify a rational social order. He taught the Athenians the value of having a clear, regular and strictly functional town plan instead of the haphazard layouts of archaic Greek towns. He lived in Athens and became a friend of Pericles, whose social ideas he appears to have shared. Though not an architect and never in charge of the actual construction of any town, he was probably responsible for the town plan of Miletos *c.*475 BC and the layout of Piraeus (founded by Themistocles *c.*470 BC) on a gridiron system with a formal, enclosed AGORA as its central feature. He possibly inspired the plan of Thourioi (founded 443 BC) as a Pan-Hellenic centre. The town plan of Rhodes has been less plausibly attributed to him. The gridiron plan was much used in later classical and Hellenistic periods. Thanks to Aristotle he has influenced writers on urbanism since the Renaissance (e.g. Sir Thomas More in *Utopia*).

F. Castagnoli, *Ippodamo di Mileto e l'urbanistica a pianta ottagonale*, Rome 1956; R. Martin, *L'Urbanisme dans la Grèce antique*, Paris 1956; J. B. Ward-Perkins, *Cities of Ancient Greece and Italy. Planning in Classical Antiquity*, New York 1974; E. Greco et al., *Storia dell'urbanistica. Il mondo Greco*, Bari 1983.

**Hippodrome**. In Ancient Greece and Rome a course for horse and horse-and-chariot races, corresponding to the STADIUM for men. Early examples were usually without masonry; for later developments *see* CIRCUS.

**Hirsau style**, *see* AUSTRIAN ARCHITECTURE; GERMAN ARCHITECTURE.

**Hirschfeld**, Christian Cay Lorenz (1742–92). Danish-born writer, professor of philosophy and aesthetics at Kiel University from 1773, whose books diffused a taste for LANDSCAPE GARDENS throughout continental Europe: *Anmerkungen über die Landhauser und die Gartenkunst* (Frankfurt-am-Main/Leipzig 1773), *Theorie der Gartenkunst* (Frankfurt-am-Main/Leipzig 1775), and the five-volume work published in German as *Theorie der Gartenkunst* and in French as *Théorie de l'Art des Jardins* (both Leipzig 1779–85). Derived largely from English writers, his theories propounded the laying out of a park as the creation of a series of views similar to those of classical landscape painters, idealizations rather than imitations of nature and each one intended to evoke a mood emphasized by a temple, ruin, cenotaph or other appropriately inscribed commemorative structure. He nevertheless advocated a specifically German national style, less close to common nature than English parks (which he had never seen) and less artificial than geometrically planned French-style gardens. More concerned than English writers with the educative and spiritually uplifting benefits to be derived from a garden, he wrote that it should be 'the favourite place to observe nature, the sanctuary of philosophy, the temple of worship of the highest wisdom'. And whereas they had been concerned only with private estates, he is notable for devoting part of his final volume to PUBLIC PARKS as places of recreation and moral improvement for all social classes. He suggested that they should have buildings adorned with didactic paintings and, an idea taken from J. J. Rousseau, statues of national heroes rather than mythological deities, fauns, etc. In order to accommodate and supervise large numbers of visitors he recommended wide straight walks rather than the meandering paths of a private garden.

W. Schepers, *H.'s Theorie der Gartenkunst*, Worms 1980; W. Kehn, *C.C.L.H.*

*1742–1792. Eine Biographie*, Worms 1992; M. Breckwoldt, *'Das Landleben' also Grundlage fur eine Gartentheorie: Eine literaturhistorische Analyse der Schriften von C.C.L.H.*, Munich 1995.

**Historical preservation**. The protection, conservation, rehabilitation and maintenance for historical and/or aesthetic reasons of buildings and built areas, also tracts of land that have acquired significance or form due to human occupation or design (LANDSCAPE ARCHITECTURE), as well as natural or wild landscape. It is to be distinguished from HISTORICAL RECONSTRUCTION and RESTORATION.

The preservation of buildings for other than religious reasons began in Antiquity. Laws to this effect were promulgated in Imperial Rome and although they lapsed in the Early Christian period it was in Renaissance Rome that the demand for preservation was revived. From the early C15 a succession of Popes issued bulls to protect Ancient Roman remains, their 'listing' was proposed, probably by RAPHAEL (appointed superintendent of antiquities in 1515) and his successor who was specifically required to 'conserve and free them from vegetation'. Later edicts restricting the exportation of works of art referred also to the preservation of ancient buildings, culminating in that of 1820 which set up an administrative structure throughout the Papal States. This was to be the basis for legislation after Italian unification, up to the law of 1939 placing the entire artistic and architectural heritage, gardens and landscape under state surveillance, irrespective of private ownership and with powers of expropriation.

Interest in medieval and later architecture had, in the meantime, enlarged the notion of what merited preservation in northern Europe. Ludwig I, Grand Duke of Hesse-Darmstadt, in 1818 ordered a survey of all historical buildings in his domain, none of which was to be altered or demolished without permission. In France where, during the Revolution, so many buildings had been destroyed and still more vandalized as relics of the 'feudal age', a campaign for preservation was launched by Romantic writers, notably by Victor Hugo in *Guerre aux démolisseurs* (1825). The French Ministry of the Interior established an Inspectorate of Historical Monuments in 1830 with the novelist Prosper Mérimée at its head 1834–60; funds were made available for conservation and restoration but no effective legislation to protect listed buildings was enacted until 1887.

The problem of preservation was publicly debated in England from the late C18 with reference to the ruthless RESTORATION of Gothic churches. In 1877 a proposal to employ George Gilbert SCOTT on restoration work at Tewkesbury Abbey, Gloucestershire, prompted MORRIS and others to found the Society for the Protection of Ancient Buildings (SPAB). The British Royal Commission on Historical Monuments was established in 1908 with the task of listing those built before 1714. In 1913 legislation for their protection was passed, despite opposition from property owners, with more stringent measures and also extensions of the chronological limits in 1914 and 1953, limiting though not preventing destruction (e.g. HARDWICK's Euston Arch). Notable archaeological sites, ruined abbeys, castles and country houses were acquired by the state, to be protected and maintained under the Ministry of Works. Meanwhile the National Trust, an association of private individuals founded in 1897 and incorporated in 1907, began to acquire and hold in trust for the nation 'places of natural beauty' which included from the 1930s onwards country houses, sometimes occupied by the heirs of their original owners, thus also preserving a way of life.

In the USA the preservation of rapidly decreasing areas of 'wilderness' came first, Yellowstone National Park (Idaho, Montana, Wyoming) in 1872 and Yosemite National Park (California) in 1890 initiating a preservation phenomenon unique in scale. The Antiquities Act of 1906 empowered the President to name areas of historic value as national monuments; in 1916 the National Parks Service was established and in 1935 the Historic Sites Act authorized the Secretary of the Interior to designate areas for protection, irrespective of ownership. The demolition of Post's New York Produce Exchange building prompted the foundation in 1965 of the Landmarks Preservation Commission, which has done much to save buildings of architectural importance. In the USA, however, the preservation of buildings has been due mainly to voluntary non-profit associations.

By the early C20 organizations for historical preservation had been established in all Western countries, also in British India (Archaeological Survey founded in 1861; Ancient Monuments Protection Act 1904) and Japan (law for the preservation of shrines and temples 1897, greatly expanded to cover other buildings in 1919 and 1929). Since the Second World War it has been increasingly recognized that buildings of major historical and architectural importance are a matter of international concern. In 1950 Unesco published a report outlining measures for co-operation between member-countries and in 1959 it launched an international campaign to save the Ancient Egyptian temples at Abu Simbel and Philae from inundation by the Aswan Dam. They were subsequently (1966–8) dismantled, moved to dry ground and reassembled. Though the campaign had cost about $80 million, half of which

was donated by some fifty countries, its success led to other campaigns and in 1972 to the international *Convention concerning the Protection of the World Cultural and Natural Heritage*. This was ratified in 1975 by some fifty countries and the World Heritage List (now covering 506 natural and cultural sites) and World Heritage Fund established. Later safeguarding campaigns promoted by Unesco included those for Mohenjodaro in Pakistan and Borobudur in Indonesia. Meantime, in 1964 the International Congress for Conservation issued the Venice Charter with guidelines for methods of preservation and founded the International Council for Monuments and Sites (ICOMOS). The following year, 1965, the World Monuments Fund (WMF, originally called the International Fund for Monuments), a private non-profit organization, was founded and incorporated in New York. It has helped to preserve many notable buildings and sites world-wide, from Nepal and Cambodia (Angkor) to Venice and the Lednice and Valtnice castles and parks in Moravia, Czech Republic. In 1995 it sponsored the World Monuments Watch programme to assess priorities for the future.

At national levels in western Europe and the USA since the 1960s the focus of attention has turned from single buildings to whole urban areas which are salvaged and revitalized as integral parts of a community (in France under the Loi Malraux of 1962 and in England the Civic Amenities Act of 1967). Areas for preservation range from the historical centres of still-growing cities (e.g. Bologna, Italy; Charleston, USA) to districts that have lost their original function (e.g. the Marais, Paris; the Vieux Carrée, New Orleans) to entire historic towns or villages (e.g. San Gimignano, Italy; Deerfield, Massachusetts).

E. R. Chamberlain, *Preserving the Past*, London 1979; J. M. Fitch, *H.P. Curatorial Management of the Built World*, New York 1982; L. Pressouyre, *The World Heritage Convention, Twenty Years Later*, Unesco, Paris 1996; S. Mark (ed.), *Concerning Buildings. Studies in Honour of Si B. Fielden*, London 1996.

**Historical reconstruction**. The re-creation of buildings and their surroundings, a development from C19 RESTORATION distinct from HISTORICAL PRESERVATION. The decision taken in 1902 to rebuild the collapsed campanile in Piazza San Marco, Venice, exactly as it had been and where it had been, was the first manifestation of a new attitude. After the First World War the centres of towns that had been devastated in Belgium and France (e.g. Ypres and Arras) were carefully reconstructed with the aid of pre-1914 photographs. After the Second World War the centre of Warsaw was reconstructed in 1948–67 using pre-1940 surveys by architectural students and other visual evidence such as Bellotto's paintings of the 1770s. In a slightly different spirit, Williamsburg, Virginia, was reconstructed from 1928 onwards as it was believed to have been at the end of the Colonial period: notable surviving buildings were restored, some 600 C19 structures demolished and replaced with C18 style houses and shops with gardens laid out by the landscape architect Arthur Asahel Shurcliff (1870–1957). Several European gardens, destroyed but known from visual images and written descriptions, have been reconstructed, e.g. in France the *jardin potager* at Villandry in 1906–24 following Du Cerceau's engravings, in England KENT's layout at Claremont, Surrey, in 1975–81, and in the Netherlands the C17 'Great Garden' at Het Loo, completed in 1984. The now popular demand for the exact replication

of buildings recently burnt down (e.g. the Fenice theatre, Venice, in 1996) is, however, opposed by many architects.

**Historicism**. From the German *Historismus*, a pejorative term coined in the 1880s for the emphasis then given to history and later, by analogy, for the C19 philosophy of history (mainly Hegelian). Later, with reference to architecture, it was used for the C19 respect for the past and revival of historical styles as a matter of religious or social responsibility, or, more loosely, simply for C19 as opposed to earlier revivals – from the GREEK and GOTHIC REVIVALS to Byzantine, Early Christian, Romanesque, Italian Renaissance, French Renaissance ('Henri Deux'), English Elizabethan and Jacobean, etc. Architects aimed to work in the spirit of a style, taking care to observe its rules and imitating ornamental details with an accuracy previously reserved for classical styles. In this they were aided by a growing number of books on architecture, with detailed and often measured illustrations, also by museum collections of architectural details or plaster casts of them. Throughout the century demands for 'an architectural style of the C19' were reiterated (first by Heinrich Hübsch, 1795–1863, in his book *In welchem Style sollen wir bauen?*, 1828), but buildings unembellished with ornament (usually historical) were rarely regarded as 'architecture' by contemporaries (e.g. PAXTON's Crystal Palace). In England from the 1860s the use of historical ornament began to diminish (e.g. Philip WEBB and Norman SHAW whose so-called 'Queen Anne style' is usually dissociated from Historicism). ART NOUVEAU was the first international reaction against historical revivals.

K. Dohmer, *In welchem Style sollen wir bauen? Architekturtheorie zwischen Klassizismus und Jugendstil*, Munich 1976; W. J.

Streich (ed.), *Der Historismus in der Architektur des 19 und 20 Jahrhunderts*, Berlin 1984; J. M. Crook, *The Dilemma of Style*, London 1988; W. Herrmann, *In What Style Should We Build? The German Debate on Architectural Style*, Chicago 1992.

**Hittite architecture**, *see* TURKISH ARCHITECTURE.

**Hittorf**, Jakob Ignaz (1792–1867). German architect, born at Cologne, who went to Paris in 1810 with GAU and placed himself under PERCIER. He then worked under BÉLANGER just at the time when the latter was busy with the glass and iron dome of the Corn Market. In 1819–23 Hittorf travelled in Germany, England and Italy. After that, till 1848, he was Royal Architect. His first major building, executed with his father-in-law Lepère, is St Vincent de Paul, Paris (1824), still with an Ionic portico, but Early Christian rather than classical inside, with its two superimposed orders and its open roof. The exterior already shows the change from the pure classical to the new, grander, more rhetorical classical of the École des Beaux Arts as it culminated in Hittorf's Gare du Nord (1859–66). He also did extensive decorative work; laid out the Place de la Concorde in its present form (1832–40) and the Champs Élysées (1834–40); built two Circuses (des Champs Élysées, 1839; Napoléon, 1851) with iron and glass domes; and, with Charles Rohault de Fleury (1801–75) and Pellechet, designed the Grand Hôtel du Louvre – all of which proves his interest in new functions and new materials. Hittorf also made a name as an archaeologist, chiefly by his discovery of the polychromy of Greek architecture (1830), a 'Victorian' discovery shocking to the older generation of Grecian purists.

D. D. Schneider, *The Works and Doctrine of J.I.H. (1792–1867)*, New York 1977; Hitchcock 1977; *J.I.H. (1792–1867). Ein Architekt aus Köln im Paris des 19 Jahrhunderts*, exh. cat., Cologne 1987.

**Hoban**, James (*c*.1762–1831), Irish architect, emigrated to America after the Revolution, and was advertising in Philadelphia in 1785. But he settled in South Carolina until 1792, designing the State Capitol at Columbia (completed 1791, burnt down 1865), based on L'ENFANT's designs for the Federal Hall in New York. But he is remembered chiefly for the White House, Washington, which he designed in 1792, basing the front on a plate in GIBBS's *Book of Architecture*. He may also have had Leinster House, Dublin, in mind, though the White House is not, as has been suggested, a mere copy. It was built 1793–1801, and Hoban also supervised its rebuilding after 1814 (completed 1829). He also designed and built the Grand Hotel (1793–5) and the State and War Offices (begun in 1818), Washington. He ended his life as a solid and much respected councillor of that city.

W. Ryan and D. Guinness, *The White House. An Architectural History*, New York 1980; Summerson 1991.

**Hoff**, Robert van't (1887–1979), *see* DE STIJL.

**Hoffmann**, Josef (1870–1956), Austrian architect, a pupil of Otto WAGNER in Vienna and one of the founders of the Vienna SECESSION with OLBRICH in 1897 and of the Wiener Werkstätte (1903). The latter was based on the William MORRIS conviction of the importance of a unity between architecture and the crafts. His style developed from ART NOUVEAU towards a new appreciation of unrelieved square or rectangular forms ('Quadratl-Hoffmann') – a change not uninfluenced by MACKINTOSH, whose furniture and other work had been exhibited by the Secession in 1900. The Convalescent Home at Purkersdorf outside Vienna (1903–11) is one of the most courageously squared buildings of its date anywhere in the world, and yet it possesses that elegance and refinement of detail which is the Viennese heritage. With his Palais Stoclet in Brussels (1904–15) Hoffmann proved that this new totally anti-period style of unrelieved shapes could be made to look monumental and lavish by means of the materials used – in this case white marble in bronze framing outside, mosaics by Gustav Klimt inside. Hoffmann later built many wealthy villas, notably the neo-classical Haus Primavesi, Vienna (1913–15), some Austrian Pavilions for exhibitions (e.g. Paris 1925) and also some blocks of flats, but his chief importance lies in his early works.

E. F. Sekler, *J.H. The Architecture*, (Vienna 1982) Princeton 1985; P. Noever and A. D'Anvia, *J.H. 1870–1956. Ornament zwischen Hoffnung und Verbrechen*, Vienna 1987.

**Höger**, Fritz (Johann Friedrich) (1877–1949), *see* EXPRESSIONISM.

**Hohenburg**, Johann Ferdinand von (1732–1816), *see* AUSTRIAN ARCHITECTURE.

**Hoist**. A primitive form of ELEVATOR for transporting freight vertically, common in English warehouse design by the early C19.

**Holabird & Roche**. William Holabird (1854–1923) went to West Point in 1873–5 and to Chicago in 1875, where he took an engineering job in the office of W. Le B. JENNEY. In 1880 he formed a partnership with Martin Roche (1855–1927). Their Tacoma building, Chicago (1887–9), following Jenney's Home Insurance and going decisively beyond it, established steel-skeleton construction

for SKYSCRAPERS and with it the CHICAGO SCHOOL style. Their Marquette building, Chicago (1895), has the same importance stylistically as the Tacoma building has structurally. Its horizontal windows and its crisp, unenriched mouldings pointed the way into the C20.

Zukowsky 1988; R. Bruegmann, *H. & R.*, New York 1990; W. Blaser (ed.), *Chicago Architecture. H. & R. 1880–1992*, Basel 1992.

**Holabird & Root**. William Holabird's son John Augur (1886–1945) and J. W. ROOT's son John Wellborn Root Jnr (1887–1963) took over HOLABIRD & ROCHE in 1928 as Holabird & Root. They made their name with spectacular ART DECO skyscrapers, notably the Palmolive Building (now the Playboy Building), Chicago (1928–9), and the Board of Trade Building, Chicago (1929–30). These were accompanied by the Daily News Building (now Riverside Plaza), Chicago (1928–9), and the Travel and Transportation Building, Chicago (1930–33), and, after the Second World War, by the Illinois Bell Telephone Company Building, Northbrook, Illinois (1973); the Hollister Incorporated Corporate HQ, Libertyville, Illinois (1981), and the Motorola Customers' Center, Schaumberg, Illinois, 1994.

W. Blaser (ed.), *Chicago Architecture. H. & R. 1880–1992*, Basel 1992.

**Holden**, Charles (1876–1960). Holden was born to poverty in Lancashire, England. When he was at last able to devote himself to architecture he joined C. R. ASHBEE in 1897 and later Percy Adams, becoming a partner in 1907. The practice specialized in hospitals. Holden's most ambitious hospital is the King Edward VII Sanatorium at Midhurst, Sussex (1903–6), and his most original work belongs to these years, i.e. Law Society annexe, London (1903–4), Bristol Public Library (1906), and British Medical Association (now Zimbabwe House), London (1906–8). In style they are not like pioneer Continental buildings of the time; nor are there direct British precedents, although MACKINTOSH and John James Joass (1868–1952) of Mappin House (1906–8) and the Royal Insurance Building, London (1907–8), might have to be named.

In 1923 Holden began working for Frank Pick of London Transport and a new phase of his development began. He designed station buildings and soon far more: stop signs for buses, shelters, platforms, etc. At first the underground stations were block-like, as were his earlier buildings (e.g. Mansion House station 1926), but from 1930 onwards they accepted the Continental Modern of e.g. Fritz Schumacher (e.g. Sudbury Town, Sudbury Hill, Southgate and Arnos Grove underground stations 1931–3). The headquarters of London Transport (55 Broadway, London), built in 1926–9, is again stocky. A noteworthy feature of this building is the external sculpture of Eric Gill, Epstein and Henry Moore. In 1932 Holden was commissioned to design the new buildings for London University in Bloomsbury. Here, alas, all his courage seems to have abandoned him. Neo-Georgian features are paired with tame modern details. In the last fifteen or twenty years of his life he was principally engaged with problems of London planning with Sir William HOLFORD.

E. Karol and F. Allibone, *C.H. Architect 1875–1960*, London (Heinz Gallery) 1988.

**Holford**, Sir William (1907–75). Leading urban designer in England, responsible with Charles HOLDEN for the post-war plan for the City of London (1946–7) and for the precinct of St Paul's Cathedral (1955–6), executed with some unfortunate modifications.

G. E. Cherry, H.: *A Study in Architecture, Planning and Civic Design*, London 1985.

**Holl**, Elias (1573–1646). The leading Renaissance architect in Germany where he holds a position parallel historically to that of his exact contemporaries Inigo JONES in England and de BROSSE in France and to the slightly younger van CAMPEN in Holland. He came of a family of Augsburg masons who had risen to prominence under the Fuggers. He travelled in Italy, visiting Venice 1600–1601 and presumably studying PALLADIO and other Italian architects. In 1602 he was appointed city architect of Augsburg, where he was responsible for a large building programme including houses, warehouses, guildhalls, market halls for the various trades, schools, gates and towers for the city walls, the arsenal and the Town Hall. As a Protestant he suffered from the religious wars and was out of office 1630–32 and finally dismissed in 1635. His first building after his nomination as city architect was the arsenal, begun 1602. He believed in symmetry and classical proportions – e.g. St Anne's School (1613) with its high arcades encircling the court, regular fenestration, horizontal emphasis and remarkably well-designed classrooms lit from both sides; and the Hospital of the Holy Ghost (1626–30), which had high arcades encircling a court. But his masterpiece is the Town Hall (1615–20, damaged in the Second World War but rebuilt), a handsome, simple, rather severe building, much in advance of anything previously built in Germany. His aim was, he said, 'to obtain a bolder, more heroic appearance' and he claimed it was well proportioned. His first, unexecuted, design for it was more advanced stylistically than that built and made much play with Palladian windows almost in the manner of Palladio's Basilica in Vicenza. As built it is distinctly German in its verticality, especially in the central section of the façade, which contrasts strikingly with the more classically pure bays on either side. His work outside Augsburg was less important but includes additions to the Willibaldsburg at Eichstätt (1608) and, probably, the designs for the Schloss at Bratislava (Pozsony: Pressburg, 1632–49).

Hempel 1965; Hitchcock 1981; B. Roeck, *E.H. Stadthaumeister und Architekt vom Europäischen Rang*, Regensburg 1984.

**Holl**, Steven (b.1947). American architect, trained in Washington, Rome and London. His neo-vernacular all-wood Berkowitz Odgis House, Martha's Vineyard, Massachusetts (1984–8), recaptured on a small scale the free spirit of MOORE's Californian Sea Ranch. But his versatility became evident with such buildings as his Void Space/Hinged Space Housing, Nexus World Kashii, Fukuoka, Japan (1991); Stretto House, Dallas, Texas (1989–92); the Minimalist offices for D. E. Shaw and Company, New York (1991), and the St Ignatius Chapel, Seattle University (1994). In 1992 he won the competition for KIASMA Contemporary Art Museum, Helsinki. He published *Anchoring* (New York, 1989).

**Holland**, Henry (1745–1806), English architect, began under his father, a Fulham builder, then became assistant to 'Capability' BROWN, whose daughter he married. His first independent work, Brooks's Club, London (1776–8), was quickly followed by his greatest, Carlton House, London, which he enlarged and altered for the Prince of Wales (1783–5, demolished 1827–8). Also for the Prince of Wales he built the Marine Pavilion at Brighton (1786–7), later transformed into the Royal Pavilion by NASH. His style owed something to both CHAMBERS and ADAM, with various Louis XVI elements added. Though lacking originality, the refined taste and 'august simplicity' of his interior decoration approached French neo-classicism in elegance. His best country houses are Southill (1796) and Berrington Hall (1778). He laid out and built Hans Town, Chelsea (1771 onwards), but this has been largely rebuilt.

D. Stroud, *H.H.*, London 1966; Summerson 1991; Colvin 1995.

**Hollein**, Hans (b.1934). Austrian architect, typically Viennese in his extreme and often ironic sophistication, as shown in the small *de luxe* commercial buildings which made his name, e.g. the Schullin jewellery shop (1974) and the Austrian State Travel Agency (1976–8), both in Vienna. His large-scale Abteilberg Museum, Mönchengladbach (1972–82), is remarkable, as are his Museum of Modern Art, Frankfurt (1991), the Neues Haas-Haus, Vienna (1991), Banco Santander, Madrid (1993) and the Assicurazioni Generali Offices, Bregenz (1993).

G. Pettena, *H.H. Opere 1960–88*, Florence and Milan 1988; Klotz 1988.

**Holmgren**, Herman Theodor (b.1842), *see* SWEDISH ARCHITECTURE.

**Holt Hinshaw Pfau Jones**, *see* UNITED STATES ARCHITECTURE.

**Holy sepulchre**. A structure imitating (sometimes only in general form) the tomb of Christ as rediscovered by Constantine. This had been encased by Constantine in a miniature temple placed in a round (or polygonal?) church, both razed and rebuilt many times. Imitations of both shrine and church followed, at first by association, as cemetery chapels (earliest at Fulda, 820–21). The shrine was most commonly imitated in Germany (e.g.

Constance CI3, Görlitz 1481–1504) and Italy (e.g. ALBERTI's in Florence, 1467), while England produced the variant of EASTER SEPULCHRES and a number of round churches (e.g. Cambridge and Northampton).

N. C. Brooks, *The Sepulchre of Christ in Art and Liturgy*, London 1921.

**Honeysuckle ornament**, *see* AN-THEMION.

**Hood**, Raymond Mathewson (1881–1934). American architect who won the competition for the Chicago Tribune Building in 1922 together with John Mead Howells (1868–1959). It was built 1923–5. This Gothic skyscraper was followed by his black and gold American Radiator Building, New York (1924). His McGraw-Hill building in New York (1931) is one of the first skyscrapers designed in the INTERNATIONAL MODERN style. In his Daily News building (1930) he stressed the closely set verticals, and this must have inspired the Rockefeller Center (begun 1931) to which the centrepiece is the RCA Building (1934) of which he was one of the participating architects.

W. H. Kilham, *R.H. Architect of Ideas*, New York 1973; R. A. M. Stern, *R.H.*, New York 1981.

**Hood-mould**. A projecting moulding to throw off the rain, on the face of a wall, above an arch, doorway or window; can be called *dripstone* or, if rectangular, a *label*. *See also* LABEL-STOP; Fig. 64.

**Hooke**, Robert (1635–1703). English scientist and WREN's closest architectural associate. His independent works were imposing but undistinguished – Royal College of Physicians (1672–7), Bethlehem Hospital (1674–6), Montagu House (1675–9), all in London and all demolished.

Summerson 1991; Colvin 1995.

Fig. 64 Hood-mould

**Hopkins**, Michael (b.1935) and Patty (b.1942). English architects in partnership since 1976. Less severe and more relaxed than FOSTER, with whom Michael Hopkins worked 1969–75, they have skilfully exploited the more 'acceptable face' of High Tech. Their own house in Hampstead, London (1975–6), was a brilliantly successful metal and glass construction of Miesian elegance and was followed by the Greene King Brewery, Bury St Edmunds, Suffolk (1977–83), of similar refinement. Their notable contribution to INDUSTRIALIZED BUILDING was realized in 1980–81, the Patera Building System, of which four prototypes were constructed at Stoke-on-Trent, Staffordshire, in 1982, and a further two at Canary Wharf, London, in 1985. Their own office in Marylebone, London, is an expanded version (1982–5). A series of remarkable and sometimes innovative buildings have followed: the Schlumberger Research Laboratories, Cambridge (1982–5); the widely acclaimed Mound Stand at Lord's Cricket Ground, London (1984–7); the Solid State Logic Building, Begbroke, Oxfordshire (1986–8); additions to Bracken House, London (1987–92); the David Mellor building, Shad Thames Street, London (1987–90); the David Mellor Cutlery Factory, Hathersage, Derbyshire (1988–9); the new opera house at Glyndebourne, Sussex (1988–94); and the New Inland Revenue Building, Nottingham (1992–4). Their New

Parliamentary Building, Westminster, London (1989), with its striking Topkapi Kitchen Wing skyline, is in course of construction. In 1989–92 they also designed the Bedfont Lakes BUSINESS PARK near Heathrow, Middlesex, with the main building, New Square. Michael Hopkins was knighted in 1995.

C. Davies, *H. The Work of M.H. and Partners*, London 1993.

**Hopper**, Thomas (1776–1856). English eclectic architect whose neo-Norman castles were bold and original – Gosford in Ireland (*c.*1820) and Penrhyn in Wales (1825–37). In 1807 he designed a cast-iron neo-Gothic conservatory and other additions to Carlton House, London (demolished 1827–8).

Colvin 1995; N. Burton in Brown 1985.

**Horeau**, Hector (1801–72), *see* CONSERVATORY.

**Hornwork**. In military architecture, an outwork of two demi-bastions connected by a curtain and joined to the main work by two parallel wings.

**Horseshoe arch**, *see* ARCH.

**Horta**, Baron Victor (1861–1947), a Belgian architect, studied in Paris in 1878–80, then at the Brussels Academy under Balat. He appeared in the forefront of European architecture with his Hôtel Tassel, Brussels, now the Mexican Embassy (designed 1892). This is the same year as that of van de VELDE's first exploration of ART NOUVEAU typography and design. The Hôtel Tassel is less startling externally, but its staircase with exposed iron supports, floral iron ornament, and much linear decoration on the wall is Art Nouveau architecture of the boldest. The Hôtel Tassel was followed by the particularly complete and lavish Hôtel Solvay (1895–1900); the Maison du Peuple (1895–9), with a curved glass and iron

façade and much structural and decorative iron inside the great hall; the store L'Innovation (1901; burnt down 1966); and several more private houses, e.g. Frissen, Uccle (1899–1900) and Furnemont, Uccle (1900–1901). His own house (1898–1901) is now the Musée Horta. Later Horta turned to a conventional Classicism (Palais des Beaux Arts, Brussels, 1922–9).

R. L. Delevoy, *V.H.*, Brussels 1958; F. Borsi and P. Portoghesi, *V.H.*, Rome 1969; A. Hoppenbrouwers *et al.*, *V.H. architectonographie*, Brussels 1975; A. Hustache, *V.H. Maisons de Campagne*, Brussels 1994; D. Dernie and A. Carew-Cox, *V.H.*, London 1995; F. Aubry and F. Vanderbreeden, *H. Art Nouveau to Modernism*, Ghent 1996.

**Hotel**. A public lodging house, a C18 development of the inn, e.g. by the addition of an assembly room as at the Lion Hotel, Shrewsbury, England (*c.*1775–80). The construction of large-scale hotels of architectural pretensions began in the C19 USA with Isaiah ROGERS and continued with POST, culminating with LAPIDUS and PORTMAN. The New York hotel architect Herbert Janeway Hardenberg (1847–1918) of the Waldorf-Astoria (1890–97, later enlarged) and the Plaza (1907), New York, should also be mentioned. Among European hotels of architectural pretensions Sir George Gilbert Scott's St Pancras Hotel, London (1868–76), and Sommaruga's Tre Croci hotel near Varese, Italy (1909–12), were notable, as was the Ritz Hotel, London (1905), by Mewés and Davis.

**Hôtel**. In France a town house of which the standard design was established by SERLIO's 'Grand Ferrare' in Fontainebleau (1544–6), i.e. a CORPS DE LOGIS with narrower wings forming a courtyard which is enclosed towards the street by a wall or by a stable and kitchen block, broken in the middle by the entrance door. The *piano nobile* with the main reception rooms was usually on the ground floor (not the first floor), with large casement windows or French doors giving on to the garden terrace. The best surviving early example is the Hôtel Carnavalet in Paris by LESCOT of *c*.1545. It was usual to have a garden or small park behind the *corps de logis*. The latter often contained a gallery on the first floor. MANSART's Hôtel de la Vrillière, Paris (1635–45), became the model for the classical type of Parisian hôtel.

Gallet 1964; Loyer 1987.

**Houber**, François (b.1955), *see* MECANOO.

**Howard**, Ebenezer (1850–1928). English urban theorist, started as a clerk in the City of London, rose to be a valued shorthand writer, and remained that nearly to the end. During a stay of five years in America (1872–7), he learned to know and admire Whitman and Emerson, and began to think of the better life and how it could be made to come true. In 1898 he read Edward Bellamy's utopian work *Looking Backward*, and this gave him the idea of his lifetime: that of the GARDEN CITY, which is an independent city and not a suburb – this is important – and is placed in the green countryside and provided with countrified housing as well as industry and all cultural amenities. His book *Tomorrow* came out in 1898, in 1899 the Garden City Association was founded, in 1902 the book was republished as *Garden Cities of Tomorrow*, and in 1903 Letchworth was started, to the design of Parker and UNWIN. This was the earliest of the garden cities and greatly influenced the post-war SATELLITE TOWNS of Britain, nor was it less influential on urban design in the USA, *see* RAD-

BURN PLANNING. Howard was knighted in 1927.

D. MacFadyen, *Sir E.H. and the Town Planning Movement*, London 1933; R. Beevers, *The Garden City Utopia. A Critical Biography of E.H.*, London 1988.

**Howard**, John Gaten (1864–1931), *see* ARTS AND CRAFTS.

**Howe**, George (1886–1955). American architect who designed in collaboration with William Lescaze (1896–1964) the Philadelphia Savings Fund Building (1929–32), one of the first skyscrapers in the INTERNATIONAL MODERN style. The partnership broke up in 1935. Of Howe's later work, Fortune Rock on Mount Desert Island, Maine (1937–9), should be mentioned.

R. Stern, *G.H. Towards a Modern Architecture*, New Haven and London 1975.

**Howells**, John Mead (1868–1959), *see* HOOD, Raymond Mathewson.

**Hua**. In Chinese roof construction a bracket, usually one of several comprising a TOU KUNG.

**Hübsch**, Heinrich (1795–1863), *see* HISTORICISM.

**Hueber**, Joseph (1716–87). Austrian Late Rococo architect working in Styria. Son of a Viennese mason, he began as a journeyman mason in Bohemia, Saxony and central and southern Germany. In 1740 he took over the architectural practice of Giuseppe Carlone in Graz on marrying his widow. He built the handsome twin towers of the Mariahilfkirche in Graz (1742–4) and two pilgrimage churches – St Veit am Vorgau (1748–51) and the Weizbergkirche (1756–8), with an elaborate interior like a stage set – and the great library at Admont Abbey (*c*.1770–74), though this has been attributed to Gotthard Hayberger (1699–

1764), who designed the library at St Florian (1744–51).

Hempel 1965; Laing 1978.

**Hültz**, Johann (d.1449), was master mason of Strasbourg Cathedral and as such designed the openwork spire with its fabulous spiral staircase. The work was completed in 1439. Hültz was the successor to Ulrich von ENSINGEN, who built the octagon (the stage below the spire).

Frankl 1972.

**Hungarian architecture**. Medieval architecture in Hungary reflects the events in various centres of the West. Sometimes inspiration came from one centre, sometimes from more than one. As in other countries the beginnings are tantalizing. A building like Feldebrö church of the C10 is mysterious in its stylistic pedigree. It is a square in plan with three apses in the middle of three sides. Should one link it with Germigny-des-Prés? Zalavár church of the C9 has three parallel east apses like the contemporary buildings in Switzerland. The Romanesque style is, as one would expect, most closely linked with south Germany and Austria and with Lombardy. The latter appears most clearly in the grand though over-restored cathedral of Pécs with its four towers flanking the west and east end of the nave. The splendid west portral of Ják has German but also north Italian and even Norman elements. The abbey churches of Ják, Lébény and Zsámbék are the most conspicuous Romanesque churches of German descent in Hungary. They have in common a relatively late date (first half C13), three east apses, two west towers and a west gallery.

As in other countries the CISTERCIANS and the Premonstratensians brought into Hungary a new plan and new details, all first developed in France. The finest

buildings are of the C13, the churches at Bélapátfalva (founded in 1232), Pannonhalma, the latter (1217–24) not Cistercian, though Cistercian in style with sexpartite rib vaults, and Osca with polygonal instead of straight-edged east chapels. Sexpartite rib vaults are a French Early Gothic feature, and the Gothic of, e.g., Noyon is also mixed with Romanesque, especially Norman, detail in the elegant chapel in the castle of Esztergom.

Of the High Gothic style Hungary possesses no major monument.

As for the Late Gothic, it is clearly dependent on south Germany and Austria. The churches are of the HALL type. They are high, with slender piers, sometimes without capitals, and they have complicated figured rib vaults. Examples are Sopron, Koloszvár and Brassó (chancel). The friars built much in Hungary during these centuries.

Among the castles of Hungary three at least must be mentioned: Buda, where much restoration and reconstruction of the great halls and the chapel has been done, Visegrád with its mighty keep of c.1260, square with triangular projections on two opposite sides, and Diósgyőr of the second half of the C14, which is oblong with an inner courtyard and four prominent angle towers.

Internationally speaking the most important phase in Hungarian architecture is that of King Matthias Corvinus (1458–90) and the decades after his death. The king was a patron of Mantegna, Verrocchio, Ercole Roberti, BENEDETTO DA MAIANO and other Italians. His library of illuminated manuscripts in the Renaissance style is unparalleled north of the Alps, and he also favoured the new style in architecture. Earlier than in any country outside Italy – including even France – are the friezes from Buda castle now in the Castle Museum and the well in Visegrád castle whose stepped terraces, still largely Gothic, are of great magnificence. In ecclesiastic art the Bakócz Chapel in Esztergom Cathedral, begun as early as 1506, is purely Italian. The architect is unknown; the altar (1519) is by Andrea Ferrucci of Fiesole.

After these years of enthusiasm Hungary settled down to a less adventurous later C16 and early C17. The fancy battlements and arcaded courtyards of houses are generally Eastern. The monuments of Turkish domination (mosques, minarets, baths, and funerary chapels at Pécs, Eger, Budapest) look odd side by side with them. As a sign of the war against the Turks some fortresses were erected (Győr, etc.) by Italian engineers on the new Italian models. The Turkish occupation ended only in the late C17, and in the C18 Austrian and Bohemian Baroque held the stage. The most interesting buildings are the Eszterházy palace at Eisenstadt across the Austrian border (1663–72) by Carl Martin Carlone (1616–67), Prince Eugene's delightful Ráckeve (1701–2) by HILDEBRANDT and then St Anne, Budapest (1740 onwards), the huge Eszterházy palace at Fertőd (1764–6) and the Lyceum at Eger (1765–85) by Jacob Fellner (1722–80).

The turn away from the Baroque in the direction of neo-classicism was taken early in Hungary. Vác Cathedral (1763–77) by Isidore Canevale (1730–86), with its giant portico of detached columns carrying a heavy attic, not a pediment, and with its central dome and coffered vaults, would be highly remarkable even if it stood in Paris. Classicism of a Romantic cast culminates in the immensely impressive cathedral of Esztergom (1822–c.1850) by Janos Páckh (1796–1839) and Jozsef Hild (1789–1867), with its central plan, its many-columned dome and its eight-column giant portico, and in the competent but more conventional neo-Greek work of Mihály POLLAK,

e.g. the National Museum, Budapest (1836–45).

The climax of C19 eclecticism is the richly Italianate Opera in Budapest (1875–84) by Miklos Ybl (1814–91), and the surprisingly late Gothic-Revival Houses of Parliament (1883–1902) by Imre Steindl (1839–1902). The ART NOUVEAU reaction against eclecticism had an unusually brilliant exponent in Ödön LECHNER. The Modern Movement set in as a branch of LOOS and HOFFMANN's Vienna with Béle Lajta (1875–1920), e.g. his Martinelli Place Emporium, Budapest (1912–14). The International Style reached Hungary in the 1930s, most notably through Farkas Molnár (1897–1945), who had studied at the Bauhaus. His own villa at Budapest (1932) and the Sanatorium at Pestujhely (1936) are exemplary. More recently Imre MAKOVECZ has attracted international attention for his Hungarian Organic Architecture.

**Hungry joint**, *see* POINTING.

**Hunt**, Richard Morris (1827–95), American architect, came of a wealthy early Colonial family. They moved to Paris in 1843, and there Hunt joined LEFUEL's *atelier* and the École des Beaux Arts. He also worked on painting with Couture and on sculpture with Barye. He travelled widely before he was made an *inspecteur* under Lefuel of the Louvre in 1854. This first-hand knowledge of the French-Renaissance Revival he took back to America in 1855. He settled in New York and, side by side with his practice, ran an *atelier* on the Parisian pattern. But he returned to Europe again in the 1860s and only in 1868 finally came to rest. His J. N. H. Griswold House, Newport, Rhode Island (1862), is a notable early example of the STICK STYLE. In 1873 he designed the Tribune building in New York (one of the first with lifts), and then rich men's residences at Newport, Rhode Island, in New York (W. K. Vanderbilt, 1878 onwards; J. J. Astor, 1893), and elsewhere (Biltmore, Ashville, North Carolina, 1895, and Ochre Court, Newport, 1892). The French Renaissance remained his favourite style. Hunt was also the designer of the Administration building at the Chicago Exposition of 1893 and the Fifth Avenue façade of the Metropolitan Museum, New York (1894–1902, renovated by ROCHE & DINKELOO 1970). He was one of the founders of the American Institute of Architects.

Hitchcock 1977; P. R. Baker, *R.M.H.*, Cambridge, Mass., 1980; S. R. Stein, *The Architecture of R.M.H. (1828–1895)*, Chicago 1986.

**Hurtado Izquierdo**, Francisco (1669–1725), one of the greatest Spanish Baroque architects, was quite the most exuberantly rich. His work is confined to interiors, which are of a fantasy unparalleled in Europe. Born and educated in Cordoba, he became a captain in the army and possibly visited Sicily. He may have designed the Victoria *camarín* above the Mausoleum of the Counts of Buenavista, Málaga (1691–3). Most of his work is in Granada, where he designed the relatively simple *sagrario* (Sacrament Chapel) for the cathedral (1704–5). The Sacrament Chapel of the Cartuja (1702–20), walled with marble, jasper and porphyry and containing a marble tabernacle supported by red and black SALOMÓNICAS, is a masterpiece of polychromatic opulence. He called it 'a precious jewel', and claimed that there was nothing like it in all Europe. In 1718 he designed the very complex *camarín*, liberally decorated with grey-and-coral-coloured marble and lapis lazuli, for the Cartuja of El Paular, Segovia. He has also been credited with the design of the still more bizarrely rich sacristy of the Granada Cartuja (executed 1730–47), where the tendency to muffle the structure in a riotous welter of ornament is taken to its final extreme.

Kubler and Soria 1959.

**Husk garland**. A FESTOON of nutshells diminishing towards the ends.

**Husley**, Jacob Otten (1738–94), *see* DUTCH ARCHITECTURE.

**Hutchinson**, Henry (1800–1831), *see* RICKMAN, Thomas.

**Huut**, Max von (b.1947), *see* ENVIRONMENTAL, GREEN OR SUSTAINABLE ARCHITECTURE.

**Hypaethral**. Without a roof, open to the sky, as in the *atrium* of an Ancient Roman house.

**Hyperbolic paraboloid roof**. A special form of double-curved shell, a construction of ANTICLASTIC curvature the geometry of which is generated by straight lines. This property makes it fairly easy to construct. The shape consists of a continuous plane developing from a parabolic arch in one direction to a similar inverted parabola in the other. It was pioneered by Matthew Nowicki (1910–51) at the Dorton Arena, Raleigh, North Carolina (1948–53) and by CANDELA in Mexico, notably at his Cosmic Ray Pavilion, University City, Mexico City (1952). *See* Fig. 65.

Mainstone 1975.

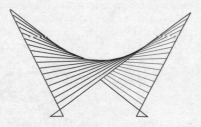

Fig. 65 Hyperbolic paraboloid

**Hypocaust**. The underground chamber or duct of the Roman system of central heating, the floor being heated by the hot air circulating below. The gases escaped up flues in the walls, thus heating these also.

**Hypogeum**. An underground room or vault.

**Hypostyle**. A hall or other large space over which the roof is supported by rows of columns like a forest.

**Hypotrachelium**. The groove round a Doric column between the SHAFT and the NECKING.

# I

**IBA** (Internationale Bauausstellung) Berlin 1979–87, *see* GERMAN ARCHITECTURE.

**Iconostasis**. A screen in Byzantine churches separating the sanctuary from the nave and pierced by three doors; originally a lattice of columns joined by a decorated PARAPET and COPING. Since the C14–15 it has become a wooden or stone wall covered with icons, hence the name.

**Ictinus**. The leading architect in Periclean Athens and one of the greatest of all time. With CALLICRATES he designed and built the Parthenon (447/6–438 BC), about which he later wrote a book, now lost, with Carpion. He was commissioned by Pericles to design the new Telesterion (Hall of Mysteries) at Eleusis, but his designs were altered by the three new architects who took over on the fall of Pericles. According to Pausanias he was also the architect of the Doric temple of Apollo at Bassae, begun after the Great Plague of 304 BC.

R. Carpenter, *The Architects of the Parthenon*, Harmondsworth 1970.

**Igloo** or **iglu**. An Inuit (Eskimo) house of packed snow cut into blocks laid in a closing spiral to form a dome. It is usually entered through a barrel-vaulted tunnel, also of snow blocks, protected with hide curtains. The snow blocks form an effective thermal barrier. See Fig. 66.

**IED**, *see* ENVIRONMENTAL DESIGN.

**Imbrex**. In Greek and Roman architecture, a convex tile to cover the join between two flat or concave roofing tiles.

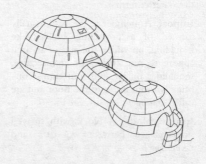

Fig. 66 Igloo

**Imbrication**. A regular overlapping of edges as of roofing tiles, or a decorative overlapping pattern resembling this.

**Imhotep**. Ancient Egyptian high priest and chief minister to King Zoser (third dynasty, 2780–2680 BC, or according to an alternative chronology 2686–2613 BC), Imhotep later acquired a mythological character as a healing deity and also as an architect. According to the C3 BC Egyptian historian Manetho, the Greeks attached some importance to Imhotep as an architect but only recently has his name been recovered in this connection (on a statue base of Zoser at Saqqara). He was architect of the Step Pyramid at Saqqara, a daring structure rising like a gigantic staircase to the heavens, and this led to the exploration of building with stone. Thus Imhotep laid the basis for the development of stone masonry on a large scale.

Smith and Simpson 1981.

**Imperial staircase**, *see* STAIRCASE.

**Impluvium**. The basin or water cistern, usually rectangular, in the centre of an ATRIUM of a Roman house to receive the rain-water from the surrounding roofs. The term is also used, loosely, for the uncovered space in the atrium as well as the water cistern.

**Impost**. A member in the wall, usually formed of a projecting bracket-like moulding, on which the end of an arch appears to rest. In Gothic architecture, mouldings on an arch sometimes continue without break to the floor and are called *continuous imposts. See* Fig. 6.

**Impost block**. A block with splayed sides placed between ABACUS and CAPITAL.

**In antis**, *see* ANTA.

**In situ**. In position or location, referring in architecture to elements or parts of a building constructed or assembled on site, i.e. at their final location.

**Inca architecture**, *see* PERUVIAN ARCHITECTURE.

**Indent**. A shape chiselled out in a stone slab to receive a brass effigy.

**Indian and Pakistani architecture and landscape architecture**. The history of architecture in the Indian sub-continent – present-day India, Pakistan and Bangladesh – is complicated by major differences in climate and availability of building materials in an area as large as Western Europe, constantly shifting internal frontiers, invasion from outside, and a diversity of religious beliefs that inspired most of the structures that survive from before the C17. It begins with the remains of cities of the Indus valley or Harappan civilization which, during its most highly developed period *c.*2100–1750 BC, extended from present-day Pakistan and Afghanistan as far south as the Gulf of Cambay and east to the Ganges valley. Mohenjo-Daro (Pakistan) is the most fully excavated site, a city about one mile across laid out on a grid plan with wide streets, sophisticated water-supply and drainage systems, numerous blocks of houses with internal courtyards built of bonded fire-burned brick of a standard size, a vast granary, a HYPOSTYLE hall and an asphalt-lined bath – none decorated. After the decline of this civilization nothing is known of Indian architecture for more than a millennium. Literary sources reveal that by the time of the birth of the Buddha *c.*563 BC there were cities in the north-east and the consecutive history of Indian architecture begins at Pataliputra (beneath modern Patna), capital of the Mauryan dynasty that came to power *c.*323 BC and, under Asoka (*c.*272–231 BC), spread its rule over the north and centre of the sub-continent. Little remains of Pataliputra (said to have covered some 36 sq. km. (14 sq. miles) apart from the foundations of a hypostyle hall with 80 stone-based pillars. Buildings were of impermanent materials but their forms were simulated in carved stone entrances to C3 BC caves in the Barabar Hills (nr Gaya) which served as retreats for ascetics during the rainy season – notably the gable end of a wooden structure with a rounded thatched roof supported on rafters and rising to a central peak, the earliest form of the horseshoe arch that was to recur in Indian architecture, notably in the entrances to CHAITYA halls. Asoka, a convert to Buddhism, promoted the erection of STUPAS which probably established their essential form – a solid brick hemisphere flattened at the top to carry a stone parasol (*chattra*) surrounded by a square railing of stone simulating woodwork. The finest early example is at Sanchi, begun under Asoka, enlarged to 40 m. (120 ft) in diameter in the C2 when it was faced with stone and surrounded by a 3 m. (10 ft) high stone railing to which four elaborate gateways were added in CI BC. Small stupas, placed in apses to permit ritual circumambulation, are features of Buddhist chaitya halls, distinguishing these caves from those of Jains and Hindus of the same period. Though excavated rather than built, these halls cut into the face of cliffs, beginning at the top with simulated rafters and descending around pillars, their entrances richly carved with figures, mark the beginning of Indian temple architecture in stone and range in date from C2 BC at Bhaja to the outstanding C5 AD examples at Ajanta and the last notable examples, at Ellora, of the C9. Caves with cells surrounding a rectangular central space were also excavated to serve as VIHARAS or monasteries. By a similar process free-standing Hindu temples were carved from the living rock – the five 'pancha rathas' each fashioned from a single boulder at Mamallapuram (C7) and the very much larger Kailasa temple with rich sculptural decoration at Ellora (mid C8). The earliest stone constructions are small cubical shrines on platforms dating from the end of the Gupta period (C3–5) in central India, at Nachna, Sanchi and Tigawa. The C6 Vishnu temple at Deogarh is more imposing, with superb carvings round the entrance and in false doors on the other three sides. Temples were also built of brick in the C5, sometimes with a more complex plan but similarly enclosing a cubical sanctuary (that at Bhitargaon is the largest and least ruined). From the C8 greater importance was given to the SIKHARA above the sanctuary and to the porch in front of it and sometimes extended to a long hall (e.g. at Aihole). Roofs were made of large stone slabs and early *sikharas* often have the appearance of one laid on top of another, diminishing in width to make a curved profile. But fully developed temples give an impression of sculptured mass rather than tectonic form. As their size increased the figurative carvings on their exteriors became ever more exuberant: the most notable examples include the Rajarana and Lingaraja temples at Bhubaneshwar; the Sasbahu temple at Gwalior; the Kandariya and Mahadeva temples at Khajuraho, all of the CII; and the Temple of the Sun at Konarak of the mid C13. These are all in northern styles (with some regional differences), brought to their highest expression at the time of the first Muslim invasions which put an end to temple building for some centuries. By this time Buddhism had lost its following in India. But the Jain religion continued to flourish (as it still does) if only in a few areas, notably Rajasthan and Gujarat; its temples differ from those dedicated to Hindu gods in that they are externally simpler but internally far richer, with more varied spaces and much intricate, mainly non-figurative, carving in the preferred medium of white marble, e.g. Adinatha temple on Mount Abu (CII), Adinatha temple at Ranakpur (mid C15).

In the south of India distinct Hindu styles emerged in the C7 (Meguti temple at Aihole and Malegitti Shivalaya temple at Badami) and continued to evolve without a break until the C18. Its distinguishing features are boldly moulded plinths, walls divided into projecting and recessed bays by pairs of pilasters, and overhanging eaves surmounted by parapets. The most notable C8 examples include the Shore temple at Mamallapuram and the richly sculptured Kailasantha temple at Kanchipuram. Under the Chola dynasty of kings who ruled in Tamil-Nadu C9–13 a vast number of temples were built, mostly small in scale but also the huge and imposing Brihadeshvara temples at Thanjavur and Gangaikondacholapuram, and the Nataraja temple at Chidambaram. To the north-west in Karnatika a distinctive style was created under the kings of the Hoysala dynasty C12–13. At Belur, Halebid and (the best preserved) Somnathpur, temples were built on very complicated plans with many angled projections, in a hard local stone which permits a sharpness of carving in their elaborate decorations which have the appearance of metalwork. From the late C13 India was under attack from Muslims, but in the C15 most of the south was united in the realm of the staunchly Hindu kings of Vijayanagara whose defiance was expressed in the massive size of buildings, many of which were added to earlier temples – towering GOPURAS which dwarf the sanctuaries in the enclosures to which they give access, long processional corridors and halls with flat roofs supported on numerous elaborately carved pillars (sometimes with horses rearing up out of them), e.g. at Kanchipuram, Srirangam and Vellore as well as the capital city of Vijayanagara (modern Hampi), which was sacked by Muslims 1565, though much survives. Temple building continued throughout the C17, most notably at Madurai, and the practice of colouring the stucco figures of deities on *gopuras* has never ceased. At Madurai the C17 royal palace, like the remains of the larger and earlier one at Vijayanagara, is in the Indo-Islamic or Mughal style.

The invasion of the Indian subcontinent by Muslims from western Asia began in the C8 when present-day Pakistan was occupied, but apart from the remains of a C8 mosque near Karachi and the undistinguished mid-C12 Solah Khambi mosque at Bhadreshwar in Kutch, the earliest Islamic buildings date from the establishment of the Delhi sultanate in 1193. The Quwwat-ul-Islam (Might of Islam) mosque, Delhi, was built 1193–7 on the site of a Hindu temple and with materials from other demolished temples as well. Surviving parts include the entrance with a 6 m. (20 ft) high

gently pointed arch carved in low relief with a distinctly Indian foliage ornament, and the Qutb minar, or tower of victory, which served also as a MINARET, originally 72.5 m. (238 ft) high (later enlarged) of four storeys diminishing in section and separated by balconies resting on brackets with stalactite mouldings. The large arch and the minaret were new to India; so too were domes and the tombs or mausolea they often crowned, one of the earliest surviving being that of Ghiyas-ud-din Tughluq, Delhi, of 1540–45, five storeys high with a central dome surrounded by little domed pavilions (the CHATRIS that became a distinguishing feature of the Indo-Islamic or Mughal style, named after the dynasty which ruled India from 1526 to 1858). The Mughals set a new standard for the magnificence of such structures, followed by the tombs of Humayun, Delhi (1565), and Akbar, Sikander, near Agra (1604–12), both set in formal gardens, the latter of red stone encrusted with geometrical patterns in marble. Akbar's main architectural achievement was the palace-city of Fatehpur Sikri (1571–85), an extraordinary complex of buildings – mosques, audience halls, the superb tomb of Shaikh Salim Chishti, living quarters for the emperor and his court etc., all in a successful amalgam of Persian–Islamic and Indian styles. The tomb of Itmad-ud-Daula at Agra (1622–8) is exquisite rather than imposing, built of white marble with grilles of lace-like carved tracery (simulating MUSHRABEYEH work) and incrustations of semi-precious stones. The much larger Taj Mahal, Agra, of 1630–53 presents an almost uniquely successful combination of delicacy and monumentality – refined in every detail of carved and inlaid work, grandiose in scale but of an opalescent colour which gives it an appearance almost of weightlessness, perfectly balanced in its proportions and the relationship of the mausoleum with its great bulbous dome to the four minarets standing out from its corners, to the red sandstone mosques on either side and to the great gateway which is separated from it by a Persian-style CHAHAR BAGH or 'paradise garden' crossed by ornamental canals. It was designed by a Persian master-builder Ustad Isa Khan Effendi with his pupil AHMAD USTAD and, for the dome, Ismail Khan, on commission from Shah Jahan as the tomb for his favourite wife. Of the Mughal rulers, Shah Jahan, who reigned 1628–57, was the most fastidious patron of architecture and garden design: the works he commissioned include the several halls and pavilions in the Red Fort at Delhi (begun 1639), the Jami Masjid in Delhi (1644–58) – the largest mosque in India – and most of the buildings in the Red Fort at Agra, notably the Moti Masjid or Pearl Mosque, also additions to the Shalamar (abode of love) Bagh, Srinagar, Kashmir, begun for his father c.1620, and the still more grandiose Shalamar Bagh, Lahore (1633–42), luxuriantly planted on three terraces with marble pavilions, cascades and fountains. The style perfected under Shah Jahan was imitated by the architects of later Mughal emperors and minor rulers in north and central India with a marked decline in form as well as detail (already evident in the Bibi-Ka-Maqbara of 1678 at Aurangabad, which was intended, but signally failed, to rival the Taj Mahal). Of C18 building the Sikh Golden Temple at Amritsar is the most interesting. By this date, however, most of India had come under European dominance.

The earliest European buildings are churches at Goa – St Francis of Assisi (begun 1527), Immaculate Conception (1541), Cathedral (1562–1619) and Bom Jesus (1594–1605), all in Portuguese styles with prominent use of the classical ORDERS. There are architectural relics of the French presence at Pondicherry laid out on a grid pattern within a circular road (1756–77) but including earlier buildings, notably the governor's palace (1752). The fantastic La Martinière boys' school at Lucknow (c.1780–1800), designed and built by Major-General Claude Martin, Lyonnais soldier, banker and political agent, is more French than anything else. British buildings appeared first in the three main stations of the East India Company – Bombay (Cathedral begun 1672, St Andrew's Kirk 1819, Town Hall 1820–23); Madras (St Mary's church 1678–80, Banqueting Hall 1802); and Calcutta (St John's church 1787; Government House, based on ADAM's Kedleston, of 1799–1802). They are all classical in style, mainly neo-PALLADIAN and GREEK REVIVAL, and, like much that followed the spread of British rule, the work of army officers who were amateur architects, as is often only too obvious. In the later C19 Gothic was adopted for churches and public buildings, most exuberantly in Bombay – High Court (1871–9) by General James Augustus Fuller and the Victoria Terminus (1878–87) by F. W. Stevens. Indo-Islamic elements were employed with equal abandon on the High Court, Madras (1888–92), by J. W. Brassington and others. The most prominent of later British buildings are those by LUTYENS and BAKER at New Delhi, mainly Imperial Roman with a few, not always very happy, references to Indian Buddhist, Hindu and Islamic traditions.

The independence and partition of India and Pakistan in 1947 brought no liberation from Western architecture. LE CORBUSIER and Maxwell FRY were commissioned to design the city of Chandigarh as a new capital of the Punjab. In Pakistan, the new capital Islamabad was laid out in 1960 by DOXIADIS Associates according to contemporary Western ideals of urban design. Though a fine mosque is by a Pakistani architect, Khwaja Zaheer-ud-Din, the huge secretariat and main hotel are by Gio PONTI. The main official buildings at Dacca, the new capital of East Pakistan (from 1971 Bangladesh), are by Louis KAHN (begun 1965). Anant Raje (b.1929) was among the notable Indian architects who inherited Kahn's great Indian legacy, e.g. Raje's Institute of Forest Management, Bhopal, begun 1984 in partnership with Achyat Kanvinde (b.1916) whose Nehru Science Centre, Bombay (1971–81), and Sher-e Kashmir Stadium, Srinagar (1984), are remarkable. Later Raje worked with DOSHI, who became with STEIN, REWALL and CORREA one of the leading Indian architects of the late C20. Uttam Jain (b.1934) should also be mentioned here for his university buildings, Jodhpur (1969–72 with additions 1983–5), his City Hall, Balotra (1985), and the Indira Gandhi Research Institute, Bombay (1987). *See also* BURMESE ARCHITECTURE; NEPALESE ARCHITECTURE; SRI LANKAN ARCHITECTURE; TIBETAN ARCHITECTURE.

**Indonesian architecture**. Stone building was introduced with Hinduism and Buddhism from India, the earliest surviving structures being small late C7 temples in central Java (Dieng plateau). Borobudor in the same region was begun *c.*780 (probably as a Hindu monument) but completed *c.*833 as the greatest Mahayana Buddhist monument anywhere – a sacred mountain of stone approximately 120 m. (360 ft) across at the base and 35 m. (115 ft) high, on a mandala plan with nine terraces linked by stairways ascending from the cardinal points and passing under corbelled arches. Figurative reliefs of high quality line the galleries which, together with statues of the Buddha, were the monument's *raison d'être*. A few other Buddhist temples of the same date survive, e.g. Candi Mendut near Borobudor. In 832 central Java came under Hindu rulers who had temples built, notably at Prambanam (835–56), dedicated to Siva, Visnu and Brahma, encrusted with much fine relief sculpture and with numerous tiers of spirelets which give a strong vertical accent in contrast to the spreading horizontality of Borobudor. Sculpture is less prominent on later temples, Kidal (*c.*1260), Singosari (*c.*1300) and Penataran (1347–75), all in eastern Java, with prominent horizontal mouldings richly carved. At Trowulan in central Java the tall temple form, divided vertically into halves and set apart, was adopted *c.*1350 to make an entrance way or 'split gate'. The latest temple in Java is Candi Sukuh, built *c.*1430 on a hill above Surakata, incorporating a truncated pyramid uncannily similar to Meso-American structures. Hinduism declined in Java after the introduction of Islam in the late C15 but survived together with local spirit cults on Bali. Bali temple architecture derived initially from Java, e.g. 'split gate' entrances to precincts, but soon acquired individuality, notably with the 'Merus', PAGODA-like towers with up to eleven roofs (Pura Taman Ayun at Mengwi, begun 1634). Mainly of wood, the temples have been frequently restored and embellished by worshippers.

On Java, Islamic architecture was mainly of wood, the earliest surviving mosques being at Demak (founded in 1478) and Kudus (begun 1549), the latter on the site of a Hindu temple of which the brick tower was converted into a minaret. Dutch-style buildings, from the period of colonial rule (1667–1949), were numerous but undistinguished. Indigenous Javanese styles survived in the kratons or palaces of the Sultans, notably at Yogyakarta and Surakarta (both mainly c18–19). The basic element was the *pendopo*, an open post-and-lintel pavilion with a pitched or hipped roof. The Batak villages of Sumatra are notable for their vernacular buildings, notably LONG-HOUSES and others, on piles with very high pitched roofs curving forward at either end and often richly painted. Of recent architecture, the vast Istiqial mosque in Jakarta was completed in 1987 and the Sukarno-Hatta airport (completed 1985) is a remarkably successful evocation of traditional Javanese architecture using modern materials and technology.

**Industrial architecture**. The mid-c18 Industrial Revolution and the development of power-driven machinery which permitted the employment of numerous unskilled workers led to new building types. Earlier factories had been conceived as expanded craft workshops, though some were very large, e.g. Lumbe's five-storey silk mill at Derby, England (1717); the Fabrica de Tobacos, Seville, Spain (1728–70), covering more than 6 hectares (15 acres). A few resembled upper-class residences, e.g. the wool mill at Linz, Austria (1722–6); the *château*-like porcelain factory at Sèvres, France (1753) and the Royal Salt Works at Arc-et-Senans, France, by LEDOUX (1775–9). But most were, like warehouses, in local vernacular styles, plain and usually tall to economize on the cost of sites near rivers which powered water-wheels and were the main transport routes for heavy materials. Power-driven machinery did not at first affect architecture, e.g. the six-storey brick cotton mill at Cromford, Derby, built in 1773 for Richard Arkwright, inventor of spinning and weaving machinery. However, the Marshall, Benyon & Bage flour mill at Ditherington, near Shrewsbury (1796–7), with iron beams and colonnettes, was the first iron-frame structure anywhere

although it has load-bearing outer walls. The large factories in England impressed foreign visitors, notably SCHINKEL in 1826, though their living and working conditions aroused concern which led to the invention of COMPANY TOWNS.

In the USA, where many mills were situated in open country, adequate housing was often provided. Machines of British origin were used from the late 1780s, installed initially in relatively small timber-framed factories, e.g. Merrimack Manufacturing Co., Lowell, Massachusetts (1822–48). In continental Europe large factories were built only after the Napoleonic wars: the Ledoux-like Grand Hornu iron foundry, Belgium (1822) and the iron and glass addition to the foundry at Sayn, near Coblenz, Germany (1824–30), were among the first. The Menier chocolate factory of 1871–80 at Noisel-sur-Marne, France, by Charles Saulnier (1828–1900), is a notable early iron-framed building without load-bearing walls, and the Charles Six spinning mill at Turcoing, France, by HENNEBIQUE in 1895, an early example of reinforced concrete construction. It was, however, in the USA that reinforced concrete was first fully exploited, notably in GRAIN ELEVATORS, after the discovery that it resists fire better than naked metals. Concrete framing also enabled architects to design factories with day-lit interiors, e.g. by RANSOME, A. KAHN and others.

Though most c19 industrial architecture was strictly utilitarian, historical styles were occasionally introduced in Europe, e.g. Ancient Egyptian at John Marshall's Temple Mills, Leeds, England, in 1842 by Joseph II BONOMI; Late Gothic for the Benedictine liqueur factory at Fécamp, France, 1893–1900; Mameluke Egyptian for the Yenidze cigarette factory at Dresden, Germany, in 1907–9. Contemporaneously with the latter BEHRENS designed a starkly functional building for turbines at the AEG factory, Berlin, and this was immediately recognized as a milestone in the development of modern architecture, not simply a feat of engineering. It was quickly followed in 1911 by the Fagus factory at Alfeld-an-der-Leine, Germany, by GROPIUS, a brick structure stripped of ornament and with wraparound windows. A year later followed the chemical works at Luban, near Poznań, Poland, by POELZIG.

After the First World War eyecatching façades were demanded by some factory owners – in the London area there was the garishly Ancient Egyptian of the Carreras cigarette factory of 1928, the lively ART DECO of the Hoover factory of 1935 and several others – and sometimes a distinguished architect might be commissioned, e.g. Giles Gilbert SCOTT for the Battersea Power Station, London, of 1929–55, with its chimneys fluted like classical columns. But there were a few notable exceptions: the Van Nelle tobacco factory, Rotterdam, Holland (1926–30), by BRINKMAN and VAN DER VLUGT and the outstanding Sunila factory near Kotka, Finland (1936–9), by AALTO.

Since the Second World War many leading architects have been involved in industrial architecture, from NERVI to FOSTER. Perhaps the most notable development in an increasingly environmentally aware society has been the INDUSTRIAL PARK.

**Industrial park**. Planned industrial districts began in the late C19, e.g. Trafford Park Estate near Manchester (1896). In the 1950s a refined version of such districts was developed in the USA for high-tech manufacturing and science-based industry, usually on the edge of an urban area and featuring a common system of utilities, a co-ordinated plan for expansion and the landscaping of open spaces, converting the suburban workplace into something resembling a university CAMPUS. Stanford Industrial Park at Palo Alto, California, is on land owned by the university, where the original campus had been designed by OLMSTED. For the Industrial Park the electronics firm of Hewlett-Packard commissioned CHURCH in 1951 and HARGREAVES in 1989–90 for landscaping.

**Industrialized building**. The massproduction of building parts may be traced from the late C18 onwards in England with Abraham Darby's Iron Bridge at Coalbrookdale, Shropshire (1775–9), and Benyon, Bage & Marshall's ironframed flax mill at Shrewsbury (1796). It was greatly developed in the C19 in both England and the USA, e.g. Boulton & Watt's seven-storey cotton mill at Salford, Lancashire (1801), BOGARDUS's cast-iron façades in New York, PAXTON's wholly prefabricated cast-iron and glass Crystal Palace, London (1851). Even BARRY's Houses of Parliament, London (1839–52), had its bronze window frames massproduced. BALLOON FRAMING was another early example. Later the CURTAIN WALL and other forms of prefabricated cladding came to typify industrialized building. However, it was not until the C20 that the idea of industrialized building systems based on massproduced factory-made prefabricated units for the construction of repetitive, identical buildings was mooted. The pioneer was GROPIUS with his Golzengüt designs of 1910, followed by LE CORBUSIER with his DOM-INO house of 1914 (see Fig. 67) and later his mass-produced housing at Pessac (1925). Prefabricated SPACE FRAME construction was developed by FULLER, PROUVÉ and others, while PRECAST CONCRETE systems were pioneered by PERRET and NERVI. Fuller's Dymaxion House project

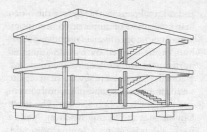

Fig. 67  Le Corbusier's Dom-ino

(1927), derived from aircraft and vehicle construction, was notable, as were, in Germany, the contemporary experiments by Konrad WACHSMANN which culminated, after he emigrated to the USA, in the 'Mobilar Structure' widespan system (1946) and, with Gropius, the General Panel System for prefabricated housing. Meanwhile, prefabricated parts, e.g. staircases, as well as complete dwellings could be bought through the catalogues of Sears Roebuck and other mail-order houses in the USA. The EAMES house (1949) was another landmark. Of later systems those developed for school building in England by Charles Herbert Aslin (1893–1959) and by the CLASP (Consortium of Local Authorities Special Programme) from 1955 onwards and, in the USA, the steel-framed SCBSD system developed in California in 1965 by Ezra Ehrenkrantz (b.1933) must be mentioned. SADIE's 'Habitat' and the HOPKINS 'Patera Building System' raised industrialized building to a new level architecturally.

B. Russell, *Building Systems, Industrialization and Architecture*, London 1981; G. Herbert, *The Dream of the Factory-Made House*, Cambridge, Mass., 1984; Klotz 1986; M. Pawley, *Theory and Design in the Second Machine Age*, London 1990.

**Inflatable architecture**, *see* PNEUMATIC ARCHITECTURE.

**Inglenook**. A draught-free recess for a bench or seat built beside a fireplace and sometimes covered by the CHIMNEY-BREAST. Traditional in English COTTAGE design, it was revived in the late C19 and early C20 with other features of vernacular architecture both in the UK and USA, usually for decorative rather than functional purposes, e.g. by GREENE & GREENE in the Gamble House.

**Ingo** or **ingoing**. The return face of a wall to provide a recess, usually for a door or window.

**Insula**, *see* ROMAN ARCHITECTURE.

**Intarsia**, *see* TARSIA.

**Integrated Environmental Design (IED)**, *see* ENVIRONMENTAL DESIGN.

**Intelligent building**. A building in which computer predictions are used in the building management system. Security, energy, environmental design systems, and structural maintenance and repair are monitored by computers. Fire detectors with a built-in memory (holding computer data about room conditions, etc.) give 'fault' and 'pre-warning' signals as well as fire alarms. The Lloyd's Building, London, by ROGERS and the Canary Wharf Tower, London, by PELLI are notable recent examples.

J. Hakser *et al.*, *I.B.: Designing and Managing the IT Infrastructure*, London (RIBA) 1992.

**Intercolumniation**. The distance between the centres of the bases of adjacent columns measured in multiples of the column diameters. Vitruvius established five main ratios, 1½D Pycnostyle, 2D Systyle, 2½D Eustyle, 3D Diastyle, 4D Araeostyle.

**International Modern** or **International Style**. Terms coined in the USA in 1932 (*see* Philip JOHNSON) for MODERNISM in architecture as created before the First World War by GROPIUS and others in central Europe and accepted elsewhere from the late 1920s onwards. The 1925–6 Bauhaus Building, Dessau, by Gropius and the 1929–33 Salvation Army Hostel, Paris, by LE CORBUSIER epitomized the style. The Californian houses of NEUTRA and SCHINDLER were early examples in the USA. As conceived in 1932, International Modern tended to divorce architecture from its social purpose and ideals which had been essential components of European Modernism. The style culminated in the USA in the immediate post-Second World War years with MIES VAN DER ROHE and others, declining in the 1960s with CORPORATE MODERNISM.

H. R. Hitchcock and P. Johnson, *The International Style*, New York (1932) 1966.

**Intrados**. The inner curve or underside of an arch; also called a *soffit. See* Fig. 6.

**Inwood**, Henry William (1794–1843). English architect, son of an architect (William Inwood, *c.*1771–1843), with whom he designed his only building of note, St Pancras Church, London (1819–22), one of the great monuments of the GREEK REVIVAL in England. Every detail is faithfully copied from the Erechtheum, Tower of the Winds, Choragic Monument, and other well-known Athenian buildings. Sometimes his archaeological material is rather recondite, but he always used it with sensibility.

Crook 1972; Summerson 1991; Colvin 1995.

**Ionic order**, *see* ORDER.

**Iranian architecture**, *see* PERSIAN ARCHITECTURE.

**Irimoya gable**. In Japanese architecture a traditional type of gable placed vertically above the end walls and marked by roofs of varying pitch.

**Irish architecture**. The most rewarding

and original phase is that before the Normans, the phase of monastic communities where coenobites lived in round or square huts, stone-vaulted by pseudo-vaults of horizontally laid stones corbelled forward gradually. There were several oratories in such communities, tapering round towers and the glorious High Crosses. The most famous sites are Skellig Michael, Nendrum, Glendalough, Clonmacnois and Monasterboyce. The buildings are mostly C10–11.

The Hiberno-Romanesque style has its most dramatic monument in Cormac's Chapel at Cashel (dated 1134); it has a tunnel-vaulted nave and a rib-vaulted chancel. There are plenty of monuments in the Norman style with only minor national characteristics. The CISTERCIANS came in the 1140s, and the east end of Christ Church Cathedral, Dublin, shows their influence. The fully Gothic style in a wholly Early English version appears in the nave of Christ Church (connected with Wells and St David's) and the largely rebuilt St Patrick's Cathedral, also in Dublin. The most conspicuous Irish contribution to Gothic architecture is her friaries, mostly rurally sited; they have the tower between nave and chancel, which is also typical of English friaries.

Medieval architecture lasted into the C17. The English promoted such new towns as Londonderry, with its Gothic cathedral of 1628–33, and such houses as Carrick-on-Suir and Strafford's Jigginstown, both of the 1630s. Gothic gradually gave place to hipped roofs or parapets, and such buildings as Beaulieu and the Kilmainham Hospital of 1679 are entirely English in style. PALLADIANISM also bore an ample harvest in Ireland, the chief architects being Sir Edward Lovett PEARCE, Richard CASTLE, James GANDON, Thomas Cooley (1740–84) and Francis Johnston (1761–1829). Examples are Castletown; Parliament House,

Dublin, by Pearce; Powerscourt by Castle; the Customs House and the Four Courts, Dublin, by Gandon; the Royal Exchange, now the City Hall, Dublin (1767–79), by Thomas Cooley; the house of the Provost of Trinity College, Dublin; Caledon, by NASH; Townley Hall, and many others. Ireland is indeed exceedingly rich in Georgian houses, though for lack of a function they are rapidly decreasing. In Dublin very much is still preserved, and the city may well claim to be the finest major Georgian city in the British Isles. If any Victorian buildings are to be singled out, they would again have to be essentially English ones: Cork Cathedral by BURGES; Queen's University, Belfast, by Lanyon; and the Trinity College Museum by Deane & WOODWARD – all Gothic in style. Among contemporary architects the best known are Michael Scott (1905–89), who built the new Abbey Theatre, Dublin (1959), and Bank of Ireland, Dublin (1973), and Kevin ROCHE, who has worked in the USA since 1948. One of the best recent buildings in Ireland is the new Library of Trinity College, Dublin, by Ahrends, Burton & Koralek (1963–7).

**Iron**. The most abundant and useful of metal elements, usually with an admixture of carbon. It is of three main kinds: *wrought iron* which is malleable and fusible at a high temperature when it can be hammered or rolled into any required shape; *cast iron* which is hard, brittle and fusible at a lower temperature; *steel* which is artificially produced with rather less carbon than most iron-alloys, and can be hardened and tempered. For the use of iron in architecture *see* METAL STRUCTURES.

**Irwin**, Robert (b.1928). American painter (initially Abstract Expressionist) and Minimalist installation artist who has

also designed notable urban plazas, e.g. Nine Spaces, Nine Trees, Public Safety Building, Seattle (1983) – a square divided by blue wire mesh fencing into nine areas each surrounding a cherry tree in a cement planter; Wave Hill Green, Bronx, New York (1986–7); and Sentinel Plaza, Pasadena, California (1990). He published *Being and Circumstance. Notes Towards a Conditional Art* (1985).

L. Wechsler, *Seeing is Forgetting the Name of the Thing One Sees. A Life of Contemporary Artist R.I.*, Berkeley 1982; M. Treib 1993.

**Isabellino style**. In Spanish architecture the style associated with Ferdinand and Isabella (1474–1516), equivalent to the MANUELINE STYLE in Portuguese architecture.

**Ishii**, Katsuhiro (b.1944), *see* JAPANESE ARCHITECTURE.

**Isidorus of Miletos** assisted ANTHEMIOS OF TRALLES in the building of Hagia Sophia, Constantinople (AD 532–7), and was, like him, a geometrician who turned his attention to architecture. He is not to be confused with a younger Isidore, who rebuilt the dome of Hagia Sophia in 558.

Krautheimer 1986.

**Islamic architecture**. A wide range of religious and secular buildings constructed for Muslims and reflecting their beliefs. The house of the Prophet Muhammed at Medina, Saudi Arabia, where he settled after leaving his native city of Mecca in AD 622 (the first year of the Muslim calendar), was a very simple range of rooms backing on to a large rectangular enclosure, along one side of which a double row of palm trunks carried a roof of palm leaves covered with mud to provide shade for himself and companions at prayer – the first MOSQUE. The Bedouin Arabs who were his original followers and responsible for the first Islamic conquests in Syria, Palestine and Persia were a nomadic people who lived in tents. In the cities they conquered they began by converting old buildings, and Christian churches became mosques; in Damascus a pagan temple transformed into a Christian church was incorporated in the Great Mosque (706–15). The earliest and one of the most beautiful of Islamic buildings is the Dome of the Rock, Jerusalem, built as a sanctuary (not as a mosque) on a circular plan (685–705, but much altered later, especially in 1561, when the exterior was cased in Persian tiles and the interior lined with marble). The first MINARETS were converted church towers in Syria, and that built at Kairouan, Tunisia (724–7), is modelled on such a tower. True to their nomadic origins the Umayyad rulers preferred country residences to town palaces. Several survive as ruins – Kas al-Khayr al Sharki (*c*.728–9), Khirbat al-Mafjar (*c*.739–44) and Mshatta near Amman, Jordan (*c*.744–50). In plan these groups of buildings were derived from Roman frontier stations. But both religious and secular buildings of the period incorporate elements which were to become distinguishing features of Islamic architecture: the horse-shoe arch, tunnel vaults of stone and brick, rich surface decoration in carved stone, mosaic and painting. During the Umayyad period the mosque took on its permanent architectural form, dictated by liturgical needs – minarets from which the faithful could be called to prayer; a wide courtyard with a central fountain for ablutions, with surrounding colonnades to give protection from the sun; a large praying chamber, marked externally by a dome (as a sign of importance) and internally by the mihrab or niche indicating the direction of Mecca, towards which the faithful must turn in prayer. The last survivor of the Umayyad

dynasty became the founder of the Emirates at Cordoba in Spain, where the early style of Islamic architecture was brought to perfection in the Great Mosque (786–990).

Under the Abbasids, who supplanted the Umayyads in 750, Persian influence began to dominate the Islamic world (*see* PERSIAN ARCHITECTURE). The main achievements in architecture were the foundation of the new capital at Baghdad, built on a circular plan (762–7, now largely destroyed), and slightly later, the smaller city of Raqqa, Syria, of which little survives except richly decorated gateways. It was at this period that Islamic architecture began to depart radically from HELLENISTIC and BYZANTINE conventions. An elaborate court etiquette, derived from Persia and contrary to Bedouin ideas of informality, was introduced, and palaces were designed for the new caliphs on more formal and grandiose lines, e.g. the palaces at Ukhaidir (*c*.764–78) and Samarra (*c*.849–59) in Iraq. These large buildings set in regularly planned gardens, with much use of water, and hunting parks, were run up very quickly: stone was abandoned in favour of brick; there was much use of decorative stucco. The main C9 achievements were the Great Mosque of Kairouan, Tunisia (836); the mosque of Bu Fatata, Susa, Tunisia (850–51); the Great Mosque of Samarra, Iraq, with its strange ZIGGURAT-like minaret (*c*.850); and the very well preserved mosque of Ibn Tulun, Cairo (876–7). Building materials were usually rough but dressed with intricate geometrical or floral surface decorations in painted stucco, mosaic, glazed tiles or shallow relief carving. Local traditions influenced the decorative style in various regions (*see* CHINESE ARCHITECTURE; INDIAN AND PAKISTANI ARCHITECTURE; INDONESIAN ARCHITECTURE; PERSIAN ARCHITECTURE; SELJUK

ARCHITECTURE; TURKISH ARCHITECTURE; UZBEK ARCHITECTURE). With the spread of Islam mosques were built also in Africa south of the Sahara, e.g. Sanskore Mosque, Timbuktu, Mali (early C14) and in towns on the east coast. Mosques and the closely associated MAUSOLEUMS and MADRASAS are the most distinctive as well as the most numerous examples of Islamic architecture; but the same systems of construction (for arches, vaults and domes) and styles of surface decoration, carved, painted or in glazed tiles – geometrical, calligraphic or foliate and floral – seldom including animals and still more rarely human figures, were adopted for palaces, smaller domestic buildings, CARAVANSERAIS, HAMMAMS and covered markets.

In the original nucleus of the Islamic world the most notable later mosques are those at Tabriz, Persia (1204), Cairo (Mosque of Sultan Barquq, 1384) and Isfahan, Persia (1585). Most of the earlier religious buildings, including the Masjid-el-Aksa and the Dome of the Rock in Jerusalem, were also altered and more richly decorated in these centuries. In southern Spain a local style of great opulence was developed: its principal monuments are the Giralda tower, Seville (1159), and the Alhambra, Granada (1309–54). And mosques are still being built not only in traditionally Islamic countries but wherever a community of Muslims has been established, notably in France, Italy, England and the USA.

**Isometric projection**. A geometrical drawing to show a building in three dimensions. The plan is set up with lines at an equal angle (usually 30°) to the horizontal, while verticals remain vertical and to scale. It gives a more realistic effect than an AXONOMETRIC PROJECTION, but diagonals and curves are distorted. See Fig. 68.

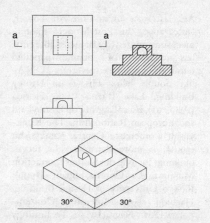

Fig. 68 Isometric projection plan; section aa; elevation

**Isozaki**, Arata (b.1931). Leading member, with KURAKAWA, MAKI and SHINOHARA, of the first post-Second World War generation of Japanese architects. He worked under TANGE until 1963 when he was briefly involved with the METABOLISTS and designed his remarkable Space City Project (1962). Four years later he made his name with the Old Oita Prefecture Library, Oita (1966), and the Fukuoka Mutual Bank, Oita (1967). These led to public commissions in which he developed a unique East–West synthesis, notably at the Gumma Prefectural Museum of Modern Art, Takasaki (1974), and the Shukosha Building, Fukuoka (1975). Simultaneously he designed a series of barrel-vaulted structures, e.g. Fujimi Country Clubhouse, Oita (1972–4), and the Central Library, Kitakyushu (1972–5). He then made a striking departure with his Tsukuba Centre Building, Tsukuba Science City (1978–83), in which historical quotations are juxtaposed in a jarring manner which Isozaki called 'schizoid'. This remarkable building was followed by his Museum of Contemporary Art, Los

Angeles (1984–6), and the Art Tower, Mito (1990), his Post-Modern masterpiece surmounted by a Brancusi-like endless column of titanium-panelled tetrahedrons whose edges create a DNA-like double helix. His Team Disney Building, Lake Buena Vista, Florida (1989–91), is a collage of Pop Disneyland and European Rationalism. The Kitakyushu Conference Centre, Kitakyushu (1991), is more dynamic. His recent buildings include the Domus Interaction Museum, La Coruña, Spain (1992); Rokyo University of Design Building, Hachioji (1993); Museum of Contemporary Art, Nagi (1994); Technology Centre, Crakow, Poland (1994), and the New Symphony Hall, Kyoto (1995). In 1996 he published *Island Nation Aesthetic* (London).

Y. Futagwa, *A.I.*, Tokyo 1991–2; D. Stewart and H. Yatsuka, *A.I. 1960–1990*, London 1991.

**Israeli architecture and landscape architecture**. Although the State of Israel was not established until 1948, the term is used for buildings constructed for Jewish settlers in the area from the early C20 onwards, at first under Ottoman Turkish rule and from 1917 under the British Mandate in Palestine. Two new cities were developed: Tel Aviv, an extension of Jaffa, and Haifa around an old Turkish fort. The Technikum university building and Reali school, Haifa (1909–13), by Alexander Baerwald (1877–1930), a German immigrant, are essays in Historicism inspired by local Islamic architecture. Under the British Mandate attempts were made by ASHBEE to preserve the visual integrity of Jerusalem by conservation and restoration and by forbidding the use of any material other than local stone in new buildings. Of the latter the Rockefeller Museum, Jerusalem (1927–8), by Austen Harrison (1891–

1976) was the most notable. Modernism was, however, demanded by immigrants intent on creating a new Zionist state and in 1920 the German architect Richard Kauffmann (1887–1958), a pupil of T. FISCHER, was invited to design new settlements or KIBBUTZIM in the open country. His remarkable centrally planned elliptical Nahala settlement (1921) was followed by several others, as well as garden suburbs in Haifa and Jerusalem. After 1930 Tel Aviv became a unique realization on a large scale of BAUHAUS ideals, a city of flat-roofed concrete blocks now called the 'White City' and listed by the World Monuments Fund. (The comprehensive garden-city plan for it by GEDDES in 1925 was only partly realized.) However, the outstanding Modernist building in Tel Aviv was indebted mainly to LE CORBUSIER, from its *pilotis* to its strip fenestration and roof-garden, the Engle House of 1933 by Ze'ev Rechter (1899–1960). Elsewhere, MENDELSOHN, who had an office in Jerusalem 1934–9, was responsible for the most distinguished buildings of the period: Chaim Weizmann's house at Rechovot (1934), the Schoken house and library, Jerusalem (1934–6), the hospital at Haifa (1937–8) and the Hadassah University Medical Centre, Mount Scopus (1937–9). Bauhaus Modernism – banned in Germany itself after 1933 – predominated under the leadership of Arieh Sharon (1902–84), who arrived from Poland in 1920, returned to Europe to study at the Bauhaus 1926–9, and collaborated with Hannes MEYER until 1931 when he set up practice in Tel Aviv, being appointed Chief Architect of the National Planning Agency of Israel in 1948. His buildings include numerous kibbutzim, co-operative housing developments and low-cost apartment blocks for workers in the 1930s. Also notable in these years was Leopold Krakauer (1890–

1954), trained under WAGNER in Vienna, who emigrated in 1925 first to Haifa and then to Jerusalem. His restaurant for the Tel-Yoseph kibbutz (1933), and Hotel Teltsch (1934–5) and Bonem residence (1935), both in Haifa, were remarkable, the Tel-Yoseph restaurant even seeming to forestall Deconstructivism in its exploitation of rotating volumes. Later buildings of note were Arieh Sharon's Hillside Housing, Upper Nazareth (1955–7), and, in collaboration with his son Eldard, a terraced convalescent home at Tiberias (1965–71) and the large new Jerusalem suburb of Gilo (1973–6). Ram Karmi (b.1931), the son of Dov Karmi (1905–62) who built the remarkable Armenian Monastery School, Jaffa (1930–39), collaborated with Yacov Rechter (b.1924, the son of Ze'ev) on the Mann Auditorium, Tel Aviv (1957), the most impressive building of its time in Israel. The Hilton Hotels in Tel Aviv and Jerusalem (1965, 1975) by Yacov Rechter have the boldness of form and intricacy of texture associated with BRUTALISM. The Supreme Court Building, Jerusalem (1986–93), by Ram Karmi and Ada Karmi Melamede (b.1936), on the other hand, is a widely spread composition of smooth cubic and cylindrical forms. A breakaway from right-angled geometry of Modernism was manifested in the Synagogue of the Military Academy campus in the Negev desert (1969), a tightly knit mass of cube-octahedrons by Svi Hecker (b.1931), who derived inspiration from crystals and organic forms and went on to design the extraordinary spiral tower of individual apartments, bright in its colours and glittering with mirrors, at Ramat Gan outside Tel Aviv (1981–90), and the remarkable Heinz Galinski School, Berlin (1992–5). The Jerusalem Centre for Near Eastern Studies (1986) by David Reznik (b.1923), with its domes, arches and courtyards, marked a different

kind of break with Modernism. Also notable is Moshe SAFDIE's work in Israel, especially for its emotive use of regional forms, e.g. Yeshivat Porat Yosef Rabbinical College (1971–9); the Hebrew Union College Campus (1972–8); the Yad Vashem Children's Holocaust Memorial (1976–87); and the Mamilla Centre (1975, 1990–96), all in Jerusalem. Safdie also designed the new town of Modi-in, between Tel Aviv and Jerusalem, begun in 1989 with Aronson as landscape architect.

Apart from garden suburbs, the most notable examples of landscape architecture are the Ida Crown Museum gardens, Jerusalem (1966), and the Walter and Else Haas Promenade, Jerusalem (1984–6), by HALPRIN and Shlomo Aronson (b.1936); the Negev Monument near Beer Sheba (1963–9) and the White Square, Kikar Levano, near Tel Aviv (1977–88), by KARAVAN; and the Kreitman Square, Ben Gurion University, Beer Sheba, the Gabriel Shereover Promenade, Jerusalem (1988), and Sapir Park in the Negev desert (1991), where open-cast phosphate mines were transformed into a huge environmental sculpture, all by Shlomo Aronson.

**Italian architecture and landscape architecture.** (For pre-Christian architecture in Italy see ETRUSCAN ARCHITECTURE; ROMAN ARCHITECTURE.) EARLY CHRISTIAN churches in Italy are mostly of the BASILICA type: nave and aisles separated by columns carrying arches or straight entablatures, and an apse, sometimes flanked by two subsidiary chambers. The best preserved of the type in Rome is S. Sabina (c.422–32). Transepts are rare but occur in the more monumental churches: Constantine's S. Giovanni in Laterano (c.313–20, later remodelled), Old St Peter's (c.320–30 with double aisles, not preserved), S. Paolo fuori le Mura (late C5 also with double aisles, rebuilt after a fire in 1823) and S. Maria Maggiore (c.432–40). Some centrally planned buildings also exist, but they are not numerous. The most notable in Rome is S. Stefano Rotondo (468–83), on a circular plan. The baptistery of S. Giovanni in Laterano (c.315 and c.432–40) is octagonal, a central plan being functionally advantageous for baptisteries. S. Costanza (c.350), one of the most beautiful Early Christian buildings, is circular, with an ambulatory. Here the explanation is that it was a mausoleum and for mausolea the Ancient Roman tradition was a circular plan.

Next to Rome, Ravenna was the most important centre (see BYZANTINE ARCHITECTURE). It became the capital of the Roman West in 404, of Odoacer in 476 and of Theodoric in 493, and of the Byzantine bridgehead in Italy in 540. Here also the majority of the churches are basilican: e.g. S. Apollinare Nuovo of c.510–20 and S. Apollinare in Classe of c.550. More original and varied are the centrally planned buildings: S. Vitale, completed in 547 and entirely Byzantine with its complex and ingenious octagonal plan, the Mausoleum of Galla Placidia of c.450 which is a Greek cross, and the two octagonal baptisteries. The Mausoleum of Theodoric, as befitted this Gothic king, is much more massive. Moreover, it is of stone, whereas the other buildings are of brick. Characteristic features of these latter are external blank arcading or LESENES connected by a small frieze of blank arches, a motif which became typical of the north Italian Romanesque style. The earliest Italian CAMPANILI are also at Ravenna. They are circular and were probably a C9 addition. The earliest campanile of which we know is the square one once attached to St Peter's in Rome, and this went back to the mid C8.

At least two Early Christian buildings not in Rome or in Ravenna must be mentioned. One is S. Salvatore at Spoleto, of the late C4–6, several times restored, with a complete façade, its details and those of the interior still strikingly Late Roman, but with an oval dome over the chancel which is a motif of Syria or Asia Minor. The other is S. Lorenzo in Milan (c.352–75, later partly remodelled), already exhibiting spatial subtleties as thrilling as those of S. Vitale. Milan possesses more early churches, at least in substantial parts, than had been known until recently, e.g. S. Simpliciano (late C4).

The transition from Early Christian to Early Medieval is imperceptible in Italy. S. Agnese in Rome of 625–38 is still entirely Early Christian, but S. Maria in Domnica and S. Maria in Cosmedin of the early C9 are in plan and elevation not essentially different. Nor is S. Prassede, although the latter has a transept, like that at Fulda probably a self-conscious reversion to Constantinian greatness. S. Maria in Cosmedin has a hall crypt, one of the earliest ever. Both Cosmedin and Domnica end in three parallel apses, and this is so in the most important early C9 churches in north Italy too: S. Pietro, Agliate (early C11), and S. Vincenzo in Prato, Milan (C11). But on the whole these and other north Italian churches continue the Early Christian type as well (S. Salvatore, Brescia, Pomposa abbey). Innovations are the square piers of e.g. S. Pietro in Silvis, Bagnacavallo, of C8–9 and the small tunnel vaults of S. Maria in Valle at Cividale of c.762–76 (the latter has also the finest early medieval sculpture in Italy). Cividale is extraordinary in plan as well, as was the interesting S. Maria delle Cinque Torre, Cassino (778–87, destroyed), which introduced the Byzantine plan of the inscribed cross and had moreover groin and tunnel vaults and three parallel apses.

It is not easy to decide where to start

using the term Romanesque in Italy. The basilican plan, the columns of the arcades, the apse continuing the nave without a transept remain the Italian norm in the C11 and into the C12. The essential innovations in plan which France and Germany introduced in the late C10 and early C11 did not at once touch Italy and remained the exception even later. Ambulatories with radiating chapels for instance are rare (S. Antimo, near Siena, begun c.1118; and Aversa Cathedral, near Naples, begun before c.1150), although vestigial ambulatories had occurred remarkably early (S. Stefano, Verona, rebuilt c.990; and Ivrea Cathedral, before 1002). The new elements which came in the C11 seem to have been derived from the Empire. Montecassino of 1066 onwards had a transept, though one not projecting. It also still had the typically Italian three parallel apses. At Salerno Cathedral, consecrated in 1084, the transept stretches out beyond the aisle lines, and S. Nicola at Bari, the most important southern building (begun immediately after 1087), has transepts, alternating supports in the nave, a gallery, two west towers placed Norman fashion outside the aisle lines and the stumps of two east towers as well. Such east towers also occur, and here clearly under German influence, at S. Abbondio at Como, consecrated in 1095. S. Fedele at Como is later but still on a trefoil plan inspired by Cologne. S. Abbondio has no transept, but Aquileia of c.1020 onwards already has, although for the rest it follows Early Christian tradition.

The C12 and the early C13 in Italy are hard to summarize. There is little of regional variation, at least in plans and elevations, though decorative motifs differ considerably from area to area. The great C12 cathedrals of the north Italian plain are truly Romanesque, though they also differ in many respects. But they have mostly alternating supports and galleries inside and the so-called dwarf galleries, small arcaded wall-passages, outside. Their towers are campanili, not integrated with the buildings themselves. Modena, begun in 1099, is the first, with a transept not projecting, and with the traditional three parallel apses. This is the same at S. Ambrogio in Milan with its solemn façade and its beautiful atrium. But the most important aspect of S. Ambrogio is the rib vaults with heavy ribs of plain rectangular section. This type occurs also in the south of France, and the several examples in Lombardy are probably all of the C12, i.e. later than the much more sophisticated ribs of Durham. The other principal north Italian cathedrals are Parma of after 1117, with a more German plan (far projecting transepts with apses and only one east apse), Piacenza of c.1120, Cremona and Ferrara. A spectacular appendix to these north Italian cathedrals is their large, detached, octagonal baptisteries. The most famous of the Italian baptisteries, however, is in central Italy, that of Pisa begun in 1153. Pisa Cathedral, exceptionally large, is exceptional in other ways as well. It was started as early as 1063 by BUSCHETO and has long-aisled transepts with end-apses, a double-aisled nave and no vaults. BON-ANNO's campanile, i.e. the leaning tower, arcaded in many tiers all round, was started in 1173. The Baptistery (1153–1265) bears an inscription to its architect, DIOTISALVI. The same predilection for outer arcading in tiers is to be found at Lucca. Florence is different. Here already in the late C11 a movement arose which deserves the name Proto-Renaissance. It favoured ancient Roman motifs and has a graceful elegance unique in Romanesque Europe. The principal examples are the Baptistery, S. Miniato and SS. Apostoli, all in Florence, and the Badia at Fiesole, none of them exactly datable. A comparable interest in Ancient Rome is found in and around Rome in the early C13 (façade, Cività Castellana Cathedral, 1210; and façade, S. Lorenzo fuori le Mura, Rome, 1220 now altered). An exception in central Italy is the church of S. Claudio al Chienti, Macerata, which is on the Byzantine inscribed-cross plan.

The relations of the Italian Romanesque to Byzantium are manifold and interesting. The major monument, totally Byzantine, is of course St Mark's in Venice (1063 onwards), with a central plan and five domes. Domes were also placed over naves in a few major south Italian churches (Canosa Cathedral, 1071 onwards; Molfetta Cathedral, c.1160 onwards). The inscribed-cross plan appears here and there in different parts of southern Italy, at Stilo, at Otranto (S. Pietro), at Trani (S. Andrea). The Byzantine elements in Sicilian architecture are fascinatingly overlaid with Saracen and Norman elements. The island had been under Byzantium from the C6, under Islam from 827, under the Normans from 1061. But during the years of the greatest Sicilian architecture, the country was one of the centres of the Hohenstaufen emperors. The Norman motifs of Cefalù and Monreale Cathedrals (1131 onwards and 1166 onwards) are patent to English visitors. On the other hand the Martorana at Palermo (1143 onwards) is on the Byzantine inscribed-cross plan, and S. Cataldo in Palermo looks wholly Arabic. This applies even more to the royal palaces and pavilions such as the Ziza and the Cuba at Palermo.

Romanesque Italy has much of secular architecture to offer. Here only a few buildings can be referred to – some byzantinizing palaces of Venice (especially the Fondaco dei Turchi) and the equally byzantinizing C11 Palazzo della Ragione at Pomposa, the slender towers of the nobility, especially famous those of San Gimignano and the two in the centre of Bologna, and the Town Halls of Como (1216), Orvieto and Massa Marittima. All these are of the C13.

But at that time the Gothic style had started on its Italian course. It had come, as in all countries, from France and, as in most countries, by means of the CISTERCIANS (Fossanova, 1187–1208, Casamari, 1203 onwards with rib vaults, both in Lazio, S. Galgano in Tuscany, 1227 onwards). The collegiate church of S. Andrea at Vercelli of c.1220 onwards is transitional between Italian Romanesque and French Gothic. The most original of the early Gothic buildings in Italy is S. Francesco at Assisi, begun in 1228 and, oddly enough, inspired by the French West and most probably by Angers Cathedral. Another early French (Burgundian) inspiration explains the splendid castles of Frederick II in the south of Italy and in Sicily (Augusta; Maniace, Syracuse; Ursino, Catania) and especially Castel del Monte of c.1240 onwards, where French Gothic structure is fascinatingly mixed with Ancient Roman detail used in a spirit of Renaissance. The plans of these castles are regular, mostly with angle towers, a plan introduced at the same time in France and thus continued in both countries (e.g. Ferrara, 1389 onwards).

Altogether the Italy of the C13 and C14 is rich in remarkable secular buildings, the public halls of Genoa, Orvieto and Piacenza, all C13 and all continuing the Romanesque type, the slightly later and less peacefully open Town Halls of Perugia (1283 onwards), Siena (1288 onwards) and Florence (Palazzo Vecchio, 1298 onwards), the Loggia dei Lanzi in Florence of 1376 with its strangely un-Gothic round arches, the Doge's Palace in Venice of 1309–1424, unique in size and composition, and some C14 palaces in Florence and Siena, and early C15 palaces in Venice (Ca' d'Oro 1424–36).

North Italian Late Gothic detail is more ornate, more northern than that further south (Porta della Carta, Doge's Palace, 1438–43).

This northern, trans-alpine character applies with much greater force to Milan Cathedral, begun in 1386 and the work of a mixture of masters from Lombardy, Germany and France, all fighting each other. The scale of Milan Cathedral incited the starting on a similar scale of the Certosa of Pavia (1396 onwards, built slowly) and S. Petronio, the largest parish church of Bologna (1390 onwards, unfinished) by Antonio di Vincenzo (c.1350–1401/2). But meanwhile, i.e. in the C13 and early C14, the Gothic style had made progress everywhere in Italy. In Bologna itself the friars' church of S. Francesco in 1236 started with a French ambulatory with radiating chapels. The friars otherwise built large but without an accepted system of plan or elevation. S. Francesco at Siena of 1326 onwards has no aisles and no vault, S. Croce in Florence, the Franciscan church there, of 1294/5 (attributed to ARNOLFO DI CAMBIO) has aisles and no vault. The east ends of both are in the Cistercian tradition. The Frari (Franciscan) and SS. Giovanni e Paolo, Venice (Dominican; both C14), have aisles, high round piers and rib vaults. The airiness of these churches is fundamentally different from the spatial feeling of the French Gothic. This Italian-ness of Italian Gothic expresses itself most strongly in S. Maria Novella in Florence (Dominican; 1278 onwards) and Florence Cathedral (begun by Arnolfo in 1296). The arcades are much more generously opened than in France so that nave and aisles appear part of one space and not three parallel vessels. The measure of each bay opening of the arcades is c.19.5 m. (64 ft); at Amiens it was c.7.5 m. (25 ft). The campanile of Florence Cathedral (by GIOTTO) is the finest of all Italian Gothic campanili. The finest Gothic façades are Siena (1284 onwards, by Giovanni PISANO) and Orvieto (c.1310 onwards, by MAITANI). As against Florence, Rome had little to contribute. The only important Gothic church is S. Maria sopra Minerva of c.1280 onwards.

For the introduction of the Renaissance also Florence took precedence over Rome, however much the Renaissance masters owed to Ancient Rome. However, even that debt is less great than C19 scholars assumed. It is certain that BRUNELLESCHI in his churches looked more to the Tuscan Proto-Renaissance (see above) than to Imperial Rome. For Florence the date of the conversion to the Renaissance is c.1420; for Venice, Milan, and also Rome it is a generation later. For Rome ALBERTI, who was more in sympathy with the Ancient Roman character in architecture than anyone else, was instrumental in establishing the Renaissance, though he had probably nothing to do with the courtyard of the Palazzo Venezia (begun 1455) which was the first to take up the ponderous motif of orders of attached columns to separate arched openings such as the Romans had used for the Theatre of Marcellus and the Colosseum. But on the whole the Quattrocento prefers arcades of slender columns carrying arches, i.e. rather delicate members, and a graceful lively decoration. Examples of the former are Brunelleschi's earliest façade, that of the Foundling Hospital in Florence (1419 onwards), and such palace courtyards as that of MICHELOZZO's Palazzo Medici in Florence (1444 onwards) or the Ducal Palace at Urbino (1460s), which also has some of the most exquisite Quattrocento decoration. Palace façades, especially in Tuscany, are still forbidding, in direct continuation of the Trecento. Heavy rustication was favoured (Palazzo Medici,

Palazzo Strozzi), though Alberti in his Palazzo Rucellai, Florence, used a more elegant articulation by tiers of pilasters, and this was taken up at the Cancelleria in Rome (c.1485). Church plans are usually longitudinal: Brunelleschi's with nave and aisles and slim arcades, Alberti's S. Andrea at Mantua aisleless, but with side-chapels, a system with a great future. But both Brunelleschi and Alberti and others as well (Giuliano da SANGALLO) favoured central plans and developed them in a variety of ways (Brunelleschi, S. Maria degli Angeli, Florence, 1434 onwards; Alberti, S. Sebastiano, Mantua, 1460 onwards; Sangallo, S. Maria delle Carceri, Prato, 1486 onwards).

Central Italians (MICHELOZZO, FILA-RETE) had introduced the Renaissance to Milan in the 1450s, and at the same time it appeared in Venice (Arsenal portal, 1457). In contrast to central Italy, however, the north of Italy went in for extremely busy decoration of façades as well as interiors (Verona and Brescia Town Halls, Certosa of Pavia, Como Cathedral, 1470s to 1490s and after 1500). These façades had considerable influence on the Early Renaissance in trans-alpine countries. Even BRAMANTE, in his early years in Milan, used this rich and playful decoration, though at S. Maria presso S. Satiro it is rather Alberti (in Mantua) who inspired him. Bramante lived in Milan in the same years as LEONARDO DA VINCI, but it is impossible to say what their relationship was. Leonardo sketched architectural ideas, but did not build. Nearly all his church plans are of central types, and he reached unprecedented complexities. Bramante clearly was attracted by the same problem, even if none of the central churches of Lombardy can with certainty be ascribed to him (Lodi, Crema).

With Bramante's move from Milan to Rome in 1499 the High Renaissance was established, with more substantial and also more Roman forms and character (St Peter's, Belvedere Court Vatican, Palazzo Caprini). RAPHAEL (Villa Madama), PERUZZI (Villa Farnesina), and GIULIO ROMANO were Bramante's successors, but the latter two soon turned away from his style to Mannerism. The solecisms of Giulio's Palazzo Te (1525 onwards) and his own house (1544), both at Mantua, are both eloquent and painful. At the same time MICHELANGELO designed in the Mannerist way (Medici Chapel and Laurentian Library, Florence, 1520s; exterior of St Peter's, 1546 onwards; and Porta Pia, Rome, 1561). Mannerism produced exquisite works (Farnese Palace, Caprarola, by VIGNOLA, 1547 onwards; Villa Giulia by Vignola, 1551 onwards, Casino of Pius IV by LIGORIO, 1559 onwards, both Rome; Uffizi, Florence, by VASARI, begun 1560), as well as perverse ones (Casa Zuccari, Rome, 1590), but it never ruled unchallenged.

During the C16 increasing importance was given to landscape architecture. Small gardens conceived as outdoor rooms had been made around Tuscan villas, e.g. Michelozzo's Villa Medici, Fiesole (c.1458–61). These were followed by far more ambitious layouts, inspired partly by Pliny the Younger's descriptions of Ancient Roman gardens and also the watery and flowery Persian style Islamic gardens which survived in Sicily. The most spectacular are at the Villa d'Este, Tivoli, on a steeply sloping site with elaborate waterworks, by LIGORIO (1550); the Boboli Gardens behind the Palazzo Pitti, Florence, planned by the scupltor Niccolo Tribolo in 1549; the Villa Lante at Bagnaia, near Viterbio, with an elaborate allegorical programme, by Vignola (1566); the Villa Aldobrandini, Frascati, with a large semicircular lake and fountains by G. della PORTA (1598–1603). They all have strong axes, hedges clipped like walls and geometrically designed open spaces. Mannerist influence is apparent mainly in their artificial grottoes and the statues that populate them. At Bomarzo, the 'sacred wood' laid out by its owner P. F. ORSINI on a narrative programme with buildings and colossal sculpture is, however, a uniquely extreme expression of Mannerist complexity, virtuosity and addiction to marvels.

In the north of Italy the Renaissance spirit was alive throughout the C16, as is demonstrated by buildings such as SANSOVINO's Library of S. Marco, Venice (1537) and Palazzo Corner, Venice (before 1561), SANMICHELI's palaces and city gates of Verona (1520s to 1550s), and PALLADIO's palaces inside and villas outside Vicenza. Though in the work of Palladio, especially his churches in Venice, Mannerist traits are easily discovered, most of his secular work must be classed as Renaissance. The problem of Vignola in Rome is similar, but whereas Palladio, where he is not Mannerist, belongs to the past, Vignola, where he is not Mannerist, points forward to the Baroque.

There can be no doubt that Vignola's Gesù, Rome (begun 1568), established a canon of church plan and elevation for the Baroque; chapels instead of aisles, transepts and a dome (S. Andrea della Valle, S. Carlo al Corso, and others in Rome). The completion of St Peter's by MADERNO was also longitudinal. But the most interesting Baroque churches are those on central or elongated central plans. Vignola had used the oval as early as 1573, but it became a standard element only in the C17, varied inexhaustibly, especially by the greatest Roman Baroque architects BERNINI and BORROMINI. Bernini uses the oval transversely at S. Andrea al Quirinale, and RAINALDI uses a grouping of elements which gives the impression of a transverse oval at S.

Agnese. The façade of this church, with its two towers and its concave centre, is by Borromini, whose façade of S. Carlino is even more complex in its use of concave and convex parts. There the interior carries the interaction of curves to the highest point it achieved in Rome, but the acme of spatial complications was reached by GUARINI at Turin. Bernini's work at St Peter's was concerned with decoration on the grandest scale (Baldacchino, Cathedra Petri) and with the forecourt in front of Maderno's façade. The elliptical colonnades and their splaying-out connection with the façade are aesthetically and from the planning point of view equally satisfying.

In the field of major urban planning Rome had already taken the lead in the late C16, when the long streets radiating from the Piazza del Popolo had been laid out. In secular architecture Rome contributed less, though the open façade of the Palazzo Barberini and the giant pilasters of Bernini's Palazzo Odescalchi had much influence. For Baroque palaces Genoa is the most interesting city, e.g. those on ALESSI's Strada Nuova.

As early as about 1700 Italy began to tone down the Baroque (FONTANA, then JUVARRA in Turin: Superga 1715–31; Palazzo Madama, 1718 onwards) and in the Veneto a Palladian revival took place (SCALFAROTTI's S. Simeone, Venice, 1718 onwards; Preti's Villa Pisani, Strà, 1735 onwards).

The C19 is more interesting in Italian architecture than most tourists realize. The neo-classical, especially neo-Greek style has produced much outstanding work. French influence is occasionally patent (S. Carlo Theatre, Naples (1820–44) by Antonio Niccolini (1722–1850)). The most monumental church is S. Francesco di Paola, Naples (1817–28), by Pietro Bianchi (1787–1849). Neo-Greek are JAPELLI's Caffè Pedrocchi, Padua

(1816–31), and the Temple at Possagno (1819–30) by the sculptor Antonio Canova; more wayward are the Cemetery at Staglieno (1835) and the Carlo Felice Theatre, Genoa (begun in 1827), which are both by Carlo Francesco Barabino (1768–1835), and the grandiose Cisternone, Livorno (1829), by Pasquale POCCIANTI. A curious anachronism is the use of classical forms and ornament by ANTONELLI in his two monster towers at Novara and Turin. In the sixties other styles had taken the place of the classical, a Super-Renaissance in MENGONI's Galleria in Milan, a Lombardo-Gothic in the Milan Cemetery by Carlo Maciachini (1818–99) and others, notably Camillo BOITO, the brother of Verdi's librettist. As in other continental countries the neo-Renaissance – e.g. the Banco d'Italia (1885–92) and Palazzo Margherita, now the American Embassy (1886–90), both in Rome, by Gaetano Koch (1849–1910) – was followed by the neo-Baroque in such prominent buildings as the Palazzo di Giustizia, Rome (1888–1910), by Guglielmo Calderini (1837–1916). And the neo-Baroque was followed by Art Nouveau, e.g. Villa Igea, Palermo (1898), by Ernesto BASILE. Italian Art Nouveau, called *stile floreale* or *stile Liberty*, was inspired at first by Vienna in the work of Raimondo d'Aronco (1857–1932) but became more original in that of SOMMARUGA and was continued with undiminished exuberance by Pietro Fenoglio (1865–1927), the creator of Casa Fenoglio, Turin (1903), and by Gino Coppedé (1866–1927) whose extraordinary apartment building in via Po, Rome, is as late as 1921. Also of these years was the remarkable Lingotto Fiat Building, Turin (1914–26) by Giacomo Matté-Trucco (1869–1934).

The C20 started with SANT'ELIA's Futurist dreams of skyscrapers. The new International Style did not make itself felt until the mid C20 and did not get a chance of showing itself in buildings until after 1930, e.g. Casa del Fascio, Como (1932), by TERRAGNI. This was the masterpiece of Italian RATIONALISM, a movement led by Terragni, FIGINI, POLLINI and a few others which produced a number of remarkable buildings – Press Pavilion for Milan Triennale 1933 by Luciano Baldessari (1896–1982), Palestra per la Scherma, Rome (1934–6), by Luigi Moretti (1907–73), Florence railway station (1933-6) by MICHELUCCI and others – before it foundered in its alliance with Fascism with such pomposities as the Foro Mussolini, Rome (1927–32), Città Universitaria, Rome (1932–5), and the 1942 Universal Exhibition buildings, now EUR, Rome (1935–41), all of which are by Marcello Piacentini (1881–1960), whose Milanese contemporary MUZIO was similarly oppressive. However, the new town of Sabaudia, south of Rome, laid out and built by Piacentini's disciple Luigi Piccinato (1899–1983) and others between 1933 and 1934 should be mentioned if only as a realization of de Chirico's paintings of eerily empty piazzas and colonnades.

The immediate post-Second World War period was notable for PONTI's Pirelli skyscraper and BBPR's Torre Velasca, both in Milan, and especially for the structurally inventive and aesthetically sensitive work of NERVI. They were followed by several remarkable architects of disparate gifts, e.g. GABETTI & ISOLA, GARDELLA, MOLLINO, PORTOGHESI, SCARPA and Gino VALLE, as well as by urban designers such as AYMONINO, DE CARLO and Giuseppe Samonà (1898–1983), influential as a theorist with his *L'Urbanistica e l'Avvenire della Città* (1959) and other writings. The experimental groups ARCHIZOOM and Superstudio, formed in 1966, had some influence, though much less than the NEO-

RATIONALISM promoted by GREGOTTI and Aldo ROSSI, also by Giorgio Grassi (b.1935), whose Students' Residence, Chieti (1979–84), was exemplary. Among younger architects are Mario BELLINI, Alessandro Mendini (b.1931), notable for his Museum at Groningen, Holland (1988–94), and, of course, Renzo PIANO, though he has had little opportunity to build in Italy apart from the Stadium at Bari (1989). Of a younger generation Massimiliano Fuksas (b.1944) and Francesco Venezia (b.1944) are outstanding, the former for his Palazzetto dello Sport and S. Giorgetto School at Anagni (1979–88) and Local Government Offices at Cassino (1985–90), followed by a remarkable series of buildings in France: the Médiathèque, Nantes-Rezé (1987–91); the College Saint-Exupéry, Noisey-le-Grand (1990–93); the Economic and Social Sciences Building, University of Tours (1991); the Maison des Arts, Michel de Montaigne University, Bordeaux (1993–5); and the Law and Economic Faculty Extension, Limoges University (1990–96). Venezia's early work was very 'site specific' and notable for its regional sensitivity, e.g. piazza at Lauro, Avellino (1972–6), Municipio, Taurano (1979–80), and his reconstructions and other work after the Belice earthquake in Sicily, e.g. the Museum at Gibellina (1980). His open-air theatre at Salemi, Sicily (1983–6), was followed by the large residential complex at San Pietro a Paterno, Naples (1988– ), and the imposing Library and University Centre at Amiens, France (1993–6).

**Ito**, Toyo (b.1941). Korean architect trained in Japan, where he settled. He made his name with the almost Zen-like introverted U-House, Tokyo (1976), and his own house, the Silver Hut, Nakano (1984), in which he exploited fragmenta-

tion and layering with perforated, semi-transparent screens of industrial materials to re-create the spatial ambiguities of traditional Japanese architecture. These were followed by the Nomad Club, Tokyo (1986), and the Tower of the Winds, Yokohama (1986, dismantled 1995), with 1,300 flickering lamps, twenty-four floodlights and twelve neo-rings in its perforated outer skin. They were computer-programmed to produce shimmering patterns modulated according to the direction and strength of the wind. The Municipal Museum, Yatsu-shiro (1991), carried his ambition to create an architecture 'as light as the wind' a stage further with its bubble-shaped 'floating' repository above vaulted stainless steel roofs and perforated metallic screens. Meantime he had designed a very different structure, the earth-covered Guest House for Sapporo Breweries, Eniwa (1989). His UFO-like Egg of Winds, Tokyo (1991), was followed by the floating UFOs of the Nagayama Amusement Complex, Tama, Tokyo (1993). The completely transparent seeming ITM Building, Matsuyama (1993), exploits every variety of glass – opaque, frosted, wire-mesh and clear – with great virtuosity; his elongated, linear Municipal Museum, Shimisuwara (1993), hovers along a narrow lakeside site with ambiguous precision, while his Fire Station, Yatsushiro (1995), floats 6 m. (20 ft) above ground.

C. Jencks, *T.I.*, London 1994.

**Iwan**. A shallow hall with a pointed vault serving as a portal or closed at the back and facing a court. The form originated in C4–6 Sassanian palatial architecture, most notably the palace at Ctesiphon, Iraq, and became an important element in Islamic architecture, first palaces (Samarra, Merv), then mosques (in Iran at Ardistan and Friday Mosque, Isfahan).

From the CII the cruciform disposition of four axial iwans around a courtyard was conventional for mosques, madrasas and caravanserais in eastern Islam, later Egypt, Syria and Turkey. The arched opening was usually enclosed in a rectangular frame and from the CI3 the vault often decorated with MUQARNAS. A portal composed of a very shallow iwan set in a rectangular frame is called a *pishtaq*. *See* Fig. 81.

**Ixnard**, Michel d' (1723–95), a French early neo-classical architect, worked mainly in the Rhineland. Born at Nîmes and trained in Paris, he became architect to the Elector of Trier. His main work is the very large, severe, and rather heavy abbey church of St Blasien in the Black Forest, Germany (1764–84, rebuilt after a fire 1874), with a Doric exterior and solemn Corinthian rotunda.

E. Franz, *P.M. d'I. 1723–1795*, Weissenhorn 1985.

**Izenour**, Steven (b.1930), *see* VENTURI, Robert.

# J

**Jacobean architecture**. Historical division of English architecture of the period 1603–25 (i.e. James I). *See* ENGLISH ARCHITECTURE.

**Jacobs**, Jane (b.1916). American activist, theorist and writer who made a notable impact on urban design with her *Death and Life of Great American Cities* (1961). Questioning the Modernist, i.e. the CIAM–LE CORBUSIER, conception of an urban utopia to be brought about by comprehensive redevelopment and functional zoning, she argued that the vitality of cities lies in their diversity, variety and human scale and vigorously opposed the URBAN RENEWAL projects of New York's powerful planner and public works official Robert Moses. As anti-suburban as she was anti-urban-order, she ridiculed all accepted planning concepts as 'the Radiant Garden City Beautiful'. Her campaign for the preservation of Manhattan's casual, pedestrian, street-oriented and densely built communities saved Soho, Greenwich Village and other threatened areas. Her influence was subsequently felt far beyond New York. She later published *The Economy of Cities* (1969) and *Systems of Survival* (1992).

**Jacobsen**, Arne (1902–71). Danish architect whose style was of the most refined, meticulous INTERNATIONAL MODERN; he was initially influenced by ASPLUND's Stockholm Exhibition of 1930 and appeared as an International Modern architect with work of 1931, at a time when Copenhagen was reaching the climax of a Classicism as refined and meticulous in its own way as Jacobsen's

architecture was to be. He built chiefly private houses and housing (notably Bellavista, Klampenborg, near Copenhagen, 1934) until shortly before the Second World War, when he was also commissioned for work on a larger scale. The Town Hall of Aarhus (with Erik Møller, 1938–42) had a concrete skeleton tower. Søllerød, an outer suburb of Copenhagen, got a town hall by Jacobsen in 1939–42. The Munkegård School at Gentofte, another outer suburb of Copenhagen, is characterized by the many small play-yards between classrooms (1952–6). The Town Hall of Rødovre, yet another outer suburb of Copenhagen, is Jacobsen's most exquisite public building (1955–6), quite unmannered, without any cliché or gimmick, nothing really but the formal apparatus of the International thirties, yet handled with an unparalleled precision and elegance. The same is true of his cylinder-boring factory at Aalborg (1957) and the SAS Hotel at Copenhagen (1960; a tower block on a podium of the Lever House type – *see* SKIDMORE, OWINGS & MERRILL). In 1964 St Catherine's College at Oxford was completed to Jacobsen's designs. During the fifties he also designed some fine and original furniture and cutlery.

T. Faber, *A.J.*, Stuttgart 1964; P. E. Shriver, *A.J.*, Copenhagen 1972; P. E. Tojner and K. Vindum, *A.J. (1902–1971) Architect and Designer*, Copenhagen 1996.

**Jadot de Ville Issy**, Jean-Nicolas (1710–61). He was trained in France and became at an early age architect to the Archduke

Franz I of Lorraine whom he accompanied to Vienna on his marriage to Maria Theresa. He built the Academy of Sciences and Letters in Vienna (1753) and the menagerie at Schönbrunn, both in an accomplished Louis XV style: and he probably provided the plan for the royal palace in Budapest (1749, greatly altered in the C19). He also designed the Arco di S. Gallo in Florence, erected to mark the Archduke's accession to the Grand Duchy of Tuscany in 1739.

Kalnein 1995.

**Jahn**, Helmut (b.1940). German-born American architect, trained in Munich and in Chicago, where he immigrated in 1966. He joined the long-established Chicago practice now called Murphy/Jahn, of which he became director of design in 1973 and president in 1982. Their notable buildings include the One South Wacker building (1979–82), the gigantic State of Illinois Center, Chicago (1980–85), with turquoise reflective and clear glass in a pinstripe pattern, the United Airlines Terminal, O'Hare International Airport, Chicago (1983–7), 425 and 750 Lexington Avenue, New York (1983–9), the spectacular Messeturm, Frankfurt-am-Main (1985–92), the tallest office building in Europe, and the Hyatt Hotel, Roissy, near Paris (1993).

N. Miller, *H.J.*, New York 1986; Klotz 1986; W. Blaser, *H.J. Transparency/Transparenz*, Berlin 1996.

**Jain**, Uttam (b.1934), *see* INDIAN ARCHITECTURE.

**Jalousie**. A blind or shutter with slats which slope upwards from without to exclude rain and sun but admit air and some light; also an open-work grille covering a gallery in a church or a box in a theatre.

**Jamb**. The vertical face of an archway, doorway or window; the part of the jamb

which lies between the glass or door and the outer wall-surface is called a *reveal*.

**Jamb shaft**. A small shaft with capital and base placed against the jamb of a door or window, mainly in medieval architecture.

**James**, John (*c.*1672–1746). English architect who built St George's, Hanover Square, London (1720–25), with its hexastyle portico of free-standing giant Corinthian columns and pediment. This idea was quickly taken up by GIBBS (St Martin-in-the-Fields). Wricklemarsh, Blackheath (1727–33), was his masterpiece, but it was demolished. He rebuilt St Mary's church, Twickenham, except for the west tower (1713–15). Appuldurcombe House, Isle of Wight, may be his. He published an English edition of Claude PERRAULT's book on the Orders in 1708.

Downes 1966; Harris 1990; Summerson 1991; Colvin 1995.

**Jami**, *see* MOSQUE.

**Japanese architecture and landscape architecture**. Temples of the indigenous Shinto religion have been periodically demolished and built anew following a design developed by the C3 AD from primitive huts, that at Ise being the best-known example. They are of stained (persimmon-orange colour) wood but unpainted, with pitched roofs of thatch supported on frames of intersecting spars which project above the ridge-pole. In the C6 an entirely different style was introduced 'ready-made' from China, with a complex system of roof construction, for the buildings in the first Japanese Buddhist monasteries – pagodas and halls for the display of images and for teaching. The earliest that survive are in the Horyuji, near Nara, founded in 607 but destroyed by fire in 670 and reconstructed with the gateway, pagoda and *kondo* (image hall) still entirely Chinese but disposed in a manner that broke away from the axial symmetry invariable in China, creating a distinctly Japanese composition of balanced solids and voids. Although most plans were bilaterally symmetrical, more emphasis was given to width than was usual in China and the size of the monasteries seems sometimes to have been greater: the Daibutsuden of the Todaiji, Nara, begun 743 though rebuilt in 1709 to the original design with a diminution in plan, is still the largest wooden building in the world (now supported on a steel skeleton inserted 1906-13). Nara, the first permanent capital of Japan, was laid out in 710 on a grid with wide avenues in emulation of Changan in China, the Tang dynasty capital. But deviations from Chinese forms began to appear in the c8 (e.g. the pagoda of the Yakushiji, Nara, with the ground storey wider than the tower, which has roofs of alternating size supported on brackets of unprecedented form) and became more pronounced after the Imperial Court moved to Kyoto in 794, especially during the Fujiwara period (898-1185), when there were few direct contacts with the Asian mainland. China proved the model for Japanese imperial administration and in the palace at Kyoto the great hall of state was placed at the end of a courtyard on axis with the main gateway to the enclosure. But living quarters and administrative buildings were disposed with more regard for convenience than symmetry and already had features that were to distinguish Japanese domestic architecture: shingles or thatch rather than ceramic tiles for roofs, veranda corridors as passages from one room or building to another, floors of wood (not of tile and stone with raised platforms as in China), and the division of interior spaces by sliding screens painted with landscapes etc. Externally, the buildings of the imperial and other palaces were

similar to temples of the same period, of which the finest surviving example is the Hondo (Phoenix Hall) dedicated to the Bodhisattva Amida, of the Byodoin at Uji, near Kyoto, founded by a Fujiwara prince in 1052. It has almost dandified elegance, with roofs so dashingly uplifted at their corners that they seem to float above the horizontal lines of the structure. Elegance is also the mark of a type of religious building peculiar to Japan, the *tahoto* or single-storey pagoda, with two wide-spreading roofs sheltering a STUPA and crowned by a tall mast (e.g. that of 1194 in the Ishiyamadera temple overlooking Lake Biwa). In these buildings the woodwork of the elaborate bracketing (more decorative than strictly functional) and of the carved ceilings is often of the greatest refinement. By the beginning of the Kamakura period (1185-1333) the main elements of Japanese religious architecture had been established (with minor variants for several different Buddhist sects) and were to be respected in numerous reconstructions, though new buildings show a tendency towards richer and heavier decoration, taken to its extreme at Nikko, in the mausoleum (1634-6) of Tokugawa Ieyasu, founder of the Shogunate that ruled Japan during the Edo period (1615-1867). The most interesting developments were, however, in domestic architecture, with an entirely different tendency.

The three-storey Kinkakuji (or Golden Pavilion), Kyoto, built in 1397 (burned down 1950 but rebuilt as an exact replica) had decorations in gold leaf on its exterior but was otherwise ostensibly simple, with a structure of squared undecorated timbers, asymmetrical grouping of supports, no elaborate bracketing and a shingle roof. The smaller two-storey Ginkakuji (called the Silver Pavilion), built in 1483, is similar but with a ground floor of more pronounced asymmetry. Both these pavilions were set in artificially 'natural' gardens and intended as places of retirement for study and meditation, commissioned by devotees of Zen Buddhism and bequeathed to Zen monasteries. A garden was an essential part of a Japanese monastery, sometimes laid out with little or no vegetation – that of the Zen sect Ryoan-ji, Kyoto (c.1500), consists of five carefully placed groups of rocks surrounded by raked gravel in an oblong walled enclosure with a veranda from which it and a view of distant hills may be contemplated. The design has been attributed to the painter and tea-ceremony master SOAMI. A different impression is given by the fortified castles built by war-lords in the late C16, e.g. at Himeji (1601–13) where the asymmetry of its several storeys may have been determined to assist defence. Within the fortifications of the Nijo Castle of the Shoguns in Kyoto, begun 1602, the single-storey buildings for reception halls are on a staggered plan, squares arranged angle to angle so that passage from one to another along the flanking corridors necessitates repeated right-angle turns – partly to foil intruders. But the more complex rambling plan of the Katsura palace outside Kyoto, begun c.1620, was determined aesthetically, to provide each room with a different view of the surrounding garden which, together with those of Nijo castle and the imperial palace in Kyoto, may have been designed by the tea-ceremony master Enshu KOBORI. At Katsura the building materials are ostentatiously simple – sometimes rough un-worked tree-trunks for posts and beams – but employed with the greatest refinement. It is a large-scale expression of the quintessentially Japanese cult of rusticity and artificial naturalness which was taken to its extreme in the small houses and rooms for the tea ceremony (which had origin-

ated in Zen monasteries). Here as elsewhere, however, freedom in planning, the articulation of walls etc. was held in check by an inviolable rule of proportions based on the double square of the *tatami* straw and rush mat – approximately $2 \times 1$ m. ($6 \times 3$ ft) (for imperial buildings $2.3 \times 1.15$ m. ($7 \times 3$ ft 6 in.)), with halves but no other fractions permitted. The rule was obeyed for housing at all levels of society but notably in *shoin* or upper-class houses of the C16, characterized by their interiors with traditional elements such as a *tokonoma* alcove and standing translucent *shoji* screens combined with asymmetry and open planning – interiors could be enlarged or reduced by sliding *fusuma* doors or screens. Such houses were to appeal strongly to European architects in the early C20, e.g. Bruno TAUT.

In the Meiji period (1868–1912), European styles were introduced as part of the government's Westernization policy, e.g. the Frenchified neo-Baroque Akasaka Detached Palace, Tokyo (1898–1909), stone-built with central heating, by Tokuma Katayama (1854–1917); and Tokyo Central Railway Station (1898–1914) by Kingo Tatsuma (1858–1919), who was responsible for some 140 public buildings, mainly banks of steel-framed red brick construction. Houses for the rich might also be given a European appearance but otherwise Japanese traditions were maintained well into the 1930s, e.g. the nationalist-traditionalist revival National Museum, Tokyo (1937), by Hitochi Watanabe (1887–1973), though he took up 'stripped Classicism' the following year for his Daiichi Life Insurance Building, Tokyo (1938). It was only after the Second World War that modern Japanese architecture – like that of Brazil slightly earlier – won international fame, and the decisive influence in Japan, as in Brazil, was LE CORBUSIER. Kunio MAEKAWA, Junzo SAKAKURA and Takamasa Yoshisaka (1917–80) all worked in his Paris office, Sakakura even contributing a Corbusian version of the traditional Japanese teahouse to the 1937 Paris Exhibition. Later they all went in for extremely massive concrete and bold, heavily fanciful forms, e.g. Maekawa's Festival Halls, Tokyo and Kyoto (both 1961); Sakakura's Town Hall, Hajima (1959); and Yoshisaka's Gotsu Town Hall (1962). The leading contemporary architect is Kenzo TANGE, whose mature works are all in concrete left as rough as possible and used for the most dramatic effects, e.g. Olympia Sports Stadium, Tokyo (1963–4), with suspended roof, and Yamanashi broadcasting centre, Kofu (1966–7). His disciples include the METABOLISM group – Kyonori KIKUTAKE, Kisho KUROKAWA, Fumihiko MAKI and Masato Otaka (b.1923) – with whom ISOZAKI and Sachio Otani (b.1924) were also briefly involved. Otani's International Conference Centre, Kyoto (1963–6), is notable.

In 1971 Takamitsu AZUMA, Takefumi AIDA and others broke with the Metabolists to form the ArchiteXt group, and the same year Team Zō (called Team Zoo from 1979) was launched and Kiko (Monta) Mozuma (b.1941) built his remarkable Anti-Dwelling Box (Mozuma House), Kushiro, Hokkaido. He and ANDO, HARA, HASEGAWA, ITO, SINOHARA and Kijo Rokkaku (b.1941) formed the second generation of Japanese post-Second World War architects. Rokkaku's Zasso Forest Kindergarten, Tana Becho (1977), and Tokyo Bundokan, Tokyo (1989), were remarkable. This second generation was followed a few years later by the third, of whom ISHII, TAKAMATSU and YAMAMOTO are outstanding. Takamatsu has transformed whole areas of Kyoto with his bold experimental buildings.

Contemporaneously the older genera-tions were in continuous and developing production, notably Tange and Isozaki, and during the last decade several outstanding European architects have been given major commissions in Japan, e.g. FOSTER and PIANO.

**Japelli** or **Jappelli**, Giuseppe (1783–1852), Italian architect and landscape gardener and a true eclectic of a type rare in Italy. Beginning at the Caffè Pedrocchi, Padua (1816–31), in a very elegant version of neo-classicism, he then turned to a severe manner derived from the astylar backs of Palladian villas – e.g. Villa Vigodarzere, Saonara (1817) – then to a bold Grecian style for the Doric slaughterhouse in Padua (1821, now the Istituto d'Arte). After a visit to France and England he added a neo-Gothic wing to the Pedrocchi (1837), and finally built the neo-Rococo Teatro Verdi, Padua (1847). His landscape parks are in the English manner; most of them in the Veneto (e.g. Saonara, Ca' Minotto, Rosà), but one of the finest was at Villa Torlonia, Rome (1840).

Meeks 1966; G. Mazza (ed.), *G.J. e il suo tempo*, Padua 1977; L. Puppi, *Il Caffè Pedrocchi di Padova*, Vicenza 1980; P. Bassadori, *Il giardino romantico e J.*, Padua 1983.

**Jardin**, Nicolas-Henri (1720–99), *see* DANISH ARCHITECTURE.

**Jardin anglo-chinois**. French term for a LANDSCAPE GARDEN coined by George-Louis Le Rouge in 1776, implying that it was not an English invention but the imitation of Chinese gardens.

**Javanese architecture**, *see* INDONESIAN ARCHITECTURE.

**Jay**, William (c.1793–1837). English architect who emigrated to the USA in 1817 and during the following seven years built in Savannah, Georgia, some of the earliest Greek Revival houses in the

USA, notably the austere Scarborough House (1818) and Telfair House (c. 1820). His Owens–Thomas House Museum, Savannah, is his best-known building. In 1822 he returned to England and worked briefly at Cheltenham and Henley-on-Thames.

Colvin 1995.

**Jean de Chelles**. Master mason to Notre Dame in Paris and responsible for the façade bays of the transepts – that to the north came first in the 1240s, that to the south was begun in 1258 to a design by PIERRE DE MONTEREAU, who succeeded him at Notre Dame in 1265. A kinsman, Pierre de Chelles, was master mason of the cathedral in the early C14 and was still active in 1316, when he was called to Chartres as a consultant.

Frankl 1972; R. Branner, *St Louis and the Court Style in Gothic Architecture*, London 1965.

**Jean d'Orbais**. The names of the first four master masons of Reims Cathedral were recorded in a maze on the floor (known from C18 transcriptions). The order was in all probability Jean d'Orbais, Jean Le Loup, Gaucher de Reims and Bernard de Soissons. Bernard's headship lasted, it seems, to c. 1290; Gaucher's from c. 1245 to 1253; Le Loup's from c. 1229 to 1245 and Jean d'Orbais's from c. 1211 to 1229. So the first total plan was by Jean d'Orbais. The cathedral was begun in 1211 and the choir was consecrated in 1241.

Frankl 1972; Bony 1983.

**Jeanneret**, Charles-Édouard (1887–1966), *see* LE CORBUSIER.

**Jeanneret**, Pierre (1896–1966). Swiss architect, cousin of LE CORBUSIER. Trained in Geneva and Paris, under PERRET, he joined his cousin as a partner in 1922. In 1940 he returned to Switzerland but in 1944 rejoined his cousin, for whom he worked at Chandigarh, India. He was

responsible for the execution of all Le Corbusier's buildings there and also designed several buildings, notably a hotel at Chandigarh (1955) and the Gandhi Bavan (1959–61), as well as housing estates, e.g. Peon Village (1952–3), all displaying great empathy with the indigenous vernacular.

G. Barbey in *Architecture, Forms, Functions*, Lausanne 1969.

**Jefferson**, Thomas (1743–1826), legislator, economist, educationalist, and third President of the United States of America (1801–9), was also an able and immensely influential architect and landscape architect. The son of a surveyor, he inherited a considerable estate in Albemarle County, Virginia, where in 1768 he chose a high romantic site for his own house, Monticello (1770–79, remodelled 1796–1808), and transformed its surroundings into an English-style landscape park. He derived the plan from Robert MORRIS's *Select Architecture*, but modified it with reference to GIBBS and Leoni's edition of PALLADIO. It had porticos front and back and a great forecourt with octagonal pavilions at the corners and square pavilions terminating the wings. It is very carefully thought out, both in its planning, on which he had strong personal views, and in its adaptation of Palladian elements. He was interested in Palladio mainly as the interpreter of Roman villa architecture, and looked back to antiquity for the 'natural' principles of his architectural theory. In 1785, while he was in Europe, he was asked to design the Virginia State Capitol for Richmond. With the help of CLÉRISSEAU, he produced a temple design based on the Maison Carrée (16 BC) at Nîmes, France, but Ionic instead of Corinthian and with pilasters in place of half-columns on the flanks and rear. The Virginia State Capitol (completed 1796 with the assistance of

LATROBE) set a pattern for official architecture in the USA. As Secretary of State to George Washington he played a leading part in planning the new federal capital in Washington from 1792 onwards. After he became President he entrusted Latrobe with the task of completing the new Capitol (1803, burnt 1814). Latrobe also assisted him with the University of Virginia, Charlottesville – a group of porticoed houses (each containing a professor's lodging and a classroom) linked by colonnades in a formal plan, with a great Pantheon at one end of the oblong composition (1817–26) – the first great CAMPUS plan.

W. H. Adams (ed.), *The Eye of T.J.*, Washington, DC, 1976, and *J.'s Monticello*, New York 1983; F. D. Nichols and R. E. Griswold, *T.J. Landscape Architect*, Charlottesville 1978; M. Braun, *University of Virginia: The Lawn*, London 1994.

**Jekyll**, Gertrude (1843–1932). English ARTS AND CRAFTS garden designer. She followed the horticulturalist William Robinson (1838–1935) in abandoning carpet-bedding, topiary work, box hedges, etc., in favour of the informality of the English cottage garden with its indigenous flowers and shrubs. For artistic rather than ecological reasons she scorned all exotica and took up the herbaceous border of hardy plants which she popularized. She often collaborated with LUTYENS, surrounding his houses with gardens in which the naturalness she aimed at in planting according to native forms and colours is offset and controlled by the formality of stonework, steps, balustrades, etc., e.g. Orchards, Godalming, Surrey (1898); Hestercombe, Taunton, Somerset (1906). Her numerous books, e.g. *Wood and Garden* (London 1890), *Home and Garden* (London 1900), had great and widespread influence in both the UK and the USA.

M. P. Tooley ed., *G.J. . . Essays*, London 1984; R. Bisgrove, *The Gardens of G.J.*, London 1992.

**Jellicoe**, Geoffrey Alan (1900–1996). English architect and landscape architect. He began as an ARTS AND CRAFTS architect but soon became active mainly as a landscape architect, e.g. at housing estates in the London suburb of Acton (1934) and at Bestwood, Nottinghamshire (1938–40), also private gardens, notably at Mottisfont Abbey, Hampshire (1936–9). In 1943 he drew up the first large-scale comprehensive plan for an industrial site – the Hope Valley cement works in the Peak District National Park, providing for the area to be returned to public recreational use and thereby initiating the concept of alternative use for industrial waste. After the Second World War he worked extensively in Zambia (1947–52) and in England planned the NEW TOWN of Hemel Hempstead, Hertfordshire (1947), with its serpentine public water garden (1957). He also designed the surroundings of factories and power stations, notably Harwell Hills for the Rutherford High Energy Laboratory, Harwell, Oxfordshire (1960). His Kennedy Memorial at Runnymede, Berkshire (1965–6), is remarkable, a simple woodland glade with a poetically placed stone slab and seats for contemplation along a path recalling the allegory of Bunyan's *Pilgrim's Progress*. From 1964 to 1972 he was consultant for the first British MOTORWAYS. His most ambitious and imaginative projects date from the 1980s, the garden at Sutton Place, Surrey (1982), which he described as 'a grand allegory of creation, life and aspiration', and the Moody Historical Gardens, Galveston, Texas (as yet unrealized), a vast THEME PARK of the history of landscape architecture. (*See* G. Jellicoe, *The Landscape of Civilization as Experienced in the Moody Gardens,*

Northiam 1988.) His work was outstanding for its continual receptiveness and response to diverse natural environments, and his and his wife Susan Jellicoe's publications had great influence on the development of landscape architecture from small private gardens to large-scale environmental design: *Studies in Landscape Design* (London (1960–70) 1990), and their classic work *The Landscape of Man* (London (1975) 1995). He was knighted in 1979.

M. Spens, *The Complete Landscape Designs and Gardens of G.J.*, London 1994.

**Jenney**, William Le Baron (1832–1907), American architect, born in Massachusetts, studied at the École Centrale des Arts et Manufactures in Paris, was an engineer in the Civil War, and opened a practice in architecture and engineering in Chicago in 1868. In 1869 he published a book called *Principles and Practices of Architecture*. By far his most important building was the Home Life Insurance building (1883–5, demolished 1931), as its iron columns, iron lintels and girders, and indeed steel beams, prepared the way for the skeleton construction of the CHICAGO SCHOOL. The Second Leiter Building, Chicago (1889–90), is an eight-storey metal-framed building.

T. Turak, *W.L.B.J. A Pioneer of Modern Architecture*, Ann Arbor 1986; Zukovsky 1988.

**Jensen**, Albert Christian (1847–1913), *see* DANISH ARCHITECTURE.

**Jensen**, Jens (1860–1951). American landscape architect. Born in Denmark, he settled in 1886 in Chicago where he worked for the city parks department and after 1920 independently. He developed a 'Prairie Style' of garden design, sometimes in collaboration with F. L. WRIGHT, e.g. Coonley House, Riverside, Illinois (1908), aiming to recreate an aboriginal, mostly mythical, Illinois landscape before the opening up of the West, using indigenous mid-West plants which he was the first to appreciate. As park superintendent in Chicago he redesigned the West Park system, upgrading Garfield, Douglas and Humboldt Parks and providing them with 'prairie' features. His chief public works were Columbus Park, Chicago, and Knickerbocker Boulevard, Hammond, Indiana.

L. K. Eaton, *Landscape Artist in America: The Life and Work of J.J.*, Chicago/London 1964; R. Grese, *J.J. Maker of Natural Parks and Gardens*, Baltimore 1992.

**Jensen-Klint**, Peter Vilhelm (1853–1930), *see* KLINT, Peter Vilhelm Jensen.

**Jersey Devil Architects**, *see* ENVIRONMENTAL, GREEN OR SUSTAINABLE ARCHITECTURE.

**Jesse window**. A window in which the tracery represents the branches of the tree of Jesse – a genealogical tree showing the ancestors of Christ ascending through Mary from the root of Jesse – as at St Denis, Canterbury and York Minster.

**Jetty**. In a TIMBER-FRAMED building the projection of an upper storey beyond the storey below made by the BEAMS and JOISTS of the lower storey oversailing the external wall. On their outer ends is placed the sill of the walling for the storey above. Buildings can be jettied on several sides, in which case a *dragon beam* is set diagonally at the corner to carry the joists to either side.

**Jib door** or **gib door**. A concealed door flush with the wall-surface painted or papered to correspond with the walls. The DADO and other mouldings are similarly carried across the door.

**Joass**, John James (1868–1952), *see* HOLDEN, Charles.

**Joggle, Joggling**. Masons' terms for joining two stones in such a way as to prevent them from slipping or sliding, by means of a notch in one and a corresponding projection in the other. It is often seen exposed on the face of a flat arch. If the joggle is concealed it is called a 'secret joggle'. *See* Fig. 69.

Fig. 69 Joggled joint

**John of Ramsey**, *see* WILLIAM OF RAMSEY.

**Johnson**, Francis (1910–96), *see* NEO-GEORGIAN.

**Johnson**, Philip Cortelyou (b.1906), American architect, invented the term INTERNATIONAL STYLE (1932, with Henry-Russell Hitchcock), but his fame was first spread by the house he built for himself in New Canaan, Connecticut (1949) – very much in the style of MIES VAN DER ROHE – a cube with completely glazed walls all round. The siting is romantic, and perhaps in the years about 1950 one should already have been able to guess that Johnson would not remain faithful to Mies's principles. In the guesthouse (1952) close to his own house vaults began to appear, inspired by SOANE, and the synagogue at Port Chester, NY (1956), made it clear that he would prefer variety, the unexpected effect, and elegance to the single-mindedness of Mies, though he collaborated with him at the Seagram Building, New York, designing the Four Seasons Restaurant (1959). He went on to design the Amon Carter Museum at Fort Worth, Texas (1961); the Art Gallery for the University of Nebraska at Lincoln (1962); the New York State Theater for the Lincoln Center in New York (1962–4); the indianizing shrine at New Harmony, Indiana (1960); and the Museum of Pre-Columbian Art, Dumbarton Oaks, Washington, DC (1963). From 1967 to 1991 he was in partnership with John Burgee (b.1933) as 'Johnson/Burgee Architects', their more notable works including the IDS Center, Minneapolis, Minnesota (1970–73); the slick and dark glass Penzoil Place, Houston, Texas (1970–76), a monument to crude oil; the sensational, star-shaped 'Crystal Cathedral' Community Church, Garden Grove, California (1976–80); the pseudo-classical AT & T (now Sony Plaza) Building, New York (1979–84); and the PPG Corporate Headquarters, Pittsburg, NJ (1979–84). The University of Houston School of Architecture, Houston, Texas (1983–6), is an essay in Ledolcian fantasy. The golden-glass-skinned Trump International Hotel and Tower, New York (1995–7, with Costas Kondylis), may be his swan-song. His *Writings*, edited by R. A. M. Stern, were published in 1979 (New York and Oxford).

N. Miller, *The Buildings and Projects of P.J.*, New York 1979; F. Schulze, *P.J. Life and Works*, New York 1994; H. Lewis and J. O'Connor, *P.J. The Architect in His Own Words*, New York 1994; D. Whitney and J. Kipnis, *P.J. The Glass House*, New York 1994; J. Kipnis, *P.J. Recent Work*, London 1996.

**Jointing**. Finishing the surface of mortar joints in brickwork or masonry while the mortar is fresh, instead of raking it out and POINTING.

**Joists**. Horizontal parallel timbers laid between the walls or the beams of a building to carry the floorboards. The undersides are either exposed to the room below and then often moulded, or have ceiling laths nailed to them for a plaster ceiling.

**Jonas**, Walter (1910–79), *see* ENGLISH ARCHITECTURE.

**Jones**, E. Fay (b.1921). American architect, apprenticed to F. L. WRIGHT, to whose 'organic' architectural principles he remained faithful. His Thorncrown Chapel, Eureka Springs, Arkansas (1979–80), notably succeeds in enhancing the spirituality of its dramatic site. Built of local wood and open to the elements, it stands on a hillside thick with oak, maple and dogwood near a stone bluff where travellers stop to admire the view.

R. A. Ivy, *F.J. The Architecture of E.F.J.*, Washington, DC 1992.

**Jones**, Edward (b.1939). English architect in partnership in London with Jeremy DIXON from 1989. Previously Jones had made his name with Mississuaga City Hall, Toronto, Canada (1986–8), in a classical style *à la* Ledoux. His later work has been less provocative but more truly innovative architecturally and notably 'site specific'; *see* DIXON, Jeremy.

**Jones**, Inigo (1573–1652), a genius far in advance of his time in England, imported the classical style from Italy to a still half-Gothic north and brought English Renaissance architecture to sudden maturity. He was the same age as Donne and Ben Jonson, and only nine years younger than Shakespeare. Born in London, the son of a Smithfield clothworker, he appears to have visited Italy before 1603, being then a 'picture-maker'. Not until 1608 is he heard of as an architect (design for the New Exchange, London); his earliest known buildings date from later still. Meantime he had become a prominent figure at Court as a

stage-designer for masques in the most lavish and up-to-date Italian manner. Many of his designs survive, of fantastic Baroque costumes and hardly less fantastic architectural sets, executed in a free, spontaneous style of draughtsmanship he had presumably picked up in Italy. In 1613 he went to Italy again, this time for a year and seven months, with the great collector Lord Arundel. He returned with an unbounded admiration for PALLADIO and a first-hand knowledge of Roman monuments unique in England at that date. (He met SCAMOZZI in Venice.) At this period he is sometimes said to have worked at Heidelberg with Salomon de CAUS, with whose nephew Isaac he was later connected in England (*see below*).

From 1615, when he became Surveyor of the King's Works, until the Civil War in 1642 he was continuously employed at the various royal palaces. Immediately he built three startlingly novel buildings which broke uncompromisingly with the Jacobean past: the Queen's House, Greenwich (1616–18 and 1629–38); the Prince's Lodging, Newmarket, Suffolk (1619–22, now destroyed); and the Banqueting House, Whitehall, London (1619–22). The Queen's House is the first strictly classical building in England, though there was a long break in its construction (the foundations were laid in 1616, but the elevations and interior date from 1632–8?). The Prince's Lodging, modest in size, set the pattern for the red-brick, stone-quoined, hipped-roof house with dormers, so popular later in the century. The Banqueting House is Jones's masterpiece; it perfectly expresses his conception of architecture – 'sollid, proporsionable according to the rules, masculine and unaffected' – as also his adoration of Palladio. But though every detail is Palladian it is not a mere imitation. Everything has been subtly transmuted and the result is unmistakably English:

solid, sturdy and rather phlegmatic. The Queen's Chapel, St James's Palace, London (1623–7), was also something new for England – a classical church, consisting of an aisleless parallelogram with a coffered segmental vault, a pedimented front, and a large Venetian window. Equally striking but more elaborate was the Bramantesque temple design he used for King James's hearse in 1625.

His principal buildings for Charles I have been destroyed, except for the Queen's House at Greenwich. This is an Italian villa sympathetically reinterpreted, whose chastity and bareness must have appeared daringly original. The upper-floor loggia is very Palladian, as is also the two-armed, curved open staircase to the terrace; but, as always with Jones, nothing is a direct copy. The proportions have been slightly altered and the general effect is long and low and very un-Italian. Inside, the hall is a perfect cube and symmetry prevails throughout. Also to the 1630s belong his great Corinthian portico at Old St Paul's, transforming the medieval cathedral into the most Roman structure in the country, and Covent Garden, the first London square, of which the church St Paul's (1630–31) and a fragment of the square survive, the latter rebuilt. The square was conceived as one composition, the houses having uniform façades with arcaded ground floors and giant pilasters above (perhaps influenced by the Place des Vosges, Paris). In about 1638 he also produced elaborate designs for an enormous Royal Palace in Whitehall. These reveal his limitations and it is perhaps fortunate for his reputation that they were never executed.

The year 1642 brought his brilliant career at Court to an end. He was with the King at Beverley, but nothing more is heard of him until 1645. Although his property was sequestrated he was par-doned in 1646 and his estate restored. From then onwards he seems to have swum quite happily with the political tide, working for the Parliamentarian Lord Pembroke. The great garden front at Wilton House was for long thought to have been built by him at about this date, but is now known to have been built c.1636 by Isaac de CAUS, whom Jones is said to have recommended and also advised. It was badly damaged by fire c.1647 and the famous state rooms therefore date from about 1649, by which time Jones was too old to give much personal attention; he put it in the hands of his pupil and nephew by marriage, John WEBB. He was responsible for the celebrated double-cube room, until recently thought to have been by Jones himself. Innumerable buildings have been attributed to Jones, of which a few may have had some connection with him, notably the pavilions at Stoke Bruerne Park (1629–35). Though profound, his immediate influence was confined to Court circles. In the early C18 he largely inspired the Palladian revival of BURLINGTON and KENT. In 1727 Kent published *The Designs of Inigo Jones*, but the designs are largely by Webb.

J. Summerson, *I.J.*, Harmondsworth (1966) 1983; J. Harris and G. Higgot, *I.J. Complete Architectural Drawings*, London 1989; Harris 1990; Summerson 1991; Colvin 1995; Mowl and Earnshaw 1995.

**Jones**, Owen (1809–74), *see* ORNAMENT.

**Jones**, Wesley (b.1958), *see* UNITED STATES ARCHITECTURE.

**Jourdain**, Frantz (1847–1935). Architect of the famous department store La Samaritaine, Paris (1901–10), a masterpiece of ART NOUVEAU though unfortunately renovated in 1926–30 in the ART DECO style.

M. L. Clausen, *F.J. and the Samaritaine*, Paris 1987; A. Barre-Despond and S. Tisé, *J. F. 1847–1935 . . .* , New York 1991.

**Juan de Álava** (d.1537), a Spanish master mason on the verge of Late Gothic and Early Renaissance, appears first as consultant at Salamanca Cathedral in 1512 (with eight others) and Seville Cathedral in 1513 (with three others), in the latter years as master to the newly restarted work at Plasencia Cathedral (first with Francisco de Colonia – *see* SIMÓN DE COLONIA – who soon quarrelled with him). Then we come across him as the designer of the cloister of Santiago Cathedral (1521 onwards) and finally as master mason to Salamanca Cathedral after the death of Juan GIL DE HONTAÑÓN in 1526. S. Esteban at Salamanca (1524 onwards) is also by him; this and the work at Plasencia round the crossing are perhaps his finest.

Kubler and Soria 1959.

**Juan de Colonia** (d.*c*.1511), *see* SIMÓN DE COLONIA.

**Jubé**. The French name for ROOD SCREEN.

**Jugendstil**, *see* ART NOUVEAU.

**Jujol**, Josip Maria (1879–1949), *see* SPANISH ARCHITECTURE.

**Jumsai**, Sumet (b.1939), *see* THAI ARCHITECTURE.

**Jussow**, Heinrich Christoph (1754–1825), German architect, born in Kassel, was given a classical education and then studied law at Marburg and Göttingen before joining the Landgräflichen Baudepartment in Kassel under Simon Louis DU RY in 1778. He later studied architecture in Paris under de WAILLY and visited Italy and England (1784–8). He completed du Ry's Schloss Wilhelmshöhe outside Kassel and built numerous ornamental buildings in the Roman, Chinese and Gothic tastes in the park. Among these is his masterpiece, the picturesque castle Löwenburg (1793–8), much influenced by the English Gothic Revival and the most elaborate C18 essay in the genre anywhere on the Continent. Built on a dramatic hillside site and approached by drawbridge across a moat, it is amply provided with ramparts, towers and (originally) guards in medieval costumes.

H. Vogel, *H.C.J.*, exh. cat., Kassel 1958–9; H. Bien, *Die Löwenburg im Schlosspark Wilhelmshöhe*, Berlin 1965; Honour 1979.

**Jutkovic**, Dusan Samo (1868–1947), *see* SLOVAK ARCHITECTURE.

**Juvarra**, Filippo (1678–1736), born in Messina of a family of silversmiths, is the greatest Italian C18 architect and a brilliant draughtsman. His elegant and sophisticated Late Baroque buildings are as typical of their period as Tiepolo's paintings and equally accomplished; they have a Mozartian gaiety and fecundity of decorative invention. Trained in Rome under FONTANA (1703/4–14), he first won fame as a stage-designer, and this theatrical experience was to leave a mark on nearly all his subsequent work.

In 1714 he was invited to Turin by Victor Amadeus II of Savoy, who appointed him 'First Architect to the King'. Apart from a trip to Portugal, London and Paris, in 1719–20, he remained in Turin for the next twenty years. His output was enormous, ranging from churches, palaces, country villas and hunting-lodges to the layout of entire new city quarters in Turin – not to mention work as an interior decorator and designer of furniture and the applied arts. Of his churches, the Superga (1715–31) and the chapel of the Venaria Reale (1716–21), both near Turin, are spectacular, the former being by far the grandest of all Italian Baroque sanctuaries, comparable with Melk in Austria and Einsiedeln in Switzerland. S. Filippo Neri (1715), S. Croce (1718 onwards), and the Carmine (1732–5, gutted during the war) in Turin are all very fine. His city palaces in Turin include Palazzo Birago della Valle (1716), Palazzo Richa di Covasolo (1730) and Palazzo d'Ormea (1730), while his work for the king is remarkable for the four great palaces and villas in or near Turin – Venaria Reale (1714–26), Palazzo Madama (1718–21), Castello di Rivoli (1718–21, but only partly executed), and his masterpiece Stupinigi (1729–33). In all these works he had the assistance of numerous highly skilled painters, sculptors and craftsmen, who were summoned from all parts of Italy to execute his designs.

Though little development is discernible in his style, which is a brilliant epitome of current ideas rather than an original invention, it reached its fine flower in Stupinigi, especially in the great central hall, whose scenic quality and skeletal structure suggest an influence from north of the Alps. In 1735 Juvarra was summoned to Spain by Philip V, for whom he designed the garden façade of S. Ildefonso near Segovia and the new Royal Palace in Madrid, executed with alterations after his death by G. B. SAC-CHETTI. He died suddenly in Madrid in January 1736.

Pommer 1967; S. Boscarino, *J. architetto*, Rome 1973; Wittkower 1982; H. Millon, *F.J. Drawings from the Roman Period 1704–1714*, Rome 1984; G. Gritella, *J. l'archittura*, Modena 1992; V. Cormoli Mandracci and A. Griseri (eds.), *F.J. (1678–1736), architetto delle capitale di Torino e Madrid 1714–1736*, Turin 1995.

# K

**Kaftanzoglou**, Lyssander (1812–62), *see* GREEK ARCHITECTURE.

**Kahn**, Albert (1869–1942). German architect who emigrated to the USA 1880. From 1905 he worked in Detroit, where he pioneered methods of standardization and team design in his factories for the Ford Motor Company, General Motors and others. His Packard Building 10, Detroit (1906) pioneered the day-lit factory interior. By the 1920s he was the leading industrial architect in the USA and his Ford Glass Plant (1922), part of Ford's Rouge River complex, Dearborn, Michigan, became a prototype for much industrial architecture. He worked in Russia 1929–32. In contrast to his factories his residential and institutional work is in various historical styles, e.g. Detroit Athletic Club (1913–15); the William L. Clement Library, Ann Arbor, Michigan (1920–21). But his last factories are among his finest, e.g. the Dodge Half-Ton Truck Assembly Plant, Detroit (1937–8), and the Ohio Steel Foundry (Whemco), Lima, Ohio (1937).

G. Hildebrand, *Designing for Industry. The Architecture of A.K.*, Cambridge, Mass. 1974; W. H. Ferry, *The Legacy of A.K.*, Detroit 1987.

**Kahn**, Louis Isadore (1901–74). Born on the island of Osel, Estonia, he went to the USA in 1905. He studied at the University of Pennsylvania, and much later taught at Yale (1947–57) and at the University of Pennsylvania (from 1957 onwards). Though now regarded as having been, after F. L. WRIGHT, the greatest American C20 architect, he was inter-nationally noticed only fairly late in life, first with the Yale University Art Gallery (with D. Orr, 1951–3), then with the Richards Medical Research Building, Philadelphia (1958–60). The Art Gallery has for its main exhibition space a SPACE-FRAME ceiling. The Medical Research Building has all ducts gathered in a number of sheer, square towers projecting from and rising above the outer walls; the reason is said to be functional, but the effect is curiously dramatic and indeed aggressive – an original version of BRUTALISM. However, Kahn's works have, with their elementary geometrical shapes and large unbroken surfaces, a majesty and severity all their own. Inspired by Ancient Roman architecture, at first combined with some Beaux Arts influence, he sought to restore a sense of civic monumentality and grandeur to American architecture that CORPORATE MODERNISM had eroded. His most significant later buildings include the Salk Institute for Biological Studies, La Jolla, California (1959–65); the First Unitarian Church and School, Rochester, NY (1959–69); the Eleanor Donnelly Erdman Hall, Bryn Mawr College, Pennsylvania (1960–65); the Indian Institute of Management, Ahmedabad, India (1962–74); and the Sher-e-Bangla Nagara Dakar, Bangladesh (1962–87), which was perhaps his finest achievement and is certainly the outstanding post-Second World War public building anywhere on a grand scale. This was followed by the Library for the Phillips Exeter Academy, Exeter, New Hampshire (1965–72); the highly acclaimed Kimbell Art Museum, Fort

Worth, Texas (1966–72); and the Yale Center for British Art, New Haven, Connecticut (1969–77). Among his unrealized projects was a remarkable design for the Palazzo dei Congressi to stand in the Giardini Pubblici in Venice (1968–74). His writings were collected and published in 1991. Among his pupils and disciples GIURGOLA was outstanding, and around him and others there formed a so-called 'Philadelphia School'.

A. Tyng, *Beginnings: L.K.'s Philosophy of Architecture*, London 1984; H. Ronner et al., *L.I.K. The Complete Works 1935–74*, Basel, Stuttgart and Boulder (1977) 1987; R. S. Wurman, *What Will Be Has Always Been. The Words of L.K.*, New York 1986; Klotz 1988; D. B. Brownlee and D. G. D. Long, *L.I.K. In the Realm of Architecture*, New York 1992; U. Büttiker, *L.I.K. Licht und Raum. Light and Space*, Basel 1993; K. K. Ashraf, *National Capital of Bangladesh, Dhaka, 1962–83. L.K.*, Tokyo 1994.

**Kampen**, Jacob van, *see* CAMPEN, Jacob van.

**Kampmann**, Hack (1856–1920), *see* DANISH ARCHITECTURE.

**Kamsetzer**, Jan Baptist (1753–95), *see* POLISH ARCHITECTURE.

**Kanvinde**, Achyat (b.1916), *see* INDIAN AND PAKISTANI ARCHITECTURE.

**Kaplicky, Jan** (b.1939), *see* FUTURE SYSTEMS.

**Karavan**, Dani (b.1930). Israeli landscape architect, sculptor and designer of environments. The Negev Monument, a group of concrete structures and 20 m. (65 ft) high tower with a wind organ in the desert near Beer Sheba (1963–8), was remarkable but he made his name internationally with his Environment for Peace in Florence (1978), followed by his White Square, Kikat Levana, Tel Aviv

(1977–88). In 1980 he was commissioned to design the Avenue Majeure for the new town of Cergy-Pontoise near Paris, a 3 km. (2 mile) long straight walk through sequences of spaces with twelve stations or stopping places, notably a terrace with twelve columns and an amphitheatre. The axiality of the layout is carried into the sky by a permanent laser beam from a tower, designed by BOFILL. Other works include 'Dialogue', Duisberg, Germany (1989), the Street of the Rights of Man, Germanisches National Museum, Nuremberg, Germany (1993), an environment in memory of Walter Benjamin at Port Bou, France/Spain (1993), and the Place for Communications Centre, Horgen, Zürich (1994–5).

P. Restany, *D.K.*, Munich 1993; Cerver 1995; Weilacher 1996.

**Karmi**, Dov (1905–64) and Ram (b.1931), *see* ISRAELI ARCHITECTURE.

**Karmi Melamede**, Ada (b.1936), *see* ISRAELI ARCHITECTURE.

**Katayama**, Tokuma (1854–1917), *see* JAPANESE ARCHITECTURE.

**Kauffmann**, Richard (1887–1958), *see* ISRAELI ARCHITECTURE.

**Kazakov**, Matvey Fyodorovich (1738–1813). Russian neo-classical architect; he worked almost entirely in the Moscow area and (unusually) neither travelled abroad nor studied at the Petersburg Academy. From a poor family, he trained under Ukhtomsky. His opportunity came as one of the team replanning and rebuilding Tver after the fire of 1763; already Baroque elements were yielding to neo-classicism in his first independent work there. Co-operation with BAZHENOV in the Kremlin palace project (1767–74) contributed to his mature style, first fully manifest in the rich yet restrained Senate building in the Kremlin (1776). His œuvre includes private houses (e.g. for the Demidov, Gubin, Razumovksy families), typically with the main porticoed façade set back between symmetrical projecting wings, public commissions (Golitsyn Hospital, 1796; Moscow 'Old' University, 1786, remodelled by Zhilyardi, 1817) and the rotunda church of St Philip (1777). His excursions into Gothic antiquarianism are less convincing than Bazhenov's (Petrovsky Palace, 1775; Palace at Tsarityno, 1786). His style tended to become plainer and more Palladian, though never puristically so; domes and their fenestration fascinated him from first to last and he created fine interiors (e.g. 'Hall of Columns' in the Nobleman's Club, 1784). He was the chief initiator of the notable tradition of Moscow neo-classical architecture culminating in D. I. Zhilyardi or Gigliardi (1788–1845). [R. Milner-Gulland]

Hamilton 1983.

**Keel moulding**. A curved moulding with a nib or arris so that in profile it resembles the keel of a ship – a pointed arch in section. *See* Fig. 70.

Fig. 70 Keel moulding

**Keeling**, Bassett (1836–86), *see* TEULON, Samuel Sanders.

**Keene**, Henry (1726–76), *see* GOTHIC REVIVAL.

**Keep**. The principal inner tower of a castle, containing sufficient accommodation to serve as the chief living-quarters permanently or in times of siege; also called a *donjon*. An early type of keep, rectangular in form, in which the great

hall and private bed-chamber were placed side by side, is called a hall-keep.

**Keldermans**, Rombout (*c.*1460–1531), *see* BELGIAN ARCHITECTURE.

**Kent**, William (1685–1748), English painter, furniture designer, and landscape gardener as well as architect, was born in Bridlington of humble parents. He contrived to study painting in Rome for ten years and was brought back to London in 1719 by Lord BURLINGTON, whose friend and protégé he remained for the rest of his life. Whimsical, impulsive, unintellectual, in fact almost illiterate, he was the opposite of his patron – and as happy designing a Gothic as a classical building. Nevertheless, he allowed Burlington to guide his hand along the correct PALLADIAN lines in all his major commissions. His interior decoration is more personal, being, like his furniture, richly carved and gilt in a sumptuous manner deriving partly from Italian Baroque furniture and partly from Inigo JONES, whose designs he published in 1727 (though they are mostly by WEBB).

He did not turn architect until after 1730, by which time he was well into his forties. His masterpiece, Holkham Hall, Norfolk (1734 onwards, executed by BRETTINGHAM), was designed partly by Burlington, whose hand is evident in the 'staccato' quality of the exterior and in such typical and self-isolating features as the VENETIAN WINDOW within a relieving arch. The marble apsidal entrance hall, based on a combination of a Roman basilica and the Egyptian Hall of VITRUVIUS, with its columns, coffered ceiling, and imposing staircase leading up to the *piano nobile*, is one of the most impressive rooms in England. His lavishly gilt and damask-hung state apartments, elaborately carved and pedimented doorframes, heavy cornices, and niches for antique marbles epitomize the English admiration for Roman magnificence. The Treasury (1733–7), 22 Arlington Street (1741), and 44 Berkeley Square (1742–4), all in London, are notable mainly for their interior decoration, especially the latter, which contains the most ingenious and spatially exciting staircase in London. Esher Place, Surrey, was the best of his neo-Gothic works (wings, now demolished, and other alterations, c.1730). His last building, the Horse Guards, London (1750–59), is a repetition of Holkham, with the unfortunate addition of a clock-tower over the centre: it was executed after his death by John VARDY. Through Burlington's influence Kent was appointed Master Carpenter to the Board of Works in 1726, and Master Mason and Deputy Surveyor in 1735. He was perhaps at his best in small park buildings, e.g. the Temple at Euston Hall, Suffolk (1746), and Worcester Lodge, Badminton House, Gloucestershire (c.1740), and was more important historically as a designer of gardens than as an architect, notably at Stowe, Buckinghamshire (from 1730) and Rousham, Oxfordshire (1738–41), the only one that survives unaltered, sometimes destroying formal layouts and greatly modifying the work of his immediate predecessor BRIDGEMAN. Although there were some precedents for his artificially natural designs with irregular lakes and clumps of trees, he virtually created the English LANDSCAPE GARDEN, being the first to have 'leap'd the fence and seen that all nature is a garden'. This revolutionized the relation of house to landscape and led to less dramatic and forceful façades. From his time onwards the country house was designed to harmonize with the landscape, rather than to dominate and control it.

M. J. Wilson, *W.K. Architect, Designer, Painter, Gardener 1685–1748*, London 1984; J. Dixon Hunt, *W.K. Landscape Garden*, London 1987; Summerson 1991; Colvin 1995.

**Kentish rag**. Hard unstratified limestone found in Kent and much used as an external building stone on account of its weather-resisting properties.

**Key**, Lieven de (c.1560–1627), the first Dutch architect of note to work in the so-called 'Dutch Renaissance' style (similar to English Jacobean). He worked for some years in England before becoming municipal architect of Haarlem (1593), where he introduced the characteristic colourful use of brick with stone dressings (horizontal bands of stone, stone voussoirs set singly in brick above windows, etc.). His masterpieces are the façade of the Leiden Town Hall (1593–7), the Weigh House, Haarlem (1598), the Meat Market, Haarlem (1602–3), and the tower of the Nieuwekerk, Haarlem (1613).

Rosenberg 1977.

**Key pattern**, *see* FRET.

**Keyser**, Hendrick de (1565–1621), the leading architect of his day in Amsterdam, where he was appointed city mason and sculptor in 1595, worked in a style somewhat similar to English Jacobean. His plain utilitarian churches had great influence on Protestant church design in the Netherlands and Germany, especially his last, the Westerkerk in Amsterdam, built on a Greek cross plan (1620). His most important secular buildings are the Amsterdam Exchange (1608) and Delft Town Hall (1618). In domestic architecture he simplified and classicized the traditional tall, gable-fronted Amsterdam house, introducing the ORDERS and reducing the number of steps in the gables. His works were engraved and published by Salomon de Bray as *Architectura moderna* (1631).

Rosenberg 1977.

**Keystone**. The central wedge-shaped stone at the crown of an arch or a rib vault, put in last, sometimes carved. *See* Fig. 6.

**Khan**. An urban CARAVANSERAI or inn for travellers located in a town.

**Khanqah**. In Islamic architecture, an endowed place of residence and hostel for Sufis – Muslim mystics – similar to a MADRASA and usually consisting of a court surrounded by a cloister giving access to individual cells on three sides and a hall for communal assembly and prayer on the QIBLA side. Of the earliest (C10) built in Iran none survives. After Sufism was introduced to Egypt in 1173, several were founded in Cairo, culminating in that in the complex of Baibars al-Jashankir (1307–10), with accommodation for 100 residents and 300 visitors, and that of Faraj b. Baruq (1400–10), an impressive structure with minarets flanking the portal and two large domes. Others were built in Syria, Anatolia, Iran, Afghanistan and Central Asia, often in association with shrines of venerated *Shaykhs* (spiritual leaders), e.g. Char Bakr outside Bukhara, Uzbekistan (1668–9), where a *khanqah* joins a mosque to a madrasa in a single architectural composition.

**Kheker cresting**. A decorative motive used by the Ancient Egyptians.

**Khmer architecture**. The architectural style of the Khmer state which was founded in northern Cambodia in the C9, expanded into present-day Vietnam, Laos and Thailand in the C11, but retracted in the C13. All the surviving buildings are religious (Hindu or Buddhist) and dedicated to a succession of god-kings, durable materials being reserved for this purpose, while all other buildings, apart from fortifications and some portions of royal palaces, were of wood and have

perished. Temples were built of stone, brick and LATERITE, without mortar but held together by iron clamps. As the only means of roofing was by corbelled vaults, interior spaces are of limited width. This is essentially an architecture of mass embellished with a jungly luxuriance of relief carving in a distinctive style often of the greatest refinement. Hinduism was introduced from India, but Indian prototypes had more influence on the ideas expressed than the means of expression. The earliest notable buildings are at Roluos, the site of Hariharalaya, the first capital, north of the Tonlé Sap (great lake): two temples partially survive, Preak Ko (879) and Lolei (893), with aligned sanctuary towers like Indian SIKHARAS, of brick covered with stucco. The nearby Bakong temple (881) is of the same materials but more grandiose, with a dominant central tower on a stepped pyramidal base, conceived like many Indian temples as a symbolic representation of Mount Meru, the centre of Hindu cosmology. The form of the temple mountain was fully developed in the Bakheng temple (*c*.900) with a logical coherence never found in India, a pyramid of five stages crowned by a quincunx of towers and a total of 104 smaller towers of exactly the same form on the platforms and surrounding the base. This was raised in a new city some 20 km. (12 miles) northwest of the group at Roluos on the edge of an area some 96 km. (60 miles) square, now known as Angkor ('capital city' in Khmer). The majority of important Khmer monuments are at Angkor, though the richest of all, Banteay Srei (968), is some 32 km. (20 miles) away. This is a relatively small temple dedicated to Vishnu, built entirely of sandstone (previously used only for attached reliefs) carved all over with figures and foliage – an extraordinarily complex work of sculpture as much as architecture. At

Angkor the most distinctive buildings are temple mountains, always on the same cosmological plan, and with *trompe l'œil* devices to make them appear still taller than they are: each of the five stages of the pyramid of diminished height, the central flight of stairs leading up to the sanctuaries slightly narrower at each level, and their risers which demand a giant's stride at the base reduced to a human scale as they reach the top. Pre Rup (961), Ta Keo (968–1000) and the Baphuon (1050–66) were followed by the finest, Angkor Wat (*c.*1115–50), where the basic scheme was expanded (covering 1,860 sq. m. (20,000 sq. ft), it is probably the largest temple in the world), enriched with vast areas of carved reliefs and much elaborated with covered galleries surrounding the base and at the upper level enclosing four courts with dramatic spatial effects unprecedented in Khmer architecture. After the sack of the city by invaders in 1177, Jayavarman VII, who became king in 1181, founded a new capital, Angkor Thom, laid out on a square plan 3 km (nearly 2 miles) across, surrounded by a moat and defensive walls, approached over a causeway flanked by giant statues and through a monumental gate. He was a Buddhist (Mahayanan) and although the Bayon (*c.*1190–1218), the temple mountain in the centre of his city, followed the same scheme as its Hindu predecessors, gigantic faces of the Bodhisattva Lokesvara (probably with his features) look out to the four points of the compass from each of its many towers. He also founded Buddhist monasteries (e.g. Ta Prohm and Preah Khan), single-storey with symmetrical disposition of cloisters, as emphatically horizontal as the temple mountains are vertical. Other buildings commissioned by Jayavarman VII include the beautiful landscape architecture complex of Neak Pean, a small temple rising in the centre of a square

reservoir surrounded by four smaller water-tanks, at Angkor; a new city, Banteay Chmar, with a temple mountain nearly as large as the Bayon (now in ruins) some 130 km. (80 miles) to the north-west, as well as roads, bridges, hospitals, rest-houses, etc. In outposts of the Khmer empire, beyond the present-day frontiers of Cambodia, there are fine though relatively small Khmer temples: in Laos, Wat Phu (C10–11), near Champasak; in Thailand, Phanom Rung (C10–12) and Khao Phra Viharn (C11), both on hill-top sites, and Muang Tam (late C10) and Phimai (late C11).

**Kibbutzim**. Self-contained and self-supporting collective settlements built in open country by and for Jewish immigrants to Palestine engaged in agriculture, hand-crafts and sometimes light industry, with communal living accommodation and all property held in common. The first was established by Russian refugees in 1909. From the 1920s they were often designed by leading architects, *see* ISRAELI ARCHITECTURE.

**Kienast**, Dieter (b.1945). Swiss landscape architect. His layouts are marked by striking simplicity of spaces and forms, influenced by Minimalist art, though he has worked mainly with plants rather than inert materials. The most notable are the Stadtpark, Wettingen, Germany (1982), and the surroundings of the Psychiatrischen Klinik, Chur, Switzerland (1994). He has also designed many private gardens.

**Kiesler**, Frederick John (1890–1965). Austrian-born American architect, trained in Vienna, who joined DE STIJL but emigrated to the USA in 1926. He specialized in theatre design (Universal Theatre, Woodstock, New Jersey, 1933; Festival Theatre, Ellenville, NY, 1955) and in endless form-continuous space designs of which his Endless House project (1958–9) and Universal Theatre Project (1961) were notable. He designed the Grotto for New Being, New Harmony, Indiana (1963), and the Shrine of the Book, Jerusalem (1959–65 with A. Bartos). His book *Inside the Endless House* was published posthumously in New York in 1966.

D. Bogner (ed.), *F.K. Architekt, Maler, Bildhauer 1890–1965*, Vienna 1988; L. Phillips, *F.K.*, New York 1989.

**Kikutake**, Kiyonori (b.1928). Leading member of the Japanese METABOLISM movement, of which his Sky House, Tokyo (1958), and Ocean City project (1962) were notable examples. The latter was partly realized at Aquapolis, Okinawa (1975), and was also taken up later by TANGE for his Tokyo Bay project. Kikutake's later work includes the Administrative Building at the Izumo Shrine, Shimane (1963); the concertina-like Civic Centre, Mijakonojo (1966); the Osaka Expo '70 Tower, Osaka (1970); the City Hall, Hagi (1974); the Tokeen Hotel, Yonago (1972); and the enormous Edo–Tokyo Museum, Tokyo (1980–92), clad in glaring white fluorine-resin coated fibre-reinforced concrete. He published *Concepts and Planning* (Tokyo 1978).

Ross 1978; Bognar 1985.

**Kiley**, Daniel Urban (b.1912). American landscape architect trained at Harvard where, with ECKBO and ROSE, he rebelled against the conservative teaching of garden design in favour of an ecological, Thoreau-inspired approach, creating a symbiosis between Man and Nature. His first major work, the landscaping for Eero SAARINEN's J. Irwin Miller House, Columbus, Indiana (1957), successfully integrated building and garden in a free-form non-orthogonal design. This was followed by more geometrically ordered

conjunctions of landscape and architecture, e.g. his layout for SOM's US Air Force Academy, Colorado Springs (1956–68). His later works range from the approaches to Saarinen's Dulles Airport, Washington, DC (1958), to the terrace and roof-gardens with 38,000 trees, shrubs and vines of varying textures and growing habits covering ROCHE's Oakland Museum, Oakland, California (1969); the 1.6 hectare (4 acre) plaza surrounding PEI's Allied Bank Tower, Dallas, Texas, transformed into a huge cascade with 263 bubbler fountains punctuated with boxed cypress trees (1987); the Henry Moore Sculpture Garden with an axial plan, terracing and long *allées* recalling vistas by Le Nôtre, for the Nelson Atkins Museum of Art, Kansas City (1987–9); the North Carolina National Bank terrace garden at Tampa, Florida (1988), and the roof-garden of indigenous plants over POLSHEK's Nashantucket Pequot Museum and Research Center (1993).

Walker and Simo 1994; Cerver 1995.

**King-post**, *see* ROOF.

**Kiosk**. A light open pavilion or summerhouse, usually supported by pillars and common in Turkey and Persia. European adaptations are used mainly in gardens, as band-stands, for example, or for small shops selling newspapers.

**Kitagawara**, Atsushi (b.1951), *see* JAPANESE ARCHITECTURE.

**Kleanthis**, Stamathios (1802–62), *see* GREEK ARCHITECTURE.

**Kleihues**, Josef Paul (b.1933), *see* GERMAN ARCHITECTURE.

**Klengel**, Wolf Caspar von (1630–91), *see* GERMAN ARCHITECTURE.

**Klenze**, Leo von (1784–1864), a north German, was a pupil of GILLY in Berlin, and then of DURAND and PERCIER and

FONTAINE in Paris. He was architect to King Jérome at Kassel in 1804–13, and to King Ludwig I in Munich from 1816. Klenze was at heart a Grecian, but he was called upon to work in other styles as well, and did so resourcefully. His chief Grecian buildings are the Glyptothek, or Sculpture Gallery (1816–34) – the earliest of all special public museum buildings – and the Propylaea, both in Munich. The Propylaea was begun in 1846, a late date for so purely Grecian a design. Grecian also, strangely enough, is that commemorative temple of German worthies, the Walhalla near Regensburg (designed 1816–21, built 1830–42), a Doric peripteral temple. Grecian, too, is his addition to the Hermitage Museum, St Petersburg (1839–49), more Ancient Roman his Befreiungshalle near Kelheim (1836–63). But as early as 1816 Klenze did a neo-Renaissance palace (Palais Leuchtenberg), the earliest in Germany, even if anticipated in France. This was followed by the Königsbau of the Royal Palace, Munich (1826) – which has affinities with the Palazzo Pitti – and the freer, more dramatic Festsaalbau of the same palace (1832). In addition, Klenze's Allerheiligen church, again belonging to the palace (1827), is – at the king's request – neo-Byzantine. *See also* GÄRTNER.

Honour 1979; O. Hederer, *L. von K. Personlichkeit und Werk*, Munich (1964) 1981; Watkin and Mellinghoff 1987.

**Klerk**, Michel de (1884–1923). Leading member of the Amsterdam School who realized their EXPRESSIONIST aims on an urban scale – largely for working-class housing in Amsterdam, e.g. the eccentric Spaarndammerburt housing (1913–19) and the more sober De Dageraad housing (1920–22).

S. S. Frank, *M. de K. 1884–1923. An Architect of the Amsterdam School*, Ann Arbor 1984; M. Bock *et al.* (eds.), *M. de K. (1884–1923) Architect and Artist of the Amsterdam School*, Rotterdam 1997.

**Klint**, Peder Vilhelm Jensen (1853–1930). Danish architect famous chiefly for his Grundtvig church at Copenhagen, won in competition in 1913 but, after further development of the design, built 1919–26. With its steeply gabled brick façade, all of a stepped organ-pipe design, and with its interior, Gothic in feeling, it stands mid-way between the HISTORICISM of the C19 and the EXPRESSIONISM of 1920, a parallel in certain ways to BERLAGE's earlier Exchange. The surrounding buildings, forming one composition with the church, are of 1924–6. Klint's son Kaare (1888–1954) was one of the most distinguished of modern Danish furniture designers.

Hitchcock 1977.

**Knapped flint**. Flint split in two and laid so that the smooth black surfaces of the split sides form the facing of a wall; found especially in East Anglia. *See also* FLUSHWORK.

**Kneeler**. The block of stone set at the top of a brick or stone wall to finish the eaves of a parapet or coping; also called a pad-stone, kneestone or skew.

**Knight**, Richard Payne (1750–1824). English country gentleman and landscape gardening theorist, began in 1772 to build Downton Castle for himself: rough, irregular (the plan is anti-symmetrical rather than asymmetrical), and boldly medieval outside, smooth, elegant and distinctly neo-classical within, it is the prototype of the picturesque country house 'castle' which was to remain popular for half a century. In 1794 he published *The Landscape – a Didactic Poem* attacking 'Capability' BROWN's smooth and artificial style of landscape gardening. It was dedicated to Uvedale PRICE, who published a lengthy reply differing on points of detail. Knight's much longer *Analytical Enquiry into the Principles of Taste* (1805) examines the PICTURESQUE philosophically.

M. Clarke and N. Penny, *The Arrogant Connoisseur*. *R.P.K.*, Manchester 1982; Summerson 1991; A. Ballantyne, *Architecture, Landscape and Liberty*. *R.P.K. and the Picturesque*, Cambridge 1997.

**Knobelsdorff**, Georg Wenzeslaus von (1699–1753). Court architect to Frederick the Great, with whom he was on terms of close friendship and whose sophisticated, eclectic tastes he faithfully mirrored although they quarrelled over the designs for Sanssouci. He was a Prussian aristocrat and began his career in the army, but in 1729 resigned his Captain's commission to train as a painter. By 1733 he was already on friendly terms with Frederick (then Crown Prince), for whom he built a little circular temple of Apollo in his garden in the garrison town of Neu-Ruppin. Frederick then enabled him to visit Italy and after his return commissioned him to enlarge the old border house of Rheinsberg, near Berlin (1737–40). Immediately after Frederick's accession to the throne in 1740 Knobelsdorff was sent off to Dresden and Paris to prepare himself for more ambitious projects. He added a wing to Monbijou for the Queen Mother (1740–42) and a wing to Charlottenburg for the king (1742–6) with a very grand, rich, colourful interior plastered with Rococo motifs (partly destroyed in the Second World War). In 1741 he began the Berlin opera house with a less exuberant interior and a severely Palladian exterior which owes much to English neo-Palladian models (burnt out 1843, renewed by K. F. Langhans; seriously damaged 1945 but now restored). While this was going forward he was appointed Surveyor General of Royal Palaces and Parks, Director in Chief of all buildings in the royal provinces, and a member of the Prussian Council of Ministers. In 1744 work began on the large Stadtschloss at Potsdam, colourful outside and in, and with one of the richest of all Rococo interiors. He began Sanssouci, Potsdam, in 1745 in close collaboration with the king, who provided the general design. (Frederick's original sketch survives.) In 1746 he quarrelled with the king, who dismissed him and thus ended his architectural career, though he made posthumous amends by writing the 'Éloge de Knobelsdorff' which was read at the Berlin Academy in 1753. (His sketch design for a palace for Prince Heinrich in Unter den Linden, Berlin, was built by J. Boumann, 1748–66. It is now the Humboldt University.)

Hempel 1965; H. J. Kaddatz, *G.W. von K.*, Leipzig and Munich 1983.

**Knöffel**, Johann Christoph (1686–1752). German architect, a contemporary in Dresden of CHIAVERI and LONGUELUNE and was much influenced by the French Classicism of the latter. His Wackerbarth Palais, Dresden (1723–8, destroyed 1945), and Kurlander Palais, Dresden (1728–9, destroyed 1945), were elegant examples of restrained pilastered town architecture. In 1734 he became Oberlandbaumeister in Dresden and in 1737 began his masterpiece, the Brühl Palais (destroyed 1899). He rebuilt the large hunting-lodge, Hubertusberg, between 1743 and 1751 and completed his rival Chiaveri's Hofkirche in Dresden after Chiaveri returned to Rome in 1748.

Hempel 1965; W. Hentschel and A. May, *J.C.K.*, Berlin 1973.

**Knotted columns**. A stone support carved in the form of two or four columns with their shafts tied into a knot, occasionally found in Romanesque architecture.

**Kobori Enshu** (1579–1649). Japanese tea-ceremony master and from 1613 principal architect of the Shogunate in Kyoto, where he rebuilt Nijo Castle (1624–6). He is said to have developed the SHOIN style and to have designed several of the finest gardens in Kyoto, including those of Nijo Castle and the east garden of the Daitoku-ji.

**Koch**, Gaetano (1849–1910), *see* ITALIAN ARCHITECTURE.

**Koenig**, Pierre (b.1925), *see* CASE STUDY HOUSES.

**Kohn Pederson Fox (KPF)**. A New York partnership formed in 1976 by A. Eugene Kohn (b.1930), William Pederson (b.1938) and Sheldon Fox (b.1930). Their dramatically curved glass and metal skyscraper at 333 Wacker Drive, Chicago (1979–83), followed by the historicizing Proctor & Gamble General Offices, Cincinnati, Ohio (1983–5), made their name. Their contributions to SOM's Canary Wharf development, London, followed, with Westendstrasse L, Frankfurt-am-Main (1990–93).

S. R. Chao and T. D. Abramson, *KPF Buildings and Projects 1976–86*, New York 1987.

**Komonen**, Markku (b.1945), *see* FINNISH ARCHITECTURE.

**Kondo**. The main hall of a Japanese Buddhist monastery.

**Koolhaas**, Rem (b.1944). Dutch architect, trained in London and New York where he won the Progressive Architecture Prize in 1974 with Laurinda Hope Spear (*see* ARQUITECTONICA). In 1975 he founded OMA (Office for Metropolitan Architecture) in London (also in Rotterdam from 1980) and became known internationally following the publication of his influential *Delirious New York* (1978, reissued 1996), promoting

the exceptional, excessive and extreme in what he called a 'culture of congestion'. His built work ranges from small private houses (Patio Villas, Rotterdam, 1984–8; Villa dall'Ava, St Cloud, France, 1985–91) to large public commissions (Netherlands Dance Theatre, The Hague, 1984–7; Kunsthalle, Rotterdam, 1987–92; Nexus World Kashii Condominium, Fukuoka, Japan, 1991). In 1988 he was appointed head architect of the Eurolille project, for which he designed the master-plan and also the Grand Palais Convention Centre (1990–94). His *S.M.L.XL. (Small, Medium, Large, Extra-Large)*, was published in New York (1996).

J. Lucan (ed.), *OMA – Rem Koolhaas*, Cambridge, Mass. 1991.

**Korb**, Hermann (1656–1735). German architect who began as a carpenter and was promoted architect by Duke Anton-Ulrich of Brunswick-Wolfenbüttel. He visited Italy in 1691, then supervised the construction of the Schloss at Salzdahlum designed by Johann Balthasar Lauterbach (1660–94) – a vast building with features anticipating DIENTZENHOFER's Pommersfelden and HILDEBRANDT's Upper Belvedere, but of mainly timber construction faced to simulate stone (demolished 1813). Also of wood was the interesting library he erected at Wolfenbüttel (1706–10). It was centrally planned (on the advice of Leibniz) with an oval interior lit by windows in the dome. His only surviving building of note is the church of the Holy Trinity, Wolfenbüttel (1705), with two tiers of galleries creating an octagonal central space.

Hempel 1965; G. Gerkens, *Das fürstliche Lustschloss Salzdahlum und sein Erbauer Herzog Anton Ulrich von Braunschweig-Wolfenbüttel*, Brunswick 1974.

**Korsmo**, Arne (1900–1986), *see* NORWEGIAN ARCHITECTURE.

**Koteřa**, Jan (1871–1923), *see* CZECH ARCHITECTURE.

**Krakauer**, Leopold (1890–1956), *see* ISRAELI ARCHITECTURE.

**Krebs**, Konrad (1491–1540), *see* GERMAN ARCHITECTURE.

**Krejcar**, Joromir (1895–1949), *see* CZECH ARCHITECTURE.

**Kremlin**. A citadel or fortified enclosure within a Russian town, notably that in Moscow.

**Krier**, Leon (b.1946). Luxembourg architect, he worked for STIRLING 1968–70 and settled in London, where his anti-modern crusade to revitalize both vernacular and classicizing architecture was influential, but his only buildings to date have been small and somewhat 'folksy', of traditional wood construction at 'Seaside' in Florida (1987). In 1989 he was chosen by the Prince of Wales to plan the Duchy of Cornwall's Poundbury development in Dorchester, a new small town which illustrates his anti-technocratic theories in a nostalgic retreat to the past. His essays and projects were published in 1993 as *L.K. Architecture and Urban Design 1967–92* (London) and in 1996 as *Architecture, choix ou fatalité* (Paris).

**Krier**, Rob (b.1938). Luxembourg architect, trained in Germany and working since 1975 in Vienna. He is as anti-modern as his brother Leon, but a number of his projects have been realized, notably in Berlin (Rauchstrasse, 1982–4, and Ritterstrasse, begun 1982 and incorporating a reconstruction of SCHINKEL's Feilnerhaus of 1828–9). He has published *Rational Architecture* (London 1978), *Architectural Composition* (London 1988) and *Monographie* (London 1993).

**Kroll**, Lucien (b.1927). Belgian architect, trained in Brussels. His Medical Faculty, University of Louvain (1968–72), is a large-scale essay in controlled anarchy in which users participated and continue to participate in the elaboration of the design. It was acclaimed as a monument to the May '68 student uprisings. His equally radical 'rehabilitations' at ZUP Perseigne, Alençon, France (1978), were followed by further participatory residential complexes at Cergy-Pontoise (1977–9) and at Marne-la-Vallée (1980). His Open School and half-submerged Maison de l'Environment, Belfort (1991), are notable. He published *Architecture of Complexity* (London 1986).

W. Pehnt, *L.K.*, Stuttgart 1987.

**Krubsacius**, Friedrich August (1718–89). German architect and architectural theorist, author of *Betrachtungen über den wahren Geschmack der Alten in der Baukunst* (Dresden 1747) attacking the Baroque style and reverting to the humanist idea that 'the noblest structure, man, the perfect proportions and graceful symmetry of his figure, were the first standards for architectural invention'. Though indebted to French theorists, he thought little of French architecture. He became royal architect and in 1764 professor of architecture at the new Academy of Arts in Dresden. But in his buildings he remained faithful to the Baroque. The most notable were the Neues Schloss at Neuwitz (1766–75; destroyed) and the Landhaus in Dresden (1770–76; burnt out 1945).

M. A. von Luttichau, *Die deutsche Ornamentkritik im 18 Jahrhundert*, Hildesheim 1983.

**Krumpper**, Hans (*c.*1570–1635), *see* GERMAN ARCHITECTURE.

**Kurakawa**, Kisho Noriaki (b.1934). Japanese architect who began in TANGE's studio and became prominent in the METABOLISM movement both for his writings, *Metabolism* (Tokyo 1960), *Con-*

*cept of Metabolism* (Tokyo 1972), *Metabolism in Architecture* (London 1977), and for his projects, of which Wall Cluster (1960) and Helix City (1961) were exemplary. Metabolism was fully expressed in his capsule buildings, e.g. Takara Beautillion, Expo '70, Osaka, and Nagakin Capsule Tower, Tokyo (1972), consisting of 144 prefabricated capsules bolted to reinforced concrete shafts, a prototype for mobile urban society residential architecture. His later buildings combine the modern and traditional, east and west, in a narrative symbiosis, e.g. Fukuoka Bank Home Offices, Fukuoka (1975); Saitama Prefectural Museum of Modern Art, Urawa (1982); National Bunraku Theatre, Osaka (1983); the Wacoal Kojimachi Building, Tokyo (1984); the Modern Art Museum, Nagoya (1987); the City Museum, Hiroshima (1988); Nara City Museum of Photography, Nara (1992). He published *New Wave Japanese Architecture* (London–Berlin 1993) and *The Philosophy of Symbiosis* (London (1990) 1994).

Ross 1978; Bognar 1985; F. Chaslin, *K.K.*, Tokyo 1988; A. Guilheux, *K.K.*, Paris 1997.

# L

**La Vallée**, Simon de (d.1642), son of a
French architect, settled in Sweden in
1637, becoming royal architect in 1639.
He designed the Riddarhus in Stockholm
(1641–2), derived from de BROSSE's
Palais Luxembourg in Paris. He was succeeded as royal architect by his son Jean
(1620–96), who travelled and studied in
France, Italy and Holland between 1646
and 1649. He completed his father's Riddarhus (with Justus VINGBOONS, who
designed the façades), built the
Oxenstjerna Palace, Stockholm (c.1650–
54), which introduced the Roman
*palazzo* style, and designed the Katheri-
nenkirka, Stockholm (1656), on a centralized plan probably derived from de
KEYSER, as well as various palaces in
Stockholm (e.g. for Field-Marshal Wran-
gel) and country houses (Castle
Skokloster).

Paulsson 1958; T. O. Nordberg, *De la
V. Ein Architektfamilij Frankrike Holland
ech Sverige*, Stockholm 1970.

**Label**, *see* HOOD-MOULD.

**Label-stop** or **head stop**. An ornamental or figural BOSS at the beginning and
end of a HOOD-MOULD.

**Labrouste**,       Pierre-François-Henri
(1801–75), French architect who won
the Grand Prix in 1824, and was in Rome
1824–30. After his return to Paris he
opened a teaching *atelier* which became
the centre of Rationalist teaching in
France. His Rationalism appears at its
most courageous in the interior of his
only famous work, the Library of Ste
Geneviève by the Panthéon in Paris

(1838–50). Here iron is shown frankly
in columns and vault, and endowed with
all the slenderness of which, in contrast
to stone, it is capable. Labrouste's is the
first monumental public building in
which iron is thus accepted. The façade
is in a nobly restrained Cinquecento style
with large, even, round-arched windows,
and there again, in comparison with the
debased Italianate or the neo-Baroque of
BEAUX ARTS type, which just then was
becoming current, Labrouste is on the
side of reason. The London architect
James Bunstone Bunning (1802–63), in
his Coal Exchange of 1846–9, since
demolished, was as bold in his use of iron,
but as an architect was lacking in the
taste and discipline of Labrouste. Between
1854 and 1875 Labrouste also built the
reading-room and the stack-rooms of the
Bibliothèque Nationale, again proudly
displaying his iron structure.

Hitchcock 1977; P. Saddy, *H.L. architecte 1801–75*, Paris 1978; Van Zanten
1987.

**Labyrinth**. An intricate, tortuous and
intentionally confusing network or maze
of pathways, usually walled or hedged,
through which it is difficult to find the
way out without a clue, as in that of the
Minotaur in Ancient Greek mythology.
One is shown on a Minoan coin and
Pliny mentioned one in the palace at
Knossos, Crete, together with others in
Egypt, notably at Hamara, as being among
the Wonders of the World. A few built
labyrinths are recorded in the Ancient
Greek world (e.g. at Epidauros and
Didyma); in Ancient Rome they figured

on mosaic pavements. In medieval Europe they acquired cosmological significance when carved on the floor or walls of cathedrals, that at Piacenza being compared to the universe in a related inscription. In the C17 and C18 cut turf labyrinths, with or without hedges, became a feature of garden design, e.g. at Versailles and Hampton Court, the latter by George London and Henry WISE (1689–1702). Labyrinths are still made as ornamental puzzles in gardens and parks.

H. Ladendorf, *L.*, Berlin 1966; H. Kern, *L.*, Munich 1982; A. Fisher, *The Art of Maze*, London 1990; A. Fisher and H. Loxton, *Secrets of the Maze*, London 1997.

**Laced windows**. Windows pulled visually together vertically by strips, usually in brick of a different colour from that of the wall, which continue vertically the lines of the window surrounds. It was a popular motif *c.*1720 in England.

**Lacing course**, *see* COURSE.

**Lacunar**. A panelled or coffered ceiling: also the sunken panels or COFFERING in such a ceiling.

**Lady chapel**. A chapel dedicated to the Virgin, usually built east of the CHANCEL and forming a projection from the main building; in England it is normally rectangular in plan.

**Lafever**, Minard (1798–1854). American architect whose illustrated books contributed, in the wake of those by HAVILAND and BENJAMIN, to the Greek Revival in the USA. He published *The Modern Building Guide* (New York 1833), *The Beauties of Modern Architecture* (New York 1835) and *The Architectural Instructor* (New York 1856). He is also notable for his churches, of which he built some forty, mostly neo-Gothic, e.g. Church of

St Ann and the Holy Trinity, Brooklyn, New York (1844–7).

J. Landy, *The Architecture of M.L.*, New York 1970.

**Lajta**, Béle (1875–1920), *see* HUNGARIAN ARCHITECTURE.

**Lambrequin**. A fringe-like ornament, popular during the Louis XIV and Régence periods. Derived from the scarf worn across a knight's helmet and its stylized representation in heraldry, it later became a deeply scalloped piece of drapery ornament.

**Lancet arch**, *see* ARCH.

**Lancet window**. A slender pointed-arched window, much used in the early C13 in England. *See* Fig. 71.

Fig. 71 Lancet window

**Land Art** or **Earth Art**. A trend of the late 1960s and 1970s, concerned with the notion of 'sites and non-sites' expressed in large-scale installations sometimes created with earth-moving equipment, e.g. Robert Smithson's Spiral Jetty in Great Salt Lake, Utah (1970). Land Art differs conceptually from LANDSCAPE ARCHITECTURE, though Christo's wrapped landscapes are sometimes ambivalent, e.g. his *Running Fence* (1976) in Sonoma and Marin County, California.

**Landmarks Preservation Commission**, *see* HISTORICAL PRESERVATION.

**Landscape architecture**. The art and science of creating open-air spaces as environments for human life, i.e. the layout of gardens and parks (*see* LANDSCAPE GARDEN; PARK; PUBLIC PARK), the planning of residential, educational, commercial and industrial sites (*see* BUSINESS PARK; CAMPUS; INDUSTRIAL PARK; URBAN DESIGN) and roads (*see* MOTORWAY; PARKWAY). *See also* LAND ART, which is conceptually different.

Gardens, as distinct from vegetable plots and orchards, were planted as adjuncts to religious and secular buildings from the 2nd millennium BC in Egypt and Mesopotamia; and large areas were enclosed and developed as royal parks, mainly but not exclusively for hunting, in Mesopotamia, Persia and China from the 1st millennium BC. The earliest recorded gardens in China and Japan are notable for their irregular planning and variety, reflecting aspects of their religious and philosophical beliefs (*see* CHINESE ARCHITECTURE; JAPANESE ARCHITECTURE); elsewhere in Asia geometrical planning prevailed, as in the symbolic CHAHAR BAGH (*see* PERSIAN ARCHITECTURE; INDIAN AND PAKISTANI ARCHITECTURE). In Ancient Greece and Rome peristyle gardens were created as open-air extensions of urban houses, as at Pompeii, and large parks were also laid out, exploiting natural features but also incorporating artificial waterworks, as at Nero's Golden House, Rome, Hadrian's Villa, Tivoli, and Pliny the Younger's two villas as described in his letters. During the European Middle Ages the gardens of Islamic Spain and Sicily were the most elaborate but large parks were laid out around castles and abbeys in England, Flanders and France, e.g. at Hesdin, France, with ingenious waterworks (begun 1295, destroyed 1553). From the C15 in Italy (later elsewhere) demands for symmetry and clear proportional relationships governed the design of gar-

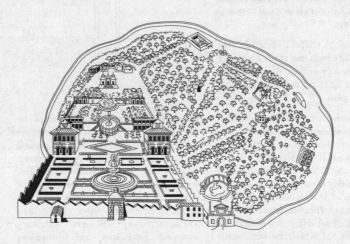

Fig. 72 Villa Lante, near Viterbo, Italy

dens as of buildings. The Florentine court
sculptor Baccio Bandinelli (1488–1560)
wrote that 'what is built should regulate
and be superior to what is planted'. Axial
plans predominated as at LIGORIO's
scenographic garden of Villa d'Este,
Tivoli (1565–72). But here as elsewhere
in Italy – e.g. Villa Lante, near Viterbo,
attributed to VIGNOLA (1566–73) (*see*
Fig. 72), and ORSINI's Bomarzo (1552–
80) – layouts were devised with water-
works, buildings and statuary to express
historical, religious or philosophical
themes according to programmes as complex as those for the cycles of wall-
paintings inside palaces of the same
period. Italian gardens were a source of
inspiration in France, where treatises on
garden design, emphasizing such decorative features as PARTERRES, were published from the early C17 by BOYCEAU
and MOLLET. At Vaux-le-Vicomte a new
standard for geometrical planning on the
grandest scale was set by LE NÔTRE,
whose guiding principles were later formulated and published by Antoine-
Joseph Dézallier d'Argenville (1680–
1765) in his *Théorie et la pratique du jardin*
*age* (Paris 1709, frequently reprinted and
translated), influencing the design of gardens and parks throughout Europe.
Reaction against the rigidity and ostentation of this style led in England to the
LANDSCAPE GARDEN, which reflected its
owner's beliefs and ideals – religious or
philosophical, social or political – in an
apparently more natural manner and by
the end of the C18 revolutionized the
Western conception of landscape architecture by subordinating buildings to
their environment. And this, in turn,
resulted eventually in an increasingly
close relationship between URBAN
DESIGN and landscape architecture, notably with such pioneers as ALPHAND,
LENNÉ, PAXTON, PENNETHORNE and
OLMSTED.

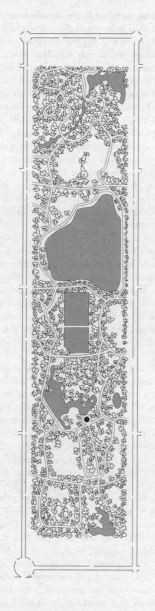

Fig. 73  Central Park, New York

The term 'landscape architecture' was first used in its present-day sense in 1840 by LOUDON in his edition of REPTON's writings. (Previously it had been used for depictions of architecture in landscape paintings, as by C. L. Meason in 1828.) But it was not until 1862 that the term 'landscape architect' was used by Olmsted and VAUX in connection with their project for Central Park, New York (see Fig. 73). Such prominent large-scale public works stimulated professionalism and the American Society of Landscape Architects, the first organization of its kind, followed in 1899. An academic course in landscape architecture was established at Harvard University in 1900 and also, as this was an all-male institution, at Groton, Massachusetts, in 1901, entitled the Lowthorpe School of Landscape Architecture, Gardening and Horticulture for Women. The British Institute of Landscape Architecture was founded in 1929 and the International Federation of Landscape Architecture in 1948. Members of these bodies, to whom the title 'landscape architect' is legally restricted in the USA and UK, are nowadays increasingly engaged in the conservation of the natural landscape and related ecological issues (see notably McHARG), as well as in the laying out of public parks, campuses, motorways, etc. by, among others, BURLE MARX, COLVIN, ECKBO, HALPRIN, JELLICOE, LASSUS, LATZ, SASAKI and WALKER.

G. and S. Jellicoe, *The Landscape of Man*, London (1975) 1995; C. Thacker, *The History of Gardens*, Berkeley 1979; G. and S. Jellicoe *et al.*, *The Oxford Companion to Gardens*, Oxford 1986; Lazzaro 1990; S. Lyall, *Designing the New Land*, London 1992; P. Walker and M. Simo, *Invisible Gardens*, Cambridge, Mass. 1994; C. Zapatka, *L'architettura del paesaggio americano*, Milan 1995; W. Weilacher, *Between L.A. and Land Art*, Basel/Berlin/Boston 1996.

**Landscape garden.** A PARK with irregular plantations of trees, usually on undulating ground with winding waterways, designed to realize an idealized vision of a natural landscape, sometimes intentionally reminiscent of the classical Virgilian landscapes of Claude's paintings. Though intended primarily for aesthetic enjoyment, it might also include farmland (see FERME ORNÉE) and game reserves. C16–17 Italian, French and English parks often included areas of woodland (*boschetti* or BOSQUETS) as adjuncts to axial vistas and flat parterres. But extensive parks in which symmetry and geometrical forms were avoided first appeared in C18 England and became the most important C18 British contribution to the visual arts, e.g. Stourhead Park, Wiltshire (begun 1743).

In 1685 Sir William Temple had contrasted the monotonous regularity of contemporary European gardens with the irregularity or SHARAWADGI of Chinese gardens. The Earl of Shaftesbury in *The Moralists* (1709) contrasted the beauties of the natural world where 'neither art nor the conceit or the caprice of man has spoiled their genuine order' with the 'formal mockery of princely gardens'. Extolling 'wilderness' as the work of God, he suggested that gardens should represent the divine order. Other writers, notably Addison and Pope, praised landscape gardens for being not only aesthetically but morally and – as expressions of 'liberty' – politically preferable to the 'unnatural' gardens of the French C17 style, most of which were subsequently destroyed in Britain as were many on the European continent as well.

SWITZER in 1715–18 was the first to publish practical advice on landscape gardening, and was followed by others, e.g. HALFPENNY, LANGLEY and R. MORRIS. But such works as the poet William Shenstone's *Unconnected Thoughts on Gardening* (1764), William Mason's *The English*

*Garden* (1772) and Horace Walpole's essay *On Modern Gardening* (1780), as well as KNIGHT's and PRICE's contributions to the PICTURESQUE controversy, were probably more influential. A landscape garden required the improvement, but not the complete transformation, of the natural terrain in accord with the *genius loci* or spirit of the place. This was carried out in various ways by BRIDGEMAN and Switzer, who are credited with the earliest landscape gardens, though they retained some geometrical elements. KENT succeeded in merging the garden with the surrounding countryside so that the country house harmonized with rather than dominated its setting, the sunken HA-HA (originally a French device) being one of the means he used. A landscape garden by Kent survives unaltered at Rousham, Oxfordshire (*see* Fig. 74), and there are several surviving landscape gardens by Capability BROWN, who evolved a distinctive style with clumps and belts of trees disposed loosely among lakes, lawns and closely cropped fields. It was criticized by CHAMBERS, who promoted a supposedly Chinese style, and by advocates of the PICTURESQUE who demanded greater ruggedness and variety. REPTON began by following Brown but later reintroduced balustraded terraces with geometrically planned flowerbeds near the house.

In continental Europe translations of Shaftesbury, Addison and Pope diffused the landscape garden concept, which was taken up by WATELET and others, notably by J. J. Rousseau with Julie's 'Elysium' or wild garden in *La Nouvelle Héloise* (1761). Theoretical writings followed: *Théorie des jardins* (Paris 1776) by Jean-Marie Morel (1728–1810), *De la composition des paysages* (Geneva 1777) by Louis-René Girardin, Marquis de Vauvray (1735–1808), *Détails de nouveaux jardins à la mode* (Paris 1776–87) in 21 parts by George Louis Le Rouge (1712–

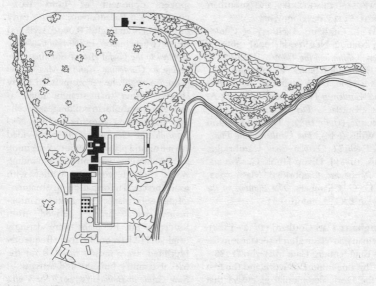

Fig. 74 Landscape garden: Rousham, Oxfordshire, by Kent

78) and HIRSCHFELD's *Theorie der Garten-kunst* (Leipzig 1779–85). Later theoretical works include those by ALPHAND, ANDRÉ, SCKELL and SILVA.

The first landscape garden in continental Europe was that at Wörlitz, Germany, laid out in 1765 by ANHALT-DESSAU, followed by Girardin's at Ermenonville, France (begun 1776 and enshrining Rousseau's tomb), CAMERON's parks at Tsarskoye Selo and Pavlovsk, Russia (1770s), Arkadia near Warsaw (1778–85), BÉLANGER's *jardin anglais* at Bagatelle, Paris (1778–80), the Giardino Inglese, Caserta, Italy (begun 1788), and RUMFORD and Sckell's Englischer Garten, Munich (begun 1789). The earliest recorded landscape garden in America was BYRD's Westover, Virginia (1742), followed by JEFFERSON's park at Monticello in the 1770s. In both the USA and Europe until the C20 the underlying principles of the landscape garden conditioned the layout of PUBLIC PARKS, CAMPUSES, CEMETERIES and suburban GARDEN CITY developments.

M. L. Gothein, *A History of Garden Art*, London/New York (1928) 1966; O. Siren, *China and the Gardens of Europe of the Eighteenth Century*, Washington, DC (1950) 1990; D. Wiebenson, *The Picturesque Garden in France*, London 1978; A. von Buttlar, *Der Landschaftsgarten*, Cologne, (1980) 1989; J. Dixon Hunt and P. Willis (eds.), *The Genius of the Place: The English L.G. 1620–1820*, Cambridge, Mass. 1988; J. Dixon Hunt, *Gardens and the Picturesque*, Cambridge, Mass. 1992; D. D. C. Chambers, *The Planters of the English L.G.*, London 1993.

**Langhans**, Carl Gotthard (1732–1808). German neo-classical architect famous for the Brandenburg Gate in Berlin (1788–91), his one important work and the first of the Doric ceremonial gateways that were to be built all over Europe in the

early C19. The Brandenburg Gate is still C18 in its elegant and rather un-Grecian proportions, as in his Belvedere of 1789–90 in the Charlottenburg park, Berlin. His later buildings were more ponderous and cubic, e.g. the Potsdam Theatre (1795) and the theatre in Gdańsk (Danzig) (1798–1801). He also did the theatre at Charlottenburg Schloss in Berlin (1788–91). His son Carl Ferdinand Langhans (1782–1869) worked under SCHINKEL in the 1830s but continued his father's style in the palace of Kaiser Wilhelm I in Berlin (1836, burnt out 1945 but now restored externally), the old Russian Embassy in Berlin (1840–41) and the theatre at Wrocław (Breslau) (1843).

T. W. Hinrichs, *C.G.L. ein schlesischer Baumeister 1732–1808*, Neudeln (1909) 1981; Watkin and Mellinghoff 1987.

**Langley**, Batty (1696–1751). English writer and illustrator of numerous books on architecture and gardens, an outspoken opponent of Lord BURLINGTON's Palladianism, an early proponent of an English Rococo style and an active Freemason. In *Practical Geometry Applied to the Useful Arts of Building, Surveying, Gardening and Mensuration* (London 1726), he recommended freely curving rather than straight lines 'as exceeding beautiful in building, as in ceilings, parquetting, painting &c.' His *New Principles of Gardening* (1728) provided advice on and plans for layouts combining formal elements with intricately winding walks through copses, together with much practical information on ornamental and useful plants. His remarks on informality were largely derived from SWITZER but his plans were daringly original. His later books, some frequently reprinted, were mostly manuals for the use of country builders and artisans: *A Sure Guide to Builders* (1729), *The Young Builder's Rudiments* (1730), *The Builder's*

*Compleat Chest-Book* (1738), *The Builder's Jewel* (1741, 19th edn 1808). But he became notorious and is now remembered mainly for *Ancient Architecture Restored and Improved* (1742), with illustrations of pavilions, chimney-pieces, door-frames, etc. in the 'Gothic mode', with details derived from Westminster Abbey and other medieval churches but 'improved' and categorized in five 'orders' with rules and proportions. Although he styled himself a practising architect he built little and nothing survives.

Harris 1990.

**Lantern**. A small circular or polygonal turret with windows all round, crowning a roof or dome admitting light to the area below. *See* Fig. 46.

**Lantern cross**. A churchyard cross with lantern-shaped top; usually with sculptured representations on the sides of the top.

**Lantern tower**. A tower open to view from the ground and lit by an upper tier of windows, often over the crossing of a church, e.g. Bell Harry Tower, Canterbury Cathedral.

**Lapidus**, Morris (b.1902). Russian-born American architect, trained in New York where he developed a showy, eye-catching version of Modernism for store fronts, e.g. Rainbow Shop, Brooklyn, New York (1941). Later he adapted this flamboyantly theatrical formula to luxury resort hotels with enormous success, notably at the Fontainebleau Hotel, Miami, Florida (1952–4), which was used as the setting for the film *Goldfinger*. This was followed by similar extravagantly decorated hotels, e.g. Eden Roc Hotel, Miami (1954), Summit Hotel, New York (1957–61), Americana Hotel, Bel Harbor, Florida (1968). He published *Architecture: A Profession and Business*

(New York 1967), *An Architecture of Joy* (Miami 1979) and *Too Much is Never Enough. M.L. – An Autobiography* (New York 1996).

M. Duttmann and F. Schneider (eds.), *M.L. Architect of the American Dream*, Basel/Berlin/Boston 1992.

**Larsen**, Hennink (b.1925), *see* DANISH ARCHITECTURE.

**Lasdun**, Denys Louis (b.1914). English architect who began under Wells COATES in 1935–7 and LUBETKIN in 1938–48 and was a member of both MARS and CIAM. He made his name in the post-Second World War London housing shortage with his technically ingenious and humanly sensitive 'cluster' blocks of flats in Bethnal Green (Usk Street, 1952 and Claredale Street, 1954), followed by the luxury apartment block at 26 St James's Place (1958). His Royal College of Physicians, Regent's Park (1959–64), subtly 'rhymed' with the neighbouring Nash terraces. At the University of East Anglia, Norwich (1962–8), he developed his concept of 'urban landscape' with a remarkable stratified composition of student and other accommodation attuned to the landscape in a development comparable to DE CARLO's contemporary university buildings at Urbino in Italy. His later buildings include the National Theatre, London (1967–76), the European Investment Bank, Luxembourg (1973), and an office block at Milton Gate, London (1986–91). He published *Architecture in the Age of Scepticism* (London 1984) and was knighted in 1977.

W. J. R. Curtis, *D.L. Architecture, City, Landscape*, London 1994.

**Lassurance**, Pierre Cailleteau, known as (1650–1724), *see* HARDOUIN-MANSART, Jules.

**Lassus**, Bernard (b.1929). French landscape architect, theorist and teacher. He began as a painter (under Léger) and from 1960 also worked as a kinetic and installation artist. As a landscape architect his major achievement to date is the Parc de la Corderie Royale, Rochefort-sur-Mer, Charente (1982–96), a uniquely sophisticated THEME PARK laid out around a former naval arsenal (designed by N.-F. BLONDEL, 1666) and ingeniously related visually to the river and old town on either side, with grand sweeping prospects, subtropical vegetation (especially specimens of exotic species introduced by French mariners C17–18), replicas of masts and rigging in a children's play area and a maze of clipped thuya hedges in which sea battles can be re-enacted. His interventions on the French autoroutes have been notable, e.g. his rest-area on the Nîmes–Caissargue autoroute, with a grass avenue terminating in the reconstructed portico of a demolished C19 theatre in Nîmes (1989–91), and the landscaping of the Angers–Tours autoroute (1996). His 1990 project for the Tuileries gardens, Paris, evoked the various levels of its previous history, including MOLLET's layout. With his book *Jardins imaginaires* (Paris 1977), on the 'pop' gardens of obsessed amateurs, and his and C. Layrit's *Autoroutes et paysages* (Paris 1994), his drawings for and extensive written descriptions of his projects including those unrealized, as well as his teaching as a professor in Paris and from 1995 in Philadelphia, he has helped to revolutionize understanding of the meaning and purpose of landscape architecture, past, present and future.

Lyall 1991; Weilach 1996.

**Lassus**, Jean-Baptiste-Antoine (1807–57), *see* VIOLLET-LE-DUC, Eugène-Emanuel.

**Laterite**. A ferruginous substance found only in tropical régions which have heavy rainfall and great heat. When freshly excavated it may be cut with an axe, but it quickly becomes iron-hard when exposed to air. Blocks ground to fit against one another without need for mortar were extensively used as a building material in Cambodia and Thailand. As the surface cannot be carved in relief it was clad with sandstone (in KHMER ARCHITECTURE) or plastered with stucco.

R. L. Pendleton in the *Geographical Review* XXXI (1941), pp. 177–202.

**Latin cross**. A cross with three short arms and a long arm. A Latin cross plan typifies many Western medieval churches, shaped like a cross with a long nave, north and south transepts and a chancel or chevet.

**Lath**. 1. A thin, narrow strip of wood or metal used in making a supporting structure for plaster, shingles, slates or tiles. 2. In Indian Buddhist architecture, a monumental free-standing pillar or *stambha*.

**Latrobe**, Benjamin Henry (1764–1820), the son of a Moravian minister in England, spent his boyhood and youth in England, in Germany, and again in England, where he worked under S. P. COCKERELL as an architect, and under Smeaton as an engineer. He must have been much impressed by SOANE's work. In 1795 he emigrated to America, where he was taken up by JEFFERSON and did the exterior of the Capitol at Richmond, Virginia. In 1798 he moved to Philadelphia, and there built the Bank of Pennsylvania (1799–1801) and in 1800 the Water Works (largely an engineering job). The architecture of these two buildings was resolutely Grecian – the first examples of the GREEK REVIVAL in America – the former Greek Doric, and the latter Ionic. Of the same year 1799 is Sedgeley, the earliest GOTHIC-REVIVAL house in America. In 1803 Latrobe was called in at the Capitol in Washington, and there did some of his noblest interiors, with much vaulting in stone. The work dated from 1803–11, but the majority had to be redone after the fire of 1814, so what one now sees is mostly of Latrobe's maturity. But his most perfect work is probably Baltimore Cathedral (1804–18). Its interior in particular, on an elongated central plan, with the shallow central dome and the segmented tunnel vaults, is as fine as that of any church in the neo-classical style anywhere. Latrobe had at the beginning submitted designs in Gothic as well as classical forms, the Gothic being the earliest Gothic church design in America. Among his other buildings were the Baltimore Exchange (1816–20, destroyed 1904), the 'Old West' of Dickenson College, Carlisle, Pennsylvania (after 1811), and the Louisiana State Bank, New Orleans (begun 1819). Latrobe was the first fully trained architect in the United States. Yet his engineering training made it possible for him, throughout his career, to work as well on river navigation, docks, etc. – a combination which was to become typical of American C19 architects. He was also an advocate of English-style LANDSCAPE GARDENS and with JEFFERSON planned that for the White House, Washington DC. His pupils included MILLS, STRICKLAND and William Small.

Hitchcock 1977; Whiffen and Koeper 1981; J. A. Cohen and C. E. Brownell, *The Papers of B.H.L. Architect and Engineer*, London 1994.

**Lattice window**. A window with diamond-shaped LEADED LIGHTS or with glazing bars arranged like an open-work screen: also, loosely, any hinged window, as distinct from a SASH WINDOW.

**Latz**, Peter (b.1939). German landscape architect, in partnership with his wife Anneliese from 1968. Their first major work was the transformation of Hafeninsel, Saarbrücken – an inland port for shipping coal destroyed in the Second World War – into a public park, retaining the remains of industrial buildings but adding an artificial symbolic ruin as well as gardens, groves of trees and an area for wild flowers (1979–89). This was a prelude to the much larger Landschaftspark Duisberg Nord, begun in 1991, where (perhaps taking a cue from HAAG's Gasworks Park, Seattle) they left intact a huge derelict iron foundry and made use of discarded industrial material, such as steel plates from casting beds, to create a 'narrative park'. This, Latz claimed, owes much to ORSINI's Bomarzo. Their arboretum and public park in Luxembourg city, begun in 1991, is outstanding for the imaginative combinations of geometrical and naturalistic spaces and forms. They have also collaborated notably with T. HERZOG on ecologically correct housing, etc.

Weilacher 1996.

**Laugier**, Marc-Antoine (1713–69) French Jesuit priest and outstanding neo-classical theorist. His *Essai sur l'architecture* (1753) expounds a Rationalist view of classical architecture as a truthful, economic expression of man's need for shelter, based on the hypothetical 'rustic cabin' of primitive man. His ideal building would have free-standing columns. He condemned pilasters and pedestals and all Renaissance and post-Renaissance elements. His book put NEO-CLASSICISM in a nutshell and had great influence, e.g. on SOUFFLOT.

Herrmann 1962; Braham 1980; Rykwert 1980.

**Laurana**, Luciano (c.1420–79). Italian architect, born in Dalmatia, he appeared in Urbino c.1466 at the humanist court of

Federigo da Montefeltro, which included Piero della Francesca and, later on, FRANCESCO DI GIORGIO. He was appointed architect of the Palazzo Ducale, Urbino (1468–72), for which he designed numerous chimney-pieces, door-cases, etc., of extreme refinement and elegance, anticipating and surpassing the C18 in delicacy. His masterpiece is the Florentine-style *cortile* in the Palazzo Ducale, with a light springy arcade of Corinthian columns echoed by shallow pilasters between the windows on the upper storey.

Lotz 1996; W. Lutz, *L.L. und der Herzogspalast in Urbino*, Berlin 1996.

**Lauterbach**, Johann Balthasar (1660–94), *see* KORB, Hermann (1656–1735).

**Lautner**, John (1911–94). American architect who went to Los Angeles in 1939 to work with F. L. WRIGHT and settled there. His imaginative residential designs became famous in the 1960s, notably Malin House or 'Chemosphere', Los Angeles (1960), an octagonal glazed pavilion mounted on a pedestal, like a spacecraft.

F. Escher (ed.), *J.L. Architect*, London 1994.

**Lauwericks**, Johannes Lodovicus Mathieu (1864–1932), *see* PROPORTION.

**Lavabo**. 1. A trough for washing in a medieval monastery, to be distinguished from a holy water STOUP. 2. A basin used by the celebrant at Mass.

**Laves**, Georg Ludwig Friedrich (1788–1864). German architect, a nephew of H. C. JUSSOW, under whom he trained in Kassel. After travelling in Italy, France and England he settled in Hanover in 1814. During the next fifty years Hanover was to be transformed by his romantic GREEK REVIVAL style almost as impressively as were Berlin and Munich by his great contemporaries SCHINKEL and KLENZE. The Leineschloss, later the Landtag (begun 1817), Wangenheim Palace (begun 1827) and the more Italianate Opera (1848–52) are his masterpieces, together with the layout of the Waterlooplatz (1855) and other new squares and streets. Laves was also an inventive and remarkably forward-looking engineer and submitted a startling design for the 1851 Exhibition Hall in London to be constructed largely of iron railway-track. It was an early attempt at prefabrication.

G. Hoeltje, *G.L.F.L.*, Hanover 1964, Watkin and Mellinghoff 1987.

**Lead**. The heaviest of the base metals, silvery-grey, durable, dense, malleable and easily fusible. The ore *galena* is the chief source. Used for plumbing by the Ancient Romans, though Vitruvius warned that water stored in lead vessels was unhealthy, it was used mainly for roofing from the Middle Ages, latterly for roof flashings, rain-water pipes, etc.

**Leaded lights**. Rectangular or diamond-shaped panes of glass set in lead CAMES to form a window. In general use in domestic architecture until the C18.

**Leaf and dart**. An OVOLO moulding decorated with a pattern of alternate leaf-like forms and darts, found especially on the ECHINUS of an Ionic capital.

**Lean-to roof**, *see* ROOF.

**Le Blond**, Jean-Baptiste-Alexandre (1679–1719). French architect and landscape architect, one of the originators of the RÉGENCE style. In Paris he built the Hôtel de Vendome (1705–6, later enlarged though his façade survives) and the Hôtel de Clermont (1708), praised by BLONDEL for the elegant simplicity of its plan. It was altered in execution and again later. He illustrated both these works in the much augmented 1710 edition of Augustin-Charles D'Aviler's *Cours* *d'Architecture* (1691), taking account of recent developments in decoration – with engravings by P. LE PAUTRE of chimney-pieces and looking-glass frames – and in planning. The separation of the public *chambres de parade* on the ground floor from the private apartments above was recommended, also the substitution of a single-storey *salon* for the previously fashionable lofty reception room, as well as ranging rooms of different sizes around a central core rather than stretching them out as an ENFILADE. *La Théorie et la pratique du jardinage* (1709) by Antoine-Joseph Dézailler d'Argenville (1680–1765) has sometimes been erroneously attributed to him, but he provided three-quarters of the illustrations, notably those of PARTERRES. In 1716 he went to St Petersburg as Architect General to Peter the Great, made a master-plan for the development of the city, planned the Summer Garden and also the park at Stelna as well as revising earlier schemes for the palace and garden at Peterhof. Although none of these works was completed before his death they helped to introduce the early C18 French style of decoration and especially of landscape architecture to Russia.

Gallet 1972; J. Cracraft, *The Petrine Revolution in Architecture*, Chicago 1988.

**Le Breton**, Gilles (d.1553). French master mason who carried out Francis I's enlargements at the Château de Fontainebleau and presumably designed them. His only surviving works are the Porte Dorée (1528–40), the north side of the Cour du Cheval Blanc, and the now greatly mutilated portico and staircase in the Cour de l'Ovale (begun 1531). The buildings around the forecourt at Fleury-en-Bière, near Fontainebleau, have been attributed to him. Le Breton's simple and austere Classicism, in his later works, derived from SERLIO and was to have

some influence on the next generation of French architects, notably LESCOT.

Blunt 1982.

**Le    Corbusier**    (Charles-Édouard Jeanneret) (1887–1966). Le Corbusier was born at La Chaux-de-Fonds in French Switzerland. He worked in PERRET's office in Paris in 1908–9, then for a short time in that of BEHRENS in Berlin. Le Corbusier was the most influential and most brilliant of C20 architects, of a fertility of formal invention to be compared only with Picasso's. But he was also restless and an embarrassingly superb salesman of his own ideas. It is no doubt relevant to an understanding of his mind and his work that he was an abstract or semi-abstract painter, comparable in some ways to Léger.

In Le Corbusier's early work three strains can be followed, continually interacting. One is the mass-production of housing (Dom-ino, 1914–15; Citrohan House, 1921–2; the abortive housing estate of Pessac, 1924/5), *see* INDUSTRIALIZED BUILDING. The second is town planning. Le Corbusier published and publicized a number of total plans for cities with a centre of identical skyscrapers, symmetrically arranged in a park setting, with lower buildings and complex traffic routes between. They are less realistic than GARNIER's Cité Industrielle of 1901, but far more dazzling (Ville Contemporaine, 1922; Plan Voisin, 1925; plan for Algiers, 1930; Ville Radieuse, 1935). The third strain of Le Corbusier's early thought tends towards a new type of private house, white, cubist, wholly or partly on PILOTIS, with rooms flowing into each other. The earliest is the villa at Vaucresson (1922). Many followed, including the exhibition pavilion of the Esprit Nouveau at the Paris Exhibition of 1925, with a tree growing through the building. The most stimulating and influential villas were probably the Villa Stein at Garches (1927) and the Villa Savoye at Poissy (1929–31). In the same years Le Corbusier did some designs for major buildings: for the League of Nations at Geneva (1927; not executed) and the Centrosojus in Moscow (1928). The designs had a great effect on progressive architects everywhere, as did his book *Vers une architecture* (Paris 1923, translated as *Towards a New Architecture*, London 1927). Of the major buildings actually erected two must be referred to: the Salvation Army Hostel in Paris (begun 1929) with its long CUR-TAIN WALL; and the Swiss House in the Paris Cité Universitaire (1930–32), introducing a random-rubble baffle wall to contrast with the usual white-rendered concrete. In 1936 Le Corbusier was called to Rio de Janeiro to advise on the new building of the Ministry of Education which was subsequently executed by COSTA, NIEMEYER, Reidy (1909–64), and others. Their contribution has never been fully distinguished from his. In 1947 Le Corbusier was one of the group of architects to come to terms with the programme of the United Nations Headquarters in New York, and the Secretariat building, a sheer glass slab with solid, windowless end walls, is essentially his design.

At the same time, however, Le Corbusier began to abandon this rational smooth glass and metal style which until then he had been instrumental in propagating, and turned to a new anti-rational, violently sculptural, aggressive style which was soon to be just as influential. The first example is the Unité d'Habitation at Marseilles (1947–52), with its heavy exposed concrete members and its fantastic roofscape. The proportions are worked out to a complicated system, called MODULOR, which Le Corbusier invented (*see* Fig. 95). The Unité was followed by another at Nantes

(1953–5) and a third at Berlin (for the Interbau Exhibition, 1956–8). Le Corbusier's most revolutionary work in his anti-rational style is the pilgrimage chapel of Ronchamp not far from Belfort (1950–54), eminently expressive, with its silo-like white tower, its brown concrete roof like the top of a mushroom, and its wall pierced by small windows of arbitrary shapes in arbitrary positions. In his villas the new style is represented by the Jaoul Houses, Neuilly-sur-Seine, Paris (1951–4), whose shallow concrete tunnel vaults soon became an international cliché. Of yet later buildings the Philips Pavilion at the Brussels Exhibition of 1958 had a HYPERBOLIC PARABOLOID ROOF, a form pioneered at Raleigh, North Carolina (1948–53). At Chandigarh, India, Le Corbusier laid out the town and built the extremely powerful Law Courts and Secretariat (1951–6), the influence of which proved to be strongest in Japan. (*See also* Pierre JEANNERET.) At the same time he did some houses at Ahmedabad, India (1954–6), which, like the buildings of Chandigarh, are of excessively heavy, chunky concrete members, notably the Millowners' Association Building (1953–6). Later he designed the Museum of Modern Art for Tokyo and the Dominican Friary of La Tourette at Eveux-sur-l'Arbresle near Lyon (1953–7), a ruthlessly hard block of immense force. His last important building was the Carpenter Art Center at Harvard.

W. Boesiger (ed.), *L.C. Œuvres complètes*, Zürich (1935–65) 1970; C. Jencks, *L.C. and the Tragic View of Architecture*, London 1973; R. Walden (ed.), *The Open Hand. Essays on L.C.*, Cambridge, Mass. 1977; S. Von Moos, *L.C. Elements of a Synthesis*, Cambridge, Mass. 1979; W. Curtis, *L.C. Ideas and Form*, Oxford 1986; J. Lucan (ed.), *L.C. une encyclopédie*, Paris 1987; C. Baker, *L.C. an Analysis of Form*, London 1989.

**Le Muet**, Pierre (1591–1669). French architect and a *retardataire* MANNERIST. He published *Manière de bien bastir pour toutes sortes de personnes* (1623), an up-to-date version of DU CERCEAU's first book of architecture, containing designs suitable for different income groups but going further down the social scale. His best surviving buildings are the Hôtels Comans d'Astry (1647), de l'Aigle and Davaux in Paris. The Hôtel Duret de Chevry (1635, now part of the Bibliothèque Nationale) was for long attributed to him but is now known to be by Jean Thiriot. His later buildings, e.g. Hôtel Tubeuf, Paris (1650), are more classical.

Blunt 1982.

**Le Nôtre**, André (1613–1700). The greatest French landscape architect, he was the son of Jean Le Nôtre (d.1655), royal gardener at the Tuileries, Paris, from 1618. André studied painting and sculpture as well as horticulture and in 1645 designed the garden of the orangerie at Fontainebleau (destroyed). The first opportunity to display his genius on a grand scale came in 1656 when he joined LE VAU, then working for the finance minister Nicolas Fouquet at Vaux le Vicomte, Seine-et-Marne. He laid out wide parterres around Le Vau's *château*, complementing and setting off its architectural form, and on its main axis created a long vista, crossing a canal and gradually descending through a succession of levels, with statuary, ponds, flowering plants and trees, to a valley with a dramatic cascade. This work, completed by 1661, excited the admiration and cupidity of Louis XIV, who sacked Fouquet, took over his team of architect, artists and gardeners and had most of the statues and trees taken to Versailles. (The gardens at Vaux-le-Vicomte were abandoned but partly reconstructed in 1875.) Le Nôtre, who

had succeeded to his father's lucrative post at the Tuileries and was appointed a Contrôleur des Bâtiments du Roi in 1657, worked from 1662 onwards at Versailles, where he transformed a vast barren site into a park on a master-plan geometrically devised yet flexible enough to permit enlargements, alterations and embellishments demanded by the king over the next three decades. On either side of a strong central axis – a vista stretching into the far distance from the centre of the *château* – every element of the French formal garden was exploited: radiating *patte d'oie* avenues, parterres, artificial lakes, a huge cruciform canal, fountains, grottoes, an amphitheatre, palisades, *bosquets* and dense woods intersected by straight paths and rides. Although much replanting was done and some additions were made in later periods, the park is still substantially as he designed it. From 1679 he laid out for the king the smaller, densely enclosed garden for Marly, Yvelines (destroyed early C19, apart from trees, but now restored to show the broad outlines of the original plan). He also reorganized the garden of the Tuileries, creating a terrace on the river side and a wide central *allée*, extended on axis beyond the wall in an avenue that was later to lead up the Champs Elysées to the Arc de Triomphe and much later to the Grande Arche de la Défense. His other works include the parks at Chantilly (1665–86, destroyed apart from the main parterre and canal restored in the C19) and the remarkable park at Dampierre (1675–86), perhaps his finest achievement, which survives with its magnificent vista across a valley and parterres, basins and cascades. Such was his fame that many gardens and parks have been erroneously attributed to him. None displays his unique ability not only to lay out grand sweeping prospects but to exploit with great sensitivity the natural features of the terrain; especially the varying ground levels. He could incorporate diverse elements without overcrowding and create both smooth transitions and welcome surprises. The main principles of his designs were formulated by Antoine-Joseph Dézailler d'Argenville (1680–1765) in his *La Théorie et la pratique du jardinage* (1709), which was translated into English and German and was issued in eleven editions by 1760.

F. Hamilton Hazlehurst, *Gardens of Illusion. The Genius of A.L.N.*, Nashville 1980; B. Jennel, *L.N.*, Paris 1985; Laird 1992; V. Scully and J. Baubion-Mackler, *French Royal Gardens, the Designs of A.L.N.*, New York 1992; A. S. Weiss, *Mirrors of Infinity*, Princeton 1995.

**Le Pautre**, Antoine (1621–81). French architect, he designed the Hôtel de Beauvais in Paris (1652–5), the most ingenious of all Parisian *hôtel* plans considering the awkward site. But he is best known for the engraved designs in his *Œuvres* (first published 1652 as *Desseins de plusieurs palais*) of vast and fantastic town and country houses, which far exceed his contemporary LE VAU in Baroque extravagance. His influence is evident in the work of WREN and SCHLÜTER.

R. W. Berger, *A.L.P. – a French Architect of the Era of Louis XIV*, New York 1969; Blunt 1982.

**Le Pautre**, Pierre (c.1648–1716), nephew of Antoine, was the leading decorator at Versailles under Jules HARDOUIN-MANSART and as influential as de COTTE and LE BLOND in the evolution of the Rococo style, e.g. his Salon de L'Œil de Bœuf (1701) and chapel (1709–10), Versailles, and the choir of Notre Dame, Paris (1711–12).

Kalnein 1995.

**Le Rouge**, George Louis (1712–78), *see* LANDSCAPE GARDEN.

**Le Vau**, Louis (1612–70), the leading Baroque architect in France, was less intellectual and refined than his great contemporary MANSART. He was also less difficult in character and headed a brilliant team of painters, sculptors, decorators, gardeners, with whom he created the Louis XIV style at Versailles. He was a great *metteur-en-scène* and could produce striking general effects with a typically Baroque combination of all the arts. Born in Paris, the son of a master mason by whom he was trained, he first revealed his outstanding gifts in the Hôtel Lambert, Paris (1642–4), where he made ingenious use of an awkward site and created the first of his highly coloured, grandiloquent interiors: the staircase and gallery are especially magnificent. In 1656 he began the Hôtel de Fontenay, Paris, and in 1657 he was commissioned by Fouquet, the millionaire finance minister, to design his country house at Vaux-le-Vicomte. This is his masterpiece and by far the most splendid of all French *châteaux*. Here grandeur and elegance are combined in a manner peculiarly French, and no expense was spared. The *château* was built in about a year and the luxurious interior, decorated by Lebrun, Guérin, and others, and the gardens laid out by LE NÔTRE were finished by 1661. In the same year Fouquet was arrested for embezzlement, whereupon his rival Colbert took over his architect and artists to work for the king. Le Vau was commissioned to rebuild the Galerie d'Apollon in the Louvre (1661–2), decorated by Lebrun (1663). In 1667 he was involved (with PERRAULT) in the design of the great east front of the Louvre in Paris. Work began on the remodelling of Versailles in 1669. Le Vau rose to the occasion, and his feeling for the grand scale found perfect expression in the new garden front. Unfortunately, this was ruined a few years later by HARDOUIN-MANSART's alterations and extensions, and nothing survives at all of the interiors he executed with Lebrun; these included the most spectacular of all, the Escalier des Ambassadeurs. In the Collège des Quatre Nations, Paris (now the Institut de France, begun 1661), which was built at the expense of Cardinal Mazarin, he came closer than any other Frenchman to the warmth and geniality of the great Italian Baroque architects. The main front facing the Seine is concave, with two arms curving forward from the domed centrepiece to end in pavilions. The sense of splendour both in planning and decoration is no less typical than the occasional lack of sensitivity in the handling of detail. Both here and at Versailles the chief member of his studio was François d'ORBAY, who carried out or completed several of his late works after his death.

Blunt 1982; R. W. Berger, *The Palace of the Sun. The Louvre of Louis XIV*, University Park, Pennsylvania, 1993; R. W. Berger, *A Royal Passion. Louis XIV as Patron of Architecture*, Cambridge 1994; J. M. Pérouse de Montclos, *Vaux-le-Vicomte*, London 1997.

**Lechner**, Ödön (1845–1914). Hungarian architect and one of the most interesting of all representatives of ART NOUVEAU architecture. He started (like GAUDÍ) in a free Gothic (Town Hall, Kecskemét, 1892, Museum of Decorative Art, Budapest, 1893–6) and developed towards a fantastic style with curvaceous gables and Moorish as well as folk-art connotations (Postal Savings Bank, Budapest, 1899–1902).

T. Bakonyi and M. Kubinsky, *O.L.*, Budapest 1981.

**Ledoux**, Claude-Nicolas (1736–1806). French architect who began as a fashionable Louis XVI architect, patronized by Mme du Barry, and developed into the most daring and extreme exponent of

neo-classicism in France. Only BOULLÉE among his contemporaries was his equal in imagination and originality, but most of Boullée's designs remained on paper. Neither was properly appreciated until recently. Despite its extreme geometrical simplicity their more advanced work is not abstract but expressive or *parlant*. Born at Dormans, Ledoux studied under J.-F. BLONDEL in Paris. He never went to Italy, though he was profoundly influenced by Italian architecture, especially by the cyclopean fantasies of PIRANESI. Though eccentric and quarrelsome, he was immediately and continuously successful and never lacked commissions. His first important buildings were the Hôtel d'Hallwyl, Paris (1766), the Château de Bénouville (1770–77), and the Hôtel de Montmorency, Paris (1770–72), the last displaying his originality in planning on a diagonal axis, with circular and oval rooms.

In 1771 he began working for Mme du Barry and the following year completed the Pavillon de Louveciennes, a landmark in the history of French taste. (It was demolished in 1930 and replaced by a copy with an added attic.) It was decorated and furnished throughout in the neo-classical style, the architectural treatment of the interior being confined to shallow pilasters, classical bas-reliefs, and delicate, honeycomb coffering. In 1776 he began the remarkable Hôtel Thélusson (demolished) in Paris, approached through an enormous triumphal arch leading into a garden laid out in the English landscape manner. This conception, in which the informality of the garden emphasized the stark simplicity and geometrical forms of the building, was repeated on a larger scale in the group of fifteen houses he built for the West Indian nabob Hosten in Paris (1792, demolished). They, too, were informally disposed in a landscape garden.

Success and official recognition appear to have stimulated rather than dulled his powers of invention, for his most advanced and original work dates from after he became an Academician and Architecte du Roi in 1773. His masterpieces are the massive and rigidly cubic theatre at Besançon (1775–84, burnt out 1957), with its unpedimented Ionic portico and, inside, a hemicycle with rising banks of seats surmounted by a Greek Doric colonnade. Odder still is his saltworks at Arc-et-Senans (1775–9), some of which still survives in a dilapidated condition. It is the supreme expression of his feeling for the elemental and primeval. The glowering entrance portico is carved inside to emulate the natural rock out of which gushes water, presumably saline though also carved in stone. Even more extreme were the buildings he envisaged for his 'ideal city' of Chaux, which were not, understandably, executed: one was to have been a free-standing sphere and another an enormous cylinder set horizontally.

His Paris toll-houses of 1785–9 are less extreme, but they illustrate the wide range of his stylistic repertoire. Of those that survive the most exciting is the Barrière de La Villette in Place de Stalingrad, consisting of a Greek cross surmounted by a cylinder – a very successful essay in pure architectural form. In 1783 he built a salt warehouse at Compiègne (only the massive arched façade survives) and in 1786 provided designs for a Palais de Justice and prison at Aix en Provence (not executed according to his designs). His career came to an end with the Revolution (he was imprisoned during the 1790s) and he spent his last years preparing his designs for publication: *L'Architecture considérée sous le rapport de l'art, des mœurs et de la législation* (1804), of which the third volume was recently discovered and published by M. Gallet and M. Mosser as *L'Architecture de Ledoux inédite: pour le tôme trois* (Paris 1991).

M. Gallet, *C.-N.L.*, Paris 1980; Braham 1980; A. Vidler, *C.-N.L.*, Cambridge, Mass. 1988; M. Gallet, *C.-N.L. Unpublished Projects*, Berlin 1992; A. Vidler, *L'Espace des lumières*, Paris 1995.

**Lefuel**, Hector-Martin (1810–80). French architect, won the Grand Prix in 1839 and in the same year went to Rome. In 1854, at the death of Louis Visconti (1791–1853), he became chief architect to the Louvre, which Napoleon III had decided to complete by connecting it with the Tuileries. The neo-Renaissance fashion originated here and soon became international (*see* HUNT). Lefuel also designed the palace for the International Exhibition of 1855.

Hitchcock 1977.

**Legeay**, Jean-Louis (d.1788). French architect and engraver. The eclectic Communs, Neues Palais, Potsdam, Germany (1767), is his only built work of note and its construction was supervised by GONTARD. But Legeay was influential on the early experimental phase of French neo-classical architecture both as a teacher and through his imaginative engravings.

Kalnein 1995.

**Legoretta**, Vilchis Ricardo (b.1931). Mexican architect, trained in Mexico City. He began with VILLAGRÁN GARCIA from 1948 to 1960 and was greatly influenced by BARRAGÁN, whose 'Mexicanidad' he later developed with his brightly coloured and dramatic wall architecture. He made his name with the Camino Real hotels in Mexico City (1968), Cancún (1975) and Ixtapa (1981). Also notable are his IBM office building, Mexico City (1975); Renault Factory, Monterrey, Mexico (1984), and 'Solana'

IBM Southlake and Villhe Center West, Dallas, Texas (1988–90). His Contemporary Art Museum, Monterrey (1989–92), sensitively develops the traditional hacienda vernacular. Dramatic and imaginative are his Greenberg House, Los Angeles, California (1991), and his transformation (with OLIN) of Pershing Square, Los Angeles (1992–4).

W. Atto (ed.), *The Architecture of R.L.*, Dallas, 1990.

**Legrand**, Jacques-Guillaume (1743–1808), *see* BÉLANGER, François-Joseph; GILLY, Friedrich.

**Leiviska**, Juha (b.1936), *see* FINNISH ARCHITECTURE.

**Lemercier**, Jacques (*c.*1585–1654). French architect, the son of a master mason who worked at St Eustache, Paris. He studied in Rome *c.*1607–14, becoming Architecte du Roi soon afterwards. With Étienne Martellange (*c.*1569–1641), who designed the Jesuit Noviciate, Paris (1630), he was the leading exponent of French Classicism as expounded by Fréart de Chambray (1606–76) in his *Parallèle de l'architecture* (1650) and ranks only just below MANSART and LE VAU. In 1624 he was commissioned by Louis XIII to plan extensions to the Louvre (the Pavillon de l'Horloge of 1641 is the most notable of his additions), in harmony with LESCOT's work of the previous century. But his principal patron was Cardinal Richelieu, for whom he designed the Palais Cardinal (Palais Royal), Paris (begun 1633); the Sorbonne, Paris (begun 1626); the *château* and church of Rueil and the *château* and town of Richelieu (begun 1631). Only a small domed pavilion of the office block survives from the enormous Château Richelieu, but the town still exists as laid out by Lemercier in a regular grid with houses of uniform design built of brick with stone quoins. As a designer

of *hôtels* he was remarkably ingenious, and his solution at the Hôtel de Liancourt, Paris (1623), became a prototype which was followed by nearly all his successors. His church of the Sorbonne (begun 1635) is perhaps his finest work and is one of the first purely classical churches in France. His dome at the Val-de-Grâce, Paris, where he took over from Mansart in 1646, is also most dramatic and effective.

J. P. Babelon, *Demeures Parisiennes. Sous Henri IV et Louis XIII*, Paris 1965; Blunt 1982.

**Lemyinge**, Robert (d.1628), *see* LIMINGE, Robert.

**L'Enfant**, Pierre Charles (1754–1825), a French architect and engineer who served as a volunteer major in the American army during the War of Independence, designed the old City Hall in New York and the Federal House in Philadelphia, but is remembered mainly for having surveyed the site and made the plan for the new federal capital in Washington, a grandiose conception based in some respects on Versailles, taking account of the natural formation of the site, with a central mall, tree-lined avenues radiating from *rond-points*, gardens, fountains and canals; but strict adherence to this plan was abandoned after 1830. He would probably have been given the commission to design the Capitol and other buildings in Washington had he not become unmanageable. He was dismissed in 1792.

Whiffen and Koeper 1981.

**Lenné**, Peter Joseph (1789–1866). The greatest German landscape architect. The son and grandson of head gardeners at Bonn, he was trained there and in Paris, becoming an ardent exponent of the English LANDSCAPE GARDEN. He often worked in association with SCHINKEL, with whom he shared patrons in the Prussian royal family and aristocracy. From 1816 onwards he was employed by the King of Prussia on the vast landscape park at Sanssouci, Potsdam, which he later enlarged to encompass Schinkel's Schloss Charlottenhof (1826–8) and PERSIUS's Schloss Lindstedt (1858–60). In 1819– 28 he created the romantic landscape park at Charlottenburg, Berlin, though he preserved the geometrical layout near the *Schloss* itself. In 1833 he began work on the Tiergarten in Berlin. This former royal game preserve of uncultivated woodland had been converted *c*.1740 into a French-style hunting forest with axial 'rides'. In 1818 Lenné had made proposals (never realized) for a public park in part of it to commemorate the war against Napoleon. Now he transformed the whole area into an informal park with winding paths and scattered lakes and clumps of trees and shrubs. It became a PUBLIC PARK in 1840 and in 1841–4 was enlarged by Lenné to include a zoological garden. He was responsible for several other public parks in Germany which are among the earliest created as such, e.g. the Friedrich-Wilhelm park at Magdeburg (1824) and the Lennépark in Frankfurt-am-Oder (1832–45). In 1846, at his suggestion, the Berlin municipality voted to create a second public park in the city, the Friedrischen park, which he designed. For private patrons he created the parks at Schloss Friedrischsfelde, Berlin (1821); Klein Glienicke, Wannsee, Berlin (1824–50); Schloss Pfaueninsel, Wannsee (1824), and at Schinkel's Schloss Babelsburg, Potsdam (1832–43), where he was succeeded by PUCKLER-MUSKAU.

G. Hinz, *P.J.L. Des Gesamtwerk des Gärten Architekter und Stadtplanner*, Hildesheim/Zürich 1989; H. Gunther, *P.J.L. Gärten, Parke, Landschaften*, Stuttgart (1985) 1991; H. Gartner *et al.*, *P.J.L. und die europaische Landschaftskunst in 19 Jahrhundert*, Griefswald 1992.

**Lennox**, Edward (1854–1933), *see* CANADIAN ARCHITECTURE.

**Leonardo da Vinci** (1452–1519). The greatest artist and thinker of the Renaissance. His wide-ranging mind embraced architecture as well as many other fields of human activity. Although he built little or nothing, he provided a model for the dome of Milan Cathedral (1487, not executed), and during his last years in France produced a vast scheme for a new city and royal castle at Romorantin (not executed). But his influence was great, especially on BRAMANTE, who took over his interest in centralized churches. Leonardo was certainly involved in Bramante's work at S. Maria delle Grazie, Milan, though his role in Bramante's Tempietto in Rome is controversial. S. Maria della Consolazione at Todi (1508), begun by Cola da Caprarola (*fl.*1499–1519), probably derived from one of his sketches by way of Bramante.

C. Pedretti, *L. da V. Architect*, London 1981, rev. edn Milan 1988; Heydenreich 1996.

**Leoni**, Giacomo (*c*.1686–1746). Italian architect, born in Venice, who settled in England some time before 1715, having previously worked in Düsseldorf. An apostle of PALLADIANISM, he published the first English edition of Palladio's *Architecture* (1715–20) and at Queensberry House (now Royal Bank of Scotland), London (1721, reconstructed 1792), provided that prototype English Palladian town house. In 1726 he published *The Architecture of L. B. Alberti*. His surviving buildings include Argyll House, London (1723); Lyme Park, Cheshire (1725–30); and Clandon Park, Surrey (1731–5).

R. Hewlings in Brown 1985; Summerson 1991; Colvin 1995.

**Leonidov**, Ivan Ilich (1902–59). Leading exponent of CONSTRUCTIVISM in Moscow, where his most notable project (unrealized) was his Lenin Institute of 1927. His only notable work to be executed was the amphitheatre etc. at the Ordzhonikidze Sanatorium, Kislovodsk (1932).

R. Koolhaus and G. Oorthuys, *I.L.*, New York 1981; A. Gozak and A. Leonidov, *I.L. The Complete Works*, London 1988.

**Leper window**, *see* LOWSIDE WINDOW.

**Lepère**, J. B. (1761–1844), *see* HITTORF.

**Lequeu**, Jean-Jacques (1757–1826). French neo-classical fantasist of neurotic power. He was born in Rouen, visited Italy in the early 1780s, and worked mainly as an architectural draughtsman until the Revolution and then as a cartographer. None of his few buildings survives. His fame rests on his drawings (Bibliothèque Nationale, Paris) in which the designs and ideas of BOULLÉE and LEDOUX appear to have gone to his head – monument to Priapus, vast and megalomaniac towers, a dairy to be built in the form of a cow, houses composed of both Gothic and antique motifs, etc., with much use of phallic and other symbols. In them he broke away from all conventions of symmetry, stylistic purity, proportion and taste.

Braham 1980; P. Duboy, *J.-J.L. An Architectural Enigma*, London 1986; J.-P. Mouillesceux and A. Jacques, *Les Architectes de la Liberté 1789–1795*, Paris 1989.

**Lesbian cymatium**. A CYMA REVERSA moulding often decorated with LEAF AND DART.

**Lescaze**, William (1896–1964). Swiss-born American architect who worked with SAUVAGE in Paris before emigrating to the USA in 1923. He made his name with the PFS Building, Philadelphia (1929–32), one of the first International

Modern skyscrapers, designed with HOWE. In 1935 his partnership with Howe broke up and his later work belongs more to Corporate Modernism, from his CBS Building, Hollywood, California (1936–8), to the US Plywood Building, New York (1963).

C. Hubert and L. S. Shapiro, *W.L.*, New York 1982.

**Lescot**, Pierre (1500/15–1578). French architect, son of a well-to-do lawyer, who gave him a good education. His only work to survive more or less intact is part of the square court of the Louvre (1546–51), which laid the foundations of French Classicism. Essentially decorative, his style is very French and entirely lacks the monumentality of his Italian contemporaries. He had the great advantage of the sculptor Jean Goujon's collaboration, and his ornamental detail is therefore of the greatest refinement and delicacy. Though much altered, parts of his Hôtel Carnavalet, Paris (*c.*1545–50), survive. The Fontaine des Innocents, Paris (1547–9), has been totally reconstructed.

Blunt 1982.

**Lesene**. A PILASTER without a base and capital, often called a pilaster-strip and usually found on the exteriors of later Anglo-Saxon and early Romanesque churches. Although they were much used as decoration during the latter period, there is evidence in some Anglo-Saxon buildings to suggest that pilaster-strips as used by the Saxons were primarily functional. They served as bonding courses in thin rubble walls, and thus split up an unbroken expanse of wall, reducing cracking in the plaster and preventing longitudinal spread. The north nave wall at Breamore church shows long stones on end between flat stones, all clearly projecting some distance into the wall. This is a crude example of LONG AND SHORT WORK, but no claim can be made that the pilaster-strip and long and short work as used for QUOINS were evolved in any particular sequence. Other examples of the structural significance of the pilaster-strip are at Worth, where they are solid stone partitions, clearly of a piece with the long and short quoins, at Sompting and at Milborne.

**Lethaby**, William Richard (1857–1931). English architect; joined the office of Norman SHAW in 1877, became his trusted principal assistant, and set up on his own in 1889, helped on by Shaw. While he thus owed much to Shaw, as an artist and a thinker he owed more to MORRIS and Philip WEBB, and he played a significant part in the ARTS AND CRAFTS movement. He was as much an educator as a scholar and an architect, and indeed built very little. Foremost among his buildings are Avon Tyrrell in Hampshire (1891) and Melsetter on Orkney (1898), the church at Brockhampton in Herefordshire (1900–1902) – probably the most original church of its date in the world – and the Eagle Insurance Building in Colmore Row, Birmingham (1899), also of a startling originality, even if influenced by Webb. Lethaby was the chief promoter and the first principal of the London Central School of Arts and Crafts, which was established in 1894 on Morris's principles. It was the first school anywhere to include teaching workshops for crafts. He published his remarkable *Architecture, Mysticism and Myth* in 1892, and in 1894 (with Swainson) brought out a learned book on Hagia Sophia in Constantinople; in 1904 a general, very deeply felt book on medieval art; in 1906 and 1925 two learned volumes on Westminster Abbey; and in 1922 a collection of brilliant, convincedly forward-looking essays called *Form in Civilisation*.

Hitchcock 1977; G. Rubens, *W.L. His Life and Work 1857–1931*, London (1978)

1985; S. Backemeyer and T. Gronberg (eds.), *W.R.L. 1857–1931. Architecture, Design, Education*, exh. cat., London 1984; G. Rubens, *W.R.L.*, London 1986; T. Garnham, *Melsetter House. W.R.L.*, London 1993.

**Levasseur**, Noël (1680–1740), *see* CANADIAN ARCHITECTURE.

**Levasseur**, Pierre-Noël (1690–1770), *see* CANADIAN ARCHITECTURE.

**Leverton**, Thomas (1743–1824). English architect, the son of an Essex builder and not highly regarded in his own day, nevertheless designed some of the most elegant interiors in London, e.g. Nos. 1 and 13 Bedford Square (1775). His 'Etruscan' hall and other rooms at Woodhall Park, Hertfordshire (1778), are equally distinguished.

Summerson 1991; Colvin 1995.

**Levi**, Rino (1901–65), *see* BRAZILIAN ARCHITECTURE.

**Levittown**. A residential suburban development for a new community named after Levitt & Son, who built the first at Hicksville, NY, in 1947–51, for house-seeking GIs. It was immediately and enormously successful and became the paradigmatic post-Second World War automobile suburb. In conception Levittown, and its successors in New Jersey and Pennsylvania, was an updated garden city with winding streets and open spaces, each of its 16,000 or more open-plan Cape Cod houses on its own site, with car-port next to the front door, recalling WRIGHT's Usonian houses. By fusing American individualism with collective planning, Levittown brought to the city office worker the advantages of the well-to-do country suburb. It was to be influential in the later development of dormitory suburbs.

H. L. Wattel in W. M. Dobrinder (ed.), *The Suburban Community*, New York

1958; H. J. Gans, *Die Levittowner. Sociographie eines Schlafenstadt*, Gutersloh 1969; D. Halberstam, *The Fifties*, New York 1993.

**Lewerentz**, Sigurd (1885–1975). Swedish architect and landscape architect. He won, with ASPLUND, the 1915 competition for Woodlands Cemetery outside Stockholm and over the next twenty years they created a masterpiece of landscape architecture combining romantic vernacular elements with Nordic Classicism. The latter is epitomized by Lewerentz's Resurrection Chapel (1922–5). The Malmö cemetery (1916–61) is also his.

J. Ahlin, *S.L. Architect 1885–1975*, Cambridge, Mass. (1985) 1987; C. Constant, *The Woodland Cemetery. Towards a Spiritual Landscape*, Stockholm 1994.

**Libera**, Adalberto (1903–63). Italian architect prominent in the RATIONALISM movement, though his Congress Building, EUR, Rome (1937–8), and other works compromised with Fascism. However, his Casa Malaparte, Capri (1938), was remarkable.

P. Garofalo and L. Versani, *A.L.*, Princeton (1989) 1992; M. Talamona, *Casa Malaparte*, New York (1990) 1992; Etlin 1991.

**Libergier**, Hugues (d.1263). A French master mason whose funerary slab is now in Reims Cathedral. He is called Maistre on it and is represented holding the model of the major parish church of Reims, St Nicaise, which he designed and began in 1231. He also has a staff, an L-square, and compasses.

Branner 1965.

**Liberty, style**, *see* ART NOUVEAU.

**Libeskind**, Daniel (b.1946). American architect, born in Poland, who emigrated to the USA in 1960. Trained in New York, he exhibited a 'lightning flash' zigzag design at the DECONSTRUCTIVIST

exhibition in 1988. His Osaka Folly Pavilion, Osaka, followed in 1989–90 and his Jewish Museum, Berlin, in 1990–96. In 1996 he won the competition for an extension to the Victoria & Albert Museum, London. He published *Line of Fire* in Milan (1988).

A. M. Müller (ed.), *D.L. Radix-Matrix*, Munich 1990.

**Liche**, *see* LYCH GATE.

**Lierne**, *see* VAULT.

**Lift**, *see* ELEVATOR.

**Lights**. Openings between the MULLIONS of a window.

**Ligorio**, Pirro (*c.*1510–83). Italian painter and archaeologist as well as architect. He built the Villa d'Este, Tivoli (1565–72), and laid out its wonderful formal gardens with elaborate fountains and water-works. His masterpiece is the exquisite little Casino di Pio IV (1559–62) in the Vatican gardens, Rome, one of the most elegant of Mannerist buildings. Also in the Vatican, he transformed the exedra in BRAMANTE's Cortile del Belvedere into a gargantuan niche.

D. R. Coffin, *The Villa d'Este at Tivoli*, Princeton 1966; G. Smith, *The Casino of Pius IV*, Princeton 1976; R. W. Gaston (ed.), *P.L. Artist and Antiquarian*, Milan 1988; Lazzaro 1990; Lotz 1996.

**Lime**. Calcium oxide, obtained by burning limestone; the main component of CEMENT and MORTAR, also of common plaster and stucco.

**Limestone**. A sandy, sedimentary rock consisting chiefly of calcium carbonate. It yields lime when burnt. Commonly used as a building stone, the crystalline variety that can be polished is known as MARBLE.

**Liminge**, **Lemyinge** or **Lyming**, Robert (d.1628). First recorded in 1607 as a carpenter, he was employed to design and supervise building at Hatfield House, Hertfordshire, in 1607–12. The loggia and frontispiece may be his, though Inigo JONES was consulted in 1609. At Blickling Hall, Norfolk (1616–17), he designed the last of the great Jacobean PRODIGY HOUSES in which Flemish ornament and planning were anglicized.

Summerson 1991; Colvin 1995.

**Lindgren**, Armas (1874–1929), *see* FINNISH ARCHITECTURE.

**Linear planning**, *see* URBAN DESIGN.

**Linenfold**. Panelling ornamented with a conventional representation of a piece of linen laid in vertical folds. One such piece fills one panel. First introduced in Flanders in the C15–16, it was much used in Tudor England for the decoration of both panelling and furniture. *See* Fig. 75.

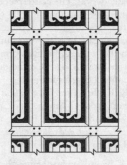

Fig. 75 Linenfold

**Linstow**, Hans Ditler Frants (1787–1851), *see* NORWEGIAN ARCHITECTURE.

**Lintel**. A horizontal beam or stone bridging an opening. Hence the term POST AND LINTEL for a simple column-and-beam structure as in an Ancient Egyptian or Greek temple.

**Lisboa**, António Francisco (1730 or 1738–1814), *see* ALEIJADINHO.

**Lissitsky**, Lazar Markovich, called El (1890–1941). Russian painter, typographer, designer and theorist as well as architect, Lissitsky became the apostle of CONSTRUCTIVISM in the West in the 1920s. He trained under Joseph OLBRICH at the College of Technology, Darmstadt (1909–14). In 1919 he became Professor of Architecture at Vitebsk, where he evolved his 'Proun' idea (Proun = 'For the New Art') which he described as an 'interchange station' between painting and architecture – an interplay between the pictorial and structural. His ideas owed something to both MALEVICH and TATLIN, then famous for his 1920 design for a spiral-shaped monument to the Third International. In 1920 Lissitsky designed his Lenin Tribune project which foreshadowed the prime Constructivist building, the Leningrad Pravda building projected by the VESNIN brothers in 1923. From 1922 until 1931 Lessitsky was in the West, where he knew and influenced the DE STIJL and other *avant-garde* architects. His 'Proun Room' for the 1923 Berlin exhibition has been reconstructed at Eindhoven (Stedelijk van Abbe-museum), and his 'Abstract Cabinet', created in 1926 for Dresden and in 1927 for Hanover and intended to 'allow abstract art to do justice to its dynamic properties', has been reconstructed in the Landesmuseum in Hanover. His most ambitious and forward-looking design – the 1924 *Wolkenbügel* project (with STAM) for office blocks in Moscow on upright or splayed legs straddling roads – never materialized. In 1939 he produced designs for the Soviet Pavilion restaurant at the New York World Fair.

S. Lissitsky-Kuppers, *E.L. Life, Letters, Texts*, London and New York 1968; *E.L.*, exh. cat., Eindhoven 1990.

**Listel**, *see* FILLET.

**Liturgical orientation**, *see* ORIEN-
TATION.

**Liwan**, *see* IWAN.

**Load-bearing** or **load-carrying construction**. Construction in which walls,
posts, columns or arcades support the
weight of the ceilings, upper floors, etc.,
as distinct from FRAME CONSTRUCTION.

**Lodge**. I. The medieval term for the
masons' workshop or tracing house, with
living-quarters, set up when a church,
castle or house was to be built. In the case
of cathedrals and great abbeys it was often
permanent, under a resident master, to
maintain the fabric of the building.

P. du Colombier, *Les Chantiers des
cathedrals*, Paris 1953; P. Booz, *Der Baumeister der Gotik*, Berlin 1956.

2. A small rustic hut or cabin in wild
country or mountains, usually for seasonal
use only, e.g. hunting lodge. 3. A small
one-storey house at the entrance to a
park, for occupation by a gatekeeper or
caretaker. Such park gate lodges became
notable features of English C18 – 19 architecture. Often designed in pairs, one on
each side of the entrance, they followed
stylistic fashions, sometimes taking fantastic forms – toy forts, Gothic chapels,
Grecian temples, etc.

T. Mowl and B. Earnshaw, *Trumpet at
a Distant Gate: The L. as a Prelude to the
Country House*, London 1985.

**Lodge books**. Medieval masons' sketch-
books or notebooks. Several survive, notably that of VILLARD DE HONNECOURT.
Bucher 1979.

**Lodoli**, Carlo (1690–1761). A Venetian
priest and architectural theorist. His neo-
classical and 'Rationalist' ideas were published after his death by A. Memmo
(*Elementi d'architettura lodoliana*, 1786) but
they had been current for many years and
were very influential, e.g. on Algarotti's
*Saggio sopra l'architettura* (1753), Piranesi's

*Della magnificenza ed architettura dei Romani*
(1761) and on LAUGIER.

Herrmann 1962; L. Grassi, *Razional-
ismo architettonico dal L. a G. Pagano*, Milan
1966; Rykwert 1980; Wittkower 1982.

**Log cabin**. Primitive hut of log construction prevalent in northern and
western frontier settlements in the USA
up to about 1830, when it was superseded
by BALLOON FRAMING. It had been introduced in the C18 by Swedes.

**Log construction**. Primitive form of
timber construction still used in regions
rich in timber. The walls are made of
tree-trunks laid horizontally on top of
one another, overlapping at the corners
where they are slotted together. If round
boles are used the joints are sealed with
moss and mud, but the logs are usually
adzed down to a plane surface. The only
surviving log church in England is
St Andrew, Greensted, of c.1013 in
which, however, the logs are set vertically
in an oak sill. *See also* SCANDINAVIAN
ARCHITECTURE.

H. J. Hansen, *Architecture in Wood: A
History of Wood Building and its Techniques
in Europe and N. America*, (Hamburg 1969)
London 1971; T. Jordan, *American L.
Building. An Old World Heritage*, Chapel
Hill 1985.

**Loggia**. A gallery or room open on one
or more sides, sometimes pillared; it may
also be a separate structure.

**Lombardo**, Pietro (c.1435–1515). A
leading sculptor and architect in late C15
Venice. He was born at Carona in Lombardy, hence his name. He appears to
have visited Florence before 1464, when
he is first recorded working in Padua as
a sculptor. Soon after 1467 he settled
in Venice. Between 1471 and 1485 he
designed and carved decorations for the
chancel of S. Giobbe, Venice, a work of
strongly Florentine character. His next

and most important work was S. Maria dei Miracoli (1481–9), in which he successfully blended the Veneto-Byzantine and Renaissance styles – marble panelling inside and out and a Byzantine dome, combined with crisply carved Renaissance ornament. To give an illusion of greater size he resorted to various *trompe l'œil* devices which he repeated on a larger scale, but with less success, on the façade of the Scuola di S. Marco (1488–90, upper storeys completed by CODUSSI). He also introduced into Venice the large architectural sepulchral monument with a classical framework and abundance of classically inspired sculpture. Here he was much assisted by his sons Antonio (*c.*1458–1516) and Tullio (*c.*1455–1532). Various Venetian palaces have been attributed to Lombardo, notably Palazzo Dario (*c.*1487).

Howard 1980; McAndrew 1980; R. Luciani, *P.L. Architetto*, Rome 1987.

**London**, George (*c.*1640–1713), *see* SWITZER, Stephen.

**Long and short work**. Saxon QUOINS, consisting of long stones on end between flat ones, all bonded into the wall. The chancel arch JAMBS at Escomb (C7 or 8) may have a bearing on the origin of the technique; it may also have been evolved simultaneously and in association with pilaster-strip work (*see* LESENE). It is the insertion of the large flat stones which makes long and short work such a good bonding technique for corners, as in many cases they extend practically through the thickness of the walls; the upright blocks alone are subject to diagonal thrust.

Superficially long and short work is of two kinds:

*a.* the 'upright and flat' type, where the full size of the horizontal stone is visible on both flanks;

*b.* the long and short strip quoin, where the horizontal stones have been cut back,

making them flush with the upright blocks.

This was a refinement in the process of finding a solid cornering for stone buildings, but is not necessarily an indication of a later date (e.g. Deerhurst of the early C10 has the 'upright and flat' type). The method of construction is the same for both kinds.

**Longhena**, Baldassare (1597–1682). Venetian Baroque architect, born in Venice of a family of stone carvers and trained under SCAMOZZI. In 1630 he won a competition for the design of the *ex voto* church of S. Maria della Salute, with which he was to be occupied off and on for the rest of his long life (it was not finally consecrated until 1687). Standing on an imposing site at the entrance to the Grand Canal, this church is a masterpiece of scenographic design, with a vast buoyant dome anchored by huge Baroque scrolls to an octagonal base, and a very complex façade which directs the eye through the main door to the high altar. The interior is conceived as a series of dramatic vistas radiating from the centre of the octagonal nave. Longhena realized a similarly theatrical concept in the design of his imposing double staircase for the monastery of S. Giorgio Maggiore (1643–5), which had considerable influence on later architects. In the domestic field he was less adventurous: Palazzo Rezzonico (begun 1667) and Palazzo Pesaro (1649/52–82, façade begun 1676) on the Grand Canal – both completed after his death – with heavily rusticated basements, abundance of carving, and deep recesses which dissolve the surface of the exterior in patterns of light and shade, are merely Baroque variations on SANSOVINO's Palazzo Corner and the Mint. (G. Massari built the top floor of Palazzo Rezzonico in 1752–6.) A tendency towards wilful exaggeration of sculptural detail in these works reaches its fantastic peak in the little church of the Ospedaletto (1670–78), with a preposterously overwrought façade bursting with *telamones*, giant heads, and lion masks. He has been credited with numerous villas on the mainland, but none is of much interest.

Wittkower 1982; L. Puppi and G. Romanelli, *B.L. 1597–1682*, Venice 1982; Howard 1987.

**Longhi**, Martino the younger (1602–60), the most important member of a family of Italian architects working mainly in Rome, was the son of Onorio Longhi (1569–1619) and the grandson of Martino Longhi the elder (d.1591). He continued his father's work on S. Carlo al Corso, Rome, and began S. Antonio de' Portoghesi, Rome (1638). His major achievement is the façade of SS. Vincenzo ed Anastasio, Rome (1646–50), a powerfully dramatic, many-columned composition in which Mannerist devices are used to obtain an overwhelming High Baroque effect of grandeur and mass.

Wittkower 1982; Varriano 1986.

**Longhouse**. 1. Type of PREHISTORIC multipurpose structure of *c*.4000 BC known only from the imprints of upright posts found at various sites in western Europe, notably Bylany, Czech Republic; Köln-Lindenthal, Germany; Elsloo, Holland. 2. Type of communal dwelling traditional in Malaysia and Indonesia, notably in Sumatra. Formed of a single wooden structure up to 180 m. (550 ft) long and 15 m. (50 ft) wide, raised off the ground by posts and with a single pitched roof, the interior being divided by partitions into apartments arranged in rows for up to fifty related families, sometimes with a communal veranda running the length of the building. 3. A similar type of communal dwelling traditional among the Iroquois tribes in north-eastern USA

until *c*.1800. The term is also used for the churches and meeting-houses of the Iroquois reservations although they do not resemble the original longhouses.

B. Dawson and J. Gallow, *The Traditional Architecture of Indonesia*, London 1994.

**Longuelune**, Zacharias (1669–1748). French-born painter-architect who collaborated with Matthaeus PÖPPELMANN in Dresden from 1715 onwards on the designs for the vast new Saxon Palace. Very few of his own projects were executed but his grandiose designs, which embodied French classicist theory, exerted considerable influence both in Saxony and as far away as Poland and Denmark. He designed the formal park at Gross-Sedlitz (1726), additions to the Japanisches Palais in Dresden (1729 onwards) and the Blockhaus terminating the Hauptstrasse in Dresden Neustadt (1731) (burnt out 1945 but now reconstructed).

Colombier 1956.

**Loop**. A small, narrow and often unglazed light.

**Loos**, Adolf (1870–1933), was born at Brno in Moravia, studied at Dresden, spent three crucial years in the United States (1893–6), partly in Chicago, where he knew SULLIVAN and WRIGHT, and then worked in Vienna, strongly influenced by the doctrines just then expounded by Otto WAGNER. From the very first his designs (Goldmann shop interior, 1898) refused to allow any decorative features or any curves, though he later relented. For Loos architecture was primarily an arrangement of spaces, consolidated as a *Raumplan* or spatial plan. This led him to create split levels and room heights in his private houses of between 1904 (Villa Karma, Lake Geneva) and 1910 (Steiner House,

Vienna). They are characterized by unrelieved cubic shapes, a total absence of ornament, and a love of fine materials. In his theoretical writings, or rather his journalism, he was a rabid anti-ornamentalist, an enemy therefore of the Wiener Werkstätten and HOFFMANN, and a believer in the engineer and in good craftsmanship, as is evident in his American Karntner Bar, Vienna (1907). His famous article called *Ornament and Crime* came out in 1908. As an architect, however, he wavered. His office building in the Michaelerplatz, Vienna (1910), has Tuscan columns, his design for the Chicago Tribune competition of 1923 is a huge closely windowed Doric column; but smaller domestic jobs, such as the house for the Dadaist Tristan Tzara in Paris (1926) and the Villa Müller, Prague (1931), remained faithful to the spirit of 1904–10. Loos was not a successful architect, but he was influential among some of the *avant-garde* in Europe and his posthumous reputation has steadily increased. His collected essays have been published in English as *Spoken into the Void* (1982).

Hitchcock 1977; B. Gravagnuolo, *A.L. Theory and Works*, New York 1982; *The Architecture of A.L.*, exh. cat., London 1986; L. v. Duzer and K. Kleinman, *Villa Müller. A Work of A.L.*, New York 1994; P. Tournikiotis, *A.L.*, New York 1994; K. Lustenberger, *A.L.*, London 1994; R. Schezen, *A.L. Architect*, New York/London 1996; K. Frampton and J. Rosa, *A.L.: Architecture 1903–1932*, New York/London 1996.

**Lorimer**, Robert Stodart (1864–1929), *see* SCOTTISH ARCHITECTURE.

**L'Orme**, Philibert de (1500/15–1570). French architect born in Lyon, the son of a master mason. Went to Rome for three years, probably 1533–6, where he moved in high diplomatic-humanist circles but misunderstood Italian architecture. He was nothing if not original and as utterly French as his friend and admirer Rabelais. His buildings are notable for their ingenuity and sometimes outrageous experimentation. Almost everything he built has been destroyed, except for parts of Anet (Diane de Poitier's house) and the tomb of Francis I in St Denis (begun 1547). The frontispiece of Anet (begun before 1550, now in the École des Beaux Arts, Paris) is a good example of his style, correct in detail and rather more monumental than that of his contemporary LESCOT. The chapel (1549–52) and entrance front (*c.*1552) are still *in situ*. For his buildings he also designed elaborate gardens with great *basins* or ponds with canals. He had a great influence on the development of French architecture, partly through his books, *Nouvelles Inventions* (1561) and *Architecture* (1567), the most practical architectural treatise of the Renaissance, containing a complete manual on the erection of a house. The decorative part of the screen in St Étienne-du-Mont, Paris, with its pierced balustrades and spiral staircase (*c.*1545), is probably by him.

A. Blunt, *P. de L'O.*, London 1958; L. Brion-Guerry, *P. de L'O.*, Milan 1965; Blunt 1982; M. Maressi, *P. de L'O.*, Milan 1997.

**Loudon**, John Claudius (1782–1843). British architect and landscape architect notably mainly for his writings. After apprenticeship to a gardener in Edinburgh, he went to London in 1803 and at once began writing on agriculture and gardening. He took up farming in Oxfordshire, made money and lost it, and travelled on the Continent (as far as Moscow in 1814, France and Italy in 1819–20). His *Encyclopedia of Gardening* came out in 1822, *Encyclopedia of Agriculture* in 1825 and his most influential works, his *Encyclopedia of Cottage, Farm and Villa Architecture* in 1833 and *The Suburban Garden and Villa Companion* in 1838. In 1840 he reprinted in a modestly priced edition the writings of REPTON, which had been one of his sources of inspiration. His ideas about garden design and architecture found expression also in the *Gardener's Magazine*, which he edited from 1826, and his short-lived *Architectural Magazine* (1834). From 1830 he had the collaboration of his wife, Jane Webb (1807–58), a no less prolific writer who addressed herself to women in *Gardening for Ladies* (1840). He was the first writer to respond to the new middle-class demand for suburban villa gardens which, he suggested, should incorporate on a reduced scale the bold groupings of trees in Repton's parks but with a greater proportion of the area given to flowering plants, the botanically interesting specimen trees and shrubs being isolated on lawns. He called this the 'gardenesque' style and it quickly spread in both Britain and the USA. He also provided designs for middle-class houses, previously neglected in architectural publications, with advice on their siting, planning, construction and embellishment. By 1816 he was experimenting with iron and glass CONSERVATORIES. His proposals for urban public parks in 1822, for a kind of greenbelt round London in 1830 and for cemeteries planned like landscape gardens in 1830 were equally precocious and forward-looking. But he had few opportunities to realize his ideas on the ground. Early in his career he worked as an architect on country houses, altering the exterior and laying out the grounds of Barnbarrow, Wigtownshire (1806, destroyed 1942), designing the neo-Gothic Garth, near Welshpool, Powys (1809–10, demolished 1947) and the Moorish style Hope End, near Ledbury, Herefordshire (1812, mostly demolished 1873). His pair of semi-detached houses (one for himself) designed to look like a single villa with a central domed conservatory, 3–5 Porchester Terrace, London (1823–4), survives. His practical ability as a landscape architect is revealed by the Arboretum, Derby, laid out in his gardenesque style as a botanical garden accessible to the general public and opened in 1840.

E. B. MacDougall, *J.C.L. and the Early Nineteenth Century in Great Britain*, Washington, DC, 1980; M. I. Simon, *L. and the Landscape; from Country Seat to Metropolis*, London 1988.

**Louis**, Victor (1731–1800). French neoclassical architect working in a somewhat florid style derived from Ancient Rome and the city palaces (rather than the villas) of PALLADIO. Born in Paris, he was trained there and at the French Academy in Rome (1756–9). In 1765 he was called to Warsaw by Stanislas-Augustus but returned the next year without having built anything. His first work of importance is also his masterpiece, the theatre at Bordeaux (1772–80), a massive structure with a dodecastyle portico (without pediment) stretching the full length of the main façade. It contains a large stage, very grand auditorium and the most monumental staircase and foyer that had been realized up to that date. He did some other work in and around Bordeaux (e.g. Hôtel Saige, now the Préfecture, 1775–7, and the Château de Bouilh, begun 1787, unfinished). He also had an extensive practice in Paris where his main work was the colonnades in the Palais Royal gardens (1780–85) and the adjoining Théâtre de la Comédie-Française (1786–90, rebuilt 1902). The original building had an iron and hollow-tile roof to reduce the danger of fires.

Braham 1980; F.-G. Pariset, *V.L.*, Bordeaux 1980; C. Taillard, *Le Grand Théâtre de Bordeaux. Miroir d'un société*, Paris 1993; Kalnein 1995.

**Louvre** or **louver**. 1. An opening, often with a LANTERN over, in the roof of a hall to let the smoke from a central hearth escape; either open-sided, or closed by slanting boards to keep out the rain. 2. One of a series of overlapping boards or slips of glass to admit air and exclude rain. *See* Fig. 76.

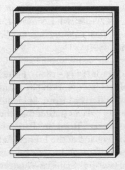

Fig. 76 Louvre

**Lowside-window**. A window usually on the south side of the chancel, lower than the others, possibly intended for communication between persons outside the chancel and the priest within; perhaps also for the sanctus bell to be heard outside the church. It was formerly, and erroneously, called a *leper window*.

**Lozenge**. A diamond shape, i.e. a flat rectilinear figure with four equal sides but two angles sharper than the others.

**Lubetkin**, Berthold (1901–90). Born in Russia, he went to Berlin in 1922, then studied and worked in Paris with PERRET before settling in London in 1931. In 1932 he formed the architectural team TECTON with ARUP, LASDUN and others. They did the freely moulded concrete Penguin Pool for the London Zoo (1934–8), also the Highpoint Flats I and II

at Highgate, London (1933–5 and 1936–8); the Finsbury Health Centre, London (1938–9); and Finsbury Council flats, London (1946–8). However, when their designs for Peterlee (1947–8), a NEW TOWN for Durham miners, were rejected, Tecton broke up and Lubetkin went into semi-retirement for the rest of his life.

P. Coe and M. Reading, *L. and Tecton. Architecture and Social Commitment*, London/Bristol 1981; J. Allen, *B.L. Architecture and the Tradition of Progress*, London 1992.

**Lucarne**. 1. A small opening in an attic or a spire. 2. A DORMER WINDOW.

**Luckhardt**, Wassili (1889–1972), *see* GLASS.

**Ludovice**, João Frederico (Johann Friedrich Ludwig, *c.*1670–1752), the leading Late Baroque architect in Portugal, was born at Hall in Swabia, the son of a goldsmith whose craft he practised first in Rome (1697–1701) then in Lisbon. In about 1711 the king of Portugal commissioned him to build a small convent at Mafra. Gradually the size of the project was enlarged, and the building finally became one of the largest in Europe (built 1717–70). It includes a royal palace, a vast church, and conventual buildings for 300 monks. Mafra derives mainly from High Baroque Rome with a few south German and Portuguese overtones: the church, liberally decorated with Italian statues, is especially impressive. His only other works of importance are the library of Coimbra University (1717–23), with a very rich *mouvementé* façade, and the apse of Évora Cathedral (1716–46).

Kubler and Soria 1959; A. de Carvalho, *Don João V e arte do seu tempo*, Lisbon 1962.

**Lundberg**, Jon, *see* NORWEGIAN ARCHITECTURE.

**Lunette**. A semicircular opening or surface, usually over a door, niche or window. When over a portal of a church it is usually called a TYMPANUM. The term can also be applied to any flat, semicircular surface.

**Lurago**, Carlo (*c.*1618–84), *see* CZECH ARCHITECTURE; GERMAN ARCHITECTURE.

**Lurçat**, André (1894–1970), *see* FRENCH ARCHITECTURE.

**Lutyens**, Edwin Landseer (1869–1944). The leading English 'Edwardian' architect and as expressive of his period as was Elgar in his music – sensitivity, imagination and impish humour being combined, not always happily, with the grandiose and majestic. After a short time with the country-house architects George & Peto, he set up on his own in 1889. His ambition was to emulate Norman SHAW but he was influenced by WEBB as well. In 1896 he designed Munstead Wood, Munstead, Surrey, for the gardener and garden designer Gertrude JEKYLL, who revived the English cottage garden. They were later to collaborate on a number of outstanding, small but usually quite opulent, houses, some of them masterpieces of ARTS AND CRAFTS architecture, notably Deanery Gardens, Sonning, Berkshire (1899–1902) for Edward Hudson, the founder of *Country Life* magazine. It is as skilful in its picturesque use of the vernacular as his reconstruction for the same client of Lindisfarne Castle, Northumberland, was to be two years later in a romantic, dramatic vein. Other examples of his early, rambling, picturesque houses are Orchards, Munstead, Surrey (1897–9); Tigbourne Court, Witley, Surrey (1899–1901); Homewood, Knebworth, Hertfordshire (1901); Marsh Court, Stockbridge, Hampshire (1901–4); Little Thakeham, Thakeham, Sussex (1902–3); and Folly Farm, Sulhamstead, Berkshire (1905). Their variety and ingenuity – especially in interior spatial play and in their imaginative interior-exterior relationships – make them comparable to Frank Lloyd WRIGHT's Prairie Houses of about the same date. They established Lutyens's reputation for originality and imaginative ability in co-ordinating vernacular forms. However, he was also attracted by Classicism, at first of a William and Mary variety (Liberal Club, Farnham, Surrey, 1894–5); then in a wilfully eccentric and grandiose Vanbrughian way (Heathcote, Ilkley, West Yorkshire, 1905–7); later more quietly neo-Georgian though on a grand scale (Nashdom, Taplow, Buckinghamshire, 1905–8, and Great Maytham, Rolvenden, Kent, 1907–9). Finally, in two late classical houses – The Salutation, Sandwich, Kent (1911), and Gledstone Hall, West Yorkshire (1922–6) – his genius achieved solutions as convincing as any of his earlier picturesque houses. In the latter style his work culminated in Castle Drogo, Drewsteignton, Devon (1910–30), an enormous and imposing feudal fantasy which was never completed.

Lutyens shared to the full the imperial *folie de grandeur* of the Edwardian heyday and this made him the ideal architect for the layout and planning on a vast scale of New Delhi in India, where his Viceroy's House (1912–31, now Rashtrapati Bhavan) has a sense of solemnity and magnificence which BAKER in his buildings for New Delhi lacked. Also notable are the four princely, domed residences begun in 1920, surrounding his All-India War Memorial Arch (1931). Though never on the scale of anything at New Delhi, some of his First World War memorials are even more impressive in their gravity and simplicity. The Cenotaph in Whitehall, London (1919–20), is the most famous, but the Memorial to the Missing of the Somme at Thiepval near Arras in France (1927–32) is overwhelming in its lonely, threnodic grandeur.

Of his later buildings – imposing in scale and as inventive and original as ever in detail – Britannic House, Finsbury Circus, London (1920–24), and the Midland Bank, Poultry, London (1924–7), should be mentioned, as also his two late, classicizing country houses: Halnaker House near Chichester, Sussex (1936), and Middleton Park, Middleton Stoney, Oxfordshire (1938). His great design for the Roman Catholic Cathedral of Liverpool (1929–44) was never to be realized – only the crypt was built (1933–41). He was knighted in 1918.

C. Hussey, *The Life of Sir E.L.*, London 1950; A. S. G. Butler, *The Architecture of Sir E.L.*, London 1950; C. Amery et al., L., exh. cat., London 1981; J. Brown, *L. and the Edwardians*, London 1996.

**Luzarches**, Robert de (d.c.1236), see ROBERT DE LUZARCHES.

**Lych gate**. A covered wooden gateway with open sides at the entrance to a churchyard, providing a resting-place for a coffin (the word *lych* is Saxon for corpse). Part of the burial service is sometimes read there.

**Lyming**, Robert (d.1628), see LIMINGE, Robert.

# M

**Machicolation**. A gallery or PARAPET projecting on brackets on the outside of castle towers and walls, with openings in the floor through which to drop molten lead, boiling oil and missiles.

**Machuca**, Pedro (d.1550). Spanish architect who began as a painter, worked in Italy and returned to Spain in 1520. His masterpiece, the Palace of Charles V with its circular courtyard in the Alhambra at Granada (1527–68), is very Italian in the RAPHAEL–GIULIO ROMANO style; indeed, it is larger than any comparable palace in Italy. But various Spanish or PLATERESQUE features crept into his design, e.g. the garlanded window frames.

E. E. Rosenthal, *The Palace of Charles V in Granada*, Princeton 1985.

**Mackay**, David John (b.1933), *see* SPANISH ARCHITECTURE.

**Mackintosh**, Charles Rennie (1868–1928), Scottish architect, studied at the Glasgow School of Art at the time when Glasgow painting had suddenly turned from a provincial past to new forms of considerable interest to people in England and even on the Continent. In 1893 and the following years he, his friend McNair, and the two Macdonald sisters, Margaret (later Mrs Mackintosh, 1865–1933) and Frances (later Mrs McNair), designed graphic work and repoussé metalwork in an ART NOUVEAU way, inspired by *The Studio* (which started in London in 1893) and especially by Jan Toorop, the Dutchman. In 1896 Mackintosh won the competition for the new building of the

Glasgow School of Art and erected a building inferior to none of its date anywhere in Europe or America – on a clear rational plan, with the basic external forms equally clear and rational (e.g. the studio windows), but with a centrepiece of complete originality and high fancifulness, influenced by VOYSEY, by the Scottish castle and manor-house tradition, and even a little by the current English 'Wrenaissance'. The metalwork of the façade and much of the interior achieve a unification of the crisply rectangular with the long, delicate, languid curves of Art Nouveau. It is in this unique harmony that Mackintosh's greatness lies, and it explains the deep impression his furniture and furnishings made on Austrian architects when they became familiar with him, first through *The Studio* and then through an exhibition at the Secession (*see* OLBRICH) in 1900. The Viennese were abandoning Art Nouveau for a clearer, saner style, and he both inspired and confirmed them.

Mackintosh had fully evolved his style in his interior work by 1899 – white lacquered chairs and cupboards, erect, elegant, clearly articulated, and with wistfully curved inlays in metal and pink, mauve or mother-of-pearl enamel. There was no one else who could combine the rational and the expressive in so intriguing a way. His capital works at or near Glasgow are the tea-rooms for Mrs Cranston (Buchanan Street, 1897 onwards; Argyle Street, 1897 and 1905; Sauchiehall Street, 1904; Ingram Street, 1901, *c.*1906 and *c.*1911), now alas mostly destroyed or disused; two houses (Windyhill, Kilmacolm,

357

1899–1901, and Hill House, Helensburgh, 1902–3); a school (Scotland Street, 1906); and the library wing of the School of Art, Glasgow (1907–9), with its sheer, towering outer wall and its bewitchingly complex interior. In 1901 he had come second in a German publisher's competition for the house of an art-lover (Baillie Scott came first), and this consolidated his reputation abroad. (His design was carried out almost a century later in Bellahouston Park, Glasgow, 1986–96.)

However, his erratic ways alienated clients. In 1913 he left the firm (Honeyman & Keppie) in which he had been a partner since 1904. He moved to Walberswick, then to London, then after the war to Port Vendres, and finally back to London, painting highly original, finely drawn landscapes and still-lifes, but never recovering an architectural practice.

T. Howarth, *C.R.M. and the Modern Movement*, London (1952) 1977; J. Cooper (ed.), *M. Architecture: The Complete Buildings and Selected Projects*, London and New York (1978) 1983; P. Nuttgens (ed.), *M. and his Contemporaries*, London 1988; P. Robertson, *C.R.M. The Chelsea Years 1915–1923*, Glasgow/London 1994; J. Steele, *C.R.M. Synthesis and Form*, London 1994; A. Crawford, *C.R.M.*, London 1995; W. Kaplan (ed.), *C.R.M.*, Glasgow 1996.

**Mackmurdo**, Arthur Heygate (1851–1942). English designer and architect. He came from a wealthy family and had plenty of leisure to evolve a style of his own. In 1874 he travelled to Italy with RUSKIN. About 1880 he seems to have built his first houses, of which 8 Private Road, Enfield (1887), is the most elegant. In 1882 he founded the Century Guild, a group of ARTS AND CRAFTS architects, artists and designers inspired by Ruskin and MORRIS. The group began in 1884

to publish a magazine, *The Hobby Horse*, which anticipated some of the features of book design recovered by Morris from the medieval past in his Kelmscott Press of 1890. As early as 1883, in the design for the cover of his book on Wren's City churches, Mackmurdo introduced those long flame-like or tendril-like curves which nearly ten years later were taken up, especially in Belgium, as a basis for ART NOUVEAU. But while in such two-dimensional designs, including a number for textiles (*c.*1884) and in some early furniture (1882–3), Mackmurdo is the lone pioneer of Art Nouveau, the furniture he designed from 1886 onwards and a stand for an exhibition at Liverpool, also of 1886, established him as the forerunner of VOYSEY in clarity of structure, elegance, and originality in the sense of independence of the past. Specially characteristic, on the exhibition stand, are the long, tapering posts with a far-projecting flat cornice. Among his later buildings the Anglo-Dutch studio-house at 15 Cadogan Gardens, London (1893–4) is notable. In 1904 Mackmurdo gave up architecture; later he concentrated on economic thought and writing, his ideas being similar to those of Social Credit.

L. Lambourne, *Utopian Craftsmen: The Arts and Crafts Movement from the Cotswolds to Chicago*, London 1980; P. Stansky, *Redesigning the World: William Morris, the 1880s and the Arts and Crafts*, Princeton 1985.

**Maclure**, Samuel (1867–1929), *see* CANADIAN ARCHITECTURE.

**MacMorran**, Donald (1914–83), *see* NEO-GEORGIAN.

**Maderno**, Carlo (*c.*1556–1629), was born at Capolago on Lake Lugano, and had settled in Rome by 1588, beginning as assistant to his uncle Domenico FON-

TANA. He was appointed architect of St Peter's in 1603, when he also completed the façade of S. Susanna, Rome, a revolutionary design with which he broke away from the current rather facile and academic MANNERISM and established his own lucid, forceful and intensely dynamic style. S. Susanna and the majestic dome of S. Andrea della Valle, Rome, are his masterpieces, though he is best known for his work at St Peter's, where he had the unenviable job of altering MICHELANGELO's centralized plan by adding a nave and façade. Work began in 1607, and the façade was finished by 1612. Its excessive length is due to the later addition of towers, of which only the substructures were built and which now appear to form part of the façade. His Confessio before the high altar and his elegant fountain in the *piazza* are more successful. His secular buildings include Palazzo Mattei, Rome (1598–1618), Villa Aldobrandini, Frascati (1603–c.1620), and Palazzo Barberini, Rome (1628, with BORROMINI), though the latter was almost entirely executed after his death by BERNINI, who made various alterations, notably to the main façade.

H. Hibbard, *C.M. and Roman Architecture 1580–1630*, London 1971; Waddy 1990.

**Madrasa**. An Islamic theological and legal college. At first instruction was given in mosques (e.g. al-Azhar, Cairo, still an intellectual centre). The first residential madrasas were built in Iran in the early C10, probably similar to Buddhist VIHARAS in Central Asia. None survives. The earliest surviving madrasa is that at Bosra, Syria, of 1136. A madrasa has a courtyard with an IWAN, serving as a classroom, on at least one side, a prayer hall and accommodation for teachers and cells for students, seldom more than twenty. The Iranian four-iwan mosque plan, with two storeys of cells around the courtyard, became usual, e.g. Nur al-Din madrasa, Damascus (1171–2), the Zahirya madrasa, Cairo (1262–3), the Imami madrasa, Isfahan, Iran (1325), the Khwaja Mahmud Gawan, Bidar, India (1472) and the three madrasas facing each other across the Registan, Samarkand, Uzbekistan (1417–1660). There are many local variants. In Anatolia from the C13 the open court was often replaced by a large domed hall, e.g. Quaratia madrasa, Konya, Turkey (1253). A prominent detached, domed prayer hall was a feature of Ottoman madrasas, e.g. Bayazid II madrasa, Istanbul (1500–1505). A small courtyard with central pool surrounded by lecture rooms and cells on two storeys was introduced in C14 Morocco, with lavish stucco, carved wood and ceramic tile decorations, e.g. Sahrij madrasa, Fez, Morocco (1321–3). Madrasas might also form part of larger complexes, e.g. the Sulemaniye complex, Istanbul (1550–57), one of SINAN's finest works.

Hillenbrand 1994.

**Maekawa**, Kunio (1905–86). Japanese architect who worked with LE CORBUSIER (1928–30) and RAYMOND (1930–35) and made his name as a pioneer of exposed concrete before the war. Later he refined its use in such buildings as the Harumi Apartments, Tokyo (1958), the Metropolitan Festival Hall, Tokyo (1961), and the Kanagawa Prefectural Youth Center, Yokohama (1962). His later work is very restrained, e.g. his 1970s extension in banded brickwork to Le Corbusier's National Museum of Western Art, Tokyo, on which he had worked as an assistant in 1955–9, or the Kumamoto Prefectural Art Museum (1977). Kenzo TANGE worked in his office (1938–42).

A. Altherr, *Drei japanische Architeckten, M., Tange, Sakakura*, Stuttgart 1968.

**Maher**, George Washington (1864–1926), *see* ARTS AND CRAFTS.

**Maiano**, Benedetto da (1442–97), *see* BENEDETTO DA MAIANO.

**Maiano**, Giuliano da (1432–90), *see* GIULIANO DA MAIANO.

**Maidan**. A term of Persian origin for an open space or square in or just outside a city, for ceremonies, military parades, etc., a notable feature of urbanism in central Asia and Mughal India.

**Maillart**, Robert (1872–1940), a Swiss engineer, studied at the Zürich Polytechnic (1890–94), and set up on his own (1902). He worked on the unexplored possibilities of REINFORCED CONCRETE, and in the course of that work, arrived at a new aesthetic for concrete, using it to span by curves. His Tavenasa Bridge in Switzerland (1905) is the first in which arch and roadway are structurally one. He built many bridges afterwards, all of them of a thoroughbred elegance; the one across the Salzinatobel, Switzerland, has a span of nearly 90 m. (300 ft) (1929–30). In 1908 he also began experimenting with 'flat-slab' concrete mushroom construction, at a time when this was being done independently in the United States; the technique involves a post and a mushroom top spreading from it that are one inseparable concrete unit, floors and roofs being constructed without supporting beams. His Federal Grain Store, Altdorf, Switzerland (1912), was the pioneer flat-slab building.

M. Bill, *R.M.*, Zürich (1949) 1962; J. R. Abel *et al.* (eds.), *The M. Papers*, Princeton 1973; D. P. Billington, *R.M.'s Bridges. The Art of Engineering*, Princeton 1979; D. P. Billington, *R.M. and the Art of Reinforced Concrete*, Cambridge, Mass. 1991.

**Maillou**, Jean (1668–1753), *see* CANADIAN ARCHITECTURE.

**Maisonette** or **duplex apartment**. A self-contained dwelling of two floors with internal stairs, in an apartment house.

**Maitani**, Lorenzo (d.1330). Sienese sculptor and architect. He was called in to advise on Orvieto Cathedral in 1310, being then described as 'universalis caput-magister', which testifies to his celebrity as an architect. From then until his death he was in complete control of all work on the façade of Orvieto Cathedral, including the sculpture, some of which is probably by him. Two drawings for the façade survive, the second being probably by Maitani (Opera del Duomo, Orvieto). In 1317 he was mentioned as working on a fountain at Perugia and in 1322 he was on the commission for the new Baptistery of Siena Cathedral.

White 1987.

**Majewski**, Hilary (1837–97), *see* COMPANY TOWN; POLISH ARCHITECTURE.

**Major**, Joshua (1787–1866), *see* PUBLIC PARK.

**Maki**, Fumihiko (b.1928). Japanese architect, trained in the USA at Harvard and worked with SOM in Chicago before returning to Japan in 1960. He was associated with METABOLISM but was to remain closer to neo-Modernist reticence and refinement, e.g. Hillside Terrace Apartments, Tokyo (1969–92). His Fujisawa Municipal Gymnasia, Fujisawa (1984–7), with its metal trusswork and stainless steel sheets in long-span shell forms, marked a complete change of course towards structural boldness, followed by his sophisticated 'fragmentary' Spiral Building, Tokyo (1985), and the vast Makuhari Exhibition Centre, Chiba Prefecture (1989). This tectonic-scenographic style culminated in the TEPIA (Technology–Utopia) Building, Tokyo (1989), and the Tokyo Metropolitan Gymnasium (1990). His Yerba Buena

Center, San Francisco, California (1993), was awarded the Pritzker Prize. Also notable was his Isar Büro Park, Munich (1995). Maki codified the MEGASTRUCTURE concept in his *Investigations in Collective Form* (St. Louis 1964). He published *Fragmentary Figures* (Tokyo 1990).

F.M. *1970–1986*, Space Design 1, Tokyo 1986; S. Salat, *F.M. Une Poétique de la Fragmentation*, Paris 1989; *F.M. 1987–1992*, Space Design 1, Tokyo 1993; *F.M. Buildings and Projects*, New York 1997.

**Makovecz**, Imre (b.1935). The outstanding exponent of Hungarian Organic Architecture. His Cultural Centre, Sarospatak (1984), Lutheran church, Siofak (1988–9), and Roman Catholic church, Paks (1989), were notable, as was his Hungarian Pavilion for the 1992 Expo in Seville.

H. Dvorszky (ed.), *Hungarian Organic Architecture*, Venice 1991; J. Cook, *Seeking Structure from Nature. I.M. and the Hungarian Organic Architecture*, Basel 1996.

**Malevich**, Kazimir (1878–1935). Russian painter, pioneer of Suprematism (hard-edged abstractionism, developed *c.*1915), who from *c.*1920 – with his pupils at *Unovis* – turned his hand to ideal architectural models which he called *Arkhitektoniki* or *Planity*. Though his aesthetic was anti-utilitarian, hence strongly opposed to CONSTRUCTIVISM, he was a seminal influence on the Modernist generations of, e.g., LISSITSKY and the BAUHAUS of the 1920s. [R. R. Milner-Gulland]

L. A. Zhadova, *M.: Suprematism and Revolution in Russian Art 1910–1930*, London 1982.

**Mallet-Stevens**, Robert (1886–1945), *see* ART DECO; FRENCH ARCHITECTURE.

**Mamluk architecture**, *see* EGYPTIAN ARCHITECTURE.

**Mandapa**. A large open hall, especially one in a Hindu temple complex.

**Mandorla**, *see* VESICA.

**Mannerism**. In its primary sense, the acceptance of a manner rather than its meaning. Now Mannerism has also become a term to denote the style current in Italy from MICHELANGELO to the end of the C16. It is characterized by the use of motifs in deliberate opposition to their original significance or context, but it can also express itself in an equally deliberate cold and rigid Classicism. The term applies to French and Spanish architecture of the C16 as well (de L'ORME; the Escorial), but how far it applies to the northern countries is controversial. Principal examples in Italy are Michelangelo's Medici Chapel and Laurentian Library, GIULIO ROMANO's works at Mantua, VASARI's Uffizi at Florence, and other works by these architects and LIGORIO, AMMANATI, BUONTALENTI, etc. PALLADIO belongs to Mannerism only in certain limited aspects of his work.

J. Shearman, *M.*, Harmondsworth 1967; Lotz 1995.

**Manning**, Warren Henry (1861–1935), *see* MOTORWAY; PARKWAY.

**Manor house**. A house in the country or a village, the centre of a manor. Architecturally the term is used to denote the unfortified, medium-sized house of the later Middle Ages in England.

M. Wood, *The Medieval English House*, London 1965; O. Cook and E. Smith, *The English House through Seven Centuries*, London 1983.

**Mansard roof**, *see* ROOF.

**Mansart**, François (1598–1666), the first great protagonist of French Classicism in architecture, holds a position parallel to Poussin in painting and Corneille in drama. He never went to Italy, and his style is extremely French in its elegance, clarity and cool restraint. Though of scrupulous artistic conscience he was unfortunately both arrogant and slippery in his business relationships, and his inability to make and keep to a final plan not unnaturally enraged his clients. As a result, he lost many commissions. For the last ten years of his life he was virtually unemployed. He was seldom patronized by the Crown and never by the great nobility; his clients belonged mainly to the newly rich bourgeoisie, who had the intelligence to appreciate and the money to pay for his sophisticated and luxurious buildings.

Born in Paris, the son of a master carpenter, he probably began under de BROSSE at Coulommiers. By 1624 he had already established himself as a prominent architect in the capital. His early work derives from de Brosse, with Mannerist overtones in the style of DU CERCEAU, but his individual style began to emerge at the Château de Balleroy (1626), where the harmonious grouping of massive blocks achieves an effect of sober monumentality. His first masterpiece, the Orléans wing of the *château* at Blois (1635–8), would have been a grander and more monumental Palais Luxembourg had it ever been completed. Only the central block and colonnades were built. But these display to the full the ingenuity of planning, clarity of disposition, and purity and refinement of detail which distinguish his work. He also introduced here the continuous broken roof with a steep lower slope and flatter, shorter upper portion that is named after him. His style reached culmination at Maisons Lafitte (1642–51), the country house near Paris which he built for the immensely wealthy René de Longueil, who apparently allowed him a completely free hand. (He pulled down part of it during construction in order to revise his designs!) It is his most complete work to survive

and gives a better idea of his genius than any other. The oval rooms in the wings and the vestibule, executed entirely in stone without either gilding or colour, epitomize his suave severity and civilized reticence in decoration. His design for the Val-de-Grâce in Paris (*c.* 1645) is contemporary with Maisons Lafitte, but he was dismissed and replaced by LEMERCIER in 1646, when the building had reached the entablature of the nave and the lower storey of the façade. The conception appears to derive from PALLADIO's Redentore.

His other important buildings are Ste Marie de la Visitation, Paris (1632–4); the Hôtel de la Vrillière, Paris (begun 1635, destroyed), wholly symmetrical and the model for the classical type of Parisian *hôtel*; the Hôtel du Jars, Paris (begun 1648, now destroyed), in which he developed a freer, more plastic disposition of rooms which was to be very influential. His last surviving work is his remodelling of the Hôtel Carnavalet in Paris (1660–61). He was consulted by Colbert in the 1660s in connection with the Louvre and a royal chapel at St Denis, but his designs were not executed.

A. Braham and P. Smith, *F.M.*, London 1973; Blunt 1982.

**Mansart**, Jules Hardouin, *see* HARDOUIN-MANSART, Jules.

**Mantelpiece**. The wood, brick, stone or marble frame surrounding a fireplace, frequently including an overmantel or mirror above; sometimes called *chimney-piece*.

**Manueline style**. An architectural style peculiar to Portugal and named after King Manuel the Fortunate (1495–1521). *See* PORTUGUESE ARCHITECTURE.

**Maqsura**. Arabic word originally signifying an area in a MOSQUE, near the MIHRAB and MINBAR, enclosed by a metal or wooden screen and reserved for a Caliph or other ruler, to emphasize his status and protect him from physical assault. It could sometimes be entered directly from an adjoining palace, e.g. at Basra, Cordoba and Kufa. A notable early CII example in wood survives in the Great Mosque, Kairouan, Tunisia. This type was seldom constructed in later mosques and from the CII the term was used for a large domed chamber incorporated in the sanctuary and intended for communal, not private, prayer – a feature of many large mosques in Iran (Great Mosque, Isfahan, c.1072–92) and Egypt (Mosque of Baybars I, Cairo, 1266–9).

**Marble**. A mineralogically imprecise term for a hard metamorphic rock or LIMESTONE that can be sawn into slabs, takes a high polish and is often veined or irregularly coloured by impurities. White marble was quarried on the Aegean island of Paros (used for the Parthenon, Athens), and since Ancient Roman times has been widely quarried in the Mediterranean area, notably at Carrara, Italy, which is still productive. Many types of coloured or variegated marbles have been used for cladding, e.g. *Giallo antico* (yellow sometimes tinged with pink, quarried by the Ancient Romans at Chemyou, Tunisia), *Rosso antico* (dark red with occasional white streaks, quarried by the Ancient Romans at Matapan, Greece).

Davey 1965; L. and T. M. Mannoni, *Il Marmo – Materia e cultura*, Genoa 1985; G. Borghini (ed.), *Marmi antichi*, Rome 1992; E. Castelnuovo, *Niveo de Marmore. L'Uso artistico del Marmo di Carrara del XI al XV Secolo*, Sarzana 1992.

**Marchionni**, Carlo (1702–86). Italian architect famous for his Villa Albani (now Torlonia), Rome (begun 1746), where the garden temples of c.1760 reflect his friend Winckelmann's neo-classicism. He also designed SS. Annunziata, Mes-sina (1763), and the Sacristy of St Peter's, Rome (1776–86).

E. Debenedetti (ed.), *C.M.*, Rome 1988.

**Markelius**, Sven Gottfrid (1889–1972). Swedish architect and urban designer. His concert hall at Hälsingborg (1925–32) is notable, but he is famous as city architect and planner to the city of Stockholm 1944–54, when he laid out the new suburb of Vällingby. Vällingby is not a SATELLITE TOWN, as it is not meant to have a completely independent existence, but is of an exemplary plan combining a truly urban-looking centre with peripheral housing of both high blocks of flats and small houses (1953–9).

S. Ray, *Il contributo svedese all'architettura contemporanea e l'opera di S.M.*, Rome 1969.

**Marot**, Daniel (c.1660–1752), was the son of a minor French architect Jean Marot (c.1619–79) who is chiefly remembered for his volumes of engravings *L'Architecture française* known as 'le grand Marot' and 'le petit Marot'. Born in Paris, Daniel emigrated to Holland after the Revocation of the Edict of Nantes (1685), becoming almost immediately architect to William of Orange. He developed an intricate style of ornamentation, similar to that of Jean Bérain (see his *Nouvelles cheminées à panneaux de la manière de France*), and was involved among other things with the design of the audience chamber or Trèveszaal in the Binnenhof, The Hague (1695–8), and the interior decoration and garden design at Het Loo. He followed William to England and designed the gardens (Grand Parterre) and perhaps some of the furnishings and interior decoration at Hampton Court, but though he later described himself as 'Architect to the King of England' no buildings can be ascribed to him (Schomberg House, London, *c.*1698, appears to have been strongly influenced by him). He died at The Hague, where he designed part of the Royal Library (1734–8) and Stadthuis (1733–9). He published his *Œuvres* in Amsterdam in 1715 but his main buildings date from the following years and are all in The Hague – the German Embassy (1715), the Hôtel van Wassenaar and the façade of the Royal Library (1734, wings by Pieter de Swart, 1761).

Rosenberg 1977; Kuyper 1980.

**Marquise**. A canopy over an entrance door, often of metal and glass.

**MARS** (Modern Architecture Research Group), *see* COATES, Wells.

**Martellange**, Étienne (d.1641), *see* LEMERCIER, Jacques.

**Martello tower**. A round, low tower, with guns mounted on the flat roof, built for coastal defence in England from 1793 onwards, mainly during the Napoleonic wars but also later and on a wide scale. There are also examples in Jersey, Orkney, Ireland, Canada, South Africa and the USA (Key West, Florida). In form they derive from the traditional Mediterranean watch tower, e.g. that on Cape Mortella, Corsica, hence the name.

S. Sutcliffe, *M.T.*, Cranberry, NJ, 1973.

**Martienssen**, Rex (1905–42), *see* SOUTH AFRICAN ARCHITECTURE.

**Martin**, Leslie (b.1908). English architect, architect to the London County Council from 1953 to 1956, in succession to Sir Robert MATTHEW, and later Professor of Architecture at Cambridge University. Under him the finest of all LCC housing estates was built, that at Roehampton for a population of about 10,000. Some of the brightest young architects in England were at that time working in the LCC office, and Martin

gave them full scope. In the course of building the style of the scheme changed from one inspired by Sweden to that of LE CORBUSIER at Chandigarh, and Martin's own work in partnership with C. A. St J. WILSON has moved in the same direction – see, for example, the new building for Caius College, Cambridge (1960–62). Other later work includes College Hall, Leicester University (1958–61), the new Oxford libraries (1961–4), Brunswick Centre, Bloomsbury, London (1962–8), and, with Peter Moro (b.1911), the re-modelled river front of MATTHEW's Royal Festival Hall, London. He was knighted in 1957.

J. Mackean, *Royal Festival Hall, LCC, L.M. and Peter Moro*, London 1992; P. Carolin and T. Dannatt (eds.), *Sir L.M. Working Papers*, London 1996.

**Martinelli**, Domenico (1650–1718). Italian quadratura painter and architect errant, who travelled widely and played an important part in the diffusion of the Italian Baroque style north of the Alps. He was born in Lucca and ordained priest, but this did nothing to interfere with his wandering artistic career. His masterpiece is the Stadtpalais Liechtenstein in Vienna (1694–1705), which introduced the elaborate triumphal staircase which was to become an essential feature of Viennese palace architecture. Martinelli also designed the large but simpler Gartenpalais Liechtenstein, Vienna (1700–1711), and probably the Harrach Palais, Vienna (*c.*1690), as well as a house for Graf von Kaunitz, Austerlitz. It is said that he also worked in Warsaw, Prague, and Holland.

He made designs for several palaces in Bohemia between 1692 and 1705 – Schloss Aussee and Schloss Landskron for Prince Liechtenstein, Schloss Austerlitz for Count Kaunitz, and for the Sternbeck Palace in Prague (1700 onwards).

H. Lorenz, *D.M.*, Vienna 1989.

**Martinelli**, Johann Baptist (1704–54), see SLOVAK ARCHITECTURE.

**Martino**, Steve (b.1947), see UNITED STATES ARCHITECTURE.

**Martorell**, (Codina) Josep (Maria) (b.1925), see SPANISH ARCHITECTURE.

**Martyrium**. A church or other building erected over a site which bears witness to the Christian faith, either by referring to an event in Christ's life or Passion, or by sheltering the grave of a martyr, a witness by virtue of having shed his or her blood. In Early Christian architecture martyria were usually circular whereas churches were rectangular (see BASILICA).

A. Grabar, *M. Recherches sur le culte des reliques et l'art chrétien antique*, Paris 1946.

**Mascaron**. A grotesque head viewed frontally. A decorative motif.

**Masjid**, see MOSQUE.

**Mask stop**, see STOPS.

**Masonry**. Work by a mason whether brickwork or stonework. See ASHLAR; BRICKWORK; RUBBLE MASONRY; RUSTICATION.

**Mason's lodge**, see LODGE.

**Mason's mark**. A symbol, monogram or initial incised in stonework by the mason responsible for the execution of the building, frequently found on Romanesque and Gothic buildings.

**Mason's mitre**. The meeting of two mouldings at right angles, the diagonal MITRE thus formed being carved on the face of one piece which butts on the other. The joint is at this point and not at the carved mitre.

**Mass**. In architecture, a term used to indicate the sense of bulk, density and weight of built forms.

**Massari**, Giorgio (1687–1766). Leading Venetian early C18 architect, a contemporary of Tiepolo with whom he often collaborated, e.g. Gesuati (1726–36), which is Palladian outside but with Rococo elements inside. His Santa Maria della Pietà (begun 1745) is more restrained, as is his Palazzo Grassi on the Grand Canal (begun 1748).

A. Massari, *G.M. architetto veneziano del settecento*, Vicenza 1971; Howard 1987.

**Mastaba**. The superstructure over an Ancient Egyptian tomb, the tomb chamber being deep underground. At first no more than a low rectangular bench-like structure of mudbrick, mastabas later became more imposing, sometimes being partly stone-built. Dynasty I and II mastabas survive at Saqqara and Gizeh outside Cairo. PYRAMIDS developed from mastabas, e.g. the step-pyramid at Saqqara (c.2700 BC) which is a mastaba enlarged by adding units of decreasing size. See Fig. 77.

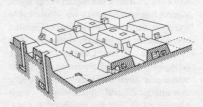

Fig. 77 Mastaba

**Matchboard**. A board with a tongue joint on one edge and a groove on the other, a series forming a panel. The joins are often beaded or V-jointed to conceal the effect of shrinkage.

**Mathematical tiles**. Small facing tiles usually the size of brick headers, applied to timber-framed walls to make them appear brick-built.

**Mathey**, Jean-Baptiste (c.1630–95). He was probably born in Dijon and trained as a painter, but was taken to Prague in

1675 as architect to the archbishop and, despite local opposition, began to work in a classicizing French manner very different from that of F. CARATTI and others there. He built Schloss Troya (1679–96), and the quietly handsome Toscana Palace in Prague (1689–90) and, in a more exuberant style, two churches which influenced FISCHER VON ERLACH – that of the Crusader Knights (1679–88) and the abbey church of St Josef Malá Strana, both in Prague.

Hempel 1965.

**Matté-Trucco**, Giacomo (1869–1934), *see* INDUSTRIAL ARCHITECTURE; ITALIAN ARCHITECTURE.

**Matthew**, Robert Hogg (1906–75). Architect to the London County Council 1946–53, i.e. the years of its notable housing and educational programmes, and of the Royal Festival Hall, London (1951, river-front remodelled 1962–4 by MARTIN). Of his and his firm's later work York University (1963) was remarkable – simple, unmonumental, and of rational construction yet pleasant to live in. The Hillingdon Civic Centre, Uxbridge (1973–8), marked a return to brick and traditional materials, the design being asymmetrical and picturesque, with pitched roofs. He was knighted in 1962.

**Matthias of Arras** (d.1352), *see* CZECH ARCHITECTURE.

**Mausoleum**. A conspicuous free-standing tomb intended as an enduring monument to the person or persons buried inside, as distinct from a CENOTAPH and a TUMULUS. The term derives from the mid-C4 BC tomb of Mausolus at Halicarnassus, some 40 m. (130 ft) high with an Ionic colonnade crowned with a stepped pyramid on a podium with much sculpture, the remains of which are in the British Museum, London. In Italy the Roman emperors preserved the Etru-

scan tradition of tomb chambers covered by tumuli, the mound being given massive architectural form and faced with marble, e.g. that of Augustus, begun 28 BC, of which only parts survive, and that of Hadrian, begun c.AD 125–30, now incorporated in Castel S. Angelo, both in Rome. From the C4 mausolea were built for Christians, e.g. that of Theodoric, Ravenna, c. AD 526. Classical style mausolea were revived by Protestants in C18 England, sometimes set in LANDSCAPE GARDENS, e.g. by HAWKSMOOR at Castle Howard, Yorkshire (1736), though more often in churchyards and CEMETERIES.

Mausolea of great architectural distinction were built for Muslims despite Muhammad's reported injunction against them. None is earlier than the late C9 (the octagonal Qubba-al-Sulabiya, Samarra, 862) but from the C10 they increased: the Tomb of the Samanids, Bukhara, Uzbekistan (c.914–43); the tomb towers of Iran, notably Gunbad-i Gabus, near Gurgan (1006–7); the vast Uljaytu at Sultaniya, Iran (1313); and, in India, those of the Mughal emperors, notably the Taj Mahal, Agra (1613–47).

The most prominent C20 mausolea are secular, notably those of Lenin, Moscow (1924–30), of Ataturk, Ankara (1944–53), and of Mao Ze Dong in Tiananmen square, Beijing (1958).

H. Colvin, *Architecture and the Afterlife*, New Haven/London 1991; Hillenbrand 1994.

**Mawson**, Thomas Hayton (1861–1933). English landscape architect, author of *The Art and Craft of Garden Making* (London 1900, 5th edn 1925), which popularized the brick or stone terrace immediately outside a house with flights of steps leading down to lawns, shrubberies and woods. From 1905 he was much employed by Lord Leverhulme at Thornton Manor, Cheshire; Rivington Hall, Lancashire; and the Leverhulme Public Park at Bolton, Lancashire. For King Constantine of Greece he planned gardens for the royal palace in Athens, and also the planting of trees round the Acropolis (1914). The grounds of Parliament House, Vancouver, Canada, were also laid out to his design. He published *The Life and Work of an English Landscape Architect* (1927).

**May**, Ernst (1886–1970). German architect and urban designer. His working-class suburbs at Frankfurt-am-Main, loosely based on GARDEN CITY principles, were notable, e.g. Römerstadt (1926–8). Between 1930 and 1933 he was in Russia with Hannes MEYER, then in Africa where he designed standardized housing at Kampala, Uganda, based on African vernacular architecture. Back in Germany after 1954 he resumed urban design, first at Hamburg where he directed the 'Neue Heimat' developments, being responsible for Neualtona among others; later he was at Wiesbaden, Bremen and Mainz.

J. Bueckschmitt, *E.M.*, Stuttgart 1963; V. Fischer *et al.*, *E.M. und das neue Frankfurt 1925–1930*, Stuttgart 1986.

**May**, Hugh (1621–84), English architect. The son of a Sussex gentleman and prominent among the virtuosi of the Restoration, he imported the placid spirit of Dutch PALLADIANISM into England and helped, with PRATT, to establish the type of house later known, erroneously, as the 'Wren' type. The east front of Cornbury House, Oxfordshire (1663–8), and Eltham Lodge, London (1663–4), are his only surviving works. He may also have designed Holme Lacy House, Hereford (begun 1673–4). His work at Windsor Castle (remodelling the Upper Ward including St George's Hall and the King's Chapel, 1675–83) was important but has

been almost completely destroyed. It was the most fully developed example of a Baroque scheme of decoration in England – achieved with the aid of the painter Verrio and the sculptor Grinling Gibbons.

Summerson 1991; Colvin 1995.

**Mayan architecture**, *see* MESOAMERICAN ARCHITECTURE.

**Maybeck**, Bernard Ralph (1862–1957). American architect trained at École des Beaux Arts, Paris, and active chiefly at Berkeley and San Francisco, California. His is a curious, highly original Californian Arts and Crafts version of the STICK STYLE. Wood was his favourite material. Examples are the Faculty Club on the Berkeley campus (1899) and the first Church of Christ Scientist at Berkeley (1910–12). The mixture of vernacular, Gothic and Japanese in this building is irresistible. Many private houses show the same qualities, the interiors often being yet more stimulating than the exteriors. Maybeck's most spectacular house is Wynton on the McCloud river, built as a fancy castle for Mrs Hearst. The Lawson House at Berkeley is remarkable for being of reinforced concrete as early as 1907. His Beaux Arts style Palace of Fine Arts, San Francisco (1915, restored 1969), foreshadowed the classical colonnades of Julia MORGAN's San Simeon.

K. H. Cardwell, *B.M. Artisan, Architect, Artist*, Salt Lake City (1977) 1986; R. Longstreth, *On the Edge of the World. Four Architects in San Francisco at the Turn of the Century*, Cambridge, Mass. 1983; S. B. Woodbridge, *B.M. Visionary Architect*, New York 1992; E. R. Bosley, *First Church of Christ Scientist, Berkeley; B.M.*, London 1994; R. Winter 1997.

**Maze**, *see* LABYRINTH.

**MBM Arquitectes SA**, *see* SPANISH ARCHITECTURE.

McHarg, Ian

**McHarg**, Ian (b.1920). Landscape architect and theorist, born in Scotland but active mainly in the USA where he founded the firm of Wallace, McHarg, Roberts and Todd in Philadelphia in 1963, engaged mainly in urban design, e.g. Inner Harbor and Municipal Center, Baltimore; the new town of Woodlands, near Houston, Texas (1970–74); and schemes for large-scale ecological planning. He is notable especially as a theorist and teacher – chairman of the Department of Landscape Architecture and Regional Planning, University of Pennsylvania (1964–86) – and was a seminal figure in the emerging environmental awareness of the 1960s which fathered a new movement not only in landscape architecture but in architecture and urban design, see ENVIRONMENTAL, GREEN OR SUSTAINABLE ARCHITECTURE; URBAN DESIGN. His classic *Design with Nature* (1969), as well as numerous periodical articles, lectures and TV interviews, had a notable impact on urban design, emphasizing the need to take into account all the ecological, climatic and historical features of a site intended for development. In place of a polluted, bulldozed, machine-dominated, dehumanized and threatened world he proposed, with passionate conviction, an ecological vision of organic vitality and balance.

Walker and Simo 1994.

**McIntire**, Samuel (1757–1811). American self-trained architect of great ability and the outstanding example of the early American craftsman-builder tradition, though most of his work dates from after the end of the Revolutionary War. He was a wood-carver by trade and lived in Salem, Massachusetts. With the help of Batty LANGLEY's and WARE's books and perhaps an edition of Palladio (which he owned at his death), he taught himself the PALLADIAN style, which he adopted

for his first houses, e.g. Pierce-Nichols House (1782) in Salem. His most ambitious effort was Salem Court House (1785, now demolished) with superimposed orders and a dome. In the 1790s he came under the influence of BULFINCH, who provided the general design for his most important private house, the Derby Mansion (1795–9, demolished 1815) and from whom he picked up the ADAM style which he used in his later and finest houses (mostly destroyed, but there are rooms from them in the Boston and Philadelphia museums).

Whiffen and Koeper, 1981.

**McKim, Mead & White**. Important American partnership formed in the 1870s by Charles Follen McKim (1847–1909), William Rutherford Mead (1846–1928) and Stanford WHITE. McKim studied first engineering at Harvard, then, in 1867–70, architecture in Paris at the École des Beaux Arts. On his return to the States he entered the office of H. H. RICHARDSON. When he set up his own practice, he went into partnership with William Rutherford Mead and a little later with Stanford WHITE. In 1878 they were all interested in Colonial architecture, a highly unusual thing at the time, and, slightly later, the SHINGLE STYLE as well, e.g. Metcalfe House, Buffalo, NY (1882–4, demolished 1980 but part now in the Metropolitan Museum, New York), and the William Low House, Bristol, Rhode Island (1887–8). To this was added almost at once a liking for the Italian Renaissance which was first introduced, it seems, by Joseph Merrill Wells, who entered the office in 1879 and died early, in 1890. The Italian Renaissance meant to them the High Renaissance, not the Baroque exuberance of classical motifs then current. A first proof of this new taste was the impressive restrained group of the Villard

Houses in Madison Avenue, New York (1882), the second the Boston Public Library (1888–95) with its façade by McKim, inspired by LABROUSTE's Ste Geneviève Library. McKim believed in interior enrichment on a grand scale, and for the library was able to call in Sargent and Puvis de Chavannes. For the Chicago exhibition of 1893, McKim did the Agriculture Building.

Later jobs include the Germantown Cricket Club (1891), decidedly American Colonial; the lavish Madison Garden (1891), Spanish with a tall tower reminiscent of Seville; the Washington Triumphal Arch in New York in the style of the Étoile; Columbia University in New York with its library rotunda (1893) inspired by the Pantheon in Rome and JEFFERSON's Charlottesville (1817–26); the Boston Symphony Hall, Boston (1892–1900), the first ever acoustically planned; the Harvard Union, Cambridge, Massachusetts (1902); the Pierpont Morgan Library, New York (1903–7); the Pennsylvania Railway Station, New York (1904–10, demolished 1963–6), a grandiose scheme echoing Imperial Roman *thermae*; and the north wing of the Metropolitan Museum, New York (1906). Although Mead's retirement in 1919 left the firm without any of its original partners, it continued until 1961.

Hitchcock 1977; G. R. Wilson, *McK., M. & W.*, London 1983; L. M. Roth, *McK., M. & W. Architects*, London 1983; S. Parissien, *Pennsylvania Station*, London 1996.

**Mead**, William Rutherford (1846–1928), *see* McKIM, MEAD & WHITE.

**Meander**, *see* FRET.

**Mecanoo**. A group of Dutch architects formed in 1983 at Delft by Christopher de Weijer (b.1956), Erik van Egerat (b.1956), Francine Houber (b.1955) and Henk Doll (b.1956). Unconventional yet unprovocative, their Boompjes Pavilion restaurant in the harbour at Rotterdam (1990), the Botanical Institute and Library, Wageningen (1992), and the IGA residential building, Stuttgart (1993), are notable.

S. Somer *et al.* (eds.), *M. Architecture*, Rotterdam 1995.

**Medrese**, *see* MADRASA.

**Meeting house**, *see* CHAPEL.

**Megalith**. A large block of stone or boulder of irregular shape, only very roughly dressed or left as found. Prehistoric megalithic monuments, mostly in northern Europe, are now dated *c.*4000–1000 BC and are of five main types: the menhir or single stone standing upright; the group or alignment of menhirs arranged in rows as at Carnac in Brittany where nearly 3,000 survive; circular settings or 'stone circles' as at Stonehenge (*c.*1800 BC), which is architecturally unique (a circle of evenly spaced uprights with a continuous curving lintel, enclosing trilithons); chamber tombs walled and roofed with megaliths, known as cairns and barrows in England and Scotland, as cromlechs in Wales, as dolmens in France and Spain, though these terms are now obsolete in this sense in English. Chamber tombs are constructed in a variety of ways, the so-called Treasury of Atreus at Mycenae, Greece, being the most sophisticated, and are usually covered with rubble or earth to form a mound or tumulus, now sometimes obliterated by natural erosion. Finally there are the apsidal megalithic temples of Malta, e.g. Mnaidra of *c.*2800–1900 BC. *See also* PASSAGE GRAVE.

G. Daniel, *M. in History*, London 1972; A. Burl, *The Stone Circles of the British Isles*, New Haven 1976; B. Rudofsky, *The Prodigious Builders*, London/New York 1977; S. van Reden, *Die M. Kulturen*,

Cologne 1978; F. Teichman, *M. in Irland, England und der Bretagne*, Stuttgart 1983; J. F. Mohen, *M. Kulturen in Europa*, 1989; A. Burl, *A Guide to the Stone Circles of Britain, Ireland and Brittany*, London 1995.

**Megalopolis**. A large urban region formed by chains of metropolitan regions (*see* METROPOLIS). The term was first used in this sense for the American urban-suburban sprawl stretching from Boston to Washington, DC, and later to similar regions in Japan, in north-western Europe and along the Great Lakes in the USA.

H. W. Eldridge (ed.), *Taming M.*, New York 1967.

**Megaron**. A square or oblong room with a central hearth and usually four columns to support the roof, the lateral walls projecting forwards beyond the entrance wall to form the sides of a porch which is usually columned. Sometimes a second entrance wall, with a single opening like the first, is added to form an anteroom. It has been traditional in Greece since Mycenaean times and is sometimes thought to be the ancestor of the Doric temple. In Greek the word means simply 'large room'. Its technical use is modern.

**Megastructure**. An urban-architectural concept defined in 1964 by MAKI as 'a large frame in which all the functions of a city or part of a city are housed', i.e. a large, permanent frame containing subordinate and possibly transient structures. It was taken up enthusiastically by the METABOLISTS in Japan and by ARCHIGRAM in England but few projects were realized except at the Montreal Expo '67, which commissioned SAFDIE's Habitat. Megastructures should be distinguished from large building complexes such as ANDREWS's Scarborough College, University of Toronto (1962–9).

J. Dahinder, *Urban Structures for the Future*, London/New York 1972; Banham 1976.

**Meier**, Richard (b.1934). American architect, who trained in New York and worked with BREUER (1960–63). He became the most prolific and purist of the NEW YORK FIVE, his work being largely responsible for their being called 'the Whites', e.g. his Smith House, Darien, Connecticut (1967); Saltzman House, East Hampton, NY (1967–9); and his one-family house at Old Westbury, NY (1969–71). With the highly acclaimed though controversial Bronx Development Center, New York (1970–76); the Atheneum, New Harmony, Indiana (1975–9); the Decorative Arts Museum, Frankfurt-am-Main (1979–84), and the High Museum, Atlanta, Georgia (1980–83), he became a leading public architect in the USA. They were all notable statements of the beauty of clear-cut slightly nautical geometries and clean, empty spaces, though sometimes questionable functionally. They were followed by the Canal Plus Headquarters, Paris (1989–92); the City Hall, The Hague (1994); the Daimler-Benz Research Center, Ulm, Germany (1993); the Ulm Townhall and Cathedral Square (1995); the Museum of Contemporary Art, Barcelona (1987–95); and the Getty Center, Santa Monica, California (1985–97).

K. Frampton and J. Ryckwert, *R.M. Architect*, New York 1993–7; P. Jodidio, *R.M.*, Cologne 1995; W. Blaser, *R.M. Details*, Basel 1996.

**Meissonnier**, Juste-Aurèle (1695–1750). Leading Rococo designer and architect, born in Turin but settled in Paris *c.*1714. Only one of his buildings survives (Chambre de Commerce, Bayonne) and his fame now rests on his engraved designs.

D. Nyberg (ed.), *Œuvres de J.-A.M.*, New York 1969.

**Meldahl**, Ferdinand (1827–1908), *see* DANISH ARCHITECTURE.

**Melnikov**, Konstantin Stepanovich (1890–1974). Russian architect who became prominent in the early 1920s for his 'Productivist' work, e.g. his wooden, demountable Sucharev Market, Moscow (1924–5), and his USSR Pavilion for the Paris 1925 exhibition which synthesized all the progressive elements in Soviet architecture. His Rusakov Workers' Club, Moscow (1927–8), and his own house in Moscow (1927–9) should be mentioned. But he was out of public life from 1934 onwards until shortly before his death.

S. F. Starr, *M. Solo Architect in a Mass Society*, Princeton (1978) 1981; S. O. Khan-Magomedev, *Pioneers of Soviet Architecture: The Search for New Solutions in the 1920s and 1930s*, London 1987; J. Pallasma and A. Gozak, *The M. House, Moskow. 1927–29. K.M.*, London 1996.

**Membrane structures**, *see* TENSILE STRUCTURES.

**Mendelsohn**, Erich or Eric (1887–1953). German architect whose bold vision of a sculptural architecture emerged early in his many small sketches for buildings that are not functionally determined but are highly expressive with their streamlined curves. In the years of German EXPRESSIONISM at and after the end of the First World War, he was just once enabled actually to build such a vision (the Einstein Tower at Potsdam, 1920–24); but vigorous curves carried round corners also characterize his remodelling of the Mosse Building in Berlin (1921), and appear much tempered by the more rational spirit of the INTERNATIONAL MODERN style of the later twenties and the thirties in his excellent Schocken stores for Stuttgart (1926) and Chemnitz (1928). As expressive as the Einstein Tower, but in terms of multiangular roof shapes instead of curves, is another early work of Mendelsohn's, a factory at Luckenwalde (1923). Mendelsohn visited the United States in 1924 and was understandably impressed by the expressive qualities of the industrial buildings and skyscrapers. Later Berlin buildings include the WOGA Bauten, Berlin (1924–6), the headquarters of the Metal Workers' Union, Berlin (1929–30); Columbushaus, Potsdam (1929–30, destroyed), and the Universum Cinema, Berlin (1927–8, rebuilt 1978–81 by Jürgen Sawade with new interior). In 1933 Mendelsohn went to London and joined Serge CHERMAYEFF. Joint work are the de la Warr Pavilion at Bexhill (1935–6) and No. 64 Old Church Street, Chelsea (1936, unhappily modified in the 1990s by FOSTER). But in 1934 he moved on to Israel (*see* ISRAELI ARCHITECTURE), and in 1941 finally settled in the United States. In Israel he built, among other things, the Hadassah University Medical Centre on Mount Scopus, Jerusalem (1936–8), in the USA the Maimonides Hospital at San Francisco (1946–50). In 1929 he published *Russland, Europa, Amerika. Ein architektonisches Querschnitt* (Berlin, reissued Basel 1990).

B. Zevi, *E.M. Opera completa*, Milan 1970; Hitchcock 1977; S. Achenback, *E.M. (1887–1953). Ideen, Bauten, Projekte*, exh. cat., Berlin 1987; K. James, *E.M. and the Architecture of German Modernism*, Cambridge 1997.

**Mendini**, Alessandro (b.1931). Italian architect, founder member of the ALCHYMIA 'new wave' design group in Milan. He made his name as an architect in the late 1980s with his museum at Gröningen, Holland (1988–94), and

Tour Paradis, Hiroshima, Japan (1989, with Yumiko Kobayashi).

R. Poletti, *Atelier M. 1988–1994*, Milan 1994.

**Mengoni**, Giuseppe (1829–77). Italian architect of the Galleria Vittorio Emanuele in Milan, won in competition in 1861. It was built in 1864–7 (though work on the decoration continued until 1877), and is the largest, highest and most ambitious of all shopping arcades. It is cruciform, and the buildings through which it runs take part in the free Renaissance design of the *galleria*. Especially impressive is the façade towards the Piazza del Duomo.

J. F. Geist, *Arcades. The History of a Building Type*, Cambridge, Mass. 1983.

**Menhir**, *see* MEGALITH.

**Meridian**. In architecture, a radial generating line of a dome surface, formed by the intersection of a plane containing the axis of revolution with the surface.

**Merlini**, Domenico (1730–97), *see* POLISH ARCHITECTURE.

**Merlon**, *see* BATTLEMENT.

**Merovingian architecture**, *see* FRENCH ARCHITECTURE.

**Merrill**, John O. (1896–1975), *see* SKIDMORE, OWINGS & MERRILL.

**Mesoamerican architecture**. The architecture of the civilizations that flourished from *c.*1000 BC until the Spanish conquest in AD 1519–21 in Central America, i.e. the area south of the Pánuco river and north of Panama, comprising part of modern Mexico, Guatemala, Honduras, Belize, El Salvador and Nicaragua. Despite differences of language and ethnic type the peoples living in this region shared similar religious beliefs and rituals, as is evident in their architecture. Nearly all surviving buildings were religious (others were of impermanent materials). The most notable are termed pyramids, though they differ from those in Egypt in both form and function – they are of varying plan (circular, oblong, square), flat-topped and conceived as artificial hills for the celebration of rites, like ZIGGURATS. Some were raised over the tombs of rulers. The earliest known *c.*C8 BC, of which only the core of layers of dried clay 30 m. (100 ft) high survives, was a truncated cone with ten ribs in a ceremonial centre of the Olmecs on the island of La Venta in the Tonolà river. At Ciucuilco (Valley of Mexico) a circular mound was raised by people of a different culture *c.*200 BC, some 140 m. (440 ft) in diameter and 21 m. (65 ft) high of four stages faced with stone slabs laid in clay, the platform approached up ramps and steps from east and west. Slightly later and much better preserved are the buildings at Teotihuacán (near present-day Mexico City), a vast city – the earliest in the Americas of which substantial traces remain – covering some 8 sq. miles (20.7 sq. km.), laid out AD C1–8 on an astronomically orientated grid plan. It has a central avenue 42 m. (130 ft) wide and 2½ km. (1½ miles) long, leading to a nearly 60 m. (200 ft) high pyramid composed of layers of clay faced with rough stones and sited on axis with the point where the sun sets on the day of its zenith passage. Later and smaller pyramids at this site were more elaborately constructed with skeleton frameworks of piers and slabs of tufa, to stabilize earth and rubble fillings, and finely dressed masonry facing – notably that dedicated to Quetzalcoatl (*c.*AD 150–250) with relief carvings of plumed serpents and menacing heads.

Pyramids, often much higher in relation to the base, were built by the Maya, who lived in city states distributed over a wide area – Honduras, Guatemala,

Belize, the whole Yucatan peninsula and the Mexican states of Tabasco and Chiapas. They were built in the ceremonial centres of cities among temples, sanctuaries, courts for the ball-game (a religious rite sometimes terminating with human sacrifice) and structures of more than one storey with many small ill-lit rooms which seem to have been intended less for habitation than for regal ceremonies and for storage. They were set on stone terraces and built of stone with a mortar composed of lime and sand. Openings have trabeated or triangular corbelled arches and interiors, corbelled vaults, which appear for the first time in the Americas early in the C4 AD at Uaxactún. Much use was made of sculpture, often of very high quality – friezes, lintels, wall-panels, the treads of pyramid stairways and their borders – intricately carved in low relief with masks, serpents or representations of religious ceremonies, as at Cerros, Uxmal, Piedras Negras, Palenque, Yaxchilán and Chichen Itzá, though many were removed and are now in American and European museums. Maya buildings date from between the C2 BC and AD 900, when many of the cities were abandoned and the territory came under the rule of a different ethnic group usually identified as the Toltecs.

In southern Mexico, outside the Maya area, the distinct culture of the Zapotecs emerged at Monte Alban, where between the C4 and C10 a whole hill was covered with somewhat severe undecorated terraces, platforms and buildings linked by great staircases. A striking contrast is provided by the contemporary Tajín, the centre of the so-called Totonac culture, where numerous buildings in a great variety of forms and with much sculptured decoration were constructed between the C5 or C6 and the C13, when the place was abandoned.

By the C10 when these early civiliza-

tions had begun to falter groups of invaders collectively known as the Chichimecs began to arrive from the north. The most important of them, the Toltecs, founded the city of Tula, where they built a grandiose pyramid dedicated to Tlahuizcalpantecuhtli, with savage sculptural decorations which include many references to human sacrifice. They appear to have taken over Chichen Itzá, where the latest buildings are sometimes said to have been erected by Toltecs, though they may be Mayan: the nine-storey pyramid called the Castillo, the Temple of the Jaguars, the Temple of the Warriors with a many-columned portico and the largest of all Mesoamerican ball courts.

The Toltec civilization was already in decline before the arrival of the Aztecs, who settled on the island of Texcoco in 1325 and soon dominated the entire Mesoamerican area. They took over the architecture of their predecessors, their only original contribution being the double pyramid. Their capital city Tenochtitlán and their holy city Cholula with many pyramids and temples were entirely destroyed by the Spaniards immediately after the conquest. Of surviving Aztec buildings the most important is the double pyramid at Tenayuca, with a monumental staircase up one side and a row of fiercely grimacing serpent heads projecting from the base on the other three sides. This pyramid appears to have been rebuilt every fifty-two years for the ceremony of the New Fire, which initiated each cycle of the Aztec calendar. The present one dates from c.1450–1500. Other notable buildings include the Pyramid at El Tepozteco (c.1502–20), constructed high on a rocky ridge, and a complex of buildings hewn from the living rock at Malinalco (1476–1520). Although the bloodthirsty and warlike Aztecs expanded their empire, in quest of prisoners for human sacrifice as well as land, one subject group maintained cultural independence – the Mixtecs, who occupied an area bordering the Pacific and roughly corresponding to the modern Mexican states of Oaxaca, Puebla and Guerrero. The only important Mixtec site is Mitla, where there are no pyramids, only palaces, notably the Palace of the Columns decorated with finely cut geometrical reliefs which provide a striking contrast to the terrifying grotesques on Aztec and Toltec buildings. For postconquest architecture in the region, *see* MEXICAN ARCHITECTURE.

**Mesopotamian architecture**, *see* SUMERIAN AND AKKADIAN ARCHITECTURE.

**Messel**, Alfred (1853–1909), *see* DEPARTMENT STORE; GERMAN ARCHITECTURE.

**Metabolism**. A Japanese movement launched in 1960 in Tokyo by TANGE with KIKUTAKE, KURAKAWA, MAKI and Masato Otaka (b.1923). ISOZAKI and others were also briefly involved. They promoted an organic, flexible architecture in reaction against the rigidity of Western Modernism, concentrating on space (not form) and changeable function. Kikutake's Ocean City Project (1962, partly realized in his Aquapolis, Okinawa, 1975) and Kurakawa's Helix City project (1961), Takara Beautillon, Osaka (1970), and Nagakin Capsule Tower, Tokyo (1972), expressed the movement's aspirations. It culminated in the Osaka Expo '70 and gradually dispersed afterwards.

K. Kurakawa, *The Concept of M.*, Tokyo 1972; K. Kurakawa, *M. in Architecture*, London 1977.

**Metal structures**. The use of metal as a building material was discussed by the Venetian theorist F. Venanzio in *Machinae Novae* (1617) but only began in practice in the late C18 with BRIDGES and the first iron-framed buildings in England (*see*

INDUSTRIALIZED BUILDING). The first instance of the use of iron beams was in RINALDI's Marble Palace, St Petersburg (1768–72). The pioneer in the use of metal for a complete structure (other than bridges) was SCHINKEL, whose cast-iron neo-Gothic Kreuzberg monument in Berlin is of 1818. Other notable architects who were early in exploiting metal include BALTARD, BÉLANGER, FONTAINE, HAVILAND, LABROUSTE, PAXTON, and STASOV, usually in conjunction with GLASS (*see also* CONSERVATORIES). In 1839 a metal flour-mill was prefabricated in London by Sir William Fairbairn and sent to Turkey, where it was erected in Istanbul in 1840. In 1843–4 a prefabricated house of iron by John Walker was erected on the Calaba river in central Africa. As early as the 1840s there were 'cast-iron districts' in American cities (*see* BOGARDUS), and though there was nothing comparable in Europe some remarkable exposed iron façades went up in Britain between 1850 and 1880, the earliest in Glasgow in 1855–6 (36 Jamaica Street) by John Baird (1798–1859) and in Liverpool by Peter ELLIS. In 1854 Sir William Fairbairn published in London *On the Application of Cast and Wrought Iron to Building Purposes* (reprinted 1970) and in 1865 Daniel D. Badger (b.1806) issued his *Illustrated Catalogue of Cast-Iron Architecture* in New York (reprinted 1981) and, contemporaneously, VIOLLET-LE-DUC published his *Entretiens* (2 vols., 1863 and 1872), in which he advocated a rational approach to construction and passionately defended new materials and techniques, especially iron. Metal was, of course, the essential element in the development of the SKYSCRAPER and the CURTAIN WALL, though it was not always exposed. In Europe metal has been largely replaced by REINFORCED CONCRETE, which is cheaper, but it continues to be used as an exposed element in the USA and Japan.

G. Roisecco, *L'architettura del ferro*, Rome 1972–3; M. Gayle and E. V. Gillo, *Cast Iron Architecture in New York City*, New York 1974; Mainstone 1975; C. Behnisch and G. Hartung, *Eisenkonstruction des 19 Jahrhunderts*, Munich 1982; B. Lemoine, *L'Architecture du fer. France XIX siècle*, Seyssel 1986; B. Marvey, *Le fer à Paris: Architecture*, Paris 1989; R. Thorne (ed.), *The Iron Revolution*, London 1990; A. Blanc *et al.* (eds.), *Architecture and Construction in Steel*, London 1993; N. Jackson, *The Modern Steel House*, London 1996.

**Métezeau**, Louis (1559/72–1615). French architect closely involved with the DU CERCEAUS in Henry IV's improvements to Paris, notably the Place des Vosges (1603 onwards) and at the Louvre, where he probably designed the south façade of the Grande Galerie. He also assisted in the interior decoration of the Petite Galerie, the Salle des Antiques and the Grande Galerie (1601–8). He collaborated with Dupérac on the interior decoration of the Hôtel de Jean de Fourcy, Paris (1601). His brother Clément or Jacques Clément Métezeau (1581–1652) may have been a more important architect. He was transitional between de BROSSE and LE VAU. He designed the Place Ducale at Charleville (1610), the portail of St Gervais, Paris (1616), the Orangerie du Louvre (1617), the Hôtel de Brienne (1630–32) and the Château de la Meilleraye (*c.*1630). He worked with de Brosse at the Luxembourg in Paris *c.*1615 and in 1611 was sent to Florence by Marie de' Medici to make drawings of Palazzo Pitti in connection with it, though they do not appear to have been used by de Brosse.

J. P. Babelon, *Demeures parisiennes. Sous Henri IV et Louis XIII*, Paris 1965.

**Metope**. The square space between two TRIGLYPHS in the FRIEZE of a Doric order; it may be carved or left plain. *See* Fig. 86.

**Metropolis**. A main city or large centre. The term is now used for the main city of a region with SUBURBS and SATELLITE TOWNS around it. Metropolitan regions are formed around several large centres.

S. R. Miles (ed.), *M. Problems*, London 1970.

**Meurtrière**. In military architecture, a small loophole, large enough for the barrel of a gun or musket and through which a soldier might fire under cover.

**Mews**. A row of stables with living accommodation above, built at the back of a town-house, especially in London. They are now nearly all converted into houses or 'mews flats'.

**Mexican architecture and landscape architecture**. (For Pre-Columbian Mexican architecture, *see* MESOAMERICAN ARCHITECTURE.) After the Spanish conquest Mexican architecture took on a Gothic (e.g. San Miguel de Actopan) or Spanish Renaissance character and then, from the late C16, Baroque (e.g. Mexico City Cathedral, 1563–1667, Puebla Cathedral, 1551–1664), sometimes of an extravagantly Churrigueresque kind (e.g. the Sanctuary at Ocotlán, *c.*1745). Indeed Mexican Baroque architecture took Spanish Baroque architecture to extremes, e.g. Governmental Palace, Guadalajara (1751–75). Mexican C20 architecture became known internationally in the 1930s with the Cardenas regime. José Villagrán Garcia (1901–82), Juan O'GORMAN and Luis BARRAGÁN all began at this time, and in 1939 Hannes MEYER, who had for a short time succeeded GROPIUS as director of the BAUHAUS, settled in Mexico. However, it was not until after the Second World War that it won international acclaim with the new university city outside the capital, planned by Mario PANI in 1947 and largely built between 1950 and 1953. Notable are the School of Architecture and Museum of Art by Villagrán Garcia, the School of Medicine by Pedro Ramírez VÁSQUEZ, the library with its vast exterior mosaics by O'Gorman and the Cosmic Ray building by CANDELA, who became, with Barragán, the best-known C20 Mexican architect. Ramírez Vásquez's programme for cheap mass-produced village schools was notable, as was also his Anthropological Museum in Mexico City of 1964. More recently the work of Ricardo LEGORRETA has been acclaimed for his imaginative use of the vernacular, as has the work of Teodoro GONZÁLEZ DE LEÓN and his intermittent partner Abraham Zabludovsky (b.1924). The landscape architecture of both Barragán and González de León is also outstanding.

**Mey**, Johann Melchior van der (1878–1949), *see* DUTCH ARCHITECTURE.

**Meyer**, Adolph (1881–1929), *see* GROPIUS, Walter.

**Meyer**, Hannes (1889–1954). Swiss architect, trained in Berlin. His Siedlung Freidorf development near Basel (1919–21) was notable and he became head of the architecture department at the BAUHAUS in 1925/6, succeeded Gropius as director the following year but was dismissed in 1930 for political reasons. He designed and built the Bundesschule des Algemeinen Deutschen Gewerkschaftsbundes, Bernau, between 1928 and 1930. For the next five years he worked in Russia, mainly on urban design, and settled in Mexico in 1939 where he became a formative influence. He retired in 1949.

C. Schnaidt, *H.M. Buildings, Projects and Writings*, London 1965; K. M. Hays, *Modernism and the Posthumanist Subject.*

*The Architecture of H.M. and L. Hilbersheimer*, Cambridge, Mass. 1992.

**Mezzanine**. A low storey between two higher ones; also called an *entresol*.

**MIAR** (Movimento Italiano per l'Architettura Razionale), *see* RATIONALISM.

**Michael of Canterbury**. A master mason working *c.* 1300, first at Canterbury for the cathedral, then in London, where he was the first master mason of St Stephen's Chapel (begun 1292) in the palace of Westminster and probably its designer. A Walter of Canterbury was in charge of work at the palace in 1322. A Thomas of Canterbury was working under him in 1324 and, in 1331, probably after Walter's death, was put in charge of work at St Stephen's Chapel. Thomas may have died in 1336.

Harvey 1984.

**Michaud**, Joseph (1822–1902), *see* CANADIAN ARCHITECTURE.

**Michelangelo Buonarroti** (1475–1564). Sculptor, painter, poet, and one of the greatest of all architects, he was the archetype of the inspired 'genius' – unsociable, distrustful, untidy, obsessed by his work, and almost pathologically proud – in fact, the antithesis of the Early Renaissance ideal of the complete man so nobly exemplified in ALBERTI and LEONARDO. Deeply and mystically religious, he was consumed by the conflicts and doubts of the Counter-Reformation. As in his life, so in his art, he rejected the assumptions of the Renaissance and revolutionized everything he touched. Nowhere was his influence so profound or so enduring as in architecture. He invented a new vocabulary of ornament, new and dynamic principles of composition, and an entirely new attitude to space. His few dicta and his drawings reveal that he conceived a building as an organic growth and in relation to the movement of the spectator. He made clay models rather than perspective drawings, and appears to have eschewed the type of highly finished design which could be turned over to the builders ready for execution. He usually made considerable modifications as the building went up, and it is now impossible to tell exactly how his many incomplete works would have looked when finished or how he would have realized in stone those compositions which remained on paper – the façade of S. Lorenzo, Florence (1516), or the centrally planned S. Giovanni dei Fiorentini, Rome (1556–60).

His first work in architecture is the exterior of the chapel of Leo X in Castel Sant'Angelo, Rome (1514). In 1515 he received his first major commission, for the façade of BRUNELLESCHI'S S. Lorenzo, Florence, which he conceived as an elaborate framework for more than life-size sculpture. In 1520, before his S. Lorenzo design was finally abandoned, he was commissioned to execute the Medici family mausoleum in the new sacristy of the same church, much of which was already built. He produced a revolutionary design in which, for the first time, the tyranny of the orders was completely rejected; windows taper sharply, capitals vanish from pilasters, tabernacles weigh down heavily on the voids of the doors beneath them. But the novelty of his design is less evident in this truculent misuse of the classical vocabulary than in the revolutionary conception of architecture which inspired it. He saw the wall not as an inert plane to be decorated with applied ornaments but as a vital, many-layered organism – hence the extraordinary form of the tabernacles with their strange elisions and recessions. The fact that he developed this new conception while the sacristy was in course of construction accounts for its many inconsistencies. The work was brought more or less to its present state by 1534 but never completed.

In 1524 he was commissioned to design a library for S. Lorenzo, Florence – the famous Biblioteca Laurenziana (reading-room designed 1525, vestibule 1526). The site determined its awkward shape and also limited the thickness of the walls. But he turned both these limitations to good effect, linking the structure to the decoration in a way never before achieved or imagined. Pilasters, which had hitherto been purely decorative elements applied to a structural wall, he used as the supports for the ceiling, while the cross-beams above the pilasters are echoed in mosaic on the floor so that the eye is drawn along the length of the room through a perspective of diminishing oblongs. He counteracted this longitudinal emphasis by stressing the verticality of the vestibule. Here the columns are set like statues in niches so that they appear to be merely decorative, though in fact they carry the roof. Other features are no less perverse – blind window-frames or aedicules with pilasters which taper towards the base, consoles which support nothing, and a staircase which pours forbiddingly down from the library on to the entrance level (executed by AMMANATI). There is no figure sculpture, but the whole interior is treated plastically as if it were sculpture.

In 1528–9 Michelangelo was employed on the fortifications of Florence, which he designed, with characteristic perversity, for offence rather than defence. In 1534 he left Florence for Rome, where he spent the rest of his life. His first Roman commission was for the reorganization of the Capitol, to provide a suitable setting for the ancient statue of Marcus Aurelius and an imposing place for outdoor ceremonies (begun 1539). He laid out the central space as an oval – the first use of this shape in the Renaissance – and designed new fronts for

Palazzo dei Conservatori and Palazzo del Senatore (neither finished before his death). His designs were strikingly original, e.g. in their use of a GIANT ORDER embracing two storeys, a device that was soon to become general. In 1546 he was commissioned to complete Antonio da SANGALLO's Palazzo Farnese. He converted the unfinished façade into one of the most imposing in Rome, redesigned the upper floors of the *cortile*, and planned a vast garden to link it with the Villa Farnesina on the far side of the Tiber (not executed). In the conception of this grandiose vista, as in his design for the Porta Pia (1561–5) at the end of a new street from the Quirinal, he anticipated the principles of Baroque town planning.

But his most important Roman commission was, of course, for the completion of St Peter's (1546–64). Here he was faced with the task of finishing a building begun by BRAMANTE and continued by Antonio da Sangallo. He reverted to the centralized plan of the former, but made it much bolder, and demolished part of the latter's additions (*see* Fig. 30). His work on the interior was entirely masked in the C17; on the exterior it is visible only on the north and south arms and the drum of the dome. (The dome itself is by della PORTA and differs substantially from Michelangelo's model.) But although his plans were much altered the church as it stands today owes more to him than to any other single architect. In his last years he designed the Cappella Sforza, S. Maria Maggiore, Rome (*c.*1560), on an ingenious plan rather coarsely executed after his death. He also provided plans for the conversion of the central hall of the Baths of Diocletian into S. Maria degli Angeli (1561), but here his work was completely overlaid in the C18.

The story of his architectural career is one of constant frustration. Not one of his major designs was complete at the time of his death. Yet his influence was none the less great. The Mannerists took from him decorative details which were gradually absorbed into the European grammar of ornament. But it was not until the C17 that architects were able to appreciate and began to emulate his dynamic control of mass and space. Significantly, his true heir was to be another sculptor architect, BERNINI.

J. S. Ackerman, *The Architecture of M.*, London 1964–6; rev. edn with J. Newman, Harmondsworth (1970) 1986; H. A. Millon and C. H. Smyth, *M. Architect*, Washington 1988; G. C. Argan and B. Contardi, *M. Architect*, New York 1993.

**Michelozzo di Bartolomeo** (1396–1471), a sculptor and architect of extreme elegance and refinement, nevertheless lacked the genius of his great contemporaries Donatello and BRUNELLESCHI. Born in Florence, the son of Bartolomeo de Gherardo, who hailed from Burgundy, he worked as assistant to Ghiberti (1417–24), then shared a studio with Donatello (1425–33). In the mid-1420s he began to turn his attention to architecture (S. Francesco al Bosco, near Florence, 1420–27) and eventually succeeded Brunelleschi as Capomaestro at the cathedral in 1446. His first important works were for the Medici family. In about 1433 he added the graceful courtyard and loggia to their castle-cum-villa at Careggi and eleven years later began the Palazzo Medici-Riccardi in Florence, the prototype Tuscan Renaissance palace, with massive rusticated basement and slightly smoother rusticated upper floors capped by a prominent cornice (*see* Fig. 50). Behind this slightly forbidding exterior there is an arcaded *cortile* derived from Brunelleschi's Ospedale degli Innocenti. His Medicean villa at Caffagiolo (1451) is again fortress-like, in contrast with his Villa Medici at Fiesole (1458–61, but considerably altered in C18), which is exquisitely light and elegant in style.

In 1437 he began work at S. Marco, Florence, where he designed the sacristy (1437–43), the cloisters and the light and harmonious library (1441). Between 1444 and 1455 he designed the tribune and sacristy of SS. Annunziata. The tribune (completed by ALBERTI, 1470–73) is centrally planned, inspired no doubt by Brunelleschi's S. Maria degli Angeli, but closer to an Ancient Roman model, the temple of Minerva Medica. This was the first centralized building to be erected in the Renaissance, and it reflects both a desire to revive an antique form and a preoccupation with the circle as a symbol of the universe and eternity. At Pistoia he built the little church of S. Maria delle Grazie (c.1452), where he employed the Early Christian and Byzantine form of a square building with central dome and subsidiary domed chapels at the four corners. In about 1462 he was in Milan, probably working on the Medici Bank. He also built the Portinari Chapel in S. Eustorgio, Milan (c.1462), which owes much to Brunelleschi's S. Lorenzo sacristy. With this chapel he introduced the Renaissance style to Lombardy. From 1462 to 1463 he was in Dubrovnik, where he designed the Palazzo dei Rettori.

H. Caplow, M., New York/London 1977; W. Ferrara and F. Quinterio, M. di B., Florence 1984.

**Michelucci**, Giovanni (1891–1990). As one of the architects of Florence railway station (1933–6) he became a leading exponent of RATIONALISM. His later work was freer and more plastically expressive, notably the Autostrada del Sole church at the Florence exit (1960–63).

F. Naldi, G.M., Florence 1978; A. Bellucci and C. Conforti, Lo spazio sacro di M., Florence 1987; M. Dezzi Bardeschi,

G.M. (1891–1990). Il Projetto continuo, Milan 1992.

**Mies van der Rohe**, Ludwig (1886–1969). German architect who worked under Bruno PAUL, and then from 1908 to 1911 in Peter BEHRENS's office in Berlin. His earliest independent designs were inspired by SCHINKEL and the Berlin Schinkel Revival of the early C20 (Kröller House, 1912). At the end of the First World War he was, like GROPIUS, caught up in the frenzy and enthusiasm of EXPRESSIONISM, and he designed then his revolutionary glass skyscrapers (1919–21). When Germany settled down to its rational responsible style of the later twenties and the early thirties, Mies van der Rohe excelled in this as well (e.g. for DEUTSCHER WERKBUND, 1927). His true greatness as an architect was first revealed in the German Pavilion for the Barcelona Exhibition (1928/9, rebuilt 1992), with its open plan and masterly spatial composition, its precious materials – marble, travertine, onyx, polished steel, bottle-green glass – a sign of a striving after the highest quality and the most immaculate finishes. The planning principles of the Barcelona Pavilion were tested for domestic purposes in the Tugendhat House at Brno, Czech Republic (1930), a private house which survives intact except for the furniture Mies designed for it.

From 1930 to 1933 Mies van der Rohe was director of the BAUHAUS, first at Dessau and then when it moved to Berlin for its last harassed phase of existence. In 1938, having emigrated to the USA, he was made Professor of Architecture at the Armour Institute (now Illinois Institute) of Technology in Chicago. In 1939 he designed a complete new campus for the Institute, whose plan has since developed and whose buildings have grown (notably Crown Hall, 1950–56, the great prototype clear-span building). They are characterized by cubic simplicity – envelopes which easily adapt to the various requirements of the Institute – and a perfect precision of details, where every member makes its own unequivocal statement. These qualities pervade all Mies van der Rohe's work. 'I don't want to be interesting, I want to be good,' he said in an interview. The volume of his work was remarkably small until after the Second World War, but then grew considerably. Among private houses the Farnsworth House at Plano, Illinois (1946–51), must be mentioned; among blocks of flats the Promontory Apartments (1947) with a concrete frame, and Lake Shore Drive (1951) with a steel frame, both in Chicago, and Lafayette Towers, Detroit (1963); among office buildings, the Seagram building in New York (1956–9), with a bronze and marble facing; the Federal Center, Chicago (1959–64); and the new National Gallery in Berlin (1963–8). They are all a final triumphant vindication of the style created in the early C20 and assimilated gradually in the thirties.

F. Schulze, *M. van der R. A Critical Biography*, Chicago 1985; J. Zukowsky (ed.), *M. Reconsidered. His Career: Legacy and Disciples*, New York 1986; J. Zukowsky and H. P. Schwartz, *M. van der R.*, exh. cat., Frankfurt 1987; F. Schulze (ed.), *M. van der R. Critical Essays*, New York 1989; F. Neumeyer, *The Artless Word. M. van der R. on the Building Art*, Cambridge, Mass. 1991.

**Migge**, Liberecht (1881–1935), *see* GERMAN ARCHITECTURE.

**Mihrab**. A niche in the QIBLA wall of a mosque, normally in the centre and often emphasized by a wide aisle from the main entrance with a dome over the last bay or a raised transept. It is not liturgically necessary and none is recorded before the early C8. Mihrabs became the most, if not the only, richly decorated part of mosque interiors. In plan they may be semicircular, rectangular or polygonal, though a recess is sometimes simulated on a flat surface. The opening usually has an arch supported on columns, the surrounding area and interior being encrusted with marble, carved woodwork, stucco and/or ceramic tiles (the earliest in the Great Mosque at Kairouan, Tunisia, 836–75), with abstract ornament and pious inscriptions. The hood of the niche was at first scalloped but later often filled with MUQARNAS.

**Milesian layout**. A city plan of regular gridiron pattern with streets of houses of approximately uniform dimensions. It probably originated in the Hittite, Assyrian and Babylonian empires and developed in Ionia in the C7 BC. It is named after the city of Miletus. Other notable examples in antiquity are Cryne in Lydia (founded 630–24 BC) and Paestum (built by Greek colonists in C6 BC). This type of plan was advocated by HIPPODAMOS, who is sometimes incorrectly said to have invented it.

**Miller**, Sanderson (1716–80), *see* GOTHIC REVIVAL.

**Mills**, Peter (1598–1670). London bricklayer who built and perhaps designed a row of Inigo JONES style houses in Great Queen Street, London, in 1637, now demolished. In 1654–6 he built Thorpe Hall, Cambridgeshire, a notable double-pile house sometimes attributed to Jones or WEBB. In 1666 he was appointed with HOOKE and Edward Jerman to be a surveyor for the rebuilding of London after the fire.

Summerson 1991; Colvin 1995.

**Mills**, Robert (1781–1855). American architect. Born in Charleston, South Carolina, he was discovered by JEFFER-

SON and articled to HOBAN and then to LATROBE, with whom he stayed from 1803 to 1808. His practice started in Philadelphia in 1808 (notably Washington Hall, perhaps influenced by LEDOUX). He designed the former State House at Harrisburg, Pennsylvania, in 1810 with a semicircular portico and a dome over the centre; a circular church at Charleston as early as 1804; an octagonal one in Richmond, Virginia (1812), another in Philadelphia in 1811–13 (the latter with 4,000 seats); and then the Washington Monument for Baltimore, an unfluted Doric column (1814–29). His principal later works are governmental buildings for Washington, all Grecian and competent (Treasury, 1836–9; Patent Office, 1836–40; Post Office, 1839, etc.), but his most famous work is the Washington Monument at Washington, won in competition in 1836 and completed only in 1884. It is an obelisk 171 m. (555 ft) high and was originally meant to have a Greek Doric rotunda at its foot. Mills also did engineering jobs and a number of hospitals. The Columbia Lunatic Asylum (1822) has none of the grimness of its predecessors. It is like a monumental hospital (Greek Doric portico), and has all wards to the south and a roof-garden. It is of fireproof construction.

Hitchcock 1977; Whiffen and Koeper 1981; R. W. Liscombe, *The Church Architecture of R.M.*, Easly, SC, 1985; J. M. Bryan (ed.), *R.M. Architect*, Washington, DC 1989; R. W. Liscombe, *Altogether American. R.M. (1781–1835) Architect and Engineer*, Oxford 1993.

**Minaret**. In ISLAMIC ARCHITECTURE a high tower from which the faithful can be called to prayer, usually attached to or near a mosque for which it served also as a visual marker. Initially the muezzin called from a roof-top or a tower (as at the Great Mosque, Damascus, of 706).

The earliest surviving purpose-built minaret is a stocky tower (begun 836) outside the courtyard of the Great Mosque, Kairouan, Tunisia. A square-based type derived from bell-towers of Christian churches was developed in Syria, North Africa and Spain, e.g. Seville (the Giralda) (1145–95); Marrakesh (c.1196); Rabat (1199). At Samarra, Iraq, the 53 m. (160 ft) high brick minaret is helicoidal with a ramp spiralling round a solid central column crowned by a kiosk (848–52), but this was unusual. Minarets normally had interior stairways. From the CII they were attached to MADRASAS and MAUSOLEA as well as mosques and some were isolated monuments rising far above the level from which the human voice is audible on the ground, e.g. 60 m. (190 ft) high at Jam, Afghanistan; 73 m. (230 ft) high at Delhi, where the Qutb Minar, begun 1199, was gradually raised to that height. They seem often to have been intended mainly to commemorate their founders' piety, the richly decorated minaret of Ma'mud III at Ghazna, Afghanistan, built on a star-shaped plan resembling a tower tomb (1099–1115). Minarets in Fatimid and Mamluk Cairo were constructed in several storeys each with a different ground-plan – square, octagonal and circular – and a different system of carved decoration on each one, e.g. Minaret of Bishtaq (1336), mosque of Sultan Hasan (1356–61) and minaret of Qu'it Bay, Al-Azhar mosque (1469). In Eastern Islam a tapering columnar form was normal, with bands of geometrical ornament and inscriptions in brickwork, e.g. Kalyan minaret, Bukhara, Uzbekistan (1127), and those built under SELJUK rule CII–13; later they were decorated with coloured glazed bricks or ceramic tiles, e.g. Friday Mosque, Yazd, Iran (1335); Madrasa of Ulugh Beg, Samarkand, Uzbekistan (1417). But a distinct cylindrical type of elegant simplicity like

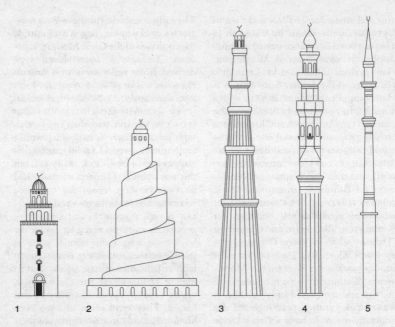

Fig. 78 Minaret: 1. Kairouan, Great Mosque   2. Samarra, Great Mosque   3. Delhi Qutb Minar   4. Cairo, Sultan Hasan Mosque   5. Cairo, Muhammed Ali Mosque

a well-sharpened pencil, girdled with balconies from which the muezzin could call, was developed in Ottoman Turkey in the C15, perfected by SINAN in the mid-C16 and established as the norm followed to the present day, as in the National Mosque, Islamabad, Pakistan, 1966–96. See Fig. 78.

J. M. Bloom, *M. Symbol of Islam*, Oxford 1989; Hillenbrand 1994.

**Minbar**. A high pulpit to the right of the MIHRAB in a congregational mosque from which an imam can deliver both religious and political instruction during the Friday prayers. The earliest surviving example of *c*.862, in the Great Mosque, Kairouan, Tunisia, is of wood with stairs flanked by intricately carved triangular walls leading up to the platform. Later examples are

usually of wood, sometimes mounted on wheels so that they could be moved into the courtyard when the congregation overfilled the prayer hall. But they were also built of mud-brick (Damghan, Iraq, probably C9), stone or marble (Selimiye Mosque, Edirne, Turkey, 1568–76).

**Minimalist architecture**. Minimalism in art, aiming at complete autonomy and purity, developed in the USA in the 1960s in reaction to Abstract Expressionism. Its leaders, Carle André, Donald Judd and Robert Morris, all constructed three-dimensional works but Minimalist architecture did not emerge until the 1980s and never developed into a defined movement. Such buildings as the Nenendorf Villa, Mallorca (1989), by John Pawson (b.1949) and Claudio Silvestrin (b.1954), and Casa Gaspar and the Drago Public School, Cadiz (1992), by Albert Campo Baeza (b.1946), were exemplary. Steven HOLL, HERZOG & De Meuron, Alvaro SIZA, O. M. UNGERS and others including such Japanese architects as ANDO, MAKI, ISOZAKI and SHINOHARA have been associated with Minimalism, the latter reflecting an indigenous and traditional aesthetic stance. Western Minimalist buildings are notable for the rarified, almost Zen-like, sense of calm and purity radiated by their uncluttered spatial clarity and serene finish, e.g. Herzog & De Meuron's Goetz Gallery, Munich (1992); Holl's D. E. Shaw and Company Office, New York (1991).

M. Toy (ed.), *Aspects of Minimal Architecture*, London 1994.

**Minoan architecture**, *see* CRETAN AND MYCENAEAN ARCHITECTURE.

**Minster**. Originally the name for any monastic establishment or its church, whether a monastery proper or a house of secular canons, it came to be applied to certain cathedral churches in England (e.g. York) and abroad and also other major churches.

**Minute**. In classical architecture a unit of measurement representing one sixtieth part of the diameter of a column at the base of its shaft. It may be either one sixtieth or one thirtieth part of a MODULE.

**Mique**, Richard (1728–94). French architect and the last of the royal architects at Versailles. He was trained under J.-F. BLONDEL in Paris, then employed by ex-King Stanislas at Nancy, who ennobled him (1761). On Stanislas's death in 1766 he returned to Paris. He built the Ursuline convent, now Lycée Hoche, at Versailles (1767–72) with quietly elegant conventual buildings and a church inspired by Palladio's Villa Rotonda, and in 1775 the Carmelite church at St Denis

(now Justice de la Paix) with an Ionic portico and cupola. The same year he succeeded GABRIEL as first architect to Louis XVI and in this capacity was responsible for numerous minor works at Versailles – the decoration of the Petits Appartements of Marie Antoinette in the main palace, the theatre at the Petit Trianon, the exquisite circular Temple de l'Amour, the Belvédère, and, his best-known work, the picturesquely rustic Hameau with exposed beams and irregular roofs (1778–82). He was guillotined.

Braham 1980; Kalnein 1995.

**Miralles**, Enric (b.1955), *see* SPANISH ARCHITECTURE.

**Misericord** or **miserere**. Bracket on the underside of the seat of a hinged choir stall which, when turned up, served as a support for the occupant while standing during long services. The undersides were usually carved, often with figures.

M. D. Anderson, *M. Medieval Life in English Woodcarving*, London 1954; G. L. Remnant, *A Catalogue of M. in Great Britain*, London 1969.

**Mission Revival**. A Californian regional style initiated by OLMSTED at Stanford University, Palo Alto (1885–91), where he used adaptations of adobe buildings left by the Franciscan Mission. Notable examples elsewhere are the A. K. Smiley Library, Redlands (1897–9); the Mission Inn, Riverside (1902–14); and Julia MORGAN's El Campanil Library, Mills College, Oakland (1904–6), all in California. The Union Station, Los Angeles (1939), is a late example.

K. J. Weitze, *California's M.R.*, Los Angeles 1984.

**Mission Style**. The Spanish Colonial Missions developed a distinctive architecture in Mexico and the southern US, usually ADOBE built, but much survives, e.g. Palace of the Governors, Santa Fé (1610–14), and San Esterán, Acoma, New Mexico (1629–42). It went on until the late C18 and C19 in California, e.g. San Carlos Borromeo, Carmel (1773, rebuilt after the 1812 earthquake); the Santa Barbara Mission, California, as rebuilt after the 1812 earthquake by Padre Antonio Ripoll. El Molino Viejo, Pasadena (1816), is a remarkably intact survival.

**Mithraeum**. A building, often semi-subterranean, for celebrating the cult of Mithras, originally a Persian demigod whose worship challenged early Christianity. A mithraeum contains a passage between broad shelves on which worshippers reclined during ceremonies, the end wall bearing a relief or fresco of Mithras. They are commonly found in the Roman provinces, e.g. Dura Europos, but also in Rome itself, e.g. below S. Clemente.

**Mitre**. The diagonal joint formed by two mouldings intersecting at right angles; *see also* MASON'S MITRE.

**Mixtec architecture**, *see* MESOAMERICAN ARCHITECTURE.

**Mnesicles**. A prominent architect in Periclean Athens. He designed the grand entrance gateway to the Acropolis, Athens (437–432 BC) but never finished; also, probably, the earlier Erechtheum of c.420 BC.

J. A. Bungaard, *M.*, Copenhagen 1957; C. Tiberi, *M. l'architetto dei propilei*, Rome 1964.

**Moat**. A wide and deep ditch, usually filled with water, surrounding a medieval town, fortress or castle as a defence against assault.

**Moderne**. Term used in the USA in the 1930s for contemporary machine-styled as opposed to traditionalist furniture and furnishings and by analogy also to architecture akin to ART DECO, especially on the West Coast.

D. Gebhard and H. von Bretton, *Kem Weber: The M. in Southern California 1920–41*, Santa Barbara 1969.

**Modernism**. Term for C20 *avant-garde* movements in architecture which shared a concern for FUNCTIONALISM and new technology, a rejection of ornament, and aspired to create new solutions for architecture and urban design appropriate to the social conditions of the C20. Originating in the late C19 with VIOLLET LE DUC and other theorists, culminating with LOOS and WAGNER whose *Modern Architektur* of 1895 pleaded for an architecture attuned to 'modern life', Modernism emerged in Europe before the First World War and reached its peak in architecture in the 1920s and 1930s with GROPIUS's Bauhaus Building, Dessau (1925–6), the DEUTSCHER WERKBUND's experimental Weissenhof Seidlung housing, Stuttgart (1926–7), and LE CORBUSIER's Salvation Army Hostel, Paris (1929). They are characterized by asymmetrical compositions, unrelieved cubic shapes, metal and glass construction resulting in large windows in horizontal bands, an absence of mouldings and a predilection for white rendering and open plans. By the 1930s the movement had reached the USA with NEUTRA and SCHINDLER and was canonized as INTERNATIONAL MODERN or INTERNATIONAL STYLE in New York in 1932. The later emigration of Bauhaus architects and others to the USA led to a second flowering there in 1945–60, notably with MIES VAN DER ROHE. It later declined into CORPORATE MODERNISM and by the 1970s Modernism was being analysed by such critics as Peter Blake in his influential *Form Follows Fiasco. Why Modern Architecture Hasn't Worked* (Boston/Toronto 1977). POSTMODERNISM followed in the 1980s.

Collins 1965; Colquhoun 1981; J. Boyd White, *What is M.?*, London 1996; Curtis 1996.

**Modernisme**. Term given to a vigorous regional style which flourished in Catalonia *c.*1880–1920 and which has influenced such recent architects as Bohigas and Martorell. *See* SPANISH ARCHITECTURE.

O. Bohigas, *Reseña y catálogo de la arquitectura modernista*, Barcelona 1971; J. L. Marfany, *Aspectes del M.*, Barcelona 1975.

**Modillion**. A small bracket or CONSOLE of which a series is frequently used to support the upper member of a Corinthian or Composite CORNICE, arranged in pairs with a square depression between each pair. *See* Fig. 51.

**Modular construction**. 1. Construction in which a selected unit or MODULE, usually a subcomponent, is consistently and repeatedly used. 2. Construction by means of large, prefabricated, mass-produced and partly pre-assembled sections or modules which are finally assembled on the building; *see also* INDUSTRIALIZED BUILDING.

**Module**. 1. A unit of measurement, usually of length, by which the proportions of a building are regulated. In classical architecture either the diameter or half the diameter of a column at the base of its shaft, in either case divided into minutes so that the full diameter represents sixty minutes. In modern architecture, any unit of measurement which facilitates prefabrication, usually based on a standard pattern of standard dimensions. 2. A uniform structural component forming part of an ordered system. 3. A repetitive unit (dimensional or functional) used in planning, recording or constructing buildings or other structures.

**Modulor**, *see* LE CORBUSIER; PROPORTION.

**Moholy-Nagy**, László (1895–1946), *see* BAUHAUS.

**Molding**, *see* MOULDING.

**Molinos**, Jacques (1743–1813), *see* BÉLANGER, François-Joseph; GILLY, Friedrich.

**Moller**, Georg (1784–1852), *see* GILLY, Friedrich.

**Mollet**, Claude (*c.*1563–1648). French garden designer, employed from 1595 onwards by Henri IV for whom he laid out geometrically planned gardens at Saint Germain-en-Laye, Fontainebleau and at the Tuileries in Paris, none of which survives. He claimed to have invented the PARTERRE DE BRODERIE, and designs for many were included in his posthumously published *Théâtre des plans et jardinages* (1652), though BOYCEAU had probably laid out the first. As royal gardener at the Tuileries he was succeeded by Jean, father of André LE NÔTRE. His son André Mollet (d.1665) was the author of *Le Jardin de plaisir* (1651), a fully illustrated summary of the principles of the French garden in which, he wrote, shrubs and trees should be treated as building materials. (There were German and Swedish editions in 1651 and an English edition in 1670.) He designed gardens for Charles I in England (St James's Palace *c.*1630; Wimbledon House 1642), for Prince Frederik Hendrik of Orange (Honselsarsdijk 1633–5), and for Queen Christina of Sweden in Stockholm (1648–53). With his brother Gabriel (d.1663) he also designed gardens for Charles II in England (St James's Park, London, and Hampton Court Palace). These gardens introduced the French style to northern Europe but none survived later changes in taste.

·K. Woodbridge, *Princely Gardens. The Origins and Development of the French Formal Style*, London 1986.

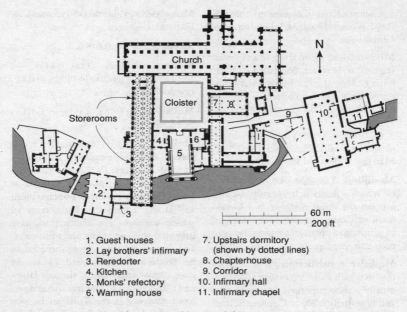

Fig. 79 Monastery: Plan of Fountains Abbey, Yorkshire

1. Guest houses
2. Lay brothers' infirmary
3. Reredorter
4. Kitchen
5. Monks' refectory
6. Warming house
7. Upstairs dormitory
   (shown by dotted lines)
8. Chapterhouse
9. Corridor
10. Infirmary hall
11. Infirmary chapel

**Mollino**, Carlo (1905–75). Italian architect. Thought a maverick in his lifetime, he became influential posthumously though his most remarkable building, the Società Ippica, Turin (1935–9), was demolished in 1960. His Teatro Regio (1973) and Business Centre, Turin (1974), are notable.

G. Brino, *C.M. (1905–75)*, London 1987.

**Molnár**, Farkas (1897–1945), *see* HUN-GARIAN ARCHITECTURE.

**Monastery.** Christian monasticism – preceded by Buddhist monasticism, *see* VIHARA – originated in Egypt, where the first men to choose a monastic life were hermits. A more organized monastic existence was conceived by St Pachomius (c.315): monks now still lived on their own like hermits, but so close together that they had a joint chapel and a joint refectory. Such monks are known as coenobites. This form of monasticism reached Europe by way of the south of France and from there entered Ireland (Skellig Michael). But the monastic architecture of medieval Europe is that created in the C6 as the expression of the rule of the order established by St Benedict at Montecassino. Its first surviving complete expression is the plan of c.830 made by a cleric of Cologne for St Gall in Switzerland; here we have the axial arrangement of ranges – the coenobites' layouts were haphazard – the cloister with its arcaded walks, the chapterhouse and dormitory or dorter in the east range, the refectory, frater or dining hall in the range opposite the church, the stores in the west range. Abbots or priors usually lived near the west end as well, while the infirmary was beyond the claustral parts to the east. There were also a guest house, kitchens, brewhouse, bakehouse, smithy, cornmills, stables, cowsheds, pigsties, and workshops. In terms of architectural composition the monastery is infinitely superior to the medieval castle. *See* Fig. 79; CISTERCIAN ARCHITECTURE; CLUNY.

Braunfels 1973; W. Horn and E. Born, *The Plan of St Gall*, Berkeley and Los Angeles 1979.

**Moneo**, José Rafael (b.1937). Spanish architect, trained in Madrid and then with UTZON in 1962–3. He made his name with Bankinter, Madrid (1970–76), and the Museo Nacional de Arte Romana, Merida (1980–86). The latter was a powerful evocation of Spanish Romanidad and marked his adherence to tradition and classical coherence, as distinct from sentimental classical revivalism. His Previsión Española Building, Seville (1982–7), and Bank of Spain, Jaén (1983–8) were followed by the Palacio de Villahermosa, Barcelona (1989–91); the San Pablo Airport Terminal, Seville (1989–91); the Atocha Station, Madrid (1991); the Miró Foundation, Palma, Mallorca (1992); the Davis Museum, Wellesley, Massachusetts (1989–93); and the Congress Building, San Sebastián (1995).

**Monier**, Joseph (1823–1906), *see* CONCRETE.

**Monitor roof**. A factory roof with a raised glazed area forming a continuous lantern light. *See* Fig. 80.

**Monolith**. A single stone, usually in the form of a monument or column.

**Monopteral**. A term applied to a building with a single row of columns on all sides, or all round it if circular.

**Monteiro**, José Luis (1849–1942), *see* PORTUGUESE ARCHITECTURE.

**Montereau**, Pierre de (d.1267), *see* PIERRE DE MONTREUIL.

**Montferrand**, August Ricard (1786–1858). French Empire architect who emigrated to Russia and became, with ROSSI and STASOV, a leading post-Napoleonic architect in St Petersburg. He was trained under PERCIER and worked at the Madeleine in Paris under VIGNON. His masterpiece is the vast and sumptuous St Isaac's Cathedral in St Petersburg (1817–57). The gilded dome (completed *c*.1842) is framed in iron – an early example of the use of metal structure, preceding the dome of the Capitol in Washington by a decade. His enormous granite Alexander Column in Winter Palace Square, St Petersburg (1829), is imposing though less original in conception than MILLS's almost contemporary Washington Monument in Washington.

G. Butikov, *St Isaac's Cathedral, Leningrad*, London 1980.

**Montigny**, A. J. V. Grandjean de (1776–1850), *see* BRAZILIAN ARCHITECTURE.

**Montoyer**, Louis Joseph (*c*.1749–1811), *see* CZECH ARCHITECTURE.

**Montreuil**, Pierre de (d.1267), *see* PIERRE DE MONTREUIL.

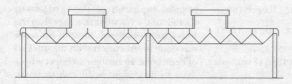

Fig. 80 Monitor roof

**Moore**, Charles Willard (1925–93). American architect whose participation with HALPRIN in the pioneering environmental-architectural project at Sea Ranch on the Californian coast north of San Francisco in 1965 established his reputation. After this striking essay in redwood cabin regionalism he turned to POST-MODERNISM with a series of colourful, convivially eclectic and often large-scale scenographic buildings and urban complexes, notably the Faculty Club, University of California, Santa Barbara (1968); Kresge College, University of California, Santa Cruz (1973); and the theatrical Piazza d'Italia, New Orleans (1979). His later work was less exuberant, e.g. St Matthew's Episcopal Church, Pacific Palisades, Los Angeles (1979–83); Extensions Center and Alumni House, University of California, Irvine (1983–5); and Wonderwall, New Orleans (1984). In 1984 his firm was renamed Centerbrook Architects and survived him. He published with K. Bloomer *Body, Memory and Architecture* (1977).

E. J. Johnson, *C.M. Buildings and Projects 1949–86*, New York 1986; S. K. Tompkins, *A Quest for Grandeur. C.M. and the Federal Triangle*, Washington, DC 1993.

**Moosbrugger**, Caspar, *see* MOSBRUGGER, Caspar.

**Morandi**, Riccardo (1902–89). Leading Italian concrete designer after NERVI. His Maracaibo bridge, Venezuela (1957), the underground automobile showroom, Turin (1959), and the autostrada bridge, Genoa (1960–67), made his name.

G. Boaga and B. Boni, *R.M.*, Milan 1962; L. V. Masini, *R.M.*, Rome 1974.

**Morava school**, *see* BYZANTINE ARCHITECTURE.

**Morel**, Jean-Marie (1728–1810), *see* LANDSCAPE GARDEN.

**Moretti**, Luigi (1907–73), *see* ITALIAN ARCHITECTURE.

**Morgan**, Julia (1872–1957). American architect trained under MAYBECK in California and in Paris at the École des Beaux Arts from 1897 to 1901. Her first buildings were in the MISSION REVIVAL style – El Campanil Library, Mills College, Oakland, California (1904–6), and the Herald Examiner Building, Los Angeles (1915). Later she developed a personal version of ARTS AND CRAFTS for the Asilomar Conference Center, Monterey, California (1913–29). From 1919 onwards she was continuously employed by William Randolph Hearst designing and building his fantastic Spanish–Moorish–Romanesque–Gothic–Renaissance castle at San Simeon, California, incorporating large fragments of Ancient Roman, medieval Spanish and other European buildings. She also designed for Hearst the Tyrolean Wyntoon in northern California (1924–42).

S. H. Boutelle, *J.M. Architect*, New York (1988) 1990; R. Winter 1997.

**Morris**, Robert (*c.*1701/2–54), a relation of Roger MORRIS, was the theoretician of English Palladianism in his *An Essay in Defence of Ancient Architecture* (1728) and *Lectures on Architecture* (1734). *Rural Architecture* (1750), reissued as *Select Architecture* (1755), also had a wide influence, e.g. on JEFFERSON's Monticello.

Kaufmann 1955; Harris 1990; Summerson 1991; Colvin 1995.

**Morris**, Roger (1695–1749). English architect and one of the most gifted and original exponents of PALLADIANISM, though of the CAMPBELL rather than the BURLINGTON school. Most of his work was done in association with the 9th Earl of Pembroke, an amateur architect whose share in his designs is difficult to assess;

works include Marble Hill, Twickenham (1724–9), White Lodge, Richmond (1727–8), and the Palladian Bridge at Wilton, Wiltshire (1736). Later he turned neo-Gothic at Inveraray Castle, Argyllshire (1746 onwards).

Kaufmann 1955; Summerson 1991; Colvin 1995.

**Morris**, William (1834–96). English poet, designer and political theorist; he was not an architect, but holds an unchallengeable place in a dictionary of architecture because of his great influence on architects. This influence acted in three ways. Morris had begun by studying divinity, then for a short time turned to architecture and worked in the Oxford office of STREET, and subsequently in a desultory way learnt to paint under Rossetti. When he furnished his digs in London, and more so when, after his marriage, he wanted a house, he found that the architecture as well as the design of his day were not to his liking. So he got his friend Philip WEBB to design Red House for him, and this straightforward, redbrick, made-to-measure house had a great deal of influence (see ARTS AND CRAFTS). Secondly, as the result of the search for satisfactory furnishings, Morris and some friends created in 1861 the firm Morris, Marshall & Faulkner (later Morris & Co.), for which enterprise Morris himself designed wallpapers, the ornamental parts (and, rarely, the figure work) of stained glass, chintzes (i.e. printed textiles), and later also carpets, tapestries and woven furnishing materials, and in the end (1890–96) even books and their type and decoration (Kelmscott Press).

All his designs shared a stylized two-dimensional quality which contrasted with the then prevailing naturalism and its unbridled use of depth; but they also possessed a deep feeling for nature which itself contrasted with the ornamental

work of a few slightly older English reformers (PUGIN; Owen Jones). These qualities impressed themselves deeply on younger architects of Norman SHAW's office and school, so much so that some of them took to design themselves. However, they might not have gone so far, if it had not been for Morris's third way of influencing architects, his lectures, which he began in 1877 and continued till his death, frequently for the SPAB (Society for the Protection of Ancient Buildings), which he founded in 1877 and which enabled him to extol the simplicity and beauty of VERNACULAR buildings. (*See also* RESTORATION). They were impassioned pleas not only for better, more considered design, but for abolishing the ugliness of towns and buildings and of all the things made to fill buildings, and for reforming the society responsible for towns, buildings and products. Morris was a socialist, one of the founders of organized socialism in England. That he was also a poet would not be of relevance here, if it were not for the fact that his poetry and his prose romances developed from an avowed medievalism to a strongly implied social responsibility for the present. At the same time the medievalism, displayed, for example, by the self-conscious use of obsolete language, is a reminder of the medievalism – admittedly adapted and even transmuted – of all his designs. There is, indeed, a medievalism even in Morris's theory, for his socialism is one of labour becoming once more enjoyable handicraft. And although Morris fervently believed, harking back again to the Middle Ages, that all art ought to be 'by the people for the people', he could never resolve the dilemma that production by hand costs more than by machine, and that the products of his own firm therefore (and for other reasons) were bound to be costly and not 'for the people'. It needed a further reform and a revision of this one essential tenet of Morris's to arrive at the C20 situation, where architects and artists design for industrial production and thereby serve the common man and not only the connoisseur. But Morris started the movement, and it was due to him that the artists such as van de VELDE or BEHRENS turned designers, and that architects like VOYSEY did likewise. It was also due to him that the criteria of two-dimensional design rose from C19 to C20 standards. Webb's work for Morris had the same effect on furniture design.

P. Thompson, *The Work of W.M.*, London 1967; P. Henderson, *W.M., his Life, Work and Friends*, London 1967; Pevsner 1972; W. Stansky, *Redesigning the World. W.M., the 1880s and the Arts and Crafts*, Princeton 1984; F. MacCarthy, *W.M. A Life for Our Time*, London 1994.

**Mortar**. A mixture of cement (or lime), sand and water, laid between courses of bricks or masonry to even out irregularities and gain greater adhesion; more loosely, any material for bedding and jointing brickwork or stonework.

**Mortice and tenon joint**. A joint formed by a rectangular projecting piece (or *tenon*) fitting into a rectangular socket (or *mortice*).

**Mosaic**. Surface decoration for walls or floors formed of small pieces or *tesserae* of glass, stone or marble set in a mastic. The design may be either geometrical or representational. CONE MOSAICS in 3500–3000 BC Sumerian temples at Uruk (Iraq) are the earliest known form of architectural ornamentation. Mosaic reached its highest pitch of accomplishment in Ancient Roman and Byzantine buildings. *See also* TERRAZZO; TESSELLATED.

E. W. Anthony, *A History of M.*, New York (1953) 1968; P. Portoghesi, *M. e architettura*, Ravenna 1959.

**Mosbrugger** or **Moosbrugger**, Caspar (1656–1723). Swiss architect, born at Au in the Bregenzerwald – the headquarters of the Vorarlberg masons' guild – and a founder of the Vorarlberg school of architects which included the BEER and THUMB families. He was apprenticed to a stone-cutter, then became a novice at the Benedictine monastery of Einsiedeln in 1682 and remained there as a lay-brother for the rest of his life. He became the greatest Swiss Baroque architect. Already in 1684 he was asked for advice at Weingarten Abbey, though building did not begin there until many years later. His masterpiece is the abbey church at Einsiedeln (begun 1719), a spatial composition of unusual complexity even for a Baroque architect. He did not live to see it completed. He also designed the parish church at Muri (1694–8). He probably played some part (even if only an advisory one) in the design of the vast Benedictine abbey church at Weingarten (1714–24), with a façade much like that at Einsiedeln, and he probably built the church at Disentis (1696–1712).

Hempel 1965; W. Oechslin (ed.), *Die Vorarlberger Barockbaumeister*, exh. cat., Einsiedeln and Bregenz 1973; N. Lieb and F. Dieth, *Die Vorarlberger Barockbaumeister*, Munich and Zürich (1960) 1983.

**Moser**, Karl (1860–1936), *see* SWISS ARCHITECTURE.

**Mosque**. In ISLAMIC ARCHITECTURE a place for prayer, strictly orientated towards Mecca. The English word is derived from the Arabic *masjid* (place of prostration), but a functional distinction is drawn between a *masjid* for daily prayers and a *jami* (*masjid al-jami*) or congregational mosque built to serve the whole adult population of a community gath-

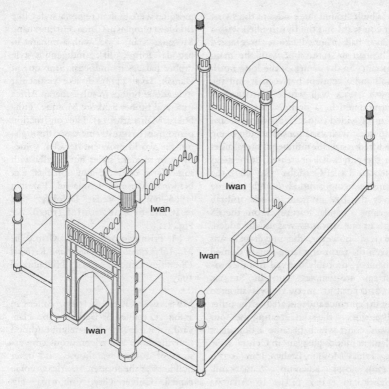

Iwan

Iwan

Iwan

Iwan

Fig. 81 A four iwan Friday mosque

ered for worship on Fridays and addressed by the imam from a MINBAR. The first mosque was built by the Prophet Muhammad at Medina, Saudi Arabia, shortly after 622 – a rectangular enclosure of some 4,200 sq. m. (45,000 sq. ft) with a double row of palm trunks carrying a roof of mud-covered palm leaves along the inner side of the southern wall, under which he and his followers could pray facing Mecca, a smaller colonnade inside the northern wall for the poorest members of the community, and along the outside of the eastern wall a range of simple rooms for himself and family. (After his death and burial in the enclosure

a succession of buildings was raised on the site, the present structure being C19.) As Islam expanded, existing buildings such as pagan temples, Zoroastrian FIRE TEMPLES and Christian CHURCHES were sometimes adapted for Muslim use. In new towns, e.g. Basra and Kufa, Iraq, mosques were planned like that at Medina but using stone columns and other spolia. (The Dome of the Rock, Jerusalem, completed in 691, was a place of pilgrimage rather than a *masjid* or *jami*.) The first great congregational mosque that survives is that at Damascus, begun in 705. Within the Ancient Roman walls of the *temenos* of a pagan temple, a two-storey arcade was built around three sides of the SAHN or courtyard and the fourth filled with a prayer-hall, planned like a three-aisled Christian BASILICA but with the main entrance in the centre of the long north wall and a transept between it and the south QIBLA wall where a MIHRAB is surmounted by a dome. This 'Arabian plan' provided a model for congregational mosques, with variations (the sahn being reduced in size, the number of lateral aisles in the prayer-hall increased, sometimes piecemeal as at Cordoba (784–987), the transept being omitted though a dome over the bay in front of the mihrab became a regular feature). From the C8 at least one MINARET was usually added. In Iran, however, the prayer-hall was given the form of a large square domed chamber, probably derived from Zoroastrian fire-temples, and in SELJUK ARCHITECTURE an IWAN was adopted for the entrance and repeated on the other three sides of the sahn, creating the 'four iwan' court which became a dominant element in mosque plans in Central Asia, e.g. Friday Mosque, Isfahan, Iran (1072–1477); Bibi Khanum, Samarkand, Uzbekistan (1399–1404). In Anatolia from the late C14 the sahn tended to be of limited size if not excluded altogether, a preference being shown for large hypo-style prayer-halls covered by domes, one above each of the bays in the Ulu Cami, Bursa, Turkey, of 1395. This type was further developed after the Ottoman conquest of Constantinople in 1453, in emulation of Hagia Sophia, culminating in centrally planned mosques with domes and half-domes of impressive dimensions covering an unobstructed space, a type perfected by SINAN (Suleimaniyeh, Istanbul, Turkey, 1550–57; Selimiye, Edirne, Turkey, 1569–74) and followed throughout Ottoman territory into the C19 (Mosque of Muhammad Ali, Cairo, 1820–57). Outside the heartlands of Islam

mosques were built in regional styles, like Buddhist temples in China (Huajuexuang Mosque, Xian, 1392, with a minaret in pagoda form), like indigenous-style timber palaces in Indonesia (mosque at Damak, Java, 1478), or like vernacular style adobe houses in sub-Saharan Africa (pisé and timber Sankore Mosque, Timbuktu, Mali, early C14). The construction of mosques has greatly increased throughout the world in recent decades, sometimes in modern styles but usually with some form of dome and minarets, e.g. National Mosque, Islamabad, Pakistan (1966–96) by Vedat Dalokay; that in Rome by PORTOGHESI (1996). See Fig. 81.

M. Frishman and H. U. Khan, *The M. Architectural Development and Regional Diversity*, London 1994; Hillenbrand 1995.

**Moss**, Eric Owen (b.1943). American architect, trained at Berkeley and Harvard, notable for his neighbourhood revivifications and adventurous conversions of disused warehouses and other buildings at the former American movie capital, Culver City, California. His imaginative use of discarded and incongruous industrial materials earned him the soubriquet of 'jeweller of junk', e.g. the Gary Group Office, Paramount Laundry and Lindblade Tower (1986–90) where the old concrete walls are draped with chains and studded with ladders of steel re-bars. His later work, often involving additions or modifications to rehabilitated buildings, includes the Box (1990–94), IRS Building (1993–4) and Samitaur Building (1993–6), all in Culver City.

E. O. Moss, *E.O.M. Buildings and Projects*, New York 1991; J. Steele, *E.O.M.*, London 1993; J. Steele, *Lawson Weston House E.O.M.*, London 1995.

**Mothe**, Jean-Baptiste Michel Vallin de la

(1729–1800), *see* VALLIN DE LA MOTHE, Jean-Baptiste Michel.

**Motorway**. A road restricted to motor traffic (i.e. excluding pedestrians, pedal-cyclists, horse-drawn vehicles, etc.) as a thoroughfare for swift transport between cities. The first were the *autostrade* of Fascist Italy in the early 1920s, followed by the more widely ranging *Autobahn* network begun in Germany in 1926 under the direction of the civil engineer Fritz Todt (1891–1942), with Alwin Seifert (1890–1972) responsible for their integration in the landscape, and BONATZ for bridges and other built installations. Extensive highways had been constructed earlier in the USA, notably the New York to San Francisco highway in 1916–19, promoted by the Packard Motor Car Company, and in 1923 Warren Henry Manning (1860–1938) published a proposal for a coast-to-coast system of national highways, but not until the 1950s was the interstate system of limited access highways begun. In the UK, France and other European countries vast networks of motorways have been constructed since the 1950s and the pre-Second World War German and Italian systems have been greatly extended. Civil engineers were in charge of their design and construction in collaboration with landscape architects (e.g. JELLICOE, LASSUS) responsible for fitting them visually into the natural environment and for planting trees, shrubs, etc. on their verges.

B. Lassus and C. Layrit, *Autoroutes et paysages*, Paris 1994.

**Motte**. A steep mound, the main feature of many C11 and C12 castles. *See* MOTTE-AND-BAILEY.

**Motte-and-bailey**. A post-Roman and Norman defence system consisting of an earthen mound (the *motte*) topped with a wooden tower, placed within a BAILEY with enclosure ditch, palisade, and, rarely, an internal bank.

**Mouchette**. A curved DAGGER motif in curvilinear TRACERY, especially popular in England in the early C14. *See* Fig. 82.

Fig. 82 Mouchette

**Moulding** or **molding**. A continuous projection or groove, used decoratively to throw shadow or to throw water away from a wall. Their contours vary. *See* BEAD MOULDING; BEAKHEAD; BILLET; BOWTELL; CABLE MOULDING; CHEVRON; DOGTOOTH; HOOD-MOULD; KEEL MOULDING; NAILHEAD; NEBULE; OGEE MOULDING; OVOLO MOULDING; ROLL MOULDING; WAVE MOULDING.

**Moving staircase**, *see* ESCALATOR.

**Moya**, John Hidalgo (1920–94), *see* POWELL & MOYA.

**Mozarabic**. The style evolved by Christians under Moorish influence in Spain from the late C9 to the early C11, e.g. S. Miguel de Escalada near León (consecrated in 913) with its arcade of arches of horseshoe shape, Santiago de Peñalba (931–7) and Sta Maria de Lebeña (also C10). The style is Christian in inspiration but Islamic in conception and has many Islamic features such as the horseshoe arch. Mozarabic churches are usually small and stand in the open countryside. They form the largest and best preserved group of pre-Romanesque buildings in Europe.

J. F. Arenas, *M. Architecture*, Greenwich, Conn. 1973.

**Mozuma**, Kiko (b.1941), *see* JAPANESE ARCHITECTURE.

**Mud-brick construction**, *see* ADOBE; PISÉ.

**Mudéjar**. Spanish Christian architecture in a purely Muslim style. (Literally, the term refers to Muslims who remained in Christian Spain after the reconquest.) The style was evolved by Muslims in Spain or by Christians working within the Spanish Muslim tradition. Notable examples are Alfonso VIII's early C13 chapel at the monastery of Las Huelgas, Burgos, and the C14 Alcázar, Seville, which has Kufic inscriptions extolling Christian rulers. Mudéjar motifs persisted in Spanish Gothic architecture and may also be found in PLATERESQUE buildings of the C16.

G. G. King, *Mudéjar*, Bryn Mawr 1927; Kubler and Soria 1959.

**Mughal architecture**, *see* INDIAN AND PAKISTANI ARCHITECTURE.

**Mullion**. A vertical post or other upright dividing a window or other opening into two or more LIGHTS.

**Mumford**, Lewis (1895–1990). American polymath and polemicist notable for his writings on urbanism in which he was influenced by GEDDES and HOWARD. Describing himself as an American humanist in the tradition of Emerson and Whitman, he argued that the physical design of cities and their economic functions were secondary to their relationship to the natural environment and to the spiritual values of the human community. He saw the city as 'a theatre of social action' and became very influential in his promotion of communitarianism and regionalism and ecological equilibrium. He was involved with C. STEIN and others in RADBURN PLANNING. In his writings he was as prolific as he was forceful, from his early *The Story of Utopias* (1922) and *The Culture of Cities* (1938) to his famous *The City in History: Its Origins,* *Its Transformation and Its Prospects* (1961). His later works include *City Development: Studies in Disintegration and Renewal* (1961) and *The Urban Prospect* (1968). He was important also for his re-evaluation of WRIGHT's organic modernism.

D. L. Miller, *L.M. A Life*, New York 1989; R. Wojtowicz, *L.M. and American Modernism. Utopian Theories for Architecture and Urban Planning*, Cambridge, Mass. 1996.

**Munday**, Richard (d.1740), *see* UNITED STATES ARCHITECTURE.

**Munggenast**, Josef (1680–1741). Austrian architect, nephew and pupil of PRANDTAUER, for whom he worked as foreman and whom he succeeded as architect at Melk. In collaboration with the Viennese sculptor, engineer and architect Matthias Steinl (1644–1727) he built the church for the Augustinian canons at Dürnstein, with a boldly *mouvementé* interior and outstandingly handsome tower (1721–7). His main independent work is the reconstruction of the monastery of Altenburg, where he provided a richly coloured, exuberantly Baroque casing for the Gothic church and created one of the best of all Baroque libraries (1730–33).

E. Munggenast, *J.M. der Stiftsbaumeister 1680–1741*, Vienna 1963; Hempel 1965; Brucker 1983.

**Muntin**. The vertical part in the framing of a door, screen, panelling, etc., butting into, or stopped by, the horizontal rails. *See* Fig. 47. In the USA a glazing bar or MULLION.

**Muqarnas**. Arabic word for a system of serried tiers of small niches or concave cells in vaults, peculiar to ISLAMIC ARCHITECTURE. It probably originated in Iran as a structural device but the earliest surviving example – fragments from a C9 secular building at Nishapur, Iran, now in the Metropolitan Museum, New York – must have been purely decorative. In a brick-built mausoleum of 977–8 at Tim near Samarkand, Uzbekistan, the octagonal zone of transition between the square chamber and dome has structural squinches framed by decorative niches and sections of domes. From the CII muqarnas became a common feature of wall and ceiling decoration throughout Islam, usually in stucco, masking the structure of a vault, e.g. the north dome chamber of the Great Mosque at Isfahan, Iran (1072–5), but sometimes carved in stone, e.g. the cornice and semi-dome in the portal of the Complex of Hassan, Cairo (1356–61). The most spectacular examples are in mid-CI4 rooms of the Alhambra, Granada, where stucco elements suspended from domes, arches and the tops of walls have the effect of stalactites, hence the English name 'stalactite vaulting'. *See* Fig. 83.

Hillenbrand 1995.

Fig. 83 Muqarnas

**Mural painting**. Decorative or figurative painting on walls, usually interior but also exterior walls, from prehistoric times onwards, e.g. interior wall-paintings in houses at Çatal Huyuk, Turkey, of *c.*5800 BC; exterior painted friezes on the Great Tomb, Vergina, Greece, of *c.*330 BC. In Europe post-medieval mural paintings were usually in FRESCO, especially in Italy. *See also* SGRAFFITO.

**Murano**, Togo (1891–1982), *see* JAPANESE ARCHITECTURE.

**Murcutt**, Glen (b.1936). Australian architect whose small-scale buildings exemplify Chermayeff and Alexander's 'Community and Privacy' principles in rural sites, realized with great sensitivity to the climatic and regional conditions, including Australian vernacular corrugated-iron construction. They range from the Short House, Kempsey (1975), to the Kempsey Museum and Tourist Information Center, Kempsey (1982); the Ball-Eastaway House, Glenorie (1983); the Bingie Bingie House, Mount Irvine (1988); and the Simpson-Lee House, Mount Wilson (1994), all in New South Wales.

P. Drew, *Leaves of Iron. G.M. Pioneer of an Australian Architectural Form*, North Ride, NSW 1985; E. M. Farrelly, *Three Houses: G.M.*, London 1993; F. Fomonot, *G.M. Works and Projects*, London 1995.

**Murphy/Jahn**, *see* JAHN, Helmut.

**Mushrabeyeh work**. Elaborate wooden lattices used to enclose the upper windows in Islamic domestic architecture.

**Mushroom construction**. A system of reinforced concrete construction whereby floor-slabs are directly supported by columns flared out at the top into circular discs, thus eliminating beams. Experiments began simultaneously in Europe and the USA *c.*1908; *see* MAILLART. The Johnson Wax

Factory, Racine, Wisconsin (1936–9), by WRIGHT, is a notable example.

**Muthesius**, Hermann (1861–1927), *see* ARTS AND CRAFTS.

**Mutule**. The projecting square block above the TRIGLYPH and under the CORONA of a Doric CORNICE.

**Muzio**, Giovanni (1893–1982). Italian architect working in Milan, where his Ca' Brutta apartment blocks (1919–23) were followed by large-scale classicizing buildings, e.g. Università Cattolica (1931) and Palazzo della Provincia (1933). His reputation has recently been reassessed together with that of his Roman contemporary PIACENTINI.

F. Irace, *G.M. 1893–1982*, Milan 1994; F. Bazzi Ceriani, *L'architettura di G.M.*, Milan 1994/5.

**Myanmar architecture**, *see* BURMESE ARCHITECTURE.

**Mycenaean architecture**, *see* CRETAN AND MYCENAEAN ARCHITECTURE.

**Mylne**, Robert (1733–1811). Scottish architect, a contemporary and rival of Robert ADAM, descended from a long line of Scottish master masons. He was trained by his father in Edinburgh, then went to Paris (1754), and Rome (1755–9), where he had amazing success by winning First Prize at the Accademia di S. Luca in 1758. But he did not fulfil this early promise. His first work after settling in London (1759) was to be his most famous, Blackfriars Bridge (1760–69, demolished), in which he introduced elliptical arches. Thereafter he worked extensively both as architect and as engineer. His largest country house, Tusmore, Oxfordshire (1766–9, demolished), was neo-Palladian. More elegant and original is The Wick, Richmond (1775), a small suburban 'box', while his façade of the Stationers' Hall, London (1800), shows him at his most neoclassical.

Harris 1990; Summerson 1991; Colvin 1995.

# N

**Nailhead**. An Early English architectural enrichment consisting of small pyramids repeated as a band. *See* Fig. 84.

**Naos**. The sanctuary or principal chamber of a Greek temple, containing the statue of the god. In Byzantine architecture, the core and sanctuary of a centrally planned church, i.e. the parts reserved for the performance of the liturgy.

**Narthex**. 1. In a Byzantine church, the transverse vestibule either preceding nave and aisles as an inner narthex (esonarthex) or preceding the façade as an outer narthex (exonarthex). An esonarthex is separated from the nave and aisles by columns, rails or a wall. An exonarthex may also serve as the terminating transverse portico of a colonnaded ATRIUM or quadriporticus. 2. In a general medieval sense, an enclosed covered ANTECHURCH at the main entrance, especially if the direction is transverse and not east–west and several bays deep; sometimes called a GALILEE. *See* Fig. 13.

**Nash**, John (1752–1835). English architect, London's only inspired urban designer and the greatest architect of the PICTURESQUE movement. He was the exact opposite of his contemporary SOANE, being self-confident and adaptable, socially successful and artistically conservative, light-handed and slipshod in detail, but with an easy mastery of general effects on a large scale. Again, unlike Soane, he was an architect of exteriors rather than interiors. The son of a Lambeth millwright, he was trained under TAYLOR, but quickly struck out on his own and by 1780 was building stucco-fronted houses, then a novelty in London. In 1783 he went bankrupt, retired to Wales and recovered, and then joined the landscape gardener REPTON, with whom he developed a fashionable country house practice. His output was enormous and in every conceivable style – classical (Rockingham, Ireland, 1810, demolished), Italian farmhouse (Cronkhill, *c.*1802), castellated Gothic (Ravensworth Castle, 1808, demolished; Caerhays Castle, 1808), even Indian and Chinoiserie (Brighton Pavilion, 1802–21). He also built thatched cottages (Blaise Hamlet, 1811). With their fancy-dress parade of styles and irregular planning and silhouettes, these buildings epitomized the picturesque in architecture. The same picturesque combination of freedom and formality marks his greatest work, the layout of Regent's Park and Regent Street in London (1811 onwards), a brilliantly imaginative conception foreshadowing the garden city of the future. He was already sixty, but still had the enthusiasm and organizing ability to carry the whole scheme through, and he lived to see it finished. The park is sprinkled with villas and surrounded by vast terraces

Fig. 84 Nailhead

and crescents of private houses built palatially with grandiose stucco façades. There are also cottage terraces and make-believe villages of barge-boarded and Italianate villas. Of his Regent Street frontages nothing now remains except the eye-catcher, All Souls, Langham Place (1822–5). During the 1820s he planned Trafalgar Square, Suffolk Street and Suffolk Place, built Clarence House and Carlton House Terrace, and began Buckingham Palace, all in London. But he shared in his royal patron's fall from public favour, was suspected of profiteering and sharp practice, and his career came to an abrupt end when George IV died in 1830. He was dismissed from Buckingham Palace (completed by Edward Blore) and from the Board of Works, of which he had been one of the Surveyors General since 1813. His reputation remained under a cloud for the next fifty years or more.

J. Summerson, *J.N.*, London (1935) 1991; M. Mansbridge, *J.N. A Complete Catalogue*, London 1991; Colvin 1995.

**Nasoni** or **Nazzoni**, Niccolò (d.1773). Italian architect, born near Florence, who settled in Portugal (1731), where he became one of the leading Baroque architects. His main work is São Pedro dos Clérigos, Oporto (1732–50), a large and impressive church on an oval plan with a very richly decorated façade, embraced by a bold pattern of ascending staircases.

Kubler and Soria 1959; R. C. Smith, *N.N. arqitecto de Porto*, Lisbon 1966.

**Navarro Baldeweg**, Juan (b.1939), *see* SPANISH ARCHITECTURE.

**Nave**. The main central body of a longitudinally planned building such as a Roman BASILICA or Christian church. In the latter it forms the western limb, i.e. the part west of the CROSSING; more usually the middle vessel of the western limb, flanked by AISLES.

**Nebule**, **nebulé** or **nebuly moulding**. A moulding with wavy or serpentine lower edge.

**Necking**. A narrow, annular MOULDING round the bottom of a CAPITAL between it and the shaft of the column. In Ancient Roman architecture it forms part of the column, in Romanesque architecture part of the capital.

**Necropolis**. An ancient burial ground in or near a town, notably the Etruscan burial complexes at Tarquinia and the Islamic necropoli around Cairo. The term was sometimes revived for C19 CEMETERIES, e.g. the Necropolis, Glasgow, begun 1831.

**Needle spire**, *see* SPIRE.

**Neo-classicism**. The radical phase of late C18 CLASSICISM. It began with GABRIEL and others and ended with BOULLÉE and LEDOUX, in an architecture of pure geometrical forms.

**Neo-Georgian**. A style inspired by British C18 town and country houses, characterized by strict symmetry, simple modular proportions, uniformity of materials – brick or stone – sash windows, fanlights and a limited use of classical details. No. 2 Palace Green, Kensington, London (1860–62), designed for himself by the novelist William Makepeace Thackeray with the aid of Frederick Hering (1800–1869), is probably the earliest example. From the 1870s it was found appropriate for the new low-cost schools of the London School Board designed by Edward Robert Robson (1835–1917), author of the influential *School Architecture* (London 1874). Until the early C20 it was less popular for domestic architecture in England than the allied but fancier QUEEN ANNE REVIVAL style and, for public buildings, than the more pretentious BEAUX ARTS style. After the accession of George V in 1910, followed by a vogue for all things Georgian, it was widely adopted in Britain, even occasionally by LUTYENS. Housing projects designed by the London County Council Architects Department were in a simplified neo-Georgian style until the Second World War. And despite attacks by Modernists it remained popular. E. Vincent Harris (1879–1971), Francis Johnson (1910–96), Donald MacMorran (1914–83) and Sir Albert Richardson (1880–1964) were prominent exponents. Raymond Erith (1904–73) was outstanding, from his early Great House, Dedham, Essex (1936), to his Provost's Lodgings, Queen's College, Oxford (1958–9). Quinlan Terry (b.1937) carried on his practice. Neo-Georgian has analogies with the COLONIAL REVIVAL architecture of Australia, South Africa and the USA.

**Neo-Gothic**, *see* GOTHIC REVIVAL.

**Neo-Palladian**, *see* PALLADIANISM.

**Neo-Rationalism**. An Italian anti-Modernist movement of the 1960s, also known as the 'Tendenza', led by Aldo ROSSI. It rejected Functionalism in favour of an autonomous architecture concerned with formal essences and not with technology. *Architettura della città* (1966) by Rossi and *La costruzione logica dell'architettura* (1967) by Giorgio Grassi (b.1935) were seminal texts, as was also GREGOTTI's *Il territorio dell'architettura* (1966). Rossi's cemetery at Modena (1971–85) is the movement's chief monument. Oswald Mathis UNGERS and Josef Paul Kleihues (b.1933) in Germany, Bruno Reichlin (b.1941) and Fabio Reinhart (b.1942) in Switzerland, as well as the KRIER brothers, have all been influenced by and loosely associated with the movement.

E. Bonfanti *et al.*, *Architettura razionale*, Milan 1973; Klotz 1986, 1988.

**Nepalese architecture**. The earliest surviving structures are STUPAS, probably c8–9 (though some may be enlargements of c3 BC originals) with later embellishments, e.g. the Svayambhu stupa near Kathmandu, a low semi-hemispherical brick mound surmounted by a square block with a huge pair of eyes inlaid on each side and a conical spire topped by a metal drum and umbrella. In Kathmandu the Kasthamandata, a pilgrims' hostel probably *c*.1100 (though much restored), is in a style followed in the region for both secular and religious buildings until the present century – mainly of wood with wide-eaved roofs of truncated pyramidal form over each of its three storeys of diminishing size. Temples called *dega*, of two or three storeys, are somewhat similar in appearance to Chinese pagodas though more importance is given to their supporting brick walls, with much woodwork elaborately carved in relief, e.g. shrine of Pasupatinatha at Deo Patan (late c14). Stone-built Hindu temples dating from the c17 and later are in northern Indian styles, but usually with a stupa-like finial crowning the SIKHARA. The royal palace on the Durbar Square, Kathmandu, mainly c17–18, with buildings surrounding some fifty courts, is the most notable example of Nepalese domestic architecture, with much fine woodwork. The many c19–20 Rana palaces in the new town are in European styles.

**Nering**, Johann Arnold (1659–95). Prussian architect who, despite his early death, laid the foundations for architectural developments in c18 Berlin. He was trained as a military architect, sent to Italy and made Oberingenieur in 1680, later (1691) Oberbaudirektor. He was much employed on urban planning and built the Leipziger Tor (1683), the covered arcade with shops on the Muhlendamm in Berlin and the Friedrichstadt suburb with 300 two-storey houses, all in military order (1688 onwards). He enlarged the Burgkirche at Königsberg, on the model of the Nieuwekerk in The Hague (pre-1687), gave the Oranienburg Palace its present appearance (1689–95), began the Charlottenburg Palace, Berlin (1695), the Arsenal, Berlin (1695, completed by SCHLÜTER and de BODT), and the Reformed Parish Church on an interesting quatrefoil plan. His style is severe and owed much to PALLADIO by way of the Dutch neo-Palladians.

Hempel 1965.

**Nervi**, Pier Luigi (1891–1979). Italian architect who took his degree in civil engineering in 1912, but had a long wait before he was allowed to establish himself as what he undoubtedly became, the most brilliant CONCRETE designer of the age. Nervi was as inventive and resourceful a technician as he was aesthetically sensitive an architect. He was moreover an entrepreneur and a university professor, a combination which would be impossible, because it is not permitted, in Britain.

The stadium in Florence was built in 1930–32; it seats 35,000, has a cantilever roof about 20 m. (70 ft) deep and an ingenious flying spiral staircase sweeping far out. In 1935, for a competition for airship hangars, he produced his idea of a vault of diagonally intersecting concrete beams with very massive flying-buttress-like angle supports. Such hangars were built at Orbetello from 1936 onwards (destroyed). A second type with trusses of precast concrete elements was carried out at Orbetello in 1940. 1948 is the date of Nervi's first great exhibition hall for Turin. The concrete elements this time are corrugated, an idea which went back to experiments of 1943–4. The second hall followed in 1950, again with a diagonal grid. The building of 1952 for the Italian spa of Chianciano is circular, and

has a grid vault. By this time Nervi's fame was so firmly established that he was called in for the structure of the Unesco building in Paris (1953–6). His also is the splendid structure of the Pirelli skyscraper in Milan (1955–8; *see also* PONTI) – two strongly tapering concrete pillars from which the floors are cantilevered. With Jean PROUVÉ he was a consultant engineer for the enormous new CNIT exhibition hall on the Rond-point de la Défense in Paris (1958): a triangle, each side (220 m. (710 ft) long, with three triangular sections of warped concrete roof, rising to a height of 45 m. (150 ft).

Nervi's last buildings were the Palazzetto dello Sport in Rome (1959), circular with V-shaped supports for the dome all round; the Palazzo dello Sport, also in Rome (1960), with a 100 m. (330 ft) span and seating 16,000; yet another exhibition hall for Turin (1961), a square with sides 160 m. (520 ft) in length, supported on sixteen enormous cross-shaped piers; and the vast audience hall for the Pope in the Vatican (1970–71). He published *Arte o scienze del costruire?* (Rome 1954), *Structures* (New York 1956) and *Aesthetics and Technology in Building* (Cambridge, Mass. 1965).

Collins 1959; A. Pica, *P.L.N.*, Rome 1969; Mainstone 1975; P. Desideri et al., *P.L.N. Pläne, Skizzen und Werkverzeichnis*, Zürich and Munich 1982.

**Nesfield**, William Eden (1835–88). English architect who began in the ARTS AND CRAFTS manner (e.g. his Regent's Park Lodge of 1864) and until 1869 was in partnership with Norman SHAW, with whom he is credited with the Queen Anne Revival. His Dutch C17 lodge at Kew Gardens (1866–7) probably inaugurated it, followed by his William and Mary–Louis XIII Kinmel Park, Clwyd (1867–74, damaged by fire 1975), and others. Some of his later buildings are in neo-Tudor and other styles, e.g. the remarkable Barclays Bank, Saffron Walden, of 1875.

A. Saint, *Richard Norman Shaw*, New Haven and London 1976; M. Girouard, *Sweetness and Light: the 'Queen Anne' Movement 1860–1900*, Oxford 1977.

**Netherlandish architecture**, *see* DUTCH ARCHITECTURE.

**Neumann**, Johann Balthasar (1687–1753), the greatest German Rococo architect, was master of elegant and ingenious spatial composition. He could be both wantonly sensuous and intellectually complex, frivolous and devout, ceremonious and playful. His churches and palaces epitomize the mid-C18 attitude to life and religion. But despite their air of spontaneity, few works of architecture have been more carefully thought out. His designs are as complex as the fugues of Bach; and for this reason he has been called an architect's architect.

The son of a clothier, he was born in Bohemia but worked mainly in Franconia, where he began in a cannon foundry and graduated to architecture by way of the Prince Bishop's artillery. He visited Vienna and Milan (1717–18) and soon after his return began the Bishop's new Residenz in Würzburg, consulting HILDEBRANDT and von Welsch in Vienna and de COTTE and BOFFRAND in Paris about his designs. The influence of Hildebrandt is very evident in the finished palace, which was executed under a succession of five bishops over some sixty years, though it was structurally complete by about 1744. Outstanding here are the Hofkirche or Bishop's Chapel (1732–41, Hildebrandt collaborating on the decoration) and the magnificent ceremonial staircase leading up to the Kaisersaal (designed 1735, ceiling decoration by Tiepolo 1752–3). This staircase is one of his most original and

ingenious conceptions, second only to his superb staircase at Bruchsal (1731–2, damaged in the Second World War but restored). He later designed the imposing staircase at Schloss Brühl near Cologne (1743–8). These ceremonial staircases formed the most important single element in each palace and are at the same time masterpieces of engineering ingenuity and exhilarating spatial play. At Schloss Werneck (1734–45) he again collaborated with Hildebrandt, but this time impressed his own stamp on all parts of the building. His secular work was by no means limited to palace architecture; he was engaged in town planning and laid out whole streets of town houses, e.g. the Theaterstrasse at Würzburg. The house he built for himself in the Kapuzinergasse (No. 7) at Würzburg reveals his ability to work in a minor key.

He was much employed as a church architect, designing the parish church at Wiesentheid (1727), the pilgrimage church at Gössweinstein (1730–39), the church of St Paulinus, Trier (begun 1734), the church of Häusenstamm near Offenbach (1739–40), the Holy Cross Chapel at Etwashausen (1741) and additions to St Peter, Bruchsal (1738) and the Dominican church at Würzburg (1741). In 1743 he began his great masterpiece, the pilgrimage church of Vierzehnheiligen (1742–53, completed 1772), where the foundations had already been built by a previous architect. His first task was to accommodate his own ideas to a somewhat inconvenient plan and this provided a spur to his genius. He worked out a remarkably complicated scheme based on the grouping of ovals, both in the vaulting and ground plan, which provides a breathtakingly exciting spatial effect, enhanced by the foaming and eddying Rococo decoration. Nowhere did the *mouvementé* quality of Rococo architecture find better expression; not only the statues but even the columns seem to be executing an elegant minuet. (The central altar, pulpit and much of the plasterwork were not completed until after Neumann's death.)

In the larger abbey church at Neresheim (begun 1747) he had a much freer hand and his plan is much simpler, though again based on ovals. By the use of very slender columns to support the large central dome he achieved an almost Gothic airiness. His last work of importance, the Marienkirche at Limbach (1747–52), is on a much smaller scale, but is unusual for him in being no less elaborately decorated on the exterior than inside.

Hitchcock 1968; C. F. Otto, *Space into Light: The Churches of B.N.*, Cambridge, Mass. 1979; T. Korth and J. Poeschke (eds.), *B.N.*, Munich 1987; E. Hubala, *B.N. – seine Kunst zu Bauen*, exh. cat., Wendlingen and Würzburg 1987–8.

**Neutra**, Richard Josef (1892–1970). He was Austrian by birth and studied in Vienna under Otto WAGNER. In 1912–14 he worked under LOOS and in 1921–3 he was with MENDELSOHN in Berlin. In 1923 he emigrated to Chicago but finally settled at Los Angeles in 1925, in partnership with SCHINDLER for a few years. With his remarkable Philip Lovell House, Los Angeles (1927–9), he became one of the chief propagators of the new European style in America. His work was predominantly domestic, and mostly of a wealthy and lavish kind. His forte was a brilliant sense for siting houses in landscape and linking buildings with nature: Desert House, Colorado (1946); Kaufmann Desert House, Palm Springs (1947); Tremaine House, Santa Barbara (1947–8); and his own house at Silverlake, Los Angeles (1933 and 1964). Neutra also designed some excellent schools – Corona School Bell, Los Angeles (1935); Emerson Junior High School, West-

wood, California (1938) – and, towards the end of his life, some religious and commercial buildings, notably the 'drive-in' church in Garden Grove, California (1959–61). His style remained essentially that of his youth; it was unchanged in its direction by the anti-rational tendencies of the last twenty years of his life. He published *Wie Baut Amerika?* (Stuttgart 1927) and *Survival Through Design* (New York 1954).

T. S. Hines, *R.N. and the Search for Modern Architecture*, New York (1982) 1994; A. Drexler, *The Architecture of R.N.*, New York 1982.

**New Brutalism**, *see* BRUTALISM.

**New Towns**. Those towns designed in the British Isles under the Act of 1946 – eight in the London region (Harlow, Crawley, Stevenage, etc.) and six in other parts of England, Scotland and Wales. More were added later. Although most of them have an existing town or village as a nucleus, they are entirely independent units, with populations of about 60,000 to 80,000. The development of these planned towns over the years has been of very great interest from sociological, architectural and planning points of view. *See also* GARDEN CITIES; RADBURN PLANNING; SATELLITE TOWNS; URBAN DESIGN.

**New York Five**. A group of five American architects: EISENMAN, GRAVES, GWATHMEY, John Hejduk (b. 1929), and MEIER, also known as the 'Whites'. They exhibited together in New York in 1969 and later published *Five Architects* (New York 1972). The group had dispersed by 1980.

Klotz 1988.

**Newel**, *see* STAIR.

**Niccolini**, Antonio (1772–1850), *see* ITALIAN ARCHITECTURE.

**Niche**. A vertical recess in a wall, pier, etc., usually arched and containing a statue, urn, or other decorative object.

**Nicola Pisano**, *see* PISANO, Nicola.

**Niemeyer**, Oscar (b.1907). Brazilian architect who studied in his home town Rio de Janeiro, then worked in the office of Lucio COSTA and received his diploma in 1934. In 1936–43 he belonged to the team of Brazilian architects working with LE CORBUSIER on the new building for the Ministry of Education at Rio. He built the Brazilian Pavilion for the New York World Fair of 1939 with Costa, but only came fully into his own with the casino, club and church of St Francis at Pampulha outside Belo Horizonte (1942–3). Here was a completely new approach to architecture, admittedly for non-utilitarian purposes: parabolic vaults, slanting walls, a porch canopy of a completely free double-curving form – a sculptural, frankly anti-rational, highly expressive style. The style suited BRAZIL, with its past of the extremest Baroque; it also became one of the elements in that general turn away from Rationalism which is principally familiar in Le Corbusier's buildings after the Second World War.

Niemeyer was made architectural adviser to Nova Cap, the organization instituted to create Brasilia, the new capital, and in 1957 became its chief architect. He designed the hotel in 1958 and the exquisite president's palace in the same year. The palace has a screen of freely and extremely originally shaped supports in front of its glass façade, and Niemeyer has varied this theme in other buildings at Brasilia as well (Law Courts). The climax of the architectural composition of the capital is the Square of the Three Powers, with the Houses of Parliament – one with a dome, the other with a saucer-shaped roof – and the sheer, quite unfanciful

skyscraper of the offices between. The slab blocks of the various ministries are also deliberately unfanciful. Niemeyer certainly varies his approach according to the spiritual function of buildings. Thus the cathedral of Brasilia (1959–70), circular, with the excelsior of a bundle of curved concrete ribs rising to the centre, is highly expressive; the block of flats for the Interbau Exhibition in Berlin (Hansa Quarter, 1957) is rational, without, however, lacking in resourcefulness; and Niemeyer's own house outside Rio (1953) is a ravishing interplay of nature and architecture. More recently he designed the Communist Party Building, Paris (1965–80), with PROUVÉ as engineer; the Mondadori Building, Milan (1968–76); the Bourse de Travail, Bobigny, Paris (1970–80), and the Maison de la Culture, Le Havre (1972–82). In the 1980s he worked again in Brazil, notably his Samba Stadium, Rio de Janeiro (1983–4); the Latin America Memorial and the Latin America Parliament Building, São Paolo (1989–92) and the Museum of Contemporary Art, Niteroi, near Rio de Janeiro (1991). In 1992 he designed the Maison Brésil-Portugal, Lisbon. He published *Minha Experiencia en Brasilia* (Rio de Janeiro 1961; Paris 1963).

S. Papadaki, *The Work of O.N.*, New York 1950–60; R. Spade, *O.N.*, London 1971; N. W. Sodre, *O.N.*, Rio de Janeiro 1978; C. Hornig, *O.N. Bauten und Projekte*, Munich 1981; A. Fils, *O.N.*, Düsseldorf 1982; D. K. Underwood, *O.N. and the Architecture of Brazil*, New York 1994.

**Nissen hut**. A prefabricated building of corrugated steel, in shape half-a-cylinder, designed by Peter N. Nissen (1871–1930). It was frequently used as a military shelter.

**Nobile**, Pietro (1773–1854). Italian neo-classicist of a rather archaeologizing tendency, working in Vienna

(Theseustempel, a miniature of the Haiphesteion, Athens, built to house a statue by Canova, 1820–23; The Burgtor, 1844) and in Trieste (S. Antonio, 1826–49).

Hitchcock 1977.

**Nodding ogee arch**, *see* ARCH.

**Nogging**, *see* BRICKWORK; TIMBER-FRAMING.

**Noguchi**, Isamu (1904–88). Sculptor and designer of environments born in California. His father was a Japanese poet, his mother American. Educated in Japan and the USA, apprenticed to Gutzon Borgium (the sculptor of gigantic portraits from living rock), he went to Paris in 1927 and worked in Brancusi's studio, returning briefly to Japan in 1930 when he saw for the first time the monastery gardens at Kyoto. All these experiences conditioned his artistic development. He began to make proposals for environmental works in 1933, notably that for a *Monument to the Plough* which would have been the first modern earthwork. His first large-scale works to be realized were two concrete bridges for TANGE's Peace Park, Hiroshima (1951–2). In 1956 he designed the gardens for SOM's Connecticut General Life Insurance headquarters, Bloomfield, Connecticut, and for BREUER's Unesco Building in Paris, the latter with mounds, biomorphic pools, grassy and paved areas, and many scattered stones and boulders, more obviously Japanese in inspiration than the former. The essential principles of Japanese dry-stone gardens (without any vegetation) were fully assimilated and expressed in his Marble Garden for the Beinecke Rare Book Library, Yale University, New Haven, Connecticut, all white with a pyramid, a cube poised on one point and a large carved ring, on flat paving (1960–64); in the Kodomo No Kuni (Children's Land), Tokyo (1964), and in the Chase Manhattan Bank Plaza, New York, with water-eroded boulders apparently emerging from geometric ripples carved on a granite pavement (1961–4) – intended to be seen from ground level or above, not to be entered. His *California Scenario* at Costa Mesa, California (1980–82), is more complex in design and in its levels of elusive meaning: a square enclosed by mirror-glass office blocks on two sides and blank stucco walls on the others, in which are placed five mounds, one of gravel planted with cactus, a meandering stream cut into the pavement, a large conical fountain, rough boulders – some isolated, others fitted together to form a monumental sculpture – and redwood trees which will alter the appearance of the space as they grow. His aim to create 'beautiful and disturbing gardens to awaken us to a new awareness of our solitude' is here realized. He designed his own sculpture gardens on the Japanese island of Shikoku (1983–5) and on Long Island, New York (opened 1985). Just before he died he planned the layout of the 160-hectare (400-acre) Moere-Ken Park, Sapporo, Japan.

M. Friedman (ed.), *N.'s Imaginary Landscapes*, exh. cat., Minneapolis 1978; S. Hunter, *I.N.*, New York 1979; D. Ashton, *N. East and West*, New York 1992; Walker and Simo 1994; Weilacher 1996.

**Noiers**, Geoffrey de, *see* GEOFFREY DE NOIERS.

**Nook-shaft**. A shaft set in the angle of a PIER, a RESPOND, a wall, or the JAMB of a window or doorway.

**Norman architecture**. In England the style corresponding to ROMANESQUE on the continent, e.g. Durham Cathedral (1093–1133); in Italy that of the Normans in Sicily, e.g. Monreale Cathedral (1174–82). French Romanesque buildings in cii–12 Normandy are also sometimes called Norman, e.g. St Étienne, Caen (c. 1060–81).

**Northlight** or **sawtooth roof**. A factory roof with rows of metal lattice girders running across the building, carrying sections of sloping roofing on triangular half-trusses from the top of one girder to the bottom of the next. The vertical sides of the girders have glazing or translucent cladding. The roofing slopes parallel to the length of the building, giving uniform, gentle natural light. In the southern hemisphere they are built facing south. *See* Fig. 85.

**Norwegian architecture**. (For medieval and earlier buildings in Norway *see* SCANDINAVIAN ARCHITECTURE.) Though Oslo was laid out regularly with a grid of streets and oblong blocks in 1824 – as was, even more regularly, Kristiansand in 1641 – Norway lagged behind Denmark and Sweden architecturally. Most Norwegian domestic architecture was still of wood, even in the c18. (The largest wooden building is Stiftsgården in Trondheim of 1774–8, nineteen windows wide with a pediment and some lacy Rococo ornament, though Danisgård at Bergen, also of the 1770s, is perhaps finer.) After 1814 Norway broke free of Denmark while remaining linked by a common monarch to Sweden, and the need for large official and public buildings led to the development in Oslo of some impressive Greek Revival monumental architecture. Apart from the Royal Palace by Hans Ditler Frants Lin-

stow (1787–1851), the most notable buildings are by Christian Henrik Grosch (1801–65), who was appointed the city architect in 1828. By him are the Stock Exchange (1828), Bank of Norway (1830) and his Schinkelesque masterpiece, the University (1839–52). The castellated and turreted Oskarshall outside Oslo of 1848 (by Johann Henrik Nevelong, 1817–71) is a notable example of the c19 Gothic Revival. Thereafter Norway followed architectural developments elsewhere in Scandinavia, though seldom with great distinction, e.g. the brick-built City Hall in Oslo of 1917–50, heavy and very unromantic in comparison with ØSTBERG's City Hall in Stockholm. However, the work of Arne Korsmo (1900–1968) should be mentioned – Dammann House (1930–32) and Hansen House (1936) in Oslo; also that of Sverre Fehn (b.1924), whose Museum, Fjaerland (1991), is remarkable, and of Jan Digerad (b.1938) and Jon Lundberg (b.1933), whose Akersverein 12–14 in Oslo is colourful.

**Nosing**, *see* STAIR.

**Notman**, John (1810–65), *see* UNITED STATES ARCHITECTURE.

**Nouvel**, Jean (b.1945). French architect, trained at the École des Beaux Arts, who made his name in 1987 with his spectacular Institut du Monde Arabe, Paris (1981–7). This was followed by the low-cost Némausus Housing, Nîmes (1985–7), the CLM/BBDO Offices, Issy-les-Moulineaux (1988–92); the refurbished

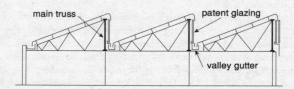

main truss — patent glazing — valley gutter

Fig. 85 Northlight roof

interior for the Opéra de Lyon (1987–93); the Vinci Palais de Congrès, Tours (1989–93), the Foundation Cartier, Paris (1991–4), and the Galeries Lafayette, Berlin (1992–5).

P. Goulet, *J.N.*, Paris (1987) 1993; P. Goulet and F. Page, *J.N.*, Paris 1994; O. Boissière, *J.N.*, Paris 1996.

**Nowicki**, Matthew (1910–51), *see* HYPERBOLIC PARABOLOID ROOF.

**Nüll**, Eduard van der (1812–68), *see* AUSTRIAN ARCHITECTURE.

**Nuraghe**. A Sardinian conical tower-like fortress used from *c.*1800 BC until Ancient Roman times. They range from single towers to more complex structures with curtain walling, all of CYCLOPEAN construction. Early examples have a single chamber, later examples have up to three floors, e.g. that at Barumini.

**Nymphaeum**. In Ancient Greece and Rome, a shrine, usually a GROTTO, dedicated to the Nymphs, female deities of nature, especially of water. Remains of Roman examples include those of CI in the ruins of Domitian's palace in Rome and at Albano near Rome. None of these, however, was known in the Renaissance when descriptions in Latin literature inspired the design of ornamental 'Nymphaea' for gardens, usually in the form of an exedra incorporating a grotto, pool, fountain and statues, e.g. Villa Giulia, Rome, by VIGNOLA (1551–5); Villa Barbaro, Maser, by PALLADIO (1560s).

A. J. Alvarez, *The Renaissance N. Its Origin and Development in Rome and Vicinity*, New York 1981.

**Nyrop**, Martin (1849–1921), *see* DANISH ARCHITECTURE.

# O

**Obbergen** or **Opbergen**, Antonius van (1543–1611), *see* DANISH ARCHITECTURE; POLISH ARCHITECTURE.

**Obelisk**. A tall tapering shaft of stone, usually granite, monolithic, of square or rectangular section, ending pyramidally and originally with a gilded apex, and usually bearing carved inscriptions in hieroglyphics. Prominent in Ancient Egypt as solar symbols, they usually stood in pairs at the entrance to tombs or temples or simply as a cult object in shrines to the sun. Only four survive on their original sites in Egypt, notably at Karnak. Several were brought to Europe under the Roman Empire (often re-erected later, as in Piazza di S. Pietro, Rome) and again in the C19 (e.g. Cleopatra's Needle, London). The form of the obelisk was taken up by architects from the Renaissance onwards, either monumentally or as a decorative termination.

L. Habachi, *Alles über O.*, Mainz 1982.

**Oberlander**, Cornelia Hahn (b.1927). Landscape architect born in Germany, who emigrated to the USA in 1939 and worked with KILEY in Philadelphia before settling in Canada in 1953. In Vancouver she laid out the grounds of ERICKSON's Museum of Anthropology (1979) and the Robson Square development (1979), incorporating pools, streams and waterfalls with rock formations and luxuriant vegetation, over 50,000 plants in all. Her later works included the grounds of the Canadian Chancery, Washington, DC (1990), and the National Gallery, Ottawa (1992).

**Obrist**, Hermann (1863–1927), *see* ART NOUVEAU.

**Octagon**. An eight equal-sided figure frequently used as a ground-plan from Roman (e.g. Nero's Golden House, atrium), Carolingian (e.g. Palatine Chapel, Aachen) and Medieval (Karlskirche, Prague; Chapterhouse, York Minster) to Renaissance and later buildings (e.g. the Octagon, Twickenham, by James GIBBS).

**Octastyle**. Of a portico with eight frontal columns.

**Oculus**. A circular opening in a wall or at the apex of a dome, e.g. Pantheon, Rome.

**ODBC** (Odile Deck, b.1953, and Benoit Cornette, b.1953), *see* FRENCH ARCHITECTURE.

**Odeon, odeion** (Gr.) or **odeum** (Lat.). In Ancient Greek and Roman architecture a small roofed theatre, for concerts and lectures.

**Odo of Metz**, *see* CAROLINGIAN ARCHITECTURE.

**O'Donnel**, James (1774–1830), *see* CANADIAN ARCHITECTURE.

**Œil-de-bœuf window**. A small round or, more usually, oval window as in the Salon de l'Œil de Bœuf at Versailles. There are three ranges of them in the dome of St Peter's, Rome.

**Œillet**. In medieval architecture, a small opening in fortifications through which missiles could be discharged.

**Off-set**. The part of a wall exposed

horizontally when the portion above it is reduced in thickness; often sloping, with a projecting drip mould on the lower edge to stop water running down the walls, e.g. in Gothic buttresses. Also called the *water-table*. *See* WEATHERING.

**Ogee**. A double-curved line made up of a convex and concave part (S or inverted S).

**Ogee arch**, *see* ARCH.

**Ogee moulding**, *see* CYMA RECTA; CYMA REVERSA.

**Ogive**. The French name for a pointed arch; hence *ogival*, a term applied to French Gothic architecture, but no longer used.

**O'Gorman**, Juan (1905–82). Mexican architect and painter who began in the International Style, e.g. houses at San Ángel, Mexico City (1929–30), but later turned to Mexican vernacular architecture for inspiration. His Central Library, National University of Mexico, Mexico City (1952–3), is his best-known building. The main block is covered with bold and colourful mosaic decoration. His own house in San Ángel, Mexico City (1950–56), also makes use of Mexican vernacular architecture.

C. B. Smith, *Builders in the Sun. Five Mexican Architects*, New York 1967.

**Oglethorpe**, James Edward (1696–1785). English army officer who founded the colony of Georgia (now USA) in 1732 and laid out the new town of Savannah on a grid-iron plan subdivided into six 'wards', each with forty sites for houses, surrounding a 1-hectare (2-acre) square market place with sites for churches, schools, etc. as well. Each family was given a triangular 2-hectare (5-acre) garden plot on the town's edge and could also have some 20 hectares (50 acres) of farmland beyond a belt of common land. The plan allowed for an expansion of twenty-five wards, the last of which was completed in 1854. Few if any such utopian urban designs have ever been realized and maintained for so long.

**Olbrich**, Joseph Maria (1867–1908). Austrian architect; studied at the Vienna Academy, gained the Rome prize in 1893, returned to work under Otto WAGNER, and in 1897–8 designed the SEZESSION Building in Vienna, the premises of a newly founded society of the young progressive artists of Austria and the work which immediately established Olbrich's reputation. The little building, with its strongly cubic walls and its delightful hemispherical openwork metal dome, is both firm in its basic shapes and fanciful in its details. It is this unusual combination of qualities which attracted Ernst Ludwig Grand Duke of Hessen to Olbrich. So in 1899 Olbrich was called to Darmstadt and there, on the Mathildenhöhe, built the studio house (Ernst Ludwig Haus) and some private houses, including one for himself. The group of houses, some of them by other members of the group of artists assembled at Darmstadt (e.g. BEHRENS), was first built and furnished and then, in 1901, presented as an exhibition, the first of the kind ever held. Later Olbrich added another exhibition building and a tower, the Hochzeitsturm (1907). His last major building was the Tietz department store (now Kaufhof) at Düsseldorf (1906–9), the closely set uprights of whose façade, deriving from Messel's Wertheim store in Berlin, were very influential.

Olbrich's historical role is among those who succeeded in overcoming the vegetable weakness of ART NOUVEAU by providing it with a firmer system of rectangular co-ordinates. The other leading architects working in this direction were HOFFMANN and MACKINTOSH. Both Mackintosh and Olbrich succeeded in preserving the fancifulness of Art Nouveau sinuosity within this new, more exacting framework, whereas Hoffmann, and of course Behrens to a still greater extent, moved right away from Art Nouveau.

l. Latham, O., London 1980; P. Haiko and B. Krimmel, *J.M.O. Architektur*, Berlin 1989.

**Oliveira**, Mateus Vicente de, *see* VICENTE DE OLIVEIRA, Mateus.

**Olmec architecture**, *see* MESOAMERICAN ARCHITECTURE.

**Olin**, Laurie (b.1939). American landscape architect, from 1976 in partnership with Bob Hanna, practising as Hanna/Olin, Philadelphia. His work is always notably site-specific in a cultural as well as biological sense (e.g. Westlake Park, Seattle, 1987–90, based on Native American patterns; World of Primates, Philadelphia Zoo, 1983–90), even when indebted overtly to C16 and C17 Italian and French garden design, e.g. his Bryant Park behind New York Public Library (1987–92). In collaboration with SOM he laid out gardens at Canary Wharf (1985–91), Bishopsgate (1986–91) and Ludgate Hill (1988–92), all in London; with SOM and GHERY the Vila Olimpica, Barcelona (1991–2), and with LEGORRETA Pershing Square, Los Angeles (1992–4). He designed sculpture gardens for the Los Angeles County Museum and National Gallery, Washington, DC, as well as the overall site design for MEIER's Getty Center, Malibu, California.

Cerver 1995.

**Olmsted**, Frederick Law (1822–1903). The greatest American landscape architect, also a social reformer and ecologist (long before the word was coined). He headed the profession after DOWNING's death and was largely responsible for establishing its status in the USA. Trained as an engineer, he worked first as a surveyor and tried farming before 1850 when he toured Europe, where he was impressed by English LANDSCAPE GARDENS and especially by PAXTON's Birkenhead Park, near Liverpool, intended for a working-class public. In 1858 he and Calvert VAUX won the competition for New York's Central Park, a 340-hectare (840-acre) site for which they planned woodlands, lakes, hills, large open spaces, a flower garden and, for pedestrians, an innovatory separation of footpaths from carriageways by means of bridges and tunnels (*see* Fig. 73). The work was soon begun but in 1863 Olmsted withdrew and went to California, where he planned the Berkeley University CAMPUS, laid out Mountain View Cemetery, Oakland, and initiated Wilderness Preservation and the National Parks by helping to ensure the protection of the Yosemite Valley and the Mariposa Grove of redwood trees. Back in New York in 1865 and again working with Vaux, he designed some fifty public parks which he called a city's lungs, notably Prospect Park, Brooklyn (1865–88). They also planned the Riverside housing estate, Illinois (1869), with sinuous curves 'to imply leisure, contemplativeness, and happy tranquillity'. After their partnership broke up in the 1870s Olmsted's office provided designs for several hundred landscape schemes, including those for the US Capitol grounds in Washington, DC (1874–91), the Niagara Falls reserve (1880s), Stanford University campus, Palo Alto, California (1886–91), and numerous private commissions, the most extensive being that for the 40,000-hectare (100,000-acre) Biltmore estate, Asheville, North Carolina, with formal gardens, parkland and much reforestation. In 1880–87 he anticipated the PARKWAY with his 'Emerald Necklace' of interconnected parks at Boston,

Massachusetts. American landscape architecture has been strongly influenced to the present day by his practice and his writings, e.g. *Public Parks and the Enlargement of Towns* (1870), in which he recommended the structuring of new towns around parks. His assistants, who continued his design office after his death, included his nephew John Charles Olmsted (1852–1920) and his son Frederick Law Olmsted Jnr (1870–1957), who was mainly responsible for giving Washington, DC, the appearance it still retains. After the latter retired in 1954 the firm was renamed the Olmsted Office Inc. and is still active.

L. W. Roper, *F.L.O.*, Baltimore 1973; C. C. McLaughlin (ed.), *The Papers of F.L.O.*, Baltimore 1983 onwards; I. D. Fisher, *F.L.O. and the City Planning Movement in the U.S.*, Ann Arbor 1986; Walker and Simo 1994; G. E. Beveridge, *F.L.O. Designing the American Landscape*, New York 1995; P. Lambert (ed.), *Viewing O.*, Cambridge, Mass. 1997.

**OMA (Office for Metropolitan Architecture)**, see KOOLHAAS, Rem (b.1944).

**Onion dome**. A pointed bulbous dome common in Russia and Eastern Europe, especially on churches and church towers. Structurally it is not a true dome, i.e. it is not vaulted.

**Opbergen** or **Obbergen**, Antonius van (1543–1611), *see* DANISH ARCHITECTURE; POLISH ARCHITECTURE.

**Open plan**. A floor plan without subdivisions and interior walls, either left free or with spaces defined by screens, furniture, columns, changes of level or ceiling heights. It was taken up by F. L. WRIGHT in the 1890s following the traditional Japanese house and SHINGLE STYLE houses in the USA. Later it was developed by LE CORBUSIER with *le plan libre* and by

other Modernist architects, notably by MIES VAN DER ROHE. Though first found in domestic architecture, it is later found mainly in office buildings, e.g. by SOM in the USA, after the introduction of air-conditioning and central-heating. There could be many work stations on each floor, usually in rows.

**Oppenordt**, Gilles-Marie (1672–1742), *see* FRENCH ARCHITECTURE; RÉGENCE ARCHITECTURE.

**Opisthodomos**. The enclosed section at the rear of a Greek temple, sometimes used as a treasury.

**Optical refinements**. Subtle modifications to profiles or surfaces to correct the illusion of sagging or disproportion in a building. *See* ENTASIS.

**Opus Alexandrinum**. Ornamental paving combining mosaic and OPUS SECTILE in guilloche design.

**Opus incertum**. Roman walling of concrete faced with irregularly shaped stones.

**Opus listatum**. Walling with alternating courses of brick and small blocks of stone.

**Opus quadratum**. Roman walling of squared stones.

**Opus reticulatum**. Roman walling of concrete faced with squared stones arranged diagonally like the meshes of a net.

**Opus sectile**. Ornamental paving or wall covering made from marble slabs cut in various, generally geometric, shapes.

**Orangery**. A garden building for growing oranges, lemons, etc., and especially for sheltering them during the winter months, with large windows on the south side, like a glazed LOGGIA. The most grandiose is that by HARDOUIN MANSART at Versailles (1685–6), though that at Kensington Palace, London

(1704–5), by HAWKSMOOR and WREN (revised by VANBRUGH), is notable. *See also* CONSERVATORY.

M. Woods and A. S. Warren, *A History of Greenhouses, O. and Conservatories*, London 1988.

**Oratory.** A small private chapel, either in a church or in a house; or a church of the Oratorian order of S. Filippo Neri, e.g. the Brompton Oratory, London.

**Orbay**, François d' (1631–97). French architect, chief assistant to LE VAU, several of whose late works he carried out, notably the Escalier des Ambassadeurs, Versailles, and the Collège des Quatre Nations (now the Institut de France), Paris. Of his independent works the Porte de Peyrou, Montpellier (*c.*1689), is notable.

A. Laprade, *F. d'O. architecte de Louis XIV*, Paris 1960; Blunt 1982.

**Orcagna** (Andrea di Cione) (active 1343–68). Italian painter – the most important in Florence after Giotto's death – but also a sculptor and architect. He was admitted to the Guild of Painters in 1343/4 and to the Guild of Stonemasons in 1352. By 1356 he was *capomaestro* at Orsanmichele, Florence, and by 1358 at Orvieto Cathedral, where he is frequently mentioned until 1362, though mainly in connection with the restoration of mosaics on the façade. In 1350 he became adviser on the construction of Florence Cathedral and until 1366 was active as a leading member of various commissions, including that which evolved the definitive design.

White 1987.

**Orchaestra** or **orchestra**. The circular 'dancing floor' of an Ancient Greek theatre, whence the corresponding semicircular space in front of the stage or PROSCENIUM of an Ancient Roman theatre.

**Orchard**, William (d.1504). English master mason, probably designer of Bishop Waynflete's Magdalen College at Oxford (1468 onwards). The initials W.O. in the ingenious vault to the Divinity School, completed in the 1480s, allow it to be attributed to him, and if the attribution is correct, the similarity in design of the vaults of the Divinity School and the chancel of Oxford Cathedral make him a likely candidate for this even more ingenious vault. Both are characterized by the pendants which look like springers built on non-existing piers between a nave and aisles. It is a technically daring, highly original, and visually most puzzling solution.

Harvey 1984.

**Order.** 1. In classical architecture, a column with base (usually), shaft, capital and entablature, decorated and proportioned according to one of the accepted modes – Doric, Tuscan, Ionic, Corinthian or Composite. The simplest is the Tuscan, supposedly derived from the Etruscan-type temple, but the Doric is probably earlier in origin and is subdivided into Greek Doric and Roman Doric, the former having no base, as on the Parthenon and the temples at Paestum. The Ionic order originated in Asia Minor in the mid C6 BC. The Ionic capital probably developed out of the earlier Aeolic capital of uncertain origin. (The Aeolic capital has an oblong top supported by two large volutes with a PALMETTE filling the space between.) The Corinthian order was an Athenian invention of C5 BC, but was later developed by the Romans, who provided the prototype for the Renaissance form. The Composite order is a late Roman combination of elements from the Ionic and Corinthian orders. The Doric, Tuscan, Ionic and Corinthian orders were described by VITRUVIUS, and in 1537 SERLIO pub-

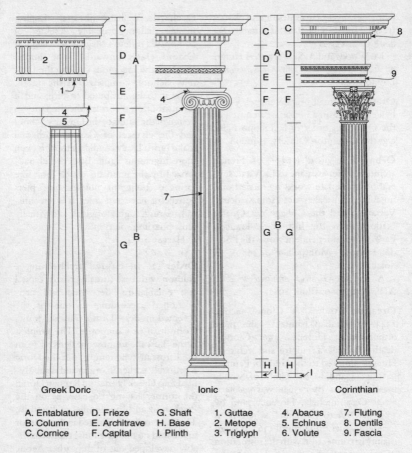

Greek Doric          Ionic          Corinthian

| A. Entablature | D. Frieze | G. Shaft | 1. Guttae | 4. Abacus | 7. Fluting |
| B. Column | E. Architrave | H. Base | 2. Metope | 5. Echinus | 8. Dentils |
| C. Cornice | F. Capital | I. Plinth | 3. Triglyph | 6. Volute | 9. Fascia |

Fig. 86  Order (see also opposite)

lished a book on the orders (coining the term Composite for what had previously been called Italic) which gave to each a range of expressive meanings as well as establishing the minutiae of proportions and embellishments for Renaissance and later architects. *See* Fig. 86; COLOSSAL ORDER. 2. Of a doorway or window, a series of concentric steps receding towards the opening.

J. Summerson, *The Classical Language*

*of Architecture*, London (1963) 1980; R. Chitham, *The Classical O. of Architecture*, London 1985; Onians 1988; J. Rykwert, *The Dancing Columns. On the O. of Architecture*, Cambridge 1996; J. Guillaume (ed.), *L'Emploi des O. à la Renaissance*, Paris 1997.

**Ordinates**. Parallel chords of conic section (in relation to bisecting diagonals) describing an ellipse: used in Renaissance

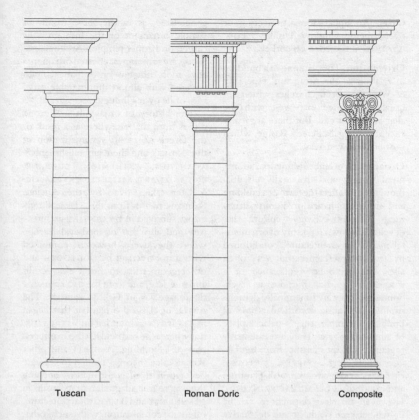

Tuscan

Roman Doric

Composite

architecture when adjusting cross-vaults of equal height but unequal span.

**Ordonnance**. The disposition of the parts of a building. In French the term was used by C17–18 theorists in allusion to the choice of an appropriate order for a building and to its application.

**Organic architecture**. 1. A term loosely applied to buildings or parts of buildings organized on a biological analogy or loosely recalling natural i.e. biomorphic forms. 2. A term used by F. L. WRIGHT, H. HÄRING and others for an architecture that is both visually and environmentally compatible, closely integrated with the site, and which reflects the architect's concern with the processes of nature and the forms they produce. Wright's first essay on the subject was of 1910. He may have influenced AALTO's later 'organic' development. Wright's *Organic Architecture: the Architecture of Democracy* was published in 1939. In Germany Häring's *Wege zur Form* (1925) was influential, notably on SCHAROUN, and led subsequently to the free-planning and spatial fluidity of G. BEHNISCH and Frei OTTO. In the USA a maverick type of organic architecture arose with GOFF and PRINCE and in Hungary a regional type with MAKOVECZ.

B. Zevi, *Towards an O.A.*, London 1951.

413

**Oriel**. An upper-storey projecting or over-hanging window. Unlike a BOW WINDOW it is carried on corbels.

**Orientation**. The planning of a building in relation to the rising sun, especially of West European churches which are usually orientated east–west with the altar at the east end. But there are many exceptions, e.g. St Peter's, Rome, which is orientated west–east.

**Ornament**. An embellishment or adornment that is not structurally essential though it may affect the form of a building and either emphasize or disguise structural elements. Every culture has developed its own repertory of ornamental motifs for architecture, conditioned by aesthetic preferences but very often also with symbolic significance or a magic, apotropaic, purpose as well. Sometimes they are functionally demonstrative, indicating a particular type of building – temple, ruler's palace, place of amusement, etc. They are essentially repetitive and thus distinct from figurative reliefs (e.g. FRIEZES, METOPES, ORTHOSTATS), narrative wall-paintings and inscriptions (*see* MURAL PAINTING). However, no clear distinctions can be drawn between symbolic and decorative ornament, as symbols often lose their original meaning in later usage.

The earliest known architectural ornaments are the geometrical patterns in CONE MOSAIC on 4th millennium BC temples in Mesopotamia. Triangles, lozenges, rectangles, chevrons and circles are found world-wide but later such abstract patterns might merge into or out of naturalistic and stylized foliage motifs, e.g. palm and papyrus columns in 3rd millennium BC Egypt. Some plant forms were given symbolic significance, e.g. the leaf of the bo tree and lotus flower on Buddhist buildings, chrysanthemum flowers in Japan. Foliage is, however, more often

generalized, as in the loose fronds of Islamic ornament or the lush growths carved on Khmer temples. Architectural motifs are sometimes repeated ornamentally, most notably on Indian temples covered with almost innumerable carvings of its own silhouette.

The history of ornament in Europe differs from that elsewhere as a result of the Greek C6–5 BC systematization of the ORDERS and their embellishments – ACANTHUS, ANTHEMION, BUCRANE, EGG AND DART, PALMETTE, PATERA, etc. – later taken over by the Ancient Romans. Motifs from this 'classical' repertory survived in BYZANTINE architecture and also that of medieval Europe where they were, however, combined with if not overlaid by DOGTOOTH and other geometrical motifs, Celtic scrolls and interlace, and from the C12 naturalistic foliage, as in Gothic capitals. The revival of classical ornament that began in C15 Italy was founded on VITRUVIUS, but whereas he had held it to be an integral part of a building, ALBERTI and other Renaissance theorists tended to separate decoration from construction, opening the way to free adaptation of its motifs in MANNERIST and BAROQUE architecture, often in combination with such other devices as FESTOONS, STRAPWORK, SWAGS, etc. In C18 Europe, despite fashions for free-flowing ROCOCO scrolls and playful CHINOISERIE, the classical repertory remained the basis of architectural ornament and from the 1750s was rendered with increasing respect for antique prototypes, illustrated in numerous publications by e.g. R. ADAM, PIRANESI, J. STUART. On GOTHIC REVIVAL buildings medieval ornament was similarly copied with increasing respect in the C19 for its various styles, from ROMANESQUE to FLAMBOYANT and their local variants.

Virtually all known styles of ornament

were imitated in the C19, Chinese, Islamic and Indian as well as European (*see* HIS-TORICISM). Specimens were illustrated in books meant for architects and designers, from *Ornamenten aller klassischen Kunstepochen* (Berlin 1831–43) by Johann Karl Wilhelm Zahn to *Analysis of Ornament* (London 1855) by Ralph Nicholson Wornum. In 1856 Owen Jones (1809–74) published the first of several editions of his world-wide *The Grammar of Ornament*, with some 3,000 motifs on 111 plates in chromo-lithography. Other encyclopedic manuals followed, e.g. Franz S. Meyer, *Handbuch der Ornamentik* (Leipzig 1888); R. Glazier, *A Manual of Historic Ornament* (London 1899); Alexander Speltz, *Der Ornamentstil* (Leipzig 1904). However, the practice of copying historic and exotic ornament eventually fell into disfavour. RUSKIN regarded ornament as a principal part of architecture but only in so far as it expressed the spiritual qualities of human labour that he felt in Gothic buildings. The main purpose of Owen Jones's *Grammar* was not to provide models for imitation but to explore the basic principles of ornamental design – in Asia and among 'savage tribes' as well as Europe – in the hope that the creation of a new style of ornament would lead to a new architecture. In a series of publications, notably *Der Stil in des technischen und tektonischen Künsten* (Frankfurt 1861–3), SEMPER deplored the current state of ornamental design and criticized historicists for their failure to develop a C19 ornamental style that would nevertheless be conditioned by traditional forms. From a similar point of view, James Fergusson (1808–86), author of the first *History of Architecture* (1862–76) to cover Asia as well as Europe, described construction as the prose and ornament as the poetry of architecture. Yet the creation of an authentically new style of ornament, ART NOUVEAU, was to be

followed by the most radical of all anti-ornament reactions. SULLIVAN, despite his own individual style of ornament, recommended in 1892 that architects refrain from using any ornament at all for some years, and with the spread of FUNCTIONALISM the total abolition of ornament in architecture was promoted, notably by LOOS. Later architects were to be less intransigent, e.g. PERRET, who held that 'one must never allow into a building any element destined solely for ornament, but rather turn to ornament all the parts necessary for the support'. Nevertheless, ornament was conspicuously absent from the INTERNATIONAL STYLE though it was to return no less conspicuously with POST-MODERNISM.

P. Meyer, *Das O. in der Kunstgeschichte*, Zürich 1944; E. H. Gombrich, *The Sense of Order*, Oxford 1979; B. Brolin, *Flight of Fancy: The Banishment and Return of O.*, New York 1985; P. Lewis and G. Darley, *Dictionary of O.*, London 1986; S. Durant, *O. A Survey of Decoration Since 1830*, London 1986; F. L. Kroll, *Das O. in der Kunsttheorie des 19 Jahrhunderts*, Hildesheim/Zürich 1987.

**Orsini**, Pier Francesco 'Vicino', Duke of Bomarzo (*c.*1513–84). Italian landowner who created, in 1552–81, a unique work of Mannerist 'narrative' landscape architecture below his castle at Bomarzo near Viterbo, Italy. He laid out this *sacro bosco* or sacred wood, as he called it, on an uneven site with a classical temple, a strange leaning house, an exedra, a grotto, fountains and, in a dense plantation of trees, colossal statues of humans, animals and monsters, with inscriptions from Dante, Petrarch and Ariosto, according to a programme with several levels of secular and religious meaning. Although famous, it was abandoned in the C17 when parts were destroyed, but was rediscovered in the late 1940s, by Salvador

Dalí among others, and much publicized.

M. J. Darnall and M. S. Weil in *Journal of Garden History*, vol. 4, no. 1, London 1984; Lazzaro 1990.

**Orthostat**. A slab of stone set upright at the base of a wall or building to form the lower section of it, sometimes carved in relief, e.g. in ancient Hittite architecture in Turkey.

**Ossuary**, *see* CHARNEL-HOUSE.

**Østberg**, Ragnar (1866–1945). Swedish architect whose international fame derives entirely from his Stockholm City Hall (begun 1909, completed 1923), a building transitional – like BERLAGE's and KLINT's work – between C19 HISTORICISM and the C20. The City Hall makes extremely skilful use of elements of the Swedish past, Romanesque as well as Renaissance. Its exquisite position by the water suggested to Østberg certain borrowings from the Doge's Palace as well. But these motifs are converted and combined in a highly original way, and the decorative details, rather mannered and attenuated, are typical of the ARTS AND CRAFTS of Germany, Austria, and central Europe in general about 1920. The City Hall was very influential in England in the twenties. Østberg had studied in Stockholm (1884–91) and travelled all over Europe as well as in America (1893–9). He also built the Patent Office (1921) and the Sea History Museum (1934–5), Stockholm, and was professor at the Stockholm Konsthögskola in 1922–32.

E. Cornell, *R.O. Svensk arkitekt*, Stockholm (1965) 1972.

**Otaka**, Masato (b.1923), *see* JAPANESE ARCHITECTURE.

**Otani**, Sachio (b.1924), *see* JAPANESE ARCHITECTURE.

**Otto**, Frei (b.1925). German architect-engineer, pioneer of TENSILE STRUCTURES. Otto's thesis, presented in 1954, was about them. He built one a year later, for an exhibition at Kassel. Further exhibitions followed: Cologne 1957, Berlin (Interbau) 1957, Lausanne 1961, Hamburg 1963, Montreal 1967. The last named – German Pavilion, Expo '67 – made him world famous. The roofs are of steel-web or polyester-web freely suspended on cable nets stretched between heavier cables attached to masts and ground anchorages. He achieves much freer tent-like forms than did earlier pioneers, e.g. Nowicki and Severund's Raleigh Arena, N. Carolina (1952), Saarinen's Yale Hockey Rink (1953). He also designed the Conference Centre, Mecca, Saudi Arabia (1971–4), with Ove ARUP, and imposing tensile structures for the Olympic Games at Munich in 1972, with Günter BEHNISCH. More recent buildings include the hotel and conference hall, Mecca (1974), and Government Offices, Riyadh, Saudi Arabia (1978–82), and the Ökohaus, Berlin (1990). He has published *Tensile Structures* (1967) and *Schriften und Reden 1951–1983* (Wiesbaden 1984).

L. Glaeser, *The Work of F.O.*, exh. cat., New York 1972; P. Drew, *F.O. Form and Construction*, London 1983; L. Sachs, *Architekten heute, Porträt F.O.*, Berlin 1984; Klotz 1986.

**Ottoman architecture**, *see* TURKISH ARCHITECTURE.

**Ottonian architecture**. The style current in Germany *c.*950–1050 under Otto the Great (reigned 936–73). The most notable surviving Ottonian buildings are Gernrode abbey church and Magdeburg Cathedral, both begun in 959, and the west choir of St Michael, Hildesheim (1010–33). *See also* CAROLINGIAN ARCHITECTURE; ROMANESQUE ARCHITECTURE.

**Oubliette**. In medieval architecture, a secret prison cell reached only through a trapdoor above, and into which a prisoner could be dropped and, presumably, forgotten.

**Oud**, Jacobus Johannes Pieter (1890–1963). Dutch architect who worked for a short time under Theodor Fischer in Germany in 1911. In 1915 he met Theo VAN DOESBURG and with him and RIETVELD he became a pillar of the group DE STIJL. Architecturally this group stood for an abstract cubism in opposition to the fanciful School of Amsterdam with its Expressionist compositions (de Klerk, Piet Kramer). There exist designs by Oud in a severely cubic manner which date from as early as 1917 and 1919. In 1918 he was made Housing Architect to the City of Rotterdam, a position he retained until 1927. (His Café de Unie, Rotterdam, of 1924/5 survives and has been recently restored.) His most important estates are one at Hoek van Holland (1924–7) and the Kiefhoek Estate (1925–30). Later Oud mellowed, abandoned the severity of his designing, and helped to create that curiously decorative, somewhat playful Dutch style which was nick- named locally Beton-Rococo. The paramount example is the Shell Building at The Hague (1938–42). Later he returned to his earlier more rigorous principles, notably at his Bio Children's Convalescent Home, Arnhem (1952–60).

G. Stamm, *J.J.P.O. Bauten und Projekte 1906–63*, Mainz and Berlin (1978) 1984; E. Mattic, *Functionalism in the Netherlands*, Amsterdam 1994.

**Outram**, John (b.1934), *see* ENGLISH ARCHITECTURE.

**Overdoor**, *see* SOPRAPORTA.

**Overhang**. Projection of the upper storey of a house.

**Oversailing courses**. A series of stone or brick courses, each one projecting beyond the one below it.

**Ovolo moulding**. A convex moulding, usually a quarter of a circle and sometimes called a quarter round. It is often ornamented with EGG AND DART or other similar patterns.

**Owen**, Robert (1771–1856), *see* COMPANY TOWN; URBAN DESIGN.

**Owings**, Nathaniel A. (1903–84), *see* SKIDMORE, OWINGS & MERRILL.

# P

**Páckh**, Janos (1796–1839), *see* HUNGARIAN ARCHITECTURE.

**Padstone**, *see* KNEELER, TEMPLATE.

**Paeschen**, Hans Hendrik van (*c*.1515–*c*.1577). Flemish architect who worked at the Town Hall, Antwerp (1561–6); the Royal Exchange, London (1566–71, burnt down 1666); Burghley House, Stamford, Lincolnshire (1564), and Kronberg Castle, Denmark (1574–7), where he was succeeded by OBBERGEN.

**Pagano** (Pogatschnig), Giuseppe (1896–1945), *see* RATIONALISM.

**Pagoda**. European name (of Portuguese origin) for a Chinese or Japanese Buddhist temple tower, usually a tiered structure of several storeys. Its origin is obscure, but it probably derived from the super-structure of an Indian Buddhist STUPA. It is called in Chinese a *ta* (*t'a*), in Japanese a *shoro* if it serves as a bell-tower or a *tahoto* if it has a single room with an elaborate superstructure. The term is also used, loosely, for Buddhist temples in Nepal and for stupas in Burma. European imitations became a feature of C18 and later parks, e.g. the Pagoda by CHAMBERS in Kew Gardens, London. *See* Fig. 87.

**P'ai lou**. A Chinese ornamental arch or gateway, commemorative or triumphal in function, with one, three or five openings. Usually built of stone but in imitation of wooden prototypes, e.g. stone beams are tenoned through the columns.

**Paine**, James (1717–89). English architect who lived in London but worked

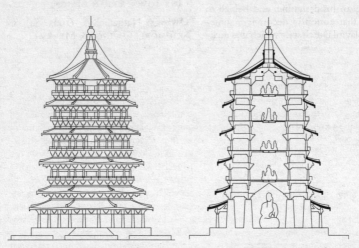

Fig. 87 Pagoda

mainly as a country-house architect in the Midlands and north. Solid and conservative, he began in the tradition of BURLINGTON and KENT and he and Sir Robert TAYLOR were said to have 'nearly divided the practice of the profession between them' in the mid C18. His houses are practically planned and very well built with dignified exteriors and excellent Rococo plasterwork, e.g. the Mansion House, Doncaster (1745–8). Later he showed more originality and preceded Robert ADAM in replacing the C17 'house of parade' plan for country houses with the compact, centrally planned 'villa with wings'. At Kedleston, Derbyshire (1759–60, later taken over by Adam), he had the brilliant idea of placing in sequence an antique basilica hall and a Pantheon-like circular saloon. At Worksop Manor, Nottinghamshire (begun 1763 but only a third built, demolished 1843), he envisaged a gigantic Egyptian Hall and at Wardour Castle, Wiltshire (1770–76), he designed a magnificent circular staircase rising towards a Pantheon-like dome. But by this date he had been superseded in the public eye by Robert Adam, and his practice declined rapidly. As a result of some domestic trouble during his last years he retired to France, where he died. Most of his work is illustrated in his two volumes of *Plans, Elevations and Sections of Noblemen's and Gentlemen's Houses* (1767 and 1783).

P. Leach, *J.P.*, London 1988; Harris 1990; Colvin 1995.

**Pakistani architecture**, *see* INDIAN AND PAKISTANI ARCHITECTURE.

**Palaestra**. An exercise ground or public building for athletes, smaller than a GYMNASIUM.

**Paliotto**. A canopy for an altar covering all four sides, as distinct from an ANTE-PENDIUM, which covers the front only.

The most famous is that of gold, silver partly gilt, enamel and semi-precious stones by Vuolvinius of the early C9 in S. Ambrogio, Milan.

**Palisade**. A fence of pales or stakes fixed deeply in the ground in a close row to form a defensive barrier, also a hedge of trees or shrubs. The French spelling *palissade* is sometimes used to distinguish a hedge clipped to form a green wall, sometimes with arched openings, or a row of trees with bare trunks and the branches pleached to make a dense leafy screen, often found in formal gardens. *See* Fig. 88.

Fig. 88 Palisade or *palissade*

**Palladian window**, *see* SERLIANA.

**Palladianism**. A style derived from the buildings and publications of PALLADIO. Its first exponent was Inigo JONES, who studied Roman ruins with Palladio's *Le antichità di Roma* and his buildings in and around Vicenza (1613–14), and introduced the style into England. Elsewhere in northern Europe, especially Holland (van CAMPEN) and Germany (HOLL), Palladian elements appear in buildings – temple fronts, the SERLIANA window, etc. – but here the leading influence was SCAMOZZI rather than Palladio. The great Palladian revival began in Italy and England in the early C18: in Italy it was confined to Venetia, but affected churches as well as secular buildings; in England it was purely domestic. The English revival, led by CAMPBELL and Lord BURLINGTON, was at the same time an Inigo Jones revival. Numerous books were published under Burlington's aegis, notably by WARE, and these provided a set of rules and exemplars which remained a dominant force in English architecture until late in the C18. From England and Venetia, Palladianism spread to Germany (KNOBELSDORFF) and Russia (CAMERON and QUARENGHI). At Potsdam accurate copies of Palladio's Palazzo Valmarana and Palazzo Thiene were built in the 1750s under the influence of Frederick the Great and his courtier, the Paduan Count Algarotti. From England the style also spread to the USA in the 1760s (JEFFERSON). Outside Italy the Palladian revival was concerned mainly with the use of decorative elements. Little attention was paid to Palladio's laws of HARMONIC PROPORTIONS except in Italy, where his ideas on this subject were examined by BERTOTTI-SCAMOZZI and elaborated by a minor architect, Francesco Maria Preti (1701–84).

R. Wittkower, *Palladio and P.*, London 1974; W. M. Whitehall and F. D. Nicholls, *P. in America*, Milan 1976; J. Harris, *The Palladians*, London 1987; R. Tavernor, *Palladio and P.*, London 1991; S. Parissien, *Palladian Style*, London 1994; J. Harris, *The Palladian Revival. Lord Burlington, His Villa and Gardens at Chiswick*, London 1995; G. Worsley, *Architecture in Britain in the Heroic Age*, London 1995.

**Palladio**, Andrea (1508–80). The most influential and one of the greatest Italian architects (*see* PALLADIANISM). Smooth, elegant, and intellectual, he crystallized various Renaissance ideas, notably the revival of Roman symmetrical planning and HARMONIC PROPORTIONS. An erudite student of Ancient Roman architecture, he aimed to recapture the splendour of antiquity. But he was also influenced by his immediate predecessors, especially BRAMANTE, GIULIO ROMANO, MICHELANGELO, RAPHAEL, SANMICHELI and SANSOVINO, and to some extent by the Byzantine architecture of Venice in his religious buildings. His style is tinged with MANNERISM, and it was understandably thought to be 'impure' by later neo-classical architects and theorists.

The son of Pietro dalla Gondola, he was born in Padua and began humbly as a stone-mason working for the Pedemura bottega, enrolled in the Vicenza guild of bricklayers and stone-masons in 1524. Then, in about 1536, he was taken up by Giangiorgio Trissino (1478–1550), the poet, philosopher, mathematician and amateur architect (entrance front of Villa Trissino, Cricoli, 1532–8), who encouraged him to study mathematics, music and Latin literature, especially VITRUVIUS, and nicknamed him Palladio (an allusion to the goddess of wisdom and to a character in a long epic poem he was then writing). Trissino took him to Rome several times between 1541 and 1547, where he studied the remains of Ancient Roman architecture. In 1546 he won a competition for the remodelling of the Early Renaissance Palazzo della Ragione or Basilica in Vicenza and work began in 1549. He surrounded it with a two-storey screen of arches employing a motive derived from SERLIO but henceforth called Palladian. This columned screen gives to the heavy mass of the old building a grandeur wholly Roman and an airy elegance no less distinctively Palladian. It established his reputation, and from 1550 onwards he was engaged in an ever-increasing series of overlapping commissions for palaces, villas and churches.

The first of his palaces in Vicenza, Casa Civena (1540–42), was followed by

Palazzo Thiene (begun 1542 perhaps on a design by Giulio Romano, modified by Palladio after Giulio Romano's death in 1546, completed 1558), which gives an impression of massive power, emphasized by the rustication of the whole wall surface with rusticated Ionic columns on either side of the windows – barely emerging from chunky bosses – heavy quoins and voussoirs which contrast with smooth Corinthian pilasters. In plan it exploits a dynamic combination of rectangular rooms with a long aspidal-ended hall and small octagons similar to those of the Roman *thermae*. Palazzo da Porto (begun *c.*1543–52) is on a symmetrical plan derived from Ancient Rome, with a façade inspired by Raphael and Bramante and much enriched with sculptured ornament. Soon afterwards he began the more original Palazzo Chiericati (1551, completed in the late C17). This was built not in a narrow street but looking on to a large square; so he visualized it as one side of a Roman forum and designed the façade as a two-storey colonnade of a light airiness unprecedented in C16 architecture. For the convent of the Carità in Venice (planned 1561, but only partly executed) he produced what he and his contemporaries supposed to be a perfect reconstruction of an Ancient Roman house; it also contains a flying spiral staircase, the first of its kind. But while his plans became ever more archaeological, his façades broke further away from classical tradition towards Mannerism, probably the result of a visit to Rome in 1554. Palazzo Valmarana (designed 1563, begun 1565) is a still more obviously Mannerist composition and introduced the Giant Order with a mass of overlapping pilasters and other elements which almost completely obscure the wall surface. The end bays are disquietingly weak, no doubt intentionally. The Loggia del Capitaniato (1571–4) is by far his richest building,

with a mass of *horror vacui* relief decoration. His last building in Vicenza was the Teatro Olimpico (begun 1580 and finished by SCAMOZZI) – an elaborate reconstruction of a Roman theatre.

His villas show a similar process of development, his flair first appearing on a substantial scale at the Villa Pisani, Bagnolo, Vicenza (1542–4). In the 1550s he evolved a formula for the ideal villa – a central block of ruthlessly symmetrical plan, decorated externally with a portico and continued by long wings of farm buildings, either extended horizontally or curved forwards in quadrants, as at La Badoera (*c.*1550–60), and linking the villa with the surrounding landscape. On this theme he composed numerous variations – from the stark severity of Poiana (*c.*1549–60), with its undecorated shafts instead of columns, to the simplicity of La Malcontenta (1559–61) and the Villa Emo, Fanzolo (1560–65), where the windows are unmarked by surrounds and the decoration is limited to a portico on the main façade, to the elaboration of La Rotonda (1567), with its hexastyle porticos on each of its four sides. The use of temple-front porticos for houses was a novelty (Palladio incorrectly supposed that they were used on Roman houses). Sometimes they are free-standing but usually they are attached or inset as at Villa Cornaro, Piombino Dese (1551–3), and Villa Pisani, Montagnana (*c.*1552–5); and at Quinto (*c.*1550) and Maser (later 1550s) he treated the whole central block as a temple front. The relation of the portico to the rest of the building and the sizes of the rooms inside were determined by harmonic proportions.

Temple fronts and harmonic proportions also play an important part in his churches, inspired by Alberti's S. Andrea in Mantua, all of which are in Venice: the façade of S. Francesco della Vigna (1562), and the churches of S. Giorgio

Maggiore (1564–80, façade 1607–11) and Il Redentore (begun 1576). The latter two appear inside to be simple basilicas, but as one approaches the high altar the curves of the transepts opening out on either hand and the circle of the dome overhead produce a unique effect of expansion and elation. Both churches terminate in arcades screening off the choirs and adding a touch of almost Byzantine mystery to the cool classical logic of the plan.

His wooden bridge at Bassano (1570) was designed in 1569 and has been reconstructed several times.

In 1554 Palladio published *Le antichità di Roma* and *Descrizione delle chiese . . . di Roma*, of which the former remained the standard guide-book for 200 years. He illustrated Barbaro's *Vitruvius* (1556) and in 1570 published his *Quattro libri dell'architettura*, at once a statement of his theory, a glorification of his achievements, and an advertisement for his practice. (His drawings of the Roman *thermae* were not published until 1730, by Lord BURLINGTON.) English translations of the *Quattro libri* by LEONI, CAMPBELL and WARE appeared in 1715–20, 1728 and 1738. Ware's remained the standard edition until 1997 when superseded by that of R. Tavernor and R. Schofield (MIT Press, Cambridge, Mass.).

He was the first great professional architect. Unlike his most notable contemporaries, Michelangelo and Raphael, he was trained to build and practised no other art. Though he was erudite in archaeology and fascinated by complex theories of proportions, his works are surprisingly unpompous and unpedantic. But the rules which he derived from a study of the ancients, and which he frequently broke in his own work, came to be accepted almost blindly as the classical canon, at any rate for domestic architecture.

Wittkower 1988; G. Zorzi (ed.), *Le opere di A.P.*, Venice 1959ff.; J. Ackerman, *P.*, Harmondsworth 1966; L. Puppi, *A.P.*, Milan (1973) 1977; P. Holberton, *P.'s Villas. Life in the Renaissance Countryside*, London 1990; R. Tavernor, *P. and Palladianism*, London 1991; B. Boucher, *A.P. The Architect of His Time*, London/ New York 1994.

**Palmer**, John (*c.*1738–1817), *see* CRESCENT.

**Palmette**. A fan-shaped decorative motif resembling a palmated leaf or a panicle of flowers. One type of Ancient Greek palmette resembles honeysuckle flowers, another is more like a palm-leaf. Both were used in bands of ANTHEMION ornament, especially on Ionic buildings (e.g. Erechtheum, Athens), and the former type is sometimes incorrectly termed an anthemion. Ancient types of palmette were revived during the Renaissance and extensively used thereafter, especially in the late C18.

**Palmstedt**, Erik (1741–1803), *see* SWEDISH ARCHITECTURE.

**Panel**. Strictly any flat surface sunk or raised within a framework, e.g. Gothic stone panelling, but more usually a framed wooden surface as used in panelling to cover a wall. A *fielded panel* has a raised central flat surface often with bevelled edges, with a frame. Panelled walls developed in northern Europe from the C15 onwards when draught-proof rooms were demanded, LINENFOLD panelling being introduced first in Flanders, perhaps in imitation of curtaining. Painted, inlaid or carved panelling followed in the C16–17 and reached great sophistication in C18 France (*see* BOISERIE).

**Pani**, Mario (1911–93). Mexican architect who trained in Paris and returned to Mexico in 1934, becoming the leading town planner. His site plan for University

City (1947), for which he later designed the Central Administrative Building (1952), was notable. His Tlatelolco City housing development, Mexico City (1964), was a gigantic URBAN RENEWAL scheme covering 80 hectares (198 acres) and providing 12,000 apartments in 101 buildings, green spaces covering half the site when completed.

M. Larrosa, *M.P. architecto de sa epocha*, Mexico City 1985.

**Pantheon dome**. A low, rather flat dome similar to that of the Pantheon in Rome, though not necessarily open in the centre.

**Pantile**. A roofing tile of curved S-shaped section, laid so that the down curve of one side overlaps the up curve of the next.

**Papworth**, John Buonarroti (1775–1847). English architect, son of John, architect (1750–99), brother of Thomas, architect (1773–1814) and of George, architect, resident in Ireland (1781–1855); father of John Woody Papworth, architect (1820–70) and Wyatt Angelicus van Sandau Papworth, architect (1822–94). John B. Papworth's most important contribution to English architecture and planning is his work at Cheltenham mostly between 1825 and 1830. This comprises the Montpellier estate with the Rotunda (1825–6), the Lansdown estate with Lansdown Place and Lansdown Crescent (1825–9) and the church of St James (completion only, 1826–32). He also designed several country houses and a palace for the King of Württemberg at Cannstadt. The palace was not built, but Papworth received the title Royal Architect for it (1820). Papworth was interested in landscape gardening as well, and also in decoration and furnishings (notably shop windows). For one year (1836–7) he was director of the Government

School of Design. Two much used picture books by Papworth were *Rural Residences* (1818) and *Hints on Ornamental Gardening* (1823).

Summerson 1991; Colvin 1995.

**Papyrus**. 1. A tall aquatic plant of the sedge family, formerly abundant in Egypt. It recurs as a decorative motif in Ancient Egyptian art and architecture, notably in columns and capitals, and similarly in EGYPTIAN REVIVAL architecture. 2. A kind of paper made from its pith or stems.

**Parabolic vault**, *see* VAULT.

**Paradise**. 1. A word derived from old Persian *pairidaeza*, meaning a park – usually for hunting – but adopted by translators of the Bible for the Hebrew *eden* (pleasure, delight). The original usage survives in the term PARADISE GARDEN. In European architecture the word 'paradise' is used for the garden or cemetery of a monastery, in particular the main cloister cemetery (e.g. Chichester Cathedral, where the cloister-garth on the south side is called the paradise). 2. An open court or ATRIUM surrounded by porticoes in front of a church. (Some medieval writers gave this name to the atrium of Old St Peter's in Rome.)

The term PARVIS(E) seems to be a corruption of *paradisus*.

**Paradise garden**. A type of enclosed garden or BAGH of Persian origin with rectangular plots divided by canals and paths, if quadripartite called a *chahar bagh*, the canals symbolizing the four rivers flowing out of the Eden of Islamic cosmography. The fine early example at Medinat al-Zahra near Cordoba (begun *c.*936) was despoiled in 1010 but is now being recovered. Later examples include the Generalife, Granada (mid-C13), the Taj Mahal, Agra (mid-C17), the Shalamar

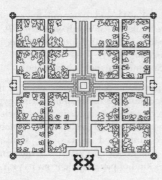

Fig. 89 Paradise garden

Bagh, Lahore (1633–45), and the Qajar Shazdeh gardens, Mahan near Kirman, Iran (C19). *See* Fig. 89.

E. B. Moynihan, *P. as a Garden in Persia and Moghul India*, London 1980; J. Brookes, *Gardens of P.: the History and Design of the Great Islamic Gardens*, London 1987; A. Petruccili (ed.), *Gardens in the Time of the Great Muslim Empires. Theory and Design*, Leiden/New York/Cologne 1997.

**Parapet**. A low wall, sometimes battlemented, placed to protect any spot where there is a sudden drop, for example, at the edge of a bridge, quay or house-top.

**Parclose**. A screen enclosing a chapel or shrine and separating it from the main body of the church so as to exclude non-worshippers.

**Parekklesion**. In Byzantine architecture, a chapel, either free-standing or attached.

**Pargeting**. Exterior plastering of a TIMBER-FRAMED building, usually modelled in designs, e.g. vine pattern, foliage, figures; also, in modern architecture, the mortar lining of a chimney flue.

**Park**. An enclosed tract of non-agricultural though sometimes pastoral land maintained for hunting or, from the early C18, laid out as a LANDSCAPE GARDEN mainly for recreational and aesthetic enjoyment. The term covers royal, private and PUBLIC PARKS and is now also used loosely for areas of preserved wilderness (notably the great National Parks of the USA, e.g. Yellowstone, Yosemite) and such park-like enclaves as the BUSINESS PARK, INDUSTRIAL PARK and THEME PARK.

**Parker**, Barry (1867–1941), *see* UNWIN, Raymond.

**Parkway**. In the USA a scenic road intended primarily for recreational motoring through an area of protected and maintained national forest or a stretch of specially planted parkland. Precedents were set by OLMSTED's approach road to Prospect Park, Brooklyn (1868), and his 'Emerald Necklace' at Boston, planned with Charles Eliot (1859–97) and completed in 1902 as a network of suburban parks connected by a winding road and terminating in a nature reserve. But the first true parkway was the 24 km (15 mile) long Bronx River Parkway planned by G. D. CLARKE (1913–23), leading from Bronx Park out into the country to Kensico Dam, with planted verges ranging in width from 60 to 310 m. (190 to 1,000 ft). It was the first road intended specifically for pleasure motoring with access restricted to private automobiles – a panoramic extension of the PUBLIC PARK. Others soon followed, notably the Milwaukee, Minneapolis and Cincinnati parkway systems designed by Warren Henry Manning (1860–1938), Merritt Parkway, Connecticut (1934–40), and the 750 km (470 mile) long Blue Ridge Parkway from the Shenandoah National Park to the Great Smoky Mountains National Park, planned in 1935 by Stanley William Abbott (1908–75) and completed in 1987. Abbott wrote that a parkway 'has as its reason none other than to reveal the charm and interest of the native American countryside'. Parkways introduced a new concept of the relationship between roads and landscape which influenced the planning of MOTORWAYS.

US Department of Commerce, *National P. Handbook*, Washington, DC 1964; US Department of Commerce, *A Proposed Programme for Scenic Roads and P.*, Washington, DC 1965; B. Rabbe, *The Merritt Parkway*, New Haven 1993; C. Zapatka, *L'architettura del paesaggio americano*, Milan 1995.

**Parker**, R. Barry (1867–1941), *see* UNWIN, Raymond.

**Parler**. The most famous family of German masons in the C14 and early C15. The name is confusing, as *Parlier* is German for the foreman, the second-in-command, in a masons' lodge and can thus occur in reference to masons not members of the family. The family worked in south Germany, chiefly Swabia, and in Bohemia, chiefly Prague. More than a dozen members are recorded. The most important ones are Heinrich I and his son Peter. Heinrich I (b.*c.*1300) was probably *Parlier* at Cologne, and then became master mason at Schwäbisch-Gmünd, one of the most important churches in Germany for the creation of the specifically German Late Gothic style (*Sondergotik*). It is likely that he designed the operative part, the chancel, a design on the HALL CHURCH principle which had great influence. A Heinrich of the same family, quite possibly he, also designed the chancel at Ulm (begun 1377).

Peter (1333–99) was called to Prague in 1352–3 to continue the cathedral begun in 1344 by Matthias of Arras (d.1352). He completed the choir by 1385 and went on to the south transept, working first on a synthesis of the French cathedral plan with the hall principle of Gmünd and its consequences. In the chapels farther west he developed interesting and fanciful lierne vaults, curiously similar to English ones built a generation and more earlier. In 1357 he began the Charles Bridge in Prague. He probably designed and worked also at Kutná Hora (Kuttenberg) and the choir of St Barthelemy, Kolin (1378).

The Parlers, and especially Peter, also exercised great influence through the sculptural work of their lodges. Another member of the family, Johann, was master mason of the town of Freiburg from 1359 and perhaps designed the chancel of the minster there (1354–63). Yet another, again called Heinrich of Gmünd, was at Milan Cathedral in 1391–2 ('Enrico da Gamondia'), but left under a cloud, having been unable to win the authorities over to his ideas. The Hans of Freiburg ('Annes de Firimburg') who, also in vain, made a report to the Milan authorities earlier in 1391 may be yet another Parler.

A. Legner (ed.), *Die P. und der schöne Stil 1350–1400. Europäische Kunst unter dem Luxemburger*, Cologne 1978–80; N. Nussbaum, *Deutsche Kirchenbaukunst der Gotik*, Cologne 1985; B. Schock-Werner in Recht 1989.

**Parpen**, **parpent** or **parbend**. A stone which passes through a wall with two smooth vertical faces. Also called a *through stone* or *bond stone*.

**Parquet**. Flooring of thin hardwood (about 0.5 cm. (¼ in.) thick) laid in patterns on a wood sub-floor and highly polished. Inlaid or plated parquet consists of a veneer of decorative hardwood glued in patterns to squares of softwood backing and then laid on a wood sub-floor. *See also* PARTERRE.

**Parris**, Alexander (1780–1852). American architect contemporary with MILLS and STRICKLAND and the leading architect in Boston after BULFINCH. His Wickham House, Richmond, Virginia (1811–13), was notable but his Greek Revival additions to Boston were outstanding, e.g. St Paul's Church (now the Anglican Cathedral) (1819–21) and the Quincy or Faneuil Hall Market (1823), which formed the centrepiece of a remarkable urban development. His Stone Temple at Quincy, Massachusetts (1828), should also be mentioned.

Hitchcock 1977.

**Parterre**. 1. In a theatre the ground-floor behind the orchestra; also called the *parquet*, of which the section under the balcony is called the *parquet circle*. 2. In a garden the level space, usually adjacent to a house and best seen from above, laid out with regularly disposed flowerbeds or a turfed lawn with a design cut into it by paths. A *parterre d'eau* or water parterre has a symmetrical arrangement of ponds usually with fountains or simple water jets. A *parterre de broderie* has paths of stone, gravel or turf and beds for plants planned in rich foliate patterns similar to those for textiles and resembling a vast panel of embroidery. BOYCEAU claimed to have designed the first for the Luxembourg gardens in Paris, c.1620 (but *see also* de VRIES). A variation popularized by MOLLET and others consisted of similar patterns made with various types of coloured earth, or sometimes with bands of turf bordered by low hedges of box. *Parterres de broderie* fell out of fashion from the mid-C18 but were revived in Victorian England, where they were filled with colourful, low-growing and often exotic plants in what was called carpet-bedding.

**Partition**. An internal wall, slighter than a wall proper, separating one part of a space from another and dividing an area into parts.

**Party walls**. A wall built on the boundary line of adjoining properties and shared equally by the two owners, each having partial rights in its use.

**Parvis(e)**. 1. In France the term for the open space in front of and around cathedrals and churches; probably a corruption of *paradisus* (*see* PARADISE). 2. In England a term wrongly applied to a room over a church porch.

**Pasqualini**, Alessandro (d. before 1559), *see* DUTCH ARCHITECTURE.

**Passage grave**. A prehistoric burial chamber covered by an earth-and-pebble cairn, entered through a long slab-lined passageway or passageways. The central space was often roofed by corbelling and was sometimes segmented into several chambers, usually with multiple burials. Usually found in Neolithic Western Europe, close to the sea, their origin is obscure. *See also* MEGALITH.

**Pastophory**. A room in an Early Christian or Byzantine church serving as a DIACONICON or PROTHESIS; as a rule, flanking the apse of the church.

**Patera**. A small, flat, circular or oval ornament in classical architecture, often decorated with ACANTHUS leaves or rose petals. *See* Fig. 90.

Fig. 90 Patera

**Patio**. In Spanish or Spanish American architecture, an inner courtyard open to the sky. In modern usage, a paved area for chairs, tables and potted plants adjacent to a house.

**Patkau**, John (b.1947) and Patricia (b.1950), *see* CANADIAN ARCHI-TECTURE.

**Patte**, Pierre (1723–1812), *see* URBAN DESIGN.

**Patte d'oie** (Fr. goose foot). Three radiating avenues, a feature of French formal parks, notably LE NÔTRE's at Versailles, perhaps derived from Baroque urban design, e.g. the three streets radiating from Piazza del Popolo, Rome.

**Paul**, Bruno (1874–1968). German architect and designer, one of the founders of the Deutsche Werkstatten in 1898 (*see* DEUTSCHER WERKBUND) and influential in industrial design up to 1933. His notable buildings include the Asiatic Museum, Berlin-Dahlem (1914–23); Auerbach House, Berlin-Dahlem (1914–25); and the Kathreiner office building, Berlin (1929–30).

A. Ziffer, *B.P.*, Munich 1992; S. Günther, *B.P.*, Berlin 1992.

**Pavilion**. An ornamental building, lightly constructed, often used as a pleasure-house or summerhouse in a garden, or attached to a cricket or other sports ground; also a projecting subdivision of some larger building, usually square and often domed, forming an angle feature on the main façade or terminating the wings.

**Pavilion ceiling** or **vault**. An arched ceiling sloping equally on all sides, as in the interior of a pavilion roof.

**Pavilion roof**, *see* ROOF.

**Pawson**, John (b.1949), *see* MINIMALISM.

**Paxton**, Sir Joseph (1803–65). English architect and landscape architect. The son of a small farmer, he became a gardener and in 1823 worked at Chiswick in the gardens of the Duke of Devonshire. The Duke discovered his exceptional ability and in 1826 made him superintendent of the gardens at Chatsworth. He became a friend of the Duke, with him visited Switzerland, Italy, Greece, Asia Minor, Spain, etc., and in 1854 became Liberal MP for Coventry. He designed greenhouses for Chatsworth, the largest being 90 m (300 ft) long (1836–40, with Decimus BURTON), tried out a new system of glass and metal roof construction in them, laid out the estate village of Edensor (1839–41), and so, in 1850–51, moved into architecture proper by submitting, uninvited, his design for a glass and iron palace for the first international exhibition ever held. The Crystal Palace was truly epoch-making, not only because this was the most direct and rational solution to a particular problem but also because the detailing of this 550 m (1,800 ft) long building was designed in such a way that all its parts could be factory-made and assembled on the site — the first ever example of PREFABRICATION and large-scale INDUSTRIALIZED BUILDING. Paxton was also nominally responsible for a few large country houses (Mentmore, Ferrières, for members of the Rothschild dynasty), but they were partly or largely designed by his son-in-law. He also designed some of the earliest PUBLIC PARKS, notably that at Birkenhead, Lancashire (1843–7), and the People's Park, Halifax, West Yorkshire (1856). In all his schemes prominence was given to flowering plants, also the subject of his contributions to periodicals of which he was the editor, *Horticultural Register* (1831–4), *Paxton's Magazine of Botany* (1834–49) and *Paxton's Flower Garden* (1850–53).

G. F. Chadwick, *The Works of Sir J.P. 1803–65*, London 1961; A. Bird, *P.'s*

*Palace*, London 1976; Hitchcock 1977; J. McKean, *Crystal Palace. J.P. and Charles Fox*, London 1994.

**Peabody**, Robert Swain (1845–1917), *see* COLONIAL REVIVAL.

**Pearce**, Sir Edward Lovett (*c*.1699–1733). He was the leading exponent of PALLADIANISM in Ireland alongside CASTLE. His father was first cousin to VANBRUGH, like whom he began his career in the army. Nothing is known of his architectural training – if he had any – but he became one of the most interesting and original architects of the BURLINGTON school. His masterpiece is the Parliament House (now the Bank of Ireland) in Dublin (1728–39). The octagonal House of Commons was burnt in 1792 and later demolished. He also built the south front of Drumcondra House (1727) and Cashel Palace (*c*.1731). He became Surveyor-General for Ireland in 1730.

Summerson 1991; Colvin 1995.

**Pearson**, John Loughborough (1817–97). English architect, a pupil of Ignatius BONOMI, SALVIN and HARDWICK. Under Hardwick he worked on the Hall of Lincoln's Inn, where one may well discover his hand in the niceness of the detailing. In 1843 he set up practice, and almost at once was commissioned to design small churches. His first important church is St Peter, Kennington Lane, Lambeth, London (1863–5), French Gothic and vaulted throughout, the ribs of stone, the webs of brick. This building displays his faith in truth in building and in a nobility to fit the religious purpose. Pearson also designed country houses – e.g. Quar Wood, Stow-on-the-Wold, Gloucestershire (1857, mostly destroyed), which is Gothic, and Westwood, Sydenham, London (1881), which is French Renaissance – but essentially he is a church architect and a Gothicist. His best

churches of the 1870s and 1880s are among the finest of their day not only in England but in Europe. Their style is C13 Franco-English, their decorative detail extremely sparing, and their spatial composition quite free and unimitative. Examples are St Augustine, Kilburn Park, London (1870–80); St Michael, Croydon (1871); St John, Red Lion Square, London (1874, demolished); Truro Cathedral, Cornwall (1879–1910); St John, Upper Norwood, London (1880–81); Cullercoats, Northumberland (1884), and St John's Cathedral, Brisbane, Australia (1887, unfinished). He was also surveyor to Westminster Abbey.

A. Quiney, *J.L.P. (1817–1897)*, New Haven and London 1979.

**Pebbledash**, *see* ROUGHCAST.

**Pedestal**. In classical architecture, the base supporting a column or colonnade; also, more loosely, the base for a statue or any superstructure. *See* Fig. 91.

**Pediment**. Not a Greek or Roman term but signifying in classical architecture a low-pitched GABLE above a PORTICO, formed by running the top member of the ENTABLATURE along the sides of the gable; also a similar feature above doors, windows, etc. It may be straight-sided or curved segmentally. The terms *open pediment* and *broken pediment* are confused and have been employed to describe pediments open or broken either at the apex or base. For clarity, a pediment where the sloping sides are returned before reaching the apex should be called an *open-topped* or *broken-apex pediment*; and one with a gap in the base moulding an *open-bed* or *broken-bed pediment*.

**Pei**, Ieoh Ming (b.1917). Chinese-born American architect, trained at MIT and Harvard. In 1948 he joined the urban developer William Zeckendorf in association with whom his first important

Fig. 91  Pedestal: Corinthian

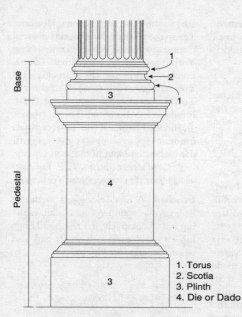

Base

Pedestal

1. Torus
2. Scotia
3. Plinth
4. Die or Dado

buildings were designed, notably the Mile High Center, Denver, Colorado (1952–6), and the Place Ville-Marie complex in Montreal (1960). In 1956 he formed I. M. Pei & Partners, New York, with Henry COBB, James FREED and others. Among their buildings are several for the new urban centre at Boston including the John Hancock Tower (1966–76); similarly for Singapore, notably the OCBC Centre (1976); the John F. Kennedy Library, Harvard University; the National Airlines Terminal at Kennedy Airport, New York; the Collins Place development at Melbourne; the extension to the National Gallery, Washington, DC, 1968–78; the Xiangshan (Fragrant Hills) Hotel, Beijing (1979–83); the El Paso Tower, Houston, Texas (1981); First Interstate Tower, Dallas, Texas (1986); the glass 'Pyramide', the new entrance to the Louvre, Paris (1989); the Morton H. Meyerson Symphony Center, Dallas (1989); the Bank of China Tower, Hong Kong (1982–9); the Rock and Roll Hall of Fame, Cleveland, Ohio (1993–5); and the remarkable Miho Museum near Kyoto, Japan (1990–97).

B. Suner, *I.M.P.*, Paris 1988; C. Wiseman, *I.M.P.*, New York 1990.

**Peichl**, Gustav (b.1928). Austrian architect who made his name with his studios for the Austrian State Radio (ORF) from 1968 onwards, e.g. those at Eidenstadt (1981–3) and Sankt Pölten (1994). Also notable were his Phosphate Elimination Plant at Berlin-Tegel (1985); his extension and school for the Stadel Museum, Frankfurt-am-Main (1990–2), and his schools at Vienna-Favoriten (Wienerberg school, 1991) and Vienna Donaustadt (Oewirkgasse school, 1993).

B. Zevi *et al.* (eds.), *G.P. Bauten, Projeckte*, Vienna 1981; Anon, *The Architecture of G.P.*, RIBA, London 1989.

**Pele-tower**. A term peculiar to northern England and Scotland, signifying a small tower or house suitable for sudden defence.

**Pelligrini**, Pellegrino known as Tibaldi (1527–96). Italian architect who began as a painter in Bologna but became the protégé of St Carlo Borromeo, who established him in Milan where he worked mainly as an architect from 1564 onwards, succeeding ALESSI as the leading architect. His more notable works include the Collegio Borromeo at Pavia, begun 1564; the austere Canonica cortile in the Archiepiscopal Palace in Milan, commissioned 1565 and begaun *c.*1572; S. Fedele in Milan, begun 1569 (the year after the Gesù in Rome) and S. Sebastiano, Milan, begun 1576. He was made chief architect of Milan Cathedral in 1567, converting the chancel from Gothic to Classical in style, and built the crypt under the choir and the high barriers between the choir and the ambulatory. From 1586 to 1594 or 1595 he was in Spain, working as a painter at the Escorial. In the 1590s he wrote a treatise, *L'Architettura* (published Milan 1990, ed. G. Panizza, intro. A. B. Mazotta).

S. della Torre and R. Schofield, *P.T. architetto e il S. Fedele di Milano. Invenzione e costruzione di una chiesa esemplare*, Como 1994; Lotz 1995.

**Pelli**, Cesar (b.1926). Argentine-born American architect who emigrated to the USA in 1952, trained in Chicago and worked for Eero SAARINEN from 1954 to 1964 when he was the project designer for the TWA Terminal, Kennedy International Airport, New York. From 1968 to 1977 he was with Gruen Associates and designed the blue-glazed Pacific Design Center, Los Angeles (1975), which made his name. His later buildings include the Residential Tower and expansion to the Museum of Modern Art, New York (1977); the Four Leaf Towers, Houston, Texas (1983–5); the four World Financial Center towers and Winter Garden, New York (1980–88); Canary Wharf Tower, London (1987–91); the Carnegie Hall Tower, New York (1987–91); the 777 Tower, Los Angeles (1991); the NTT Headquarters Building, Tokyo (1991–5), and the Petronas Twin Towers, Kuala Lumpur (1991–7), at 455 m. (1,483 ft) the highest building in the world.

P. Goldberger (intro.), *C.P. Buildings and Projects 1965–1990*, New York 1990.

**Pendant**. A BOSS elongated so that it hangs down; found in Late Gothic vaulting and, decoratively, in French and English C16 and early C17 vaults and also stucco ceilings. *See* Fig. 92.

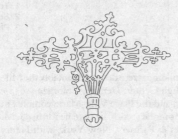

Fig. 92 Pendant

**Pendentive**. A concave SPANDREL leading from the angle of two walls to the base of a circular DOME. It is one of the means by which a circular dome is supported over a square or polygonal compartment (*see also* SQUINCH), and is used in Byzantine (Hagia Sophia, Istanbul) and occasionally Romanesque architecture (Périgueux), and often in Renaissance, Baroque, and later architecture. *See* Fig. 46.

**Pennethorne**, James (1801–71). As chief Government architect in London from 1845 onwards he was responsible for the Victoria Embankment, Commercial

Road, Southwark Street and Victoria Street (1852–70) as well as New Oxford Street (1843–7) and other new roads off the royal parks, e.g. Kensington Palace Gardens (1843), intended for upper-class development. Victoria Park, Hackney (1842–5), and Battersea Park with a serpentine lake (1851–63), both laid out in working-class districts, were his most notable works. His buildings ranged from the academic Classicism of the University of London Senate House (1867–70, now the Museum of Mankind) to the robust neo-Gothic of the Public Record Office in Fetter Lane (1851–6). He was knighted in 1870.

G. Tyack, *Sir J.P. and the Making of Victorian London*, Cambridge 1992.

**Penthouse**. A subsidiary structure with a lean-to roof (*see* ROOF); also a separately roofed structure on the roof of a high block of flats.

**Percier**, Charles (1764–1838). French architect who studied in Paris under A.-F. Peyre and in Rome (1786–92) with his future partner P.-F.-L. FONTAINE. They worked together from 1794 until 1814, becoming the leading architects in Paris under Napoleon and creating the Empire style in decoration. For their joint works and publications, *see* FONTAINE.

**Peressutti**, Enrico (1908–73), *see* ROGERS, Ernesto Nathan.

**Pergola**. A covered walk in a garden usually formed by a double row of posts or pillars with BEAMS above and covered with climbing plants.

**Peribolos**. In Ancient Greek architecture the wall or colonnade surrounding a temple or sacred enclosure, hence sometimes applied to the enclosure itself.

**Perimeter block**. An apartment block built round an internal court laid out as a garden with trees. A feature of late C19 and early C20 URBAN DESIGN, e.g. Berlage's 'new south' area of Amsterdam (1902–20).

**Peripteral**. Of a building, surrounded by a single row of columns.

**Peristyle**. A range of columns surrounding a building, open court or garden.

**Perpend**. A large stone extending through a wall and finished at both ends.

**Perpendicular style** or **Perp**. Historical division of English Gothic architecture from *c.*1335–50 to *c.*1530. The last phase of Gothic in England, characterized by emphasis on vertical elements, e.g. window tracery with straight verticals and horizontals, flattened arches and complex vaulting such as fan-vaulting. *See* ENGLISH ARCHITECTURE.

**Perrault**, Claude (1613–88). A French doctor by profession and amateur architect. He was partly if not mainly responsible for the great east front of the Louvre in Paris (begun 1667), one of the supreme masterpieces of the Louis XIV style. LE VAU and the painter Lebrun were also members of the committee appointed to design this façade. It owes something to BERNINI's rejected project for the Louvre, and is notable for its great colonnade or screen of paired columns with an unusual, perhaps unprecedented, system of iron reinforcement (probably due to Perrault). He also designed the Observatoire, Paris (1667), and brought out an edition of VITRUVIUS (1674). In 1683 he published *Ordonnance des cinq espèces de colonnes* (English translation by J. K. McEver, Chicago 1992). His brother Charles (1626–1703) was a theorist and Colbert's chief assistant in the Surintendance des Bâtiments.

M. Soriano, *Le Dossier C.P.*, Paris 1972; W. Herrmann, *The Theory of C.P.*, London 1973; Blunt 1982; A. Picon, *C.P. 1613–1688*, Paris 1988; R. W. Berger, *The*

*Palace of the Sun: The Louvre of Louis XIV*, University Park 1993; R. W. Berger, *A Royal Passion. Louis XIV as Patron of Architecture*, Cambridge 1994.

**Perrault**, Dominique (b.1953). French architect who made his name with his functionally controversial glazed towers for his new Bibliothèque Nationale, Paris (1992–6). He had previously displayed his skilful use of industrial materials at the Hôtel Industrielle Berlier, Paris (1986–90). His Velodrome and Swimming Pool, Berlin (1992–8) should be mentioned.

**Perret**, Auguste (1874–1954). French architect, the son of the owner of a building and contracting firm. After studies under Guadet he and two brothers joined the firm which was known from 1905 as Perret Frères. His first outstanding job was the house No. 25b rue Franklin near the Trocadéro in Paris (1903–4), a block of flats on an interesting plan; it has a CONCRETE structure with the concrete members displayed and ART NOUVEAU faience infillings. Next came a garage in the rue Ponthieu (1905), even more demonstratively expressing its concrete frame. The Théâtre des Champs Élysées (1911–14) was originally designed by van de VELDE, but in its final form it is essentially Perret's, and its distinguishing feature is again the proud display of its concrete skeleton. Details, however, are decidedly classical, even if with a minimum of traditional motifs, and Perret was subsequently to develop in that direction. Nevertheless, until the mid-twenties bold concrete experiments still prevailed: the 20-m (65-ft) arches across the vast workroom of the Esders tailoring establishment, Paris (1919), and the decorative concrete grilles of the windows and the concrete excelsior of the steeple of the churches of Notre Dame du Raincy (1922–3) and of Montmagny (1926). Examples of Perret at his most classical –

basically the successor to the most restrained French C18 style – are the Museum of Public Works (1937, though with a brilliant curved flying concrete staircase inside) and the post-war work for Amiens (skyscraper 1947) and Le Havre (1945 onwards). The latter includes Perret's last work, the strange centrally planned church of St Joseph (1952–5). He published *Une Contribution à une théorie de l'architecture* (Paris 1952).

B. Champigneulle, *P.*, Paris 1959; M. Zahar, *D'une doctrine d'architecture: A.P.*, Paris 1959; Collins 1959; E. Goldfinger, *A.P. Writings on Architecture*, London 1972.

**Perron**. An exterior platform ascended by steps and leading to the (usually first-floor) entrance to a house, church, etc. The door opens on to it. More loosely, the flight or flights of steps ascending to the platform.

**Persian architecture**. A term describing not only buildings in present-day Iran but also those in adjacent territories under Sassanian and Ilkhanid rule (but *see also* SELJUK ARCHITECTURE). The nomadic peoples of Persia produced no architecture until after their conquest of Babylon in 539 BC. The only notable example of the succeeding Achaemenid period is the palace at Persepolis (518–*c*.460 BC), which reveals Assyrian influence in the extensive use of animal sculpture for the capitals of columns and in the use of large-scale relief decorations. Relief decorations in brightly coloured glazed brickwork (now in the Louvre, Paris) were also employed at Susa. The *apadana* or Hall of a Hundred Columns at Persepolis, so far as it can be reconstructed, shows that other elements were derived from Egypt though treated with greater lightness and elegance. Under the Sassanian dynasty (226 BC to AD 642), whose empire extended to the West through Mesopotamia (modern

Iraq), palaces and Zoroastrian FIRE TEMPLES were constructed of brick, with vaults and domes, and decorated with carved stucco. The remains of the magnificent palace in the capital city, Ctesiphon near Baghdad (probably 531–79), include the IWAN whose vault has the widest span of any pre-modern brick building. Other partially surviving buildings of note include the palaces of Firuzabad (*c*.226–41), Sarvistan (420–40) and Qaar-i-Shirin, Kurdistan (*c*.590).

Sassanian buildings and their decorations provided a starting point for ISLAMIC ARCHITECTURE in the region after its conquest by the Muslims (649–51), further developed when Persia came under the rule of the Samanid dynasty (874–999), the SELJUKS to the mid-C12 and the Mongol Ilkhanid to 1335. This is evident in the design of the characteristically Persian mosque with an iwan on each side of the courtyard and a dome over the chamber in front of the MIHRAB – most imposingly in the Friday Mosque, Isfahan (probably begun late C11). The domed mausoleum, probably derived from Zoroastrian fire temples, was another Persian building type. The earliest survival is the C10 'Tomb of the Samanids', Bukhara (now Uzbekistan), a cube constructed of bricks laid in intricate geometric patterns; the most grandiose is the octagonal mausoleum of Oljietu, Sultaniya (*c*.1309–13). From the C11 increasing use was made of glazed tiles for revetments, predominantly a very beautiful turquoise blue.

Some of the most impressive mosques were built under the Safavid dynasty (1502–1736), most notably in Isfahan, where the Masjid-i-Shah (1612–30) and Masjid-i-Shaykh Lutfullah (1602–4) stand on either side of a large square which is itself a fine example of urban planning. During this period many restorations of and additions to older buildings were

carried out. Other achievements included bridges, notably the two-storey Pul-i-Khaj, Isfahan (1643–4), which serves also as a dam. Domestic architecture, especially pavilions in gardens, was developed with a refinement matching the decorative arts (notably carpets) of the period, e.g. Chihil Sutun, Isfahan.

After the fall of the Safavid dynasty there was little architectural activity until the rule of the Qajar (1794–1925), when conflicting tendencies – Islamic and Western – became evident, e.g. Gulistan Palace, Tehran. Tehran was further Westernized under Riza Shah Pahlavi (1925–41), *see* GUÉVREKIAN, Gabriel.

**Persico**, Edoardo (1900–1936), *see* RATIONALISM.

**Persius**, Ludwig (1803–45). German architect, follower of SCHINKEL with whom he collaborated on several buildings at Potsdam, e.g. Nikolaikirche (1830–37). He was equally refined and accomplished, e.g. his Fasanerie, Potsdam-Sanssouci (1844), even when working in other historical styles, e.g. Friedenskirche (1845–54) or the elegant Moorish Pumphouse (1841–2), both in Potsdam.

E. Börsch-Supan, *L.P. Das Tagebuch des Architekten Friedrich Wilhelms IV, 1840–45*, Berlin 1980; S. Bohle-Heintzenberg and M. Haman, *L.P. 1840–45. Architekt des Königs*, Berlin 1993.

**Perspective**. Several systems have been evolved for the representation on a flat surface of the appearance of a three-dimensional object, such as a building, in spatial recession. Linear perspective, as used by BRUNELLESCHI in about 1415 and codified by ALBERTI in 1435 in his treatise on painting, was based on the observation that all receding parallel lines at right angles to the field of vision – called orthogonals – appear to converge on a single distant vanishing point. *See also* AXONOMETRIC PROJECTION; ISON-OMETRIC PROJECTION; RENDERING.

J. Mohrle, *Architecture in P. Construction, Representation, Design and Colour*, London 1994.

**Peruvian architecture**. Remains of the earliest known buildings on the American continent are in Peru, notably at Chuqui-tanta in the centre of the coast – a *c.*2000–1800 BC temple of stone-faced adobe walls on an artificial mound flanked by long wings. A ceremonial group at Chavin de Huantar in a valley of the central Andes built *c.*900 BC is more impressive, with platforms surrounding a sunken court dominated by a square block about 75 m. (240 ft) wide and still standing 15 m. (45 ft) high, faced with well-cut stone, windowless but enclosing three storeys of galleries connected by stairs and ramps and ingeniously ventilated by air shafts. The Mochica peoples in the north built *c.*250 BC–AD 700 huge pyramids and also clustered dwellings of moulded adobe (e.g. at Moche). In the far south (modern Bolivia) at Tiahuanaco there is a large ceremonial centre begun AD *c.*400 with the remains of buildings constructed from blocks of stone ingeniously dressed so that they could be bonded by grooves, slots or mortice and tenon joints but sometimes linked also by pouring molten copper into matching cavities. A new phase in the architectural history of Peru was initiated by the Incas, whose empire (founded in the C13) gradually expanded over most of the country and flourished until the Spanish conquest in 1532. At their capital Cuzco there are huge walls of polygonal masonry, tenoned together, of regular courses of rectangular blocks fixed by grinding the surface of one against those beneath and beside it. Both methods of construction were used *c.*1500 at the fortified town of Machu Picchu,

on a saddle of the Andes, which survives remarkably complete. Other notable Inca buildings are on the islands of Lake Titi-caca, Pachacamac and Ollantayambo. Types of buildings were simple and stan-dardized, rectangular and circular with windows and doors of trapezoid shape. Architectural decoration was sparse. Of colonial period buildings the cathedrals at Cuzco (1582–1654) and Lima (1582–1602), both largely by Francisco Becerra (*c.*1545–1605), are in the austere Spanish style of the mid C16 apart from the façade of the former, which is in the rather heavy Baroque style that was developed in the church of the Compañia, Cuzco, and elsewhere. A more classical style was introduced by the amateur architect Manuel Amat, who was viceroy 1761–76 and designed the Nazarenas church at Lima. After the declaration of independence in 1821 the main influences were French for official buildings and a kind of South American vernacular for others. Recent buildings in Lima by ARQUITEC-TONICA are notable.

**Peruzzi**, Baldassare (1481–1536). One of the best High Renaissance architects in Rome. His works are much indebted to BRAMANTE and RAPHAEL, but have an almost feminine delicacy which con-trasts with the monumentality of the former and the gravity of the latter. Born in Siena, he began as a painter under Pinturicchio. In 1503 he went to Rome, where he was employed by Bramante and assisted him with his designs for St Peter's. He probably built S. Sebastiano in Valle Piatta, Siena (*c.*1507), a centralized Greek cross church derived from Bramante. His first important work was the Villa Farnesina, Rome (1508–11), one of the most exquisite of all Italian houses both for its architecture and for its interior decoration (frescos by Peruzzi himself, Raphael, GIULIO ROMANO, Sodoma and Ugo da Carpi), which combine to make it the outstanding secular monument of the High Renaissance. The plan is unusual: a square block with an open loggia in the centre of the garden front and projecting wings. The main rooms are on ground level. The façade decoration is rich with two superimposed orders of pilasters crowned with a boldly carved frieze of *putti* and swags in which the attic windows are set.

On Raphael's death (1520) Peruzzi completed his S. Eligio degli Orefici, Rome, and succeeded him as architect of St Peter's. In 1527 he fled from the Sack of Rome to Siena, where he was appointed city architect. In Siena he was mainly engaged on fortifications (near Porta Laterina and Porta S. Viene), but he also built Palazzo Polini and, outside Siena, the Villa Belcaro (now much altered). His last work, Palazzo Massimo alle Colonne, Rome (1532–6), is perhaps his most interesting, for its unorthodox design seems to echo the uneasy atmosphere of Rome in the years after the Sack. The façade is curved; there is a disturbing contrast between the ground floor with its deeply recessed loggia and the papery-thin upper part, with shallow window surrounds on the first floor and curious flat leathery frames round those on the floors above. In the *cortile* the sacrosanct orders are wilfully misused. The self-confidence of the High Renaissance has here given way to the sophisticated elegance and spiritual disquiet of MANNERISM.

Lotz 1977; H. Wurm, *B.P. Architekturzeichnungen*, Tübingen (1981) 1984; M. Fagiolo and M. L. Madonna (eds.), *B.P. pittura, scena e architettura nel cinquecento*, Rome 1987; C. Tessari, *B.P. Il Progretto dell'Antico*, Milan 1995; Lotz 1995.

**Petersen**, Carl (1874–1923), *see* DANISH ARCHITECTURE.

**Petschnigg**, Hubert (b.1913), *see* HENTRICH, Helmut.

**Pew**. A fixed wooden seat in a church, in use at least by the C14. In medieval times pews were partially enclosed at the ends next to the aisles with *bench-ends*, which sometimes rise above the WAINSCOT and terminate in carved FINIALS (*see* POPPYHEAD). A *box-pew* is one with a high wooden enclosure all round and a small door; it is essentially a Georgian type.

**Peyre**, Marie-Joseph (1730–85), *see* WAILLY, Charles de.

**Pharos**. An ancient Roman lighthouse.

**Philadelphia School**, *see* GIURGOLA, Romnaldo; KAHN, Louis.

**Piacentini**, Marcello (1881–1960), *see* ITALIAN ARCHITECTURE; RATIONALISM.

**Piano**, Renzo (b.1937). Italian architect who made his name with the Centre Pompidou (Beaubourg), Paris (1971–7), in partnership with Richard ROGERS. With its exposed structure and brightly coloured functional mechanism visible externally, it became an emblematic populist building and made a major impact world-wide. Piano broke with Rogers afterwards and his later work owes less to HIGH TECH, e.g. rehabilitation of the Schlumberger Industrial Site, Paris (1980–84) and the ultra-refined, cool and formal Menil Museum, Houston, Texas (1980–87). A small de-mountable construction of glass, wood, aluminium and plastic designed as a travelling pavilion for IBM Europe in 1982–4 illustrates his remarkable versatility. This was followed by the Bercy II Shopping Centre, Paris (1987–90), an innovative example of highway architecture; the 60,000-seat San Nicola Football Stadium, Bari, Italy (1987–90), and the Kansai International

Airport on a man-made island in Osaka Bay, Japan (1988–94). This mile-long stainless steel construction in the form of an arc looks like an immense glider and outdoes SAARINEN's TWA Terminal at Kennedy International Airport, New York, as a symbol of flight. The vast curved roof was made possible by sophisticated CAD calculations using new toroidal and other geometries. In 1992 he won the competition for the overall plan for the new Potsdamer Platz, Berlin, and in 1995 construction began on his Beyeler Museum, Rieden, Basel, Switzerland.

M. Dini, *R.P. Projects and Buildings 1964–83*, New York 1983; P. Goldberger, *R.P. Buildings and Projects 1971–89*, New York 1989; P. Buchanan, *R.P. Building Workshop*, London 1993; V. N. Lampugnani, *R.P. Projetti e Architetture 1987–1994*, Milan 1994.

**Piano nobile**. The main floor of an Italian (Renaissance or later) palace, containing the reception rooms. It is usually higher than the other floors, with a basement or ground floor below and one or more shallower storeys above.

**Piazza**. 1. In Italy an open space, usually oblong, surrounded by buildings. 2. In C17 and C18 England, a long covered walk or LOGGIA with a roof supported by columns.

**Piccinato**, Luigi (1899–1983), *see* ITALIAN ARCHITECTURE.

**Picturesque**. Originally a landscape or building which looked as if it had come out of a picture in the style of Claude or Gaspar Poussin. In the late C18 it was defined in a long controversy between Payne KNIGHT and Uvedale PRICE as an aesthetic quality between the Sublime and the Beautiful, characterized in the LANDSCAPE GARDEN by wild ruggedness (chasms, dark impenetrable woods, rushing streams, etc.), and in architecture by

interesting asymmetrical dispositions of forms and variety of texture – as in the COTTAGE ORNÉ and the Italianate or castellated Gothic country houses of John NASH and later in the mid-C19 Domestic Revival in England. The notion of the 'picturesque' was the most important English aesthetic idea to have influenced architecture.

C. Hussey, *The P.*, London 1927; Pevsner 1968; N. Pevsner (ed.), *The P. Garden and its Influence*, Dumbarton Oaks, Washington, DC, 1974; D. Watkin, *The English Vision*, London 1982; J. Dixon-Hunt, *Gardens and the Picturesque*, Cambridge, Mass. 1992.

**Pier**. 1. A solid masonry support, as distinct from a COLUMN. 2. The solid mass between doors, windows, and other openings in buildings. 3. A name frequently given to Romanesque and Gothic pillars varying from a square to a composite section (*see* COMPOUND PIER).

**Piermarini**, Giuseppe (1734–1808). Leading Italian neo-classical architect in Milan, he was trained in Rome under VANVITELLI and settled in Milan in 1769, then under Austrian rule. His most famous work is the façade of the Teatro alla Scala, Milan (1776–8). He also built several vast palaces, all rather severe with long façades, e.g. Palazzo Reale, Milan (1769–78), Palazzo Belgioioso, Milan (1772–81), and Villa Reale, Monza (1777–80).

Meeks 1966; D. Cesarini, *G.P. Architetto neoclassico*, Milan 1983.

**Pierre de Chelles**, *see* JEAN DE CHELLES.

**Pierre de Montreuil** (or **Montereau**) (d.1267). He may have been trained at Amiens. His early work for St Germain des Prés, Paris (1239–45), is destroyed. He is said to have been master mason at St Denis in the 1230s and 1240s, and the Sainte Chapelle in Paris has been attributed to him. But his sole surviving work is the upper part of the south arm terminal of the transept of Notre Dame, Paris (1258–67), where he took over from JEAN DE CHELLES. He succeeded Jean de Chelles as architect at Notre Dame in 1265. On his tombstone he is called *doctor lathomorum*.

D. Kimpel and R. Suckale, *Die gotische Architektur in Frankreich 1130–1270*, Munich 1985; R. Suckale in Recht 1989.

**Pietilä, Reima** (1923–93), *see* FINNISH ARCHITECTURE.

**Pietra serena**. A fine-grained pale grey SANDSTONE from Fiesole near Florence. A darker and slightly brown coloured version is called *pietra bigia*. Both were used prominently in Florentine Renaissance architecture, e.g. by BRUNELLESCHI in S. Lorenzo and S. Spirito where the cool grey *pietra serena* columns, pilasters, etc. are set off against white plaster, or by MICHELANGELO in the vestibule of the Laurentian Library where the columns, consoles, tabernacles, stairs and balustrade are of *pietra serena* similarly set off against white plaster.

F. Rodolico 1953; N. Penny 1993.

**Pietre dure**. Italian term for semi-precious stones, such as agate, jasper and lapis lazuli, used from the C16 onwards for mosaics, sometimes covering complete interiors. The Cappella dei Principi, S. Lorenzo, Florence (begun 1604), is the most notable example. Such work was more usual on a small scale, to decorate altar frontals, furniture, etc. Sometimes called *commesso di pietre dure* or Florentine mosaic.

U. Baldini *et al.*, *La Cappella dei Principi e le P.D. a Firenze*, Milan 1979.

**Pietro da Cortona** (1596–1669), *see* CORTONA, Pietro Berretini da.

**Pigage**, Nicolas de (1723–96). French architect born at Lunéville and trained in Paris, visited Italy and probably England, and in 1749 became architect to the Elector Palatine Carl Theodore in Mannheim, Germany, for whom his best work was done. His masterpiece is Schloss Benrath near Düsseldorf (1755–69), a large pavilion, apparently of one storey (but in fact of three), somewhat similar to Sanssouci at Potsdam, and decorated internally in the most exquisitely refined and restrained Rococo manner that hovers on the verge of Louis XVI Classicism. At Schwetzingen he laid out the Elector's garden (1766), and built a miniature theatre and various follies, including a mosque, a romantic water castle, and a bath-house with a mirror ceiling.

Colombier 1956; W. Heber, *Die Arbeiten des N. de P. (1723–96) in der Residenzen Mannheim und Schwetzingen*, Worms 1986.

**Pikionis**, Dimitris (1887–1968), *see* GREEK ARCHITECTURE.

**Pilaster**. A shallow PIER or rectangular column projecting only slightly from a wall and, in classical architecture, conforming with one of the ORDERS.

**Pilaster-strip**, *see* LESENE.

**Pile**. A heavy timber or shaft of metal or concrete driven into the ground, sometimes underwater (e.g. at Venice), to provide support for foundations by translating building loads through weak soils to strong soils or through skin friction to the surrounding soil. Groups of piles may be driven in a close pattern to support a *spread* or *raft* foundation; *see* FOUNDATION.

**Pilgram**, Anton (d.*c.*1515), was mason and sculptor first at Brno, Czech Republic, *c.*1502 and Heilbronn, Germany (at Heilbronn he did the high-spired tabernacle for the Holy Sacrament), and later at St Stephan in Vienna, where the organ foot (1513) and the pulpit (1514–15) are his, both very intricate in their architectural forms and both including a self-portrait of the master.

K. Oettinger, *A.P. und die Bildhauer von St Stephan*, Vienna 1951; R. Feuchtmüller, *Die spätgotische Architektur und A.P.*, Vienna 1952.

**Pilgram**, Franz Anton (1699–1751), *see* SLOVAK ARCHITECTURE.

**Pilgrimage church**. 1. A type of Romanesque church built on the roads across France and Spain to Santiago de Compostela, where the shrine of St James had attracted pilgrims from as early as 844. Most were built or rebuilt in the C11 and are spacious with long naves and wide transepts, often with notable sculptured reliefs. Common features are apses surrounded by an ambulatory with radiating chapels (e.g. St Sernin, Toulouse), tribunes or galleries above the aisles opening on to the nave or choir, and ribbed barrel-vaults over the nave. St Martin at Tours may have been the first, but little now survives. Apart from the great church at Santiago de Compostela the finest surviving examples are St Foy, Conques; St Etienne, Nevers; and St Sernin, Toulouse. 2. The term is also used for later churches to which pilgrimages were made, e.g. COLA DA CAPRAROLA's S. Maria della Consolazione, Todi, Italy; ZIMMERMANN's Wieskirche near Füssen, Germany; NEUMANN's Vierzehnheiligen, Bavaria, Germany.

**Pilier cantonné**. In medieval architecture, the combination of a simple mono-cylindrical support and engaged colonnettes rising from floor to vault.

**Pillar**. A free-standing upright member which, unlike a COLUMN, need not be cylindrical or conform with any of the orders.

**Pillar piscina**, *see* PISCINA.

**Pilotis**. French term for a pile or support. It was adopted and canonized by LE CORBUSIER for the cylindrical concrete stilts or pillars he used to carry a building, raising it to first floor level and leaving the ground floor free and open.

**Pinnacle**. A small turret-like termination crowning spires, buttresses, the angles of parapets, etc.; usually of steep pyramidal or conical shape and ornamented, e.g. with CROCKETS. *See* Fig. 108.

**Pinós**, **Carme** (b.1954), *see* SPANISH ARCHITECTURE.

**Piper**, Fredrik Magnus (1746–1824), *see* SWEDISH ARCHITECTURE.

**Piranesi**, Giovanni Battista (1720–78). Italian engraver of views of Roman antiquities and an architectural theorist who exerted a profound influence on the development of the neo-classical and Romantic movements. Born in Venice, he was trained as an engineer and architect, and settled in Rome *c*.1745. His highly dramatic views of Roman ruins and imaginative reconstructions of Ancient Rome helped to inspire a new attitude to antiquity. In *Della magnificenza ed architettura dei Romani* (1761) he championed the supremacy of Roman over Greek architecture and in *Parere sull'architettura* (1765) advocated a free and imaginative use of Roman models for the creation of a new architectural style. He put his theories into practice only once, not very successfully, at S. Maria del Priorato, Rome (1764–6), which combines an antique flavour with allusions to the Knights of Malta, who owned the church; but it lacks the power and imagination of his engravings.

J. Wilton-Ely, *The Mind and Art of P.*, London 1978; Rykwert 1980; J. Wilton-Ely and J. Connors, *P. Architetto*, Rome 1992; J. Wilton-Ely, *P. as Architect and Designer*, London 1993; A. Lütgens,

*G.B.P. Bilder von Orten und Räumen*, Stuttgart 1994; T. Bloomer, *Architecture and the Text. The (S)crypts of Joyce and P.*, London 1995.

**Pisano**, Andrea (d.1348/9). Not a relation of Giovanni PISANO but the finest Italian sculptor of the next generation and also an architect. As such he is traceable in records of Florence Cathedral as master mason, probably after GIOTTO's death in 1337 (the niche stage of the campanile is probably his). He was succeeded *c.*1343 by TALENTI and from 1347 was master mason at Orvieto Cathedral, though by that time the most important sculptural and architectural work on its façade was over.

Trachtenberg 1971; White 1987.

**Pisano**, Nicola (d.*c.*1280), and his son Giovanni (d. shortly after 1314), the greatest Italian sculptors of their generations, are also recorded as architects. In the case of Nicola we have no documents, but tradition (VASARI) and some stylistic arguments; in the case of Giovanni we are on firmer ground. He appears as master mason of Siena Cathedral in 1290 and at Siena some years earlier, during the time when the cathedral received its Gothic façade. About 1296 he moved to Pisa and was there probably also master mason. White 1987.

**Piscina**. A stone basin in a niche near the altar for washing the Communion or Mass vessels; provided with a drain and usually set in or against the wall south of the altar. A free-standing piscina on a pillar can be called a *pillar piscina*.

**Pisé** or **terre pisé**. Clay or earth kneaded or mixed with gravel and used for building cottages, walls, etc. by being rammed between boards or formwork which is removed as it hardens. It was a building material common in the ancient Near East. *See also* ADOBE; COB.

**Pishtaq**, *see* IWAN.

**Pitched roof**, *see* ROOF.

**Plaisance**. A summerhouse or pleasure-house near a mansion.

**Plan**. The horizontal arrangement of the parts of a building or a drawing or diagram showing such arrangement as a horizontal section. *See also* AXIAL PLAN; CENTRALLY PLANNED.

**Planes**. Flat two-dimensional surfaces. They may be vertical (walls) or horizontal.

**Plaster**, *see* STUCCO.

**Plastics**. Artificial substances containing natural or synthetic *polymers*, usually divided into two main classes – *thermoplastics* and *thermosets* – which require different jointing methods in building. They can be moulded under pressure and usually set in an irreversible form on cooling. Invented in the mid-C19, they were manufactured in quantity from the 1930s mainly for small household utensils. After the Second World War, when they were used in aircraft and their durability was proved, they were employed in buildings for wall and ceiling cladding, joinery and stucco mouldings, tubes, gutters, etc., often in imitation of wood and metal. Sandwich panels with foam plastic cores which are lightweight and provide insulation were much employed for internal walls and high-strength moulded panels reinforced with glass-fibre for larger wall and roof components. The US Exhibition Building in Moscow (1959), constructed of interconnected fibreglass umbrellas, demonstrated that enclosures could be made entirely of plastics. Although they continued to be used mainly as substitutes for traditional materials, plastics were also exploited to create new architectural forms: nylon polyester and glass-fibre for OTTO's tensile structures from 1967; transparent acrylic or polycarbonate that can be heat-formed in curves and is virtually unbreakable for R. B. FULLER's geodesic domes and to cover the exterior escalators of the Centre Pompidou, Paris, by PIANO and ROGERS. The manufacture of plastics is, however, a source of pollution and as they cannot be recycled nor are they biodegradable, their use is discouraged by advocates of ENVIRONMENTAL ARCHITECTURE.

T. R. Newman, *P. as Design Form*, Philadelphia 1972.

**Plat band**, *see* BAND.

**Plate**. A longitudinal timber set on top of a foundation or wall. An *arcade plate* is placed on top of wall posts in an aisled construction. A *flying plate* is set in from the plane of the wall and carried by brackets or by horizontal timbers set perpendicular to the wall plates.

**Plate tracery**, *see* TRACERY.

**Plateresque**. Literally 'silversmith-like', the name is given to an ornate architectural style popular in Spain during the C16. It is characterized by a lavish use of ornamental motifs – Gothic, Renaissance, and even Moorish – unrelated to the structure of the building to which it is applied. The main practitioners, many of whom were sculptors as well as architects, included Diego de SILOE, Alonso de COVARRUBIAS, Rodrigo GIL DE HONTAÑÓN.

Kubler and Soria 1959.

**Platform framing**, *see* BALLOON FRAMING.

**Platt**, Charles Adams (1861–1933). American architect and landscape architect. He began as a painter but turned to laying out gardens in emulation of those of the C16–18 he had seen in Italy and illustrated in his *Italian Gardens* (1894),

breaking away from the English style hitherto popular in the US. To create integrated 'country places' – house and grounds – he evolved an eclectic Renaissance-Georgian style for the houses as well, e.g. Faulkner Farm, Brookline, Massachusetts (1897); Timberline, near Philadelphia (1907–8). Subsequently he designed several prominent public buildings, notably the Freer Gallery of Art (1913–20) and a large extension to the Corcoran Gallery of Art (1925–8), both in Washington, DC.

K. N. Morgan, *Shaping the American Landscape, the Art and Architecture of C.A.P.*, Hanover, NH 1995.

**Playfair**, William Henry (1790–1857). Scottish architect, the leading GREEK REVIVAL architect in Edinburgh alongside T. HAMILTON. He was the son of James Playfair (1755–94) who designed Melville Castle (1786) and Cairness House (1791–7), the latter in an advanced neo-classical style with neo-Egyptian features inside. W. H. Playfair may have studied under SMIRKE in London but returned to Scotland in 1817 on being commissioned to complete R. ADAM's Edinburgh University. This established him professionally. He followed Adam's designs closely, but the interiors are his, notably the Library (*c.*1827), which is among his finest works. In 1818 he also began the Academy at Dollar and the New Observatory on Calton Hill, Edinburgh, where he also built the National Monument (1824–9, unfinished), a Doric monument to his uncle John (1825) and another to Dugald Stewart (1831). His best-known works are the Royal Scottish Academy (1822, enlarged and modified 1831) and the National Gallery of Scotland (1850), Doric and Ionic respectively. The Surgeons' Hall (begun 1829), with its elegant and crisp Ionic portico, is perhaps his masterpiece.

Though essentially a Greek Revival architect Playfair worked in other styles as well, e.g. neo-Gothic at New College, Edinburgh (1846–50) and neo-Elizabethan at Donaldson's Hospital, Edinburgh (1841–51).

A. J. Youngson, *The Making of Classical Edinburgh*, Edinburgh 1966; Crook 1972; Macaulay 1975; Glendinning, MacInnes and Mackechnie 1997.

**Pleasance** or **pleasaunce**. Old English word for a garden, now used to describe the park of a medieval castle or monastery.

**Pleasure garden**. Strictly any garden intended primarily to give pleasure, as distinct from a plot for vegetables or fruit. In the C18 the term was used also for a commercially run entertainment place with promenades and buildings for musical performances, refreshments, etc., set among trees. The first of note was Spring Gardens, later known as Vauxhall, in London, with statuary and, in the buildings, paintings by Hogarth and others, a fashionable resort from 1732 until the end of the century, finally closed in 1859. Its rival was Ranelagh, London, a huge rotunda for concerts set in a formally planned garden, opened in 1742 and closed in 1805. Both were much imitated elsewhere in England and in France.

**Plečnik**, Jože (1872–1957). Slovenian architect, trained in Vienna under Otto WAGNER for whom he worked as an assistant and through whom he knew HOFFMANN, OLBRICH and KOTĚRA. In Vienna he built the Zacherlhaus (1903–5) and the Church of the Holy Spirit (1910–13). In 1920 he was commissioned to remodel Prague Castle, formerly a great Habsburg symbol, into a new national or regional one. His terraces, gardens, monumental stairways and interiors, such as the St Matthias Hall (1928–30), are remarkable. Also in Prague he built the Church of the Sacred Heart, Vinhrady (1922–33). But his most notable works are in his native Ljubljana, where pan-Slavic nationalism favoured his mixture of local Slovenian vernacular forms with modern, classical and Byzantine in a style expressive of his passionate regionalism. Outstanding are the Chamber of Commerce, Crafts and Industry (1924–7), the Flat Iron Building (1933–4), the National University Library (1936–41), St Michael's church (1937–8), Zale cemetery (1938–40) and the bridges and river-bank promenades, all at Ljubljana.

F. Burckhardt, C. Eveno and B. Podrecca, *J.P. Architect 1872–1957*, Cambridge, Mass. 1989; D. Prelovšck, *J.P. 1872–1957. Architektur perennis*, (1992) London 1997; P. Krešic, *P. The Complete Works*, London 1993; J. Margolius, *Church of the Sacred Heart, Prague, 1922–33. J.P.*, London 1995.

**Plinth**. The projecting base of a wall or column pedestal, generally CHAMFERED or moulded at the top. *See* Figs. 86, 91.

**Plinth block**. A block at the base of the architrave of a door, chimney piece, etc., against which the skirting of the wall is stopped.

**Plough share twist**. The irregular or winding surface of a vault caused by the wall ribs starting at a higher level than the other, diagonal, ribs, due to the position of the clerestory windows.

**Plywood**. Three or more thin sheets of wood glued or cemented together, face to face, the grain of the alternating sheets running in different directions.

**Pneumatic structures** or **inflatable architecture**. A special type of TENSILE or MEMBRANE STRUCTURE supported by the difference in pressure between the air inside and outside. Air is usually pumped in through fans, acting also for ventilation, the membrane being sealed to prevent its escape. Entrance is through an airlock. The membrane has to be in sufficient tension to withstand wind and other natural loads. Pneumatic structures are used mostly for temporary buildings, being quickly erected and dismantled, e.g. the Pepsi Cola Pavilion at Expo '70, Osaka.

R. N. Dent, *Principles of P. Architecture*, London 1971; T. Herzog, *P.S. A Handbook of I.A.*, New York 1976; Klotz, 1986.

**Poccianti**, Pasquale (1774–1858). Italian neo-classical architect notable for his Cisternone, Livorno (1829–42), with a façade reminiscent of BOULLÉE.

D. Matteoni, *P.P. e L'Acquedotto di Livorno*, Rome/Bari 1992.

**Pod**. A VOLUMETRIC BUILDING such as a bathroom pod.

**Podium**. 1. A continuous base or plinth supporting columns or a wall. 2. The platform enclosing the arena in an ancient amphitheatre.

**Podrecca**, Boris (b.1940), *see* AUSTRIAN ARCHITECTURE.

**Poelaert**, Joseph (1817–79), *see* BELGIAN ARCHITECTURE.

**Poelzig**, Hans (1869–1936). German architect, studied at the College of Technology in Berlin, and in 1899 was appointed to a job in the Prussian Ministry of Works. In the next year, however, he became Professor of Architecture in the School of Arts and Crafts at Breslau (Wroclaw), and in 1903 its director. He stayed till 1916, then became City Architect of Dresden (till 1920), and after that Professor of Architecture in the College of Technology and the Academy of Arts in Berlin. In 1936 he accepted a chair at Ankara, but died before emigrating.

His first building of note was the water tower at Posen (Poznań), built in 1910 as an exhibition pavilion for the mining industry. It is of iron framing with brick infilling and details of exposed iron inside. Of 1911–12 are an office building at Breslau, with the motif of bands of horizontal windows curving round the corner – a motif much favoured in the 1920s and 1930s – and a chemical factory at Luban, equally advanced in its architectural seriousness and its grouping of cubic elements. During and immediately after the First World War Poelzig was one of the most fertile inventors of EXPRESSIONIST forms, chiefly of a stalagmite or organ-pipe kind. These fantastic forms characterize his House of Friendship (1916), designed for Istanbul, his designs for a town hall for Dresden (1917), and those for a Festival Theatre for Salzburg (1919–20), none of which was executed. However, he did carry out the conversion of the Grosses Schauspielhaus in Berlin (1918–19, destroyed), with its stalactitic vault and its highly Expressionist corridors and foyer. Later buildings were more conventionally modern (the enormous office building of 1928–31 for the Dye Trust, I. G. Farben, at Frankfurt (later the US Army headquarters) and the equally enormous building (1930–31) for the German Broadcasting Company in Berlin, now Radio Free Berlin).

T. Heus, *H.P. Bauten und Entwurfe. Das Lebensbild eines deutschen Baumeisters*, Stuttgart (1939) 1985; B. Miller-Lane, *Architecture and Politics in Germany 1918–1945*, Cambridge, Mass. 1968; J. Posener (ed.), *H.P. Gesammelte Schriften und Werke*, Berlin 1970; J. Posener, *H.P. Reflections in His Life and Work*, Cambridge 1992; C. Marquart, *H.P. Painter–Designer–Architect–Maler–Zeichner*, Tübingen/Berlin 1995.

**Point-block**. A high-rise block of simple geometry (not of pyramidal skyscraper form) as in LE CORBUSIER's plan for a city for 3 million people. The centre is usually reserved for staircases, elevators, etc., and the apartments fan out from it. *See also* TOWER BLOCK.

**Pointed arch**, *see* ARCH.

**Pointing**. The exposed mortar finishing to brick or masonry joints raked out to receive it. JOINTING is more durable. Old brickwork has to be 'repointed' by renewing decayed mortar. Pointing is usually flush at the edges ('flush pointing') or slightly recessed ('recessed pointing'). If flush but gently recessed in the middle, it is called 'bag-rubbed pointing'. If deeply recessed to display the outline of each stone or brick, it is called 'hungry joint pointing'. If the joints are formed with a trowel, it is called 'ribbon pointing'.

**Policy**. A C18 term for an enclosed garden, often some distance from the house. The word is still used in Scotland in this sense.

**Polish architecture**. The oldest surviving building in Poland is the small quatrefoil Chapel of St Mary on the Wawel at Cracow. It is of the C10 and in this and other ways the exact parallel to the oldest building of Bohemia, the Rotunda on the Prague Hradshin. The Romanesque style in Poland is part of that of Germany. Italian connections are largely explicable via Germany. The cathedral on the Wawel has its (German) crypt and parts of the west towers. At Gniezno splendid bronze doors of *c*.1175 survive, at Strzelno some columns decorated with small figures under arches.

As in other countries the way was paved for the Gothic style by the CISTERCIANS. Their first abbey was at Jedrzejow near Wroclaw in Silesia (1140 onwards), and there are a number of other abbeys. More determinedly Gothic are the buildings of the friars, starting with that of the Blackfriars at Sandomierz (1227

onwards). The east part of Wroclaw (Breslau) Cathedral, of 1244–72, has the straight ambulatory of Cistercian tradition. The nave followed in the C14, the century in which Cracow Cathedral on the Wawel was also rebuilt. Gniezno Cathedral of 1342–1415 has an ambulatory and a ring of straight-sided radiating chapels on the pattern of Cistercian architecture.

Late Gothic Polish churches have the high proportions and the ornate figured rib vaults of Germany. Wroclaw, Gdańsk (Danzig), Torun (Thorn), the Cistercian abbeys of Oliva and Pelplin, were of course all German. A characteristic Eastern feature however – though even this originated in Germany – is the so-called folded vaults, i.e. complicated space frames without ribs. Basilican sections are more frequent than halls. There are also a few two-naved halls. The church at Goslawice is an octagon with four cross-arms.

Of secular buildings by far the proudest is the Town Hall at Torun of about 1250, but mainly late C14, a bold oblong with blank giant arcading, an inner courtyard and one mighty tower. The surviving early buildings of Cracow University are also among the most interesting buildings of their kind anywhere in Europe.

The Renaissance reached Poland early, and probably by way of Hungary and Bohemia. The Early Renaissance parts of the Wawel (castle) of Cracow were begun as early as 1502 and the domed chapel of King Sigismond attached to Cracow Cathedral in 1517–38; the architects in both cases were Italians. Yet closest to the windows of the Wawel palace is the Vladislav Hall at Prague, closest to the chapel that of 1507 at Esztergom. Specially characteristic of the indigenous later C16 and early C17 style are lively top crestings instead of battlements (Cracow, Cloth Hall, 1555) and courtyards or façades with arcading at two or three levels (Poznań, i.e. Posen, Town Hall, 1550–61, partially destroyed 1945, rebuilt). The former also occurs in the other East European countries, the latter in them and Germany. Castles in the country were often square or oblong with courtyards and with or without angle towers (Niepolomice, 1550 onwards; Baranow, 1579 onwards; Ujazdow, 1606 onwards). The Arsenal at Gdańsk (Danzig) of 1602–5 by the Flemish architect Antonius van Opbergen (1543–1611) is one of the great Netherlandish Renaissance buildings in this city. The remarkable new town of Zamość, on the other hand, was built by a Venetian architect in 1587–1605.

Much interesting church work went on as well, with stuccoed tunnel vaults, their decoration being either Gothic Survival or simple geometrical patterns (Pultusk, 1556–63) or strapwork. Architects continued to be Italian and that remained so in the C17 as well. Poland has proportionately more churches of Italian inspiration in the C16 and early C17 than Germany.

The Italian church type of the Gesù in Rome was taken over before 1600 (Jesuit Church, Cracow, 1597 onwards, by J. M. Bernardone and J. Trevano); and Poland contributed much to the Italianate Baroque of the later C17 (Cracow University church, 1689). Besides longitudinal there are central churches. Klimontov (1643 onwards) is oval, Gostyn (1677 onwards) octagonal, and the church of the Holy Sacrament in Warsaw (1688) round with four short arms. The latter is by the Dutch TYLMAN VAN GAMEREN, who became the leading Polish architect in the second half of the C17.

The plans of the C18, with their predilection for elongated central themes, show affinities with Bohemia and once more south Germany (Lwów, or Lvov,

Dominicans, 1749–64, Berezwecz, with its curvaceous twin-tower façade, 1750 onwards). The principal country house of the first half of the C17 is Podhorce (1635–40), still square with angle towers, and with the pedimented windows and superimposed orders of pilasters which one would find at the same time in Austria and Bohemia. The full-blown Baroque came with Wilanow near Warsaw (1681 etc. by August Locci). In opposition to it was van Gameren's Franco-Dutch style (Warsaw, Krasiński Palace, 1682–94). This however did not apply to his ecclesiastical architecture throughout. St Anne at Cracow (1689 onwards) is thoroughly Italian and Baroque. The C18 saw a large activity both by the Saxon court and the native nobility. They culminated in PÖPPELMANN's designs for the Royal Palace. Style again varies from his exuberant Baroque to the classical French restraint of others.

Neo-classicism came early, and its earliest and finest phase corresponds with the reign of King Stanislaw Augustus Poniatowski (1764–85). Earlier still is the chapel belonging to the country palace of Podhorce. This is of 1752–66, by an architect signing himself C. Romanus. It is round, with a giant portico and a dome. Round and domed also, with a Roman Doric portico and decidedly French, is the Protestant Church at Warsaw of 1777 by Simon Gottlieb Zug (1733–1807). The leading court architects of Stanislaw were Giacomo Fontana (1710–73) and Domenico Merlini (1730–97). Theirs is the Ujazdow Palace (1768 onwards). By Merlini and the younger Jan Baptist Kamsetzer (1753–95) are the remodelling of the Lazienki Palace of Ujazdow (1788) and the excellent interiors of the Royal Palace (1780–85). Kamsetzer's church at Petrykosy of 1791 is wholly of the French Revolution type. At the same time the grounds of the country houses were converted in the English picturesque way (Arcadia, 1778 onwards, Natolin, Warsaw Belvedere). Between c.1780 and c.1825 Poland produced a number of spacious country houses in the classicist style and also the two Town Halls of Wilno and Grodno with detached giant porticos. But the most monumental of the giant porticos is that of Wilno Cathedral of 1777–1801, and that is by the Polish architect Wawrzyniec Gucewicz (1753–98). Antonio Corazzi (1792–1877) designed the Polish Bank (1828–30), which is very French, and the Grecian Grand Theatre (1826–33). The later C19 went through the same Historicist motions as all European countries, though the huge Poznanski textile factory and housing complex at Lodz, built from 1872 onwards by Hilary Majewski (1837–97), should be mentioned as a major 'historicizing' example of industrial architecture (it combines a BEAUX ARTS style palace for the owner with the factory and blocks of workers' flats in earlier styles). In the early C20 Poland had a kind of national (in this case free neo-Romanesque) romanticism more characteristic of Russia, Finland and Sweden than of the West. It is exemplified by the enormous 'Kaiserhaus', Poznań (1905–10), by Franz Schwechten (1841–1924) and by the church of St James, Warsaw (1909–23), by the leading Polish architect of the inter-war period, Oscar Sosnowski (1880–1939), whose Expressionist church of St Roche, Bialystok (1927–39) should be mentioned. (For the remarkable buildings in Wroclaw, formerly Breslau, of these years, see Max BERG and Hans POELZIG.) The *avant-garde* was less evident in Poland than in Bohemia during these years despite contact with Russian Constructivism, e.g. the Warsaw Sanatorium of 1931 by Helen and Szymon Syrkus (1900–1982 and 1893–1967). Since the Second World

War several Polish architects have made their name, e.g. Henryk Buszko (b.1924) in partnership with Aleksander Franta (b.1925) in Katowice, Wojciech Zablocki (b.1930), whose Sports Centre, Warsaw (1974), may be mentioned. The post-war rebuilding of the Old Town of Warsaw from 1948 to 1957 was a notable achievement in HISTORICAL RECONSTRUCTION.

**Polish parapet.** A decorative device consisting of a large-scale cresting of blind arcades, pinnacles, pyramids, etc., used to crown the façades and mask the roofs of many Polish buildings, notably the Cloth Hall at Cracow (1555) and Town Halls of Poznań (c.1550–61) and Culm (1567–97). It also occurs in Bohemia.

**Polk**, Willis Jefferson (1867–1924), *see* CURTAIN WALL; UNITED STATES ARCHITECTURE.

**Pollak**, Leopoldo (1751–1806). He was born and trained in Vienna, settled in Milan in 1775 and became an assistant to PIERMARINI. His masterpiece is the Villa Belgioioso Reale (1793), now the Galleria d'Arte Moderna, a very large and grand but strangely frenchified version of PALLADIO, with a rusticated basement, giant Ionic order, and lavish use of sculpture. He built villas near Milan and laid out their gardens in the English style, e.g. Villa Pesenti Agliardi, Sombreno (c.1800).

Meeks 1966; P. Mezzanotte, *Architettura neoclassica in Lombardia*, Naples 1966.

**Pollak**, Mihály (1773–1855), the leading Hungarian classicist, was born in Vienna. His father was an architect, and his stepbrother was Leopoldo POLLAK. He studied under his brother in Milan and settled in Budapest in 1798. His style is moderate, never *outré*, and not very personal. Occasionally he also used Gothic features (Pécs, or Fünfkirchen Cathedral, 1805 onwards). He built large private houses and country houses, but his *chefs-d'œuvre* are public buildings at Budapest, notably the Theatre and Assembly Room (completed 1832), the Military Academy (Ludoviceum, 1829–36), and the National Museum with its Corinthian portico and its splendid staircase (1836–45).

A. Zador, *M.P.*, Budapest 1960.

**Pollini**, Gino (1903–82), *see* FIGINI, Luigi.

**Polshek**, James Stewart (b. 1930). American architect, trained under L. KAHN but never belonged to the Philadelphia School. A sensitive response to context combined with remarkable versatility have marked his work from the early Teijin Research Institutes I and II in Tokyo and Osaka, Japan (1963–71), to his Rochester Riverside Convention Center, Rochester, NY (1980); 500 Park Avenue, New York (1980); Seamen's Church Institute, New York (1991); Arts Theatre Center, Yerba Buena Gardens, San Francisco (1993); Inventure Place, Akron, Ohio (1992–5); and the innovative Mashantucket Pequot Museum and Research Center, Mashantucket Pequot Reserve, Connecticut (1993–7). With H. Searing and G. Wright he published *Context and Responsibility* (New York 1988).

**Polychromy**. The ancient Greek use of many colours in architecture, especially on the exterior, was 'discovered' in 1830 by HITTORF, to the dismay of Greek purists. It was taken up in their own buildings by Hittorf and others, notably BINDESBØLL, DUBAN, LABROUSTE, KLENZE and SEMPER.

D. Van Zanten, *The Architectural P. of the 1830s*, New York 1977.

**Polygonal masonry**. Masonry composed of blocks of stone dressed to fit one another with irregular polygonal exposed faces, rather than rectangular ones as in ASHLAR masonry. If some of the edges are curved it is called 'curvilinear'.

**POMO**, *see* POST-MODERNISM.

**Pompeiian Style**. Of the few buildings erected in imitation of those unearthed at Pompeii and Herculaneum in the C18, that by GÄRTNER at Aschaffenburg, Germany (1841–6), is outstanding. The Pompeian Style is predominantly a decorative style derived from the frescoed rooms found at Pompeii which are marked by the use of rather flimsy architectural motifs of a fantastic kind and a preference for dark terracotta red colour, called 'Pompeiian red'. It became popular soon after Pompeii was discovered in the C18 and remained so into the C19. It is not to be confused with the similar 'Etruscan Style' invented by Robert ADAM, e.g. the Etruscan Room, Osterley Park, near London (1775).

P. Werner, *Pompeii und der Wanddekoration der Goethezeit*, Munich 1970.

**Pontelli**, Baccio (1450–92/4). Florentine architect who worked at Urbino 1479–82, then in Rome until 1492. His most important work was the fortifications at Ostia. The Cancellaria, Rome (*c.* 1485), and S. Pietro in Montorio, Rome (*c.* 1490), have been attributed to him.

G. de Fiore, *B.P. architetto fiorentino*, Rome 1963; Heydenreich 1996.

**Ponti**, Gio (1891–1979), Italian designer, architect, and also a painter and draughtsman in the twenties. His drawing reflects the style of the Vienna Secession (*see* OLBRICH), and his designs for porcelain of around 1925 may also be inspired by the Wiener Werkstätte. Ponti was a universal designer; his œuvre includes ships' interiors, theatrical work, light fittings, furniture and products of light industry. Much of his best work in these fields dates from after the war, e.g. the famous very delicately detailed rush-seated chair (1951). His fame as an architect rested for a long time on three buildings: the Faculty of Mathematics in the Rome University City, dated 1934 and one of the *incunabula* of INTER-NATIONAL MODERN architecture in Italy (though preceded by TERRAGNI's few buildings); and then the two twin office buildings (1936 and 1951) designed for the Montecatini Company, both in Milan. The first, with its subdued modernity and its elegant detail, was a pioneer work and very personal. Ponti's finest building is the Pirelli skyscraper in Milan (1955–8, with NERVI); the building is 135 m. (415 ft) high, a slender slab of curtain walling with the long sides tapering to the slenderest ends. His Villa Planchart, Caracas (1955), is also remarkable, as are his neo-Expressionist Taranto Cathedral and Denver Art Museum, Colorado. He published *In Praise of Architecture* (Milan 1957; New York 1960), and was for many years editor of the influential periodical *Domus*, which he founded.

L. L. Ponti, *G.P. The Complete Works*, London 1989.

**Ponzio**, Flaminio (1560–1613), official architect to Pope Paul V (Borghese), was able but rather unadventurous; he never developed far beyond the Late MANNERIST style in which he was trained. His most notable work is the Cappella Paolina in S. Maria Maggiore, Rome (1605–11), very richly decorated with sculpture and panels of coloured marbles and semiprecious stones. He also built the courtyard and loggia of Palazzo Borghese, Rome (1605–14), and the handsome Acqua Paolo fountain on the Janiculum (1610–14, with G. FONTANA). Early in the C17 he rebuilt, with a new dome, RAPHAEL and PERUZZI's S. Eligio degli Orefici, Rome.

H. Hibbard, *The Architecture of the Palazzo Borghese*, Rome 1962, and C. Maderno and *Roman Architecture 1580–1630*, London 1971; P. Waddy, *Seventeenth-Century Roman Palaces: Use and the Art of the Plan*, Cambridge, Mass. 1990.

**Pope**, John Russell (1874–1937), *see* UNITED STATES ARCHITECTURE.

**Pöppelmann**, Matthaeus Daniel (1662–1736). He was the architect of the Zwinger at Dresden, a Rococo masterpiece. He was born at Herford in Westphalia and settled in Dresden in 1686, being appointed Kondukteur in the Landbauamt in 1691, and eventually, in 1705, succeeding Marcus Conrad Dietze as Landbaumeister to the Elector of Saxony and King of Poland, Augustus the Strong. In 1705–15 he built the Taschenberg Palais in Dresden for the Elector's mistress. For a state visit in 1709 he built a temporary wooden amphitheatre which the Elector then decided to replace with a stone construction (the Zwinger) which could be incorporated in the great new royal palace which Pöppelmann was commissioned to design. In 1710 he was appointed Geheim Cämmeriere and sent off to study and gather ideas in Vienna and Italy. His designs for the palace show some influence from both the Viennese Baroque of HILDEBRANDT and the Roman Baroque of Carlo FONTANA. But the Zwinger itself could hardly be more original in general conception: a vast space surrounded by a single-storey gallery linking two-storey pavilions and entered through exuberant frothy gateways – the whole composition resembling a giant's Meissen table-centre. Only a section was ever built (1711–20; the Kronentor in 1713, the Wallpavillon in 1716. It was damaged in 1944 but is now rebuilt). The sculptural decoration was executed by Balthasar Permoser and the brilliance of the total effect is largely due to the successful collaboration between sculptor and architect. Pöppelmann's other buildings are far less exciting: the 'Indian' Wasserpalais at Schloss Pillnitz on the Elbe (1720–23) with CHINOISERIE roofs and painted figures of Chinamen under the eaves; the Bergpalais at Schloss Pillnitz (1724); Schloss Moritzberg, begun 1723, but executed under the direction of LONGUELUNE; and, from 1727 onwards, extensions to the Japanisches Palais in Dresden, executed under the direction of de BODT. His designs for the Dreikönigskirche in Dresden Neustadt (1732–9) were executed by Georg BÄHR. From 1728 onwards Pöppelmann collaborated with Longuelune in Warsaw on the designs for a vast new Saxon Palace of which only the central section was built (c.1730). His son Carl Friedrich (d.1750) succeeded him in Warsaw.

Hempel 1965; H. Heckmann, *M.D.P. (1662–1736) Leben und Werk*, Munich and Berlin 1972, and *M.D.P. und die Barockbaukunst in Dresden*, Berlin and Stuttgart 1986; H. Marx, *M.D.P. (1662–1736)*, Leipzig 1989.

**Poppyhead**. An ornamental termination to the top of a bench or stall-end, usually carved with foliage and fleur-de-lis type flowers, animals or figures. A poppyhead is in fact a FINIAL.

**Porch**. The covered entrance to a building; called a PORTICO if columned and pedimented like a temple front.

**Porphyry**. Strictly a hard igneous rock ranging in colour from green to red, but the term is usually restricted to a deep reddish-purple variety known as *porfido rosso antico*, found only on Mount Porphyrites in Egypt. It was quarried there from C4–3 BC but after 30 BC the quarries became Imperial Roman property and porphyry was reserved for imperial use,

being carved into columns and slabs for wall cladding as well as sarcophagi and smaller objects. The quarries went out of use in the C5 AD and porphyry has subsequently been rarely used in architecture except for discs cut from antique columns and set in walls etc., notably in COSMATI work and C15 Venice.

R. Delbrueck, *Antike Porphyrwerke*, Berlin 1932; S. B. Butters, *The Triumph of Vulcan*, Florence 1996.

**Porta**, Giacomo della (c.1533–1602). Italian MANNERIST architect of Lombard origin working in Rome, notable mainly as a follower of MICHELANGELO, whom he succeeded as architect of the Capitol. Here he finished the Palazzo dei Conservatori to Michelangelo's design with slight alterations (1578) and also built the Palazzo del Senatore (1573–98) with rather more alterations. He followed VIGNOLA as architect of the Gesú, Rome, designing the façade (1571–84), which was destined to be copied for Jesuit churches throughout Europe. In 1573–4 he became chief architect at St Peter's, where he completed Michelangelo's exterior on the garden side and built the minor domes (1578 and 1585) and the major dome (1588–90) to his own design. The large dome is his masterpiece, though it is rather more ornate and much nearer in outline to the dome of Florence Cathedral than Michelangelo's would have been. He also built the Palazzo della Sapienza (begun c.1575); S. Maria ai Monti (begun 1580); the nave of S. Giovanni del Fiorentini (1582–92); S. Andrea della Valle (1591, completed by MADERNO 1608–23); Palazzo Marescotti (c.1590), and the very splendid Villa Aldobrandini, Frascati (1598–1603).

V. Tiberia, *G. della P. Un architetto tra manierismo e barocco*, Rome 1974; Lotz 1996.

**Portal**. An imposing door or entrance,

notably in Romanesque and Gothic architecture when they were usually very richly sculptured, e.g. at Chartres and Reims Cathedrals.

**Portcullis**. A gate of iron or iron-reinforced wooden bars made to slide up and down in vertical grooves in the JAMBS of a doorway; used for defence in castle gateways.

**Porte-cochère**. A porch large enough for wheeled vehicles to pass through.

**Portico**. A roofed space, open or partly enclosed, forming the entrance and centrepiece of the façade of a temple, house or church, often with detached or attached columns and a PEDIMENT. It is called *prostyle* or *in antis* according to whether it projects from or recedes into a building; in the latter case the columns range with the front wall. According to the number of front columns it is called *tetrastyle* (4), *hexastyle* (6), *octastyle* (8), *decastyle* (10), or *dodecastyle* (12). If there are only two columns between pilasters or antae it is called *distyle in antis*. *See* Fig. 93.

**Porticus**. A room or porch leading off the central vessel of a medieval church.

**Portland cement**, *see* CEMENT.

**Portman**, John Calvin (b. 1924). American architect who revolutionized luxury hotel design with his Hyatt Regency Hotel, Atlanta, Georgia (1964–7). This has a spectacular sky-lighted ATRIUM with interior elevators overlooking a garden-like central space with sidewalk café, coffee shops, lounges, etc. which provide the animation of an open-air plaza. The formula was very successful and was followed all over the world as well as by Portman himself in his later Hyatt hotels, e.g. at O'Hare Airport, Chicago (1971); Embarcadero Center, San Francisco (1974); Westin Bonaventura Hotel, Los Angeles (1976); and Renaissance Center, Detroit (1977). In the 1980s he became an influential figure in urban planning following the publication of his and Jonathan Barnett's manifesto *The Architect as Developer* (1976), in which they pleaded for the entrepreneur-builder and against the architectural profession's over-specialization.

P. Riani, *J.P.*, Milan 1990.

**Portoghesi**, Paolo (b. 1931). Italian architect of eclectic taste who first took up Organic Architecture, as expounded by Zevi, and then a historicizing Post-Modernism. He is notable also as a historian of Italian Renaissance, Baroque and later architecture. His built work ranges from his early 'Organic' Casa Baldi, Rome (1959–61), to the more

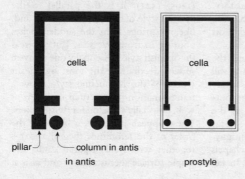

pillar — column in antis
in antis

prostyle

Fig. 93 Portico

freely eclectic Casa Papanica, Rome (1966–70), followed by the Chiesa della Santa Famiglia, Salerno (1969–74); ENEL residential building, Tarquinia (1980–87); and the controversial Post-Modern Islamic Mosque in Rome (1975–91).

C. Norberg-Schulz, *Architetture di P.P. e Vittorio Gigliotti*, Rome 1982; G. Priori, *Architettura ritrovata. Opere recenti di P.P.*, Bologna 1985; M. Pisani, *P.P. Opere e projetti*, Milan 1992.

**Portuguese architecture**. Until about 1500 Portugal participates in the development of Spanish architecture: there are Roman remains (temple at Évora); S. Frutuoso de Montélios is a C7 church on a Greek cross plan with horseshoe apses and domes, clearly inspired by Byzantium; Lourosa is MOZARABIC of 920; and the principal monuments of the Romanesque style also have their closest parallels in Spain. They are the cathedrals of Braga (begun *c.*1100) and Coimbra (begun after 1150), inspired by Santiago de Compostela, in the style of the so-called pilgrimage churches of France: high tunnel-vaulted naves, arcades and galleries, and no clerestory lighting. On the other hand, they have no ambulatories. Individual buildings of special interest are the Templars' church of Tomar of the late C12, with a domed octagonal centre and a lower sixteen-sided ambulatory, and the Domus Municipalis of Braganza, a low irregular oblong with rows of short arched windows high up.

The Romanesque style died hard; the cathedral of Évora (begun 1186) is still pre-Gothic. The Gothic style was introduced by the Cistercians, and the outstanding Early Gothic building is the abbey of S. Maria Alcobaça (1178–1252) on the pattern of Clairvaux and Pontigny, i.e. with ambulatory and radiating chapels forming an unbroken semicircle. Its tall rib-vaulted interior is one of the noblest of the order in all Europe. The monastic quarters are well preserved and very beautiful too. But Alcobaça is an exception; for, generally speaking, the Gothic style does not begin in Portugal until the mid C13. Among the most important buildings are a number of friars' churches (S. Clara, Santarém) and a number of cathedral cloisters (Coimbra, Évora, Lisbon – all early C14).

But Portuguese architecture comes properly into its own only with the great enterprise of Batalha, a house of Blackfriars commemorating the battle of Aljubarrota. It was begun in 1388 with a vaulted nave of steep Spanish proportions and an east end of the type peculiar to the Italian friars. But after 1402 a new architect appeared, called Huguet or Ouguete, who continued the work until 1438. He introduced a full-blown Flamboyant, i.e. a Late Gothic style mixed with many reminiscences of the English PERPENDICULAR. The façade, the vaults of the cloister and chapterhouse, and the chapel of João I are his work. He also began a large octagon with seven radiating chapels east of the old east end, but this was never completed. Here, as in the link with the old east end, the vaults are of complex English types. The climax of the Late Gothic in Portugal is the MANUELINE STYLE, named after King Manuel I (1495–1521). It is the parallel to the Spanish style of the Reyes Católicos and, like it, springs from the sudden riches pouring in from overseas. But whereas the Spanish style is essentially one of lavish surface decoration, the most significant works of the Manueline style show a transformation of structural members as well, especially a passion for twisted piers. These appear at Belém, a house of the order of the Jerónimos (begun 1502) – together with richly figured vaults and ample surface incrustation – and also at

Setúbal (1494–8). In addition there are the wildly over-decorated doorways and windows of Golegã and Tomar (1510 onwards). The portal to the unfinished east chapels of Batalha suggests East Indian inspiration. The leading masters were Diogo Boytac (*fl.*1490–1525), a Frenchman, at Setúbal and Belém, Mateus Fernandes (*fl.*1480–1515) in the portal of Batalha, and Diogo ARRUDA in the nave and windows of Tomar (1510–14).

But Tomar also contains the most important example in Portugal of the Italian Renaissance in its Roman Cinquecento forms. The building in question is the Great Cloister of the Cristo Monastery, Tomar (begun 1557), by Diego de TORRALVA. But, as in Spain, the Renaissance had arrived earlier and in playful Quattrocento forms. Among cathedrals the Cinquecento style is represented by Leiria (begun 1551), the work of Afonso Álvares (*fl.*1551–75). His nephew Baltasar (*fl.*1570–1620) designed the Jesuit church of Oporto (*c.*1590–1610) with its typically Mannerist, high and restless twin-tower façade. Also as in Spain, the Baroque was long in coming, but when it came it was less wild than in the neighbouring country; it influenced Brazil considerably (e.g. the Seminary at Santarém, 1676). The leading Baroque architects are João Turriano (1610–79) and João Antunes (1683–1734), and the most completely Baroque town is Aveiro. Octagonal and round plans are typical of Portuguese Baroque churches. The climax of the Baroque is well within the C18. It appears in the buildings of Niccolò NASONI (d.1773), a native of Italy – such as the palace of Freixo and several churches at Oporto, notably S. Pedro dos Clérigos (1732–50) – and the buildings of J. F. LUDOVICE (*c.*1670–1752), a native of Germany – such as the grand abbey of Mafra (1717–70) and the chancel of Évora Cathedral

(1716–46). His pupil VICENTE DE OLIVIERA designed the main block of the palace at Queluz (1747–52).

Opposition to the Baroque set in about the middle of the C18. There were two centres: Oporto, where the large hospital is by John CARR of York (designed 1796) and the Terceiros church has decoration inspired by Robert ADAM; and Lisbon, where rebuilding (to a plan) after the disastrous earthquake of 1755 was done on French principles. The most spectacular piece of the rebuilding is the Terreiro do Paço, the large square facing the Tejo. The whole area between the square and O Rocio was laid out by Eugenio dos Santos de Carvalho (1711–60) and is one of the most splendid surviving examples of C18 urbanism. Early C19 Portuguese architecture was dominated by several, not very distinguished, Italian architects; later C19 buildings are strongly Italian or French influenced, e.g. the Municipal Camera, Lisbon, of 1867–75, by Domingos Penente da Silva (1836–1901), and other public buildings in Lisbon by José Luis Monteiro (1849–1942), who had worked under BALLU on the rebuilding of the Hôtel de Ville, Paris. The metal structures by EIFFEL at Oporto and Lisbon – Ponte Maria Pia (1877) and Santa Justa Lift (1898–1901) – are exceptional.

In the conservative climate of pre-revolutionary C20 Portugal the tentative Modernism of the Igreja do Sagrado Coração de Jesus in Lisbon (1962–7) by Nuno Porta and Castelo Branco, and the sensitive AALTO-influenced buildings by Alvaro SIZA VIEIRA such as the Pinto e Sotto Mayor Bank in Oliveira de Azemeis (1971–4) were outstanding. Since 1974 Siza has designed several notable buildings including the internationally acclaimed Museum of Contemporary Galician Art, Santiago de Compostela, Spain (1988–94).

**Portzamparc**, Christian de (b.1944). French architect trained at the École des Beaux Arts, Paris. His evocative, romantic approach to architecture was seen first in his Château d'Eau, Marne-la-Vallée (1974), a converted water-tower with spiralling vegetation. This was followed by his soaring Piranesi-like 209 Logements, rue des Hautes Formes, Paris (1975–9) and the Conservatoire de Musique, Paris (1984). He made his name with the Cité de la Musique (1985–95) in TSCHUMI's Parc de la Villette, Paris, one of President Mitterrand's 'grands travaux', followed by his Crédit Lyonnais Tower, Lille (1992–5); the ZAC housing complex, Bercy, Paris (1991–4); and the LVMH Tower, New York (1995–8). He published *Christian de Portzamparc Architecte* (Paris 1984).

J. P. Dantec, *P.*, Paris 1995; S. Wright, *C. de P. Genealogy of Forms*, Paris 1996.

**Posokhin**, Mikhail N. (1919–89), *see* RUSSIAN ARCHITECTURE.

**Post**, George Browne (1837–1913). American architect who graduated in civil engineering and then worked in HUNT's office. He conducted his own practice from 1860 and started again after the war in 1868. Post was an eclectic, without commitment to any one style in particular. He was interested in structure and planning, and late in life was partly responsible for evolving the standard American hotel plan with a bath to every room, a system which is complete in the Statler Hotel at Buffalo (1911–12). He did a number of millionaires' residences (Cornelius Vanderbilt, 1889 and 1895) and several prominent office buildings in New York, notably the Equitable building of 1869–71 (the first with lifts, demolished), the high-domed Republic Bank for Savings (originally the Williamsburg Savings Bank), Brooklyn (1870–1905), the New York Produce Exchange

(1881–5, demolished *c*.1953), the New York Times and Pulitzer buildings (both 1889), the St Paul building (1897–9), which, with its twenty-two storeys, was the tallest in New York at that time, and the richly ornamented classical New York Stock Exchange (1904).

Condit 1961; Whiffen and Koeper 1981.

**Post**, Pieter (1608–69). Dutch architect who began as van CAMPEN's right-hand man at the Mauritshuis and Amsterdam Town Hall. He became a leading exponent of Dutch PALLADIANISM, an unpretentious, placid and economic form of Classicism, characterized by its use of brick with stone dressings and straightforward, almost diagrammatic use of pilasters. His masterpiece was the Huisten-Bosch near The Hague (1645–51; exterior ruined by C18 additions; interior decoration supervised by van Campen and C. Huygens), but the small Weighhouse at Leiden (1657), with its Tuscan pilasters on a rusticated base and supporting a simple pediment, is more typical. The Town Hall of Maastricht (begun 1659) is more ambitious. His style had great influence, and was later imported into England by Hugh MAY and others.

Kuyper 1980; J. J. Terwen and K. A. Ottenheym, *P.P. (1608–69)*, Zutphen 1993.

**Post and lintel construction**. An ancient and, structurally, the simplest type of construction: vertical members (columns, posts, piers or walls) support horizontal members (beams or lintels) as in Ancient Egyptian or Greek temples. *See also* TRABEATED.

**Postern**. A small gateway, sometimes concealed at the back of a castle, town or monastery.

**Post-Modernism**. A term coined in the 1940s but given currency by Charles

Jencks in the 1970s for the reaction, primarily in architecture but also in the decorative arts, to Modernism and to Modernism's rational, functionalist ideals associated with the Bauhaus. Pop Art had led the way in America towards an anti-rational, pluralist aesthetic and this encouraged eclectism of a brash, uninhibited kind favouring 'elements which are hybrid rather than pure' and 'messy vitality over obvious unity', as VENTURI wrote in 1966. Post-Modernism, or POMO as it was later called, emerged soon afterwards in the USA (GRAVES, MOORE), in Europe (BOFILL) and in Japan (ISOZAKI, TAKEYAMA, TANGE). Later the term was adopted by a variety of architects who had little in common apart from their opposition to Modernism and a tendency to relapse into pastiche, becoming almost the accepted style of late C20 capitalism until DECONSTRUC-TIVISM was promoted as an alternative.

C. Jencks, *The Language of P.M. Architecture*, London 1977; Klotz 1988; Frampton 1992; M. S. Larson, *Behind the P.M. Façade*, Los Angeles/London 1993; C. Jencks, *What is P.M.?*, London 1996.

**Posts**. In TIMBER-FRAMED buildings the main vertical timbers of the walls. In ROOF construction vertical timbers which carry longitudinal ones.

**Powell & Moya** (A. J. Philip Powell, b.1921, and John Hidalgo Moya, 1920–94), English architects, established themselves by winning the City of Westminster competition for the large housing estate in Pimlico, later named Churchill Gardens (1946). Moya also did the Skylon for the Festival of Britain, London, in 1951. The clarity, precision and directness of their style has been maintained in all their later work, such as the Mayfield School in Putney, London (1956), the ingenious sets for Brasenose College, Oxford (1956 onwards), the Princess

Margaret Hospital at Swindon, Wiltshire (1957 onwards), the Festival Theatre at Chichester, Sussex (1962), large additions to St John's College, Cambridge (completed 1967), Christ Church, Oxford (completed 1968), Wolfson College, Oxford (1974), and the London Museum (1976).

Maxwell 1972.

**Poyet**, Bernard (1742–1824), *see* FRENCH ARCHITECTURE.

**Pozzo**, Andrea (1642–1709). Erroneously known as 'Padre Pozzo', he was an Italian lay brother who entered the Jesuit order in 1665. Architect and painter, he was famous for illusionistic ceiling paintings, notably that in S. Ignazio, Rome (1691–4), and also those in the Chiesa della Missione, Mondovi (1676–7), and the Palais Liechtenstein, Vienna (1704–8). Born in Trento, he was trained in Milan and from 1681 worked in Rome (for a time in RAINALDI's studio) until 1702 when he settled in Vienna. He was extremely influential in the spread of the Baroque style from Italy to central Europe, through his engraved designs. His *Perspectivum pictorum et architectorum* (Rome 1693–1702) was frequently reprinted and had several foreign language editions as well. He designed the S. Ignazio altar in the Gesú, Rome (1697–8). His buildings are unexciting compared to his engraved designs. They include S. Ignazio, Dubrovnik (1699–1725), the Gesú and the interior of S. Maria dei Servi at Montepulciano (1702), the university church at Vienna (1705) and S. Francesco Saverio at Trento (begun 1708).

B. L. Kerber, *A.P.*, Berlin and New York 1971; Wittkower 1982; V. de Feo, *A.P. Architettura e illusione*, Rome 1988; F. de Feo and V. Martinelli, *A.P.*, Milan 1995.

**Prairie School**. Architectural movement in American Midwest between *c.*1900 and 1916, mainly in residential building. Inspired initially by SULLIVAN, it was given direction by Frank Lloyd WRIGHT. Horizontality, open plans and emphasis on the natural qualities of materials typified Prairie School buildings. After the first decade they became more varied and personal in expression and less local in scope, e.g. W. B. GRIFFIN. The landscape architect J. JENSEN developed a so-called Prairie Style of garden design.

H. A. Brooks, *The P.S.*, Toronto 1972.

**Prandtauer**, Jakob (1660–1726). Austrian architect, notably of Melk, Austria (1702–14), perhaps the most impressive of all Baroque abbeys. The church, with its undulating façade, many-pinnacled towers, and bold dome, is clasped between two long ranges of monastic buildings which stretch forward to form a courtyard. Prandtauer took every advantage of the unusually dramatic site above the Danube to create a picturesque group of buildings which seems to rise out of the rock. The interior of the church (completed by other architects) is rich and *mouvementé*, with an almost Gothic sense of height. Prandtauer's other works are less exciting: the church at Sonntagberg (1706–17), a smaller version of Melk; completion of CARLONE's church at Christkindl; the magnificent stairway (1706–14), entrance portal (1712) and Marble Hall (1718–24) at St Florian near Vienna; the priory of Dürnstein (begun 1717); the little hunting-lodge of Hohenbrunn (1725–9); alterations to the Gothic cathedral at St Pölten (1722) and town houses in St Pölten. He belonged to an ancient tradition of master masons and (unlike HILDEBRANDT) supervised every stage of the works entrusted to him. Close sympathy with his religious patrons is suggested by his buildings no less than by his personal piety. He was a member of a lay confraternity and contributed handsomely to the expense of building his parish church at St Pölten (1722) and town houses in St Pölten. He was succeeded at Melk by his nephew Josef MUNGGENAST.

R. Feuchtmuller in *J.P. und sein Kunstkreis*, exh. cat., Vienna 1960; Brucker 1983.

**Prang**. Thai term for a type of spire with a rounded top. The form derives from structures symbolizing Mount Meru above the sanctuaries of Indian and Khmer temples. But in THAI ARCHITECTURE the free-standing *prang* appears in Buddhist monasteries from the C13. The *prang* differs from a *chedi* (or STUPA) in that it has a small sanctuary for an image either at ground level or some way up and reached by external stairs. The most prominent example (mid-C19) is that of Wat Arun (Bangkok), encrusted with pieces of glazed pottery.

**Pratt**, Sir Roger (1620–85). An English gentleman amateur, learned and widely travelled, the most gifted of JONES's followers. His few buildings were very influential, but have all been destroyed or altered. At Coleshill, Berkshire (1650, now destroyed), Kingston Lacy, Dorset (1663–5, altered by BARRY), and Horseheath, Cambridgeshire (1663–5, destroyed), he invented the type of house later erroneously called the 'Wren' type. Clarendon House, London (1664–7, destroyed), was the first great classical house in London and was widely imitated and copied, e.g. at Belton House, Lincolnshire (1684–6). His role and importance have recently been questioned.

Summerson 1991; Colvin 1995; T. Mowl and B. Earnshaw, *Architecture without Kings. The Rise of Puritan Classicism under Cromwell*, Manchester 1995.

**Precast concrete**. Concrete components cast in a factory or on the site before being placed in position.

**Pre-Columbian architecture**, *see* MESOAMERICAN ARCHITECTURE; PERUVIAN ARCHITECTURE.

**Predock**, Antoine (b.1936). American architect trained in New Mexico and New York, the leading exponent of an ecologically oriented architecture with a strong sense of place and time. He goes beyond earlier regionalisms and contextualisms in responding not only to 'native' American traditions, such as the adobe architecture of the south-west, but to wider themes, even reaching out to the geological and cosmic. His concern with the ecosystem found notable expression in his Rio Grande Nature Center, Albuquerque, New Mexico (1982), which was followed by a series of remarkable buildings: Nelson Fine Arts Center, Arizona State University, Tempe (1986–9); Zuber House, Phoenix, Arizona (1986–9); Las Vegas Central Library and Children's Discovery Museum, Las Vegas, Nevada (1987–90); Hotel Santa Fé, Euro-Disney, Marne-la-Vallée, France (1992); American Heritage Center, Laramie, Wyoming (1987–93); Civic Arts Plaza, Thousand Oaks, California (1989–94); Ventata Vista Elementary School, Tucson, Arizona (1992–4).

B. Collins and J. Robbins, *A.P. Architect*, New York 1994.

**Prefabrication**. The manufacture of building components or whole buildings in a factory for subsequent assembly at the site. If the building is factory-assembled, requiring only connection to services on delivery to the site, it is called a *volumetric building*. The factory may be distant from the site, making complete buildings or complete units, e.g. bathroom pods, or it may be on or near the site making cladding panels or other building elements. Prefabrication began in the C19, PAXTON's Crystal Palace, London (1850–51), being the first notable instance though not recognized as such at the time. *See* INDUSTRIALIZED BUILDING.

B. Kelly, *The P. of Houses*, London/New York 1951; R. B. White, *P. A History of Its Development in Great Britain*, London 1965; G. Herbert, *Pioneers of P.*, Baltimore 1978.

**Prefabs**. Prefabricated bungalows erected in the UK under the Temporary Housing Programme 1944–8. Less than a third of the promised half-million were built, but they were popular. Exteriors were of concrete, asbestos sheeting or aluminium and they contained fully fitted bathrooms and kitchens, including refrigerators. Many are still in use.

D. Hard and C. Ward, *Arcadia for All*, London 1984; B. Vale, *P. A History of the UK Temporary Housing Programme*, London 1985.

**Prehistoric architecture**. The earliest evidence of building comes from the *c.*16,000–13,000 BC remains of oval and round huts constructed of mammoth bones and tusks, probably covered with animal skins or turf, on the Central Asian steppes, at Kostienki, near Voronez, Russia, and at Mezeric, Mezin and Moldova, Ukraine. There are less substantial *c.*12,000 BC remains of buildings with wooden posts supporting roofs of animal skins at Monte Verde, Chile. Round habitations up to 6 m. (20 ft) in diameter were built in France, partly of stone *c.*11,000 BC at Etoilles (Essonne) and of wood *c.*10,000 BC at Pincevent (Seine-et-Marne). Such palaeolithic structures, providing simple interior spaces with hearths, appear to have been occupied seasonally by nomads who otherwise sheltered in movable TENTS. When hunting and gathering was supplemented by agriculture in

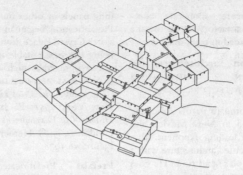

Fig. 94 Çatal Hüyük, Turkey (reconstruction drawing after Mrs G. Huxtable)

neolithic cultures, houses intended for permanent habitation were built in villages. Those of the Natufian culture, *c.*8000–6000 BC, were on curvilinear plans, e.g. at Muteybet, Syria; Haymonin and Mellaha, Israel. Houses on rectangular plans, subdivided internally with spaces for animals and storage as well as human habitation, were built of ADOBE, PISÉ, WOOD and sometimes a limited use of stone at Jericho, Jordan, *c.*7000 BC; at Bouqras, Syria, *c.*6400–5900 BC; at Çatal Hüyük, Turkey, *c.*6250–5500 BC, some including cult-shrines unknown elsewhere at this date (*see* Fig. 94); Dzejtun, Turkmenistan, *c.*5000 BC; Merimde, Egypt, *c.*4000 BC, where they were aligned on roads; Iblis, Iran, *c.*4000–3000 BC, some exceptionally large with several rooms on two storeys. (For proto-historical buildings in south and west Asia *see* INDIAN AND PAKISTANI ARCHITECTURE; SUMERIAN ARCHITECTURE.)

Housing was developed during the same millennia in China. At Banpo, near Xi'an, and at other sites in the north, the remains of farming communities reveal that from *c.*6000 BC round, oval and rectangular habitations with their floors sunk below ground level and construction confined to conical or pyramidal roofs of wood and thatch were sited facing streets, open spaces or larger communal buildings. In the marshy delta of the Yangzijang, notably at Hemdu, rectangular houses were built on wooden stilts with sophisticated mortice and tenon joinery *c.*5000–3400 BC. Japanese fishing and farming communities had semi-subterranean dwellings from *c.*3500 BC. Buildings on stilts with overhanging thatched roofs for habitation and grain storage were evolved by CI BC at Toro and provided the model for the Shinto temples at Ise, Japan.

Prehistoric architecture was predominantly domestic and its materials were mainly wood and earth, e.g. the neolithic LONGHOUSE. On the Atlantic coasts of Europe, however, large stones (MEGALITHS) were used from *c.*4000 BC to construct chamber-tombs, long passages sometimes with corbelled vaults, e.g. Newgrance, Eire; Barnenez off the coast of Brittany; and also stone circles in Brittany, England and Scotland. Exceptionally large megaliths supporting lintels were used for cult centres in England, notably Stonehenge (*c.*2100–2000 BC). At Skara Brae on the treeless island of Orkney a village of six or seven houses and workshops linked by covered alleyways was built entirely of local stone (*c.*2400–1800 BC). On the Mediterranean islands of Malta and Gozo temples on approximately oval or trefoil plans were built of regularly shaped slabs of limestone (*c.*3000–2000 BC).

For prehistoric architecture in the Americas *see* MESOAMERICAN ARCHITECTURE; PERUVIAN ARCHITECTURE.

**Presbytery**. The part of the church which lies east of the choir and where the high altar is placed.

**Preservation**, *see* HISTORICAL PRESERVATION.

**Prestressed concrete**. A development of ordinary REINFORCED CONCRETE by FREYSSINET from *c.*1926. The reinforcing steel is replaced by wire cables in ducts, so positioned that compression can be induced in the tension area of the concrete before it is loaded. This is done by stretching or tensioning the cables before or after casting the concrete. It results in more efficient use of materials and greater economy.

A. H. Allen, *P.C.*, London 1978.

**Preti**, Francesco Maria (1701–74), *see* PALLADIANISM.

**Price**, Bruce (1843–1903). American architect whose houses notably developed the loose open plans with ample verandas of the SHINGLE STYLE, e.g. The Craigs, Newport, RI (1879), and especially his houses at Tuxedo Park, New York, of the mid-1880s. Less interesting are his later Renaissance style skyscrapers in New York City.

**Price**, Sir Uvedale (1747–1829). English landscape gardening theorist, a friend of REPTON and R. P. KNIGHT, whom he joined in a revolt against the 'Capability' BROWN style. In reply to Knight's poem *The Landscape* he published a three-volume *Essay on the Picturesque* (1794), which defined the PICTURESQUE as an aesthetic category distinct from the Sub-

lime and the Beautiful as defined by Burke. His approach was more practical than Knight's and laid great stress on the need for landscape gardeners to study the works of the great landscape painters. He practised what he preached in the improvements of his own estate, Foxley, Herefordshire (where some of his plantings survive), and encouraged landowning friends to do likewise.

N. Pevsner, *Studies in Art, Architecture and Design*, vol. I, London 1968.

**Primaticcio**, Francesco (1504/5–70). Italian decorative painter and sculptor and, as such, head of the First School of Fontainebleau. His few buildings date from towards the end of his career, notably the Aile de la Belle Cheminée at Fontainebleau (1568) and the Chapelle des Valois at St Denis, largely built after his death by BULLANT and now destroyed.

Blunt 1982.

**Prince**, Bart (b.1947), *see* GOFF, Bruce.

**Principal**, *see* ROOF.

**Prior**, Edward Schroeder (1852–1932), *see* ARTS AND CRAFTS.

**Prix**, Wolf D. (b.1942), *see* COOP HIMMELBAU.

**Prodigy houses**. Recently coined term for a group of extravagant country houses built in England around 1600, e.g. Robert SMYTHSON's Wollaton Hall.

Summerson 1991.

**Profile**. The section of a MOULDING or, more generally, the contour or outline of a building or any part of it.

**Projection**. A geometrical drawing of a building in three dimensions, but not as seen in perspective; *see* AXONOMETRIC PROJECTION; ISOMETRIC PROJECTION.

**Promenade**. A paved public walk, usually shaded by trees, a feature of urban improvement from the C17, sometimes on obsolete city fortifications, especially in France and Germany (*see* BOULEVARD). It was a predecessor of the PUBLIC PARK. The Promenade de Peyrou, Montpellier, France (1683–93, extended 1765), was created as a formal garden for public enjoyment. The C19 development of coastal towns as seaside holiday resorts included the construction of promenades above and along the beaches, e.g. Promenade des Anglais, Nice.

**Pronaos**. The vestibule of a Greek or Roman temple, enclosed by side walls and a range of columns in front.

**Proportion**. In architecture, the relationship between the dimensions of a building and of its parts to the whole. A sense of good or harmonious proportions, like an ear for musical harmony, is acquired unconsciously from a cultural environment, but in many parts of the world proportions have also been determined mathematically in relation to geometrical figures. In Ancient Egypt from the 3rd millennium BC a cord with twelve units marked with knots, used to make right-angled triangles with sides 3:4:5, was adopted as the MODULE for plans and elevations. If numbers were endowed with occult significance – usually 3 and its multiples – ratios had symbolic significance. Babylonian concern with numerology and astronomy, especially the presumed orbits of related planets, appears to have determined the proportions of ZIGGURATS intended to reflect cosmic order. The Hebrew Bible records the divinely prescribed dimensions of Noah's Ark, the Tabernacle and Solomon's Temple, with simple ratios, 1:2, 2:3, 3:5. In India by the C6 BC rules had been laid down for the proportions of sacrificial altars. More complex systems were later devised for the construction of temples in the belief that they could function only if their proportions were in harmony with the mathematical basis of the universe. All measurements from overall plan and height to doorways and base mouldings were related to those of cult statues, as prescribed in such manuals as the C7 AD *Mansara Silpasastra*. But proportional systems may sometimes have been derived simply from aesthetic preferences, as in Japan where from the C14 the standard 1:2 *tatami* mat served as the module for the construction of Zen monasteries and domestic buildings.

In the West, visual proportions were related to aural harmony by the C6 BC Pythagorean philosophers, who observed that if two resonant strings are struck the difference in pitch is an octave when one is half the length of the other, a fifth when one is two-thirds the length of the other and a fourth when the relationship is 3:4. The consonance on which the musical system was based could thus be expressed by the progression 1:2:3:4, which contains the simple octave, fifth and fourth and also the composite consonances: octave plus fifth (1:2:3) and two octaves (1:2:4). This was the basis for the theory of cosmic order and harmony elaborated by Plato, who took into account irrational and incommensurable ratios, e.g. $\sqrt{2}$, and gave cosmological significance to the five regular solids (cube, tetrahedron, etc.) as forms of absolute beauty united by proportion. The principles of Greek geometry were given definitive statement *c*.300 BC by Euclid, who regarded them as exclusively philosophical without practical utility. And surviving buildings suggest that the notion of harmonic, as distinct from visually harmonious or pleasing, proportions had little direct influence on construction in Ancient Greece, the Hellenistic kingdoms or Ancient Rome. VITRUVIUS, who had access to Greek architectural treatises (lost

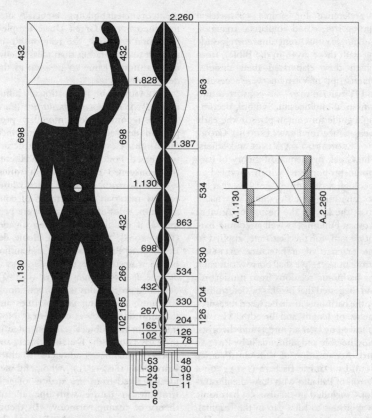

Fig. 95 Le Corbusier's Modulor

to us), recommended musical education for architects. But his concept of proportions was anthropomorphic: he likened the *symmetria* or harmonious relationship between the parts of a building to those of the human body, remarking that a well-formed man with arms and legs extended fits into the two perfect geometrical figures, circle and square – later to be called 'Vitruvian man'. Apart from his statement that a domed space should have the height of its diameter, he provided measurements only

for the ORDERS, ruling that the heights of the sturdy 'male' Doric column and the more slender 'female' Ionic column should be respectively six and eight times the diameter of the base or module. These rules were not, however, strictly observed in practice by Ancient Roman architects.

Ancient Greek notions of proportion, as of geometry in general, were preserved and developed in Islam and account for the recurrence of clearly defined ratios, especially 2:3, in mosque designs. In medieval Christendom architects showed a preference for simple geometrical figures, square and equilateral triangles, and simple ratios (sometimes corresponding with those given in the Bible), from which they elaborated their designs. Manuscripts of Vitruvius were accessible and 'Vitruvian man' was converted into a mystical microcosmic symbol, becoming a guide for church plans in the early Renaissance for FRANCESCO DI GIORGIO, LEONARDO DA VINCI and others. The Greek mathematical theory of harmonic proportions, which survived in theological literature, notably that of St Augustine and Boethius, was taken up as the key to the beauty of Ancient Roman buildings as well as cosmic harmony and, for the first time, applied to the practice of architecture. ALBERTI wrote in 1452: 'we shall borrow our rules for harmonic relations from musicians', and suggested that heights be determined by the harmonic mean between measurements of length and breadth. He was followed by later architects and theorists, most notably and influentially by PALLADIO. A translation of Vitruvius (Venice 1556) by Daniele Barbaro (1513–70), a patron of Palladio who drew the illustrations, included an excursus on harmonic proportions to fill a gap in the original. The subject continued to be discussed by e.g. Henry WOTTON, *Elements of Architecture* (London 1624), F. BLONDEL, *Cours d'architecture* (Paris 1675–83), R. MORRIS, *Lectures on Architecture* (London 1734), B. A. VITTONE, *Istruzione elementare* (Lugano 1760). It was, however, pointed out that mathematically calculated ratios are rarely apparent when a building is seen in perspective and are therefore irrelevant visually in architecture. And although Vitruvius was respected as the authority on classical architecture, his rules for the orders, as codified by SERLIO and VIGNOLA, were found to be at odds with the measurements of ancient buildings, especially after the discovery of Greek Doric temples. Structural exigence, the relationship of support to load, rather than ideas of cosmic harmony, came to be seen as the determining factor.

DURAND, in his internationally influential *Précis des leçons d'architecture* (Paris 1802), recommended modular proportions derived from the grid on which the plan and elevation of a single structure were based. For C19 architects and theorists, concerned mainly with historical styles and ornament or the potentialities of new materials and methods of construction, rules of proportion were peripheral if not irrelevant. Julien Guadet (1834–1908), teacher at the École des Beaux Arts, Paris, from 1872 and author of the magisterial textbook *Éléments et théories de l'architecture* (Paris 1901–4), described proportions as a 'compositional attribute', dismissing general rules and the musical analogy as chimerical. New interest in the subject was generated in the early C20 by the Dutch architect and teacher Johannes Ludovicus Mathieu Lauweriks (1864–1932), who combined ideas derived from the analysis of cell-structure in nature with the ancient theory of cosmic harmony. His theory was developed in the Netherlands by architects seeking a way out of historicism – BERLAGE, OUD, RIETVELD – and in Germany at the BAUHAUS. They also influenced LE CORBUSIER, who evolved a complex, Platonic but unmetaphysical theory published in two volumes as *Le Modulor* (Boulogne-sur-Seine 1948 and 1955), relating anthropomorphic dimensions to the GOLDEN SECTION, illustrated by the figure of a 2 m. (6 ft) man beside metric and British scales of measurement and a Fibonacci series of numbers, from which ratios could be derived (*see* Fig. 95). He had this image inset in the walls of his Unité d'Habitation, Marseille (1947–52), as a declaration of the proportional system underlying its design. At about the same time the Renaissance notion of harmonic proportions expounded in Rudolf Wittkower's *Architectural Principles in the Age of Humanism* (London 1949) stimulated young architects dissatisfied with FUNCTIONALISM.

P. H. Scholfield, *The Theory of P. in Architecture*, Cambridge 1958; Kruft 1994.

**Propylaeum**. The entrance gateway to an enclosure (usually temple precincts), as on the Acropolis at Athens.

**Propylon**. A free-standing classical gateway.

**Proscenium**. 1. In a Greek or Roman theatre, the stage on which the action took place. 2. In a modern theatre, the space between the curtain and orchestra, sometimes including the arch and frontispiece facing the auditorium.

**Prost**, Henri (1874–1959), *see* FORESTIER, J.-C.-N.

**Prostyle**. Having free-standing columns in a row, as often in a PORTICO.

**Prosthesis**. In Byzantine architecture, the room attached to or enclosed in the church and serving for the preparation and storage of the species of the Eucharist before Mass; generally used for the storage of the Eucharist after Mass.

**Proto-Renaissance**, *see* ITALIAN ARCHITECTURE.

**Prouvé**, Jean (1901–84). French architect and leading exponent of INDUSTRIALIZED BUILDING, he was trained as a metal craftsman in Nancy, where his father was a prominent Art Nouveau designer. A pioneer of the CURTAIN WALL, e.g. his Roland Garros Aeroclub, Buc (1936, dismantled 1940), Maison du Peuple, Clichy, Paris (1939), he

developed systems of metal cladding and replaceable wall components which were used by many architects, e.g. LE CORBUSIER, CANDILIS and notably NIEMEYER at the Communist Party Headquarters in Paris. His modifiable Maison du Peuple, Clichy (1937–9), and his housing estate of small units, made of aluminium, at Meudon (1949), were remarkable, as were his prefabricated 'Sahara' houses of 1958. His buildings could be very elegant, e.g. his Spa building at Évian of 1957. In 1953–8 he was associated with ZEHRFUSS and others at the gigantic CNIT building at La Défense, Paris, and in 1969, again with Zehrfuss, in the Unesco V building, Paris.

B. Huber and J. C. Steinegger, *J.P. Prefabrication – Structural Elements*, Zürich and London 1971; D. D. Clayssen, *J.P. L'Idée constructive*, Paris 1983; P. Sulzer, *J.P. (1901–1984)*, Tübingen 1993; C. Coley, *J.P.*, Paris 1993.

**Pseudo-dipteral**. In classical architecture, a temple planned to be DIPTERAL but lacking the inner range of columns.

**Pseudo-peripteral**. In classical architecture, a temple with porticos at either end and engaged columns or pilasters along the sides.

**Pteroma**. In a Greek temple, the space between the walls and colonnades.

**Pteron**. An external colonnade as in a Greek temple.

**Public park**. A PARK made for and usually maintained at the expense of an urban population. From the C17 public PROMENADES had been created in many European cities and royal parks were often made accessible to the public, e.g. London's St James's Park, Hyde Park and Kensington Gardens, called in the early C18 the 'lungs' of the city. The Prater just outside Vienna was designated a 'place for the pleasure of all men' by the emperor Joseph II in 1766. WATELET in 1774 suggested that French royal parks be opened to the public. And in 1785 HIRSCHFELD published proposals for new parks as places of recreation and moral improvement for all social classes. The first true public park, designed and created as such, was the Englischer Garten in Munich begun in 1789, see RUMFORD; SCKELL, Friedrich. In 1818 LENNÉ made proposals for a public park and his Friedrich-Wilhelm Park, Magdeburg (1824), was among the earliest to be realized. In 1840 the king of Prussia handed over Lenné's Tiergarten, Berlin, to the municipality who voted that year to create a VOLKSPARK as well for the working-class. Meantime in the USA, BIGELOW had designed in 1831 Mount Auburn Cemetery, Boston, as a landscape garden that could serve also as a place of quiet public recreation. In England, where LOUDON and others had been calling for public parks since the early C19, the first laid out at public expense were Victoria Park, Hackney, London, by PENNETHORNE (1842); Birkenhead Park, Cheshire, by PAXTON (1843–7) and three in Manchester (1845) by the landscape architect Joshua Major (1787–1866). These parks, created in heavily industrialized districts for the health, enjoyment and moral improvement of the inhabitants, impressed OLMSTED, who went on to design with VAUX the much larger Central Park, New York (planned 1858, begun 1863), the first of many in the USA, notably HALL's Golden Gate Park, San Francisco (1871–8). In France the transformation of Paris under Napoleon III, with HAUSSMANN in charge, included ALPHAND's conversion of the Bois de Boulogne into a public park (from 1853) and his creation of the Butte-Chaumont in an industrial district

(1864–9), followed by FORESTIER's parks in the late C19 and early C20.

By the end of the C19 most European and North American cities had public parks, and from the 1920s they increasingly included areas for athletics and sports, e.g. Bos Park near Amsterdam, conceived in 1928 by a team of landscape architects, botanists, zoologists, engineers and sociologists to include sports grounds, a hippodrome, a swimming-pool, a toboggan slope, a canal for rowing races and an open-air theatre as well as densely planted woodland and a wild nature reserve (begun 1934). Since the Second World War THEME PARKS have stimulated innovation, e.g. HAAG's Gasworks Park, Seattle, USA (begun 1973); LASSUS's Parc de la Corderie Royale, Rochefort-sur-Mer, France (begun 1988); LATZ's Hafeninsel, Saarbrucken (1979–89), and Duisberg Nord (begun 1991), both Germany, and Bernard TSCHUMI's Parc de la Villette, Paris (1983–95). The need for open spaces in cities has also been increasingly answered by PLAZAS and VEST-POCKET PARKS.

C. F. Chadwick, *The Park and the Town*, London 1966; H. Conway, *People's Parks: the Design and Development of Victorian Parks in Britain*, Cambridge 1991.

**Pückler-Muskau**, Hermann Ludwig Heinrich, Fürst von (1785–1871). German landscape architect and theorist. After visiting many late-C18 LANDSCAPE GARDENS in England he began in 1816 to lay out in the same style his own park at Muskau on the Prussian–Polish border, and later, after 1846, another smaller park at Branitz. His theoretical work *Andeutungen über Landschaftsgärtenerei* (Stuttgart 1834) helped to keep alive in Europe the style advocated by REPTON after it had fallen out of favour in England. In 1843 he succeeded LENNÉ at Babelsberg, Potsdam, and in 1852 he was called to Paris by Napoleon III to advise on the city's public parks and probably influenced ALPHAND's design for the Bois de Boulogne.

R. B. Ende and W. Herman, *Fürst P. und sein Gärten*, Dortmund 1995.

**Pueblo**. A communal dwelling, usually of ADOBE, built by Native Americans in the south-western USA, who were named after it. (*Pueblo* is Spanish for 'village'.) For thermal protection in the hot summer months they were often built in excavated hollows in cliff faces (as at the Anasazi village, Mesa Verde, Colorado, of *c*.1100) or, if on a plain, one above the other with thick mud-brick roofs (as at Taos, New Mexico). A pueblo is usually entered from above by means of ladders.

**Pugin**, Augustus Welby Northmore (1812–52). His father, Augustus Charles Pugin (*c*.1769–1832), came from France to London in 1792, became a draughtsman in the office of NASH and later a draughtsman and editor of books on Gothic architecture (*Specimens*, 1821 onwards; *Gothic Ornaments*, 1828–31). The son helped on these, but soon received decorative and then architectural commissions. He designed furniture for Windsor Castle when he was only fifteen years old and stage sets for the theatre (*Kenilworth*, 1831) before he was twenty. He found himself shipwrecked off the Firth of Forth in 1830, got married in 1831, lost his wife one year later, got married again in 1833, lost his second wife in 1844, got married once more in 1848, and lost his mind in 1851.

He had a passion for the sea, and, after his conversion to Catholicism in 1835, a greater, more fervent passion for Catholic architecture, which had to be Gothic of the richest 'Second Pointed', i.e. late C13 to early C14 in style. He leaped to fame and notoriety with his book *Contrasts* (1836), a plea for Catholicism illustrated

by brilliant comparisons between the meanness, cruelty and vulgarity of buildings of his own day – classicist or minimum Gothic – and the glories of the Catholic past. Later he wrote more detailed and more closely considered books (*The True Principles of Pointed or Christian Architecture*, 1841, etc.), and in them showed a deeper understanding than anyone before of the connections between Gothic style and structure and of the function of each member. From these books he even appears a founder father of FUNCTIONALISM, though this is true only with qualifications.

His buildings mostly suffer from lack of means. He was rarely allowed to show in stone and wood the sparkling lavishness he could achieve on paper. He was as interested in furnishings, altars, screens, stained glass, metalwork, as in the building itself. This is how BARRY got him to work for the Houses of Parliament, where not only the Gothic details of the façades but even such fitments as inkstands and hatstands were designed by Pugin (1844–55/6). He was a fast and ardent draughtsman. Perhaps his best churches are St Giles, Cheadle, Staffordshire (1841–6), the cathedral of Nottingham (1841–4), and St Augustine, Ramsgate (1845–51), which he paid for himself and which stands next to his own house. As against earlier neo-Gothic churches, Pugin's are usually archaeologically correct, but often have their tower asymmetrically placed, and this started the calculated asymmetry of most of the best English C19 church design.

P. B. Stanton, *A.W.N.P.*, London (1967) 1971; Pevsner 1972; H. M. Port, *The Houses of Parliament*, London 1976; Hitchcock 1977; P. Atterbury and C. Wainwright (eds.), *P.A. Gothic Passion*, London 1994.

**Puig i Cadafalch**, Josep (1869–1956), *see* SPANISH ARCHITECTURE.

**Puigdomènech**, Albert (b.1944), *see*
SPANISH ARCHITECTURE.

**Pullman**, George M. (1831–97), *see*
COMPANY TOWN.

**Pulpit**. An elevated stand of stone or
wood for a preacher or reader, which first
became general in the later Middle Ages
(the AMBO was used in the early Middle
Ages). Often elaborately carved, and
sometimes with an acoustic canopy above
the preacher called a *sounding board* or
TESTER. Occasionally found against the
outside wall of a church. The Anglican
*three-decker pulpit* combines a reading desk
and a clerk's stall with the preacher's
stand, one on top of the other.

**Pulpitum**. A stone screen in a major
church erected to shut off the choir from
the nave. It could also be used as a backing
for the return choir stalls.

**Pulvin**. In Byzantine architecture, a
DOSSERET above the capital supporting
the arch above.

**Pulvinated**. Convex in profile; a term
usually applied to a FRIEZE.

**Pumice** or **pumice stone**. A porous
lightweight igneous rock derived from
volcanic lava, used as an abrasive for
smoothing and polishing, also as an
absorbent. It was used by the Ancient
Romans as a building stone and also
occurs later in Byzantine and Romanesque structures.

**Purbeck marble**. A dark fossiliferous
limestone, called after the Isle of Purbeck,
Dorset. Not a marble but used as one on
account of its capacity to take a high
polish. In fashion in England from the
later C12 onwards and favoured particularly in the C13. Used for COMPOUND
PIERS in churches. Purbeck shafts in conjunction with shafts of normal limestone
give a striking effect of light and dark.
Also used for effigies all over England.

**Purlin**, *see* ROOF.

**Putlock holes**, **putlog holes** or
**putholes**. Holes in a wall to support
scaffolding during construction. They are
frequently left after construction is
finished. Putlocks or putlogs are the short
horizontal timbers which bear the
scaffolding boards.

**Pycnostyle**. With an arrangement of
columns set 1½ times their diameter apart.
*See also* ARAEOSTYLE; DIASTYLE;
EUSTYLE; SYSTYLE.

**Pylon**. In Ancient Egyptian architecture,
the rectangular, truncated, pyramidal
towers flanking the gateway of a temple;
also, more loosely, any high isolated
structure used decoratively or to mark a
boundary.

**Pyramid**. A term, probably of Ancient
Egyptian origin, used in Ancient Greece
for an Egyptian royal tomb and subsequently for a geometric solid of the
same form, i.e. with a square base and
sloping sides meeting at the apex. The
earliest type of royal tomb in Egypt was
a MASTABA; that of Zoser at Saqqara near
Cairo of *c*.2770 BC was heightened with
five solid units of decreasing size to form

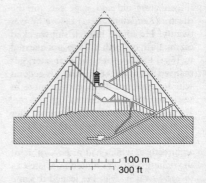

Fig. 96 Section of Great Pyramid of Khufu
(Cheops), Giza, Egypt

a STEP PYRAMID. The first true pyramids were built for Sneferu at Dashur (c.2720 BC), one broadly based with a 43° 36" inclination, the other – the 'bent pyramid' – with a 54° 15" inclination at the base changing about halfway up to 43°. The classic form, with a 52° inclination, was achieved in the largest, built for Khufu (or Cheops) and Khafra at Giza near Cairo c.2650–2590 BC, the former originally 148 m. (485 ft) high on a base 233 m. (764 ft) square, the other slightly less. That of Khufu (see Fig. 96) contains a system of passages and chambers reached from entrance shafts which were sealed after the body of the pharaoh or king was placed inside (an ineffectual attempt to prevent robbery); that of Khafra has a simpler interior arrangement of two passages leading to the burial chamber at the centre of the base. Both were originally surfaced with blocks of polished limestone which survive only at the apex of the pyramid of Khafra. Smaller pyramids were built for later rulers of the Old and Middle Kingdoms and also much later (c3 BC to AD c4) for the kings of Meroë in the far south.

Originally Egyptian pyramids did not stand in solitary isolation as they do today. Surrounded by a walled enclosure, they formed part of a complex of buildings offering chapels, mortuary temples, etc. Their purpose was to mark and protect the mummified body of the dead king secreted inside it, ensuring his eternal welfare, on which that of the kingdom was believed to depend. In the New Kingdom, however, the same form was adopted for private tombs. Later, pyramidal forms were used mainly for decorative effect or structural convenience. But their meaning and association with the afterlife survived in those built as MAUSOLEA in Rome, where that of Caius Cestius (d.12 BC) was probably the source of inspiration for the many constructed from

the C18 in Britain, Germany and North America.

The term pyramid is also loosely applied to similarly tapering but usually terraced or stepped structures, notably in MESOAMERICAN ARCHITECTURE, built as temple substructures (not tombs), with steps up to the platform carrying the temple building as at Teotihuacan, Mexico (AD C1–7), or at Tikal, Guatemala (before AD 800).

I. E. S. Edwards, *The P. of Egypt*, Harmondsworth (1947) 1985; A. Fakhry, *The P.*, Chicago 1969; W. S. Smith (rev. W. K. Simpson) 1981; R. Stadelmann, *Die Ägyptischen P.*, Mainz 1985; P. Hodges, *How the P. Were Built*, Shaftesbury 1989.

**Pythius** (*fl.*353–334 BC). Architect and theorist working in Asia Minor. With Satyros he designed and wrote an account of the most famous and elaborate sepulchral monument of antiquity, the richly sculptured Mausoleum built for the Carian satrap Mausolos at Halicarnassus and numbered among the seven wonders of the world (begun before 353 BC and finished after 350; sculptured fragments now in the British Museum). He was also the architect of the large temple of Athena Pollas at Priene (dedicated 334; fragments now in Berlin and in the British Museum) in which the Ionic order was thought to have achieved its canonical form. In a treatise on this building (known to Vitruvius but now lost) he extolled the perfection of its proportions, criticized the Doric order and, apparently for the first time, recommended a wide training for the architect who, he said, 'should be able to do more in all the arts and sciences than those who, by their industry and exertions, bring single disciplines to the highest renown'.

Lawrence 1996.

# Q

**Qasr**. In Islamic architecture a castle, palace or mansion.

**Qavam Al-Din Shirazi** (d.1438), *see* UZBEK ARCHITECTURE.

**Qibla**. The direction in which every Muslim must turn when praying. Originally Jerusalem, but in 624 Mohammed changed it to the Black Stone in the Ka'ba in Mecca. In MOSQUES it is indicated by the qibla wall, usually with one or more MIHRABS.

**Quadrangle**. A rectangular courtyard enclosed by buildings on all sides and sometimes within a large building complex. The arrangement is often found in colleges and schools.

**Quadrant**. A quarter of a circle. A quadrant moulding is a quarter-round moulding (*see* OVOLO). In urban planning a quadrant is a street or space of similar form.

**Quadratura**. *Trompe l'œil* architectural painting of walls and ceilings. In the C17 and C18 it was frequently executed by travelling painters who specialized in it and were known as *quadraturisti*.

**Quadrifrons**. A four-arched structure, often placed by the Ancient Romans at an intersection of right-angled thoroughfares. It was usually on a square plan.

**Quadriga**. A sculptured group of a chariot drawn by four horses, often used to crown a monument or façade.

**Quadripartite vault**, *see* VAULT.

**Quarenghi**, Giacomo (1744–1817). Italian architect much admired and patronized by Catherine II of Russia. Born near Bergamo, he went to Rome in 1763 to study painting, but soon turned to architecture. He designed the interior of S. Scolastica, Subiaco (1770–76), in a light, elegant vein of neo-classicism. In 1779 he accepted an invitation to St Petersburg, where he spent the rest of his life. His first important building is the English Palace, Peterhof (1781–9, destroyed), a sternly aloof Palladian house with no decoration apart from a vast projecting portico on one side and a recessed loggia on the other. He employed a similar formula for the State Bank (1783–90) and the Academy of Sciences (1783–9), both in St Petersburg. The Hermitage Theatre, St Petersburg (1783–7), is smaller and richer. His later work is more accomplished and excellent in its precision and clarity of mass, e.g. Imperial Pharmacy, St Petersburg (1789–96), Yusopov Palace, St Petersburg (begun 1790), Alexander Palace, Tsarskoe Selo (1792–6), the Riding School (1805–7) and Smolny Institute (1806–8), both in St Petersburg.

Hamilton 1983; M. F. Kovsunova, *G.Q.*, Bergamo 1986; V. Zanella, *G.Q. Architetto a Pietroburgo. Lettere e altri scritti*, Venice 1988.

**Quarry** or **quarrel**. A small, usually diamond-shaped pane, or a square one placed diagonally, with which medieval leaded windows were glazed. The term can also apply to any small quadrangular opening in the TRACERY of a window. The word probably derives from the French *carré*. Various devices and patterns were painted on quarries, particularly during the Perpendicular period. The lead supports are called *cames*.

**Quarry faced**. Ashlar left as it comes from the quarry, squared off only for the joints. *See also* RUSTICATION.

**Quatrefoil**, *see* FOIL.

**Queen Anne architecture**. Period of English architecture typified by the sensible, plain brick domesticity of Queen Anne's reign (1707–14).

**Queen Anne Revival Style**, *see* SHAW, Richard Norman; NESFIELD, William.

**Queen-post**, *see* ROOF.

**Quincunx**. An arrangement of five verticals, with four at the angles of a rectangle and the fifth in the centre. The term is also applied to a Christian (usually Byzantine) church on a CROSS-IN-SQUARE plan with a central dome, four rectangular bays covered by barrel vaults and four smaller bays covered by domes at the angles of the cross.

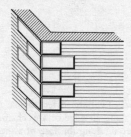

Fig. 97   Quoins

**Quirk**. A sharp V-shaped incision in a moulding and between mouldings.

**Quoins**. The dressed stones at the corners of buildings, usually laid so that their faces are alternately large and small. From the French *coin* (corner). *See* Fig. 97.

**Quonset hut**. A prefabricated portable hut with a semicircular roof of corrugated metal that curves down to form walls. Named after Quonset, Rhode Island, USA, where it was first made.

# R

**Rabbet** or **rebate**. A rectangular recess made along an edge or any channel or groove cut along the face of a piece of stone, wood, etc., so as to receive a tongue or edge of another piece.

**Rabirius** (*fl.*AD 81–96). Roman architect who, according to Martial, was employed by Domitian to build the palace on the Palatine in Rome which became the permanent residence of Roman emperors (the word palace is derived from it) and was still in use in the late C6. Enough survives to reveal the grandeur of this vast building or complex of buildings, erected on two levels of the hill and incorporating a hippodrome, libraries and courtyard gardens as well as innumerable state and private apartments. It was both a symbol of the Emperor's power and a perfect setting for the ceremony of his court (poets were quick to associate the several domes above the official rooms with the arc of the heavens). With its rich decorations and many fountains splashing in marble-lined courtyards it was the epitome of luxurious opulence. He has been credited with many other buildings, without evidence, but was probably responsible for Domitian's villa near Albano, of which little survives.

MacDonald 1965; Ward-Perkins 1981.

**Radburn planning**. A planning idea conceived in the United States after the First World War by a group including Lewis MUMFORD, Clarence STEIN, Henry Wright (1878–1936), and others. It was first tried out at Radburn, New Jersey, in 1929, which was intended to be a self-contained new town (not a com-

muter suburb as it became). The main object of the plan is the complete segregation of traffic and pedestrians. Areas known as superblocks, containing a complex of houses, shops, schools, offices, etc., around a central green or pedestrian space, are ringed by roads from which cul-de-sac service roads provide access. All paths and walks linking the blocks with each other and the town centre pass over or under the roads. Examples of towns planned under some such system are Vällingby, near Stockholm, and Cumbernauld, one of the NEW TOWNS in Scotland.

D. Schaffer, *Garden Cities of America: The R. Experience*, Philadelphia 1982.

**Radiating chapels**. Chapels projecting radially from an AMBULATORY or APSE. *See also* CHEVET.

**Raft foundation**, *see* FOUNDATION.

**Rafters**, *see* ROOF.

**Raggle**. A groove cut in masonry, e.g. to receive the edge of a roof.

**Ragstones**, *see* RUBBLE MASONRY.

**Raguzzini**, Filippo (*c*.1680–1771). The most original and spirited Rococo architect in Rome, where he built the hospital and church of S. Gallicano (1725–6) and Piazza di S. Ignazio (1727–8). The latter is a masterpiece of scenic town planning.

D. T. Metzger, *Piazza S. Ignazio, Rome, in the Seventeenth and Eighteenth Centuries*, London 1981; M. Rotili, *F.R. nel terzo centenario della nascità*, Naples 1982.

**Rail**. A horizontal member in the frame of a door, window, panel, etc.

**Rainaldi**, Carlo (1611–91), was born and lived in Rome. Son of a minor architect, Girolamo Rainaldi (1570–1655), he came into his own only after his father's death. He evolved a typically Roman grand manner notable for its lively scenic qualities and for its very personal mixture of MANNERIST and north Italian features with the High Baroque style of his great contemporaries, especially BERNINI. With his father he began S. Agnese in Piazza Navona, Rome, on a conservative Greek cross plan in 1652, but was dismissed in the following year when BORROMINI took over the work. His principal buildings are all in Rome – S. Maria in Campitelli (1663–7); the façade of S. Andrea della Valle (1661–5); the exterior apse of S. Maria Maggiore (1673); and the artfully symmetrical pair of churches in Piazza del Popolo, S. Maria in Monte Santo and S. Maria de' Miracoli (1662–79), which punctuate the beginning of the three main streets radiating into the centre of the city (Bernini replaced him as architect of the former in 1673).

Wittkower 1982.

**Rainwater head**. A box-shaped structure of metal, usually cast iron or lead, and sometimes elaborately decorated, in which water from a gutter or parapet is collected and discharged into a down-pipe.

**Raje**, Anant (b.1929), *see* INDIAN AND PAKISTANI ARCHITECTURE.

**Ramée**, Joseph-Jacques (1763–1842). French landscape architect, trained as an architect under BÉLANGER. In 1790 he designed the monumental altar for the Fête de la Fédération in Paris. Later, as a Royalist, he emigrated to Germany and in 1811 to the USA, where he planned in 1813 the landscape setting for Union College, Schenectady, NY, the first CAMPUS in America, and went on to design the layouts of Parishtown in upstate New York and several informal private parks. In 1816 he returned to Europe and illustrated his work, of which little survives, in *Jardins irreguliers, maisons de campagne de tous genres et de toutes dimensions* (1823) and *Parcs et Jardins composées dans differens contrées de l'Europe et des Etats Unis d'Amérique* (1830).

P. V. Turner, *J.R. International Architect in the Age of Revolution*, Cambridge 1996.

**Ramirez Vazquez**, Pedro (b.1919), *see* MEXICAN ARCHITECTURE.

**Rammed earth construction**, *see* PISÉ.

**Ramp**. 1. A slope joining two different levels. 2. Part of a staircase handrail which rises at a steeper angle than normal, usually where winders (*see* STAIR) are used.

**Rampart**. A stone or earth wall surrounding a castle, fortress or fortified city for defence purposes.

**Ramping arches**. Arches which are made asymmetrical to follow the ramp of a staircase.

**Ramsey**, *see* WILLIAM OF RAMSEY.

**Random ashlar**. Masonry composed of rectangular stones set without continuous joints.

**Ransome**, Ernest Leslie (1844–1917). Emigrated to the USA in 1869 from England, bringing a CONCRETE patent with which he pioneered reinforced concrete construction in America, notably at the Pacific Coast Borax Factory, Bayonne, NJ (1897–1903), and the United Shoe Machinery Plant, Beverley, Massachusetts (1903–5). The latter was the first mature example of a large factory of reinforced concrete construction, contemporary with Albert KAHN's Packard Motor Car Company Factory, Detroit

(1905), and the great GRAIN ELEVATORS. Collins 1959; Banham 1986.

**Raphael** (Raffaello Sanzio, 1483–1520). The greatest exponent of High Renaissance Classicism in architecture as well as in painting. His buildings are few, but they quickly took their place beside Ancient Roman buildings and the late works of BRAMANTE as architectural models. Though he owed much to Bramante, his style is sweeter, softer and simpler. Born in Urbino, he was trained as a painter under Pietro Perugino at Perugia. An early painting of *The Betrothal of the Virgin* (1504, Brera Gallery, Milan) is dominated by a domed building, which reveals an exquisite sensitivity to architecture and a particular interest in centrally planned structures. In 1508 he settled in Rome, where he was almost immediately employed by Pope Julius II to paint the Stanza della Segnatura in the Vatican, including *The School of Athens* with its wonderful architectural perspective of coffered vaults. His first building was S. Eligio degli Orefici, Rome (designed *c.*1511–12, construction begun 1514). The dome was begun, probably under PERUZZI, in 1526 and completed in 1542: but the whole church was rebuilt, with a new dome, by Flaminio PONZIO in the early C17). He designed the Palazzo Bresciano-Costa, Rome (*c.*1515, now demolished), the Palazzo Pandolfini, Florence (*c.*1517, but executed by Giovanni Francesco Sangallo and, after 1530, by Aristotile Sangallo) and Palazzo Branconio dell'Aquila (Rome 1518–20, demolished). These derive from Bramante's Palazzo Caprini with notable variations, e.g. unbroken horizontal lines of rustication on the basement, and at Palazzo Costa alternate triangular and segmental pediments above the windows on the first floor, between clusters of three pilasters. (Palazzo Vidoni-Caffarelli,

Rome, of *c.*1525 has often been attributed to Raphael but is not by him.)

In 1515 he was appointed Superintendent of Roman Antiquities and probably proposed a scheme (also attributed to Bramante) for measuring and drawing all the Roman remains and restoring a large number of them. The most notable result of his archaeological interests was the design for Villa Madama, Rome (begun 1517, but never completed), with a circular courtyard and numerous apsed and niched rooms inspired by the Roman *thermae* and Pliny's description of his villa at Laurentium. It greatly impressed PALLADIO. The only part completed was decorated with exquisitely subtle stucco reliefs and GROTESQUE paintings by Giovanni da Udine and GIULIO ROMANO, who worked in his studio and may have assisted in some of his architectural designs also. Raphael here re-created the elegance of Roman interior decoration as effectively as Bramante had reproduced the solemnity and monumental grandeur of Roman architecture. He was appointed architect of St Peter's (1514) with Fra GIOCONDO and A. da SANGALLO, and drew up a basilican variant to Bramante's plan. His centrally planned Chigi Chapel in S. Maria del Popolo, Rome, of *c.*1513 onwards, represents his reply to Bramante's more restricted view of ancient architecture. The chapel was completed, with some modifications, by BERNINI.

C. L. Frommel, *R. architetto*, Rome 1984; C. L. Frommel *et al.*, *R. Das architektonisch Werk*, Stuttgart 1987; Lotz 1996.

**Rastrelli**, Bartolomeo Francesco (Varfolomey Varfolomeevich, 1700–1771). Italian architect, the leading exponent of the 'Petersburg Baroque' period. He came to Russia from France at fifteen with his father, Bartolomeo Carlo (*c.*1675–1744), a sculptor and occasional architect, and both settled there. Rastrelli probably studied in Paris but dates and details are unclear. His first independent buildings date from the 1720s; the earliest to have survived (1730s) were for Biron (Bühren) at Mitau (Yelgava, Latvia). Thereafter follow twenty years of uninterrupted work on a series of major commissions, mostly for the Empress Elizabeth, during which Rastrelli as chief court architect headed a large *atelier* of architects and designers, and the characteristic features of 'Rastrellian Baroque' – which had repercussions far beyond St Petersburg – were established. The chief surviving works are St Andrew's church, Kiev (1747–67, realized by I. Michurin); extensions and remodelling of Peterhof (1745 onwards); the Vorontsov and Stroganov palaces, St Petersburg (1750s); the *ensemble* of the Smolny Cathedral (1748–57) and Convent, St Petersburg (not realized as originally planned – a belfry was intended); the Great Palace of Tsarskoe Selo, now Pushkin (1749–52), incorporating CHEVAKINSKY's palace; and finally the Winter Palace, St Petersburg (1754–62).

Most of his interiors, Rococo in spirit, have been lost or altered. His exteriors, exuberant as they are with their colourwashed stucco, rhythmically massed columns and delicate fenestration, nevertheless have the solid monumentality of the High Baroque rather than the curvilinear lightness of true Rococo. The origins of his style, variously attributed to France, Italy, south Germany and Russia, are still obscure: his lesser works have affinities with FISCHER VON ERLACH's domestic buildings. His grander commissions achieve a uniquely Russian synthesis: gigantic as they are, they are cheerful rather than overwhelming. The modest three storeys of the Winter Palace set a ceiling on subsequent St Petersburg building that has helped to preserve the city's remarkable visual wholeness.

With the rejection of his plans for the Market Building (Gostiny Dvor) in St Petersburg in 1761 (*see* VALLIN DE LA MOTHE), Rastrelli's dominance in Russian architecture was abruptly terminated and a new generation of neo-classically orientated architects associated with the Academy of Arts (founded 1759) swept his influence away in the subsequent reign of Catherine. His last years were embittered by an unsuccessful search for commissions. [R. R. Milner-Gulland]

M. Orsyannikov, *F.B.R.*, Leningrad 1982; Hamilton 1983.

**Ratha**. A Hindu monolithic, rock-cut temple, notably in south India, e.g. the Bhima Ratha and Dharmaraja Ratha of 630–70 at Mamallapuram. *Ratha* means literally a 'car' or 'chariot', which they sometimes resemble.

**Rationalism**. Italian movement led by the 'Gruppo 7' founded in 1926 by FIGINI, POLLINI, TERRAGNI and a few others, notably Marcello Piacentini (1881–1960), and expanded in 1928 by Giuseppe Pagano (Pogatschnig, 1896–1945), Edoardo Persico (1900–1936) and others to form MIAR (Movimento Italiano per l'Architettura Razionale). Its ostensibly 'modern' programme derived partly from SANT'ELIA's Futurist projects. Terragni was its outstanding exponent with the Novocomun apartments and the Casa del Fascio at Como, but the movement foundered in its alliance with Fascism, which led to the eclecticism of Piacentini's buildings for Rome University (1932) and eventually to the nationalistic and reactionary monumentality of the buildings for the 1942 Universal Exhibition, now EUR, Rome.

E. Mantero (ed.), *Il R. italiano*, Bologna 1984; R. A. Etlin, *Modernism in Italian Architecture 1890–1940*, Cambridge, Mass.

1989; T. Schumacher, *Surface and Symbol. G. Terragni and the Italian R. Movement*, Princeton 1990.

**Rauch**, John (b.1930), *see* VENTURI, Robert.

**Ravelin**. In military architecture, an out-work formed of two faces of a salient angle and constructed beyond the main ditch and in front of the CURTAIN WALL.

**Raymond**, Antonin (1889–1976). American architect who emigrated in 1910 from Prague, where he was trained under Otto WAGNER. From 1912–20 he worked for F. L. WRIGHT, latterly on the Imperial Hotel, Tokyo, Japan, where he settled and played a notable part in introducing the International Style with his own house in Reinanzaka, Tokyo (1924); the Rising Sun Petroleum Co. Building, Yokohama (1926); the Tokyo Golf Club, Saitama (1930); Akaboshi House (1932) and Kawasaki House (1934), Tokyo. In 1937 he went to India, where his dormitories for the Sri Aurobindo Ashram, Pondicherry (1938), are notable. During the Second World War he worked in the USA but returned to Japan in 1949 and built the Reader's Digest Building, Tokyo (1951, demolished 1964), the first outstanding post-war building in Japan together with SAKAKURA's Museum of Modern Art, Kamakura (1951). In 1953 he abandoned Western architectural forms in favour of traditional Japanese vernacular features such as exposed logs, e.g. his own house at Azuba. Later his St Anselm Meguro Church, Tokyo (1956), and Gumma Music Center, Takasaki (1961), exploit modern materials, the latter with folded reinforced concrete zigzag walls. He published *An Autobiography* (Rutland, Vermont 1973).

**Raymond du Temple** (active *c.*1360–1405). French master mason to Charles V and Charles VI (Maître des Œuvres de Maçonnerie du Roi). He was held in high esteem. The king made presents to him and was godfather to a son of his. In 1363 he became master mason at Notre Dame. In 1367–70 he built the Chapel of the Célestins, of which some outstanding sculpture is now in the Louvre. In the seventies the Vis du Louvre, the famous external spiral staircase, was added by him to the Louvre. In 1387 he contracted to build the Collège de Beauvais, a university college in Paris. He was also active in the country.

Ph. Henwood in *Bulletin de la Société de l'histoire* 105, 1978/9.

**Rayonnant**. The Gothic style prevailing in France from *c.*1230 to *c.*1350, named after the radiating arrangement of lights in rose windows. Ste Chapelle, Paris (1241–8), epitomizes the style.

Branner 1965.

**Rear arch**. The arch on the inside of a wall spanning a doorway or window opening.

**Rear vault**. The small vaulted space between the glass of a window and the inner face of the wall, when the wall is thick and there is a deep SPLAY.

**Rebate**, *see* RABBET.

**Rechter**, Yacov (b.1924), *see* ISRAELI ARCHITECTURE.

**Rechter**, Ze'ev (1899–1960), *see* ISRAELI ARCHITECTURE.

**Redan**. A small RAVELIN.

**Redman**, Henry (d.1528), was the son of the master mason of Westminster Abbey, London, and is first found working there in 1496. He succeeded his father at the Abbey in 1516 and also worked for the king, holding the post of King's Master Mason from 1519, jointly with William VERTUE, and in the end alone. He was called in with Vertue for an opinion at

King's College Chapel, Cambridge, in 1509, and again appears with him at Eton for the design of Lupton's Tower in 1516. He was also Cardinal Wolsey's architect, and may have designed Hampton Court. At Christ Church, Oxford (Cardinal College), he was, jointly with John Lebons or Lovyns, in charge from the beginning (1525).

Harvey 1984.

**Redoubt**. A detached outwork of a fortification.

**Reeding**. Parallel convex mouldings of equal width, touching one another, the inverse of FLUTING. The fluting of the lower third of column shafts was sometimes infilled with reeding to strengthen them.

**Re-entrant corners**. Corners with angles pointing inwards.

**Refectory**, *see* MONASTERY.

**Régence Style**. The first phase of French ROCOCO, e.g. interior of the Palais Royale, Paris (1716–20) by Gilles-Marie Oppenord (1672–1742); AUBERT's Hôtel de Lassay, Paris (*c*.1728).

**Regency architecture**. A modern and imprecise term for the predominant style in English architecture from the 1790s until the early Victorian 1840s, its most notable exponents being Henry HOLLAND and John NASH whose Regent Street and Regent's Park developments in London epitomize it. Strictly, the term should be reserved for the style current between 1811, when George, Prince of Wales, became Regent, and 1820 when he succeeded as George IV (or 1830 when he died), but these dates are without architectural significance.

S. Parissien, *R. Style*, London 1992; J. Morley, *R. Design 1790–1840 Gardens, Buildings, etc.*, London 1993.

**Reginald of Ely** (d.1471). First master mason, and so probably the designer, of King's College Chapel, Cambridge (begun 1446). However, his design did not include the present fan vaulting; it seems that he intended a lierne vault (*see* VAULT) instead. Reginald in all probability designed Queens' College too (1446 onwards), and perhaps the archway of the Old Schools (begun 1470), now at Madingley Hall.

Harvey 1984.

**Regulus**. The short band between the TENIA and GUTTAE on a Doric ENTABLATURE.

**Reichlin**, Bruno (b.1941), *see* SWISS ARCHITECTURE; NEO-RATIONALISM.

**Reidy**, Affonso Eduardo (1909–64), *see* BRAZILIAN ARCHITECTURE.

**Reinforced concrete**. Since concrete is strong in compression and weak in tension, steel mesh or rods are inserted to take the tensile stresses which, in a simple beam, occur in the lower part; the concrete is thus reinforced. Also called *ferro-concrete*, introduced by Joseph Monier in 1849. It resists fire better than naked metal, hence its importance in SKYSCRAPER and SHELL construction. *See* CONCRETE.

J. Faber and D. Alsop, *R.C. Simply Explained*, London 1979; A. Allen, *R.C. Design to BS 8110*, London 1988.

**Reinhardt**, Fabio (b.1942), *see* SWISS ARCHITECTURE; NEO-RATIONALISM.

**Relieving arch**, *see* ARCH.

**Renaissance**. The Italian word *rinascimento* (rebirth) was already being used by C15 Italian (i.e. Renaissance) writers to indicate the restoration and reintroduction of Ancient Roman standards and motifs, notably the ORDERS. Today the term means, first of all, Italian art and architecture from *c*.1420 (BRUNELLESCHI) to the mid-C16, followed by

MANNERISM and the BAROQUE. The old practice is still occasionally found, however, of extending the term Renaissance to include Mannerism and the Baroque. In countries other than Italy the Renaissance started with the adoption of Italian Renaissance motifs, but the resulting styles – French Renaissance, German Renaissance, etc. – have little in common with the qualities of the Italian Renaissance, which are a sense of stability and poise as well as Ancient Roman forms and ornament. For Proto-Renaissance, *see* ITALIAN ARCHITECTURE. *See also* CLASSICISM; BELGIAN ARCHITECTURE; CZECH ARCHITECTURE; DUTCH ARCHITECTURE; FRENCH ARCHITECTURE; GERMAN ARCHITECTURE; HUNGARIAN ARCHITECTURE; ITALIAN ARCHITECTURE; POLISH ARCHITECTURE; RUSSIAN ARCHITECTURE; SPANISH ARCHITECTURE; SWISS ARCHITECTURE.

**Renard**, Bruno (1781–1861), *see* COMPANY TOWN.

**Rendering**. 1. Plaster or stucco applied to an exterior wall; a first coat of plaster on an internal wall. 2. A perspective or elevation drawing of a building or project or part of it, the materials and their textures and colours being shown as well as shadows. The natural and other features of the site are also delineated.

R. Gill, *Basic R.*, London 1991.

**Rennie**, John (1761–1821). Scottish architect, the son of a farmer. He was trained by an inventive millwright and then at Edinburgh University. In 1784 he was put in charge of installing the new Boulton & Watt steam engine at the Albion Works in London. In 1791 he set up in business on his own. He was first interested in canals (Kennet and Avon), later also in fen drainage, harbours and docks, lighthouses, and also bridges. He designed Kelso Bridge (1800–1803), Waterloo Bridge (1811–17, demolished), Southwark Bridge (1815–19, demolished) and London Bridge (1824–31), built by his sons George (1791–1866) and Sir John (1794–1874), which was demolished in 1967 and re-erected at Lake Havasu City, Arizona.

C. T. G. Boucher, *J.R. 1761–1821. The Life and Work of a Great Engineer*, Manchester 1963; Summerson 1991; Colvin 1995.

**Renwick**, James (1818–95), the son of an English engineer who emigrated to America and became the most prominent man in his field in the United States, graduated at Columbia College, New York, and became famous as an architect of churches (Grace Church, Broadway, 1843 onwards, St Patrick's Cathedral, 1853–87). His other best-known buildings are the sweetly picturesque neo-Norman Smithsonian Institution in Washington, DC (1847–55), and Vassar College, an essay in a free Renaissance mixture (1865).

S. Rattner, *R.'s Design for Grace Church. Religious Doctrine and the Gothic Revival*, New York 1969; Hitchcock 1977; Whiffen and Koeper 1981.

**Repton**, Humphry (1752–1818), the leading English landscape gardener of the generation after BROWN, was a contemporary of PRICE and KNIGHT, with whose defence of wildness and ruggedness, however, he did not agree. The innovation of his layouts, an innovation which pointed forward into the C19, is the treatment of the garden close to the house not naturally and picturesquely, but formally with parterres and terraces, to which in his late work he added such 'Victorian' motifs as rose-arbours, aviaries, etc. He also was responsible for a certain amount of architectural work though this was mostly left to his sons

John Adey (1775–1860) and George (1786–1858). Repton had lived as a country gentleman until a financial setback forced him to make a living out of his passion for gardening. He was at once successful, and the total of parks and gardens treated by him is in the neighbourhood of 200. Those that survive include Brocklesby, Lincolnshire; Corsham, Wiltshire; Longleat, Wiltshire; Moccas, Herefordshire; Sheffield Park, Sussex; and Wimpole, Cambridgeshire. He provided for clients albums of watercolours, known as 'red books' from their bindings, with before-and-after views to suggest how landscapes could be 'improved'. Similar drawings were reproduced in his books, which had international influence (an allusion to them is made in Goethe's *Elective Affinities*). He published *Sketches and Hints on Landscape Gardening* (1795), *Observations on the Theory and Practice of Landscape Gardening* (1803), *An Inquiry into the Changes of Taste in Landscape Gardening* (1806), and *Fragments on the Theory and Practice of Landscape Gardening* (1816). They were collected and republished by LOUDON (1840). The term 'landscape gardening' is his.

D. Stroud, *H.R.*, London 1962; G. Carter *et al.*, *H.R. Landscape Gardener 1752–1818*, Norwich 1982; Summerson 1991; Dixon Hunt 1992; Colvin 1995.

**Reredos**. A wall or screen, usually of wood or stone, rising behind an altar, and as a rule decorated.

**Respond**. A half-PIER bonded into a wall and carrying one end of an arch; often at the end of an ARCADE.

**Restoration**. The treatment of an old building to recover its prior or 'original' condition by removing later accretions (such as Baroque additions to Gothic churches or Gothic additions to Romanesque churches), by recreating elements believed to have been lost and by reworking weathered surfaces. It is to be distinguished from HISTORIC PRESERVATION. The practice of restoration, and also opposition to it, began in England with J. WYATT's restoration in 1788–96 of Hereford Cathedral and of Salisbury Cathedral in 1789–92 according to his interpretation of Gothic, which provoked an outcry from antiquaries. In Rome the surviving central part of the CI Arch of Titus was dismantled and rebuilt by Raffaello Stern and VALADIER in 1818–24 with the addition of sides and superstructure in different stone to distinguish new work from old – the earliest example of an archaeologically sensitive practice rarely followed until the C20. Most of the buildings restored in the CI9 were medieval: castles such as Windsor, restored by WYATVILLE in 1824–37, the Tower of London, restored by SALVIN in 1845, and especially churches. RICKMAN's *An Attempt to Discriminate the Styles of Architecture in England* (London 1817) was intended to help 'the guardians of our ecclesiastical edifices . . . to judge with considerable accuracy of the restorations necessary', as well as to select styles for new churches, thus linking restoration with HISTORICISM. Church restoration in mid-CI9 England often reflected current religious movements, e.g. the Cambridge Camden Society, founded in 1839, which promoted the re-introduction of much Catholic ritual into Anglican worship and thus necessitated alterations to existing buildings to bring them back to their former arrangement. In 1841 it engaged Salvin to restore the church of the Holy Sepulchre, Cambridge, in the Norman style. In the same year it founded the *Ecclesiologist* periodical which monitored ecclesiastical architecture in Britain for the next quarter-century, during which many Anglican churches were stripped of such CI8 features as box-pews and three-decker pulpits, if not completely remodelled. Most of the leading Victorian architects were at some time employed on such work, none more actively than George Gilbert SCOTT. The leading French C19 restorer was VIOLLET LE DUC, an agnostic whose ideals were purely aesthetic but similarly aimed at giving a building an appearance of stylistic integrity, derived from its earliest surviving parts, to present it in a 'complete state' such as, he wrote in 1866, 'it may never have been at any one time'. At Carcassonne (from 1844) and the Château de Pierrefonds (1858–70) his restoration work verged on HISTORICAL RECONSTRUCTION. Restorations in his manner were carried out all over Europe; the 1858–69 restoration of the semi-ruined C12 Fondaco dei Turchi, Venice, in a supposedly Byzantine style, was a notorious instance, as was ABADIE's restoration of St Front, Périgueux.

'Restoration, so-called, is the worst manner of Destruction,' Ruskin declared in 1849. Inspired by his writings, MORRIS, Philip WEBB and their friends founded in 1877 the Society for the Protection of Ancient Buildings (SPAB), which helped in promoting 'historic preservation' and immediately supported Venetians in their campaign to halt the restoration of S. Marco, Venice. In response the influential BOITO issued from 1883 a series of publications setting limits to restoration. Attempts to restore buildings to their original state continued nonetheless, especially in Italy, e.g. the church of S. Maria in Cosmedin, Rome, where a Baroque façade was replaced in 1894–9 by one in the Romanesque style. The less ruthless and more scholarly attitude of later restorers can be seen at the same Roman church where the campanile was restored in 1958 by reopening blocked windows and supplying new columns accurately copied from the few originals that survived. However, controversy over the principles and methods of restoration continues to the present day.

N. Pevsner, *Some Architectural Writers of the Nineteenth Century*, London 1972; J. Fawcett (ed.), *The Future of the Past*, London 1976; E. R. Chamberlin, *Preserving the Past*, London 1978.

**Restoration architecture**. Historical division of English architecture from the restoration of Charles II in 1660 to the death of William and Mary in 1707. The period includes the careers of WREN, HAWKSMOOR and others but Restoration architecture is typified by a red-brick stone-quoined Dutch style of domestic building.

**Retable**. A superstructure found since C11, either painted or carved, on the rear of the altar or on its own pedestal behind the altar, especially one with carved figures in the *corpus* or central part, flanked by carved and/or painted wings.

**Retaining wall**. A wall, usually battered, which supports or retains a weight of earth or water, also called a *revetment*.

**Reticulated**, *see* TRACERY.

**Retro-choir**. The space behind the high altar in a major church.

**Return**. The side or part which falls away, usually at right angles, from the front or direct line of a structure. Two particular uses of the term are: (a) that part of a dripstone or HOOD-MOULD which, after running downwards, turns off horizontally; (b) the western row of choir stalls which runs north–south, set against the screen at the west end of the choir.

**Reveal**. That part of a JAMB which lies between the glass or door and the outer wall surface. If cut diagonally, it is called a SPLAY.

**Revell**, Viljo (1910–64), *see* CANADIAN

ARCHITECTURE; FINNISH ARCHI-
TECTURE.

**Revetment**. 1. *See* RETAINING WALL.
2. The facing (e.g. of marble) applied to
a wall built of some other material.

**Revett**, Nicholas (1720–1804), *see*
STUART, James 'Athenian'.

**Rewal**, Raj (b.1934). Indian architect,
trained in Delhi, London and Paris and
notable for his skilful and imaginative use
of traditional Indian vernacular forms and
materials with modern technology
together with a sensitive adaptation of
indigenous building types, e.g. the *haveli*
or Rajasthan courtyard house, to concrete and metal construction, notably in
housing for mass urbanization. His Asian
Games Housing, New Delhi (1980–82),
was outstanding, an aggregation of courts,
precincts and terraces (not free-standing
blocks of flats in open spaces) with standard units combined in ways to create a
variety of forms and aspects. This was
followed by the campus for the National
Institute of Immunology, New Delhi
(1988), which recalls, in its varying layers
of transition from public to private space,
such Rajasthan citadels as Jaisalmer. A
similar reconciliation of modern technology with vernacular forms marks his office
and administrative buildings, e.g. the
CIET buildings, New Delhi (1991); the
World Bank, New Delhi (1993); and the
new Parliament Library, New Delhi
(1995).

B. B. Taylor, *R.R.*, Ahmedabad 1992.

**Reyns**, *see* HENRY OF REYNS.

**Reznik**, David (b.1923), *see* ISRAELI
ARCHITECTURE.

**Rez de chaussée**. Fr. for ground floor
(in UK) or first floor (in USA).

**Rib**. A projecting band on a ceiling or
vault, usually structural but sometimes

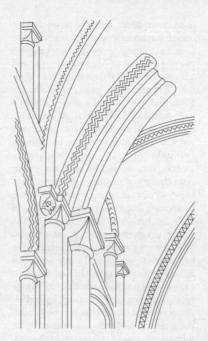

Fig. 98 Rib

purely decorative, separating the CELLS
of a groined VAULT. *See* Fig. 98.

**Ribat**. A fortified religious outpost on
the Muslim frontier. The term is also used
loosely for a CARAVANSERAI.

**Ribbon development**. The construction of continuous strings of houses along
main roads. This was responsible for
much spoliation of the English countryside during the first quarter of this century, but was largely halted by the passing
of the Ribbon Development Act of 1935.

**Ribera**, Pedro de (*c*.1683–1742), the
leading Late Baroque architect in Madrid,
carried the CHURRIGUERESQUE style to
its ultimate point of elaboration. In the
neo-classical period he was held up for
derision by one authority, who published
a complete list of his buildings as an object

lesson to students, with the result that his œuvre is unusually well documented. Of Castilian origin, he began working for the city council of Madrid in 1719, and became its official architect in 1726. With the exception of the tower of Salamanca Cathedral (c.1738) and a chapel attached to S. Antonio, Ávila (1731), all his buildings are in Madrid. His most celebrated work is the doorway to the Hospico S. Fernando (c.1722), an overpowering extravaganza of boldly and somewhat coarsely carved draperies, festoons, top-heavy ESTÍPITES, urns, and flames rising in staccato leaps above the roofline. In 1718 he built the little church of the Virgen del Puerto, which has an exterior like a garden pavilion, with a picturesque bell-shaped spire, and an octagonal interior with a CAMARÍN behind the altar. Other works include the Toledo Bridge (designed 1719, built 1723–4), with elaborately carved tabernacles perched above the arches; the Montserrat church (1720, incomplete); and S. Cayetano (1722–32, incomplete).

Kubler and Soria 1959.

**Ricardo**, Halsey (1854–1928), *see* ARTS AND CRAFTS; TILES.

**Ricchino**, Francesco Maria (1583–1658). The most important Lombard architect of the Early Baroque. His S. Giuseppe in Milan (1607–30) broke away from the prevailing academic MANNERISM as decisively as did MADERNO's S. Susanna in Rome (1603). Both in its plan (a fusion of two centralized units) and in its aedicule façade S. Giuseppe is entirely forward-looking. Nearly all his later churches have been destroyed. Of his surviving works the best are the concave façades of the Collegio Elvetico, Milan (1627), and the Palazzo di Brera, Milan (1651–86), with its noble courtyard. His vast central cortile of the Ospedale Mag-

giore, Milan, was designed with G.-B. Pessina (1625–49, restored 1950s).

Wittkower 1982.

**Rice**, Peter (1935–92). English structural engineer who began with ARUP and contributed notably not only to the realization but also the conception and design of such buildings as UTZON's Sydney Opera House; PIANO and ROGERS's Pompidou Centre, Paris; FOSTER's Stansted airport terminal and a number of buildings at La Défense, Paris, in the late 1980s and the 1990s. In 1982 he formed RFR Design Engineering with Ian RITCHIE and Martin Francis. Their bioclimatic façades for the National Museum of Science, Technology and Industry, La Villette, Paris (1985), were notable. He published, with H. Dutton, *Le Verre structurel* (Paris (1990) 1995), and, posthumously, *An Engineer Imagines* (London 1994).

**Richardson**, Sir Albert E. (1886–1964), *see* NEO-GEORGIAN.

**Richardson**, Henry Hobson (1838–86). American architect; studied at Harvard, and then studied architecture at the École des Beaux Arts in Paris (1859–62), where, after the Civil War, he returned to work under LABROUSTE and then HITTORF. Back at Boston in 1865 he started a practice, and in 1870 won the competition for the Brattle Square church (1871–3), in 1872 that for Trinity church (1873–7). These established him as an original, and at the same time a learned, architect. His favourite style was a very massive, masculine Romanesque, inspired by architects such as VAUDREMER. But the tower of the Brattle Square church, with its frieze of figures right below the machicolated top, is Romanesque only in so far as it is round-arched. In 1882 he travelled in Europe, and only then saw French and north-Spanish Romanesque buildings at first hand. The Romanesque suited him as a style: it was direct and powerful, thus capable of fulfilling American requirements. Rockfaced rustication was also a favourite with him. In fact, he was always attracted by utilitarian jobs. The most monumental of these were the Marshall Field Wholesale Warehouse in Chicago (1885–7, demolished *c.*1935) and the Allegheny Court House and Gaol, Pittsburg (1884–7). He also designed small railway stations in the eighties (e.g. South Framingham Station, Massachusetts, 1883–5). Before then he had done some small libraries (Win Memorial Library, Woburn, Massachusetts, 1876–9), two buildings for Harvard (Sever Hall, 1878, which is remarkably independent of any stylistic imitation; Austin Hall, 1881, which is Romanesque), and also some private houses (the SHINGLE-faced, very original and forward-pointing Stoughton House at Cambridge, Massachusetts, 1882–3; the Glessner House at Chicago, 1885–7) which illustrate his ARTS AND CRAFTS affiliations. Richardson was a *bon vivant*, a designer of zest and conviction. His Romanesque was soon widely imitated – to its detriment – but helped greatly in liberating America from the indiscriminate imitation of European revivals. Among his pupils were McKIM and WHITE, and he also influenced ROOT and SULLIVAN decisively.

Hitchcock 1977; J. K. Ochsner, *H.H.R. (1838–1886). Complete Architectural Works*, Cambridge, Mass. 1984; J. F. O'Gorman, *H.H.R. Architectural Forms for an American Society*, Chicago 1987; E. Harrington, *H.H.R. J.J. Glessner House, Chicago, 1885–87*, Tübingen/Berlin 1993; M. H. Floyd, *H.H.R.*, New York 1997.

**Rickman**, Thomas (1776–1841). English architect, moved late from medicine and business into architecture. From sketching and writing about old churches he went on to open a practice as an architect in London. This was in 1817, the year in which he also published some lectures under the title *An Attempt to Discriminate the Styles of Architecture in England*; *see* RESTORATION. This little book established our terms Early English, Decorated and Perpendicular. As a church architect Rickman could be remarkably conscientious in trying to create credible Gothic interiors. Such churches as St George, Birmingham (1819–22, demolished) and those at Hampton Lucy, Warwickshire (1822–6), and Oulton, Yorkshire (1827–9), must have struck his contemporaries as archaeologically convincing. The latter were done in partnership with Henry Hutchinson (1800–1831), his former pupil, who was also largely responsible for Rickman's most familiar building: New Court, St John's College, Cambridge (1826–31), with the attached so-called Bridge of Sighs. Rickman was a Quaker, but late in life turned Irvingite.

Hitchcock 1977; Colvin 1995.

**Ridge pole**, *see* ROOF.

**Ridge-rib**, *see* VAULT.

**Ridinger** or **Riedinger**, Georg (1568–after 1616). Leading German Renaissance architect, a contemporary of Elias HOLL, Heinrich SCHICKHARDT and Jacob WOLFF. His masterpiece was Schloss Aschaffenburg (1605–14, destroyed but rebuilt) built for the Archbishop of Mainz, Ulrich von Gemmingen (the patron of Matthias Grünewald), and his successor Johann Schickard von Kronberg. The square ground-plan of four wings and corner towers round a central courtyard was probably derived from French *château* design through DU CERCEAU's engravings. Though still rather medieval and fortress-like, the elevations were articulated with strong horizontal mouldings and occasional Netherlandish ornamentation. Ridinger thought it 'heroic'. It had great and long-lasting influence in Germany, e.g. on Petrini's (1624–1701) Marquardsburg of almost a hundred years later.

Hitchcock 1981; B. von Rode, *Schloss Aschaffenburg und Pompeijanum*, Munich 1982.

**Ried von Piesting**, Benedikt, *see* RIETH VON PIESTING, Benedikt.

**Riemerschmid**, Richard (1868–1957). German architect, more important as a designer, being one of the earliest to work for industrialized mass-production. But in 1907 he planned the first German GARDEN CITY at Hellerau near Dresden (begun 1909) for which he also designed several buildings (1910–13). His small theatre in the Munich Schauspielhaus (1901 with Max Littmann) is a notable late ART NOUVEAU work. His Reckendorf pavilion for the Cologne Werkbund in 1928 was also remarkable.

W. Nerdinger (ed.), *R.R. Vom Jugendstil zum Werkbund*, Munich and Nuremberg 1982; M. Rammert, *R.R. Möbel und Innenräume von 1895–1900*, Munich 1987.

**Rieth von Piesting**, Benedikt (*c.*1454–1534). German mason, Master of the King's Works in Bohemia. His *chefd'œuvre* at Prague is the Vladislav Hall in the castle with its intricate lierne vault, including curved ribs, and its curious italianizing details of windows and doorways, Quattrocento in style, but including strange Gothic twists. This work belongs to the years 1493–1502. By Rieth also may be the Organ Gallery in Prague Cathedral, fancifully Late Gothic (*c.*1490–93). It has ribs in the form of naturalistically imitated branches. At St Barbara, Kutná Hora, Rieth altered the existing plans for the nave and aisles,

and designed the vault, a vault whose ribs form a net of lozenges (executed after his death, 1540–48). Equally intricate is the vault of Laun city church, his last work.

G. Fehr, *B.R.*, Munich 1961; Hitchcock 1981; F. Seibt (ed.), *Renaissance in Böhmen*, Munich 1985.

**Rietveld**, Gerrit Thomas (1888–1964). Dutch designer, famous for his Red-Blue chair (1918), he became the leading DE STIJL architect. His paradigmatic masterpiece is the Schroeder House, Utrecht (1924), which epitomized the style and incorporated most of the features of the INTERNATIONAL STYLE – asymmetrical composition, unrelieved cubic shapes, slab roof cantilevered out at the corners, white rendering and large windows in horizontal strips with flexible continuous interior spaces made possible by steel skeleton construction. His later buildings include terrace houses and the Vreeburg Cinema, Utrecht (1930 and 1934). He enjoyed a revival in his old age, designing the sculpture pavilion for Sonsbeck Park, Arnhem (1954, re-erected at Otterlo 1964), and the Rijksmuseum Vincent van Gogh, Amsterdam, built posthumously with modifications (1963–72).

T. M. Brown, *The Work of G.R. Architect*, Cambridge and Utrecht 1958; A. Buffinga, *G.T.R.*, Amsterdam 1971; P. Overy *et al.*, *Das Rietveld-Schröder Haus*, Brunswick and Wiesbaden 1988; M. Kuper and I. van Zijl, *G.R. (1888–1960) The Complete Works*, Utrecht 1992.

**Rinaldi**, Antonio (*c.*1709–94). Italian architect who became one of the leading Late Rococo architects in Russia. His main works are the Peter III Palace and the Chinese Palace (1758–62 and 1762–8), Oranienbaum, now Lomonosov, with a pretty CHINOISERIE interior, and the Marble Palace, St Petersburg (1768–72), derived from JUVARRA's Palazzo d'Ormea, but rather more austere and classical, faced with red granite and grey Siberian marble. It is of interest also as the first ever example of the use of iron beams in architecture. The Gatchina Palace (1766–81) is tentatively classicizing.

Hamilton 1983.

**Rinceau**. An ornamental motif of scrolls of foliage, usually vine.

**Rise**. Of an arch or vault, the vertical distance between the SOFFIT at the crown and the level of the SPRINGING LINE.

**Riser**, *see* STAIR.

**Ritchie**, Ian (b.1947), *see* ENGLISH ARCHITECTURE.

**Robert de Luzarches** (d.*c*.1236). The master mason who began the nave of Amiens Cathedral in 1220. He was succeeded by Thomas de Cormont, who built the choir and aisles *c*.1236–40.

Branner 1965.

**Roberto**, Marcelo (1908–64) and Milton (1914–53), *see* BRAZILIAN ARCHITECTURE.

**Roberts**, Henry (1803–76). Designed the Fishmongers' Hall, London (1832–5), in a Greek Revival style in the manner of SMIRKE, but is notable as a pioneer in improving working-class housing. He built model working-class houses in London from the 1840s onwards and published extensively on the subject.

J. S. Curl, *The Life and Works of H.R. 1803–76*, London 1983; Colvin 1995.

**Robinson**, William (1838–1935), *see* JEKYLL, Gertrude.

**Robson**, Edward Robert (1835–1917), *see* NEO-GEORGIAN ARCHITECTURE.

**Rocaille**. The amorphous, rock-like material used in grottoes, and on fountains, hence suggestive of water and mutability, which together with shells was

perhaps the main inspiration and origin of ROCOCO ornament. The name is used especially for this type of Rococo ornament.

H. Bauer, *R., zur Herkunft und zum Wesen eines Ornament-Motivs*, Berlin 1962.

**Roche**, Eamon Kevin (b.1922). Born in Dublin, he went to the USA in 1948 and worked with Eero SAARINEN from 1951 to his death in 1961, when Roche took over his practice in partnership with John Dinkeloo (1918–81). The Cummins Engine Factory, Darlington, Co. Durham (1962–6), was an early building, followed by the Oakland Museum, Oakland, California (1962), almost entirely covered at varying levels by a remarkable roof-garden by KILEY (1965–9). The Ford Foundation Headquarters, New York (1963–8), made their name. It foreshadowed with its great ATRIUM many office buildings in New York and elsewhere of the following decades. A year later came the headquarters of the Knights of Columbus, New Haven, Connecticut (1965–9), then the College Life Insurance Company of America, Indianapolis (1967); the Creative Arts Center, Wesleyan University, Middletown, Connecticut (1971); extension to the Metropolitan Museum, New York (1967–78); the General Foods Corp. Headquarters, Rye Brook, NY (1977–83), and Yarakucho I-chono B, Tokyo (1984).

F. Dallo, *K.R.*, London 1986.

**Rococo architecture and landscape architecture**. The Rococo is not a style in its own right, like the BAROQUE, but the last phase of the Baroque. The great breaks in European art and thought take place at the beginning of the Baroque and again at the beginning of NEOCLASSICISM. The Rococo is chiefly represented by a type of decoration initiated in France (*see* RÉGENCE STYLE; BOF-FRAND; MEISSONNIER), by lightness in colour and weight, where the Baroque had been dark and ponderous, and, in south Germany and Austria, by a great spatial complexity (notably NEUMANN), which, however, is the direct continuation of the Baroque complexity of BORROMINI and GUARINI. The new decoration is often asymmetrical and abstract – the term for this is ROCAILLE – with shell-like, coral-like forms and many C- and S-curves. Naturalistic flowers, branches, trees, whole rustic scenes, and also Chinese motifs are sometimes playfully introduced into *rocaille*. In French external architecture the Rococo is only noticeable by a greater elegance and delicacy. In the design of gardens in France, Germany and the Netherlands, formality was maintained but with less emphasis on wide terraces and sweeping prospects than the creation of varied intimate spaces. The finest surviving example is the Hofgarten at Veitshöchheim, Germany, begun 1763, with a succession of diversely planned areas and a large population of elegantly poised statues by Ferdinand Dietz and other sculptors. England has no Rococo, apart from occasional interiors. But the playful use of Chinese, Indian, and also Gothic forms in garden furnishings can well be ascribed to Rococo influence.

**Rodriguez Tizon**, Ventura (1717–85), the leading Spanish Late Baroque architect, began under SACCHETTI at the Royal Palace, Madrid, and was employed by the Crown until 1759. His first important work was the church of S. Marcos, Madrid (1749–53), built on an oval plan derived from BERNINI's S. Andrea al Quirinale, Rome. In 1753 he built the Transparente in Cuenca Cathedral. In 1760 he became professor at the Madrid academy and his work began to assume a

more dogmatic appearance under French neo-classical influence. The Royal College of Surgery, Barcelona (1761), is almost gaunt in its severe renunciation of ornament. His noblest work is the façade of Pamplona Cathedral (1783), with a great Corinthian portico flanked by square towers, archaeologically correct in detail yet still reminiscent of early C18 Rome.

T. F. Reese, *The Architecture of V.R. (1717–1785)*, New York 1976.

**Roebling**, John Augustus (1806–69), *see* BRIDGE.

**Rogers**, Ernesto Nathan (1909–69), Italian architect who founded BBPR in Milan in 1932 with Enrico Peressutti (1908–73). The Torre Velasca, Milan (1957–60), made his name, followed by the Chase Manhattan Bank, Milan (1969), but he was also influential as editor of *Domus* and *Casabella*.

**Rogers**, Isaiah (1800–1869). American architect, born in Massachusetts and a pupil of WILLARD in Boston. His first important job was a hotel, the Tremont House, Boston (built 1828–9), which was immediately followed by the Astor House, New York (1832–6). Other major hotels by Rogers were the Exchange, Richmond, Virginia (1841), the Charleston, Charleston, South Carolina (opened 1839), with a memorable Corinthian colonnade, the St Charles, New Orleans (*c.*1851), Maxwell House, Nashville (1859–69), and Burnet House, Cincinnati (1854–6). He also designed the Romanesque St John Episcopal Church, Cincinnati, with its diagonally placed towers, the Bank of America, New York (1835), whose façade became the entrance feature of Pine Lodge Park, Methuen Hall and the Mercantile Exchange, New York (1836–42), with its central rotunda and long colonnade, now part of the National City Bank. Hitchcock 1977.

**Rogers**, Richard (b.1933). Leading English HIGH TECH architect, cousin of Ernesto N. ROGERS, was in partnership with Norman FOSTER in Team 4 until 1967 and became known internationally in the 1970s with the Centre Pompidou, Paris (1971–7), designed with Renzo PIANO with whom he was in partnership. The Centre Pompidou, with its exposed structure and brightly coloured functional mechanism, made a major impact on architects all over the world. His later independent buildings include the Fleetguard Building, Quimper, France (1979–81); the PA Technology Laboratories and Offices, Princeton, NJ (1982–3); the Inmos Microprocessor Factory, Newport, Wales (1982); Lloyd's of London Headquarters, London (1978–86); Channel 4 TV Headquarters, London (1990–94); the European Court of Human Rights, Strasbourg (1989–95). His large-scale urban schemes for London and Shanghai, the latter covering nearly 4 km. (2½ miles) square, were notably imaginative but await realization. In 1990 he published *Architecture: a Modern View*, London. He was knighted in 1991 and ennobled as Baron Rogers of Riverside in 1996.

K. Powell, *R.R.*, London 1994; D. Sudjic, *The Architecture of R.R.*, London 1994; N. Silver, *The Making of Beaubourg. A Building Biography of the Centre Pompidou*, Paris, Cambridge, Mass. 1994; R. Burdett, *R.R. Partnership*, London/New York 1995.

**Rohault de Fleury**, Charles (1801–75), *see* HITTORF, Jakob Ignaz.

**Rokkaku**, Kijo (b.1941), *see* JAPANESE ARCHITECTURE.

**Roman architecture**. Whereas GREEK ARCHITECTURE is tectonic, built up from a logical series of horizontals and verticals (the Doric temple has been called 'sublimated carpentry'), Roman architecture is plastic with much use of rounded forms (arch, vault and dome), so that buildings tend to look as if they had been made of concrete poured into a mould. In Greek and HELLENISTIC ARCHITECTURE the column was the most important member; in Rome the column was frequently degraded to merely decorative uses, while the wall became the essential element. Hence the Roman predilection for the PSEUDO-PERIPTERAL (Temple of Fortuna Virilis, Rome, late C2 to mid C1 BC; Maison Carrée, Nîmes, begun *c.*19 BC), for the Corinthian order, and for elaborately carved ENTABLATURES and other ornamentation. It was the development of CONCRETE used in conjunction with brick that made possible the construction of the great Roman domes and vaults. Concrete proved as economical of materials as of labour, since the masons' rubble could be used for filling. Surfaces were either stuccoed or clad in marble. The earliest concrete dome is C2 BC (Stabian Baths, Pompeii), while the earliest large-scale concrete vault is that of the Tabularium in Rome of 78 BC, where the half-columns are used ornamentally – the first important instance of the divorce of decoration and function. The concrete barrel vault on a large scale appears in Nero's Golden House, Rome, by the architect SEVERUS (mid C1 AD) and in the palace buildings by RABIRIUS for Domitian on the Palatine in Rome (late AD C1). Later vaulted buildings of importance include the Baths of Caracalla (*c.*AD 215), Baths of Diocletian (AD 306), and the Basilica Nova of Maxentius (AD 310–13), all in Rome.

Roman architecture reaches its apogee in the Pantheon, Rome (*c.*AD 100–125, with a dome 43 m. (141 ft) in diameter), which is both a feat of engineering and a masterpiece of simple yet highly satisfying proportions – it is based on a sphere, the heights of the walls being equal to the radius of the dome. Comparison of the Pantheon with the Parthenon reveals the contrast between the tectonic and extrovert nature of Roman architecture. This is equally evident in the most typically Roman of all buildings, the BASILICA, which, with its interior colonnades, is like a Greek temple turned outside in. Other typically Roman buildings are: THERMAE, with their rich decoration and complicated spatial play; AMPHITHEATRES, of which the Colosseum, Rome (AD 69–79), is the largest; and TRIUMPHAL ARCHES, a purely decorative type of building of which the earliest recorded examples were temporary structures of the C2 BC. Always of the Corinthian or Composite ORDER, these arches vary from the relative severity of that at Susa near Turin to the elaboration of that at Orange in the south of France (c. 30 BC). City gateways were hardly less profusely decorated, e.g. Porta Nigra at Trier, Germany (late C3 or early C4 AD).

In domestic architecture three types were developed: the *domus* or townhouse; the *insula* or multi-storey apartment house or tenement block; and the *villa* or suburban or country house. The *domus* derived from the Greek and Hellenistic house and was usually of one storey only and inward-looking, the rooms being grouped axially and symmetrically around an atrium and one or more peristyle courts. The street façade was plain and without windows, or was let off as shops, as can still be seen at Pompeii. The *insula* had several identical but separate floors and was often vaulted throughout with concrete construction. A decree of Augustus limited their height in Rome to 23 m. (75 ft). During the Neronian rebuilding of Rome after the fire of AD 64 new quarters of *insulae* were laid out symmetrically along arcaded streets and round public squares. The *villa* derived from the traditional farmhouse and was more casual and straggling in plan than the *domus*. It was also more outward-looking, and great variety in planning and room shapes was attained in the more luxurious examples. The exteriors were enlivened with porticos and colonnades, rooms were designed to catch the view, or the sun in winter or the shade in summer, as at Pliny's villa at Laurentum.

Hadrian's fantastic sprawling villa at Tivoli (c. AD 123) illustrates almost the whole range of Imperial Roman architecture at its sophisticated best. Indeed it is perhaps over-sophisticated already. The last great architectural monument of the Roman Empire is Diocletian's Palace at Split in Croatia (c. AD 300), built after the Pax Romana had begun to disintegrate. Yet even here the Roman genius for experimentation was still at work. Certain decorative elements, e.g. engaged columns standing on isolated corbels, anticipate the language of BYZANTINE ARCHITECTURE.

**Romanesque architecture**. The style current until the advent of GOTHIC. Some experts place its origins in the C7, others in the C10: the former view includes CAROLINGIAN in Romanesque architecture, the latter places the beginning of Romanesque at the time of the rising of the Cluniac order in France and the Ottonian Empire in Germany. The first view includes Anglo–Saxon architecture, the second identifies the Romanesque in Britain with the Norman.

The Romanesque in the northern countries is the style of the round arch. It is also characterized by clear, easily comprehended schemes of planning and elevation, the plan with staggered apses (*en échelon*) at the east end of churches, the plan with an ambulatory and radiating chapels, plans (mainly in Germany) with square bays in nave, transepts and chancel, and square bays in the aisles one quarter the area. The compositions of the walls also stress clearly marked compartments, e.g. in the shafts which in Norman churches run from the ground right up to the ceiling beams.

The Early Romanesque had not yet the skill to vault major spans. Experiments began about 1000, but remained rare till after 1050. Then various systems were developed which differentiated regional groups: tunnel vaults in France, often pointed (Burgundy, Provence), and also in Spain; groin vaults in Germany; domes in the south-west of France; rib vaults at Durham and in Italy. The spread of the rib vault and the pointed vault, however, is usually a sign of the approaching Gothic style. In the exteriors the two-tower façade plus a tower over the crossing is most typical of England and Normandy, whereas screen façades with no towers are characteristic of the south of France, and a multitude of towers over the west as well as the east parts is typical of Germany. *See also* ENGLISH ARCHITECTURE; GERMAN ARCHITECTURE; ITALIAN ARCHITECTURE; SPANISH ARCHITECTURE.

**Roll moulding**. Moulding of semicircular or more than semicircular section.

**Roman**, Jacob (1640–*c*.1716). Dutch sculptor and architect who designed the Town Halls at Deventer (1693) and de Voorst (1695–1700) and succeeded MAROT at Het Loo.

Kuyper 1980.

**Romanian architecture**, *see* BYZANTINE ARCHITECTURE.

**Romano**, *see* GIULIO ROMANO.

**Rond-point**. French term for a circular space at the convergence of four or more rides or *allées* in a park or streets in a town.

**Rood**. Originally the Saxon word for a cross or crucifix. In churches this was set at the east end of the nave, flanked by figures of the Virgin and St John. It was usually wooden, and fixed to a special beam stretching from RESPOND to respond of the CHANCEL ARCH, above the ROOD LOFT. Sometimes the rood is painted on the wall above the chancel arch.

**Rood loft**. A gallery built above the ROOD SCREEN, often to carry the ROOD or other images and candles; approached by stairs either of wood or built in the wall. Rood lofts were introduced in the C15 in England, and many were destroyed in the Reformation.

**Rood screen**. A screen below the ROOD, set across the east end of the nave and shutting off the chancel. In French, a JUBÉ.

**Roof**
*Construction*

Roofs are generally called after the principal structural component, e.g. *crown-post, hammerbeam, king-post*, etc. *See below* under *Elements*.

A *single-framed* roof is constructed with no main trusses. The rafters may be fixed to a wall-plate or ridge, or longitudinal timbers may be absent altogether. A *common rafter* roof is one in which pairs of rafters are not connected by a collar-beam. A *coupled rafter* roof is one in which the rafters are connected by collar-beams.

A *double-framed* roof is constructed with longitudinal members such as purlins. Generally there are principals or principal rafters supporting the longitudinal members and dividing the length of the roof into bays.

A *slab roof* is a flat roof composed either of single slabs stretching from one side of an enclosed space to another, or one of

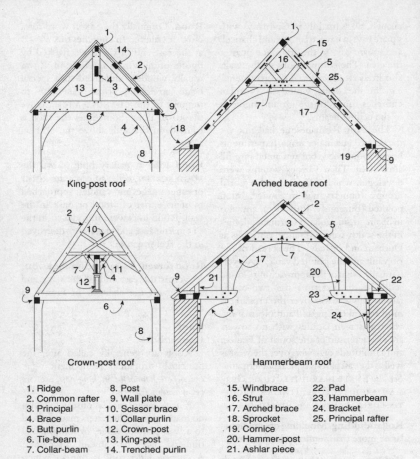

King-post roof

Arched brace roof

Crown-post roof

Hammerbeam roof

| 1. Ridge | 8. Post | 15. Windbrace | 22. Pad |
|----------|---------|---------------|---------|
| 2. Common rafter | 9. Wall plate | 16. Strut | 23. Hammerbeam |
| 3. Principal | 10. Scissor brace | 17. Arched brace | 24. Bracket |
| 4. Brace | 11. Collar purlin | 18. Sprocket | 25. Principal rafter |
| 5. Butt purlin | 12. Crown-post | 19. Cornice | |
| 6. Tie-beam | 13. King-post | 20. Hammer-post | |
| 7. Collar-beam | 14. Trenched purlin | 21. Ashlar piece | |

Fig. 99 Roofs

concrete which has the appearance of a thick slab.

*Elements*

*Ashlar piece.* A short vertical timber connecting an inner wall-plate or timber pad to a rafter above.

*Blades, see* CRUCKS.

*Braces.* Subsidiary timbers set diagonally to strengthen the frame. *Arch braces*: a pair of curved braces forming an arch, usually connecting the wall or post below with the tie- or collar-beam above. *Passing braces*: straight braces of considerable length, passing across other members of the truss. *Scissor braces*: a pair of braces which cross diagonally between pairs of rafters or principals. *Wind-braces*: short, usually curved braces connecting side purlins with principals. They are sometimes decorated with cusping.

*Collar-beam*. A horizontal transverse timber connecting a pair of rafters or principals at a height between the apex and the wall-plate.

*Crown-post*. A vertical timber standing centrally on a tie-beam and supporting a collar purlin. Longitudinal braces usually rise from the crown-post to the collar purlin. When the truss is open lateral braces generally rise to the collar-beam, and when the truss is closed they go down to the tie-beam.

*Crucks*, *see* CRUCK CONSTRUCTION; CRUCKS.

*Hammerbeam*. Horizontal brackets projecting at wall-plate level on opposite sides of the wall like a tie-beam with the centre cut away. The inner ends carry vertical timbers called hammer-posts and braces to a collar-beam. The famous hammerbeam roof in Westminster Hall, London, of 1394–1406 was devised by the king's carpenter, Hugh Harland.

*Hammer-post*. A vertical timber set on the inner end of a hammerbeam to support a purlin; it is braced to a collar-beam above.

*King-post*. A vertical timber standing centrally on a tie- or collar-beam and rising to the apex of the roof where it supports a ridge.

*Principals*. The pair of inclined lateral timbers of a truss which carry common rafters. Usually they support side purlins and their position corresponds to the main bay division of the space below.

*Purlin*. A horizontal longitudinal timber. *Collar purlin*: a single central timber which carries collar-beams and is itself supported by crown-posts. *Side purlins*: pairs of timbers occurring some way up the slope of the roof, they carry the common rafters and are supported in a number of ways: *butt purlins* are tenoned into either side of the principals; *clasped purlins* rest on queen-posts or are carried in the angles between the principals and

the collar; *laid-on purlins* lie on the backs of the principals; *trenched purlins* are trenched into the backs of the principals.

*Queen-posts*. A pair of vertical, or near vertical, timbers placed symmetrically on a tie-beam and supporting side purlins.

*Rafters*. Inclined lateral timbers sloping from wall-top to apex and supporting the roof covering. *Common rafters*: rafters of equal scantling found along the length of a roof or sometimes interrupted by main trusses containing principal rafters. *Principal rafters*: rafters which act as principals but also serve as common rafters.

*Ridge*, *ridge-piece*. A horizontal, longitudinal timber at the apex of a roof supporting the ends of the rafters.

*Sprocket*. A short timber placed on the back, and at the foot of a rafter to form projecting eaves.

*Strut*. A vertical or oblique timber which runs between two members of a roof truss but does not directly support longitudinal timbers.

*Tie-beam*. The main horizontal, transverse timber which carries the feet of the principals at wall plate level. A *baulk-tie* joins the wall posts of a timber roof and prevents the walls from spreading.

*Truss*. A rigid framework of timbers which is placed laterally across the building to carry the longitudinal roof timbers which support the common rafters.

*Wall-plate*. A timber laid longitudinally on the top of a wall to receive the ends of the rafters. In a timber-framed building the posts and studs of the wall below are tenoned into it.

*See* Fig. 99.

Shape

The following terms are used to describe the shape rather than the construction of roofs. In principle most of these shapes can be formed by more than one type of construction.

A *Belfast* or *bowstring roof* is constructed

with curved timber trusses and horizontal tie-beams, connected by light diagonal lattices of wood.

A *coupled* roof is constructed without ties or collars, the rafters being fixed to the wall-plates and ridge pieces.

A roof is *double-framed* if longitudinal members (such as ridge beam and purlins) are used. Generally the rafters are divided into stronger ones called principals and weaker subsidiary rafters.

A *gable roof* is a *pitched roof* (*see below*).

A *gambrel roof* terminates in a gablet at the ridge; in the USA a gambrel roof is simply a *mansard roof*.

A *helm roof* has four inclined faces joined at the top, with a gable at the foot of each.

A *hipped roof* has sloped instead of vertical ends.

A *lean-to roof* has one slope only and is built against a vertical wall.

A *mansard roof* has a double slope, the lower being steeper than the upper; named after François MANSART.

A *pavilion roof* slopes, or is hipped, equally on all four sides.

A *pitched roof* is the commonest type of

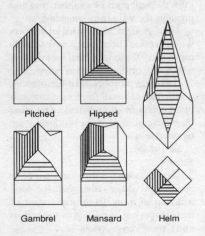

Pitched    Hipped

Gambrel    Mansard    Helm

Fig. 100 Roof; types

roof with gables at both ends. Also called a *gable roof*.

A *saddleback roof* is the name given to a normal pitched roof, when used over a tower.

*Suspended roof, see* OTTO, Frei.

In a *wagon roof*, by closely set rafters with arched braces, the appearance of the inside of a canvas over a wagon is achieved. Wagon roofs can be panelled or plastered (ceiled), or left uncovered. Also called a *cradle roof*.

*See* Fig. 100; *see also* HYPERBOLIC PARABOLOID ROOF; MONITOR ROOF, Fig. 80; NORTHLIGHT ROOF, Fig. 85.

**Roof-garden**. The famous Hanging Gardens of Babylon, one of the Seven Wonders of the Ancient World, were probably terraces constructed within rather than on top of the royal palace. Descriptions may, nevertheless, have inspired the planting of gardens on roofs in Ancient Roman times (e.g. Pompeii) and from the Renaissance onwards, though few are recorded. Large roof-gardens were a byproduct of the C18 development of structural systems strong enough to support the necessary earth and of waterproofing material to protect the rooms underneath. LE CORBUSIER in 1923 advocated roof-gardens in cities and provided space for them above many of his buildings. But the earliest large roof-garden was that on top of Derry & Toms department store, London, 1931–3, divided into areas in different historical styles of garden layout, also with a woodland glade and stream. In Brazil BURLE MARX created the first of a number of notable roof-gardens on the Ministry of Education building, Rio de Janeiro, 1938. Since the Second World War roof-gardens planted for ecological as well as aesthetic motives have become widespread throughout the West. Notable examples include those by KILEY completely covering the Oakland Museum, California, 1965–9; by Masao Kinoshita of SASAKI & Associates over the Place Bonaventure Hotel, Montreal, Canada, 1967; and by S. CROWE over the Scottish Widows' Fund and Life Assurance Offices, Edinburgh.

G. Gollwitzer, *Dachflächen*, Munich 1971.

**Root**, John Wellborn (1850–91). American architect, born in Georgia, USA, who went to school near Liverpool and studied at Oxford. He then took an engineering degree at the University of New York. In 1871 he went to live in Chicago. There he met BURNHAM and went into partnership with him, a suitable partnership to which Burnham contributed his organizational acumen and interest in planning, Root his resourcefulness and his aesthetic accomplishments, which included not only drawing but also music. On the work of the partnership *see* BURNHAM. For John Wellborn Root Jnr (1887–1963) *see* HOLABIRD & ROOT.

D. Hoffmann (ed.), *The Meaning of Architecture: Buildings and Writings by J.W.R.*, New York 1967; D. Hoffmann, *The Architecture of J.W.R.*, Baltimore 1973; Zukowsky 1988.

**Root house**. A small building constructed mainly of stumps and roots of dead trees as a picturesque feature for an English C18–19 LANDSCAPE GARDEN.

**Roriczer** or **Roritzer**. A family of C15 German masons, master masons of Regensburg Cathedral for three generations. Wenzel died in 1419. His style was so clearly influenced by Prague and the PARLERS that he must have been trained in their lodge. The surviving drawing of the west front of the cathedral may be his. Konrad, his son (d.1477), is mentioned as master mason to the cathedral in 1456 and 1474. Concurrently, he had the same

job at St Lorenz in Nuremberg (*see* HEINZELMANN) from 1439 onwards. At Regensburg he probably designed the triangular porch. He was consulted for St Stephan in Vienna in 1462, and for the Frauenkirche in Munich in 1475. His son Matthäus or Mathes (1430–*c.*1495) worked under his father at S. Lorenz, Nuremberg, becoming master mason there 1463–6. Between 1466 and 1473 he was a member of the Brotherhood of Masons at Regensburg and worked with Hans BÖBLINGER at Esslingen. He was in Munich in 1473 and in 1476 became a citizen of Regensburg, where in 1477 he followed his father as master mason at the cathedral, of which the west façade, the Eichel turret (1487–8) and the tabernacle (1493) are his. He published an important booklet on how to set out Gothic finials, *Büchlein vor des fialen Gerechtigkeit* (Regensburg 1486); also *Winpergbüchlein* and *Geometria deutsch*, (Regensburg 1486–90). His brother Wolfgang was appointed his successor. Wolfgang was executed for political reasons in 1514.

L. R. Shelby, *Gothic Design Techniques: The Fifteenth Century Design Booklets of M.R. and Hans Schluttermayer*, Carbondale 1977; A. Hubel in Recht 1989.

**Rose**, James C. (1910–91). Influential American landscape architect. With ECKBO and KILEY he rebelled against the Historicist teaching at Harvard 1936–8 and set out to evolve garden designs in key with the free flow of interior space in buildings by GROPIUS, MIES VAN DER ROHE, etc. He was influenced by the paintings of Mondrian and VAN DOESBURG and inspired by Zen Buddhism. Although employed mainly on private gardens, he had great influence through his writings in periodicals from 1938 onwards as well as with his books, *Creative Gardens* (1958), *Gardens Make Me Laugh*

(1965) and *The Heavenly Environment* (1990).

M. Snow, *Modern American Gardens Designed by J.R.*, 1967.

**Rose window** or **wheel window**. A circular window with FOILS of patterned TRACERY arranged like the spokes of a wheel.

**Rosette**. A rose-shaped PATERA. *See* Fig. 90.

**Rossellino**, Bernardo di Matteo Gamberelli called (1409–64). Italian architect and sculptor. Precocious, he was still only in his twenties when he completed the Misericordia at Arezzo (1433) and the Chiostro degli Aranci in the Badia, Florence (1436–7). In the 1440s he was concerned mainly with sculpture, but in the 1450s in Rome he became *ingegnere di palazzo* to Pope Nicholas V and also knew ALBERTI. Later, back in Florence, he superintended the building of Alberti's Palazzo Rucellai and completed the lantern on BRUNELLESCHI's *duomo*. His chief works in architecture are the piazza and surrounding buildings at Pienza (1460–62), commissioned by Pope Pius II (Piccolomini), notably the cathedral and Palazzo Piccolomini. It was the first ideal city of the Renaissance to be realized.

C. R. Meek, *Studies in the Architectural Career of B. di M.G. called R.*, Ann Arbor and London 1980; C. R. Mack, *Pienza. The Creation of a Renaissance City*, London 1987; A. Tonnesmann, *Pienza-Stadtebau und Humanismus*, Munich 1990; Heydenreich 1996.

**Rossetti**, Biagio (*c.*1447–1516). Italian architect and town planner, responsible for the expansion of Ferrara under Duke Ercole I by a planned extension to the north on a site enclosed by a wall – the Addizione Erculea. It is the most important piece of systematic Renaissance town planning in Italy, and contains four churches and eight palaces by Rossetti. He is first recorded working at Palazzo Schifanoia, Ferrara, under Pietro Benvenuti (d.1483), whom he succeeded as ducal architect. In 1492 he began work on the Addizione Erculea. His most important building is the Palazzo dei Diamanti (after 1498), but the Casa Rossetti and the Palazzi Bevilacqua and Rondinelli in Piazza Nuova (1490s) are very accomplished too. His Palazzo di Lodovico Moro is *c.*1500. S. Francesco and S. Cristoforo are the best preserved of his four churches, S. Maria in Vado and S. Benedetto being much altered or damaged.

B. Zevi, *B.R. architetto ferrarese*, Turin 1960; A. F. Marcianò, *L'età di B.R. Rinascimento di casa d'Este*, Rome 1991; Heydenreich 1996.

**Rossi**, Aldo (1931–97). Italian architect and stimulating theorist, notable also for his colourful drawings. He was the leading proponent of the Italian anti-Modernist NEO-RATIONALISM movement, of which his book *L'architettura della città* (1966, English edn 1982) was the seminal text. With its study of the morphology of cities founded on typologies of basic pre-industrial patterns reinterpreted in a language of simple geometries, it made a notable contribution to URBANISM. His San Cataldo Cemetery, Modena (designed 1971–6, built 1980–5), was the movement's masterpiece, though his residential block for AYMONINO's Gallaratese complex, Milan (1970–73) should be mentioned along with his school at Fagnano Olona (1974–7) and the floating demountable theatre for Venice (1979). Outstanding among his later works were the renovations and additions to the Carlo Felice Theatre, Genoa (1981–91, with GARDELLA); the Centro Torri, Parma (1985–8); the Südliche Friedrichstadt Housing, Berlin (1981–8); the Palazzo Hotel, Fukuoka,

Japan (1987–8); the University of Castellanza building, Italy (1990, renovation of an abandoned textile factory); the Bonnefanten Museum, Maastricht, Netherlands (1990–95); Celebration Place, Celebration, Florida (1991–95). He published *A Scientific Autobiography* (Cambridge, Mass. 1981).

A. Ferlin, *A.R. Architecture 1959–87*, Cambridge, Mass. 1989; A. Ferlenga, *A.R. Architecture 1988–92*, Milan 1993; H. Geisert (ed.), *A.R. Architect*, London 1994.

**Rossi**, Giovanni Antonio de (1616–95), *see* DE ROSSI, Giovanni Antonio.

**Rossi**, Karl Ivanovich (1775–1849). The leading architect in post-1815 St Petersburg, where he was responsible for replacing the Greek Revival style of THOMON, VORONIKHIN and ZAKHAROV with a much juicier Rome-inspired brand of Classicism. The son of an Italian ballerina, he was trained in Russia and visited Italy only in 1802. Until 1816 he worked mainly in Moscow, but his principal buildings are in St Petersburg: the New Michael Palace (now the Russian Museum), 1819–28, together with the square and surrounding buildings, the huge and richly Roman General Staff Arch and the vast hemicycle of office buildings on either side; the Alexander, now Pushkin, Theatre (1827–32); and the Senate and Synod (1829–34). But he is perhaps less important for these than for the town planning around them.

M. Z. Taranovskaya, *K.R.*, Leningrad 1980; Hamilton 1983.

**Rostral column**, *see* COLUMNA ROSTRATA.

**Rostrum**. A raised platform, stand or dais for public speaking. That in the Ancient Roman forum was decorated with the prows (*rostra*) of captured ships, hence the name.

**Roth**, Emery (1871–1948). Born in Hungary, he emigrated to the USA in 1884 and worked under BURNHAM before setting himself up in New York in 1898. He made his name with the Ritz Tower, Park Avenue (1925), followed by the Art Deco twin-towered San Remo and Eldorado Buildings, New York (1930). His sons Robert (b.1928) and Julian carried on after 1948 as Emery Roth & Sons, with their Look Building, Madison Avenue (1949), and became the outstanding exponents of CORPORATE MODERNISM in the 1950s and 1960s, e.g. 460 Park Avenue (1955); 415 Madison Avenue (1956) and 400 and 410 Park Avenue, New York (1958 and 1959). Between 1950 and 1970 they built seventy or more major office buildings in New York City.

S. Ruttenbaum, *Mansions in the Clouds: The Skyscraper Palazzi of E.R.*, New York 1986.

**Rotunda**. A building (often surrounded by a colonnade) or room circular in plan and usually domed, e.g. the Pantheon.

**Roughcast, slapdash, wetdash** (*harl* in Scotland). An external rendering of rough material, usually applied in two coats of cement and sand on to which gravel, crushed stone or pebbles are thrown before the second coat is dry; also called *pebbledash*.

**Rousseau**, Pierre (1751–1810), *see* FRENCH ARCHITECTURE.

**Royston**, Robert (b.1918), *see* ECKBO, Garrett.

**Rubble masonry**. Rough unhewn building stones or flints, generally not laid in regular courses. *Coursed rubble* is walling with the stones or flints roughly dressed and laid in deep courses. *Snecked* or *speckled rubble* is walling with stones of varying sizes with small rectangular fillings or snecks between them.

**Rudnyev**, Lev Vladimirovich (1885–1956), *see* RUSSIAN ARCHITECTURE.

**Rudolph**, Paul (1918–97). American architect, trained under GROPIUS at Harvard. He began in Florida in 1946 and a series of small houses with slim columns and airy canopies followed, many in Siesta Key. In 1957 he became head of the school of architecture at Yale and designed the new Art and Architecture Building, New Haven, Connecticut (1958–63), which, with its massive striated concrete columns and rugged interlocking planes, belonged unmistakably to BRUTALISM. But Rudolph, like Eero SAARINEN and JOHNSON, was not one of those who felt compelled to adhere to one style in all their buildings, even those of the same years, e.g. the dynamic expressionist Temple Street Parking Garage, New Haven (1959–62). His notable buildings of these years include the mannered Jewett Arts Center, Wellesley College, Massachusetts (1955–9), and the Tuskegee Institute Chapel, Tuskegee, Alabama (1969), as well as the 'Brutalist' Endo Laboratories, Garden City, NY (1961–4), and the major URBAN RENEWAL project for the Government Center, Boston (1961–3, 1967–72). However, his reputation declined after the 1960s and his often remarkable later buildings were mostly outside the US, e.g. the Diaei Company Building, Nagoya, Japan (1971); the Pan-Lion Hotel, Jerusalem (1974); the Dharmala Building, Jakarta, Indonesia (1982), partly inspired by indigenous forms as were his Grand Road Condominium, Singapore (1987), and the twin octagonal towers of the Lippo Center, Hong Kong (1988).

S. Moholy-Nagy, *Introduction to the Architecture of P.R.*, New York 1970; R. Spade, *P.R.*, London/New York 1971.

**Rumford**, Benjamin Thompson, Count von (1753–1814). American scientist, inventor, soldier and landscape architect. He was born in Massachusetts but spent most of his life in Europe, where he was made a count of the Holy Roman Empire. In Munich in 1789 he advised on and perhaps initiated the Englischer Garten laid out by F. SCKELL. It was the first PUBLIC PARK designed as such and a notable example of the English LANDSCAPE GARDEN style. It survives intact, though enlarged. This park and his essay on the value of public parks in his *Philosophical Papers* (London 1802) influenced DOWNING and OLMSTED among others.

**Rundbogenstil**. German C19 'round-arched style' derived in various degrees from Early Christian, Byzantine, German and Italian Romanesque and even Italian Early Renaissance styles. It corresponds to the neo-Romanesque of C19 France and the USA and to the neo-Norman of C19 England but is much more prominent, having been used by GÄRTNER, KLENZE, SCHINKEL and many other architects. The term seems to have been coined by H. Hübsch in 1828. *See also* HISTORICISM.

**Running dog**. A classical ornament often used in a frieze, similar to the wave ornament. It is sometimes called a *Vitruvian scroll*. *See* Fig. 101.

Fig. 101 Running dog

**Ruskin**, John (1819–1900). English writer, not an architect, but the source of an influence as strong on architecture as it was on the appreciation of art. This influence made itself felt in two ways: by the principles which Ruskin tried to establish, and by the styles whose adoption he pleaded for.

As for the former, they are chiefly the principles of the *Seven Lamps of Architecture*, which came out in 1849: Sacrifice (architecture, as against mere building, takes into account the venerable and beautiful, however 'unnecessary'); Truth (no disguised supports, no sham materials, no machine work for handwork); Power (simple grand massing); Beauty (only possible by imitation of, or inspiration from, nature); Life (architecture must express a fullness of life, embrace boldness and irregularity, scorn refinement, and also be the work of men as men, i.e. handwork); Memory (the greatest glory of a building is its age, and we must therefore build for perpetuity); Obedience (a style must be universally accepted: 'We want no new style', 'the forms of architecture already known are good enough for us'). From this last point, Ruskin proceeded to list the styles of the past which are perfect enough to be chosen for universal obedience. They are the Pisan Romanesque, the Early Gothic of west Italy, the Venetian Gothic, and the earliest English Decorated. This last, the style of the late C13 to early C14, had in fact been the choice of PUGIN, of the Cambridge Camden Movement (*see* BUTTERFIELD), and of SCOTT. But Ruskin's next book on architecture was *The Stones of Venice* (1851–3), which, being in praise of the Venetian Gothic, led admirers of Ruskin to imitate that style – G. F. BODLEY, J. P. SEDDON, J. Prichard, early STREET, early GODWIN and the Irish architects Benjamin WOODWARD and Thomas Deane (1792–1871), whose University Museum, Oxford (1854–60), was a notable essay in Ruskinian Gothic. But *The Stones of Venice* also contains the celebrated chapter *On the Nature of Gothic*, which for the first time equated the beauties of medieval architecture and decoration with the pleasure taken by the workman in producing them. This was the mainspring that released the work of MORRIS as creator of workshops and as social reformer. *See also* RESTORATION.

Hitchcock 1954; Pevsner 1972; E. Blau, *R. Gothic: The Architecture of Deane and Woodward 1845–61*, Princeton 1982; M. Swenarton, *Artisans and Architects. The R. Tradition in Architectural Thought*, London 1989; M. W. Brooks, *J.R. and Victorian Architecture*, London 1990; M. Wheeler and N. Whitels (eds.), *The Lamp of Memory. R. Tradition and Architecture*, Manchester 1992.

**Russian architecture**. The architectural history of Russia is conditioned by Orthodox Eastern Europe: unlike the West, yet similarly, if tenuously, linked with the traditions of classical antiquity (through Byzantium), and experiencing from time to time westernizing movements that culminated in the comprehensive reforms of Peter the Great (*c.*1700). Uniquely among Orthodox lands, Russia has preserved buildings of aesthetic significance from all periods in nearly 1,000 years of architectural development. Since Russia did not experience the Renaissance, the first seven centuries of its architectural history after the official conversion to Christianity (AD 988) may broadly be termed medieval. Thereafter the same standard categories of periodization (Baroque, neo-classical, etc.) are applied as in the rest of Europe.

From prehistoric times the material of vernacular Russian architecture was wood, used until this century not only for domestic buildings but in quite elaborate structures (fortresses, churches, palaces). The early development of such architecture is hard to establish, since no surviving building appears to be older than the church of the Muromsky monastery on Lake Onega (standing in 1391), and few antedate the C17. Literary evidence suggests an elaborate wooden architecture as early as the C10 (any links with Viking Scandinavia are so far unelucidated).

With the transplanting of Byzantine Orthodox culture into Kievan Russia at the Conversion, ambitious brick and stone buildings begin to be commissioned (masonry may indeed have appeared earlier, in the Kiev Prince's palace). Excavations of the so-called Tithe church in Kiev (late C10) revealed a cross-in-square BYZANTINE cathedral with rich decoration. The earliest standing churches, of the C11, are located on or near the great trade route 'from the Vikings to the Greeks', axis of the Old Russian state. The Transfiguration Cathedral at Chernigov (c.1036) is unique in showing the longitudinal tendencies of a domed basilica. All other Old Russian churches are based on the classic middle-Byzantine CROSS-IN-SQUARE plan, generally a cross-vaulted and centrally domed quincunx with apses to east and narthex to west. Santa Sophia ('Holy Wisdom') – the 'Great Church' of Kiev, begun in 1037 – is uniquely elaborate with its seven naves, staircase-towers, thirteen domes on elongated drums grouped pyramidally, and mixed fresco and mosaic decoration. Santa Sophia of Novgorod (1045) is starker and the vertical tendency more emphatic.

Russian C11–12 architecture (particularly in Novgorod) is characterized by simple forms and a craggy monumentality; exterior decorative effect is often achieved through mixed brick-and-stonework set in prominent bands of pink (brick-dust) mortar – later concealed by whitewash and (in the south) stuccoed Baroque accretions. Around the mid C12 new strivings towards refinement and decorative complexity appear, and considerable variegation in architectural patterns is seen within the fragmented Russian principalities. The shift of the Grand Prince's capital from Kiev to Vladimir in the north-eastern forest zone is marked by the construction of a splendid group of churches in fine white local limestone, some of which (notably St Demetrius, Vladimir, 1199, and Yuryev-Polsky, 1230) are covered externally with low-relief figurative sculpture, of complex iconography and uncertain provenance. (Scholars have attempted to demonstrate variously Romanesque, Transcaucasian, Serbian, Byzantine and native Russian elements in these remarkable structures, without definitive conclusions.) A portion of the royal palace at Bogolyubovo near Vladimir (1158) is the earliest surviving Russian domestic building. Meanwhile architectural innovation proceeded in a different direction in the west Russian lands, and subsequently Novgorod; the Yefrosinyev monastery cathedral at Polotsk (mid-C12) and the church of St Michael at Smolensk (1191) add a central element with curved gable-ends (bochka, 'barrel') beneath the central drum, thus creating the outline of a stepped pyramid – a development that was crucially to affect the history of the cross-domed church in Russia in the later Middle Ages. The brick-built Pyatnitsky church in Chernigov (c.1200) takes the process further; superposed gable-ends (pointed, though Gothic influence is unlikely) rise in a dramatic series of steps that clearly foreshadow the later Muscovite kokoshniki (small tiered decorative arches). Ogees are seen at Yuryev-Polsky and Suzdal (1222), their form reminiscent of the characteristic Russian 'onion dome' (whose early history is obscure, though it had evolved out of the 'helmet' dome by the C13, probably in Novgorod).

The Tatar invasion (sack of Kiev, 1240) and 240 years of occupation checked but did not completely arrest building activity. Novgorod recovered its prosperity before the turn of the century, and numerous small churches – inventively varying the trefoil-gabled roof-line – testify to its merchants' patronage. The C14 rise of Moscow as successor to Vladimir leads to a series of 'white stone' churches (Zvenigorod, c.1399; Trinity Cathedral, north-east of Moscow, 1422; Andronikov Monastery, Moscow, before 1427), carrying the use of *kokoshniki* to daring heights. From c.1480, with the sack of Novgorod and liberation from the Tatars, Moscow's dominance in Russia is complete, and architectural patronage is concentrated there. Ivan III embarked on a grand programme of construction in his capital: from 1475 to 1505 there successively appear the Dormition Cathedral, the 'Faceted Chamber', the Kremlin walls, the Annunciation Cathedral, the Ordination church, the first stages of the great belfry and the Cathedral of the Archangel Michael. Mistrustful of Moscow masons, Ivan employed a team of builders from Pskov (in several smaller churches) and a succession of Italian engineers (notably Aristotele Fioravanti (c.1415–86), who arrived via Hungary in 1474) to oversee the main Moscow works, e.g. the Dormition Cathedral. Nevertheless the basic forms of the cross-domed church are reaffirmed, and Italianisms are noticeable only in certain applied features: faceted stonework on the Chamber; Renaissance cornices, scallops and stucco decoration on the Archangel Cathedral; swallowtail battlements on the walls.

Official church architecture of the centralized Muscovite state (C16–17) is grandiose, styleless and perfunctory: whitewashed brick replaces white stone, flat metal roofs vulgarize the subtly curved façades of earlier times, proportions become dumpy, decorative features coarsened and huddled. But an astonishing architectural development from (probably) the 1520s gives rise to a small number of bizarrely impressive 'spire' or 'tent' churches that at last move away from the tenacious cross-in-square ground-plan; techniques of popular wooden architecture are demonstrably influential. The most *outré* of these structures, the amalgam of nine churches on Red Square known as St Basil's (1555), weirdly combines elements used earlier at Kolomenskoe (1532) and Dyakovo (1547); it had no successors, though variations on the 'tent' principle (declared uncanonical in the 1650s) continue. Particularly on smaller churches decorative features (window surrounds, porches, polychrome masonry and ceramic inlays) multiply wildly; the treatment is Manneristic, calculatedly picturesque and unstructural. From the C15 secular masonry architecture slowly evolves: palaces (Moscow, Novgorod, Uglich); fine monastic complexes; domestic buildings (not numerous from before 1700, but good surviving examples in Moscow, Pskov, Gorokhovets); above all great brick fortresses patterned on the Moscow Kremlin (Smolensk, Tula, Novgorod). But wood continues to be the dominant material for all building purposes: a culmination of this architecture is reached in the multi-domed C18 churches of Kizhi.

The complex westernization of Russian architecture begins before Peter's reforms, with the adoption of isolated RENAISSANCE and BAROQUE decorative motifs (e.g. pediments over window surrounds) from the mid C17 (Residential Palace, Moscow Kremlin, 1635). The moment of transition comes with the 'Moscow Baroque' of the 1680s–90s – sometimes called Naryshkin Baroque – an original and impressive style, already showing some understanding of the orders and classical symmetry, but still medieval in fundamental respects. Among notable surviving buildings are Dubrovitsy church (1690–1704), with free-standing sculpture, Fili church

(1693) and the *ensemble* of the Novo-devichy Convent, Moscow. The re-incorporation of the west Russian lands (under Poland since the Tatar period) provided a pool of culturally westernized personnel; Ukrainian Baroque has its own characteristics, however, and stylistically the interaction with Muscovy is less significant than was once thought. In the 1700s rule-of-thumb methods of design are superseded and Western textbooks become better known; with the foundation of St Petersburg (1703) enormous architectural opportunities are opened, though till 1714 Moscow continues to be the chief 'laboratory' for new trends.

'Petrine Baroque' is generally stylistically rather restrained. Prototypes seem to be largely north European, but there are some idiosyncratic developments (e.g. towers of several diminishing storeys, often topped with a flèche). Peter imported Western architects (LE BLOND, SCHÄDEL, SCHLÜTER, Mattarnovi, Konrad, D. TREZZINI, etc., of whom the last had the greatest impact), but certain native architects show individual personality: O. Startsev and Y. Bukhvostov in the 1690s, D. Aksamitov (Lefortovo Palace, 1697) and above all I. Zarudny (d.1727), whose work is poised remarkably between the old and the new. Peter's death (1725) heralds a decline in the fortunes of St Petersburg and building activity generally; it picks up again with the reign of Elizabeth (1741–62) and the last, grandest stage of the Baroque in Russia, associated above all with the name of RASTRELLI (though CHEVAKINSKY, Michurin, D. Ukhtomsky, A. Kvasov, and F. Argunov have their own importance). Save for interior work and some house-plans of Argunov and K. I. Blank it is not really appropriate to designate this architecture Rococo. It was an age of immense palaces (Winter Palace, etc. in St Petersburg; Tsarskoe Selo; Peterhof;

Apraksin House in Moscow), but also of revived church architecture: monastic *ensembles* with tall belfries and cross-domed churches recall Old Russia.

'Petersburg Baroque' terminated with startling abruptness in the last year of Elizabeth's reign; even in the provinces it scarcely lingered beyond the 1760s. Neo-classicism found an early exponent in J.-B. M. VALLIN DE LA MOTHE. Catherine II (1762–96), consciously emulating Peter, commissioned large-scale urban building schemes in the capital and provinces, tempting leading progressive European architects (CAMERON and QUARENGHI) to settle in Russia. The last-named was an influential proponent of PALLADIANISM, yet already before his arrival native-born architects (KAZAKOV, STAROV, Yegov Velten, 1730–1801) had evolved a neo-classical manner of exceptional purity and unforced grace. BAZHENOV, one of the most original figures of the period, stands slightly apart. He and Kazakov also reflected the antiquarian tastes of the age in a number of inventive mock-Gothic buildings (with Old Russian features) from as early as the 1760s.

By the end of the century the stark primitivism associated with LEDOUX and BOULLÉE had a foothold in Russia (cf. THOMON, ZAKHAROV, STASOV), and the reign of Alexander I saw the next great age of Russian neo-classicism — more vigorous and cheerful perhaps than most in Western Europe. From Kazakov to Zhilyardi (Domenico Gigliardi, 1788–1845) several major architects concentrated on work in Moscow, particularly after the fire of 1812; in the provinces this was the classic age of the Russian country house with its park and outbuildings. Meanwhile St Petersburg was taking on its final shape (with the vast schemes of ROSSI) as one of the most consistently neo-classical cities of Europe, its stuccoed and colour-washed façades, with details picked out in white, giving a theatrical yet delicate effect.

Eclecticism, visible in church architecture (VORONIKHIN, MONTFERRAND) before vernacular neo-classicism had lost its hold on the townscape, led to the characteristic mid-C19 mixing of motifs and loss of sense of scale (prominently seen in the work of Konstantin Andrejevich Thon or Ton (1794–1881), e.g. Great Kremlin Palace, Moscow, 1838). Medieval revivalism during the rest of the century seldom led to convincing results, perhaps through sheer lack of knowledge of the character of Old Russian building (cf. the misapprehensions of VIOLLET-LE-DUC, one of its keenest proponents, in his *L'Art russe*, 1877), until the church at Abramtsevo by A. Vasnetsov and others (1882) and the Yaroslavl railway terminus in Moscow (1903) by Fedor Osipovich Shekhtel (1859–1926).

There is some interesting ART NOUVEAU work in Moscow and St Petersburg (Ryabushinsky House, Moscow (1900–1902) by Shekhtel), associated with the pioneers of the Modern Movement in art, often featuring external ceramic work (e.g. by Vrubel on Metropole Hotel, Moscow, 1899). More characteristic of turn-of-the-century building, however, was an 'Edwardian' mannered eclecticism giving rise to occasionally quite successful pastiche buildings in various classical (sometimes *style russe*) idioms. Architects such as V. A. Shchuko, Lev Vladimirovich Rudnyev (1885–1956), Ivan Fomin (1872–1936) and Ivan Zholtovsky (1867–1959), characteristically adaptable, not only made their mark at this period but were on hand much later, when Stalin's Russia rejected modernism in the 1930s, to re-establish the heavy classical motifs that dominated building of *c*.1934–55.

War and revolution disrupted architectural activity; when it resumed a new generation of radically modern theorists

was ready. Ambitions towards the total remodelling of townscape in the spirit of an exalted proletarian consciousness (Mayakovsky: 'Streets are our brushes, squares our palettes') found expression first in street décor for huge popular pageants, then in TATLIN's and LISSITSKY's visionary schemes; the notion of architectural design as a sort of aesthetic 'laboratory for the future' (MALEVICH) was eventually to clash with functionalist principles and practical needs. Meanwhile revolutionary Russia gave the world the name (coined by A. Gan, 1919) and early theory of CONSTRUCTIVISM, a utilitarian Modernism of great subsequent importance (e.g. at the BAUHAUS). Resources for large-scale building became available only in the mid-1920s, and some of the most forward-looking Constructivist designs (e.g. by LEONIDOV) remained on paper. Nevertheless the achievements of a decade or so of Modernist architecture were considerable: in public buildings (e.g. *Izvestiya* offices, Moscow, by G. Barkhin, 1927), workers' clubs (e.g. the Rusakov Club, Moscow, by MELNIKOV and the Zuyev Club, Moscow, 1926–8, by Ilya A. Golosov, 1883–1945, and others by the VEZNIN brothers), collective housing (e.g. Narkomfin building, Moscow, 1928–30 by Moisei Ginzburg (1893–1946), monuments (Lenin's Mausoleum in Red Square (1930) by Alexie V. Shchusev, 1873–1949), houses (e.g. Melnikov's in Moscow of 1929), exhibition design (Lissitsky) and, most interestingly, in large integrated schemes incorporating factories, housing, theatres, etc., notably the Likhachev Car Works in Moscow of 1934 by the Vesnins, also, for example, in Kharkov and St Petersburg.

The anti-modernist reaction of the 1930s may partially correspond to an international shift in taste, but the rhetorical architecture of the late 1940s and early 1950s is like nothing anywhere else:

notably, the half-dozen skyscrapers facetiously dubbed 'Stalinist Gothic' that encircle the centre of Moscow, culminating in the New University (1949–53) by Rudnyev. Unfortunately this period also witnessed unimaginative reconstruction in the major Soviet cities (many war-damaged). From the later 1950s simplicity and modern methods of construction have been dominant, sometimes with successful results (Palace of Congresses, Moscow Kremlin, 1964–7, and mass prefabricated housing schemes, e.g. the Kalinin Prospekt or New Arbat development, Moscow 1962–7, by Mikail Posokhin (1910–89), have led to a more sensitive approach to town planning. An interesting locale in which to assess changes of Soviet style over forty years is the Moscow Underground railway, whose stations evolve from Constructivist reminiscences through unimaginable ornateness to contemporary Functionalism. [R. R. Milner-Gulland]

**Rusticated column.** A BLOCKED column whose SHAFT is interrupted by rusticated square blocks. *See* Fig. 102.

**Rustication.** Masonry cut in massive blocks (sometimes in its crude, quarry-dressed state) separated from each other by deep joints, employed to give a rich and bold texture to an exterior wall and normally reserved for the lower part of it. Various types have been used: *banded*, with only the horizontal joints emphasized; *chamfered*, with smooth stones separated by V joints, as in *smooth* rustication described below; *cyclopean* (or *rock-faced*), with very large rough-hewn blocks straight from the quarry (or artfully carved to look as if they were); *diamond-pointed*, with each stone cut in the form of a low pyramid; *frosted*, with the surface of the stones carved to simulate icicles; *smooth*, with blocks, neatly finished to present a flat face, and chamfered edges to emphasize the joints; *vermiculated*, with the blocks carved with shallow curly channels like worm tracks. Sometimes it is simulated in stucco or other compositions, e.g. by PALLADIO. *See* Fig. 103.

**Ry**, Paul du, *see* DU RY, Paul.

**Rybarcak**, Albert (b.1958), *see* SLOVAK ARCHITECTURE.

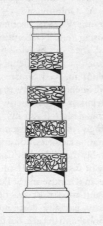

Fig. 102 Rusticated column

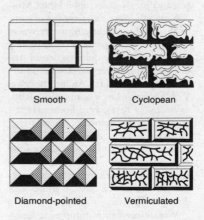

Smooth     Cyclopean

Diamond-pointed     Vermiculated

Fig. 103 Rustication

# S

**Saarinen**, Eero (1910–61), the son of Eliel SAARINEN, went with his father to the United States, but spent part of his study years in Paris (1929–30). In 1931–4 he was at Yale, in 1935–6 back in Finland and from 1936 onwards he taught at his father's Cranbrook Academy of Art together with Charles EAMES. They were to pioneer a new approach to architecture and furniture design. As an architect his important works are all of the post-war years, and taken together they are admirable for their variety and sense of visual and structural experiment, beginning with the huge stainless steel parabolic arch designed for the Jefferson National Expansion Memorial at St Louis, Missouri (1947). The General Motors' Technical Center at Warren, Michigan (1948–56), has severely rectangular buildings in the style of MIES VAN DER ROHE, plus a circular auditorium with a shallow aluminium-roofed dome, and a highly original water-tower 40 m. (132 ft) high as a vertical accent. The Kresge Auditorium of the Massachusetts Institute of Technology at Cambridge (1950–55) has a warped roof on three supports, and the chapel there has undulating inner brick walls and a central opening in a dome whose top is of an abstract sculptural form. The chapel of Concordia Senior College (1953–8) has a steeply pointed, decidedly Expressionist roof, while the David Ingalls Ice Hockey Rink, Yale University, New Haven, Connecticut (1956–9), has a central arch of double curve spanning the length, not the width of the building. The Trans-World Airline's Kennedy Terminal, New York (1956–62), with its two dramatically outward-swinging arches, is consciously symbolic of flight and has elements inside of almost GAUDÍ-like heavy curving. After that the T. J. Watson Research Center at Yorktown, NY (1957–61), is, with its 300 m. (1,000-ft) curved shape, perfectly crisp and unemotional; but the Ezra Stiles and Morse Colleges at Yale (1958–62), a unified composition, have the stepping-forward-backward-and-upward movements so characteristic of Louis KAHN's Medical Research Building in Philadelphia, begun one year earlier. Saarinen's last fling was the Dulles International Airport for Washington, DC (1958–63), with a long down-curving roof ridge on lines of closely set, heavy and outward-leaning concrete supports. He had the collaboration here of the landscape architect Dan KILEY, with whom he had worked elsewhere from 1947 onwards at the St Louis Memorial Arch. Saarinen also designed the United States Embassies in London (1955–61) and Oslo (1959 onwards). His CBS Building, Sixth Avenue, New York (1961–5), was designed just before his death and carried out by ROCHE and DINKELOO, who took over his practice in 1961.

A. Temko, *E.S.*, New York and London 1962; R. Spade, *E.S.*, London and New York 1971; R.A. Kuhner, *E.S. His Life and Work*, Monticello 1975.

**Saarinen**, Eliel (1873–1950). Finnish architect whose early buildings, notably his 1902 Arts and Crafts log and granite house Hvittrask, near Helsinki, and his more Nordic romantic National

Museum, Helsinki (1904–10), were built in collaboration with Armas Lindren (1874–1929) and Hermann Gesellius (1874–1916). His most famous building in Finland is the railway station at Helsinki, which was built in 1905–14 after a competition he won in 1904. The style is inspired by the Vienna Secession (*see* OLBRICH), but in a highly original version, and the building takes its place in the series of outstanding central European railway stations characteristic of the years from the end of the C19 to the First World War (Hamburg, begun 1903; Leipzig, 1905; Karlsruhe, 1908; Stuttgart, 1911). Saarinen took part in the Chicago Tribune competition of 1922, and his design, though placed second, was much admired. As a result he left Finland and emigrated to the United States in 1923, where his great achievement was the Cranbrook Academy. He designed the buildings for it at Bloomfield Hills, Michigan (1926–43), and became president of the academy of art in 1932, attracting there Charles EAMES and his own son Eero as teachers. It had great influence in the USA. With Eero he designed the Kleinhaus Music Hall, Buffalo, NY (1940), and Christ Church Lutheran, Minneapolis (1949). Independently he designed the First Christian Church, Columbus, Indiana (1942). He published *The Cranbrook Development* (1931), *The Search for Form in Art and Architecture* (1939, New York 1985), and *The City: Its Growth, Its Decay, Its Future* (1943).

A. Christ-Janer, *E.S. (1873–1950). Finnish-American Architect and Educator*, Chicago and London 1979; M. Hansen *et al.*, *E.S. Projects 1893–1923*, Cambridge, Mass. 1990.

**Sacchetti**, Giovanni Battista (1700–1764). Italian architect, a pupil of JUVARRA, whom he followed to Spain

and whose designs he executed for the garden façade of the palace La Granja at S. Ildefonso (1736–42). His main work is the Royal Palace, Madrid (begun 1738), where he greatly enlarged Juvarra's scheme by reference to BERNINI's Louvre project: the result is imposing, almost overpowering and rather top-heavy. He also laid out the area of the city surrounding the palace.

Kubler and Soria 1959; Pommer 1967.

**Sacconi**, Count Giuseppe (1854–1905). Italian architect whose *magnum opus* is the National Monument to Victor Emmanuel II in the centre of Rome, won in competition in 1884 (completed 1911). Among other works the Assicurazioni Generali in Piazza Venezia, Rome (1902–7), and the tomb of Umberto I (Pantheon, 1900) might be mentioned.

Meeks 1966; P. Portoghesi, *L'eclettismo a Roma 1870–1922*, Rome 1968; P. R. David, *G.S. (1854–1905) architetto restauratore*, Rome/Reggio Calabria 1990.

**Sacristy** or **vestry**. A room in a church, usually adjacent to the choir, for storing sacred vessels and vestments, sometimes used also as a chapel or meeting-room.

**Saddle bars**. In CASEMENT glazing, the small iron bars to which the leaded panels are tied.

**Saddle stone**, *see* APEX STONE.

**Saddleback roof**, *see* ROOF.

**Saénz de Oiza**, Francisco (b.1918), *see* SPANISH ARCHITECTURE.

**Safdie**, Moshe (b.1938). Israeli architect, trained under KAHN, who settled in 1964 in Montreal, Canada, where his 'Habitat' at the 1967 Expo made his name. Its dramatic approach to 'assembly' raised prefabricated building to a new architectural level. His later work is no less remarkable in its emotive use of vernacular forms, e.g. Yeshivat Porat Yosef Rabbinical College (1971–9); the Hebrew Union College Campus (1972–8); the Yad Vashem Children's Holocaust Memorial (1976–87); the Mamilla Centre (1975; 1990–96); all in Jerusalem. His Museum of Civilization, Quebec (1981–6) was followed by the National Gallery of Canada, Ottawa (1983–8), and a dramatic extension to the Montreal Museum (1987–92). More recently he has realized the vast Skirball Cultural Center, Los Angeles (1985–95); the Rosovsky Hall, Harvard University, Cambridge, Massachusetts (1991–4); and the Library Square and Federal Tower, Vancouver, Canada (1992–5). In 1989 he began the new town of Modi – in between Tel Aviv and Jerusalem in Israel – with ARONSON as landscape architect. He has published *Beyond Habitat* (Cambridge, Mass. 1970); *For Everyone a Garden* (Cambridge, Mass. 1974); *Form and Purpose* (Boston 1982); *The Harvard Jerusalem Studio: Urban Designs for the Holy City* (Cambridge, Mass. 1986); *Jerusalem: The Future of the Past* (Boston 1989).

W. Kohn (ed.), *M.S.*, London 1996.

**Sahn**. The courtyard of a MOSQUE, in front of the sanctuary or prayer hall, usually surrounded by colonnades and with a fountain for ablutions.

**Sail vault**, *see* DOME.

**Sakakura**, Junzo (1904–69). Japanese architect who followed MAEKAWA in LE CORBUSIER's Paris office (1931–6) and made his name with his Japanese Pavilion for the World's Fair, Paris (1937). His Museum of Modern Art, Kamakura (1951), was, with RAYMOND's Reader's Digest Building, the first prominent post-Second World War Japanese building and he became a notable exponent of the 'New Japan Style', e.g. the City Hall, Hajima (1959), though Corbusian influences can be felt in his work as late as the 1960s, e.g. City Hall and Civic Center, Kure (1962).

A. Altherr, *Drei japanische Architekte, Maekawa, Tange, S.*, Stuttgart 1968.

**Sala terrena**. A ground-floor room opening directly on to the garden, a feature especially of C17–18 palaces. They were often decorated with *trompe l'œil* painted vegetation or like a grotto to suggest their intermediary function between the built and the natural world.

**Saljuq architecture**, *see* SELJUK ARCHITECTURE.

**Sally-port**. A POSTERN gate or passage underground from the inner to the outer works of a fortification.

**Salomónica**. Spanish term for SOLOMONIC COLUMN, much used in Spanish Baroque architecture.

**Salone**. Italian term for a large hall or reception room.

**Salvi**, Nicola (1697–1751). Italian architect who designed the Trevi Fountain in Rome (1732–62), a Late Baroque masterpiece. It consists of a classical palace-façade, based on a Roman TRIUMPHAL ARCH; this is set on an enormous artificial outcrop of rock out of which fountains gush into a lake-size basin at the bottom. Marble tritons and Neptune in a shell preside over the whole fantastic composition.

J. A. Pinto, *The Trevi Fountain*, New Haven and London 1986.

**Salvin**, Anthony (1799–1881). English architect who came of an old North Country family and was the son of a general. A pupil of NASH, he became an authority on the RESTORATION and improvement of castles, and his work in that field includes the Tower of London, Windsor, Caernarvon, Durham, Warwick, Alnwick and Rockingham. But he by no means devoted himself exclusively to castles, though he was emphatically a domestic rather than an ecclesiastical architect. The range of styles used by him includes the sober Tudor of Mamhead in Devon (1826–38, a remarkably early use of the Tudor style), the ecclesiological of Kilndown church, Kent (1839–40), the C13 fortress of Peckforton Castle, Cheshire (1846–50), the lush Italian Renaissance interiors of Alnwick (1854 etc., not designed but approved by him), and the elaborate Jacobean of Thoresby, Nottinghamshire (1864–75). But his most stunning building is quite an early one: Harlaxton in Lincolnshire (1835–43), which is in an elaborate, indeed grossly exuberant, Elizabethan style. The building was carried on by W. Burn.

J. Allibone, *A.S. Pioneer of Gothic Revival Architecture*, Cambridge 1988.

**Salvisberg**, Otto Rudolf (1882–1940), *see* SWISS ARCHITECTURE.

**Sambin**, Hugues (1515/20–1601/2). French Mannerist architect, sculptor and furniture designer. He worked in Burgundy, where he led a school of gifted provincial architects who indulged in rich surface effects with elaborately cut rustication (e.g. Petit Château at Tanlay, *c.*1568) or with high-relief sculpture (e.g. Maison Milsand, Dijon, *c.*1561). Sambin also built the Palais de Justice at Besançon and his style had considerable influence, even in Paris, e.g. Hôtel de Sully. He published *Œuvre de la diversité des termes* (1572).

A. Castan, *L'Architecteur H.S.*, Besançon and Dijon 1891; Blunt 1982.

**Samonà**, Giuseppe (1898–1983), *see* ITALIAN ARCHITECTURE.

**Sanctuary**. A sacred place or building set apart for the worship of one or more deities, e.g. a church, temple or mosque, especially the most holy part of that place or building, e.g. in a Christian church the altar and the area immediately around it. *See also* PRESBYTERY.

**Sandstone**. A sedimentary rock, composed of particles of grit or sand with a high silica content bound in a natural cement. Sandstone is usually soft and easily eroded, but some, such as Yorkshire grit stones, the fine-grained Italian *pietra bigia* and *pietra serena* of Fiesole, or Indian sandstones of various types, are hard and durable. Some can be polished.

**Sanfelice**, Ferdinando (1675–1748), a leading Neapolitan architect of his day, was spirited, light-hearted, and unorthodox. He is notable especially for his ingenious scenographic staircases, e.g. Palazzo Sanfelice, Palazzo Serra di Cassano (1720–38).

G. A. Ward, *The Architecture of F.S.*, New York and London 1988.

**Sangallo**, Antonio da (Antonio Giamberti), the elder (1455–1534), was born in Florence. His only notable building is one of the great masterpieces of Renaissance architecture, S. Biagio, Montepulciano (1518–34). It was inspired by BRAMANTE's plan for St Peter's, i.e. a Greek cross with central dome and four towers (only one of which was built) between the arms.

Lotz 1977; G. Satzinger, *A. da S. des Ältere und die Madonna di San Biagio bei Montepulciano*, Tübingen 1991; M. Cozzi, *A. da S. il Vecchio e l'architettura del Cinquecento in Valdichiana*, Genoa, 1992; Lotz 1996.

**Sangallo**, Antonio da (Antonio Cordiani), the younger (1483–1546), who was born in Florence, was the most notable member of the Sangallo family: nephew of Antonio the elder and Giuliano. He became the leading High Renaissance architect in Rome for two decades after RAPHAEL's death. He began as an architectural draughtsman, employed first by

BRAMANTE then by PERUZZI. In 1516 he became Raphael's assistant as architect at St Peter's, and was employed there to strengthen Bramante's work. He designed Palazzo Palma-Baldassini, Rome (1515?-46). His masterpiece is Palazzo Farnese, Rome (begun c.1519, completed after 1546 by MICHEL-ANGELO), the most monumental of Renaissance palaces. The façade is astylar and the walls are smooth except for string courses dividing the storeys and bold quoins, which combine to give a horizontal emphasis stressing the gravity of the composition. It is at once sober, elegant and restful. Several other palaces have been attributed to him, notably Palazzo Sacchetti, Rome (begun 1542), which was his own palace. In 1539 he became chief architect of St Peter's, and supplied designs for the alteration of Bramante's plan (not executed). He designed the interior of the Cappella Paolina in the Vatican (1540-46). For many years he was employed as a military engineer on the fortifications around Rome. On his death he was succeeded as architect of St Peter's by Michelangelo, whose dynamic style makes a striking contrast to Sangallo's suave, self-confident classicism.

G. Giovannoni, *A. da S. il Giovane*, Rome 1959; Frommel 1973; Lotz 1977; G. Spagnesi (ed.), *A. da S. il Giovane: La vita e l'opera*, Rome 1986; C. Frommel and N. Adams (eds.), *The Architectural Drawings of A. da S. the Younger and His Circle*, New York 1994; Lotz 1996.

**Sangallo**, Giuliano da (Giuliano Giamberti, 1445–1516), military engineer and sculptor as well as architect, was born in Florence. The brother of Antonio da Sangallo the elder, he was one of the best followers of BRUNELLESCHI, and maintained the Early Renaissance style into the age of BRAMANTE and RAPHAEL.

Most of his buildings are in and around Florence: Villa del Poggio a Caiano (1485–97?, later altered internally); S. Maria delle Carceri, Prato (1484–91), the first Renaissance church on a Greek cross plan, with marble-clad exterior, Brunelleschian interior; the atrium of S. Maria Maddalena de' Pazzi, Florence (c.1490–95); the sacristy of S. Spirito, Florence (in collaboration with CRONACA, 1492–4); probably Palazzo Corsi, Florence (now the Museo Horne); and Palazzo Gondi, Florence (1490–94), with a rusticated façade deriving from Palazzo Medici-Riccardi and a monumental staircase rising from the interior courtyard. Between 1489 and 1490 he made a model for Palazzo Strozzi, Florence, in which the Florentine city palace found its perfect expression. It was later executed by BENEDETTO DA MAIANO and Cronaca, but its conception was probably his. He left Florence after the death of Lorenzo the Magnificent. His Palazzo Rovere at Savona (now much altered) dates from these years. He also worked in Rome, where he built S. Maria dell'Anima (1514) and provided a project for St Peter's (c.1514).

Lotz 1977; S. Bardazzi and E. Castellani, *La villa medicea a Poggio a Caiano*, Prato 1981; P. Morselli and G. Corti, *La chiesa di S. Maria delle Carceri in Prato*, Florence 1982; A. Tönnesmann, *Der Palazzo Gondi in Florenz*, Worms 1983; A. Belluzzi, *G. da S. La chiesa della Madonna a Pistoia*, Florence 1993; Heydenreich 1996.

**Sanmicheli**, Michele (c.1487–1559), the leading MANNERIST architect in Verona, was famous as a military engineer; most of his works have a rather fortress-like appearance, and the façade he designed for S. Maria in Organo, Verona (1547–59), might almost be mistaken for one of the fortified gateways to the city. He is often compared with PALLADIO, who was indebted to him and succeeded him as the leading architect in the Veneto, but there is a striking contrast between the massive muscularity of Sanmicheli's works and the far more intellectual and polished buildings of Palladio.

Born in Verona, the son of an architect, he went to Rome c.1505. He supervised work on the Gothic façade of Orvieto Cathedral (1510–24 – the crowning gable is his, begun 1513), where he also designed the altar of the Magi (1514–28). In 1526 he was employed by the Pope on the fortifications of Parma and Piacenza, and in the following year he settled in Verona. He was much in demand as a military architect, fortifying Legnago (1529), in charge of the fortifications at Verona (from 1530) and Venice (from 1535), and also in Corfu and Crete. The buildings he designed in this capacity are among his best – boldly rusticated gateways and whole fortresses with robust Doric columns and a few strongly effective ornaments such as coats of arms and giant heads frowning out of keystones, e.g. Forte di S. Andrea a Lido, Venice (1535–49), Porta Nuova, Verona (1539–50), Porta S. Zeno, Verona (c.1540), and most forceful of all, the Porta Palio, Verona (c.1547).

His Veronese palaces, beginning with Palazzo Canossa (begun c.1530) with a high rusticated base and simplified SERLIAN windows on the first floor, explored variations on the tradition of Bramante and Raphael, anticipating and influencing Palladio's domestic architecture in Vicenza a decade later. Palazzo Pompei (c.1530–40) and Palazzo Bevilacqua (c.1530), both in Verona, followed. Palazzo Bevilacqua, a recasting of a large medieval house round a courtyard and planned to have a façade of fifteen bays, has an elaborate pattern of windows, spiral columns, and a rather oppressive use of

sculpture. Here he adopted a device which later became popular, projecting the triglyphs to form consoles for a balcony. In his later palaces he strove towards the elimination of the wall surface, and at Palazzo Grimani, Venice (begun 1556, later altered), he almost entirely filled the spaces between pilasters and columns with windows. He was little employed for churches but the Cappella Pellegrini which he added to S. Bernardino, Verona (c.1527–50), and Madonna di Campagna, Verona (1559), are of interest for their domes, rather squat, on high drums decorated with alternating groups of two blank arches and three windows.

Lotz 1977; L. Puppi, *M.S. architetto. Opera completa*, Rome 1986; H. Burns *et al.*, *M.S. Architetto, linguaggio e cultura artistica nel cinquecento*, Milan 1995; Lotz 1996.

**Sansovino**, Jacopo d'Antonio Tatti, called (1486–1570) who was primarily a sculptor, introduced the High Renaissance style of architecture to Venice. Born in Florence, the son of Antonio Tatti, he was trained under Andrea Sansovino, whose name he took. From 1505 he worked mainly in Rome as a sculptor and restorer of antique statues. In 1517 he quarrelled with MICHELANGELO, and at the Sack of Rome (1527) he fled to Venice, intending to go to France, but he was commissioned to repair the main dome of S. Marco, appointed Protomagister of S. Marco in 1529, and then stayed on in Venice for the rest of his life. Friendship with Titian and Aretino introduced him into the Venetian 'establishment', and he soon became the leading architect, a position he maintained until the arrival of PALLADIO, who owed much to him.

Apart from Palazzo Gaddi, Rome (1518), his main buildings are all in Venice: the Library and Mint (1537–45) facing the Doge's Palace, and the nearby Loggetta (1537–42) at the foot of the Campanile. They show a happier fusion of architecture and figure sculpture than had previously been achieved in Venice and together make a remarkable urbanistic contribution to the city. Probably influenced by SERLIO's theories, he used the orders expressively to indicate the functions of the buildings – rusticated Doric for the Mint, Composite for the Loggetta (a meeting place for patricians) and so on. Palladio called the Library the richest building erected since classical times. Sansovino built several churches, notably S. Francesco della Vigna (1534, completed by Palladio) and the façade of S. Giuliano (1553–5), also one of the finest of the *scuole*, the Scuola Grande della Miseracordia (begun 1532, never completed). In Palazzo Corner on the Grand Canal he adapted a Roman-type palace to Venetian requirements (before 1561). On the mainland he built Villa Garzoni, Pontecasale (1535–45), a somewhat severe structure surrounding a wide courtyard, a radical though uninfluential attempt to create a villa type in the C16 Veneto.

D. Howard, *J.S.*, London (1975) 1987; G. Romanelli, *Ca' Corner della Ca' Grande*, Venice 1993.

**Sant'Elia**, Antonio (1888–1916), the architect of Italian FUTURISM. He was killed in the war, too early to have had a chance to do any actual building. However, his drawings, notably his 1914 *Città Nuova* series, and those of Mario Chiattone (1891–1957) create a remarkable vision of the industrial and commercial metropolis of the future, with stepped-back skyscrapers, traffic lanes at different levels, factories with boldly curved fronts. The forms are influenced by the Vienna Secession (*see* OLBRICH), but are also curiously similar to those of

MENDELSOHN's sketches of the same years. The metropolitan content, however, is Futurist.

L. Caramel, *A. S.'E. Complete Works*, New York 1988; E. da Costa Meyer, *The Work of A. S.'E. Retreat into the Future*, London 1995.

**Santini-Aichel**, Jan Blazej (1667–1723). A Bohemian architect of Italian extraction born in Prague but trained in Italy. He also made visits to England and Holland. He worked sometimes in a Baroque (derived from BORROMINI and GUARINI) and sometimes in a neo-Gothic or rather a Baroque–Gothic style of his own devising. His secular work was in the former style, e.g. town palaces in Prague and Schloss Karlskrone (1721–2), his ecclesiastical work in the latter style – gay, naïve and very personal, with a predilection for star-shaped forms in his elegant and airy vaulting. His Baroque–Gothic churches include those at Sedlec (1702–6), at Kladruby (1712–26) and the pilgrimage church on Zelena Hora (Green Hill), Žd'ár (1720–22), all in Bohemia. But he was a freak and had no influence at all.

Hempel 1965; B. Queysanne, *J.B. S.-A. Un architecte baroque-gothique en Bohème (1667–1723)*, Paris 1986.

**Saracenic architecture**, *see* ISLAMIC ARCHITECTURE.

**Sarcophagus**. A stone or terracotta coffin, usually embellished with relief sculptures and inscriptions and often of arcaded form, used by the Ancient Greeks, Etruscans, Romans, Phoenicians, etc. The term is derived from an Ancient Greek word for a type of stone believed to have the property of consuming the flesh of a dead body. The sarcophagus was revived, for ornamental purposes, in the Renaissance and later.

**Sasaki**, Hideo (b.1919). American landscape architect born in California of Japanese parents. After graduating (1948) he began teaching and continued at Harvard from 1958 to 1968, meanwhile establishing his own practice. In 1957 he founded with Peter WALKER the first of a succession of partnerships which expanded, as Sasaki Associates from 1978, into a corporation that now has design offices in nine US cities, with some 300 employees including architects, town planners, engineers and ecologists as well as landscape architects, similar in structure to SOM with which it collaborated at Golden Gateway Center, San Francisco (1960); Upjohn Company Headquarters, Kalamazoo, Michigan (1961); Weyerhaeuser World Headquarters, near Seattle (1963–72). Sasaki's role became increasingly that of co-ordinator, critic and supervisor while encouraging individual expression, e.g. Masao Kinoshita's 2-hectare (5-acre) roof-garden, Place Bonventure Hotel, Montreal, Canada (1967), conceived as a Canadian landscape with streams, waterfalls and lakes; the 'vestpocket' Greenacres Park, New York (1971). The firm's notable large-scale works include Constitution Plaza, Hartford, Connecticut (begun 1959); Foothills College, Los Altos, California (1960); Deere and Company Headquarters, Moline, Illinois, with building by Eero SAARINEN (1963); Waterfront Park, Boston (1980s).

P. Walker and M. Simo, *Invisible Gardens*, Cambridge, Mass. 1994.

**Sash**. A wooden, metal or plastic frame for glazing. It can be hinged, fixed or sliding in a window. A CASEMENT is a hinged sash.

**Sash window**. A window formed with sashes, i.e. double-hung, with usually wooden sashes sliding up and down in vertical grooves with pulleys. It can be opened or partly opened at the top and/

or bottom. Imported from Holland into England in the late C17. *See* WINDOW.

**Sassanian architecture**, *see* PERSIAN ARCHITECTURE.

**Satellite town**. A self-contained town which is nevertheless dependent upon a larger centre for certain facilities, such as higher education. Though distinct from them they were greatly influenced by GARDEN CITIES such as Letchworth. The inhabitants usually work in the central town, with which communications are easy and frequent. However, a *consumer satellite* (i.e. a dormitory suburb or town) is to be distinguished from a *production satellite* in which some provision is made for industrial or commercial employment of its inhabitants independently from that provided by the central town, e.g. the NEW TOWNS in England.

V. G. Davidovich and B. S. Khorev (eds.), *S.T.*, Washington, DC 1962; J. Beaujeu-Garnier and G. Chabet, *Urban Geography*, London/New York 1967.

**Saucer dome**, *see* DOME.

**Saulnier**, Charles (1828–1900), *see* INDUSTRIAL ARCHITECTURE.

**Sauvage**, Henri-Frédéric (1873–1932), *see* FRENCH ARCHITECTURE.

**Sawtooth roof**, *see* NORTHLIGHT ROOF.

**Scagliola**. A material used since Ancient Roman times to imitate MARBLE and other coloured stones, especially popular in the C17 and C18 for columns, pilasters and other interior architectural features. It is composed of pulverized selenite, applied to a wet gesso ground, fixed under heat and highly polished, hence sometimes called *stucco lustro*. It was also developed from the C16 onwards in Italy, especially for table-tops etc., in imitation of Florentine mosaic work.

**Scalfarotto**, Giovanni Antonio (*c.*1690–

1764). Venetian architect notable for his San Simeon Piccolo (begun 1718), which greets visitors to Venice arriving by rail. The solemnity of its prototype – the Pantheon – is treated with light-hearted Venetian elegance.

Howard 1987.

**Scallop**. An ornament carved or moulded in the form of a shell.

**Scalloped capital**, *see* CAPITAL.

**Scamozzi**, Ottavio Bertotti (1719–90), *see* BERTOTTI-SCAMOZZI, Ottavio.

**Scamozzi**, Vincenzo (1552–1616). Italian architect, the most important of PALLADIO's immediate followers, a conservative and rather pedantic formalist who maintained the principles of the C16 into the age of the Baroque. But he designed a handful of buildings of outstanding merit. Born in Vicenza, he was the son of a carpenter-cum-architect, from whom he received his training. In 1575–8 he built his masterpiece, the Rocca Pisana at Lonigo, a villa perched on a hilltop and commanding spectacular views which the windows were designed to frame in an unprecedented manner. The villa is an 'improved' version of Palladio's Rotonda (which Scamozzi had completed), with an inset portico on the main façade and Venetian windows on the others. (Lord BURLINGTON took elements from both villas for Chiswick House.) His masterpiece as a town palace is Palazzo Trissino, now the Palazzo del Comune, Vicenza (1592), where he was indebted to PERUZZI as well as Palladio. His later houses, e.g. Villa Molin alla Mandria near Padua (1597), tended to be enlargements and elaborations of Palladian themes. From 1578 to 1580 he travelled in south Italy, visiting Naples and Rome, where he gathered material for his *Discorsi sopra le antichità di Roma* (1582). After Palladio's death he took over several of his unfinished works, notably S. Giorgio Maggiore, Venice. At the Teatro Olimpico, Vicenza, he added the elaborate permanent stage set (1585). In 1588 he designed a similar theatre at Sabbioneta, predecessor of the Teatro Farnese, Parma (1618–28), by Giovanni Battista Aleotti (1546–1636). In 1582 he began the somewhat overweighted church of S. Gaetano, Padua. The same year he won the competition for the Procuratie Nuove in Piazza S. Marco, Venice, with a design based on Sansovino's Library – later much elongated and heightened by a third storey. Also in Venice, in 1595, he began S. Nicolo dei Tolentini, a derivation from Palladio's Redentore. In 1599 he went to Prague, then across Germany to Paris, returning to Venice in 1600; four years later he visited Salzburg, where he made designs for the cathedral (not executed), a cross between the Redentore and S. Giorgio Maggiore. In Venice his late buildings include S. Lazzaro dei Mendicanti (1601–34) and Palazzo Contarini (1609–16). The fruits of his travels were incorporated in his *L'idea dell'architettura universale* (1615), the last and most academic of the theoretical works of the Renaissance and the first to mention medieval as well as classical and Renaissance buildings. It also provided the final codification of the ORDERS and thus exercised a wide and lasting influence especially in northern Europe.

F. Barbieri, *V.S.*, Vicenza 1952; M. Muraro, *Venetian Villas*, Milan 1986; Howard 1987.

**Scandinavian architecture**. The beginnings are auspicious: the ship-shaped houses of *c.*1000 near Trelleborg in Denmark, sixteen of them, each nearly 30 m. (100 ft) long, and with an outer veranda all round, arranged in four squares of four, all in one round enclosure, and the superb and frightening decoration of the Oseberg ship, cart and sledges, all superb Viking work of c.800. The Vikings were heathens and intrepid explorers. They conquered parts of England, settled down in Normandy, and reached Iceland, Greenland and America. At the same time the Swedes conquered Russia and reached the Dnieper. The christianization of Denmark and Sweden took place from north Germany in the C9 and C10, of Norway only at the end of the C10. The style of the intricate Viking ornamentation continued in the next outstanding contribution of Norway, the STAVE CHURCHES of the C12 (Urnes, Borgund, Sogne) with their timber arcading structurally as ingenious as it is visually fascinating. Apart from stave churches there were also straightforward log churches of the type of Greensted in Essex. The best examples are Hedared and St Mary Minor at Lund in Sweden of c.1020. But the most impressive Swedish contribution to timber architecture is her detached bell-towers of unboarded skeletal construction. Where stone was used, the northern countries looked primarily to Germany for guidance (cf. for an early example the C11 WESTWORK of Husaby Skaraborg). Another secure, though less pronounced, is Anglo-Saxon England (e.g. Sigtuna, St Peter). The principal C12 cathedrals were Lund (in Sweden) which became an archbishop's see in 1104, Viborg and Ribe (in Denmark). Their twin west towers, their projecting transepts, their hall crypts and their details all derive from Germany. Lund is the most interesting. Its origin is Speier in Germany and via Speier, Lombardy. A master Donatus working at Lund may well have been Italian himself. At Ribe the dome over the crossing seems south-west French in origin, but the mid-C13 sexpartite rib vaults of the nave are Early French Gothic. Brick may have reached Denmark from Lombardy and was at once

adopted (Ringsted, 1160 onwards, the Cistercian Sorø, 1161 onwards). The most interesting Danish building of the Middle Ages is of brick: the church of Kalundborg, a centrally planned late C12 building with a centre on the Byzantine (Russian?) inscribed-cross plan, but with four arms of equal length, projecting and crowned by four towers, which with the broader and higher central tower creates a splendid skyline.

Of brick also is Roskilde Cathedral, much changed by picturesque later additions. Its ambulatory is French Romanesque, but other elements mark the transition to the Gothic style. The two most important Norwegian cathedrals point unmistakably to England. Stavanger has a nave of c.1130 onwards with typically English short round piers and a Gothic chancel of 1272 onwards, equally English. Trondheim has a singular east end in which the straight-ended chancel is continued by an octagon to house the shrine of St Olav. The corona of St Thomas at Canterbury, evidently the source for the centrally planned east shrine, had been completed in 1185. Trondheim must have been begun just about then. The details of octagon and choir are derived from Lincoln, begun in 1192. The screen between chancel and octagon is of c.1330 and has its parallels also in England. The west front, left incomplete, is entirely English too, of the screen type with late C13 sculpture and two west towers set outside the aisle fronts. The finest secular building of the Middle Ages in Scandinavia is King Haakon's Hall at Bergen, completed in 1261. The largest Scandinavian cathedral is that of Uppsala, begun c.1270 and with a French Gothic ambulatory and radiating chapels and continued from 1287 by Étienne de Bonneuil. Linköping Cathedral, also C13, has a nave of hall type more probably derived from English hall choirs such as those of Salisbury and the Temple Church than from Germany. But German HALL CHURCHES, more and more the favourite church type in that country, also had an impact on the north, and an increasing impact (Malmö St Peter, Aarhus Cathedral). The friars, settling from the 1230s onwards, preferred halls. One of the earliest friars' churches is that of the Dominicans at Sigtuna (*c.*1240), one of the finest is that of the Carmelites at Elsinore (Helsingborg) of the late C15. Both have brickwork in the decoratively enriched patterns so dear to the north German builders. Altogether the churches of the Late Gothic period depend on north Germany and especially Westphalia. Examples are the cathedrals of Strängnäs and Västerås in Sweden with their figured rib vaults. Swedish parish churches are notable for the survival of a large number of Late Gothic wall-paintings. For later Scandinavian architecture, *see* DANISH ARCHITECTURE; NORWEGIAN ARCHITECTURE; SWEDISH ARCHITECTURE.

**Scantling.** 1. A small piece of timber, usually no more than 13 cm (5 in.) square in cross-section. 2. A STUD or small upright piece of timber in the FRAME of a building.

**Scarp,** *see* ESCARP.

**Scarpa,** Carlo (1906–78). Italian architect remarkable for his sensitivity to materials and fluid spatial effects, in which his admiration for DE STIJL and F. L. WRIGHT were combined. He made his name with exhibition and museum designs, e.g. Klee Pavilion, Venice Biennale (1948); Gipsoteca Canoviana extension, Possagno (1956–7); F. L. Wright Pavilion, Milan Triennale (1960); Fondazione Querini Stampalia, Venice (1961–3); Museo del Castelvecchio, Verona (1964); Italian Pavilion, Venice Biennale (1968). His Olivetti shop, Venice (1959),

and Gavina shop, Bologna (1960), were notable, as was his Banca Populare, Verona (1974). Outstanding was the Brion Cemetery complex at San Vito d'Altivole, Treviso (1970–72).

F. Dal Co and G. Mazzariol, *C.S. The Complete Works*, London 1986; M. A. Crippa, *C.S. Theory, Design, Projects*, Cambridge 1987; P. Noever (ed.), *C.S. The Other City – Die Andere Stadt . . .*, Vienna 1989; B. Albertini and S. Bagnoli, *S. Museen und Ausstellungen*, Tübingen 1992; S. Los, *C.S.*, Cologne 1993; S. Watari *et al.*, *C.S. Villa 'Palazzeto'*, Tokyo 1993.

**Scarpagnino,** Antonio Abbondi, called, *see* BON or BONO, Bartolomeo.

**Schädel,** Gottfried (1680–1752). German architect who went to St Petersburg with SCHLÜTER in 1713 and built the vast, exuberantly Baroque palace for Prince Menshikov at Oranienbaum (1713–25), the first large Western-style palace in Russia. In 1735 he settled in Kiev, where he worked on the Sophia Cathedral and St Andrew's Cathedral (1747–52).

Hamilton 1983.

**Scharoun,** Hans (1893–1972). German architect who presents us with the curious case of an architect who, because of his style, stood in the forefront when he was thirty, who through a shift in style among others fell into oblivion, and who, with a return to something approaching the style which had been his in his youth and which he had never felt compelled to change, found himself in the forefront once again at the age of sixty-five to seventy. Scharoun belongs among the EXPRESSIONISTS and fantasts of post-1918 Germany; like them he freely penned his dreams. In the later twenties and thirties he built some houses and flats (e.g. Haus Schminke, Löbau, 1932–3; Haus Baensch, Berlin-Gatow, 1934–5;

in 1929–32 he planned the Siemensstadt, Berlin), but major jobs were offered him only in the post-Second World War years when sympathy with the twenties played such an important part; then the *Wirtschaftswunder* made it possible to build what had remained on paper forty years earlier. Among his last jobs were an estate at Charlottenburg-North, Berlin (1955–61); Romeo and Juliet, a twin scheme of flats at Stuttgart (1955–9); the Berlin Philharmonie (1956–63); the German Embassy, Brasilia (1970); the Maritime Museum, Bremen (1970); and the spacious new National Library, Berlin (finished 1978), opposite the new National Gallery by MIES VAN DER ROHE.

E. Janofske, *Die Architekturauffassung H.S.*, Darmstadt 1982, and *Architektur-Räume: Idee und Gestalt bei H.S.*, Brunswick 1984; C. Hoh-Siodczyk *et al.*, *H.S. Architect in Deutschland 1893–1972*, Munich 1992; J. C. Kirschenmann and E. Syriny, *H.S.*, Stuttgart 1993; J. C. Bürkle, *H.S.*, Zürich 1993; J. F. Geist, *H.S. Chronik zu Leben und Werk*, Berlin 1993; P. Pfaukuch, *H.S. Bauten, Entwurfe, Texte*, Berlin 1993; P. B. Jones, *H.S.*, London 1995.

**Schickhardt**, Heinrich (1558–1635). One of the first German Renaissance architects, less well known than Elias HOLL because none of his buildings survives, but of great historical importance. He was trained by Georg Beer (d.1600), whom he helped to design the Neues Lusthaus at Stuttgart (1584–93, demolished). In 1590 he became official architect to the Duke of Württemberg, with whom he visited Italy (1598–1600). His newly acquired knowledge of Italian Renaissance architecture was manifested in the new wing he added to the Schloss at Stuttgart on his return (1600–1609, destroyed 1777) – a symmetrical building

with some sixty Tuscan columns in the ground-floor stables. He also designed and laid out the small town of Freudenstadt around a large central arcaded square with church, town hall, market hall and hospital at the corners (destroyed in the Second World War but rebuilt) – an unusually progressive example of north European town planning. The church (1601–9) is L-shaped, with altar and pulpit in the corner.

Hitchcock 1981; *Der Württembergische Baumeister H.S. 1558–1635*, exh. cat., Herrenberg and Freudenstadt 1982.

**Schindler**, Rudolph Michael (1887–1953). Born and trained in Vienna. In 1913 he emigrated to America, where in 1918 he began to work under Frank Lloyd WRIGHT. In 1921 he started practising on his own in Los Angeles. By about 1925 he had developed his personal style inspired by Wright and the INTERNATIONAL MODERN, especially OUD, e.g. his own house in Hollywood (1922), the El Pueblo Ribera Courts, La Jolla (1923–5), and the How House, Los Angeles (1925). Cubism also must have inspired him. From 1925 onwards, for a few years, he worked in partnership with NEUTRA. Like Neutra, Schindler specialized in expensive private houses. His *magnum opus* is Beach House (Lovell House) at Newport Beach (1925–6), the prototypical Californian beach-house. Of his later buildings, Oliver House (1933), Buck House (1934), McAlmon House (1935), Fitzpatrick House (1937), the Falk Apartments (1939), Los Angeles and the Tischler House, Bel Air (1949–50), should be mentioned.

D. Gebhard, *S.*, New York 1972; A. Sarnitz, *R.M.S. Architect 1887–1953*, New York 1989; L. March and J. Sheine, *R.M.S. Composition and Construction*, London 1993; J. Steele, *How House, R.M.S.*, London 1996.

**Schinkel**, Karl Friedrich (1781–1841), the greatest German architect of the C19, was Prussian and worked almost exclusively in Prussia. He was the son of an archdeacon, went to school in Berlin, and received his architectural training there too, under GILLY, in whose father's house he boarded, and at the newly founded Academy. He was powerfully influenced by the original and francophile style of Gilly. He stayed in Italy and in Paris in 1803–5, then worked as a painter of panoramas and dioramas, and a little later (chiefly *c.*1810–15) did independent paintings too, in an elevated Romantic style (landscapes and Gothic cathedrals). This led on to theatrical work, and Schinkel designed for the stage from 1816 right into the thirties (forty-two plays, including *The Magic Flute, Undine, Käthchen von Heilbronn*). Meanwhile, however, he had begun to submit architectural designs, hoping to attract attention to himself. The first was for a mausoleum for the much beloved Prussian Queen Luise. This was eminently romantic in the Gothic style, with coloured glass in the windows and life-size white angels by the head of the sarcophagus. It was followed by church designs, e.g. a cathedral in the trees, centrally planned with a steep Gothic dome. In 1810 Schinkel had secured a job in the administration of Prussian buildings, with the help of Wilhelm von Humboldt. In 1815 he was made Geheimer Oberbaurat in the newly created Public Works Department, a high title for so young a man, and in 1830 he became the head of the department.

All his principal buildings were designed between 1816 and 1830. The earliest are pure Grecian, yet always serviceable, functionally planned, and with the motifs of the façade, in the spirit of Gilly, modified with originality to ensure that the stylistic apparatus does not interfere with the use of the building.

The Neue Wache or New Guard House in Unter den Linden, Berlin, came first (1816–18; Greek Doric portico, transformed internally 1966), then the Theatre (1818–21), large, with a raised Ionic portico and excellent interiors (badly damaged 1945, restored but interior converted to a concert-hall), and after that the Old Museum (1823–30, interior partly destroyed 1945), with its unbroken row of slender Ionic columns along the façade, its Pantheon-like centre rotunda, taken obviously from DURAND, and its staircase open to the portico and picturesquely introducing a degree of interpenetration of spaces not to be expected from outside. This is the first sign of hidden resources in Schinkel, making it impossible to label him a Grecian and leave it at that. Side by side with these major buildings, Schinkel designed the War Memorial on the Kreuzberg (1818), Gothic and of cast iron, Tegel, Humboldt's country house (1822–4), in a characteristic domestic Grecian, Schloss Glienicke, Wannsee, Berlin (1824–7) and the Werdersche Kirche, Berlin (1824–31, restored, now a sculpture museum). The design for this last was submitted in a classical and a Gothic version, both vaulted; the Gothic version won, evidently inspired by the English type of Late Gothic Royal Chapels with their four angle turrets.

Schinkel was, indeed, keenly interested in England and in 1826 travelled through the country, after staying for a while in Paris. It was not his first major journey since Italy: in 1816 he had been to the Rhine, where he developed an interest in the preservation of monuments, and in 1824 he went again to Italy. In England he was more interested in industrial developments than in architecture proper, the promotion of crafts and industry being part of his official responsibilities.

# Schlaun, Johann Conrad

His principal late works show a remarkable change of style and widening of possibilities. They include unexecuted designs for an exchange or merchants' hall with warehouse (1827?) and for a library (1830s), both utilitarian without any period trimmings. Among executed works, the Nikolaikirche at Potsdam (1830–37, badly damaged 1945 but restored) is classical, whereas the building for the Academy of Architecture is only vestigially period (north Italian Quattrocento), but essentially also unenriched Functional (1831–6, demolished). A widening in another direction led to projects for centrally and longitudinally planned churches in arcuated styles, vaguely Early Christian or Italian Romanesque (the so-called RUNDBOG-ENSTIL of Lombardy; see GÄRTNER), while a broadening of yet another kind is represented by two small buildings in LENNÉ's park at Potsdam–Charlottenhof and the Roman Bath (1826 and 1833) – and the costly projects for a palace on the Acropolis, Athens (1834) and in the Crimea (1838), in all of which Grecian motifs are applied to picturesquely irregular compositions where architecture and nature collaborate. Of his immediate followers Ludwig PERSIUS was outstanding.

E. Forssmann, *K.F.S. Bauwerk und Baugedanken*, Munich 1981; A. Haus, *K.F.S. Bauten, Gemälde, Industriedesign, Bühnenbilder*, Munich 1987; Watkin and Mellinghoff 1987; M. Snodin (ed.), *K.F.S. A Universal Man*, London 1991; B. Bergdoll, *K.F.S. An Architecture for Prussia*, New York 1994; J. Zukowsky (ed.), *K.F.S. The Drama of Architecture*, Chicago 1994.

**Schlaun**, Johann Conrad (1695–1773). A German (Westphalian) Baroque architect who began with small and simple churches for Capuchin friars, e.g. Brakel (1715–18). He then studied under NEU-

MANN at Würzburg (1720–21), travelled to Rome and returned to Münster by way of France and Munich (1724). In 1725 he was appointed architect to Clemens August, Elector of Cologne, for whom he began Schloss Brühl (1725–8, later altered by CUVILLIÉS) and the very elegant little cruciform hunting-lodge Clemenswerth, near Sögel (1735–47). For the Elector's minister, Graf von Plettenberg, he erected various buildings in the park at Nordkirchen, notably the Oranienburg (from 1725). Still clinging to the Baroque style, by then rather *démodé*, he built the Clemenskirche, cleverly inserted into a corner of the House of the Brethren of Mercy at Münster (1745–53), the Borrominesque church of St Johann Nepomuk at Rietberg (1744–8), the Erbdrostenhof in Münster (1749–51) and the Residenz at Münster (1732 and 1766–73). The two houses he built for himself are remarkably original: the Rüschhaus outside Münster (1743–49) in the Westphalian rustic tradition with a few sophisticated Baroque flourishes, and a town house in Münster (1753–5) stylistically similar.

Hempel 1965; *J.C.S.*, exh. cat., Münster 1973; *J.C.S. Sein Leben, seine Zeit, sein Werk*, exh. cat., Munich 1994; K. Bussmann et al., *J.C.S. 1695–1773. Architektur des Spätbarock in Europa*, Stuttgart 1995; F. Matzner and U. Schulze, *J.C.S. Das Gesamtwerk*, Stuttgart 1995.

**Schlüter**, Andreas (*c.*1659–1714). German architect, equally distinguished as a sculptor. As an architect he ranks slightly below his great contemporaries HILDE-BRANDT and FISCHER VON ERLACH. He was trained in Danzig (and was probably born there) but is first heard of in Warsaw in 1689–93 as the sculptor of pediments on the Krasiński Palace. He does not seem to have worked as an architect in Poland. In 1694 he was called to Berlin by the

Elector Friedrich III, who sent him to France and Italy to study. On his return in 1696 he was commissioned to carve the very elaborate sculptural keystones for windows and doors on the Berlin Arsenal designed by NERING. He succeeded Nering as architect at the Arsenal in 1698. In the same year he was put in charge of the building of the Royal Palace in Berlin, and in 1698 became its Surveyor General. The Royal Palace (1698–1706, completed by Eosander; bombed 1945, demolished 1950) was his masterpiece. Only the portal now survives, by EOSANDER after Schlüter's design. Some of his sculptural decoration on the Lustgarten façade, on the great staircase and Baronial Hall, was fortunately removed before demolition in 1950. The influence of BERNINI and LE PAUTRE is evident in the design, as well as that of Fischer von Erlach and Nicodemus TESSIN, both of whom were in Berlin while it was being built. In 1701–4 he also built the Old Post Office in Berlin (demolished 1889), but he fell into disgrace shortly afterwards as a result of the collapse of the Münzturm water-tower at the northwest corner of the Royal Palace. He was dismissed from his appointments in 1707. In 1711–12 he built the Villa Kamecke in Dorotheenstadt, Berlin (destroyed 1945, but fragments preserved in the Bode Museum, Berlin). After the king's death he left Berlin and settled in St Petersburg in 1713, where he died.

Hempel 1965; G. Peschken and W. Klunner, *Das Berliner Schloss*, Berlin 1982; G. Peschken, *Das Königliche Schloss zu Berlin*, vol. I, Munich 1993.

**Schmidt**, Friedrich von (1825–91), *see* AUSTRIAN ARCHITECTURE.

**Schmuzer**, Joseph (1683–1752). The best known of a dynasty of Bavarian stuccadors and architects in Wessobrunn. His Rococo interiors of the parish church at Oberammergau (1736–42), the abbey church of Rottenbuch (1737–42) and at Ettal (1744–52) are notable.

Hitchcock 1968.

**Schneider-Esleben**, Paul (b.1915), *see* GERMAN ARCHITECTURE.

**Schoch**, Johann Georg (1758–1826), *see* ANHALT-DESSAU, Leopold Friedrich Franz, Fürst von.

**Schoch**, Johannes or Hans (c.1550–1631). German architect whose masterpiece is the Friedrichsbau in Heidelberg Castle (1601–7) in which the architectural elements are closely knit and vigorously moulded though still somewhat heavy-handed as compared with later and more accomplished German Renaissance buildings, e.g. Jacob WOLFF's Pellerhaus in Nuremberg of the same years. Schloch may have worked with Speckle (1536–89) on the Neuer Bau at Strasbourg (1582–5) and perhaps also on the Grosse Metzig in Strasbourg (1586). The Fleischhalle at Heilbronn (c.1600) and the south wing of the Arsenal at Amberg (1604) may derive from designs by Schoch.

Hitchcock 1981.

**Schultes**, Axel (b.1943), *see* GERMAN ARCHITECTURE.

**Schuricht**, Christian Friedrich (1753–1832), *see* CZECH ARCHITECTURE.

**Schutze**, Philip Trammell (1890–1982), *see* CLASSICISM.

**Schwartz**, Martha (b.1950). American landscape architect in SASAKI's office (1976–82) and in partnership with WALKER (1984–90) but maintaining an independent approach inspired by Minimal Art (especially by Carl André), Pop Art and Land Art. She made her name with the temporary 53 sq. m. (64 sq. yard) 'Bagel Garden' with low box hedges, purple pebbles and 96 bagels coated with shellac, outside her own house in Back

Bay, Boston, Massachusetts (1979). Her King County Jail Plaza, Seattle (1982–7), is a spatially enigmatic composition of geometrical solids in pastel-coloured ceramics; her 'Splice Garden' on the roof of the Whitehead Institute for Biomedical Research, Cambridge, Massachusetts (1986), is all green with painted walls and arcs and circles of plastic resembling clipped box. On a larger scale and in a startling range of primary colours she designed the plaza for ARQUITECTON-ICA's Rio Shopping Center, Atlanta, Georgia (1988), with ferns, bamboos and fountains and several hundred gilded fibreglass frogs squatting on grass and hovering above a rectangular pool. In contrast, at Rocklin, California, she replanted meadows of local wild flowers and grasses at GEHRY's Herman Miller Western Region Manufacturing and Distribution Facility (1989). For the Citadel, City of Commerce, California (1990–91), she surrounded a former rubber tyre factory with some 200 date palms planted inside what look like gigantic white inner-tubes. For the entrance courtyard to the International Housing Site at Fukuoka, Japan, she created a circular mound of ceramic tiles (repeated in 1992 in Javitz Plaza, New York). In 1994 she began a remarkable project for the inner harbour at Baltimore.

Lyall 1991; Weilacher 1996.

**Schwechten**, Franz (1841–1924), *see* POLISH ARCHITECTURE.

**Sckell**, Friedrich Ludwig von (1750–1823). German landscape architect employed by Karl Theodor, Elector Palatine and from 1777 Elector of Bavaria. After studying landscape gardens by 'Capability' BROWN in England, he laid out the Elector's park at Schwetzingen, Baden-Württemberg, in a similar manner (begun 1776). In Munich he laid out the Englischer Garten as a PUBLIC PARK, the first designed specifically as such, initially with the advice of Count RUMFORD, from 1789 onwards. He also created the landscape park around the old French-style garden of the summer palace, Nymphenburg, Munich (1804–23). His other works include the transformation of the Mannheim city fortifications into a public promenade (1799) as well as the layout of several private parks in the Rhineland and Bavaria. He published his theories, developed from HIRSCHFELD with reservations about sentimental monuments and exotic buildings, in his *Beiträgen zur Bildenen Gartenkunst* (Munich 1818).

A. van Buttlar, *Der Landschaftsgarten*, Cologne 1989; V. Hennwacker, *F.L. von S. Der Begründer des Landschaftsgartens in Deutschland*, Stuttgart 1992.

**Sconce**. In military architecture, a small fort or earthwork, usually built as a counter-fort or to defend a pass, castle gate, etc.

**Scotia**. A concave moulding which casts a strong shadow, as on the base of a column between the two TORUS mouldings. *See* Figs. 91, 104.

Fig. 104 Scotia

**Scott**, Sir George Gilbert (1811–78). English architect, the son of a clergyman and himself an evangelical; he regarded himself as an architect of the multitude, not of the chosen few, and his sturdy stand on the *juste milieu* secured him an unparalleled multitude of buildings. He started with workhouses – a speciality of Sampson Kempthorne, the architect under whom he had worked – and he did them in partnership with W. B. Moffatt. The Royal Wanstead School at Wanstead, Essex, formerly an Orphan Asylum, is their first important work; it is Jacobean in style. But one year later they built St Giles, Camberwell, London (1841–3), and here Scott found his feet. This is a Gothic church which was substantial, no longer papery as the earlier neo-Gothic churches had been, and which was, moreover, both knowledgeable and, with its properly developed chancel, ritualistically acceptable to the Cambridge Camden group. In the same year Scott began to restore Chesterfield church, and so started on his career as a busy, undaunted restorer (*see* RESTORATION). In the next year, 1844, he won the competition for St Nicholas at Hamburg with a competent German Gothic design which established him internationally. He restored more cathedrals and parish churches in England than can be remembered, was made surveyor of Westminster Abbey in 1849, and built – to name but a few – the grand Doncaster parish church (1854 onwards), the chapels of Exeter College, Oxford (1856), and St John's College, Cambridge (1863–9), and the parish church of Kensington, London (1869–72). His style is Anglo-French High Gothic (late C13 to early C14).

He was also active as a secular architect. Examples are Kelham Hall, Nottinghamshire (1857 onwards), the St Pancras Station Hotel in London (1868–74), the Albert Memorial (1863–72), the group of houses in Broad Sanctuary, just west of Westminster Abbey (1854), and Glasgow University buildings (begun 1868). Scott even wrote a persuasive book to prove that the Gothic style was as suited to secular as to clerical C19 tasks (*Remarks on Secular and Domestic Architecture*, 1858), and was deeply hurt when he found himself forced by Lord Palmerston to do the new Government offices, now the Foreign Office, in Whitehall in the Renaissance style (1862–73). Scott was ambitious and fully convinced he was as good an architect as any; this comes out clearly in his *Personal and Professional Recollections* (1879). He was, in fact, a highly competent architect, but he lacked genius. As a restorer he believed in careful preservation, but was ruthless in action. In spite of this he was quite a medieval scholar, as is demonstrated by his *Gleanings from Westminster Abbey* (1862).

His sons George Gilbert (1839–97) and John Oldrid (1842–1913) were both Gothicists too, competent and careful like their father, but they had in addition a sensitivity which belongs to the Late as against the High Victorian milieu. George Gilbert's *chef-d'œuvre* was St Agnes, Kennington, London (1877), remarkably bare and grand; John Oldrid, following his brother, did the grand Catholic church of Norwich (1884–1910).

Pevsner 1972; D. Cole, *The Work of Sir G.S. (1811–78)*, London 1980; G. Fisher, G. Stamp *et al.*, *Catalogue of the Drawings Collection of the R.I.B.A. The Scott Drawings*, London 1981; I. Toplis, *The Foreign Office. An Architectural History*, London and New York 1987.

**Scott**, Sir Giles Gilbert (1880–1960), the son of George Gilbert and grandson of Sir George Gilbert, rose to sudden and very early fame with his design for Liverpool Cathedral, won in competition in 1904 and very evidently inspired by BODLEY. This means that it is still Gothicist in the C19 manner. However, it has an originality of plan and a verve of verticals which promised much. Scott's early ecclesiastical buildings, such as St Joseph, Lower Sheringham, Norfolk (1909–35), and the Charterhouse School Chapel (1922–7), are indeed both original and bold, and in addition much less dependent on a style from the past. Scott exploited a surprising variety of possibilities. The results included Battersea Power Station in London (1932–4), which became the pattern for post-war brick-built power stations all over England, culminating in his Bankside Power Station, London (1957–60), and the new Waterloo Bridge (1939–45), with the fine sweep of its shallow arches. However, his official representational architecture lost the early tensions and turned commonplace: Cambridge University Library (1931–4), the new building for the Bodleian Library, Oxford (1936–46), Guildhall Building, London (1954–8).

V. L. Cotton, *The Book of Liverpool Cathedral*, London 1964.

**Scott**, Mackay Hugh Baillie (1865–1945), *see* ARTS AND CRAFTS.

**Scott**, Michael (1905–89), *see* IRISH ARCHITECTURE.

**Scott-Brown**, Denise (b.1931), *see* VENTURI, Robert.

**Scottish architecture**. Prehistory is characteristically represented by Neolithic chamber-tombs (Maes Howe, Orkney), a Bronze Age stone circle (Callanish), hut circles and round WHEELHOUSES and defensive BROCHS. Roman occupation lasted from AD 58 to 100 and from 140 to 200 and was superficial. Several forts were built, but the most familiar monument is the Antonine Wall of 143. The Dark Ages produced beehive huts and high crosses. The Ruthwell Cross of *c*.700 is the most accomplished in Britain. The figure sculpture surpasses anything of the same date in all Europe. Round church towers, an Irish feature, begin in Scotland as in Ireland in the C10 (Brechin, Egilsay). The Romanesque style starts in the C11, but the major Norman works belong to the C12: Dunfermline (*c*.1150) under

Durham influence, Jedburgh Abbey of the same date with the so-called giant arcading of Romsey and Oxford, and Kelso of the late C12 with the west transept of Ely and Bury St Edmunds. Castles of stone appeared in the late C12; but Scotland did not go in for keeps. To the Transitional from Norman to Gothic belong the Cistercian Dundrennan Abbey and the elegant nave of Jedburgh. Fully Gothic are the choir of Glasgow Cathedral with its vaulted undercroft, the beautiful west end of Elgin and the nave of Dunblane. The paramount example of the C14 and C15 is Melrose, which has some French features. We shall find such direct inspiration from France again later. As for the C15 and early C16 the climax in ecclesiastic architecture is Rosslyn Chapel (*c*.1450), in its abundance of decoration reminiscent of Spain, and in secular architecture Borthwick (*c*.1430) with its majestic Great Hall covered by a pointed tunnel vault. In the C15 and C16 secular architecture is on the whole more eventful than church architecture. As for the latter, it is enough here to mention St Giles at Edinburgh, with a fine tierceron vault and a so-called crown on its tower and a few other town parish churches (Linlithgow, Stirling, Dundee). Concerning castles, Inverlochy of the C13 has a nearly square *enceinte* with four round corner towers, Caerlaverock has a big C13 to C15 gatehouse, and there are many TOWERHOUSES. They are high and forbidding. Characteristic of them are the many TOURELLES, a French not an English feature. Elphinstone, the oldest part of Glamis and Affleck represent the type. The Great Hall of Edinburgh Castle dates from *c*.1505 and has a wooden roof. Of about the same date is the impressive gatehouse of Stirling Castle.

As in England the Renaissance comes in the first half of the C16 as a mode of decoration applied to indigenous buildings or elements. Such is the case of the Great Halls of Edinburgh Castle and Stirling Castle and later of Falkland Palace (c.1540). In all these cases the source is not the Renaissance of Italy but of France and her Loire châteaux. Equally French is, for example, Huntly Castle (1602), whereas Crichton Castle (1581–91) derived its façade of diamond-cut ashlar blocks from Ferrara or Spain. The castles and tower houses of the Elizabethan and Jacobean decades are Scotland's most memorable contribution to pre-Victorian architecture. Half-a-dozen names are all that can be given here: Kellie of 1573, Balmanno of about the same time, Dundarave of 1596, Cawdor of about the same time, Crathes of 1595 and Fyvie also mostly late C16. Jacobean and after are the north quarter of Linlithgow Palace (1618–21) and the east quarter of Caerlaverock (c.1620–35). Inside such buildings is often good plasterwork and far more often than in England ceiling painting (mostly of folk quality). The most monumental Scottish building of the mid C17 is Heriot's Hospital in Edinburgh of 1628–59 by William Wallace (d.1631), who was the chief exponent of a 'Jacobean-Netherlandish' version of the Scottish castle style which culminated at Drumlanrig Castle, Dumfries and Galloway (1675–89).

A Scottish C17 speciality is reformed churches of more monumental intentions than they are in England. Burntisland is square with a square tower above the middle (1592); Lauder is a Greek cross (1673); Dairsie (1621) and several others are Gothic Survival.

The Inigo Jones–Christopher Wren style took some time to get entry into Scotland. The interpreter was William BRUCE. An early example is Holyrood House (1671 onwards). It has superimposed pilasters and a pediment, once again more French than English. A pedimented centre was also introduced by Bruce at Hopetoun House in 1703. This part of the mansion and also a house like Kinross belong to the English group round Coleshill. After Scotland had thus submitted to the London taste, Scottish Georgian is on the whole the same as English Georgian. The ADAMS worked in the north as they did in the south – see the major parts of Hopetoun and Robert Adam's Mellerstain (1778) and his Edinburgh University (1789–94). His Culzean (1777–92) is the most dramatically sited of the several remarkable, almost astylar, castles which he designed towards the end of his life for Scottish clients, e.g. Seton Castle near Edinburgh. (They are very different from his earlier neo-Gothic work in England.) The most important architectural event in C18 Scotland however is the laying-out of Edinburgh's New Town. The design is of 1767, by James Craig (1744–95). But Charlotte Square was built to designs by Robert Adam (1791).

So to the C19. Scotland was stronger in the Grecian than in the Gothic mode. Of Gothic buildings reference might be made to the gorgeous Taymouth of 1806–10 by Archibald and James Elliot (1760–1823 and 1770–1810) and St John at Edinburgh of 1816–18 by William Burn (1789–1870), who initiated the 'Scottish Baronial' style for country houses c.1830, though it was his pupil David Bryce (1803–76) who became its most celebrated exponent. As for Grecian, the Edinburgh High School of 1825 (by T. HAMILTON) is one of the most serious Doric compositions in Britain. Also at Edinburgh are PLAYFAIR's Royal Scottish Academy (Doric, 1822–36) and National Gallery (1850). The Perth Waterworks of 1832 (by W. Anderson) deserve to be better known. But the most interesting neo-Greek phenomenon in Scotland is the work of Greek THOMSON, who expressed himself in that style at a time when it was thoroughly unpopular all over Europe (but cf. the Vienna Parliament of 1873–83 by HANSEN). His churches handle the Greek amazingly freely, with a dash of Egyptian, whereas his terraces of well-to-do houses such as Moray Place, Glasgow, of 1859 are clearly derived from SCHINKEL. Thomson also did commercial premises, though in that field the most interesting building is the house at the corner of Argyll Street and Jamaica Street, Glasgow, which is of 1855–6 by John Baird (1798–1859) and has an arcuated cast-iron front. Other styles used in the mid C19 are the Gothic (Glasgow Stock Exchange of 1877 by John Burnet, 1814–1901) and the Elizabethan (Donaldson's Hospital, Edinburgh, of 1841–51, by Playfair).

Nothing in such buildings would have led anybody to expect that by the 1890s Scotland would possess the most brilliant architect in Europe, Charles Rennie MACKINTOSH. His synthesis of sinuous Art Nouveau decoration with precisely rectangular panels, his synthesis (in the Glasgow School of Art of 1907–9) of functional considerations with freely playing ornament, his synthesis of sympathy for the Scottish past and daring innovation, his sense of spatial interpenetrations – all this was nowhere else to be seen combined in one man. His almost exact contemporary, Robert Stodart Lorimer (1864–1929), began as an ARTS AND CRAFTS architect and went on, like Lutyens, to work in various styles from the classical, e.g. his distinguished and elegant New Library, St Andrews University, St Andrews (1907–9), to the Gothic, e.g. Thistle Chapel, St Giles's Cathedral, Edinburgh (1910), to the Scottish Baronial, often with a touch of the vernacular sensitively used. His Scottish National War Memorial in Edinburgh Castle was his last and best-known work.

Among recent buildings the controversial megastructure town centre at Cumbernauld New Town near Glasgow (1963), St Bride at East Kilbride (1958) by Jack Coia (1898–1981) and the student accommodation (1964–9) and Arts Centre (1974–5) at St Andrews University, St Andrews, by STIRLING were notable. Ian Hamilton FINLAY has made a unique contribution to landscape architecture.

**Screen.** A partition wall of wood or stone, with one or more doors, as at the kitchen end of a medieval hall where it usually supports a gallery. *See also* PARCLOSE; ROOD SCREEN.

**Screens passage.** The space at the service end of a medieval hall between the screen and the buttery, kitchen and pantry entrances.

**Scriptorium.** The place where manuscripts were written and illuminated in a monastery, cathedral or secular workshop.

**Scroll.** 1. An ornament in the form of a scroll of paper partly rolled. 2. In classical architecture, the VOLUTE of an Ionic or Corinthian CAPITAL. 3. In Early English and Decorated Gothic architecture, a moulding in such a form. *See* Fig. 105.

Fig. 105 Scroll

**Scuola.** Italian for 'school' but in Venice the term for religious confraternities of laymen and their premises, which often comprise imposing ceremonial spaces, usually large halls, one above the other. Several are notable architecturally: Scuola

Grande di S. Marco by LOMBARDO and CODUSSI (begun 1485); di S. Giovanni Evangelista, staircase by Codussi (begun 1496); di S. Rocco by BON (begun 1516); della Misericordia by SANSOVINO (begun 1532); and the Scuola dei Carmine by LONGHENA of 1668. They are unique to Venice.

**Secession** or **Sezession**. A group of architects and artists who seceded from the conservative academy in Vienna and established the Wiener Sezession in 1897. Notable among them were the painter Klimt and the architects HOFFMANN and OLBRICH. Olbrich designed their exhibition building in Vienna in 1898. They were later joined by Otto WAGNER and became very influential, Austrian and German ART NOUVEAU (or *Jugendstil*) being sometimes called *Sezessionstil*.

R. Weissenberger, *Die Wiener Sezession*, Vienna 1972.

**Section**. A diagrammatic drawing of a vertical plane cut through a building.

**Sedding**, John Dando (1838–91), *see* ARTS AND CRAFTS; ENGLISH ARCHITECTURE.

**Seddon**, John Pollard (1827–1906). English architect in partnership with John Pritchard 1852–62. His most spectacular work is the former hotel (now university) at Aberystwyth, Wales (1867–after 1872). This displays a rather wild Gothic. Gothic and rather capricious too is the church of Ayot St Peter, Hertfordshire (1875). Much quieter is Chigwell Row, Essex (1867). The Powell Almshouses, Fulham, London (1869), are small and engaging. Finally, and unexpectedly, the beautiful church of Hoarwithy, Herefordshire (1880s), in the Italian Romanesque style with detached campanile. Seddon was on friendly terms with the Pre-Raphaelites and MORRIS.

M. Darby, *J.P.S. (1827–1906)*, London 1984.

**Sedilia**. Seats for the clergy, generally three (for priest, deacon and subdeacon), and of masonry, in the wall on the south side of the CHANCEL.

**Segal**, Walter (1907–85), *see* COMMUNITY ARCHITECTURE.

**Segment**. Part of a circle smaller than a semicircle.

**Segmental**. Of an arch or other curved member, having the profile of a circular arc substantially less than a full circle.

**Segmental arch**, *see* ARCH.

**Seidl**, Gabriel von (1848–1913). German architect and a notable exponent of HISTORICISM in Munich. His work ranged from the neo-Renaissance of the Lenbachhaus (1887–1900) to the neo-Romanesque of St Anna church (1887–92) and finally to his Deutsches Museum in reinforced concrete (1906–16), completed by his brother Emanuel (1856–1919) though not open to the public until 1925.

**Seidler**, Harry (b.1923). Born in Vienna, studied under GROPIUS at Harvard and settled in Australia in 1948. His early domestic work is smooth and efficient, e.g. Rose Seidler House, Sydney (1949); his later large-scale urban developments were more notable, e.g. Australia Square, Sydney (1960–71 with NERVI as engineer); the MLC Centre, Sydney (1978); Grosvenor Place, Sydney (1982–7); and the Riverside Centre, Brisbane (1983–7). Among individual buildings his Australian Embassy, Paris (1977–9); Hamilton House, Vaucluse, Australia (1989–91); and Marshallhof project, Vienna, of the 1990s should be mentioned.

K. Frampton and P. Drew, *H.S. Four Decades of Architecture*, London 1992.

**Seifert**, Alwin (1890–1972), *see* MOTORWAY.

**Seljuk** (or **Saljuq**) **architecture**. C11–13 Islamic architecture built by the Turkish Seljuk clan who founded *c.*1025 a Central Asian empire which eventually included Mesopotamia and most of Anatolia. It is characterized by great vigour and outstandingly fine brickwork laid in bold geometrical patterns, brick vaults with simple MUQARNAS and sharply cut stucco inscriptions. A type of mosque with four IWANS facing the courtyard and a dome behind that on the qibla side was developed (e.g. Friday Mosque, Isfahan, Iran, 1072–92, but much altered) which became standard throughout eastern Islam, also for MADRASAS. The most distinctive Seljuk buildings are tower tombs derived from earlier Iranian MAUSOLEA (e.g. the spectacular Gunbad i-Qabus, Gurgan, Iran, 1006–7), circular or star-shaped in plan with geometrical ornament and inscriptions in brickwork on the exterior (e.g. at Damghan, 1027, and Rayy, 1139, both Iran). Prominence was given to minarets as symbols of Islam more than as platforms for the call to prayer, gently tapering with bands of ornamental brickwork, sometimes with turquoise glazed bricks (e.g. the Chehel Dukhtaran, Isfahan, Iran, 1107–8). After the death in 1157 of Sanjar, the last Sultan of the main line, whose imposing mausoleum survives at Merv, Turkmenistan, the Seljuk empire disintegrated, Baghdad being sacked by the Mongols in 1258. However, Seljuk buildings were to influence later PERSIAN ARCHITECTURE under the Ilkhanids from 1295. The Seljuk Sultanate of Rum survived in Anatolia, where the last great Seljuk mosques, minarets and numerous madrasas were built, often with richer ornamentation than those in the East and with more stone masonry (e.g. minaret, Yivli Mosque, Antalya, Turkey, 1219–36; the Ince Minareli madrasa, Konya, Turkey, 1258, and the Cifte Minareli madrasa, Erzerum, Turkey, 1253; see TURKISH ARCHITECTURE).

**Selva**, Giovanni Antonio (1753–1819), a leading neo-classical architect in Venice, trained under TEMANZA, then visited Rome, Paris and London (1779–83). His early works are in a simplified neo-Palladian style, e.g. Teatro La Fenice, Venice (1788–92, burnt down 1836 but rebuilt to his design with some modifications, notably the auditorium; burnt out again 1996). But he developed a much stronger neo-classical manner later on, e.g. Duomo, Cologna Veneta (1806–17), with its vastly imposing octastyle Corinthian portico.

E. Bassi, *G. S. architetto veneziano*, Padua 1936; Howard 1987.

**Semi-detached house** or **double house**. One of a pair, built simultaneously with a common or party wall between them, i.e. attached on one side, unlike a TERRACE HOUSE.

**Semper**, Gottfried (1803–79), the most important German architect of the mid-C19, was born at Hamburg and studied at Göttingen, and then in Munich (under GÄRTNER). In 1826, after fighting a duel, he fled to Paris, where he worked under GAU and HITTORF. The years 1830–33 were spent in Italy and Greece, and after that journey Semper published a pamphlet on polychromy in Greek architecture, immediately influenced by Hittorf. In 1834 he was appointed to a chair at the Dresden Academy and there built his finest buildings. The Opera came first (1838–41; redesigned 1871 after a fire; burnt out 1945, restored). It was, in its original form, neo-Cinquecento, with subdued ornamentation and an exterior that expressed clearly its interior spaces. The semicircular front was inspired by

Moller's theatre at Mainz (*see* GILLY). After that followed the synagogue, a mixture of Lombard, Byzantine, Moorish and Romanesque elements (1839–40); the Quattrocento Villa Rose (1839); and the Cinquecento Oppenheim Palace (1845). Then came the Picture Gallery, closing with its large arcuated façade the Baroque Zwinger at the time left open to the north (1847–54), and the Albrechtsburg, a grand terraced Cinquecento villa above the river Elbe (1850–55), symmetrical, yet the German equivalent of, say, Osborne. After the revolution of 1848 Semper fled Germany and went first to Paris (1849–51) – an unsuccessful time, which made him contemplate emigration to America – and then to London (1851–5), where he did certain sections of the 1851 Exhibition and advised Prince Albert on the tasks for the museum which is now the Victoria and Albert.

Semper was, in fact, keenly interested in art applied to industry, and his *Der Stil* (1861–3, only two volumes published) is the most interesting application of materialist principles to craft and design, an attempt at proving the origin of ornament in certain techniques peculiar to the various materials used. In architecture Semper believed in the expression of the function of a building in its plan and exterior, including any decorative elements.

In 1855 Semper went to the Zürich Polytechnic and taught there till 1871. During that time he made designs for the Wagner National Theatre (1864–6) which considerably influenced the building as it was erected at Bayreuth (by O. Brückwald, 1841–1904; opened 1876). Semper's last years were spent in Vienna. His style then, as is clearly seen in the Dresden Opera (as redesigned 1871), was more Baroque, less disciplined, and looser. This is also evident in the two large identical museum buildings for Vienna,

forming a forum with the Neue Hofburg (1872 and 1881 onwards), and in the Burgtheater (1873). These last buildings were executed by Karl von Hasenauer (1833–94), but the well-thought-out, clearly articulated plans are Semper's. His writings on architecture have been translated as *The Four Elements of Architecture and Other Writings*. G.S., ed. H. F. Mallgrave (Cambridge 1989).

Pevsner 1972; W. Herrmann, *G.S. (1803–1879). In Search of Architecture*, Cambridge, Mass., and London 1984; F. Frölich, *G.S.*, Zürich 1991; H. Laudel, *Architektur und Stil. Zum theoretischen Werk*. G.S., Munich 1991; H. F. Mallgrave, *G.S. Architect of the C19*, New Haven/London 1996.

**Senmut** (*fl.c.*1520 BC), *see* EGYPTIAN ARCHITECTURE.

**Sens**, *see* WILLIAM OF SENS.

**Sepulchre**, *see* EASTER SEPULCHRE; HOLY SEPULCHRE.

**Serbian architecture**, *see* BYZANTINE ARCHITECTURE.

**Serliana** or **Serlian motif**. An archway or window with three openings, the central one arched and wider than the others: so called because it was first illustrated in SERLIO's *Architettura* (1537), though it probably derived from BRAMANTE. It was much used by PALLADIO, and it became one of the hallmarks of PALLADIANISM, especially in C17–18 England. It is more commonly known as a Venetian or Palladian window. *See* Fig. 106.

**Serlio**, Sebastiano (1475–1554). Italian painter and architect, more important as the author of *L'Architettura*, published posthumously in 1584, which had appeared in six parts between 1537 and 1551 (augmented from his drawings 1575). This was the first book on architecture whose aim was practical as well as

Fig. 106 Serliana

theoretical, and the first to codify the five ORDERS: it diffused the style of BRAMANTE and RAPHAEL throughout Europe, and provided builders with a vast repertory of motifs. (The first English translation appeared in 1611 as *The Five Books of Architecture*.) His approach to classical architecture was more critical than that of earlier theorists, he paid great attention to the meanings that different styles could convey and virtually created a vocabulary to describe aesthetic responses to buildings. Born and trained in Bologna, he went to Rome *c.*1514, and remained there until the sack of 1527 as a pupil of PERUZZI, who bequeathed him plans and drawings used extensively in his book. He then went to Venice until 1540, when he was called to France, and advised on building operations at Fontainebleau. Here he built a house for the Cardinal of Ferrara, known as the Grand Ferrare (1544–6, destroyed except for the entrance door) and the *château* at Ancy-le-Franc, near Tonnerre (begun 1546), which survives. The Grand Ferrare established the standard form for the HÔTEL or town house in France for more than a century. The fantastic designs, especially for rusticated portals, in the later parts of his books, published in France, were much imitated by French MANNERIST architects.

M. N. Rosenfeld, *S.S. On Domestic Architecture*, Cambridge and New York 1978; Onians 1988; C. Thoenes (ed.), *S.S. Sesto Seminario internazionale di storia dell'architettura, Vicenza*, Milan 1989; Harris 1990; V. Hart and P. Hicks (eds.), *S.S.*, New Haven/London 1996; Lotz 1996.

**Sert**, José Luis (1902–83). Spanish architect from Barcelona who worked from 1929 to 1932 for LE CORBUSIER, then returned to Barcelona, where he built the Dispensari Antituberolosi (1934–6). His Spanish Republican Pavilion for the Paris International Exhibition (1937, demolished) was notable not only for Picasso's *Guernica* which it housed. In 1939 he emigrated to America and succeeded GROPIUS at Harvard 1953–69. He designed the Students' Hall of Residence for Harvard in 1962 – a restless design. Other works are the US Embassy, Baghdad (1959–60), the Fondation Maeght, St Paul de Vence, near Nice (1959–64), and the Fundación Miró, Barcelona (1972–5).

M. L. Borràs (ed.), *S: Mediterranean Architecture*, Boston 1975; J. Freixa (ed.), *J.L.S.*, Zürich 1980; E. Mannino and I. Paricio, *J.L.S.: construccion y architectura*, Barcelona 1983; X. Costa *et al.* (eds.), *J.L.S. Architect in New York*, Barcelona 1997.

**Servandoni**, Giovanni Niccolò (1695–1766), born in Florence and trained as a painter under Pannini, began as a stage designer in France in 1726, but soon turned to architecture. In 1732 he won the competition for the west façade of St Sulpice, Paris. Though not executed until 1737, and revised meanwhile, this is among the earliest manifestations of a reaction against the Rococo. He later worked in England, designing the gallery of Roger MORRIS's Brandenburg House, Hammersmith (1750, demolished 1822).

Rykwert 1980; Colvin 1995.

**Setback**. An upper section of a building, especially of a skyscraper, which is recessed, usually in more than one stage, in order to admit light and air to the floors and street below. Designs for setback skyscrapers were published by SULLIVAN in 1891, anticipating the consequences of urban zoning laws in the USA from 1916 onwards.

**Severus** (*fl.*AD 64). Roman architect employed by Nero to build the Domus Aurea on the Esquiline after the disastrous fire of AD 64. Tacitus and Suetonius testify to the grandeur of the whole concept, the spacious gardens with which the buildings were integrated, the size, number and richness of the rooms decorated with gold, gems, mother of pearl and ivory, the baths of sea water and sulphur water, the dining-rooms fitted with devices for sprinkling the guests with scent from the ceiling. Nero is reported to have remarked that he was 'beginning to be housed like a human being'. The parts which survive reveal the architect's genius in designing a large series of rooms of contrasting forms and creating ingenious systems of indirect lighting. He was assisted by the engineer Celer in this work and also in a project to build a canal from Lake Avernus to the Tiber. It is probable that he was also in charge of the rebuilding of Rome after the fire and the author of the new city building code.

MacDonald 1965.

**Severy**. A compartment or bay of a vault.

**Sexpartite vault**, *see* VAULT.

**Sezession**, *see* SECESSION.

**Sgraffito**. Decoration on plaster of incised patterns, the top coat being cut through to show a differently coloured coat beneath; used mainly on exterior walls, notably in C16 Italy.

C. Pericoli-Ridolfini, *Mostra delle case Romane con facciate graffite e dipinte*, Rome 1960.

**Shaft**. The trunk of a column between the base and CAPITAL. *See* Fig. 86. Also, in medieval architecture, one of several slender columns attached (in a cluster) to a pillar or pier, door jamb or window surround. *See* COMPOUND PIER; Fig. 35.

**Shaft-ring** or **annulet** or **corbel-ring**. A motif of the C12 and C13 consisting of a ring round a SHAFT.

**Shaft grave**, *see* PREHISTORIC ARCHITECTURE.

**Shaker architecture**. The 'Shaking Quakers' or Shakers were members of a Christian communal sect (the United Society of Believers in Christ's Second Appearance) founded in England in 1747. They landed in America in 1774 and in 1782 founded their first community at New Lebanon, NY. Their statutes or

Millennial Laws (1821) laid down precise instructions for their buildings, which were to be planned as the expression of identified needs, economically and almost without ornament. Their architecture is very distinctive. Quaker ideals of simple living and scrupulous honesty are evident in the sound workmanship and strictly functional design, of which the spare clean lines and austere elegance were much admired by C20 architects. Hancock, Massachusetts, is a remarkable surviving Shaker village with several late C18 and early C19 buildings, notably the Round Barn of 1826 and Church Family house of 1830–31. Pleasant Hill and South Union, Kentucky, are also remarkable.

D. Laskin, P. Rocheleau and J. Sprigg, *S. Built. The Form and Function of S. Architecture*, London 1994.

**Sharawadgi**. Artful irregularity in garden design and, more recently, in town planning. The word, probably derived from the Japanese, was first used in 1685 by Sir William Temple in *The Garden of Epicurus* to describe the irregularity of Chinese gardens; it was taken up again and popularized in mid-C18 England and, in connection with town planning, some sixty years ago.

**Sharon**, Arieh (1902–84), *see* ISRAELI ARCHITECTURE.

**Shaw**, Richard Norman (1831–1912). English architect, a pupil of William Burn (1789–1870), a very successful, competent and resourceful architect of country houses. Shaw won the Academy Gold Medal in 1854, after having travelled in Italy, France and Germany. He published a hundred of the travel sketches in 1858 as *Architectural Sketches from the Continent* and in the same year went as chief draughtsman to STREET, following WEBB in this job. He started in practice with a friend from Burn's office, W. Eden NESFIELD, but they mostly worked separately. Shaw began in Gothic style, and did a number of churches, some of them remarkably powerful (Bingley, Yorkshire, 1864–8; Batchcott, Shropshire, 1891–2), and one at least partaking of his happily mixed, mature style (Bedford Park, London, 1877). But this style was not reached by Shaw and Nesfield at once. A few years intervened of highly picturesque, still somewhat boisterous country mansions, timber-framed as well as of stone (Leys Wood, Sussex, 1868; Cragside, Northumberland, 1870). At the same time, however, a change took place to a more intimate style, simpler details, and local materials (Glen Andred, Sussex, 1868; Grim's Dyke, Harrow, now a hotel, 1870–72). This was called their 'Old English style' and influenced the ARTS AND CRAFTS movement. This both architects have entirely in common. Shaw published *Sketches of Cottages and Other Buildings* (London 1878).

Shaw and Nesfield's mature style is much more subdued, and its period sources are mid-C17 brick houses under Dutch influence and the William and Mary style, rather than Gothic and Tudor. It was popularly known as the 'Queen Anne style'. Decoration is more refined than was usual, and interior decoration was here and there left to MORRIS's firm. Which of the two architects really started this style is not certain. Nesfield is the more likely – see his Dutch C17 lodge at Kew Gardens (1866) and his William-and-Mary-cum-Louis-XIII Kinmel Park, Denbighshire (begun 1867) – but Shaw made an international success of it. That some inspiration from Webb stands at the beginning is indubitable. The key buildings were New Zealand Chambers in the City of London (1871–3, now demolished), Lowther Lodge, Kensington (1873, now Royal Geographical

Society), Shaw's own house, 6 Ellerdale Road, Hampstead (1875), Swan House, Chelsea Embankment (1876), and 170 Queen's Gate, London (1888–90). At the same time Shaw was associated with Bedford Park, Turnham Green, London, as the earliest garden suburb ever. It was not until the 1880s that he received his first public commission, New Scotland Yard, London (1887–90), a vigorous and impressive red-brick and stone building with TOURELLES and a lively skyline. A second block was added in 1890, which Shaw is said to have regretted. About 1890 (e.g. Bryanston, Dorset, 1889–94) Shaw turned away from the dainty elegance of his earlier domestic style towards a grand Classicism with giant columns and Baroque details (Chesters, Northumberland, 1891; Piccadilly Hotel, 1905); this also was very influential.

A. Saint, *R.N.S.*, New Haven and London 1976; M. Girouard, *Sweetness and Light: the 'Queen Anne' Movement 1860–1900*, Oxford 1977.

**Shchusev**, Aleksei V. (1873–1949), *see* RUSSIAN ARCHITECTURE.

**Shear**. A force or stress acting transverse to the axis of a structural member in a building, thus tending to cause sliding between its constituent elements.

**Sheet glass**. A clear transparent glass with a fire-finished surface. The surfaces are never perfectly flat or parallel and a certain degree of distortion of vision and reflection results.

**Shekhtel**, Fedor Osipovich (1859–1926), *see* RUSSIAN ARCHITECTURE.

**Shell**. A thin, self-supporting membrane on the eggshell principle (*see* STRESSED-SKIN CONSTRUCTION), developed in the early C20 by FREYSSINET and other CONCRETE designers, notably TORROJA and MAILLART, whose Cement Industry Pavilion at Zürich (1938–9) is a paradig-matic shell structure, and above all, NERVI, Eero SAARINEN and CANDELA, who pioneered HYPERBOLIC PARABOLOID vaulting in Mexico in the early 1950s.

J. Joedicke, *S. Architecture*, New York 1963; J. A. Starezewski, *Felix Candela. The Structure and Form of Reinforced Concrete S.*, Anne Arbor 1993.

**Shepheard**, Edward (d.1747), *see* WOOD, John.

**Sheppard**, Richard (1910–82). English architect whose partnership, Richard Sheppard, Robson & Partners, designed Churchill College, Cambridge (1961–8), with a number of small and medium-sized courts grouped loosely round the towering concrete-vaulted hall; hostels for Imperial College, London (1961–3); Digby Hall, Leicester University (1958–62); the School of Navigation of Southampton University (1959–61); the West Midland Training College at Walsall (1960–63); and the City University, St John Street, London (1976).

**Shingle style**. The American term for the Domestic Revival of the 1870s and 1880s, based on the traditional STICK STYLE, influenced initially by Norman SHAW but replacing his tile-hanging by SHINGLE-hanging. The pioneer building is the Sherman House at Newport, Rhode Island, by RICHARDSON (1874). McKIM, MEAD & WHITE also participated, e.g. the Wilson Low House, Bristol, Rhode Island (1887–8), as well as other Eastern US architects such as J. Lyman Silsbee (1848–1919) in Chicago and Wilson EYRE in Philadelphia. The masterpiece is Richardson's Stoughton House at Cambridge, Massachusetts (1882–3). The shingle style is almost exclusively a style of the medium-sized private house, and its most interesting and most American feature, not implied in the name, is open internal planning.

V. Scully, *The S.S. and the Stick Style*, New Haven 1971, and *The Architecture of the American Summer. The Flowering of the S.S.*, New York (1971) 1988.

**Shingles**. Wooden tiles for covering roofs, walls and spires. They were sometimes of other materials (e.g. asbestos, cement) but were always cut to standard shapes and sizes.

**Shinohara**, Kazuo (b.1925). Leading member of the first generation of post-Second World War Japanese architects. He began by exploring vernacular Japanese forms and spaces in small-scale domestic buildings, e.g. Umbrella House, Tokyo (1962) and House with an Earthen Floor, Karuizawa (1963), and went on to 'abstract' these traditional qualities and elements, sometimes with symbolic intent, e.g. House in White, Tokyo (1966); Prism House, Yamanaka-ko (1972). Later he turned away from this aesthetic approach towards what he termed the 'progressive anarchy' of urban chaos, abruptly inserting large-scale brutal structures in suburban city-scapes, notably his TIT Centennial Hall, Tokyo (1986–8). This was followed by his Clinic, Hanayama (1988); Hanegi Complex, Tokyo (1988); K2-Building, Osaka (1990); and the inverted pyramidal Police HQ, Kumamoto (1991). He published *Chaos and the Machine* (London 1988).

T. Matsunaga, *K.S.*, New York 1982; A. Menge, *K.S.*, Berlin 1994.

**Shoin**. An upper-class Japanese house, notably of the C16; *see* JAPANESE ARCHITECTURE.

**Shoji**. A Japanese standing screen of translucent paper or other similar material.

**Shopping arcade**. A covered passage with shops on one or both sides, or a complex of such passages; in function a European version of an Islamic BAZAAR. The Burlington Arcade, London (1815–18), by Samuel Ware (1781–1860), and the Galerie d'Orléans, Paris (1828–30, demolished 1935), by FONTAINE, were notable early examples. The development of glass and metal structures led to the construction of large-scale shopping arcades, e.g. Galleria Vittorio Emmanuele II, Milan (1864–7) by MENGONI; the Galleria Umberto I, Naples (1887–90); the Cleveland Arcade, Cleveland, Ohio (1887–90); and the GUM building, Moscow (1888–93), which originally covered sixteen blocks on a grid plan with shops on four floors linked by glazed arcades.

J. F. Geist, *A. The History of a Building Type*, Cambridge, Mass. 1983; W. Lauter, *Passagen*, Dortmund 1984; M. Mackeith, *The History and Conservation of S.A.*, London 1986; B. Lemoine, *Les Passages couverts en France*, Paris 1989.

**Shopping centre** or **supermarket**. A mid-C20 invention, sited out-of-town for automobile users, pioneered in the USA by John Graham at the Northgate Shopping Center, near Seattle (1950), and notably by GRUEN at the Northland Shopping Center, Detroit (1952–4), which was surrounded by several acres of parking lots.

V. Gruen and L. Smith, *Shopping Towns USA. The Planning of S.C.*, New York 1960.

**Shopping mall**. The urban counterpart to the out-of-town shopping centre, accommodating a wide range of activities (cultural, civic, etc.) within a predominantly commercial, consumer context. GRUEN's Fox Hills Mall, Los Angeles (1975), is exemplary. The shopping mall culminated in the Eaton Center, Toronto, Canada (1981), covering five city-blocks; the West Edmonton Mall,

Edmonton, Canada (1986); and the even larger Mall of America, Minneapolis, Minnesota (1992). Notable architecturally were Gruen and PELLI's Pacific Design Center, Los Angeles (1974 and 1990), and GEHRY's small but distinguished Edgema Center, Santa Monica, California (1989), which, unlike most shopping malls, are marked by their exteriors. Among European shopping malls the Olivandenhof, Cologne (1988), by HENTRICH and the Haas Haus, Vienna (1991), by HOLLEIN are outstanding. The shopping mall is related to the UEC or Urban Entertainment Center, a hybrid complex of retail, high tech and entertainment contained within a comprehensive themed environment.

B. Maitland, *S.M. Planning and Design*, Harlow 1985.

**Shore**. A timber or metal prop set obliquely against a wall, building or other structure (e.g. a ship in dry dock) as a temporary support, notably when it is being altered or repaired.

**Shoring**. A temporary framework of SHORES set up to support an unstable building or a building undergoing or adjacent to restructuring or other repair work; also the framework used to support the sides of an excavation.

**Shoulder**. The end of a timber member from which a TENON projects, as if the tenon were a head with shoulders.

**Shouldered arch**, *see* ARCH.

**Shurcliff** (né Shurtleff), Arthur Asahe (1870–1957), *see* HISTORICAL RECONSTRUCTION.

**Shute**, John (d.1563), the author of the first English architectural book, *The First and Chief Groundes of Architecture* (1563), described himself as a painter and architect, and was a member of the household of the Duke of Northumberland, who

sent him to Italy about 1550. His book included illustrations of the five orders, derived mainly from SERLIO. It went into four editions before 1587 and must have been widely used.

Summerson 1983; Harris 1990.

**Shuttering**, *see* FORMWORK.

**Shutze**, Philip Trammel (1890–1982), *see* UNITED STATES ARCHITECTURE.

**Sicard von Sicardsburg**, August (1813–68), *see* AUSTRIAN ARCHITECTURE.

**Sick building syndrome**, *see* ENVIRONMENTAL DESIGN.

**Siegel**, Robert (b.1939), *see* GWATHMEY, Charles.

**Sikhara**. The spire or tower of a Hindu temple, over the sanctuary.

**Sill** or **cill**. The horizontal member at the base of a timber-framed wall into which the posts and studs are normally tenoned. Also the horizontal member at the bottom of a window-opening or door-frame.

**Silo**. A tall cylindrical structure for storage of fodder, *see* GRAIN ELEVATOR.

**Siloe**, Diego de (*c*.1495–1563). Spanish architect and sculptor, one of the main practitioners of the PLATERESQUE style. Born in Burgos, he studied in Italy (Florence and possibly Rome), where he acquired a Michelangelesque style of sculpture and picked up the vocabulary of Renaissance architecture. His finest work as both sculptor and architect is the Escalera Dorada in Burgos Cathedral (1519–23) – a very imposing interior staircase rising in five flights and derived from that designed by BRAMANTE to link the terraces of the Belvedere Court. To decorate it *putti*, portraits in roundels, winged angel heads and other Renaissance motifs are used with a still Gothic profusion. In 1528 Siloe began his masterpiece, Granada Cathedral, where his main innovation was a vast domed chancel very skilfully attached to the wide nave. Here he adopted a purer and more severe manner which was to have wide influence in Spain. His other buildings include the tower of S. Maria del Campo, near Burgos (1527); Colegio Fonseca courtyard, Salamanca (1529–34); the Salvador church, Ubeda (1536); Guadix Cathedral (1549); and S. Gabriel, Loja (1552–68), with its unusual trefoil *chevet*.

Kubler and Soria 1959; E. E. Rosenthal, *The Cathedral of Granada*, Princeton 1961.

**Silsbee**, J. Lyman (1848–1913), *see* SHINGLE STYLE; WRIGHT, Frank Lloyd.

**Silva**, Ercole (1756–1840). Italian landscape architect who, from 1799, laid out a notable English-style LANDSCAPE GARDEN for himself at Cinisello, near Milan, of which nothing survives. He wrote the first Italian book on landscape gardening, *Dell'arte dei giardini inglesi* (1801, expanded 1813, reprinted Milan 1976), based on English ideas of irregularity derived mainly from HIRSCHFELD but recommending a wider range of plants including exotica.

G. Venturi (ed.), *E.S.: Dell'arte dei giardini inglesi*, Milan 1976.

**Silva**, Domingos Penente da (1836–1901), *see* PORTUGUESE ARCHITECTURE.

**Silvestrin**, Claudio (b.1954), *see* MINIMALIST ARCHITECTURE.

**Sima recta**, *see* CYMA RECTA.

**Sima reversa**, *see* CYMA REVERSA.

**Simatium**, *see* CYMATIUM.

**Simon**, Jacques (b.1930), *see* FRENCH ARCHITECTURE.

**Simón de Colonia** (d.*c.*1511). Spanish architect, the son of Juan de Colonia

(d.1481), and father of Francisco de Colonia (d.1542). Juan no doubt came from Cologne, and, indeed, the spires of Burgos Cathedral (1442–58) look German Late Gothic. Juan was also the designer of the Charterhouse of Miraflores outside Burgos (1441 onwards). Simón, sculptor as well as architect, followed his father at Burgos Cathedral and Miraflores and designed, in a typically Spanish wild Late Gothic, the Chapel of the Constable of the cathedral (1486 onwards) and the façade of S. Pablo at Valladolid (1486–99). He became master mason of Seville Cathedral in 1497. Francisco, who probably completed the façade of S. Pablo, is responsible (with Juan de Vallejo) for the crossing tower of Burgos Cathedral (1540 onwards), still essentially Gothic, though Francisco had done the Puerta de la Pellejería of the cathedral in the new Early Renaissance in 1516. Francisco was made joint master mason with JUAN DE ÁLAVA at Plasencia Cathedral in 1513, but they quarrelled over the job and also over Álava's work at Salamanca Cathedral. Álava commented on Francisco's '*poco saber*'.

Kubler and Soria 1959; M. Dezzi Bardeschi, *La cattedrale di Burgos*, Florence 1965.

**Sinan** (1489–1578 or 1588), the greatest Turkish architect. He worked for Suleiman I 'The Magnificent' throughout the Ottoman Empire, from Budapest to Damascus, and, according to himself, built no less than 334 mosques, schools and hospitals, public baths, bridges, palaces, and so on. His mosques developed from Hagia Sophia, the most famous being the enormous Suleymaniye in Istanbul (1551–8), though the Hushrev Pasha mosque, Aleppo, Syria (1536–7); the Haseki Hurrem Kulliye, Istanbul (1539); the Shezade mosque (1544–8); the Selimaniye Kulliye, Istanbul (1550–

57); the Mihrimah Mery, Istanbul (1562–5); and the small Sokollu Mehmet Pasha mosque, Istanbul (1570–74), should be mentioned. He considered his masterpiece to be the Selimiye at Edirne (Adrianople, 1569–74).

A. Stratton, *S.*, New York 1972; E. Egli, *S.*, Zürich 1976; A. Kuran, *S. The Grand Old Master of Ottoman Architecture*, Washington, DC and Istanbul 1987; J. Freely and A. R. Burelli, *S. Architect of Suleyman the Magnificent and the Ottoman Golden Age*, London 1992; G. Goodwin, *S. Ottoman Architecture and its Values Today*, London 1992; U. Vogt-Gökuil, *S.*, Tübingen 1992.

**Singhalese** or **Sinhalese architecture**, *see* SRI LANKAN ARCHITECTURE.

**Site** (Sculpture in the Environment). An *avant-garde* American group formed in New York in 1970 by James Wines (b.1932) and Michelle Stone (b.1949). Approaching architecture as a form of Conceptual Art, they propounded a 'de-architecturization' theory and in 1972 were commissioned by Best Products to design a series of showrooms. They began with a built ruin, the Indeterminate Façade Showroom, Houston, Texas (1975), which appears to be in a state of demolition. Later, at the Forest Building Showroom, Richmond, Virginia (1978–80), nature was allowed to take over with trees and shrubs penetrating the structure. Few of their later projects have been realized, e.g. their Tennessee Aquarium Imax Building project, Chattanooga, Tennessee (1993), and the Trausfynydd Nuclear Power Station Decommissioning project in Wales (1994). Their built work includes the undulating water wall, Avenue 5 at the Universal Expo, Seville (1992), and Ross's Landing Plaza and Park, Chattanooga, Tennessee (1992).

T. Nakamura, *S.*, Tokyo 1986; H. Muschamp, *S.*, New York 1989.

**Sitte**, Camillo (1843–1903), Austrian town-planner and architect, was director of the Trades' School of Salzburg (1875–93), and then of Vienna (1893 onwards). His fame rests entirely on his book *Der Städtebau* (1889, English tr. *City Planning According to Artistic Principles*, London 1965), which is a brilliant essay in visual urban planning. Sitte, with the help of a large number of diagrammatic plans, analyses open spaces in towns and the many ways in which irregularities of plan can cause attractive effects. No writer did more to encourage a reaction against the monotonous uniformity and geometrical severity of C19 urban planning.

G. R. Collins, *C.S. and the Birth of Modern City Planning*, New York 1965.

**Six-light window**, *see* WINDOW.

**Siza Vieira**, Alvaro (b.1933). Portuguese architect, trained at Oporto where he developed an Aalto-influenced but highly personal Minimalist style, e.g. Pinto e Sotto Mayor Bank, Oliveira de Azemeis (1971–4); Casa Beires, Povo do Varzim (1973–6). Some notable mass-housing developments followed, e.g. Bouça housing, Oporto (1973–7); Quinta da Malaguerra, Evora (1977). His sensitive response to site and local building traditions combined with modern construction techniques and materials is evident in his remarkable Museum of Contemporary Galician Art, Santiago de Compostela, Spain (1988–94), and the University Library, Aveira (1988–95).

P. Testa, *Arquitectura de A.S.*, Oporto 1988; J. P. Santos, *A.S.*, Barcelona 1993; B. Fleck (ed.), *A.S. Stadtskizzes*, Basel 1994; M. Dubois, *A.S.*, Milan 1997; A. Angelico (ed.), *A.S. Writings on Architecture*, London 1997.

**Skeleton construction**. A method of construction consisting of a load bearing framework (*see* FRAMED BUILDING) and an outer covering which takes no load (*see* CLADDING). The skeleton, usually of metal or reinforced concrete (or wood), may be visible from the outside.

W. Blaser, *Filigrane Architecture. Metall- und Glaskonstruktion Skin und Skeleton in Europa und den USA*, Basel and New York 1980.

**Skew**, *see* KNEELER.

**Skewback**. That portion of the ABUT-MENT which supports an arch.

**Skidmore, Owings & Merrill** (known as SOM). One of the largest and best-known architectural firms in the USA, named after the founding partners Louis Skidmore (1897–1962), Nathaniel A. Owings (1903–84) and John O. Merrill (1896–1975). SOM has branches in New York, Chicago and other centres, each with its own head of design. Gordon BUNSHAFT, a partner in 1945, was an especially distinguished designer. Outstanding among the works of the firm, which later tended to decline into what is now known as CORPORATE MODERN-ISM, were the following: Lever House, New York (completed 1952), which started the international vogue for curtain-walled SKYSCRAPERS rising on a podium of only a few storeys, and which has, moreover, a garden-court in the middle of the podium; the Hilton Hotel at Istanbul (begun 1952); the United States Air Force Academy at Colorado Springs (begun 1955), with its remarkable chapel (1962). Other important buildings are the Manufacturers' Hanover Trust Company Bank in New York (1952–4), memorably low in a city of high buildings and (although a bank and in need of security) largely glazed to the outside; the Connecticut General Life Insurance at Hartford (1953–7), beautifully land-scaped and detailed; the Inland Steel Building, Chicago (1958); the Pepsi-Cola World Headquarters, New York (1960); and the Chase Manhattan Bank, New York (1961). SOM's style developed from that of MIES VAN DER ROHE and, for many years, rarely departed from its crispness and precision. For some time the firm went in for concrete used in pre-cast members. In this field their Banque Lambert in Brussels of 1959 and the Heinz Headquarters, Hayes Park, England (1962–5) have proved as influential as Lever House less than a decade before. In some of their later buildings a playfulness – even though a structural playfulness – has appeared which is less convincing. Among their more notable buildings are the John Hancock Center, Chicago (1970), the Hirschorn Museum, Washington, DC (1973), 33 West Monroe Building, Chicago (1980), Columbus City Hall, Columbus, Indiana (1981), the National Commercial Bank Building and International Airport buildings at Jeddah, Saudi Arabia (1982), and the Canary Wharf Scheme, Isle of Dogs, and Broad-gate development, Liverpool Street, both in London, of the 1990s. Their Islamic Cultural Center (1992) is New York's first mosque. Owings published *The Spaces in Between, an Architect's Journey* (Boston 1973).

E. Danz, *Architecture of SOM 1950–1962*, New York 1962; A. Drexler and A. Menges, *Architecture of SOM 1963–1973*, New York 1974; A. Bush-Brown, *Architecture of SOM 1973–1983*, New York 1984; C. H. Krinsky, *Gordon Bunshaft of SOM*, Cambridge, Mass. 1988; R. Bruegmann (ed.), *Modernism at Mid-Century: The Architecture of the US Air Force Academy*, Chicago 1994.

**Skirting**. The edging, usually of wood, fixed to the base of an internal wall.

**Skylight**. A window set into a roof or ceiling to provide top-lighting.

**Skyscraper**. A multi-storey building constructed on a steel skeleton, provided with high-speed electric elevators and combining extraordinary height with ordinary room-spaces such as would be used in low buildings. The term originated in the United States in the late 1880s, about ten or twelve years after office buildings in New York had reached the height of ten or twelve storeys or $c.75$ m. (250 ft). It was the ELEVATOR that had made them possible. The Equitable Building, New York (1869–71), by POST was the first to have an elevator and the first skyscrapers followed soon afterwards, notably Post's Western Union Telegraph Building (1873–5, demolished) and HUNT's New Tribune Building (1873). To go much beyond these so-called New York 'elevator buildings' was impossible with traditional building materials, and further development was based on the introduction of metal framing. This took place at Chicago in 1883 (*see* JENNEY). Steel skeleton construction for skyscrapers was first established by HOLABIRD & ROCHE's Tacoma Building in Chicago (1887–8), which had twenty-two storeys and a complete steel skeleton. BURNHAM & ROOT's Reliance Building, Chicago (1891), and SULLIVAN's Guaranty Building, Buffalo, NY (1890–95), are other notable early skyscrapers. The *Chicago Tribune* competition of 1922, to which GROPIUS, LOOS, Eliel SAARINEN and others submitted notable designs, initiated the great flowering of skyscraper design in the 1920s and 1930s even though HOOD's winning design was uninspired. The highest skyscraper before the First World War was C. Gilbert's Woolworth building in New York at 241 m. (792 ft). The Empire State Building, New York (1930–32), is 381 m.

(1,250 ft) high; the twin towers of the World Trade Center, New York (1970–74, by YAMASAKI), are 411 m. (1,350 ft). The Sears Tower, Chicago (completed 1974 by SKIDMORE, OWINGS & MERRILL), is 443 m. (1,454 ft). The Petronas Twin Towers, Kuala Lumpur (1996), by PELLI are 455 m. (1,483 ft).

Condit 1964; P. Goldberger, *The S.*, New York 1981; Hart 1985; Zukowsky 1988; T. A. P. van Leeuwen, *The Skyward Trend of Thought*, Cambridge, Mass. 1988; S. B. Landau and C. W. Condit, *Rise of the New York S. 1865–1913*, New Haven/London 1996; C. Willis, *Form Follows Finance*, New York 1996.

**Slab roof**, *see* ROOF.

**Slate**. A dark grey metamorphic rock which splits easily into thin slabs and has been widely used in northern Europe for roofing, and for paving, cladding and flooring.

F. J. North, *S. of Wales*, London (1927) 1946.

**Slate-hanging**. A wall covering of overlapping rows of slates on a timber substructure.

**Sleeper wall**. An underground wall either supporting SLEEPERS, or built between two PIERS, two walls, or a pier and a wall, to prevent them from shifting. The foundation walls of an ARCADE between nave and aisle would thus be sleeper walls.

**Sleepers**, *see* BEAM.

**Slovak architecture**. Slovakia in Central Europe was on the frontier of the Roman empire C1–2, was later invaded from the East, Christianized in C9 and in 1030 became part of the kingdom of Hungary with which it was absorbed into the Habsburg empire in 1526. In 1918 it joined with Bohemia and Moravia to form Czechoslovakia, from which it seceded as an independent republic in 1992. The earliest church, St Emeranus at Nitra, was built in 833 and partly survives in the apse of a C12 Romanesque basilica built on the site. Other Romanesque buildings include the Premonstratensian church of the Virgin, Bina (remodelled in C17), the twin-towered basilica at Diakovce (1228) and notable charnel-houses at Banská Stiavnica, Bratislava (1221) and Kremnika. Gothic was introduced in the mid-C13 in the churches of the Assumption, Banská Bystrica, and of Sts Peter and Paul, Holice, also the town hall of Bratislava. Later Gothic structures include the magnificent belfry of the Franciscan church, Bratislava, and the cathedrals of Nitra (1333) and Kosice (begun 1382), also several C15–16 churches, notably St James, Levoca. Italian Renaissance influence was initially limited to such decorative details as the portal of the town hall, Bardenjow (1508–9), and the addition of arcaded courtyards to earlier buildings, e.g. the town hall at Bratislava (1558). The most notable C16 and C17 secular as well as religious buildings are in Bratislava, which was the capital of Hungary from 1586 to 1683. The most distinguished C18 buildings were by Austrian architects – the church of St Elizabeth, Bratislava (1739–42), and the Premonstratensian abbey, Jasov (begun 1745), both by Franz Anton Pilgram (1699–1751); the castle of Antol and the Appony, Esterhazy and Grassalkovich palaces, as well as major additions to the royal castle, Bratislava, by Johann Baptist Martinelli (1704–54). Austrian influence remained strong until the disintegration of the Austro-Hungarian empire. A distinctly Slovak style inspired by vernacular wooden buildings was, however, developed by Dusan Samo Jutkovic (1868–1947) for private houses, hotels, etc., not only in his native Slovakia, e.g. thermal building,

Lubokovice, Moravia, Czech Republic (1902). Jutkovic subsequently veered towards the International Modern style (Sanatorium of Dr Koch, Bratislava, 1929–32), later more wholeheartedly taken up by Emil Bellus (1899–1979), whose covered bridge for the thermal station at Piestany (1929) and National Bank, Bratislava (1938), are notable. Of recent buildings the church of St Bartholomew, Vojkovce (1993), by Albert Rybarcak (b.1958) is outstanding.

**Slype.** A covered way or passage, especially in a cathedral or monastic church, leading east from the cloisters between transept and chapterhouse.

**Smeaton,** John (1724–92). Scottish civil engineer notable as an architect for his arched bridges (Perth, Banff and Coldstream) and for the third Eddystone lighthouse (1756–9).

A. W. Skempton (ed.), *J.S.*, *F.R.S.*, London 1981.

**Smirke,** Sir Robert (1780–1867), the leading GREEK REVIVAL architect in England, nevertheless lacked the genius of his almost exact contemporary in Germany, SCHINKEL, by whom he may have been influenced. The son of a painter and Academician, he was articled to SOANE, but quarrelled after a few months. From 1801 to 1805 he travelled in Italy, Sicily and Greece, sketched most of the ancient buildings in the Morea, and on his return to London published the first and only volume of his projected *Specimens of Continental Architecture* (1806). His first buildings were medieval in style – Lowther Castle, Cumbria (1806–11), and Eastnor Castle, Herefordshire (c.1810–15). He made his name with Covent Garden Theatre (1808, destroyed), the first Greek Doric building in London and as such very influential. It showed with what simple means gravity and grandeur might be achieved. His cool businesslike efficiency quickly brought him fame and fortune, and in 1813 he reached the head of his profession when he joined Soane and NASH as Architect to the Board of Works. His masterpieces came in the next decade, first the British Museum (1823–47), then the General Post Office (1824–9, demolished), both large in scale and massively Grecian in style. Though less uncompromising and less impressive than Schinkel's Altes Museum in Berlin (1823–30) the British Museum with its tremendous Ionic colonnade has a noble dignity and illustrates his admirable directness and scholarly detailing at their best. Knighted in 1832, he retired in 1845.

J. M. Crook, *The British Museum*, London 1972; Crook 1972; Colvin 1978.

**Smithson**, Peter (b.1923) and Alison (1928–94). English architects, prominent members of Team 10 in the early 1950s (*see* CIAM) when their Secondary Modern School, Hunstanton, Norfolk (1950–57), was one of the most influential buildings of the time. It was not informal but a symmetrical group, and in its details is inspired by MIES VAN DER ROHE. The Smithsons then turned in the direction of BRUTALISM, but their biggest and most mature building, for the *Economist* in London (1962–4), has none of the quirks of that trend. It is a convincingly grouped scheme of various heights, with a façade to St James's Street that succeeds in establishing a *modus vivendi* with the C18 clubs around, and with two high blocks of different heights behind. Their more recent Robin Hood Gardens, London (1968–72), is less successful. They have published *Urban Structuring* (London 1967), *Without Rhetoric: An Architectural Aesthetic 1955–1972* (London 1973), *The Shift* (London 1981) and *Changing the Art of Inhabitation* (London 1994).

Banham 1966; D. Dunster (ed.), *A.*

*and P.S.*, London 1982; M. Vidotto, *A. and P.S.*, Genoa 1991.

**Smythson**, Robert (*c.*1535–1614). English architect – the only Elizabethan architect of note – who perfected the spectacular if rather outlandish country-house style developed by the courtiers and magnates of the period. First heard of at Longleat, Wiltshire, where he worked as principal freemason (1568–75), he built his masterpiece, Wollaton Hall, Nottinghamshire, during the next decade (1568/72–80). This was a revolutionary building – a single pile with corner towers and a central hall, planned symmetrically on both axes. The plan probably derives from SERLIO and the whimsical Flemish carved ornamentation of banded shafts, strapwork, etc., from de VRIES, but the fantastic and romantic sham-castle silhouette is his own invention and wholly English. He settled near Wollaton, acquiring property there and the style of a 'gentleman'. But he almost certainly had a hand in the design of three later houses of note, Worksop Manor, Nottinghamshire (*c.*1585, now destroyed), Hardwick Hall, Derbyshire (1590–97), and Burton Agnes, Yorkshire (1601–10). His son John (d.1634) designed Bolsover Castle, Derbyshire (*c.*1612–34), perhaps the most romantic of all the sham castles.

M. Girouard, *R.S. and the Elizabethan Country House*, London 1983.

**Snozzi**, Luigi (b.1932), *see* SWISS ARCHITECTURE.

**Soami** (1472–1523). Japanese painter, art connoisseur and tea master in the service of the Shoguns in Kyoto. He has been credited with the design of the Ryoan-ji garden, Kyoto (*c.*1500), perhaps the finest as well as the most celebrated of the Zen inspired dry stonework gardens – an oblong enclosure with fifteen stones arranged in five groups on a bed of raked gravel.

**Soane**, Sir John (1753–1837). The most original English architect after VAN-BRUGH. His extremely personal style is superficially neo-classical but, in fact, romantic or 'picturesque' in its complicated and unexpected spatial interplay. Intense, severe, and sometimes rather affectedly odd, his buildings reflect his tricky character. He was always slightly unsure of himself and, despite his genius, never achieved complete confidence and authority even in his own style. The son of a Berkshire builder, he trained under DANCE and HOLLAND, then studied for three years in Italy, where he probably knew PIRANESI; but French influence, especially that of PEYRE and LEDOUX, was more profound. He returned to London in 1780, but his career only really began with his appointment as Surveyor to the Bank of England in 1788. His work at the Bank, now destroyed, was among the most advanced in Europe. The Stock Office (begun 1792) and the Rotunda (begun 1796) must have seemed shockingly austere, with their shallow domes and general emphasis on utility and structural simplicity, not to mention his reduction of classical ornamentation to rudimentary grooved strips and diagrammatic mouldings. The romantic or picturesque element in his work is felt increasingly after 1800, notably in Pitshanger Manor (Ealing Public Library, 1800–1803) and in the Dulwich College Art Gallery (1811–14, restored 1953), a 'primitivist' construction in brick with each element curiously detached by some slight break or recession, and, above all, in his own house, No. 13 Lincoln's Inn Fields, London (1812–13), now Sir John Soane's Museum. This is highly eccentric and personal to the point of perversity, especially inside, with congested, claus-trophobic planning, complicated floor-levels, ingenious top-lighting, hundreds of mirrors to suggest receding planes and blur divisions, and hanging, Gothic-inspired arches to detach ceilings from walls. The exterior perfectly illustrates his linear stylization and emphasis on planes rather than masses. His last buildings of note are the astylar utilitarian stables of Chelsea Hospital, London (1814–17), St Peter's, Walworth (1822), and Pell Wall House, Staffordshire (1822–8) with curious features reminiscent of VAN-BRUGH. He was made Professor of Architecture at the Royal Academy in 1806 and knighted in 1831. He published *Designs in Architecture* (London, 1778, reissued 1790).

P. de la Ruffinière du Prey, *J.S. The Making of an Architect*, London 1982; J. Summerson *et al.*, *J.S.*, London 1983; D. Stroud, *Sir J.S.*, London 1984; E. Schumann-Bacia, *Die Bank von England und ihr Architekt J.S.*, Munich 1989; E. M. Schumann-Bacia, *J.S. und die Bank des England*, Hildesheim–Zürich–New York 1990; D. Watkin, *Sir J.S. Enlightened Thought and the Royal Academy Lectures*, Cambridge 1996.

**Socle**. A low, plain pedestal or plinth base, or the lower part of a wall.

**Soffit**. The underside of any architectural element, e.g. an INTRADOS.

**Soffit cusps**. Cusps springing from the flat soffit or INTRADOS of an arched head, and not from its chamfered sides or edges.

**Solar**. A private chamber on an upper floor of a medieval house, usually a bedroom or living-room on the first floor adjoining the hall at the high-table end.

**Solar design**, *see* ENVIRONMENTAL GREEN OR SUSTAINABLE ARCHITECTURE.

**Solari**, Guiniforte (1429–81), a Milanese

'last-ditch' Gothic conservative, completed FILARETE's Renaissance Ospedale Maggiore in the Gothic style, built the simplified Gothic nave of S. Maria delle Grazie, Milan (1465–90, completed by BRAMANTE), and worked on the Gothic Milan Cathedral.

F. Welch, *Art and Authority in Renaissance Milan*, New Haven/London 1995; Heydenreich 1996.

**Solari**, Santino (1576–1646), one of the first Italian architects to work extensively in Germany and Austria, came of a large family of artists from Como. His main work is Salzburg Cathedral (1614–28), an entirely Italian basilican church with dome and with twin towers flanking the west façade. For the Bishop of Salzburg he built the Italianate Lustschloss at Hellbrunn, outside Salzburg (1613–19). He also designed (*c.*1620) the solemn little shrine of the black-faced Virgin at Einsiedeln, Switzerland, later surrounded by MOOSBRUGGER's fantastic Baroque abbey church.

Hempel 1965.

**Solarium**. A sun terrace or LOGGIA.

**Solea**. In an Early Christian or Byzantine church, a raised pathway projecting from the BEMA to the AMBO.

**Soleri**, Paolo (b.1919). Italian architect trained in Turin, worked with Frank Lloyd WRIGHT 1947–8, returned to Italy and built the Solimene ceramic factory, Vietri, near Salerno, 1951–4, then returned to the USA and started the Cosanti Foundation, Scottsdale, Arizona, in 1955 to pursue alternative urban planning. In 1969 he published *Arcology: The City in the Image of Man* (Cambridge, Mass., and London) and by 1970 had designed thirty Arcologies – a series of high-density mega-metropolises up to 800 m. (2,600 ft) high of which one, Arcosanti, at Cordes Junction, Arizona,

has been under construction since 1970. In 1973 he published *The Bridge Between Matter and Spirit is Matter Becoming Spirit. The Arcology of P.S.* (New York).

D. Wall, *Visionary Cities: The Arcology of P.S.*, London 1971; Banham 1976; *P.S. Architectural Drawings*, exh. cat., New York 1981.

**Solomonic column**. A spirally fluted or shaped column commonly called a 'barley-sugar column'. Such columns in St Peter's, Rome, were traditionally believed to have come from Solomon's Temple, hence the name.

**SOM**, *see* SKIDMORE, OWINGS & MERRILL.

**Sommaruga**, Giuseppe (1867–1917). Milanese architect, studied under the historicizing architects Luca Beltrami (1854–1933) and Camillo BOITO but turned to ART NOUVEAU and became, side by side with Ernesto Basile (1857–1932; Casa Basile, Palermo, 1904) and Raimondo d'Aronco (1857–1932; buildings for the Turin exhibition 1902), its most important representative in Italy. His principal works are the Palazzo Castiglioni, Milan (1901), the Clinica Colombo, Milan (1909), and the Hotel Tre Croci, Campo dei Fiori, near Varese (1909–12).

Pevsner and Richards 1973; Nicoletti 1978.

**Sonck**, Lars (1870–1956), *see* FINNISH ARCHITECTURE.

**Sondergotik**, *see* GERMAN ARCHITECTURE.

**Sopraporta**. A painting above the door of a room, usually framed in harmony with the door-case to form a decorative unit.

**Sorensen**, Carl Theodor (1893–1979). Danish landscape architect who made his name with his park-like layout for the university buildings by Kay FISKER at Aarhus (1931–47). This was followed by similar layouts at Klempenberg (1931–5); the Bellahoj quarter, Copenhagen (1947–58); Angli V, Herning, Jutland (1963–8); and the museum at Herning (1965–77).

S. L. Anderson and S. Hoyer, *C.T.S. en Havekunster Arkitektens*, Copenhagen 1993.

**Soria y Mata**, Arturo (1844–1920), *see* URBAN DESIGN.

**Soufflot**, Jacques Germain (1713–80), the greatest French neo–classical architect, was the son of a provincial lawyer against whose wishes he went off to Rome to study architecture in 1731. He stayed seven years, settling on his return in Lyon, where he was commissioned to build the enormous Hôtel Dieu (1741 onwards). This made his reputation, and in 1749 he was chosen by Mme de Pompadour to accompany her brother, M. de Marigny, to Italy, where he was to spend two years preparing himself for his appointment as Surintendant des Bâtiments. The tour was very successful and may be regarded as marking the beginning of NEO-CLASSICISM in France, of which the great masterpiece was to be Soufflot's Ste Geneviève (called the Panthéon since the Revolution) in Paris (begun 1757). This was a revolutionary building for France and was hailed by the leading neo-classical critic and theorist, LAUGIER, as 'the first example of perfect architecture'. It perfectly expresses a new, more serious, not to say solemn attitude towards antiquity, and combines Roman regularity and monumentality with a structural lightness derived from Gothic architecture. Soufflot himself said (1762) that one should combine the Greek orders with the lightness one admired in Gothic buildings. He continued working on his masterpiece to the end of his life,

but did not live to see it finished. His other buildings are of less interest, e.g. École de Droit, Paris (designed 1763, built 1771 onwards) and various follies in the Château de Menars park (1767 onwards) including a rotunda, nymphaeum and orangery, all in an elegant but rather dry neo-classical style.

Braham 1980; Rykwert 1980; M. Gallet *et al.*, *S. et son temps*, Paris 1980; D. Ternois and F. Perez, *L'Œuvre de S. à Lyon*, Lyon 1982; B. Bergdoll (ed.), *Le Panthéon. Symbole des revolutions*, Paris 1989; Kalnein 1995.

**Sounding board**, *see* PULPIT.

**South African architecture**. There is no unified, consistent representative of South African architecture any more than there is a unified South African culture; the reasons are of course the same. In typical colonial fashion, indigenous traditions were neglected and models from the countries of origin (Holland and Britain) were copied, imperfectly but sometimes with happy results. South Africa is no longer colonial but foreign influences, now American rather than European, continue to prevail.

The first of these influences, following on the occupation of the Cape by the Dutch East India Company in 1652, was Dutch–Flemish, resulting in a regional style of mainly domestic architecture known as Cape Dutch. This style was based on short-span, symmetrical, rectangular-plan forms, usually with E, H, T or U configurations. The houses were single-storeyed, with thick lime-washed walls and relatively narrow, economically disposed door- and window-openings, thatched with reeds and adorned with local versions of Baroque and then Rococo gables, e.g. Groot Constantia (altered *c.* 1792) in Constantia; Stellenberg House (1790) in Kenilworth; and Morgenster House (1786) in Somerset West.

More sophisticated influences were brought to the Cape by particular individuals, notably Anton Anreith (1754–1822), a skilled sculptor and woodcarver from Germany who arrived in 1776, and Louis Michel Thibault (1750–1815), who had studied under GABRIEL c.1775 and came as a military engineer with the French occupying forces in 1783. In their work they maintained the continuity of the Cape Dutch tradition, but added new ideas and elements, and a great deal of refinement, e.g. Lutheran church, Cape Town, which Anreith refaced 1787–92.

After the Napoleonic wars, the British found themselves the reluctant masters of a strategically important but otherwise unprofitable colony. Expenditure on development was small, but a style based on English Georgian architecture gradually established itself in Cape Town, while a modified English vernacular tradition was planted in the Eastern Cape, where about 4,000 British immigrants were settled in 1820 in an effort to stabilize the troubled frontier.

British imperialism with its concomitant colonial technology developed rapidly in the C19 and when, in the 1870s, first diamonds and then gold were discovered in South Africa, there was available a 'ready-made' political and administrative apparatus accompanied by a literally ready-made architecture. Victorian patterns, executed in Victorian corrugated- and cast-iron, proliferated throughout the country. At the same time, the new prosperity attracted original talents and Cecil Rhodes's architect, Herbert BAKER (strongly influenced by LUTYENS), was the central figure in a new wave of external influence on South African architecture.

Baker was appreciative of the Cape Dutch tradition and sought, in his early work in Cape Town (e.g. Groot Schuur, 1890), to incorporate its elements into his already eclectic but sensitive and skilful architecture. His major works, after the Second Anglo-Boer War, included the Rhodes Memorial in Cape Town (1905–8), the Pretoria railway station (1908), the Supreme Court Buildings, Johannesburg (1911), and the Urban Buildings, Pretoria (1910–13). His former associates and other architects influenced by him, notably J. M. Solomon, who designed the University of Cape Town campus (1915), and Gordon Leith, who practised in the Transvaal and Orange Free State, exerted a powerful influence on all South African architecture until the beginnings of the Modern Movement in the 1920s.

From about 1925 the influence of contemporary movements abroad became evident, mainly through the architectural schools and the *South African Architectural Record*. A. Stanley Furner, editor of the *SAAR* from 1926–9, introduced most contemporary movements to the profession. His students, under the leadership of Rex Martienssen (1905–42) and recent immigrants from Europe, responded to these influences, mainly from the heroic period of the INTERNATIONAL MODERN style. House Munro, Pretoria (1932 by McIntosh) was followed by others of which House Harris, Johannesburg (1933 by Hanson, Tomkin and Finkelstein) is a good example, a two-storey white cube showing formal and spatial characteristics derived from GROPIUS and MIES VAN DER ROHE. A rapid development of domestic architecture followed, culminating in Caso Bedo, Johannesburg (1936 by Cowin and Ellis), a free-plan form and Miesian spatial organization adapted to local conditions by wide eaves and a hipped roof reminiscent of Sir Herbert Baker and Frank Lloyd WRIGHT. This adaptation is typical and produced a model for many houses of the next two decades.

A similar pattern of development

occurred in other building types. Early International Style buildings gave the lead for buildings in Johannesburg such as Hotpoint House (1934), Reading Court (1936) and Denstone Court (1937 by Hanson, Tomkin and Finkelstein), Aiton Court (1938 by W. R. Stewart, A. Stewart and Bernard Cooke), Peterhouse (1936 by Fassler, Martienssen and Cooke) and in Cape Town the Cavalla Factory (1938 by Policansky).

Local conditions, technology, and inventiveness led to adaptations towards a contemporary vernacular: examples in Johannesburg include the 20th Century Fox Cinema and offices (1936 by Hanson, Tomkin and Finkelstein) and the innovative work of W. B. Pabst; in Cape Town the work of P. E. Pahl, M. Policansky, Prof. L. Thornton Whyte and others; in Durban such buildings as the Technical College Clubhouse (1943 by Jackson and Park Ross).

By the 1950s a fairly widespread contemporary vernacular had emerged albeit with regional differences and notwithstanding attempts by Fassler, Hanson and others to establish a neo-classical style based on the work of PERRET. The country was growing rapidly, commercialism was the order of the day, and in general architecture and the cities were eroded by pragmatic immediacy. There were notable exceptions. Norman Eaton (1902–55) developed a fine regional architecture, e.g. Greenwood House and Village, Pretoria (1951), Wachthuis, Pretoria (1960), and the Netherlands Bank, Durban (1965). Other examples of regionally sensitive and appropriate architecture are the Club Building, Pretoria (1963 by John Templar), houses in Durban by Biermann and Hallen, and the houses of Revel Fox in the Cape.

The next discernible wave of influence occurred in the early 60s with the return of young architects who had done graduate study under Louis KAHN, Romualdo Giurgola, Paul RUDOLPH, Robert VENTURI and others in America. Examples of this influence are, in Cape Town, the Truworths Factory (1968 by R. S. Uytenbogaardt), in Johannesburg, House Robinson (1966 by Meyer and Gallagher) and House Britz (1972 by Britz) and in Durban, the work of Hallen and Theron.

With continued prosperity foreign architects were commissioned to design major buildings, mainly in Johannesburg, e.g. Carlton Centre (1966–72 by SKIDMORE, OWINGS & MERRILL), Standard Bank (1971 by HENTRICH) and JAHN's glittering 11 Diagonal Street, Johannesburg (1981–3), and 88 Field Street, Durban (1982–5). These years also have seen the emergence of diverse local talents attempting a revalidation of architectural language, e.g. in the Cape, the Naude House (1968 by A. and A. de Sousa Santos) and Werdmuller Centre (1976 by R. S. Uytenbogaardt) and in Johannesburg, the RAU University (Meyer *et al.*) and the Miller House (1974 by Stan Field). Outstanding is the Portuguese-born Amancio d'Alpoim Miranda Guedes (b.1925), who has developed a highly individual and exhilarating style combining Gaudí and Kahn with the local vernacular. Though long resident in South Africa and since 1975 professor and head of the department of architecture at Witwatersrand University, Johannesburg, most of his work has been in Mozambique, e.g. the Smiling Lion Hotel, Lourenço Marques (1956–8), with Ndebele-inspired external murals, and the Governor's Palace, Vila Pery (1973). [I. Prinsloo and J. Moyle]

**Space-frame**. A three-dimensional truss framework for enclosing spaces, in which all members are interconnected and act as a single entity, resisting loads applied in any direction. It can be supported at

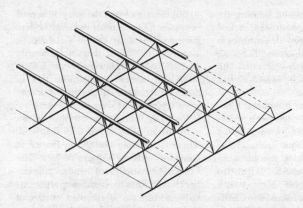

Fig. 107 Space-frame

virtually any of the points where the members are joined. Systems can be designed to cover very large spaces, uninterrupted by support from the ground, and the surface covering can be integrated to play its part in the structural whole. Some types have the appearance of egg-boxes (pyramidal in their elements), others are based on hexagonal or other geometric figures. The chief exponents to date are Zygmunt S. Makowski (*space-grid*), Bruno TAUT, Konrad WACHSMANN, Jean PROUVÉ, and Buckminster FULLER, whose dome, designed for the Union Tank Car Co., Baton Rouge (1958), has a diameter of 117 m. (384 ft). *See* Fig. 107.

Z. S. Makowski, *Steel Space Structures*, London 1965.

**Span**. The horizontal distance between the supports of an arch, beam or roof.

**Spandrel**. The triangular space between the side of an arch, the horizontal drawn from the level of its apex, and the vertical of its springing; also applied to the surface between two arches in an arcade, and the surface of a vault between adjacent ribs.

**Spanish architecture and landscape architecture**. After the Ancient Roman aqueducts, the first noteworthy monu-

ments in Spain are a few relics of the Visigothic age, notably S. Juan de Baños (661), originally with a very odd plan with a square chancel and square chapels of the same size attached to the long narrow transepts. The plan of S. Miguel at Tarrasa (C9 or earlier) – Tarrasa being one of the rare surviving examples of a 'church family' – is of the Early Christian and Byzantine inscribed-cross plan, that of S. Pedro de Nave (C7) a composition of square or oblong compartments like the English *porticus*. This latter scheme became that of the eminently interesting Asturian churches of the C9 such as S. Julián de los Prados, Oviedo (*c.*830), with its astonishing Pompeian interior decoration, Sta Cristina de Lena and S. Miguel de Linio. One of them, now a church, was originally a royal hall (Sta Maria de Naranco, 843–50).

Meanwhile the Muslims had captured most of Spain (711), and the Mosque of Cordoba had been begun in 786. It grew to be in the end a vast rectangle of *c.*167 × 128 m. (550 × 420 ft), filled with a forest of columns so as to form nineteen parallel naves. The most ornate parts date from *c.*970. A few miles outside Cordoba, Madinat al-Zahra, a palace city with accommodation for the Caliph, gardens, hunting park, mosque and housing for the court, was founded 936–40, sacked in 1010 but remembered for centuries as an exemplar of palatial luxury. (The site has recently been partly excavated and the magnificently rich audience hall restored.)

The structure of the mosque at Cordoba, especially the vaults with intersected ribs, may have inspired some Gothic and some Baroque vaults. However, Islamic architecture also immediately inspired Spanish Christian architecture. The term MOZARABIC means such mixtures of Islamic and Christian elements as are exemplified by S. Miguel de Escalada (consecrated in 913), with its arcade arches of horseshoe shape, Santiago de Penalba (931–7) and Santa Maria de Lebeña (also C10). The term MUDÉJAR refers to Christian architecture in a purely Muslim style, and this remained characteristic of secular architecture in Spain nearly to the end of the Middle Ages. No wonder, considering the glories and luxurious comforts of the Alhambra of Granada and the Generalife, a summer villa set in an extensive formally laid-out terraced garden with canals, pools and fountains, hedges and sunken flowerbeds, which – in the one remaining Islamic part of the peninsula – were created as late as the C14. Among the Christians such Mudéjar towers of the C13 as those of Teruel look back at the splendour of the Giralda at Seville of c.1172–90, and palaces of Christian rulers established Islamic forms of decoration, of plan and of life. The palace of Tordesillas is of the 1340s, the Alcázar at Seville of the years of Pedro the Cruel (1349–68), and at Seville the so-called House of Pilate carried Mudéjar right into the C16, even if the last-built parts of the house (which was not completed in 1553) take full note of Gothic as well as developed Renaissance motifs.

But this anticipates the story by several centuries. The Romanesque style had started in the early C11 in Catalonia in a version similar to that of Lombardy (Ripoll, 1020–32, heavily restored; Cardona, consecrated 1040). The C11 in Spain is particularly important for decorative sculpture. It seems that ever since S. Pedro de Nave in the C10 the Spanish were ahead of the French in this field. There is certainly nothing in France to compare with the capitals of Jaca. The French Romanesque of the great pilgrimage churches has an outstanding representative in the far north-west corner of Spain in the celebrated church of Santiago de Compostela (begun c.1075 and completed with the splendidly sculptured Pórtico de la Gloria in 1188). Other Romanesque churches are S. Martin de Frómista of c.1060, S. Isidoro at León with its antechurch known as the Panteón de los Reyes also of c.1060, and Lugo Cathedral, a direct descendant of Santiago, and S. Vicente at Ávila, both of the C12. The Late Romanesque of Spain is best represented by the Old Cathedral of Salamanca and the Cathedral of Zamora, both with curious domes of west and south-west French affinities, but essentially original.

To determine the date when the Gothic style arrived is as difficult for Spain as for England. The Old Cathedral of Salamanca for instance has pointed arches almost entirely. But pointed arches are not necessarily Gothic. The CISTERCIANS who came directly or indirectly from Burgundy brought the pointed arch as a Burgundian Romanesque motif. The Cistercians arrived in Spain in 1131, and soon large buildings were erected by them in many places: Moreruela, Meira, La Oliva, Huerta, Veruela, Poblet, Santas Creus have the standard French plan with chancel and transeptal east chapels. But while these are mostly straight-ended it is also usual in Spain to have the chancel apsed (Oliva, Huerta, Meira) or even an ambulatory and apsed radiating chapels (Moreruela, Poblet, Veruela). Whereas in many of these churches one can be in doubt as to what to regard as Romanesque, what as Gothic, La Oliva must clearly be considered Gothic, and the date of the beginning is 1164.

With the C13 the north French cathedral style entered Spain. The most French cathedrals of the C13 are those of Burgos (1221 onwards), Toledo (1226 onwards), and León, but the most original version of the Spanish Gothic is Catalan (Barcelona Cathedral, 1298 onwards; Sta María del Mar, Barcelona, 1329 onwards; Palma Cathedral, Majorca), with very wide and high naves and very high aisles or with aisles replaced by chapels between internal buttresses (Sta Catalina, Barcelona, 1223 onwards; Sta Maria del Pino, Barcelona, c.1320; and Gerona Cathedral, whose nave, with a span of 23 m. (74 ft) is the widest in Europe). The Late Gothic style was much influenced by Germany and the Netherlands, as is shown by such works as the towers of Burgos Cathedral by Juan de Colonia (*see* SIMÓN DE COLONIA) (begun 1442). Late Gothic vaults with their lierne rib patterns also have German origins. Spatially, however, Spain was entirely Spanish: the vast rectangles of her cathedrals hark back to the mosques of Islam, but their height and the height of the aisles are her own. Seville Cathedral was begun in 1402 and is 131 m. (430 ft) long and 76 m. (250 ft) wide, with a nave 39 m. (130 ft) high and aisles 20 m. (65 ft) high. Spain continued to embark on new cathedrals on this scale right up to the time of the Reformation. Salamanca was started in 1512, Segovia in 1525. In Spain those were the years of greatest wealth, resulting in the many funerary monuments and the excessively lavish decoration of such buildings as the

Constable's Chapel at Burgos Cathedral (1482 onwards) and S. Juan de los Reyes, Toledo (1476 onwards), or of such façades as those of S. Pablo (1486 onwards) and S. Gregorio (c.1492), both at Valladolid. No square inch must lack its complicated and lacy carving. The spirit of Islam reasserted itself in this, and the desire to overdecorate surfaces was carried on with Renaissance details in the C16 (PLATERESQUE style) and with Baroque details in the C18 (CHURRIGUERESQUE style).

Spain is the country of the most spectacular castles. For the C12 the most magnificent display is the walls of Ávila, for the C13 the castle of Alcalá de Guadaira, for the C14 Bellver on Majorca (1309–14), which is round and has a round courtyard, for the C15 Coca, vast and all of brick.

The Italian Renaissance had actually reached Spain early, and such monuments as the courtyard of the castle of La Calahorra (1509–12) or the staircase of the Hospital of Toledo (1504 onwards) are pure and perfectly at ease. But almost at once the crowding of motifs started again, and the façade of the University of Salamanca (c.1515 onwards) is no more than a furnishing of the Late Gothic façade with new motifs. Soon, however, the pure Italian High Renaissance also entered Spain. The first and for a while the only example is Charles V's unfinished palace on the Alhambra (1527–86 by MACHUCA), with its circular courtyard and its motifs reminiscent of RAPHAEL and GIULIO ROMANO. The severest and vastest palace in the Italian style is Philip II's Escorial (1563 onwards by Juan Bautista de TOLEDO and HERRERA). Ecclesiastical architecture in the C16 reached its climax in the east end of Granada Cathedral by SILOE (1528 onwards), and the parts of Valladolid Cathedral by Herrera of 1585 onwards. But such austerity remained rare, and Spain came once again into her own when, in the late C17, she developed that style of excessive Baroque surface decoration which culminated in such buildings as the façade of Santiago de Compostela (1738 onwards), the sacristy of the Charterhouse of Granada (1727 onwards), the Transparente by TOMÉ in Toledo Cathedral (1721–32), the portal of the Hospital of S. Ferdinand in Madrid (1722) and that of the Dos Aguas Palace at Valencia (1740–44). Greater sobriety in an Italian and French sense characterizes the circular Sanctuary of St Ignatius of Loyola, begun in 1689 and designed by Carlo FONTANA, the Royal Palace in Madrid by G. B. SACCHETTI begun in 1738, the Royal Palace of La Granja, partly by Filippo JUVARRA (1719 onwards), and the Royal Palace at Aranjuez, rebuilt in 1748–68 after Herrera's designs by Santiago Bonavia (d.1759). Among the Spanish academics Ventura RODRÍGUEZ TIZON was the most conspicuous figure; his giant portico for Pamplona Cathedral was built in 1783. Of 1787 is the even more neo-classical design for the Prado in Madrid by Juan de VILLANUEVA.

C19 conservatism was broken only towards the end of the century by the lively Catalonian version of Art Nouveau known in Spain as 'Modernisme'. GAUDÍ was the great genius of the movement, but Lluis Doménech i Montaner (1850–1923), Josep Puig i Cadafalch (1869–1956) and Josep Maria Jujol (1879–1949) were hardly less eccentrically individual, e.g. Doménech's Palau de la Musica (1904–8), Puig i Cadafalch's Casaramona factory (1912) and Jujol's Casa Torre de la Creu (1913–16), all in Barcelona. The 1929 Barcelona International Exhibition introduced the INTERNATIONAL MODERN style with one of its masterpieces, MIES VAN DER ROHE's Barcelona Pavilion (now restored), and in the 1930s TORROJA and SERT designed several not-

able buildings. Barcelona has remained the centre of innovative architecture, with José Antonio Coderch (1913–84), whose Casa Ugalde (1952), Cocheras flats (1968) and Trade Office Building (1965) in Barcelona are notable; followed by MBM Arquitectes SA, formed in Barcelona in 1962 by Josep Martorell (b.1925), Oriol Bohigas (b.1925), David Mackay (b.1933) and Albert Puigdoménech (b.1944), whose free-ranging experimentation extends from the vernacular to the 'machine-age' (Santa Aguada Housing, Benicassim, of 1966, Thau School, Barcelona, of 1972–4 and plan for the Olympic Village, Barcelona, 1992). In 1962, also, Ricardo BOFILL founded his Taller de Arquitectura and has since become famous internationally – indeed most of his recent work has been outside Spain. In 1962, again, Francisco Saénz de Oíza (b.1918) built his remarkable Wrightian Torres Blancas apartment tower in Madrid. More recently José Rafael MONEO has made his name with a series of notable buildings, and Santiago CALATRAVA likewise with his remarkable bridges and railway stations in Spain and Switzerland. More recently Eric Miralles (b.1955) and Carmen Pinós (b.1954) attracted international attention with their Igualada Cemetery, Barcelona (1985–90), and subsequently with their Civic Centre (Els Hosralets de Balanya), Barcelona (1988–98), and National Training Centre for Rhythmic Gymnastics, Alicante (1989–93). Also notable is the Minimalist work of Alberto Campo Baeza (b.1946).

**Speckle** or **Specklin**, Daniel (1536–89). German military architect, trained in Vienna (1555), who designed fortifications in Flanders, Scandinavia, Prussia and Poland. His *Architectura von Vestungen* (Strasbourg 1589), written from a staunchly Germanic viewpoint, scorning

Italian theories, served as a practical manual on fortification until the C18 (the last reprint was in 1736), providing also down-to-earth advice on the structure of houses and the design for a centrally planned octagonal city.

Kruft 1994.

**Speer**, Albert (1905–81). German architect and, after 1942, armaments minister. Imprisoned 1945–66. He made his name with his spectacular settings for Nazi Party rallies in the 1930s, notably by his dramatic use of massed flags and searchlights creating 'bowls of light'. His buildings were on an increasingly grand and eventually megalomaniac scale – Zeppelin Field, Nuremberg (1934–7, partly demolished), the New Reich Chancellery, Berlin (1938–9, demolished), and many unrealized projects for Berlin. In comparison TROOST almost seems refined. His reputation has been re-assessed by certain POST-MODERN architects. He published *Inside the Third Reich* (New York–London 1970) and *Spandau: The Secret Diaries* (New York–London 1976).

B. Miller-Lane, *Architecture and Politics in Germany 1918–1945*, Cambridge, Mass. 1968; L. Krier (ed.), *A.S.*, Brussels 1985; S. Scarrocchia, *Piacentini e S.*, Milan 1995.

**Spence**, Sir Basil Urwin (1907–76), *see* ENGLISH ARCHITECTURE.

**Spere**. A fixed structure which serves as a screen at the lower end of an open (medieval) hall between the hall proper and the SCREENS PASSAGE. It has a wide central opening between posts and short screen walls, and there is often a movable screen in the opening. The top member is often the tie-beam of the roof truss above; screen and truss are then called a *spere-truss*.

**Spezza**, Andrea (d.1628), *see* CZECH ARCHITECTURE.

**Spiral stairs**, *see* STAIR.

**Spire**. A tall pyramidal, polygonal or conical structure rising from a tower, turret or roof (usually of a church) and terminating in a point. It can be of stone, or of timber covered with SHINGLES, or lead. A *broach spire* is usually octagonal in plan, placed on a square tower and rising without an intermediate parapet. Each of the four angles of the tower not covered by the base of the spire is filled with an inclined mass of masonry or broach built into the oblique sides of the spire, carried up to a point, and covering a SQUINCH. A broach spire is thus the interpenetration of a lower-pitch pyramid with a much steeper octagon. A *needle spire* is a thin spire rising from the centre of a tower roof, well inside a parapet protecting a pathway upon which scaffolding could be erected for repairs. *See* Fig. 108.

**Spirelet**, *see* FLÈCHE.

**Splay**. A sloping, chamfered surface cut into the walls. The term usually refers to the widening of doorways, windows or other wall-openings by slanting the sides. *See also* REVEAL.

**Spoerry**, François (b.1912), *see* FRENCH ARCHITECTURE.

**Spolia**. Materials removed from buildings of an earlier period than that in which they are incorporated, e.g. reliefs on the Arch of Constantine, Rome; Roman columns in the Great Mosque, Cordoba.

J. Poeseke (ed.), *Antike Spolie in der Architektur des Mittelalters und der Renaissance*, Munich 1995.

**Spread footing**, *see* FOUNDATION.

**Spread foundation**. A foundation constructed like a pyramid to spread the weight of a column or pier over a large area, sometimes built over a cluster of piles. Spread foundations can be extended in a line to support wall loads.

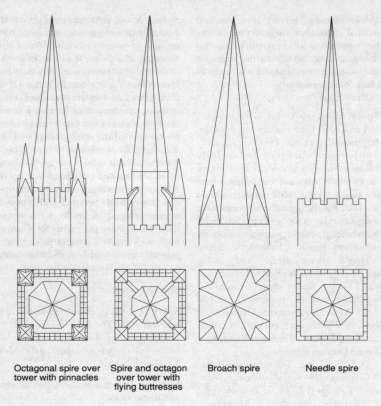

Octagonal spire over tower with pinnacles

Spire and octagon over tower with flying buttresses

Broach spire

Needle spire

Fig. 108 Spire

**Spreckelsen**, Johan Otto von (1929–87), *see* DANISH ARCHITECTURE.

**Springer**, *see* SPRINGING LINE.

**Springing line**. The level at which an arch springs from its supports. The bottom stone of the arch resting on the IMPOST each side can thus be called a *springer. See also* SKEWBACK; Fig. 6.

**Sprocket**, *see* ROOF.

**Spur**. An ornament, usually of foliage, on the corner of a square plinth surmounted by a circular PIER; also called a *griffe*.

**Spur stone**. A stone projecting from the angle of a corner or arch to prevent damage by passing traffic: it is usually circular in section.

**Spur wall**. The transverse, triangular wall above the side aisle of a church that provides lateral support to the piers as well as to the side-aisle roofs at each bay.

**Square**. 1. A rectangular urban space surrounded by buildings; equivalent to a French *place*, Italian *piazza* or Spanish *plaza*. 2. A special type developed in Britain from the late C17 (as recommended by EVELYN), surrounded by dwellinghouses of a superior kind and with a central enclosed garden planted with trees and shrubs for the exclusive use of the residents who were jointly responsible for its maintenance, e.g. Russell Square, London, designed by REPTON *c.*1800 (though this is now a public space). Such squares became a prominent feature of London and other English and Scottish cities and from the C19 were imitated in Continental Europe and North America.

**Squinch**. An arch or corbelling system of concentrically wider and gradually projecting arches, placed diagonally at the internal angles of towers to fit a polygonal or round superstructure on to a square plan. *See* Fig. 46.

**Squint**. An obliquely cut opening in a wall or through a PIER to allow a view of the main altar of a church from places whence it could not otherwise be seen; also called a *hagioscope*.

**Squint corner**. A corner of a building not at a right angle.

**Sri Lankan architecture**. The earliest surviving buildings in Sri Lanka (formerly Ceylon) are Buddhist STUPAS, locally called dagobas. Buddhism was introduced from India in the mid C3 BC and the Thuparama dagoba in the ancient capital city of Anuradhapura dates back to this time, though the original hemisphere was subsequently enlarged. The building of dagobas has continued to the present day, the Sinhalese majority being Buddhist: there are slight variations in form, bell-shaped, bulbous or spreading (likened to a heap of rice), each with a spire rising from a rectangular block. They are set on terraced bases and some were originally surrounded by colonnades. Remains of early monastic buildings and, perhaps, palaces are limited to stone supports which give no indication of the form of their wooden superstructures. But steps to the platforms of the more important ascend from semicircular slabs called moonstones, often very delicately carved, and also have carvings on their risers and balustrades. At Polonnaruwa, the capital *c.*1055–1270, there are more substantial remains of monastic and palatial buildings. Here much use was made of brick for piers, walls and also tunnel vaults. The most impressive structure is the Tivanka image house (*c.*1160–1200), with much relief sculpture, similar to south Indian work, on the exterior but quite unlike any Indian temple in form. Another type of monument indigenous to the island, called a vatadage, consists of a raised stepped circular platform with a small dagoba or statue of the Buddha in the centre, surrounded by at least one ring of monolithic columns and sometimes a wall, usually said to have been roofed, though its structure is uncertain. Notable examples are at Tiriyai on the east coast (founded C8), Polonnaruwa and nearby Medirigiriya (both C11). At Yapahuwa there is an impressive stone-built gate-house, all that remains of a royal palace of 1273–84, perched on a mountain side and approached up a very long and steep flight of steps. Later buildings are mainly of wood – the temple of the Holy Tooth at Kandy (the royal capital 1592–1815) and others nearby – apart from those constructed by the Dutch from 1658 (fortifications and churches at Jaffna, Galle and Colombo) and throughout the island during the British occupation of 1815–1948. Of recent buildings those of Geoffrey BAWA are outstanding.

**Staddle stones**. Mushroom-shaped stones used as bases to support timber-built granaries or hay barns, especially in Sussex.

**Stadium**. In Ancient Greece a running-track; now a large, usually unroofed, sports ground for athletic events.

**Stained glass**, *see* GLASS.

**Stair**, **staircase**. There are special names for the various parts of a stair: the *tread* is the horizontal surface of a step; the *nosing* is the overhanging edge of a tread, usually a half-round; the *riser* is the vertical surface; a *winder* is a tread wider at one end than the other. A *newel*, *spiral*, *vice*, *winding* or *turnpike* (Scot.) *staircase* is a circular or winding staircase with a solid central post in which the narrow ends of the steps are supported. The *newel* is also the principal post at the end of a flight of stairs; it carries the *handrails* and the *strings* which support the steps. A *dog-leg staircase* consists of two flights at right angles, with a half landing. *See* Fig. 109. A *flying stair* is cantilevered from the stairwell without a newel. A *geometric stair* is a flying stair whose inner edge describes a curve; it can be built on either a circular or elliptical plan. A *well stair* is a stair within an open well, especially a *half-turn stair* which climbs up three sides of the well with corner landings.

Staircases seem to have existed as long as monumental architecture: a staircase of *c*.6000 BC has been discovered in the excavations of Jericho. Monumental staircases also existed at Knossos in Crete and Persepolis in Iran. The Greeks and the Romans were not apparently much interested in making an architectural feature of the staircase, and medieval staircases were also utilitarian as a rule. In the Middle Ages the accepted form was the newel staircase, which could assume a monumental scale (Vis du Louvre, Paris, late C14), but only did so to any extent after 1500 (Blois). The standard form of the Italian Renaissance is two flights, the upper at an angle of 180° to the lower, and both running up between solid walls. However, a few architects, notably FRANCESCO DI GIORGIO and LEONARDO DA VINCI, worked out on paper a number of other, more interesting types, and these seem to have been translated into reality in the C16, mostly in Spain. There is the staircase which starts in one flight and returns in two, the whole rising in one well, called *double-return stairs*; the staircase which starts in one and turns at right angles into two (BRAMANTE's Belvedere Court in the Vatican; Escalera Dorada, Burgos); and, the most frequent type, the staircase which runs up in three flights at right angles round an open well, i.e. a squared spiral stair with intermediate

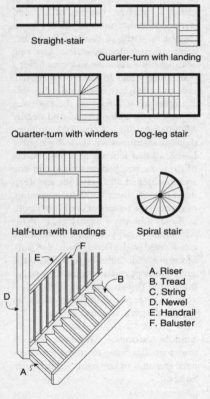

Straight-stair

Quarter-turn with landing

Quarter-turn with winders

Dog-leg stair

Half-turn with landings

Spiral stair

A. Riser
B. Tread
C. String
D. Newel
E. Handrail
F. Baluster

Fig. 109 Stair

landings. But Bramante in the Vatican still built a normal spiral stair, though also with an open well, and BERNINI (Palazzo Barberini) made this oval, a characteristically Baroque turn. PALLADIO invented the geometrical or flying staircase (Academy, Venice), a spiral staircase without any support other than the bonding of the steps into the outer wall.

The Baroque is the great age of monumental and inventive staircases. The finest of all are in Germany (Würzburg, Brühl and especially Bruchsal, all by NEUMANN), but there are excellent ones also in France (MANSART at Blois) and in Italy (Naples).

In C20 architecture the staircase has assumed a new significance as the element in a building which is most expressive of spatial flow. The earliest staircase in a glass cage is GROPIUS's at the Cologne Werkbund exhibition (1914). Since then much has been made of flying staircases, staircases without risers, and similar effects.

A. Chastel and J. Guillaume, *L'Escalier dans l'architecture de la Renaissance*, Paris 1988; C. Baldon and I. Melchior, *Steps and Stairways*, New York 1989; G. Gambardella, *L'architettura delle scale. Disegno, teoria e tecnica*, Genoa 1993; J. Templer, *The S. History and Theories*, Cambridge Mass. 1993.

**Stalactite vaulting**, *see* MUQARNAS.

**Stall**. A carved seat of wood or stone in a row of similar seats; if hinged, often carved on the underside (*see* MISERICORD).

**Stam**, Mart or Martinus Adrianus (1899–1986). Dutch architect, associated with the BAUHAUS and the Russian Constructivists but not with DE STIJL. In 1926–31 he was involved with BRINKMAN and VAN DER VLUGT in the influential Van Nelle Factory, Rotterdam, and in 1927 he contributed to the DEUTSCHER WERKBUND's Weissenhofsiedlung at Stuttgart. From 1930 he was

in Russia with MAY and, after 1948, in East Germany. He is famous as the inventor of the tubular steel chair (1924).

R. Blijstra, *M.S. Documentation of his Work 1920–1965*, London 1970; G. Dorthuys, *M.S.*, London 1970; S. Rümmele, *M.S.*, Zürich/Munich 1992; W. Moller, *M.S. (1899–1986)*, Tübingen/Berlin 1997.

**Stanchion**. A vertical supporting member, nowadays mainly of steel.

**Starck**, Philippe (b.1949), *see* FRENCH ARCHITECTURE.

**Starling**. A pointed projection on the PIER of a bridge to break the force of the water. *See* CUTWATER.

**Starov**, Ivan Yegorovich (1744–1808). Russian neo-classical architect. Unlike the older BAZHENOV and KAZAKOV, with their predominantly urban commissions, he frequently worked in the provinces and may be considered the initiator of the classic age of Russian country-house architecture. Born in Moscow, he trained at the Academy in St Petersburg and in Paris under de WAILLY (1762–8). Outstanding among his early works are the *ensemble* of Nikolskoye-Gagarino (Moscow Province, 1773 – its notable columned rotunda belfry destroyed 1941) and Taitsy (1774) near St Petersburg; in each the main house has an un-Palladian dynamism reminiscent of Bazhenov. Later came grander, more sober buildings: the somewhat heavy cathedral of the Alexander Nevsky Monastery in St Petersburg (1778); the hugest of all Russian country houses at Pella on the Neva (1785, soon afterwards dismantled); and his masterpiece, the Tauride Palace in St Petersburg (1783), very extensive but (with its single-storeyed galleries) not overwhelming. From 1771 to the 1790s he was extremely influential in the planning of new and reconstructed towns throughout the Russian Empire. [R. R. Milner-Gulland]

Hamilton 1983.

**Stasov**, Vasily Petrovich (1769–1848). Russian architect who was, with ROSSI, the leading architect of the later neo-classical period in St Petersburg, but more experimental. Some of his work has the stark geometricity of LEDOUX. Public commissions included vast military and cavalry complexes (incorporating five domed churches) in St Petersburg; the laconic Victualling Store in Moscow (1832, designed 1821) and his last St Petersburg masterpiece, the triumphal Moscow Gate (1834), a Greek Doric pro-pylaea in cast iron. He rebuilt much of the interior of the Winter Palace after a fire (1837). Outside the capitals his best-known work is at Arakcheev's estate of Gruzino, with beacon-towers and a belfry (destroyed in the last war) that looked like an even more aggressively geometric variant of the Admiralty spire, St Peters-burg (see ZAKHAROV). [R. R. Milner-Gulland]

Hamilton 1983.

**Stave church**. A timber-framed and timber-walled church; the walls are of upright planks with corner-post columns. The term is applied exclusively to Scandi-navian churches built from the early or mid C11 onwards e.g. the Hoaltälen church now in the Folk Museum, Trond-heim. Later stave churches usually have inner rows of posts or piers, sometimes an external covered arcade, and roofs arranged in tiers. A third system was also used from c.1200, incorporating a central column from the floor to the roof, e.g. Borgund church (c.1150) and Urnes church (early C12), both Sogne Fjord.

A. Bugge, *Norwegian S.C.*, Oslo 1953; D. Lindholm, *S.C. in Norway*, London 1970.

**Steel**. A refined, strong alloy of IRON of which an inexpensive version became available in the 1870s. It was used for build-ing from the mid-1880s, first in Chicago (see SKYSCRAPER). The non-corrosive Cor-Ten Steel which oxidizes to a rust-brown finish can be used for exterior work. *See also* METAL STRUCTURES.

A. Blanc *et al.*, *Architecture and Construc-tion in S.*, London 1993; N. Jackson, *The Modern S. House*, London 1996.

**Steele**, Fletcher (1885–1971). American landscape architect who began with con-ventional Italianate and/or English-style private gardens but went on, in the 1920s when influenced by GUÉVRÉKIAN and others, to seek a synthesis of modern and traditional elements, notably at Naumkeag, Stockbridge, Massachusetts (1925–38). Here he combined a Chinese garden, a rose garden with serpentine beds curving through a lawn and the frequently illustrated flight of steps painted pale blue with white metal hand-rails, rising on either side of cascades through a plantation of silver birches – a Modernist interpretation of a Renais-sance idea. His books, in which he dis-cussed the management of space, form, texture and colour, inspired a younger and more radically inclined generation: *New Pioneering in Garden Design* (1930); *Landscape Design for the Future* (1932); *Modern Garden Design* (1936).

R. Karson, *F.S. Landscape Architect*, New York 1989.

**Steenwinckel**, Hans the elder (c.1545–1601), Hans the younger (1587–1639), and Lourens van (c.1585–1619), *see* DANISH ARCHITECTURE.

**Steeple**. The tower and spire of a church taken together.

**Stein**, Clarence (1882–1975). American landscape architect and urban designer, responsible with Henry Wright (1878–

1936) and others for Radburn, New Jersey (1929); *see* RADBURN PLANNING. Radburn had been partially anticipated by his and Wright's Sunnyside Gardens, Queens, New York (1927), and they went on to design Chatham Village, Pittsburgh, NJ (1930–32). In the late 1930s Stein designed several green-belt new towns as part of the New Deal welfare programme. In 1941 he designed Baldwin Hills Village, Los Angeles. He published *Towards New Towns in America* (Liverpool 1951).

D. Schaffer, *Garden Cities of America: The Radburn Experience*, Philadelphia 1982; Walker and Simo 1994.

**Stein**, Joseph Allen (b.1912). American architect; worked with NEUTRA and later in San Francisco, where he collaborated with ECKBO with whom he was also to work after he settled in India in 1952, especially at the Lodhi Park, New Delhi, near or in which many of his buildings are sited, notably the International Center (1959–62), the Ford Foundation (1968) and the Unicef Building (1981). From 1977 he was in partnership with DOSHI. His Kashmir Conference Center, Srinagar (1977–89), followed, notable for its sensitive response to regional and vernacular influences.

S. White, *Building in the Garden. The Architecture of J.A.S. in India and California*, Delhi/Oxford 1993.

**Steindl**, Imre (1839–1902), *see* HUNGARIAN ARCHITECTURE.

**Steiner**, Rudolf (1861–1925), *see* SWISS ARCHITECTURE.

**Stella**, Paolo della (d.1552), *see* CZECH ARCHITECTURE.

**Step pyramid**. A tapering, stepped or terraced structure, usually terminating in a platform, e.g. that of Zoser at Saqqara near Cairo of *c*.2770 BC, a mastaba heightened with five solid storeys of decreasing size. It is to be distinguished from a PYRAMID, which has smoothly shaped sides rising to a point.

**Stereobate**. A solid mass of masonry serving as a base, usually for a wall or a row of columns.

**Stereotomy**. The art and science of cutting, or making sections of, solids, e.g. pre-cutting stones to fit in their allocated place, especially in an arch or vault, where the geometry of their planes is complex.

**Stern**, Robert A. M. (b.1939). American architect and architectural historian and polemicist. His early buildings shared VENTURI's sophisticated populism and eclecticism, e.g. Wiseman residence, Montauk, NY (1961–8); Lang residence, Washington, Connecticut (1974), but his search for a meaningful synthesis of tradition and innovation led to a wide historical-associational range, e.g. Observatory Hill Dining Hall, University of Virginia, Charlottesville (1982–4); Prospect Point, La Jolla, California (1983–5); Copperflagg Development, Staten Island, New York (1983 onwards); Norman Rockwell Museum, Stockbridge, Massachusetts (1987–92); culminating in his work for the Walt Disney Company – Casting Center, Walt Disney World, Orlando, Florida (1987–9), the Newport Bay Club (1988–90); Cheyenne Hotel, Disneyland, Paris (1988–90) and Disney Feature Animation Building, Burbank (1994). His Banana Republic, Chicago (1991), a make-believe tropical plantation villa, is also notable. He published *New Directions in American Architecture* (New York (1969) 1977); *Modern Classicism* (New York 1988), and, with T. Mellins and D. Fishman, a three-volume history of New York architecture or urbanism, *New York 1900; 1930; 1960* (New York 1983–95).

P. Arnell and E. Bickford (eds.), *R.A.M.S. Buildings and Projects 1965–80*, New York 1981; L. F. Rneda (ed.), *R.A.M.S. Buildings and Projects 1981–85*, New York 1986.

**Stethaimer** or **Stettheimer**, Hans (d.1432). German architect working at Landshut in Bavaria. He came from Burghausen, is usually called Hans von Burghausen and may not have been called Stethaimer. He began St Martin's, the chief parish church of Landshut, in 1387. On his funerary monument other works of his are mentioned: they include the chancel of the Franciscan church at Salzburg (begun 1408). He was one of the best of the German Late Gothic architects, believed in the HALL CHURCH, in brick as a material, where he could use it, and in a minimum of decoration. At Salzburg the most fascinating motif is that of the long slender piers of the chancel with one of them placed axially, due east, so that the eye faces not an interstice but a pier with the light from the east playing round it. Stethaimer's monument may indicate that he was also concerned with sculpture. His source is the style of the PARLER family.

T. Herzog, *Meister Hans von Burghausen, gen. S. Sein Leben und sein Werk*, Landshut 1958; Frankl 1972.

**Stick style**. Popular C19 type of timber-built house in the USA, picturesque and rustic, derivative partly from BALLOON-FRAME buildings and also from other vernacular forms, e.g. the Swiss *chalet*, but usually with wide surrounding verandas as well. It reached its height between 1850 and 1875, notably with HUNT's Griswold House, Newport, Rhode Island (1863). *See also* SHINGLE STYLE.

V. Scully, *The Shingle Style and the S.S.*, New Haven 1971.

**Stiff-leaf**. A late C12 and early C13 type of sculptured foliage, found chiefly on CAPITALS and BOSSES, a development from the CROCKETS of crocket capitals; almost entirely confined to Britain. *See* Fig. 110.

Fig. 110 Stiff-leaf capital

**Stijl, De**, *see* DE STIJL.

**Stile**. The vertical member to which the RAILS of a door, window or other frame are joined.

**Stile floreale**. Italian term for ART NOUVEAU, especially that of the early, Flamboyant buildings by D'ARONCO and SOMMARUGA.

**Stile Liberty**. The Italian term for ART NOUVEAU.

**Stilted arch**, *see* ARCH.

**Stirling**, James Frazer (1926–92). British architect, trained in Liverpool. His early buildings, designed in partnership with James Gowan (b.1923), moved from a mild BRUTALISM (Ham Common Flats, Richmond, London, 1955–8) to a highly original and imposing proto-HIGH TECH style (Engineering Department, Leicester University, 1959–63). The latter established his reputation. His later buildings were less impressive, e.g. History Faculty, Cambridge University (1965–8); Florey Building, Queen's College, Oxford (1966–71); Student Lodgings, St Andrew's University (1968). In 1971 he was joined by Michael Wilford (b.1938) as a partner and in 1977 they won the competition for the New Art Gallery, Stuttgart, with a design that combined a sense of grandeur with a new, more colourful sophistication and historical allusiveness which perhaps owed something to POST-MODERNISM, as did their Wissenschaftscentrum, Tiergarten, Berlin (1979–87). Completed in 1984, the Stuttgart gallery is more imaginative and accomplished than their Sackler Gallery for Harvard University, Cambridge, Massachusetts (1979–84), or the Clore Gallery extensions to the Tate Gallery, London (1980–87). The Performing Arts Center, Cornell University, NY (1983–8), was followed by the vast and impressive factory complex at Melesangen near Frankfurt, Germany (1986–92). He was knighted in 1992.

P. Arnell and T. Bickford, *J. S. Buildings and Projects*, London 1984; R. Maxwell and T. Muirhead, *J.S. and Michael Wilford. Buildings and Projects 1975–1992*, London 1994.

**Stoa**. In Greek architecture, a covered colonnade, sometimes detached. In Byzantine architecture, a covered hall, its roof supported by one or more rows of columns parallel to the rear wall; in Latin, *porticus*.

J. J. Coulton, *The Architectural Development of the Greek S.*, Oxford 1976.

**Stock brick**. A hard, moulded brick that has been burnt in a clamp during manufacture. London stock brick is of yellowish clay mixed with ground chalk.

**Stoep**. The Dutch term for a veranda, as often found in South African architecture.

**Stone circles**, *see* MEGALITHS.

**Stone**, Edward Durell (1902–78). American architect who designed with Philip Goodwin (1885–1958) the Museum of Modern Art, New York (1939), of which only the façade now

survives. It was the first International Style public building in the USA. His later work became more fanciful, usually including arched elements, e.g. US Embassy, New Delhi (1954–8); the Huntington Hartford Museum, New York (1958–64); the Kennedy Center for the Performing Arts, Washington, DC (1971). He published *Recent and Future Architecture* (New York 1967).

**Stonework**. Geologically there are three families of stones: igneous, e.g. GRANITE; sedimentary, e.g. LIMESTONE; and metamorphic, e.g. SLATE. Masonry techniques vary from RUBBLE MASONRY to precisely laid ASHLAR. Though the earliest arches and vaults of *c.*3000 BC in Mesopotamia were probably of brick, stone was widely used in the ancient world for arches, domes and vaults as well as walls. In medieval Europe it was handled with great skill, stone voussoirs in the three-dimensional curved surfaces of complex Gothic vaults requiring geometrical precision (*see* STEREOTOMY). Stone is now used mainly for cladding and not structurally.

**Stoop**. In the USA a small porch, platform or staircase leading to the entrance of a house. (From the Dutch *stoep*.)

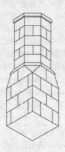

Fig. 111 Stop-chamfer

**Stop-chamfer**. An ornamental termination to a CHAMFER, common in the Early

English period and very much favoured by Victorian architects bringing the edge of the pared-off stone or beam back to a right angle; also called a *broach-stop*. See Fig. 111.

**Stops**. Projecting stones at the ends of HOOD-MOULDS, STRING COURSES, etc., against which the mouldings finish: often carved, e.g. a *mask stop*. *See also* LABEL-STOP.

**Storey** or **story**. The space between any two floors or between the floor and roof of a building. In England the ground-level storey is usually called the ground floor, in America the first floor, in France the *rez-de-chaussée*.

**Storey posts**. The principal posts of a timber-framed wall.

**Stoup**. A vessel to contain holy water, placed near the entrance of a church; usually in the form of a shallow dish set against a wall or pier or in a niche. To be distinguished from a FONT.

**Strainer arch**, *see* ARCH.

**Strapwork** or **rollwork**. Ornament consisting of interlaced bands, reminiscent of leather thongs or carved fretwork. Its origin is uncertain (*see* ARABESQUE) but it appears in the Galerie de François I at Fontainebleau (1533–5). It became popular in northern Europe, especially the Netherlands, where fantastic, typically MANNERIST, variations of it were published by DIETTERLIN, FLORIS and de VRIES. It was generally used on ceilings, screens and panelling and was popular in Elizabethan England. *See* Fig. 112.

P. Ward-Jackson, in *Victoria & Albert Museum Bulletin*, April 1967.

**Street**, George Edmund (1824–81). English architect, a pupil of George Gilbert SCOTT. He was in practice in 1849, after having already designed some

Fig. 112 Strapwork

churches in Cornwall. In 1850–51 he travelled in France and Germany, in 1853 in north Italy (resulting in a book on the marble and brick buildings of north Italy which came out in 1855), in 1854 in Germany again, in 1861–3 three times in Spain (his important book on Spanish Gothic architecture was published in 1865). In 1852 Street started a practice at Oxford and among his first assistants were WEBB and MORRIS. The first important building is the Cuddesdon Theological College. Street was a High Church man much appreciated by the Cambridge Camden group (*see* BUTTERFIELD), a tremendous worker and a fertile draughtsman who liked to design all details himself. His first large church was St Peter, Bournemouth (1853 onwards).

The practice was moved to London in 1855, and there Street's most characteristic early church is St James the Less, off Vauxhall Bridge Road (1860–61), a very strong design encouraged no doubt by Butterfield but not imitating him, and inspired by RUSKIN. The Gothic is continental rather than English. Among Street's most notable churches are Oakengates, Shropshire (1855); Boyne Hill, Berkshire (1859); St Philip and St James, Oxford (1860–62); All Saints, Clifton, Bristol (1863–8); St John, Torquay (1861–71); St Mary Magdalen, Paddington, London (1868–78); St Paul's, Rome (1872–6); and Holmbury St Mary, Surrey, built at his own expense (1879). Street is always unconventional and inventive, yet hardly ever as aggressive as Butterfield. His principal secular work is the Law Courts, London, won in competition in 1866. It is a high-minded essay in C13 Gothic, yet picturesque in grouping. The Great Hall inside is particularly impressive.

Meeks 1966; Hitchcock 1977; D. Brownlee, *The Law Courts. The Architecture of G.E.S. (1824–1881)*, Cambridge, Mass., and London 1984.

**Street furniture**. Benches, bollards, bus and tram-stop shelters, Métro entrances and exits, pillar-boxes, public urinals, telephone kiosks, etc., usually of cast-iron or other metal and sometimes notable in design, e.g. the Paris Métro entrances and exits by GUIMARD and those in Vienna by WAGNER; the Dutch 'telefoon' booths by BRINKMAN and the British telephone kiosks by Sir G. G. SCOTT (model 2 of 1926 and model 6 of 1936).

S.F., Design Council catalogue, London 1979; G. Stamp, *Telephone Boxes*, London 1989; N. Johannessen, *Telephone Boxes*, Princes Risborough 1994; P. Borhan, *Charles Marville: Vespasiennes*, Paris 1994.

**Stressed-skin construction**. A form of construction in which the outer skin or SHELL acts with the frame members to contribute to the flexural strength of the unit as a whole.

**Stretcher**, *see* BRICKWORK.

**Strickland**, William (1788–1854). American architect, a pupil of LATROBE in Philadelphia, who rose to fame with the Second Bank of the United States, Philadelphia, now the Custom House. This had first been designed by Latrobe, but was then built to a modified design by Strickland (1818–24). It is Grecian in style, whereas Strickland's earlier Masonic Temple (1810) had been Gothic. His finest buildings are the Philadelphia Merchants' Exchange (1832–4), with its elegant corner motif crowned by a copy

of the Lysicrates Monument, and the Tennessee State Capitol at Nashville (1845–59). He also built the United States Mint, Washington, DC (1829–33), in a style similar to MILLS's, and the United States Naval Asylum (1827) with an Ionic portico and tiers of long balconies left and right. Strickland was a very versatile man: in his early days he painted and did stage design, and he was also throughout his later life engaged in major engineering enterprises (canals, railways, the Delaware Breakwater).

A. A. Gilchrist, *W.S. Architect and Engineer*, Philadelphia 1950; Hitchcock 1977.

**String course**. A continuous horizontal band set in the surface of an exterior wall or projecting from it and usually moulded.

**Strings**. The two sloping members which carry the ends of the treads and risers of a STAIRCASE. *See* Fig. 109.

**Strut**, *see* ROOF.

**Stuart**, James 'Athenian' (1713–88), a minor English architect, is nevertheless important in the history of GREEK REVIVAL architecture for his temple at Hagley (1758), the earliest Doric Revival building in Europe. He and Nicholas Revett (1720–1804) went to Greece in 1751–5 and in 1762 published the *Antiquities of Athens* (2nd vol. 1789), which had little immediate influence except on interior decoration. Indolence and unreliability lost him many commissions, and he built very little. He designed several important rooms at Spencer House, London (1760 onwards). His No. 15 St James's Square, London (1763–6), was later altered internally by James WYATT (*c*.1791). The Triumphal Arch, Tower of the Winds and Lysicrates Monument in the park at Shugborough Staffordshire, are his best surviving works

(1764–70). His chapel at Greenwich Hospital (1779–88) seems to have been designed largely by his assistant William Newton.

D. Watkin, *Athenian S. Pioneer of the Greek Revival*, London 1982; Harris 1990; J. Friedman, *Spencer House: Chronicle of a Great London Mansion*, London 1993.

**Stuart architecture**. Late Renaissance architecture in England of the period 1625–1702; *see* ENGLISH ARCHITECTURE.

**Stübben**, Joseph (1845–1936), *see* URBAN DESIGN.

**Stucco**. A slow-setting plaster composed basically of gypsum, sand and slaked lime with other substances to facilitate modelling and ensure durability. The term is used in English for a type introduced from Italy in the C18, with marble dust as a binder and strengthener; also, more loosely, for various types of fine plaster used both as a medium for internal decorative work and externally as a rendering or protective coating and for architectural features, in lieu of stone.

Of ancient but unknown origin, stucco was developed by the Ancient Romans for ceiling decorations etc. and later by Islamic architects for both external and internal decorative work, e.g. MUQARNAS niches and domes as at the Alhambra, Granada. In Renaissance and Baroque Europe it was used on a large scale for interior decorative schemes, e.g. at the Château de Fontainebleau, reaching great refinement in C17–18 Germany, where it was often combined with BOISERIES, e.g. by Dominikus ZIMMERMANN in the Residenz, Munich, and, more typically of German Rococo, at his country church at die Wies, with the addition only of occasional paint and gilding. In England such craftsmen as Joseph Rose (1745–99) carried out decorative schemes in stucco, especially ceilings, to designs by the ADAM brothers. The use of stucco for large-scale decorative schemes was revived briefly by ART NOUVEAU architects, notably August ENDELL's Elvira Studio, Munich (1897–8). For its use as an exterior facing, notably in England by ADAM, NASH and others, *see* CEMENT.

Laing 1978; G. Beard, *S. and Decorative Plasterwork in Europe*, London 1983; D. Garsting, *Giacomo Serpotta and the Stuccatori of Palermo 1560–1790*, London 1984; W. Jahn, *Stukkatoren des Rokoko. Bayreuther Hofkünstler in markgräflichen Schlössern und in Würzburg*, Sigmaringen 1988; H. Schnell and U. Schedler, *Lexikon der Wessobrunner Künstler und Handwerker*, Munich and Zürich 1988.

**Stucco lustro**, *see* SCAGLIOLA.

**Studs**. In TIMBER-FRAMED buildings secondary vertical timbers of the walls. See Fig. 116.

**Stupa**. The earliest Indian Buddhist (and Jain) religious monument, in origin a hemispherical funerary mound. The first were built to enshrine the cremated remains of Buddha and his disciples; later they commemorated the teaching of Buddha (or of Mahavira, the founder of Jainism) though enshrining the relics of other teachers. Early stupas, such as those at Sanchi of C3–1 BC, consist of hemispheres of earth and rubble raised on low cylindrical bases and faced with bricks or stone. Miniature stone railings mark the square platform at the summit, with a central stone mast supporting a finial with one or more umbrella-like tiers, called a *chattra*. A relic casket is embedded below. A paved pathway for worshippers to perform the rite of *pradakshina* by circumambulation surrounded the stupa, usually with a stone railing and four gateways, often bearing elaborate sculptural decor-

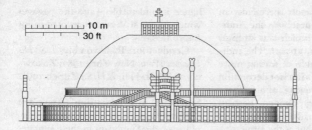

ations. The stupa itself is undecorated, but it is imbued with complex cosmological and/or Buddhist symbolism.

The stupa is called a *chorten* in Bhutan, Nepal and Tibet and a *dagoba* in Sri Lanka, where it became bell-shaped. The bell-shape form evolved several variants in Burma, Thailand, Cambodia and Indonesia. *See* Fig. 113.

A. Snodgrass, *The Symbolism of the S.*, Ithaca 1985; J. W. Glanche, *Des S. Kultbau der Buddhismus*, Cologne 1995.

**Stylobate**. The substructure on which a colonnade stands; more correctly, the top step of the structure forming the CREPIDOMA.

**Suardi**, Bartolomeo, called Bramantino (*fl.* 1503–36). Italian painter responsible for one outstanding building in his native Milan, the octagonal Trivulzio chapel, S. Nazaro Maggiore. It is a masterpiece of classical restraint and geometrical purity. It was begun in 1512.

W. Suida, *Bramante e il Bramantino*, Milan 1955.

**Suburb**. An outlying built area or urban fringe to a town, in origin a middle-class residential expansion providing a village-like arcadian alternative to the urban environment. It is to be distinguished from a SATELLITE TOWN. The Stockholm suburb of Vallingby designed by MARKELIUS is exemplary. *See also* GARDEN CITY AND GARDEN SUBURB; LEVITTOWN; RADBURN PLANNING.

**Suger**, Abbot (1081–1151), was not an architect; neither does he seem to have been responsible, even as an amateur, for any architectural work. But as he was abbot of St Denis, outside Paris, when the abbey church was partly rebuilt (*c.* 1135–44) and as this was the building where the Gothic style was to all intents and purposes invented, or where it finally evolved out of the scattered elements already existing in many places, his name must be recorded here. He wrote two books on the abbey in which the new building is commented on, but nowhere refers to the designer or indeed explicitly to the innovations incorporated in the building.

E. Panofsky, *S. Abbot of Saint-Denis 1081–1151*, Princeton 1979; S. McK. Crosby, *The Royal Abbey of Saint Denis from its Beginnings to the Death of S. 475–1151*, New Haven 1987.

**Sullivan**, Louis Henry (1856–1924), was of mixed Irish, Swiss and German descent. He was born in Boston, studied architecture briefly at the Massachusetts Institute of Technology, and moved to Chicago in 1873. He worked there under JENNEY, then, after a year in Paris in VAUDREMER'S *atelier*, returned to Chicago. In 1879 he joined the office of Dankmar Adler (1844–1900), who had emigrated from Germany in 1854 and was established as an architect in Chicago by 1869. The firm became Adler & Sullivan in 1881. Their first major building, and no doubt the most spectacular in Chicago up to that time, was the Auditorium (1886–90), which was strongly influenced by RICHARDSON. The auditorium itself is capable of seating more than 4,000. Sullivan's interior decoration is exceedingly interesting, of a feathery vegetable character, derived perhaps partly from the Renaissance in an ARTS AND CRAFTS spirit but at the same time pointing forward to the licence of ART NOUVEAU. Similarly fantastic was their Garrick Theatre, Chicago (1892, demolished 1962). His two most familiar skyscrapers, the Wainwright building, St Louis (1890), and the Guaranty building, Buffalo (1894), have not the exclusively functional directness of HOLABIRD & ROCHE's Marquette building of 1894, but they do express externally the SKELETON structure and the cellular interior arrangements. However, Sullivan, though pleading in his *Kindergarten Chats* (1901) for a temporary embargo on all decoration, was himself as fascinated by ornament as by functional expression, and this appears even in the entrance motifs of his major building, the Carson, Pirie & Scott Store (1899–1904), which is most characteristic of the CHICAGO SCHOOL. For the Chicago Exhibition of 1893 Sullivan designed the Transportation building, with its impressively sheer giant entrance arch. He recognized the setback which the Classicism otherwise prevailing at the exhibition would mean to the immediate future of American architecture.

Adler died in 1900, and after that time Sullivan's work grew less until it dried up almost entirely, though his National Farmers' Bank, Owatonna, Minnesota (1907–8), should be mentioned. Though modest in scale, it is monumental in effect and shows him at his most authentically 'American'. He was a difficult man, uncompromising and erratic, but his brilliance is undeniable – see the passages which his pupil WRIGHT devoted to his *Lieber Meister*.

Condit 1964; R. Twombly, *L.S. His Life and Work*, New York 1987; Zukowsky 1988; H. Frei, *L.H.S.*, Zürich 1992.

**Sumerian and Akkadian (Assyrian) architecture**. As early as the 4th millennium BC the Sumerians in the Euphrates delta had evolved a complex architecture. The main material was brick; techniques included the arch, the dome and the vault (though the latter appears to have been used only for underground burial chambers). Having solved these basic problems of construction, architects applied themselves to decoration. An astonishing proof of their ability is provided by the great ZIGGURAT temple of the Uruk period (late 4th millennium) at Warka (Biblical Erech): the surface was decorated with a mosaic of red-, black- and buff-coloured terracotta cones arranged in geometrical patterns; *see* CONE MOSAIC. The façades were further articulated by a succession of decorative buttresses – a device that was to distinguish sacred buildings in Mesopotamia until Hellenistic times. The temple at Al 'Ubaid near Ur, built by King A-annipadda, *c.*2600 BC, shows that by this date painted and relief decorations were used not merely as ornaments but to emphasize the structure. But perhaps the most remarkable of these early constructions is the vast ziggurat at Ur, built *c.*2200 BC – an extremely sophisticated building with dramatic staircases ascending to the shrine on top and with every line subtly curved to correct optical illusions. The principles of this architecture were taken over by the Assyrians of northern Mesopotamia towards the end of the 2nd millennium. So far as may be judged from the excavated sites (unfortunately their great cities at Nineveh and Nimrud yield little for the student of architecture), the Assyrians could not make any technical advances of importance on the Sumerians, but they demanded effects of greater grandeur with lavish use of brilliant colour and much sculpture in the round as well as in relief. The Palace of Sargon at Khorsabad reveals that they achieved their effects of splendour by the multiplication of units rather than bold overall designing.

**Superblocks**, *see* RADBURN PLANNING.

**Superimposed orders**. The ORDERS used one above the other in an arcaded or colonnaded building, using Doric, Ionic and Corinthian in that order upwards, as on the Colosseum in Rome, which is a notable early example.

**Supermarket**, *see* SHOPPING CENTRE.

**Superstudio**, *see* ITALIAN ARCHITECTURE.

**Surcharge**. The mass placed over the haunches of an arch or vault or a pendentive in order to increase structural stability.

**Suspended roofs**, *see* HENTRICH, Helmut; OTTO, Frei.

**Sustainable architecture**, *see* ENVIRONMENTAL, GREEN OR SUSTAINABLE ARCHITECTURE.

**Sustris**, Friedrich (1524–99 or 91?). Netherlandish MANNERIST painter and architect working in Munich at the same time as Peter CANDID and the Mannerist sculptor Hubert Gerhard. He studied in Italy, where he acquired a sophisticated Mannerist style derived from VASARI. His main work in architecture is the chancel and transept of St Michael's church in Munich (1592, built after the collapse of a tower in that year). He probably designed the Grotto Court (c.1581) in the Residenz, very Florentine Mannerist in style. In 1584 he remodelled the parish

church of Dachau. The court and interior decoration of Schloss Landshut survive (1573–8); the Akademie der Wissenschaften (1585–97, formerly the Jesuit College) in Munich is attributed to him.

Hitchcock 1981.

**Swag**. A FESTOON in the form of a piece of cloth draped over two supports.

**Swan-neck**. An OGEE-shaped member, e.g. the curve in a staircase handrail where it rises to join the newel post.

**Swedish architecture and landscape architecture**. (For medieval and earlier architecture in Sweden, *see* SCANDINAVIAN ARCHITECTURE.) Though the present-day centre of Stockholm was laid out on a grid shortly after 1625 (as were also Kalmar, after 1647, and Karlskrona, after 1679), the Renaissance made itself felt slowly and reached Sweden mainly from the Netherlands. Justus VINGBOONS visited Sweden in 1653–7, but already before then the style of van CAMPEN and POST had been developed. The de Geer House in Stockholm of 1646 is a perfect example of it. The initiator may have been Simon de LA VALLÉE, who had arrived in 1637 and died in 1642, or his son Jean. The Riddarhus in Stockholm of c.1641–71 was begun by Simon de la Vallée and completed by Vingboons and Jean de la Vallée. At the same time Jean provided in the Oxenstjerna Palace of c.1650–54 an example of the Roman *palazzo* façade.

Churches are of course all Protestant and hence all variations on Dutch types. There are a remarkable number of them, starting with St Katherine in Stockholm by the younger LA VALLÉE begun in 1656. It is a Greek cross with a dome and four corner turrets. Kalmar Cathedral by Nicodemus TESSIN the Elder of 1660 onwards is also basically a Greek cross with corner turrets, but the west and east arms are lengthened and apsed. To the churches must be added the Kagg Mausoleum at Floda of 1661, again a Greek cross, and the grand Carolean Mausoleum attached to the Riddarholm church at Stockholm by the elder Tessin with its splendid columnar exterior. This was designed in 1671.

Openness to influences from several countries remained characteristic of Scandinavia in the C18, or rather of Denmark and Sweden; for Norway had been left behind ever since the Middle Ages. The most monumental building of Scandinavia, the Royal Palace in Stockholm by the younger TESSIN, begun in 1697, reflects more powerfully than any other palace in Europe the impact made by BERNINI's plans for the Louvre in Paris. In 1693 Tessin had made a similar design for the King of Denmark. Tessin knew both Rome and Paris. His country house Steninge of 1694–8 has an entirely French plan, derived from Vaux-le-Vicomte. His father's Drottningholm of the 1660s and Eriksberg had been French throughout, as was also Svartsjö – a completely French *maison de plaisance* – of 1735–9 by Carl Hårleman (1700–1753), the architect of the great East India Company Warehouse at Göteborg of *c.*1740 – an outstanding example of early industrial architecture, nineteen windows wide and four storeys high. About the middle of the C18 the PICTURESQUE movement made its mark in Sweden, inspired by England, which had been visited by Fredrik Magnus Piper (1746–1824) before he designed the landscape park at Haga and followed an English *jardinier* in dealing with the landscape park at Drottningholm, both near Stockholm.

The outstanding neo-classical buildings in Sweden are the theatre of Gripsholm Castle (1782) by Erik Palmstedat (1741–1803) and the Uppsala Botanicum (1788) and other buildings by Jean-Louis Desprez (1743–1804), who had belonged to the most advanced Parisian artistic circles before settling in Sweden in 1784. Between that year and the death of Gustavus III in 1792 he was the fount of the strictest Scandinavian classicism. However, such was the mood of the later C18 that he also designed in the Chinese style for the park at Haga, near Stockholm. The work of Carl August Ehrensvard (1745–1800) was much more severe – indeed his are among the most radical neo-classical designs anywhere. For C19 HISTORICISM the best examples in Sweden are late, e.g. the grandiose Renaissance-style university buildings at Uppsala of 1879–87 by Herman Theodor Holmgren (b.1842) and the Nordisk Museum, Stockholm, of 1890–1907 by Isak Gustaf Clason (1856–1930) in what might be called a northern Renaissance style. But already from the 1890s onwards Swedish architects, such as Ferdinand Boberg (1860–1945), whose post office in Stockholm dates from these years, had begun to join the vanguard of those who tried to get away from Historicism by some 'modern' fusion of styles, both historical and vernacular. ØSTBERG's City Hall in Stockholm of 1909–23 is the best-known exemplar of this trend, though the earlier Engelbrekst church, Stockholm, of 1906–14 by Lars Israel Wahlman (1870–1952) is an even more strikingly romantic fantasy. Sweden was to reach its own distinctive and distinguished C20 style through a conjunction of national sources: the large-scale and carefully designed industrial (usually hydro-electric) installations, such as those at Trollhättan of 1906–16, followed by ALMQUIST's power-stations near Hammersfors and Krangfors of 1925–8 combined with the so-called 'Nordic Classicism' of Ivar Tengbom (1878–1968), the most prolific Swedish architect of his day, whose Stockholm concert-hall of 1920–26 is typical of the style which culminated in ASPLUND's Stockholm City Library of 1920–28. Asplund collaborated with Sigurd LEWERENTZ at the Woodlands Cemetery, Stockholm, where Lewerentz's Resurrection Chapel of 1927 was followed in 1935–40 by Asplund's famous crematorium. By that date Asplund had achieved his unique brand of the INTERNATIONAL MODERN – delicate, refined, with thin steel and much glass, and eminently tactful, as in his lawcourts addition to the Göteborg Town Hall of 1934–7. Later Lewerentz was to break away from its restraints towards a more personal and uncompromising, almost Brutalist, idiom in his two late churches of St Mark, Stockholm (1956–60), and St Peter's, Klippan (1963–6).

The new town of Vällingby, an outer suburb of Stockholm, not a satellite town, was planned by MARKELIUS in 1949 and began to be built in 1953. It has something of the informality and freshness of a carnival. Among the more recent buildings of note in Sweden those by ERSKINE should be mentioned – his Ski Resort hotel at Borgafjäll of 1948–54 and his Stockholm Universrsity library, students' centre and sports hall of 1973–83. With Asplund, Lewerentz, Erik GLEMME and Sven Hermelin (1900–1984), Sweden made a notable contribution to landscape architecture. Hermelin's park at Sundbyberg near Stockholm (1937) for the Marabon Chocolate Factory was outstanding for its social commitment.

**Swiss architecture and landscape architecture**. Switzerland has all the architectural advantages and disadvantages of a position between three large countries (Germany, France and Italy): the advantage of variety of styles, the disadvantage of little visual identity.

The country is uncommonly rich (given its small size) in early buildings. At Romainmôtier a small, aisleless C5 church with two transeptal porticos (in the English sense of the word) has been excavated, and a larger church consecrated in 753 and still of the same archaic plan. Chur has the C8 east end of St Lucius with a ring-crypt and above it three parallel apses on Italian Early Christian precedent. The same east end is at St Martin at Chur, Müstair and Disentis. The famous ideal plan for the monastery of St Gall is of c.820 (the surviving church and library are C18).

The earliest Romanesque churches are inspired by Burgundy and especially the second church of Cluny. They are the third building of Romainmôtier with a typically Burgundian antechurch, and Payerne. Both are C11. Schaffhausen on the other hand of the late C11 and early C12 looks to Germany and the chief German Cluniac centre Hirsau. The Romanesque style culminates in the cathedral of Basel, connected closely with Alsace. It contains a little of the early C11, but dates mostly from c.1180 and later.

At that same time the cathedral of Lausanne had already been begun, and this as well as Geneva Cathedral are again orientated towards France and now a Gothic France. Lausanne Cathedral in particular actually belongs to the Burgundian school of the C13. The principal Late Gothic churches on the other hand are an outlier of south Germany: Berne Minster (1421 onwards), St Oswald at Zug (1478 onwards) and St Leonard at Basel (1489 onwards).

It is understandable that the Renaissance appears first in the cantons bordering on Italy. The portal of St Salvator at Lugano of 1517 is close to Como in style. Of later C16 buildings it is enough to refer to the three-storeyed courtyard arcades of the Ritter House at Lucerne (1556–61) and to the Geltenzunft (1578) and Spiesshof (late C16) at Basel, both more classical than such buildings usually are in Germany. The Spiesshof in particular with its SERLIANA windows is indeed closely dependent on SERLIO.

The C17 gives a mixed impression. There is the fascinating Gothicism of the church of the Visitandes at Fribourg, a quatrefoil in plan but with the most intricate rib vaults (1653–6), there is the Zürich Town Hall, still Renaissance rather than Baroque, though as late as 1694–8, and there are the beginnings of a German Baroque in such a church as that of Muri, designed by MOSBRUGGER and begun in 1694. Its centre is a spacious octagon. Mosbrugger then designed the spatially complex Einsiedeln abbey church (1719–23).

The C18 in Switzerland stands under the sign of the contrast between the dazzling and melodramatic south German Baroque (abbey church of St Gallen of 1748–60 by Peter THUMB and others) and the cool restrained French Dix-huitième (private houses, Geneva). There is in this of course also a contrast between Catholic and Protestant. Typically Protestant churches of unusual interior are the entirely French Temple at Geneva (1707–10 by Vennes), and Holy Ghost, Berne (1726–9 by Schildknecht). The church at Berne is oblong and has four entries in the middle of the four sides and as its only asymmetrical accents a (German) west tower and the pulpit inside close to the east end. The cathedral of Solothurn of 1762 onwards (by G. M. Pisoni) is mildly classicist, the noble west portico of Geneva Cathedral of 1752–6 (by Count ALFIERI) much more radically so. But the most exactingly neo-classicist building of the late C18 in Switzerland is the town hall of Neufchâtel of 1782–90, by Pierre-Adrien Pâris (1745–1819).

For the C19 the most interesting series of buildings are the *hôtels*. For the C20 Switzerland contributed good architecture in the pre-first-war years, e.g. the

Kunsthaus, Zürich (1907–10), and the Badischer Bahnhof, Basel (1912–13), by Robert Curjel (1859–1925) and Karl Moser (1860–1936); also some outstanding EXPRESSIONISM of the same and the immediate post-first-war years, e.g. Goetheanum Dornach, 1913 and again after a disastrous fire 1923–8, by Rudolf Steiner (1861–1925), and much good and early work in the INTERNATIONAL MODERN of the twenties and thirties, notably by Hannes MEYER and Otto Rudolf Salvisberg (1882–1940), whose Lory Hospital, Berne (1924–9) was notable. Outstanding was the work of Robert MAILLART in concrete construction, especially for bridges. Some of the churches were highly influential abroad, e.g. St Anthony, Basel (1925–31), by Karl Moser. LE CORBUSIER, who was born at La Chaux-de-Fonds, contributed one block of flats at Geneva (1931–2) and the Centre Le Corbusier at Zürich (1964–6). The domestic work in wood by Max Bill (1908–94) of the 1940s was remarkable, but his most distinguished building is in Germany (Hochschule für Gestaltung, Ulm, 1953–5). To these years also belong the Halen Housing near Berne (1955–60) by Atelier 5 (founded 1955). Two late Expressionist buildings are of note: the pilgrimage church at Neviges (1963–8) by Gottfried BÖHM and the church centre at Hérémence (1963–71) by Walter-Maria Förderer (b.1928). More recently the so-called Ticino School made its name internationally with such distinguished small buildings as the Casa Tonino, Torricella, of 1972–4, by Bruno Reichlin (b.1941) and Fabio Reinhart (b.1942), and especially work by Mario BOTTA. More recently the Deconstructivist Bernard TSCHUMI and the Jacques HERZOG and De Meuron partnership have been acclaimed internationally, also the landscape architect Dieter KIENAST.

**Switzer**, Stephen (1682–1745). English landscape architect who began as an apprentice to George London (c.1640–1713) and Henry WISE, designers of French-style gardens, but became one of the initiators of the English LANDSCAPE GARDEN. He worked in close collaboration with his patrons, the Earl of Carlisle at Castle Howard, Yorkshire, where from 1706 a mature wood near the house was transformed into a much admired 'wilderness' with winding walks, many statues and fountains, and the Earl of Bathurst at Cirencester Park, Gloucestershire, laid out from c.1714 with woodlands and arable fields linked by straight avenues intersecting at *ronds-points*. At Grimsthorpe Castle, Lincolnshire, he modernized c.1722 a geometrical scheme to make a smooth transition from parterres around the house to an informal park with a view of distant hills. He was influential as the author of *The Nobleman, Gentleman and Gardener's Recreation*, the first part of his three-volume *Ichonographia Rustica* (London 1715–18), in which he advocated 'mixing the useful and profitable parts of gardening with the pleasurable' in what he later called a FERME ORNÉE. A whole estate with farmland, woods and pleasure grounds should, he wrote, be laid out with respect to natural features and also to improvements in agriculture and forestry, on a single masterplan with a few great axial lines.

D. Jacques, *Georgian Gardens*, London 1983.

**Synagogue**. A Jewish place of worship, in origin a meeting-house, not a temple. The earliest of which traces survive seem to have developed from the ancient Roman BASILICA, like EARLY CHRISTIAN churches. The Ark of the Covenant (*Aron Hakodesh*), for the Scrolls of the Law, originally had no fixed position but a niche (as at Dura Europos) or an apse (as at Beth Alpha) became usual, generally in front of the end wall. Later the Ark and the reading desk were raised on steps (*see* TEBAM). Architecturally, synagogues have adopted the styles current wherever they were built – Romanesque, Gothic, Renaissance, Baroque, Rococo, etc. The C14 Gothic synagogue in Prague, the Altneuschule, is one of the oldest to survive intact. Erich MENDELSOHN's domed synagogue in Cleveland, Ohio, 1945, and L. KAHN's Mikvch Israel Synagogue, Philadelphia (1961–72), are recent notable examples.

J. S. M. Chiat, *Handbook of S. Architecture*, Chicago 1982; C. H. Krinsky, *S. of Europe. Architecture, History, Meaning*, Cambridge, Mass./London (1985) 1996; H. Meek, *The S. The Complete History of the Art and Architecture of the S.*, London 1994.

**Synclastic**. Of a surface, having curvatures in the same sense (concave or convex) in all directions through any point, as in a simple DOME and in contrast to an ANTICLASTIC surface.

**Synthronon**. In Early Christian and Byzantine churches, the bench or benches reserved for the clergy in the semicircle of the apse or in rows on either side of the BEMA.

**Syrkus**, Helen and Szymon (1900–1982 and 1893–1967), *see* POLISH ARCHITECTURE.

**Systems, industrialized building**. Either complete prefabricated assemblies, e.g. VOLUMETRIC BUILDINGS, or only the outer walls and their cladding for erection on the site, *see* INDUSTRIALIZED BUILDING.

**Systyle**. With an arrangement of columns spaced two diameters apart. *See also* ARAEOSTYLE; DIASTYLE; EUSTYLE; PYCNOSTYLE.

**T'a**, *see* PAGODA.

**Tabby**. Concrete made with lime mixed with shells, gravel or small stones in equal proportions; very hard when dry.

**Tabernacle**. A canopied recess to contain an image; an ornamental receptacle for the consecrated host, usually in the form of a miniature building placed on an altar in a Catholic church; the portable shrine in which the Jewish Ark of the Covenant was housed.

**Tablinum**. In Ancient Roman architecture, a room with one side open to the ATRIUM or central courtyard.

**TAC (The Architects' Collaborative)**, *see* GROPIUS, Walter.

**Taenia**, *see* TENIA.

**Tahoto**, *see* PAGODA.

**Takamatsu**, Shin (b.1948). Japanese second-generation 'New Wave' architect, trained in Kyoto. He began with a remarkable series of science-fiction-like buildings in which, he said, 'function follows form', notably the three Origin Buildings, Kyoto (1981−2 and 1986), and the Ark (Nishina Dental Clinic), Kyoto (1983). These were followed by several bizarre urban structures, e.g. Kirin Plaza, Osaka (1987); Solaris, Amagasaki (1990); and Syntax, Kyoto (1990). With the Zeus, Nima Sand Museum, Nima-cho (1990), he initiated a more geometrical phase in his development which culminated with the Kunibiki Messe Convention Hall, Matsue, Shimane Prefecture (1993), and the Quasar Building, Frankfurter Allée, Berlin (1994). In 1991 he formed Taka-matsu & Lahyani Architects Assn in Berlin and Geneva.

P. Polledri (ed.), *S.T.*, New York 1993; N. Ueshina (ed.), *Die Japanische Herausforderung. T. und Gabriel Lahyani Architects Assn*, Zürich 1994; Bognar 1995.

**Takeyama**, Minoru (b.1934). Japanese architect, trained in Tokyo and the USA (Harvard), later working with SERT and UTZON. On returning to Japan in 1965 he broke with METABOLISM. With AIDA, AZUMA and others he founded ArchiteXt to pursue urban semiology and what he called architectural 'heterology'. He made his name internationally at the same time with his spectacularly garish populist Ichiban-Kan (1969) and Niban-Kan (1970) buildings, Tokyo, which were hailed as Post-Modern in the West. They were followed by his equally striking Hotel Beverly Tom (now Hotel East Japan), Tomakomai (1973). With AIDA and others he changed course in the 1980s, e.g. his Renaissance commercial centre, Kyoto (1986). His recent Tokyo International Port Terminal (1991) is his major work to date.

Ross 1978; Bognar 1995.

**Talenti**, Francesco (*fl.*1340−69). Florentine architect who completed the windowed upper storeys of the campanile after he succeeded Andrea PISANO there in *c.*1343. From 1350 he was *capomastro* at the Duomo (*see* ARNOLFO DI CAMBIO), of which little was built until after 1357, to an enlarged and modified plan by Talenti; his final design of 1366−7 included the octagon (*see* BRUNEL-

LESCHI). Francesco Talenti's son Simone (1340/45–81) was the principal architect of the Loggia dei Lanzi, Florence (1376–82).

Trachtenberg 1971; White 1987.

**Tall building**, *see* SKYSCRAPER.

**Taller de Arquitectura**, *see* BOFILL, Ricardo.

**Talman**, William (1650–1719). English architect and WREN's most distinguished contemporary. He was the leading country-house architect until eclipsed by VANBRUGH. Little is known about him personally, though he seems to have been difficult and quarrelsome. His country houses are by far the largest and most lavish of their period in England, and display a mixed French and Italian Baroque character. They were very influential, e.g. in the use of giant pilasters with architrave and frieze to frame a façade, the cornice alone continuing across. Thoresby, Nottinghamshire (1683–5, destroyed), the south and east fronts and state rooms inside at Chatsworth, Derbyshire (1687–96), Dyrham Park, Gloucestershire (1698–1704), Dorchester House, Surrey (*c.*1700), and the new front at Drayton, Northamptonshire (*c.*1701), were his main works, all country houses. He probably designed the state apartments at Burghley House, Northamptonshire (1688, destroyed). He succeeded Hugh MAY as Comptroller of the Office of Works in 1689, serving under Wren, whose design for Hampton Court he probably revised and altered in execution.

J. Harris, *W.T. Maverick Architect*, London 1982.

**Talon**. An ogee moulding; *see* CYMA RECTA; CYMA REVERSA.

**Talus**. In military architecture, the enlarged, sloped base of a wall or fortification.

**Tambour**. 1. The core of a Corinthian or Composite CAPITAL. 2. The circular wall carrying a DOME or CUPOLA (*see* DRUM).

**Tange**, Kenzo (b.1913). Japanese architect who studied at Tokyo University (1935–8), then under MAYEKAWA, returning to Tokyo University 1942–5 as a graduate. In 1949 he won the competition for the Peace Centre, Hiroshima (built 1950–55), with a light and elegant structure, but his mature buildings are all dramatically plastic: the Kagawa prefectural offices at Takamatsu (1958) with a ruthlessly expressed post-and-beam structure; the civic complex of City Hall and Public Hall, Imabari (1958), combining the influence of Le Corbusier's plastic style with elements from traditional Japanese architecture in a way that initiated a trend in Japanese architecture; the waterfront Dentsu offices at Osaka (1960); the Atami Gardens Hotel, Atami (1961); the challenging Old Kurashiki City Hall, now Art Museum (1960), standing four-square and quakeproof; St Mary's Roman Catholic Cathedral, Tokyo (1965), a cruciform arrangement of paraboloids; and the joyful Golf Club, Totsuka (1962), in which an upswept traditional roof is contrasted with aluminium curtain walls. With Yoshokatsu Tsuboi as engineer, Tange designed the magnificent tensile catenary roof spanning the 15,000-seat National Gymnasium for the Tokyo Olympic Games in 1964. Tange's leadership of the younger generation resulted from his research work into urban design at Tokyo University, the absence of which had reduced Japan's expanding industrial cities to a critical state of congestion. Tange's plan for Tokyo (1960) showed a logical hierarchy of rapid transit roads within connecting ring roads, enclosing environmental areas of high-density housing; his idea was to extend the city in this way on piles over Tokyo Bay. In 1961 he founded URTEL, a team of architects and urbanists with whom he developed planning methods applicable to both towns and buildings, and in 1965 won the international competition for replanning Skopje in Yugoslavia with a system of multi-purpose blocks. He designed prototypes of these for the Dentsu Building and Tsukiji area, Tokyo (1965), with flying bridges clad in criss-cross concrete grilles, and for the Yamanashi Communications Centre, Kofu (built 1966–7), which is held together by sixteen cylindrical towers of lifts and services. Tsuboi was engineer for Dentsu and Fugaku Yokoyama for the astonishing Yamanashi project. This was followed by the smaller but no less startling Shizuoko Press and Broadcasting Office, Tokyo (1967). In 1967 Tange was also appointed (with Uzo Nikiyama) master planner of the 1970 exhibition at Osaka. Thereafter he changed course. At the Akasaka Prince Hotel, Tokyo (1983), visual delicacy and metallic precision replace his former plastic exuberance, while his enormous New Tokyo City Hall complex (1986–91) and the United Nations University, Tokyo (1992), might be called the last Post-Modern buildings on a grand scale to be realized.

Banham 1976; H. R. von der Moll et al., *K.T.*, Zürich 1978; R. Miyake, *K.T. et ses disciples. Tokyo Project*, Brussels 1989; Bognar 1985; Bognar 1995.

**Taniguchi**, Yoshio (b.1937), *see* JAPANESE ARCHITECTURE.

**Tarsia**. A form of mosaic or inlay made up of different coloured woods popular in C15–16 Italy especially for the decoration of studies and small rooms in palaces and for the choirs of churches.

**Tas-de-charge**. The lowest courses of a vault or arch, laid horizontally and bonded into the wall.

**Tatami**. A Japanese mat of rice-straw used as a floor-covering and made to a standard size (approximately 180 × 90 cm. or 70 × 35 in.); multiples of this determine the size and proportions of Japanese rooms.

**Tatlin**, Vladimir (1885–1953). Russian artist and architect who began and ended his career as a painter, but became famous as a pioneer of abstract sculpture, theatre designer and creator of a single major architectural model, one of the most visionary, perhaps notorious, of modern times; his activity provided much of the inspiration for CONSTRUCTIVISM. Acquaintance with Picasso's early collages (1914) inspired his 'counter-reliefs', utilizing *objets trouvés*, that take on architectonic significance in his décor (with G. Yakulov) for the Moscow Café Pittoresque (1917). He was closely associated with the literary Futurists, for whom artistic and political revolution were complementary. In 1919 he embarked on his project for a monument to the Third International: a 400 m. (1,300 ft) building, straddling the river Neva, in the form of a double skew spiral of open-work girders, with revolving halls suspended at various levels. Unrealized and probably unrealizable, this great symbol of revolutionary Modernism – an 'answer' to the Eiffel Tower – was endlessly discussed, and several scale models have been constructed. Tatlin's organic theories of art and society led after 1930 to many years' work on *Letatlin*, a glider with movable wings, and to various utilitarian projects and educational activities. But his 'culture of materials' smacked of aestheticism to extreme Constructivists and of formalism to traditionalists, and he became a lonely figure; from the mid-1930s his only public activity was in theatre design, and from *c.*1944 until 1962 his heritage was virtually ignored in Russia. [R. R. Milner-Gulland]

J. Milner, *V.T. and the Russian Avant-Garde*, New Haven and London 1983; L. A. Zsadova (ed.), *T.*, London 1988; J. Harten (ed.), *V.T. Leben, Werk, Wirkung – Ein Symposium*, Cologne 1990; A. Strigalev, *V.T. Retrospective*, Cologne 1993.

**Tatsuma**, Kingo (1858–1919), *see* JAPANESE ARCHITECTURE.

**Taut**, Bruno (1880–1938). German architect. A pupil of Theodor Fischer, he settled in Berlin in 1908 and was first noticed for his steel industry pavilion at the Leipzig Fair (1913) and his highly original glass pavilion at the 1914 WERKBUND exhibition in Cologne, a polygonal building with walls of thick glass panels and a glass dome, the elements set in lozenge framing (a SPACE-FRAME). In the years of the wildest Expressionism he wrote his *Alpine Architektur* (1917–18, English edn 1972) and *Die Stadtkrone* (1919) and designed fantastic buildings for imprecisely formulated purposes. Later he developed functional theories for mass-housing, e.g. his housing at Hufeisen, Berlin, 1925–31, with Martin Wagner (1885–1957). In 1929 he published *Modern Architecture* (London) and in 1933 he emigrated to Japan (1933–6) and then to Turkey (1936–8).

R. H. Bletter, *B.T. and Paul Schubart's Vision. Utopian Aspects of German Expressionist Architecture*, New York 1979; I. Boyd-White, *B.T. and the Architecture of Activism*, Cambridge, Mass. 1983.

**Taut**, Max (1884–1967). He worked with MIES VAN DER ROHE 1906–11 and then with his brother Bruno, 1914–31. His most notable buildings were concrete-frame office blocks in Berlin, e.g. Verband der Deutschen Buchdrucker (1922–5) with Mart STAM and his Alex-

ander von Humboldt high school, Berlin Köpernick (1928–9). Some of his post-1945 housing is notable, e.g. Reuther Siedlung, Bonn (1949–52), and August-Thyssen Siedlung, Duisberg (1955–64).

*M.T.*, exh. cat., Berlin 1964.

**Taylor**, Sir Robert (1714–88). English architect, son of a mason-contractor, trained as a sculptor under Cheere and visited Rome *c.*1743. Though sufficiently successful to be commissioned by Parliament to design and carve the monument to Captain Cornewall in Westminster Abbey (1744), he soon abandoned sculpture for architecture and by assiduity and businesslike methods quickly built up a large practice. He and PAINE were said to have 'nearly divided the practice of the profession between them' during the mid-century. He was highly competent and worthily carried on the neo-Palladian tradition of BURLINGTON and KENT; indeed he went some way beyond it in his late work. Most of his work has been destroyed, notably that in the Bank of England, which included his last and by far his most original work, the Reduced Annuities Office, a top-lit hall with circular clerestory carried on shallow segmental arches which anticipate his pupil SOANE. (The Court Room of 1767–70 has been reconstructed.) Asgill House, Richmond (1758–67), and Stone Building, Lincoln's Inn, London (begun 1775), are the best of his surviving buildings. He was knighted when sheriff of London, 1782–3, and left the bulk of his large fortune to found the Taylorian Institute in Oxford.

M. Binney, *Sir R.T.: From Rococo to Neo-Classicism*, London 1984; Colvin 1995.

**Team 4**, *see* FOSTER, Sir Norman.

**Team 10**, *see* CIAM.

**Team Zoo**, *see* JAPANESE ARCHI-TECTURE.

**Tebam**. A dais or rostrum for the reader in a synagogue. Adjoining it to the east is the Chief Rabbi's seat.

**Tecton**. A team established in London in 1932 by Berthold LUBETKIN to which among others LASDUN belonged. They did the Highpoint Flats I and II at High-gate, London, in 1936 and 1938, the Fins-bury Health Centre in 1938–9, and the blocks of flats in Rosebery Avenue in 1946–9. Their most popular work was for the London Zoo (1934–8). The details here of freely moulded concrete are prophetic of the 1950s. The group disbanded in 1948. Their plans for Peterlee, a new town for miners in County Durham, were never realized.

P. Coe and M. Reading, *Lubetkin and T. Architecture and Social Commitment*, London and Bristol 1981.

**Telamones**, *see* ATLANTES.

**Telford**, Thomas (1757–1834), son of a Scottish shepherd, trained as a mason, worked in Edinburgh, then in London, and by 1784 had been made supervisor of works on Portsmouth Dockyard. In 1788 he became surveyor to the county of Shropshire. He built several churches in the county, notably Bridgnorth (1792), and several bridges, notably Buildwas Bridge (1795–8, demolished), which was of iron (the Coalbrookdale Bridge had been built in iron in 1777) and had a 40 m. (130 ft) span. In 1793 work started on the Ellesmere Canal, and Telford was put in charge. He built the Chirk Aque-duct at Ceiriog, 210 m. (700 ft) long and 21 m. (70 ft) high (1796–1801), and the Pont Cysylltau Aqueduct, 300 m. (1,000 ft) long and 35 m. (120 ft) high (1795–1805). In 1800 he suggested the rebuilding of London Bridge with a single span of 183 m. (600 ft). Telford was

responsible for other canals (Caledonian, 1804; Göta, 1808), for the St Katherine's Docks (1827; *see* HARDWICK), for fen drainage, for roads, and for further bridges, including the beautiful Dean Bridge, Edinburgh, of stone (1829), the Menai Straits Suspension Bridge, of iron, with a 170 m. (530 ft) span (1819–26), and the Conway Suspension Bridge, also of iron (1821–6).

L. T. C. Rolt, *T.T.*, London 1958; Colvin 1978; A. Penfold (ed.), *T.T. Engineer*, London 1980.

**Temanza**, Tommaso (1705–89). The most sensitive of Venetian neo-Palladians. His masterpiece is the little church of the Maddalena, Venice (begun 1763), with its interior freely derived from PALLADIO's chapel at Maser. He wrote *Le vite dei più celebri architetti e scultori veneziani* (1778).

Meeks 1966; Howard 1987; Wittkower 1982; P. Valle, *T.T. e l'archit-ettura civile a Venezia e il settecento diffusione e funzionalisazione dell'architettura*, Venice 1989.

**Temenos**. The ground surrounding or adjacent to an Ancient Greek temple or sanctuary, hence any sacred enclosure or precinct.

**Template**. 1. The block of stone set at the top of a brick or rubble wall to carry the weight of the JOISTS or roof-trusses; also called a *pad stone*. 2. A pattern used to control the profile of cut stone or other material.

**Temple**, Raymond du (active *c.*1360–1405), *see* RAYMOND DU TEMPLE.

**Tempietto**. Italian for a small temple, usually referring to an ornamental build-ing in a park or garden though the most famous *tempietto*, that by BRAMANTE in S. Pietro in Montorio, Rome, is a MARTYRIUM.

**Tenement block**. An APARTMENT block of small and inexpensive apartments, usually for tenants of modest means.

**Tengbom**, Ivar (1878–1968), *see* SWEDISH ARCHITECTURE.

**Tenia**. The small moulding or fillet along the top of the ARCHITRAVE in the Doric ORDER.

**Tenon**, *see* MORTICE AND TENON JOINT.

**Tensile or membrane structures**. Generally flexible and temporary structures of thin pliable tissue or new-technology fabrics such as coated glass-fibre or other PLASTICS, supported by masts or props and stabilized by cables, like a TENT. Pioneered by Frei OTTO from 1954 onwards. They are often used only as roofing, detached from any enclosures beneath. *See also* PNEUMATIC STRUCTURES.

F. Otto, *The Suspended Roof*, Berlin 1954; P. Drew, *T. Architecture*, London 1979; H. J. Schock, *Soft Shells . . .* , Basel 1997.

**Tent**. A portable shelter of two basic types. 1. A tensile structure with upright posts held in place by a membrane – woven material or animal skin – stretched tightly over them and attached to the ground with ropes. 2. An armature of rods to which a protective covering is attached.

Tents were made by nomads from very early times. They may be represented in the 4th to 3rd millennium BC rock paintings at Sefar (Tassili-n-Ajjer), Algeria. There are references to them in Ancient Egyptian writings from the 3rd millennium BC and in the Hebrew Bible (notably the temporary shelter for the Ark of the Covenant, Exodus 28–40). Those used in military campaigns are represented in carvings on the C13 BC Ram-

asseum, Luxor, Egypt, and in C7 BC Assyrian reliefs. Many, including some richly decorated, are depicted in medieval European and Islamic miniatures. The oldest and also the most elaborate surviving examples are tensile tents with finely woven membranes, made for Ottoman generals in C17–19 (Military Museum, Istanbul; Army Museum, Vienna). Tents still in permanent use include the yurts of Central Asia with coverings of felt; several regionally distinct types with intricately bent meshed wooden armatures made by nomads in sub-Saharan Africa; and the conical tepees covered with skins of bark of native Americans of the Plains. A symbiotic relationship between the early developments of tent construction and building is often suggested. But not until recently have architects exploited large-scale TENSILE STRUCTURES.

P. Drew, *Tensile Architecture*, London 1979; T. Faegre, *T. Architecture of the Nomad*, New York 1979; L. Prussin, *Nomadic Architecture*, Washington, DC 1995.

**Term**. A pedestal tapering towards the base and usually supporting a bust; also a pedestal merging at the top into a sculptured human, animal or mythical figure; also called *terminal figures* or *termini* (*see also* CARYATID). *See* Fig. 114.

**Terrace**. 1. A level promenade in front of a building. 2. A row of attached houses designed as a unit, flat-faced and flush with those on either side, a feature of Victorian England, though their kinship with Georgian Bath and London is apparent, e.g. Bedford Square, London.

S. Muthesius, *The English T. House*, New Haven and London 1982.

**Terracotta**. Literally 'baked earth': clay moulded and kiln-fired to make a hard compact material used for bricks, roof-tiling, cladding and ornament, especially

# Terracotta

Fig. 114 Term

with motifs repeated by casting from a single matrix, but also hand-modelled figurative sculpture. Whether left in its raw brownish-red, sometimes yellow or blue, state or coloured with paint or slip (diluted clay that is more ductile), it is to be distinguished from FAÏENCE and GLAZED BRICKS (*see also* TILES). Ancient Greek temples had terracotta roof-tiles, antifixae, metopes and friezes from the C8–7 BC, later only where stone was in short supply. Terracotta was used for facing woodwork and for all ornament on temples in Etruria from C5 BC (*see* ETRUSCAN ARCHITECTURE). But the Ancient Romans regarded it as a material inferior to stone, suitable only for buildings of minor importance. In Central Asia decorative reliefs incorporated in the brickwork of Islamic buildings from

AD C9 were sometimes of terracotta, though STUCCO was more usual.

The use of terracotta was resumed in areas of medieval Europe where brick was the main building material, e.g. in *Backsteingotik* architecture (see GERMAN ARCHITECTURE), notably Katherinen Kirche (1357–1411) and Rathaus (1470–80), Brandenburg; and in north Italy, notably the cathedrals of Crema and Cremona before 1400 and FILARETE's Ospedale Maggiore, Milan (1451). However, not until the C19 was its decorative as well as utilitarian potentiality reassessed. (COADE STONE is to be distinguished from terracotta.) In Germany HÜBSCH incorporated a large terracotta relief in his Trinkhalle, Baden-Baden (1839–42). In England, Edmund Sharpe (1809–77), at the suggestion of a brick manufacturer, built the church of St Stephen, Bolton, Lancashire, entirely of terracotta, including the pews and organ-case (1842–5), and used it for cladding Holy Trinity, Fallowfield, Manchester (1845–6). These buildings were derided as 'pot-churches' but terracotta returned to favour as a result of the mid-C19 cult of medieval and Early Renaissance brick architecture. Hermann Friedrich Waesmann (1813–79) used it for friezes on the Berlin Rathaus (1863–9), as did FOWKE still more lavishly on the façade (now inner courtyard) of the Victoria and Albert Museum, designed 1864. The publication of *The Terracotta Architecture of North Italy* (London 1867), with illustrations by Ludwig Gruner (1801–82), set a seal of aesthetic approval on terracotta which was to be widely used on Historicist buildings throughout the West, e.g. WATERHOUSE's Natural History Museum, London (1873–8), with cladding in yellow and blue panels as well as figurative sculpture; CUYPERS's Rijksmuseum (1876–85) and Railway Station (1885–9), Amsterdam; McKIM's Boston

Public Library, USA (1888–95). SULLI-
VAN's eminently original ornamental
reliefs were also cast in terracotta, e.g. the
Wainwright Building, St Louis (1890–
91), and the Guaranty Building, Buffalo
(1894–5), both USA. In the US terracotta was favoured as a fireproof as well
as a decorative material to sheathe steel
skeleton constructions, and both relief
and flat panels in a wide range of colours
were manufactured on a large scale from
the 1870s until the 1930s, after its use
in architecture had been abandoned in
Europe.

Elliot 1992; N. A. Winter, *Greek Archi-
tectural T.*, Oxford 1993; M. Stratton, *The
T. Revival. Building, Innovation and the
Image of the Industrial City in Britain and
N. America*, London 1993.

**Terragni**, Giuseppe (1904–43). Italian
architect, the leading exponent of Italian
RATIONALISM. He began with a five-
storey concrete block of flats in Como,
'Novocomun', in 1928–9. His masterpiece, the Casa del Fascio, Como, followed in 1933–6. The Asilo Sant'Elia,
Como (1936–7), the Casa Bianca, Seveso
(1936–7), the Casa del Fascio, Lissone
(1938–9), and the Casa Giuliani, Como
(1939–40), are only slightly less distinguished. His Danteum library and
museum project for Rome (1937) was
never built.

B. Zevi (ed.), *G.T.*, Bologna 1980;
A. F. Marcianò, *G.T. L'opera completa
1925–1943*, Rome 1987; Etlin 1989; S.
Germer and A. Preis, *G.T. 1904–43, Mod-
erne und Faschismus in Italien*, Munich
1990; T. Schumacher, *Surface and Symbol,
G.T. and the Italian Rationalist Movement*,
Princeton 1990; T. L. Schumacher, *T.
The Danteum*, Princeton 1993; G. Cucci
(ed.), *G.T. Opera completa*, Milan 1996.

**Terrazzo**. A flooring finish of marble
chips mixed with cement mortar and laid

*in situ*; the surface is then ground and
polished.

**Terry**, Quinlan (b.1937), *see* ENGLISH
ARCHITECTURE; NEO-GEORGIAN ARCHI-
TECTURE.

**Tessellated**. Of a cement floor or wall
covering, having TESSERAE embedded in
it.

**Tessenow**, Heinrich (1876–1950), *see*
GERMAN ARCHITECTURE.

**Tesserae**. The small cubes of glass, stone
or marble used in MOSAIC.

**Tessin**, Nicodemus, the elder (1615–
81), a leading Baroque architect in
Sweden, was born at Stralsund and began
by working under Simon LA VALLÉE. In
1651–2 he made a tour of Europe and
in 1661 was appointed city architect of
Stockholm. His main work is
Drottningholm Palace (begun 1662),
built in an individual Baroque style,
derived from Holland, France and Italy.
His other works include Kalmar
Cathedral (1660), Göteborg Town Hall
(1670), the Carolean Mausoleum
attached to the Riddarholm church,
Stockholm (designed 1671), and numerous small houses in Stockholm. His son
Nicodemus the younger (1654–1728)
succeeded him as the leading Swedish
architect. Trained under his father, he
travelled in England, France and Italy
(1673–80), and completed his father's
work at Drottningholm. His main building is the vast royal palace in Stockholm
(begun 1697), where he adopted a
Baroque style reminiscent of, and probably influenced by, BERNINI's Louvre
project.

Paulsson 1958; B. R. Kommer, *N.T.
der Jüngere und das Stockholmer Schloss*,
Heidelberg 1974.

**Tester**. A canopy suspended from the

ceiling or supported from the wall above a bed, throne, pulpit, etc.

**Tetrastyle**. Of a PORTICO with four frontal columns.

**Teulon**, Samuel Sanders (1812–73). English architect. Goodhart-Rendel called Teulon a rogue-architect, together with Edward Buckton Lamb (1806–69) and Bassett Keeling (1836–86). Teulon was a Gothicist, but the motifs he used – motifs of the late C13 and early C14 – are treated freely and with a heaviness not to be found c.1300. His churches are domineering, his details coarse. These qualities are already fully exhibited in so early a mansion as Tortworth Court (1849–52), Avon. Teulon's most overpowering country house is Shadwell Park, Norfolk (1856–60), an addition to an older building. Of the churches designed by Teulon the most characteristic are St Mary, Ealing (1866–73), St Stephen, Hampstead (1869–76), and Silvertown (1859), all in London, though St John, Huntley, Gloucestershire (1861–3), is more enterprising.

M. Saunders in Brown 1985.

**Thai architecture**. Buddhist STUPAS (called *chedis* in Thai) were built in the valley of the Chao Phraya river from the C7, but only fragments of their relief sculptures survive. The earliest surviving buildings are Hindu and Mahayana Buddhist temples in the north-east, dating from C11–13 when this area was under Khmer rule, fine but relatively small examples of KHMER ARCHITECTURE (Phanom Rung, Khao Phra Vihara, Muang Tam and Phimai). Little is known of the history of architecture or of the rise and fall of the kingdoms on which it was dependent until the C17. (A chronology based on a supposedly late C13 inscription recently shown to be a C19 fabrication, and on royal chronicles written in the late C18, can no longer be accepted.) Remains of extensive cities in the Chao Phraya valley – Sukhothai, Si Satchanalai and Kamphaeng Phet – include numerous religious buildings constructed of LATERITE, originally covered with carved and painted stucco, which soon decays in the tropical climate even if not damaged as when the wooden buildings surrounding them were destroyed in recurrent wars. They are probably of the same date as similar buildings further south at Ayudhya, capital of a kingdom extending at times into Burma and Cambodia: Wat Phra Ram with a bold Khmer style PRANG, the three great *chedis* of Wat Phra Sri Samphet, and the daringly elegant Chedi Phukhao Thong, which although on the sites of C14–15 structures were not given their present form until the C17–18. In the north of Thailand at Lamphun, the capital of a small kingdom, the imposing five-storey pyramidal *chedi* of Wat Ku Kut is traditionally believed to have been founded in the C8, though the present structure with rich stucco relief decorations may be no earlier than the C18. At Chiang Mai, capital of Lannan, another northern kingdom, Wat Chet Yot is on the site of a building founded in 1455 but apparently reconstructed much later. In form a cube decorated with fine reliefs, it supports five *prangs* in emulation of the great Buddhist shrine at Bodh Gaya in India. This northern area was conquered by the king of Pegu, Burma, in the mid-C16 and until the mid-C19 its architecture was BURMESE.

Ayudhya was sacked by the Burmese in 1767 and a new capital was founded some 50 km. (30 miles) to the south at Bangkok, where from the early C19 the royal palace and monastic complexes were built in a richly ornamented style, with much use of strong colours and of glittering inlays of ceramics and glass, adopted throughout the kingdom which spread over the whole area of present-day Thailand. In the main cities old buildings were replaced rather than restored and at Nakhon Pathom, near Bangkok, the highest of all *chedis* was raised over ancient rubble from 1853 onwards. The most numerous as well as the most notable buildings are monastic halls – for daily prayers, ordinations and the display of images – with very steeply pitched ceramic-tile roofs constructed in such a way that the uppermost, with the longest ridge-pole, seems to float above the others that extend the building at either end. Prominent upward-curving *naga*, or snake-head finials, terminating the ridge-poles are often elaborately carved and add notably to the buildings' distinctive character. Such halls are still being built on the same model, though ferro-concrete for supports and iron girders for beams are now used instead of stuccoed brick and wood. Western techniques and (for secular buildings) historical styles were introduced in the late C19 as part of a royally instigated campaign of modernization. But nearly all houses continued to be built of wood in traditional vernacular styles, varying from region to region (many examples are preserved in the open-air museum, 'Ancient City', near Bangkok). The INTERNATIONAL MODERN style was introduced in the 1960s for offices, blocks of flats, shops, hotels, etc. Economic growth from the mid-1970s, after the end of the Vietnam war, financed a nation-wide building boom, and the Bangkok of canals and monasteries rising above low wooden houses was transformed into a city of traffic-clogged and polluted streets, multi-storey shopping malls and sky-scrapers, sometimes of an uninhibited Post-Modern eclecticism. Some buildings of this period were, however, architecturally distinguished, notably those in

Bangkok by Sumet Jumsai (b.1939): the School for the Blind (1973) and the Science Museum (1974–6), inspired by Le Corbusier but well adapted to local conditions; the six-storey Bank of Asia (1986–7) in the form of a giant robot, and the *Nation* newspaper offices (1990–91); more restrained were his Thammasat University (1986) and International School of Bangkok (1993), which successfully assimilate features from Thai vernacular architecture. Plan Architect Co., an agency founded by five young architects in Bangkok in 1973, has developed a distinctive Thai modern style, e.g. their apartment houses Suan Paritchat (1981) and Bean Suan Rim Klong (1993), high-rise blocks Sithakarn (1984) and Ben Yoke (1987), and the Pridi Banomyong Foundation (1993), all in Bangkok though the group has been employed throughout the country.

**Thatch**. A roof covering of straw, reeds or other vegetable material, held in place by stones, ropes or poles, or interspersed with layers of mud. Thatch of even the best materials lasts no more than eighty years. Very little is known about ancient methods of thatching.

Davey 1961; R. West, *T. A Manual for Owners, Surveyors, Architects and Builders*, London 1987.

**Theatre**. A place for viewing dramas or other spectacles, open-air in Ancient Greece and Rome, usually covered in Europe since the C16.

**Theme park**. An amusement PARK organized round a unifying idea or group of ideas. Ideas or themes from history, geography or narrative are represented by buildings, statuary, landscape and layout. The term 'theme park' was first used in 1960 with reference to Disneyland. This opened in 1955 at Anaheim, California, to give three-dimensional visible form to the world of Walt Disney's films in a setting more salubrious and attractive to a middle-class public than an amusement park such as New York's Coney Island. Designed by Disney's 'Imagineers', its central and evocative recreation of a *c*.1900 Main Street, the soul of the traditional American town, leads past the Sleeping Beauty Castle to Frontierland and Adventureland and on to Tomorrowland and Fantasyland. The manipulation of scale and limitation to pedestrians together with nostalgic and admiring if rose-tinted reconstructions of American vernacular styles combined to produce, in the heyday of International Modernism, a subversive influence comparable to VENTURI's populism. As Charles MOORE wrote in 1965, 'this incredibly energetic collection of environmental experiences offers enough lessons for a whole architectural education in all the things that matter'. It reaffirmed the importance of architecture's symbolic content and the effectiveness of storytelling in built forms, while its celebration of traditional urbanism led not only to widespread support in the USA for HISTORICAL PRESERVATION but also to what became known as the New Urbanism; *see* DUANG & PLATER ZYBERG ARCHITECTS INC. Disneyland was followed by the much larger Walt Disney World at Orlando, Florida (1971), and Disneyland Paris or EuroDisneyland at Marne-la-Vallée, France (1992), to both of which ISOZAKI, GRAVES, MOORE, PREDOCK, Aldo ROSSI, SCOTT BROWN, STERN, VENTURI and others contributed. Disneyland set a standard for 'narrative' theme parks everywhere, e.g. Parc Astérix, Ermenonville, France, and the Parco di Pinocchio, Collodi, Italy (begun 1963). It also led to the development in the USA of UECs or Urban Entertainment Centers, hybrid complexes of retail, high tech and entertainment contained within a comprehensive themed environment.

The term 'theme park' may also be used to refer to open-air architectural museums, the first of which, Skansen near Stockholm, Sweden, opened in 1895. It was followed by others similarly illustrating national building types: New England of 1790–1840 at Old Sturbridge Village, Massachusetts; Dutch at the Netherlands Openluchtmuseum, Arnhem (1918); Thai at Ancient City, Bangkok. Buildings and streets of biblical Palestine have been reconstructed at the Bijbels Openluchtmuseum, Berg-an Dal, Holland; a whole Dutch town with accurate replicas of churches and houses was begun in 1989 on the Japanese island of Kyushu; *see also* HISTORICAL RECONSTRUCTION. The Moody Gardens, a park demonstrating how plants have been integrated into human life at different times and places, was designed for Galveston, Texas, by JELLICOE in 1985.

J. M. Findlay, *Magic Lands*, Berkeley, 1992; M. Sorkin (ed.), *Variations on a T.P.*, New York 1992; B. Dunlop, *Building a Dream. The Art of Disney Architecture*, New York 1996; Ghirardo 1996.

**Thermae**. In Roman architecture public baths, sometimes of great size and splendour, e.g. the Baths of Caracalla, Rome (AD 212–16), and containing libraries and other amenities as well as every provision for bathing, from the huge, lofty *frigidarium* (cold room) to the smaller and lower *tepidarium* (warm room) and circular, domed *caldarium* (hot room). Their remains in Rome were studied by architects from PALLADIO onwards and had great influence on planning.

W. Heinz, *Römische T.: Badewesen und Badeluxus in Römischen Reich*, Munich 1983.

**Thermal window**. A semicircular window divided into three lights by two

·vertical mullions, also known as a Diocletian window because of its use in the Thermae of Diocletian, Rome. Its use was revived in the C16 especially by PALLADIO and is a feature of PALLADIANISM.

**Tholos**. A beehive-shaped circular chamber of stone and roofed by CORBELLING entered from the DROMOS, an uncovered narrow passage, e.g. 'Treasury of Atreus' at Mycenae. *See* Fig. 115.

**Thomas**, William (1799–1860), *see* CANADIAN ARCHITECTURE.

**Thomas of Canterbury** (*fl.* 1324–31), *see* MICHAEL OF CANTERBURY.

**Thomon**, Thomas de (1754–1813). Leading neo-classical architect in Russia. He was born in Berne, probably studied under LEDOUX in Paris and completed his training in Rome *c.* 1785. In 1789 he followed the Comte d'Artois into exile to Vienna, where he found a patron in Prince Esterhazy. From there he went to Russia. His designs for the Kazan Cathedral were rejected (1799) but in 1802 he became architect to the Court of Alexander I in St Petersburg and immediately obtained important commissions – the Grand Theatre (1802–5, demolished) and the Bourse (designed 1801–4, built 1805–16), a Tuscan Doric temple with blank pediments, great segmental lunettes and flanking *columna rostrata*. The Bourse is his masterpiece and a major neo-classical building of the most severe and radical kind, more advanced than anything in Paris at that date. In 1806–10 he built a Doric mausoleum to Paul I in the park at Pavlovsk. He published *Recueil de plans et façades des principaux monuments construits à St Petersburg* (1808, republished in Paris 1819 with an amended title).

Hamilton 1983.

**Thompson**, Benjamin, Count von Rumford (1753–1814), *see* RUMFORD, Benjamin Thompson, Count von.

**Thompson**, Benjamin (b. 1918), *see* URBAN RENEWAL.

**Thomson**, Alexander (1817–75). Scottish architect, lived and worked in Glasgow, and was in practice from about 1847. He was known as 'Greek' Thomson, and rightly so, for to be a convinced Grecian was a very remarkable thing for a man belonging to the generation of PUGIN, SCOTT and RUSKIN. The formative influence on his style was SCHINKEL rather than English Grecians. This comes out most clearly in such monumental terraces as Moray Place (1859), where the purity of proportion and the scarcity of enrichment suggest a date some thirty years earlier. His churches, on the other hand, though essentially Grecian, are far from pure: they exhibit an admixture of the Egyptian, even the Hindu, as well as a boldness in the use of iron, which combine to produce results of a fearsome originality. The three churches – all United Presbyterian – are the Caledonian Road church (1856), the St Vincent Street church (1859), and the Queen's Park church (1869, burnt 1942). They are among the most forceful churches of their

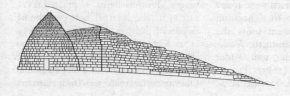

Fig. 115 Tholos, with dromos or uncovered entry passage: Treasury of Atreus, Mycenae, Greece

date anywhere in Europe. Equally interesting are Thomson's warehouses, especially the Egyptian Halls.

A. Gomme and D. Walker, *The Architecture of Glasgow*, London 1969; Crook 1972; Pevsner 1972; R. McFadzean, *The Life and Works of A.T.*, London 1979; G. Stamp and S. McKinstry (eds.), *Greek T. Neo-classical Architectural Theory, Buildings and Interiors*, Edinburgh 1994.

**Thon** or **Ton**, Konstantin Andrejevich (1794–1881), *see* RUSSIAN ARCHITECTURE.

**Thornton**, William (1759–1828), was an English physician who emigrated from the West Indies to the USA and became an American citizen in 1788. He designed the Philadelphia Library Company building in 1789 and in 1793 won the competition for the Capitol, Washington, though his runner-up, Stephen Hallet (*c.*1760–1825), was put in charge of the execution of his designs. The foundation stone was laid by George Washington in the same year. Hallet modified Thornton's designs and was replaced in 1795 by James HOBAN who proposed further alterations and was dismissed in 1798. But by 1800 the north wing containing the Senate had been completed substantially to Thornton's designs. In 1803 LATROBE took charge and completed the south wing by 1807. He also supervised the rebuilding after the Capitol had been sacked and burnt by British troops in 1814. Latrobe followed Thornton's designs for the exterior though not for the interior. In 1827 BULFINCH connected the two wings, again following the original design. (The dome and further extensions were added by T. U. WALTER, 1857–63.) Thornton also designed the Octagon (now the American Institute of Architects), Washington, DC (1799–1801), and Tudor Place, Georgetown, DC (1815).

E. Stearns and D. N. Yerkes, *W.T.*

*A Renaissance Man in the Federal City*, Washington, DC, 1976; B. S. Jenkins, *W.T.: Small Star of the American Enlightenment*, San Luis Obispo, California 1982.

**Thorpe**, John (*c.*1563–1655), an unimportant clerk in the Office of Works in London and later a successful land surveyor, was not, as is sometimes thought, the architect of Longleat, Kirby, Wollaton, Audley End, and other great Elizabethan and Jacobean houses. Plans and a few elevations of these and many other Elizabethan buildings are in a volume of drawings by him in the Sir John Soane Museum, London.

Summerson 1991; Colvin 1995.

**Through stone**, *see* PARPEN.

**Thrust**. The outward force of an ARCH or VAULT counterbalanced if necessary by BUTTRESSES.

**Thumb**, Michael (d.1690). He was born at Bezau (Austria) in the Bregenzerwald and was a founder of the Vorarlberger school of architects which included, beside the Thumb family, the MOSBRUGGER family and the BEER family. The latter intermarried with the Thumb family. The long series of buildings of this school, mostly for Benedictine monasteries in south-west Germany and Switzerland, was eventually to mark the triumph of German over Italian elements in south German Baroque architecture (i.e. over the domination of such Italians as ZUCCALLI and VISCARDI from the Grisons). Michael Thumb's pilgrimage church of Schönenberg near Ellwangen (begun 1682) is a prototype of the Vorarlberger Münsterschema – a pillared HALL CHURCH, the internal buttresses being faced with pilasters and projecting so deep as to form chapels, usually connected above by a gallery. He continued the type at the Premonstratensian abbey church of Obermarchtal (1686–92). Both churches

are notable for their plain-spoken dignity.
His son Peter (1681–1766) worked as a
foreman for Franz BEER from 1704 and
married his daughter. He later occupied
an influential position at Constance. As
an architect he developed a much more
sophisticated manner than his father and
achieved a wonderfully light and sparkling Rococo unity of effect in his best
interiors. In 1738 he built the library of
the monastery of St Peter in the Black
Forest, successfully adapting the Vorarlberger Münsterschema of internal buttresses with columns and a balcony
swirling round them. His masterpiece is
the pilgrimage church of Birnau on Lake
Constance (1746–58), where he had the
collaboration of Feuchtmayer on the decoration. At the great Benedictine abbey
of St Gallen he worked for eleven years
(1748–58) but the extent of his contribution to the abbey church is uncertain.
He was probably mainly responsible for
the great central rotunda and he probably
influenced the design of the two-towered
east façade, built by Johann Michael BEER
in 1760–69. For the library in the monastery at St Gallen (1758–67) he employed
the same system as at St Peter in the Black
Forest.

Christian    Thumb    (1683–1726)
worked    with    Michael    Thumb    at
Schönenberg and at Obermarchtal,
where he continued after Michael's death
in 1690. His masterpiece is the Schlosskir-
che at Friedrichshafen (1695–1701). He
probably collaborated with Andreas
Schreck at the abbey church at Weingarten (1716–24).

Hitchcock 1968; H. M. Gubler, *Der
Barockmeister P.T. 1681–1766*, Sigmaringen 1972; N. Lieb and F. Dieth, *Die
Vorarlberger Barock Baumeister*, Munich
and Zürich (1960) 1983.

**Thura**, Laurids de (1706–59), *see*
DANISH ARCHITECTURE.

**Tibaldi**, Pellegrino Pellegrini (1527–
96), *see* PELLEGRINI, Pellegrino.

**Tibetan architecture**. The earliest permanent buildings were c8 Buddhist
temples and STUPAS (e.g. Samye near
Lhasa). In the C11 Buddhism was revived
or reintroduced and many monastic complexes date back to this period, notably
at Toling and Mangnang. Indian and,
after the C13, Chinese influences are evident (the latter in the form of roofs),
but a highly distinctive Tibetan style was
developed in connection with tantric
Buddhism. No architecture is more
obsessively symbolic, in orientation,
planning (based on mandalas), proportions and the number of columns,
openings, storeys, etc., as well as ornament. Tibetan stupas, called *chorten*, have
interior spaces and vary in form: that
begun 1425 in the Palkhor monastery,
Gyantse, is unique – octagonal in plan,
four storeys high with 73 interior shrines.
The famous Potala dominating Lhasa was
built mainly in the C17 (on the site of
earlier structures) as the palace of the Dalai
Lama and a monastery with a very severe
exterior rising to nine storeys and with
innumerable richly decorated – though
often very small – rooms inside.

**Ticino School**, *see* SWISS ARCHI-
TECTURE.

**Tie-beam**, *see* ROOF.

**Tierceron**, *see* VAULT.

**Tigerman**, Stanley (b.1930). Chicago
architect who has exploited the meta-
phorical possibilities of architecture, e.g.
Daisy House, Porter, Indiana (1977), for
the owner of a striptease club. He published *The Architecture of Exile* (New York
1988).

R. Miller and D. M. Habel, *Versus.
An American Architect's Alternatives*. S.T.,
New York 1982; S. M. Underhill (ed.),

Tile-hanging

*S.T. Buildings and Projects 1966–89*, New York 1989.

**Tile-hanging**. A wall covering of overlapping rows of tiles on a timber structure, like SLATE-HANGING.

**Tiles**. The use of glazed pottery tiles for pavement or wall decoration is of ancient Near Eastern origin, like that of GLAZED BRICKS. Glazed tiles survive from C9 BC Ashur (East Berlin) and C7 BC Susa (Louvre, Paris). They were not used by the Ancient Greeks or Romans but were revived on a large scale with the rise of Islam, and both the interior and exterior walls of mosques were frequently clad with them, as were also domes. In the C15, tilework was transplanted from Islamic North Africa to Spain, where it is called ALICATADOS, and also Portugal (*see* AZULEJOS). The export to Italy of Spanish tiles led to their production there and in Holland and France in the C15–17. ENCAUSTIC TILES were much used in medieval Europe for flooring. After a decline in the early C19 tiles returned to favour in both Europe and the USA in the late C19, the Industrial Revolution having transformed the manufacture of ceramics, notable use being made of them for exterior wall cladding by both ARTS AND CRAFTS architects, e.g. Debenham House, 8 Addison Road, London (1905–7), by Halsey Ricardo (1854–1928), and ART NOUVEAU architects, e.g. Otto WAGNER. *See also* PANTILES.

A. Barendsen, *T.*, London 1967; A. Vallet, *La Céramique architecturale*, Paris 1982; H. van Lemmen, *T. in Architecture*, London 1993; T. Herbert and K. Huggins, *The Decorative T. in Architecture and Interiors*, London 1995.

**Timber** or **lumber**. Until the introduction of METAL CONSTRUCTION in the late C18, wood was the only material available for structural framing, and in many parts of the world it was and often still is the standard building material for floors and roof construction. For complete buildings in wood *see* BARNS; LOG CONSTRUCTION; STAVE CHURCH. *See also* TIMBER-FRAMING. The largest surviving building of wood construction is the Daibutsuden, Todaiji, Nara, Japan, of the C8 but frequently rebuilt and now supported on a steel skeleton inserted 1906–13.

Timber may be classified in two groups: softwoods (e.g. pine, spruce), derived from conifers and native to the Northern Temperate Zone; and hardwoods (e.g. oak, teak), derived from broad-leaved, mainly deciduous trees and widely distributed throughout the world.

J. Sunley and A. B. Beddington (eds.), *T. in Construction*, London 1985.

**Timber-framing**. A method of construction (called colloquially *half-timbering*) in which walls are built of interlocking vertical and horizontal timbers. The spaces are filled with non-structural walling of wattle and daub, lath and plaster (known as nogging), etc. Sometimes the timber-frame is covered by plaster, boarding laid horizontally (*see* WEATHERBOARDING) or MATHEMATICAL TILES to make it seem brick-built. *See also* BEAM; BRACE; BRESSUMER; CROSS-RAIL; CRUCKS; JETTY; JOISTS; POSTS; SILL; STUDS; WEALDEN HOUSE. *See* Fig. 116.

R. W. Brunskill, *T. Building in Britain*, London 1985; R. J. Brown, *T.F. Buildings of England*, London 1986.

**Tithe barn**, *see* BARN.

**Todd**, Frederick G. (1876–1948). American landscape architect who began by working under OLMSTED. In 1900 he settled in Canada, where he designed in emulation of Olmsted the 'necklace of parks' and garden suburbs round Mon-

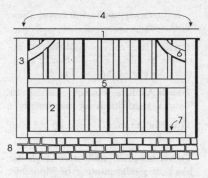

1. Wall plate
2. Stud
3. Post
4. Bay
5. Bressumer
6. Brace
7. Sill beam
8. Ground wall

Fig. 116 Timber-framing

treal as well as the Assiniboine Park and Tuxedo Park, Winnipeg (1904–6); the Parc des Champs de Bataille, Quebec (1909–14); St Helen's Island, Montreal (1938); and the Chemin de la Croix for the St Joseph Oratory, Montreal (1945).

**Todt**, Fritz (1891–1942), *see* GERMAN ARCHITECTURE; MOTORWAY.

**Tokonoma**. The alcove in which a painting or print is hung and a flower vase placed in a Japanese house.

**Toledo**, Juan Battista de (d.1567). Spanish philosopher and mathematician as well as architect; spent many years in Italy and for some time before 1559 was architect to the Spanish Viceroy in Naples. In 1562 he was appointed architect of the Escorial, drew up the entire ground-plan, but built only the two-storeyed Court of the Evangelists, modelled on SANGALLO's Palazzo Farnese, Rome, and the vast severe south façade.

Kubler and Soria 1959; G. Kubler, *Building the Escorial*, Princeton 1982; J. J. Riviera Blanco, *J.B. de T. y Felipe II. La implantacion del clasicismo en España*, Valladolid 1984.

**Toltec architecture**, *see* MESOAMERICAN ARCHITECTURE.

**Tomb**. A memorial structure, over or beside a grave, as distinct from a CENOTAPH and MAUSOLEUM which may contain more than one tomb. A tomb is usually inside a building and often decorated with sculpture.

**Tomb-chest**. A chest-shaped stone coffin, the most usual medieval form of funerary monument. *See also* ALTAR-TOMB.

**Tomé**, Narciso (active 1715–42). Spanish sculptor with his father and brothers on the façade of Valladolid University (1715). His famous Transparente in Toledo Cathedral (1721–32) is the most stupefying of all Baroque extravaganzas in spatial illusionism. It goes farther than anything invented by Italian Baroque architects and is exceptional even for Spain.

Kubler and Soria 1959.

**Ton** or **Thon**, Konstantin A. (1794–1881), *see* RUSSIAN ARCHITECTURE.

**Tongue and groove**. Alternative term for MORTICE AND TENON JOINT, especially that used for joining flat boards.

**Torana**. Indian gateway, especially one of the enclosure of a Buddhist STUPA. *See* Fig. 113.

**Torii**. Ceremonial entrance gateway to a Shinto shrine in Japan. Of great simplicity, it consists of two upright posts embedded directly in the ground with a beam projecting widely across the top and another, often not projecting, slightly below. The posts are cylindrical, the beams rectangular in section, the upper surface of the top beam being bevelled. Some *torii* have slightly splayed posts and curved beams resembling the eaves in temple architecture. *See* Fig. 117.

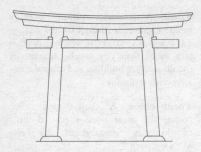

Fig. 117 Torii

**Torp**, Niels (b.1940), *see* NORWEGIAN ARCHITECTURE.

**Torralva**, Diego de (1500–1566), the leading Portuguese Renaissance architect, was the son-in-law of ARRUDA but abandoned his rich MANUELINE style for one much simpler, sterner and more Italianate. His main work is the cloister of the Cristo Monastery, Tomar (1557), with the SERLIAN MOTIF used as an open arcade on the upper floor. He designed the apse for the Jeronimite Church at Belém (1540–51). Several other buildings have been attributed to him, notably the octagonal church of the Dominican Nuns at Elvas (1543–57).

Kubler and Soria 1959; Smith 1968.

**Torroja (y Miret)**, Eduardo (1899–1961). Spanish concrete engineer and architect and a pioneer of SHELL construction. The Algeciras Market Hall (1933) made his name internationally, followed by his Zarzuela racecourse grandstand and the SHELL roof of the Fronton Recoletos (destroyed), both of 1935. The sinuous roof of the Las Cortes football stadium, Barcelona, of 1943 is also remarkable. He published *Philosophy of Structure* (Berkeley, California, 1958) and *The Structures of E.T.* (New York 1958).

I. Joedicke, *Shell Architecture*, New York 1963.

**Torus**. A large convex moulding of semicircular profile, e.g. at the base of a column. *See also* ASTRAGAL; Fig. 91.

**Touch**. A soft black marble quarried near Tournai, used chiefly for monuments.

**Tourelle**. A turret CORBELLED out from the wall.

**Tower block**. A multi-storey high-rise block of public housing of Modernist design. Though later denigrated, its widespread adoption in post-Second World War UK contributed notably to the Welfare State's abolition of slum dwellings and their replacement with better public housing. Trellick Tower, London (1966–73), by Ernö Goldfinger (1902–87), is outstanding for its effective and dramatic design.

M. Glendinning and S. Muthesius, *T.B. Modern Public Housing in England, Scotland, Wales and Northern Ireland*, London 1994.

**Tower house**. A medieval Scots type of fortified house with the main hall raised above the ground and with one or more storeys above. It continued into the C17 with modifications and elaborations, e.g. Glamis Castle. *See also* SCOTTISH ARCHITECTURE.

**Town**, Ithiel (1784–1844), *see* DAVIS, Alexander Jackson.

**Town planning**, *see* URBAN DESIGN.

**Townsend**, Charles Harrison (1851–1928). English Late Victorian 'rogue' architect whose small-scale public buildings challenge those of his more successful, pompous contemporaries such as Aston WEBB. Outstanding are the Bishopsgate Institute (1892–4), Whitechapel Art Gallery (1895–9) and, most original of all, the Horniman

Museum (1898–1901), all in London.
Service 1977.

**Trabeated**. Constructed on the POST
AND LINTEL principle, as Greek buildings
were, in contrast to ARCUATED.

**Tracery**. The ornamental intersecting
work in the upper part of a window,
screen or panel, or used decoratively in
blank arches and vaults. The earliest use of
the term so far traced is in Sir Christopher
WREN, the medieval word being *form-
pieces* or *forms*.

In windows of more than one light
in Early Gothic churches the SPANDREL
above the lights is often pierced by a
circle, a quatrefoil, or some such simple
form. This is known as *plate tracery*. Later,
and first at Reims (1211), the circle is no
longer pierced through a solid spandrel;
instead the two lights are separated by a
moulded MULLION and the mouldings of
this are continued at the head forming
bars of circular, quatrefoil, etc., forms and
leaving the rest of the spandrels open.
This is called *bar tracery*, and throughout
the later Middle Ages it was one of the
principal decorative elements of
churches. The patterns made by the bars
were first the simple geometrical forms
already indicated (*geometrical tracery*), later
fantastical forms including double curves
(*flowing tracery*), and later still – at least in
England – plain, vertical, arched panels
repeated more or less exactly (*panel
tracery*). In Germany, France and Spain
forms similar to the English flowing
tracery became the rule in the late Middle
Ages. With the end of the Middle Ages
tracery generally disappeared.

*Bar tracery*, introduced at Reims and
brought to England *c.*1240, consists of
intersecting ribwork made up of slender
shafts continuing the lines of the mullions
up to a decorative mesh in the window-
head.

*Flowing tracery* is made up of compound

or OGEE curves, with an uninterrupted
flow from curve to curve; also called *curvilinear* or *undulating tracery*. It was used from
the beginning of the C14 in England, and
throughout the C15 in France, where it
rapidly became fully developed and
FLAMBOYANT, with no survival of the
geometrical elements of the early flowing
tracery of England.

*Geometrical tracery* is characteristic of
*c.*1250–1300 and consists chiefly of circles
or foiled circles.

In *intersecting tracery* each mullion of a
window branches into curved bars continuous with the mullions. The outer arch
of the window being of two equal curves
(*see* ARCH), all subdivisions of the
window-head produced by these tracery
bars following the curves of the outer
arch must of necessity be equilateral also.
The bars and the arch are all drawn from
the same centre with a different radius.
Such a window can be of two, or usually
more, lights, with the result that every
two, three or four lights together form a
pointed arch. Additional enrichment, e.g.
circles, CUSPING, is always of a secondary character. The form is typical of
*c.*1300.

*Kentish tracery* is FOILED tracery in a
circle with barbs between the foils.

*Panel tracery* is Perpendicular tracery
formed of upright, straight-sided panels
above the lights of a window, also called
*rectilinear*.

*Plate tracery* is a late C12 and early C13
form where decoratively shaped openings
are cut through the solid stone infilling
in a window-head.

*Reticulated tracery*, a form used much in
the early to mid C14, is made up entirely
of circles drawn at top and bottom into
OGEE shapes resulting in a net-like
appearance.

In *Y-tracery* a mullion branches into
two forming a Y shape; typical of *c.*1300.
*See* Fig. 118.

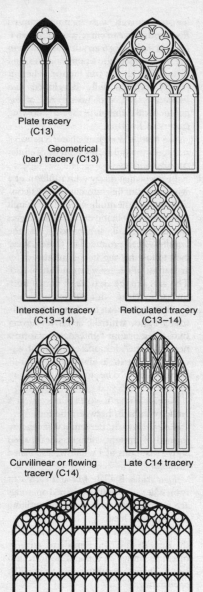

Plate tracery
(C13)

Geometrical
(bar) tracery (C13)

Intersecting tracery
(C13–14)

Reticulated tracery
(C13–14)

Curvilinear or flowing
tracery (C14)

Late C14 tracery

Panel tracery (C14)

Fig. 118 Tracery

**Trachelion.** The neck of a Greek Doric column, between the SHAFT-RING and HYPOTRACHELIUM.

**Tracing house.** The house or room in which the medieval mason drew or scratched details of mouldings and other details as instructions to those working under him (*super moldas in trasura*). The tracing could also be done on sand on the floor of the room. *See also* LODGE AND LODGE BOOKS.

**Tramello,** Alessio (*c.*1470/5–*c.*1529). Italian architect who worked for most of his life in and around Piacenza in a style which owes much to the Milanese buildings of BRAMANTE. His more notable buildings include S. Sisto (1499) and the centrally planned Madonna di Campagna (1522), both at Piacenza. In 1525 he was consulted about the Steccata at Parma which had been begun in 1521 by Giovanfrancesco Zaccagni (1491–1543), who resigned in 1525.

Lotz 1996.

**Transenna.** An openwork screen or lattice, usually of marble, in an Early Christian church.

**Transept.** The transverse arms of a cross-shaped church, usually between NAVE and CHANCEL, but also occasionally at the west end of the nave as well, and also doubled, with the eastern arms farther east than the junction of nave and chancel. The latter form is usual in English Gothic cathedrals.

In Islamic architecture a heightened area in the prayer hall of a MOSQUE, between the central entrance and the MIHRAB, with an axis at right angles to the much longer QIBLA wall.

**Transitional architecture.** A term usually referring to the period of transition from the ROMANESQUE to the GOTHIC, or in Britain from the NORMAN to the EARLY ENGLISH style. Sometimes details of the later styles are used on the general forms of the earlier.

**Transom**. A horizontal bar of stone or wood across the opening of a window or across a panel.

**Transparente**, *see* TOMÉ, Narciso.

**Transverse arch**, *see* VAULT.

**Transverse rib**. A rib extending at right angles to the wall across a bay or other space.

**Travertine**. A cream-coloured Italian limestone with small, irregular holes which give it the appearance of Gruyère cheese. Formed by the direct precipitation of the calcium carbonate found in spring water upon exposure to the air, it abounds in the Tiber valley and was used for dressed masonry in Rome from ancient times. It was and still is exported in large quantities and is widely used as a finishing material and for cladding and paving.

F. Rodolico, *Le pietre delle città d'Italia*, Florence 1953.

**Tread**, *see* STAIR.

**Tree-house**. Shelters constructed in the branches of living trees, notably in Oceania, South-East Asia, Africa, Meso-america and South America, usually as refuges from predatory animals or as observation posts. There is no known connection between them and the ornamental tree-houses constructed in European gardens from the C16, which became popular in the C18 (a large example survives at Pitchford Hall, Shropshire). They are still made today, mainly for children.

**Trefoil**, *see* FOIL.

**Trezzini** or **Tressini** (spelt in Russian Trezini), Domenico (1670–1734), a Swiss, was one of the first foreign architects to come to Russia at the invitation of Peter the Great; he was engaged (by the Russian ambassador in Copenhagen, where he had been working on Frederick IV's palace) just before St Petersburg was founded (1703), and with his character-istic adaptability and compliance to Peter's wishes he was extremely active in the city's early construction. Of the numerous buildings his *atelier* designed, there survive: Peter's modest Summer Palace (1711); the Cathedral of SS. Peter and Paul (1714), replacing a wooden pre-decessor and likewise sporting a dramatic flèche, gilded and topped with an angel, designedly higher than the Moscow belfry 'Big John' – the cathedral as a whole a somewhat awkwardly articulated domed basilica with prominent volutes on the west front, though it is now hard to envisage it with its original Baroque detail (note the magnificent carved-wood ICONOSTASIS by Zarudny); and Trez-zini's masterpiece, the 'Twelve Colleges' – i.e. Government ministries, sub-sequently housing the University – strung end-to-end across the tip of Vasilyev Island, each with a colossal order of pil-asters under a high hipped roof, linked originally by a continuous open gallery and a 600 metre (2,000 ft) long corridor. His younger relative (once thought to be his son) Pietro Antonio (in Russia 1726–51) was also a busy architect, notable for pioneering the reintroduction of the Old Russian five-domed centralized church-plans to St Petersburg Baroque. [R. R. Milner-Gulland]

Hamilton 1983; *D. T. e la Costruzione di San Pietroburgo*, Milan 1994.

**Triangulation**. The achievement of rigidity, or at least the prevention of com-pletely free relative movement, in an assembly of struts and ties, by arranging them in a continuous series of triangles in one or more planes.

**Tribune**. 1. A raised platform in an Ancient Roman BASILICA, sometimes in a semicircular addition to the end of the building. 2. The apse in a basilican church. 3. A platform inside a church, usually raised on columns and overlooking the interior.

**Triclinium**. The dining-room in an Ancient Roman house.

**Triconch**. Clover-leaf or trefoil in plan, e.g. a church ending in three apsidally ended arms at right-angles to one another.

**Triforium**. An arcaded wall-passage facing on to the NAVE, at a level above the arcade and below the CLERESTORY windows (if there are any). The term is often wrongly applied to a TRIBUNE or GALLERY.

**Triglyphs**. Blocks separating the MET-OPES in a Doric FRIEZE. Each one has two vertical grooves or glyphs in the centre and half grooves at the edges. If the half grooves are omitted (as occasionally in post-Renaissance architecture), the block is called a diglyph. *See* Fig. 86.

**Trilithon**. A prehistoric monument consisting of a horizontal MEGALITH resting on two upright ones, as at Stonehenge.

**Trim**. The framing or edging of openings and other features on a façade or indoors. It is usually of a colour and material (wood, stucco or stone) different from that of the adjacent wall surface.

**Triquetra**. A symmetrical ornament formed of three interlaced arcs or lobes.

**Trissino**, Giangiorgio (1478–1550), *see* PALLADIO, Andrea.

**Triumphal arch**. A free-standing monumental gateway of a type which originated in Rome in the C2 BC in richly decorated temporary structures erected by Roman magistrates for such festive occasions as the triumphs decreed to victorious generals. From the late C1 BC similar structures were erected in stone, and often richly decorated with sculpture, as city gates or as entrances to *fora* but also frequently as urban decorations with no more than a commemorative purpose: some twenty survive from the reign of Augustus, mostly in Italy and Gaul. They were built throughout the Roman Empire and numerous AD C2 and C3 examples survive in North Africa. There are two main types – those with a single archway (Arch of Augustus at Susa, Piedmont, 9–8 BC, Arch of Titus in Rome, *c.* AD 82) and those with a large archway flanked by two small archways (Arch of Septimius Severus in Rome, AD 203, and Arch of Constantine in Rome, AD 315). Sometimes they seem to have been designed primarily as richly ornamented bases for gilt bronze statues. The form was revived in the Italian Renaissance, once again as a type of temporary festival architecture, which remained popular until the late C18. Many were built in stone during the C18 and C19 often in direct imitation of Roman prototypes, e.g. Arco di S. Gallo, Florence, by J.-N. JADOT DE VILLE ISSY (1739), Arc du Carrousel, Paris, by PERCIER and FONTAINE (1806–7), Arc de Triomphe, Paris, by CHALGRIN (1806–35), the Marble Arch, London, by J. NASH (1828), etc. By extension the term 'triumphal arch' is sometimes applied to structures with one large and two small doorways, e.g. the choir screen in a medieval church. A Chinese type of triumphal or commemorative arch is called a P'AI LOU.

M. P. Nilsson, *The Origin of the T.A.*, Lund 1932; U. Westfehling, *Triumphbogen in 19 und 20 Jahrhunderts*, Munich 1975; G. A. Mansuelli *et al.*, *Studi sull'arco onorario romano*, Rome 1979.

**Triumphal column**. A massive column erected as a public monument. The first were set up in Republican Rome but these appear to have been relatively small and simple in comparison with Trajan's column completed AD 113 and 43 m. (125 ft) high. It is adorned with a continuous spiral of low relief carving illustrating Trajan's two Dacian wars. This and the similar Antonine Column (or Column of Marcus Aurelius), probably completed in AD 193, set a pattern for such monuments. Their progeny included the columns of Theodosius the Great of 386 and of Arcadius of 403, both in Constantinople (and both destroyed), and in much later times the pair of columns flanking the Karlskirche in Vienna by FISCHER VON ERLACH (begun 1716) and the Vendôme Column in Paris with bronze reliefs (1806–10, thrown down 1871 and re-erected 1874). The majority of commemorative columns, though often on bases imitated from the Roman prototypes, have plain shafts, e.g. the Monument, London (1671–7), by WREN, the Washington Monument in Baltimore (1814–29) by Robert MILLS, and Nelson's Column, Trafalgar Square, London, designed by William Railton (1839–42).

G. Becatti, *La colonna coclide istoriata*, Rome 1960.

**Troost**, Paul Ludwig (1878–1934), *see* GERMAN ARCHITECTURE.

**Trophy**. A sculptured group of arms or armour used as a memorial to victory, sometimes with floreated motifs intermingled to form a FESTOON.

**Trulli**, *see* BEEHIVE HOUSE.

**Trumeau**. The stone MULLION supporting the middle of a TYMPANUM of a doorway, a notable feature in French Romanesque churches, e.g. La Madeleine, Vézelay, of *c.*1120–32. The *trumeau* was sometimes very elaborately carved, as at the abbey church, Souillac, Périgord, *c.*1125.

**Truss**. A rigid frame (to bridge a space, form a bracket or carry other structural elements) constructed of timber or metal struts and/or ties forming triangles. It cannot be deflected without deforming one of its components. The trusses of a roof are usually named after the particular feature of their construction, e.g. king-post, queen-post, etc.; *see* ROOF.

**Tschumi**, Bernard (b.1944). Swiss architect, trained in Zürich, who settled in New York in 1976. His Parc de la Villette, Paris, of 1984–9 was the first work to explore DECONSTRUCTIVE concepts of dissociation. (The philosopher Jacques Derrida was involved with him in its plan.) He exhibited at the 1988 Deconstructivist exhibition in New York. In 1990 he designed the small but remarkable Glass Video Gallery, Gröningen, Netherlands. A fluent theorist, he has published *Manhattan Transcripts* (New York 1981); *Event Cities* (New York 1994); and *Architecture and Disjunction* (Cambridge, Mass. 1994).

**Tudor arch**, *see* ARCH.

**Tudor architecture**. Historical division of English architecture from *c.*1485 to *c.*1558 (Henry VII to Mary I), partly overlapping the late Gothic style of PERPENDICULAR when Renaissance influence began to be felt in ornament; *see* ELIZABETHAN ARCHITECTURE.

**Tudor flower**. An upright ornamental motif, rather like a formalized ivy leaf, often used in English Late Gothic and Tudor architecture, especially for BRATTISHING.

**Tufa**. The commonest Roman building stone, formed from volcanic dust; it is porous and grey.

**Tumulus**. A mound covering an ancient burial or tomb, usually of earth but sometimes of stones. The latter is called a *cairn*. Earth mounds, round or elongated, are called *barrows* or *long barrows*, and in England belong to the Early and Middle Neolithic period, though burial under a round mound continued occasionally until Roman and Anglo-Saxon times.

**Tunnard**, Christopher (1910–79). Canadian-born landscape architect. He settled in England in 1928, collaborated on the MARS group's rational urban plans, and pioneered the 'modern garden style' for INTERNATIONAL STYLE houses at CHERMAYEFF's Bentley Wood, Halland, Sussex, and his own St Ann's Hill, Chertsey, Surrey (both 1936–7). These layouts with wide expanses of lawn and geometrically planned paths were illustrated in his *Gardens in the Modern Landscape* (1938), in which he ridiculed Victorian gardens with their ornaments and herbaceous borders. It led to his invitation by GROPIUS to Harvard where his pupils included HALPRIN. In his foreword to the second edition (1948), however, he called for a revaluation of C19 garden design and launched the first attack on Modernist architecture written by an insider. He was subsequently engaged in site analysis rather than design, teaching at Yale University, campaigning for HISTORICAL PRESERVATION and writing, notably *The City of Man* (1953), an influential history of urbanism in America.

**Tunnel vault**, *see* VAULT.

**Turba**. Arabic term for an Islamic MAUSOLEUM.

**Turkish architecture**. The *c.*7000 BC Neolithic settlements at Çatal Hüyük and Hacilar are among the earliest known, consisting of rectangular mud-brick buildings, *see* Fig. 94. Access is through the roofs only. Impressive remains of Hittite buildings survive at Boghazköy (*c.*1360 BC), notably monumental gateways with figurative reliefs. C7 BC Urar-

tian temples and fortresses at Altintepe and Kofkalesi are impressive. (For later pre-Islamic architecture in Turkey, *see* HELLENISTIC ARCHITECTURE; BYZANTINE ARCHITECTURE.)

The battle of Manzikert in 1071 opened Anatolia to Islam, but not until the turn of the C13 were the Seljuks sufficiently established to begin sponsoring monumental architecture. Notable among SELJUK buildings in Anatolia are the mosque of Khuand Khatun, Kayseri (1237–8), the mosque and hospital, Divrik (1228–9), the Cifte Minareli MADRASA, Erzerum (1253), and the Karatay madrasa (1252) and Ince Minareli madrasa (1258) at Konya. With the advent of the Ottomans a distinctive style developed typified by lead-covered domes, pencil-thin minarets and lavish tilework and marble relief decorations in limestone. The Yeshil mosque, Iznik (1378–92), the Ulu mosque (1395–9) and Yeshil mosque (1421), Bursa, and especially the Uch Sherefeli mosque, Edirne (1438–47), are outstanding early Ottoman buildings. After the conquest of Constantinople in 1453 Hagia Sophia and other Christian churches were converted into mosques and Byzantine influence is felt in later Ottoman architecture, notably in that of the greatest Ottoman architect, SINAN, of whose numerous buildings the Shezade mosque (1544–8), Suleymaniye mosque (1551–8) and Sokollu Mehmet mosque (1570–74) in Istanbul and his great Selimiye mosque (1569–74) in Edirne may be mentioned. Of later Ottoman mosques that of Sultan Ahmed in Istanbul (1610–16) is outstanding. Of secular Ottoman buildings the kiosk is typical, though the famous Chinli Kiosk, Istanbul (1472), is unique. Most domestic architecture was of wood and little survives. Of C19 buildings the Dolmabahçe Palace, Istanbul (1852), is an unusually lavish example of an orientalized Louis XVI and French Empire style.

In the early C20 the Italian *stile Liberty* architect Raimondo d'ARONCO (1857–1932) and the German Functionalist Bruno TAUT both worked in Turkey, but the most notable contemporary buildings are by the Turkish architect Sedad Hakki Eldem (1908–88), whose work ranges from his rather stern but imposing university buildings in Istanbul (1942) and Ankara (1943) to the notable Social Security Agency Complex at Zehreh, Istanbul (1962–4), and the genial Koç Foundation, Ataturk Library, Istanbul (1973). His luxurious waterside country houses or *yalis* along the Bosphorus – e.g. the Rahmi Koç villa at Tarabya (1975–80) – and his embassy buildings at Ankara (1964–77) are also notable. The distinctly Turkish–Ottoman character which marks his work is all the more effective for being so unforced.

**Turkish bath**, *see* HAMMAM.

**Turnpike stair**, *see* STAIR.

**Turret**. A small and slender tower, sometimes corbelled out from the corner of a building. A feature of medieval architecture.

**Tuscan order**, *see* ORDER.

**Tusking**. Stones left projecting from a wall for subsequent bonding into another wall.

**Tylman van Gameren** (*c.*1631–1706). Dutch architect chiefly responsible for introducing the Baroque style into Poland, where he settled in 1665. His three centralized churches in Warsaw – Holy Sacrament (1688), St Casimir (1688–9) and St Boniface (1690–92) – reveal him as a somewhat stolid, classicizing master of the Baroque. St Anne, Cracow (1689–1705), is livelier, but this may be due to collaboration with Baldassare Fontana. He rebuilt the palace of Prince Sanguszko, Warsaw (enlarged C18), designed Castle Nieborów (1680–83) and completed the Krasinski Palace, Warsaw (1682–94).

Hempel 1965; S. Mossakowski, *T.G.*, Munich 1994.

**Tympanum**. The area between the LINTEL of a doorway and the arch above it, sometimes very elaborately carved in French Romanesque architecture, e.g. that by Gislebertus at Autun Cathedral of *c.*1130; also the triangular or segmental space enclosed by the mouldings of a pediment.

# U

**UEC (urban entertainment center)**, *see* SHOPPING MALL; THEME PARK.

**Undercroft**. A vaulted room, sometimes underground, below an upper room such as a chapel or church.

**Ungers**, Oswald Mathias (b.1926). German architect, trained under EIERMANN to whose Rationalism the disciplined simplicity of his early work owed much, e.g. housing at Cologne-Braunsfeld (1951), Cologne-Nippes (1957) and Cologne-Seeberg (1965–6), as also later in his Architectural Museum, Frankfurt-am-Main (1979–83), a building inside a building, and his Alfred-Wegener Institute, Bremerhaven (1980–84). His Torhaus skyscraper, Frankfurt-am-Main (1983–5), was controversial, but his acclaimed, though rejected, Potsdamer Platz project for Berlin (1991–4) was remarkable. Also notable were his own house in Belvederestrasse, Cologne (1958–9; 1990), followed by that at Kämpchenweg, Cologne (1994–5), and his Minimalist Gallery of Contemporary Art, Hamburg (1996). He has published *Morphologie. City Metaphors* (Cologne 1986).

M. Kieren, *O.M.U. Architektur 1951–1994*, Zürich 1994.

**Unit system**. Large factory-assembled glazed units forming a curtain wall. They are lifted into place by cranes and bolted to the building structure.

**United States architecture and landscape architecture**. Apart from PUEBLOS the earliest permanent buildings were those erected by Spanish settlers in what is now New Mexico, e.g. Governor's Palace, Santa Fe (1610–14), *see* MISSION STYLE. In C17 New England architecture was modest, first Dutch in inspiration, then English, e.g. St Luke's, Isle of Wight County, Virginia (1632), Bacon's Castle, Surrey County, Virginia (c.1655, rebuilt), Capen House, Topsfield, Massachusetts (1683). Original and unique to New England were the meeting houses, square halls serving both secular and religious functions. The Old Ship Meeting House, Hingham, Massachusetts (1681 with C18 additions), survives. The most complete surviving example of Colonial architecture is Williamsburg, Virginia, though it is much restored (*see* HISTORICAL RECONSTRUCTION) – the Capitol (1701–5, rebuilt 1928–34), the College of William and Mary (1716–1859) and the Palace of the Governors (1749–51, rebuilt 1928–34). In Philadelphia the Independence Hall of 1731–91 was rebuilt by STRICKLAND in 1832. C18 churches are entirely Georgian, often influenced in their spires by GIBBS. Houses are equally Georgian, in the country as well as the towns, e.g. Colony House, Newport, Rhode Island (1739), by Richard Munday (d.1740) (*see also* Peter HARRISON and Samuel McINTIRE). But in both houses and churches timber plays a prominent part alongside, or instead of, brick. Among the best churches are Christ Church, Philadelphia (1727 and 1754); St Michael, Charleston (1753); Christ Church, Cambridge (1759–61); and the Baptist Church at Providence (1775). The finest Early Georgian house is BYRD's Westover, Virginia (1726–30), with the earliest landscape garden in America. From the mid C18 notable examples are Mount Airey, Virginia (perhaps by John ARISS), Mount Pleasant, Philadelphia, and Whitehall, Maryland, with giant Corinthian portico. Later porticos tend to have attenuated columns (Homewood, Baltimore). As town *ensembles* Salem and Nantucket (Massachusetts) and Charleston (South Carolina) may be singled out. The United States has still quite a few C18 public buildings: Old State House, Boston (1710); Faneuil Hall, Boston (1742); and so to the Capitol in its original form (1792) and the Boston State House by BULF-INCH (1795–8). The earliest university buildings are also Georgian: at Yale (1750–52); and then Thomas JEFFER-SON's University of Virginia at Charlottesville (1817–26), the second American CAMPUS, i.e. with buildings composed round a spacious lawn. Jefferson's own house, Monticello, was built 1770–79, remodelled 1796–1808. In the wide diffusion of this Georgian style in the late C18 and early C19 such books as *The Country Builder's Assistant* (1797), *The American Builder's Companion* (1806) and others by Asher Benjamin (1773–1845) played a significant part. His works are illustrated with contemporary American buildings and he assumed that his readers would probably build in wood.

The Greek Revival starts with LATROBE's Doric Bank of Pennsylvania of 1799–1801. From 1803 he did much in a Grecian taste inside the Capitol in Washington (begun by William THORN-TON and finished by T. U. WALTER). His finest work, comparable with that of SOANE in elegance and originality, is Baltimore Cathedral (begun 1804). But for this building he also submitted a Gothic design; a country house of his (Sedgeley, Philadelphia) was Gothic too. His near contemporary Maximilien

GODEFROY was similarly ambidextrous. However, except in church design, Gothic made slow progress, and the most thoroughly Grecian years are the 1820s and 1830s, with HAVILAND and STRICKLAND in Philadelphia, JAY in Savannah, PARRIS and WILLARD in Boston, the big government buildings in Washington by HADFIELD, HOBAN and, above all, MILLS and several state capitols by Town & DAVIS (North Carolina, Connecticut, Illinois, Indiana, Ohio) and Strickland (Tennessee). Davis experimented in many styles, including the Egyptian and the Old-English cottage. The most prominent Gothic churches are RENWICK's Grace Church, New York (1846), UPJOHN's Church of the Holy Trinity, Brooklyn (1841–6), and others in New York by Minard LAFEVER. (*See also* WARE & VAN BRUNT; CRAM; GOODHUE.) Contemporaneously DOWNING began promoting not only a picturesque type of landscaping which was to lead with OLMSTED and others later in the C19 to the great US contribution to landscape architecture, but also to an original type of small house or villa, later taken up by such architects as DAVIS and NOTMAN. Henry Austin (1804–91) deserves a special mention; if ever there was a rogue architecture, his New Haven railway station (1848–9) is it. Its style cannot be derived from any clear direction. The USA has been rich in such highly gifted eccentrics and loners, e.g. Frank FUR-NESS, Bernard MAYBECK and Bruce GOFF.

Already in the second quarter of the century certain American specialities began to appear. One is hotels, especially of the size and type that became standard in Europe later (*see* Isaiah ROGERS and George Browne POST); another is such technical equipment as AIR-CONDITIONING, ELEVATORS and ESCA-

LATORS. Later C20 developments in hotel design by LAPIDUS and PORTMAN may also be mentioned here.

The United States moved from a marginal to a central position with the work of H. H. RICHARDSON, both in the field of the massive uncompromising commercial building for which his style was a French-inspired Romanesque (Marshall Field Wholesale Warehouse, Chicago, 1885–7) and in the field of the informal, comfortable, moderately dimensioned private house (Sherman House, Newport, 1874–6 – see SHINGLE STYLE). Even more independent are some of the houses designed in their early years by McKIM, MEAD & WHITE, notably one at Bristol, Rhode Island (1887, demolished). Otherwise that firm is principally remembered for their Italian Renaissance Revival (Villard Houses, New York, 1885; Boston Public Library, 1888–95), Colonial Revival, and also Palladian Revival, the latter on a grand scale (Pennsylvania Station, New York, 1904–10, demolished). Their assistant Henry Bacon (1861–1924) and disciple John Russell Pope (1874–1937) carried on the tradition into the C20 with, respectively, the Lincoln Memorial (1917) and Jefferson Memorial (1934–43) in Washington, where Paul CRET worked in a freer BEAUX ARTS style during the same years.

Meanwhile, however, Chicago had established a style of commercial architecture all her own and vigorously pointing forward into the C20 (CHICAGO SCHOOL). It started from the introduction of the principle of steel framing (*see* SKYSCRAPER) in 1883 with JENNEY's Home Insurance building (demolished) and reached its climax in such buildings as the Tacoma (1887–8) by HOLABIRD & ROCHE, the Marquette (1894) by the same firm, the Masonic Temple (1892, demolished) by BURNHAM and ROOT and, most personal, the Wainwright

building at St Louis (1890) by SULLIVAN. With Sullivan's Carson, Pirie & Scott Store, Chicago (1899–1904), a totally unhistoricist style of unrelieved verticals and horizontals was reached, though Sullivan was perhaps at his most original in his feathery, decidedly ART NOUVEAU ornament. BEMAN's pioneering COMPANY TOWN for Pullman should be mentioned here as well as the landscape architecture of JENSEN.

Sullivan's principal pupil was Frank Lloyd WRIGHT, the greatest American architect to date, who bridges the whole period from *c*.1890 to nearly 1960. His early PRAIRIE houses culminated in his first, brilliantly original, style of sweeping horizontals and of intercommunication between spaces inside a house and between inside and outside spaces. Almost contemporaneously in California another pupil of Sullivan, Irving GILL, developed a new domestic style which was taken further, again partly under Wright's inspiration, by GREENE & GREENE and others, including Rudolph SCHINDLER. In the East the influence of Europe still predominated with the so-called INTERNATIONAL MODERN style, introduced by such prominent buildings as the Philadelphia Savings Fund building by HOWE & Lescaze (1929–32 – relatively late in European terms) and the McGraw-Hill building, New York, by Raymond HOOD (1931); but the spectacular development of C20 architecture in the United States belongs to the years after the Second World War. The flowering was fostered by such distinguished immigrants as GROPIUS, MIES VAN DER ROHE, NEUTRA and BREUER. The first stage belongs to the rational, cubic, crisp so-called International Modern and culminates in Mies van der Rohe's houses and blocks of flats of *c*.1950 onwards and much of the work of SKIDMORE, OWINGS & MERRILL. Their more routine jobs and those of ROTH and others which earned the soubriquet CORPORATE MODERNISM marked the 1950s and 1960s in the north-east and mid-West. In California some remarkable and internationally influential experiments were made in INDUS-TRIALIZED BUILDING, most notably by Charles EAMES in 1949 for John Entenza's CASE STUDY programme. Case Study House No. 18, Beverly Hills (1955–8), by Craig Ellwood (b.1922), and the work of SCBSD (State of California Building Systems Development) under Ezra Ehrenkrantz (b.1933) are also notable. The West Coast architect WURSTER should also be mentioned here, together with the very influential CALIFORNIA SCHOOL of landscape architects, notably BAYLIS, CHURCH, ECKBO and HALP-RIN, with whom HARGREAVES, KILEY, SASAKI, SCHWARTZ and WALKER should also be mentioned. More recently Steve MARTINO (b.1947) has created such remarkable works as the Papago Park between Phoenix and Scottsdale, Arizona (1990).

The second stage was that of the neo-sculptural, anti-rational, highly express-ive style current in many countries in the 1960s. The United States is richer than any other part of the world in such build-ings, from a love of novelty as well as from a prosperity that encourages display. Trends within this trend cannot here be separated: they run from the powerful concrete curves of Eero SAARINEN to the smooth professionalism of Ieoh Ming PEI. They include such mercurial and controversial figures as Philip JOHNSON, Paul RUDOLPH, Louis KAHN, Minoru YAMASAKI, Kevin ROCHE and Robert VENTURI. The intellectual sophistication of the latter has earned him the (perhaps unwanted) position of high priest to POST-MODERNISM, whose chief exponents in the USA are Michael

GRAVES, Charles MOORE, Robert A. M. STERN and Stanley TIGERMAN. Partly in reaction to this trend the NEW YORK FIVE emerged in 1969, of whom Peter EISENMAN and Richard MEIER are not-able. Outside these two currents flourish several notable architects among whom GEHRY is outstanding though several others should be mentioned: ARQUITEC-TONICA, HOLL, LIBESKIND, MOSS, POLSHEK and PREDOCK, some of whom contributed to the creation of the THEME PARKS following on the first Disneyland at Anaheim, California.

A postscript on American technical achievements: first FULLER's geodesic domes, of which the largest has a diameter of 117 m. (384 ft); second the SKY-SCRAPERS of New York, Chicago, Hous-ton and other cities; and finally roadworks. The American MOTORWAYS and PARKWAYS have no competitors, the latter being an American invention com-parable to the great public parks (Central Park, New York; Golden Gate Park, San Francisco) and National Parks (Yellow-stone, Yosemite or the Grand Canyon). Their boldness of conception and their intricacy of junction are stupendous. But they place the motor vehicle above man. They led to the invention by Victor GRUEN of the out-of-town shopping centre or supermarket marooned in an enormous car-park.

**Universal design**, *see* BARRIER FREE DESIGN.

**Unwin**, Sir Raymond (1863–1940). The leading English town planner of his day and the man who – in partnership from 1896 to 1914 with R. Barry Parker (1867–1941) – translated into reality the GARDEN CITY scheme conceived by Ebe-nezer HOWARD. The 'First Garden City', as the company for its realization was actually called, was Letchworth in Hert-fordshire (begun 1903), though it had a prelude at New Earswick near York, a 'garden village' for which they provided the plan in 1902. Unwin published *The Garden City* (London 1905). However, while the growth of Letchworth did not progress as rapidly or as smoothly as had been anticipated, two garden suburbs did extremely well, Hampstead Garden Suburb outside London (begun 1907), and Wythenshawe outside Manchester (begun 1927). The Hampstead Garden Suburb in particular must be regarded as the *beau idéal* of the garden city principles of domestic and public planning, with its formal centre – the two churches and the institute designed by LUTYENS – its pattern of straight main and curving minor vehicular roads and its occasional pedestrian paths, its trees carefully preserved and its architectural style controlled in no more than the most general terms of a free neo-Tudor. Unwin also showed his sense of subtle visual planning effects in his *Town Planning in Practice*, first published in 1909. He was knighted in 1932.

Mumford 1961; W. L. Creese, *The Search for Environment. The Garden City: Before and After*, New Haven and London (1960) 1966, and *The Legacy of R.U. A Human Pattern for Planning*, Cambridge, Mass., and London 1967; F. Jackson, *Sir R.U. (1863–1940)*, London 1985; M. Miller, *R.U. Garden Cities and Town Planning*, Leicester 1992.

**Upjohn**, Richard (1802–78), was born at Shaftesbury, England, where he was later in business as a cabinet-maker. He emigrated to America in 1829 and opened a practice as an architect at Boston in 1834. His speciality was Gothic churches: the first came in 1837, and the principal ones are Trinity Church, New York (1844–6), an effort in a rich Anglo-Gothic, and Trinity Chapel, West 25th Street (1853), also Anglo-Gothic. Later he specialized in small parish churches emulating those of English villages, e.g. St Paul's in Brookline, Massachusetts, of 1851–2. He built in other styles (Trinity Building, New York, 1852, is Italianate). Upjohn was first president of the American Institute of Architects.

E. Upjohn, *R.U. Architect and Churchman*, New York 1939; P. B. Stanton, *The Gothic Revival and American Church Architecture. An Episode in Taste 1840–56*, New York 1968.

**Urban design**. The earliest known permanent human settlements were huddles of dwellings, notably Jericho (Jordan) from *c.*7000 BC and Çatal Hüyük (Turkey) *c.*6000–5600 BC, *see* Fig. 94. Basic elements of urban design began to appear in the 4th millennium BC at Ur (Iraq) – paths or streets, approximately rectangular and equal-sized plots for housing, division into districts and the demarcation of a boundary with surrounding country. Grid planning, the simplest means of apportioning land for building, was developed in the Indus Valley (*c.*2300–1750 BC, *see* INDIAN AND PAKISTANI ARCHITECTURE), in Egypt at Kahun (1897–78 BC) and Akhetaten (1379–62 BC), in China at Zhengzou from *c.*1600 BC and Anyang from 1300 BC. Housing in close set plots might be combined with the monumental architecture of widely spaced palaces and temples, e.g. Khorsabad, Iraq (*c.*700 BC), Babylon, Iraq, with its magnificent processional way (605–562 BC), and Teotihuacán, Mexico (AD C1–7), where the grid was oriented to reflect cosmic order.

Grid planning, often called Hippodamian after HIPPODAMUS OF MILETOS who evolved a social theory of urbanism transmitted to posterity by Aristotle, could be realized only for new towns and urban extensions. Where property rights had been established, urban design was limited to the incorporation of monumental architecture in an existing urban fabric. Athens was by the C5 BC distinguished for the number and architectural quality of its public buildings but they were informally related to one another, even around the trapezoid AGORA. Later, in the royal and sacred areas of Hellenistic capitals, e.g. Pergamon, Turkey (from 240 BC) (*see* HELLENISTIC ARCHITECTURE), monumental effects were achieved by siting, grouping and the creation of vistas. Under the Roman empire this was further developed. In Rome itself, a sprawl of mud-brick buildings until the mid-C1 BC, campaigns of urban renewal promoted by successive emperors inserted marble-clad forums, temples, arenas and THERMAE of unprecedented magnificence in a city of narrow streets where the mass of the population lived in tall concrete-built INSULAE. This fortuitous mixture of public and private building was rationalized in new towns founded throughout the empire, based on the CASTRUM plan with the forum sited off the crossing of the two main, sometimes colonnaded, streets, and public baths, temples, theatres, etc. distributed among the uniformly square plots for housing, e.g. Timgad, Algeria (*c.*AD 100). In the eastern Mediterranean Greek and Hellenistic cities were enlarged and embellished under Roman rule, most extensively Constantinople from 330.

During the following centuries notable urban designs were realized in Islamic lands. The Calif al-Mansur founded a new capital city at Baghdad on a circular plan of cosmic significance, with his palace surrounded by a park in the centre (762 destroyed 1259). Near Cordoba, Spain, in 936, Medinet al-Zahra was laid out on a hillside – a double square about 1.5 km. (1 mile) wide with the Caliph's palace on the upper level and, below,

rectangular plots for houses decreasing in size according to the status of their occupants. Elsewhere urban design was limited to the layout of palatial and administrative compounds, e.g. those in Egypt from 641 onwards, now absorbed into the urban sprawl of Cairo. In India the Mughal emperor Akbar founded in 1571 the city of Fatehpur Sikri near Agra, with its centre on the ridge of a hill that determined a linear plan with a series of buildings and open spaces all based on the same proportional module though informally interrelated. Urban developments in Central Asia are among the most remarkable of their time. At Samarkand, Uzbekistan, the spacious Registan (ceremonial square) begun in 1417–21 was given in the C17 its definitive form with lofty ceramic-tile clad façades of madrasas on three sides. Isfahan, Iran, was transformed from 1590 onwards into the capital city of Shah Abbas, with the Maidan, an 8 hectare (20 acre) elongated rectangular piazza surrounded by ranges of uniform two-storey shops, and the 4 km. (2½ mile) long Chahar Bagh boulevard with a canal and gardens along the centre and houses for the nobility on either side.

In Christendom, Roman cities were sacked as the empire disintegrated. Their basic rectilinear patterns of streets sometimes survived, though not until the C10 did urban life begin to revive. From the mid-C12 BASTIDES in France and similar small settlements in Spain and England were laid out on grids. But, with increasing populations and economic prosperity, the main cities grew within their fortifications until they were tightly packed with buildings around which narrow lanes twisted and turned. There were usually main thoroughfares from the gates and always an open, sometimes rectangular, space for a market – in north-eastern France and Flanders surrounded by houses for the richer citizens, town hall, guild premises, etc. of varying heights, e.g. Antwerp, Arras, Bruges, Brussels. Civic pride found expression in public buildings, especially in free cities, nowhere more conspicuously than in the republican communes of Tuscany. A remarkable campaign of urban improvement was initiated in Florence in 1284: the cathedral and baptistery were linked by a wide straight street (which necessitated some demolition) with the grain market and town hall. (Or San Michele and Palazzo Vecchio.) Laws controlled the maximum heights of buildings but here as elsewhere attention was focused on façades, e.g. BRUNELLESCHI's Foundling Hospital (begun 1418), which determined more than a century later the design of buildings around the piazza in front of it.

That a new concept of urban design began to emerge in the mid-c15 was due mainly to ALBERTI. From VITRUVIUS's recommendation that a town be centrally planned for easy defence and to benefit from the eight winds, he derived the idea of an octagonal scheme that was to obsess designers for two centuries, from FILARETE and CATANEO to SPECKLE and VAUBAN, though only a few were realized, notably Koevorden, Netherlands (1580), and Palmanova, near Udine, Italy (1593). With greater practical consequences, he developed from Vitruvius's descriptions of a FORUM the idea of a PIAZZA, prescribing the proportional ratios of its length and breadth to the height of surrounding buildings, which should have porticos raised slightly above ground level. His painter's eye for scenographic effects led him to remark that streets should be broad and straight only in great cities, otherwise winding to make them appear longer and present a different view at every turn.

The first fully realized Renaissance piazza was that in Pienza, Italy (1460–

62) by ROSSELLINO, who was close to Alberti, as was also his patron Pope Pius II Piccolomini. The much larger Piazza Ducale in Vigevano near Milan, surrounded by buildings with uniform, porticoed façades, was begun in 1494, probably with the collaboration of BRAMANTE. In Rome, where urban design on a grand scale was facilitated by a magistracy empowered to expropriate land, a succession of authoritarian Popes from Eugenius IV (1431–47), advised by Alberti, to Sixtus V (1585–90) imposed on the urban fabric a great network of streets which introduced the 'trivium', an unprecedented element in planning consisting of three long streets radiating out from a point, as from the Piazza del Popolo. With its vast new palaces built along them and such open spaces as the Piazza del Popolo, Piazza Farnese, Piazza Navona and most notably Piazza del Campidoglio, designed by MICHELANGELO, Rome became by the end of the c16 the most imposing example of urban design in Europe.

Similar developments followed in France, where in 1605–10 Henri IV set out to transform medieval Paris by using royal land to create the Place des Vosges (a combination of Flemish style marketplace and an Italian piazza) for upper-class habitation, the triangular Place Dauphine for artisans and the semicircular Place de France (unrealized) for trade. Louis XIV commissioned HARDOUIN MANSART to design the grandiose Place Vendôme, Paris (1698). By the mid-c18 every major French city had a Place Royale dominated by a royal statue, inserted into the urban fabric usually with the regularization of surrounding areas, e.g. Bordeaux (1730–55) and Rennes (1736–44), both by J. GABRIEL, and in Paris (now the Place de la Concorde) (1757–72) by A.-J. GABRIEL. At Nancy, capital of Lorraine, King Stanislas engaged HÉRÉ DE CORNY to design the Place Royale (1752 onwards) with the Place de la Carrière leading to the Hemi-cycle. The Late Rococo architect Pierre Patte (1723–1812) discussed urban design in his *Mémoires sur les objets plus important de l'architecture* (Paris 1769), rejecting recti-linear grids, 'monotony and excessive uni-formity'. He recommended that a city display variety in its parts, while insisting that sanitation and traffic control should be determining factors. But the rigidity of grid planning and the resulting uniformity of buildings were just what appealed to absolutist rulers in Germany (e.g. Karls-ruhe, 1739), Portugal (Lisbon from 1755) and Russia (St Petersburg from 1703, but mainly after 1762).

Different approaches to urban design were explored elsewhere in Europe. On a plan made in 1613 for the extension of Amsterdam, the richest city in the newly established Dutch Republic, marshy land surrounding the old centre was drained, building lots facing three concentric canals with wide quays were laid out, and carried by the 1680s tall houses each designed according to the wishes of its occupant. English urban development, on the other hand, was controlled by private landowners and speculative builders. In London the first Italianate piazza was built on the property of the Earl of Bedford by Inigo JONES in 1630; the first streets of houses with classical orders (of which Lindsey House, Lin-coln's Inn Fields, is the only survivor) were financed by a property developer in 1640; and the first SQUARE to be named as such was laid out for the Earl of South-ampton in 1661. After the Great Fire that devastated the city of London in 1666, regulations were introduced to stan-dardize structures and a few streets were widened, but projects for comprehensive replanning, including that by WREN, were rejected in order to preserve prop-erty rights. The building of uniform ter-races and squares took place on the surrounding farmland, into which the population expanded. Similarly, it was outside the city of Bath that John WOOD and his son built on leasehold land from 1727 the square, circus and crescent which alone or in combination for long remained the basic elements in British urban design, e.g. New Town, Edin-burgh by R. and J. ADAM (1791), Regent's Park and Regent Street, London by NASH from 1811. In British North American colonies grid layouts with London-style squares were the rule, e.g. Philadelphia, planned by William Penn with Thomas Hulme in 1682, and OGLETHORPE's Savannah, Georgia (1733). However, L'ENFANT's partly realized plan for Washington, DC, of 1792 cut through a grid with a net-work of diagonal streets radiating from *ronds-points*, reminiscent of the Rome of Sixtus V, still the pre-eminent capital city.

By the early C19 in Europe, especially Britain, the agricultural and industrial revolutions had led to overcrowding and an uncontrolled sprawl of slum dwellings which impelled Robert Owen (1771–1858) to found the first COMPANY TOWN in 1816 and to acquire land for a co-operative industrial town in the USA at New Harmony, Indiana, designed by Thomas Stedman Whitwell (1784–1840) but never realized. The French social theorist Charles Fourier (1772–1837) projected in 1822 a radially planned town, probably influenced by LEDOUX's plan for Chaux but intended to express the harmony of the socialist world he envis-aged. Yet none of the new industrial towns built at this period had any such ambitions, e.g. Decazeville in France (1830); Middlesbrough in England (from 1831). Throughout the West, however, attempts were made to alleviate con-ditions in overcrowded, smoke-polluted de-naturized cities by the creation of PUBLIC PARKS and tree-lined BOULEVARDS.

Large-scale urban design in early C19 Europe was limited to the aggrandizement of old cities and their expansion. Munich was extended from 1816 by GÄRTNER and KLENZE, who broke away from the tradition of uniform terracing by lining streets and squares with detached buildings in different historical styles, unified only by an underlying sense of scale. In Vienna the Ringstrasse, projected in the 1830s and begun in 1858 on a plan by Ludwig Förster (1797–1863), surrounded the city with public buildings and houses outside the glacis of obsolete fortifications made into a public park to separate the new from the old city. The most extensive campaign of modernization was carried out in Paris, begun by Napoleon I (rue de Rivoli by FONTAINE and Percier 1801) and more fully carried out by Napoleon III, who from 1853 employed HAUSSMANN to impose a system of wide boulevards on the old urban fabric, much of which was demolished, and ALPHAND to create several notable public parks. By the end of the C19 virtually every European city had been similarly transformed. In the USA the CITY BEAUTIFUL MOVEMENT had analogous effect. Other notable C19 developments were the creation of suburban housing estates for the middle class, e.g. by BURTON and NASH in England, by DAVIS in the USA, and the laying out of PUBLIC PARKS. The idea of surrounding a city with a GREEN BELT was first realized at Adelaide, South Australia, from 1817 (*see* AUSTRALIAN ARCHITECTURE).

Theories of urban design proliferated from the mid-C19. In 1867 the Spanish civil engineer Ildefonso Cerdà (1815–76) published his two-volume *Teoría general de la urbanización*, coining the word that passed into English as urbanization, to signify the concentration of population in a physically expanding city. In Germany, Richard Baumeister (1833–97) laid the basis for a scientific approach to urban design in his *Stadt-Erweiterungen in technischer, baupolizeilicher und wirtschaftlicher Beziehung* (Berlin 1876); and Joseph Stübben (1845–1936), responsible for the layout of more than thirty urban complexes, surveyed the subject more comprehensively in *Der Stadtbau* (Darmstadt 1890, revised 1907, 1924). Their orthodox planning was opposed by SITTE, who extolled the irregular informality of medieval towns. His writings were a source of inspiration for the British theorist GEDDES, who brought a fresh approach to the problems of restructuring old cities and their surroundings – in practice one of the main activities of urban designers though it has recently become controversial; *see* URBAN RENEWAL.

More radical proposals were put forward in plans for ideal cities. In 1882 the Spanish architect Arturo Soria y Mata (1844–1920) published a project for the 'linear city', elaborated from 1894 in *La Ciudad Lineal*, the first periodical devoted to urban design. This was to be developed from an existing city through farmland as a 510 m. (550 yard) strip for alternating groups of housing, factories, etc., with a central spine for railways and roads and the supply of water, gas and electricity, that might eventually be extended from, he suggested, Cadiz to St Petersburg or even Beijing to Brussels. Although such linear planning was to be realized only in Russia and on a limited scale (Magnitogorsk, 1928), the basic notion of a city in which every inhabitant would be within walking distance of open country and of transport to workplaces was pervasive and long-lasting. The tradition of centralized planning was nevertheless maintained in projects for new cities zoned to separate industry from housing (*see* ZONING), with ample space for gardens and surrounded by green belts, published almost simultaneously, though diametrically opposed ideologically, by Theodor Fritsch (1844–1933), a campaigner for German moral regeneration and racial purity, in *Die Stadt der Zukunft* (Leipzig 1896) and E. HOWARD, inspired by the social criticism of Ruskin and Morris, in *Tomorrow: A Peaceful Path to Real Reform* (London 1898). With R. UNWIN, Howard was to create the first GARDEN CITY.

The French architect T. GARNIER, believing that cities of the future would inevitably be industrial, worked out a comprehensive scheme for the *Cité industrielle*, exhibited 1904 and published 1917. In 1914 SANT'ELIA designed high-rise buildings which would exploit modern structural techniques for an Italian Futurist city. The Bauhaus teacher HILBERSHEIMER, in *Hochhausstadt* (Hanover 1924), envisaged a city of identical rectangular glass-fronted twenty-storey blocks separated by a wide straight street for traffic at ground level but linked above the fifth floor by walkways and bridges. In contrast F. L. WRIGHT's Broadacre City plan of 1931–5 was laid out on a vast decentralized grid with some high-rise buildings several miles apart but most of the space occupied by single-family 'Usonian' houses, each with an acre of land for subsistence farming. None of these visionary schemes was realized. Nor were those projected by LE CORBUSIER – his master-plan for Chandigarh, India (1951–6), was far less ambitious – though his ideas were encapsulated in CIAM's Athens Charter of 1933 recommending functional zones divided by green belts, housing with shops, restaurants, etc. in widely spaced blocks rising above parkland, no conventional streets but ringroads for fast automobile circulation. This was to provide the programme for International Modern urban design world-wide.

Alongside these grand schemes, attention was also given from the early C20 to relatively small-scale and often stylistically conservative, municipally financed urban extensions to house the working-class population in healthy, airy surroundings, notably in the Netherlands by BERLAGE, DUDOK, de KLERK and OUD, in Germany around Frankfurt-am-Main by E. MAY, and around Berlin by B. TAUT and Martin Wagner (1885–1957). In the USA the new town of Radburn NJ was built from 1929 as a garden city with an ingenious system to separate pedestrian from motor traffic; *see* RADBURN PLANNING. It was followed in 1937 by the GREEN-BELT towns in Maryland financed by President F. D. Roosevelt's New Deal and, later, by LEVITTOWN. After the Second World War the Welfare State in Britain sponsored Le Corbusian housing estates in the London area by MARTIN and assistants and also the creation of NEW TOWNS planned in collaboration with landscape architects, notably CROWE and JELLICOE. From 1945 an increasingly important role in urban design was played by landscape architects, in Brazil by BURLE MARX at Brasilia, in the USA by HALPRIN, SASAKI, P. WALKER and many others. McHARG especially made a notable impact worldwide with his demand that urban development should not simply include green spaces but should take into account all the ecological, climatic and historical features of the site.

Reactions against the orthodoxies of International Modern urban design (never popular with the general public), and also the Garden City ideal, gathered force from the 1950s onwards. The tenth meeting of CIAM in 1956 recommended 'cluster planning', a new concept of complex, closely knit aggregations of buildings. Yona Friedman (b.1923) anticipated later developments (*see* C. ALEXANDER; COMMUNITY ARCHITECTURE) by founding in 1958 the Groupe d'Étude d'Architecture Mobile to promote the idea that buildings and whole urban complexes should be designed by their future occupants in collaboration with an architect responsible only for the infrastructure. Three years later J. JACOBS published *The Death and Life of Great American Cities*, a passionate appeal for a return to traditional urban life which was being destroyed, she believed, by urban planners. Contemporaneously, the Disneyland THEME PARK in California, with its diverse human-scale buildings informally laid out, came to be seen as a possible model for the future, while R. VENTURI revealed the benefits to be gained from *Learning from Las Vegas* (Cambridge, Mass. 1972).

In a climate in which Main Street might be thought to be 'nearly all right', the influence of theorists such as A. ROSSI (*Architettura della Città*, Padua 1966), R. KRIER (*Stadtraum in Theorie und Praxis*, Stuttgart 1975), C. Rowe and R. Koetter (*Collage City*, London 1978) and L. KRIER (*Reconstruction of the European City*, Brussels 1978) was muted. L. Krier went on to propose a classical never-never land in *Atlantis* (1988). Architects continued nevertheless to design cities of the future with utopian technology, e.g. TANGE's project to extend Tokyo out over the sea (1960) and ARCHIGRAM's science-fiction *Walking City* and *Plug-in City* (1962–4), while the problem of housing the world's rapidly increasing population and eliminating atmospheric pollution was confronted by urban designers, notably DOXIADIS and SOLERI. In the USA the 'New Urbanism', a term coined for the work of Peter Anthony Calthorpe (b.1949), author of *The Next American*

*Metropolis: Ecology, Community and the American Dream* (New York 1993), and DUANY & PLATER-ZYBERG ARCHITECTS INC., focused on closely integrated urban complexes with a strong neighbourhood identity from which automobile traffic is excluded. Although urban designers continue to be much engaged in urban renewal, the emergence of a post-industrial information-based economy has led, especially in the USA, to the growth of self-contained Edge City suburbs or 'technoburbs' connecting with each other rather than with the older cities they surround.

L. Mumford, *The Culture of Cities*, New York 1938; P. Lavedan, *Histoire de l'urbanisme*, rev. edn Paris 1959, 1966; E. A. Gutkind, *International History of City Development*, New York 1964–72; W. Braunfels, *U.D. in Western Europe* (1977), Chicago 1988; S. Kostof, *The City Shaped*, Boston/London 1991; S. Kostof, *The City Assembled*, Boston/London 1992; M. Sorkin (ed.), *Variations on a Theme Park*, New York 1992; V. Vercelloni, *Atlante storico della città ideale*, Milan 1994; F. Katz, *The New Urbanism*, New York 1994; R. T. Le Gates and F. Stout, *The City Reader*, London 1996.

**Urban entertainment center (UEC)**, *see* SHOPPING MALL; THEME PARK.

**Urban renewal**. The rehabilitation and/or rebuilding of decaying urban areas through large-scale planning schemes, usually with government and/or municipal finance. It tends to reduce inexpensive and often well-liked housing and other buildings (shops and workshops) by upgrading them, a process resulting in the displacement of the urban poor and later called 'gentrification'. Criticized for this reason, especially in the USA, urban renewal has become suspect though defended as an inevitable result of modern urban transport and other facilities. The

Government Center, Boston, by Paul RUDOLPH (1961–3, 1967–72), the Philadelphia City Center by Edmund BACON (1963 onward) and Mario PANI's Tlatelolco development in Mexico City (1964 onwards) were among the more ambitious schemes to be carried out. The redevelopment of more limited areas has usually been less controversial, e.g. Faneuil Hall Marketplace, Boston, in 1978 by Benjamin Thompson (b.1918) and Fulton Market and South Street Seaport, New York, in 1984.

J. Jacobs, *The Death and Life of Great American Cities*, New York 1961; C. Doxiadis, *U.R. and the Future of the American City*, New York 1996.

**Utzon**, Jørn (b.1918). Danish architect, trained in Copenhagen and influenced by both ASPLUND and F. L. WRIGHT, whom he visited in the USA. His early Kingo housing near Elsinore (1956–60) was followed by that at Fredensborg (1959–62), both in Denmark, in which he explored themes and forms of 'anonymous' vernacular architecture he had studied in Mexico and North Africa. His project layout for Birkehoj, Elsinore (1963), introduced standardized elements. In 1956 he won the competition for the Sydney Opera House, and this building (designed 1956–66), on which ARUP collaborated, was completed in 1973 in a modified form after his resignation. However, it made his name internationally. His Bagsvaerd Church, Copenhagen (1969–76) is perhaps his finest and certainly his most fully realized achievement. Also notable is his National Assembly Building, Kuwait (1972–82).

J. Utzon in D. Lasdun (ed.), *Architecture in an Age of Scepticism*, London 1984; T.

Faber, *J.U. Houses in Fredensborg*, Berlin 1991.

**Uzbek architecture**. Notable Islamic buildings in Uzbekistan date from before the Uzbeks took possession of the Timurid empire in Transoxiana in the early C16. In Bokhara the remarkable C10 brick-built Samanid mausoleum and the gigantic Kalyan minaret of 1127 survive intact. At Shahr-i Sabz a great iwan partially survives with its polychrome ceramic tile decorations from the great palace of Timur Lang (Tamerlane 1336–1406), and at Samarkand his gigantic Bibi Khanum mosque (1399–1404) and magnificent mausoleum Gur-i Mir (1403), with a ribbed double dome rising high above the interior semispherical ceiling, both survive, the mosque in a semiruined state. After Timur's death his son Shahruk employed the architect Qavam al-Din Shirazi (d.1438) to design the mosque at Mashad, Persia (1416–18), and the complex of mosque, madrasa (both destroyed) and mausoleum at Herat, Afghanistan. At Gazargah, Afghanistan, he designed for Shahruk the shrine of 'Abdallah Ansari (1425–7). Shahruk's son Ulugh Beg (1394–1449) built the magnificent madrasa (1417–21) and kanaqh (later replaced) facing each other across the Registan, Samarkand, one of the finest city squares anywhere. In 1616–36 the kanaqh was replaced with a second madrasa balancing and complementing Ulugh Beg's, with a façade of the same proportions and similarly clad in polychrome brick mosaic and ceramic tiles. In 1646–60 a third madrasa was built on the north side, with a similar central iwan portal framed with two-storey arched wings, recalling in design the Qul Baba Kukaltach madrasa (1560) and Lab-i Hawz madrasa (1620) in Bokhara.

# V

**Vaccarini**, Giovan Battista (1702–68). Italian architect, born in Palermo. He studied under Carlo FONTANA in Rome and settled in Catania (1730), where his exuberant Sicilian Rococo style is seen in the façade of the cathedral (begun 1730), Palazzo Municipale (1732), Collegio Cutelli (1754) and S. Agata (begun 1735).

G. Alajmo Alessandro, *G.B.V. e le sconosciute vicende della sua vita*, Palermo 1950; A. Blunt, *Sicilian Baroque*, London 1968.

**Vaccaro**, Domenico Antonio (1681–1750). With SANFELICE, a leading Neapolitan architect of his day. His small ingeniously planned churches are notable, e.g. SS. Concezione, Montecalvario (1720); S. Maria delle Grazie, Calvizzano, near Naples (*c.*1743). But he is known mainly for his maiolica cloister at S. Chiara, Naples (1739–42).

Blunt 1975; S. Pisani, *D.-A.V.'s SS. Concezione a Montecalvario*, Frankfurt/Berlin 1994.

**Valadier**, Giuseppe (1762–1839). Italian archaeologist, town planner, and a prolific though rather reactionary architect. His main buildings are neo-Palladian rather than neo-classical, e.g. interior of Spoleto Cathedral (1784), interior of Urbino Cathedral (1789), and façade of S. Rocco, Rome (1833), though the boldly simple S. Pantaleo, Rome (1806), is more in tune with his times. His masterpiece is the reorganization of Piazza del Popolo, Rome, for which he published a design in 1794 and which he began in 1813 (executed 1816–20). *See also* RESTORATION.

P. Marconi, *G.V.*, Rome 1964.

**Valle**, Gino (b.1923). Italian architect trained under SCARPA and in the USA at Harvard. He made his name with the Zanussi building, Pordenone (1959–60), followed by the Fantoni building, Osoppo (1973–8), a notable essay in prefabrication; his popular housing development on the Giudecca, Venice (1980–86); the Banca Commerciale Italiana, New York (1981–6), and the Palazzo di Giustizia, Padua (1984–94).

P. A. Croset, *G.V. progetti e architetture*, Milan 1989.

**Vallin de la Mothe**, Jean-Baptiste Michel (1729–1801). French architect who came to Russia in 1759 at the invitation of Count I. I. Shuvalov to teach architecture at the newly founded St Petersburg Academy of Arts. The Academy itself (1765), very French and rather cold in contrast with the near-contemporary Russian Palladian buildings in its neighbourhood, was apparently designed by de la Mothe in collaboration with A. F. Kokorinov (1726–72), Director of the Academy, and himself a considerable architect whose work was already adumbrating the turn away from the Baroque. For the Academy building – the first prominent neo-classical structure of Petersburg – they seem to have reworked a plan previously commissioned from J.-F. BLONDEL, de la Mothe's uncle. But de la Mothe had earlier (1761) produced a more humdrum but historically significant contribution to the overthrow of RASTRELLI's Baroque in his Market Building on Nevsky Prospekt. Continuing his role of neo-classical pioneer, de la Mothe built the 'small' Hermitage next to the Winter Palace for Catherine (1764), and undertook the construction of the great classical archway to the port area of 'New Holland' begun by CHEVAKINSKY. He left Russia in 1776. [R. R. Milner-Gulland]

Hamilton 1983.

**Valode et Pistre** (founded 1977), *see* FRENCH ARCHITECTURE.

**Valsamakis**, Nikos (b.1924), *see* GREEK ARCHITECTURE.

**Van Alen**, William (1882–1954), *see* ART DECO.

**Van Berkel**, Ben (b.1957), *see* DUTCH ARCHITECTURE.

**Van Brunt**, Henry (1832–1903), *see* WARE & VAN BRUNT.

**Van Campen**, Jacob (1595–1657), *see* CAMPEN, Jacob van.

**Van de Velde**, Henry (1863–1957), *see* VELDE, Henry van de.

**Van den Broek**, Johannes Hendrik (1898–1978), *see* DUTCH ARCHITECTURE.

**Van der Swaelmen**, Louis (1883–1929), *see* BELGIAN ARCHITECTURE; GARDEN CITY.

**Van Doesburg**, Theo (Christian Emil Maria Küpper, 1883–1931). Dutch painter, architect and theorist associated with Mondrian, OUD and RIETVELD in founding the DE STIJL movement in 1917. He became its spokesman and lectured at the Bauhaus in the 1920s. His notable buildings include the interior of the Café l'Aubette, Strasbourg (1926–8), with the painter Hans Arp, and his own house and studio at Meudon-Val-Fleury in France (1929–30). His death marked the end of De Stijl.

E. van Straaten, *T.V.D. peintre et architecte*, Paris 1993; E. van Straaten, *T.V.D. Constructor of the New Life*, Otterlo 1994.

**Van Eesteren**, Cornelis (1897–1988), *see* DUTCH ARCHITECTURE.

**Van Egeraat**, Erik (b.1956), *see* DUTCH ARCHITECTURE.

**Van Eyck**, Aldo (b.1918). Dutch architect, trained in Zürich (1938–42), who settled in Amsterdam after 1945. He joined Team 10 in 1953 with HERTZBERGER, the SMITHSONS and others, forming a dissident group in CIAM. His first important building, the Municipal Orphanage, Amsterdam (1957–60), a cellular cluster of domed spaces and open courts, was a key work of the 1960s comparable to the Smithsons' Hunstanton Secondary School. From 1959 onwards his magazine *Forum* was influential in promoting an architecture that is 'user friendly', environmentally adaptable and open to a wide range of vernacular, non-European and other influences, e.g. his Sculpture Pavilion, Arnhem (1966), a circular building of what he called 'labyrinthine clarity' recalling his interest in the cosmic symbolism of Dogon and other sub-Saharan African architecture. From 1971 to 1982 he was in partnership with Theo Bosche (1940–94), with whom he designed the Reienhaus housing, Zwolle (1971–5). At the Humbertus Home (for single parents and their children), Amsterdam (1982–7), Van Eyck achieved a notable balance between rationality and seemingly unsystematic ad hoc improvisation. Also notable are his Church for the Moluccan Community, Deventer (1984–92); the Conference Centre and other facilities for ESTEC (European Space Research and Technology Centre), Noordwijk (1989); Padua Psychiatric Hospital residential block, Boekelo, Eindhoven (1989), and the Tripolis office block, Amsterdam (1991–4).

P. Buchanan *et al.*, *H.V.E. Recent Work*, Amsterdam 1989; F. Strauven, *Relativiteit en verbeelding*, Amsterdam 1994; Ibelings 1995.

**Vanbrugh**, Sir John (1664–1726), soldier, adventurer, playwright, and herald, was also the outstanding English Baroque architect. His father was a Flemish refugee who became a rich sugar-baker and married the daughter of Sir Dudley Carleton. He was brought up as a gentleman and commissioned in the Earl of Huntingdon's regiment in 1686. In 1690 he was arrested in Calais for spying and imprisoned for two years, part of the time in the Bastille. After his release he took London by storm with his witty and improper comedies *The Relapse* and *The Provok'd Wife*. Then he switched his talents to architecture – 'without thought or lecture', said Swift – having been invited by the Earl of Carlisle to try his hand at designing Castle Howard (1699). Lord Carlisle also had him appointed Comptroller at the Office of Works (1702), and thus he became, without any training or qualifications, WREN's principal colleague. But he turned out to be an architect of genius. The Tories later deprived him of his Comptrollership, but he was reinstated after the death of Queen Anne and knighted (1714). Witty and convivial, a friend of Tonson and Congreve and a member of the Kit Cat Club, he lived on familiar terms with the great men who became his clients.

His style derives from Wren at his grandest – e.g. Greenwich Hospital – and probably owes much to HAWKSMOOR, his assistant from 1699 onwards. But every building that he designed is stamped with his own unique personality – expansive, virile, and ostentatious, more Flemish than English and often rather coarse and theatrical. Castle Howard (1699–1712), is an amazing trial of strength by a young undisciplined genius. His great opportunity came in 1705 at Blenheim Palace (1705–24), the nation's gift to Marlborough in honour of his victories. Here he had almost unlimited funds at his disposal and the whole megalomaniac conception suited his temperament perfectly. He was always at his best on the largest possible scale, and his genius for the dramatic and heroic, for bold groupings of masses and for picturesque recessions and projections and varied skylines had full play.

His style reached sudden maturity at Blenheim – indeed, English Baroque architecture culminates there – and it changed little afterwards. The best of his later houses are Kimbolton, Huntingdonshire (1707–9), King's Weston, Gloucestershire (1711–14), Seaton Delaval, Northumberland (1720–28), Lumley Castle, County Durham (entrance front and interior alterations, 1722), and Grimsthorpe, Lincolnshire (north range only, *c.*1722–6). He said he wanted his architecture to be 'masculine' and to have 'something of the Castle Air', and nowhere does his peculiar version of the Baroque come closer to the massiveness of a medieval fortress than at Seaton Delaval. Sombre and cyclopean, this extraordinary house is unlike any other building in England or anywhere else. His strong sense of the picturesque led him to further and more explicit medievalisms elsewhere, notably at his own house at Greenwich (after 1718), which is castellated and has a fortified-looking round tower. He seems here to have foreshadowed the romantic spirit of later Gothic revivals.

G. Beard, *The Work of J.V.*, London 1986; K. Downes, *Sir J.V. A Biography*, London 1987; C. Saumarez Smith, *The Building of Castle Howard*, London 1990;

F. McCormick, *Sir J. V. The Playwright as Architect*, University Park, Pennsylvania 1991; Summerson 1991; Colvin 1995.

**Van't Hoff,** Robert (1887–1979), *see* DE STIJL.

**Vantini**, Rodolfo (1791–1856), *see* CEMETERY.

**Vanvitelli**, Luigi (1700–1773). Italian architect, born in Naples, the son of the painter Gasper van Wittel, studied painting under his father in Rome, and emerged as an architect only in the 1730s. He worked at Pesaro, Macerata, Perugia, Loreto, Siena, Ancona and Rome (monastery of S. Agostino and remodelling of S. Maria degli Angeli) before he was summoned to Naples by Carlo III in 1751 to build the enormous 1,200-room palace at Caserta. This is the last great Italian Baroque building. Its immense internal vistas, ceremonial staircase and central octagonal vestibule rival the most extravagant stage-set in scenographic fantasy, though the exterior already veers towards neo-classical restraint. Almost equally impressive are his Chiesa dell'Annunziata (1761–82), Piazza Dante (1757–63), and 40 km. (25 mile) long Acquedotto Carolino (1752–64).

Blunt 1975; F. Strazzullo (ed.), *Le lettere di L.V.*, Galatina 1976–7; Wittkower 1982.

**Vardy,** John (1718–65). Friend and close associate of KENT, whose designs for the Horse Guards, London, he carried out (with W. Robinson, 1751–8). His most important surviving work is Spencer House, London (1756–65), an excellent example of PALLADIANISM freely interpreted.

R. White in Brown 1985; Summerson 1991; J. Friedman, *Spencer House*, London 1994; Colvin 1995.

**Vasari**, Giorgio (1511–74). Italian painter and author of the famous *Vite de'*

*più eccellenti architetti, pittori e scultori italiani* (1550, revised 1568), which by its eulogistic account of MICHELANGELO exerted an important influence on architectural taste. As an architect he had a hand, with VIGNOLA and AMMANATI, in designing the Villa Giulia, Rome (1551–5). His most important independent work is the Uffizi, Florence (begun 1560), with a long narrow courtyard stretching down towards the river and closed by a range with two superimposed Serlian arcades – an adaptation of Michelangelo's Laurentian Library to external architecture – completed by BUONTALENTI, who designed the famous *tribuna* (1584). In his native town, Arezzo, he designed the abbey church of SS. Fiora e Lucilla (begun 1566), and the imposing Logge Vasariane (1573). In Florence his renovations of the interiors of S. Maria Novella in 1565–72 and S. Croce in 1566–84 were important. Following the ideas of the Council of Trent, he 'purified' them to create open, clarified interior spaces, removing the medieval screens, choir stalls, etc.

L. Satkowski, *Studies on V.'s Architecture*, New York 1977; C. Conforti, *G.V. Architetto*, Milan 1994; L. Satkowski, *G.V. Architect and Courtier*, Princeton; Lotz 1995.

**Vásquez** **(Vázquez)**, Lorenzo (*fl.* 1489–1512), to whom the earliest works of the Renaissance in Spain are now attributed, was master mason to Cardinal Mendoza and for the Cardinal the Colegio de Santa Cruz at Valladolid, begun in 1486, was transformed in 1491 by Vásquez, with its Quattrocento frontispiece medallion. The next buildings in order of date were also commissioned by the Mendoza family: the palace at Cogolludo (probably 1492–5), with windows still floridly Late Gothic; the palace at Guadalajara (before 1507); and the castle of La Calahorra, Granada (1509–12). In the latter case, however, it is known that Michele Carlone of Genoa was called in to take charge. For other early major Renaissance designs in Spain *see* EGAS.

Kubler and Soria 1959.

**Vásquez**, Pedro Ramírez (b.1919), *see* MEXICAN ARCHITECTURE.

**Vauban**, Sébastien le Prestre de (1633–1707). French architect, town planner and the most famous of all military engineers. According to Voltaire he constructed or repaired the fortifications of 150 'places du guerre' and he was said to have directed some 53 sieges. A close friend of Louvois (minister of war 1666–91) and of Colbert, he became Commissaire Général des Fortifications in 1677. In 1703 he was made a Maréchal de France. His genius as a military engineer lay in the resourcefulness with which he used and adapted traditional means rather than in the invention of new ones. His ingenuity is well displayed at difficult sites, e.g. Mont-Louis in the Pyrenees and Mont-Dauphin and Château Queyras on the Savoy frontier. But his most famous fortifications are those of Lille (1668–74), Maubeuge (1683–5) and Neuf-Brisach (1697–1708). Some of his fortresses were in effective military use up to the 1914–18 war, notably Langwy (built 1678). He laid out the new towns he brought into being, such as Neuf-Brisach, and occasionally designed individual buildings, e.g. the governor's house, church and arsenal at Lille and churches at Givet and Briançon. He restored the *châteaux* of Auney and Ussé. But his merit as an architect is best appreciated in the massive simplicity of such ramparts as those of Oléron, Gravelines and Bayonne and in his monumental gateways which range from the Baroque splendour of the Porte de Paris at Lille, enriched with columns, entablatures, trophies and sculptured panels, to the simple grandeur of the Mons Gate at Maubeuge. In these Vauban approached the noble severity and grandeur achieved by his contemporaries Libéral BRUANT and François BLONDEL. His memoirs, *Plusieurs maximes bonnes à observer pour tous ceux qui font bâtir*, contain a complete treatise on building. He also published *Véritable manière de bien fortifier. De Mr de Vauban* (Amsterdam 1702).

M. Parent and J. Verroust, *V.*, Paris 1971.

**Vaudoyer**, Léon (1803–72). French architect. With Félix Duban, LABROUSTE and VIOLLET LE DUC, he was one of the 'romantic' historicizing Beaux Arts architects. His *chef-d'œuvre* is Marseille Cathedral (begun in 1852), which combines convincingly a Romanesque plan with a Byzantine elevation and the polychrome horizontal striping of, e.g., Siena Cathedral.

Hitchcock 1977; Van Zanten 1987; B. Bergdoll, *L.V. Historicism in the Age of Industry*, Cambridge, Mass. 1994.

**Vaudremer**, Joseph-Auguste-Émile (1829–1914). French architect who, after a training under the sober utilitarian architects Blouet and Gilbert, started with the large Santé Prison, Paris (1862 onwards), in the same spirit. However, in 1864 he was commissioned to build the church of St Pierre de Montrouge in Paris (1864–70), and here his very sobriety and directness made him choose the Romanesque rather than the Gothic style. The building must have impressed H. H. RICHARDSON. Romanesque also, but internally with much grander stone vaults, is Notre Dame, rue d'Auteuil, Paris (1876 onwards). The much larger and more famous Sacré Cœur on Montmartre is by Paul ABADIE.

Hitchcock 1977; *Entre archéologie et*

*modernité. Paul Abadie architecte*, exh. cat., Paris 1988/9.

**Vault**. An arched ceiling or roof of stone, brick or concrete, sometimes imitated in wood or plaster.

*Barrel vault, see* tunnel vault.

*Cloister vault, see* domical vault.

*Cross-vault, see* groin vault.

*Domical vault*. A dome rising direct on a square or polygonal base, the curved surfaces separated by GROINS. *See* DOME. In America called a *cloister vault*. *See* Figs. 41, 46.

A *fan vault* consists of solid concave-sided semi-cones, meeting or nearly meeting at the apex of the vault. The areas between are flat and, if the cones meet, form concave-sided lozenges. The cones and centres are decorated with panelling so as to give the appearance of a highly decorated rib vault. *See* Fig. 119.

A *groin vault* is produced by the intersection at right angles of two tunnel vaults of identical shape. *See* Fig. 119.

*Handkerchief vault, see* DOME.

*Hyperbolic paraboloid vault, see* HYPERBOLIC PARABOLOID ROOF.

*Lierne*. A tertiary rib, that is, one which does not spring either from one of the main springers or from the central BOSS. *See* Fig. 119. A *lierne vault* is a ribbed vault with liernes.

For *net vault* see definition under RIETH.

*Parabolic vault*. A thin shell covering, usually of reinforced concrete, of parabolic section, i.e. in form a cone cut parallel to one edge. Such vaults are light and little subject to tensional stresses. *See also* HYPERBOLIC PARABOLOID ROOF; SHELL.

A *ploughshare vault* or *stilted vault* has the wall ribs sprung from a higher level than the diagonal ribs, in order to increase the light from a clerestory window.

In a *quadripartite vault* one bay is divided into four quarters or CELLS.

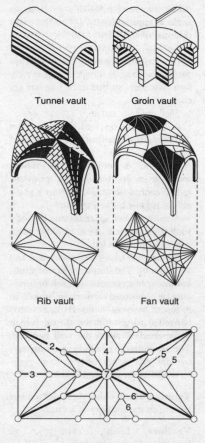

Tunnel vault    Groin vault

Rib vault    Fan vault

1. Transverse rib
2. Diagonal rib
3. Transverse ridge-rib
4. Longitudinal ridge-rib
5. Tiercerons
6. Liernes
7. Boss

Fig. 119 Vault

A *rampart vault* is a wagon vault with abutments at different heights.

A *rib vault* is a framework of diagonal arched ribs carrying the cells which cover in the spaces between them. *See* Fig. 119.

*Ridge-rib*. The rib along the longitudinal or transverse ridge of a vault, at an angle of approximately 45° to the main diagonal ribs. *See* Fig. 119.

*Sail vault, see* DOME.

In a *sexpartite vault* one bay of quadripartite vaulting is divided transversely into two parts so that each bay has six compartments.

*Shell vault, see* SHELL.

A *stellar vault* is one with the ribs, liernes and tiercerons arranged in a star-shaped pattern.

*Tierceron*. A secondary rib, which springs from one of the main springers, or the central boss, and leads to a place on the ridge-rib. *See* Fig. 119.

A *transverse arch* separates one bay of a vault from the next. It can be either plain in section or moulded.

*Tunnel vault* (also called *barrel vault* and *wagon vault*). The simplest form of vault, consisting of a continuous vault of semicircular or pointed sections, unbroken in its length by cross-vaults. BUTTRESSING is needed to ground the thrust, which is dispersed all along the wall beneath. Tunnel vaults can be subdivided into bays by transverse arches. *See* Fig. 119.

*Wagon vault, see* tunnel vault.

**Vaulting shaft**. The vertical member leading to the springer of a vault.

**Vauthier**, Louis (*c.*1810–77), *see* BRAZILIAN ARCHITECTURE.

**Vaux**, Calvert (1824–95). English-born architect and landscape architect who emigrated in 1850 to the USA, where he worked in partnership with DOWNING until 1852 and then with OLMSTED (1857–72). He collaborated with Olmsted on Central Park, New York, where he designed the Belvedere, bridges, etc., as well as on Prospect Park, Brooklyn, and private gardens. With Jacob Wray Mould he designed the Metropolitan Museum, New York

(completed 1880). The grounds of Parliament House, Ottawa, were laid out by him in 1873 and he later designed several notable private parks, e.g. Olana for the painter Frederick Edwin Church, exploiting spectacular views over the Hudson River valley. He published *Villas and Cottages* (New York 1857, reprinted 1970).

W. Alex, *C.V. Architect and Planter*, New York 1994.

**Vázquez**, Lorenzo (*fl.*1489–1512), *see* VÁSQUEZ, Lorenzo.

**Velarium**. An awning hung over a courtyard or, in Ancient Rome, over an amphitheatre.

**Velde**, Henry van de (1863–1957). Belgian architect and designer, born at Antwerp of a well-to-do family and was first a painter influenced aesthetically by the neo-Impressionists (Pointillists), socially by the ideals which at the time also inspired van Gogh. About 1890, under the impact of RUSKIN and MORRIS, he turned from painting to design and in 1892 produced the first works that are entirely his own and at the same time are entirely representative of ART NOUVEAU, the anti-historical movement just then emerging. They are works of typography and book decoration, with long flexible curves, and an appliqué panel called *The Angels Watch*. Their stylistic source seems to be the Gauguin of Pont Aven and his circle, especially Émile Bernard.

In 1895 van de Velde designed a house and furnishings at Uccle near Brussels for his own young family. It was his first achievement in architecture and interior design, and both now became his principal concerns. He was commissioned to design interiors for Bing's newly established shop L'Art Nouveau in Paris (1895) and then showed most of this work at an exhibition in Dresden (1897). In both centres its impact was great, but whereas reactions were largely hostile in France, they were enthusiastic in Germany, and so van de Velde decided to leave Brussels and settle in Berlin. In the next years he did much furnishing work for the wealthy and the refined, including the shop of the imperial barber (Haby, 1901). In 1901 he was called to Weimar as consultant on the co-ordination of crafts, trades and good design. He furnished the Nietzsche-Archiv there (1903), and rebuilt the Art School and the School of Arts and Crafts (1904, 1907), of which latter he became director. He also did the interior of the Folkwang Museum at Hagen (1901–2) and the Abbe Monument at Jena (1908).

His style is characterized by the long daring curves of Art Nouveau, which he endowed with a peculiar resilience, and in architecture also by the use of the curve rather than the angle – e.g. for roofs, notably at the Springmannhaus, Hagen (1913). For the Werkbund Exhibition at Cologne in 1914 (see GROPIUS; TAUT) he did the theatre, also with curved corners and a curved roof.

Being Belgian he left his job in Germany during the war, lived through restless years of émigré life and only in 1925 settled down again, now back in Brussels. However, the years of his great successes and his European significance were over. His late style is less personal, close to that of the Amsterdam School, notably his University Library, Ghent (1936), and the Kröller-Müller Museum at Otterlo in Holland, beautifully coordinated with the heath scenery around (1937–54).

He published Déblaisement d'art (Brussels 1894); Aperçus en vue d'une synthèse d'art (Brussels 1895); Vom neuen Stil (Leipzig 1907); and, posthumously, his autobiography, Geschichte meines Lebens (Munich 1962).

A. M. Hammacher, Le Monde de H.

van de V., Antwerp and Paris 1967; K. J. Sembach, H. van de V., London 1989; K. T. Sembach and B. Schulte (eds.), H. van de V. (1863–1957). Ein europäische Kunstler seine Zeit, Cologne 1992; A. van Loo and F. van der Kererkhove (eds.), H. van de V. Récit de ma Vie, Paris 1992.

**Velten**, Yegor (1730–1801), see RUSSIAN ARCHITECTURE.

**Venetian door**. An adaptation of the SERLIANA to a doorway, i.e. with the central opening arched and flanked by tall narrow square-topped windows.

**Venetian window**, see SERLIANA.

**Venezia**, Francesco (b.1944), see ITALIAN ARCHITECTURE.

**Vennecool**, Steven Jacobs (1657–1719), see DUTCH ARCHITECTURE.

**Venturi**, Robert (b.1925). Leading American architect whose theoretical writings have had a world-wide influence. He was in partnership from 1964 with John Rauch (b.1930) and from 1967 with his wife Denise Scott-Brown (b.1931) and later with Steven Izenour (b.1930) as Venturi, Scott-Brown and Associates. His early buildings were built at low cost, notably his mother's house at Chestnut Hill, Pennsylvania (1961–5), the Guild House (old people's home), Philadelphia (1960–65), and the Fire Station, Columbus, Indiana (1966). In 1966 he published Complexity and Contradiction in Architecture, in which he argued for complexity, contradiction, ambiguity and paradox in place of the purity, clarity and simplicity of the INTERNATIONAL STYLE. To MIES VAN DER ROHE's dictum 'less is more' Venturi replied 'less is a bore'. In 1972 he published, with Denise Scott-Brown and Steven Izenour, Learning from Las Vegas. These books provided a theoretical basis for a populist Post-Modernism and made Venturi famous internationally. His occasional writings were collected and published as *Iconography and Electronics upon a Generic Architecture: A View from the Drafting Room* (Cambridge, Mass. 1997).

His later buildings have the provocativeness and scholarly refinement of his writings, notably the Dixwell Fire Station, New Haven (1970–74); extension to the Allen Memorial Art Gallery, Oberlin, Ohio (1976); Brant Johnson House, Vail, Colorado (1975–7); Busco Showroom, Philadelphia (1979); Gordon Wu Hall, Princeton University Campus, Princeton, NJ (1983); Seattle Art Museum, Seattle, Washington (1984–91); Sainsbury Wing extension to the National Gallery, London (1986–91); and Museum of Contemporary Art, San Diego, California (1996).

C. Mead, *The Architecture of R.V.*, Cambridge, Mass. 1989; C. Vaccaro and F. Schwartz, *R.V. – D.S.B. and Associates*, Zürich 1992.

**Veranda**. An open gallery or balcony with a roof supported by light, usually metal, supports, a notable feature of the STICK STYLE in the USA and of the BUNGALOW in England.

**Verge**, John (1782–1861), *see* AUSTRALIAN ARCHITECTURE.

**Vergeboard**, *see* BARGEBOARD.

**Vermiculation**. Decoration of masonry blocks with irregular shallow channels like worm tracks. *See* Fig. 103.

**Vernacular architecture**. A term of recent usage indicating, by analogy with language (native or local dialects), buildings in indigenous styles constructed from locally available materials following traditional building practice and patterns and not architect-designed – e.g. North American farm houses, often of CLAPBOARD, without any or with only a few superficial classical features; or in England

medieval BARNS or timber-framed houses of which the WEALDEN HOUSE was a notable type. The C16–17 Kelmscott Manor, owned by William MORRIS, is a prime example of English, specifically Oxfordshire, vernacular architecture. Although a taste for such buildings formed a part of the PICTURESQUE from the late C18 (e.g. the COTTAGE ORNÉ), they were generally scorned until the mid to late C19, when professional architects associated with Morris and the ARTS AND CRAFTS movement (notably DEVEY, Philip WEBB, Norman SHAW and VOYSEY) drew inspiration from them in their search for a way out of HISTORICISM while preserving contact with national or local history and traditions. More recently, vernacular architecture has been emulated and its materials – brick, rubblemasonry, knapped flint, wood, etc. – favoured in contrast to the impersonal concrete and glass of the INTERNATIONAL MODERN style. The vernacular has also been studied more closely than before in reaction against an elitist approach to history. There are, nevertheless, underlying connections between buildings in vernacular and 'polite' styles, the latter usually preceding the former, and since, until the C20, both were conditioned by local aesthetic preferences, the difference between them is often no more than one of degree. When used in a global context the term 'vernacular architecture' indicates what has been called, more appropriately, 'architecture without architects'.

R. W. Brunskill, *Illustrated Handbook of V.A.*, London 1987; A. Clifton-Taylor, *The Pattern of English Building*, London 1987; J. Kemp, *American V.*, New York 1988; R. W. Brunskill, *Traditional Buildings of England: an Introduction to V.A.*, London 1994.

**Vertue**, Robert (d.1506) and William

(d.1527), English masons and brothers. Robert, the elder, appears at Westminster Abbey from 1475. About 1501 both brothers were master masons for Bath Abbey, begun at that time by Bishop King. This grandly Perpendicular building has a fan VAULT which, so they told the bishop, would be such that 'there shall be none so goodly neither in England nor in France'; and as at that moment neither the vault of King's College Chapel, Cambridge, nor that of Henry VII Chapel in Westminster Abbey, nor that of St George's Chapel, Windsor, existed (though the latter was building), the claim was just. The Vertues' precise connection with these three works cannot be proved, but as they were jointly the King's Master Masons, with Robert Janyns and John Lebons (*see* REDMAN), it is likely that a connection existed. William, in any case, signed a contract with another (John Aylmer) to vault the chancel at Windsor, and visited King's College Chapel once in 1507, once (with Redman) in 1509, and once (with WASTELL) in 1512, if not more often.

In 1516 William appeared at Eton (with Redman), where he made a design (the design?) for Lupton's Tower. From 1515 he was joint King's Mason with Redman. In 1526 he probably designed the fan-vaulted cloister chapel in the Palace of Westminster.

Harvey 1984.

**Vesica**. An upright almond shape; found chiefly in medieval art to enclose a figure endowed with divine light, usually Christ or the Virgin. Also called a mandorla.

**Vesnin**, Aleksandr (1883–1959). Russian architect who almost always worked with one or both of his brothers – Leonid (1880–1933) and Viktor (1882–1950) – as the most successful architectural partnership (in terms of buildings actually erected) of the era of Russian CON-

STRUCTIVISM; Aleksandr was their theoretician and editor of the influential journal *Contemporary Architecture*. Already initiators of modernistic simplicity of design by 1914, the Vesnins' major opportunities came in the 1920s and early 1930s: as well as various monumental projects and stage-designs, they particularly specialized in workers' clubs and theatres. Their largest commissions included the great Dnieper dam and ancillary works at Zaporozhye, and the replanning of the whole region around the Simonov Monastery and Likhachyov Car Works in Moscow (1930–37). [R. R. Milner-Gulland]

S. O. Khan-Magomedov, *A.V. and Russian Constructivism*, London 1987.

**Vestibule**. An anteroom or entrance hall.

**Vest-pocket park**. A very small urban park, often fitted into 'space left over after planning' or sloap. *See* SASAKI, Hideo; ZION, Robert.

**Vestry**, *see* SACRISTY.

**Viaduct**. A long series of arches carrying a road or railway. *See* BRIDGE.

**Vice**. *See* STAIR.

**Vicente de Oliveira**, Mateus (1710–86), the leading Portuguese ROCOCO architect, began under LUDOVICE but forsook his grandiose manner for one more delicate and intimate. His masterpiece is the palace of Queluz (1747–52, interior destroyed), where a large building is disguised behind an exquisitely frivolous façade swagged with garlands of carved flowers. He also designed the very large Estrêla church in Lisbon (1778).

Kubler and Soria 1959; Smith 1968.

**Victorian architecture**, *see* ENGLISH ARCHITECTURE.

**Vigano**, Vittoriano (b.1919), *see* ITALIAN ARCHITECTURE; RATIONALISM.

**Vignola**, Giacomo (or Jacopo) Barozzi da (1507–73), the leading architect in Rome after the death of MICHEL-ANGELO, was born at Vignola, near Modena, and studied painting and architecture at Bologna. In 1530 he settled in Rome. He seems to have played the leading part in designing the Villa Giulia, Rome (1551–5), in collaboration with AMMANATI and VASARI. It is a masterpiece of Mannerist architecture and garden design, with much play with vistas from one courtyard to another, hemicycles echoing each other, a curious rhythmical use of the orders, and very shallow relief decorations applied to the surfaces.

In 1559 he began work on the Palazzo Farnese at Caprarola, which had already been started on a pentagonal plan. He designed the rather stern façades, the elegant circular interior courtyard and the ingenious arrangement of rooms. The famous circular staircase is also his, and he probably designed the gardens as well. In about 1550–c.1553 he built the little Tempietto di S. Andrea in via Flaminia, Rome, for Pope Julius III, using for the first time in church architecture an oval plan which he was to repeat on a larger scale in his design for S. Anna dei Palafrenieri, Rome (begun 1565), and which was to be used extensively by Baroque architects. His most influential building was the Gesù, Rome (begun 1568); it has probably had a wider influence than any church built in the last 400 years. The plan, which owes something to ALBERTI's S. Andrea, Mantua, combines the central scheme of the Renaissance with the longitudinal scheme of the Middle Ages. The aisles are replaced by a series of chapels opening off the nave, and various devices – e.g. lighting and the placing of the nave pilasters – direct attention to the high altar. (The facade was by della PORTA, 1571–84; the

interior was redecorated in 1668–73.) In 1558 he designed Palazzo Farnese in Piacenza, on which work stopped soon after 1560 so that barely a third was built. He may also have designed the Portico dei Banchi at Bologna (begun c.1561).

Vignola was architect to St Peter's (1567–73) and continued Michelangelo's work there faithfully. In 1562 he published *Regole delle cinque ordini*, a simple MODULAR interpretation of the architectural ORDERS which, on account of its straightforward approach, enjoyed immense popularity. It became one of the most important textbooks ever written (translated into English in 1655).

J. Coolidge, W. Lotz et al., *La vita e le opere di J.B. da V.*, Vignola 1974; Harris 1990; Lazzaro 1990; Lotz 1995.

**Vignon**. Pierre-Alexandre (1762–1828). French Empire architect famous for the Madeleine in Paris (1806–45), his one important building. He was trained under J.-D. Leroy and LEDOUX and in 1793 became Inspecteur Général des Bâtiments de la République. His Madeleine is an enormous peripteral Corinthian temple on a high podium, as imposingly and imperially Roman in scale as in its slightly vulgar ostentation. It superseded a building designed by Pierre Contant d'Ivry (1698–1777) in 1764, revised c.1777 by G. M. Couture (1732–99). This had hardly begun to be built when Napoleon called in Vignon in 1806, having decided that it should be a *Temple de la Gloire* and not a church. But he reversed this decision in 1813 after the Battle of Leipzig and the loss of Spain. Vignon did not live to see his masterpiece completed and it was finished by J.-J.-M. Huvé (1783–1852).

M. L. Biver, *Le Paris de Napoléon*, Paris 1963.

**Vihara**. A residential building for monks and other ascetic groups in an Indian

Buddhist or Jain monastery. Viharas followed a standard pattern, small cells opening off a square or rectangular court. In the middle of one side is the entrance. The cell opposite usually accommodates a votive STUPA or Buddha image. Like CHAITYA HALLS, the earliest were rock-cut, but brick remains of structural monasteries have survived. Indian Buddhist monasteries are essentially groups of viharas, as at Ajanta and Nalanda.

J. Prip-Möller, *Chinese Buddhist Monasteries. Their Plan and Function as a Setting for Buddhist Monastic Life*, Copenhagen 1937.

**Villa**. In Roman architecture, the landowner's residence or farmstead on his country estate; in Renaissance architecture, a country house; in C19 England, a detached house 'for opulent persons', usually on the outskirts of a town; in modern architecture, a small detached house. The basic type developed with the growth of urbanization: it is of five bays, on a simple corridor plan with rooms opening off a central passage. The next stage is the addition of wings. The courtyard villa fills a square plan with subsidiary buildings and an enclosure wall with a gate facing the main corridor block. As a building-type the Palladian villa was to have enormous influence (*see* PALLADIANISM).

G. A. Mansuelli, *Le V. del mondo romano*, Milan 1958; J. Ackerman, *The V. Form and Ideology of Country Houses*, London 1990; D. Arnold (ed.), *The Georgian V.*, Stroud 1996.

**Villagrán Garcia**, José (1901–82), *see* MEXICAN ARCHITECTURE.

**Villanueva**, Carlos Raúl (1900–1975). Notable Venezuelan architect working in Caracas, to whose rapid growth he contributed several remarkable housing projects on a very large scale, e.g. the Dos de Diciembre estate (1943–5) for over 12,000 people and the El Paraiso complex (1954). But he is best known for his stadium, auditorium and other buildings for Caracas University (1950–57).

S. Moholy-Nagy, *C.R.V.*, New York 1964.

**Villanueva**, Juan de (1739–1811), the leading Spanish neo-classical architect, was the son of a sculptor under whom he trained. He began in the CHURRIGUERESQUE tradition, then became a draughtsman to SACCHETTI in Madrid and adopted an Italianate Baroque style. He was sent by the Royal Academy to Rome (1759–65), and on his return his brother Diego (1715–74) published his *Colección de papeles críticos sobre la arquitectura* (1766), the first neo-classical attack on the Churrigueresque and Rococo to appear in Spain. Rather tentatively he began to put these ideas into practice in the Palafox Chapel in Burgo de Osma Cathedral (1770), Casita de Arriba at the Escorial (1773), and Casita del Principe at El Pardo (1784). His outstanding work is the Prado Museum, Madrid, designed (1787) as a museum of natural history but later adapted to house the royal collection of pictures. With its sturdy Tuscan portico in the centre and its boldly articulated wings with Ionic colonnades at first-floor level, it is an effective and undoctrinaire essay in neo-classicism.

Kubler and Soria 1959.

**Villard de Honnecourt**, a French architect who was active around 1225–35 in the north-west of France and probably worked at Cambrai Cathedral, which no longer exists, and perhaps at Reims *c.*1228–33. Villard is known to us by the book of drawings with short texts compiled for learners in his LODGE, the masons' workshop and office. The most famous of LODGE BOOKS, it is in the Bibliothèque Nationale in Paris and contains plans of buildings (both copied and invented), elevational details, figure sculpture, figures drawn *au vif*, foliage ornament, a lectern, a stall end, a *perpetuum mobile*, and in addition many small technical drawings, more of an engineering kind, which were added to the book by two successors of Villard. From the text and the examples illustrated it is certain that Villard knew Reims, Laon, Chartres, Lausanne, and that he travelled as far as Hungary. The sculptural style of his figures connects him with work of about 1230 at Reims. Villard's book gives us the clearest insight we can obtain into the work of a distinguished master mason and the atmosphere of a lodge. It has been suggested that he was an artist, not an architect or mason, but this seems improbable.

H. R. Hahnloser, *V. de H.*, Vienna (1937) 1972; T. Bowie (ed.), *The Sketchbook of V. de H.*, Bloomington and London 1968; Bucher 1979; C. F. Barnes, *V. de H. the Artist and his Drawings*, Boston, Mass. 1982, and in Recht 1989; R. Bechman, *V. de H. La pensée technique aux XIII siècle et sa communication*, Paris 1991.

**Vimana**. In Hindu temples the shrine proper and its superstructure, but also, more loosely, a Hindu temple comprising sanctuary and attached porches.

**Vincidor**, Tommaso (*c.*1495–1560), *see* DUTCH ARCHITECTURE.

**Vingboons** or **Vinckeboons**, Philip (1607/8–78), was the leading exponent of van CAMPEN's Dutch Classicism for middle-class domestic architecture in Amsterdam. He worked for the prosperous merchants while Pieter POST was patronized by the upper class. Being Roman Catholic he obtained no commissions for public buildings or churches. He created a new type of town house,

sober, unpretentious and eminently practical, with strictly symmetrical planning and severely simple elevations. His designs, published as *Œuvres d'architecture* in two volumes (1648 and 1674), were very influential especially in England. His brother Justus (*fl.*1650–70) designed the façades of LA VALLÉE's Riddarhus in Stockholm (1653–6) and built the imposing Trippenhuis in Amsterdam (1662).

Kuyper 1980; K. Ottenheym, *P.V. (1607–1678)*, Zutphen 1989.

**Viollet-le-Duc**, Eugène-Emanuel (1814–79). French theorist, restorer and architect, born into a wealthy, cultured and progressive family. His opposition to the 'establishment' began early: he helped to build barricades in 1830 and refused to go to the École des Beaux Arts for his training. In 1836–7 he was in Italy studying buildings with industry and intelligence. His future was determined by his meeting with Prosper Mérimée (1803–70), author of *Carmen* and Inspector in the newly founded Commission des Monuments Historiques. Viollet-le-Duc, inspired by Victor Hugo's enthusiasm on the one hand and by Arcisse de Caumont's scholarship on the other, now turned resolutely to the French Middle Ages and soon established himself both as a scholar and as a restorer; *see* RESTORATION. His first job was Vézélay (1840). He then did the Sainte Chapelle in Paris with Félix-Jacques Duban (1797–1870), and Notre Dame with Jean-Baptiste-Antoine Lassus (1807–57). The number of his later restorations is legion, e.g. the whole town of Carcassonne (1844 onwards). Some of his restorations have recently been removed in the course of further 'restoration', notably at St Sernin, Toulouse.

As a scholar he developed new and highly influential ideas on the Gothic style, which to him is socially the outcome of a lay civilization succeeding the sinister religious domination of the earlier Middle Ages. The Gothic style to Viollet-le-Duc is also a style of rational construction based on the system of rib vault, flying buttress, and buttress. The ribs are a skeleton, like a C19 iron skeleton; the webs or cells are no more than light infilling. All thrusts are conducted from the ribs to the flying buttresses and buttresses, and thin walls can be replaced by large openings. These ideas were laid down and made universal property by Viollet-le-Duc's *Dictionnaire raisonné de l'architecture française* (published 1854–68). A comparison between Gothic skeleton and C19 iron skeleton building was drawn, or rather implied, in Viollet-le-Duc's *Entretiens* (2 vols., published 1863 and 1872), and especially in the second volume. Here Viollet-le-Duc appears as a passionate defender of his own age, of engineering, and of new materials and techniques, especially iron for supports, for framework, and for ribs. The plates to the *Entretiens* are extremely original, but aesthetically they are none too attractive. As an architect Viollet-le-Duc had in fact little merit. Time and again one is struck by the discrepancy between the consistency and daring of his thought and the looseness and commonplace detailing of his original buildings, e.g. St Denys-de-l'Estrée, St Denis (1864–7).

Pevsner 1972; Van Zanten 1987; F. Bercé *et al.*, *V.-le-D. Architect*, Washington, DC, 1988; M. F. Heard (ed.), *The Architectural Theory of V.-le-D. (1814–1879). Readings and Commentary*, Cambridge, Mass. 1990; E. Vassallo, *E.V.-le-D. (1814–1879)*, Milan 1997.

**Viscardi**, Giovanni Antonio (1647–1713). Italian architect born in Switzerland who went, like his compatriot and bitter rival ZUCCALLI, to work in Munich, where he became master mason to the Court in 1678 and chief architect in 1685. Zuccalli helped to oust him from this post in 1689 but he was in charge of enlarging Nymphenburg palace from 1702 onwards (he began the saloon and added pavilions etc.) and he was reinstated as chief architect 1706–13. His most important building is the Mariahilfkirche at Freystadt (1700–1708), with a very high central dome, on a plan that was to have widespread influence even beyond Bavaria (BÄHR used it as a model for the Frauenkirche in Dresden). He also designed the Cistercian church of Fürstenfeld (1701–47). His last works were the Jesuit assembly hall or Bürgersaal, Munich (1709–10), and the church of the Holy Trinity in Munich (1711–14).

Hempel 1965; K.-L. Lippert, *G.A.V.*, Munich 1969.

**Visconti**, Louis-Tullius-Joachim (1791–1853), *see* LEFUEL, Hector-Martin.

**Vitozzi**, Ascanio (*c.*1539–1615). Italian architect who began as an officer and military engineer, serving at Lepanto in 1571 and later in Tunis and in Spain and Portugal. In 1584 he was called by Duke Carlo Emanuele I of Savoy to Turin, where he built S. Maria del Monte or dei Cappuccini (begun 1585) and the Trinità (begun 1598), but his masterpiece is the enormous centrally planned pilgrimage church at Vicoforte di Mondoví, in Piedmont (begun 1596).

Wittkower 1982.

**Vitruvian opening**. A doorway or window of which the sides incline slightly inwards towards the top, giving it a heavy, Egyptian look. It was described by Vitruvius.

**Vitruvian scroll**, *see* RUNNING DOG.

**Vitruvius Pollio**, Marcus (active 46–30 BC). Ancient Roman architect and theorist of slight importance in his own time but of enormous influence from the Early Renaissance onwards, served under Julius Caesar in the African War (46 BC), built the basilica at Fano (destroyed), and in old age composed a treatise on architecture in ten books *De architectura*, written in a somewhat obscure style and dedicated to Augustus. This is the only complete treatise on architecture to survive from antiquity. Several manuscript copies were known and used in the Middle Ages. In 1414 Poggio Bracciolini drew attention to a copy at St Gall, and the treatise soon came to be regarded as a vade-mecum for all progressive architects. Both ALBERTI and FRANCESCO DI GIORGIO derived much from it for their writings and buildings. The first printed text was published in Rome *c.*1486 and the first illustrated edition by Fra GIOCONDO in 1511; an Italian translation was prepared under RAPHAEL's direction *c.*1520, and another translation was printed in 1521 with an extensive commentary by Cesare Cesariano and numerous illustrations. A vast number of subsequent editions and translations in nearly all European languages appeared (into English in 1692). The obscurity of the text, which made a strong appeal to the Renaissance intellect, enabled architects to interpret its gnomic statements in a variety of ways.

MacDonald 1965; Ward-Perkins 1981; H. Knell (ed.), *V. – Kolloquien des Deutschen Archäologen-Verbandes*, Darmstadt 1984; Harris 1990.

**Vittone**, Bernardo (1702–70). Italian architect of real if rather freakish genius, worked exclusively in Piedmont, where he was born. He studied in Rome and edited GUARINI's posthumous *Architettura civile* (1737). His secular buildings are dull; not so his numerous churches, mostly small and scattered in remote vil-

lages, in which the unlikely fusion of Guarini and JUVARRA had surprising and original results in a Rococo vein. Of his structural inventions the pendentive-squinch (e.g. S. Maria di Piazza, Turin, 1751–4) and fantastic three-vaulted dome are the most successful. His churches at Vallinotto (1738–9), Brà (1742), and Chieri (1740–44) show his structural ingenuity at its prettiest. Later churches – Borgo d'Ale, Rivarolo Canavese, Grignasco – are larger, less frivolous, but suavely calm and sinuous. He had several followers and disciples in Piedmont, but no influence whatever farther afield.

Pommer 1967; Wittkower 1982; Varriano 1986.

**Voit**, August von (1801–70). German architect, pupil of GÄRTNER, notable for his Neuen Pinakothek (1846–53, destroyed 1945) and Glaspalast (1853–4, destroyed 1931), both in Munich. *See* GLASS.

**Volksgarten** or **Volkspark**. German term used in the mid-C19 for a PUBLIC PARK designed specifically for a working-class public; given more precise significance from the 1920s to designate one intended for popular recreations including sports, e.g. Bos Park, Amsterdam (begun 1928).

**Volumetric building**, *see* PREFABRICATION.

**Volute**. A spiral scroll on an Ionic CAPITAL; smaller versions appear on Composite and Corinthian capitals. *See* Fig. 86.

**Vorarlberger School**, *see* BEER, MOSBRUGGER and THUMB families.

**Voronikhin**, Andrei Nikiforovich (1760–1814). Russian architect and one of the leading figures in the neo-classical transformation of St Petersburg, was born a serf on the estates of Count Stroganov, who sent him to study in Moscow, then on a European tour (1786–90), and finally employed him to design the state apartments in his palace. His main works are in St Petersburg, e.g. Cathedral of the Virgin of Kazan (1801–11), with striking colonnades derived from Bernini's in Rome, and the Academy of Mines (1806–11), with a dodecastyle Paestum portico.

Hamilton 1983.

**Voussoir**. A brick or wedge-shaped stone forming one of the units of an arch. *See* Fig. 6.

**Voysey**, Charles Francis Annesley (1857–1941). English architect who worked first under SEDDON and from 1880 with DEVEY, on whose vernacular manner his own early work was based. He set up in practice in 1882. He was as interested in design as in architecture, under the general influence of MORRIS and of MACKMURDO in particular, and became a leading member of the ARTS AND CRAFTS movement. His earliest designs for wallpapers and textiles are of 1883 and are indeed very reminiscent of Mackmurdo. His first commissions for houses date from 1888–9, and from then until the First World War he built a large number of country houses and hardly anything else. They are never extremely large, never grand, never representational; instead they are placed in intimate relation to nature – perhaps an old tree preserved in the courtyard – and developed informally. They spread with ease and, having lowish comfortable rooms, are often on the cosy side. The exteriors are usually rendered with pebbledash and have horizontal windows. They are no longer period imitations at all – in fact, more independent of the past than most architects ventured to be before 1900 – but they never lack the admission

of a sympathy for the rural Tudor and Stuart traditions. Voysey designed the furniture and all the details, such as fireplaces, metalwork, etc., himself, and the furniture is again inspired by Mackmurdo's (and in its turn inspired MACKINTOSH's). It is reasonable, friendly, and in the decoration not without a sweet sentimentality; the same is true of textiles and wallpapers.

Among his houses which had a tremendous influence in England (right down to the caricatures produced between the wars by speculative builders) and abroad, the following may be listed: Cottage, Bishops Itchington, Warwickshire, 1888; Perrycroft, Colwall, Herefordshire, 1893; Annesley Lodge, Hampstead, London, 1896; Merlshanger (Grey Friars), Hog's Back, Guildford, Surrey, 1896; Norney, Shackleford, Surrey, 1897; Broadleys (now the Windermere Motor Boat Club) and Moor Crag, both Gill Head, Windermere, Cumbria, 1898; The Orchard, Chorley Wood, Hertfordshire, 1900–1901, designed for himself, and the Homestead, Frinton-on-Sea, Essex, 1905. After the war Voysey was rarely called upon to do any architectural work.

D. Gebhard, *C.F.A.V. Architect*, Los Angeles 1975; J. Brandon-Jones, *C.F.A.V. Architect and Designer 1857–1941*, exh. cat., Brighton 1978; D. Simpson, *C.F.A.V. (1857–1941). An Architect of Individuality*, London 1979; S. Durant, *C.F.A.V.*, London 1992; W. Hitchmough, *C.F.A.V.*, London 1995.

**Vries**, Hans Vredeman de (1527–1606). Flemish painter who settled in Antwerp, and published fantastic ornamental pattern-books – *Architectura* (1565), *Compertimenta* (1566), *Hortorum viridariorumque elegantes et multiplicis formae* (1583), *Variae Architecturae Formae* (1601) – which had enormous influence on architecture all over northern Europe including England (e.g. SMYTHSON's Wollaton). His style lacks FLORIS's grace and wit but well represents the Flemish and Dutch contribution to MANNERISM and expresses the northern feeling for flat pattern in STRAPWORK or carved decoration of interlaced bands and forms similar to fretwork or cut leather. His designs for PARTERRES were widely followed, e.g. for the *Hortus Palatinus* at Heidelberg (1615–20).

Gerson and ter Kuile 1960.

**Vyse**. A spiral staircase or a staircase winding round a central column.

# W

**Wachsmann**, Konrad (1901–80). German architect and pioneer of INDUSTRIALIZED BUILDING, he was experimenting with standardized elements for prefabricated buildings by 1925 and after emigrating to the USA he developed his General Panel System with GROPIUS in the 1940s. In 1946 he launched his Mobilar Structures and in 1961 published *The Turning Point in Building. Structures and Design* (New York).

G. Herbert, *The Dream of the Factory Made House: Walter Gropius and K.W.*, Cambridge, Mass. 1985; Klotz 1986; T. Herzog *et al.*, *Vom Sinn des Detail. Zum Gesamtwerk von K.W.*, Cologne 1988.

**Wagner**, Martin (1885–1957), *see* TAUT, Bruno.

**Wagner**, Otto (1841–1918). Austrian architect who became professor at the Academy in Vienna in 1894, and delivered an inaugural address pleading for a new approach to architecture, for independence of the past, and for Rationalism ('Nothing that is not practical can be beautiful'). Before that time he had himself designed in the neo-Renaissance style. His most familiar achievement is some stations for the Vienna Stadtbahn (1894–1901), ART NOUVEAU with much exposed iron, though more restrained than Hector GUIMARD's contemporary ones for the Paris Métro. But his most amazingly modern and C20-looking job is the Post Office Savings Bank, Vienna (1904–6), the exterior faced with marble slabs held in place by aluminium bolts and the interior featuring a glass barrel vault realized with a clarity and economy hardly matched by anyone else at so early a date. Wagner had a decisive influence on the best younger architects of Vienna (*see* HOFFMANN, LOOS, OLBRICH) and outside Austria through his pupil and assistant Jan Koteřa (1871–1923) in Czechoslovakia and through his assistant Jože PLEČNIK in Prague and Ljubliana in the 1930s. Wagner's most monumental building, close to the style of the Secession, is the Steinhof Asylum chapel, Vienna (1906). He published *Moderne Architektur* (Vienna 1896; English translation by H. F. Mallgrave, Chicago 1989).

H. Geretsegger and M. Peifner, *O.W. 1841–1918*, London (1964) 1979; O. A. Graf, *O.W.*, Vienna 1985; I. B. Whyte, *O.W.*, Oxford 1985; P. Haiko (ed.), *Sketches, Projects and Executed Buildings by O.W.*, London 1987; G. Kolb, *O.W. und die Wiener Stadtbahn*, Vienna 1990; H. F. Mallgrave (ed.), *O.W. Reflections on the Raiment of Modernity*, Chicago/Malibu 1994.

**Wagon roof**, *see* ROOF.

**Wagon vault**, *see* VAULT.

**Wahlman**, Lars Israel (1870–1952), *see* SWEDISH ARCHITECTURE.

**Wailly**, Charles de (1730–98). Notable French architect trained under BLONDEL, SERVANDONI and at the French Academy in Rome (1754–6). His talent ranged from interiors of a somewhat theatrical opulence (salone of Palazzo Spinola, Genoa, 1772–3) to the austerity of his most celebrated building, the Odéon, Paris (1779–82), designed in collaboration with Marie-Joseph Peyre (1730–85). It was twice burnt but little altered in rebuilding (1807 and 1818). De Wailly's other works are no less remarkable, e.g. the Château de Montmusard near Dijon (1764–72, unfinished), the first *château* in France in which the influence of antiquity is preponderant, and various *hôtels* in Paris.

Gallet 1964; M. Mosser and D. Rabreau, *C. de W. 1730–1798: Peintre architecte dans l'Europe des lumières*, exh. cat., Paris 1979; Braham 1980.

**Wainscot**. The timber lining to walls. The term is also applied to the wooden panelling of PEWS.

**Walker**, Peter (b.1932). American landscape architect in partnership with SASAKI from 1957, collaborating with him at Foothills College, Los Altos, California (1957–60), Upjohn Company Headquarters, Kalamazoo, Michigan (1961), etc., and from 1975 to 1983 principal of the Sasaki Walker Associates design office, San Francisco, when he designed South Coast Plaza Town Center, Orange County, California. He was in partnership with M. SCHWARTZ (1983–92), when his work became more innovative, e.g. Tanner Fountain, Harvard University, Cambridge, Massachusetts (1985), and at Solana, a 344-hectare (850-acre) office park for IBM at Westlake/Southlake, Texas, where he embedded buildings by LEGORETTA in a combination of geometrically rigid spaces, informal plantations and wild prairie (1984–9). For ISOZAKI's Centre for Advanced Technology in the Harima Science Garden City, Hyogo, Japan, he designed a Zen-inspired garden (1993). His setting for JAHN's Kempinski Hotel at Munich airport (1994) has a slightly skewed geometrical parterre with topiary, metal pyramids for climbing plants and 5.5 m. (18 ft) high glass walls enclosing

shelves with pots of artificial (plastic) scarlet pelargoniums, a feature he repeated beside palm trees in the hotel atrium. With Melanie Simo he wrote *Invisible Gardens: The Search for Modernism in the American Landscape* (1994).

Lyall 1991; Cerver 1995; Weilacher 1996.

**Walker**, Ralph Thomas (1889–1973). American architect, notable for his powerful, fortress-like skyscrapers of the 1920s, sometimes with remarkable Art Deco interiors, e.g. the Barclay-Vesey Building (1923–6); the NY Telephone Company Building (1926); and the Irving Trust Building, Wall Street (1929), all in New York. Of his later buildings the Bell Telephone Laboratories (1937–49) should be mentioned.

Anon., *R.W. Architect*, New York 1957.

**Wall arcade**. A blind arcade.

**Wall-plate**, *see* ROOF.

**Wall rib**, *see* FORMERET.

**Wallace**, William (d.1631), *see* SCOTTISH ARCHITECTURE.

**Wallis, Gilbert & Partners**, *see* ART DECO; INDUSTRIAL ARCHITECTURE.

**Wallot**, Paul (1841–1912), *see* GERMAN ARCHITECTURE.

**Walsingham**, Alan of, *see* ALAN OF WALSINGHAM.

**Walter**, Thomas Ustick (1804–87). American architect of German descent, born in Philadelphia, where his father was a mason. He studied under STRICKLAND and started on his own in 1830. As early as 1833 he was commissioned to design Girard College, an ambitious, wholly peripteral (and thus functionally dubious) white marble building. In 1851 he began the completion of the Capitol in Washington: he added the wings, and the dominant dome on a cast-iron framing is his. He also completed MILLS's Treasury. Like nearly all the leading American architects, Walter was also capable of major engineering works – e.g. a breakwater he built in Venezuela (1843–5).

Hitchcock 1977; Whiffen and Koeper 1981.

**Walter of Canterbury** (*fl.c.*1322), *see* MICHAEL OF CANTERBURY.

**Walton**, George (1867–1933). Scottish architect and designer who anticipated MACKINTOSH to some extent. He moved to London from Glasgow in 1897, and designed shopfronts for Kodak throughout Europe, though The Leys, Elstree, England, is his most notable building.

K. Moon, *G.W. Designer and Architect*, London 1993.

**Warchavchik**, Gregori (1896–1972), *see* BRAZILIAN ARCHITECTURE.

**Ward**. The courtyard of a castle; also called a *bailey*.

**Ward**, William E. (1821–1900), *see* CONCRETE.

**Wardell**, William Wilkinson (1823–99), *see* AUSTRALIAN ARCHITECTURE.

**Ware**, Isaac (c.1717–66). English architect, a protégé of Lord BURLINGTON and a strict Palladian. His buildings are competent but uninspired, e.g. Chesterfield House, London (1749, destroyed), and Wrotham Park (*c.*1754). However, his *Complete Body of Architecture* (1756) was very influential and became a standard textbook.

Harris 1990; Summerson 1991; Colvin 1995.

**Ware**, Samuel (1781–1860), *see* SHOPPING ARCADE.

**Ware & van Brunt**. American architect William Robert Ware (1832–1915) took a Harvard BS degree and was then a pupil of HUNT. Henry van Brunt (1832–1903) also took a Harvard degree and was also a pupil of Hunt. The two were in partnership from 1863 to 1881. Ware created the first American school of architecture (1865) at the MIT and the second (1881) at Columbia. The educational system was influenced by the École des Beaux Arts in Paris. Both Ware and van Brunt started at Gothicists, inspired by RUSKIN. Their best Gothic churches are First Church, Boston (1865–7), St John, Cambridge, Massachusetts (1869–70), and – more original – Third Universalist, Cambridge (1875), and St Stephen Lynn, Massachusetts (1881). Ware often judged competitions and took a great interest in the affairs of the American Institute of Architects, whereas van Brunt was a brilliant architectural writer. He translated VIOLET-LE-DUC's *Entretiens* in 1875, and when Ware was commissioned to do internal alterations to the Harvard Library, he took his inspiration from LABROUSTE. Van Brunt moved to Kansas City in 1884. In his last phase he designed many railway stations. His Electricity Building at the Chicago Exhibition of 1893 is classical. His partner on this was Frank Howe.

Hitchcock 1977; Whiffen and Koeper 1981.

**Wastell**, John (d.*c.*1515). English mason who lived at Bury St Edmunds, Suffolk, and, though evidently highly appreciated, was not in the King's Works. He had probably started under and with Simon CLERK, and followed him both at the abbey of Bury and at King's College Chapel, Cambridge, where he appears from 1486 and was master mason throughout the years when the glorious fan VAULT was built and the chapel completed. The vault can therefore with some probability be considered his design, though the King's Masons, William VERTUE and Henry REDMAN, visited the building in 1507, 1509 and 1512. Wastell was also Cardinal Morton's mason and then the master mason of Canterbury Cathedral, where he was presumably the designer for Bell Harry, the crossing tower of the cathedral (built 1494–7). Other buildings have been attributed to him on stylistic grounds.

Harvey 1984.

**Watanabe**, Hitoshi (1887–1973), *see* JAPANESE ARCHITECTURE.

**Watanabe**, Toyokaza (b.1938), *see* JAPANESE ARCHITECTURE.

**Watelet**, Claude-Henri (1718–86). French painter, writer and landscape architect. He was a rich man (tax farmer), painted landscapes in the style of his friend François Boucher, and realized them in the park he laid out for himself, Le Moulin Joli, on the Seine near Paris (1754–72). It was much visited and admired until destroyed during the Revolution. He combined parterres and long straight radiating *allées* with irregular plantations of trees, winding walks and areas of wild plants. In his *Essai sur les jardins* (1774), which begins with a tribute to J. J. Rousseau, he advocated plans neither as rigid as French gardens nor as artificially natural as English parks, with pleasure grounds in which cultivated fields, barns, pigsties, duckponds, etc. should be disposed for aesthetic effect – true FERMES ORNÉES. Marie-Antoinette's notorious rustic village, the *hameau* at Versailles (1785), may owe something to his ideas.

**Waterhouse**, Alfred (1830–1905). English architect who started in practice at Manchester in 1856 and moved to London in 1865. In Manchester he won the competitions for the Assize Courts (1859) and Town Hall (1869–77), both excellently planned and externally in a free, picturesque Gothic which yet does not depart too far from symmetry. Soon after, his style hardened and assumed that odd character of sharp forms and harsh imperishable materials (terracotta, encaustic tiles, best red brick) which one connects with him. He remained a planner of great clarity and resourcefulness and used ironwork freely for structural purposes. But he was a Historicist all the same, happiest in a rigid matter-of-fact Gothic, but also going in for a kind of Romanesque (Natural History Museum, London 1873–81) and for French Renaissance (Caius College, Cambridge, 1868 onwards). Of his many buildings the following may be mentioned: some very interestingly planned Congregational churches (Lyndhurst Road, Hampstead, 1883; King's Weigh House Chapel, 1889–91); the headquarters of the Prudential Assurance in Holborn (1876 onwards); The City and Guilds Institute in Kensington (1881); St Paul's School (1881–4, demolished); the National Liberal Club (1884); and a number of country mansions (Hutton Hall, Yorkshire, 1865, enlargement of Eaton Hall, Cheshire, 1870–83, demolished 1961).

Hitchcock 1977; M. Girouard, *A.W. and the Natural History Museum*, New Haven and London 1980; C. Cunningham and R. P. Waterhouse, *A.W. (1830–1905). Biography of a Practice*, Cambridge 1992.

**Water-leaf.** A leaf shape used in later C12 CAPITALS. The water-leaf is broad, unribbed and tapering, curving out towards the angle of the ABACUS and turned in at the top. *See* Fig. 27.

**Water-table**, *see* OFF-SET.

**Water wall.** A curtain of falling water within a rectangular framework, a device used by late C20 landscape architects, especially for urban plazas in the USA. It was used notably by SITE for their 300 m. (975 ft) long Avenue 5 at the Seville Expo in 1992.

**Wattle and daub**. A method of wall construction consisting of branches or thin laths (wattles) roughly plastered over with mud or clay (daub), sometimes used as a filling between the vertical members of TIMBER-FRAMED houses.

**Wave moulding**. A compound moulding formed by a convex curve between two concave curves; typical of the Decorated style.

**Wayss**, Gustav Adolf (1850–1917), *see* CONCRETE.

**Wealden house**. A medieval TIMBER-FRAMED house of distinctive form. It is peculiar to England and found mainly in the south-east. It has a central open hall flanked by bays of two storeys. The end bays are JETTIED to the front but a single roof covers the whole building, thus producing an exceptionally wide overhang to the eaves in front of the hall. They are supported by diagonal, usually curved, braces starting from the short inner sides of the overhanging wings and rising parallel with the front wall of the hall towards the centre of the eaves.

**Weatherboarding**. Overlapping horizontal boards covering a TIMBER-FRAMED wall; the boards are wedge-shaped in section, the upper edge being the thinner.

**Weathering**. A sloping horizontal surface on sills, tops of buttresses, etc., to throw off water. *See* OFF-SET.

**Web**. A compartment or bay of a VAULT, between the ribs, also called a cell or *severy*.

**Webb**, Sir Aston (1849–1930). English architect, perhaps the most successful of the providers of large public buildings in suitable styles around 1900, together with his partner Edward Ingress Bell (1837–1914). His favourite style, especially earlier in his career, was a free François I. Later there are also buildings in the Imperial-Palladian of the years of Edward VII. Chief buildings: Law Courts, Birmingham (with Ingress Bell, 1886–91); Metropolitan Life Assurance, Moorgate, London (with Bell, 1890–93), one of his best; Victoria and Albert Museum, London (1891–1909); Royal Services Institute, Whitehall (with Bell, 1893–5); Christ's Hospital, Horsham, Sussex (with Bell, 1894–1904); Royal Naval College, Dartmouth (1899–1904); Royal College of Science, London (1900–1906); University, Birmingham (1900–1909), Byzantino-Italian; Imperial College, Kensington (1900–1906); Admiralty Arch, London (1908–9). His layout of the Mall, from his curving Admiralty Arch at one end to his refronted Buckingham Palace at the other (1901–14), epitomizes Edwardian architecture at its most Imperial.

Service 1977.

**Webb**, John (1611–72). English architect, pupil and nephew by marriage of Inigo JONES, whose right-hand man he appears to have been from the 1630s onwards. He was responsible for the reconstruction of the staterooms at Wilton in 1649 after a fire, including the famous double-cube room which was for long thought to be one of Jones's masterpieces. However, Webb's independent work mostly dates from after his master's death and much of it has been destroyed, e.g. Gunnersbury House, Middlesex (*c.*1658–63, demolished) and Amesbury House, Wiltshire (*c.*1600, rebuilt). The portico of the Vine (1654–6) and the King Charles block at Greenwich Palace (1664–9) survive. His reputation has been overshadowed, unjustly, by that of Jones.

J. Bold, *J.W.: Architectural Theory and Practice in the Seventeenth Century*, Oxford 1989; Summerson 1991; Colvin 1995; Mowl and Earnshaw 1995.

**Webb**, Philip Speakman (1831–1915). English architect who hardly ever designed anything but houses, all outstanding examples of the ARTS AND CRAFTS movement, of which he became the main theorist. Among the architects of the English Domestic Revival, he and Norman SHAW stand supreme: Shaw much more favoured, more inventive, more voluble, more widely influential; Webb harder, more of a thinker, totally deficient in any architectural bedside manner, and perhaps more deeply influential, even on Shaw himself. Webb chose his clients and never agreed to having a stable of assistants. His style is strangely ruthless: from the first he mixed elements from the Gothic and the C18, not for the fun or devilry of it, but because one should use the most suitable motifs regardless of their original contexts. He also liked to expose materials and show the workings of parts of a building. For Webb, LETHABY wrote, architecture was first of all a common tradition of honest building. Though he did not publish or exhibit he was very influential largely through his work for the SPAB (*see* MORRIS; RESTORATION). His buildings showed how traditional building crafts could be used inventively.

His first job was Red House (1859) for William Morris, whose closest friend he remained throughout. For Morris's firm he designed furniture of a rustic Stuart kind, and also table glass and metalwork. He also joined in the stained glass work. His principal town houses are No. 1 Palace Green (1868) and No. 19 Lincoln's Inn Fields (1868–9). Of his country houses Joldwyns, Surrey (1873), Smeaton

Manor, Yorkshire (1878), and Conyhurst, Surrey (1885), come nearest to Shaw in character – gabled, cheerful, with weatherboarding, tilehanging, and white window trim. Standen, East Grinstead, Sussex (1892–4), is best preserved. Clouds, Wiltshire (1876–91), is the largest and least easy to take, strong no doubt, but very astringent indeed, designed, as it were, in a take-it-or-leave-it mood. Webb's interiors from the later seventies onwards often have white panelling and exhibit a marked sympathy with the C18 vernacular. In 1901 he retired to a country cottage and ceased practising.

H. Lethaby, *P.W. and His Work*, Oxford 1935; S. Kirk, *P.W. (1831–1915). Domestic Architecture*, London 1985; O. Garnett, *Standen (Built by P.W. 1892–4)*, London 1993.

**Webbing**. The stone surface of a vault seen as infilling between the ribs.

**Weijer**, Christopher de (b.1956), *see* MECANOO.

**Weinbrenner**, Johann Jacob Friedrich (1766–1826). German architect born at Karlsruhe, visited Berlin (1790–92) and Rome (1792–7). His major achievement is the transformation of Karlsruhe into a neo-classical city, rather like a miniature version of St Petersburg. The Marktplatz (1804–24), with balancing but not identical buildings and a pyramid in the centre, and the circular Rondellplatz (1805–13), with the Markgräfliches Palais are masterpieces of neo-classical town planning. He also built a handsome circular Catholic church (1808–17).

D. B. Brownlee (ed.), *F.W. (1766–1826) Architect of Karlsruhe*, exh. cat., Philadelphia, Karlsruhe, Cambridge, Mass. 1986/7; C. Elbert, *Die Theater F.W. Bauten und Entwurfe*, Karlsruhe 1988; G. Leiber, *F.W., sein städtebauliche . . .*, Karlsruhe 1991.

**Wells**, Joseph Merrill (d.1890), *see* McKim.

**Wells Coates** (1895–1958), *see* Coates, Wells.

**Welsch**, Johann Maximilien von (1671–1745). German Baroque architect who preceded Johann Dientzenhofer at Schloss Pommersfelden, Hildebrandt and Neumann at the Residenz, Würzburg, and at Bruchsal. The abbey church at Amorbach (1742–7) was his last work.

J. Meintzschel, *Studien zu M. von W.*, Würzburg 1963.

**Werkbund**, *see* Deutscher Werkbund.

**Westwork**. The west end of a Carolingian or Romanesque church, consisting of a low entrance hall and above it a room open to the nave and usually flanked or surrounded by aisles and upper galleries. The whole is crowned by one broad tower, and there are occasionally stair turrets as well. In the main upper room stood an altar as a rule.

**Wheel window**, *see* rose window.

**Wheelhouse**. Prehistoric Scottish stone-built house, circular in plan with partition walls projecting inwards like the spokes of a wheel. They preceded and survived alongside the defensive brochs.

**White**, Stanford (1853–1906). American architect, a pupil of Richardson and from 1879 joined the McKim, Mead & White partnership. White became a rich *bon vivant*, a man who entertained sumptuously, and exuberant in other ways as well. He was a brilliant and effortless designer, his range stretching from magazine covers to a railway carriage, including Gordon Bennett's yacht, and houses more original than any by anyone anywhere at the time. The temerity of the Low House at Bristol, Rhode Island (1887, demolished), with its enormous spreading pitched roof, is almost beyond belief. For other buildings *see* McKim, Mead & White. White was shot dead at the opening night of a musical farce at the dinner theatre on the roof of the old Madison Square Garden.

L. M. Roth, *McKim, Mead & W. Architects*, London 1978; L. Wodehouse, *W. of McKim Mead & W.*, London and New York 1988; P. Baker White, *Stanny. The Gilded Life of S.W.*, New York 1989; S. Lessard, *The Architect of Desire: Beauty and Danger in the S.W. Family*, London 1997.

**White**, Stanley (1891–1979). American landscape architect who worked under Steele and then Olmsted but is notable mainly as a charismatic teacher at Illinois University, where his pupils included Sasaki and P. Walker.

**Whitwell**, Thomas Stedman (1784–1844), *see* urban design.

**Widow's walk**. A railed rooftop gallery, usually on a coastal dwelling for the observation of vessels at sea, notably on the east coast of the USA.

**Wiener Werkstatte**. A craft studio founded in Vienna in 1903 by Joseph Hoffmann, based on the William Morris conviction of the importance of a unity between architecture and the crafts. It survived until 1932.

W. J. Schweiger, *W.W. Design in Vienna 1903–1932*, London 1984; G. Fahr-Becker, *W.W.*, Cologne 1995.

**Wigwam**, *see* tent.

**Wilkins**, William (1778–1839). English architect, son of a Norwich architect, was educated at Caius College, Cambridge, where he was elected Fellow in 1802. He travelled in Greece, Asia Minor and Italy (1801–4) and published *Antiquities of Magna Graecia* (1807) on his return. He pioneered the Greek Revival in England with his designs for Downing

College, Cambridge (begun 1806), Haileybury College (1806–9), and the temple-style country house Grange Park (1809), with its Theseum peristyle and other rather pedantically Athenian references. In fact, he was rather priggish and doctrinaire, and his rival SMIRKE had little difficulty in overtaking his lead in the movement. But Downing College is important historically as the first of all university CAMPUSES – separate buildings round a park-like expanse of lawn – preceding JEFFERSON's Charlottesville. His other university buildings in Cambridge were neo-Gothic, e.g. New Court, Trinity (1821–3), and the screen and hall-range at King's (1824–8). He had greater opportunities in London to develop his neo-Greek style but muffed them – University College (1827–8), St George's Hospital (1828–9), and finally the National Gallery (1834–8), which ruined his reputation. Only the main block of University College is his, and though the portico itself is very imposing he seems to have been unable to unite it satisfactorily with the rest of the composition. This inability to subordinate the parts to the whole resulted at the National Gallery in a patchy façade unworthy of its important site.

R. W. Liscombe, *W.W. 1778–1839*, Cambridge 1980; Colvin 1995.

**Willard**, Salomon (1783–1861). Massachusetts architect. First a carpenter and as such in 1808 built the ingenious spiral staircase in the Exchange Coffee House in Boston. He was also busy as a carver in wood (e.g. ships' figureheads) and stone. However, he moved into architecture – e.g. the Bunker Hill Monument, mostly by him (1825–42), the Doric United States Bank in Boston (1824–6), two County Court Houses at Boston (Suffolk County) and Dedham (Norfolk County) and the Town Hall at Quincy (1844).

Whiffen and Koeper 1981.

**William of Ramsey** (d.1349). A member of a family of English masons who worked in Norwich and London from about 1300 onwards, William appears first in 1325 as a mason working on St Stephen's Chapel in the Palace of Westminster (*see* MICHAEL OF CANTERBURY). In 1332 he became master mason of the new work at St Paul's Cathedral, which meant the chapterhouse and its cloister. In 1336 he was appointed Master Mason to the King's castles south of Trent, which included the Palace of Westminster and St Stephen's Chapel. William was also commissioned in 1337 to give his *sanum consilium* on Lichfield Cathedral. In the early thirties he may have been master mason to Norwich Cathedral also: the cloister there was taken over by one William of Ramsey from John of Ramsey, probably his father, who was already master mason to the cathedral in 1304. William was evidently an important man, and what we know from an old illustration and surviving fragments of the chapterhouse of St Paul's indicates that the creation of the Perpendicular style was due to him, or at least that he made a style out of elements evolved in London and especially at St Stephen's Chapel in the decade preceding 1330.

Harvey 1984.

**William of Sens** (d.*c*.1180). Designer and master mason of the chancel of Canterbury Cathedral, rebuilt after a fire had destroyed it in 1174. He was a Frenchman (or else his successor would not have been known as William the Englishman) and came from Sens Cathedral, which was begun *c*.1140 and which contained features repeated at Canterbury (also in the Englishman's work, no doubt on the strength of drawings left in the lodge by William of Sens). He was, however, also familiar with more recent French work, notably Notre Dame in Paris (begun 1163), St Rémi at Reims, Soissons, and buildings in the north-west such as Valenciennes. William, as a true master mason of the Gothic Age (*see also* VILLARD DE HONNECOURT), was familiar with wood as well as stone and with devices to load stone on to ships. He had been chosen at Canterbury from a number of English and French masons assembled for consultation on action to be taken after the fire.

Webb 1965.

**William of Wynford** (d.*c.*1405–10). English mason who was made master mason of Wells Cathedral in 1365, after having worked at Windsor Castle, where William of Wykeham (later bishop of Winchester and Chancellor of England) was then clerk of the works. Wynford remained in the royal service and in 1372 received a pension for life. He also remained William of Wykeham's protégé, and worked for him at Winchester College and from 1394 at Winchester Cathedral, where he probably designed the new nave and west front. New College, Oxford, has also been attributed to him. He was obviously a much appreciated man; he dined with William of Wykeham, at the high table of Winchester College, and at the prior's table at the cathedral, and received a furred robe once a year from the cathedral. On several occasions he appeared, no doubt for consultations, together with YEVELE.

Harvey 1984.

**Williams**, E. A. (b.1914), *see* ECKBO, Garrett.

**Williams**, Owen (1890–1969). English architect notable for his early use structurally of reinforced concrete with overall glazing. His two Boots factories at Beeston, Nottinghamshire (1930–32 and 1935–8), were his outstanding works, though his Daily Express Building, Fleet Street, London (1931–3), is striking with its opaque black glass cladding, which he repeated at his Daily Express Building, Glasgow (1937). His Empire Pool, Wembley, London (1933–4), should also be mentioned.

D. Cottam, *Sir O.W. 1890–1969*, London 1986.

**Wilson**, Colin St John (b.1922). English architect trained in Cambridge, where he later taught and practised with MARTIN, under whom he worked in the LCC office from 1950 onwards. These were the years of the remarkable Roehampton housing estates, combining Swedish modernism with LE CORBUSIER's *ville radieuse*. From 1956 he was in partnership with Martin at Cambridge, where their new court for Gonville and Caius College (1960–62) was notable, as was their Manor Road Library, Oxford (1961–4). The first project for a British Library dates from these years also. Further designs by Wilson followed from 1970–75 onwards but construction did not begin on the Euston Road, London, site until 1982. The great brick-clad building was completed only in 1996, a monument to its architect's single-minded tenacity and to his belief in architecture's social/humanitarian role – to provide an image of wholeness and of structure in the environment and thereby make its users feel more at home in the world.

K. Frampton *et al.*, *C. St J.W.*, London 1997.

**Wilson**, William Hardy (1881–1955), *see* COLONIAL REVIVAL.

**Wind-brace**, *see* ROOF.

**Wind scoop**. A feature of C16–19 Persian domestic architecture consisting of a tower-like funnel which carries air down into a building, often to an underground cellar with water-tanks for cooling, and thence upwards into the living quarters.

Notable examples survive at Yazd and elsewhere.

**Winde**, William (d.1722). English architect, born in Holland, the son of a Royalist exile. He followed GERBIER as architect of Hampstead Marshall (1662–88), of which only the gate piers survive, and became, with PRATT and MAY, a leader of the Anglo-Dutch school. His Buckingham House, London (1705, destroyed), with its unpedimented attic storey, forebuildings and quadrant colonnades, was very influential. None of his buildings survives unless Belton House, Lincolnshire (1685–8), is his.

Summerson 1991; Colvin 1995.

**Winder**, *see* STAIR.

**Winding stair**, *see* STAIR.

**Window**. 1. An opening made in a wall to light or ventilate an enclosed space. Early windows, from considerations of security and architectural stability, were little more than incisions in the wall. Their SILLS and the REVEAL of the JAMBS might be SPLAYED to increase the flow of light. They became much larger in Roman times, when glazing was introduced (by AD 65 according to Seneca). The spread of glazing and developments in skeletal vaulting in the Middle Ages both made larger windows possible. These would be divided into LIGHTS by MULLIONS (and later horizontally divided by TRANSOMS), whose heads in Gothic architecture were elaborated into steadily more complex TRACERY. Gothic windows are usually protected externally by a HOOD-MOULD, and the reveals may be enriched by colonnettes and MOULDINGS. In classical architecture a window may be framed externally by a simple ARCHITRAVE, with or without a crowning ENTABLATURE or PEDIMENT, or it may be more richly set in an AEDICULE.

2. *Window* is also used to refer to the glass held in wood or metal frames within the opening. Such frames, with QUARRIES of glass held in lead CAMES braced by SADDLE BARS, were originally hinged when required to open inwards or outwards – the CASEMENT WINDOW. When larger panes of *crown glass* became available in the C17, these were incorporated in wooden SASH WINDOWS sliding up and down one in front of the other. These were at first held in place by pegs, and then (the *'double-hung' sash*) by cords with counter-balancing weights inside the jambs. These were invented in Holland in the 1680s, and on their introduction to England (first recorded as replacements in the Banqueting House, Whitehall, in 1685) they rapidly replaced casements in all but the smallest houses. In the course of the C18 the *glazing bars* became slenderer and the panes of glass larger, but only in the C19 did the ready availability of large panes of *sheet glass* allow the abandonment of glazing bars, and thus a delicate relationship between the proportions of the glazing and those of the building as a whole.

The need for light in the factories and ever more mammoth office blocks of the C19 and C20 has made windows steadily more prominent in relation to the wall. (Repeal of the excise duty on glass in England was in 1845, and of the window tax in 1851.) The development of SKELETON CONSTRUCTION, together with more efficient heating systems and the invention of air-conditioning, have removed the traditional constraints upon this process; and much of modern architecture can be seen as the acceptance, followed by the aesthetic exploitation, of the new relationship of the window to the *skeleton frame*. Modern buildings employ metal-frame windows which, where they open at all, are usually sliding, or of the side and vertical *pivot-hung* type.

*Double-glazing* is becoming common.

Special types of window include: *bay*, *bow* and *oriel windows*, which are all forms of projection from a house front containing fenestration. *Oriel windows* generally project from an upper storey (though not necessarily, viz. college halls), supported on some form of CORBELLING or BRACKET. *Bay windows* are canted projections rising from the ground; *bow windows* are rounded projections, often only of the window frame itself. *Biforate windows*, common in Italian medieval architecture and called *bifore*, are divided vertically by a column to form two separate arched openings. *French windows* are, as the French name (*croisée*) for them suggests, casement windows carried down to the floor so as to open like doors. They made their appearance at Versailles in the 1680s. *Dormer windows* are windows placed vertically in a sloping roof with a roof of their own. The name derives from the fact that they usually lighted sleeping quarters. For the *Palladian* or *Venetian window*, *see* SERLIANA. The *Diocletian* or *thermal window*, whose use was revived by PALLADIO himself and became another feature of PALLADIANISM, is a semicircular window divided into three lights by two vertical mullions. It derives its name from its use in the THERMAE of Diocletian at Rome. *Picture window* is a name often used to describe a large window in a house, containing a single uninterrupted pane of glass. A *Wyatt window* has three lights recessed under a segmental relieving arch. *See also* CHICAGO WINDOW; FANLIGHT; GLASS; LANCET; LATTICE; LOW-SIDE; ŒIL-DE-BŒUF; SKYLIGHT. [A. Laing]

**Wines**, James (b.1932), *see* SITE.

**Wise**, Henry (1653−1738). An enterprising English nurseryman, in partnership with George London (*c*.1640−1713), with whom he laid out gardens in the French style, all subsequently destroyed apart from that at Melbourne Hall, Derbyshire, with its parterre, *allées*, geometrically designed pools, bosquets and much statuary (1704−6). The Privy Garden they made for William III at Hampton Court, London (probably after a design by MAROT), is now being recreated. Their apprentices included, however, two of the initiators of the English style of LANDSCAPE GARDENING, BRIDGEMAN and SWITZER.

D. Green, *Gardener to Queen Anne. H.W. and the Formal Garden*, London 1956.

**Wit** or **Witte**, Peter de, *see* CANDID.

**Wohlmut** **(Wolmuet)**, Bonifaz (d.1579), *see* CZECH ARCHITECTURE.

**Wolff**, Jacob, the elder (*c*.1546−1612). German master mason to the city of Nuremberg. His most notable work was the *überherrliche* (super-magnificent) house which he and Peter Carl built for Martin Peller in Nuremberg (1602−7, destroyed in the Second World War but partially rebuilt). Martin Peller had been a consul in Venice and the Pellerhaus is a curious compromise between Venetian and German taste, its three heavily rusticated storeys being crowned with a rich three-storey German gable. On the Marienberg, above Würzburg, he connected the wings of the existing castle to make a vast elongated rectangular court (1600−1607) very sparingly decorated. His son Jacob Wolff the younger (1571−1620) travelled and studied in Italy and brought back a more highly developed Italian Renaissance style which he used in a striking manner in his additions to the Nuremberg Town Hall (1616−22, destroyed in the Second World War but rebuilt).

Hempel 1965; Hitchcock 1981.

**Wood**, *see* TIMBER.

**Wood**, John, the elder (1704–54). English architect and urban designer, a competent exponent of PALLADIANISM (e.g. Prior Park near Bath, 1735–48), and the author of the eccentric *The Origin of Building* (1741), revolutionized town planning with his scheme for Bath (1727), unfortunately only partly executed. He began with Queen Square (1729–36), treating the north side as a palace front with a rusticated ground floor and attached central pediment. (This had recently been attempted in Grosvenor Square, London, c.1730, by Edward Shepheard (d.1747) but only partially realized.) Entirely original was the Circus (1754), a circular space with three streets radiating out of it; the elevations have superimposed orders so that it looks like the Colosseum turned outside in. He intended to follow the Circus with a Forum, of which North and South Parades are fragments, and an enormous Gymnasium (unexecuted), and thus make Bath once more into a Roman city. He died soon after placing the first stone of the Circus, but his work was carried on by his son John Wood the younger (1728–81), who took it a step further towards open planning with his Royal Crescent (1767–75), the first of its kind and an artistic conception of great originality and magnificence. It has been widely copied ever since (*see* CRESCENT), though usually without emulating the most original feature of Wood's plan, i.e. its facing what appears to be unlimited open parkland, trees being planted to conceal the city beyond. His other buildings – e.g. the Assembly Rooms (1769–71) and Hot Baths (1773–8) – are excellent late examples of Palladianism.

T. Mowl and B. Earnshaw, *J.W. Architect of Obsession*, Bath 1988; Harris 1990; Summerson 1991; Colvin 1995.

**Woods**, Shadrach (1923–73), *see* CANDILIS, Georges.

**Woodward**, Benjamin (1815–61). Irish architect associated with Sir Thomas Deane (1792–1871), knighted as mayor of Cork. They built Queen's College, Cork, in 1846–8 and the New Library and Museum, Trinity College, Dublin, in 1853–7, the latter with Venetian Gothic detailing. Their best-known building followed in 1855–60, the University Museum, Oxford, in which Ruskin took a close interest despite its skeletal glass and iron structure only slightly later in date than LABROUSTE's Ste Geneviève Library, Paris. Their Crown Life Office, New Bridge Street, London (1855–7), is notable for its arcaded façade.

T. Garnham, *Oxford Museum. Deane and Woodward*, London 1992.

**Wotton**, Sir Henry (1563–1639). English diplomat and author of *The Elements of Architecture* (1624), for long the classic statement in English of architectural fundamentals, recognizing the architect's philosophical status, independent of the artisan. It influenced PRATT, Inigo JONES and the English Palladians. Wotton had been ambassador in Venice between 1604 and 1624, collected Palladio's drawings and knew his patron Daniele Barbaro.

Harris 1990.

**Wren**, Sir Christopher (1632–1723). The greatest English architect. His father was Dean of Windsor and his uncle Bishop of Ely, both pillars of the High Church. He was educated at Westminster School and at fifteen became a demonstrator in anatomy at the College of Surgeons; then he went up to Oxford. Experimental science was just then coming to the fore, and he found himself in company with a group of brilliant young men who were later to found the Royal Society. He was entirely engrossed in scientific studies. Evelyn called him 'that miracle of a youth' and Newton thought him one of the best geometricians of the day. In 1657 he was made Professor of Astronomy in London, in 1661 in Oxford; but two years later his career took a different turn with his appointment to the commission for the restoration of St Paul's. After the Great Fire of London he was appointed one of the Surveyors under the Rebuilding Act (1667) and in 1669 became Surveyor General of the King's Works. Then he resigned his Oxford professorship and was knighted (1673). He was twice MP (1685–7 and 1701–2) and, despite his Tory connections, survived the Whig revolution of 1688, but on the accession of George I in 1714, he lost his office. He was twice married, first to a daughter of Sir John Coghill, and secondly to a daughter of Lord Fitzwilliam of Lifford. He died aged ninety-one having, as he wrote, 'worn out (by God's Mercy) a long life in the Royal Service and having made some figure in the world'.

If Wren had died at thirty he would have been remembered only as a figure in the history of English science. His first buildings, the Sheldonian Theatre, Oxford (1664–9), and Pembroke College Chapel, Cambridge (1663–5), are the work of a brilliant amateur though the trussed roof of the Sheldonian already displays his structural ingenuity. In 1665–6 he spent eight or nine months studying French architecture, mainly in Paris, and may well have visited Flanders and Holland as well. He met BERNINI in Paris, but learnt more from MANSART and LE VAU, whom he probably knew and whose works he certainly studied. French and Dutch architecture were to provide the main influences on his own style. The Fire of London in 1666 gave him his great opportunity. Though his utopian city plan was rejected, every facet of his empirical genius found scope for expression in the rebuilding of St Paul's and the fifty-one city churches. The latter

especially revealed his freshness of mind, his bounding invention and his adventurous empiricism. There were, of course, no precedents in England for classical churches except in the work of Inigo JONES. Wren's city churches were built between 1670 and 1686, nearly thirty being under construction in the peak year of 1677. Plans are extremely varied and often daringly original, e.g. St Stephen, Walbrook (1672–9), which foreshadows St Paul's, and St Peter's, Cornhill (1675–81), in which his two-storeyed gallery church with vaulted nave and aisles was first adumbrated. This type was later perfected at St Clement Danes (begun 1680) and St James's, Piccadilly (1676–84). But his originality and fertility of invention are best seen in the steeples, which range from the neo-Gothic of St Dunstan in the East to the Borrominesque fantasy of St Vedast and St Bride.

More scholarly and refined in detail than his sometimes rather hastily conceived and crudely executed city churches is his masterpiece, St Paul's Cathedral. Nothing like it had ever before been seen in England. It was a triumph of intellectual self-reliance, and the dome is one of the most majestic and reposeful in the world, purely classical in style. Baroque influences are evident elsewhere in the building, notably in the towers, the main façade, and such illusionist features as the sharm-perspective window niches and the false upper storey in the side elevations to conceal the nave buttresses. The interior is ostensibly classical, but contains many Baroque gestures. It was begun in 1675, and Wren lived to see it finished in 1709.

His secular buildings range from the austere Doric barracks at Chelsea Hospital (1682–92) to the grandest and most Baroque of all his works, Greenwich Hospital (1696 onwards), where the Painted Hall (1698) is the finest room of its kind in England. Of his vast and elaborate additions and alterations to Whitehall Palace, Winchester Palace and Hampton Court only a fragment of the latter survives (and this was probably revised and altered by his assistant William TALMAN). Like nearly all his work, these great schemes were carried out for the Office of Works. (The question of his delegation of designs to assistants and associates, notably to Robert HOOKE, is controversial.) Of his few independent commissions the best are Trinity College Library, Cambridge (1676–84), and Tom Tower, Christ Church, Oxford (1681–2). Apart from Marlborough House, London (1709–10, now much altered), no town or country house can be certainly attributed to him, though his name has been optimistically given to many, e.g. Winslow Hall, Buckinghamshire. HAWKSMOOR was his only pupil of note, but he had a wide and profound influence through his long reign at the Office of Works.

E. F. Sekler, *W. and His Place in European Architecture*, London 1956; K. Downes, *The Architecture of W.*, London 1982; Summerson 1991; Colvin 1995.

**Wright**, Frank Lloyd (1869–1959). The greatest American architect to date, a generation younger than LE CORBUSIER and MIES VAN DER ROHE. His œuvre ranges over more than sixty years and is never repetitive, routine or derivative. He first worked with Joseph Lyman Silsbee (1848–1913), a SHINGLE STYLE architect, then with SULLIVAN, whom he never ceased to admire, and was responsible for much of his master's domestic work until 1893. In 1894 he helped found the Chicago ARTS AND CRAFTS Society. The first type of building he developed as an independent architect is what he called the PRAIRIE house – low, spreading, with rooms running into each other,

terraces merging with the gardens, and roofs far projecting. Houses of this type are located in the outer suburbs of Chicago (Oak Park, Riverside, etc.). The development was extremely consistent, ending up with designs more daringly novel than any other architect's in the same field. The series was heralded by houses before 1900 (notably his own house and studio, Oak Park, Illinois, 1889–1909) and was complete by about 1905 (e.g. Darwin D. Martin House, Buffalo, NY, 1904); its climax is the Robie House, Chicago (1908). Concurrently he had done one church, Unity Temple, Oak Park (1905–6), and one office building, Larkin Building, Buffalo (1904, demolished 1950) – both with the same stylistic elements and the same freshness of approach as the private houses. The Larkin Building might well be called the most original office building of its date anywhere.

Some bigger jobs came along about the time of the First World War: Midway Gardens, Chicago (1913, demolished), a lavish and short-lived entertainment establishment, and the no longer surviving Imperial Hotel at Tokyo (1916–23, demolished 1965, partially reconstructed 1980 in the Meiji-mura Village Museum, Inuyama, Japan). His assistant here, Antonin RAYMOND, then settled in Japan. Both these buildings were very heavily decorated, and the elements of this decoration, polygonal and sharp-angled forms, are entirely Wright's, favoured by him from the very beginning, but less in evidence in the prairie houses, at least externally. The houses of the twenties introduced a new technique which allowed Wright to use surface decoration on the outside as well: precast concrete blocks. A remarkable series of Californian houses followed, heralded by the Barnsdall House (Hollyhock House), Los Angeles (1921), where the walls were battered inward like a Mayan pyramid. The Mrs G. M. Millard House, Pasadena (1923), broke away from the long-low Prairie Style with a tall, vertical house of compact plan, built of concrete blocks cast with geometrical patterns, sometimes pierced to introduce light and an element of openness and airiness. Steel rods knit the whole building together. The Storer House, Hollywood (1923), was his second experiment in this so-called 'knit-block' construction with Aztec imagery, followed by the large Mexican-fortress-like Ennis House, Los Angeles (1924).

In fact, from then onwards, Wright went more and more his own way, and it is very rare for his work to run parallel to international developments and conventions. One exception is Falling Water, Bear Run, Pennsylvania (1937–9), which is closer to the so-called INTERNATIONAL MODERN of Europe (and by then of America) than anything else Wright designed. His own work which, about 1914–17, influenced GROPIUS as well as the Dutch DE STIJL group is not represented in Europe at all, as his harmless little Memorial Hostel for Venice was prevented from being executed. In his auto-biography Wright tells of many such calamities, but as a writer he was biased and monotonously convinced that he was always right and blameless. This attitude seems to have distinguished his Taliesin Community in Wisconsin from the frater-nity ideals of RUSKIN: it was more of a master-and-disciples than a guild relation-ship. Wright built at Taliesin three times (1911, 1914, and 1925 onwards), and then added a Taliesin Winter Camp at Scottsdale, Arizona (1927 onwards), emi-nently fantastical and very exciting.

These years were also marked by his urban project, Broadacre City (1931–5), a decentralized automobile-oriented segment of rural America rather than a city (see URBAN DESIGN) – and his lower-

middle income residential schemes, not-ably the Usonian (United Statesian) house. This was a simplified development of his prairie house, first realized at the Hoult House, Wichita, Kansas (1935). With the Jacobs House, Madison, Wis-consin (1937) he introduced standardiz-ation to simplify design and construction. Examples built 1947–50 survive at Mount Pleasant, NY, and illustrate the openness and variety he could achieve on a small budget.

World-wide recognition came late to Wright, and only in his last twenty years or so, that is from the time when he was nearly seventy, did large commissions come his way fairly evenly. The first was the Johnson Wax Factory at Racine, Wis-consin (1936–9). Here he built an office block with walls of brick and glass tubes, and an interior with reinforced concrete mushroom columns (see MAILLART). The laboratory tower was added in 1949. The chapel of Florida Southern College dates from 1940, the Unitarian Church at Madison from 1947, the design for the Guggenheim Museum in New York from 1942 (completed 1960), the H. C. Price Tower, Bartlesville, Oklahoma (1956), and the posthumously completed Marin County Civic Center, San Rafael, California (1958–72). The museum, designed as a spiral ramp on a circular plan, is functionally indefensible but formally certainly startling, the masterpiece of the 'Organic Architecture' about which he had first written in 1910 though his Organic Architecture: the Architecture of Democracy was published in 1939. The skyscraper and the two ecclesiastical buildings display Wright's inborn passion for sharp angles more radically than any of his earlier buildings, and it is interesting to observe that the later turn of architec-ture towards aggressive sharp angles (see BREUER; Eero SAARINEN) gave this pre-1900 passion of Wright's new topicality.

He lived through three phases of free decorative play in international architecture: the Arts and Crafts, Expressionism, and the most recent anti-rationalism.

Wright's writings on architecture have been collected and edited by F. Gutheim as *F.L.W. on Architecture: Selected Writings 1894–1940* (New York 1941) and as *In the Cause of Architecture: Essays by F.L.W. for the Architectural Review 1908–1952* (New York 1975).

N. K. Smith, *F.L.W. a Study in Architectural Context*, Englewood Cliffs, NJ 1966; R. C. Twombly, *F.L.W. His Life and Architecture*, New York 1979; W. A. Storrer, *The Architecture of F.L.W. A Complete Catalogue*, Cambridge, Mass., and London (1974) 1982; B. Gill, *Many Masks. A Life of F.L.W.*, New York 1988; C. Bolon, R. Nelson and L. Seidel (eds.), *The Nature of F.L.W.*, Chicago 1988; N. Levine, *The Architecture of F.L.W.*, Princeton 1996.

**Wright**, Henry (1878–1936), *see* RADBURN PLANNING.

**Wu**, Liang yong (b.1922), *see* CHINESE ARCHITECTURE.

**Wurster**, William Wilson (1895–1973). American architect, trained at Berkeley, California. He worked in San Francisco from 1926 onwards and pioneered American regionalism, notably of the Bay Area school, combining early local Hispanic and Yankee influences with modern materials and techniques, e.g. his Gregero Farmhouse, Santa Cruz (1927), Butler House, Pasatiempo (1934–6), and Cowell College, University of California, Santa Cruz (1965). His Valencia Public Housing, San Francisco (1939–43), and renovation and remodelling of Ghirardelli Square, San Francisco (1961–3) – both with HALPRIN – were also notable.

M. Treib, *An Everyday Modernism. The Houses of W.W.*, San Francisco 1995.

**Wyatt**, Benjamin Dean (1775–c.1855). English architect, son of James WYATT. He was notable for his lavish Louis XV interiors at Lancaster House, London (1825, begun by SMIRKE 1820) and Apsley House, London (1828). He also designed Drury Lane Theatre (1811, present portico later) and the Duke of York's Column (1831–4), both in London.

J. M. Robinson, *The W.s. An Architectural Dynasty*, London 1979; Colvin 1995.

**Wyatt**, James (1746–1813). English architect, the most successful of his day, rivalled the ADAM brothers and even overshadowed CHAMBERS, whom he succeeded as Surveyor-General in 1796. But his brilliance was superficial, and his reputation now rests mainly on his neo-Gothic extravaganzas, though the best of these have been destroyed. The son of a Staffordshire timber-merchant and builder, he went to Italy in 1762. He was in Venice for two years studying under the painter-architect Visentini, then in Rome. He leapt to fame on his return to London in about 1768 with the Pantheon in Regent Street (1772, now destroyed), an astonishing neo-classical version of Hagia Sophia in Constantinople. He was inundated with commissions from then onwards, despite his outrageously bad manners to clients and his general unreliability. His classical houses, smooth and elegant, include Heaton Hall, Manchester (1772), Heveningham, Suffolk (interior c.1780–84), Castle Coole, Northern Ireland (1790–97), and Dodington, Gloucestershire (1798–1813), the latter very solemn and severe. Sober but more genial is his library at Oriel College, Oxford (1780). His neo-Gothic work ranges from the exquisite miniature Lee Priory (1785–90, destroyed, but one room survives in the Victoria and Albert Museum) to the fabulous Fonthill Abbey (1796–1812, destroyed) for William

Beckford and the almost equally extravagant Ashridge, Hertfordshire (1808–13). His numerous and ruthless RESTORATIONS and 'improvements' to Gothic buildings include work at Salisbury, Durham and Hereford Cathedrals, and earned him the name of 'Wyatt the Destroyer'.

J. M. Robinson, *The W.s. An Architectural Dynasty*, London 1979; Summerson 1991; Colvin 1995.

**Wyatt**, Sir Matthew Digby (1820–77), *see* WYATT, Thomas Henry.

**Wyatt**, Samuel (1737–1807). English architect, the elder brother of James WYATT. He began under Robert ADAM at Kedleston in 1759 and later worked with his brother on the Pantheon in London. His country houses are austere versions of his brother's – e.g. Doddington Hall, Cheshire (1777–98). He is notable for his structural innovations. His Albion Mills, London (1783–6), was founded on a structural raft and he was experimenting with cast-iron construction in the 1780s, taking out a patent in 1800 for building cast-iron bridges, warehouses, etc. Trinity House, Tower Hill, London (1792–4), with its robust Ionic façade, is outstanding.

J. M. Robinson, *The W.s. An Architectural Dynasty*, London 1979; Colvin 1995.

**Wyatt**, Thomas Henry (1807–80). English architect. Neither he nor his brother Sir Matthew Digby (1820–77), was related to James WYATT. Thomas Henry's *chef-d'œuvre* is Wilton Church, Wiltshire (1842–3), in an Early-Christian-Italian-Romanesque manner; it is perhaps the finest example of that style of the 1840s, rarer in England than in Germany. He also designed many Gothic churches (for a time in partnership with

David Brandon). Sir Matthew Digby Wyatt belonged to the circle of Henry Cole and Owen Jones, who were responsible for much of the work on the Exhibition of 1851; Wyatt himself was Secretary of the Executive Committee. He was a poor architect (*see* the architectural parts of Paddington Station, 1854–5), but an extremely intelligent and far-seeing architectural journalist, a believer in the new materials of his century and the possibilities of machine production.

Hitchcock 1954; Pevsner 1972.

**Wyatt window**, *see* WINDOW.

**Wyatville**, Sir Jeffry (1766–1840). English architect, the nephew of James WYATT, under whom he trained and whose work at Ashridge he completed in 1817 (adding the north entrance, east wing and stables). Although a competent classical architect (e.g. his entrance hall and stable court at Longleat, 1806–13), he specialized in neo-Gothic and 'Tudor collegiate' mansions. His masterpiece is Windsor Castle, which he 'restored' for George IV between 1824 and 1837, giving it a picturesque silhouette by raising the Round Tower 10 m. (33 ft) to make it a dominant feature around which to group his newly battlemented and machicolated towers. He added the George IV Gateway and Lancaster Tower and rebuilt the Chester and Brunswick Towers. His Waterloo Gallery and new royal apartments are still in use. He changed his name to Wyatville when he began work at the Castle and was knighted in 1828,

D. Linstrum, *Sir J.W.*, Oxford 1972; J. M. Robinson, *The W.s. An Architectural Dynasty*, London 1979; Colvin 1995.

**Wynford** (d.c.1405–10), *see* WILLIAM OF WYNFORD.

# X

**Xystus**. In a church, an AMBULATORY. In Greek architecture, a long portico used for athletic contests; in Roman architecture, a long covered or open walk bordered by colonnades or trees.

# Y

**Yagi**, Koji (b.1944), *see* JAPANESE ARCHITECTURE.

**Yamamoto**, Riken (b.1945). Japanese architect trained in Tokyo, notable for his light and airy, semi-transparent, small-scale residential buildings with eccentric roof construction, e.g. Rotunda Building, Yokohama (1987), Hamlet Residential Complex, Tokyo (1988) and the low-cost Hotakubo Public Housing (KAP), Kumamoto (1991), innovative both as apartment units and in their assembly into an urban composition. His Ryokuen-toshi Inter-junction City, Yokohama (1992–4), succeeds in recreating in galvanized steel and painted metal something of the easy indoors-outdoors unpredictable quality of a traditional Asian townscape.

**Yamasaki**, Minoru (1912–86). Born in Seattle, USA, he trained there and in New York. The St Louis Airport (1953–5), designed with Hellmut and Leinweber, made him famous. Its crossing concrete vaults are eminently impressive. Later buildings tended to be playful and weak: American Concrete Institute, Detroit, Michigan (1958); the Pruitt-Igoe public housing, St Louis, Missouri (1958, demolished 1972); Reynolds Metals Building, Detroit (1959); Conference Center and Education Building, Wayne State University, Detroit (1958 and 1961); Michigan Consolidated Gas Company, Detroit (1962); School of Music, Oberlin College, Ohio (1964). But his twin-towered World Trade Center, New York, 1970–74, is a land-mark. He published *A Life in Architecture* (New York 1979).

**Ybl**, Miklos Nikolaus (1814–91), *see* HUNGARIAN ARCHITECTURE.

**Yevele**, Henry (*c.*1320/30–*c.*1400). English architect, admitted a citizen of London in 1353, and became mason to the Black Prince about 1357, to the king (for Westminster, the Tower, and other palaces and castles) from 1360, and to Westminster Abbey from 1388 at the latest. It is probable that he had designed the nave of the abbey (as begun *c.*1375), and that of Canterbury Cathedral, built *c.*1379–1405, has also been attributed to him. He designed parts of New College, Oxford (*c.*1381), and remodelled Westminster Hall, London (1395). He was a wealthy man with property in many places, and he engaged in business both in connection with and apart from his duties as the king's Master Mason.

J. H. Harvey, *H.Y. c.1320–1400. The Life of an English Architect*, London 1944; J. H. Harvey, *H.Y. Reconsidered*, London 1952; Harvey 1984.

**Yorke**, Francis Reginald Stevens (1906–62), *see* ENGLISH ARCHITECTURE.

**Yorkshire lights**. In a mullioned window, a pair of lights, one fixed and the other sliding horizontally.

**Yoshisaka**, Takamasa (1917–80), *see* JAPANESE ARCHITECTURE.

**Yugoslav architecture**, *see* BYZANTINE ARCHITECTURE.

**Yurt**. Turkic word for a territory or campsite, applied to a type of felt-covered armature TENT with a conical roof, constructed from early times to the present day by nomads in Central Asia. From the

CII its form was imitated in brick-built Islamic MAUSOLEA.

# Z

**Zablocki**, Wojciech (b.1930), *see* POLISH ARCHITECTURE.

**Zabludovscy**, Abraham (b.1924), *see* MEXICAN ARCHITECTURE.

**Zaccagni**, Giovanfrancesco (1491–1543), *see* TRAMELLO, Alessio.

**Zakharov**, Andreyan Dmitrievich (1761–1811), a leading Russian neo-classicist and one of the great Russian architects, was trained at the St Petersburg Academy of Arts, then in Paris under CHALGRIN (1782–6), and travelled in Italy. His masterpiece is the Admiralty, St Petersburg (1806–20), vast, bold, and solid, with a façade 400 m. (a quarter of a mile) long, a huge columned tower supporting a needle-like spire (preserved from the original Admiralty building by I. Korobov of 1732) over the central gate, and dodecastyle Tuscan porticos at the ends. To give expression to such an immense frontage without breaking its unity was a major achievement. But the end blocks are still more successful, the nearest approach to BOULLÉE's architecture of geometrical shapes on a grand scale: each is in the form of a cubic pavilion capped by a low cylindrical drum, pierced by a vast semicircular portal, and flanked by colonnades. Another of his notable works is the cathedral of St Andrew in Kronstadt. He and VORONIKHIN were the leading architects in the committee that planned the Petersburg Bourse and adjacent townscape (*see* THOMON).

G. G. Grimm, *Arkhitekton A. Z.*, Moscow 1940; Hamilton 1983.

**Zapotec architecture**, *see* MESOAMERICAN ARCHITECTURE.

**Zehrfuss**, Bernard-Louis (1911–96). French architect who was associated with BREUER and NERVI in the design of the Unesco building, Paris (1953–8), and with Robert Camelot (1903–92) and Jean de Mailly (1911–75) in planning the La Défense development in Paris from the 1950s onwards. With Camelot, de Mailly and PROUVÉ he designed the gigantic shell-structure CNIT building at La Défense (1953–8). However, he was later involved in the high-rise development of Super-Montparnasse in the 1980s.

**Zenetos**, Takis (1926–77), *see* GREEK ARCHITECTURE.

**Zhilyardi** (or **Gigliardi**), Domenico (1788–1845), *see* RUSSIAN ARCHITECTURE.

**Zholtovsky**, Ivan (1867–1959), *see* RUSSIAN ARCHITECTURE.

**Ziggurat** or **zikkurat**. A rectangular temple-tower in the form of a truncated pyramid built in diminishing stages, each stage being reached by ramps, erected by the Sumerians and their successors. The best-known examples are those of Ur and Babylon, the fabled Tower of Babel. The largest and best preserved is that at Choga Zanbil (Iran) of 1250 BC. *See* Fig. 120.

**Zimbalo**, Giuseppe (active 1659–86). Italian architect, the chief exponent of the wildly exuberant and rather coarse Baroque style developed at Lecce, e.g. Prefettura (1659–95), Cathedral (1659–

Fig. 120 Ziggurat

82), S. Agostino (1663), and Chiesa del Rosario (1691). His pupil Giuseppe Cino (1645–1722) carried his style on into the C18.

M. Calvesi and M. Manieri-Elia, *Architettura barocca a Lecce e in terra di Puglia*, Rome 1971.

**Zimmermann**, Dominikus (1685–1766), one of the greatest south German Rococo architects, but a craftsman before he was an architect, retained to the last his peasant vitality, spontaneity, and unquestioning piety. It is significant that his masterpiece, the die Wies church, was built neither for a great prince nor for the abbot of a rich monastery but for a simple rustic community. Born at Wessobrunn, he began there as a stucco worker, then settled at Füssen (1698), and finally at Landsberg (1716), where he eventually became mayor. He continued to work as a stuccoist after becoming an architect and frequently collaborated with his brother Johann Baptist (1680–1758), who was a painter. His earliest building is the convent church at Mödigen (1716–18), but his mature style first becomes apparent in the pilgrimage church of Steinhausen (1728–31), which is the first wholly Rococo church in Bavaria. It broke away decisively from its Baroque predecessors, the mystical indirect lighting and rich velvety colour of ASAM giving place to flat even lighting and a predominantly white colour scheme – bright, brittle, and porcellaneous. The colours used are all symbolical, as are the motifs in both painted and carved decoration. At the Frauenkirche, Günzberg (1736–41), he adopted an oblong plan, and at die Wies (1745–54) he combined an oval with an oblong, using the former for the nave with its wide ambulatory (necessary for a pilgrimage church), and the latter for the rather long chancel, which is treated with an intensified, predominantly pink colour scheme. Here stucco work, white-painted wooden statues, and frescos combine with architecture to delight and instruct the pilgrim, be he never so humble or so sophisticated. In more ways than one it is the meeting-place of the courtly Rococo style and an ancient tradition of craftsmanship which stretches back to the Middle Ages.

H.-R. Hitchcock, *German Rococo. The Z. Brothers*, London 1968; H. and A. Bauer, *J.B. and D.Z.*, Regensburg 1985.

**Zion**, Robert (b.1921). American landscape architect in partnership from 1957 with Harold A. Breen. They designed the first and still most notable of New York's 'vest-pocket parks': the 13 × 30 m. (42 × 100 ft) Paley Park on East 53rd Street, an outdoor room paved with grey granite, planted with twelve honey locust trees and with ivy climbing over two brick walls framing a 6 m. (20 ft) high WATER WALL. Other works include the landscape environment for the apartment blocks of Co-Op City, New York (1965–70), and the redevelopment of the plaza around the base of the Statue of Liberty (1986).

**Zitek**, Josef (1832–1909), see CZECH ARCHITECTURE.

**Zone of transition**. In ISLAMIC ARCHI-TECTURE the area of wall between a square or polygonal chamber and a dome, either incorporating or concealing with MUQARNAS a structural system of SQUINCHES.

**Zoning**. A legal restriction affecting URBAN DESIGN, parts of cities being deemed to be for particular uses – e.g. for business, housing, etc. – and the heights and volumes of buildings being prescribed. New zoning laws were passed in the USA in 1916.

**Zoomorph**. A boulder carved by the Maya with animal and other forms, as distinct from a megalith cut and carved into the form of a STELE.

**Zoophorus**. A frieze with animal reliefs, as on the Theseum in Athens.

**Zoroastrian fire temple**, *see* FIRE TEMPLE.

**Zuccalli**, Enrico (1642–1724). Baroque architect, born in the Grisons, who settled in Munich where he and his rival VIS-CARDI dominated the architectural scene for several years. He succeeded BARELLI as architect to the Elector in 1672. In Munich he completed Barelli's Theatine church of St Cajetan, reducing the size of the dome. He supervised the decoration of the Residenz (Imperial suite 1680–1701; Alexander and Summer suite 1680–85) and built the Portia Palace (1694). Outside Munich, at Schleissheim, he built the Lustheim or Banqueting House (1684–9) and began the main palace (1701, completed by EFFNER). In 1695 he began rebuilding the palace at Bonn (completed after 1702 by de COTTE). He rebuilt the abbey church of Ettal (1709–26, partly burnt and rebuilt 1742). His kinsman Giovanni Gaspare (active 1685) built two Italianate churches at Salzburg: St Erhard (1586–9) and St Cajetan (1685–1700).

Brucker 1983; S. Heym, *H.Z. (1642–1724). Der kurbayerische Hofbaumeister*, Munich 1984.

**Zug**, Gottlieb Simon (1733–1807), *see* POLISH ARCHITECTURE.

# BIBLIOGRAPHICAL ABBREVIATIONS

| | |
|---|---|
| Banham 1960 | R. Banham, *Theory and Design in the First Machine Age*, London 1960 |
| Banham 1976 | R. Banham, *Megastructures*, London 1976 |
| Baum 1956 | J. Baum, *German Cathedrals*, London 1956 |
| Benevolo 1971 | L. Benevolo, *History of Modern Architecture*, London (1960) 1971 |
| Blair and Bloom 1994 | S. S. Blair and J. M. Bloom, *The Art and Architecture of Islam 1250–1800*, London and New Haven 1994 |
| Blunt 1975 | A. Blunt, *Neapolitan Baroque and Rococo Architecture*, London 1975 |
| Blunt 1982 | A. Blunt, *Art and Architecture in France: 1500–1700*, Harmondsworth (1953) 1982 |
| Boethius 1978 | A. Boethius, *Etruscan and Early Roman Architecture*, Harmondsworth (1970) 1978 |
| Bognar 1985 | B. Bognar, *Contemporary Japanese Architecture*, London 1985 |
| Bognar 1995 | B. Bognar, *The Japan Guide*, Princeton 1995 |
| Bony 1979 | J. Bony, *The English Decorated Style*, Oxford 1979 |
| Bony 1983 | J. Bony, *French Gothic Architecture Twelfth to Thirteenth Century*, Berkeley and London 1983 |
| Braham 1980 | A. Braham, *The Architecture of the French Enlightenment*, London 1980 |
| Branner 1965 | R. Branner, *St. Louis and the Court Style in Gothic Architecture*, London 1965 |
| Braunfels 1973 | W. Braunfels, *Monasteries of Western Europe*, Princeton 1973 |
| Broadbent 1990 | G. Broadbent, *Emerging Concepts in Urban Space Design*, London 1990 |
| Brown 1985 | R. Brown (ed.), *The Architectural Outsiders*, London 1985 |
| Brucker 1983 | G. Brucker, *Barockarchitektur in Österreich*, Cologne 1983 |
| Bucher 1979 | F. Bucher, *Architector. The Lodge Books and Sketchbooks of Medieval Architects*, New York 1979 |
| Cerver 1995 | F. A. Cerver, *The World of Landscape Architecture*, Barcelona 1995 |
| Clarke 1969 | B. F. L. Clarke, *Church Builders of the Nineteenth Century*, Newton Abbot (1938) 1969 |
| Collins 1959 | P. Collins, *Concrete. The Vision of a New Architecture. A Study of Auguste Perret and his Precursors*, New York and London 1959 |
| Collins 1965 | P. Collins, *Changing Ideals in Modern Architecture (1750–1950)*, London 1965 |
| Colombier 1956 | P. du Colombier, *L'Architecture française en Allemagne au XVIIIe siècle*, Paris 1956 |

Colvin 1995      H. Colvin, *Biographical Dictionary of British Architects 1600–1840*, London (1954) 1995

Conant 1979      K. J. Conant, *Carolingian and Romanesque Architecture: 800–1200*, Harmondsworth (1959) 1979

Condit 1961      C. Condit, *American Building Art – The Twentieth Century*, New York 1961

Condit 1964      C. Condit, *The Chicago School of Architecture*, Chicago 1964

Condit 1968      C. Condit, *American Building Materials*, Chicago 1968

Crook 1972       J. M. Crook, *The Greek Revival*, London 1972

Crook 1987       J. M. Crook, *The Dilemma of Style*, London and Chicago 1987

Curtis 1996      W. J. R. Curtis, *Modern Architecture Since 1900*, London 1996

Davey 1961       N. Davey, *A History of Building Materials*, London 1961

Davies 1988      C. Davies, *High Tech Architecture*, London 1988

*DBI*            *Dizionario biografico degli italiani*, Rome 1960 onwards

Dixon and        R. Dixon and S. Muthesius, *Victorian Architecture*, London 1978
  Muthesius 1978

Dixon-Hunt 1992  J. Dixon-Hunt, *Gardens and the Picturesque. Studies in the History of Landscape Architecture*, Cambridge, Mass. 1992.

Downes 1966      K. Downes, *English Baroque Architecture*, London 1966

Elliott 1992     C. D. Elliott, *Technics and Architecture*, Cambridge, Mass. 1992

Etlin 1991       R. A. Etlin, *Modernism in Italian Architecture*, Cambridge, Mass. 1991

Ettinghausen and R. Ettinghausen and O. Grabar, *The Art and Architecture of Islam*
  Grabar 1988    *650–1250*, Harmondsworth 1988

Frankfort 1970   H. Frankfort, *The Art and Architecture of the Ancient Orient*, Harmondsworth 1970

Frankl 1962      P. Frankl, *Gothic Architecture*, Harmondsworth 1962

Frankl 1977      P. J. Frankl, *The Gothic*, Princeton (1960) 1977

Frommel 1973     C. L. Frommel, *Der Römischen Palastbau des Cinquecento*, Tübingen 1973

Gallet 1964      M. Gallet, *Demeures Parisiennes à la époque de Louis XVI*, Paris 1964

Gerson and       H. Gerson and E. H. ter Kuile, *Art and Architecture in Belgium*
  ter Kuile 1960 *1600–1800*, Harmondsworth 1960

Ghirardo 1996    D. Ghirardo, *Architecture after Modernism*, London 1996

Giedion 1967     S. Giedion, *Space, Time and Architecture: The Growth of a New Tradition*, Cambridge, Mass., and Oxford (1941) 1967

Goldthwaite 1980 R. A. L. Goldthwaite, *The Building of Renaissance Florence*, Baltimore and London 1980

Goodwin 1971     G. Goodwin, *A History of Ottoman Architecture*, London 1971

Hamilton 1983    G. H. Hamilton, *The Art and Architecture of Russia*, Harmondsworth (1954) 1983

Harris 1990      E. Harris and N. Savage, *British Architectural Books and Writers 1556–1785*, Cambridge 1990

Hart 1985        F. Hart, W. Henn and H. Sontag, *Multi-Storey Buildings in Steel*, London 1985

Harvey 1984      J. Harvey, *English Medieval Architects. A Biographical Dictionary down to 1580*, London (1954) 1984

Hempel 1965          E. Hempel, *Baroque Art and Architecture in Central Europe*, Harmondsworth 1965

Herrmann 1962        W. Herrmann, *Laugier and Eighteenth Century French Theory*, London 1962

Heydenreich 1996     L. Heydenreich, *Architecture in Italy 1400–1500*, London and New Haven 1996

Hillenbrand 1994     R. Hillenbrand, *Islamic Architecture*, Edinburgh 1994

Hitchcock 1954       H.-R. Hitchcock, *Early Victorian Architecture in Britain*, New Haven and London 1954

Hitchcock 1968       H.-R. Hitchcock, *Rococo Architecture in Southern Germany*, London 1968

Hitchcock 1977       H.-R. Hitchcock, *Architecture: Nineteenth and Twentieth Centuries*, Harmondsworth (1958) 1977

Hitchcock 1981       H.-R. Hitchcock, *German Renaissance Architecture*, Princeton 1981

Holden 1996          R. Holden, *International Landscape Design*, London 1996

Honour 1977          H. Honour, *Neo-Classicism*, Harmondsworth (1968) 1977

Honour 1979          H. Honour, *Romanticism*, Harmondsworth 1979

Howard 1987          D. Howard, *Architectural History of Venice*, London (1980) 1987

Ibelings 1995        H. Ibelings, *Twentieth Century Architecture in the Netherlands*, Rotterdam 1995

Jencks 1988          C. Jencks, *Architecture Today*, London 1988

Kalnein 1995         W. v. Kalnein, *Architecture in France in the Eighteenth Century*, London and New Haven 1995

Kaufmann 1955        E. Kaufmann, *Architecture in the Age of Reason*, Cambridge, Mass. 1955

Klotz 1986           H. Klotz (ed.), *Vision der Moderne*, Munich 1986

Klotz 1988           H. Klotz, *The History of Postmodern Architecture*, Cambridge, Mass. 1988

Krautheimer 1986     R. Krautheimer, *Early Christian and Byzantine Architecture*, Harmondsworth (1965) 1986

Kruft 1994           H. W. Kruft, *A History of Architectural Theory*, London 1994

Kubler 1984          G. Kubler, *Art and Architecture of Ancient America*, Harmondsworth (1962) 1984

Kubler and           G. Kubler and M. Soria, *Art and Architecture in Spain and Portugal
  Soria 1959          and their American Dominions 1500–1800*, Harmondsworth 1959

Kuyper 1980          W. Kuyper, *Dutch Classicist Architecture*, Delft 1980

Laing 1978           A. Laing in A. Blunt (ed.), *Baroque and Rococo Architecture and Decoration*, London 1978

Laird 1992           M. Laird, *The Formal Garden*, London 1992

Lawrence 1996        A. W. Lawrence, *Greek Architecture*, New Haven and London (1957) 1996

Lazzaro 1990         C. Lazzaro, *The Italian Renaissance Garden*, London and New Haven 1990

LeGates and          R. T. LeGates and F. Stout (eds.), *The City Reader*, London
  Stout 1996          and New York 1996

| | |
|---|---|
| Lieberman 1982 | R. Lieberman, *Renaissance Architecture in Venice*, New York 1982 |
| Lotz 1977 | W. Lotz, *Studies in Renaissance Architecture*, Cambridge, Mass. 1977 |
| Lotz 1995 | W. Lotz, *Architecture in Italy 1500–1600*, London and New Haven 1995 |
| Loyer 1979 | F. Loyer, *Art Nouveau Architecture*, London 1979 |
| Loyer 1982 | F. Loyer, *Architecture of the Industrial Age 1789–1914*, New York 1982 |
| Loyer 1987 | F. Loyer, *Paris XIX siècle. L'immeuble et la rue*, Paris 1987 |
| Lyall 1991 | S. Lyall, *Designing the New Landscape*, London 1991 |
| McAndrew 1980 | J. McAndrew, *Venetian Architecture of the Early Renaissance*, Cambridge, Mass. 1980 |
| Macaulay 1975 | J. Macaulay, *The Gothic Revival 1745–1845*, Glasgow 1975 |
| MacDonald 1965 | W. L. MacDonald, *The Architecture of the Roman Empire*, Vol. 1, New Haven and London 1965 |
| MacDonald 1986 | W. L. MacDonald, *The Architecture of the Roman Empire*, Vol. 2, New Haven and London 1986 |
| Mainstone 1975 | R. Mainstone, *Developments in Structural Form*, London 1975 |
| Mark 1993 | R. Mark (ed.), *Architectural Technology*, Cambridge, Mass. 1993 |
| Maxwell 1972 | R. Maxwell, *New British Architecture*, London 1972 |
| Meeks 1966 | C. L. V. Meeks, *Italian Architecture 1750–1914*, New Haven and London 1966 |
| Middleton and Watkin 1977 | R. D. Middleton and D. Watkin, *Neo-Classical and Nineteenth Century Architecture*, London 1977 |
| Middleton 1982 | R. D. Middleton, *The Beaux-Arts and Nineteenth Century French Architecture*, London 1982 |
| Miller Lane 1968 | B. Miller Lane, *Architecture and Politics in Germany 1918–1945*, Cambridge, Mass. 1968 |
| Mumford 1961 | L. Mumford, *The City in History. Its Origins, its Transformations and its Prospects*, London 1961 |
| Nicoletti 1978 | G. M. Nicoletti, *L'architettura liberty in Italia*, Bari and Rome 1978 |
| Onians 1988 | J. Onians, *Bearers of Meaning. The Classic Orders in Antiquity, the Middle Ages and the Renaissance*, London 1988 |
| Paulsson 1958 | T. Paulsson, *Scandinavian Architecture*, London 1958 |
| Pevsner 1968 | N. Pevsner, *Studies in Art, Architecture and Design*, London 1968 |
| Pevsner 1972 | N. Pevsner, *Some Architectural Writers of the Nineteenth Century*, Oxford 1972 |
| Pevsner and Richards 1973 | N. Pevsner and J. M. Richards (eds.), *The Anti-Rationalists*, Wisbech 1973 |
| Pierson and Jordy 1970 | W. H. Pierson and W. Jordy, *American Builders and their Architects. The Colonial and Neo-Classical Styles*, New York 1970 |
| Pommer 1967 | R. Pommer, *Eighteenth Century Architecture in Piedmont: The Open Structures of Juvara, Alfieri and Vittone*, New York and London 1967 |
| Recht 1989 | R. Recht (ed.), *Les Bâtisseurs des cathédrales gothiques*, Strasbourg 1989 |

Robertson 1969 · D. S. Robertson, *A Handbook of Greek and Roman Architecture*, Cambridge (1943) 1969

Rosenberg 1977 · J. Rosenberg, S. Slive and E. H. ter Kuile, *Dutch Art and Architecture 1600–1800*, Harmondsworth (1966) 1977

Ross 1978 · M. F. Ross, *Beyond Metabolism. The New Japanese Architecture*, Cambridge. Mass. 1978

Roth 1979 · L. M. Roth, *A Concise History of American Architecture*, New York 1979

Rykwert 1980 · J. Rykwert, *The First Moderns*, London 1980

Service 1977 · A. Service, *Edwardian Architecture*, London 1977

Smith 1968 · R. C. Smith, *The Art of Portugal 1500–1800*, London 1968

Smith and Simpson 1981 · W. S. Smith and W. K. Simpson, *The Art and Architecture of Ancient Egypt*, Harmondsworth 1981

Steenbergen and Reh 1996 · C. Steenbergen and W. Reh, *Architecture and Landscape*, Munich 1996

Summerson 1983 · J. Summerson, *Architecture in Britain 1530–1830*, Harmondsworth (1953) 1983

Tafuri 1966 · M. Tafuri, *L'architettura del Manierismo nel cinquecento europeo*, Rome 1966

Tischler 1989 · W. H. Tischler, *American Landscape Architecture*, Washington, DC, 1989

Trachtenberg 1971 · M. Trachtenberg, *The Campanile of Florence Cathedral. 'Giotto's Tower'*, New York 1971

Van Zanten 1987 · D. Van Zanten, *Designing Paris. The Architecture of Duban, Labrouste, Le Duc and Vaudoyer*, Cambridge, Mass. 1987

Varriano 1986 · J. Varriano, *Italian Baroque and Rococo Architecture*, New York and Oxford 1986

Walker and Simo 1994 · P. Walker and M. Simo, *Invisible Gardens*, Cambridge Mass. 1994

Ward-Perkins 1981 · J. B. Ward-Perkins, *Roman Imperial Architecture*, Harmondsworth 1981

Watkin and Mellinghoff 1987 · D. Watkin and T. Mellinghoff, *German Architects and the Classical Ideal 1740–1840*, London 1987

Webb 1965 · G. Webb, *Art and Architecture in Britain: The Middle Ages*, Harmondsworth 1965

Weilacher 1996 · U. Weilacher, *Between Landscape Architecture and Land Art*, Basel, Berlin and Boston 1996

Whiffen and Koeper 1981 · M. Whiffen and F. Koeper, *American Architecture 1607–1976*, London 1981

White 1987 · J. White, *Art and Architecture in Italy 1250–1400*, Harmondsworth (1966) 1987

R. Winter 1997 · R. Winter (ed.), *Towards a Simple Way of Life. The Arts and Crafts Architects of California*, Los Angeles 1997

Wittkower 1974 · R. Wittkower, *Palladio and Palladianism*, London 1974

Wittkower 1982 · R. Wittkower, *Art and Architecture in Italy 1600–1750*, Harmondsworth (1965) 1982

Bibliographical Abbreviations

Wittkower 1988   R. Wittkower, *Architectural Principles in the Age of Humanism*, London (1949) 1988

Zukowsky 1988   J. Zukowsky, *Chicago Architecture 1872–1922. The Building of a Metropolis*, Chicago 1988

# READ MORE IN PENGUIN

In every corner of the world, on every subject under the sun, Penguin represents quality and variety – the very best in publishing today.

For complete information about books available from Penguin – including Puffins, Penguin Classics and Arkana – and how to order them, write to us at the appropriate address below. Please note that for copyright reasons the selection of books varies from country to country.

**In the United Kingdom**: Please write to *Dept. EP, Penguin Books Ltd, Bath Road, Harmondsworth, West Drayton, Middlesex UB7 0DA*

**In the United States**: Please write to *Consumer Sales, Penguin Putnam Inc., P.O. Box 12289 Dept. B, Newark, New Jersey 07101-5289*. VISA and MasterCard holders call 1-800-788-6262 to order Penguin titles

**In Canada**: Please write to *Penguin Books Canada Ltd, 10 Alcorn Avenue, Suite 300, Toronto, Ontario M4V 3B2*

**In Australia**: Please write to *Penguin Books Australia Ltd, P.O. Box 257, Ringwood, Victoria 3134*

**In New Zealand**: Please write to *Penguin Books (NZ) Ltd, Private Bag 102902, North Shore Mail Centre, Auckland 10*

**In India**: Please write to *Penguin Books India Pvt Ltd, 11 Community Centre, Panchsheel Park, New Delhi 110017*

**In the Netherlands**: Please write to *Penguin Books Netherlands bv, Postbus 3507, NL-1001 AH Amsterdam*

**In Germany**: Please write to *Penguin Books Deutschland GmbH, Metzlerstrasse 26, 60594 Frankfurt am Main*

**In Spain**: Please write to *Penguin Books S. A., Bravo Murillo 19, 1° B, 28015 Madrid*

**In Italy**: Please write to *Penguin Italia s.r.l., Via Benedetto Croce 2, 20094 Corsico, Milano*

**In France**: Please write to *Penguin France, Le Carré Wilson, 62 rue Benjamin Baillaud, 31500 Toulouse*

**In Japan**: Please write to *Penguin Books Japan Ltd, Kaneko Building, 2-3-25 Koraku, Bunkyo-Ku, Tokyo 112*

**In South Africa**: Please write to *Penguin Books South Africa (Pty) Ltd, Private Bag X14, Parkview, 2122 Johannesburg*

# READ MORE IN PENGUIN

## REFERENCE

### The Penguin Dictionary of the Third Reich
James Taylor and Warren Shaw

This dictionary provides a full background to the rise of Nazism and the role of Germany in the Second World War. Among the areas covered are the major figures from Nazi politics, arts and industry, the German Resistance, the politics of race and the Nuremberg trials.

### The Penguin Biographical Dictionary of Women

This stimulating, informative and entirely new Penguin dictionary of women from all over the world, through the ages, contains over 1,600 clear and concise biographies on major figures from politicians, saints and scientists to poets, film stars and writers.

### Roget's Thesaurus of English Words and Phrases
Edited by Betty Kirkpatrick

This new edition of Roget's classic work, now brought up to date for the nineties, will increase anyone's command of the English language. Fully cross-referenced, it includes synonyms of every kind (formal or colloquial, idiomatic and figurative) for almost 900 headings. It is a must for writers and utterly fascinating for any English speaker.

### The Penguin Dictionary of International Relations
Graham Evans and Jeffrey Newnham

International relations have undergone a revolution since the end of the Cold War. This new world disorder is fully reflected in this new Penguin dictionary, which is extensively cross-referenced with a select bibliography to aid further study.

### The Penguin Guide to Synonyms and Related Words
S. I. Hayakawa

'More helpful than a thesaurus, more humane than a dictionary, the *Guide to Synonyms and Related Words* maps linguistic boundaries with precision, sensitivity to nuance and, on occasion, dry wit' *The Times Literary Supplement*

# READ MORE IN PENGUIN

## REFERENCE

**The Penguin Dictionary of Troublesome Words**  Bill Bryson

Why should you avoid discussing the *weather conditions*? Can a married woman be celibate? Why is it eccentric to talk about the aroma of a cowshed? A straightforward guide to the pitfalls and hotly disputed issues in standard written English.

**Swearing**  Geoffrey Hughes

'A deliciously filthy trawl among taboo words across the ages and the globe' Valentine Cunningham, *Observer*, Books of the Year. 'Erudite and entertaining' Penelope Lively, *Daily Telegraph*, Books of the Year.

**Medicines: A Guide for Everybody**  Peter Parish

Now in its seventh edition and completely revised and updated, this bestselling guide is written in ordinary language for the ordinary reader yet will prove indispensable to anyone involved in health care: nurses, pharmacists, opticians, social workers and doctors.

**Media Law**  Geoffrey Robertson QC and Andrew Nichol

Crisp and authoritative surveys explain the up-to-date position on defamation, obscenity, official secrecy, copyright and confidentiality, contempt of court, the protection of privacy and much more.

**The Penguin Careers Guide**
Anna Alston and Anne Daniel; Consultant Editor: Ruth Miller

As the concept of a 'job for life' wanes, this guide encourages you to think broadly about occupational areas as well as describing day-to-day work and detailing the latest developments and qualifications such as NVQs. Special features include possibilities for working part-time and job-sharing, returning to work after a break and an assessment of the current position of women.

# READ MORE IN PENGUIN

## DICTIONARIES

Abbreviations
Ancient History
Archaeology
Architecture
Art and Artists
Astronomy
Biographical Dictionary of
  Women
Biology
Botany
Building
Business
Challenging Words
Chemistry
Civil Engineering
Classical Mythology
Computers
Contemporary American History
Curious and Interesting Geometry
Curious and Interesting Numbers
Curious and Interesting Words
Design and Designers
Economics
Eighteenth-Century History
Electronics
English and European History
English Idioms
Foreign Terms and Phrases
French
Geography
Geology
German
Historical Slang
Human Geography
Information Technology

International Finance
International Relations
Literary Terms and Literary
  Theory
Mathematics
Modern History 1789–1945
Modern Quotations
Music
Musical Performers
Nineteenth-Century World
  History
Philosophy
Physical Geography
Physics
Politics
Proverbs
Psychology
Quotations
Quotations from Shakespeare
Religions
Rhyming Dictionary
Russian
Saints
Science
Sociology
Spanish
Surnames
Symbols
Synonyms and Antonyms
Telecommunications
Theatre
The Third Reich
Third World Terms
Troublesome Words
Twentieth-Century History
Twentieth-Century Quotations